T0305277

Nonparametric Econometrics

Nonparametric Econometrics

Theory and Practice

Qi Li and Jeffrey Scott Racine

Princeton University Press
Princeton and Oxford

Published by Princeton University Press,
41 William Street, Princeton, New Jersey 08540
In the United Kingdom: Princeton University Press,
3 Market Place, Woodstock, Oxfordshire OX20 1SY

Library of Congress Cataloging-in-Publication Data

Li, Qi, 1956–
    Nonparametric econometrics : theory and practice / Qi Li &
        Jeffrey S. Racine.
        p. cm.
    Includes index.
    ISBN-13: 978-0-691-12161-1 (cloth : alk. paper)
    ISBN-10: 0-691-12161-3 (cloth : alk. paper)
    1. Econometrics. 2. Nonparametric statistics. I. Racine, Jeffrey S.
    1962– II. Title.
    HB139.L55 2006
    330.01'51954-dc22

                                                        2006044989

British Library Cataloging-in-Publication Data is available

The publisher would like to acknowledge the authors of
this volume for providing the camera-ready copy from
which this book was printed.

Cover design by Carmina Alvarez-Gaffin

press.princeton.edu

Contents

Preface

Throughout this book, the term "nonparametric" is used to refer to statistical techniques that do not require a researcher to specify a functional form for an object being estimated. Rather than assuming that the functional form of an object is known up to a few (finite) unknown parameters, we substitute less restrictive assumptions such as smoothness (differentiability) and moment restrictions for the objects being studied. For example, when we are interested in estimating the income distribution of a region, instead of assuming that the density function lies in a parametric family such as the normal or log-normal family, we assume only that the density function is twice (or three times) differentiable. Of course, if one possesses prior knowledge (some have called this "divine insight") about the functional form of the object of interest, then one will always do better by using parametric techniques. However, in practice such functional forms are rarely (if ever) known, and the unforgiving consequences of parametric misspecification are well known and are not repeated here.

Since nonparametric techniques make fewer assumptions about the object being estimated than do parametric techniques, nonparametric estimators tend to be slower to converge to the objects being studied than *correctly specified* parametric estimators. In addition, unlike their parametric counterparts, the convergence rate is typically inversely related to the number of variables (covariates) involved, which is sometimes referred to as the "curse of dimensionality." However, it is often surprising how, even for moderate datasets, nonparametric approaches can reveal structure in the data which might be missed were one to employ common parametric functional specifications. Nonparametric methods are therefore best suited to situations in which (i) one knows little about the functional form of the object being estimated, (ii) the number of variables (covariates) is small, and (iii) the researcher has a reasonably large data set. Points (ii) and (iii) are closely related because, in nonparametric settings, whether or not one has a sufficiently large sample depends on how many covariates are present. Silverman (1986, see Table 4.2, p. 94) provides an excellent illustration on the relationship between the sample size and the covariate dimension required to obtain accurate nonparametric estimates. We use the term "semiparametric" to refer to statistical techniques that do not require a researcher to specify a parametric functional form for some part of an object being estimated but do require parametric assumptions for the remaining part(s).

As noted above, the nonparametric methods covered in this text offer the advantage of imposing less restrictive assumptions on functional forms (e.g., regression or conditional probability functions) as compared to, say, commonly used parametric models. However, alternative approaches may be obtained by relaxing restrictive assumptions in a conventional parametric setting. One such approach taken by Manski (2003) and his collaborators considers probability or regression models in which some parameters are not identified. Instead of imposing overly strong assumptions to identify the parameters, it is often possible to find bounds for the permissible range for these parameters. When the bound is relatively tight, i.e., when the permissible range is quite narrow, one can *almost* identify these parameters. This exciting line of inquiry, however, is beyond the scope of this text, so we refer the interested reader to the excellent monograph by Manski (2003); see also recent work by Manski and Tamer (2002), Imbens and Manski (2004), Honoré and Tamer (2006) and the references therein.

Nonparametric and semiparametric methods have attracted a great deal of attention from statisticians in the past few decades, as evidenced by the vast array of texts written by statisticians including Prakasa Rao (1983), Devroye and Györfi (1985), Silverman (1986), Scott (1992), Bickel, Klaassen, Ritov and Wellner (1993), Wand and Jones (1995), Fan and Gijbels (1996), Simonoff (1996), Azzalini and Bowman (1997), Hart (1997), Efromovich (1999), Eubank (1999), Ruppert, Carroll and Wand (2003), and Fan and Yao (2005). However, the number of texts tailored to the needs of applied econometricians is relatively scarce, Härdle (1990), Horowitz (1998), Pagan and Ullah (1999), Yatchew (2003), and Härdle, Müller, Sperlich and Werwatz (2004) being those of which we are currently aware.

In addition, the majority of existing texts operate from the presumption that the underlying data is strictly continuous in nature, while more often than not economists deal with categorical (nominal and ordinal) data in applied settings. The conventional frequency-based nonparametric approach to dealing with the presence of discrete variables is acknowledged to be unsatisfactory. Building upon Aitchison and Aitken's (1976) seminal work on smoothing discrete covariates, we recently proposed a number of novel nonparametric approaches; see, e.g., Li and Racine (2003), Hall, Racine and Li (2004), Racine and Li (2004), Li and Racine (2004a), Racine, Li and Zhu (2004), Ouyang, Li and Racine (2006), Hall, Li and Racine (2006), Racine, Hart and Li (forthcoming), Li and Racine (forthcoming), and Hsiao, Li and Racine (forthcoming) for recent work in this area. In this text we emphasize nonparametric techniques suited to the rich array of data types (continuous, nominal, and ordinal) encountered by an applied economist within one coherent framework.

Another defining feature of this text is its emphasis on the properties of nonparametric estimators in the presence of potentially irrelevant variables. Existing treatments of kernel methods, in particular, bandwidth selection methods, presume that all variables are relevant. For example, existing treatments of plug-in or cross-validation methods presume that all covariates in a regression model are in fact relevant, i.e., that all covariates help explain variation in the outcome (i.e., the dependent variable). When this is not the case, however, existing results such as rates of convergence and the behavior of bandwidths no longer hold; see, e.g., Hall et al. (2004), Hall et al. (2006), Racine and Li (2004), and Li and Racine (2004a). We feel that this is an extremely important aspect of sound nonparametric estimation which must be appreciated by practitioners if they are to wield these tools wisely.

This book is aimed at students enrolled in a graduate course in nonparametric and semiparametric methods, who are interested in application areas such as economics and other social sciences. Ideal prerequisites would include a course in mathematical statistics and a course in parametric econometrics at the level of, say, Greene (2003) or Wooldridge (2002). We also intend for this text to serve as a valuable reference for a much wider audience, including applied researchers and those who wish to familiarize themselves with the subject area.

The five parts of this text are organized as follows. The first part covers nonparametric estimation of density and regression functions with independent data, with emphasis being placed on mixed discrete and continuous data types. The second part deals with various semiparametric models again with independent data, including partially linear models, single index models, additive models, varying coefficient models, censored models, and sample selection models. The third part deals with an array of consistent model specification tests. The fourth part examines nearest neighbor and series methods. The fifth part considers kernel estimation of instrumental variable models, simultaneous equation models, and panel data models, and extends results from previous Chapters to the weakly dependent data setting.

Rigorous proofs are provided for most results in Part I, while outlines of proofs are provided for many results in Parts II, III, IV, and V. Background statistical concepts are presented in an appendix.

An R package (R Development Core Team (2006)) is available and can be obtained directly from http://www.R-project.org that implements a number of the methods discussed in Part I, II, and some of those discussed in Parts III, IV, and V. It also contains some datasets used in the book, and contains a function that allows the reader to easily implement new kernel-based tests and kernel-based estimators.

Exercises appear at the end of each chapter, and detailed hints are provided for many of the problems. Students who wish to master the material are encouraged to work out as many problems as possible. Because some of the hints may render the questions almost trivial, we strongly encourage students who wish to master the techniques to work on the problems without first consulting the hints.

We are deeply indebted to so many people who have provided guidance, inspiration, or have laid the foundations that have made this book possible. It would be impossible to list them all. However, we ask each of you who have in one way or another contributed to this project to indulge us and enjoy a personal sense of accomplishment at its completion.

This being said, we would like to thank the staff at Princeton University Press, namely, Peter Dougherty, Seth Ditchik, Terri O'Prey, and Carole Schwager, for their eye to detail and professional guidance through this process.

We would also like to express our deep gratitude to numerous granting agencies for their generous financial support that funded research which forms the heart of this book. In particular, Li would like to acknowledge support from the Social Sciences and Humanities Research Council of Canada (SSHRC), the Natural Sciences and Engineering Research Council of Canada (NSERC), the Texas A&M University Private Research Center, and the Bush School Program in Economics. Racine would like to acknowledge support from SSHRC, NSERC, the Center for Policy Research at Syracuse University, and the National Sciences

Foundation (NSF) in the United States of America.

We would additionally like to thank graduate students at McMaster University, Syracuse University, Texas A&M University, the University of California San Diego, the University of Guelph, the University of South Florida, and York University, who, as involuntary subjects, provided valuable feedback on early drafts of this manuscript.

We would furthermore like to thank numerous coauthors for their many and varied contributions. We would especially like to thank Peter Hall, whose collaborations on kernel methods with mixed data types and, in particular, whose singular contributions to the theoretical foundations for kernel methods with irrelevant variables have brought much of this work to fruition.

Many people have provided feedback that has deepened our understanding and enhanced this book. In particular, we would like to acknowledge Chunrong Ai, Zongwu Cai, Xiaohong Chen, David Giles, Yanquin Fan, Jianhua Huang, Yiguo Sun, and Lijian Yang.

On a slightly more personal note, Racine would like express his deep-felt affection and personal indebtedness to Aman Ullah, who not only baptized him in nonparametric statistics, but also guided his thesis and remains an ongoing source of inspiration.

Finally, Li would like to dedicate this book to his wife, Zhenjuan Liu, his daughter, Kathy, and son, Kevin, without whom this project might not have materialized. Li would also like to dedicate this book to his parents with love and gratitude. Racine would like to dedicate this book to the memory of his father who passed away on November 22, 2005, and who has been a guiding light and will remain an eternal source of inspiration. Racine would also like to dedicate this book to his wife, Jennifer, and son, Adam, who continue to enrich his life beyond their ken.

Part I

Nonparametric Kernel Methods

Chapter 1

Density Estimation

The estimation of probability density functions (PDFs) and cumulative distribution functions (CDFs) are cornerstones of applied data analysis in the social sciences. Testing for the equality of two distributions (or moments thereof) is perhaps the most basic test in all of applied data analysis. Economists, for instance, devote a great deal of attention to the study of income distributions and how they vary across regions and over time. Though the PDF and CDF are often the objects of direct interest, their estimation also serves as an important building block for other objects being modeled such as a conditional mean (i.e., a "regression function"), which may be directly modeled using nonparametric or semiparametric methods (a conditional mean is a function of a conditional PDF, which is itself a ratio of unconditional PDFs). After mastering the principles underlying the nonparametric estimation of a PDF, the nonparametric estimation of the workhorse of applied data analysis, the conditional mean function considered in Chapter 2, progresses in a fairly straightforward manner. Careful study of the approaches developed in Chapter 1 will be most helpful for understanding material presented in later chapters.

We begin with the estimation of a univariate PDF in Sections 1.1 through 1.3, turn to the estimation of a univariate CDF in Sections 1.4 and 1.5, and then move on to the more general multivariate setting in Sections 1.6 through 1.8. Asymptotic normality, uniform rates of convergence, and bias reduction methods appear in Sections 1.9 through 1.12. Numerous illustrative applications appear in Section 1.13, while theoretical and applied exercises can be found in Section 1.14

We now proceed with a discussion of how to estimate the PDF

$f_X(x)$ of a random variable X. For notational simplicity we drop the subscript X and simply use $f(x)$ to denote the PDF of X. Some of the treatments of the kernel estimation of a PDF discussed in this chapter are drawn from the two excellent monographs by Silverman (1986) and Scott (1992).

1.1   Univariate Density Estimation

To best appreciate why one might consider using nonparametric methods to estimate a PDF, we begin with an illustrative example, the parametric estimation of a PDF.

Example 1.1. *Suppose X_1, X_2,..., X_n represent independent and identically distributed (i.i.d.) draws from a normal distribution with mean μ and variance σ^2. We wish to estimate the normal PDF $f(x)$.*

By assumption, $f(x)$ has a known parametric functional form (i.e., univariate normal) given by $f(x) = (2\pi\sigma^2)^{-1/2} \exp\left[-\frac{1}{2}(x - \mu)^2/\sigma^2\right]$, where the mean $\mu = \mathrm{E}(X)$ and variance $\sigma^2 = \mathrm{E}[(X - \mathrm{E}(X))^2] = \mathrm{var}(X)$ are the only unknown parameters to be estimated. One could estimate μ and σ^2 by the method of maximum likelihood as follows. Under the i.i.d. assumption, the joint PDF of $(X_1, \ldots, X_n)$ is simply the product of the univariate PDFs, which may be written as

$$f(X_1, \ldots, X_n) = \prod_{i=1}^{n} \frac{1}{\sqrt{2\pi\sigma^2}} e^{-\frac{(X_i - \mu)^2}{2\sigma^2}} = \frac{1}{(2\pi\sigma^2)^{n/2}} e^{-\frac{1}{2\sigma^2} \sum_{i=1}^{n}(X_i - \mu)^2}.$$

Conditional upon the observed sample and taking the logarithm, this gives us the log-likelihood function

$$\mathcal{L}(\mu, \sigma^2) \equiv \ln f(X_1, \ldots, X_n; \mu, \sigma^2)$$
$$= -\frac{n}{2} \ln(2\pi) - \frac{n}{2} \ln \sigma^2 - \frac{1}{2\sigma^2} \sum_{i=1}^{n}(X_i - \mu)^2.$$

The method of maximum likelihood proceeds by choosing those parameters that make it most likely that we observed the sample at hand given our distributional assumption. Thus, the likelihood function (or a monotonic transformation thereof, e.g., $\ln$) expresses the plausibility of different values of μ and σ^2 given the observed sample. We then maximize the likelihood function with respect to these two unknown parameters.

The necessary first order conditions for a maximization of the log-likelihood function are $\partial \mathcal{L}(\mu, \sigma^2)/\partial \mu = 0$ and $\partial \mathcal{L}(\mu, \sigma^2)/\partial \sigma^2 = 0$. Solving these first order conditions for the two unknown parameters μ and σ^2 yields

$$\hat{\mu} = \frac{1}{n} \sum_{i=1}^{n} X_i \quad and \quad \hat{\sigma}^2 = \frac{1}{n} \sum_{i=1}^{n} (X_i - \hat{\mu})^2.$$

$\hat{\mu}$ and $\hat{\sigma}^2$ above are the maximum likelihood estimators of μ and σ^2, respectively, and the resulting estimator of $f(x)$ is

$$\hat{f}(x) = \frac{1}{\sqrt{2\pi\hat{\sigma}^2}} \exp\left[-\frac{1}{2} \left(\frac{x - \hat{\mu}}{\hat{\sigma}} \right)^2 \right].$$

The "Achilles heel" of any parametric approach is of course the requirement that, prior to estimation, the analyst must specify the exact parametric functional form for the object being estimated. Upon reflection, the parametric approach is somewhat circular since we initially set out to estimate an unknown density but must first assume that the density is in fact known (up to a handful of unknown parameters, of course). Having based our estimate on the assumption that the density is a member of a known parametric family, we must then naturally confront the possibility that the parametric model is "misspecified," i.e., not consistent with the population from which the data was drawn. For instance, by assuming that X is drawn from a normally distributed population in the above example, we in fact impose a number of potentially quite restrictive assumptions: symmetry, unimodality, monotonically decreasing away from the mode and so on. If the true density were in fact asymmetric or possessed multiple modes, or was nonmonotonic away from the mode, then the presumption of distributional normality may provide a misleading characterization of the true density and could thereby produce erroneous estimates and lead to unsound inference.

At this juncture many readers will no doubt be pointing out that, having estimated a parametric PDF, one can always test whether the underlying distributional assumption is valid. We are, of course, completely sympathetic toward such arguments. Often, however, the rejection of a distributional assumption fails to provide any clear alternative. That is, we can reject the assumption of normality, but this rejection leaves us where we started, perhaps having ruled out but one of a large number of candidate distributions. Against this backdrop, researchers might instead consider nonparametric approaches.

Nonparametric methods circumvent problems arising from the need to specify parametric functional forms prior to estimation. Rather than presume one knows the exact functional form of the object being estimated, one instead presumes that it satisfies some regularity conditions such as smoothness and differentiability. This does not, however, come without cost. By imposing less structure on the functional form of the PDF than do parametric methods, nonparametric methods require more data to achieve the same degree of precision as a *correctly specified* parametric model. Our primary focus in this text is on a class of estimators known as "nonparametric kernel estimators" (a "kernel function" is simply a weighting function), though in Chapters 14 and 15 we provide a treatment of alternative nonparametric methodologies including nearest neighbor and series methods.

Before proceeding to a formal theoretical analysis of nonparametric density estimation methods, we first consider a popular example of estimating the probability of a head on a toss of a coin which is closely related to the nonparametric estimation of a CDF. This in turn will lead us to the nonparametric estimation of a PDF.

Example 1.2. *Suppose we have a coin (perhaps an unfair one) and we want to estimate the probability of flipping the coin and having it land heads up. Let $p = \mathrm{P}(H)$ denote the (unknown) population probability of obtaining a head. Taking a relative frequency approach, we would flip the coin n times, count the frequency of heads in n trials, and compute the relative frequency given by*

$$\hat{p} = \frac{1}{n}\left\{\#\ of\ heads\ \right\}, \tag{1.1}$$

which provides an estimate of p. The $\hat{p}$ defined in (1.1) is often referred to as a "frequency estimator" of p, and it is also the maximum likelihood estimator of p (see Exercise 1.2). The estimator $\hat{p}$ is, of course, fully nonparametric. Intuitively, one would expect that, if n is large, then $\hat{p}$ should be "close" to p. Indeed, one can easily show that the mean squared error (MSE) of $\hat{p}$ is given by (see Exercise 1.3)

$$\mathrm{MSE}\,(\hat{p}) \overset{\mathrm{def}}{=} \mathrm{E}\left[(\hat{p} - p)^2\right] = \frac{p(1-p)}{n},$$

so $\mathrm{MSE}\,(\hat{p}) \to 0$ as $n \to \infty$, which is termed as $\hat{p}$ converges to p in mean square error; see Appendix A for the definitions of various modes of convergence.

We now discuss how to obtain an estimator of the CDF of X, which we denote by $F(x)$. The CDF is defined as

$$F(x) = \mathrm{P}[X \leq x].$$

With i.i.d. data $X_1, \ldots, X_n$ (i.e., random draws from the distribution $F(\cdot)$), one can estimate $F(x)$ by

$$F_n(x) = \frac{1}{n} \{ \, \# \text{ of } X_i\text{'s} \leq x \, \}. \tag{1.2}$$

Equation (1.2) has a nice intuitive interpretation. Going back to our coin-flip example, if a coin is such that the probability of obtaining a head when we flip it equals $F(x)$ ($F(x)$ is unknown), and if we treat the collection of data $X_1, \ldots, X_n$ as flipping a coin n times and we say that a head occurs on the ith trial if $X_i \leq x$, then $\mathrm{P}(H) = \mathrm{P}(X_i \leq x) = F(x)$. The familiar frequency estimator of $\mathrm{P}(H)$ is equal to the number of heads divided by the number of trials:

$$\hat{\mathrm{P}}(H) = \frac{\# \text{ of heads}}{n} = \frac{1}{n}\{ \, \# \text{ of } X_i\text{'s} \leq \mathrm{x} \, \} \equiv F_n(x). \tag{1.3}$$

Therefore, we call (1.2) a frequency estimator of $F(x)$. Just as before when estimating $\mathrm{P}(H)$, we expect intuitively that as n gets large, $\hat{\mathrm{P}}(H)$ should yield a more accurate estimate of $\mathrm{P}(H)$. By the same reasoning, one would expect that as $n \to \infty$, $F_n(x)$ yields a more accurate estimate of $F(x)$. Indeed, one can easily show that $F_n(x) \to F(x)$ in MSE, which implies that $F_n(x)$ converges to $F(x)$ in probability and also in distribution as $n \to \infty$. In Appendix A we introduce the concepts of convergence in mean square error, convergence in probability, convergence in distribution, and almost sure convergence. It is well established that $F_n(x)$ indeed converges to $F(x)$ in each of these various senses. These concepts of convergence are necessary as it is easy to show that the ordinary limit of $F_n(x)$ does not exist, i.e., $\lim_{n\to\infty} F_n(x)$ does not exist (see Exercise 1.3, where the definition of an ordinary limit is provided). This example highlights the necessity of introducing new concepts of convergence modes such as convergence in mean square error and convergence in probability.

Now we take up the question of how to estimate a PDF $f(x)$ without making parametric presumptions about it's functional form. From the definition of $f(x)$ we have[1]

$$f(x) = \frac{d}{dx} F(x).\tag{1.4}$$

From (1.2) and (1.4), an obvious estimator of $f(x)$ is[2]

$$\hat{f}(x) = \frac{F_n(x+h) - F_n(x-h)}{2h},\tag{1.5}$$

where h is a small positive increment.

By substituting (1.2) into (1.5), we obtain

$$\hat{f}(x) = \frac{1}{2nh}\{ \# \text{ of } X_1,\ldots,X_n \text{ falling in the interval } [x-h, x+h] \}.\tag{1.6}$$

If we define a uniform kernel function given by

$$k(z) = \begin{cases} 1/2 & \text{if } |z| \leq 1 \\ 0 & \text{otherwise,} \end{cases}\tag{1.7}$$

then it is easy to see that $\hat{f}(x)$ given by (1.5) can also be expressed as

$$\hat{f}(x) = \frac{1}{nh} \sum_{i=1}^{n} k\left(\frac{X_i - x}{h}\right).\tag{1.8}$$

Equation (1.8) is called a uniform kernel estimator because the kernel function $k(\cdot)$ defined in (1.7) corresponds to a uniform PDF. In general, we refer to $k(\cdot)$ as a kernel function and to h as a smoothing parameter (or, alternatively, a bandwidth or window width). Equation (1.8) is sometimes referred to as a "naïve" kernel estimator.

In fact one might use many other possible choices for the kernel function $k(\cdot)$ in this context. For example, one could use a standard normal kernel given by

$$k(v) = \frac{1}{\sqrt{2\pi}} e^{-\frac{1}{2}v^2}, \quad -\infty < v < \infty.\tag{1.9}$$

This class of estimators can be found in the first published paper on kernel density estimation by Rosenblatt (1956), while Parzen (1962) established a number of properties associated with this class of estimators

---

[1]We only consider the continuous X case in this chapter. We deal with the discrete X case in Chapters 3 and 4.

[2]Recall that the definition of the derivative of a function $g(x)$ is given by $d\,g(x)/dx = \lim_{h\to 0} \frac{g(x+h)-g(x)}{h}$, or, equivalently, $d\,g(x)/dx = \lim_{h\to 0} \frac{g(x+h)-g(x-h)}{2h}$.

and relaxed the nonnegativity assumption in order to obtain estimators which are more efficient. For this reason, this approach is sometimes referred to as "Rosenblatt-Parzen kernel density estimation."

We will prove shortly that the kernel estimator $\hat{f}(x)$ defined in (1.8) constructed from any general nonnegative bounded kernel function $k(\cdot)$ that satisfies

$$
\begin{array}{ll}
(i) & \displaystyle\int k(v)\,dv = 1 \\[2mm]
(ii) & k(v) = k(-v) \\[2mm]
(iii) & \displaystyle\int v^2 k(v)\,dv = \kappa_2 > 0
\end{array}
\tag{1.10}
$$

is a consistent estimator of $f(x)$. Note that the symmetry condition (ii) implies that $\int v k(v)\,dv = 0$. By consistency, we mean that $\hat{f}(x) \to f(x)$ in probability (convergence in probability is defined in Appendix A). Note that $k(\cdot)$ defined in (1.10) is a (symmetric) PDF. For recent work on kernel methods with asymmetric kernels, see Abadir and Lawford (2004).

To define various modes of convergence, we first introduce the concept of the "Euclidean norm" ("Euclidean length") of a vector. Given a $q \times 1$ vector $x = (x_1, x_2, \ldots, x_q)' \in \mathbb{R}^q$, we use $||x||$ to denote the Euclidean length of x, which is defined by

$$
||x|| = [x'x]^{1/2} \equiv \sqrt{x_1^2 + x_2^2 + \cdots + x_q^2}.
$$

When $q = 1$ (a scalar), $||x||$ is simply the absolute value of x.

In the appendix we discuss the notation $O(\cdot)$ ("big Oh") and $o(\cdot)$ ("small Oh"). Let a_n be a nonstochastic sequence. We say that $a_n = O(n^\alpha)$ if $|a_n| \le C n^\alpha$ for all n sufficiently large, where α and C (> 0) are constants. Similarly, we say that $a_n = o(n^\alpha)$ if $a_n/n^\alpha \to 0$ as $n \to \infty$. We are now ready to prove the MSE consistency of $\hat{f}(x)$.

Theorem 1.1. *Let $X_1, \ldots, X_n$ denote i.i.d. observations having a three-times differentiable PDF $f(x)$, and let $f^{(s)}(x)$ denote the sth order derivative of $f(x)$ $(s = 1, 2, 3)$. Let x be an interior point in the support of X, and let $\hat{f}(x)$ be that defined in (1.8). Assume that the kernel function $k(\cdot)$ is bounded and satisfies (1.10). Also, as $n \to \infty$, $h \to 0$ and $nh \to \infty$, then*

$$
\begin{aligned}
\mathrm{MSE}\left(\hat{f}(x)\right) &= \frac{h^4}{4}\left[\kappa_2 f^{(2)}(x)\right]^2 + \frac{\kappa f(x)}{nh} + o\left(h^4 + (nh)^{-1}\right) \\
&= O\left(h^4 + (nh)^{-1}\right),
\end{aligned}
\tag{1.11}
$$

where $\kappa_2 = \int v^2 k(v)\, dv$ and $\kappa = \int k^2(v)\, dv$.

Proof of Theorem 1.1.

$$
\begin{aligned}
\mathrm{MSE}\left(\hat{f}(x)\right) &\equiv \mathrm{E}\left\{\left[\hat{f}(x) - f(x)\right]^2\right\} \\
&= \mathrm{var}\left(\hat{f}(x)\right) + \left[\mathrm{E}\left(\hat{f}(x)\right) - f(x)\right]^2 \\
&\equiv \mathrm{var}\left(\hat{f}(x)\right) + \left[\mathrm{bias}\left(\hat{f}(x)\right)\right]^2.
\end{aligned}
$$

We will evaluate the bias($\hat{f}(x)$) and var($\hat{f}(x)$) terms separately.

For the bias calculation we will need to use the Taylor expansion formula. For a univariate function $g(x)$ that is m times differentiable, we have

$$
\begin{aligned}
g(x) =\,&g(x_0) + g^{(1)}(x_0)(x - x_0) + \frac{1}{2!}g^{(2)}(x_0)(x - x_0)^2 + \\
&\cdots + \frac{1}{(m-1)!}g^{(m-1)}(x_0)(x - x_0)^{m-1} + \frac{1}{m!}g^{(m)}(\xi)(x - x_0)^m,
\end{aligned}
$$

where $g^{(s)}(x_0) = \frac{\partial^s g(x)}{\partial x^s}|_{x=x_0}$, and ξ lies between x and x_0.

The bias term is given by

$$
\begin{aligned}
\text{bias}\left(\hat{f}(x)\right) &= \mathrm{E}\left\{\frac{1}{nh}\sum_{i=1}^{n}k\left(\frac{X_i - x}{h}\right)\right\} - f(x) \\
&= h^{-1}\mathrm{E}\left[k\left(\frac{X_1 - x}{h}\right)\right] - f(x) \\
&\quad \text{(by identical distribution)} \\
&= h^{-1}\int f(x_1)k\left(\frac{x_1 - x}{h}\right)dx_1 - f(x) \\
&= h^{-1}\int f(x + hv)k(v)h\,dv - f(x) \\
&\quad \text{(change of variable, } x_1 - x = hv\text{)} \\
&= \int\left\{f(x) + f^{(1)}(x)hv + \frac{1}{2}f^{(2)}(x)h^2v^2 + O(h^3)\right\}k(v)\,dv \\
&\quad - f(x) \\
&= \left\{f(x) + 0 + \frac{h^2}{2}f^{(2)}(x)\int v^2 k(v)\,dv + O\left(h^3\right)\right\} - f(x) \\
&\quad \text{by (1.10)} \\
&= \frac{h^2}{2}f^{(2)}(x)\int v^2 k(v)\,dv + O\left(h^3\right),
\end{aligned}
\tag{1.12}
$$

where the $O\left(h^3\right)$ term comes from

$$
(1/3!)h^3\left|\int f^{(3)}(\tilde{x})v^3 k(v)\right|dv \le Ch^3\int\left|v^3 k(v)dv\right| = O\left(h^3\right),
$$

where C is a positive constant, and where $\tilde{x}$ lies between x and $x + hv$.

Note that in the above derivation we assume that $f(x)$ is three-times differentiable. We can weaken this condition to $f(x)$ being twice differentiable, resulting in ($O(h^3)$ becomes $o(h^2)$, see Exercise 1.5)

$$
\begin{aligned}
\text{bias}\left(\hat{f}(x)\right) &= \mathrm{E}\left(\hat{f}(x)\right) - f(x) \\
&= \frac{h^2}{2}f^{(2)}(x)\int v^2 k(v)\,dv + o\left(h^2\right).
\end{aligned}
\tag{1.13}
$$

Next we consider the variance term. Observe that

$$\text{var}\left(\hat{f}(x)\right) = \text{var}\left[\frac{1}{nh}\sum_{i=1}^{n} k\left(\frac{X_i - x}{h}\right)\right]$$

$$= \frac{1}{n^2 h^2}\left\{\sum_{i=1}^{n} \text{var}\left[k\left(\frac{X_i - x}{h}\right)\right] + 0\right\}$$

(by independence)

$$= \frac{1}{nh^2}\text{var}\left(k\left(\frac{X_1 - x}{h}\right)\right)$$

(by identical distribution)

$$= \frac{1}{nh^2}\left\{\text{E}\left[k^2\left(\frac{X_1 - x}{h}\right)\right] - \left[\text{E}\left(k\left(\frac{X_1 - x}{h}\right)\right)\right]^2\right\}$$

$$= \frac{1}{nh^2}\left\{\int f(x_1)k^2\left(\frac{x_1 - x}{h}\right)dx_1\right.$$

$$\left. - \left[\int f(x_1)k\left(\frac{x_1 - x}{h}\right)dx_1\right]^2\right\}$$

$$= \frac{1}{nh^2}\left\{h\int f(x + hv)k^2(v)\,dv\right.$$

$$\left. - \left[h\int f(x + hv)k(v)\,dv\right]^2\right\}$$

$$= \frac{1}{nh^2}\left\{h\int \left[f(x) + f^{(1)}(\xi)hv\right]k^2(v)\,dv - O\left(h^2\right)\right\}$$

$$= \frac{1}{nh}\left\{f(x)\int k^2(v)\,dv + O\left(h\int |v|k^2(v)\,dv\right) - O(h)\right\}$$

$$= \frac{1}{nh}\left\{\kappa f(x) + O(h)\right\}, \tag{1.14}$$

where $\kappa = \int k^2(v)\,dv$.

Equations (1.12) and (1.14) complete the proof of Theorem 1.1. □

Theorem 1.1 implies that (by Theorem A.7 of Appendix A)

$$\hat{f}(x) - f(x) = O_p\left(h^2 + (nh)^{-1/2}\right) = o_p(1).$$

By choosing $h = cn^{-1/\alpha}$ for some $c > 0$ and $\alpha > 1$, the conditions required for consistent estimation of $f(x)$, $h \to 0$ and $nh \to \infty$, are clearly satisfied. The overriding question is what values of c and α should be used in practice. As can be seen, for a given sample size n, if h is small, the resulting estimator will have a small bias but a large variance. On the other hand, if h is large, then the resulting estimator will have a small variance but a large bias. To minimize $\text{MSE}(\hat{f}(x))$, one should balance the squared bias and the variance terms. The optimal choice of h (in the sense that $\text{MSE}(\hat{f}(x))$ is minimized) should satisfy $d\text{MSE}(\hat{f}(x))/dh = 0$. By using (1.11), it is easy to show that the optimal h that minimizes the leading term of $\text{MSE}(\hat{f}(x))$ is given by

$$h_{\text{opt}} = c(x)n^{-1/5}, \qquad (1.15)$$

where $c(x) = \left\{ \kappa f(x)/[\kappa_2 f^{(2)}(x)]^2 \right\}^{1/5}$.

$\text{MSE}(\hat{f}(x))$ is clearly a "pointwise" property, and by using this as the basis for bandwidth selection we are obtaining a bandwidth that is optimal when estimating a density *at a point* x. Examining $c(x)$ in (1.15), we can see that a bandwidth which is optimal for estimation at a point x located in the tail of a distribution will differ from that which is optimal for estimation at a point located at, say, the mode. Suppose that we are interested not in tailoring the bandwidth to the pointwise estimation of $f(x)$ but instead in tailoring the bandwidth globally *for all points* x, that is, for all x in the support of $f(\cdot)$ (the support of x is defined as the set of points of x for which $f(x) > 0$, i.e., $\{x : f(x) > 0\}$). In this case we can choose h optimally by minimizing the "integrated MSE" (IMSE) of $\hat{f}(x)$. Using (1.11) we have

$$\text{IMSE}(\hat{f}) \overset{\text{def}}{=} \int \text{E}\left[\hat{f}(x) - f(x)\right]^2 dx = \frac{1}{4}h^4\kappa_2^2 \int \left[f^{(2)}(x)\right]^2 dx$$
$$+ \frac{\kappa}{nh} + o\left(h^4 + (nh)^{-1}\right). \qquad (1.16)$$

Again letting h_{opt} denote the optimal smoothing parameter that minimizes the leading terms of (1.16), we use simple calculus to get

$$h_{\text{opt}} = c_0 n^{-1/5}, \qquad (1.17)$$

where $c_0 = \kappa_2^{-2/5}\kappa^{1/5}\left\{\int \left[f^{(2)}(x)\right]^2 dx\right\}^{-1/5} > 0$ is a positive constant. Note that if $f^{(2)}(x) = 0$ for (almost) all x, then c_0 is not well defined. For example, if X is, say, uniformly distributed over its support, then $f^{(s)}(x) = 0$ for all x and for all $s \geq 1$, and (1.17) is not defined in this case. It can be shown that in this case (i.e., when X is uniformly distributed), h_{opt} will have a different rate of convergence equal to $n^{-1/3}$; see the related discussion in Section 1.3.1 and Exercise 1.16.

An interesting extension of the above results can be found in Zinde-Walsh (2005), who examines the asymptotic process for the kernel density estimator by means of generalized functions and generalized random processes and presents novel results for characterizing the behavior of kernel density estimators when the density does not exist, i.e., when the density does not exist as a locally summable function.

1.2   Univariate Bandwidth Selection: Rule-of-Thumb and Plug-In Methods

Equation (1.17) reveals that the optimal smoothing parameter depends on the integrated second derivative of the unknown density through c_0. In practice, one might choose an initial "pilot value" of h to estimate $\int \left[f^{(2)}(x) \right]^2 dx$ nonparametrically, and then use this value to obtain h_{opt} using (1.17). Such approaches are known as "plug-in methods" for obvious reasons. One popular way of choosing the initial h, suggested by Silverman (1986), is to assume that $f(x)$ belongs to a parametric family of distributions, and then to compute h using (1.17). For example, if $f(x)$ is a normal PDF with variance σ^2, then $\int \left[f^{(2)}(x) \right]^2 dx = 3/[8\pi^{1/2}\sigma^5]$. If a standard normal kernel is used, using (1.17), we get the pilot estimate

$$ h_{\mathrm{pilot}} = (4\pi)^{-1/10} \left[(3/8)\pi^{-1/2} \right]^{-1/5} \sigma n^{-1/5} \approx 1.06\sigma n^{-1/5}, \qquad (1.18) $$

which is then plugged into $\int [\hat{f}^{(2)}(x)]^2 dx$, which then may be used to obtain h_{opt} using (1.17). A clearly undesirable property of the plug-in method is that it is not fully automatic because one needs to choose an initial value of h to estimate $\int [f^{(2)}(x)]^2 dx$ (see Marron, Jones and Sheather (1996) and also Loader (1999) for further discussion).

Often, practitioners will use (1.18) itself for the bandwidth. This is known as the "normal reference rule-of-thumb" approach since it is the optimal bandwidth for a particular family of distributions, in this case the normal family. Should the underlying distribution be "close" to a normal distribution, then this will provide good results, and for exploratory purposes it is certainly computationally attractive. In practice, σ is replaced by the sample standard deviation of $\{X_i\}_{i=1}^n$, while Silverman (1986, p. 47) advocates using a more robust measure of spread which replaces σ with A, an "adaptive" measure of spread given by

$$A = \min(\text{standard deviation}, \text{interquartile range}/1.34).$$

We now turn our attention to a discussion of a number of fully automatic or "data-driven" methods for selecting h that are tailored to the sample at hand.

1.3 Univariate Bandwidth Selection: Cross-Validation Methods

In both theoretical and practical settings, nonparametric kernel estimation has been established as relatively insensitive to choice of kernel function. However, the same cannot be said for bandwidth selection. Different bandwidths can generate radically differing impressions of the underlying distribution. If kernel methods are used simply for "exploratory" purposes, then one might undersmooth the density by choosing a small value of h and let the eye do any remaining smoothing. Alternatively, one might choose a range of values for h and plot the resulting estimates. However, for sound analysis and inference, a principle having some known optimality properties must be adopted. One can think of choosing the bandwidth as being analogous to choosing the number of terms in a series approximation; the more terms one includes in the approximation, the more flexible the resulting model becomes, while the smaller the bandwidth of a kernel estimator, the more flexible it becomes. However, increasing flexibility (reducing potential bias) necessarily leads to increased variability (increasing potential variance). Seen in this light, one naturally appreciates how a number of methods discussed below are motivated by the need to balance the squared bias and variance of the resulting estimate.

1.3.1 Least Squares Cross-Validation

Least squares cross-validation is a fully automatic data-driven method of selecting the smoothing parameter h, originally proposed by Rudemo (1982), Stone (1984) and Bowman (1984) (see also Silverman (1986, pp. 48-51)). This method is based on the principle of selecting a bandwidth that minimizes the integrated squared error of the resulting estimate, that is, it provides an optimal bandwidth tailored to *all* x in the support of $f(x)$.

The integrated squared difference between $\hat{f}$ and f is

$$\int \left[\hat{f}(x) - f(x) \right]^2 dx = \int \hat{f}(x)^2 \, dx - 2 \int \hat{f}(x) f(x) \, dx + \int f(x)^2 \, dx.$$
(1.19)

As the third term on the right-hand side of (1.19) is unrelated to h, choosing h to minimize (1.19) is therefore equivalent to minimizing

$$\int \hat{f}(x)^2 \, dx - 2 \int \hat{f}(x) f(x) \, dx$$
(1.20)

with respect to h. In the second term, $\int \hat{f}(x) f(x) \, dx$ can be written as $E_X[\hat{f}(X)]$, where $E_X(\cdot)$ denotes expectation with respect to X and not with respect to the random observations $\{X_j\}_{j=1}^n$ used for computing $\hat{f}(\cdot)$. Therefore, we may estimate $E_X[\hat{f}(X)]$ by $n^{-1} \sum_{i=1}^n \hat{f}_{-i}(X_i)$ (i.e., replacing E_X by its sample mean), where

$$\hat{f}_{-i}(X_i) = \frac{1}{(n-1)h} \sum_{j=1, j \neq i}^n k \left(\frac{X_i - X_j}{h} \right)$$
(1.21)

is the leave-one-out kernel estimator of $f(X_i)$.[3] Finally, we estimate the first term $\int \hat{f}(x)^2 \, dx$ by

$$\int \hat{f}(x)^2 \, dx = \frac{1}{n^2 h^2} \sum_{i=1}^n \sum_{j=1}^n \int k \left(\frac{X_i - x}{h} \right) k \left(\frac{X_j - x}{h} \right) dx$$

$$= \frac{1}{n^2 h} \sum_{i=1}^n \sum_{j=1}^n \bar{k} \left(\frac{X_i - X_j}{h} \right),$$
(1.22)

where $\bar{k}(v) = \int k(u) k(v-u) \, du$ is the twofold convolution kernel derived from $k(\cdot)$. If $k(v) = \exp(-v^2/2)/\sqrt{2\pi}$, a standard normal kernel, then $\bar{k}(v) = \exp(-v^2/4)/\sqrt{4\pi}$, a normal kernel (i.e., normal PDF) with mean zero and variance two, which follows since two independent $N(0,1)$ random variables sum to a $N(0,2)$ random variable.

---

[3]Here we emphasize that it is important to use the leave-one-out kernel estimator for computing $E_X(\cdot)$ above. This is because the expectations operator presumes that the X and the X_j's are independent of one another. Without using the leave-one-out estimator, the cross-validation method will break down; see Exercise 1.6 (iii).

Least squares cross-validation therefore chooses h to minimize

$$CV_f(h) = \frac{1}{n^2 h} \sum_{i=1}^{n} \sum_{j=1}^{n} \bar{k}\left(\frac{X_i - X_j}{h}\right)$$

$$- \frac{2}{n(n-1)h} \sum_{i=1}^{n} \sum_{j\neq i, j=1}^{n} k\left(\frac{X_i - X_j}{h}\right), \quad (1.23)$$

which is typically undertaken using numerical search algorithms.

It can be shown that the leading term of $CV_f(h)$ is CV_{f0} given by (ignoring a term unrelated to h; see Exercise 1.6)

$$CV_{f0}(h) = B_1 h^4 + \frac{\kappa}{nh}, \quad (1.24)$$

where $B_1 = (\kappa_2^2/4)\left[\int [f^{(2)}(x)]^2\, dx\right]$ ($\kappa_2 = \int v^2 k(v)\, dv$, $\kappa = \int k^2(v)\, dv$). Thus, as long as $f^{(2)}(x)$ does not vanish for (almost) all x, we have $B_1 > 0$.

Let h^0 denote the value of h that minimizes CV_{f0}. Simple calculus shows that $h^0 = c_0 n^{-1/5}$ where

$$c_0 = [\kappa/(4B_1)]^{1/5} = \kappa^{1/5} \kappa_2^{-2/5} \left\{\left[\int f^{(2)}(x)\right]^2 dx\right\}^{-1/5}.$$

A comparison of h^0 with h_{opt} in (1.17) reveals that the two are identical, i.e., $h^0 \equiv h_{\text{opt}}$. This arises because h_{opt} minimizes $\int \mathrm{E}[\hat{f}(x) - f(x)]^2\, dx$, while h^0 minimizes $\mathrm{E}[CV_f(h)]$, the leading term of $CV_f(h)$. It can be easily seen that $\mathrm{E}[CV_f(h)] + \int f(x)^2\, dx$ is an alternative version of $\int \mathrm{E}[\hat{f}(x) - f(x)]^2\, dx$; hence, $\mathrm{E}[CV_f(h)] + \int f(x)^2\, dx$ also estimates $\int \mathrm{E}[\hat{f}(x) - f(x)]^2\, dx$. Given that $\int f(x)^2\, dx$ is unrelated to h, one would expect that h^0 and h_{opt} should be the same.

Let $\hat{h}$ denote the value of h that minimizes $CV_f(h)$. Given that $CV_f(h) = CV_{f0} + (s.o.)$, where $(s.o.)$ denotes smaller order terms (than CV_{f0}) and terms unrelated to h, it can be shown that $\hat{h} = h^0 + o_p(h^0)$, or, equivalently, that

$$\frac{\hat{h} - h^0}{h^0} \equiv \frac{\hat{h}}{h^0} - 1 \to 0 \text{ in probability.} \quad (1.25)$$

Intuitively, (1.25) is easy to understand because $CV_f(h) = CV_{f0}(h) + (s.o.)$, thus asymptotically an h that minimizes $CV_f(h)$ should be close to an h that minimizes $CV_{f0}(h)$; therefore, we expect that $\hat{h}$ and h^0 will be close to each other in the sense of (1.25). Härdle, Hall and Marron (1988) showed that $(\hat{h} - h^0)/h^0 = O_p(n^{-1/10})$, which indeed converges to zero (in probability) but at an extremely slow rate.

We again underscore the need to use the leave-one-out kernel estimator when constructing CV_f as given in (1.23). If instead one were to use the standard kernel estimator, least squares cross-validation will break down, yielding $\hat{h} = 0$. Exercise 1.6 shows that if one does not use the leave-one-out kernel estimator when estimating $f(X_i)$, then $h = 0$ minimizes the objective function, which of course violates the consistency condition that $nh \to \infty$ as $n \to \infty$.

Here we implicitly impose the restriction that $f^{(2)}(x)$ is not a zero function, which rules out the case for which $f(x)$ is a uniform PDF. In fact this condition can be relaxed. Stone (1984) showed that, as long as $f(x)$ is bounded, then the least squares cross-validation method will select h optimally in the sense that

$$\frac{\int [\hat{f}(x, \hat{h}) - f(x)]^2 \, dx}{\inf_h \int [\hat{f}(x, h) - f(x)]^2 \, dx} \to 1 \text{ almost surely,} \qquad (1.26)$$

where $\hat{f}(x, \hat{h})$ denotes the kernel estimator of $f(x)$ with cross-validation selected $\hat{h}$, and $\hat{f}(x, h)$ is the kernel estimator with a generic h. Obviously, the ratio defined in (1.26) should be greater than or equal to one for any n. Therefore, Stone's (1984) result states that, asymptotically, cross-validated smoothing parameter selection is optimal in the sense of minimizing the estimation integrated square error. In Exercise 1.16 we further discuss the intuition underlying why $\hat{h} \to 0$ even when $f(x)$ is a uniform PDF.

1.3.2 Likelihood Cross-Validation

Likelihood cross-validation is another automatic data-driven method for selecting the smoothing parameter h. This approach yields a density estimate which has an entropy theoretic interpretation, since the estimate will be close to the actual density in a Kullback-Leibler sense. This approach was proposed by Duin (1976).

Likelihood cross-validation chooses h to maximize the (leave-one-out) log likelihood function given by

$$\mathcal{L} = \ln L = \sum_{i=1}^{n} \ln \hat{f}_{-i}(X_i),$$

where $\hat{f}_{-i}(X_i)$ is the leave-one-out kernel estimator of $f(X_i)$ defined in (1.21). The main problem with likelihood cross-validation is that it is severely affected by the tail behavior of $f(x)$ and can lead to inconsistent results for fat tailed distributions when using popular kernel functions (see Hall (1987a, 1987b)). For this reason the likelihood cross-validation method has elicited little interest in the statistical literature.

However, the likelihood cross-validation method may work well for a range of standard distributions (i.e., thin tailed). We consider the performance of likelihood cross-validation in Section 1.3.3, when we compare the impact of different bandwidth selection methods on the resulting density estimate, and in Section 1.13, where we consider empirical applications.

1.3.3   An Illustration of Data-Driven Bandwidth Selection

Figure 1.1 presents kernel estimates constructed from $n = 500$ observations drawn from a simulated bimodal distribution. The second order Gaussian (normal) kernel was used throughout, and least squares cross-validation was used to select the bandwidth for the estimate appearing in the upper left plot of the figure, with $h_{\text{lscv}} = 0.19$. We also plot the estimate based on the normal reference rule-of-thumb ($h_{\text{ref}} = 0.34$) along with an undersmoothed estimate ($1/5 \times h_{\text{lscv}}$) and an oversmoothed estimate ($5 \times h_{\text{lscv}}$).[4]

Figure 1.1 reveals that least squares cross-validation appears to yield a reasonable density estimate for this data, while the reference rule-of-thumb is inappropriate as it oversmooths somewhat. Extreme oversmoothing can lead to a unimodal estimate which completely obscures the true bimodal nature of the underlying distribution. Also, undersmoothing leads to too many false modes. See Exercise 1.17 for an empirical application that investigates the effects of under- and oversmoothing on the resulting density estimate.

1.4   Univariate CDF Estimation

In Section 1.1 we introduced the empirical CDF estimator $F_n(x)$ given in (1.2), while Exercise 1.4 shows that it is a $\sqrt{n}$-consistent estimator

---

[4]Likelihood cross-validation yielded a bandwidth of $h_{\text{mlcv}} = 0.15$, which results in a density estimate virtually identical to that based upon least squares cross-validation for this dataset.

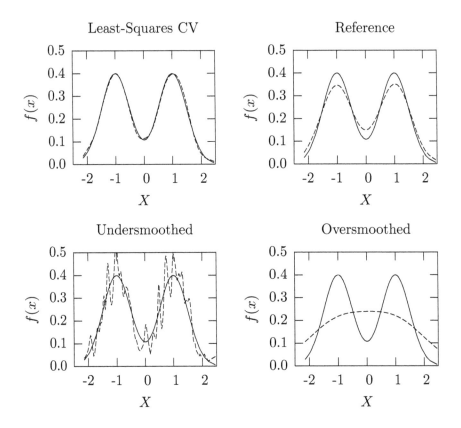

Figure 1.1: Univariate kernel estimates of a mixture of normals using least squares cross-validation, the normal reference rule-of-thumb, undersmoothing, and oversmoothing ($n = 500$). The correct parametric data generating process appears as the solid line, the kernel estimate as the dashed line.

of $F(x)$. However, this empirical CDF $F_n(x)$ is not smooth as it jumps by $1/n$ at each sample realization point. One can, however, obtain a smoothed estimate of $F(x)$ by integrating $\hat{f}(x)$. Define

$$\hat{F}(x) = \int_{-\infty}^{x} \hat{f}(v)\, dv = \frac{1}{n}\sum_{i=1}^{n} G\left(\frac{x - X_i}{h}\right), \qquad (1.27)$$

where $G(x) = \int_{-\infty}^{x} k(v)\, dv$ is a CDF (which follows directly because $k(\cdot)$ is a PDF; see (1.10)). The next theorem provides the MSE of $\hat{F}(x)$.

Theorem 1.2. *Under conditions given in Bowman, Hall and Prvan (1998), in particular, assuming that $F(x)$ is twice continuously differentiable, $k(v) = d\,G(v)/dv$ is bounded, symmetric, and compactly supported, and that $d^2 F(x)/dx^2$ is Hölder-continuous, $0 \leq h \leq Cn^{-\epsilon}$ for some $0 < \epsilon < \frac{1}{8}$, then as $n \to \infty$,*

$$\mathrm{MSE}(\hat{F}) = \mathrm{E}\left[\hat{F}(x) - F(x)\right]^2$$
$$= c_0(x)n^{-1} - c_1(x)hn^{-1} + c_2(x)h^4 + o\left(h^4 + hn^{-1}\right),$$

where $c_0 = F(x)(1 - F(x))$, $c_1(x) = \alpha_0 f(x)$, $\alpha_0 = 2\int vG(v)k(v)\,dv$, $f(x) = d\,F(x)/dx$, $c_2(x) = [(\kappa_2/2)F^{(2)}(x)]^2$, $\kappa_2 = \int v^2 k(v)\,dv$, and where $F^{(s)}(x) = d^s F(x)/dx^s$ is the sth derivative of $F(x)$.

Proof. Note that $\mathrm{E}\left[\hat{F}(x)\right] = \mathrm{E}\left[G\left(\frac{x-X_i}{h}\right)\right]$. Then we have $(\int = \int_{-\infty}^{\infty})$

$$\mathrm{E}\left[G\left(\frac{x - X_i}{h}\right)\right] = \int G\left(\frac{x - z}{h}\right) f(z)dz$$
$$= h\int G(v)f(x - hv)\,dv = -\int G(v)dF(x - hv)$$
$$= -\left[G(v)F(x - hv)\right]\big|_{v=-\infty}^{v=\infty} + \int k(v)F(x - hv)\,dv$$
$$= \int k(v)\left[F(x) - F^{(1)}(x)hv + (1/2)h^2 F^{(2)}(x)v^2\right]dv$$
$$+ o(h^2)$$
$$= F(x) + (1/2)\kappa_2 h^2 F^{(2)}(x) + o(h^2), \qquad (1.28)$$

where at the second equality above we used

$$-\int_{\infty}^{-\infty}[\ldots]\,dv = \int_{-\infty}^{\infty}[\ldots]\,dv.$$

Also note that we did not use a Taylor expansion in $\int G(v)F(x-hv)\,dv$ since $\int v^m G(v)\,dv = +\infty$ for any $m \geq 0$. We first used integration by parts to get $k(v)$, and then used the Taylor expansion since $\int v^m k(v)\,dv$ is usually finite. For example, if $k(v)$ has bounded support or $k(v)$ is a standard normal kernel function, then $\int v^m k(v)\,dv$ is finite for any $m \geq 0$.

Similarly,

$$
\mathrm{E}\left[G^2\left(\frac{x-X_i}{h}\right)\right] = \int G^2\left(\frac{x-z}{h}\right)f(z)dz = h\int G^2(v)f(x-hv)\,dv
$$
$$
= -\int G^2(v)dF(x-hv)
$$
$$
= 2\int G(v)k(v)F(x-hv)\,dv
$$
$$
= 2\int G(v)k(v)[F(x)-F^{(1)}(x)hv]\,dv + O(h^2)
$$
$$
= F(x) - \alpha_0 h f(x) + O(h^2),
$$

$$(1.29)$$

where $\alpha_0 = 2\int vG(v)k(v)\,dv$, and where we have used the fact that

$$
2\int_{-\infty}^{\infty} G(v)k(v)\,dv = \int_{-\infty}^{\infty} dG^2(v) = G^2(\infty) - G^2(-\infty) = 1,
$$

because $G(\cdot)$ is a (user-specified) CDF kernel function.

From (1.28) we have $\mathrm{bias}[\hat{F}(x)] = (1/2)\kappa_2 h^2 F^{(2)}(x) + o(h^2)$, and from (1.28) and (1.29) we have

$$
\mathrm{var}\left[\hat{F}(x)\right] = n^{-1}\mathrm{var}\left[G\left(\frac{x-X_i}{h}\right)\right]
$$
$$
= n^{-1}\left\{\mathrm{E}\left[G^2\left(\frac{x-X_i}{h}\right)\right] - \left[\mathrm{E}\,G\left(\frac{x-X_i}{h}\right)\right]^2\right\}
$$
$$
= n^{-1}F(x)[1-F(x)] - \alpha_0 f(x)hn^{-1} + o(h/n).
$$

Hence,

$$
\mathrm{E}\left(\hat{F}(x)-F(x)\right)^2 = \left[\mathrm{bias}\left(\hat{F}(x)\right)\right]^2 + \mathrm{var}\left[\hat{F}(x)\right]
$$
$$
= n^{-1}F(x)\left[1-F(x)\right] + h^4(\kappa_2/2)^2\left[F^{(2)}(x)\right]^2
$$
$$
- \alpha_0 f(x)\frac{h}{n} + o(h^4 + n^{-1}h).
$$

$$(1.30)$$

This completes the proof of Theorem 1.2. $\qquad\square$

From Theorem 1.2 we immediately obtain the following result on the IMSE of $\hat{F}$:

$$\text{IMSE}(\hat{F}) = \int \text{E}\left[\hat{F}(x) - F(x)\right]^2 dx$$
$$= C_0 n^{-1} - C_1 h n^{-1} + C_2 h^4 + o\left(h^4 + h n^{-1}\right), \quad (1.31)$$

where $C_j = \int c_j(x)\,dx$ $(j = 0, 1, 2)$. Letting h_0 denote the value of h that minimizes the leading term of IMSE, we obtain

$$h_0 = a_0 n^{-1/3},$$

where $a_0 = [C_1/(4C_2)]^{1/3}$, hence the optimal smoothing parameter for estimating univariate a CDF has a faster rate of convergence than the optimal smoothing parameter for estimating a univariate PDF ($n^{-1/3}$ versus $n^{-1/5}$). With $h \sim n^{-1/3}$, we have $h^2 = O(n^{-2/3}) = o(n^{-1/2})$. Hence, $\sqrt{n}[\hat{F}(x) - F(x)] \to N(0, F(x)[1 - F(x)])$ in distribution by the Liapunov central limit theorem (CLT); see Theorem A.5 in Appendix A for this and a range of other useful CLTs.

As is the case for nonparametric PDF estimation, nonparametric CDF estimation has widespread potential application though it is not nearly as widely used. For instance, it can be used to test stochastic dominance without imposing parametric assumptions on the underlying CDFs; see, e.g., Barrett and Donald (2003) and Linton, Whang and Maasoumi (2005).

1.5   Univariate CDF Bandwidth Selection: Cross-Validation Methods

Bowman et al. (1998) suggest choosing h for $\hat{F}(x)$ by minimizing the following cross-validation function:

$$CV_F(h) = \frac{1}{n}\sum_{i=1}^{n} \int \left\{\mathbf{1}(X_i \leq x) - \hat{F}_{-i}(x)\right\}^2 dx, \qquad (1.32)$$

where $\hat{F}_{-i}(x) = (n-1)^{-1}\sum_{j\neq i}^{n} G\left(\frac{x-X_j}{h}\right)$ is the leave-one-out estimator of $F(x)$.

Bowman et al. (1998) show that $CV_F = \text{E}[CV_F] + (s.o.)$ and that

(see Exercise 1.9)

$$\mathrm{E}[CV_F(h)] = \int F(1-F)\,dx + \frac{1}{n-1}\int F(1-F)\,dx - C_1 h n^{-1}$$
$$+ C_2 h^4 + o\left(hn^{-1} + h^4\right).$$

$$(1.33)$$

We observe that (1.33) has the same leading term as $\mathrm{IMSE}(\hat{F})$ given in (1.31). Thus, asymptotically, selecting h via cross-validation leads to the same asymptotic optimality property for $\hat{F}(x)$ that would arise when using h_0, the optimal deterministic smoothing parameter. If we let $\hat{h}$ denote the cross-validated smoothing parameter, then it can be shown that $\hat{h}/h_0 \to 1$ in probability. Note that when using $\hat{h}$, the asymptotic distribution of $\hat{F}(x, \hat{h})$ is the same as $\hat{F}(x, h_0)$ (by using a stochastic equicontinuity argument as outlined in Appendix A), that is,

$$\sqrt{n}\left(\hat{F}(x) - F(x)\right) \xrightarrow{d} N\left(0, F(x)(1 - F(x))\right), \qquad (1.34)$$

where $\hat{F}(x)$ is defined in (1.27) with h replaced by $\hat{h}$. Note that no bias term appears in (1.34) since $\mathrm{bias}(\hat{F}(x)) = O(h_0^2) = O(n^{-2/3}) = o(n^{-1/2})$, which was not the case for PDF estimation. Here the squared bias term has order smaller than the leading variance term of $O(n^{-1})$ (i.e., $\mathrm{var}(\hat{F}(x)) = O(n^{-1})$).

We now turn our attention to a generalization of the univariate kernel estimators developed above, namely multivariate kernel estimators. Again, we consider only the continuous case in this chapter; we tackle discrete and mixed continuous and discrete data cases in Chapters 3 and 4.

1.6 Multivariate Density Estimation

Suppose that $X_1, \ldots, X_n$ constitute an i.i.d. q-vector ($X_i \in \mathbb{R}^q$, for some $q > 1$) having a common PDF $f(x) = f(x_1, x_2, \ldots, x_q)$. Let X_{is} denote the sth component of X_i ($s = 1, \ldots, q$). Using a "product kernel function" constructed from the product of univariate kernel functions, we estimate the PDF $f(x)$ by

$$\hat{f}(x) = \frac{1}{nh_1 \ldots h_q} \sum_{i=1}^{n} K\left(\frac{X_i - x}{h}\right), \qquad (1.35)$$

where $K\left(\frac{X_i-x}{h}\right) = k\left(\frac{X_{i1}-x_1}{h_1}\right) \times \cdots \times k\left(\frac{X_{iq}-x_q}{h_q}\right)$, and where $k(\cdot)$ is a univariate kernel function satisfying (1.10).

The proof of MSE consistency of $\hat{f}(x)$ is similar to the univariate case. In particular, one can show that

$$\text{bias}\left(\hat{f}(x)\right) = \frac{\kappa_2}{2}\sum_{s=1}^{q} h_s^2 f_{ss}(x) + O\left(\sum_{s=1}^{q} h_s^3\right), \qquad (1.36)$$

where $f_{ss}(x)$ is the second order derivative of $f(x)$ with respect to x_s, $\kappa_2 = \int v^2 k(v)\,dv$, and one can also show that

$$\text{var}\left(\hat{f}(x)\right) = \frac{1}{nh_1\ldots h_q}\left[\kappa^q f(x) + O\left(\sum_{s=1}^{q} h_s^2\right)\right] = O\left(\frac{1}{nh_1\ldots h_q}\right), \qquad (1.37)$$

where $\kappa = \int k^2(v)\,dv$. The proofs of (1.36) and (1.37), which are similar to the univariate X case, are left as an exercise (see Exercise 1.11).

Summarizing, we obtain the result

$$\text{MSE}\left(\hat{f}(x)\right) = \left[\text{bias}\left(\hat{f}(x)\right)\right]^2 + \text{var}\left(\hat{f}(x)\right)$$

$$= O\left(\left(\sum_{s=1}^{q} h_s^2\right)^2 + (nh_1\ldots h_q)^{-1}\right).$$

Hence, if as $n \to \infty$, $\max_{1\leq s\leq q} h_s \to 0$ and $nh_1\ldots h_q \to \infty$, then we have $\hat{f}(x) \to f(x)$ in MSE, which implies that $\hat{f}(x) \to f(x)$ in probability.

As we saw in the univariate case, the optimal smoothing parameters h_s should balance the squared bias and variance terms, i.e., $h_s^4 = O\left((nh_1\ldots h_q)^{-1}\right)$ for all s. Thus, we have $h_s = c_s n^{-1/(q+4)}$ for some positive constant c_s ($s = 1,\ldots,q$). The cross-validation methods discussed in Section 1.3 can be easily generalized to the multivariate data setting, and we can show that least squares cross-validation can optimally select the h_s's in the sense outlined in Section 1.3 (see Section 1.8 below).

We briefly remark on the independence assumption invoked for the proofs presented above. Our assumption was that the data is independent across the i index. Note that no restrictions were placed on the s index for each component X_{is} ($s = 1,\ldots,q$). The product kernel is used simply for convenience, and it certainly *does not* require that the X_{is}'s are independent across the s index. In other words, the multivariate kernel density estimator (1.35) is capable of capturing general dependence among the different components of X_i. Furthermore, we shall relax the "independence across observations" assumption in Chapter 18, and will see that all of the results developed above carry over to the weakly dependent data setting.

1.7   Multivariate Bandwidth Selection: Rule-of-Thumb and Plug-In Methods

In Section 1.2 we discussed the use of the so-called normal reference rule-of-thumb and plug-in methods in a univariate setting. The generalization of the univariate normal reference rule-of-thumb to a multivariate setting is straightforward. Letting q be the dimension of X_i, one can choose $h_s = c_s X_{s,sd} n^{-1/(4+q)}$ for $s = 1, \ldots, q$, where $X_{s,sd}$ is the sample standard deviation of $\{X_{is}\}_{i=1}^n$ and c_s is a positive constant. In practice one still faces the problem of how to choose c_s. The choice of $c_s = 1.06$ for all $s = 1, \ldots, q$ is computationally attractive; however, this selection treats the different X_{is}'s symmetrically. In practice, should the joint PDF change rapidly in one dimension (say in x_1) but change slowly in another (say in x_2), then one should select a relatively small value of c_1 (hence a small h_1) and a relatively large value for c_2 (h_2). Unlike the cross-validation methods that we will discuss shortly, rule-of-thumb methods do not offer this flexibility.

For plug-in methods, on the other hand, the leading (squared) bias and variance terms of $\hat{f}(x)$ must be estimated, and then $h_1, \ldots, h_q$ must be chosen to minimize the leading MSE term of $\hat{f}(x)$. However, the leading MSE term of $\hat{f}(x)$ involves the unknown $f(x)$ and its partial derivative functions, and pilot bandwidths must be selected for *each* variable in order to estimate these unknown functions. How to best select the initial pilot smoothing parameters can be tricky in high-dimensional settings, and the plug-in methods are not widely used in applied settings to the best of our knowledge, nor would we counsel their use other than for exploratory data analysis.

1.8 Multivariate Bandwidth Selection: Cross-Validation Methods

1.8.1 Least Squares Cross-Validation

The univariate least squares cross-validation method discussed in Section 1.3.1 can be readily generalized to the multivariate density estimation setting. Replacing the univariate kernel function in (1.23) by a multivariate product kernel, the cross-validation objective function now becomes

$$CV_f(h_1, \ldots, h_q) = \frac{1}{n^2} \sum_{i=1}^{n} \sum_{j=1}^{n} \bar{K}_h(X_i, X_j)$$

$$- \frac{2}{n(n-1)} \sum_{i=1}^{n} \sum_{j \neq i, j=1}^{n} K_h(X_i, X_j), \quad (1.38)$$

where

$$K_h(X_i, X_j) = \prod_{s=1}^{q} h_s^{-1} k \left(\frac{X_{is} - X_{js}}{h_s} \right),$$

$$\bar{K}_h(X_i, X_j) = \prod_{s=1}^{q} h_s^{-1} \bar{k} \left(\frac{X_{is} - X_{js}}{h_s} \right),$$

and $\bar{k}(v)$ is the twofold convolution kernel based upon $k(\cdot)$, where $k(\cdot)$ is a univariate kernel function satisfying (1.10).

Exercise 1.12 shows that the leading term of $CV_f(h_1, \ldots, h_q)$ is given by (ignoring a term unrelated to the h_s's)

$$CV_{f0}(h_1, \ldots, h_q) = \int \left[\sum_{s=1}^{q} B_s(x) h_s^2 \right]^2 dx + \frac{\kappa^q}{n h_1 \ldots h_q}, \quad (1.39)$$

where $B_s(x) = (\kappa_2/2) f_{ss}(x)$.

Defining a_s via $h_s = a_s n^{-1/(q+4)}$ $(s = 1, \ldots, q)$, we have

$$CV_{f0}(h_1, \ldots, h_q) = n^{-4/(q+4)} \chi_f(a_1, \ldots, a_q), \quad (1.40)$$

where

$$\chi_f(a_1, \ldots, a_q) = \int \left[\sum_{s=1}^{q} B_s(x) a_s^2 \right]^2 dx + \frac{\kappa^q}{a_1 \ldots a_q}. \quad (1.41)$$

Let the a_s^0's be the values of the a_s's that minimize $\chi_f(a_1, \ldots, a_q)$. Under the same conditions used in the univariate case and, in addition, assuming that $f_{ss}(x)$ is not a zero function for all s, Li and Zhou (2005) show that each a_s^0 is uniquely defined, positive, and finite (see Exercise 1.10). Let $h_1^0, \ldots, h_q^0$ denote the values of $h_1, \ldots, h_q$ that minimize CV_{f0}. Then from (1.40) we know that $h_s^0 = a_s^0 n^{-1/(q+4)} = O\left(n^{-1/(q+4)}\right)$.

Exercise 1.12 shows that CV_{f0} is also the leading term of $E[CV_f]$. Therefore, the nonstochastic smoothing parameters h_s^0 can be interpreted as optimal smoothing parameters that minimize the leading term of the IMSE.

Let $\hat{h}_1, \ldots, \hat{h}_q$ denote the values of $h_1, \ldots, h_q$ that minimize CV_f. Using the fact that $CV_f = CV_{f0} + (s.o.)$, we can show that $\hat{h}_s = h_s^0 + o_p(h_s^0)$. Thus, we have

$$\frac{\hat{h}_s - h_s^0}{h_s^0} = \frac{\hat{h}_s}{h_s^0} - 1 \to 0 \quad \text{in probability, for } s = 1, \ldots, q. \quad (1.42)$$

Therefore, smoothing parameters selected via cross-validation have the same asymptotic optimality properties as the nonstochastic optimal smoothing parameters.

Note that if $f_{ss}(x) = 0$ almost everywhere (a.e.) for some s, then $B_s = 0$ and the above result does not hold. Stone (1984) shows that the cross-validation method still selects $h_1, \ldots, h_q$ optimally in the sense that the integrated estimation square error is minimized; see also Ouyang et al. (2006) for a more detailed discussion of this case.

1.8.2   Likelihood Cross-Validation

Likelihood cross-validation for multivariate models follows directly via (multivariate) maximization of the likelihood function outlined in Section 1.3.2, hence we do not go into further details here. However, we do point out that, though straightforward to implement, it suffers from the same defects outlined for the univariate case in the presence of fat tail distributions (i.e., it has a tendency to oversmooth in such situations).

1.9   Asymptotic Normality of Density Estimators

In this section we show that $\hat{f}(x)$ has an asymptotic normal distribution. The most popular CLT is the Lindeberg-Levy CLT given in

Theorem A.3 of Appendix A, which states that $n^{1/2}[n^{-1}\sum_{i=1}^{n} Z_i] \to$ $N(0,\sigma^2)$ in distribution, provided that Z_i is i.i.d. $(0,\sigma^2)$. Though the Lindeberg-Levy CLT can be used to derive the asymptotic distribution of various semiparametric estimators discussed in Chapters 7, 8, and 9, it cannot be used to derive the asymptotic distribution of $\hat{f}(x)$. This is because $\hat{f}(x) = n^{-1}\sum_i Z_{i,n}$, where the summand $Z_{i,n} = K_h(X_i, x)$ depends on n (since $h = h(n)$). We shall make use of the Liapunov CLT given in Theorem A.5 of Appendix A

Theorem 1.3. *Let $X_1, \ldots, X_n$ be i.i.d. q-vectors with its PDF $f(\cdot)$ having three-times bounded continuous derivatives. Let x be an interior point of the support of X. If, as $n \to \infty$, $h_s \to 0$ for all $s = 1, \ldots, q$, $nh_1 \ldots h_q \to \infty$, and $(nh_1 \ldots h_q)\sum_{s=1}^{q} h_s^6 \to 0$, then*

$$\sqrt{nh_1 \ldots h_q}\left[\hat{f}(x) - f(x) - \frac{\kappa_2}{2}\sum_{s=1}^{q} h_s^2 f_{ss}(x)\right] \xrightarrow{d} N(0, \kappa^q f(x)).$$

Proof. Using (1.36) and (1.37), one can easily show that

$$\sqrt{nh_1 \ldots h_q}\left[\hat{f}(x) - f(x) - \frac{\kappa_2}{2}\sum_{s=1}^{q} h_s^2 f_{ss}(x)\right]$$

has asymptotic mean zero and asymptotic variance $\kappa^q f(x)$, i.e.,

$$\sqrt{nh_1 \ldots h_q}\left[\hat{f}(x) - f(x) - \frac{\kappa_2}{2}\sum_{s=1}^{q} h_s^2 f_{ss}(x)\right]$$

$$= \sqrt{nh_1 \ldots h_q}\left[\hat{f}(x) - \mathrm{E}\left(\hat{f}(x)\right)\right]$$

$$\quad + \sqrt{nh_1 \ldots h_q}\left[\mathrm{E}\left(\hat{f}(x)\right) - f(x) - \frac{\kappa_2}{2}\sum_{s=1}^{q} h_s^2 f_{ss}(x)\right]$$

$$= \sqrt{nh_1 \ldots h_q}\left[\hat{f}(x) - \mathrm{E}\left(\hat{f}(x)\right)\right]$$

$$\quad + O\left(\sqrt{nh_1 \ldots h_q}\sum_{s=1}^{q} h_s^3\right) \quad \text{(by (1.36))}$$

$$= \sum_{i=1}^{n}(nh_1 \ldots h_q)^{-1/2}$$

$$\quad \times \left[K\left(\frac{X_i - x}{h}\right) - \mathrm{E}\left(K\left(\frac{X_i - x}{h}\right)\right)\right] + o(1)$$

$$\equiv \sum_{i=1}^{n} Z_{n,i} + o(1) \xrightarrow{d} N\left(0, \kappa^q f(x)\right),$$

by Liapunov's CLT, provided we can verify that Liapunov's CLT condition (A.21) holds, where

$$Z_{n,i} = (nh_1 \ldots h_q)^{-1/2} \left[K \left(\frac{X_i - x}{h} \right) - \mathrm{E} \left(K \left(\frac{X_i - x}{h} \right) \right) \right]$$

and

$$\sum_{i=1}^{n} \sigma_{n,i}^2 \overset{\text{def}}{=} \sum_{i=1}^{n} \mathrm{var}(Z_{n,i}) = \kappa^q f(x) + o(1)$$

by (1.37). Pagan and Ullah (1999, p. 40) show that (A.21) holds under the condition given in Theorem 1.3. The condition that $\int k(v)^{2+\delta} \, dv < \infty$ for some $\delta > 0$ used in Pagan and Ullah is implied by our assumption that $k(v)$ is nonnegative and bounded, and that $\int k(v) \, dv = 1$, because $\int k(v)^{2+\delta} \, dv \leq C \int k(v) \, dv = C$ is finite, where $C = \sup_{v \in \mathbb{R}^q} k(v)^{1+\delta}$. $\square$

1.10   Uniform Rates of Convergence

Up to now we have demonstrated only the case of pointwise and IMSE consistency (which implies consistency in probability). In this section we generalize pointwise consistency in order to obtain a stronger "uniform consistency" result. We will prove that nonparametric kernel estimators are uniformly almost surely consistent and derive their uniform almost sure rate of convergence. Almost sure convergence implies convergence in probability; however, the converse is not true, i.e., convergence in probability may not imply convergence almost surely; see Serfling (1980) for specific examples.

We have already established pointwise consistency for an interior point in the support of X. However, it turns out that popular kernel functions such as (1.9) may not lead to consistent estimation of $f(x)$ when x is at the boundary of its support, hence we need to exclude the boundary ranges when considering the uniform convergence rate. This highlights an important aspect of kernel estimation in general, and a number of kernel estimators introduced in later sections are motivated by the desire to mitigate such "boundary effects." We first show that when x is at (or near) the boundary of its support, $\hat{f}(x)$ may not be a consistent estimator of $f(x)$.

Consider the case where X is univariate having bounded support. For simplicity we assume that $X \in [0, 1]$. The pointwise consistency result $\hat{f}(x) - f(x) = o_p(1)$ obtained earlier requires that x lie in the interior of its support. Exercise 1.13 shows that, for x at the boundary of its support, MSE($\hat{f}(x)$) may not be $o(1)$. Therefore, some modifications may be needed to consistently estimate $f(x)$ for x at the boundary of its support. Typical modifications include the use of boundary kernels or data reflection (see Gasser and Müller (1979), Hall and Wehrly (1991), and Scott (1992, pp. 148–149)). By way of example, consider the case where x lies on its lowermost boundary, i.e., $x = 0$, hence $\hat{f}(0) = (nh)^{-1} \sum_{i=1}^{n} K((X_i - 0)/h)$. Exercise 1.13 shows that for this case, $E[\hat{f}(0)] = f(0)/2 + O(h)$. Therefore, bias$[\hat{f}(0)] = E[\hat{f}(0)] - f(0) = -f(0)/2 + O(h)$, which will not converge to zero if $f(0) \neq 0$ (when $f(0) > 0$).

In the literature, various boundary kernels are proposed to overcome the boundary (bias) problem. For example, a simple boundary corrected kernel is given by (assuming that $X \in [0,1]$)

$$
k_h(x,y) = \begin{cases}
h^{-1}k\left(\frac{y-x}{h}\right) / \int_{-x/h}^{\infty} k(v)\,dv & \text{if } x \in [0,h) \\
h^{-1}k\left(\frac{y-x}{h}\right) & \text{if } x \in [h, 1-h] \\
h^{-1}k\left(\frac{y-x}{h}\right) / \int_{-\infty}^{(1-x)/h} k(v)\,dv & \text{if } x \in (1-h, 1],
\end{cases}
\tag{1.43}
$$

where $k(\cdot)$ is a second order kernel satisfying (1.10). Now, we estimate $f(x)$ by

$$
\hat{f}(x) = \frac{1}{n} \sum_{i=1}^{n} k_h(x, X_i),
\tag{1.44}
$$

where $k_h(x, X_i)$ is defined in (1.43). Exercise 1.14 shows that the above boundary corrected kernel successfully overcomes the boundary problem.

We now establish the uniform almost sure convergence rate of $\hat{f}(x) - f(x)$ for $x \in \mathcal{S}$, where $\mathcal{S}$ is a bounded set excluding the boundary range of the support of X. In the above example, when the support of x is $[0,1]$, we can choose $\mathcal{S} = [\epsilon, 1 - \epsilon]$ for arbitrarily *small* positive ϵ $(0 < \epsilon < 1/2)$. We assume that $f(x)$ is bounded below by a positive constant on $\mathcal{S}$.

Theorem 1.4. *Under smoothness conditions on $f(\cdot)$ given in Masry (1996b), and also assuming that $\inf_{x \in \mathcal{S}} f(x) \geq \delta > 0$, we have*

$$
\sup_{x \in \mathcal{S}} \left| \hat{f}(x) - f(x) \right| = O\left(\frac{(\ln(n))^{1/2}}{(nh_1 \ldots h_q)^{1/2}} + \sum_{s=1}^{q} h_s^2 \right) \quad \textit{almost surely.}
$$

A detailed proof of Theorem 1.4 is given in Section 1.12.

Since almost sure convergence implies convergence in probability, the uniform rate also holds in probability, i.e., under the same conditions as in Theorem 1.4, we have

$$\sup_{x \in \mathcal{S}} \left| \hat{f}(x) - f(x) \right| = O_p \left(\frac{(\ln(n))^{1/2}}{(nh_1 \ldots h_q)^{1/2}} + \sum_{s=1}^{q} h_s^2 \right).$$

Using the results of (1.36) and (1.37), we can establish the following uniform MSE rate.

Theorem 1.5. *Assuming that $f(x)$ is twice differentiable with bounded second derivatives, then we have*

$$\sup_{x \in \mathcal{S}} \mathrm{E} \left\{ \left[\hat{f}(x) - f(x) \right]^2 \right\} = O \left(\sum_{s=1}^{q} h_s^4 + (nh_1 \ldots h_q)^{-1} \right).$$

Proof. This follows from (1.36) and (1.37), by noting that $\sup_{x \in \mathcal{S}} f(x)$ and $\sup_{x \in \mathcal{S}} |f_{ss}(x)|$ are both finite ($s = 1, \ldots, q$). $\square$

Note that although convergence in MSE implies convergence in probability, one cannot derive the uniform convergence rate in probability from Theorem 1.5. This is because

$$\mathrm{E} \left\{ \sup_{x \in \mathcal{S}} \left[\hat{f}(x) - f(x) \right]^2 \right\} \neq \sup_{x \in \mathcal{S}} \mathrm{E} \left[\hat{f}(x) - f(x) \right]^2,$$

and

$$\mathrm{P} \left[\sup_{x \in \mathcal{S}} \left| \hat{f}(x) - f(x) \right| > \epsilon \right] \neq \sup_{x \in \mathcal{S}} \mathrm{P} \left[\left| \hat{f}(x) - f(x) \right| > \epsilon \right].$$

The sup and the $\mathrm{E}(\cdot)$ or the $\mathrm{P}(\cdot)$ operators do not commute with one another.

Cheng (1997) proposes alternative (local linear) density estimators that achieve automatic boundary corrections and enjoy some typical optimality properties. Cheng also suggests a data-based bandwidth selector (in the spirit of plug-in rules), and demonstrates that the bandwidth selector is very efficient regardless of whether there are non-smooth boundaries in the support of the density.

1.11 Higher Order Kernel Functions

Recall that decreasing the bandwidth h lowers the bias of a kernel estimator but increases its variance. Higher order kernel functions are devices used for bias reduction which are also capable of reducing the MSE of the resulting estimator. Many popular kernel functions such as the one defined in (1.10) are called "second order" kernels. The order of a kernel, ν ($\nu > 0$), is defined as the order of the first nonzero moment. For example, if $\int uk(u)\,du = 0$, but $\int u^2 k(u)\,du \neq 0$, then $k(\cdot)$ is said to be a second order kernel ($\nu = 2$). A general νth order kernel ($\nu \geq 2$ is an integer) must therefore satisfy the following conditions:

$$(i) \int k(u)\,du = 1,$$

$$(ii) \int u^l k(u)\,du = 0, \quad (l = 1,\ldots,\nu - 1), \qquad (1.45)$$

$$(iii) \int u^\nu k(u)\,du = \kappa_\nu \neq 0.$$

Obviously, when $\nu = 2$, (1.45) collapses to (1.10).

If one replaces the second order kernel in $\hat{f}(x)$ of (1.35) by a νth order kernel function, then as was the case when using a second order kernel, under the assumption that $f(x)$ is νth order differentiable, and assuming that the h_s's all have the same order of magnitude, one can show that

$$\text{bias}\left(\hat{f}(x)\right) = O\left(\sum_{s=1}^{q} h_s^\nu\right) \qquad (1.46)$$

and

$$\text{var}\left(\hat{f}(x)\right) = O\left((nh_1 \ldots h_q)^{-1}\right) \qquad (1.47)$$

(see Exercise 1.15). Hence, we have

$$\text{MSE}\left(\hat{f}(x)\right) = O\left(\sum_{s=1}^{q} h_s^{2\nu} + (nh_1 \ldots h_q)^{-1}\right) \qquad (1.48)$$

and

$$\hat{f}(x) - f(x) = O_p\left(\sum_{s=1}^{q} h_s^\nu + (nh_1 \ldots h_q)^{-1/2}\right).$$

Thus, by using a νth higher order kernel function ($\nu > 2$), one can reduce the order of the bias of $\hat{f}(x)$ from $O\left(\sum_{s=1}^{q} h_s^2\right)$ to $O\left(\sum_{s=1}^{q} h_s^\nu\right)$, and the optimal value of h_s may once again be obtained by balancing the squared bias and the variance, giving $h_s = O\left(n^{-1/(2\nu+q)}\right)$, while the rate of convergence is now $\hat{f}(x) - f(x) = O_p(n^{-\nu/(2\nu+q)})$. Assuming that $f(x)$ is differentiable up to any finite order, then one can choose ν to be sufficiently large, and the resulting rate can be made arbitrarily close to $O_p(n^{-1/2})$. Note, however, that for $\nu > 2$, no nonnegative kernel exists that satisfies (1.45). This means that, necessarily, we have to assign negative weights to some range of the data which implies that one may get *negative* density estimates, clearly an undesirable side-effect. Furthermore, in finite-sample applications nonnegative second order kernels have often been found to yield more stable estimation results than their higher order counterparts. Therefore, higher order kernel functions are mainly used for theoretical purposes; for example, to achieve a $\sqrt{n}$-rate of convergence for some finite dimensional parameter in a semiparametric model, one often has to use high order kernel functions (see Chapter 7 for such an example).

Higher order kernel functions are quite easy to construct. Assuming that $k(u)$ is symmetric around zero,[5] i.e., $k(u) = k(-u)$, then $\int u^{2m+1} k(u)\, du = 0$ for all positive integers m. By way of example, in order to construct a simple fourth order kernel (i.e., $\nu = 4$), one could begin with, say, a second order kernel such as the standard normal kernel, set up a polynomial in its argument, and solve for the roots of the polynomial subject to the desired moment constraints. For example, letting $\Phi(u) = (2\pi)^{-1/2} \exp(-u^2/2)$ be a second order Gaussian kernel, we could begin with the polynomial

$$k(u) = (a + bu^2)\Phi(u), \qquad (1.49)$$

where a and b are two constants which must satisfy the requirements of a fourth order kernel. Letting $k(u)$ satisfy (1.45) with $\nu = 4$ ($\int u^l k(u)\, du = 0$ for $l = 1, 3$ because $k(u)$ is an even function), we therefore only require $\int k(u)\, du = 1$ and $\int u^2 k(u)\, du = 0$. From these two restrictions, one can easily obtain the result $a = 3/2$ and $b = -1/2$. For readers requiring some higher order kernel functions, we provide a few examples based on the second order Gaussian and Epanechnikov kernels, perhaps the two most popular kernels in applied nonparametric estimation. As noted, the fourth order univariate Gaussian kernel

---

[5]Typically, only symmetric kernel functions are used in practice, though see Abadir and Lawford (2004) for recent work involving optimal asymmetric kernels.

is given by the formula

$$k(u) = \left(\frac{3}{2} - \frac{1}{2}u^2\right) \frac{\exp(-u^2/2)}{\sqrt{2\pi}},$$

while the sixth order univariate Gaussian kernel is given by

$$k(u) = \left(\frac{15}{8} - \frac{5}{4}u^2 + \frac{1}{8}u^4\right) \frac{\exp(-u^2/2)}{\sqrt{2\pi}}.$$

The second order univariate Epanechnikov kernel is the *optimal* kernel based on a calculus of variations solution to minimizing the IMSE of the kernel estimator (see Serfling (1980, pp. 40–43)). The univariate second order Epanechnikov kernel is given by the formula

$$k(u) = \begin{cases} \frac{3}{4\sqrt{5}}\left(1 - \frac{1}{5}u^2\right) & \text{if } u^2 < 5.0 \\ 0 & \text{otherwise,} \end{cases}$$

the fourth order univariate Epanechnikov kernel by

$$k(u) = \begin{cases} \frac{3}{4\sqrt{5}}\left(\frac{15}{8} - \frac{7}{8}u^2\right)\left(1 - \frac{1}{5}u^2\right) & \text{if } u^2 < 5.0 \\ 0 & \text{otherwise,} \end{cases}$$

while the sixth order univariate Epanechnikov kernel is given by

$$k(u) = \begin{cases} \frac{3}{4\sqrt{5}}\left(\frac{175}{64} - \frac{105}{32}u^2 + \frac{231}{320}u^4\right)\left(1 - \frac{1}{5}u^2\right) & \text{if } u^2 < 5.0 \\ 0 & \text{otherwise.} \end{cases}$$

Figure 1.2 plots the second, fourth, and sixth order Epanechnikov kernels defined above. Clearly, for $\nu > 2$, the kernels indeed assign negative weights which can result in negative density estimates, not a desirable feature.

For related work involving exact mean integrated squared error for higher order kernels in the context of univariate kernel density estimation, see Hansen (2005). Also, for related work using iterative methods to estimate transformation-kernel densities, see Yang and Marron (1999) and Yang (2000).

1.12   Proof of Theorem 1.4 (Uniform Almost Sure Convergence)

The proof below is based on the arguments presented in Masry (1996*b*), who establishes uniform almost sure rates for local polynomial regression with weakly dependent (α-mixing) data; see Chapter 18 for further details on weakly dependent processes. Since the bias of the kernel

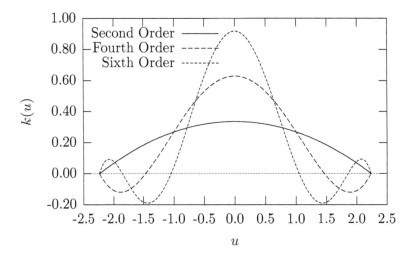

Figure 1.2: Epanechnikov kernels of varying order.

density estimator is of order $O(\sum_{s=1}^{q} h_s^2)$ and the variance is of order $O((nh_1 \ldots h_q)^{-1})$, it is easy to show that the optimal rate of convergence requires that all h_s should be of the same order of magnitude. Therefore, for expositional simplicity, we will make the simplifying assumption that

$$h_1 = \cdots = h_q = h.$$

This will not affect the optimal rate of convergence, but it simplifies the derivation tremendously. We emphasize that, in practice, one should always allow h_s $(s = 1, \ldots, s)$ to differ from each other, which is of course always permitted when using fully data-driven methods of bandwidth selection such as cross-validation. Only for the theoretical analysis that immediately follows do we assume that all smoothing parameters are the same.

Proof. Let $W_n = W_n(x) = |\hat{f}(x) - f(x)|$. To prove that the random variable W_n is of order (η) almost surely (a.s.), we can show that $\sum_{n=1}^{\infty} \mathrm{P}\left(|W_n/\eta| > 1\right)$ is finite (for some $\eta > 0$). Then by the Borel-Cantelli lemma (see Lemma A.7 in Appendix A), we know that $W_n = O(\eta)$ a.s. Here, the supremum operator complicates the proof because $\mathcal{S}$ is an uncountable set. Letting L_n denote a countable set, then we have

$$P\left(\max_{x\in L_n} W_n(x) > \eta\right) \le (\# \text{ of } L_n) \max_{x\in L_n} P(W_n(x) > \eta). \qquad (1.50)$$

But in our case, $x \in \mathcal{S}$ is uncountable and we cannot simply use an inequality like (1.50) to bound $P\left(\sup_{x\in\mathcal{S}} W_n(x) > \eta\right)$.

However, since $\mathcal{S}$ is a bounded set we can partition $\mathcal{S}$ into countable subsets with the volume of each subset being as small as necessary. Then $P(\sup_{x\in\mathcal{S}} |W_n(x)| > \eta)$ can be transformed into a problem like $P\left(\max_{x\in L_n} |W_n(x)| > \eta\right)$ and the inequality of (1.50) can be used to handle this term. Using this idea we prove Theorem 1.4 below.

We write

$$\left|\hat{f}(x) - f(x)\right| = \left|\hat{f}(x) - E\left(\hat{f}(x)\right) + E\left(\hat{f}(x)\right) - f(x)\right|$$
$$\le \left|\hat{f}(x) - E\left(\hat{f}(x)\right)\right| + \left|E\left(\hat{f}(x)\right) - f(x)\right|.$$

We prove Theorem 1.4 by showing that

$$\sup_{x\in\mathcal{S}} \left|E\left(\hat{f}(x)\right) - f(x)\right| = O\left(h^2\right), \qquad (1.51)$$

and that

$$\sup_{x\in\mathcal{S}} \left|\hat{f}(x) - E\left(\hat{f}(x)\right)\right| = O\left(\frac{(\ln(n))^{1/2}}{(nh^q)^{1/2}}\right) \text{ almost surely.} \qquad (1.52)$$

We first prove (1.51). Because the compact set $\mathcal{S}$ is in the interior of its support, by a change-of-variables argument, we have, for $x \in \mathcal{S}$,

$$E\left(\hat{f}(x)\right) - f(x) = \int f(x + hv)K(v)\,dv - f(x)$$
$$= h^2 \int v' f^{(2)}(\tilde{x})vK(v)\,dv$$
$$\le C_1 h^2 \int v'vK(v)\,dv \le Ch^2 = O\left(h^2\right)$$

uniformly in $x \in \mathcal{S}$. Thus, we have proved (1.51).

We now turn to the proof of (1.52). Since $\mathcal{S}$ is compact (closed and bounded), it can be covered by a finite number $L_n = L(n)$ of (q-dimensional) cubes $I_k = I_{k,n}$, with centers $x_{k,n}$ and length l_n ($k =$

$1, \dots, L(n)$). We know that $L_n = \text{constant}/(l_n)^q$ because $\mathcal{S}$ is compact, which gives $l_n = \text{constant}/L_n^{1/q}$. We write

$$
\sup_{x \in \mathcal{S}} \left| \hat{f}(x) - \mathrm{E}\left(\hat{f}(x)\right) \right| = \max_{1 \le k \le L(n)} \sup_{x \in \mathcal{S} \cap I_k} \left| \hat{f}(x) - \mathrm{E}\left(\hat{f}(x)\right) \right|
$$

$$
\le \max_{1 \le k \le L(n)} \sup_{x \in \mathcal{S} \cap I_k} \left| \hat{f}(x) - \hat{f}(x_{k,n}) \right|
$$

$$
+ \max_{1 \le k \le L(n)} \left| \hat{f}(x_{k,n}) - \mathrm{E}\left(\hat{f}(x_{k,n})\right) \right|
$$

$$
+ \max_{1 \le k \le L(n)} \sup_{x \in \mathcal{S} \cap I_k} \left| \mathrm{E}\left(\hat{f}(x_{k,n})\right) - \mathrm{E}\left(\hat{f}(x)\right) \right|
$$

$$
\equiv Q_1 + Q_2 + Q_3.
$$

Note that Q_2 does not depend on x, so $\sup_{x \in \mathcal{S} \cap I_k}$ does not appear in the definition of Q_2.

We first consider Q_2. Write $W_n(x) = \hat{f}(x) - \mathrm{E}\left(\hat{f}(x)\right) = \sum_i Z_{n,i}$, where $Z_{n,i} = (nh^q)^{-1}\{K((X_i - x)/h) - \mathrm{E}[K((X_i - x)/h)]\}$. For any $\eta > 0$, we have

$$
\mathrm{P}[Q_2 > \eta] = \mathrm{P}\left[\max_{1 \le k \le L(n)} |W_n(x_{k,n})| > \eta\right]
$$

$$
\le \mathrm{P}[W_n(x_{1,n}) > \eta \text{ or } W_n(x_{2,n}) > \eta, \dots, \text{or } W_n(x_{L(n),n}) > \eta]
$$

$$
\le \mathrm{P}\left(W_n(x_{1,n}) > \eta\right) + \mathrm{P}\left(W_n(x_{2,n}) > \eta\right) + \dots
$$

$$
+ \mathrm{P}\left(W_n(x_{L(n),n}) > \eta\right)
$$

$$
\le L(n) \sup_{x \in \mathcal{S}} \mathrm{P}\left[|W_n(x)| > \eta\right]. \tag{1.53}
$$

Since $K(\cdot)$ is bounded, and letting $A_1 = \sup_x |K(x)|$, we have $|Z_{n,i}| \le 2A_1/(nh^q)$ for all $i = 1, \dots, n$. Define $\lambda_n = (nh^q \ln(n))^{1/2}$. Then $\lambda_n |Z_{n,i}| \le 2A_1[\ln(n)/(nh^q)]^{1/2} \le 1/2$ for all $i = 1, \dots, n$ for n sufficiently large.[6] Using the inequality $\exp(x) \le 1 + x + x^2$ for $|x| \le 1/2$, we have $\exp(\pm \lambda_n Z_{n,i}) \le 1 + \lambda_n Z_{n,i} + \lambda_n^2 Z_{n,i}^2$. Hence,

$$
\mathrm{E}\left[\exp(\pm \lambda_n Z_{n,i})\right] \le 1 + \lambda_n^2 \mathrm{E}\left[Z_{n,i}^2\right] \le \exp\left[\mathrm{E}\left(\lambda_n^2 Z_{n,i}^2\right)\right], \tag{1.54}
$$

where we used $\mathrm{E}(Z_{n,i}) = 0$ while for the second inequality we used $1 + v \le \exp(v)$ for $v \ge 0$ ($v = \mathrm{E}[\lambda_n^2 Z_{n,i}^2]$).

---

[6]For now, any choice of $\lambda_n \le (nh^q)/(4A_1)$ will lead to $|\lambda_n Z_{n,i}| \le 1/2$. Later on we will show that, in order to obtain the optimal rate for Q_2, one needs to choose $\lambda_n = (nh^q \ln(n))^{1/2}$.

By the Markov inequality (see Lemma A.23 with $\phi(x) = \exp(ax)$) we know that

$$P[X > c] \leq \frac{E[\exp(Xa)]}{\exp(ac)}, \quad (a > 0). \tag{1.55}$$

Using (1.55) we have

$$P[|W_n(x)| > \eta] = P\left[\left|\sum_{i=1}^{n} Z_{n,i}\right| > \eta\right]$$

$$= P\left[\sum_{i=1}^{n} Z_{n,i} > \eta\right] + P\left[\sum_{i=1}^{n} Z_{n,i} < -\eta\right]$$

$$\leq P\left[\sum_{i=1}^{n} Z_{n,i} > \eta\right] + P\left[-\sum_{i=1}^{n} Z_{n,i} > \eta\right]$$

$$\leq \frac{E\left[\exp(\lambda_n \sum_{i=1}^{n} Z_{n,i})\right] + E\left[\exp(-\lambda_n \sum_{i=1}^{n} Z_{n,i})\right]}{\exp(\lambda_n \eta_n)}$$

(by (1.55), $a = \lambda_n, c = \eta$)

$$\leq 2\exp(-\lambda_n \eta)\left[\exp\left(\lambda_n^2 \sum_{i=1}^{n} E(Z_{n,i}^2)\right)\right]$$

(by (1.54))

$$\leq 2\exp(-\lambda_n \eta)\left[\exp\left(A_2 \lambda_n^2/(nh^q)\right)\right], \tag{1.56}$$

where we used

$$E\left[Z_{n,i}^2\right] \leq (nh^q)^{-2} E\left[K^2((X_i - x)/h)\right] \leq A_2(n^2 h^q)^{-1}[1 + o(1)].$$

Because the last bound in (1.56) is independent of x, it is also the uniform bound, i.e.,

$$\sup_{x \in \mathcal{S}} P[|W_n(x)| > \eta] \leq 2\exp\left(-\lambda_n \eta + \frac{A_2 \lambda_n^2}{nh^q}\right). \tag{1.57}$$

We want to have $\eta \to 0$ as fast as possible, and at the same time we need $\lambda_n \eta \to \infty$ at a rate which ensures that (1.57) is summable.[7] We can choose $\lambda_n \eta = C_4 \ln(n)$, or $\lambda_n = C_4 \ln(n)/\eta$. Finding the fastest rate for which $\eta \to 0$ is equivalent to finding the fastest rate for which $\lambda_n \to \infty$. We also need the order of $\lambda_n \eta \geq \lambda_n^2/(nh^d)$, or $\ln(n) \geq \lambda_n^2/(nh^d)$.

---

[7]A sequence $\{a_n\}_{n=1}^{\infty}$ is said to be summable if $|\sum_{j=1}^{\infty} a_j| < \infty$.

Thus, we simply need to maximize the order of $\lambda_n \to \infty$ subject to $\lambda_n^2 \leq (nh^q)\ln(n)$. Doing so, we get

$$\lambda_n = [(nh^q)\ln(n)]^{1/2} \text{ and } \eta = C_4 \ln(n)/\lambda_n = C_4 \left[\ln(n)/(nh^q)\right]^{1/2}. \tag{1.58}$$

Using (1.58) we get

$$-\lambda_n \eta/2 + A_2 \lambda_n^2/(nh^q) = -C_4 \ln(n) + A_2 \ln(n)$$
$$= -\alpha \ln(n),$$

where $\alpha = C_4 - A_2$. Substituting this into (1.57) and then into (1.53) gives us

$$P[Q_2 > \eta_n] \leq 2L(n)/n^\alpha. \tag{1.59}$$

By choosing C_4 sufficiently large, we can obtain the result that $L(n)/n^a$ is summable by properly choosing the order of $L(n)$, i.e., $\sum_{n=1}^\infty P(|Q_2/\eta_n| > 1) \leq 4\sum_{n=1}^\infty L(n)/n^a < \infty$. Therefore, by the Borel-Cantelli lemma we know that

$$Q_2 = O(\eta_n) = O\left((\ln(n))^{1/2}/(nh^q)^{1/2}\right) \text{ almost surely.} \tag{1.60}$$

We now consider Q_1 and Q_3. Recall that $\|\cdot\|$ denotes the usual Euclidean norm of a vector. By the Lipschitz condition on $K(\cdot)$, we know that

$$\sup_{x \in S \cap I_k} |K((X_i - x)/h) - K((X_i - x_{k,n})/h)| \leq C_1 h^{-1} \sup_{x \in S \cap I_k} \|x - x_{k,n}\|$$
$$\leq C_2 h^{-1} l_n.$$

Therefore, by choosing $l_n = (\ln(n))^{1/2} h^{(q+2)/2}/n^{1/2}$, we have

$$|Q_1| \leq C_2 h^{-(q+1)} l_n = O\left((\ln(n)/(nh^q))^{1/2}\right). \tag{1.61}$$

By exactly the same argument we can show that

$$|Q_3| \leq C_3 h^{-(q+1)} l_n = O\left((\ln(n)/(nh^q))^{1/2}\right). \tag{1.62}$$

Equations (1.60) through (1.62) prove (1.52), and this completes the proof of Theorem 1.4. $\square$

1.13   Applications

We now consider a number of applications of univariate and multivariate density estimation that illustrate the flexibility and power of the kernel approach.

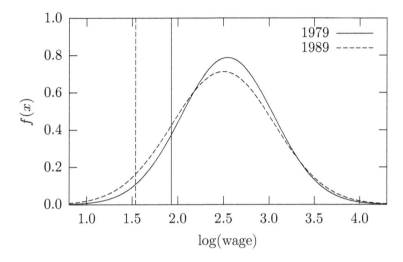

Figure 1.3: Parametric density estimate (vertical lines represent (log) minimum wages in 1979 and 1989).

1.13.1   Female Wage Inequality

DiNardo and Tobias (2001, p. 12) used nonparametric kernel methods to investigate the phenomenon of female wage inequality which grew from 1979 to 1989. Sometimes the scale of a parametric distribution is used as a crude measure of inequality, and the standard deviation of log wages increased 25% from 0.41 to 0.50 over this period.[8] One might think that common culprits underlying such changes would include international trade, technical change, or perhaps organizational change. As we will see below, DiNardo and Tobias show that the kernel estimator can help reveal who the true culprit is.

If one used a parametric model and assumed, say, a normal distribution for log wages, one would arrive at the description of the data presented in Figure 1.3.

Use of nonparametric kernel methods and a simple "normal refer-

---

[8]The minimum wages in 1979 and 1989 were $2.90/hour and $3.35/hour, while the CPI was 72.6, 124.0, and 172.2 in 1979, 1989, and 2000 respectively. Wages were taken from the Current Population Survey (CPS). There were 140,284 and 167,863 observations in the 1979 and 1989 samples respectively. The Gaussian kernel was used, and the normal reference rule-of-thumb bandwidths were 0.050 and 0.053 for the 1979 and 1989 samples respectively. Wage values appearing in Figures 1.3 and 1.4 are in current (2000) dollars.

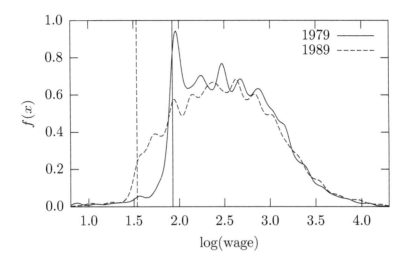

Figure 1.4: Nonparametric density estimate (vertical lines represent (log) minimum wages in 1979 and 1989).

ence rule-of-thumb" ($h = 1.06\sigma n^{-1/5}$) bandwidth along with a second order Gaussian kernel yields the estimates plotted in Figure 1.4.

The two kernel density estimates based on the normal reference rule-of-thumb presented in Figure 1.4 appear to be undersmoothed. However, these estimates clearly reveal a feature not captured by parametric methods: a binding modal minimum wage for 1979 that is no longer binding in 1989 for most women. This finding suggests that the growing wage inequality can be explained by truncation induced by a binding real minimum wage in 1979. That is, in 1979, unlike 1989, employers were paying minimum wage to many employees, which distorts and *reduces* the variance of the wage distribution. The real value of the minimum wage falls over time, becoming nonbinding in 1989. Thus, the nonparametric estimator readily reveals the true reason underlying growing wage inequality, and focuses attention away from other possible explanations, such as international trade, technical change, or possibly organizational change. This example serves simply to underscore the fact that traditional parametric approaches may mask important characteristics present in data.

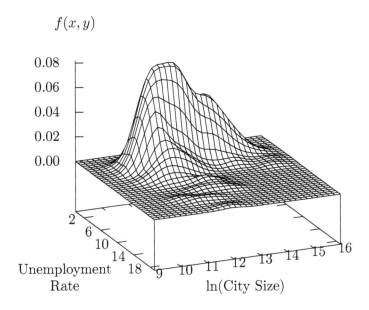

$f(x, y)$

Figure 1.5: Unemployment rate and ln(city size) joint density estimate.

1.13.2   Unemployment Rates and City Size

For this example we use U.S. data on city population (ln(city size)) and unemployment rates based upon a sample of $n = 295$ cities. Gan and Zhang (2006) present a theory predicting that the larger the city, the smaller the unemployment rate (on average). In Figure 1.5 we plot the estimated joint PDF using least squares cross-validated bandwidth selection and a second order Gaussian kernel. The cross-validated bandwidths are 0.665 and 0.351 for the unemployment rate and population respectively.

The joint density estimate presented in Figure 1.5 is consistent with the hypothesis that large cities tend to have low unemployment rates and vice versa. That is, Figure 1.5 reveals a somewhat "right-angled" distribution having probability mass at low unemployment rates and large city sizes, while as the city size falls we observe the probability mass shifting first toward the origin and then, as city size falls further, the mass shifts toward higher unemployment rates.

1.13.3   Adolescent Growth

Abnormal adolescent growth can provide an early warning that a child has a medical problem. For instance, too rapid growth may indicate the presence of a hydrocephalus (an accumulation of liquid within the cavity of the cranium), a brain tumor, or other conditions that cause macrocephaly (having an unusually large head), while too slow growth may indicate malformations of the brain, early fusion of sutures or other problems. Insufficient gain in weight, height or a combination may indicate failure-to-thrive, chronic illness, neglect or other problems.

We consider data from the population of healthy U.S. children obtained from the Center for Disease Control and Prevention's (CDC) National Health and Nutrition Examination Survey. We combine data and use two recent cross-sectional nationally representative health examination surveys for the years 1999/2000 and 2001/2002. For each cross section, two separate datasets must be linked (a body measurement dataset and a demographic variable dataset). The combined linked datasets contains $8,399$ complete observations for children and youths ages 2-20 years of age. We model the joint distribution of height and weight by sex.

Figures 1.6 and 1.7 reveal that the joint distribution of height and weight is similar for males and females; however, that for males contains greater probability mass at higher values of both weight and height. That is, one is more likely to observe both taller and heavier boys than girls. Such data lays the foundation for the construction of adolescent growth charts, for instance, weight for stature charts.[9] See also Wei and He (2006) for related work on conditional growth charts.

1.13.4   Old Faithful Geyser Data

The Old Faithful Geyser is a tourist attraction located in Yellowstone National Park. This famous dataset containing $n = 272$ observations consists of two variables, eruption duration (minutes) and waiting time until the next eruption (minutes). This dataset is used by the park service to model, among other things, expected duration conditional upon the amount of time that has elapsed since the previous eruption. Modeling the joint distribution is, however, of interest in its own right. The underlying bimodal nature of the joint PDF is readily revealed by

---

[9]See http://www.cdc.gov/growthcharts for official growth charts developed by the National Center for Health Statistics.

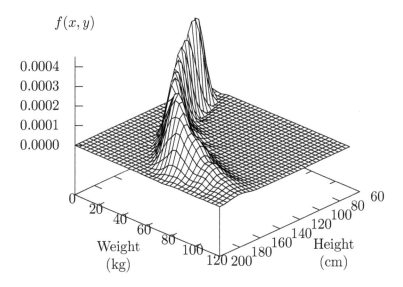

Figure 1.6: Weight and height joint density estimate for males.

the kernel estimator graphed in Figure 1.8 constructed using likelihood cross-validated bandwidths and a second order Gaussian kernel.[10]

If one were to instead model this density with a parametric model such as the bivariate normal (being symmetric, unimodal, and monotonically decreasing away from the mode), one would of course fail to uncover the underlying structure readily revealed by the kernel estimate.

1.13.5 Evolution of Real Income Distribution in Italy, 1951–1998

Baiocchi (2006) recently considered the evolution of the distribution of real income in Italy using kernel methods. He considers a series of

---

[10]Likelihood cross-validated bandwidths were computed and were equal to (h_1, h_2) $= (0.368\sigma_1 n^{-1/6}, 0.764\sigma_2 n^{-1/6})$, while least squares cross-validated bandwidths were $(h_1, h_2) = (0.307\sigma_1 n^{-1/6}, 0.733\sigma_2 n^{-1/6})$ where h_1 is that for eruption duration and h_2 that for waiting time.

$f(x,y)$

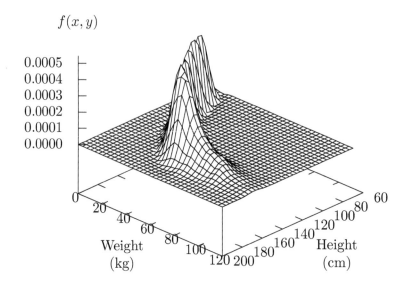

Figure 1.7: Weight and height joint density estimate for females.

"stacked" univariate kernel density estimates of the income distribution for 21 regions and plots the resulting evolution of the univariate kernel density estimates over time. We are indebted to Giovanni Baiocchi for providing the data containing observations for the period 1951–1998 (millions of lire, 1990 = base) used to generate a series of univariate kernel estimates using likelihood cross-validation. Figure 1.9 presents the evolution of real GDP per capita (millions of 1990 lire) by stacking the series of annual (i.e., cross section) univariate kernel estimates in a 3D plot.

Figure 1.9 reveals that the distribution of income has evolved from a unimodal one in the early 1950s to a markedly bimodal one in the 1990s. This result is robust to bandwidth choice, and is observed whether using simple rules-of-thumb or data-driven methods such as likelihood cross-validation. The kernel method readily reveals this evolution which might easily be missed were one to use parametric models of the income distribution (e.g., the lognormal distribution commonly found in

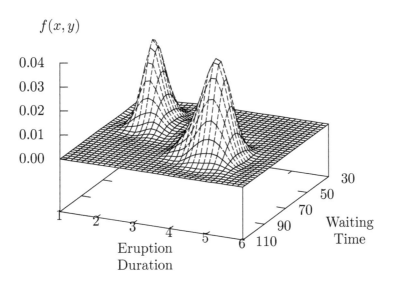

Figure 1.8: Joint density estimate for the Old Faithful data.

applied work).

1.14 Exercises

Exercise 1.1. Consider the following sample of continuous data:

$$\{-0.57, 0.25, -0.08, 1.40, -1.05, -1.00, 0.37, -1.15, 0.73, 1.59\},$$

(e.g., the real seasonally adjusted GDP gap in trillions of dollars).
Recall that the parametric normal density function is given by

$$f(x) = \frac{1}{\sqrt{2\pi\sigma^2}} e^{-\frac{1}{2}\left(\frac{x-\mu}{\sigma}\right)^2}.$$

(i) Compute and graph the parametric density function for this data
(i.e., compute $\hat{\mu}$ and $\hat{\sigma}^2$) assuming an underlying normal distribution.

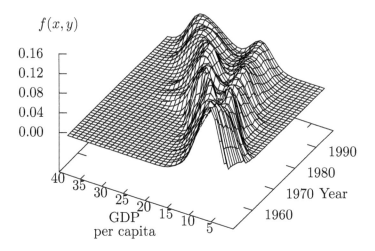

$f(x,y)$

Figure 1.9: Evolution of the income distribution in Italy, 1951–1998 (series of univariate cross section kernel estimates).

(ii) Compute and graph a histogram for this data using bin widths of 0.5 ranging from -1.5 through 2.0.

Recall that the kernel estimator of a univariate density function for continuous data can be expressed as

$$\hat{f}(x) = \frac{1}{nh} \sum_{i=1}^{n} K\left(\frac{X_i - x}{h}\right)$$

and that a common (optimal) kernel is the Epanechnikov kernel given by

$$K\left(\frac{X_i - x}{h}\right) = \begin{cases} \frac{3}{4\sqrt{5}}\left(1 - \frac{1}{5}\left(\frac{X_i - x}{h}\right)^2\right) & \text{if } \left|\frac{X_i - x}{h}\right| < \sqrt{5} \\ 0 & \text{otherwise,} \end{cases}$$

where h is a smoothing parameter restricted to lie in the range $(0, \infty]$.

(iii) Using the same tiny sample of data, compute the kernel estimator of the density function for every sample realization using the bandwidth $h = 1.5$. Show all steps.

(iv) Using the same data, compute the kernel estimator of the density function for every sample realization using the bandwidth $h = 0.5$. Show all steps.

(v) On the same axes, graph your estimates of the density functions using a smooth curve to "connect the dots" for each function.

(vi) Describe the effect of *increasing* the smoothing parameter on the estimated density function.

Exercise 1.2. Let $\hat{p}$ be defined as in (1.1). Show that $\hat{p}$ is the maximum likelihood estimator of $p = \mathrm{P}(H)$.

Hint: Define $X_i = 1$ if the ith trial is H, and $X_i = 0$ if it is T. Then the likelihood function is $\prod_{i=1}^{n} f(X_i) = \prod_{i=1}^{n} p^{X_i}(1-p)^{1-X_i}$. The log-likelihood function is $\ln L = (\sum_{i=1}^{n} X_i) \ln p + [\sum_{i=1}^{n}(1-X_i)] \ln(1-p)$.

Exercise 1.3.

(i) Show that $\mathrm{MSE}\,(\hat{p}_n) = p(1-p)/n$, where $p = \mathrm{P}(H)$.

(ii) Show that $\mathrm{plim}_{n\to\infty}\,\hat{p} = p$.

(iii) Supposing that $p = \mathrm{P}(H) \in (0,1)$, show that the ordinary limit $\lim_{n\to\infty}\hat{p}$ does not exist.

Note that the ordinary limit is defined as follows. Letting a_n be a sequence of real numbers, we write $\lim_{n\to\infty} a_n = c$ if for all (small) $\epsilon > 0$, there exists a positive integer n_0 such that $|a_n - c| < \epsilon$ for all $n \geq n_0$.

Hint: For (ii) use the result from (i) along with Theorem A.3 of Appendix A.

Hint: For (iii) argue by contradiction.

Exercise 1.4. Let $F(x)$ be defined as in (1.2).

(i) Show that $\mathrm{MSE}[F_n(x)] = O(n^{-1})$ (note that this implies that $F_n(x) - F(x) = O_p(n^{-1/2})$ by Theorem A.7 of Appendix A.

(ii) Prove that

$$\sqrt{n}(F_n(x) - F(x)) \overset{d}{\to} N(0, F(x)(1 - F(x))).$$

Hint: First show that $\mathrm{E}[F_n(x)] = F(x)$ and $\mathrm{var}(F_n(x)) = F(x)(1 - F(x))$. Then use the Lindeberg-Levy CLT.

Exercise 1.5. Prove (1.13) under the assumption that $f(x)$ has a continuous second order derivative at x.

Hint: Use the dominated convergence theorem given by Lemma A.26 in Appendix A.

Exercise 1.6. Write $k_{ij} = k\left(\frac{X_i - X_j}{h}\right)$ and $\bar{k}_{ij} = \bar{k}\left(\frac{X_i - X_j}{h}\right)$. Using $n^{-2} = (n(n-1))^{-1} - (n^2(n-1))^{-1}$, we obtain from (1.23)

$$CV_f(h) = \frac{1}{n(n-1)h}\sum_{i=1}^{n}\sum_{j=1}^{n}\bar{k}_{ij} - \frac{2}{n(n-1)h}\sum_{i=1}^{n}\sum_{j\neq i}^{n}k_{ij}$$

$$- \frac{1}{n^2(n-1)h}\sum_{i=1}^{n}\sum_{j=1}^{n}\bar{k}_{ij}$$

$$= \frac{1}{(n-1)h}\bar{k}(0) + \frac{1}{n(n-1)h}\sum_{i=1}^{n}\sum_{j\neq i}^{n}[\bar{k}_{ij} - 2k_{ij}] + O_p(n^{-1})$$

$$= \frac{\kappa}{(n-1)h} + J_n + O_p(h(nh)^{-1}), \qquad (1.63)$$

where $J_n = [n(n-1)h]^{-1}\sum_{i=1}^{n}\sum_{j\neq i}^{n}[\bar{k}_{ij} - 2k_{ij}]$ and $\kappa = \int k^2(v)\, dv \equiv \bar{k}(0)$.

(i) Show that $\mathrm{E}(J_n) = B_0 + B_1 h^4 + O(h^5)$, where $B_0 = -\int f(x)^2\, dx$, and $B_1 = (\kappa_2^2/4)\{\int [f^{(2)}(x)]^2\, dx\}$.

(ii) Accept the fact that $J_n = \mathrm{E}(J_n) +$ smaller order terms. So, asymptotically, minimizing $CV_f(h)$ is equivalent to minimizing $I(h) \overset{\mathrm{def}}{=} (nh)^{-1}\kappa + \mathrm{E}(J_n)$. Obtain that $\hat{h}$ which minimizes $I(h)$.

(iii) Assume that $k(0) \geq k(v)$ for all v (which is usually true for kernel estimation). If we do not use the leave-one-out estimator, then we would instead have the objective function $V(h) \overset{\mathrm{def}}{=} (nh)^{-1}[\kappa - 2k(0)] + \mathrm{E}(J_n)$. Show that $h = 0$ minimizes $V(h)$, which obviously violates the requirement that $nh \to \infty$ as $n \to \infty$. This shows that we *must* use the leave-one-out estimator when constructing $CV_f(h)$.

(iv) In deriving (1.63) we used

$$A_n \overset{\text{def}}{=} (n^2(n-1)h)^{-1} \sum_i \sum_{j \neq i} \bar{k}((X_i - X_j)/h) = O_p(n^{-1}).$$

Prove this result.

(v) Using the U-statistic H-decomposition given in Lemma A.15 of Appendix A, show that $J_n = E(J_n) + O_p(h^{1/2}(nh)^{-1} + n^{-1/2}h^4) +$ terms unrelated to h. Therefore, we indeed have $J_n = E(J_n) +$ (s.o.) (for a given value of h).

Hints: Note that $\bar{k}(\cdot)$ is also a nonnegative, symmetric PDF, i.e., $\int \bar{k}(v)\, dv = 1$, $\int v^s \bar{k}(v)\, dv = 0$ when s is an odd positive integer.

(i)

$$E[\bar{k}_{12}] = h^{-1} E \int k\left(\frac{X_1 - x}{h}\right) k\left(\frac{X_2 - x}{h}\right) dx$$

$$= h^{-1} \int \left[Ek\left(\frac{X_1 - x}{h}\right)\right] \left[Ek\left(\frac{X_2 - x}{h}\right)\right] dx$$

$$= h^{-1} \int \left[Ek\left(\frac{X_1 - x}{h}\right)\right]^2 dx$$

$$= h \int \left[f(x) + 0 + (\kappa_2/2)f^{(2)}(x)h^2 + 0\right.$$

$$\left. + (\kappa_4/4!)f^{(4)}(x)h^4 + O(h^5)\right]^2 dx.$$

$$E[k_{12}] = Ek\left(\frac{X_1 - X_2}{h}\right)$$

$$= \int k\left(\frac{x_1 - x_2}{h}\right) f(x_1) f(x_2)\, dx_1\, dx_2$$

$$= h \int f(x)\Big\{ f(x) + 0 + (\kappa_2/2)f^{(2)}(x)h^2 + 0$$

$$+ (\kappa_4/4!)f^{(4)}(x)h^4 \Big\}\, dx + O(h^5).$$

(ii) Note that $\bar{k}(0) = \int k^2(v)\, dv > 0$.

(iii) Show that $h \to 0$ produces a value of the objective function $V(h) = -\infty$. Thus, $h = 0$ minimizes $V(h)$.

(iv) Show that $\mathrm{E}[|A_n|] = \mathrm{E}(A_n) = O(n^{-1})$, then apply Theorem A.7.

(v) Using the U-statistic H-decomposition (again, see Appendix A), show that the last two terms in the H-decomposition are of order $O_p(n^{-1/2}h^4)$ (plus terms unrelated to h) and $O_p(h^{1/2}(nh)^{-1})$, respectively.

Exercise 1.7. Derive (1.27), i.e., show that

$$\int_{-\infty}^{x} \hat{f}(v)\, dv = n^{-1} \sum_{i=1}^{n} G\left(\frac{x - X_i}{h}\right).$$

Hint: Use $\hat{f}(v) = (nh)^{-1} \sum_{i=1}^{n} k\left(\frac{X_i - v}{h}\right)$ and do a change of variable $(x_i - v)/h = t$ and $dx_i = h\, dv$.

Exercise 1.8.

(i) Discuss the relationship between the kernel and empirical CDF estimators, i.e., $\hat{F}(x)$ and $F_n(x) = n^{-1} \sum_{i=1}^{n} \mathbf{1}(X_i \leq x)$.

(ii) Discuss whether or not one can use $h = 0$ in $\hat{F}(x)$ defined in (1.27), i.e., can one let $h \to 0$ arbitrarily fast in $\hat{F}(x)$?

(iii) $\hat{F}(x)$ and $F_n(x)$ have the same asymptotic distribution. What is the advantage of using $\hat{F}(x)$ over $F_n(x)$? Which estimator do you expect to have smaller *finite-sample* MSE? Explain.

Exercise 1.9. Derive (1.33).
Hint: Write $\mathbf{1}_i(x) = \mathbf{1}(X_i \leq x)$ and $G_{x,x_j} = G((x - X_j)/h)$, then

$$
\begin{aligned}
\mathrm{E}[CV_F(h)] &= \frac{1}{n(n-1)^2} \sum_{i=1}^{n} \sum_{j \neq i}^{n} \sum_{l \neq i}^{n} \int \mathrm{E}\left\{\left[\mathbf{1}_i(x) - G_{x,x_j}\right]\right. \\
&\qquad \times \left.\left[\mathbf{1}_i(x) - G_{x,x_l}\right]\right\} dx \\
&= \frac{1}{n-1} \int \mathrm{E}\left\{\left[\mathbf{1}_i(x) - G_{x,x_j}\right]^2\right\} dx \\
&\qquad + \frac{n-2}{n-1} \int \mathrm{E}\left\{\mathrm{E}\left[\mathbf{1}_i(x) - G_{x,x_j}|X_i\right]\right\}^2 dx \\
&= CV_1 + CV_2,
\end{aligned}
$$

then show that

$$CV_1 = (n-1)^{-1} \left\{ 2 \int F(1-F)\, dx - C_1 h + O(h^2) \right\} \quad \text{and}$$

$$CV_2 = \left[1 - \frac{1}{n-1} \right] \left\{ \int F(x)(1-F(x))\, dx + h^4 \int C_2(x)^2\, dx \right\}.$$

Exercise 1.10. Define a $q \times q$ matrix A with its (t,s)th element given by $A_{t,s} = (\kappa_2/2) \int B_t(x) B_s(x)\, dx$.

  (i) Show that A is positive semidefinite.

 (ii) Show that if A is positive definite, then the a_s^0's defined in (1.41) are all uniquely determined, positive, and finite.

     A necessary condition for A to be positive definite is that $f_{ss}(x)$ is not a zero function for all $s = 1, \ldots, q$.

  Hint:

  (i) Note that for any $q \times 1$ vector $z = (z_1, \ldots, z_q)'$ that $z'Az = \int [\sum_{s=1}^q B_s(x) z_s]^2\, dx \geq 0$.

 (ii) Define $z_s = a_s^2$, then $\chi_f = z'Az + \kappa^q/\sqrt{z_1 \ldots z_q}$, and let z_s^0 denote values of z_s that minimize χ_f. It is easy to argue that $\infty > \inf_{z_1,\ldots,z_q} \chi_f > 0$. This implies that $z_s^0 > 0$ for all s. The fact that A is positive definite implies that $z_s^0 < \infty$ for all s. Finally, z_s^0 is uniquely determined by a result given in Li and Zhou (2005). Therefore, $a_s^0 = \sqrt{z_s^0}$ is uniquely determined, positive and finite for all $s = 1, \ldots, q$.

     Note that A being positive definite is a sufficient condition. Li and Zhou (2005) provide a weaker necessary and sufficient condition for this result.

Exercise 1.11. Prove (1.36) and (1.37).

  Hint: For a multivariate Taylor expansion, we have $f(x_0 + x) = f(x_0) + \sum_{s=1}^q f_s(x_0)(x_s - x_{s0}) + (1/2) \sum_{s=1}^q \sum_{s'=1}^q f_{ss'}(\tilde{x})(x_s - x_{s0})(x_{s'} - x_{s'0})$, $\tilde{x}$ is on the line segment between x and x_0.

Exercise 1.12. For the multivariate case, we have

$$CV_f(h_1, \ldots, h_q) = \frac{\kappa^q}{nh_1 \ldots h_q} + J_n + O_p\left(\left(n^2 h_1 \ldots h_q \right)^{-1} \right)$$

where $J_n = [n(n-1)]^{-1} \sum_i \sum_{j \neq i} \left[\bar{K}_n(X_i, X_j) - 2K_n(X_i, X_j) \right]$.

(i) Show that $E(J_n) = \int \left[\sum_{s=1}^{q} B_s(x) h_s^2 \right]^2 dx + o\left(\sum_{s=1}^{q} h_s^4 \right)$, where the definition of $B_s(x)$ is given in Section 1.8.

(ii) Use the U-statistic H-decomposition to show that (ignoring the term unrelated to the H_s's)

$$J_n = E(J_n) + O_p\left(n^{-1/2} \left(\sum_{s=1}^{q} h_s^2 \right)^2 \right)$$

$$+ O_p\left((h_1 \ldots h_q)^{1/2} (nh_1 \ldots h_q)^{-1} \right).$$

Note that (i) and (ii) together imply that

$$CV_f = \sum_{s=1}^{a} B_s h_s^4 + \kappa^q (nh_1 \ldots h_q)^{-1} + o_p\left(\eta_2^2 + \eta_1 \right)$$

where $\eta_2 = \sum_{s=1}^{q} h_s^2$ and $\eta_1 = (nh_1 \ldots h_q)^{-1}$.

Hint: Using H-decomposition, show that the second moments of the second and third terms are of order $O(n^{-1/2} \eta_2^2)$ and $O\left((h_1 \ldots h_1) \eta_1^2 \right)$, respectively.

Exercise 1.13. Assuming that $X \in [0,1]$ and $f(0) > 0$, show that $E[\hat{f}(0)] = f(0)/2 + O(h)$ so that $\hat{f}(0)$ is a biased estimator of $f(0)$ even asymptotically.

Hint: $\hat{f}(0) = (nh)^{-1} \sum_{i=1}^{n} k((X_i - 0)/h)$, and

$$E[\hat{f}(0)] = h^{-1} E[k(X_i/h)] = h^{-1} \int_0^1 f(x_1) k(x_1/h) \, dx_1$$

$$= \int_0^{1/h} f(hv) k(v) \, dv$$

$$\to f(0) \int_0^{\infty} k(v) \, dv = f(0)/2.$$

Exercise 1.14. With the boundary-corrected kernel defined in (1.43), and with $\hat{f}(x)$ defined in (1.44) and with the support of X being $[0,1]$, show that for $x \in [0,h]$ at the boundary region, we have $E[\hat{f}(x)] = f(x) + O(h)$. Explicitly state the conditions that you need to derive this result.

Therefore, bias$[\hat{f}(x)] = O(h) \to 0$ as $n \to \infty$, and the boundary-corrected kernel restores the asymptotic unbiasedness for $\hat{f}(x)$ for x at the boundary region.

Hint: One can write $x = \alpha h$ with $0 \leq \alpha \leq 1$. One can assume that $|f(x) - f(z)| \leq C|x - z|$ for all $x, z \in [0, 1]$, where C is a positive constant. Then

$$
\begin{aligned}
\mathrm{E}[\hat{f}(x)] &= h^{-1} \int_{-x/h}^{\infty} \frac{k\left(\frac{x_1 - x}{h}\right)}{\int_{-x/h}^{\infty} k(v)\, dv} f(x_1)\, dx_1 \\
&= \int_{-\alpha}^{\infty} \frac{k(w)}{\int_{-\alpha}^{\infty} k(v)\, dv} f(\alpha h + wh)\, dw \quad \text{(used } x/h = \alpha \text{ and } x = \alpha h\text{)} \\
&= f(0) \frac{\int_{-\alpha}^{\infty} k(w)\, dw}{\left[\int_{-\alpha}^{\infty} k(v)\, dv\right]} + O(h) \\
&= f(0) + O(h).
\end{aligned}
$$

Exercise 1.15. With a νth order kernel, prove (1.46) and (1.47) for the univariate x case (i.e., $q = 1$).

Exercise 1.16. Intuitively, one might think that when $f(x)$ is a uniform density, say on $[0, 1]$, then one can choose a nonshrinking value of h to estimate $f(x)$ for some $x \in [0, 1]$ (i.e., h does not go to zero as $n \to \infty$). This intuition is correct when x is an interior point of $[0, 1]$. However, at (or near) the boundary of $[0, 1]$, estimation bias will not go to zero even for uniform $f(x)$.

(i) Show that if h does not converge to 0 as $n \to \infty$, then $\int_0^1 [\hat{f}(x, h) - f(x)]^2\, dx$ will not go to zero, where $f(x)$ is the uniform PDF.

(ii) Show that if $h \to 0$ as $n \to \infty$, then $\int_0^1 [\hat{f}(x, h) - f(x)]^2\, dx \to 0$ as $n \to \infty$, where $f(x)$ is the uniform PDF.

(i) and (ii) above explain why the cross-validated selection of h, $\hat{h}$, must converge to zero as $n \to \infty$, and why one does not need the condition that $f^{(2)}(x)$ is not a zero function. Of course when $f(x)$ is a uniform PDF, $\hat{h}$ will no longer have the usual order $(n^{-1/5})$. Instead it has an order equal to $n^{-1/3}$ since the bias now is of order h rather than h^2.

Exercise 1.17. Consider the Italian income data from Section 1.13.5. For the two samples of size $n = 21$ for the years 1951 and 1998, compute the density estimates using the reference rule-of-thumb in (1.17) presuming an underlying normal distribution. How many times larger than this would the bandwidth have to be to remove the bimodal feature present in the 1998 sample? Next, compute the density estimates using least squares cross-validation. Presuming that these bandwidths represent the "optimal" bandwidths, how much larger would the bandwidth for 1998 have to be to produce an apparently unimodal distribution? Finally, compare your least squares cross-validated density estimates with a naïve histogram. Do your estimates appear to be sensible, i.e., do they reflect features you believe are in fact present in the data?

Chapter 2

Regression

Regression analysis is perhaps the most widely used tool in all of applied data analysis. Regression methods model the expected (average) behavior of a dependent variable typically denoted by Y given a vector of covariates typically denoted by X (which are often commonly referred to as "regressors" or "explanatory variables"). In other words, regression analysis is designed to address questions such as, What is the expected wage of a black female college graduate working in the transportation sector? Furthermore, practitioners are often interested in how the dependent variable responds to a change in one or more of the covariates ("response") and whether this response differs significantly from zero ("test of significance"). We first briefly outline parametric regression, and then quickly move on to the study of nonparametric regression.

By far the most popular parametric regression model is the linear regression model given by

$$Y_i = \beta_0 + X_i'\beta + u_i, \quad i = 1, \ldots, n, \tag{2.1}$$

where $X_i \in \mathbb{R}^q$, and β is a $q \times 1$ vector of unknown parameters, while a more general nonlinear regression model is given by

$$Y_i = g(X_i, \beta) + u_i, \quad i = 1, \ldots, n, \tag{2.2}$$

where $g(.,.)$ has a known functional form with β again being a vector of unknown parameters. For example, we might posit a model of the form $g(x, \beta) = \exp(x'\beta)$. Having specified the functional form of the regression model up to a finite number of unknown parameters, methods such as ordinary least squares or nonlinear least squares could then be used to estimate the unknown parameter vector β in (2.1) or (2.2) respectively.

As was the case when modeling a PDF with parametric methods (see Chapter 1), in practice the true regression functional form is rarely if ever known. Since parametric methods require the user to specify the exact parametric form of the model prior to estimation, one must confront the likelihood that the presumed model may not be consistent with the data generating process (DGP), and in practice one must address issues that arise should the parametric regression model be severely misspecified. For valid inference, one must correctly specify not only the conditional mean function, but also the heteroskedasticity and serial correlation functions. The unforgiving consequences of estimation and inference based on incorrectly specified models are well established, and include inconsistent parameter estimates and invalid inference. As noted in Chapter 1, one could of course test whether the presumed parametric model is correct, but rejection of one's parametric model typically offers nothing in the way of alternative models. That is, rejection of the presumed model does not thereby produce a correctly specified model.

Nonparametric regression models do not require practitioners to make functional form presumptions about the underlying DGP. Rather than presume one knows the exact functional form of the object being estimated, one instead presumes the object exists and satisfies some regularity conditions such as smoothness (differentiability) and moment conditions. We again point out that this does not, however, come without a cost. By imposing less structure on the problem, nonparametric methods require more data to achieve the same degree of precision as a *correctly specified* parametric model. However, if one suspects that a parametric model is misspecified to some degree, and the sample at hand is not too small to meaningfully apply nonparametric techniques, practitioners might instead wish to consider nonparametric regression methods.

We begin by considering the nonparametric regression model

$$Y_i = g(X_i) + u_i, \quad i = 1, \ldots, n. \tag{2.3}$$

We assume for the moment that the sample realizations (Y_i, X_i) are i.i.d., though we relax this assumption in Chapter 18. The functional form $g(\cdot)$ is of course unknown. If $g(\cdot)$ is a smooth function, then we can estimate $g(\cdot)$ nonparametrically using kernel methods. We will interpret

$g(x)$ as the conditional mean of Y given $X = x$, i.e., $g(x) = \mathrm{E}[Y_i|X_i = x]$ due to the following result.

Theorem 2.1. *Let $\mathcal{G}$ denote the class of Borel measurable (or continuous) functions having finite second moment (see Appendix A for the definition of Borel measurable functions). Assume that $g(x) \equiv \mathrm{E}(Y|X = x)$ belongs to $\mathcal{G}$, and that $\mathrm{E}(Y^2)$ is finite. Then $\mathrm{E}(Y|X)$ is the optimal predictor of Y given X, in the following MSE sense:*

$$\mathrm{E}\{[Y - r(X)]^2\} \geq \mathrm{E}\{[Y - \mathrm{E}(Y|X)]^2\} \text{ for all } r(\cdot) \in \mathcal{G},$$

or, equivalently,

$$\min_{\{r(\cdot)\in\mathcal{G}\}} \mathrm{E}\{[Y - r(X)]^2\} = \mathrm{E}\{[Y - \mathrm{E}(Y|X)]^2\}.$$

Proof. First we observe that $g(x) = \mathrm{E}(Y|x)$ is a function of x. Next let $f_{y,x}(x, y)$, $f(x)$ and $f_{y|x}(y|x)$ denote the joint PDF of (Y, X), the marginal PDF of X, and the conditional PDF of $Y|X$, respectively. From $f_{y|x}(x, y) = f_{y,x}(x, y)/f(x)$, we have

$$\mathrm{E}(Y|X = x) = \int y f_{y|x}(y|x)\, dy = \frac{\int y f_{y,x}(x, y)\, dy}{f(x)} \overset{\text{def}}{=} g(x), \qquad (2.4)$$

which is obviously a function of x. Now, for any function $r(x)$, we have

$$\begin{aligned}
\mathrm{E}\{[Y - r(X)]^2\} &= \mathrm{E}\{[Y - \mathrm{E}(Y|X) + \mathrm{E}(Y|X) - r(X)]^2\} \\
&= \mathrm{E}\{[Y - \mathrm{E}(Y|X)]^2\} + \mathrm{E}\{[\mathrm{E}(Y|X) - r(X)]^2\} \\
&\quad + 2\mathrm{E}\{[(Y - \mathrm{E}(Y|X))(\mathrm{E}(Y|X) - r(X))]\} \\
&= \mathrm{E}\{[Y - \mathrm{E}(Y|X)]^2\} + \mathrm{E}\{[\mathrm{E}(Y|X) - r(X)]^2\} \\
&\geq \mathrm{E}\{[Y - \mathrm{E}(Y|X)]^2\},
\end{aligned}$$

where we used the fact that

$$\begin{aligned}
\mathrm{E}\{[Y - \mathrm{E}(Y|X)][\mathrm{E}(Y|X) - r(X)]\} &\equiv \mathrm{E}\{[Y - \mathrm{E}(Y|X)][g(X) - r(X)]\} \\
&= \mathrm{E}\{[g(X) - r(X)] \\
&\quad \times \mathrm{E}[Y - \mathrm{E}(Y|X)|X]\} = 0
\end{aligned}$$

by the law of iterated expectations (see Appendix A, Lemma A.11). $\square$

Theorem 2.1 says that $\mathrm{E}(Y|X)$ is the optimal function of X for predicting Y in the sense that the prediction MSE will be minimized in the class of all Borel measurable (or continuous) functions $r(x)$. Thus we will interpret $g(x)$ in (2.3) as $E(Y|x)$. In light of (2.4), it is clear that once one knows how to estimate $f_{y,x}(x,y)$ and $f(x)$ using the methods presented in Chapter 1, one can easily obtain an estimator for $g(x) = E(Y|x)$. This leads directly to the "local constant" kernel estimator, originally proposed by Nadaraya (1965) and Watson (1964), which is often referred to simply as the "Nadaraya-Watson kernel estimator."

2.1   Local Constant Kernel Estimation

We considered the estimation of $f_{y,x}(x,y)$ and $f(x)$ in detail in Chapter 1, and so the only additional step required for estimating a conditional mean is integration with respect to y to obtain $\int y f_{y,x}(x,y)\,dy$. Note that we can estimate $\int y f_{y,x}(x,y)\,dy$ by replacing the unknown PDF $f_{y,x}(x,y)$ with its kernel estimate yielding $\int y \hat{f}_{y,x}(x,y)\,dy$, where

$$\hat{f}_{y,x}(x,y) = \frac{1}{nh_0h_1\ldots h_q}\sum_{i=1}^{n} K\left(\frac{X_i-x}{h}\right) k\left(\frac{y-Y_i}{h_0}\right),$$

where $K\left(\frac{X_i-x}{h}\right) = k\left(\frac{X_{i1}-x_1}{h_1}\right) \times \ldots \times k\left(\frac{X_{iq}-x_q}{h_q}\right)$ and where h_0 is the smoothing parameter associated with Y. Thus we have

$$\int y\hat{f}_{y,x}(x,y)\,dy = \frac{1}{nh_0h_1\ldots h_q}\sum_{i=1}^{n} K\left(\frac{X_i-x}{h}\right) \int yk\left(\frac{y-Y_i}{h_0}\right)dy$$

$$= \frac{1}{nh_0h_1\ldots h_q}\sum_{i=1}^{n} K\left(\frac{X_i-x}{h}\right) \int (Y_i+h_0v)k(v)h_0\,dv$$

(change of variables: $(y-Y_i)/h_0 = v$)

$$= \frac{1}{nh_1\ldots h_q}\sum_{i=1}^{n} K\left(\frac{X_i-x}{h}\right) Y_i,$$

$$(2.5)$$

where we used $\int k(v)\,dv = 1$ and $\int vk(v)\,dv = 0$.
Based on (2.4) and (2.5) we thereby estimate $E(Y|x) \equiv g(x)$ by

$$\hat{g}(x) = \frac{\int y\hat{f}_{y,x}(x,y)\,dy}{\hat{f}(x)} = \frac{\sum_{i=1}^{n} Y_i K\left(\frac{X_i-x}{h}\right)}{\sum_{i=1}^{n} K\left(\frac{X_i-x}{h}\right)}, \qquad (2.6)$$

which is simply a weighted average of Y_i because we can rewrite (2.6) as

$$\hat{g}(x) = \sum_{i=1}^{n} Y_i w_i,$$

where $w_i = K\left(\frac{X_i - x}{h}\right) / \sum_{j=1}^{n} K\left(\frac{X_j - x}{h}\right)$ is the weight attached to Y_i. Note that the weights are nonnegative and sum to one.

Along the lines of the analysis given in Chapter 1, one can show that

$$\hat{g}(x) - g(x) = O_p\left(\sum_{s=1}^{q} h_s^2 + (nh_1 \ldots h_q)^{-1/2}\right),$$

the proof of which is similar to the proof of

$$\hat{f}(x) - f(x) = O_p\left(\sum_{s=1}^{q} h_s^2 + (nh_1 \ldots h_q)^{-1/2}\right),$$

which was presented in Section 1.6 of Chapter 1. An easy way to establish the consistency of $\hat{g}(x)$ is to handle its numerator and denominator separately. First we write

$$\hat{g}(x) - g(x) = \frac{(\hat{g}(x) - g(x)) \hat{f}(x)}{\hat{f}(x)} \equiv \frac{\hat{m}(x)}{\hat{f}(x)}, \qquad (2.7)$$

where $\hat{m}(x) = (\hat{g}(x) - g(x)) \hat{f}(x)$. Using $Y_i = g(X_i) + u_i$, we have

$$\hat{m}(x) = \hat{m}_1(x) + \hat{m}_2(x),$$

where

$$\hat{m}_1(x) = (nh_1 \ldots h_q)^{-1} \sum_{i=1}^{n} (g(X_i) - g(x)) K\left(\frac{X_i - x}{h}\right)$$

and

$$\hat{m}_2(x) = (nh_1 \ldots h_q)^{-1} \sum_{i=1}^{n} u_i K\left(\frac{X_i - x}{h}\right).$$

Using the notation $r(x + hv) = r(x_1 + h_1 v_1, \ldots, x_q + h_q v_q)$ and using the same arguments as in the derivation of (1.36), we can easily show that

$$E[\hat{m}_1(x)] = (h_1 \ldots h_q)^{-1} \int f(x_1) \left[g(x_1) - g(x) \right] K\left(\frac{x_1 - x}{h} \right) dx_1$$

$$= \int f(x + hv) \left[g(x + hv) - g(x) \right] K(v) \, dv$$

$$= \frac{\kappa_2}{2} \sum_{s=1}^{q} h_s^2 \left\{ \left[2f_s(x)g_s(x) + f(x)g_{ss}(x) \right] \right\} + O\left(\sum_{s=1}^{q} h_s^3 \right)$$

$$\equiv f(x) \sum_{s=1}^{q} h_s^2 B_s(x) + O\left(\sum_{s=1}^{q} h_s^3 \right),$$

(2.8)

where $\kappa_2 = \int v^2 k(v) \, dv$, $B_s(x) = \frac{\kappa_2}{2} \{ 2f_s(x)g_s(x) + f(x)g_{ss}(x) \} / f(x)$, and $r_s(x)$ and $r_{ss}(x)$ are the first and second order derivatives of $r(x)$ with respect to x_s, respectively ($r = g$ or $r = f$). Also,

$$\text{var}\left(\hat{m}_1(x) \right) = (nh_1^2 \ldots h_q^2)^{-1} \text{var}\left[(g(X_1) - g(x)) K\left(\frac{X_1 - x}{h} \right) \right]$$

$$= (nh_1^2 \ldots h_q^2)^{-1} \left(\text{E}\left\{ \left[(g(X_1) - g(x)) K\left(\frac{X_1 - x}{h} \right) \right]^2 \right\} \right.$$

$$\left. - \left\{ \text{E}\left[(g(X_1) - g(x)) K\left(\frac{X_1 - x}{h} \right) \right] \right\}^2 \right)$$

$$= (nh_1^2 \ldots h_q^2)^{-1} \left((h_1 \ldots h_q) \int f(x + hv) \right.$$

$$\left. \times \left[g(x + hv) - g(x) \right]^2 K(v)^2 \, dv - (s.o.) \right)$$

$$= O\left((nh_1 \ldots h_q)^{-1} \sum_{s=1}^{q} h_s^2 \right),$$

(2.9)

where ($s.o.$) denotes terms of smaller order.

Equations (2.8) and (2.9) lead to

$$\hat{m}_1(x) = f(x) \sum_{s=1}^{q} B_s(x) h_s^2 + O_p\left(\eta_2^{3/2} + \eta_2^{1/2} \eta_1^{1/2} \right), \qquad (2.10)$$

where $\eta_1 = (nh_1 \ldots h_q)^{-1}$ and $\eta_2 = \sum_{s=1}^{q} h_s^2$ (see Exercise 2.1). Next, we observe that $E[\hat{m}_2(x)] = 0$, and that

$$E\Big\{ [\hat{m}_2(x)]^2 \Big\} = (nh_1^2 \ldots h_q^2)^{-1} E\left[u_i^2 K^2 \left(\frac{X_i - x}{h} \right) \right]$$

$$= (nh_1^2 \ldots h_q^2)^{-1} E\left[\sigma^2(X_i) K^2 \left(\frac{X_i - x}{h} \right) \right]$$

$$= (nh_1 \ldots h_q)^{-1} \left\{ f(x)\sigma^2(x) \int K(v)^2 \, dv + O\left(\sum_{s=1}^{q} h_s^2 \right) \right\}$$

$$\equiv (nh_1 \ldots h_q)^{-1} \Omega(x) + O\left((nh_1 \ldots h_q)^{-1} \sum_{s=1}^{q} h_s^2 \right), \qquad (2.11)$$

where $\Omega(x) = \kappa^q f(x)\sigma^2(x)$, $\kappa = \int k(v)^2 \, dv$ and $\sigma^2(x) = E(u_i^2|X_i = x)$. Equations (2.10) and (2.11) lead to

$$\hat{m}(x) = \hat{m}_1(x) + \hat{m}_2(x) = O_p\left(\eta_2 + \eta_1^{1/2} \right). \qquad (2.12)$$

Therefore, given that $\hat{g}(x) - g(x) = \hat{m}(x)/\hat{f}(x)$ and that $\hat{f}(x) = f(x) + o_p(1)$, we just proved the following result (assuming that $f(x) > 0$):

$$\hat{g}(x) - g(x) = O_p\left(\frac{\hat{m}(x)}{[f(x) + o_p(1)]} \right)$$

$$= O_p\left(\sum_{s=1}^{q} h_s^2 + (nh_1 \ldots h_q)^{-1/2} \right). \qquad (2.13)$$

From (2.13) it is easy to see that if each bandwidth (h_s) has the same order of magnitude, then the optimal choice of h_s that minimizes $\text{MSE}[\hat{g}(x)]$ is $h_s \sim n^{-1/(q+4)}$, and the resulting MSE is therefore of order $O(n^{-4/(q+4)})$.

The asymptotic normality of $\hat{g}(x)$ can also be established at this stage by using Liapunov's CLT.

Theorem 2.2. *Under the assumption that x is an interior point, $g(x)$ and $f(x)$ are three-times continuously differentiable, and $f(x) > 0$, then as $n \to \infty$, $h_s \to 0$ (for all s), $nh_1 \ldots h_q \to \infty$ and $(nh_1 \ldots h_q)\sum_{s=1}^{q} h_s^6 \to 0$, we have*

$$\sqrt{nh_1 \ldots h_q} \left(\hat{g}(x) - g(x) - \sum_{s=1}^{q} h_s^2 B_s(x) \right) \xrightarrow{d} N\left(0, \kappa^q \sigma^2(x)/f(x) \right),$$

$$(2.14)$$

where $B_s(x)$ is defined immediately following (2.8).

Proof. $(nh_1 \ldots h_q)^{1/2} \hat{m}_2(x)$ has mean zero and (2.11) shows that it has asymptotic variance $\Omega(x)$. Using Liapunov's CLT, one can easily show that

$$\sqrt{nh_1 \ldots h_q} \hat{m}_2(x) \overset{d}{\to} N\left(0, \Omega(x)\right). \qquad (2.15)$$

Combining (2.10) and (2.15), we have

$$\sqrt{nh_1 \ldots h_q} \left(\hat{m}(x) - \sum_{s=1}^{q} h_s^2 B_s(x) \hat{f}(x) \right) = \sqrt{nh_1 \ldots h_q} \hat{m}_2(x) + o_p(1)$$

$$\overset{d}{\to} N\left(0, \Omega(x)\right)$$

$$(2.16)$$

because $(nh_1 \ldots h_q)^{1/2} \eta_2^{3/2} \sim (nh_1 \ldots h_q)^{1/2} \sum_{s=1}^{q} h_s^3 = o(1)$.

From (2.16), and also noting that $\hat{f}(x) = f(x) + o_p(1)$, we immediately obtain

$$\sqrt{nh_1 \ldots h_q} \left(\hat{g}(x) - g(x) - \sum_{s=1}^{q} h_s^2 B_s(x) \right)$$

$$\equiv \frac{\sqrt{nh_1 \ldots h_q} \left(\hat{g}(x) - g(x) - \sum_{s=1}^{q} h_s^2 B_s(x) \right) \hat{f}(x)}{\hat{f}(x)}$$

$$= \frac{\sqrt{nh_1 \ldots h_q} \left(\hat{m}(x) - \sum_{s=1}^{q} h_s^2 B_s(x) \hat{f}(x) \right)}{\hat{f}(x)}$$

$$\overset{d}{\to} \frac{1}{f(x)} N\left(0, \Omega(x)\right) = N\left(0, \kappa^q \sigma^2(x)/f(x)\right). $$

$$(2.17)$$

This completes the proof of Theorem 2.2.   □

2.1.1 Intuition Underlying the Local Constant Kernel Estimator

In order to master nonparametric kernel regression methods, one should not only master basic skills such as deriving rates of convergence, but in addition seek to cultivate an intuitive understanding of why kernel methods work as they do.

Fortunately, the intuition underlying $\hat{g}(x) \overset{p}{\to} g(x)$ is really quite simple. The basic idea is that $g(x)$ is simply a "local average," which can perhaps best be explained in a simple one regressor setting ($X_i \in \mathbb{R}$) employing a uniform kernel. In this case ($h_1 = h$) we see that

$$
\begin{aligned}
\hat{g}(x) &= \frac{\sum_{i=1}^{n} Y_i K\left(\frac{X_i - x}{h}\right)}{\sum_{i=1}^{n} K\left(\frac{X_i - x}{h}\right)} \\
&= \frac{\sum_{|X_i - x| \leq h} Y_i(1/2)}{\sum_{|X_i - x| \leq h}(1/2)} \\
&= \frac{\sum_{|X_i - x| \leq h} [g(X_i) + u_i]}{\sum_{|X_i - x| \leq h} 1} \\
&= \{ \text{ average of } g(X_i)\text{'s} + \text{ average of } u_i\text{'s with } |X_i - x| \leq h \} \\
&\xrightarrow{p} g(x) + 0 = g(x),
\end{aligned}
$$

because $|g(X_i) - g(x)| = O(h) = o(1)$ for $|X_i - x| \leq h$ by the assumption that $g(x)$ has a bounded derivative at x. In fact, given the symmetry of the kernel function, we have $n^{-1} \sum_{|X_i - x| \leq h}(g(X_i) - g(x)) = O_p\left(h^2\right)$. The condition $nh \to \infty$ ensures that asymptotically, infinitely many observations appear in each interval with length h (or $2h$, i.e., within distance h either side of the point $X = x$ at which we evaluate our estimate of $g(x)$). This is because the number of intervals is of the order $O(1/h)$. On average, we would expect to have $n/O(1/h) = O(nh)$ observations in an interval with length h. Azzalini and Bowman (1997) refer to nh as the "local sample size," which is a nice way of thinking about things, as this is the sample relevant for estimating the regression function at a fixed point x. Consistency therefore requires that the size of the "local sample" must increase ($nh \to \infty$) with the overall sample size ($n \to \infty$) while at the same time the interval width must shrink to zero in the limit ($h \to 0$). The average of the u_i's in each interval converges to their population mean value $E(u_i) = 0$ (in probability) by a law of large numbers argument because $nh \to \infty$ as $n \to \infty$. We therefore see that, for the uniform kernel, $\hat{g}(x)$ uses a simple local average of the Y_i's (based upon those X_i lying close to x) to estimate $g(x)$.

Summarizing, we estimate the conditional mean function by locally averaging those values of the dependent variable which are "close" in terms of the values taken on by the regressors. The amount of local information used to construct the average is controlled by a window width. By controlling the amount of local information used to construct the estimate (the "local sample size") and allowing the amount of local averaging to become more informative as the sample size increases, while also shrinking the neighborhood in which the averaging occurs, we can ensure that our estimates are consistent under standard regularity conditions.

The estimator $\hat{g}(x)$ is often called the "local constant" estimator of $g(x)$, though one could just as easily use local linear/polynomial methods to estimate $g(x)$, and for a more in-depth treatment of local polynomial methods we refer the reader to Fan and Gijbels's (1996) well-written monograph. Local linear estimators also automatically provide an estimator of response, i.e., the derivative of $g(x)$, while a pth order local polynomial method can estimate derivatives up to order p. We discuss local linear and local polynomial methods in Section 2.4 below, but first we address a fundamental aspect of nonparametric local constant regression, namely, bandwidth selection.

2.2   Local Constant Bandwidth Selection

In this section we discuss various approaches to smoothing parameter selection for the estimation of the unknown regression function $g(\cdot)$ by the local constant estimator given by (2.6). We discuss three different methods of smoothing parameter selection, (i) rule-of-thumb and plug-in methods, (ii) the least squares cross-validation method, and (iii) a modified AIC procedure.

2.2.1   Rule-of-Thumb and Plug-In Methods

When using a second order kernel, it can be shown that the optimal smoothing parameter should be of order $O(n^{-1/(4+q)})$. A popular rule-of-thumb procedure is therefore to choose h_s by $c_s X_{s,sd} n^{-1/(4+q)}$ $(s = 1, \ldots, q)$, where c_s is a constant and $X_{s,sd}$ is the sample standard deviation of $\{X_{is}\}_{i=1}^n$. In practice, c_s is often chosen to be 1 or some other constant close to 1. The argument underlying this rule-of-thumb is related to the so-called normal reference rule for density estimation discussed in Chapter 1. Rules-of-thumb are attractive to practitioners because they are simple, computationally speaking. However, one disadvantage of such approaches is that that they treat all components (covariates) of x symmetrically. In practice, a regression function $g(x)$ may change slowly with respect to one component, say x_1, but quite rapidly with respect to another component, say x_2. In this case, one ought to use a relatively large smoothing parameter for x_1 and a relatively small smoothing parameter for x_2. Clearly the rule-of-thumb method lacks this flexibility.

An alternative method is the so-called plug-in method which is usually based on minimizing a "weighted integrated MSE" (WIMSE) of the form $\int E[\hat{g}(x) - g(x)]^2 \nu(x)\,dx$, where the expectation is taken with respect to the random sample $\{X_i, Y_i\}_{i=1}^n$, and where $\nu(x)$ is a nonnegative weight function which ensures that asymptotically, the WIMSE is finite.

The leading bias and variance terms of $\hat{g}(x)$ are derived in (2.14). Thus, the leading term of the WIMSE $\int E[\hat{g}(x) - g(x)]^2 \nu(x)\,dx$ is given by

$$
\begin{aligned}
\text{WIMSE} &= \int \left\{ \left[\sum_{s=1}^{q} h_s^2 B_s(x) \right]^2 + \frac{\kappa^q}{nh_1 \dots h_q} \frac{\sigma^2(x)}{f(x)} \right\} \nu(x)\,dx \\
&= O\left(\left(\sum_{s=1}^{q} h_s^2 \right)^2 + (nh_1 \dots h_q)^{-1} \right).
\end{aligned}
\tag{2.18}
$$

Note that the use of a weighting function here is important since $\int \sigma^2(x) f(x)^{-1}\,dx$ does not exist for many well-known distributions (e.g., the normal distribution).

By defining a_s via $h_s = a_s n^{-1/(q+4)}$, (2.18) becomes

$$
\text{WIMSE} = n^{-4/(q+4)} \chi_\nu(a_1, \dots, a_q),
\tag{2.19}
$$

where

$$
\chi_\nu(a_1, \dots, a_q) = \int \left\{ \left[\sum_{s=1}^{q} a_s^2 B_s(x) \right]^2 + \frac{\kappa^q}{a_1 \dots a_q} \frac{\sigma^2(x)}{f(x)} \right\} \nu(x)\,dx.
\tag{2.20}
$$

We let $a_1^0, \dots, a_q^0$ denote the values of $a_1, \dots, a_q$ that minimize $\chi_\nu(a_1, \dots, a_q)$. If one of the a_s^0 is zero, we must have $a_t^0 = \infty$ for some $t \neq s$. This implies that $h_t = \infty$. If $h_t = \infty$, we readily see that $k((X_{it} - x_t)/h_t) = k(0)$ becomes a constant, and this constant cancels in the numerator and the denominator of $\hat{g}(x)$ so that $\hat{g}(x)$ is then unrelated to x_t (if $h_t = \infty$). In this section we assume that all the components in x are relevant regressors and hence we rule out the case for which $a_t^0\,(h_t)$ is infinity and assume that[1]

Each a_s^0 is uniquely defined, positive, and *finite*.   (2.21)

Letting the h_s^0's denote the smoothing parameters that minimize (2.18), we have

$$h_s^0 = n^{-1/(q+4)} a_s^0 \quad \text{for } s = 1, \ldots, q. \quad (2.22)$$

Equation (2.22) implies that $h_s^0 = O(n^{-1/(q+4)})$. We observe that a_s^0 depends on the unknown functions $g(\cdot)$, $f(\cdot)$, and their derivatives (because $B_s(x)$ depends on these functions). Obtaining explicit expressions for the a_s^0 when $1 \leq q \leq 2$ is fairly straightforward (see Exercise 2.2). However, for general high dimensional cases, closed form expressions for the a_s^0's do not exist, even though the a_s's are well defined (again, see Exercise 2.2).

When a closed form expression for a_s^0 exists, one can obtain a consistent estimator for a_s^0. Letting $\hat{a}_s^0$ denote a consistent estimator of a_s^0, one can estimate h_s^0 by $\hat{h}_s^0 = \hat{a}_s^0 n^{-1/(q+4)}$ $(s = 1, \ldots, q)$. This approach is called a plug-in method for selecting the smoothing parameters. Even when a closed form expression for a_s^0 does not exist, in principle one can still obtain consistent estimates for a_s^0. For example, one can replace $B_s(x)$ by some consistent estimator, say $\hat{B}_s(x)$, compute the integration involving χ_ν, and then minimize χ_ν numerically over $a_1, \ldots, a_q$ to obtain $\hat{a}_1^0, \ldots, \hat{a}_q^0$. Such a procedure can be computationally intensive. As we discuss in Section 2.2.2, one can use an alternative *cross-validation* procedure to optimally select the smoothing parameters in such situations.

Even if a closed form expression for a_s^0 exists, one still requires initial nonparametric estimates of $B_s(x)$ and $\sigma^2(x)$, which in turn requires one to select some initial or "pilot" smoothing parameters in order to estimate these unknown quantities. The initial smoothing parameters may be chosen by rule-of-thumb methods such as $h_s = x_{s,sd} n^{-1/(q+4)}$ as discussed above $(s = 1, \ldots, q)$. However, if the initially chosen smoothing parameters lie far from their optimal values (h_s^0's), the second-step plug-in $\hat{h}_s^0$'s can also lie far from h_s^0's, as discussed in Loader (1999). Finally, when condition (2.21) fails, the plug-in method is no longer well defined. We show in the next section that a least squares cross-validation approach is immune to each of the aforementioned problems.

---

[1]We discuss the "irrelevant regressor" case in Section 2.2.4. There we shall see that the optimal smoothing parameter for an irrelevant regressor should be infinity.

Perhaps for these reasons, plug-in methods are infrequently used in multivariate nonparametric empirical applications.

2.2.2 Least Squares Cross-Validation

In this section we introduce a completely data-driven method of smoothing parameter selection known as "local constant (lc) least squares cross-validation." We choose $h_1, \ldots, h_q$ to minimize the objective function

$$CV_{lc}(h_1, \ldots, h_q) = n^{-1} \sum_{i=1}^{n} (Y_i - \hat{g}_{-i}(X_i))^2 M(X_i), \qquad (2.23)$$

where $\hat{g}_{-i}(X_i) = \sum_{l \neq i}^{n} Y_l K((X_i - X_l)/h) / \sum_{l \neq i}^{n} K((X_i - X_l)/h)$ is the leave-one-out kernel estimator of $g(X_i)$ and $0 \leq M(\cdot) \leq 1$ is a weight function which serves to avoid difficulties caused by dividing by zero or by the slow convergence rate caused by boundary effects (defined in Section 1.10).

In Section 2.7 we show that

$$CV_{lc}(h_1, \ldots, h_q) = n^{-4/(q+4)} \chi(a_1, \ldots, a_q) + o\left(n^{-4/(q+4)}\right)$$

$$+ \text{(terms unrelated to } h), \qquad (2.24)$$

where the a_s are defined via $h_s = a_s n^{-1/(q+4)}$ $(s = 1, \ldots, q)$, and

$$\chi(a_1, \ldots, a_q) = \int \left\{ \sum_{s=1}^{q} B_s(x) a_s^2 \right\}^2 f(x) M(x) \, dx$$

$$+ \frac{\kappa^q}{a_1 \ldots a_q} \int \sigma^2(x) M(x) \, dx. \qquad (2.25)$$

Comparing χ_ν given in (2.20) with χ of (2.25), we observe that if $\nu(x) = f(x)M(x)$ in (2.20), then $\chi_\nu = \chi$. This is not surprising as χ_ν is related to the leading term of

$$\int \mathrm{E}[\hat{g}(x) - g(x)]^2 \nu(x) \, dx, \qquad (2.26)$$

while χ is related to the leading term of $\mathrm{E}[CV_{lc,0}]$, where $CV_{lc,0} = n^{-1} \sum_i (g_i - \hat{g}_i)^2 M_i$ is the leading term of CV_{lc}, $g_i = g(X_i)$ and $\hat{g}_i =$

$\hat{g}_{-i}(X_i)$. Thus, we have

$$
\begin{aligned}
\mathrm{E}[CV_{lc,0}] &= \mathrm{E}\left\{[\hat{g}_i - g_i]^2 M_i\right\} = \mathrm{E}\left\{\mathrm{E}\left[(\hat{g}_i - g_i)^2 M_i | X_i\right]\right\} \\
&= \int \mathrm{E}\left[(\hat{g}_i - g_i)^2 M_i | X_i = x\right] f(x)\, dx \\
&= \int \mathrm{E}\left[\hat{g}(x) - g(x)\right]^2 M(x) f(x)\, dx,
\end{aligned}
\tag{2.27}
$$

where the last equality uses the fact that $\hat{g}_i$ is a leave-one-out estimator so that $\{X_j, Y_j\}_{j=1, j\neq i}^n$ is independent of X_i by assumption. Comparing (2.26) and (2.27), we see that they are identical if $\nu(x) = f(x)M(x)$.

Along the lines of the analysis outlined in Section 2.2.1, let $a_1^0, \ldots, a_q^0$ denote values of $a_1, \ldots, a_q$ that minimize χ subject to each of them being nonnegative. As was the case for (2.21) we assume that

Each a_s^0 is uniquely defined, positive, and *finite*.   (2.28)

Let h_s^0 denote values of h_s $(1 \leq s \leq q)$ that minimize the leading term of $\mathrm{E}[CV_{lc,0}(h)]$; then

$$
h_s^0 = a_s^0 n^{-1/(q+4)} \text{ for } s = 1, \ldots, q.
\tag{2.29}
$$

If we let $\hat{h}_s$ $(s = 1, \ldots, q)$ denote the values of h_s selected by cross-validation, then, since $CV_{lc}(h) = \mathrm{E}[CV_{lc,0}(h)] + (s.o.) + $ terms related to h, we can show that $\hat{h}_s = h_s^0 + o_p(h_s^0)$. Thus, we have the main result of this section.

Theorem 2.3. *Under conditions given in Section 2.7 and (2.28),*

$$
n^{1/(q+4)} \hat{h}_s \to a_s^0 \text{ in probability for } 1 \leq s \leq q, \text{ and}
$$

$$
n^{4/(q+4)} \left\{ CV_{lc}(\hat{h}_1, \ldots, \hat{h}_q) - n^{-1} \sum_i u_i^2 M(X_i) \right\}
$$

$$
\to \inf_{a_1, \ldots, a_q} \chi(a_1, \ldots, a_q) \text{ in probability.}
$$

For applied researchers, cross-validation methods are quite appealing since they need not know the explicit expressions for the optimal smoothing parameters; rather, all they need is to minimize the objective function CV_{lc} defined in (2.23), which can be done using any standard numerical optimization procedure. Even if the h_0^s's $\left(a_s^0\right)$ do not have closed form expressions, Theorem 2.3 states that smoothing parameters selected via cross-validation (the $\hat{h}_s$'s) are optimal in the sense of being asymptotically equivalent to the deterministic optimal smoothing parameters, the h_s^0's.

A rigorous proof of Theorem 2.3 is very involved because the smaller order terms must be shown to be uniformly small in $(h_1, \ldots, h_q) \in H_n$, defined in Section 2.7, and in $x \in \operatorname{supp} M$ (the support of M; see Hall et al. (2006) for details). However, by sacrificing rigor and glossing over some details when proving the uniformity for some smaller order terms, Theorem 2.3 is intuitively easy to understand. Equation (2.29) implies that $n^{1/(q+4)}h_s^0 \to a_s^0$, and the fact that $CV_{lc} = \mathrm{E}[CV_{lc,0}] + (s.o.)$ implies that $n^{1/(q+4)}\hat{h}_s = n^{1/(q+4)}h_s^0 + (s.o.) = a_s^0 + o_p(1) \to a_s^0$ in probability.

Assumption (2.28) is the most important condition required for Theorem 2.3 to hold. We now discuss this condition in some detail. Defining $z = (a_1^2, \ldots, a_q^2)'$, $C_0 = \int \sigma^2(x)M(x)\,dx$, and letting A denote a $q \times q$ matrix with its (t, s)th element given by

$$\int B_t(x)B_s(x)f(x)M(x)\,dx,$$

we can write (2.82) as

$$\chi_z(z_1, \ldots, z_q) \stackrel{\text{def}}{=} z'Az + \frac{C_0}{\sqrt{z_1 \cdots z_q}}. \qquad (2.30)$$

Let $z_1^0, \ldots, z_q^0$ denote the values of $z_1, \ldots, z_q$ that minimize χ_z subject to the constraint that they are all nonnegative. We want to find conditions which guarantee that $z_1^0, \ldots, z_q^0$ are all positive and finite (which is equivalent to (2.28)). It can be shown that[2]

$z_1^0, \ldots, z_q^0$ are all positive and finite if A is positive definite.   (2.31)

Note that A is a positive semidefinite matrix since

$$z'Az = \int \left[\sum_{s=1}^{q} B_s(x)z_s \right]^2 f(x)M(x)\,dx \geq 0$$

for all z. Condition (2.31) states that A being positive definite is sufficient for $z_1^0, \ldots, z_q^0$ to be finite. We give an intuitive proof of (2.31)

---

[2]Note that (2.31) is a sufficient condition. A (weak) necessary and sufficient condition for $z_1^0, \ldots, z_q^0$ to all be positive and finite can be found in Li and Zhou (2005).

here and relegate a more rigorous proof to Exercise 2.2. First, note that A being positive definite implies that $z_s^0 < \infty$ for all s, for otherwise we will have $\chi_z = \infty$. Next, we have $z_s^0 > 0$ for all s, otherwise we have $C_0/(z_1^0 \ldots z_q^0)^{1/2} = \infty$. Thus, we must have $0 < z_s^0 < \infty$ for all $s = 1, \ldots, q$.

Theorem 2.3 only covers the case whereby all components of x are relevant. As we discussed in Section 2.2.1, when $q = 2$ and $g(x_1, x_2) = \theta(x_1)$ for all $(x_1, x_2) \in \mathbb{R}^2$ (x_2 is an irrelevant regressor), then (2.28) does not hold. However, we can show that the cross-validation method still leads to optimal smoothing parameter selection, as the optimal smoothing in this case should have the property that $\hat{h}_1 = O_p\left(n^{-1/5}\right)$ and $\hat{h}_2 \to \infty$, as we demonstrate in Section 2.2.4.

2.2.3 AIC_c

An alternative bandwidth selection method having impressive finite-sample properties was proposed by Hurvich, Simonoff and Tsai (1998). Their approach is based on an improved Akaike information criterion (AIC; see Akaike (1974)). Hurvich et al.'s criterion provides an approximately unbiased estimate of expected Kullback-Leibler information for nonparametric models. Akaike's original information criterion was designed for parametric models, while Hurvich et al.'s approach is valid for estimators that can be written as linear combinations of the outcome, hence is directly applicable to a wide range of nonparametric estimators. Their criterion is given by

$$\text{AIC}_c = \ln(\hat{\sigma}^2) + \frac{1 + \text{tr}(H)/n}{1 - \{\text{tr}(H) + 2\}/n},$$

where

$$\hat{\sigma}^2 = \frac{1}{n}\sum_{i=1}^{n}\{Y_i - \hat{g}(X_i)\}^2 = Y'(I - H)'(I - H)Y/n$$

with $\hat{g}(X_i)$ being a nonparametric estimator and H being an $n \times n$ weighting function (i.e., the matrix of kernel weights) with its (i,j)th element given by $H_{ij} = K_{h,ij}/\sum_{l=1}^{n} K_{h,il}$, $K_{h,ij} = \prod_{s=1}^{q} h_s^{-1}k((X_{is} - X_{js})/h_s)$.

Through simulation experiments, Hurvich et al. (1998) show that the AIC_c bandwidth selector performs quite well compared with the plug-in method (when it is available) and with a number of generalized cross-validation methods (Craven and Wahba (1979)). While there is no rigorous theoretical result available for the optimality of the AIC_c selector, Hurvich et al. conjecture that the AIC_c selector shares the same asymptotic optimality properties as the least squares cross-validation method outlined in Section 2.2.2. Indeed, simulation results reported in Li and Racine (2004a) show that, for small samples, AIC_c tends to perform better than the least squares cross-validation method, while for large samples there is no appreciable difference between the two approaches.

2.2.4 The Presence of Irrelevant Regressors

We now consider the case wherein (i.e., allow for the possibility that) some of the regressors are irrelevant. Without loss of generality, we assume that only the first q_1 components of x are relevant in the sense defined below. For integers $1 \leq q_1 \leq q$, $0 \leq q_2 \leq q - 1$ satisfying $q_1 + q_2 = q$, let $\bar{X}$ consist of the first q_1 components of X and let $\tilde{X} = X/\bar{X}$ denote the remaining components of X (i.e., its complement). We assume that

$$(Y, \bar{X}) \text{ is independent of } \tilde{X}. \tag{2.32}$$

A consequence of (2.32) is that $\text{E}[Y|\bar{X}, \tilde{X}] = \text{E}[Y|\bar{X}]$ almost surely, so that $\bar{X}$ contains only relevant regressors while $\tilde{X}$ contains only irrelevant regressors. It is important to note, however, that we do not assume that this is known a priori. In practice we proceed to estimate $\text{E}(Y_i|X_i)$, rather than $\text{E}(Y_i|\bar{X}_i)$, nonparametrically. We will show that if least squares cross-validation is used to select the smoothing parameters, then asymptotically the irrelevant variables can be automatically smoothed out. To be more specific about what we mean by "smoothing out irrelevant variables," note that

$$\hat{g}(x) = \frac{\sum_{i=1}^n Y_i \prod_{s=1}^{q_1} k\left(\frac{X_{is}-x_s}{h_s}\right) \prod_{s=q_1+1}^q k\left(\frac{X_{is}-x_s}{h_s}\right)}{\sum_{i=1}^n \prod_{s=1}^{q_1} k\left(\frac{X_{is}-x_s}{h_s}\right) \prod_{s=q_1+1}^q k\left(\frac{X_{is}-x_s}{h_s}\right)}. \tag{2.33}$$

If $h_s = \infty$ for $s = q_1 + 1, \ldots, q$, then $k\left((X_{is} - x_s)/h_s\right) = k(0)$ for $s = q_1 + 1, \ldots, q$, and (2.33) reduces to

$$\hat{g}(x) = \frac{\sum_{i=1}^n Y_i \prod_{s=1}^{q_1} k\left(\frac{X_{is}-x_s}{h_s}\right)}{\sum_{i=1}^n \prod_{s=1}^{q_1} k\left(\frac{X_{is}-x_s}{h_s}\right)}, \tag{2.34}$$

as $k(0)^{q-q_1}$ cancels from the numerator and denominator of $\hat{g}(x)$. Therefore, $\hat{g}(x)$ will be unrelated to the irrelevant variables x_s ($s = q_1 + 1, \ldots, q$). We show in Theorem 2.4 below that bandwidths selected via cross-validation indeed possess this property, i.e., as $n \to \infty$, $\hat{h}_s \to \infty$ for $s = q_1 + 1, \ldots, q$. Thus, asymptotically, cross-validation is capable of automatically removing irrelevant variables. In other words, cross-validation in conjunction with the local constant kernel estimator is capable of automatic dimensionality reduction when some of the regressors are in fact irrelevant.

The cross-validation objective function is the same as that defined in Section 2.2.2 except that now $Y_i = \bar{g}(\bar{X}_i) + u_i$ with $\mathrm{E}(u_i|X_i) = 0$, that is, the conditional mean function now depends only on the relevant regressors $\bar{X}$.

The analogue of the function χ defined in Section 2.2.2 is now modified to (see Exercise 2.5):

$$\bar{\chi}(a_1, \ldots, a_{q_1}) = \int \left[\sum_{s=1}^{q_1} \bar{B}_s(\bar{x}) a_j^2 \right]^2 \bar{f}(\bar{x}) \bar{M}(\bar{x}) d\bar{x}$$

$$+ \frac{\kappa^{q_1}}{a_1 \ldots a_{q_1}} \int \bar{\sigma}^2(\bar{x}) \bar{M}(\bar{x}) d\bar{x} \qquad (2.35)$$

where

$$\bar{M}(\bar{x}) = \int \tilde{f}(x_{q_1+1}, \ldots, x_q) M(\bar{x}, x_{q_1+1}, \ldots, x_q) \, dx_{q_1+1} \ldots dx_q,$$

and the "bar" notation refers to functions involving only the first q_1 components of x. $\bar{f}$ ($\tilde{f}$) is the marginal density of $\bar{X}$ ($\tilde{X}$) and $\bar{B}_s$ is defined in the same way as B_s except that it is only a function of $\bar{X}$. Note that the irrelevant components do not appear in the definition of $\bar{\chi}$.

As before, let $a_1^0, \ldots, a_{q_1}^0$ denote values that minimize $\bar{\chi}$ subject to each of them being nonnegative. We require

For $s = 1, \ldots, q_1$, each a_s^0 is uniquely defined and is finite. $\qquad (2.36)$

Since we should allow the smoothing parameters for irrelevant variables to diverge from zero as $n \to \infty$, conditions used in Section 2.7 cannot be imposed here. We impose the following conventional restrictions on the bandwidth and kernel function. Define

$$H_{2n} = \left(\prod_{s=1}^{q_1} h_s \right) \prod_{s=q_1+1}^{q} \min(h_s, 1).$$

Let $0 < \epsilon < 1/(q+4)$. Assume that

$$n^{\epsilon-1} \leq H_{2n} \leq n^{-\epsilon}; \quad \min(h_1, \dots, h_q) > n^{-C} \text{ and}$$
$\max(h_1, \dots, h_q) < n^C$ for some $C > 0$; the kernel k is a symmetric, compactly supported, Hölder-continuous PDF;
$$k(0) > k(\delta) \text{ for all } \delta > 0. \tag{2.37}$$

If ϵ is arbitrarily small, the above conditions on $h_1, \dots, h_q$ are in essence that $nh_1 \dots h_{q_1} \to \infty$, $h_1 \dots h_{q_1} \to 0$ and $h_1 \dots h_q \to 0$ as $n \to \infty$, and that the fastest rate at which h_s goes to zero cannot exceed n^{-a} (for some $a > 0$) and that the fastest rate at which h_s (for irrelevant variables) goes to ∞ is contained by n^b (for some $b > 0$). With these conditions we obtain the following result.

Theorem 2.4. *Under conditions (2.32), (2.36), and (2.37), letting $\hat{h}_1, \dots, \hat{h}_q$ denote the smoothing parameters that minimize CV_{lc}, then*

$$n^{1/(q_1+4)}\hat{h}_s \to a_s^0 \text{ in probability, for } 1 \leq j \leq q_1;$$
$$P(\hat{h}_s > C) \to 1 \text{ for } q_1 + 1 \leq s \leq q \text{ and all } C > 0. \tag{2.38}$$

Theorem 2.4 states that the smoothing parameters for the irrelevant components diverge to infinity in probability, therefore, all of the irrelevant variables can be (asymptotically) automatically smoothed out, while the smoothing parameters for the relevant variables continue to inherit the same optimality properties that would prevail if the irrelevant variables did not exist.

Here we mention that (2.32) is a sufficient, not a necessary, condition for Theorem 2.4 to hold. Simulation results reported in Hall et al. (2006) suggest that the conclusion of Theorem 2.4 still holds true if (2.32) is replaced by the condition "conditional on $\bar{X}$, Y is independent of $\tilde{X}$," although a rigorous proof for this seems quite challenging and remains a topic for future research.

The complicated proof of Theorem 2.4 is given in Hall et al. (2006). Here we present some intuitive reasons to expect the results of Theorem 2.4 to hold.

We call the terms of order $\eta_2 = \sum_{s=1}^{q_1} h_s^2$ the leading bias term, and the terms of order $\eta_1 = (nh_1 \dots h_{q_1})^{-1}$ the leading variance term. Hall et al. (2006) show that the presence of irrelevant variables does not contribute to the leading bias term in CV_{lc} because, by (2.32), the irrelevant components cancel in the ratio $\bar{\mu}_g(\bar{x}) = E[\hat{m}(x)]/E[\hat{f}(x)]$. Therefore, for the leading bias squared terms of order $O(\eta_2^2)$, the h_ss

$(q_1 + 1 \leq s \leq q)$ do not show up. Their contribution to the leading variance term (the $O(\eta_1)$ order term) is a multiplicative factor of the following kernel ratio arising due to the existence of the irrelevant components (see Exercise 2.5):

$$R(\tilde{x}, h_{q_1+1}, \ldots, h_q) = \frac{\mathrm{E}\left[\left\{\prod_{s=q_1+1}^{q} k\left(\frac{\tilde{x}_s - \tilde{X}_{is}}{h_s}\right)\right\}^2\right]}{\left(\mathrm{E}\left[\prod_{s=q_1+1}^{q} k\left(\frac{\tilde{x}_s - \tilde{X}_{is}}{h_s}\right)\right]\right)^2} \qquad (2.39)$$

Therefore, the leading terms of $CV_{lc}(h_1, \ldots, h_q)$ are of the following form (see Exercise 2.5):

$$\int \left\{ \left[\sum_{s=1}^{q_1} \bar{B}_s(\tilde{x}) h_s^2\right]^2 \right. \\ \left. + \left[\frac{\kappa^{q_1} \bar{\sigma}^2(\tilde{x})}{nh_1 \ldots h_{q_1} \bar{f}(\tilde{x})}\right] R(\tilde{x}, h_{q_1+1}, \ldots, h_q) \right\} f(x) M(x) \, dx. \qquad (2.40)$$

By Hölder's inequality, $R \geq 1$ for all choices of $h_{q_1+1}, \ldots, h_q$. Obviously, $R \to 1$ as $h_s \to \infty$ $(q_1 + 1 \leq s \leq q)$. In fact we have the following result:

Result 2.1. *The only values for which* $R(\tilde{x}, h_{q_1+1}, \ldots, h_q) = 1$ *for some* $\tilde{x} \in \mathrm{supp}\, w$ *are* $h_s = \infty$ *for* $q_1 + 1 \leq s \leq q$. *To see this let us define* $Z_n = \prod_{j=q_1+1}^{q} K\left(\frac{\tilde{x}_s - \tilde{X}_{is}}{h_s}\right)$. *Then* $\mathrm{var}(Z_n) = \mathrm{E}[Z_n^2] - [\mathrm{E}(Z_n)]^2 > 0$ *so that* $R = \mathrm{E}[Z_n^2]/[\mathrm{E}(Z_n)]^2 > 1$, *unless in the definition of* Z_n, *all* $h_s = \infty$, *in which case* $Z_n \equiv k(0)^{q-q_1}$ *and* $\mathrm{var}(Z_n) = 0$ *so that* $R = 1$ *in this and only this case.*

Therefore, to minimize (2.40) (the leading term of $CV_{lc}(h_1, \ldots, h_q)$), noting that both the squared bias and the variance terms are positive, we must have $R \to 1$ as $n \to \infty$, which implies that we *must* have the smoothing parameters for irrelevant components diverging to infinity. Thus, the irrelevant components are asymptotically smoothed out. Using $R = 1$ in (2.40) leads to (2.35), which in turn implies that the smoothing parameters for the relevant variables retain their optimality property as given in Theorem 2.4.

If $\hat{g}$ is computed using the asymptotically optimal *deterministic* smoothing parameters, then it is easy to show that

$$(nh_1^0 \ldots h_{q_1}^0)^{1/2} \left(\hat{g}(x) - \bar{g}(\bar{x}) - \sum_{s=1}^{q} \bar{B}_s(\bar{x})(h_s^0)^2 \right) \to N(0, \bar{\sigma}_g^2(\bar{x}))$$

(2.41)

in distribution, where

$$B_s(\bar{x}) = \frac{\kappa_2}{2} \sum_{s=1}^{q_1} \left\{ \bar{g}_{ss}(\bar{x}) + 2\frac{\bar{f}_s(\bar{x})\bar{g}_s(\bar{x})}{\bar{f}(\bar{x})} \right\} \quad \text{and}$$

$$\bar{\sigma}_g^2(\bar{x}) = \frac{\kappa^{q_1}\bar{\sigma}_u^2(\bar{x})}{\bar{f}(\bar{x})},$$

(2.42)

with $\bar{\sigma}_u^2(\bar{x}) = \mathrm{E}(u_i^2 | \bar{X}_i = \bar{x})$.

The next theorem shows that when the cross-validated smoothing parameters are used rather than the asymptotically optimal deterministic ones, the asymptotic normality result given in (2.41) still holds.

Theorem 2.5. *Under the same conditions found in Theorem 2.4, (2.41) remains true if $\hat{g}(x)$ is computed using the smoothing parameters chosen by cross-validation, i.e.,*

$$\sqrt{n\hat{h}_1 \ldots \hat{h}_{q_1}} \left(\hat{g}(x) - \bar{g}(\bar{x}) - \sum_{s=1}^{q_1} \hat{h}_s^2 \bar{B}_s(\bar{x}) \right) \xrightarrow{d} N\left(0, \kappa^{q_1}\bar{\sigma}^2(\bar{x})/\bar{f}(\bar{x})\right).$$

The proof of Theorem 2.5 is given in Hall et al. (2006). It can be understood intuitively as follows: First, note that as $\hat{h}_s \to \infty$ for $s = q_1 + 1, \ldots, q$, we have $\hat{g}(x, \hat{h}_1, \ldots, \hat{h}_q) = \hat{g}(\bar{x}, \hat{h}_1, \ldots, \hat{h}_{q_1}) + (s.o.)$, where $\hat{g}(\bar{x}, \hat{h}_1, \ldots, \hat{h}_{q_1})$ is a kernel estimator of $\bar{g}(\bar{x})$ using only the relevant regressors. Next, given the fact that $\hat{h}_s - h_s^0 = o_p(h_s^0)$ $(s = 1, \ldots, q_1)$, we expect that $\hat{g}(x, \hat{h}_1, \ldots, \hat{h}_{q_1}) = \hat{g}(\bar{x}, h_1^0, \ldots, h_{q_1}^0) + o_p\left(\sum_{s=1}^{q_1}(h_s^0)^2\right)$. Theorem 2.5 follows from this result and (2.41).

Note that the condition (2.32) is quite strong. It not only assumes that $\tilde{X}$ is independent of Y, but also requires that $\tilde{X}$ is independent of $\bar{X}$. Ideally, one would like to relax this condition to either (i) $\mathrm{E}[Y|\bar{X}, \tilde{X}] = \mathrm{E}[Y|\bar{X}]$ almost surely, or to (ii) conditional on $\bar{X}$, Y is independent of $\tilde{X}$. Hall et al. (2006) conjecture that Theorem 2.4 remains true when (2.32) is relaxed and replaced by condition (i) or (ii) above. The simulation results reported in Hall et al. provide some evidence in support of this conjecture.

2.2.5   Some Further Results on Cross-Validation

Racine and Li (2004) also established the rate of convergence of $\hat{h}_s/h_s^0 - 1$, which is given by

$$\frac{\hat{h}_s - h_s^0}{h_s^0} \equiv \frac{\hat{h}_s}{h_s^0} - 1 = O_p\left(n^{-\alpha/(4+q)}\right), \qquad (2.43)$$

where $\alpha = \min\{q/2, 2\}$. When $q = 1$, we get $(\hat{h}_s - h_s^0)/h_s^0 = O_p\left(n^{-1/10}\right)$, which coincides with the result obtained by Härdle et al. (1988), among others. Equation (2.43) implies that $\hat{h}$ converges to the nonstochastic optimal smoothing parameter h_s^0 in probability.

Equation (2.43) shows that $(\hat{h}_s - h_s^0)/h_s^0 = O_p\left(n^{-q/[2(4+q)]}\right)$ for $q \leq 4$, and $(\hat{h}_s - h_s^0)/h_s^0 = O_p\left(n^{-2/(4+q)}\right)$ for $q \geq 4$. The reason for having two different expressions for $(\hat{h}_s - h_s^0)/h_s^0$ (depending on whether or not $q \geq 4$) is that, in the higher order expansions of the cross-validation function $CV_{lc}(h_1, \ldots, h_q)$, we have terms of order $O_p\left(\sum_{s=1}^{q} h_s^6\right)$ and a second order degenerate U-statistic of the form

$$(n(n-1))^{-1} \sum_i \sum_{j \neq i} v_i v_j K_h(X_i, X_j),$$

where $\mathrm{E}(v_i|X_i) = 0$, which has an order $O_p\left(n(h_1 \ldots h_q)^{1/2}\right)^{-1}$); see Appendix A for a general treatment of degenerate U-statistics. When $q \leq 4$, the $O_p\left(n(h_1 \ldots h_q)^{1/2})^{-1}\right)$ term dominates the $O_p\left(h_s^6\right)$ term since $h_s \sim O_p\left(h_s^0\right) = O_p\left(n^{-1/(4+q)}\right)$, while when $q \geq 5$, the $O_p\left(h_s^6\right)$ term becomes the dominating term. Therefore, the rate of convergence differs depending on whether $q \leq 4$ or $q \geq 5$ (see Racine and Li (2004) for a detailed proof).

2.3   Uniform Rates of Convergence

Proceeding along lines similar to those used when deriving the uniform almost sure rate for the density estimator discussed in Section 1.12 of Chapter 1, we can establish the uniform almost sure convergence rate of $\hat{g}(x)$ to $g(x)$ for $x \in \mathcal{S}$, where $\mathcal{S}$ is a compact subset of $\mathbb{R}^q$ that excludes the boundary range of the support of X.

Condition 2.1. *Assume that*

(i) $f(x)$ is differentiable and $g(x)$ is twice differentiable, and that the derivative functions all satisfy the Lipschitz condition $|m(x) - m(v)| \leq C|x - v|$ for some $C > 0$ $(m(\cdot) = g_{ss}(\cdot)$ or $f_s(\cdot))$.

(ii) $\sigma^2(x) = \mathrm{E}(u_i^2|x)$ is a continuous function, and $\inf_{x \in \mathcal{S}} f(x) \geq \delta > 0$.

(iii) The kernel $k(\cdot)$ is symmetric, bounded and has compact support (say $k(v) = 0$ for $|v| > 1$). Defining $H_l(v) = |v|^l K(v)$, we assume that $|H_l(v) - H_l(u)| \leq C_2|u - v|$ for all $0 \leq l \leq 3$.

Theorem 2.6. *Under Condition 2.1, we have*

$$\sup_{x \in \mathcal{S}} |\hat{g}(x) - g(x)| = O\left(\frac{(\ln n)^{1/2}}{(nh_1 \ldots h_q)^{1/2}} + \sum_{s=1}^{q} h_s^2\right) \quad almost\ surely.$$

$$(2.44)$$

The proof of (2.44) is quite similar to the proof of Theorem 1.4 of Chapter 1. By writing $\hat{g}(x) - g(x) = \hat{m}(x)/\hat{f}(x)$, where $\hat{m}(x) = (\hat{g}(x) - g(x))\hat{f}(x)$, one can show that

$$\sup_{x \in \mathcal{S}} |\hat{m}(x)| = O\left(\sum_{s=1}^{q} h_s^2 + (\ln n)^{1/2}/(nh_1 \ldots h_q)^{1/2}\right) \quad a.s.$$

Also, the fact that the density is bounded away from zero in $\mathcal{S}$ and Theorem 1.4 imply that $\inf_{x \in S} \hat{f}(x) \geq \delta' > 0$ a.s., where δ' is a positive constant. Hence,

$$\sup_{x \in \mathcal{S}} |\hat{g}(x) - g(x)| = \sup_{x \in \mathcal{S}} \left|\hat{m}(x)/\hat{f}(x)\right| \leq \sup_{x \in \mathcal{S}} |\hat{m}(x)|/|\inf_{x \in D} \hat{f}(x)|$$

$$= O\left((\ln n)^{1/2}/(nh_1 \ldots h_q)^{1/2} + \sum_{s=1}^{q} h_s^2\right) \quad a.s.$$

Having examined the local constant kernel estimator in detail, we now turn to another popular method, the local polynomial approach.

2.4 Local Linear Kernel Estimation

Though the local constant estimator is the workhorse of kernel regression, it is not without its idiosyncrasies. In particular, it has potentially large bias when estimating a regression function near the boundary of support. The local linear estimator proposed by Stone (1977) and Cleveland (1979), on the other hand, shares many of the properties of the local constant approach (e.g., their variances are identical), while it is one of the best known approaches for boundary correction as its bias is not a function of the design density $f(x)$; see Fan (1992), Fan (1993), and Fan and Gijbels (1992). For an extensive treatment of the local linear estimator see the excellent monograph by Fan and Gijbels (1996).

We again consider a regression model of the form

$$Y_j = g(X_j) + u_j, \quad j = 1, \ldots, n. \tag{2.45}$$

Recall that the local constant kernel estimator discussed in Section 2.1 was given by

$$\hat{g}(x) = \frac{\sum_{j=1}^n Y_j K\left(\frac{X_j - x}{h}\right)}{\sum_{j=1}^n K\left(\frac{X_j - x}{h}\right)}, \tag{2.46}$$

which can also be obtained as the solution of a in the following minimization problem:

$$\min_a \sum_{j=1}^n (Y_j - a)^2 K\left(\frac{X_j - x}{h}\right). \tag{2.47}$$

Letting $\hat{a} = \hat{a}(x)$ be the solution that minimizes (2.47), one can easily see that $\hat{a} \equiv \hat{g}(x)$ as defined in (2.46).

Note, however, that (2.47) uses a constant a to approximate $g(x)$ (or Y) in the neighborhood of x, since (2.47) only uses a local (X_j's close to x) average of Y_j's to estimate $g(x)$. For this reason, $\hat{g}(x)$ defined in (2.46) is called a "local constant" kernel estimator. However, one could instead use a "local linear" (or higher order polynomial) estimator to estimate $g(x)$. One feature of a local linear method is that it automatically provides an estimator for $g^{(1)}(x) \stackrel{\text{def}}{=} \partial g(x)/\partial x$, the first order derivative of $g(x)$, though the local constant partial derivative estimator is well-studied; see, for example, Vinod and Ullah (1988), Rilstone and Ullah (1989), Härdle and Stoker (1989) and Pagan and Ullah (1999, Section 4.2) for further details.

The local linear method is based on the following minimization problem:

$$\min_{\{a,b\}} \sum_{j=1}^n \left(Y_j - a - (X_j - x)'b\right)^2 K\left(\frac{X_j - x}{h}\right). \tag{2.48}$$

Let $\hat{a} = \hat{a}(x)$ and $\hat{b} = \hat{b}(x)$ be the solutions to (2.48). We will show in this section that $\hat{a}(x)$ is a consistent estimator of $g(x)$ and $\hat{b}(x)$ is a consistent estimator of $g^{(1)}(x) = \partial g(x)/\partial x$ (both b and $g^{(1)}(x)$ are $q \times 1$ vectors). The local linear approach given in (2.48) is easily understood because it is analogous to a "local least squares" estimator. Hence the slope estimator $\hat{b}$ estimates the local slope $g^{(1)}(x)$.

Let $\delta = \delta(x) = (a(x), (b(x))')'$, let $\mathcal{Y}$ be the $n \times 1$ vector having ith component Y_i, let $\mathcal{X}$ be an $n \times (1+q)$ matrix with the ith row being $(1, (X_i - x)')$, and let $\mathcal{K}(x)$ be an $n \times n$ diagonal matrix having ith diagonal element $K\left(\frac{X_i-x}{h}\right)$. Then in vector-matrix notation, (2.48) can be written as

$$\min_{\{a,b\}} (\mathcal{Y} - \mathcal{X}\delta)' \mathcal{K}(x)(\mathcal{Y} - \mathcal{X}\delta). \qquad (2.49)$$

Equation (2.49) is a standard generalized least squares (GLS) problem. Let $\hat{\delta} = (\hat{a}, \hat{b}')'$ be the solution of (2.49). Then using the standard formula for a GLS estimator, we get

$$\hat{\delta}(x) = (\mathcal{X}'\mathcal{K}(x)\mathcal{X})^{-1}\mathcal{X}'\mathcal{K}(x)\mathcal{Y}$$

$$= \left[\sum_{j=1}^{n} K\left(\frac{X_j - x}{h}\right) \binom{1}{X_j - x} (1, (X_j - x)') \right]^{-1}$$

$$\times \sum_{j=1}^{n} K\left(\frac{X_j - x}{h}\right) \binom{1}{X_j - x} Y_j. \qquad (2.50)$$

The following condition is needed to establish the consistency and asymptotic normality of $\hat{\delta}(x)$ given in (2.50).

Condition 2.2.

(i) $\{X_j, Y_j\}_{j=1}^{n}$ are i.i.d., $g(x)$ and $f(x)$ and $\sigma^2(x) = \mathrm{E}(u_i^2|x)$ are twice differentiable.

(ii) K is a bounded second order kernel.

(iii) As $n \to \infty$, $nh_1 \ldots h_q \sum_{s=1}^{q} h_s^2 \to \infty$ and $nh_1 \ldots h_q \sum_{s=1}^{q} h_s^6 \to 0$.

The next theorem establishes the asymptotic normality of $\hat{\delta}(x)$.

Theorem 2.7. *Recall that* $\kappa = \int k(v)^2\,dv$, $\kappa_2 = \int k(v)v^2\,dv$, *define* $\kappa_{22} = \int v^2 k(v)^2\,dv$, *and let*

$$D(n) = \begin{pmatrix} \sqrt{nh_1\ldots h_q}, & 0 \\ 0, & \sqrt{nh_1\ldots h_q}D_h \end{pmatrix},$$

$$\Sigma = \begin{pmatrix} \kappa^q \sigma^2(x)/f(x), & 0 \\ 0, & \kappa^{q-1}\kappa_{22}\sigma^2(x)I_q/[\kappa_2^2 f(x)] \end{pmatrix},$$

where D_h *is a* $q \times q$ *diagonal matrix with the sth diagonal element given by* h_s, *and where* I_q *is an identity matrix of dimension* q. *Then under Condition 2.2 we have*

$$D(n)\left(\hat{\delta}(x) - \delta(x) - \begin{pmatrix} \frac{\kappa_2}{2}\sum_{s=1}^q h_s^2 g_{ss}(x) \\ 0 \end{pmatrix}\right) \xrightarrow{d} N\,(0,\Sigma)\,. \qquad (2.51)$$

The proof of Theorem 2.7 is given in Section 2.7.2.

Note that Theorem 2.7 implies the following different rates of convergence:

$$(nh_1\ldots h_q)^{1/2}\left[\hat{a}(x) - g(x) - \frac{\kappa_2}{2}\sum_{s=1}^q h_s^2 g_{ss}(x)\right] \xrightarrow{d} N\left(0,\frac{\kappa^q \sigma^2(x)}{f(x)}\right),$$
$$(2.52)$$

and

$$(nh_1\ldots h_q)^{1/2}h_s\left[\hat{b}_s(x) - g_s(x)\right] \xrightarrow{d} N\left(0,\frac{\kappa^{q-1}\kappa_{22}\sigma^2(x)}{\kappa_2^2 f(x)}\right), \qquad (2.53)$$
$$\text{for } s = 1,\ldots,q,$$

where $g_s(x) = \partial g(x)/\partial x_s$ is the sth component of $g(x)$.

Let $\hat{g}(x) = \hat{a}(x)$ and $\hat{g}_s(x) = \hat{b}_s(x)$ denote the local-linear kernel estimates of $g(x)$ and $g_s(x)$, respectively. Then $\hat{g}(x) - g(x) = O_p\left(\eta_2 + \eta_1^{1/2}\right)$, and $\hat{g}_s(x) - g_s(x) = O_p\left(\eta_2 + \eta_1^{1/2}h_s^{-1}\right)$ ($\eta_2 = \sum_{s=1}^q h_s^2$, $\eta_1 = (nh_1\ldots h_q)^{-1}$). This is a standard result, i.e., that the convergence rate for derivative estimation is slower than that for regression function estimation. For estimating the lth order derivative of $g(x)$, the rate of convergence will be $O_p\left(\eta_2 + \eta_1^{1/2}\left(\sum_{s=1}^q h_s^{2l}\right)^{-1/2}\right)$. We discuss higher order derivative estimators in Section 2.5.

Consistent estimation of $g(x)$ requires that $h_s \to 0$ ($s = 1,\ldots,q$) and $nh_1\ldots h_q \to \infty$ in order for the bias and the variance to both converge to zero, while consistent estimation of $g_s(x)$ requires an even stronger condition, namely, $nh_1 \ldots h_q \sum_{s=1}^{q} h_s^2 \to \infty$, in order for the variance term of the derivative estimator to converge to zero.

Note that when the underlying regression function is in fact linear in x (i.e., $g(x) = \alpha_0 + x'\alpha_1$, where the scalar α_0 and $q \times 1$ vector α_1 are constants), then the local linear estimator exhibits the property that the bias term is zero for *any* value of $(h_1, \ldots, h_q)$ (see Exercise 2.10). Thus, the local linear estimator becomes unbiased when $g(x)$ is linear in x. When the bias is zero we could allow $h_s = \infty$ ($s = 1, \ldots, q$), and it is easy to show in this instance that the local linear estimator collapses to $\hat{a}(x) = \hat{\alpha}_0 + x'\hat{\alpha}_1$, where $\hat{\alpha}_0$ and $\hat{\alpha}_1$ are the ordinary least squares estimators of α_0 and α_1, respectively (see Exercise 2.6). Thus, the local linear estimator nests the least squares estimator as a special case if one allows for h_s to assume sufficiently large values for all $s = 1, \ldots, q$. We come back to this point when we discuss cross-validated smoothing parameter selection for the local linear estimator in the next section, since this has important implications for both bandwidth selection and rates of convergence.

2.4.1 Local Linear Bandwidth Selection: Least Squares Cross-Validation

Let $\hat{g}_{-i,L}(X_i)$ denote the leave-one-out local linear estimator. That is, let $(\hat{a}_i, \hat{b}_i)$ be the solution of (a, b) in the following minimization problem:

$$\min_{\{a,b\}} \sum_{j \neq i, j=1}^{n} \left[Y_j - a - (X_j - X_i)'b\right]^2 K\left(\frac{X_i - X_j}{h}\right),$$

where $K\left(\frac{X_i - X_j}{h}\right) = \prod_{s=1}^{q} k\left(\frac{X_{is} - X_{js}}{h_s}\right)$. Then $\hat{a}_i \equiv \hat{g}_{-i,L}(X_i)$ is the leave-one-out local linear kernel estimator of $g(X_i)$.

The local linear cross-validation approach to bandwidth selection chooses those h_s's which minimize

$$CV_{ll}(h_1, \ldots, h_q) = \min_{h} \frac{1}{n} \sum_{i} [Y_i - \hat{g}_{-i,L}(X_i)]^2 M(X_i), \qquad (2.54)$$

where $M(\cdot)$ is a weight function. Note that the objective function (2.54) only involves estimation of $g(\cdot)$ and not its derivatives, therefore we only need the conditions on $h_1, \ldots, h_q$ stated in (2.74), that is, we do not need the stronger conditions on the smoothing parameters that ensure consistent estimation of the derivatives of $g(\cdot)$.

For fixed $x \in \mathbb{R}^q$, we have derived the asymptotic bias and variance terms of $\hat{g}(x) = \hat{a}(x)$ of the local linear estimator, while (2.52) implies that

$$
\mathrm{E}[\hat{g}(x) - g(x)]^2 = \left[\frac{\kappa_2}{2} \sum_{s=1}^{q} g_{ss}(x) h_s^2 \right]^2 + \frac{\kappa^q}{nh_1 \dots h_q} \frac{\sigma^2(x)}{f(x)} + o(\eta_2^2 + \eta_1).
$$

(2.55)

As we discussed in Section 2.2.2, the cross-validation objective function is asymptotically equivalent to $\int \mathrm{E}[\hat{g}(x) - g(x)]^2 f(x) M(x)\, dx$. Using (2.55) one might conjecture that the leading term of CV_{ll} would be

$$
\begin{aligned}
CV_{ll,0} &\sim \int \mathrm{E}[\hat{g}(x) - g(x)]^2 f(x) M(x)\, dx \\
&= \int \left[\frac{\kappa_2}{2} \sum_{s=1}^{q} g_{ss}(x) h_s^2 \right]^2 f(x) M(x)\, dx + \frac{\kappa^q \int \sigma^2(x) M(x)\, dx}{nh_1 \dots h_q} \\
&\quad + o(\eta_2^2 + \eta_1),
\end{aligned}
$$

(2.56)

and this conjecture turns out to be correct as the leading term of CV_{ll} is indeed given by (2.56) (see Li and Racine (2004a) for a detailed proof).

Closely following the approach presented in Section 2.2, we express the leading term of (2.56) as $n^{-4/(q+4)} \chi_{ll}(a_1, \dots, a_q)$, where the a_s's are defined by $h_s = a_s n^{-1/(q+4)}$ $(s = 1, \dots, q)$, and

$$
\begin{aligned}
\chi_{ll}(a_1, \dots, a_q) &= \int \left[\frac{\kappa_2}{2} \sum_{s=1}^{q} g_{ss}(x) a_s^2 \right]^2 f(x) M(x)\, dx \\
&\quad + \frac{\kappa^q}{a_1 \dots a_q} \int \sigma^2(x) M(x)\, dx.
\end{aligned}
$$

(2.57)

Let $a_{1,l}^0, \dots, a_{q,l}^0$ denote those values of $a_1, \dots, a_q$ that minimize χ_{ll}, and assume that

Each $a_{s,l}^0$ is uniquely defined and is positive and finite.   (2.58)

Assumption (2.58) rules out the case for which $a_{s,l}^0 = \infty$, which implies that $g_{ss}(x)$ cannot be a zero function. That is, we explicitly rule out cases for which $g(x)$ is linear in any of its components x_s.

Letting the $\hat{h}_s$'s denote those values of the h_s's that minimize (2.54), Li and Racine (2004a) showed that

$$
n^{1/(q+4)} \hat{h}_s \to a_{s,l}^0 \text{ in probability for } s = 1, \dots, q.
$$

(2.59)

Equation (2.59) states that the local linear cross-validation smoothing parameters converge to the optimal smoothing parameters, and that the *rate of convergence* of the resulting local linear estimator is the same as the local constant cross-validation case *when the underlying regression function is not linear in any of its components.*

When $g(x)$ is linear in some component of x, say x_s, then (2.58) does not hold. In this case we also need to modify the conditions imposed on the smoothing parameters as was done in Section 2.2.4 so that we allow those smoothing parameters corresponding to those regressors entering $g(x)$ linearly to diverge to infinity. Then we would expect that local linear least squares cross-validation should have the ability to select a large value of h_s when $g(x)$ is linear in x_s while selecting relatively small values of h_t for regressors that enter nonlinearly. The simulation results reported in Li and Racine (2004a) show that this is indeed the case, though we are not aware any work that provides a rigorous theoretical proof of this result.

Specifically, let us consider the case for which $q = 2$ and where the underlying regression function $g(x_1, x_2) = \theta(x_1) + x_2\alpha$ is a partially linear function (e.g., linear in x_2). In this case, local linear cross-validation will tend to select a very large value of $\hat{h}_2$ ($\hat{h}_2 \to \infty$), while $\hat{h}_1 = O_p\left(n^{-1/5}\right)$ (rather than $O_p\left(n^{-1/6}\right)$). Thus, local linear cross-validation would suggest that $g(\cdot)$ is linear in x_2.

2.5 Local Polynomial Regression (General pth Order)

2.5.1 The Univariate Case

As was the case when we derived the local linear kernel estimator, we can use a higher order local polynomial estimator to estimate $g(x)$. When x is *univariate*, a pth order local polynomial kernel estimator is based on minimizing the following objective function:

$$\min_{\{b_0,b_1,\ldots,b_q\}} \sum_{j=1}^{n} (Y_j - b_0 - b_1(X_j - x) - \cdots - b_p(X_j - x)^p)^2$$
$$\times K\left(\frac{X_j - x}{h}\right). \tag{2.60}$$

Let $\hat{b}_l$ denote the values of b_l ($l = 0, 1, \ldots, p$) that minimize (2.60).

Then $\hat{b}_0$ estimates $g(x)$, and $l!\hat{b}_l$ estimates $g^{(l)}(x)$, where $g^{(l)}(x) = d^l g(x)/dx^l$ is the lth order derivative of $g(x)$ ($l = 1, \ldots, p$).

Once again, (2.60) is a standard weighted least squares regression problem. Letting $\mathcal{X}_i = (1, (X_j - x), \ldots, (X_j - x)^p)'$, then

$$
\hat{b} = \begin{pmatrix} \hat{b}_0 \\ \hat{b}_1 \\ \cdots \\ \hat{b}_p \end{pmatrix} = \left[\sum_j \mathcal{X}_j \mathcal{X}_j' K \left(\frac{X_j - x}{h} \right) \right]^{-1} \sum_j \mathcal{X}_j Y_j K \left(\frac{X_j - x}{h} \right).
$$

(2.61)

Ruppert and Wand (1994) study the leading conditional bias and conditional variance of $\hat{b}_0$, which we summarize in the following theorem.

Theorem 2.8. *Let $\hat{g}(x) \equiv \hat{b}_0(x)$, and let $\mathcal{Z}_n = \{X_i\}_{i=1}^n$.*
If p is odd,

$$
\mathrm{E}\left[\hat{g}(x)|\mathcal{Z}_n\right] - g(x) = h^{p+1} c_{1,p} \left[\frac{m^{(p+1)}(x)}{(p+1)!} \right] + o\left(h^{p+1}\right),
$$

(2.62)

and if p is even,

$$
\mathrm{E}\left[\hat{g}(x)|\mathcal{Z}_n\right] - g(x) = h^{p+2} \left\{ c_{2,p} \left[\frac{m^{(p+1)}(x) f^{(1)}(x)}{f(x)(p+1)!} \right] \right.
$$
$$
\left. + c_{3,p} \left[\frac{m^{(p+2)}(x)}{(p+2)!} \right] \right\} + o(h^{p+2}). \quad (2.63)
$$

In either case,

$$
\mathrm{var}\left(\hat{g}(x)|\mathcal{Z}_n\right) = \left[\frac{c_{4,p}\sigma^2(x)}{nhf(x)} \right] + o\left(\frac{1}{nh}\right),
$$

(2.64)

where $c_{j,p}$ ($j = 1, 2, 3, 4$) are some constants defined in Ruppert and Wand (1994).

Theorem 2.8 shows that the leading conditional bias term depends upon whether p is odd or even. By a Taylor series expansion argument, we know that when considering $|X_j - x| \leq h$, the remainder term from a pth order polynomial expansion should be of order $O(h^{p+1})$, so the result for odd p is quite easy to understand. When p is even, $(p+1)$ is odd; hence the term h^{p+1} is associated with $\int K(v)v^l \, dv$ for l odd, and this term is zero because $K(v)$ is an even function. Therefore, the h^{p+1} term disappears, while the remainder term becomes $O(h^{p+2})$. Since p is either odd or even, we see that the bias term is an even power of h. This is similar to the case where one uses higher order kernel functions based upon a symmetric kernel function (an even function) for the local constant estimator, where the bias is always an even power of h.

Summarizing, conditional on $\mathcal{X}_n$ we have

$$\text{When } p \text{ is odd } \hat{g}(x) - g(x) = O_p\left(h^{p+1} + (nh)^{-1/2}\right).$$
$$\text{When } p \text{ is even } \hat{g}(x) - g(x) = O_p\left(h^{p+2} + (nh)^{-1/2}\right). \tag{2.65}$$

Let $\hat{g}^{(l)}(x) = l!\hat{b}_l(x)$ denote the estimator of $g^{(l)}(x)$ based on a pth order local polynomial fit ($l \leq p$). The following theorem states the leading bias and variance of $\hat{g}^{(l)}(x)$.

Theorem 2.9. *When $p - l$ is odd,*

$$\mathrm{E}\left[\hat{g}^{(l)}(x)|\mathcal{X}_n\right] - g^{(l)}(x) = h^{p-l+1}c_{1,l,p}\left[\frac{m^{(p+1)}(x)}{(p+1)!}\right] + o\left(h^{p-l+1}\right).$$

When $p - l$ is even,

$$\mathrm{E}\left[\hat{g}^{(l)}(x)|\mathcal{X}_n\right] - g^{(l)}(x) = h^{p-l+2}\left\{c_{2,l,p}\left[\frac{m^{(p+2)}(x)}{(p+2)!}\right]\right.$$
$$\times \int v^{p+2}K_{(l,p)}(v)\,dv$$
$$\left. + c_{3,l,p}\left[\frac{m^{(p+1)}(x)f^{(1)}(x)}{f(x)(p+1)!}\right]\right\}.$$

In either case,

$$\mathrm{var}\left(\hat{g}^{(l)}(x)|\mathcal{X}_n\right) = \left[\frac{c_{4,l,p}\sigma^2(x)}{nh^{2l+1}f(x)}\right] + o\left((nh^{2l+1})^{-1}\right),$$

where $c_{j,l,p}$ ($j = 1, 2, 3, 4$) are constants defined in Ruppert and Wand (1994).

Note that $f^{(1)}(x)/f(x)$ does not appear in the conditional bias term if $p - l =$ is odd. Ruppert and Wand (1994) also show that when $p - l$ is odd, the bias at the boundary is of the same order as that for points on the interior. Thus, the appealing boundary behavior of local polynomial mean estimation extends to derivative estimation *when $p - l$ is odd.* However, when $p - l$ is even, the bias at the boundary is *larger* than in the interior, and the bias can also be large at points where $f(x)$ is discontinuous. For these reasons, we recommend strictly setting $p - l$ to be odd when estimating $g^{(l)}(x)$.

Theorem 2.9 implies that, conditional on $\mathcal{X}_n$,

$$\text{When } p - l \text{ is odd } \hat{g}^{(l)}(x) - g^{(l)}(x) = O_p\left(h^{p-l+1} + (nh^{2l+1})^{-1/2}\right).$$

$$\text{When } p - l \text{ is even } \hat{g}^{(l)}(x) - g^{(l)}(x) = O_p\left(h^{p-l+2} + (nh^{2l+1})^{-1/2}\right).$$

$$\tag{2.66}$$

Using Liapunov's CLT, we can also establish the asymptotic normality of $\hat{g}(x)$ and $\hat{g}^{(l)}(x)$. We postpone our discussion of asymptotic normality results until the next section, in which we discuss general multivariate local polynomial regression.

2.5.2 The Multivariate Case

A general pth order local polynomial estimator for the *multivariate* regressor case is more cumbersome notationally speaking. The general multivariate case is considered by Masry (1996*a*, 1996*b*), who develops some carefully considered notation and establishes the uniform almost sure convergence rate and the pointwise asymptotic normality result for the local polynomial estimator of $g(x)$ and its derivatives up to order p. Borrowing from Masry (1996*b*), we introduce the following notation:

$$r = (r_1, \ldots, r_q), \quad r! = r_1! \times \cdots \times r_q!, \quad \bar{r} = \sum_{j=1}^{q} r_j, \tag{2.67}$$

$$x^r = x_1^{r_1} \times \cdots \times x_q^{r_q}, \quad \sum_{0 \leq \bar{r} \leq p} = \sum_{j=0}^{p} \sum_{r_1=0}^{j} \cdots \sum_{r_q=0}^{j}, \tag{2.68}$$

$$(\text{with } \bar{r} \equiv r_1 + \cdots + r_q = j)$$

and

$$(D^r g)(x) = \frac{\partial^r g(x)}{\partial x_1^{r_1} \ldots \partial x_q^{r_q}}. \tag{2.69}$$

Using this notation, and assuming that $g(x)$ has derivatives of total order $p + 1$ at a point x, we can approximate $g(z)$ locally using a multivariate polynomial of total order p given by

$$g(z) \cong \sum_{0 \leq \bar{r} \leq p} \frac{1}{r!}(D^r)g(v)|_{v=x}(z-x)^r. \tag{2.70}$$

Define a multivariate weighted least squares function by

$$\sum_{i=1}^{n} \left\{ Y_i - \sum_{0 \leq \bar{r} \leq p} b_r(x)(X_i - x)^r \right\}^2 K\left(\frac{X_i - x}{h}\right). \tag{2.71}$$

Minimizing (2.71) with respect to each b_r gives an estimate $\hat{b}_r(x)$, and by (2.70), we know that $r!\hat{b}_r(x)$ estimates $(D^r g)(x)$ so that $(D^r\hat{g})(x) = r!\hat{b}_r(x)$. For a general treatment of multivariate bandwidth selection for the local linear kernel estimator, see Yang and Tschernig (1999).

2.5.3   Asymptotic Normality of Local Polynomial Estimators

Local pth order polynomial regression can be used to estimate the derivatives of $g(x)$ up to order p. We use N_l to denote the number of distinct lth order derivatives of $g(x)$. For example, $N_0 = 1$, $N_1 = q$ (q different first order derivatives), and $N_2 = q(q+1)/2$ (q second own derivatives and $q(q-1)/2$ cross second order derivatives). The general formula is

$$N_l = \binom{q+l-1}{q-1} = \frac{(q+l-1)!}{(q-1)!l!}, \quad l = 0, 1, \ldots, p.$$

There are N_l distinct lth order derivatives of $g(x)$, and we use $\nabla^{(l)}g(x)$ to denote the $N_l \times 1$ vector of these lth order derivatives using a lexicographic order. For example, when $l = 2$, we have the $N_2 = q(q+1)/2$ distinct second order derivatives, and $\nabla^{(2)}g(x)$ is defined by

$$\left(\nabla^{(2)}g\right)(x) = \begin{pmatrix} \frac{\partial^2 g(x)}{\partial x_1^2} \\ \frac{\partial^2 g(x)}{\partial x_1 \partial x_2} \\ \vdots \\ \frac{\partial^2 g(x)}{\partial x_q^2} \end{pmatrix}.$$

Masry (1996a) uses the following condition to establish the asymptotic normality result for the local polynomial estimator.

Condition 2.3.

(i) $g(x)$ *has continuous derivatives of total order* $(p+1)$.

(ii) $k(v)$ *is a bounded second order kernel function having compact support.*

(iii) *For expositional simplicity, letting* $h_1 = \cdots = h_q = h$, *assume that* $h = O\left(n^{-1/(q+2p+2)}\right)$.

Theorem 2.10. *Under Condition 2.3, we have for* $0 \le l \le p$

$$\left(nh^{q+2l}\right)^{1/2}\left[\nabla^{(l)}\hat{g}(x) - \nabla^{(l)}g(x) - A_{l,p+1}(x)h^{p+1-l}\right]$$

$$\xrightarrow{d} N\left(0, \frac{\sigma^2(x)}{f(x)}V_l\right)$$

at continuous points of $\sigma^2(x)$ *and* $f(x)$ *with* $f(x) > 0$, *where the definitions of* $m_{p+1}(x)$, A_l *and* V_l *are given in Section 2.7.*

Proof. See Theorem 5 of Masry (1996*a*).   □

If we compare Theorem 2.10 with Theorems 2.8 and 2.9, we observe that Theorem 2.10 does not yield differing bias expressions depending on whether $p - l$ is odd or even. It can be shown that when $q = 1$ (the single regressor case), the bias expression of Theorem 2.10 matches that of Theorems 2.8 and 2.9 for the case when $p - l$ is odd. When $p - l$ is even, the leading bias term given in Theorem 2.10 is in fact zero. Thus, the leading nonzero bias term will be of the next order with $O(h^{p-l+2})$ when $p - l$ is even. We verify this for the case of $p = 1$ (local linear) in Section 2.7, where we show that $A_{l,p+1}(x) = A_{1,2}(x) = 0$, and so the nonvanishing leading bias term will be of order $O(h^{p+2-l}) = O\left(h^2\right)$ rather than $O(h^{p+1-l}) = O(h)$ $(p = l = 1)$. This matches the result of Theorem 2.7, hence the results given in Theorem 2.10 are consistent with those given in Theorems 2.8 and 2.9.

Assuming that $p - l$ is odd, we have

$$\text{MSE}\left(\hat{g}^{(l)}(x)\right) = O\left(h^{2(p-l+1)} + (nh^{q+2l})^{-1}\right),$$

$$\text{or } \hat{g}^{(l)}(x) = O_p\left(h^{p-l+1} + (nh^{q+2l})^{-1/2}\right).$$

Masry (1996*b*) established the uniform almost sure convergence rate of the local polynomial estimator, and we present his results in the next theorem.

Theorem 2.11. *For each $0 \le l \le p$ we have*

$$\sup_{x \in \mathcal{S}} \left| \nabla^{(l)} \hat{g}(x) - \nabla^{(l)} g(x) \right| = O\left(\left(\frac{\ln(n)}{nh^{q+2l}} \right)^{1/2} + h^{p-l+1} \right) \quad (2.72)$$

almost surely.

Proof. See Theorem 6 of Masry (1996*b*). □

As was the case for our earlier discussion on this issue, the above results show that when $p - l$ is even, the order of the bias is not as small as it could be. For example, when $p - l$ is even, Theorem 2.11 provides a bias of order $O(h^{p-l+1})$. Given the pointwise rate of order $O\left(h^{p-l+2} \right)$ when $p - l$ is even, it should be possible to reduce the bias term from $O\left(h^{p-l+1} \right)$ to $O\left(h^{p-l+2} \right)$ when $p - l$ is even, although this may be quite complicated given the general structure of the model.

Based on (minimax) efficiency arguments, Ruppert and Wand (1994) suggest that $p - l$ should be chosen to be odd. When $p - l$ is odd, the order of the bias in Theorem 2.11 matches the order of the bias for the pointwise rate result.

For $l = 0$, Theorem 2.11 gives the uniform rate of

$$\left| \nabla^{(0)} \hat{g}(x) - \nabla^{(0)} g(x) \right| \equiv |\hat{g}(x) - g(x)|$$
$$= O\left((\ln(n)/(nh^q))^{1/2} + h^{p+1} \right),$$

where $\hat{g}(x)$ is the pth order local polynomial estimator of $g(x)$. We see that the bias in a pth order local polynomial regression is of order $O(h^{p+1})$, and it can be further reduced to $O\left(h^{p+2} \right)$ for p even. For $p \ge 2$, the bias term is similar to that arising from the use of a higher order kernel function for the local constant estimator.

For $l = 1$, Theorem 2.11 provides the uniform almost sure rate for first order derivative estimators,

$$\left| \nabla^{(1)} \hat{g}(x) - \nabla^{(1)} g(x) \right| \equiv \left| \hat{g}^{(1)}(x) - g^{(1)}(x) \right|$$
$$= O\left(\left(\ln(n)/\left(nh^{q+2} \right) \right)^{1/2} + h^p \right).$$

Similarly, one can obtain the uniform almost sure rate for higher order derivative estimators from Theorem 2.11.

Throughout this chapter we assume that the data $\{X_i, Y_i\}_{i=1}^n$ is observed without error. In practice, however, data may be contaminated or measured with error. There is a rich literature on how to handle measurement error in nonparametric settings. Though it is beyond the scope of this book to cover this vast literature, we direct the interested reader to Fan and Truong (1993), Carroll and Hall (2004), and Carroll, Maca and Ruppert (1999) and the references therein.

2.6 Applications

2.6.1 Prestige Data

We consider the following example using data from Fox's (2002) `car` library in R (R Development Core Team (2006)). The dataset consists of 102 observations, each corresponding to a particular occupation. The dependent variable is the prestige of Canadian occupations, measured by the Pineo-Porter prestige score for occupation taken from a social survey conducted in the mid-1960s. The explanatory variable is average income for each occupation measured in 1971 dollars. Figure 2.1 plots the data and five local linear regression estimates each differing in their window widths, the window widths being undersmoothed, oversmoothed, Ruppert, Sheather and Wand's (1995) direct plug-in, Hurvich et al.'s (1998) corrected AIC (AIC_c), and cross-validation (CV) (Li and Racine (2004a)). A second order Gaussian kernel was used throughout.

The oversmoothed local linear estimate in Figure 2.1 is globally linear, and in fact is exactly simple linear least squares regression of Y on X as expected, while the AIC_c and CV criterion appears to provide the most reasonable fit to this data.

2.6.2 Adolescent Growth

In Section 1.13.3 we noted that abnormal adolescent growth can provide an early warning that a child has a medical problem. We used data from the population of healthy U.S. children obtained from the Center for Disease Control and Prevention's (CDC) National Health and Nutrition Examination Survey to model the joint distribution of height and weight by sex.

We now consider the regression function underlying the relationship between height and age for males and females using the mixed data local linear estimator to be introduced shortly in Chapter 4 to model "stature for age means." The local linear estimator was used

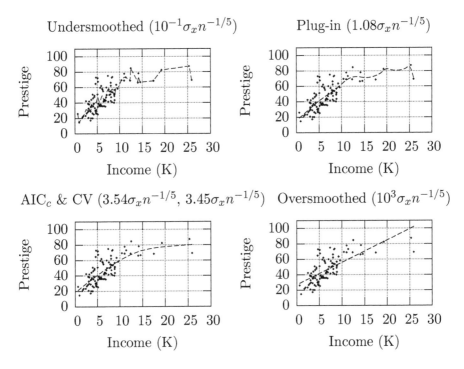

Figure 2.1: Local linear kernel estimates with varying window widths (note that the AIC_c and CV bandwidths are almost identical, hence the two curves appear as one in the lowerleft figure).

with bandwidths selected by Hurvich et al.'s (1998) AIC_c criterion using a second order Gaussian kernel. The bandwidth for age is 7.63, while that for sex is 0.

Figure 2.2 presents mean height by age and sex. It is interesting to note that mean height is virtually indistinguishable by sex until roughly 10–12 years of age, and then diverges significantly. This behavior would be particularly difficult to model in a parametric setting without resorting to sample splitting, while the nonparametric approach readily reveals this structure.

2.6.3 Inflation Forecasting and Money Growth

The conventional wisdom prevalent in monetary circles is that money growth should have predictive power for forecasting inflation. How-

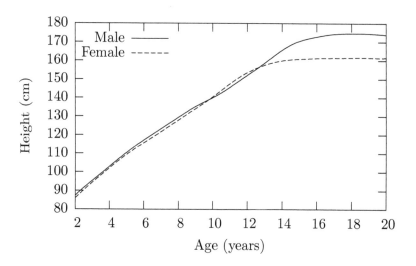

Figure 2.2: Stature-for-age means.

ever, empirical results overwhelmingly suggest just the opposite, i.e., that money growth has no predictive power for forecasting inflation whatsoever. Moreover, this finding has been robust to changes in the sample period and econometric methodology (see Leeper and Roush (2003) and Stock and Watson (1999)). This inconsistency between theory and empirics is a well-known puzzle in macroeconomics. Much of the empirical work in this area has focused on forecasts obtained from linear vector autoregressive (VAR) models of the form

$$X_t = \alpha + \beta(L)X_{t-1} + \epsilon_t,$$

where $X_t = (\pi_t, Z_t)'$, π_t is the inflation rate at time t, and Z_t is the growth rate of a monetary aggregate.

Bachmeier, Leelahanon and Li (forthcoming) revisit this issue from a nonparametric perspective using monthly data for the period January 1959 through May 2002. The monetary aggregates used are M1, M2, and M3, and the corresponding M1, M2, and M3 Divisia monetary services index, while inflation is measured with the consumer price index.

Using data from Bachmeier et al. (forthcoming), we first consider parametric forecasts of inflation obtained from a bivariate VAR model of inflation and money growth, which are made using a recursive estimation procedure with an increasing window of data; each forecast

Table 2.1: Relative parametric MSPE (including/excluding each monetary aggregate with 1 lag)

Horizon	M1	M2	M3	M1D	M2D	M3D
1 Month	1.05	1.02	1.06	1.00	1.00	1.00
6 Months	0.90	1.00	1.11	1.00	1.04	1.06
12 Months	0.93	0.96	1.09	1.00	1.02	1.04

Table 2.2: Relative parametric MSPE (including/excluding each monetary aggregate with 2 lags)

Horizon	M1	M2	M3	M1D	M2D	M3D
1 Month	1.04	0.99	1.04	1.00	1.00	1.00
6 Months	0.91	1.00	1.10	0.99	1.04	1.07
12 Months	0.92	0.94	1.06	1.00	1.01	1.05

was made based on a model estimated using all data available through the date that forecast would have been made. Forecasts were made for each model and forecast horizon (January 1994 through April 2002). The mean squared prediction error (MSPE) was calculated for each model for forecast horizons of $s = 1, 6$, and 12 months. SIC-optimal lag length selection was employed resulting in two lags of inflation and money growth, so that the forecasting equation of interest is

$$\pi_t = \alpha_0 + \alpha_1 \pi_{t-s} + \alpha_2 \pi_{t-s-1} + \alpha_3 \Delta m_{t-s} + \alpha_4 \Delta m_{t-s-1} + \varepsilon_t,$$

where m_t can be any one of the six monetary aggregate measures ($\Delta m_t = m_t - m_{t-1}$). For the sake of robustness, we report results for 1 and 2 lags of the monetary aggregate, and Tables 2.1 and 2.2 report the ratio of MSPE of the VAR model with each monetary aggregate *included* to that with each monetary aggregate *excluded* for the given horizon for 1 and 2 lags of the monetary aggregate respectively; values less than 1.00 imply that including the monetary aggregate improves the forecast for a given forecast horizon.

Tables 2.1 and 2.2 reveal no apparent systematic gain from including money as a predictor. With 1 lag of the monetary aggregate included, 9/18 forecasts worsen, 3/18 improve, and 6/18 are unchanged; with 2 lags, 8/18 worsen, 5/18 improve, and 5/18 are unchanged. Overall, the case for using money growth as an inflation predictor can be

Table 2.3: Relative MSPE of the nonparametric AR(2)/parametric AR(2)

Horizon	
1 Month	0.98
6 Months	1.01
12 Months	0.88

seen to be rather weak in a parametric setting as inclusion of the monetary aggregate leads to less efficient forecasts on balance.

Next we compare a parametric AR(2) model's forecasts with that for a local constant nonparametric AR(2) model of the form

$$\pi_t = g(\pi_{t-s}, \pi_{t-s-1}) + \varepsilon_t,$$

where $g(\cdot)$ is unknown. We conduct leave-one-out cross-validation on the estimation sample, and then use cross-validated bandwidths to generate our out-of-sample forecasts.[3] Table 2.3 presents the relative MSPE of the nonparametric AR(2) model with that for the parametric AR(2) model.

Table 2.3 reveals that the cross-validated local constant AR(2) model is generating predictions that are comparable to that from the parametric model for the 1 and 6 month horizon and are substantially improved for the 12 month horizon. This suggests misspecification of the parametric model since the nonparametric model is less efficient than a *correctly specified* parametric model. One then wonders whether the conclusion about the forecast inefficacy of monetary aggregates may in fact be an artifact of parametric misspecification. We therefore consider a local constant nonparametric model of the form

$$\pi_t = g(\pi_{t-s}, \pi_{t-s-1}, \Delta m_{t-s}, \Delta m_{t-s-1}) + \varepsilon_t, \qquad (2.73)$$

where $g(\cdot)$ is again unknown and we again use leave-one-out cross-validation for our bandwidth selector.

Tables 2.4 and 2.5 present the relative MSPE of the nonparametric model which utilizes the monetary aggregate to the nonparametric

---

[3]Note that Bachmeier et al. (forthcoming) use a more complicated two-step cross-validation procedure. Therefore, the results reported here differ slightly from those reported in Bachmeier et al. (forthcoming) due to the different bandwidth selection procedures being used.

Table 2.4: Relative nonparametric MSPE (including/excluding monetary aggregate with 1 lag)

Horizon	M1	M2	M3	M1D	M2D	M3D
1 Month	1.07	1.00	0.85	0.92	0.89	0.89
6 Months	0.96	0.95	1.15	1.00	1.00	1.00
12 Months	0.96	0.84	0.98	1.00	1.00	1.00

Table 2.5: Relative nonparametric MSPE (including/excluding monetary aggregate with 2 lags)

Horizon	M1	M2	M3	M1D	M2D	M3D
1 Month	1.07	0.98	1.06	1.00	1.00	0.88
6 Months	1.00	0.96	1.07	1.00	1.00	1.00
12 Months	0.99	0.83	0.98	1.00	0.97	0.93

model which excludes the monetary aggregate. These tables reveal that with 1 lag of the monetary aggregate included, 2/18 forecasts worsen (in the parametric setting we had 9/18), 9/18 improve (in the parametric setting we had 3/18), and 7/18 are unchanged (in the parametric setting we had 6/18); with 2 lags, 3/18 worsen, 8/18 improve, and 7/18 are unchanged. In a nonparametric setting, the case for using money growth as an indicator variable for inflation is in fact quite favorable as inclusion of the monetary aggregate leads to more accurate forecasts on balance.

Thus, the robust nonparametric method suggest that money growth affects inflation nonlinearly. The early puzzle appears therefore to be an artifact arising from the use of a misspecified linear relationship.

2.7 Proofs

In this section we provide some omitted proofs for earlier material in this chapter.

2.7.1   Derivation of (2.24)

Since we only consider the case in which all regressors are relevant, we assume therefore that

$$(h_1, \ldots, h_q) \in H_n = \Big\{ (h_1, \ldots, h_q) | (h_1, \ldots, h_q) \in [0, \eta_n]^q, $$
$$\text{and } nh_1 \ldots h_q \geq t_n \Big\}, \tag{2.74}$$

where η_n is a positive sequence that converges to zero at a rate slower than the inverse of any polynomial in n, and t_n is a sequence of constants that diverges to infinity. Equation (2.74) basically requires that $nh_1 \ldots h_q \to \infty$ and that $h_s \to 0$ $(s = 1, \ldots, q)$.

Let $\mathcal{S}$ denote the support of w. We also assume that

$g(\cdot)$, $f(\cdot)$ and σ^2 have two continuous derivatives; w is continuous, nonnegative and has compact support; $f(\cdot)$ is

bounded away from zero for $x \in \mathcal{S}$. $\tag{2.75}$

Using (2.23) with $g_i = g(X_i)$, $\hat{g}_i = \hat{g}_{-i}(X_i)$, and $M_i = M(X_i)$, we have

$$CV_{lc}(h_1, \ldots, h_q) = n^{-1} \sum_{i=1}^{n} (g_i - \hat{g}_i)^2 M_i + 2n^{-1} \sum_{i=1}^{n} u_i (g_i - \hat{g}_i) M_i$$
$$+ n^{-1} \sum_{i=1}^{n} u_i^2 M_i. \tag{2.76}$$

The third term on the right-hand side of (2.76) does not depend on $(h_1, \ldots, h_q)$. It can be shown that the second term has an order smaller than the first term (see Exercise 2.3). So, asymptotically, minimizing $CV_{lc}(h)$ is equivalent to minimizing $\sum_{i=1}^{n} [g_i - \hat{g}_i]^2 M_i$, the first term on the right-hand side of (2.76).

We next analyze the leading term of CV_{lc}. Note that

$$\hat{g}_i - g_i = (\hat{g}_i - g_i) \hat{f}_i / \hat{f}_i$$
$$= (\hat{g}_i - g_i) \hat{f}_i / f_i + (s.o.)$$
$$\equiv \hat{m}_i / f_i + (s.o.),$$

where $\hat{m}_i = (\hat{g}_i - g_i) \hat{f}_i$. Define

$$\hat{m}_{1i} = (n-1)^{-1} \sum_{l \neq i}^{n} g_l K_{h,il} - g_i \hat{f}_i$$

and

$$\hat{m}_{2i} = (n-1)^{-1} \sum_{l \neq i}^{n} u_l K_{h,il},$$

where $K_{h,ij} = \prod_{s=1}^{q} h_s^{-1} k((x_{is} - x_{js})/h_s)$. Then $\hat{m}_i = \hat{m}_{1i} + \hat{m}_{2i}$. Thus, $[\hat{m}_i - \hat{f}_i g_i] f_i^{-1} = (\hat{m}_{1i} + \hat{m}_{2i}) f_i^{-1}$ is the leading component of $\hat{g}_i - g_i$. Therefore, the leading term of $CV_{lc}(h)$ is $CV_{lc,0}(h) = \sum_{i=1}^{n} [\hat{m}_{1i} + \hat{m}_{2i}]^2 f_i^{-2} M_i$. It can be further shown that $CV_{lc,0}(h) = \mathrm{E}[CV_{lc,0}(h)] + (s.o.)$. Hence, $\mathrm{E}[CV_{lc,0}(h)]$ is the leading term of $CV_{lc}(h)$. Now,

$$\mathrm{E}[CV_{lc,0}(h_1, \ldots, h_q)] = \mathrm{E}\left\{ \left[(\hat{m}_{1i} + \hat{m}_{2i})^2 f_i^{-2} \right] M_i \right\}$$
$$= \mathrm{E}\left[\hat{m}_{1i}^2 f_i^{-2} M_i \right] + \mathrm{E}\left[\hat{m}_{2i}^2 f_i^{-2} M_i \right], \quad (2.77)$$

where we have used $\mathrm{E}[\hat{m}_{1i} \hat{m}_{2i} f_i^{-2} M_i] = 0$ (since $\mathrm{E}(u_i | \{X_j\}_{j=1}^{n}) = 0$). Then

$$\mathrm{E}\left[\hat{m}_{1i}^2 f_i^{-2} | X_i \right] = \mathrm{E}\left[(g_j - g_i) K_{h,ij} (g_l - g_i) K_{h,il} f_i^{-2} | X_i \right]$$
$$+ n^{-1} \mathrm{E}\left[(g_j - g_i)^2 K_{h,ij}^2 f_i^{-2} | X_i \right]$$
$$= \left\{ \mathrm{E}\left[(g_j - g_i) K_{h,ij} | x_i \right] f_i^{-1} \right\}^2$$
$$+ O\left((nh_1 \ldots h_q)^{-1} \sum_{s=1}^{q} h_s^2 \right)$$
$$= \left\{ \frac{1}{f(X_i)} \int (g(X_i + hv) - g(v)) K(v) f(X_i + hv)\, dv \right\}^2$$
$$+ O(\eta_1 \eta_2)$$
$$= \left\{ \sum_{s=1}^{q} B_s(X_i) h_s^2 \right\}^2 + O(\eta_2^3 + \eta_1 \eta_2), \quad (2.78)$$

where $B_s(x)$ is the same as that defined in (2.8), $\eta_1 = (nh_1 \ldots h_{q_1})^{-1}$, and $\eta_2 = \sum_{s=1}^{q_1} h_s^2$.

Using (2.78) we have

$$\mathrm{E}\left[\hat{m}_{1i}^2 f_i^{-2} M_i \right] = \int \left\{ \sum_{s=1}^{q} B_s(x) h_s^2 \right\}^2 f(x) M(x)\, dx$$
$$+ O\left(\eta_2^3 + \eta_1 \eta_2 \right). \quad (2.79)$$

Next,

$$
\begin{aligned}
\mathrm{E}\left[\hat{m}_{2i}^2 f_i^{-2} M_i\right] &= \mathrm{E}\left\{f_i^{-2} M_i \mathrm{E}\left[\hat{m}_{2i}^2 | X_i\right]\right\} \\
&= n^{-1}\mathrm{E}\left\{f_i^{-2}M_i\mathrm{E}\left[u_j^2 K_{h,ij}^2|X_i\right]\right\} \\
&= (nh_1\ldots h_q)^{-1} \\
&\qquad \times \mathrm{E}\left\{f_i^{-2}M_i\int f(X_i+hv)\sigma^2(X_i+hv)K^2(v)\,dv\right\} \\
&= (nh_1\ldots h_q)^{-1} \\
&\qquad \times \mathrm{E}\left\{f_i^{-2}M_i\left[\kappa^q f(X_i)\sigma^2(X_i)+O(\eta_2)\right]\right\} \\
&= \frac{\kappa^q}{nh_1\ldots h_q}\int \sigma^2(x)M(x)\,dx + O(\eta_1\eta_2). \qquad (2.80)
\end{aligned}
$$

Substituting (2.79) and (2.80) into (2.77) we obtain

$$
\begin{aligned}
\mathrm{E}[CV_{lc,0}(h_1,\ldots,h_q)] &= \int\left\{\sum_{s=1}^{q}B_s(x)h_s^2\right\}^2 f(x)M(x)\,dx \\
&\quad + \frac{\kappa^q}{h_1\ldots h_q}\int\sigma^2(x)M(x)\,dx + o\left(\eta_2^2+\eta_1\right) \\
&= n^{-4/(q+4)}\chi(a_1,\ldots,a_q) + o\left(n^{-4/(q+4)}\right), (2.81)
\end{aligned}
$$

where the a_ss are defined via $h_s = a_s n^{-1/(q+4)}$ $(s=1,\ldots,q)$ and

$$
\begin{aligned}
\chi(a_1,\ldots,a_q) &= \int\left\{\sum_{s=1}^{q}B_s(x)a_s^2\right\}^2 f(x)M(x)\,dx \\
&\quad + \frac{\kappa^q}{a_1\ldots a_q}\int\sigma^2(x)M(x)\,dx. \qquad (2.82)
\end{aligned}
$$

2.7.2   Proof of Theorem 2.7

We sketch an outline of the proof of Theorem 2.7, while leaving certain details as exercises.

One problem arising from working with (2.50) is that

$$
\frac{1}{n}\sum_i K_h(X_i,x)\binom{1}{X_i-x}(1,(X_i-x)')
$$

is an (asymptotically) singular matrix and thus is not invertible. We could rewrite (2.50) in an equivalent form by inserting an identity matrix $I_{q+1} = G_n^{-1} G_n$ in the middle of (2.50), and where $G_n = \begin{pmatrix} 1, & 0 \\ 0, & D_h^{-2} \end{pmatrix}$, where D_h^{-2} is a $q \times q$ diagonal matrix with the sth diagonal element given by h_s^{-2}, giving us (applying $B^{-1}C = B^{-1}G_n^{-1}G_n C = (G_n B)^{-1} G_n C$)

$$\hat{\delta}(x) = \left[\sum_i K_h(X_i, x) G_n \begin{pmatrix} 1 \\ X_i - x \end{pmatrix} (1, (X_i - x)') \right]^{-1}$$

$$\times \sum_i K_h(X_i, x) G_n \begin{pmatrix} 1 \\ X_i - x \end{pmatrix} y_i$$

$$= \left[\sum_i K_h(X_i, x) \begin{pmatrix} 1 \\ D_h^{-2}(X_i - x) \end{pmatrix} (1, (X_i - x)') \right]^{-1}$$

$$\times \sum_i K_h(X_i, x) \begin{pmatrix} 1 \\ D_h^{-2}(X_i - x) \end{pmatrix} y_i. \tag{2.83}$$

The advantage of using (2.83) in the proof is that

$$\frac{1}{nh_1 \dots h_q} \sum_i K_h(X_i, x) \begin{pmatrix} 1 \\ D_h^{-2}(X_i - x) \end{pmatrix} (1, (X_i - x)')$$

converges in probability to a nonsingular matrix. Therefore, we can analyze the denominator and numerator of (2.83) separately and thus greatly simplify the analysis.

Using a Taylor expansion given by

$$g(X_i) = g(x) + (X_i - x)' g^{(1)}(x) + (X_i - x)' g^{(2)}(x)(X_i - x)/2$$
$$+ R_m(x, X_i)$$
$$= (1, (X_i - x)')\delta(x) + (X_i - x)' g^{(2)}(x)(X_i - x)/2 + R_m(x, X_i),$$

where $R_m(x, X_i)$ is the remainder term, we have

$$
\hat{\delta}(x) = \left[\frac{1}{n} \sum_i K_{h,ix} \left(\frac{1}{D_h^{-2}(X_i - x)} \right) (1, (X_i - x)') \right]^{-1}
$$

$$
\times \left\{ \frac{1}{n} \sum_i K_{h,ix} \left(\frac{1}{D_h^{-2}(X_i - x)} \right) [g(X_i) + \epsilon_i] \right\}
$$

$$
= \delta(x) + \left[\frac{1}{n} \sum_i K_{h,ix} \left(\begin{matrix} 1, & (X_i - x)' \\ D_h^{-2}(X_i - x), & D_h^{-2}(X_i - x)(X_i - x)' \end{matrix} \right) \right]^{-1}
$$

$$
\times \left\{ \frac{1}{n} \sum_i K_{h,ix} \left(\frac{1}{D_h^{-2}(X_i - x)} \right) \right.
$$

$$
\left. \times \left[(X_i - x)' g^{(2)}(x)(X_i - x)/2 + \epsilon_i + R_m(x, X_i) \right] \right\}
$$

$$
\equiv \delta(x) + \left[A^{1,x} \right]^{-1} \left\{ A^{2,x} + A^{3,x} \right\} + (s.o.), \qquad (2.84)
$$

where

$$
A^{1,x} = \frac{1}{n} \sum_i K_{h,ix} \left(\begin{matrix} 1, & (X_i - x)' \\ D_h^{-2}(X_i - x), & D_h^{-2}(X_i - x)(X_i - x)' \end{matrix} \right), \quad (2.85)
$$

$$
A^{2,x} = \frac{1}{2n} \sum_i K_{h,ix} \left(\frac{1}{D_h^{-2}(X_i - x)} \right) (X_i - x)' g^{(2)}(x)(X_i - x), \quad (2.86)
$$

$$
A^{3,x} = \frac{1}{n} \sum_i K_{h,ix} \left(\frac{1}{D_h^{-2}(X_i - x)} \right) \epsilon_i, \qquad (2.87)
$$

and the smaller order (s.o.) term comes from

$$
[A^{1,x}]^{-1} \frac{1}{n} \sum_i K_{h,ix} R_m(x, X_i),
$$

which has an order smaller than $[A^{1,x}]^{-1} A^{2,x}$.

Exercise 2.7 shows that $A^{1,x} = Q + o_p(1)$, where

$$
Q = \begin{pmatrix} f(x), & 0 \\ \kappa_2 f^{(1)}(x), & \kappa_2 f(x) I_q \end{pmatrix}.
$$

Using the partitioned inverse, we get

$$
Q^{-1} = \begin{pmatrix} 1/f(x), & 0 \\ -f^{(1)}(x)/f^2(x), & I_q/(\kappa_2 f(x)) \end{pmatrix}.
$$

Next, rewrite (2.84) as

$$D(n)\left(\hat{\delta}(x) - \delta(x)\right) = D(n)\left[A^{1,x}\right]^{-1}\left[A^{2,x} + A^{3,x}\right] + (s.o.), \quad (2.88)$$

and define diagonal matrices

$$R = \text{diag}(Q^{-1}) = \begin{pmatrix} 1/f(x), & 0 \\ 0, & I_q/(\kappa_2 f(x)) \end{pmatrix}$$

and

$$V = \begin{pmatrix} \kappa^q \sigma^2(x) f(x), & 0 \\ 0, & \kappa^{q-1}\kappa_{22}\sigma^2(x)f(x)I_q \end{pmatrix}.$$

The proof of Theorem 2.1 follows if we can show the following:

(i) $D(n)[A^{1,x}]^{-1}[A^{2,x} + A^{3,x}] = D(n)Q^{-1}[A^{2,x} + A^{3,x}] + o_p(1)$,

(ii) $D(n)Q^{-1}[A^{2,x} + A^{3,x}] = RD(n)[A^{2,x} + A^{3,x}] + o_p(1)$,

(iii) $D(n)A^{2,x} = \begin{pmatrix} (nh_1 \dots h_q)^{1/2}(\kappa_2/2)f(x)\sum_{s=1}^{q} g_{ss}(x)h_s^2 \\ 0 \end{pmatrix} + o_p(1)$,

(iv) $D(n)A^{3,x} \to N(0, V)$ in distribution.

The proofs of (i)–(iv) are given in four lemmas below. Statements (i)–(iv) imply that

$$D(n)\left[\hat{\delta}(x) - \delta(x) - \begin{pmatrix} (\kappa_2/2)f(x)\sum_{s=1} g_{ss}(x)h_s^2 \\ 0 \end{pmatrix}\right]$$

$$= RD(n)[A^{2,x} + A^{3,x}] - \begin{pmatrix} (nh_1 \dots h_q)^{1/2}(\kappa_2/2)\sum_{s=1}^{q} g_{ss}(x)h_s^2 \\ 0 \end{pmatrix}$$

$$+ o_p(1)$$

$$= RD(n)A^{3,x} + o_p(1) \to RN(0, V) + o_p(1) \to N(0, \Sigma)$$

in distribution, where $\Sigma = RVR$ is the same Σ as that given in Theorem 2.7.

Lemma 2.1. $D(n)[A^{1,x}]^{-1}[A^{2,x}+A^{3,x}] = D(n)Q^{-1}[A^{2,x}+A^{3,x}]+o_p(1)$.

Proof. Writing $D(n)[A^{1,x}]^{-1}[A^{2,x} + A^{3,x}] = D(n)Q^{-1}[A^{2,x} + A^{3,x}] + D(n)[(A^{1,x})^{-1} - Q^{-1}][A^{2,x} + A^{3,x}]$, it is sufficient to show that

$$D(n)\left[\left(A^{1,x}\right)^{-1} - Q^{-1}\right]\left[A^{2,x} + A^{3,x}\right] = o_p(1). \quad (2.89)$$

From $A^{1,x} = Q + o_p(1)$ (see Exercise 2.7) we know that

$$\left(A^{1,x}\right)^{-1} = Q^{-1} + o_p(1). \tag{2.90}$$

Let $J \stackrel{\text{def}}{=} (A_{11}^{1,x})^{-1} - Q^{-1} \equiv \begin{pmatrix} J_{11}, & J_{12} \\ J_{21}, & J_{22}I_q \end{pmatrix}$. Equation (2.90) implies that $J_{ij} = o_p(1)$ for $i, j = 1, 2$. To prove (2.89), we need a sharp (i.e., fast) rate for J_{12}. Below we show that $J_{12} = O_p(\eta_2)$.

Define $G = \left(A_{22}^{1,x} - A_{21}^{1,x}(A_{11}^{1,x})^{-1}A_{12}^{1,x}\right)^{-1}$. Using the partitioned inverse and the results of Exercise 2.7, we obtain

$$(A^{1,x})^{-1} = \begin{pmatrix} \left(A_{11}^{1,x}\right)^{-1}\left(I_q + A_{12}^{1,x}GA_{21}^{1,x}\left(A_{11}^{1,x}\right)^{-1}\right), & -(A_{11}^{1,x})^{-1}A_{12}^{1,x}G \\ -GA_{21}^{1,x}\left(A_{11}^{1,x}\right)^{-1}, & G \end{pmatrix}$$

$$= \begin{pmatrix} (1/f(x))I_q + O_p(\eta_2), & O_p(\eta_2) \\ -f^{(1)}(x)/f(x)^2 + o_p(1), & I_q/[\kappa_2 f(x)] + o_p(1) \end{pmatrix}, \tag{2.91}$$

because $A_{12}^{1,x} = O_p(\eta_2)$ by Exercise 2.7 (ii). Equation (2.91) leads to

$$J = (A_{11}^{1,x})^{-1} - Q^{-1} = \begin{pmatrix} O_p(\eta_2), & O_p(\eta_2) \\ o_p(1), & o_p(1)I_q \end{pmatrix}, \tag{2.92}$$

which proves that $J_{12} = O_p(\eta_2)$. Using (2.92) we immediately have

$$D(n)\left[(A^{1,x})^{-1} - Q^{-1}\right]\left[A^{2,x} + A^{3,x}\right] = (nh_1 \ldots h_q)^{1/2}\begin{pmatrix} 1, & 0 \\ 0 & D_h \end{pmatrix}$$

$$\times \begin{pmatrix} O_p(\eta), & O_p(\eta_2) \\ o_p(1), & o_p(1)I_q \end{pmatrix}\left[\begin{pmatrix} A_1^{2,x} \\ A_2^{2,x} \end{pmatrix} + \begin{pmatrix} A_1^{3,x} \\ A_2^{3,x} \end{pmatrix}\right]$$

$$= o_p(1),$$

because

$$(nh_1 \ldots h_q)^{1/2}O_p(\eta_2)A_2^{2,x} = O_p\left((nh_1 \ldots h_q)^{1/2}\eta_2^2\right) = o_p(1)$$

and

$$(nh_1 \ldots h_q)^{1/2}O_p(\eta_2)A_2^{3,x} = (nh_1 \ldots h_q)^{1/2}\eta_2 O_p\left((nh_1 \ldots h_qh_s)^{-1/2}\right)$$

$$= O_p\left(\eta_2^{1/2}\right)$$

by Exercises 2.8 and 2.9.

This proves (2.89). $\square$

Lemma 2.2. $D(n)Q^{-1}\left[A^{2,x} + A^{3,x}\right] = RD(n)\left[A^{2,x} + A^{3,x}\right] + o_p(1)$.

Proof. Noting that R is a diagonal matrix with $R = \text{diag}(Q^{-1})$, we have

$$D(n)Q^{-1}\left[A^{2,x} + A^{3,x}\right] = RD(n)\left[A^{2,x} + A^{3,x}\right] + o_p(1)$$

because the terms associated with the off-diagonal element of Q^{-1} are all $o_p(1)$:

$$(nh_1\ldots h_q)^{1/2}h_s A_1^{2,x} = \sqrt{nh_1\ldots h_q}O_p(h_s\eta_2) = o_p(1)$$

and

$$(nh_1\ldots h_q)^{1/2}h_s A_1^{3,x} = O_p(h_s) = o_p(1).$$

$\square$

Lemma 2.3.

$$D(n)A^{2,x} = \begin{pmatrix} (nh_1\ldots h_q)^{1/2}(\kappa_2/2)f(x)\sum_{s=1}^{q}g_{ss}(x)h_s^2 \\ 0 \end{pmatrix} + o_p(1).$$

Proof. By Exercise 2.9, we have

$$(nh_1\ldots h_q)^{1/2}A_1^{2,x} = \sqrt{nh_1\ldots h_q}(\kappa_2/2)f(x)\sum_{s=1}^{q}g_{ss}(x) + o_p(1),$$

and

$$(nh_1\ldots h_q)^{1/2}D_h A_2^{2,x} = \sqrt{nh_1\ldots h_q}O_p\left(\eta_2^{3/2}\right) = o_p(1).$$

Hence

$$D(n)A^{2,x} = \begin{pmatrix} (nh_1\ldots h_q)^{1/2}A_1^{2,x} \\ (nh_1\ldots h_q)^{1/2}D_h A_2^{2,x} \end{pmatrix}$$

$$= \begin{pmatrix} (nh_1\ldots h_q)^{1/2}(\kappa_2/2)f(x)\sum_{s=1}^{q}g_{ss}(x)h_s^2 \\ 0 \end{pmatrix} + o_p(1).$$

$\square$

Lemma 2.4. $D(n)A^{3,x}\rightarrow N(0,V)$ *in distribution, where*

$$V = \begin{pmatrix} \kappa^q f(x)\sigma^2(x), & 0 \\ 0, & \kappa^{q-1}\kappa_{22}f(x)\sigma^2(x)I_q \end{pmatrix}.$$

Proof. By Exercise 2.9, var $\left((nh_1 \dots h_q)^{1/2} A_1^{3,x} \right) = \kappa^q f(x)\sigma^2(x) + o(1)$, var $\left((nh_1 \dots h_q)^{1/2} D_h A_2^{3,x} \right) = \kappa^{q-1}\kappa_{22} f(x)\sigma^2(x) I_q + o(1)$ and

$$\text{cov}\left((nh_1 \dots h_q)^{1/2} A_1^{3,x}, (nh_1 \dots h_q)^{1/2} D_h A_2^{3,x} \right) = o(1).$$

Hence, var $\left(D(n) A^{3,x} \right) = V + o(1)$. Also note that $A^{3,x}$ has mean zero. Thus $D(n) A^{3,x} \xrightarrow{d} N(0, V)$ by the Liapunov CLT. $\qquad\square$

2.7.3 Definitions of $A_{l,p+1}$ and V_l Used in Theorem 2.10

We use the notation introduced in (2.67) to (2.69) to define

$$\mu_j = \int v^j K(v)\, dv, \quad \gamma_j = \int v^j K^2(v)\, dv. \tag{2.93}$$

$$M = \begin{pmatrix} M_{0,0} & M_{0,1} & \dots & M_{0,p} \\ M_{1,0} & M_{1,1} & \dots & M_{1,p} \\ \vdots & & & \vdots \\ M_{p,0} & M_{p,1} & \dots & M_{p,p} \end{pmatrix}, \quad \Gamma = \begin{pmatrix} \Gamma_{0,0} & \Gamma_{0,1} & \dots & \Gamma_{0,p} \\ \Gamma_{1,0} & \Gamma_{1,1} & \dots & \Gamma_{1,p} \\ \vdots & & & \vdots \\ \Gamma_{p,0} & \Gamma_{p,1} & \dots & \Gamma_{p,p} \end{pmatrix},$$
$$\tag{2.94}$$

where $M_{i,j}$ and $\Gamma_{i,j}$ are $N_i \times N_j$ dimensional matrices. For example, $M_{1,2} = \mu_{(1)} \times \mu_{(2)}$, where $\mu_{(1)}$ and $\mu_{(2)}$ are of dimension $N_1 \times 1$ and $N_2 \times 1$ and are defined from μ_j with the lexicographic order

$$\mu_{(1)} = \begin{pmatrix} \int v_1 K(v)\, dv \\ \int v_2 K(v)\, dv \\ \vdots \\ \int v_p K(v)\, dv \end{pmatrix}, \quad \mu_{(2)} = \begin{pmatrix} \int v_1^2 K(v)\, dv \\ \int v_1 v_2 K(v)\, dv \\ \vdots \\ \int v_p^2 K(v)\, dv \end{pmatrix}. \tag{2.95}$$

Similarly, $\Gamma_{i,j}$ can be obtained from $M_{i,j}$ with $K(\cdot)$ replaced by $K^2(\cdot)$.

For two $m \times 1$ vectors C_1 and C_2 we use $C_1 \otimes C_2$ to denote an $m \times 1$ vector with its jth element being $C_{1,j} C_{2,j}$ $(j = 1, \dots, m)$, i.e., $\otimes$ denotes element by element product.

The V_l matrix introduced in Theorem 2.10 is defined via the following $N \times N$ matrix V $(N = \sum_{j=1}^p N_j)$:

$$V = M^{-1} \Gamma M^{-1}.$$

Then V_l is an $N_l \times N_l$ dimensional matrix, consisting of rows and columns from $\sum_{j=0}^{l-1} N_j + 1$ to $\sum_{j=0}^{l} N_j$. For example, V_0 is the first diagonal element of V. V_1 consists of rows and columns from 2 to $N_1 + 1 = q+1$ of V. V_2 consists of rows and columns from $N_0 + N_1 + 1 = q + 2$ to $N_0 + N_1 + N_2 = 1 + q + q(q+1)/2$ of V, etc.

We can easily check that when $p = 1$ (the local linear case), we get

$$M = \begin{pmatrix} 1 & 0 \\ 0 & \kappa_2 I_q \end{pmatrix},$$

$$\Gamma = \begin{pmatrix} \kappa^q & 0 \\ 0 & \kappa^{q-1}\kappa_{22} I_q \end{pmatrix}, \qquad (2.96)$$

$$V = M^{-1}\Gamma M^{-1}$$

$$= \begin{pmatrix} \kappa^q & 0 \\ 0 & (\kappa^{q-1}\kappa_{ss}/\kappa_2^2) I_q \end{pmatrix},$$

where $\kappa_2 = \int v^2 k(v) \, dv$, $\kappa = \int k^2(v) \, dv$, and $\kappa_{22} = \int v^2 k^2(v) \, dv$. Thus, $V_0 = \kappa^q$ and $V_1 = (\kappa^{q-1}\kappa_{ss}/\kappa_2^2) I_q$. The variance $[\sigma^2(x)/f(x)]V_l$ exactly matches the result of Theorem 2.7 for $l = 0$ and $l = 1$.

Define an $N_l \times 1$ vector $l_{(r)}$ whose elements vary with different forms of $1/(r!) = 1/(r_1! \times r_2! \times \cdots \times r_q!)$, $\bar{r} = l$, in the lexicographic order. For example 2_j is an $N_2 \times 1$ vector given by

$$2_{(r)} = \begin{pmatrix} 1/2 \\ \iota_{q-1} \\ 1/2 \\ \iota_{q-2} \\ \vdots \\ 1/2 \end{pmatrix}, \qquad (2.97)$$

where ι_m is a vector of ones of dimension m.

Then define

$$\mathcal{A} \equiv \begin{pmatrix} A_0 \\ A_1 \\ \vdots \\ A_p \end{pmatrix} \overset{\text{def}}{=} \begin{pmatrix} M_{0,p+1} \\ M_{1,p+1} \\ 2_{(r)} \otimes M_{1,p+1} \\ \vdots \\ p_{(r)} \otimes M_{p,p+1} \end{pmatrix}. \qquad (2.98)$$

There are N_{p+1} distinct derivatives like $(1/j!)(D^j g)(x)$ of total order $\bar{j} = p + 1$: we put them in an $N_{p+1} \times 1$ vector using the lexicographic order, and we denote this vector by $m_{(p+1)}(x)$. For example, when $p = 1$ (the local linear case), we have

$$m_{(2)}(x) \equiv \begin{pmatrix} \frac{1}{2}\frac{\partial^2 g(x)}{\partial x_1^2} \\ \frac{\partial^2 g(x)}{\partial x_1 \partial x_2} \\ \vdots \\ \frac{1}{2}\frac{\partial^2 g(x)}{\partial x_q^2} \end{pmatrix}. \tag{2.99}$$

Then $A_{l,p+1}$ introduced in Theorem 2.10 is defined via $(l = 0, \ldots, p)$ the following equation:

$$\mathcal{B} \stackrel{\text{def}}{=} M^{-1}\mathcal{A}m_{(p+1)}(x) \equiv \begin{pmatrix} A_{0,p+1} \\ A_{1,p+1} \\ \vdots \\ A_{p,p+1} \end{pmatrix}, \tag{2.100}$$

where M and $\mathcal{A}$ are defined in (2.94) and (2.98), respectively, and $m_{(p+1)}(x)$ is defined immediately following (2.98).

When $p = 1$ (the local linear case), using (2.96), (2.99), and (2.98) we have

$$\mathcal{B} = M^{-1}\mathcal{A}m_{(2)}(x) = \begin{pmatrix} (1/2)\kappa_2 \operatorname{tr}[g^{(2)}(x)] \\ 0 \end{pmatrix} \equiv \begin{pmatrix} A_{0,2} \\ A_{1,2} \end{pmatrix}. \tag{2.101}$$

Using the above $A_{0,2}$ and $A_{1,2}$ in Theorem 2.10 leads to results identical to those in Theorem 2.7, as of course they should.

2.8   Exercises

Exercise 2.1. Prove (2.10).

   Hint: Note that $\mathrm{E}[\hat{m}_1(x) - f(x)\sum_{s=1}^{q} B_s(x)h_s^2]^2 = \{\mathrm{E}[\hat{m}_1(x) - f(x)\sum_{s=1}^{q} B_s(x)h_s^2]\}^2 + \operatorname{var}(\hat{m}_1(x))$, then apply (2.8) and (2.9).

Exercise 2.2.

(i) Consider (2.82) for $q = 2$:

$$\chi(a_1, a_2) = \int \left\{ \left[a_1^2 B_1(x) + a_2^2 B_2(x)\right]^2 + \frac{\sigma^2(x)}{a_1 a_2 f(x)} \right\} f(x)M(x)\,dx.$$

Derive the explicit expressions of a_1^0 and a_2^0 that minimize $\chi(a_1, a_2)$.

(ii) For the general multivariate case, χ_w can be written as (see (2.30))

$$\chi_z(z_1, z_2, \ldots, z_q) = z'Az + \frac{C_0}{\sqrt{z_1 z_2 \ldots z_q}},$$

where A is a $q \times q$ positive semidefinite matrix and $C_0 > 0$ is a constant.

Show that when A is positive definite, then $\inf \chi_\nu > 0$. This will imply that $a_1^0, \ldots, a_q^0$ are all positive and finite.

Hint for (ii): This follows the same analysis as those used in Exercise 1.10.

Exercise 2.3. Show that

$$n^{-1} \sum_{i=1}^n u_i(g(X_i) - \hat{g}_{-i}(X_i)) M(X_i) = o_p\left(\eta_2 + \eta_1^{1/2}\right).$$

Hint: Write $n^{-1} \sum_{i=1}^n u_i(g_i - \hat{g}_{-i}) M_i = n^{-1} \sum_{i=1}^n u_i(g_i - \hat{g}_{-i}) \hat{f}_i M_i / f_i + (s.o.)$. Then show that the second moment of this leading term is $O(n^{-1}(\eta_2^2 + \eta_1))$.

Exercise 2.4. Suppose one does not use the leave-one-estimator in the cross-validation procedure.

(i) Show that, in this case, $CV(h)$ approaches its lower bound (zero) as $h \to 0$, i.e., $\lim_{h \to 0+} CV(h) = 0$. That is, $h \to 0$ minimizes $CV(h)$.

(ii) What is the resulting estimator if h is arbitrarily close to zero, roughly say, $\hat{g}(X_i, h = 0)$?

We know that $h \to 0$ too fast violates the condition $nh_1 \ldots h_q \to \infty$ as $n \to \infty$. The variance of such an estimator goes to infinity as $n \to \infty$.

Exercise 2.5. This problem explains $R(\tilde{x}, h_{q_1+1}, \ldots, h_q)$ defined in (2.39). Write $\hat{g}(x) - \bar{g}(\bar{x}) = [\hat{g}(x) - \bar{g}(\bar{x})] \hat{f}(x) / \hat{f}(x) = \hat{m}(x) / \hat{f}(x)$, where $\hat{m}(x) = \hat{m}_1(x) + \hat{m}_2(x)$, $\hat{m}_1(x) = n^{-1} \sum_{i=1}^n (\bar{g}_i - \bar{g}(\bar{x})) K_{h,xi}$, and $\hat{m}_2(x) = n^{-1} \sum_{i=1}^n u_i K_{h,xi}$. Write $K_{h,xi} = \bar{K}_{h,xi} \tilde{K}_{h,xi}$, $\bar{K}_{h,xi} = \prod_{s=1}^{q_1} k\left((X_{is} - X_s)/h_s\right)$, and $\tilde{K}_{h,xi} = \prod_{s=q_1+1}^q k\left((X_{is} - X_s)/h_s\right)$, where the bar and tilde refer to relevant and irrelevant variables, respectively.

Define $\eta_{2,q_1} = \sum_{s=1}^{q_1} h_s^2$ and $\eta_{1,q_1} = (nh_1 \ldots h_{q_1})^{-1}$.

(i) Show that

$$\mathrm{E}[\hat{f}(x)] = \bar{f}(\bar{x})\mathrm{E}[\tilde{K}_{h,xi}] + O(\eta_{2,q_1}), \text{ and that}$$
$$\mathrm{var}(\hat{f}(x)) = O(\eta_{1,q_1}) = o(1).$$

Therefore,

$$\hat{f}(x) = \bar{f}(\bar{x})\mathrm{E}[\tilde{K}_{h,xi}] + o_p(1). \qquad (2.102)$$

Note that (2.102) implies the following:

$$\hat{g}(x) - \bar{g}(\bar{x}) = \frac{\hat{m}(x)}{\hat{f}(x)} = \frac{\hat{m}(x)}{\bar{f}(\bar{x})\mathrm{E}[\tilde{K}_{h,xi}]} + (s.o.) \equiv A_n(x) + (s.o.),$$

where $A_n(x) = \hat{m}(x)/[\bar{f}(\bar{x})\mathrm{E}(\tilde{K}_{h,xi})]$ is the leading term of $\hat{g}(x) - \bar{g}(\bar{x})$.

(ii) Show that

$$\mathrm{E}[\hat{m}_1(x)] = \sum_{s=1}^{q_1} h_s^2 \bar{B}_s(\bar{x})\bar{f}(\bar{x})\mathrm{E}[\tilde{K}_{h,xi}] + o(\eta_{2,q_1}\mathrm{E}(\tilde{K}_{h,xi})), \text{ and that}$$

$$\mathrm{var}(\hat{m}_1(x)) = O(\eta_{2,q_1}\eta_{1,q_1}[\mathrm{E}(\tilde{K}_{h,xi})]^2) = o(\eta_{1,q_1}[\mathrm{E}(\tilde{K}_{h,xi})]^2).$$

Therefore,

$$\mathrm{E}[\hat{m}_1(x)^2] = \left\{ \sum_{s=1}^{q_1} h_s^2 \bar{B}_s(\bar{x})\bar{f}(\bar{x})\mathrm{E}[\tilde{K}_{h,xi}] \right\}^2$$
$$+ o\left((\eta_{2,q_1}^2 + \eta_{1,q_1}) \left[\mathrm{E}(\tilde{K}_{h,xi}) \right]^2 \right). \qquad (2.103)$$

(iii) Show that

$$\mathrm{E}[\hat{m}_2(x)^2] = \eta_{1,q_1}\kappa^{q_1}\bar{\sigma}^2(\bar{x})\bar{f}(\bar{x})\mathrm{E}\left[\tilde{K}_{h,xi}^2 \right] [1 + o(1)]. \qquad (2.104)$$

(iv) Show that (2.102) to (2.104) imply that

$$\mathrm{E}[A_n(x)^2] = \left[(\kappa_2/2)\sum_{s=1}^{q_1} \bar{B}_s(\bar{x})h_s^2 \right]^2$$
$$+ \frac{\kappa^{q_1}\bar{\sigma}^2(\bar{x})}{nh_1 \dots h_{q_1}\bar{f}(\bar{x})} R(\tilde{x}, h_{q_1+1}, \dots, h_q) + (s.o.),$$
$$\qquad (2.105)$$

where $R(\cdot)$ is defined by (2.39).

(v) Using (2.105) and

$$CV = \int \mathrm{E}[\hat{g}(x) - \bar{g}(\bar{x})]^2 f(x) M(x)\, dx \sim \mathrm{E}[A_n^2(x)],$$

we have

$$CV \sim \int \left\{ \left[\sum_{s=1}^{q_1} \bar{B}_s(\bar{x}) h_j^2 \right]^2 \right.$$
$$\left. + \left[\frac{\kappa^{q_1} \bar{\sigma}^2(\bar{x})}{n h_1 \ldots h_{q_1} \bar{f}(\bar{x})} \right] R(\tilde{x}, h_{q_1+1}, \ldots, h_q) \right\} f(x) M(x)\, dx$$

$$(2.106)$$

Show that $h_s \to \infty$ $(s = q_1 + 1, \ldots, q)$ minimizes (2.106). This will result in $R(\cdot) = 1$. Using $R = 1$ show that (2.106) leads to (2.35). Note that $f(x) = \bar{f}(\bar{x})\tilde{f}(\tilde{x})$ by (2.32).

Give an intuitive proof of Theorem 2.4 based on the above results.

Exercise 2.6.

(i) Show that if one uses $h_s = \infty$ for all $s = 1, \ldots, q$, then the local linear estimator $\hat{g}(x)$ is identical to the least squares estimator $\hat{\alpha}_0 + x'\hat{\alpha}_1$, where $\hat{\alpha}_0$ and $\hat{\alpha}_1$ are the least squares estimators of α_0 and α_1 based on $Y_i = \alpha_0 + X_i'\alpha_1 + $ error. (Note that we do not necessarily assume that the true regression function $g(\cdot)$ is linear in x for this problem.)

(ii) Show when $g(x) = \alpha_0 + x'\alpha_1$ is linear in x, then the local linear estimator is unbiased (note that you should not assume $h_s = \infty$ in this problem).

Exercise 2.7. Let $A_{ts}^{1,x}$, $(t, s = 1, 2)$ be defined as in Section 2.7. Prove the following results:

(i) $A_{11}^{1,x} = f(x) + o_p(1)$.

(ii) $A_{12}^{1,x} = O_p(\eta_2) = o(1)$.

(iii) $A_{21}^{1,x} = \kappa_2 f^{(1)}(x) + o_p(1)$.

(iv) $A_{22}^{1,x} = \kappa_2 f(x) I_q + o_p(1)$.

Note that (i)-(iv) imply that

$$A^{1,x} = Q + o_p(1), \quad \text{where } Q = \begin{pmatrix} f(x), & 0 \\ \kappa_2 f^{(1)}(x), & \kappa_2 f(x) I_q \end{pmatrix}.$$

Hint: Show that $\mathrm{E}[A^{1,x}] = Q + o(1)$ and that $\mathrm{var}(A^{1,x}) = o(1)$.

Exercise 2.8. Let $A_t^{2,x}$ $(t = 1, 2)$ be defined as in Section 2.7. Prove the following results:

(i) $A_1^{2,x} = (\kappa_2/2) f(x) \sum_{s=1}^q g_{ss}(x) h_s^2 + o_p(\eta_2)$.

(ii) $A_2^{2,x} = O_p(\eta_2)$.

Hint:

(i) Show that $\mathrm{E}\left[A_1^{2,x}\right] = (\kappa_2/2) f(x) \sum_{s=1}^q g_{ss}(x) h_s^2 + o(\eta_2)$ and that $\mathrm{var}\left(A_1^{2,x}\right) = o(\eta_2^2)$.

(ii) Show that $\mathrm{E}\left[\left|A_{2,s}^{2,x}\right|\right] = O(\eta_2)$ for all $s = 1, \ldots, q$, where $A_{2,s}^{2,x}$ is the sth component of $A_2^{2,x}$.

Exercise 2.9. Let $A_t^{3,x}$ $(t = 1, 2)$ be defined as in Section 2.7. Prove the following results $(\eta_1 = (nh_1 \ldots h_q)^{-1})$:

(i) $\mathrm{var}\left((nh_1 \ldots h_q)^{1/2} A_1^{3,x}\right) = \kappa^q \sigma^2(x) f(x) + o(1)$.

(ii) $\mathrm{var}\left((nh_1 \ldots h_q)^{1/2} D_h A_2^{3,x}\right) = \kappa_{22} \kappa^{q-1} f(x) \sigma^2(x) I_q + o(1)$.

(iii) $\mathrm{cov}\left((nh_1 \ldots h_q)^{1/2} A_1^{3,x}, (nh_1 \ldots h_q)^{1/2} D_h A_2^{3,x}\right) = O(\eta_2^{1/2}) = o(1)$.

Note that (i) - (iii) above imply that

$$\mathrm{var}\left(D(n) A^{3,x}\right) = \begin{pmatrix} \kappa^q \sigma^2(x) f(x) & 0 \\ 0 & \kappa_{22} \kappa^{q-1} f(x) \sigma^2(x) I_q \end{pmatrix} \equiv V.$$

Exercise 2.10. Show that when $g(x)$ is linear in x $(g(x) = a + x'b)$, then the local linear estimator of $g(x)$ is an unbiased estimator of $g(x)$.

Note: Unbiasedness is a *finite-sample* concept (no asymptotics). Thus, one should not use change-of-variable and Taylor expansion methods to prove this result, as these methods assume $h \to 0$ and $n \to \infty$.

Exercise 2.11. Pagan and Ullah (1999, pp. 154–155) present a local constant kernel estimate of an earnings profile (log income versus age) based on Canadian data (1971 Canadian Census Public Use Tapes) for $n = 205$ males having common education (high school). While the parametric quadratic specification is globally concave, the nonparametric fit reflects a "dip" around the median age (approximately 38 years).

(i) Compute and plot the local constant, local linear, and parametric quadratic estimates using least squares cross-validated bandwidths for the kernel estimators.

(ii) Is the dip present in the resulting nonparametric estimates?

(iii) Plot the nonparametric estimates along with their error bounds using the asymptotic formulas for the standard errors (i.e., $\hat{g}(x) \pm 2\hat{\sigma}(\hat{g}(x))$). Without conducting a formal test, does the dip appear to be significant?

(iv) Which nonparametric estimator (i.e., the local constant or local linear) appears to provide the most "appropriate" fit to this data?

Chapter 3

Frequency Estimation with Mixed Data

Traditional kernel methods typically presume that the underlying data is continuous in nature. When encountering a dataset containing a mix of continuous and discrete data, the conventional nonparametric approach is to split the data into "cells" corresponding to the values assumed by the discrete variables, then use the data in each cell to estimate a probability or a regression function according to the problem at hand. We shall refer to this approach as a "frequency-based" method from now on. However, strong theoretical and practical reasons support the application of kernel smoothing methods to a mix of continuous and discrete (i.e., nominal and ordinal categorical) data types, where both the continuous *and* the discrete data are smoothed in a particular fashion. This smooth approach, as opposed to the frequency approach considered below, is discussed in Chapter 4.

To set the stage for the material presented in Chapter 4, we first discuss traditional (i.e., frequency-based) nonparametric estimation of probability functions and regression functions strictly for the discrete variable case, and then we discuss the frequency-based mixed discrete and continuous variable case in Section 3.3. Throughout this chapter we use the frequency (nonsmoothing) method to handle the presence of discrete variables. From a theoretical perspective, the frequency method is easy to work with since establishing rates of convergence and asymptotic normality is quite straightforward. However, one quickly realizes that the frequency method can be problematic in practice when the sample size is not large relative to the number of discrete cells, which then leads naturally to the approach outlined in Chapter 4 where we demonstrate how, by smoothing discrete variables in a particular manner, one can often obtain estimation results superior to those produced by the frequency method, especially when the number of cells is large.

3.1 Probability Function Estimation with Discrete Data

When a random variable X takes on discrete values with probabilities $p(x)$, the function $p(x)$ is commonly referred to as a "probability function" (recall that we referred to the continuous X counterpart as a "probability density function," denoted by $f(x)$). Using the superscript d to denote a discrete variable, we consider an r-dimensional discrete random variable X_i^d, and let X_{is}^d denote its sth component $(s = 1, \ldots, r)$. Assuming that X_i^d has finite support, then without loss of generality we assume that the support of X_{is}^d is $\{0, 1, 2, \ldots, c_s - 1\}$, so that the support of X_i^d is $\mathcal{S}^d = \prod_{s=1}^r \{0, 1, 2, \ldots, c_s - 1\}$, where $c_s \geq 2$ is a positive integer $(s = 1, \ldots, r)$. We use $\mathbf{1}(\cdot)$ to denote the usual indicator function, which assumes the value 1 if $(\cdot)$ is true, 0 otherwise. Defining the indicator function $(x^d \in \mathcal{S}^d)$

$$\mathbf{1}(X_i^d = x^d) = \begin{cases} 1 & \text{if } X_i^d = x^d \\ 0 & \text{otherwise,} \end{cases} \tag{3.1}$$

then, for any $x^d \in \mathcal{S}^d$, we estimate the probability function $p(x^d)$ by

$$\tilde{p}(x^d) = \frac{1}{n} \sum_{i=1}^n \mathbf{1}(X_i^d = x^d). \tag{3.2}$$

Equation (3.2) is the standard and well-known "frequency estimator" for $p(x^d)$. Note that this estimator indeed bears a strong resemblance to the kernel estimator for continuous data given in (1.8) if we view $\mathbf{1}(X_i^d = x^d)$ to be a nonsmoothing kernel function. It is easy to see that

$$\begin{aligned} \mathrm{E}\left[\tilde{p}(x^d)\right] &= \mathrm{E}[\mathbf{1}(X_1^d = x^d)] \\ &= \sum_{x_1^d \in \mathcal{S}^d} \mathbf{1}(x_1^d = x^d) p(x_1^d) \\ &= p(x^d). \end{aligned}$$

Thus, $\tilde{p}(x^d)$ is unbiased. Also,

$$
\begin{aligned}
\operatorname{var}\left(\tilde{p}(x^d)\right) &= n^{-1}\operatorname{var}\left(\mathbf{1}(X_1^d = x^d)\right) \\
&= n^{-1}\left[\mathrm{E}(\mathbf{1}(X_1^d = x^d)) - (E\mathbf{1}(X_1^d = x^d))^2\right] \\
&= n^{-1}\left[p(x^d) - p(x^d)^2\right] \\
&= n^{-1}p(x^d)(1 - p(x^d))
\end{aligned}
$$

(where we use the fact that $\mathbf{1}^2(\cdot) = \mathbf{1}(\cdot)$). Hence,

$$
\mathrm{MSE}\left(\tilde{p}(x^d)\right) = n^{-1}p(x^d)(1 - p(x^d)) = O\left(n^{-1}\right),
$$

which implies that

$$
\tilde{p}(x^d) - p(x^d) = O_p\left(n^{-1/2}\right). \tag{3.3}
$$

Moreover, by the Lindeberg-Levy CLT, we have

$$
\sqrt{n}\left(\tilde{p}(x^d) - p(x^d)\right) \xrightarrow{d} N\left(0, p(x^d)(1 - p(x^d))\right). \tag{3.4}
$$

Note that the above calculation is identical to the MSE computation we obtained in Chapter 1 when considering the coin toss probability estimator ($\hat{p} = \mathrm{P}(H)$). Equations (3.3) and (3.4) show that, for nonparametric estimation involving discrete variables, the rate of convergence is faster than the case of nonparametric estimation involving continuous variables. The reason for this result is quite simple, and it follows from our assumption that the support of x^d is finite. Hence, for any $x^d \in \mathcal{S}^d$, we have $p(x^d) > 0$, and among the n independent random draws $X_1^d, \ldots, X_n^d$, there are on average $np(x^d) = O(n)$ observations that assume the value x^d. Therefore, our estimator $\hat{p}(x^d)$ is expected to converge to $p(x^d)$ at the parametric rate of $O_p\left((np(x^d))^{-1/2}\right) = O_p\left(n^{-1/2}\right)$. The finite support assumption implies that we have only finitely many parameters ($p(x^d), x^d \in \mathcal{S}^d$) to be estimated. This is essentially a parametric model (since the number of parameters does not increase as sample size increases); therefore, we naturally obtain the $\sqrt{n}$-rate, i.e., the standard *parametric* rate of convergence. There is also a large literature in statistics that deals with the case in which the number of discrete cells grows as the sample size increases, with the number of observation in each cell being finite even as $n \to \infty$. This is the so-called sparse asymptotics framework, and we refer the interested reader to Simonoff (1996). We do not pursue this case further in this book.

3.2   Regression with Discrete Regressors

Consider a nonparametric regression model having only discrete regressors given by

$$Y_i = g(X_i^d) + u_i, \tag{3.5}$$

where $X_i^d \in \mathcal{S}^d$, u_i is i.i.d. with zero mean and $\mathrm{E}(u_i^2 | X_i^d = x^d) = \sigma^2(x^d)$. We allow the error process to be conditionally heteroskedastic and of unknown form. For any $x^d \in \mathcal{S}^d$, we estimate $g(x^d)$ by

$$\tilde{g}(x^d) = \frac{1}{n} \sum_{i=1}^{n} Y_i \mathbf{1}(X_i^d = x^d) / \tilde{p}(x^d), \tag{3.6}$$

where $\tilde{p}(x^d)$ is defined in (3.2).

One can easily show that

$$\tilde{g}(x^d) - g(x^d) = O_p\left(n^{-1/2}\right), \tag{3.7}$$

and also that

$$\sqrt{n}\left(\tilde{g}(x^d) - g(x^d)\right) \xrightarrow{d} N\left(0, \sigma^2(x^d)/p(x^d)\right), \tag{3.8}$$

by observing that $\sum_{i=1}^{n} \left[g(X_i^d) - g(x^d)\right] \mathbf{1}(X_i^d = x^d) = 0$. The proofs of (3.7) and (3.8) are fairly straightforward and are left to the reader as an exercise (see Exercise 3.1).

3.3   Estimation with Mixed Data: The Frequency Approach

We now turn our attention to the mixed discrete and continuous variables case. We use X_i^c to denote a continuous variable, and therefore write $X_i = (X_i^c, X_i^d) \in \mathbb{R}^q \times \mathcal{S}^d$. We define $f(x) = f(x^c, x^d)$ to be the joint PDF of (X_i^c, X_i^d).

3.3.1   Density Estimation with Mixed Data

Suppose that we have independent observations $X_1, X_2, \ldots, X_n$ drawn from $f(\cdot)$. A nonparametric kernel estimator of $f(x)$ is given by

$$\tilde{f}(x) = \frac{1}{n} \sum_{i=1}^{n} W_h(X_i^c, x^c) \mathbf{1}(X_i^d = x^d), \tag{3.9}$$

where $W_h(X_i^c, x^c) = \prod_{s=1}^q h_s^{-1} w((X_{is}^c - x_s^c)/h_s)$, with $w(\cdot)$ being a standard univariate second order kernel function satisfying (1.10). We state the rate of convergence and the asymptotic distribution of $\tilde{f}(x)$ in the next theorem.

Theorem 3.1. *For all $x^d \in \mathcal{S}^d$, assume that $f(x^c, x^d)$ satisfies the same conditions as $f(x^c)$ given in Theorem 1.3. Also assume that, as $n \to \infty$, $h_s \to 0$ $(s = 1, \ldots, q)$, $n(h_1 \ldots h_q)(\sum_{s=1}^q h_s^6) \to 0$, and $nh_1 \ldots h_q \to \infty$. Then*

(i) $\tilde{f}(x) - f(x) = O_p\left(\sum_{s=1}^q h_s^2 + (nh_1 \ldots h_q)^{-1/2}\right).$

(ii) $(nh_1 \ldots h^q)^{1/2}\left(\tilde{f}(x) - f(x) - (\kappa_2/2)\sum_{s=1}^q f_{ss}(x)h_s^2\right)$ *converges in distribution to $N(0, \kappa^q f(x))$, where $f_{ss}(x) = \partial^2 f(x^c, x^d)/\partial(x_s^c)^2$ is the second order derivative of $f(\cdot)$ with respect to x_s^c, and where $\kappa_2 = \int v^2 w(v)\, dv$ and $\kappa = \int w^2(v)\, dv$.*

The proof of Theorem 3.1 is given in Section 3.5. From Theorem 3.1 we see that the rate of convergence of $\tilde{f}(x)$ for the mixed variable case is the same as the case involving only the subset of q purely continuous variables. This follows simply because estimation with purely discrete variables has an $O_p\left(n^{-1/2}\right)$ rate of convergence, which is faster than the rate of convergence for the q purely continuous variables case. Hence, the rate of convergence of $\tilde{f}(x)$ for the mixed variables case is determined by the rate of convergence arising from the presence of the subset of q continuous variables, the slower of the two rates.

3.3.2 Regression with Mixed Data

The above frequency method can also be used to estimate regression functions with mixed discrete and continuous regressors. For $x = (x^c, x^d) \in \mathbb{R}^q \times \mathcal{S}^d$, we estimate $g(x) = \mathrm{E}(Y|X = x)$ by

$$\tilde{g}(x) = n^{-1}\sum_{i=1}^n Y_i W_h(X_i^c, x^c)\mathbf{1}(X_i^d = x^d)/\tilde{f}(x), \qquad (3.10)$$

where $\tilde{f}(x)$ is defined in (3.9). The following theorem gives the asymptotic distribution of $\tilde{g}(x)$.

Theorem 3.2. *For any fixed $x^d \in \mathcal{S}^d$, assuming that $g(x^c, x^d)$ satisfies the same conditions as $g(x^c)$ given in Theorem 2.2, and also assuming that, as $n \to \infty$, $h_s \to 0$ $(s = 1, \ldots, q)$, $nh_1 \ldots h_q \to \infty$ and*

$n(h_1 \ldots h_q)(\sum_{s=1}^{q} h_s^6) \to 0$, *then we have*

$$\sqrt{nh_1 \ldots h_q} \left(\tilde{g}(x) - g(x) - \sum_{s=1}^{q} B_s(x)h_s^2 \right) \xrightarrow{d} N \left(0, \kappa^q \sigma^2(x)/f(x) \right),$$

where $B_s(x) = (\kappa_2/2)\{2f_s(x)g_s(x) + f(x)g_{ss}(x)\}/f(x)$ is the same as that defined in Theorem 2.2 except that now $x = (x^c, x^d)$, and $g_s(x)$ ($f_s(x)$) and $g_{ss}(x)$ are the first and second order derivatives of g (f) with respect to x_s^c, where again $\kappa_2 = \int v^2 w(v)\, dv$ and $\kappa = \int w^2(v)\, dv$.

The proof is similar to the proof of (2.14) (the case with purely continuous variables only), and is left as an exercise (see Exercise 3.2).

From Theorem 3.2 we once again see that the rate of convergence is solely determined by the rate associated with the continuous variables.

Following the analysis in Chapter 2, one can again choose the smoothing parameters (h_s's) by the cross-validation (CV) method, generalized CV method, or plug-in method (when a closed form expression is available). In order for the nonparametric *frequency* estimation method to yield reliable results in the mixed variables case, one needs a reasonable amount of data in each discrete cell. Should the number of discrete cells be large relative to the sample size, nonparametric frequency methods may, as expected, be quite unreliable.

3.4 Some Cautionary Remarks on Frequency Methods

In this chapter we have shown that, *theoretically*, there is no problem whatsoever with adding discrete variables (with finite support) to a nonparametric estimation framework because the nonparametric frequency method (with only discrete variables) has an $O_p(n^{-1/2})$ rate of convergence, which is faster than the rate of convergence associated with the subset of q purely continuous variables. However, nonparametric frequency methods will clearly be useful only when one has a large sample size and when the discrete variables assume a limited number of values, i.e., in situations where the number of discrete cells is much smaller than the sample size. For many economic datasets, however, one often encounters cases for which the number of discrete cells is close to or even larger than the sample size. Obviously, the sample splitting frequency estimator cannot be used in such situations.

To further illustrate this point, let M denote the number of cells associated with the discrete variables. In even simple applications, M can be in the hundreds and even tens of thousands. For example, if one has data which includes a person's sex (0/1), industry of occupation (say, 1–20), and religious affiliation (say, 1–5), then the simple presence of three discrete variables gives rise to $2 \times 20 \times 5 = 200$ cells. The average number of observations (the effective sample size) in each cell is $n_{eff} = n/M$. Since M is a fixed finite number (no matter how large), asymptotically we have $n/M = O(n)$. Therefore, the effective sample size is of order n. Even if $M = 1,000,000$, n/M is still of order $O(n)$. For a univariate continuous variable, however, the effective sample size used in estimation is of order $nh = O(n^{4/5})$ (if $h = O(n^{-1/5})$). *Asymptotically, $cn^{4/5}$ is of smaller order than n/M for any positive constants c and M.* Therefore, asymptotically the effective sample size for discrete variables is larger than that for continuous variables, Consequently, nonparametric estimation with discrete variables has a faster rate of convergence than that with continuous variables.

In finite-sample applications, however, the story can be quite different. The $\sqrt{n}$ rate for the discrete variable case can provide a misleading impression regarding its usefulness in small sample applications. Let us consider some artificial data having a sample size $n = 500$ with five discrete variables, and further suppose that the five discrete variables assume 2, 2, 5, 5, and 5 different values, respectively. In this example, the number of discrete cells arising from the presence of these five discrete variables is $2 \times 2 \times 5 \times 5 \times 5 = 500$. Therefore, the average number of observations (the effective sample size) in each cell is $n/500 = 500/500 = 1$, which is too small to yield any meaningful nonparametric estimates (were one to use the frequency method, that is). However, $n = 500$ is certainly large enough to ensure accurate nonparametric estimation with one continuous variable. If $q = 1$ ($r = 0$, i.e., no discrete variables), then the effective sample size used in nonparametric estimation with a continuous variable is $n^{4/5} = 500^{4/5} \sim 144$, which is much larger than the effective sample size of 1 in the above discrete variable example (with the number of cells equal to 500).

In Chapter 4, we discuss an alternative approach where we also smooth the discrete variables in a particular manner first suggested by Aitchison and Aitken (1976). We extend Aitchison and Aitken's approach to cover nonparametric regression and conditional density estimation with mixed discrete and continuous variables. We also present several empirical applications where we show that such smoothing approaches can also provide superior out-of-sample predictions when compared with some commonly used parametric methods.

3.5 Proofs

3.5.1 Proof of Theorem 3.1

Proof. For what follows, we use the following shorthand notation:

$$f(x^c + hv, x^d) = f(x_1^c + h_1v_1, \ldots, x_q^c + h_qv_q, x^d).$$

By the same argument used in the proof of Theorem 1.3, we have

$$
\begin{aligned}
\mathrm{E}[\tilde{f}(x)] &= \mathrm{E}[W_h(X_i^c, x^c)\mathbf{1}(X_1^d = x^d)] \\
&= (h_1 \ldots h_q)^{-1} \sum_{x_1^d \in \mathcal{S}^d} \int f(x_1^c, x_1^d) W\left(\frac{x_1^c - x^c}{h}\right) \mathbf{1}(x_1^d = x^d) dx^c \\
&= (h_1 \ldots h_q)^{-1} \int f(x_1^c, x^d) W\left(\frac{x_1^c - x^c}{h}\right) dx^c \\
&= \int f(x^c + hv, x^d) W(v)\, dv \\
&= f(x^c, x^d) + (\kappa_2/2) \sum_{s=1}^{q} f_{ss}(x) h_s^2 + O\left(\sum_{s=1}^{q} h_s^3\right).
\end{aligned}
$$

Next, by the same argument as in the proof of Theorem 1.4, we

have

$$\text{var}(\tilde{f}(x)) = n^{-1}\text{var}[W_h(X_1, x^c)\mathbf{1}(X_1^d = x^d)]$$

$$= (nh_1^2 \ldots h_q^2)^{-1}\left\{ \text{E}\left[W\left(\frac{X_1^c - x^c}{h}\right)^2 \mathbf{1}(X_1^d = x^d)\right]\right.$$

$$\left. - \left\{ \text{E}\left[W\left(\frac{X_1^c - x^c}{h}\right)\mathbf{1}(X_1^d = x^d)\right]\right\}^2\right\}$$

$$= (nh_1^2 \ldots h_q^2)^{-1}\left\{ \sum_{x_1^d \in \mathcal{S}^d} \int f(x_1^c, x_1^d)\right.$$

$$\times W\left(\frac{x_1^c - x^c}{h}\right)^2 \mathbf{1}(x_1^d = x^d)\, dx_1^c$$

$$\left. - \left[\sum_{x_1^d \in \mathcal{S}^d} \int f(x_1^c, x_1^d) W\left(\frac{x_1^c - x^c}{h}\right)\mathbf{1}(x_1^d = x^d)\, dx_1^c\right]^2\right\}$$

$$= (nh_1 \ldots h_q)^{-1}\left\{ f(x^c, x^d)\int W^2(v)\, dv + O\left(h_1 \ldots h_q\right)\right\}$$

$$\equiv (nh_1 \ldots h_q)^{-1}\{\kappa^q f(x) + O(h_1 \ldots h_q)\}$$

$$\left(\text{since} \int^2 W(v)\, dv = \left[\int w^2(v)\, dv\right]^q = \kappa^q\right).$$

The above results show that $\text{bias}(\tilde{f}(x)) = O(\sum_{s=1}^q h_s^2)$ and that $\text{var}(\tilde{f}(x)) = O\left((nh_1 \ldots h_q)^{-1}\right)$. Hence, $\text{MSE}(\tilde{f}(x)) = O((\sum_{s=1}^q h_s^2)^2 + (nh_1 \ldots h_q)^{-1})$, which implies Theorem 3.1 (i).

Part (ii) follows by the same argument given above, and the application of Liapunov's CLT (see the proof of Theorem 1.3) proves Theorem 3.1 (ii). ☐

3.6   Exercises

Exercise 3.1. Prove (3.7) and (3.8).

Hint: Write

$$\tilde{g}(x^d) - g(x^d) = (\tilde{g}(x^d) - g(x^d))\tilde{p}(x^d)/\tilde{p}(x^d) \equiv \tilde{m}(x^d)/\tilde{p}(x^d).$$

Now $(Y_i = g(X_i^d) + u_i)$,

$$\tilde{m}(x^d) = n^{-1} \sum_i [g(X_i^d) + u_i - g(x^d)]\mathbf{1}(X_i^d = x^d)$$

$$= n^{-1} \sum_i U_i \mathbf{1}(X_i^d = x^d), \qquad (3.11)$$

because $\sum_i [g(X_i^d) - g(x^d)]\mathbf{1}(X_i^d = x^d) = 0$.

From (3.11), it is easy to see that $\mathrm{E}[\tilde{m}(x^d)] = 0$ and $\mathrm{E}[\tilde{m}(x^d)^2] = O(n^{-1})$, which implies $\tilde{m}(x^d) = O_p(n^{-1/2})$.

Also, $\tilde{p}(x^d) = p(x^d) + O_p(n^{-1/2})$. Together we have $\tilde{g}(x^d) - g(x^d) = O_p(n^{-1/2})$.

Using (3.11), it is easy to see that $\mathrm{E}\{[\tilde{m}(x^d)]^2\} = n^{-1}\sigma^2(x^d)p(x^d)$. Hence, $n^{1/2}\tilde{m}(x^d) \xrightarrow{d} N(0, \sigma^2(x^d)p(x^d))$ by the Lindeberg-Levy CLT. Hence,

$$\sqrt{n}(\tilde{g}(x^d) - g(x^d)) = \sqrt{n}\tilde{m}(x^d)/\tilde{p}(x^d) \xrightarrow{d} (1/p(x^d))N(0, \sigma^2(x^d)p(x^d))$$

$$= N(0, \sigma^2(x^d)/p(x^d)).$$

Exercise 3.2. Prove Theorem 3.2.

Hint: Similar to the proof of (2.14), write $\tilde{g}(x) - g(x) = (\tilde{g}(x) - g(x))\tilde{f}(x)/\tilde{f}(x) \equiv \tilde{m}(x)/\tilde{f}(x)$. Write $\tilde{m}(x) = \tilde{m}_1(x) + \tilde{m}_2(x)$, where $\tilde{m}_1(x)$ and $\tilde{m}_2(x)$ are defined the same ways as $\hat{m}_1(x)$ and $\hat{m}_2(x)$ of Chapter 1. Show that

$$\tilde{m}_1(x) = (\kappa_2/2) \sum_{s=1}^{q} [f(x)f_{ss}(x) + 2f_s(x)g_s(x)]h_s^2$$

$$+ o_p\left(\sum_{s=1}^{q} h_s^2 + (nh_1 \ldots h_q)^{-1/2}\right),$$

and that

$$(nh_1 \ldots h_q)^{1/2}\hat{m}_2(x) \to N(0, \kappa^q \sigma^2(x)f(x))$$

in distribution. These results and $\tilde{f}(x) = f(x) + o_p(1)$ lead to Theorem 3.2.

Chapter 4

Kernel Estimation with Mixed Data

In Chapter 3 we discussed the traditional frequency-based approach to nonparametric estimation in the presence of discrete variables, and also outlined the pros and cons associated with such approaches. We now turn our attention to an alternative nonparametric approach which can be deployed when confronted with discrete variables where, instead of using the conventional frequency method described in Chapter 3, we elect to *smooth* the discrete variables in a particular fashion.

By smoothing the discrete variables when estimating probability and regression functions rather than adopting the traditional cell-based frequency approach, we can dramatically extend the reach of nonparametric methods. From a statistical point of view, smoothing discrete variables may introduce some bias; however, it also reduces the *finite-sample* variance resulting in a reduction in the *finite-sample* MSE of the nonparametric estimator relative to a frequency-based estimator.

A particularly noteworthy feature of this approach is developed in Section 4.5, where the smoothing method is used in conjunction with a data-driven method of bandwidth selection, such as cross-validation, to automatically remove "irrelevant variables" (a specific definition of irrelevant variables is given in Section 4.5). This is an important result as we have observed that irrelevant variables appear surprisingly often in practice. When irrelevant variables exist, the conventional frequency method outlined in Chapter 3 still splits the sample into many discrete cells including those cells arising from the presence of the irrelevant variables. In contrast, the smoothing-cross-validation method can (asymptotically) automatically remove these irrelevant variables, thereby reducing the dimension of the nonparametric model to that associated with the relevant variables only. In such cases, impressive efficiency gains often arise by smoothing the discrete variables. Sections 4.1, 4.2 and 4.3 discuss the discrete-variable-only case, and Sections 4.4 and 4.5 cover the general mixed discrete and continuous variable case.

4.1 Smooth Estimation of Joint Distributions with Discrete Data

We now consider the kernel estimation of a probability function defined over discrete data $X^d \in \mathcal{S}^d$, the support of X^d. As before we use x_s^d and X_{is}^d to denote the sth component of x^d and X_i^d $(i = 1, \ldots, n)$, respectively. Following Aitchison and Aitken (1976), for x_s^d, $X_{is}^d \in \{0, 1, \ldots, c_s - 1\}$, we define a discrete univariate kernel function

$$l(X_{is}^d, x_s^d, \lambda_s) = \begin{cases} 1 - \lambda_s & \text{if } X_{is}^d = x_s^d \\ \lambda_s/(c_s - 1) & \text{if } X_{is}^d \neq x_s^d. \end{cases} \qquad (4.1)$$

Note that when $\lambda_s = 0$, $l(X_{is}^d, x_s^d, 0) = \mathbf{1}(X_{is}^d = x_s^d)$ becomes an indicator function, and if $\lambda_s = (c_s - 1)/c_s$, then $l\left(X_{is}^d, x_s^d, \frac{c_s-1}{c_s}\right) = 1/c_s$ is a constant for *all* values of X_{is}^d and x_s^d. The range of λ_s is $[0, (c_s - 1)/c_s]$.

For multivariate data we use a standard product kernel function given by

$$L(X_i^d, x^d, \lambda) = \prod_{s=1}^{r} l(X_{is}^d, x_s^d, \lambda_s)$$

$$= \prod_{s=1}^{r} \{\lambda_s/(c_s - 1)\}^{N_{is}(x)} (1 - \lambda_s)^{1 - N_{is}(x)}, \qquad (4.2)$$

where $N_{is}(x) = \mathbf{1}\left(X_{is} \neq x_s^d\right)$ is an indicator function, which equals 1 if $X_{is}^d \neq x_s^d$, and 0 otherwise.

For a given value of the vector $\lambda = (\lambda_1, \ldots, \lambda_r)$, we estimate $p\left(x^d\right)$ by

$$\hat{p}\left(x^d\right) = \frac{1}{n} \sum_{i=1}^{n} L(X_i^d, x^d, \lambda). \qquad (4.3)$$

Note that the weight function $l(., ., .)$ defined in (4.1) adds up to one, which ensures that $\hat{p}\left(x^d\right)$ defined in (4.3) is a proper probability measure, i.e., $\sum_{x^d \in S^d} \hat{p}\left(x^d\right) = 1$. Note also that if $\lambda_s = 0$ for all $1 \leq s \leq r$, (4.3) collapses to the frequency estimator defined in (3.2) of Chapter 3. Therefore, our smoothed estimator $\hat{p}\left(x^d\right)$ nests the frequency estimator $\tilde{p}\left(x^d\right)$ as a special case. Another interesting case arises when λ_s assumes its upper bound value $(c_s - 1)/c_s$, since then $\hat{p}\left(x^d\right)$ becomes unrelated to x_s^d. In this case we say that x_s^d is "smoothed out," and the resulting estimator $\hat{p}\left(x^d\right)$ is uniformly distributed with respect to x_s^d, i.e., $\hat{p}\left(x_{-s}^d, x_s^d\right) = \hat{p}(x_{-s}^d, z_s^d)$ for all $x_s^d, z_s^d \in S_s^d = \{0, 1, \dots, c_s - 1\}$, where $x_{-s}^d = (x_1^d, \dots, x_{s-1}^d, x_{s+1}^d, \dots, x_r^d)$. We say that X^d is uniformly distributed with respect to x_s if, for all $x_{-s}^d \in S^d/S_s^d$ (where $x \in A/B$ means that $x \in A$ but $x \notin B$),

$$p\left(x_{-s}^d, x_s^d\right) = p\left(x_{-s}^d, z_s^d\right) \text{ for all } x_s^d, z_s^d \in \{0, 1, \dots, c_s - 1\}. \quad (4.4)$$

There are at least two reasons for smoothing categorical variables when estimating a joint probability function. First, although $\lambda_s \neq 0$ introduces some estimation bias, it reduces the variance, hence the *finite-sample* MSE can be reduced. Second, when X^d is uniformly distributed with respect to x_s^d, $\lambda_s = (c_s - 1)/c_s$ effectively uses this information, i.e., it does not introduce bias but reduces variance.

The above arguments underscore the desirability of data-driven bandwidth selection methods having the ability to select a large value of λ_s if X^d is uniformly distributed with respect to x_s^d, and a small value for λ_s otherwise. It turns out that least squares cross-validation indeed has a high probability of selecting a large value for λ_s when x_s^d is uniformly distributed.

In many economic data sets, the number of discrete cells is close to or even larger than the sample size, rendering the frequency method unreliable or simply impossible to apply. In such situations, however, one can sensibly apply the smoothed estimator defined in (4.3) because in (4.3) we avoid splitting the data into different cells when estimating $p\left(x^d\right)$.

Assuming that $\lambda_s \to 0$ as $n \to \infty$ $(s = 1, \dots, r)$, it is straightforward to show that (see Exercise 4.3)

$$
\begin{aligned}
\mathrm{E}\left[\hat{p}\left(x^d\right)\right] &= p\left(x^d\right) + \sum_{s=1}^{r} B_{p,s}\lambda_s + O\left(\sum_{s=1}^{r}\lambda_s^2\right), \\
\mathrm{var}\left(\hat{p}\left(x^d\right)\right) &= \frac{p\left(x^d\right)\left(1 - p\left(x^d\right)\right)}{n} + O\left(n^{-1}\sum_{s=1}^{r}\lambda_s\right),
\end{aligned}
\tag{4.5}
$$

where the $B_{p,s}$'s are some constants defined in Exercise 4.3. From (4.5) it is easy to see that if $\lambda_s = o_p\left(n^{-1/2}\right)$, then we will have $\sqrt{n}\left(\hat{p}\left(x^d\right) - p\left(x^d\right)\right) \xrightarrow{d} N\left(0, p\left(x^d\right)\left(1 - p\left(x^d\right)\right)\right)$, i.e., if $\lambda = o_p\left(n^{-1/2}\right)$, then $\hat{p}\left(x^d\right)$ has the same asymptotic distribution as the frequency estimator of $\tilde{p}\left(x^d\right)$ defined in defined in (3.2) of Chapter 3.

As was the case when dealing with continuous variables, the selection of smoothing parameters is of crucial importance. We suggest choosing the smoothing parameters $\lambda_1, \ldots, \lambda_r$ by minimizing a criterion function that is based on the squared difference between $\hat{p}(\cdot)$ and $p(\cdot)$, which is given by ($\sum_{x^d} \equiv \sum_{x^d \in \mathcal{S}^d}$)

$$
\begin{aligned}
I_n &= \sum_{x^d}\left[\hat{p}\left(x^d\right) - p\left(x^d\right)\right]^2 \\
&= \sum_{x^d}\left[\hat{p}\left(x^d\right)\right]^2 - 2\sum_{x^d}\hat{p}\left(x^d\right)p\left(x^d\right) + \sum_{x^d}\left[p\left(x^d\right)\right]^2 \\
&\equiv I_{1n} - 2I_{2n} + \sum_{x^d}\left[p\left(x^d\right)\right]^2,
\end{aligned}
\tag{4.6}
$$

where $I_{1n} = \sum_{x^d}\left[\hat{p}\left(x^d\right)\right]^2$ and $I_{2n} = \sum_{x^d}\hat{p}\left(x^d\right)p\left(x^d\right)$. Note that $I_{2n} = \mathrm{E}_X\left[\hat{p}\left(X^d\right)\right]$, where $\mathrm{E}_X(\cdot)$ denotes expectation with respect to X^d, and not to the random observations $\{X_j^d\}_{j=1}^n$ that are used in defining $\hat{p}(\cdot)$. Therefore, we estimate I_{2n} by replacing the population mean $\mathrm{E}_X(\cdot)$ with the sample mean,

$$
\hat{I}_{2n} = \frac{1}{n}\sum_{i=1}^{n}\hat{p}_{-i}\left(X_i^d\right) = n^{-2}\sum_{i=1}^{n}\sum_{j\neq i}^{n}L_{\lambda,ij},
\tag{4.7}
$$

where $L_{\lambda,ij} = L(X_i^d, X_j^d, \lambda)$ and $\hat{p}_{-i}\left(X_i^d\right) = n^{-1}\sum_{j=1,j\neq i}^{n}L_{\lambda,ij}$ is the leave-one-out kernel estimator of $p\left(X_i^d\right)$.

The last term on the right-hand side of (4.6) is unrelated to $\lambda_1, \ldots, \lambda_r$. Therefore, we choose $\lambda_1, \ldots, \lambda_r$ to minimize

$$CV_p(\lambda) = I_{1n} - 2\hat{I}_{2n} = \sum_{x^d \in S^d} \left[\hat{p}\left(x^d\right) \right]^2 - 2n^{-2} \sum_{i=1}^{n} \sum_{j \neq i}^{n} L_{\lambda, ij}. \quad (4.8)$$

Let $\hat{\lambda}_1, \ldots, \hat{\lambda}_r$ denote the cross-validated λ_s's that minimize (4.8). Ouyang et al. (2006) showed that as long as x_s^d is not uniformly distributed, then $\hat{\lambda}_s = o_p(1)$ $(s = 1, \ldots, r)$. Let $\lambda_{(r)} = (\lambda_1, \ldots, \lambda_r)'$ denote the $r \times 1$ vector of the smoothing parameters. To derive the limiting behavior of the $\hat{\lambda}_s$'s, Ouyang et al. use the U-statistic H-decomposition and expand $CV_p(\lambda)$ as a polynomial in λ_s to obtain the following result:

$$CV_p(\lambda) = \lambda_{(r)}' \Omega_r \lambda_{(r)} - n^{-1} A_r' \lambda_{(r)} + o_p \left(n^{-1} \sum_{s=1}^{r} \lambda_s + \sum_{s=1}^{r} \lambda_s^2 \right)$$

$$+ \text{ terms not related to } \lambda, \quad (4.9)$$

where Ω_r is an $r \times r$ positive semidefinite matrix and A_r is an $r \times 1$ $O_p(1)$ random vector. The explicit expression for Ω_r is given in Exercise 4.4. If Ω_r is positive definite, then by minimizing (4.9) over $\lambda_{(r)}$, we obtain

$$\hat{\lambda}_{(r)} = n^{-1} \Omega_r^{-1} A_r + o_p(n^{-1}). \quad (4.10)$$

Equation (4.10) shows that $\hat{\lambda}_s = O_p(n^{-1})$ for $s = 1, \ldots, r$. The crucial condition needed for (4.10) to hold is that Ω_r is positive definite. Below we show that Ω_r is positive definite if and only if X^d is not uniformly distributed with respect to x_s for all $s = 1, \ldots, r$.

Ouyang et al. (2006) show that

$$B_\lambda \overset{\text{def}}{=} \lambda_{(r)}' \Omega_r \lambda_{(r)} = \sum_{x^d \in S^d} \left\{ \sum_{s=1}^{r} \lambda_s \left[p\left(x^d\right) - p_{1,s}\left(x^d\right) \right] \right\}^2, \quad (4.11)$$

where $P_{1,s}$ is defined in Exercise 4.4.

Equation (4.11) shows that Ω_r is positive semidefinite, which follows because $\lambda_{(r)}' \Omega_r \lambda_{(r)} \geq 0$ for all $\lambda_{(r)}$. It can be shown that if X^d is uniformly distributed with respect to any of its components, say x_s^d, then $p_{1,s}\left(x^d\right) = p\left(x^d\right)$ hence $B(\lambda)$ will not depend on λ_s (λ_s drops out since its coefficient in B_λ is zero). Thus, Ω_r is not positive definite in this case. Ouyang et al. (2006) further show that the converse is true, i.e., that if X^d is not uniformly distributed in all x_s^d's, then Ω_r is positive definite.

We use $\hat{\lambda}_1, \ldots, \hat{\lambda}_r$ to denote the cross-validated choices of $\lambda_1, \ldots, \lambda_r$ that minimize (4.8). The next result follows immediately from (4.10).

Theorem 4.1. *Assuming that X^d is not uniformly distributed with respect to x_s for all $s = 1, \ldots, r$, then*

$$\hat{\lambda}_s = O_p\left(n^{-1}\right) \quad for\ s = 1, \ldots, r.$$

Proof. The conditions of Theorem 4.1 imply that Ω_r is positive definite. Hence, Theorem 4.1 follows from (4.10). With the fast n^{-1} rate of convergence of the $\hat{\lambda}_s$'s given in Theorem 4.1, the following results follow immediately from (4.5). $\qquad\qquad\qquad\qquad\qquad\qquad\square$

Theorem 4.2. *Under the same conditions as in Theorem 4.1, we have*

(i) $\hat{p}\left(x^d\right) - p\left(x^d\right) = O_p(n^{-1/2})$.

(ii) $n^{1/2}\left(\hat{p}\left(x^d\right) - p\left(x^d\right)\right) \xrightarrow{d} N\left(0, p\left(x^d\right)\left(1 - p\left(x^d\right)\right)\right)$.

The proof of Theorem 4.2 follows from Theorem 4.1 and is left as an exercise (see Exercise 4.6).

Theorem 4.2 reveals that the *asymptotic* distribution of $\hat{p}\left(x^d\right)$ is the same as that of the frequency estimator $\tilde{p}\left(x^d\right)$. This is exactly what one should expect since, asymptotically, we have an infinite-sample size, hence even with sample splitting we still have an infinite amount of data lying in each cell, again asymptotically. Therefore, if the sample size is sufficiently large, $\hat{\lambda}_1, \ldots, \hat{\lambda}_r$ should all be close to zero, and our cross-validated estimator $\hat{p}\left(x^d\right)$ will be quite close to the frequency estimator $\tilde{p}\left(x^d\right)$. However, in finite-sample applications, the two approaches can be expected to yield very different results.

Theorem 4.2 shows that the cross-validated $\hat{\lambda}_s$ converge to zero at the rate n^{-1}, which is the same convergence rate as the maximum likelihood cross-validation choice of λ_s (see Hall (1981)).

An important case not covered by Theorem 4.2 occurs when X^d is uniformly distributed with respect to x_s for some $s \in \{1, \ldots, r\}$. Without loss of generality, assume that X^d is not uniformly distributed with respect to x_s^d for $s = 1, \ldots, r_1$ and that X^d is uniformly distributed with respect to x_s^d for $s = r_1 + 1, \ldots, r$ $(1 \leq r_1 < r)$. The following theorem shows that the asymptotic behavior of $\hat{\lambda}_s$ differs depending on whether x_s^d is uniformly distributed or not.

Theorem 4.3. *Assuming that $p\left(x^d\right)$ does not have a uniform distribution with respect to $x_1, \ldots, x_{r_1}$, and that $p\left(x^d\right)$ has a uniform distribution with respect to $x_{r_1+1}, \ldots, x_r$, then*

(i) $\hat{\lambda}_s = O_p\left(n^{-1}\right)$ *for $s = 1, \ldots, r_1$.*

(ii) For $s = r_1 + 1, \ldots, r$, $\lim_{n\to\infty} \mathrm{P}\left[\hat{\lambda}_s = \frac{c_s-1}{c_s}\right] \geq \delta$ for some $0 < \delta < 1$.

Theorem 4.3 is proved in Ouyang et al. (2006). Theorem 4.3 states that the smoothing parameters associated with uniformly distributed variables will not converge to zero; rather, they have a high probability of assuming their upper extreme values so that the estimated probability function satisfies the uniform distribution condition of (4.4) for $s = r_1 + 1, \ldots, r$ and is more efficient than an estimator that does not impose this restriction. It is difficult to determine the exact value of δ. The simulation results reported in Ouyang et al. suggest that δ is around 0.6 for a wide range of data generating processes.

4.2   Smooth Regression with Discrete Data

We now consider a nonparametric regression model given by

$$Y_i = g\left(X_i^d\right) + u_i,$$

where $g(\cdot)$ is an unknown function, $X_i^d \in \mathcal{S}^d$, $\mathrm{E}(u_i|X_i^d) = 0$ and $\mathrm{E}(u_i^2|X_i^d) = \sigma^2(X_i^d)$ is of unknown form. Although the kernel function defined in (4.2) can be used to estimate $g\left(x^d\right)$, we suggest using the following simple alternative kernel function in regression settings:

$$l(X_{is}^d, x_s^d, \lambda_s) = \begin{cases} 1 & \text{when } X_{is}^d = x_s^d \\ \lambda_s & \text{otherwise.} \end{cases} \tag{4.12}$$

When $\lambda_s = 0$, $l(X_{is}^d, x_s^d, 0)$ becomes an indicator function, and when $\lambda_s = 1$, $l(X_{is}^d, x_s^d, 1) \equiv 1$ is a uniform weight function. Therefore, the range of λ_s is $[0,1]$. Note that the kernel weight function defined in (4.12) does not add up to 1 and therefore would be inappropriate for estimating a probability function. However, this does not affect the nonparametric estimator $\hat{g}(x)$ defined in (4.14) below, because the kernel function appears in both the numerator and the denominator of

(4.14), and obviously the kernel function can therefore be multiplied by any nonzero constant leaving the definition of $\hat{g}(x)$ intact.

By using (4.12), the product kernel function is given by

$$L(X_i^d, x^d, \lambda) = \prod_{s=1}^r \lambda_s^{N_{is}(x)}, \qquad (4.13)$$

where $N_{is}(x) = \mathbf{1}\left(X_{is}^d \neq x_s^d\right)$ (the indicator function). We estimate $g\left(x^d\right)$ by

$$\hat{g}\left(x^d\right) = \frac{n^{-1} \sum_{i=1}^n Y_i L(X_i^d, x^d, \lambda)}{\hat{p}\left(x^d\right)}, \qquad (4.14)$$

where $\hat{p}\left(x^d\right) = n^{-1} \sum_{i=1}^n L(X_i^d, x^d, \lambda)$. When $\lambda_s = 0$ for all $s = 1, \ldots, r$, our estimator collapses to the frequency estimator given in (3.6).

Under the assumption that $\lambda_s \to 0$ as $n \to \infty$ ($s = 1, \ldots, r$), one can easily show that $\hat{g}\left(x^d\right) - g\left(x^d\right) = O_p\left(\sum_{s=1}^r \lambda_s + n^{-1/2}\right)$. For example, as was the case for the proof of the purely continuous variable estimator discussed in Chapter 2, we could write $\hat{g}\left(x^d\right) - g\left(x^d\right) = [\hat{g}\left(x^d\right) - g\left(x^d\right)]\hat{p}\left(x^d\right)/\hat{p}\left(x^d\right) \equiv \hat{m}\left(x^d\right)/\hat{p}\left(x^d\right)$. One can show that $\mathrm{E}[\hat{m}(x^d)] = O(\sum_{s=1}^r \lambda_s)$ and $\mathrm{var}[\hat{m}(x^d)] = O(n^{-1})$. These imply that $\mathrm{E}\left(\hat{m}\left(x^d\right)^2\right) = O\left(\sum_{s=1}^r \lambda_s^2 + n^{-1}\right)$, which in turn implies that $\hat{m}\left(x^d\right) = O_p\left(\sum_{s=1}^r \lambda_s + n^{-1/2}\right)$, while it can easily be shown that $\hat{p}\left(x^d\right) = p\left(x^d\right) + O_p\left(\sum_{s=1}^r \lambda_s + n^{-1/2}\right)$ by the same arguments that lead to (4.5). Hence, we have

$$\hat{g}\left(x^d\right) - g\left(x^d\right) = \frac{\hat{m}\left(x^d\right)}{\hat{p}\left(x^d\right)} = \frac{O_p\left(\sum_{s=1}^r \lambda_s + n^{-1/2}\right)}{p\left(x^d\right) + o_p(1)}$$

$$= O_p\left(\sum_{s=1}^r \lambda_s + n^{-1/2}\right). \qquad (4.15)$$

We now discuss the use of cross-validation for selecting the λ_s's. We choose $\lambda_1, \ldots, \lambda_r$ to minimize the cross-validatory sum of squared residuals

$$CV_d(\lambda) = n^{-1} \sum_{i=1}^n \left[Y_i - \hat{g}_{-i}(X_i^d)\right]^2, \qquad (4.16)$$

where

$$\hat{g}_{-i}(X_i^d) = \frac{n^{-1} \sum_{j \neq i}^n Y_j L(X_i^d, X_j^d, \lambda)}{\hat{p}_{-i}(X_i^d)} \qquad (4.17)$$

is the leave-one-out kernel estimator of $g(X_i^d)$, and $\hat{p}_{-i}(X_i^d)$ is the leave-one-out estimator of $p(X_i^d)$. We use $\hat{\lambda}_1,\ldots,\hat{\lambda}_r$ to denote the cross-validation choices of $\lambda_1,\ldots,\lambda_r$ that minimize (4.16).

In this section we consider only the case for which all of the components of X^d are relevant, and we postpone the discussion of potentially irrelevant regressors until the next section. Also, in Section 4.5 we discuss the more general case with mixed categorical and continuous regressors. We start with the following assumption.

Assumption 4.1.

(i) $\mathrm{E}(Y_i^2|X_i^d)$ is finite.

(ii) The only values of $(\lambda_1,\ldots,\lambda_r)$ that make

$$\sum_{x^d \in S^d} p(x^d) \left\{ \sum_{z^d \in S^d} p(z^d)[g(x^d) - g(z^d)]L(x^d, z^d, \lambda) \right\}^2 = 0$$

are $\lambda_s = 0$ for all $s = 1,\ldots,r$.

Assumption 4.1 (ii) implies that $g(x)$ is not a constant function for any component $x_s \in D_s$ (see Exercise 4.11) and it also implies that $\hat{\lambda}_s = o_p(1)$ for all $s = 1,\ldots,r$.

The next theorem establishes the convergence rate of $\hat{\lambda}_1,\ldots,\hat{\lambda}_r$.

Theorem 4.4. *Under Assumption 4.1 we have*

$$\hat{\lambda}_s = O_p(n^{-1}) \text{ for all } s = 1,\ldots,r.$$

Theorem 4.4 is proved in Li, Ouyang and Racine (2006). Exercise 4.7 asks the reader to prove that Theorem 4.4 holds for the simple case for which x^d is univariate (hints are also provided).

Theorem 4.4 shows that $\hat{\lambda}_s$ converges to zero at the rate $O_p(n^{-1})$. With this fast rate of convergence it is easy to establish the asymptotic distribution of $\hat{g}(x)$, as the next theorem shows.

Theorem 4.5. *Under Assumption 4.1, we have*

$$\sqrt{n}\left(\hat{g}\left(x^d\right) - g\left(x^d\right)\right) / \sqrt{\hat{\sigma}^2\left(x^d\right)/\hat{p}\left(x^d\right)} \to N(0,1) \text{ in distribution,}$$

where $\hat{\sigma}^2\left(x^d\right) = n^{-1}\sum_i[Y_i - \hat{g}\left(X_i^d\right)]^2 L(X_i^d, x, \hat{\lambda})/\hat{p}(x)$ *is a consistent estimator of* $\sigma^2\left(x^d\right) = \mathrm{E}[u_i^2|X_i^d = x^d]$.

Proof. Recall that the frequency estimator $\tilde{g}\left(x^d\right)$ can be obtained from $\hat{g}\left(x^d\right)$ with $\lambda_s = 0$ for all $s = 1,\ldots,r$. Using $\hat{\lambda}_s = O_p(n^{-1})$, it is easy to see that $\hat{g}(x) = \tilde{g}(x) + O_p(n^{-1})$. Therefore, $\sqrt{n}(\hat{g}(x) - g(x)) = \sqrt{n}(\tilde{g}(x) - g(x)) + O_p(n^{-1/2}) \xrightarrow{d} N\left(0, \sigma^2\left(x^d\right)/p\left(x^d\right)\right)$ by (3.8). Finally, Exercise 4.8 shows that $\hat{\sigma}^2\left(x^d\right) = \sigma^2\left(x^d\right) + o_p(1)$. Theorem 4.5 follows directly. □

In the next section we discuss the case in which a subset of regressors is irrelevant.

4.3   Kernel Regression with Discrete Regressors: The Irrelevant Regressor Case

In this section we allow for the possibility that some of the regressors are in fact irrelevant in the sense that they are independent of the dependent variable. Without loss of generality we assume that the first r_1 ($1 \le r_1 < r$) components of X_i^d are relevant, while the remaining $r_2 = r - r_1$ components of X_i^d are irrelevant. Let $\bar{X}_i^d$ denote the r_1-dimensional relevant components of X_i^d and let $\tilde{X}_i^d$ denote the r_2-dimensional irrelevant components. Similar to the approach taken in Li et al. (2006), we assume that

$$(Y, \bar{X}^d) \text{ and } \tilde{X}^d \text{ are independent of each other.} \qquad (4.18)$$

The kernel estimator of $g(x^d)$ as well as the definition of the CV objective function are the same as that given in Section 4.2. We still use $(\hat{\lambda}_1,\ldots,\hat{\lambda}_r)$ to denote the CV-selected smoothing parameters. In Theorem 4.6 below we show that (i) the smoothing parameters associated with the relevant regressors converge to zero at the rate of $n^{-1/2}$, which differs from the n^{-1} rate of convergence when no irrelevant components exist, and (ii) the smoothing parameters associated with the irrelevant components will not converge to zero, but have a high probability of converging to their upper extreme values, so that these irrelevant regressors are smoothed out with high probability. Furthermore, there is also a positive probability that these smoothing parameters do not converge to their upper extreme values even as $n \to \infty$.

Mirroring the notation used for $\bar{x}^d$ and $\tilde{x}^d$, we shall use $\bar{\lambda}$ to denote the smoothing parameters associated with the relevant regressors, and $\tilde{\lambda}$ for the irrelevant ones. Thus, we have $\bar{\lambda}_s = \lambda_s$ for $s = 1,\ldots,r_1$, and $\tilde{\lambda}_s = \lambda_{r_1+s}$ for $s = 1,\ldots,r_2$ ($r_2 = r - r_1$). Also, using $\bar{p}(\cdot)$ and $\tilde{p}(\cdot)$

to denote the marginal probability functions of $\bar{X}$ and $\tilde{X}$, respectively, then by (4.18) we know that $p(x^d) = \bar{p}(\bar{x}^d)\tilde{p}(\tilde{x}^d)$, and using $\bar{S}^d$ to denote the support of $\bar{x}^d$, Assumption 4.1 is modified as follows.

Assumption 4.2. *The only values of $\lambda_1, \ldots, \lambda_{r_1}$ that make*

$$\sum_{\bar{x}\in\bar{S}^d} p(\bar{x}^d) \left\{ \sum_{\bar{z}^d\in\bar{D}} p(\bar{z}^d)[g(\bar{x}^d) - g(\bar{z}^d)] L(\bar{x}^d, \bar{z}^d, \lambda) \right\}^2 = 0$$

are $\lambda_s = 0$ for all $s = 1, \ldots, r_1$.

Assumption 4.2 ensures that the CV-selected smoothing parameters associated with the relevant regressors will converge to zero, while we do not impose any assumption on the smoothing parameters associated with the irrelevant regressors except that they take values in the unit interval $[0, 1]$.

The next theorem provides the asymptotic behavior of the CV-selected smoothing parameters.

Theorem 4.6. *Assume that $r_1 \geq 1$ and $r_2 \geq 1$ (with $r = r_1 + r_2 \geq 2$). Then under Assumption 4.2, we have*

$$\hat{\lambda}_s = O_p(n^{-1/2}) \text{ for } s = 1, \ldots, r_1;$$

$$\lim_{n\to\infty} \mathrm{P}\left(\hat{\lambda}_{r_1+1} = 1, \ldots, \hat{\lambda}_r = 1\right) \geq \alpha \text{ for some } \alpha \in (0, 1).$$

The proof of Theorem 4.6 can be found in Li et al. (2006).

Theorem 4.6 states that the smoothing parameters associated with the relevant regressors all converge to zero at the rate of $n^{-1/2}$, while the smoothing parameters for the irrelevant regressors have a positive probability of assuming their upper bound value of 1. That is, there is a positive probability that the irrelevant regressors will be smoothed out. It is difficult to determine the exact value of α for the general case. The simulation results reported in Li et al. (2006) show that there is usually about a 60% chance that $\hat{\lambda}_s$ takes the upper extreme value 1 and a 40% chance that $\hat{\lambda}_s$ takes values between 0 and 1, for $s = r_1 + 1, \ldots, r$.

Note that when x_s^d is an irrelevant regressor, the asymptotic behavior of $\hat{\lambda}_s$ is difficult to characterize in further detail since $\hat{\lambda}_s$ does not converge to zero in this case. The asymptotic distribution of the resulting $\hat{g}(x^d)$ will also be difficult to obtain. When one obtains a relatively large value for $\hat{\lambda}_s$ and suspects that this may reflect the fact that x_s^d is an irrelevant regressor, one may perform a formal test of the null hypothesis that x_s^d is indeed an irrelevant regressor, say, using the bootstrap based test suggested by Racine et al. (forthcoming) (see Chapter 12). If one fails to reject the null hypothesis, one may remove this regressor from the model. In this way only relevant regressors are expected to remain in the model, and one can recompute the cross-validated bandwidths using only those regressors deemed to be relevant. Then the results of Theorem 4.4 and Theorem 4.5 apply as no irrelevant regressors are expected to remain in the model.

We now proceed to the general case of smooth nonparametric estimation with mixed discrete and continuous data.

4.4   Regression with Mixed Data: Relevant Regressors

4.4.1   Smooth Estimation with Mixed Data

In this section we consider a nonparametric regression model where a subset of regressors are categorical while the remaining are continuous. As in Chapter 3, we use X_i^d to denote an $r \times 1$ vector of regressors that assume discrete values and let $X_i^c \in \mathbb{R}^q$ denote the remaining continuous regressors. We again let X_{is}^d denote the sth component of X_i^d. We assume that X_{is}^d assumes $c_s \geq 2$ different values, i.e., that $X_{is}^d \in \{0, 1, \ldots, c_s - 1\}$ for $s = 1, \ldots, r$, and define $X_i = (X_i^d, X_i^c)$.

The nonparametric regression model is given by

$$Y_i = g(X_i) + u_i, \tag{4.19}$$

with $\mathrm{E}(u_i|X_i) = 0$. We use $f(x) = f(x^c, x^d)$ to denote the joint PDF of (X_i^c, X_i^d).

For the discrete variables X_i^d, we first consider the case for which the variables possess no natural ordering. The extension to the general case whereby some of the discrete regressors have a natural ordering is discussed at the end of this section.

For $x^c = (x_1^c, \ldots, x_q^c)$, define

$$W_h(x^c, X_i^c) = \frac{1}{h_1 \ldots h_q} W\left(\frac{x^c - X_i^c}{h}\right) \equiv \prod_{s=1}^r \frac{1}{h_s} w\left(\frac{x_s^c - X_{is}^c}{h_s}\right),$$

where w is a symmetric, nonnegative univariate kernel function. $0 < h_s < \infty$ is the smoothing parameter for x_s^c, and for $x^d = (x_1^d, \ldots, x_r^d)$

define

$$L(x^d, X_i^d, \lambda) = \prod_{s=1}^{r} \lambda_s^{N_{is}(x)},$$

where $N_{is}(x) = \mathbf{1}\left(X_{is}^d \neq x_s^d\right)$ is an indicator function which equals one when $X_{is}^d \neq x_s^d$, and zero otherwise. The smoothing parameter for x_s^d is $0 \leq \lambda_s \leq 1$. Note that when $\lambda_s = 1$, $L(x^d, X_i^d, 1)$ becomes unrelated to (x_s^d, X_{is}^d) (i.e., x_s^d is smoothed out).

The kernel function for the vector of mixed variables $x = (x^c, x^d)$ is simply the product of $W_h(\cdot)$ and $L(\cdot)$, i.e., defining $K_\gamma(x, X_i) = W_h(x^c, X_i^c)L(x^d, X_i^d, \lambda)$ ($\gamma = (h, \lambda)$), we estimate $g(x)$ by

$$\hat{g}(x) = \frac{n^{-1}\sum_{i=1}^{n} Y_i K_\gamma(x, X_i)}{n^{-1}\sum_{i=1}^{n} K_\gamma(x, X_i)}. \tag{4.20}$$

Note that the denominator $n^{-1}\sum_{i=1}^{n} K_\gamma(x, X_i)$ is the kernel estimator of the joint density $f(x) = f(x^c, x^d)$. It can be shown that $\hat{g}(x) - g(x) = O_p\left(\sum_{s=1}^{q} h_s^2 + \sum_{s=1}^{r} \lambda_s + (nh_1 \ldots h_q)^{-1/2}\right)$. Defining $\hat{m}(x) = [\hat{g}(x) - g(x)]\hat{f}(x)$, one can then show that (see Exercise 4.9)

$$\mathrm{E}[\hat{m}(x)] = \sum_{s=1}^{q} B_{1s}(x)f(x)h_s^2 + \sum_{s=1}^{r} B_{2s}(x)f(x)\lambda_s + o(\eta_2), \tag{4.21}$$

$$\mathrm{var}(\hat{m}(x)) = \frac{\kappa^q \sigma^2(x)f(x)}{nh_1 \ldots h_q}\left[1 + O(\eta_2)\right], \text{ and} \tag{4.22}$$

$$\hat{f}(x) = f(x) + O_p(\eta_2 + \eta_1^{1/2}), \tag{4.23}$$

where

$$B_{1s}(x) = \frac{\kappa_2}{2}\left[g_{ss}(x) + 2g_s(x)f_s(x)f(x)^{-1}\right],$$

$$B_{2s}(x) = \frac{1}{c_s - 1}\sum_{z^d \in \mathcal{S}^d} \mathbf{1}_s\left(x^d, z^d\right)\left[g(x^c, z^d) - g(x)\right]f(x^c, z^d)f(x)^{-1},$$

$$\kappa = \int w(v)^2\, dv, \quad \eta_2 = \sum_{s=1}^{q} h_s^2 + \sum_{s=1}^{r} \lambda_s,$$

$$\eta_1 = (nh_1 \ldots h_q)^{-1},$$

and

$$\mathbf{1}_s\left(x^d, z^d\right) \stackrel{\text{def}}{=} \mathbf{1}\left(x_s^d \neq z_s^d\right)\prod_{s' \neq s}^{r} \mathbf{1}\left(x_s^d = z_s^d\right). \tag{4.24}$$

$\mathbf{1}_s \left(x^d, z^d\right)$ takes the value 1 if x^d and z^d differ only in their sth component, 0 otherwise.

Equations (4.21) and (4.22) are equivalent to $\mathrm{E}[\hat{m}(x)^2] = O\left(\eta_2^2 + \eta_1\right)$, which implies that $\hat{m}(x) = O_p\left(\eta_2 + \eta_1^{1/2}\right)$ and that

$$\hat{g}(x) - g(x) = \frac{\hat{m}(x)}{\hat{f}(x)} = \frac{O_p(\eta_2 + \eta_1^{1/2})}{f(x) + o_p(1)} = O_p\left(\eta_2 + \eta_1^{1/2}\right).$$

If, in addition to $\eta_1 = o(1)$ and $\eta_2 = o(1)$, one also assumes that $(nh_1 \ldots h_q)^{1/2}\eta_2^{3/2} = o(1)$, then using (4.21) to (4.23) one can establish the asymptotic normal distribution of $\hat{g}(x)$ using Liapunov's CLT:

$$\sqrt{nh_1 \ldots h_q} \left[\hat{g}(x) - g(x) - \sum_{s=1}^{q} B_{1s}(x)h_s^2 - \sum_{s=1}^{r} B_{2s}(x)\lambda_s\right]$$
$$\xrightarrow{d} N\left(0, \kappa^q \sigma^2(x)/f(x)\right). \tag{4.25}$$

4.4.2   The Cross-Validation Method

Least squares cross-validation selects $h_1, \ldots, h_q, \lambda_1, \ldots, \lambda_r$ to minimize the following cross-validation function:

$$CV_r(h, \lambda) = \sum_{i=1}^{n} (Y_i - \hat{g}_{-i}(X_i))^2 M(X_i), \tag{4.26}$$

where $\hat{g}_{-i}(X_i) = \sum_{l \neq i}^{n} Y_l K_\gamma(X_i, X_l) / \sum_{l \neq i}^{n} K_\gamma(X_i, X_l)$ is the leave-one-out kernel estimator of $g(X_i)$, and $0 \leq M(\cdot) \leq 1$ is a weight function which serves to avoid difficulties caused by dividing by zero or by the slow convergence rate induced by boundary effects.

We assume that

$$(h_1, \ldots, h_q, \lambda_1, \ldots, \lambda_r) \in [0, \eta]^{q+r}, \text{ and } nh_1 \ldots h_q \geq t_n, \tag{4.27}$$

where $\eta = \eta_n$ is positive sequence that converges to zero at a rate slower than the inverse of any polynomial in n, and t_n is a sequence of constants that diverges to infinity.

Let $\mathcal{S}$ denote the support of $M(\cdot)$. We also assume that

$g(\cdot)$ and $f(\cdot)$ have two continuous derivatives; $M(\cdot)$ is continuous, nonnegative and has compact support; $f(\cdot)$ is

bounded away from zero for $x = (x^c, x^d) \in \mathcal{S}$. $\qquad$ (4.28)

It can be shown that the leading term of CV_r is CV_{r0}, given by (ignoring the terms unrelated to (h, λ))

$$CV_{r0}(h, \lambda) = \sum_{x^d} \int \left\{ \left[\sum_{s=1}^{q} B_{1s}(x)h_s^2 + \sum_{s=1}^{r} B_{2s}(x)\lambda_s \right]^2 f(x) \right.$$
$$\left. + \frac{\kappa^q \sigma^2(x)}{nh_1 \dots h_q} \right\} M(x)\, dx^c. \tag{4.29}$$

The relationship between CV and $\mathrm{MSE}[\hat{g}(x)]$ can also be used to derive (4.29). In Chapter 2 we argued that the leading term of CV is related to the pointwise MSE by

$$CV \sim \sum_{x^d} \int \mathrm{MSE}[\hat{g}(x)] f(x) M(x)\, dx^c. \tag{4.30}$$

Equation (4.25) implies that

$$\mathrm{MSE}[\hat{g}(x)] \sim \left[\sum_{s=1}^{q} B_{1s}(x)h_s^2 + \sum_{s=1}^{r} B_{2s}(x)\lambda_s \right]^2$$
$$+ \kappa^q \sigma^2(x) f(x)^{-1} (nh_1 \dots h_q)^{-1}.$$

Substituting this into (4.30), and ignoring the terms unrelated to (h, λ) and the smaller order terms, we obtain $CV_r(a, b) = n^{-4/(4+q)} \chi_r$, where

$$\chi_r(a, b) = \sum_{x^d} \int \left\{ \left[\sum_{s=1}^{q} B_{1s}(x)a_s^2 + \sum_{s=1}^{r} B_{2s}(x)b_s \right]^2 f(x) \right.$$
$$\left. + \frac{\kappa^q \sigma^2(x)}{a_1 \dots a_q} \right\} M(x)\, dx^c, \tag{4.31}$$

where $a_s = n^{1/(4+q)} h_s$ and $b_s = n^{2/(4+q)} \lambda_s$. Equation (4.31) indeed gives the leading term of CV_r as stated in (4.29).

Let $a_1^0, \dots, a_q^0, b_1^0, \dots, b_r^0$ denote values that minimize χ_r subject to each of them being nonnegative. We exclude the case for which some a_s^0 or b_s^0 are infinite, and require that

The a_s^0's and b_s^0's are uniquely defined, and each of them is finite. (4.32)

This implies that $0 < a_s^0 < \infty$ for each s, but it is possible for b_s^0 to vanish for some s. Exercise 4.10 derives the explicit expression for a^0 and b^0 for the simple case of $q = r = 1$.

Let h_s^0 $(1 \leq j \leq q)$ and λ_s^0 $(1 \leq s \leq r)$ denote values of h_s and λ_s that minimize $CV_{r0}(h, \lambda)$; then (4.32) implies the following:

$$h_s^0 \sim n^{-1/(q+4)} a_s^0 = O\left(n^{-1/(q+4)}\right) \qquad \text{for } 1 \leq s \leq q,$$
$$\lambda_s^0 \sim n^{-2/(q+4)} b_s^0 = O\left(n^{-2/(q+4)}\right) \qquad \text{for } 1 \leq s \leq r. \tag{4.33}$$

Let $\hat{h}_s$ $(s = 1, \ldots, q)$ and $\hat{\lambda}_s$ $(s = 1, \ldots, r)$ denote the values of h_s and λ_s chosen via cross-validation, respectively. The next theorem shows that (4.33) holds true when h_s^0 and λ_s^0 are replaced by $\hat{h}_s$ and $\hat{\lambda}_s$, respectively.

Theorem 4.7. *Under conditions (4.27), (4.28) and (4.32),*

$$n^{1/(q+4)} \hat{h}_s \to a_s^0 \quad \text{for } 1 \leq s \leq q,$$
$$n^{2/(q+4)} \hat{\lambda}_s \to b_s^0 \quad \text{for } 1 \leq s \leq r,$$

and $\inf n^{4/(q+4)} [CV_r(h, \lambda) - n^{-1} \sum_{i=1}^n u_i^2 M_i] \to \inf \chi$ *in probability.*

The proof of Theorem 4.7 can be found in Hall et al. (2006). Theorem 4.7 follows from (4.33) and the fact that

$$CV_r(h, \lambda) - \int \sigma^2(x) M(x) \, dx = CV_{r0}(h, \lambda) + (s.o.)$$

uniformly in $(x^c, x^d) \in w \times \mathcal{S}^d$, $(h, \lambda) \in [0, \eta_n]^{q+r}$, where $\eta_n > 0$ and $\eta_n \to 0$ as $n \to \infty$.

Intuitively, one should expect that the $\hat{h}_s$'s and $\hat{\lambda}_s$'s that minimize $CV_r(\cdot, \cdot)$ have the same asymptotic behavior as the h_s^0's and λ_s^0's that minimize $CV_{r0}(\cdot, \cdot)$, the leading term of $CV_r(h, \lambda)$. Therefore, one expects that $\hat{h}_s = h_s^0 + (s.o.)$ and $\hat{\lambda}_s = \lambda_s^0 + (s.o.)$.

4.5 Regression with Mixed Data: Irrelevant Regressors

In this section we consider the case in which (i.e., allow for the possibility that) some of the regressors may be irrelevant. Without loss of generality, we assume that only the first q_1 components of X^c and the first r_1 components of X^d are "relevant" regressors in the sense defined below. For integers $0 \leq q_1, q_2 \leq q$ and $0 \leq r_1, r_2 \leq r$ satisfying $q_1 + q_2 = q$ and $r_1 + r_2 = r$, let $\bar{X}$ contain the first q_1 components of

X^c and the first r_1 components of X^d, and let $\tilde{X} = X/\bar{X}$ denote the remaining components of X. In this section we assume that

$$(Y, \bar{X}) \text{ is independent of } \tilde{X}. \tag{4.34}$$

A consequence of (4.34) is that $\mathrm{E}[Y|\bar{X}, \tilde{X}] = \mathrm{E}[Y|\bar{X}]$ so that only $\bar{X}$ are relevant in (4.19) (hence $\tilde{X}$ contains only irrelevant regressors). However, we do not assume that this information is known a priori, and in practice we therefore proceed to nonparametrically estimate $\mathrm{E}(Y_i|X_i)$ rather than $\mathrm{E}(Y_i|\bar{X}_i)$. We shall demonstrate that if one smooths both the discrete and the continuous variables, and uses the least squares cross-validation method to select the smoothing parameters, then asymptotically the irrelevant variables can be automatically smoothed out. To be more specific as to what we mean by "smoothing out the irrelevant variables," note that

$$\hat{g}(x) = \frac{\sum_{i=1}^n Y_i \prod_{s=1}^{q_1} w\left(\frac{X_{is}-x_s}{h_s}\right) \prod_{s=q_1+1}^{q} w\left(\frac{X_{is}-x_s}{h_s}\right)}{\sum_{i=1}^n \prod_{s=1}^{q_1} w\left(\frac{X_{is}-x_s}{h_s}\right) \prod_{s=q_1+1}^{q} w\left(\frac{X_{is}-x_s}{h_s}\right)}$$
$$\times \frac{\prod_{s=1}^{r_1} l(X_{is}^d, x_s^d, \lambda_s) \prod_{s=r_1+1}^{r} l(X_{is}^d, x_s^d, \lambda_s)}{\prod_{s=1}^{r_1} l(X_{is}^d, x_s^d, \lambda_s) \prod_{s=r_1+1}^{r} l(X_{is}^d, x_s^d, \lambda_s)}. \tag{4.35}$$

If $h_s = \infty$ for $s = q_1 + 1, \ldots, q$ and $\lambda_s = 1$ for $s = r_1 + 1, \ldots, r$, then $w((X_{is} - x_s)/h_s) = w(0)$ for $s = q_1 + 1, \ldots, q$, $l(X_{is}^d, x_s^d, 1) = 1$ for $s = r_1 + 1, \ldots, r$, and (4.35) reduces to

$$\hat{g}(x) = \frac{\sum_{i=1}^n Y_i \prod_{s=1}^{q_1} w\left(\frac{X_{is}-x_s}{h_s}\right) \prod_{s=1}^{r_1} l(X_{is}^d, x_s^d, \lambda_s)}{\sum_{i=1}^n \prod_{s=1}^{q_1} w\left(\frac{X_{is}-x_s}{h_s}\right) \prod_{s=1}^{r_1} l(X_{is}^d, x_s^d, \lambda_s)}, \tag{4.36}$$

because $w(0)^{q-q_1}$ cancels out in the numerator and the denominator of $\hat{g}(x)$ and, as a result, $\hat{g}(x)$ is no longer related to the irrelevant variables x_s^c ($s = q_1 + 1, \ldots, q$) and x_s^d ($s = r_1 + 1, \ldots, r$). We show in Theorem 4.8 below that cross-validation possesses this property, i.e., as $n \to \infty$, $\hat{h}_s \to \infty$ for $s = q_1 + 1, \ldots, q$ and $\hat{\lambda}_s \to 1$ for $s = r_1 + 1, \ldots, r$. Thus, asymptotically, cross-validation can automatically remove irrelevant variables.

The cross-validation objective function is the same as that defined in Section 4.4 except that now $Y_i = \bar{g}(\bar{X}_i) + u_i$ with $\mathrm{E}(u_i|X_i) = 0$, that is, the conditional mean function depends only on the relevant regressors $\bar{x}$. The definitions of m_i, $\hat{m}_i$ and $\hat{f}_i$ all remain unchanged except that one needs to replace $g_i = g(X_i)$ by $\bar{g}_i = \bar{g}(\bar{X}_i)$ wherever it occurs.

The modified analogue of the function χ defined in Section 4.4 is

$$
\bar{\chi}(a_1, \ldots, a_{q_1}, b_1, \ldots, b_{r_1})
$$

$$
= \sum_{\bar{x}^d} \int \left\{ \left(\sum_{s=1}^{r_1} b_s \sum_{\bar{v}^d} I_s(\bar{v}^d, \bar{x}^d) \left\{ \bar{g}(\bar{x}^c, \bar{v}^d) - \bar{g}(\bar{x}) \right\} \bar{f}(\bar{x}^c, \bar{v}^d) \bar{f}(\bar{x})^{-1} \right. \right.
$$

$$
\left. + \frac{1}{2} \kappa_2 \sum_{s=1}^{q_1} a_s^2 \left\{ \bar{g}_{ss}(\bar{x}) + 2 \bar{f}_s(\bar{x}) \bar{g}_s(\bar{x}) \bar{f}(\bar{x})^{-1} \right\} \right)^2 \bar{f}(\bar{x})
$$

$$
+ \sum_{\bar{x}^d} \int \frac{\kappa^q \bar{\sigma}^2(\bar{x})}{a_1 \ldots a_{q_1}} \right\} \bar{w}(\bar{x}) d\bar{x}^c \tag{4.37}
$$

where

$$
\bar{w}(\bar{x}^c, \bar{x}^d) = \sum_{x_{r_1+1}^d, \ldots, x_r^d} \int \tilde{f}(x_{q_1+1}^c, \ldots, x_q^c, x_{r_1+1}^d, \ldots, x_r^d)
$$

$$
\times w(\bar{x}^c, x_{q_1+1}^c, \ldots, x_q^c) \, dx_{q_1+1}^c \ldots dx_q^c,
$$

and the bar (tilde) notation refers to functions of vectors involving only the relevant (irrelevant) regressors $\bar{x}$, $(\tilde{x})$. $\bar{f}$ $(\tilde{f})$ is the joint density of $\bar{x} = (\bar{x}^c, \bar{x}^d)$ $(\tilde{x} = (\tilde{x}^c, \tilde{x}^d))$ and $\bar{m}_{ss}$ $(\bar{f}_{ss})$ are second order derivatives of $\bar{m}$ $(\bar{f})$ with respect to $\bar{x}_s^c$, $\bar{m} = \bar{g}\bar{f}$.

As before, let $a_1^0, \ldots, a_{q_1}^0, b_1^0, \ldots, b_{r_1}^0$ denote values that minimize $\bar{\chi}$ subject to each of them being nonnegative. We require that the a_s^0's and b_s^0's are uniquely defined, and that each is finite.

Note that the irrelevant components do not appear in the definition of $\bar{\chi}$. This is because the irrelevant components cancel each other in the ratio $E[\hat{m}(x)]/E[\hat{f}(x)]$, which we denote by $\bar{\mu}_g(\bar{x}) = E[\hat{m}(x)]/E[\hat{f}(x)]$. For the relevant variables $\bar{x}$ we require that

$$
\sum_{\bar{x}^d} \int_{\text{supp } w} [\bar{\mu}_g(\bar{x}) - \bar{g}(\bar{x})]^2 \bar{w}(\bar{x}) \bar{f}(\bar{x}) d\bar{x}^c, \tag{4.38}
$$

interpreted as a function of $h_1, \ldots, h_{q_1}, \lambda_1, \ldots, \lambda_{r_1}$, vanishes if and only if all of these smoothing parameters vanish.

Since we should allow the smoothing parameters for irrelevant variables to diverge from zero, we can no longer impose the requirement that $h_s = o(1)$ and $\lambda_s = o(1)$ for all s. Rather, we impose the following conventional conditions on the bandwidth and kernels. Define

$$H = \left(\prod_{s=1}^{q_1} h_s \right) \prod_{s=q_1+1}^{q} \min(h_s, 1).$$

Let $0 < \epsilon < 1/(q+4)$. Assume that

$$n^{\epsilon-1} \;\leq\; H \;\leq\; n^{-\epsilon}; \; \min(h_1, \ldots, h_q) \;>\; n^{-C} \text{ and}$$
$\max(h_1, \ldots, h_q) < n^C$ for some $C > 0$; the kernel K is a symmetric, compactly supported, Hölder-continuous PDF; $w(0) > w(\delta)$ for all $\delta > 0$. \hfill (4.39)

If ϵ is arbitrarily small, the above conditions on $h_1, \ldots, h_q$ are basically that $n h_1 \ldots h_{q_1} \to \infty$, $h_1 \ldots h_{q_1} \to 0$ and $h_1 \ldots h_q \to 0$ as $n \to \infty$. In addition, we require that the fastest rate at which h_s goes to zero cannot exceed n^{-C} and the fastest rate at which h_s (for irrelevant variables) goes to ∞ cannot exceed n^C.

With these conditions we obtain the following result.

Theorem 4.8. *Under conditions (4.28), (4.34), (4.38), (4.39), and letting $\hat{h}_1, \ldots, \hat{h}_q, \hat{\lambda}_1, \ldots, \hat{\lambda}_r$ denote the smoothing parameters that minimize CV_r, then*

$$n^{1/(q_1+4)} \hat{h}_s \to a_s^0 \text{ in probability, for } 1 \leq s \leq q_1;$$
$$P(\hat{h}_s > C) \to 1 \text{ for } q_1+1 \leq s \leq q \text{ and for all } C > 0;$$
$$n^{2/(q_1+4)} \hat{\lambda}_s \to b_s^0 \text{ in probability, for } 1 \leq s \leq r_1;$$
$$\lambda_s \to 1 \text{ in probability, for } r_1+1 \leq s \leq r;$$

$$n^{4/(q_1+4)} \inf \left[CV_r(\hat{h}, \hat{\lambda}) - \frac{1}{n} \sum_i u_i^2 M_i \right] \xrightarrow{p} \inf \bar{\chi}. \hfill (4.40)$$

The proof of Theorem 4.8 is quite involved and is given in Hall et al. (2006). Theorem 4.8 states that the smoothing parameters for the irrelevant components converge in probability to the upper extremities of their respective ranges; therefore, all of the irrelevant variables can be (asymptotically) automatically smoothed out, while the smoothing parameters for the relevant variables possess the same optimality properties that would prevail were the irrelevant variables not present. This stands in stark contrast to the results for the discrete-regressor-only case that we discussed in Section 4.3 where there is also a positive probability that the irrelevant regressors may not be smoothed out.

The next theorem presents the asymptotic normality result for $\hat{g}(x)$ when cross-validation is used to select the smoothing parameters.

Theorem 4.9. *Under the same conditions as in Theorem 4.8, letting* $\mathcal{S}^c = \operatorname{supp} w$ *and letting* $x = (x^c, x^d) \in \mathcal{S}^c \times \mathcal{S}^d$, *then*

$$(n\hat{h}_1 \ldots \hat{h}_{q_1})^{1/2} \left[\hat{g}(x) - \bar{g}(\bar{x}) - \sum_{s=1}^{q_1} \bar{B}_{1s}(\bar{x})\hat{h}_s^2 - \sum_{s=1}^{r_1} \bar{B}_{rs}(\bar{x})\hat{\lambda}_s \right]$$

$$\xrightarrow{d} N\left(0, \frac{\kappa^{q_1}\bar{\sigma}^2(\bar{x})}{\bar{f}(\bar{x})}\right), \qquad (4.41)$$

where

$$\bar{B}_{1s}(\bar{x}) = \frac{1}{2}\kappa_2 \sum_{s=1}^{q_1} \left\{ g_{ss}(\bar{x}) + 2\frac{\bar{f}_s(\bar{x})\bar{g}_s(\bar{x})}{\bar{f}(\bar{x})} \right\},$$

$$\bar{B}_{2s}(\bar{x}) = \sum_{\bar{v}^d} \mathbf{1}_s(\bar{v}^d, \bar{x}^d) \left\{ g(\bar{x}^c, \bar{v}^d) - \bar{g}(\bar{x}) \right\} \bar{f}(\bar{x}^c, \bar{v}^d)\bar{f}(\bar{x})^{-1}, (4.42)$$

and $\bar{\sigma}^2(\bar{x}) = \mathrm{E}(u_i^2 | \bar{X}_i = \bar{x})$.

The proof of Theorem 4.9 is given in Hall et al. (2006). Intuitively, it can be understood as follows. First, note that as $\hat{h}_s \to \infty$ for $s = q_1 + 1, \ldots, q$ and as $\hat{\lambda}_s \to 1$ for $s = r_1 + 1, \ldots, r$, we have $\hat{g}(x, \hat{h}_1, \ldots, \hat{h}_q, \hat{\lambda}_1, \ldots, \hat{\lambda}_r) = \hat{g}(\bar{x}, \hat{h}_1, \ldots, \hat{h}_{q_1}, \hat{\lambda}_1, \ldots, \hat{\lambda}_{r_1}) + (s.o.)$. Next, from the fact that $\hat{h}_s - h_s^0 = o_p(h_s^0)$ $(s = 1, \ldots, q_1)$ and $\hat{\lambda}_s - \lambda_s^0 = o_p(\lambda_s^0)$ $(s = 1, \ldots, r_1)$, we have that $\hat{g}(\bar{x}, \hat{h}_1, \ldots, \hat{h}_{q_1}, \hat{\lambda}_1, \ldots, \hat{\lambda}_{r_1}) = \hat{g}(\bar{x}, h_1^0, \ldots, h_{q_1}^0, \lambda_1^0, \ldots, \lambda_{r_1}^0) + (s.o.)$. Theorem 4.9 then follows.

4.5.1 Ordered Discrete Variables

Up to now we limited our attention to the case for which the discrete variables are unordered. If, however, some of the discrete variables are ordered (i.e., are "ordinal categorical variables"), then we should use a kernel function which is capable of reflecting the fact that these variables are ordered. Assuming that x_s^d can take on c_s different ordered values, $\{0, 1, \ldots, c_s - 1\}$, Aitchison and Aitken (1976, p. 29) suggested using the kernel function given by $l(x_s^d, v_s^d, \lambda_s) = \binom{c_s}{j} \lambda_s^j(1 - \lambda_s)^{c_s - j}$

when $|x_s^d - v_s^d| = j$ $(0 \le s \le c_s)$, where $\binom{c_s}{j} = c_s!/[j!(c_s-j)!]$. Observe that these weights add up to 1; however, when $c_s \ge 3$, this weight function is deficient since there is no value of λ_s that can make $l(x_s^d, v_s^d, \lambda_s)$ equal to a constant function. Thus, even if x_s^d turned out to be an irrelevant regressor, it could never be smoothed out if one were to use this kernel. Therefore, we suggest the use of the following alternative kernel function:

$$l(x_s^d, v_s^d, \lambda_s) = \lambda_s^{|x_s^d - v_s^d|}. \tag{4.43}$$

The range of λ_s is $[0, 1]$. Again, when λ_s assumes its extreme upper bound value ($\lambda_s = 1$), we see that $l(x_s^d, v_s^d, 1) \equiv 1$ for all values of x_s^d, $v_s^d \in \{0, 1, \dots, c_s - 1\}$, and in this case x_s^d is completely smoothed out of the resulting estimate.

It can be easily shown that when some of the discrete variables are ordered, then all of the results established above continue to hold provided one uses the kernel function given by (4.43).

Of course, if an ordered discrete variable assumes a large number of different values, one might simply treat it as if it were a continuous variable. In practice this may well lead to estimation results similar to those arising were one to treat the variable as an ordered discrete variable and use the kernel function given by (4.43).

Bierens (1983, 1987) and Ahmad and Cerrito (1994) also consider smoothing both the discrete and continuous variables for the nonparametric estimation of a regression function. But they do not study the fundamental issue of data-driven selection of smoothing parameters. As we have shown in this section, it is important to use automatic data-driven methods to select smoothing parameters. Moreover, least squares cross-validation has the attractive property that it can automatically (asymptotically) remove irrelevant explanatory variables. In nonparametric settings with mixed discrete and continuous variables, least squares cross-validation stands alone and appears to be without any obvious peers.

4.6 Applications

4.6.1 Food-Away-from-Home Expenditure

Prior to the 1980s, the value added in China's food sector that was accounted for by food-away-from-home (FAFH) consumption was negligible. Household production of most meals used grain, raw vegetables, and meat produced at home, purchased from state-run food stores, or purchased directly from farmers. Mirroring China's rapid income growth after 1980, Chinese consumers increasingly ate more meals in restaurants, cafeterias and dining halls. The FAFH share of total food expenditure has steadily increased from 5.03% in 1992 to 14.70% at 2000. In 2000, per capita annual FAFH expenditure reached 288 yuan with total FAFH expenditure of 132 billion yuan in urban China ($15.9 billion US dollars). In the application below, it will be seen that nonparametric methods suggest that the FAFH expenditure growth in China is expected to continue, due to the rising middle class, rapid urbanization, and to its relatively low FAFH share compared with the United States (40.3% in 2001, Economic Research Service, USDA), Canada (35.6% in 2001, Statistic Canada), and other developed countries (see Jensen and Yen (1996)). This stands in contrast to conclusions obtained from a popular linear model that has been used to model such expenditure.

The data is obtained from urban household surveys conducted by the State Statistical Bureau of the People's Republic of China in 1992 and 1998. The dependent variable is household per capita FAFH expenditure (in 1992 yuan). The explanatory variables include household per capita income (in 1992 yuan), household size, education level of the household head (seven categories)[1], age of the household head, a 0-1 dummy variable indicating that the household is in a large city, and a gender dummy for the household head. The total sample size in this study is 3,459 for 1992 and 3,359 for 1998. Min, Fang and Li (2004) also estimated a popular linear model to be used for comparison purposes. They presented some graphs that show the relationship between FAFH expenditure and income (holding all other regressors fixed at their sample median). Both 1992 and 1998 nonparametric FAFH expenditure curves show that FAFH consumption stops increasing after a high income level has been attained. This is quite different from the parametric results, where the linear model predicts higher FAFH consumption for higher income households. To check which results appear to provide a better description of the data, Min et al. computed goodness-of-fit (R^2) for both the parametric and nonparametric models. The R^2 from the linear models for the 1992 and 1998 data are 0.128

---

[1] 1. below elementary school, 2. elementary school, 3. middle school, 4. high school, 5. middle level specialized training, 6. two-year college, 7. bachelor degree or above.

and 0.170, while the R^2 for the nonparametric models are 0.382 and 0.348 for 1992 and 1998, respectively.

Table 4.1 gives the average FAFH expenditure for different income intervals, along with the predicted average values using the parametric (ordinary least squares, OLS) and nonparametric models. High income households indeed spent less on FAFH than those households with slightly lower income. In 1992 households with income exceeding 5,000 yuan spent about 11 yuan less on FAFH than those with income between 3,000 and 5,000 yuan. In 1998 households with income exceeding 9,000 yuan spent 52 yuan less on FAFH than those with income between 4,000 and 9,000 yuan. We observe that for low and middle income levels, both the parametric and the nonparametric models predict the average FAFH expenditure well. However, for high income levels, the parametric model appears to give misleading predictions, while the nonparametric method performs much better in this case.

Table 4.2 reports estimated mean and median income elasticities. For the nonparametric model, the elasticity η_i for house i is computed via $\eta_i = \frac{\partial \hat{g}(x_i, z_i)}{\partial x_{1i}} \frac{x_{1i}}{y_i}$, where x_{1i} is the income of the ith household, while for the linear model, $\eta_i = \beta_1 \frac{x_{1i}}{y_i}$. Table 4.2 reveals some interesting phenomena. Comparing the elasticities of 1992 and 1998, the nonparametric results show that both the mean and median income elasticities have increased for both large city and middle-small city households. In contrast, the parametric model shows only that the mean elasticity for middle-small city has increased, while the mean elasticity for large cities and the median elasticity for both large and middle-small cities fell from 1992 to 1998. The conflicting estimates are likely due to the misspecification of the linear model. As we discussed earlier, the linear model overestimates FAFH expenditure for high income households due to its imposing an incorrect linear income (trend) component on FAFH consumption. The misspecified linear model also overestimates the elasticities for high income families, leading to the erroneous prediction that the median elasticity has decreased from 1992 to 1998.

4.6.2   Modeling Strike Volume

We consider a panel of annual observations used to model strike volume for 18 Organization for Economic Cooperation and Development (OECD) countries. The data consist of observations on the level of strike volume (days lost due to industrial disputes per 1,000 wage salary earners) and their regressors in 18 OECD countries from 1951 to

Table 4.1: Average FAFH expenditure by income category

1992

Income	Data Ave.	OLS Ave.	NP Ave.
Below 3K	82.78	82.12	83.26
3K-5K	154.9	152.0	148.0
Above 5K	143.9	221.7	144.9

1998

Income	Data Ave.	OLS Ave.	NP Ave.
Below 4K	119.40	120.1	121.9
4K-9K	257.0	250.0	254.0
Above 9K	205.2	441.1	232.9

Table 4.2: Mean and median income elasticities (η_i denotes income elasticity of household i)

Parametric Results	Large City		Mid-Small City	
	1992	1998	1992	1998
Mean	0.878	0.848	1.274	1.351
Median	0.848	0.832	1.074	0.994
% of $\eta_i > 1$	18.5%	13.9%	69.6%	48.8%
Nonparametric Results	Large City		Mid-Small City	
	1992	1998	1992	1998
Mean	0.626	0.826	0.900	0.947
Median	0.751	0.851	0.938	0.960
% of $\eta_i > 1$	35.0%	39.9%	45.9%	45.8%

1985. The average level and variance of strike volume vary substantially across countries. The data distribution also features a long right tail and several large values of volume. We make use of the following regressors: 1) country code; 2) year; 3) strike volume; 4) unemployment; 5) inflation; 6) parliamentary representation of social democratic and labor parties; 7) a time-invariant measure of union centralization. The data are publicly available (see StatLib, http://lib.stat.cmu.edu). As one country had incomplete data we analyze only the 17 countries having complete records.

These data were analyzed by Western (1996), who considered a

Table 4.3: Regressor standard deviations and bandwidths for the proposed method for the training data, $n_1 = 561$

	1	2	3	4	5	6
$\hat{\sigma}$	9.53	2.84	4.75	13.31	0.31	NA
$\hat{h}/\hat{\lambda}$	102565846.11	4800821.61	5.84	30.56	408328.03	0.12

Key: 1) year; 2) unemployment; 3) inflation; 4) parliamentary representation; 5) union centralization; 6) country code.

linear panel data model with country-specific fixed effects and a time trend. We consider a nonparametric model which treats country code as categorical and the remaining regressors as continuous. To assess each model's performance we estimate each on data for the period 1951–1983, and then evaluate each based on its out-of-sample predictive performance for the period 1984–1985, again using predictive squared error as our criterion. We begin by considering the cross-validated bandwidths, which are summarized in Table 4.3.

As can be seen from Table 4.3, the continuous regressors year, unemployment, and union centralization are effectively smoothed out of the resulting nonparametric estimate, having bandwidths that are orders of magnitude larger than the respective regressor's standard deviation. This suggests that the continuous regressors inflation and parliamentary representation and the discrete regressor country code are relevant in the sense outlined earlier.

We next compare the out-of-sample forecasting performance of each model. The relative *predictive* MSE of the parametric panel model (all variables enter the model linearly) versus the NP *CV* approach is 1.33. We note that varying the forecast horizon has little impact on the relative predictive performance. We have also tried a parametric model with interaction terms (quadratic in the continuous regressors) and the resulting out-of-sample predictive MSE is larger than even the linear model's MSE prediction (the ratio of its predictive MSE over NP *CV*'s is 1.44), while a parsimonious parametric model having only a constant, unemployment, and inflation has a predicted MSE 15% larger than that of the NP *CV* approach (the relative predictive MSE is 1.15), suggesting that a linear parametric specification is inappropriate.

4.7 Exercises

Exercise 4.1. Derive the MSE of the nonsmoothing estimator of $p(x)$ given by

$$\tilde{p}(x) = \frac{1}{n} \sum_{i=1}^{n} \mathbf{1}(X_i = x),$$

where $\mathbf{1}(\cdot)$ is an indicator function defined by

$$\mathbf{1}(X_i = x) = \begin{cases} 1 & \text{if } X_i = x \\ 0 & \text{otherwise,} \end{cases}$$

and where $X_i \in \mathcal{S} = \{0, 1, \ldots, c - 1\}$ is a discrete random variable having finite support.

Exercise 4.2. Consider the kernel estimator of $p(x)$ given by

$$\hat{p}(x) = \frac{1}{n} \sum_{i=1}^{n} L(X_i, x, \lambda),$$

where x is a scalar and $L(\cdot)$ is a kernel function defined by

$$L(X_i, x, \lambda) = \begin{cases} 1 - \lambda & \text{if } X_i = x \\ \lambda/(c - 1) & \text{otherwise,} \end{cases}$$

where $\lambda \in [0, (c - 1)/c]$.

(i) Derive the bias of this estimator, then demonstrate that if X has a (discrete) uniform distribution, so that $p(x) = 1/c$ for all X, then the kernel estimator $\hat{p}(x)$ is unbiased for *any* admissible value of λ.

(ii) Show that

$$\text{var}(\hat{p}(x)) = \frac{p(x)(1 - p(x))}{n} \left(1 - \lambda \frac{c}{(c - 1)} \right)^2.$$

Demonstrate that if X has a (discrete) uniform distribution, so that $p(x) = 1/c$ for all X, then the variance of $\hat{p}(x)$ is zero when $\lambda = (c - 1)/c$, its upper bound.

(iii) Given your results above, is it possible for the kernel estimator $\hat{p}(x)$ to have an MSE of zero when the underlying distribution is uniform? What are the conditions that λ must satisfy for this to occur? Demonstrate your result.

Exercise 4.3.

(i) Show that $\mathrm{E}[\hat{p}\left(x^d\right)]$ and $\mathrm{var}(\hat{p}\left(x^d\right))$ are indeed given by (4.5) with $B_{p,s} = \sum_{z^d} \frac{1}{c_s-1} \mathbf{1}_s \left(x^d, z^d\right) p\left(z^d\right) - p(x^d)$, where $\mathbf{1}_s \left(x^d, z^d\right)$ is defined in (4.24).

(ii) Show that $\mathrm{E}(\hat{m}\left(x^d\right)^2) = O\left(\sum_{s=1}^r \lambda_s^2 + n^{-1}\right)$, where $\hat{m}\left(x^d\right)$ is defined above (4.15). Note that $O\left((\sum_{s=1}^r \lambda_s)^2\right) = O\left(\sum_{s=1}^q \lambda_s^2\right)$.

Exercise 4.4. Ω_r is an $r \times r$ matrix with its (s,t)th element given by

$$\sum_{x^d \in \mathcal{S}^d} \left[p\left(x^d\right) - p_{1,s}\left(x^d\right)\right] \left[p\left(x^d\right) - p_{1,t}\left(x^d\right)\right],$$

where

$$p_{1,s}\left(x^d\right) = \frac{1}{c_s-1} \sum_{z^d \in \mathcal{S}^d} p\left(z^d\right) \mathbf{1}_s \left(x^d, z^d\right). \tag{4.44}$$

Note that $p_{1,s}\left(x^d\right)$ is also a probability measure since $p_{1,s}\left(x^d\right)$ is the average probability over the $c_s - 1$ z^d's $\in \mathcal{S}^d$ that differ from x^d only in the sth component, i.e., $p_{1,s}\left(x^d\right) = \frac{1}{c_s-1} \sum_{z_s^d \neq x_s^d} p(z_s^d, x_{-s}^d)$.

Consider the simple case of $r = 2$. Then

$$\lambda'_{(2)} \Omega_2 \lambda_{(2)} = \sum_{x^d} \left\{ \lambda_1 \left[p\left(x^d\right) - p_{1,1}\left(x^d\right)\right] + \lambda_2 \left[p\left(x^d\right) - p_{1,2}\left(x^d\right)\right] \right\}^2.$$

Show that Ω_2 is positive definite if and only if there exists $x^d, z^d \in \mathcal{S}^d$ such that $p\left(x^d\right) \neq p_{1,1}\left(x^d\right)$ and that $p\left(z^d\right) \neq p_{1,2}\left(z^d\right)$.

Exercise 4.5. Using (4.3), we have

$$I_{1n} = \sum_{x^d} \left[\hat{p}\left(x^d\right)\right]^2 = \frac{1}{n(n-1)} \sum_{i=1}^n \sum_{j=1}^n \sum_{x^d} L_{\lambda,ix} L_{\lambda,jx}$$

$$= n^{-2} \sum_{i=1}^n \sum_{j=1}^n L_{\lambda,ij}^{(2)},$$

where $L_{\lambda,ij}^{(2)} = \sum_{x^d} L_{\lambda,ix} L_{\lambda,jx}$.

Thus we have

$$CV_p(\lambda) = n^{-2} \sum_{i=1}^n L_{\lambda,ii}^{(2)} + \frac{1}{n(n-1)} \sum_i \sum_{j \neq i} \left[L_{\lambda,ij}^{(2)} - 2L_{\lambda,ij}\right]$$

$$- \frac{1}{n^2(n-1)} \sum_i \sum_{j \neq i} L_{\lambda,ij}^{(2)}. \tag{4.45}$$

Let $CV_p(\lambda)$ be defined in (4.45) and assume that x^d is univariate taking values in $\{0, 1, \ldots, c-1\}$. Show that (λ is a scalar)

$$\mathrm{E}(CV_p(\lambda)) = D_1\lambda^2 - D_2\lambda n^{-1} + o\left(\lambda^2 + \lambda n^{-1}\right)$$
$$+ \text{ terms independent of } \lambda, \qquad (4.46)$$

where the D_j's are (positive) constants. Derive explicit expressions for the D_j's.

Note that minimizing (4.46) over λ leads to $\tilde{\lambda} = n^{-1}D_2/(2D_1) = O(n^{-1})$.

Exercise 4.6.

(i) Prove Theorem 4.2 (i).

Hint: Use Theorem 4.1 and the result in (3.3).

(ii) Prove Theorem 4.2 (ii).

Hint: Use Theorem 4.1 and the result in (3.4).

Exercise 4.7. Prove Theorem 4.4 for the case when x^d is univariate.

Hint: When x^d is univariate, $L_{ij,\lambda} = \mathbf{1}_{d_{ij}=0} + \lambda \mathbf{1}_{d_{ij}\neq 0}$, where $d_{ij} = |x_i^d - x_j^d|$. Write

$$\hat{p}_{-i}(X_i^d) = n^{-1}\sum_{j\neq i}[\mathbf{1}_{d_{ij}=0} + \lambda\mathbf{1}_{d_{ij}\neq 0}] \equiv \hat{p}_{i0} + \lambda\hat{p}_{i1}.$$ Then

$$\frac{1}{\hat{p}_{-i}(X_i^d)} = \frac{1}{\hat{p}_{i0}}\left[1 - \lambda\frac{\hat{p}_{i1}}{\hat{p}_{i0}}\right] + O(\lambda^2)$$

One can expand $CV_d(\lambda)$ in a power series of λ, i.e.,

$$CV_d = A_1\lambda^2 + A_{2n}\lambda n^{-1} + o(\lambda n^{-1} + \lambda^2) + \text{(terms not related to } \lambda),$$

where $A_1 > 0$ is a positive constant, and A_{2n} is an $O_p(1)$ random variable.

Exercise 4.8. In the proof of Theorem 4.5 we have used $\hat{\sigma}^2\left(x^d\right) = \sigma\left(x^d\right) + o_p(1)$. Prove this result.

Hint: Write $\hat{\sigma}^2\left(x^d\right) - \sigma^2\left(x^d\right) = [\hat{\sigma}^2\left(x^d\right) - \sigma^2\left(x^d\right)]\hat{p}\left(x^d\right)/\hat{p}\left(x^d\right)$. Use $\hat{\lambda}_s = O_p(n^{-1})$. Show that $\hat{\sigma}^2\left(x^d\right)\hat{p}\left(x^d\right) = n^{-1}\sum_{i=1}^{n}u_i^2\mathbf{1}(X_i^d = x^d) + O_p(n^{-1}) \xrightarrow{p} \sigma^2\left(x^d\right)p\left(x^d\right)$ by a law of large numbers argument.

Exercise 4.9. Derive (4.21) through (4.23).

Exercise 4.10. The a_s^0's and b_s^0's are defined as the unique finite values that minimize χ defined in (4.31). Consider the case of $q = 1$ and $r = 1$. Solve for a_1^0 and b_1^0 by minimizing (4.31).

Hint: Note that $\chi(a_1, b_1) = C_1 a_1^4 + C_2 b_1^2 - C_3 a_1^2 b_1 + C_0/a_1$, where $C_j > 0$ for $j = 0, 1, 2$. This can be written as

$$\chi(a_1, b_1) = C_2 \left[b_1 - A_1 a_1^2 \right]^2 + A_2 a_1^4 + C_0/a_1,$$

where $A_1 = C_3/(2C_2)$, and where $A_2 = C_1 - C_3^2/(4C_2) > 0$. Thus, we have $b_1^0 = \max\{0, A_1(a_1^0)^2\}$ (since b_1^0 is nonnegative) and $a_1^0 = [C_0/(4A_2)]^{1/5}$ if $A_1 \geq 0$, and $a_1^0 = [C_0/(4C_1)]^{1/5}$ if $A_1 < 0$.

Exercise 4.11. Considering the simple case for which $r = 1$, show that Assumption 4.1 holds true if and only if $g(x^d)$ is not a constant function (when x^d is univariate).

Hint: Assumption 4.1 becomes, for all $x^d \in S^d$ (x^d is univariate since $r = 1$), $\sum_{z^d \in S^d} \left\{ [g(x^d) - g(z^d)] \left[\mathbf{1}(x^d = z^d) + \lambda \mathbf{1}(x^d \neq z^d) \right] \right\}^2 = 0$, which is equivalent to $\lambda^2 \sum_{z^d \in S^d} [g(x^d) - g(z^d)]^2 \mathbf{1}(x^d \neq z^d) = 0$ because $[g(x^d) - g(z^d)] \mathbf{1}(x^d = z^d) \equiv 0$. However, since $g(x^d)$ is not a constant function, we know that $\sum_{z^d \in S^d} [g(x^d) - g(z^d)]^2 \mathbf{1}(x^d \neq z^d) > 0$. Thus, we must have $\lambda = 0$. Thus, Assumption 4.1 holds true if and only if $g(x^d)$ is not a constant function when x^d is univariate.

Chapter 5

Conditional Density Estimation

Conditional PDFs form the backbone of most popular statistical methods in use today, though they are not often modeled directly in a parametric framework. They have perhaps received even less attention in a kernel framework. Nevertheless, as will be seen, they are extremely useful for a range of tasks including modeling count data or predicting consumer choice (see Cameron and Trivedi (1998) for a thorough treatment of count data models). In this chapter we discuss the nonparametric estimation of conditional PDFs. Throughout this chapter, we emphasize the practically relevant mixed discrete and continuous data case. Given the theoretical and practical advantages associated with smoothing discrete variables in a particular manner versus using a frequency-based approach, which we covered in Chapters 3 and 4, we shall proceed directly with smoothing both the discrete and continuous variables for what follows. Note that we may refer to conditioning variables as regressors even though we are estimating a conditional density rather than a regression function

5.1 Conditional Density Estimation: Relevant Variables

Let $f(\cdot)$ and $\mu(\cdot)$ denote the joint and marginal densities of (X, Y) and X, respectively. For what follows we shall refer to Y as a dependent variable (i.e., Y is explained), and to X as covariates (i.e., X is the explanatory variable). We use $\hat{f}$ and $\hat{\mu}$ to denote kernel estimators thereof, and we estimate the conditional density $g(y|x) = f(x, y)/\mu(x)$ by

$$\hat{g}(y|x) = \hat{f}(x, y)/\hat{\mu}(x). \tag{5.1}$$

We begin by considering the case for which Y is a univariate continuous random variable, and then we discuss the case for which Y is a univariate discrete variable. We treat the multivariate Y case in Section 5.4. Our estimators of $f(\cdot)$ and $\mu(\cdot)$ are given by

$$\hat{f}(x, y) = n^{-1} \sum_{i=1}^{n} K_\gamma(x, X_i) k_{h_0}(y, Y_i), \tag{5.2}$$

$$\hat{\mu}(x) = n^{-1} \sum_{i=1}^{n} K_\gamma(x, X_i), \tag{5.3}$$

where h_0 is the smoothing parameter associated with Y, $\gamma = (h, \lambda)$, and

$$K_\gamma(x, X_i) = W_h(x^c, X_i^c) L(x^d, X_i^d, \lambda),$$

$$W_h(x^c, X_i^c) = \prod_{s=1}^{q} \frac{1}{h_s} w\left(\frac{x_s^c - X_{is}^c}{h_s}\right),$$

$$L(x^d, X_i^d, \lambda) = \prod_{s=1}^{r} [\lambda_s/(c_s - 1)]^{N_{is}(x)} (1 - \lambda_s)^{1 - N_{is}(x)},$$

$N_{is}(x) = \mathbf{1}(X_{is}^d \neq x_s^d)$ is an indicator function that equals one when $X_{is}^d \neq x_s^d$, zero otherwise, and $k_{h_0}(y, Y_i) = h_0^{-1} k((y - Y_i)/h_0)$.

As we emphasized in previous chapters, data-driven methods of bandwidth selection such as cross-validation are required in applied settings. Below we discuss two different cross-validation methods. The first is based on minimizing a weighted integrated squared difference between $\hat{g}(y|x)$ and $g(y|x)$, and the second is a likelihood approach. As will be seen, the first method has some desirable optimality properties but can be computationally burdensome for large samples. The second method is computationally less costly but can lead to inconsistent estimates if the distribution for the continuous variables has fat tails.

5.2 Conditional Density Bandwidth Selection

5.2.1 Least Squares Cross-Validation: Relevant Variables

As was the case for unconditional density estimation, when estimating conditional densities with kernel methods we could pursue a least squares cross-validation approach to selecting smoothing parameters. We consider the following criterion based upon a weighted integrated square error ($\int dx = \sum_{x^d} \int dx^c$),

$$
\begin{aligned}
ISE &= \int \{\hat{g}(y|x) - g(y|x)\}^2 \, \mu(x) M(x^c) \, dxdy \\
&= I_{1n} - 2I_{2n} + I_{3n},
\end{aligned}
\tag{5.4}
$$

where $M(\cdot)$ is a weight function,

$$
I_{1n} = \int \hat{g}(y|x)^2 \mu(x) M(x^c) \, dxdy, \quad I_{2n} = \int \hat{g}(y|x) f(x,y) M(x^c) \, dxdy,
$$

and where $I_{3n} = \int g^2(y|x)\mu(x)M(x^c)\,dxdy$ does not depend on the smoothing parameters used to compute $\hat{f}$ and $\hat{\mu}$. Observe that

$$
I_{1n} = \int \hat{G}(x) \frac{\mu(x)}{\hat{\mu}(x)^2} M(x^c) \, dx = \mathrm{E}_X \left[\frac{\hat{G}(X)}{\hat{\mu}(X)^2} M(X^c) \right],
$$

where the expectation is with respect to X, not to the random observations $\{X_i, Y_i\}_{i=1}^n$ that are used to compute $\hat{G}(\cdot)$ and $\mu(\cdot)$, $\hat{G}(x) = \int \hat{f}(x,y)^2 dy$, and where $G(\cdot)$ is defined as

$$
\hat{G}(x) = \frac{1}{n^2} \sum_{i_1=1}^n \sum_{i_2=1}^n K_\gamma(x, X_{i_1}) K_\gamma(x, X_{i_2}) \int w_{h_0}(y, Y_{i_1}) w_{h_0}(y, Y_{i_2}) dy.
$$

Similarly, I_{2n} can be written as

$$
\mathrm{E}_Z[\hat{g}(Y|X)M(X^c)] = E_Z[\hat{f}(Y,X)M(X^c)/\hat{\mu}(X)],
$$

where the expectation is with respect to $Z = (Y, X)$. Therefore, the following cross-validation approximations, $\hat{I}_{1n}$ and $\hat{I}_{2n}$, for I_{1n} and I_{2n}, respectively, are adopted:

$$
\hat{I}_{1n} = \frac{1}{n} \sum_{i=1}^n \frac{\hat{G}_{-i}(X_i) M(X_i^c)}{\hat{\mu}_{-i}(X_i)^2}, \quad \hat{I}_{2n} = \frac{1}{n} \sum_{i=1}^n \frac{\hat{f}_{-i}(X_i, Y_i) M(X_i^c)}{\hat{\mu}_{-i}(X_i)},
$$

where the subscript $-i$ denotes leave-one-out estimators, for example,

$$\hat{G}_{-i}(X_i) = \frac{1}{(n-1)^2} \sum_{i_1=1, i_1 \neq i}^{n} \sum_{i_2=1, i_2 \neq i}^{n} K_n(X_i, X_{i_1}) K_n(X_i, X_{i_2})$$

$$\times \int w_{h_0}(y, Y_{i_1}) w_{h_0}(y, Y_{i_2}) dy.$$

Thus, our cross-validation objective function is given by

$$CV_g(h_0, h, \lambda) = \hat{I}_{1n}(h_0, h, \lambda) - 2\hat{I}_{2n}(h_0, h, \lambda),$$

where $(h, \lambda) = (h_1, \ldots, h_q, \lambda_1, \ldots, \lambda_r)$.

Along the lines of the analysis presented in Section 4.4.2, again using $\hat{\mu}(x)^{-1} = \mu(x)^{-1} + (\mu(x) - \hat{\mu}(x))/[\mu(x)\hat{\mu}(x)]$ to handle the presence of the random denominator, it is easy to see that the leading term of $\hat{g}(y|x) - g(y|x)$ is $[\hat{g}(y|x) - g(y|x)]\hat{\mu}(x)/\mu(x) = [\hat{f}(x,y) - \hat{\mu}(x)g(y|x)]/\mu(x)$. Hall et al. (2004) have further shown that the leading term of CV_g is

$$CV_{g0} = \int \left\{ \mathrm{E}\left[\hat{f}(x,y) - \hat{f}(x)g(y|x)\right]^2 M(x^c)/\mu(x)^2 \right\} dx dy. \quad (5.5)$$

Letting $\rho_s = \lambda_s/\{(1-\lambda_s)(c_s - 1)\}$, and letting $f_{00}(x^c, x^d, y)$ and $f_{ss}(x^c, x^d, y)$ denote the second derivative of $f(x^c, x^d, y)$ with respect to y and x_s^c respectively, we may write

$$\mathrm{E}\left\{\hat{f}(x,y)\right\} = \sum_{v^d} \left\{ \prod_{s=1}^{r} (1-\lambda_s)\rho_s^{1(v_s^d \neq x_s^d)} \right\} \left\{ \int \prod_{s=1}^{q} k(z_s) \right\} M(v)$$

$$\times f(x^c - hz, x^d, y - h_0 v) dz_1 \ldots dz_q dv$$

$$= f(x,y) + \sum_{s=1}^{r} \lambda_s \left\{ \frac{1}{c_s - 1} \sum_{v^d} 1_s(v^d, x^d) f(x^c, v^d, y) - f(x,y) \right\}$$

$$+ \frac{1}{2}\kappa_2 h_0^2 f_{00}(x, y) + \frac{1}{2}\kappa_2 \sum_{s=1}^{q} h_s^2 f_{ss}(x, y) + o(\eta_2),$$

$$(5.6)$$

where $\mathbf{1}_s(v^d, x^d)$ is defined in (4.24) and $\eta_2 = \sum_{s=1}^r \lambda_s + \sum_{s=0}^q h_s^2$, and

$$
E\{\hat{\mu}(x)\} = \sum_{v^d} P(X^d = v^d) \left\{ \prod_{s=1}^r (1-\lambda_s)\rho_s^{\mathbf{1}(v_s^d \neq x_s^d)} \right\}
$$

$$
\times \left\{ \int \prod_{s=1}^q k(z_s) \right\} M(v) f\left(x^c - hz, x^d, y - h_0 v\right) dz_1 \ldots dz_q dv
$$

$$
= \mu(x) + \sum_{s=1}^r \lambda_s \left\{ \frac{1}{c_s - 1} \sum_{v^d} \mathbf{1}_s(v^d, x^d)\mu(x^c, v^d) - \mu(x) \right\}
$$

$$
+ \frac{1}{2}\kappa_2 \sum_{s=1}^q h_s^2 \mu_{ss}(x, y) + o(\eta_2).
$$

$$(5.7)$$

Therefore, (5.6) and (5.7) lead to

$$
E\left\{\hat{f}(x,y) - \hat{\mu}(x)g(y|x)\right\}
$$

$$
= \prod_{s=1}^r (1-\lambda_s)\rho_s^{\mathbf{1}(v_s^d \neq x_s^d)} \left\{ f(x^c, v^d, y) - \frac{\mu(x^c, v^d)}{\mu(x)} f(x, y) \right\}
$$

$$
+ \frac{1}{2}\kappa_2 h_0^2 f_{00}(x,y) + \frac{1}{2}\kappa_2 \sum_{s=1}^q h_s^2 \left\{ f_{ss}(x,y) - \frac{\mu_{ss}(x)}{\mu(x)} f(x,y) \right\} + o(\eta_2).
$$

$$(5.8)$$

Note that

$$
\text{var}\left(\hat{f}(x,y) - \hat{\mu}(x)g(y|x)\right) = n^{-1}\text{var}\left[K_n(x, X_i)\left\{k_{h_0}(y, Y_i) - g(y|x)\right\}\right]
$$

$$
= n^{-1}E\left[\left\{K_n(x, X_i)k_{h_0}(y, Y_i)\right\}^2\right] + o(\eta_1)
$$

$$
= \kappa^{q+1} f(x,y)\eta_1 + o(\eta_1),
$$

$$(5.9)$$

where $\eta_1 = (nh_1 \ldots h_q)^{-1}$.

Combining (5.8) and (5.9) we can see that that

$$
CV_{g0}(h_0, h, \lambda) = n^{-q/(q+4)}\chi_g(a_0, a, b)
$$

$$(5.10)$$

where

$$
\chi_g(a_0, a, b) = \sum_{x^d} \int \left(\left[\sum_{s=1}^{r} \frac{b_s}{c_s - 1} \sum_{v^d} \mathbf{1}_s(v^d, x^d) \right. \right.
$$

$$
\times \left\{ f(x^c, v^d, y) - \frac{\mu(x^c, v^d)}{\mu(x)} f(x, y) \right\} + \frac{1}{2} \kappa_2 a_0^2 f_{00}(x, y)
$$

$$
\left. + \frac{1}{2} \kappa_2 \sum_{s=1}^{q} a_s^2 \left\{ f_{ss}(x, y) - \frac{\mu_{ss}(x)}{\mu(x)} f(x, y) \right\} \right]^2
$$

$$
\left. + \frac{\kappa^{q+1} f(x, y)}{a_1 \ldots a_q} \right) \frac{M(x^c)}{\mu(x)} \, dx^c dy, \tag{5.11}
$$

where the a_s's and b_s's are defined via $h_s = n^{-1/(q+5)} a_s$ and $\lambda_s = b_s n^{-2/(q+5)}$, respectively.

Letting $a_0^0, a_1^0, \ldots, a_q^0, b_1^0, \ldots, b_r^0$ denote those values that minimize χ_g, we assume that the a_s^0's and b_s^0's are uniquely determined and that each is finite. Let $h_1^0, \ldots, h_q^0, \lambda_1^0, \ldots, \lambda_r^0$ denote the values of $h_1, \ldots, \lambda_r$ that minimize CV_{g0}. Then $h_s^0 \sim n^{-1/(q+5)} a_s^0$ and $\lambda_s^0 \sim n^{-2/(q+5)} b_s^0$. Also, given that $CV_g = CV_{g0} + (s.o.)$, we expect that $\hat{h}_s = h_s^0 + (s.o.)$ and $\hat{\lambda}_s = \lambda_s^0 + (s.o.)$, which is indeed true as the next theorem shows.

Theorem 5.1.

$$
n^{1/(q+5)} \hat{h}_s \to a_s^0 \ \text{for } s = 0, 1, \ldots, q;
$$

$$
n^{2/(q+5)} \hat{\lambda}_s \to b_s^0 \ \text{for } s = 1, \ldots, r; \tag{5.12}
$$

$$
n^{4/(q+5)} \inf CV_g \to \inf \chi_g \ \text{in probability}.
$$

The proof of (5.12) is given in Hall et al. (2004).

Using Theorem 5.1, we can derive the asymptotic distribution of $\hat{g}(y|x)$. We postpone this result until Section 5.3 where we discuss a more general case that allows for the existence of irrelevant covariates.

5.2.2 Maximum Likelihood Cross-Validation: Relevant Variables

The least squares cross-validation approach discussed in Section 5.2.1 has some desirable optimality properties, which were given in Theorem 5.1. However, least squares cross-validation in the context of conditional PDFs is computationally costly, particularly when the sample size is large. This is because the objective function CV_g (i.e., $\hat{I}_{1n}$) involves three summations. When the sample size is small, one can realize substantial speed improvements by storing temporary weight matrices in computer memory rather than recomputing their components when computing CV_g, but for even moderate sample sizes, the memory required for storage of these weight matrices will quickly overwhelm the memory capacity of most computers. This is a classical computational trade-off – memory versus speed. In contrast, however, likelihood cross-validation has a substantial advantage from a computational perspective, as we show below.

The likelihood cross-validation method involves choosing h_1, ..., h_q, λ_1, ..., λ_r by maximizing the log-likelihood function

$$\mathcal{L} = \sum_{i=1}^{n} \ln \hat{g}_{-i}(Y_i | X_i), \tag{5.13}$$

where $\hat{g}_{-i}(Y_i | X_i) = \hat{f}_{-i}(X_i, Y_i) / \hat{m}_{-i}(X_i)$, and $\hat{f}_{-i}(X_i, Y_i)$ and $\hat{m}_{-i}(X_i)$ are the leave-one-out kernel estimators of $f(X_i, Y_i)$ and $\mu(X_i)$, respectively. The objective function (5.13) involves one less summation than that for least squares cross-validation, and is therefore less computationally burdensome. One problem with likelihood cross-validation arises when the continuous variables are drawn from fat tailed distributions. In such cases, likelihood cross-validation tends to oversmooth the data, and may lead to inconsistent estimation results (see Hall (1987a, 1987b)).

Two practical methods can be used to prevent this from happening. First, one can compare the likelihood cross-validatory smoothing parameters with some ad hoc formula (say, $h_s = x_{cd} n^{-1/(q+4)}$), and if the two sets of smoothing parameters are comparable, then it is unlikely that the cross-validation method has oversmoothed. When likelihood cross-validation oversmooths the data, there are two possibilities: either it leads to inconsistent estimation, or the related variable is irrelevant. We note that, in the latter case, oversmoothing is in fact highly desirable. To distinguish between these two cases, one can therefore use a second method that compares the out-of-sample predictions based on likelihood cross-validation with those based upon a parametric method. If the nonparametric method behaves better than or is comparable to its parametric counterpart on the hold-out data, this indicates that likelihood cross-validation has probably not fallen victim to the potential inconsistency problem. Of course, should the least squares cross-validation method be computationally feasible, the least squares cross-validated smoothing parameters should also be computed and they then can be used to judge whether likelihood cross-validation has produced unreasonably large smoothing parameters.

5.3 Conditional Density Estimation: Irrelevant Variables

We now consider the case for which some of the covariates may be irrelevant. Using notation defined in Section 4.5, for integers $0 \leq q_1, q_2 \leq q$ and $0 \leq r_1, r_2 \leq r$ satisfying $q_1 + q_2 = q$ and $r_1 + r_2 = r$, let $\bar{X}$ be composed of the first q_1 components of X^c and the first r_1 components of X^d, and $\tilde{X} = X/\bar{X}$ denote the remaining components of X. We assume that

$$(Y, \bar{X}) \text{ is independent of } \tilde{X}. \tag{5.14}$$

Condition (5.14) implies that $g(y|\bar{x}, \tilde{x}) = g(y|\bar{x})$, i.e., that the irrelevant variable $\tilde{x}$ does not affect $g(y|\bar{x})$. Again we do not assume this information is known a priori, and in practice we estimate $g(y|x)$ rather than $g(y|\bar{x})$. We will show that by selecting smoothing parameters via the cross-validation approach, the irrelevant variables can be (asymptotically) smoothed out.

The χ_g function now needs to be modified as follows:

$$
\begin{aligned}
\bar{\chi}_g(a_0, a, b) = \sum_{\bar{x}^d} \int \Bigg(\Bigg[& \sum_{s=1}^{r_1} \frac{b_s}{c_s - 1} \sum_{\bar{v}^d} \mathbf{1}_s(\bar{v}_s^d, \bar{x}_s^d) \\
& \times \left\{ \bar{f}(\bar{x}^c, \bar{v}^d, y) - \frac{\bar{\mu}(\bar{x}^c, \bar{v}^d)}{\bar{\mu}(\bar{x})} \bar{f}(\bar{x}, y) \right\} + \frac{1}{2} \kappa_2 a_0^2 \bar{f}_{00}(\bar{x}, y) \\
& + \frac{1}{2} \kappa_2 \sum_{s=1}^{q_1} a_s^2 \left\{ \bar{f}_{ss}(\bar{x}, y) - \frac{\bar{\mu}_{ss}(\bar{x})}{\bar{\mu}(\bar{x})} \bar{f}(\bar{x}, y) \right\} \Bigg]^2 \\
& + \frac{\kappa^{q_1+1} \bar{f}(\bar{x}, y)}{a_1 \dots a_{q_1}} \Bigg) \frac{\bar{w}(\bar{x})}{\bar{\mu}(\bar{x})} d\bar{x}^c dy,
\end{aligned}
\tag{5.15}
$$

where

$$
\bar{w}(\bar{x}^c, \bar{x}^d) = \\
\sum_{x_{r_1+1}^d, \dots, x_r^d} \int \frac{w(\bar{x}^c, x_{q_1+1}^c, \dots, x_q^c)}{f(\bar{x}^c, x_{q_1+1}^c, \dots, x_q^c, \bar{x}^d, x_{r_1+1}^d, \dots x_r^d)} dx_{q_1+1}^c \dots dx_q^c.
$$

We know from Theorem 4.8 that for nonparametric regression, least squares cross-validation asymptotically smooths out irrelevant variables. The next theorem shows that similar results hold true for cross-validated conditional density estimation.

Theorem 5.2. *Under conditions similar to those given in Theorem 4.8 and letting $\hat{h}_1,\ldots,\hat{h}_q,\hat{\lambda}_1,\ldots,\hat{\lambda}_r$ denote the smoothing parameters that minimize CV_g, then*

$$n^{1/(q_1+5)}\hat{h}_s \overset{p}{\to} a_s^0 \text{ for } 1 \leq j \leq q_1;$$

$$\mathrm{P}(\hat{h}_s > C) \to 1 \text{ for } q_1+1 \leq s \leq q \text{ and for all } C > 0;$$

$$n^{2/(q_1+5)}\hat{\lambda}_s \overset{p}{\to} b_s^0 \text{ for } 1 \leq s \leq r_1;$$

$$\hat{\lambda}_s \overset{p}{\to} \frac{c_s - 1}{c_s} \text{ for } r_1+1 \leq j \leq r;$$

$$n^{4/(q_1+5)}\inf CV_r(\hat{h},\hat{\lambda}) \overset{p}{\to} \inf \bar{\chi}. \tag{5.16}$$

The proof of Theorem 5.2 is given by Hall et al. (2004). Like Theorem 4.8, Theorem 5.2 states that cross-validated smoothing parameter selection is asymptotically capable of removing irrelevant conditioning variables. The following theorem provides the asymptotic normal distribution of $\hat{g}(y|x)$.

Theorem 5.3. *Letting $\hat{g}(y|x)$ be computed using the cross-validation smoothing parameters $\hat{h}_0,\ldots,\hat{h}_q,\hat{\lambda}_1,\ldots,\hat{\lambda}_r$, then*

$$\left(n\hat{h}_1\ldots\hat{h}_{q_1}\right)^{1/2}\left(\tilde{g}(y|x) - g(y|x) - \sum_{s=1}^{q_1}B_{1s}(\bar{x},y)\hat{h}_s^2 - \sum_{s=1}^{r_1}B_{2s}(\bar{x},y)\hat{\lambda}_s\right)$$

$$\to N\left(0,\sigma_g^2(\bar{x},y)\right) \text{ in distribution,}$$

$$\tag{5.17}$$

where

$$B_{1s}(\bar{x},y) = \frac{1}{2}\kappa\hat{h}_0^2\bar{g}_{00}(y|\bar{x}) + \frac{1}{2}\kappa_2\sum_{s=1}^{q_1}\hat{h}_s^2\left\{\frac{\bar{f}_{ss}(y|\bar{x})}{\bar{\mu}(\bar{x})} - \frac{\bar{\mu}_{ss}(\bar{x})}{\bar{\mu}(\bar{x})}\bar{g}(y|\bar{x})\right\},$$

$$B_{2s}(\bar{x},y) = \sum_{s=1}^{r_1}\frac{\hat{\lambda}_s}{c_s-1}\sum_{\bar{v}^d}1_s(\bar{v}^d,x_s^d)\left\{\bar{g}(y|\bar{x}^c,\bar{v}^d) - \frac{\bar{\mu}(\bar{x}^c,\bar{v}^d)}{\bar{\mu}(\bar{x})}\bar{g}(y|\bar{x})\right\},$$

$$\sigma_g^2(\bar{x},y) = \kappa^{q_1+1}\bar{g}(y|\bar{x})/\bar{\mu}(\bar{x}).$$

So far we have assumed that Y is a continuous random variable. Now we turn our attention to the case for which Y is discrete. If Y assumes c_0 different values, then we replace the continuous kernel $k_{h_0}(y, Y_i) = h_0^{-1} k((y - Y_i)/h_0)$ by the categorical kernel $l(y, Y_i, \lambda_0) = \lambda_0^{N_i(y)}(1 - \lambda_0)^{1-N_i(y)}$, where $N_i(y) = \mathbf{1}(Y_i \neq y)$. Theorem 5.2 can be modified by replacing $q_1 + 5$ with $q_1 + 4$, and by replacing $n^{1/(q_1+5)}\hat{h}_0 \to a_0^0$ with $n^{2/(q_1+4)}\hat{\lambda}_0 \to b_0^0$, where b_0^0 is defined in a way similar to b_s^0 for $s = 1, \dots, r$. Theorem 5.3 also requires minor modification (see Exercise 5.1).

Theorems 5.2 and 5.3 are quite powerful results, particularly for data containing a mix of discrete and continuous data, having the potential to extend the reach of nonparametric methods. In Section 5.5 we show, via several empirical applications, that "irrelevant" variables occur quite often for various datasets and that cross-validated conditional density estimates can outperform some commonly used parametric methods in terms of their out-of-sample predictions, even for situations in which the number of discrete cells is comparable to the sample size.

5.4 The Multivariate Dependent Variables Case

In this section we consider the estimation of the conditional PDF of Y given X when Y is also a general multivariate vector. Let $Z = (X, Y)$, and we shall also write $Z = (Z^c, Z^d)$, where Z^d consists of r discrete variables, and where $Z^c \in \mathbb{R}^q$ represents the continuous components. For expositional simplicity, we first consider the case where Z^d is a vector of nominal variables (i.e., having no natural ordering) with $Z^d \in \prod_{s=1}^{r}\{0, 1, \dots, c_s - 1\}$. We write $Y = (Y^c, Y^d)$, $X = (X^c, X^d)$, and assume that Y^c contains the first q_y continuous components of Z^c while Y^d contains the first r_y discrete components of Z^d. Thus, $Y^c \in \mathbb{R}^{q_y}$, $Y^d \in \prod_{s=1}^{r_y}\{0, 1, \dots, c_s - 1\}$, $X^c \in \mathbb{R}^{q-q_y}$. Similarly, $X^d \in \prod_{s=r_y+1}^{r}\{0, 1, \dots, c_s - 1\}$.

As before, let $f(z) = f(y, x)$ denote the joint PDF of (Y, X),[1] $\mu(x)$ the marginal PDF of X, and $g(y|x) = f(y, x)/\mu(x)$ the conditional PDF of Y given $X = x$.

---

[1] Depending on the situation, we sometimes may write the joint density as $f(z^c, z^d)$ rather than $f(y, x)$, where $z^c = (y^c, x^c)$ and $z^d = (y^d, x^d)$.

We use Z_{is}^d to denote the sth component of Z_i^d. As in Section 5.1, for Z_{is}^d, $Z_{js}^d \in \{0, 1, \ldots, c_s - 1\}$, we define a univariate kernel function $l(Z_{is}^d, Z_{js}^d, \lambda_s) = 1 - \lambda_s$ if $Z_{is}^d = Z_{js}^d$, and $l(Z_{is}^d, Z_{js}^d, \lambda_s) = \lambda_s/(c_s - 1)$ if $Z_{is}^d \neq Z_{js}^d$. The product kernel is given by $L_{\lambda, Z_i^d, Z_j^d} = \prod_{s=1}^{r} l(Z_{is}^d, Z_{js}^d, \lambda_s)$.

Letting Z_{is}^c denote the sth component of Z_i^c, $w(\cdot)$ denote a univariate kernel function, and $W(\cdot)$ denote a product kernel function for Z^c, we write $W_{h, Z_i^c, Z_j^c} \overset{\text{def}}{=} \prod_{s=1}^{q} h_s^{-1} w((Z_{is}^c - Z_{js}^c)/h_s)$.

To avoid introducing too much notation, we shall use the same notation $L(\cdot)$ and $W(\cdot)$ to denote the product kernel for Y^d and Y^c, i.e., $L_{\lambda_y, Y_i^d, Y_j^d} = \prod_{s=1}^{r_y} l(Y_{is}^d, Y_{js}^d, \lambda_s)$ and $W_{h_y, Y_i^c, Y_j^c} = \prod_{s=1}^{q_y} h_s^{-1} w((Y_{is}^c - Y_{js}^c)/h_s)$. Similarly, we define $L_{\lambda_x, X_i^d, X_j^d} = \prod_{s=1}^{r_x} l(X_{is}^d, X_{js}^d, \lambda_{r_y+s})$ and $W_{h_x, X_i^c, X_j^c} \overset{\text{def}}{=} \prod_{s=1}^{q-q_y} h_{q_y+s}^{-1} ((X_{is}^c - X_{js}^c)/h_{q_y+s})$.

We estimate $f(z)$ and $\mu(x)$ by

$$\hat{f}(y, x) = \hat{f}(z) = \frac{1}{n} \sum_{i=1}^{n} K_{\gamma, Z_i, z} \text{ and } \hat{\mu}(x) = \frac{1}{n} \sum_{i=1}^{n} K_{\gamma_x, X_i, x}, \qquad (5.18)$$

where $K_{\gamma, Z_i, z} = L_{\lambda, z_i^d, z^d} W_{h, Z_i^c, z^c}$ and $K_{\gamma_x, X_i, x} = L_{\lambda_x, X_i^d, x^d} W_{h_x, X_i^c, x^c}$. Therefore, we estimate $g(y|x) = f(x, y)/m(x)$ by

$$\hat{g}(y|x) = \frac{\hat{f}(x, y)}{\hat{\mu}(x)}. \qquad (5.19)$$

We choose the smoothing parameters by cross-validation methods which minimize a sample analogue of a weighted integrated square error I_n, where ($\int dz = \sum_{z^d} \int dz^c$) $I_n = \int [\hat{g}(y|x) - g(y|x)]^2 \mu(x) \, dz = I_{1n} - 2I_{2n} + I_{3n}$, $I_{1n} = \int [\hat{g}(y|x)]^2 \mu(x) \, dz$, $I_{2n} = \int \hat{g}(y|x) g(y|x) \mu(x) \, dz$, and $I_{3n} = \int [g(y|x)]^2 \mu(x) \, dz$. As before I_{3n} is independent of (h, λ). Therefore, minimizing I_n over (h, λ) is equivalent to minimizing $I_{1n} - 2I_{2n}$.

Define the leave-one-out estimators for $\hat{f}(X_l, Y_l)$ and $\hat{\mu}(X_l)$ to be

$$\hat{f}_{-l}(X_l, Y_l) = \frac{1}{n} \sum_{i=1, i \neq l}^{n} K_{Z_i, Z_l} \text{ and}$$

$$\hat{\mu}_{-l}(X_l) = \frac{1}{n} \sum_{i=1, i \neq l}^{n} K_{X_i, X_l}. \qquad (5.20)$$

Also define $G_{-l}(X_l)$ to be

$$\hat{G}_{-l}(X_l) = n^{-2} \sum_{i \neq l} \sum_{j \neq l} K_{X_i, X_l} K_{X_j, X_l} K^{(2)}_{Y_i, Y_j}, \qquad (5.21)$$

where $K^{(2)}_{Y_i, Y_j} = \sum_{y^d} \int K_{\gamma_y, Y_i, y} dy^c$.

Then by arguments similar to those used in Section 5.1, Racine et al. (2004) show that a consistent estimator of $I_{1n} - I_{2n}$ is given by

$$CV(h, \lambda) \stackrel{\text{def}}{=} \frac{1}{n} \sum_{l=1}^{n} \frac{\hat{G}_{-l}(X_l)}{[\hat{\mu}_{-l}(X_l)]^2} - \frac{2}{n} \sum_{l=1}^{n} \frac{\hat{f}_{-l}(X_l, Y_l)}{\hat{\mu}_{-l}(X_l)}, \qquad (5.22)$$

where $\hat{f}_{-l}(X_l, Y_l)$, $\hat{\mu}_{-l}(X_l)$, and $\hat{G}_{-l}(X_l)$ are defined in (5.20) and (5.21).

We then choose $(h, \lambda) = (h_1, \ldots, h_q, \lambda_1, \ldots, \lambda_r)$ to minimize the objective function $CV(h, \lambda)$ defined in (5.22). Let $(\hat{h}, \hat{\lambda})$ denote the cross-validation choices of (h, λ). Since we know that irrelevant independent variables will be asymptotically smoothed out, in the analysis below we will only consider the case where the independent variables are all relevant. Racine et al. (2004) show that $\hat{h}_s/h_s^0 \overset{p}{\to} 1$ and $\hat{\lambda}_s/\lambda_s^0 \overset{p}{\to} 1$, where

$h_s^0 = c_{1s} n^{-1/(4+q)}$ for $s = 1, \ldots, q$, and $\lambda_s^0 = c_{2s} n^{-2/(4+q)}$ for $s = 1, \ldots, r$, where c_{1s} and c_{2s} are some constants. (h^0, λ^0) are the nonstochastic optimal smoothing parameters that minimize the leading term of the cross-validation function. (5.23)

Theorem 5.4, proved in Racine et al. (2004), establishes the rate of convergence of $(\hat{h}, \hat{\lambda})$ to (h^0, λ^0).

Theorem 5.4. *Under assumptions given in Racine et al. (2004), we have $(\hat{h}_s - h_s^0)/h_s^0 = O_p(n^{-\alpha/(4+q)})$ for $s = 1, \ldots, q$, and we have $\hat{\lambda}_s - \lambda_s^0 = O_p(n^{-\beta})$ for $s = 1, \ldots, r$, where $\alpha = \min\{2, q/2\}$ and $\beta = \min\{1/2, 4/(4+q)\}$.*

Given Theorem 5.4, one can further show the following:

Theorem 5.5. *Define*

$$B_{1s}(z) = (1/2)\kappa_2 f_{ss}(y|x)/\mu(x)$$

for $s = 1, \dots, q_y$, *and let*

$$B_{1s}(z) = (1/2)\kappa_2[f_{ss}(z) - \mu_{ss}(x)g(y|x)]/\mu(x)$$

for $s = q_y + 1, \dots, q$. *Also, define*

$$B_{2s} = \frac{1}{c_s - 1} \sum_{v^d \in \mathcal{D}} I_s(v^d, z^d)f(z^c, v^d)$$

for $s = 1, \dots, r_y$,

$$B_{2s}(z) = \frac{1}{c_s - 1} \sum_{u^d \in \mathcal{D}_x} I_s(u^d, x^d)[f(z^c, y^d, u^d) - g(y|x)\mu(x^c, u^d)]/\mu(x)$$

for $s = r_y + 1, \dots, r$, *and* $\Omega(z) = \kappa^q g(y|x)/\mu(x)$. *Then*

$$\sqrt{n\hat{h}_1 \dots h_q} \left[\hat{g}(y|x) - g(y|x) - \sum_{s=1}^{q} \hat{h}^2 B_{1s}(z) - \sum_{s=1}^{r} \hat{\lambda}_s B_{2s}(z) \right]$$

converges to $N(0, \Omega(z))$ *in distribution.*

The proof of Theorem 5.5 is given in Section 5.4.2.

We now discuss how to extend the above analysis to also cover the case for which Z^d contains ordered categorical variables.

5.4.1 The General Categorical Data Case

For ordered categorical variables, Aitchison and Aitken (1976, p. 29) suggest using the kernel weight function given by

$$l_{AA}(Y_{is}^d, Y_{js}^d, \lambda_s) = \binom{c_s}{t} \lambda_s^t (1 - \lambda_s)^{c_s - t} \text{ when } |Y_{is}^d - Y_{js}^d| = t, \quad (5.24)$$

for $0 \le t \le c_s$, where $\binom{c_s}{t} = c_s!/[t!(c_s - t)!]$. As discussed previously, this kernel function has the advantage that it leads to a proper density estimator (the kernel l_{AA} sums to one), but it has the disadvantage that it cannot smooth out irrelevant variables. Since irrelevant discrete variables can occur only among the covariates X^d, we suggest using the l_{AA} kernel defined in (5.24) only for the dependent discrete ordered variables (Y^d), while for the independent ordered discrete variables X^d, we suggest using the following kernel function:

$$l(X_{s,i}^d, X_{s,j}^d, \lambda_s) = \lambda_s^t \text{ when } |X_{s,i}^d - X_{s,j}^d| = t, \quad (5.25)$$

for $0 \le t \le c_s$, where $\lambda_s \in [0,1]$. When $\lambda_s = 1$, we obtain a uniform weight of 1, so with this choice of kernel function, irrelevant components of X^d can automatically be removed. Note that we do not need the kernels associated with X^d to sum to one, since the kernel associated with X^d appears in both the numerator and denominator in the conditional density estimate, hence any nonzero constant multiplying the kernel function will cancel out from the numerator and the denominator, leaving the estimator unchanged.

The results of Theorem 5.4 and Theorem 5.5 can also be easily extended to cover the case for which some of the discrete variables have natural orderings while others do not, except that $\frac{1}{c_s-1}\mathbf{1}_s(u^d, x^d)$ must be replaced by $\mathbf{1}(|u_s^d - x_s^d| = 1)\prod_{t \ne s}\mathbf{1}(u_t^d = x_t^d)$ when x_s^d has a natural ordering, and $\frac{1}{c_s-1}\mathbf{1}_s(v^d, y^d)$ must be replaced by $\frac{1}{c_s}\mathbf{1}(|y_s^d - v_s^d| = 1)\prod_{t \ne s}\mathbf{1}(y_t^d = v_t^d)$ when y_s^d has an natural ordering (since $\binom{c_s}{1} = 1/c_s$).

5.4.2 Proof of Theorem 5.5

Proof. By using stochastic equicontinuity arguments, we know that the asymptotic distribution of $\hat{g}(y|x)$ remains the same whether we use the stochastic smoothing parameters $\hat{h}_s$, $\hat{\lambda}_s$, or the nonstochastic smoothing parameters $h_s = c_{1s}n^{-1/(4+q)}$ and $\lambda_s = c_{2s}n^{-2/(4+q)}$ defined in (5.23). Therefore, we consider only the nonstochastic smoothing parameter case in this proof.

Letting

$$K_{\gamma_y, y_i, y} = W_{h_y, y_i^c, y^c} L_{\lambda_y, y_i^d, y^d} \text{ and } K_{\gamma_x, y_i, y} = W_{h_x, x_i^c, x^c} L_{\lambda_x, x_i^d, x^d},$$

we estimate $f(y, x)$, $\mu(x)$ and $g(y|x)$ by

$$\hat{f}(y, x) = \frac{1}{n}\sum_{i=1}^{n} K_{\gamma_y, y_i, y} K_{\gamma_x, x_i, x},$$

$$\hat{\mu}(x) = \frac{1}{n}\sum_{i=1}^{n} K_{\gamma_x, x_i, x}, \text{ and}$$

$$\hat{g}(y|x) = \frac{\hat{f}(y, x)}{\hat{\mu}(x)},$$

respectively.

To derive the asymptotic normality of $\hat{g}(y|x) - g(y|x)$, we write

$$\hat{g}(y|x) - g(y|x) = \frac{[\hat{g}(y|x) - g(y|x)]\hat{\mu}(x)}{\hat{\mu}(x)} \equiv \frac{\hat{m}(y,x)}{\hat{\mu}(x)},$$

where $\hat{m}(y,x) = [\hat{g}(y|x) - g(y|x)]\hat{\mu}(x) \equiv \hat{f}(y,x) - g(y|x)\hat{\mu}(x)$.

We compute $\mathrm{E}[\hat{m}(y,x)]$ and $\mathrm{var}(\hat{m}(y,x))$ below. Note that

$$\mathrm{E}[\hat{m}(y,x)] = \mathrm{E}[\hat{f}(y,x)] - g(y|x)\mathrm{E}[\hat{\mu}(x)], \tag{5.26}$$

while

$$\mathrm{E}[\hat{f}(y,x)] = f(y,x) + \frac{\kappa_2}{2}\sum_{s=1}^{q} h_s^2 f_{ss}(y,x)$$

$$+ \sum_{s=1}^{r} \frac{\lambda_s}{c_s - 1} \sum_{v^d \in \mathcal{D}} I_s(v^d, z^d) f(z^c, v^d) + o\left(|h|^2 + |\lambda|\right), \tag{5.27}$$

where $f_{ss}(z) = \partial f^2(z)/\partial(z_s^c)^2$ for $s = 1, \dots, q$, $\kappa_2 = \int k(v)^2\, dv$, $|h|^2 = \sum_{s=1}^{q} h_s^2$ and $|\lambda| = \sum_{s=1}^{r} \lambda_s$.

Similarly,

$$\mathrm{E}[\hat{\mu}(x)] = \mu(x) + \frac{\kappa_2}{2}\sum_{s=q_y+1}^{q} h_s^2 \mu_{ss}(x)$$

$$+ \sum_{s=r_y+1}^{r} \frac{\lambda_s}{c_s - 1} \sum_{u^d \in \mathcal{D}_x} I_s(u^d, x^d)\mu(x^c, u^d) + o\left(|h_x|^2 + |\lambda_x|\right), \tag{5.28}$$

where $|h_x|^2 = \sum_{s=q_y+1}^{q} h_s^2$ and $|\lambda_x| = \sum_{s=r_x+1}^{r} \lambda_s$.

Substituting (5.27) and (5.28) into (5.26), we obtain

$$\mathrm{E}[\hat{m}(y,x)] = \sum_{s=1}^{q} h_s^2 B_{1s}(z) + \sum_{s=1}^{r} \lambda_s B_{2s}(z) + o\left(|h|^2 + |\lambda|\right). \tag{5.29}$$

Next, using the notation $H_q = h_1 \ldots h_q$, $\int dz = \sum_{z^d} \int dz^c$, we have

$$
\begin{aligned}
\operatorname{var}[\hat{m}(y,x)] &= \operatorname{var}\left[\hat{f}(y,x) - g(y|x)\hat{\mu}(x)\right] \\
&= \frac{1}{n}\left\{\operatorname{var}\left(\left[K_{\gamma_y,y_i,y} - g(y|x)\right]K_{\gamma_x,x_i,x}\right)\right\} \\
&= \frac{1}{n}\left\{\mathrm{E}\left\{\left[K_{\gamma_y,y_i,y} - g(y|x)\right]^2 K_{x_i,x}^2\right\} + O(1)\right\} \\
&= \frac{1}{n}\left\{\mathrm{E}\left[K_{\gamma_y,y_i,y}^2 K_{\gamma_x,x_i,x}^2\right] + O(1)\right\} \\
&= n^{-1}\left\{\int f(z_i) K_{\gamma,z_i,z}^2\, dz_i + O(1)\right\} \\
&= n^{-1}\left\{H_q^{-1}\int f\left(z^c + hv, z^d\right) W^2(v)\, dv + o\left(H_q^{-1}\right)\right\} \\
&= (nH_q)^{-1}\kappa^q f(y,x) + (s.o.).
\end{aligned}
$$

$$(5.30)$$

Equations (5.29) and (5.30) give the leading bias and leading variance terms for $\hat{m}(y,x)$. With optimal smoothing, i.e., $h_s \sim n^{-1/(4+q)}$ for $s = 1, \ldots, q$ and $\lambda_s \sim n^{-2/(4+q)}$ for $s = 1, \ldots, r$, then by (5.29), (5.30) and applying the Liapunov CLT, we know that

$$
\sqrt{nH_q}\left\{\hat{m}(y,x) - \left[\sum_{s=1}^{q} h_s^2 B_{1s}(z) + \sum_{s=1}^{r} \lambda_s B_{2s}(z)\right]\right\}
$$
$$
\xrightarrow{d} N\left(0, \kappa^q f(y,x)\right).
$$

$$(5.31)$$

Note that it is well established that

$$
\hat{\mu}(x) - \mu(x) = O_p\left(\sum_{s=g_y+1}^{q} h_s^2 + (nh_{g_y+1}\ldots h_q)^{-1/2}\right).
$$

$$(5.32)$$

Combining (5.31) and (5.32) we immediately have

$$\sqrt{nH_q}\left[\hat{g}(y|x) - g(y|x) - \sum_{s=1}^{q}h_s^2 B_{1s}(z) - \sum_{s=1}^{r}\lambda_s B_{2s}(z)\right]$$

$$\equiv \sqrt{nH_q}\left\{\hat{m}(y,x) - \hat{\mu}(x)\left[\sum_{s=1}^{q}h_s^2 B_{1s}(z) + \sum_{s=1}^{r}B_{2s}(z)\right]\right\}/\hat{\mu}(x)$$

$$= \sqrt{nH_q}\left\{\hat{m}(y,x) - \mu(x)\left[\sum_{s=1}^{q}h_s^2 B_{1s}(z) + \sum_{s=1}^{r}B_{2s}(z)\right]\right\}/\mu(x) + o_p(1)$$

$$\xrightarrow{d} \frac{1}{\mu(x)}N\left(0, \kappa^q f(y,x)\right) = N\left(0, \kappa^q g(y|x)/\mu(x)\right).$$

$$(5.33)$$

$\square$

5.5 Applications

5.5.1 A Nonparametric Analysis of Corruption

Political corruption (or the perception thereof) plays a central role in political theory and in the theory of economic development. Whether or not there is convergence in corruption across countries over time, or whether similarities in the distribution of corruption persist over time remains a subject of ongoing debate.

The Corruption Perception Index (CPI)[2] ranks countries in terms of perceived corruption. The CPI lies in the range 0–10 with 10 indicating the absence of corruption. In the spirit of analysis done by McAdam and Rummel (2004), who considered a panel of 40 countries having full records for the years 1995–2002, we create a balanced panel of 45 countries having full records for the nine year period 1996–2004. For this panel of $n = 405$ observations, we estimate the conditional PDF of CPI conditional upon year using the approach discussed in this chapter. The estimated conditional PDF is plotted in Figure 5.1.

We treat year as an ordered categorical variable, and the LSCV bandwidths are $\hat{h}_{\text{CPI}} = 0.224$ and $\hat{\lambda}_{\text{year}} = 1.00$ (the upper bound value for λ_{year}). The cross-validated value of $\hat{\lambda}_{\text{year}}$ suggests that pooling of the data for all years is appropriate, i.e., that there has been no appreciable change in the distribution over time. This finding supports

---

[2]http://www.transparency.org/cpi/.

$\hat{f}(\text{CPI}|\text{Year})$

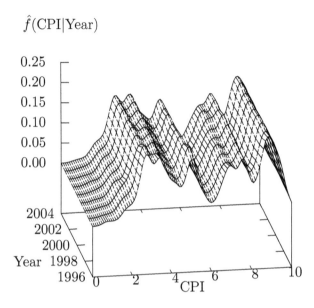

Figure 5.1: The conditional PDF of the Corruption Perception Index for 1996–2004, $n = 405$.

the persistence hypothesis (i.e., distributional stability across time), while the shape of the estimated PDF is consistent with multiple equilibria (i.e., multiple modes). These results are consistent with those of McAdam and Rummel (2004, p. 509), who report that "our findings lend support to concerns expressed in the theoretical literature - namely, that corruption can be highly persistent, and characterized by multiple equilibria."

5.5.2   Extramarital Affairs Data

In a widely cited paper, Fair (1978) proposes a "theory of extramarital affairs" and considers the allocation of an individual's time among work and two types of leisure activities, time spent with one's spouse and time spent with one's "paramour." The unique dataset is taken from two magazine surveys, and Fair considers a parametric Tobit estimator for modeling the number of extramarital affairs per year. This dataset and the econometric methodology continue to generate interest, as witnessed by Pagan and Vella's (1989), Chernozhukov and Hong's (2002), Wells's (2003), and Li and Racine's (2004b) reexaminations of the evidence and econometric methodology used in the original study.

One of the rather fascinating aspects of this study is the potential influence of an individual's personal characteristics on propensity to engage in extracurricular activities. In particular, Fair (1978) found that infidelity increased significantly with the number of years married. Pagan and Vella (1989) questioned the validity of this finding via numerous diagnostic tests, and also suggested that a discrete count model is more appropriate than the Tobit model used by Fair, while the analysis undertaken by Wells (2003) concluded that perhaps people do tend to "play around" the longer they have been married.

The data consist of 601 observations on 9 variables, sex (0/1), age (9 groups), years married (8 groups), children (0/1), how religious (1–5), level of education (7 groups), occupation (7 groups), marriage rating (1–5), and number of times subject engaged in extramarital sexual intercourse during the past year (0 = none, 1 = once, 2 = twice, 3 = three times, 7 = 4–10 times, 12 = monthly or more frequent). Clearly each of these variables is categorical by nature.

The Tobit specification employed by Fair (1978) has a positive and significant parameter associated with number of years married, as does a Poisson count model and a simple linear model. However, these models share a common feature, the linear index specification. The discrete and unordered nature of some of the variables would call into question the appropriateness of such specifications, as would the lack of interaction terms.

One of the features of automatic bandwidth selection methods such as cross-validation is their ability to remove irrelevant variables by choosing a large value for the associated bandwidths. We therefore apply the cross-validated conditional density estimator and examine the performance of the cross-validated bandwidths. We treat sex, children, and occupation as unordered and the remaining variables as ordered categorical variables.

We observe from Table 5.1 that the cross-validated smoothing parameter associated with number of years married lies at its upper bound value, indicating that number of years married is not relevant for the prediction of the number of affairs. In fact, the only variables that appear to be relevant from a predictive standpoint are age, how religious a respondent claims to be and, not surprisingly, how respondents rate

Table 5.1: Conditional density, LSCV

Variable	$\hat{\lambda}$	Upper Bound
Number of affairs	0.019	0.833
Sex	0.500	0.500
Children	0.500	0.500
Occupation	0.857	0.857
Age	0.886	1.000
Years married	1.000	1.000
Religious	0.290	1.000
Education	1.000	1.000
Marriage rating	0.329	1.000

their marriage.

To better understand why nonparametric and parametric methods yield differing results, we consider the nonparametric estimation results in more detail. Figure 5.2 plots the expected number of affairs conditional upon age from the nonparametric model when all remaining covariates are held constant at their median values. We observe that the relationship between age and number of affairs is nonlinear, being flat and/or upward sloping for younger ages, and exhibiting a downward trend for people over 40. Thus, the nonparametric results suggest that age has a nonlinear effect on the number of affairs, while the number of years of marriage is independent of the number of affairs conditional on age and other relevant covariates. Years of marriage and age are highly correlated covariates, and simple parametric models assume that each covariate has either a globally positive or negative effect only. When the true relationship is nonlinear, say in age, age has a positive effect over one range and a negative effect over another. The parametric models appear to erroneously attribute a negative effect to the age covariate, and in an attempt to model nonlinearity in age with a linear index function (the upward sloping portion for younger ages), the parametric model picks an irrelevant covariate (which is highly correlated with young age) and assigns a significant positive sign to it.

The above analysis is based on the assumption that the nonparametric approach is more faithful to the data than the parametric specifications. In order to assess whether this is indeed the case, we consider the in-sample predictions for the kernel method and best-performing

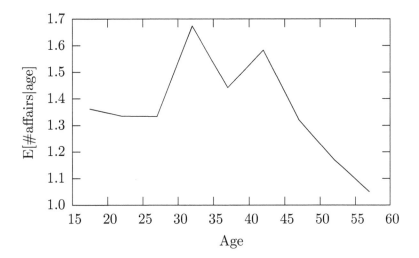

Figure 5.2: Expected number of affairs conditional on age, remaining variables held constant at their median values.

parametric model (ordered Logit specification). The nonparametric method and the ordered Logit give 79.2% and 75.0% correct predictions for the number of affairs, respectively. Also, for the 150 people recording a positive number of affairs, the nonparametric method correctly predicts the number of affairs for 25 of them (16.7%), where the ordered logit model correctly predicts those for only 3 (2.0%). The prediction results indicate that the parametric models are misspecified.

The extramarital affairs data studied by Fair (1978) is a rich dataset that continues to generate controversy. Existing work has focused mainly on specification tests based on *parametric* linear single index models. The possible nonlinearity of relevant covariates is largely ignored. We focus instead on the impact of parametric misspecification on assessing predictor relevance, and conclude that one covariate long thought to be a significant predictor of affairs, the number of years married, does not in fact appear to be associated with an increase in one's propensity to engage in these types of extracurricular activities.

5.5.3   Married Female Labor Force Participation

We now consider a simple application in which we model the labor force participation decision of married Swiss females solely based on

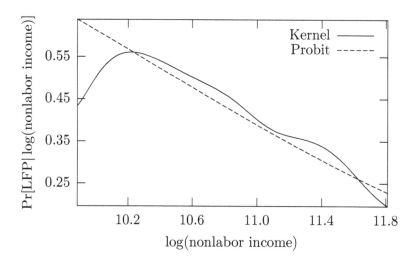

Figure 5.3: Kernel estimate of the conditional probability of labor force participation for Gerfin's data ($\mathrm{P}[Y = 1|x]$).

their nonlabor income. We use the data of Gerfin (1996), who models the labor market participation of married Swiss women using a cross-sectional data set of size $n = 872$. For present purposes, we simply consider applying kernel estimates to obtain the conditional probability of participation as a function of nonlabor income. We also present a Probit model with a linear index which is that used by Gerfin. For the kernel method, the Aitchison and Aitken (1976) kernel is used for the binary labor force participation variable, the Gaussian kernel is used for the continuous nonlabor income variable, and bandwidths were selected via likelihood cross-validation ($\lambda_{\mathrm{lfp}} = 0.07$, $h_{\mathrm{nonlaborinc}} = 0.16$). To guard against the potential oversmoothing by the likelihood method, we also computed the least squares cross-validation bandwidth ($\lambda = 0.03$, $h = 0.11$) and an ad hoc value of $h = x_{sd}n^{-1/5} = 0.11$, where x_{sd} is the sample standard deviation of the log of nonlabor income. Different methods lead to similar values of h supporting the use of likelihood cross-validation in this application (i.e., one obtains similar results when using a variety of methods for selecting λ and h).

First, in Figure 5.3 we note that the parametric and nonparametric methods are in broad agreement, suggesting that one's probability of labor force participation falls from over 50% to around 20% as one's nonlabor income increases. However, the kernel method detects a rising participation probability for low levels of nonlabor income, which then begins to fall as nonlabor income rises. One possible explanation for this is suggested in Juhn and Murphy (1997), who argue that low-ability women tend to marry low-ability men; furthermore, low-ability men have low earnings, which implies that their wife's nonlabor income tends to be low. For low levels of nonlabor income these women are more productive at home than in the labor market because of their low unobservables (e.g., ability); however, as men's earnings increase the unobservables (ability) of women tend to improve, leading to higher female participation. At some point, the nonlabor income effect (wealth effect) begins to dominate as expected, and female participation begins its decline.

5.5.4   Labor Productivity

We consider an unbalanced panel measuring labor productivity for Indonesian pulp and paper companies from 1975 to 1997 reported in van Dijk and Szirmai (2003). This dataset contains a number of interesting features. The first Indonesian paper mill was established in 1923, and until 1974 only six state-owned mills were founded. The market for printing and writing paper developed rapidly between 1974 and 1984, with the number of mills increasing from 7 to 33, with all new mills being privately owned. For this panel, some years (cells) are quite sparse, containing as few as 8 observations, while the largest cell contains only 52 observations, and there are $n = 783$ observations in total. We therefore consider modeling the conditional PDF for labor productivity conditional on the discrete covariate year. The Gaussian kernel was used for labor productivity and Aitchison and Aitken's (1976) kernel was used for year. Likelihood cross-validation was used for bandwidth selection with $h_{\mathrm{labor}} = 1044.07$ and $\lambda_{\mathrm{year}} = 0.28$.

A major policy change intended to foster growth in this industry was introduced in 1983, and it is therefore interesting to see whether productivity appears to differ pre- versus post-1983. In Figure 5.4, we observe a shift in labor productivity mass in the late 1980s on through the 1990s. This example highlights the potential benefits which can arise from smoothing discrete data when the number of cells is large relative to the sample size.

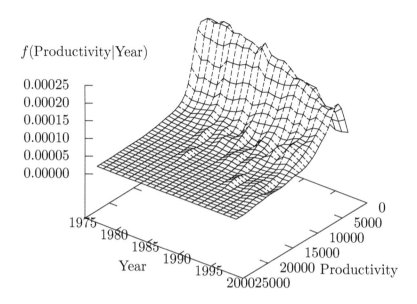

Figure 5.4: Kernel estimate of the PDF for labor productivity conditional on time.

5.5.5 Multivariate Y Conditional Density Example: GDP Growth and Population Growth Conditional on OECD Status

We consider the dataset used in Maasoumi, Racine and Stengos (forthcoming), who examined issues surrounding economic growth rates and the existence of "convergence clubs." For the present example, our goal is simply to demonstrate that estimating multivariate Y conditional PDFs with data-driven methods of bandwidth selection is straightforward. By way of example, we pool panel data on 88 countries over seven 5-year periods: 1960–1964, 1965–1969, 1970–1974, 1975–1979, 1980–1984, 1985–1989 and 1990–1994, for a total of $n = 616$ observations. We consider the following variables: y_1, the growth rate of income per capita during each period; y_2, the annual rate of population growth during each period; x, OECD status (0/1). The average annual growth rate of per capita GDP and population for each period are

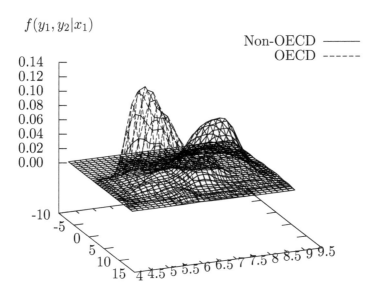

Figure 5.5: Multivariate Y conditional PDF with Y consisting of GDP and population growth rates and X being OECD status.

from the World Bank. We estimate the conditional density $f(y_1, y_2|x)$ and present the resulting conditional PDF in Figure 5.5, that is, we plot $\hat{f}(y_1, y_2|X = 0)$ and $\hat{f}(y_1, y_2|X = 1)$. Hall et al.'s (2004) least squares cross-validation method was used to obtain the bandwidths, with $\hat{h}_{\text{GDP}} = 0.96$ $\hat{h}_{\text{Pop}} = 0.21$, and $\hat{\lambda}_{\text{OECD}} = 0.00$.

Figure 5.5 presents a clear picture of this multivariate Y conditional PDF. The joint PDF for non-OECD countries has a modal population growth rate of roughly 7.3% while that for OECD countries has modal population growth rate that is roughly 5.7% during this period, while the modal GDP growth rate for non-OECD countries is roughly 1.8% with that for OECD countries being roughly 2.7%.

5.6   Exercises

Exercise 5.1. When Y is a discrete variable, say,

$$Y \in \mathcal{S}_0^d = \{0, 1, \ldots, c_0 - 1\},$$

show that (5.17) should be modified to

$$(n\hat{h}_1 \ldots \hat{h}_{q_1})^{1/2}(\tilde{g}(y|x) - g(y|x) - \sum_{s=1}^{q_1} B_{1s}(\bar{x}, y)\hat{h}_s^2 - \sum_{s=1}^{r_1} B_{2s}(\bar{x}, y)\hat{\lambda}_s)$$

$$\rightarrow N(0, \sigma_g^2(\bar{x}, y)),$$

where

$$B_{1s}(\bar{x}, y) = \frac{1}{2}\kappa_2 \sum_{s=1}^{q_1} \hat{h}_s^2 \left\{ \frac{\bar{f}_{ss}(y|\bar{x})}{\bar{\mu}(\bar{x})} - \frac{\bar{\mu}_{ss}(\bar{x})}{\bar{\mu}(\bar{x})}\bar{g}(y|\bar{x}) \right\},$$

$$B_{2s}(\bar{x}, y) = \frac{\hat{\lambda}_0}{c_0 - 1} \sum_{z^d \in \mathcal{S}_0^d} \mathbf{1}_0(z^d, y) \left\{ \bar{g}(z|\bar{x}^c, \bar{v}^d) - \frac{\bar{\mu}(\bar{x}^c, \bar{v}^d)}{\bar{\mu}(\bar{x})}\bar{g}(y|\bar{x}) \right\}$$

$$+ \sum_{s=1}^{r_1} \frac{\hat{\lambda}_s}{c_s - 1} \sum_{\bar{v}^d} \mathbf{1}_s(\bar{v}^d, x_s^d) \left\{ \bar{g}(y|\bar{x}^c, \bar{v}^d) - \frac{\bar{\mu}(\bar{x}^c, \bar{v}^d)}{\bar{\mu}(\bar{x})}\bar{g}(y|\bar{x}) \right\},$$

$$\sigma_g^2(\bar{x}, y) = \kappa^{q_1}\bar{g}(y|\bar{x})/\bar{\mu}(\bar{x}),$$

where $\hat{\lambda}_0$ is the cross-validation selected smoothing parameter that is associated with y.

Exercise 5.2. Using the data underlying the local constant kernel estimate of an earnings profile (log income versus age) presented in Pagan and Ullah (1999, pp. 154–155) that we used in Exercise 2.11, generate the PDF of earnings conditional on age using least squares cross-validation.

    Next, plot the resulting conditional PDF and compare your estimate with the conditional mean function you generated in Exercise 2.11. Can you readily visualize the conditional mean function from the conditional PDF function?

Chapter 6

Conditional CDF and Quantile Estimation

The estimation of conditional mean functions (i.e., regression functions) that we considered in Chapter 2 is undoubtedly the most popular activity in all of applied data analysis. However, a conditional mean is sometimes not the most appropriate object that one might consider. For example, if the dependent variable is censored, the conditional mean function based on the censored data may deviate substantially from the true conditional mean function associated with the uncensored population, and it is the latter that is typically of interest to applied economists. In such cases, the so-called quantile regression function may be more robust and thus provide a viable alternative to the conditional mean regression function. In addition to being robust to the presence of censoring, a more comprehensive picture of the conditional distribution of a dependent variable can often be obtained by estimating a set of conditional quantiles rather than by simply presenting the conditional mean itself. For a complete treatment of quantile regression methods, we direct the reader to Koenker (2005).

In this chapter we begin by studying how to estimate a conditional CDF in nonparametric settings. We first discuss the estimation of a conditional CDF having only continuous covariates. The conditional quantile function that is often of direct interest can be obtained directly from the conditional CDF, and is obtained by simply inverting the conditional CDF. Having considered the case with continuous data only, we then show that the results can be easily extended to the mixed discrete and continuous covariate case that is often encountered in applied settings.

6.1 Estimating a Conditional CDF with Continuous Covariates without Smoothing the Dependent Variable

We first consider an estimator of a conditional CDF that does not smooth the dependent variable. This estimator is similar in spirit to the local constant regression estimator developed in Chapter 2. We use $F(y|x)$ to denote the conditional CDF of Y given $X = x$, while $\mu(x)$ is the marginal density of X. Note that $F(y|x) = \mathrm{E}[\mathbf{1}(Y_i \leq y)|X_i = x]$ is the conditional mean function of $\mathbf{1}(Y_i \leq y)$ conditional on $X_i = x$, which suggests one can use the conditional mean (regression) function estimator discussed in Chapter 4 to estimate $F(y|x)$. Thus, we estimate $F(y|x)$ by

$$\tilde{F}(y|x) = \frac{n^{-1}\sum_{i=1}^{n}\mathbf{1}(Y_i \leq y)W_h(X_i, x)}{\hat{\mu}(x)}, \tag{6.1}$$

where $\hat{\mu}(x) = n^{-1}\sum_{i=1}^{n}W_h(X_i, x)$ is the kernel estimator of $\mu(x)$, $W_h(X_i, x) = \prod_{s=1}^{q}h_s^{-1}w((X_{is} - X_s)/h_s)$, and $w(\cdot)$ is a univariate kernel function.

We make the following assumptions:

Assumption 6.1. *Both $\mu(x)$ and $F(y|x)$ have continuous second order derivatives with respect to x^c. $w(\cdot)$ is a symmetric, bounded and compactly supported PDF.*

Assumption 6.2. *We assume that as $n \to \infty$, $nh_1 \ldots h_q \to \infty$ and $h_s \to 0$ for all $s = 1, \ldots, q$.*

For $s = 1, \ldots, q$, let $A_s(y, x) = \partial A(y, x)/\partial x_s$ and $A_{ss}(y, x) = \partial^2 A(y, x)/\partial x_s^2$, $A_0(y, x) = \partial A(y, x)/\partial y$, $A_{00}(y, x) = \partial A^2(y, x)/\partial y^2$, $\kappa_2 = \int w(v)v^2 dv$, and $\kappa = \int w(v)^2 dv$, where $\kappa^q = \prod_{s=1}^{q}\int w(v_s)^2 dv_s = \int W(v)^2 dv$.

We write $\tilde{F}(y|x) - F(y|x) = \tilde{M}(y, x)/\hat{\mu}(x)$, where $\tilde{M}(y, x) = [\tilde{F}(y|x) - F(y|x)]\hat{\mu}(x)$. The next theorem gives the asymptotic distribution of $\tilde{F}(y|x)$.

Theorem 6.1. *Under Assumptions 6.1 and 6.2, and also assuming that $\mu(x) > 0$ and $F(y|x) > 0$, we have*

(i) $\mathrm{E}[\tilde{M}(y,x)] = \mu(x)\left[\sum_{s=1}^{q} h_s^2 B_s(y,x)\right] + o(\sum_{s=1}^{q} h_s^2)$, where

$$B_s(y,x) = (1/2)\kappa_2[F_{ss}(y|x) + 2\mu_s(x)F_s(y|x)/\mu(x)].$$

(ii) $\mathrm{var}[\tilde{M}(y,x)] = (nh_1 \ldots h_q)^{-1}\mu(x)^2 \Sigma_{y|x} + o\left((nh_1 \ldots h_q)^{-1}\right)$, where $\Sigma_{y|x} = \kappa^q F(y|x)[1 - F(y|x)]/\mu(x)$.

(iii) If $(nh_1 \ldots h_q)^{1/2} \sum_{s=1}^{q} h_s^3 = o(1)$, then

$$(nh_1 \ldots h_q)^{1/2}\left[\tilde{F}(y|x) - F(y|x) - \sum_{s=1}^{q} h_s^2 B_s(y,x)\right] \overset{d}{\to} N(0, \Sigma_{y|x}).$$

The proof of Theorem 6.1 is given in Section 6.9.
By using

$$\tilde{F}(y|x) - F(y|x) = \tilde{M}(y,x)/\hat{\mu}(x)$$

$$= \tilde{M}(y,x)/\mu(x) + O_p\left(\sum_{s=1}^{q} h_s^2 + (nh_1 \ldots h_q)^{-1/2}\right),$$

Theorem 6.1 implies that

$$\mathrm{MSE}[\tilde{F}(y|x)] = \left[\sum_{s=1}^{q} h_s^2 B_s(y,x)\right]^2 + \frac{\Sigma_{y|x}}{nh_1 \ldots h_q} + (s.o.),\qquad (6.2)$$

where $(s.o.)$ denotes (omitted) smaller order terms.

If we choose $h_1, \ldots, h_q$ to minimize a weighted integrated MSE given by $\int \mathrm{MSE}[\tilde{F}(y|x)]s(y,x)dxdy$, where $s(y,x)$ is a nonnegative weight function, then from (6.2) it is easy to show that the optimal smoothing parameters that minimize the integrated MSE should be $h_s \sim n^{-1/(4+q)}$ for $s = 1, \ldots, q$. However, there does not exist a closed form expression for the optimal h_s's. Though one can compute plug-in h_s's, it is computationally challenging to say the least. Li and Racine (forthcoming) recommend using a least squares cross-validation method of bandwidth selection designed for the estimation of conditional PDFs. We showed in Chapter 5 that, for conditional PDF estimation, optimal smoothing yields bandwidths of the form $h_0 \sim h_s \sim n^{-1/(5+q)}$ for all $s = 1, \ldots, q$. Note that the exponential factor is $-1/(5+q)$ because the dimension of (y,x) is $q + 1$ since we assumed that Y is a continuous variable. We can also multiply the conditional LSCV smoothing parameters by the factor $n^{(5+q)/(4+q)}$ to obtain the correct optimal rate for the conditional CDF optimal smoothing parameters. The simulations reported in Li and Racine indicate that this approach performs well.

6.2 Estimating a Conditional CDF with Continuous Covariates Smoothing the Dependent Variable

In this section we discuss an alternative estimator that also smooths the dependent variable Y as we did for the unconditional CDF estimator developed in Section 1.4. That is, we can also estimate $F(y|x)$ by

$$\hat{F}(y|x) = \frac{n^{-1}\sum_{i=1}^{n} G\left(\frac{y-Y_i}{h_0}\right) W_h(X_i, x)}{\hat{\mu}(x)}, \tag{6.3}$$

where $G(\cdot)$ is a kernel CDF chosen by the researcher, say, the standard normal CDF, and h_0 is the smoothing parameter associated with Y.

In addition to Assumption 6.1, we also need to assume that as $n \to \infty$, $h_0 \to 0$. Defining $\hat{M}(y,x) = \left[\hat{F}(y|x) - F(y|x)\right]\hat{\mu}(x)$, then $\hat{F}(y|x) - F(y|x) = \hat{M}(y,x)/\hat{\mu}(x)$. We have the following result.

Theorem 6.2. *Define $B_0(y,x) = (1/2)\kappa_2 F_{00}(y|x)$ and let $\Omega(y,x) = \kappa^q F_0(y|x)/\mu(x)$. Note that $\Sigma_{y|x}$ and $B_s(x)$ are the same as those defined in Theorem 6.1. Letting $|\bar{h}|^2 = h_0^2 + \sum_{s=1}^{q} h_s^2 = \sum_{s=0}^{q} h_s^2$, then under conditions similar to those given in Theorem 6.1, we have*

(i) $\mathrm{E}[\hat{M}(y,x)] = \mu(x)\sum_{s=0}^{q} h_s^2 B_s(y,x) + o(|\bar{h}|^2).$

(ii) $\mathrm{var}[\hat{M}(y,x)] = (nH_q)^{-1}\mu(x)^2[\Sigma_{y|x} - h_0 C_k \Omega(y,x)] + o\left((nH_q)^{-1}\right),$
where $H_q = h_1 \ldots h_q$ and $C_k = 2\int G(v)w(v)v\,dv.$

(iii) *If $(nh_1 \ldots h_q)^{1/2}\sum_{s=0}^{q} h_s^3 = o(1)$, then*

$$(nh_1 \ldots h_q)^{1/2}\left[\hat{F}(y|x) - F(y|x) - \sum_{s=1}^{q} h_s^2 B_s(y,x)\right] \xrightarrow{d} N(0, \Sigma_{y|x}).$$

The proof of Theorem 6.2 is given in Section 6.9.

Theorem 6.2 implies that

$$\mathrm{MSE}[\hat{F}(y|x)] = \left[\sum_{s=0}^{q} h_s^2 B_s(y,x)\right]^2 + \frac{\Sigma_{y|x} - h_0 C_k \Omega(y,x)}{nh_1 \ldots h_q} + (s.o.). \tag{6.4}$$

One may choose the smoothing parameters to minimize the leading term of a WIMSE of $F(y|x)$ given by

$$
\text{WIMSE} = \int \left\{ \left[\sum_{s=0}^{q} h_s^2 B_s(y,x) \right]^2 \right. \\
\left. + \frac{[\Sigma_{y|x} - h_0 C_k \Omega(y,x)]}{nh_1 \dots h_q} \right\} s(y,x)\, dydx,
\tag{6.5}
$$

where $\int dxdy = \sum_{x^d \in D} \int dx^c dy$.

Were one to adopt a plug-in method of bandwidth selection, one would first estimate $B_s(y,x)$, $\Sigma_{y|x}$ and $\Omega(y,x)$, which requires one to choose initial "pilot" smoothing parameters, while the accurate numerical computation of a $q+1$ dimensional integration can be extremely difficult. However, well developed automatic data-driven methods do exist for selecting the smoothing parameters for estimating a conditional PDF. Given the lack of data-driven methods for conditional CDF estimation having desirable properties, we again suggest using the cross-validation methods that have been developed for conditional PDF estimation. As discussed in Chapter 5 for conditional PDFs, optimal smoothing gives $h_0 \sim h_s \sim n^{-1/(5+q)}$ for all $s = 1, \dots, q$. Below we show that optimal smoothing for conditional CDFs requires that $h_0 = o(h_s)$ for $s = 1, \dots, q$ and that $h_s \sim n^{-1/(4+q)}$. For the sake of clarity, we first consider the case of $q = 1$ and then turn to the general case.

Consider the case for which $q = 1$. From (6.4) we know that the weighted MSE is given by

$$
\text{WIMSE} = \int \text{MSE}[\hat{F}(y|x)]s(y,x)dydx \\
= A_0 h_0^4 + A_1 h_0^2 h_1^2 + A_2 h_1^4 \\
+ A_3 (nh_1)^{-1} - A_4 h_0 (nh_1)^{-1} + O(\eta_n),
\tag{6.6}
$$

where $\eta_n = h_1^6 + h_0^6 + (h_1^2 + h_0^2)(nh_1)^{-1}$, and the A_j's are some constants given by

$$A_0 = \int B_0(y,x)^2 s(y,x) dy dx,$$

$$A_1 = 2 \int B_0(y,x) B_1(y,x) s(y,x) dy dx,$$

$$A_2 = \int B_1(y,x)^2 s(y,x) dy dx,$$

$$A_3 = \Sigma_{y|x} s(y,x) dy dx, \text{ and}$$

$$A_4 = \Omega(y,x) s(y,x) dy dx.$$

All the A_j's, except A_1, are positive, while A_1 can be positive, negative or zero.

The first order conditions are

$$\frac{\partial \text{WIMSE}}{\partial h_0} = 4 A_0 h_0^3 + 2 A_1 h_0 h_1^2 - A_4 (n h_1)^{-1} + (s.o.) = 0, \qquad (6.7)$$

$$\frac{\partial \text{WIMSE}}{\partial h_1} = 2 A_1 h_0^2 h_1 + 4 A_2 h_1^3 - A_3 (n h_1^2)^{-1} + (s.o.) = 0, \qquad (6.8)$$

where $(s.o.)$ denotes smaller order terms.

From (6.7) and (6.8), we can easily see that h_0 and h_1 cannot have the same order. Furthermore, it can be shown that h_0 must have an order smaller than that of h_1. Assuming that $h_0 = c_0 n^{-\alpha}$ and $h_1 = c_1 n^{-\beta}$, then we must have $\alpha > \beta$. Then, from (6.8) we get $\beta = 1/5$, and substituting this into (6.7) we obtain $\alpha = 2/5$. Thus, optimal smoothing requires that $h_0 \sim n^{-2/5}$ and $h_1 \sim n^{-1/5}$.[1]

For the general case of $q > 1$, by symmetry, all h_s's should have the same order, say, $h_s \sim n^{-\beta}$ for $s = 1, \ldots, q$ and $h_0 \sim n^{-\alpha}$. Then it is easy to show that $\beta = 1/(4+q)$ and $\alpha = 2/(4+q)$. Thus, the optimal $h_s \sim n^{-1/(4+q)}$ for $s = 1, \ldots, q$, and $h_0 \sim n^{-2/(4+q)}$.

Up to now we have focused on a local constant estimator of $F(y|x)$. We can also use local linear methods to estimate $F(y|x)$. As we discussed earlier, $F(y|x) = \text{E}[\mathbf{1}(Y_i \le y)|X_i = x]$ is the conditional mean function of $\mathbf{1}(Y_i \le y)$ conditional on $X_i = x$. Thus, we can also use the local linear method to estimate this conditional mean function by regressing $\mathbf{1}(Y_i \le y)$ on $(1, (X_i - x)')$ using kernel weights. The resulting

---

[1]One can also try to use $\alpha = \beta$, which will lead to $\beta = 1/5$ from (6.8) and $\beta = 1/4$ from (6.7), a contradiction. Similarly, assuming that $\alpha < \beta$ also leads to a contradiction. Therefore, we must have $\alpha > \beta$.

intercept estimator will be the local linear estimator of $F(y|x)$. It can be shown that this estimator has a leading bias term given by

$$(\kappa_2/2) \sum_{s=1}^{q} h_s^2 F_{ss}(y|x) \tag{6.9}$$

and a leading variance term of $\Sigma_{y|x}$, which is the same as that of the local constant estimator given in Theorem 6.1. However, as pointed out by Hall, Wolff and Yao (1999), two undesirable properties are associated with the local linear estimator: (i) it may not be monotone in Y, and (ii) it is not be constrained to take values in $[0, 1]$.

Motivated by the empirical likelihood approach, Hall et al. (1999) and Cai (2002) introduce a weighted local constant estimator to overcome problems arising from the use of a local linear approach. A weighted local constant estimator is given by

$$\bar{F}(y|x) = \frac{\sum_{i=1}^{n} p_i(x) K_h(X_i, x) \mathbf{1}(Y_i \le y)}{\sum_{i=1}^{n} p_i(x) K_h(X_i, x)}, \tag{6.10}$$

where $p_i(x)$, for $i = 1, \ldots, n$, denotes the weight functions of the data $X_1, \ldots, X_n$ and the design point x satisfying the properties $p_i(x) \ge 0$, $\sum_{i=1}^{n} p_i(x) = 1$, and

$$\sum_{i=1}^{n} (X_i - x) p_i(x) K_h(X_i, x) = 0. \tag{6.11}$$

Condition (6.11) is motivated by the local linear estimator, which ensures that the estimation bias has the same order of magnitude in the boundary and interior regions. It also reduces the number of leading bias terms in the Taylor expansion. However, $p_i(x)$'s satisfying these conditions are not uniquely defined (since we have n parameters of $p_i(x)$, only $q + 2$ restrictions). Hall et al. and Cai suggest choosing the $p_i(x)$'s by maximizing $\prod_{i=1}^{n} p_i(x)$ subject to these constraints. This leads to the following optimization problem:

$$\max_{p_i(x)'s} \sum_{i=1}^{n} \ln p_i(x), \text{ subject to (6.11), } p_i(x) \ge 0 \text{ and } \sum_{i=1}^{n} p_i(x) = 1. \tag{6.12}$$

Letting γ be the Lagrangian multiplier associated with condition (6.11), then (see the hints given in Exercise 6.5)

$$\hat{p}_i(x) = \frac{1}{n[1 + \hat{\gamma}(X_i - x) K_h(X_i, x)]}, \tag{6.13}$$

where

$$\hat{\gamma} = \arg\max_{\gamma} \frac{-1}{nh} \sum_{i=1}^{n} \ln\left[1 + \gamma(X_i - x)K_h(X_i, x)\right]. \tag{6.14}$$

Equation (6.14) does not have a closed form solution. Cai (2002) recommends using the Newton-Raphson scheme to find the root (solution) of γ based on (6.14). Under regularity conditions similar to those given in Theorem 6.2, Cai establishes the asymptotic distribution of $\bar{F}(y|x)$, which is given by

$$(nh)^{1/2}\left[\bar{F}(y|x) - F(y|x) - \sum_{s=1}^{q} h_s^2 \bar{B}_s(y, x)F_{ss}(y|x)\right] \xrightarrow{d} N(0, \Sigma_{y|x}),$$
$$\tag{6.15}$$

where $\bar{B}_s(y, x) = (1/2)\kappa_2 F_{ss}(y|x)$.

Equation (6.15) shows that $\bar{F}(y|x)$ has the same (first order) asymptotic distribution as a local linear kernel estimator of $F(y|x)$. It also has the additional advantage of being monotone in Y and taking values only in $[0, 1]$. A disadvantage is that numerical optimization routines are required for its computation.

When X has bounded support, Cai (2002) further shows that $\bar{F}(y|x)$ has the same order of bias ($\sum_{s=1}^{q} h_s^2$) and variance at the boundary of the support of X, i.e., this approach is immune to boundary effects in bounded support settings.

We observe that the above weighted local constant estimator has properties similar to that of the local linear estimator. One disadvantage mentioned above is that computation requires nonlinear optimization procedures, while the local constant and local linear estimators possess closed form solutions and can be readily computed. The problem arising with the local linear estimator is that the local weight function may assume negative values, hence the resulting estimator of $F(y|x)$ may assume values lying outside the unit interval $[0, 1]$. Hansen (2004) proposes a modified local linear estimator of $F(y|x)$ in which he replaces the negative weight (when it occurs) by 0. This modification is asymptotically negligible, but it constrains the resulting local linear estimator of $F(y|x)$ to assume values in $[0, 1]$ leading to a valid conditional CDF estimator. Hansen shows that the asymptotic distribution of his modified local linear estimator is first order equivalent to $\bar{F}(y|x)$ given in (6.15).

The nonparametric estimation of conditional CDFs has widespread potential application in economics. For example, such estimators have been used to identify and estimate nonadditive and nonseparable functions; see Matzkin (2003) and Altonji and Matzkin (2005).

Up to now we have focused on nonparametric estimation of a conditional CDF. When the dimension of the covariates is high, the curse of dimensionality may prevent accurate nonparametric estimation. Hall and Yao (2005) propose using dimensionality reducing methods to approximate the conditional PDF. Specifically they use $F(Y|X'\beta)$ to approximate the true conditional CDF $F(Y|X)$, where X is of dimension q and β is a vector of $q \times 1$ unknown parameters. Their estimation method is similar in spirit to the single index model method (see Chapter 8). Since $X'\beta$ is a scalar (i.e., univariate), it involves one-dimensional nonparametric estimation only and hence is immune to the curse of dimensionality critique.

6.3 Nonparametric Estimation of Conditional Quantile Functions

Quantile regression methods are being widely used by practitioners. For a comprehensive analysis of a range of parametric methods we direct the reader to Koenker (2005). One reason for the popularity of these methods is that they more fully characterize the conditional CDF of a variable of interest, in contrast to regression models that provide the conditional mean only.

The unconditional αth quantile of a CDF $F(\cdot)$ is defined as

$$q_\alpha = \inf\{y : F(y) \geq \alpha\} = F^{-1}(\alpha), \qquad (6.16)$$

where $\alpha \in (0, 1)$.

For example, let $Y \sim N(0,1)$ and let $F(\cdot)$ be the associated standard normal CDF. Then $q_{.5} = 0$ since $F(0) = 0.5$ and $F(0-\epsilon) < 0.5$ for any $\epsilon > 0$. To determine a quantile, say, $q_{.95}$, we work with the inverse CDF. That is, since $q_{.95} = F^{-1}(.95)$ and $F(q_{.95}) = F(F^{-1}(.95)) = 0.95$, we obtain $q_{.95} = 1.645$ because $P[N(0,1) \leq 1.645] = F(1.645) = 0.95$.

In general, if we let X denote a random variable with CDF $F(\cdot)$, then the method for finding q_α involves applying F on $q_\alpha = F^{-1}(\alpha)$ to get

$$F(q_\alpha) \equiv P[X \leq q_\alpha] = \alpha,$$

i.e., applying F on (6.16).

Again by way of example, suppose that X represents family income in a given year. Then $q_{.25}$ is that level of income such that 25% of all family incomes lie below it.

Often, it is a conditional rather than unconditional quantile that is of interest. The conditional αth quantile is defined by ($\alpha \in (0, 1)$)

$$q_\alpha(x) = \inf\{y : F(y|x) \geq \alpha\} = F^{-1}(\alpha|x). \qquad (6.17)$$

For example, suppose that X represents age and Y represents individual incomes. Then $q_{.25}(x = 30)$ is that level of income for 30 year olds such that 25% of 30 year olds have incomes below it.

In practice, we can estimate the conditional quantile function $q_\alpha(x)$ by inverting an estimated conditional CDF function. Using the estimators with a smooth function and an indicator function respectively for Y, we would obtain

$$\hat{q}_\alpha(x) = \inf\{y : \hat{F}(y|x) \geq \alpha\} \equiv \hat{F}^{-1}(\alpha|x), \qquad (6.18)$$

$$\tilde{q}_\alpha(x) = \inf\{y : \tilde{F}(y|x) \geq \alpha\} \equiv \tilde{F}^{-1}(\alpha|x). \qquad (6.19)$$

Because $\hat{F}(y|x)$ ($\tilde{F}(y|x)$) lies between zero and one and is monotone in Y, $\hat{q}_\alpha(x)$ ($\tilde{q}_\alpha(x)$) always exists. Therefore, once one obtains $\hat{F}(y|x)$ ($\tilde{F}(y|x)$), it is trivial to compute $\hat{q}_\alpha(x)$ ($\tilde{q}_\alpha(x)$) using (6.18) ((6.19)).

We interpret (6.18) to mean that, for a given value of α and x, we solve for $q_\alpha(x)$ by choosing q_α to minimize the objective function

$$\hat{q}_\alpha(x) = \arg\min_q |\alpha - \hat{F}(q|x)|. \qquad (6.20)$$

That is, the resulting value of q that minimizes (6.20) is $\hat{q}_\alpha(x)$.

We assume that $F(y|x)$ has a conditional PDF $f(y|x)$, $f(y|x)$ is continuous in x^c, and $f(q_\alpha(x)|x) > 0$. Note that $f(y|x) \equiv F_0(y|x)$ since $F_0(y|x) = \partial F(y|x)/\partial y$.

The next two theorems give the asymptotic distribution of $\tilde{q}_\alpha(x)$ and $\hat{q}_\alpha(x)$.

Theorem 6.3. *For $s = 1, \ldots, q$, define*

$$B_{\alpha,s}(y, x) = \frac{B_s(y, x)}{f(q_\alpha(x)|x)},$$

where $B_s(y, x)$ is defined in Theorem 6.1. Then under conditions similar to those given in Theorem 6.1, we have

$$(nh_1 \ldots h_q)^{1/2} \left[\tilde{q}_\alpha(x) - q_\alpha(x) - \sum_{s=1}^{q} h_s^2 B_{\alpha,s}(x) \right] \xrightarrow{d} N(0, V_\alpha(x)),$$

where $V_\alpha(x) = \alpha(1-\alpha)\kappa^q / \left[f^2(q_\alpha(x)|x)\mu(q_\alpha(x)) \right]$.

Theorem 6.4. *Define $B_{\alpha,0}(x) = F_0(y|x)/\mu(x)$ and $B_{\alpha,s}(x)$ is the same as in Theorem 6.3 for $s = 1,\ldots,q$. Then under conditions similar to those given in Theorem 6.2, we have*

$$(nh_1 \ldots h_q)^{1/2} \left[\hat{q}_\alpha(x) - q_\alpha(x) - \sum_{s=0}^q h_s^2 B_{\alpha,s}(x) \right] \xrightarrow{d} N(0, V_\alpha(x)),$$

where $B_{\alpha,s}$ ($s = 1,\ldots,q$) and $V_\alpha(x)$ are the same as defined in Theorem 6.3.

The proof of Theorem 6.3 is left as an exercise and the proof of Theorem 6.4 is given in Section 6.9.1.

One can also estimate $q_\alpha(x)$ by inverting the weighted local constant estimator of $F(y|x)$ given in (6.10), i.e.,

$$\bar{q}_\alpha(x) = \inf\{y : \bar{F}(y|x) \geq \alpha\} \equiv \bar{F}^{-1}(\alpha|x). \qquad (6.21)$$

Cai (2002) shows that

$$(nh_1 \ldots h_q)^{1/2} \left[\bar{q}_\alpha(x) - q_\alpha(x) - \sum_{s=0}^q h_s^2 \bar{B}_s(q_\alpha(x), x)/f(q_\alpha(x)|x) \right]$$
$$\xrightarrow{d} N(0, V_\alpha(x)),$$
$$\qquad (6.22)$$

where the $\bar{B}_s(.,.)$'s are defined in (6.15) and where $V_\alpha(x)$ is the same as that defined in Theorem 6.4.

6.4 The Check Function Approach

A popular alternative estimator for $q_\alpha(x)$ can be derived using the so-called check function; see Chaudhuri (1991), Chaudhuri, Doksum and Samarov (1997), Jones and Hall (1990), Yu and Jones (1997, 1998), Honda (2000), Cheng and Peng (2002), Whang (2006), and the references therein. The check function gets its name from the shape of the underlying objective function. Note that L_2-norm objective functions such as those based on least squares methods yield U-shaped objective functions, while L_1-norm objective functions such as those based on least absolute deviations yield a V-shaped or "check-shaped" objective function.

The popular parametric linear quantile regression model (Koenker and Bassett (1978)) is of the form

$$Y_i = X_i'\beta + u_i, \tag{6.23}$$

and from (6.23) we obtain $q_\alpha(Y_i|X_i) = X_i'\beta + q_\alpha(u_i|X_i)$. One cannot separately identify β and $q_\alpha(u_i|X_i)$, just as one cannot separately identify the intercept and $E(u_i)$ in a least squares regression model (i.e., where we *impose* $E(u_i) = 0$). We can rewrite this model as

$$Y_i = q_\alpha(Y_i|X_i) + v_{\alpha,i} = X_i'\beta_\alpha + v_{\alpha,i}, \tag{6.24}$$

where $v_{\alpha,i} = u_i - q_\alpha(u_i|X_i)$. By definition $q_\alpha(v_{\alpha,i}|X_i) = 0$. Basically, we impose the condition that the conditional αth quantile of the error process is equal to zero.

It is well known that one can estimate β_α in (6.24) by minimizing the following objective function:

$$\hat{\beta}_\alpha = \arg\min_\beta \sum_{i=1}^n \rho_\alpha(Y_i - X_i\beta), \tag{6.25}$$

where $\rho_\alpha(z) = z[\alpha - \mathbf{1}(z \leq 0)]$, the check function; see Koenker and Bassett (1978) for details. Also, see He and Zhu (2003) for a lack-of-fit test for parametric quantile regression models. Equation (6.25) can be shown to be equivalent to

$$\hat{\beta} = \arg\min_\beta \left\{ \alpha \sum_{Y_i \geq X_i'\beta} |Y_i - X_i'\beta| + (1-\alpha) \sum_{Y_i < X_i'\beta} |Y_i - X_i'\beta| \right\}, \tag{6.26}$$

where we make use of the fact that $-z = |z|$ for $z < 0$.

Koenker and Bassett (1978) showed that

$$\sqrt{n}(\hat{\beta}_\alpha - \beta_\alpha) \xrightarrow{d} N\left(0, \sigma_\alpha^2 [E(X_i X_i')]^{-1}\right)$$

where $\sigma_\alpha^2 = \alpha(1-\alpha)f_{v_\alpha}(0)$, and $f_{v_\alpha}(\cdot)$ is the PDF of v_α.

This check function approach can also be adopted for the estimation of a nonparametric quantile regression model. We use a local constant method (or, alternatively, we could use a local linear method), and we choose a to minimize the following objective function:

$$\min_a \sum_{j=1}^{n} \rho_\alpha(Y_j - a) W_h(X_i, x), \qquad (6.27)$$

where $\rho_\alpha(v) = v[\alpha - \mathbf{1}(v \leq 0)]$. By letting $\hat{q}_{\alpha,lc}(x)$ denote the value of a that minimizes (6.27), it can be shown that $\hat{q}_{\alpha,lc}(x)$ is a consistent estimator for $q_\alpha(x)$.

The leading MSE of $\hat{a}_{\alpha,lc}(x)$ can be found in Jones and Hall (1990) and Yu and Jones (1997). The leading bias and variance terms of $\hat{q}_{\alpha,lc}(x)$ are exactly the same as those for $\tilde{q}_\alpha(x)$ given in Theorem 6.3. Therefore, $\hat{q}_{\alpha,lc}(x)$ has the same asymptotic distribution as that of $\tilde{q}_\alpha(x)$ presented in Theorem 6.3.

One can also use a local linear method by replacing (6.27) by the following objective function:

$$\min_{a,b} \sum_{j=1}^{n} \rho_\alpha(Y_j - a - (X_j - x)'b) W_h(X_j, x), \qquad (6.28)$$

where the minimizer a is the local linear estimator of $q_\alpha(x)$, and b estimates the derivative of $q_\alpha(x)$.

Let $\hat{q}_{\alpha,ll}(x)$ denote the resulting estimator of $q_\alpha(x)$. The leading MSE term of $\hat{q}_{\alpha,ll}(x)$ can be found in Fan, Hu and Truong (1994) and Yu and Jones (1997). The leading variance term is the same as that for the local constant estimator (hence identical to that given in Theorem 6.3), while the leading bias term is given by

$$\text{bias}(\hat{q}_{\alpha,ll}(x)) = \frac{1}{2} \kappa_2 \sum_{s=1}^{q} h_s^2 q_{\alpha,ss}(x), \qquad (6.29)$$

where $q_{\alpha,ss}(x) = \partial^2 q_\alpha(x)/\partial x_s^2$.

6.5 Conditional CDF and Quantile Estimation with Mixed Discrete and Continuous Covariates

When X is a vector of mixed discrete and continuous variables, we need to replace the kernel function by a generalized product kernel appropriate for mixed data types. We first discuss estimating a conditional CDF without smoothing the dependent variable Y. We estimate $F(y|x)$ by

$$\tilde{F}(y|x) = \frac{n^{-1}\sum_{i=1}^{n} \mathbf{1}(Y_i \leq y)K_\gamma(X_i, x)}{\hat{\mu}(x)}, \qquad (6.30)$$

where $\hat{\mu}(x) = n^{-1}K_\gamma(X_i, x)$ is the kernel estimator of $\mu(x)$, $K_\gamma(X_i, x)$ $= W_h(X_i^c, x^c)L_\lambda(X_i^d, x^d)$, $W_h(X_i^c, x^c) = \prod_{s=1}^{q} h_s^{-1}w((X_{is} - x_s)/h_s)$, $L_\lambda(X_i^d, x^d) = \prod_{s=1}^{r} l(X_{is}^d, x_s^d, \lambda_s)$, and $l(X_{is}^d, x_s^d, \lambda_s) = \mathbf{1}(X_{is}^d = x_s^d) + \lambda_s\mathbf{1}(X_{is}^d \neq x_s^d)$.

Should we elect to smooth the dependent variable Y, we obtain another estimator of $F(y|x)$ given by

$$\hat{F}(y|x) = \frac{n^{-1}\sum_{i=1}^{n} G\left(\frac{y-Y_i}{h_0}\right) K_\gamma(X_i, x)}{\hat{\mu}(x)}, \qquad (6.31)$$

where $G(\cdot)$ is a CDF, say, the standard normal CDF, and h_0 is the smoothing parameter associated with Y.

Define $\tilde{M}(y, x) = [\tilde{F}(y|x) - F(y|x)]\hat{\mu}(x)$ and also let $\hat{M}(y, x) = [\hat{F}(y|x) - F(y|x)]\hat{\mu}(x)$. The following two theorems give the asymptotic distributions of $\tilde{F}(y|x)$ and $\hat{F}(y|x)$, respectively.

Theorem 6.5. *Under regularity conditions similar to those given in Theorem 6.1 but with the differentiability condition changed with respect to x^c (see Li and Racine (forthcoming) for details), we have*

(i) *Letting $\eta_n = |\bar{h}|^6 + (nh_1 \ldots h_q)^{-1}|\bar{h}|^2$, then*

$$\mathrm{MSE}[\tilde{M}(y, x)] = \left\{\sum_{s=1}^{q} h_s^2 B_{1s}(y|x) + \sum_{s=1}^{r} \lambda_s B_{2s}(y|x)\right\}^2$$
$$+ V_0(y|x)(nh_1 \ldots h_q)^{-1} + O(\eta_n),$$

where

$$B_{1s}(y, x) = (1/2)\kappa_2[2F_s(y|x)\mu_s(x) + \mu(x)F_{ss}(y|x)] \text{ and}$$
$$B_{2s}(y, x) = \mu(x)^{-1} \sum_{z^d \in \mathcal{S}^d} \mathbf{1}_s(z^d, x^d)\Big[F(y|x^c, z^d)\mu(x^c, z^d)$$
$$- F(y|x)\mu(x)\Big],$$

where $\mathbf{1}_s(v^d, x^d)$ is defined in (4.24).

(ii) Letting $\Sigma_{y|x} = F(y|x)[1 - F(y|x)]/\mu(x)$, then

$$(nh_1 \ldots h_q)^{1/2}\left[\tilde{F}(y|x) - F(y|x) - \sum_{s=1}^{q} h_s^2 B_{1s}(y|x)\right.$$

$$\left. - \sum_{s=1}^{r} \lambda_s B_{2s}(y|x)\right] \xrightarrow{d} N(0, \Sigma_{y|x}).$$

Theorem 6.6. *Define* $|\lambda| = \sum_{s=1}^{r} \lambda_s$, $B_{10}(y|x) = (1/2)\kappa_2 F_{00}(y|x)$, $\Omega(y, x) = \kappa^q F_0(y|x)/\mu(x)$, *and let* $\Sigma_{y|x}$, $B_{1s}(y, x)$ *and* $B_{2s}(y, x)$ *be the same as those defined in Theorem 6.5. Then under assumptions given in Li and Racine (forthcoming), we have*

$$\mathrm{MSE}[\hat{M}(y, x)] = \mu(x)\left\{\sum_{s=0}^{q} h_s^2 B_{1s}(y, x) + \sum_{s=1}^{r} \lambda_s B_{2s}(y, x)\right\}^2$$

$$+ \frac{\mu(x)^2[\Sigma_{y|x} - h_0\Omega(y, x)]}{nh_1 \ldots h_q} + O(\eta_n),$$

where $\eta_n = |\bar{h}|^6 + |\lambda|^2 + (nh_1 \ldots h_q)^{-1}(|\bar{h}|^2 + |\lambda|)$, *and*

$$(nh_1 \ldots h_q)^{1/2}\left[\hat{F}(y|x) - F(y|x) - \sum_{s=1}^{q} h_s^2 B_{1s}(y, x) - \sum_{s=1}^{r} \lambda_s B_{2s}(y|x)\right]$$

$$\xrightarrow{d} N(0, \Sigma_{y|x}).$$

The proofs of Theorems 6.5 and 6.6 are given in Section 6.9.2. As discussed above, to obtain a quantile estimator, invert $\hat{F}(\cdot)$:

$$\hat{q}_\alpha(x) = \hat{F}^{-1}(\alpha|x).$$

In practice we compute $\hat{q}_\alpha(x)$ via

$$\hat{q}_\alpha(x) = \arg\min_q |\alpha - \hat{F}(q|x)|.$$

The asymptotic distribution of $\hat{q}_\alpha(x)$ is given in the next theorem.

Theorem 6.7. *Define* $B_{n,\alpha}(x) = B_n(q_\alpha(x)|x)/f(q_\alpha(x)|x)$, *where* $(y = q_\alpha(x))$ $B_n(y|x) = [\sum_{s=0}^{q} h_s^2 B_{1s}(y|x) + \sum_{s=1}^{r} \lambda_s B_{2s}(y|x)]$ *is the leading bias term of* $\hat{F}(y|x)$. *Then under the same conditions as those used in Theorem 6.6, we have*

(i) $\hat{q}_\alpha(x) \to q_\alpha(x)$ in probability, and

(ii) $(nh_1 \ldots h_q)^{1/2}[\hat{q}_\alpha(x) - q_\alpha(x) - B_{n,\alpha}(x)] \to N(0, V_\alpha(x))$ in distribution, where $V_\alpha(x) = \alpha(1 - \alpha)\kappa^q/[f^2(q_\alpha(x)|x)\mu(q_\alpha(x))] \equiv V(q_\alpha(x)|x)/f^2(q_\alpha(x)|x)$ (since $\alpha = F(q_\alpha(x)|x)$).

The proof of Theorem 6.7 is similar to the proof of Theorem 6.4 and is therefore omitted here.

In Exercise 6.4 the reader is asked to show that the optimal smoothing parameters for estimating $\hat{F}(y|x)$ should satisfy $h_s \sim n^{-1/(4+q)}$ for $s = 1, \ldots, q$, $\lambda_s \sim n^{-2/(4+q)}$ for $s = 1, \ldots, r$, and $h_0 \sim n^{-2/(4+q)}$. Unfortunately, to the best of our knowledge, there does not exist an *automatic* data-driven method for optimally selecting bandwidths when estimating a conditional CDF in the sense that a weighted integrated MSE is minimized. Given the close relationship between the conditional PDF and the conditional CDF, Li and Racine (forthcoming) recommend using the least squares cross-validation method based on conditional PDF estimation when selecting bandwidths and using them for estimating the conditional CDF function $\hat{F}(y|x)$ and the conditional quantile function $\hat{q}_\alpha(x)$.

Let $\bar{h}_s$ and $\bar{\lambda}_s$ denote the values of h_s and λ_s selected by minimizing the PDF cross-validation function (see Chapter 5). Recall that in Chapter 5 we showed that the optimal bandwidths are of order $\bar{h}_s \sim n^{-1/(5+q)}$ for $s = 0, 1, \ldots, q$, and $\bar{\lambda}_s \sim n^{-2/(5+q)}$ for $s = 1, \ldots, r$ (assuming that Y is a continuous variable). To obtain bandwidths that have the correct optimal rates for $\hat{F}(y|x)$, Li and Racine (forthcoming) recommend using $\hat{h}_0 = \bar{h}_0 n^{\frac{1}{5+q} - \frac{2}{4+q}}$, $\hat{h}_s = \bar{h}_s n^{\frac{1}{5+q} - \frac{1}{4+q}}$ ($s = 1, \ldots, q$), and $\hat{\lambda}_s = \bar{\lambda}_s n^{\frac{2}{5+q} - \frac{2}{4+q}}$ ($s = 1, \ldots, r$).

Theorems 6.6 and 6.7 hold true with the above (stochastic) bandwidths $\hat{h}_0, \hat{h}_s, \hat{\lambda}_s$.

6.6   A Small Monte Carlo Simulation Study

We briefly investigate the finite-sample performance of the conditional quantile estimator defined in (6.18) and (6.19), following Li and Racine (forthcoming). The DGP we consider is given by

$$Y_i = \beta_0 + \beta_1 X_{i1}^d + \beta_2 X_{i2}^d + \beta_3 \sin(X_i^c) + \epsilon_i$$

where $X_i^c \sim \text{uniform}[-2\pi, 2\pi]$, X_{i1}^d and X_{i2}^d are both binomial (the total number of discrete cells is $c = 4$), and $\epsilon_i \sim N(0, \sigma^2)$ with $\sigma = 0.50$ and

Table 6.1: MSE performance of the nonsmooth and smooth quantile estimators

h_{x^c}	$(\lambda_{x_1^d}, \lambda_{x_2^d})$	$h_y = h_0$	MSE
$1.06\sigma_x n^{-1/6}$	0	Indicator	0.49
$1.06\sigma_x n^{-1/6}$	0	$1.06\sigma_y n^{-1/6}$	0.41
$1.06\sigma_x n^{-1/6}$	LSCV	$1.06\sigma_y n^{-1/6}$	0.33
LSCV	LSCV	LSCV	0.25

$n = 100$.

We consider the estimator given in (6.18) that treats Y using an indicator function, i.e., $\mathbf{1}(y - Y_i \geq 0)$, and the estimator given in (6.19) that uses a smooth function, $G((y - Y_i)/h_0)$, where $G(\cdot)$ is the Gaussian CDF kernel. Regardless of the kernel function chosen for $G((y - Y_i)/h_0)$, as $h_0 \to 0$, $G((y - Y_i)/h_0) \to \mathbf{1}(y - Y_i \geq 0)$, hence to generate results for $\mathbf{1}(y - Y_i \geq 0)$ we simply set $h_y = 0$ (choosing a sufficiently small h_0).

We conduct 1,000 Monte Carlo replications, each time computing the MSE of the quantile estimator with $\alpha = 0.50$. We report the median relative MSE over the 1,000 replications, and investigate the relative performance of the nonsmooth and smooth quantile approaches based on a variety of bandwidth selectors. Results are summarized in Table 6.1, where numbers less than one indicate superior performance of the smooth quantile estimator, (6.19).

From Table 6.1 we observe that by smoothing Y with an ad hoc formula $h_y = 1.06\sigma_y n^{-1/6}$, MSE is reduced by 20% compared with the estimator that uses a nonsmooth indicator function for Y. Next, smoothing over the discrete covariates by LSCV reduces the MSE by another 20%. Finally, choosing h_x and h_y also by LSCV (rather than using the ad hoc formula) reduces the MSE by a further 25%. Using LSCV reduces the MSE by half compared with ad hoc choices of h_y or indicator functions for the dependent variable and the discrete covariates. Note that in the above experiment, all covariates are relevant. In practice it is often the case that some covariates are in fact irrelevant (i.e., are independent of the dependent variable), and in such cases, the efficiency gains achieved by using LSCV will be even larger since the LSCV approach can automatically smooth out irrelevant covariates.

Nonparametric quantile regression with dependent data was considered by Cai (2002). See also Koenker and Xiao (2002), who discuss inference regarding the quantile regression process.

6.7 Nonparametric Estimation of Hazard Functions

By combining the results on conditional CDF estimation discussed above and the conditional PDF estimator discussed in Chapter 5, nonparametric estimators of hazard functions can easily be obtained. We first provide a formal definition of a hazard function.

Definition 6.1. *Let T denote a random variable that stands for the time of exit from a state (e.g., no longer unemployed). The probability that a person who, having occupied a state up to time t, leaves it in the short time interval of length dt after t is $\mathrm{P}(t \leq T < t + dt | T \geq t)$. The* **hazard function** *is defined as*

$$h(t) = \lim_{dt \to 0} \frac{\mathrm{P}(t \leq T < t + dt | T \geq t)}{dt},$$

which is the instantaneous rate of exit.

Roughly speaking, the hazard function can be interpreted so that $h(t)dt$ is the probability of exit from a state in a short time interval of length dt after t, conditional on the state still being occupied at t.

Hazard functions are often used to describe the probability of exiting from unemployed status (i.e., getting a job) in an immediate future time interval (say, next week), conditional on the individual being unemployed at present (up to this week). They are also often used to describe the probability of death of a patient in the next time period (say, next week) conditional on the patient being alive up to this week.

It can be shown that the hazard function can be written as (see the hint in Exercise 6.6)

$$h(t) = \frac{f_T(t)}{1 - F_T(t)} = -\frac{d}{dt} \ln[1 - F_T(t)], \ t > 0. \tag{6.32}$$

Hence, $f_T(t) = h(t) \exp(- \int_0^t h(v)dv)$.

$1 - F_T(t)$ is called the "survival function." This is because $F_T(t) = \mathrm{P}(T \leq t)$ is the probability of exit (say, death) before t, hence $1 - F_T(t) = \mathrm{P}(T > t)$ is the probability of survival beyond period t.

One commonly used parametric PDF in hazard and duration analysis is the Weibull distribution, whose PDF is given by

$$f_T(t; a, b) = abt^{b-1} \exp(-at^b), \ t > 0, a, b > 0.$$

The hazard function is given by

$$h(x) = bat^{b-1}.$$

Hence the hazard function is strictly increasing if $b > 1$ and strictly decreasing if $b < 1$. When $b = 1$, the Weibull distribution reduces to the exponential distribution with constant hazard. The Weibull distribution is often used to model unemployment data.

Often interest lies in a hazard rate conditional on the outcome of a set of variables x. The conditional hazard function is defined as

$$h(t|x) = \frac{f_T(t|x)}{1 - F_T(t|x)}, \ t > 0. \tag{6.33}$$

For example, T may be the time of death of cancer patients and x contains treatment type and individual characteristics. We assume that x contains q continuous and r discrete variables. Nonparametric estimation of $h(t|x)$ can be readily obtained by replacing $f_T(t|x)$ and $F_T(t|x)$ by their nonparametric estimators,

$$\hat{h}(t|x) = \frac{\hat{f}_T(t|x)}{1 - \hat{F}_T(t|x)}, \tag{6.34}$$

where $\hat{f}_T(t|x)$ and $\hat{F}_T(t|x)$ are defined in Chapter 5 and Section 6.5, respectively. From $\hat{F}_T(t|x) = \hat{F}_T(t|x) = O_p(\sum_{s=0}^{q} h_s^2 + \sum_{s=1}^{r} \lambda_s + (nh_1 \dots h_q)^{-1})$, it is easy to see that the asymptotic distribution of $\hat{h}(t|x)$ is the same as that of $\hat{f}_T(t|x)/a_{t,x}$, where $a_{t,x} = 1 - F_T(t|x)$. Hence, by Theorem 5.3 we immediately know that

$$(nh_1 \dots h_q)^{1/2} \left\{ \hat{h}(t|x) - h(t|x) \right.$$

$$\left. - a_{t,x}^{-1} \left[\sum_{s=1}^{q} B_{1s}(t, x) h_s^2 + \sum_{s=1}^{r} B_{2,s}(t, x) \right] \right\}$$

$$\xrightarrow{d} N \left(0, \frac{V(t|x)}{a_{t,x}^2} \right), \tag{6.35}$$

where $B_{1s}(t, x)$ and $B_{2s}(t, x)$ are defined in Theorem 5.3.

In the discussion above we assume that the data is not censored. In applications such as follow-up surveys for patients having received a particular treatment, a patient may fail to respond to a survey before dying and the data will thereby be censored. We will discuss how to handle censored data in nonparametric and semiparametric settings in Chapter 11.

Also, when one estimates a hazard function in high dimensional settings, the curse of dimensionality may preclude accurate nonparametric estimation. In such cases, one may choose to instead estimate a semiparametric hazard model as proposed by Horowitz (1999), who considered semiparametric proportional hazard models. See also Linton, Nielsen and van de Geer (2003) for kernel-based approaches to the estimation of multiplicative and additive hazard models.

6.8   Applications

6.8.1   Boston Housing Data

We consider the 1970s era Boston housing data that has been extensively analyzed by a number of authors. For what follows, we report on the application outlined in Li and Racine (forthcoming). This dataset contains $n = 506$ observations, and the response variable Y is the median price of a house in a given area. Following Chaudhuri et al. (1997, p. 724), we focus on three important covariates: RM = average number of rooms per house in the area (rounded to the nearest integer), LSTAT = percentage of the population having lower economic status in the area, and DIS = weighted distance to five Boston employment centers. An interesting feature is that the data is right censored at \$50,000 (1970s housing prices), which makes this particularly well suited to quantile methods.

We first shuffle the data and create two independent samples of size $n_1 = 400$ and $n_2 = 106$. We then fit a linear parametric quantile model and nonparametric quantile model using the estimation sample of size n_1, and generate the predicted median of Y based upon the covariates in the independent hold-out data of size n_2. Finally, we compute the mean square prediction error defined as MSPE $= n_2^{-1} \sum_{i=1}^{n_2} (Y_i - \hat{q}_{0.5}(X_i))^2$ where $q_{0.5}(X_i)$ is the predicted median generated from either the parametric or nonparametric model, and Y_i is the actual value of the response in the hold-out dataset. To deflect potential criticism that our

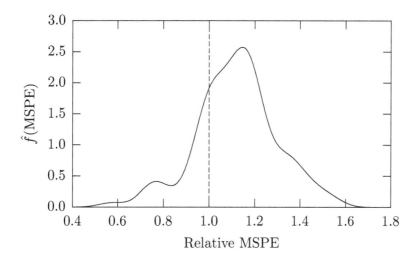

Figure 6.1: Density of the relative MSPE over the 100 random splits of the data. Values > 1 indicate superior out-of-sample performance of the kernel method for a given random split of the data (lower quartile=1.03, median=1.13, upper quartile=1.20).

result reflects an unrepresentative split of the data, we repeat this process 100 times, each time computing the relative MSPE (i.e., the parametric MSPE divided by the nonparametric MSPE). For each split, we use the method of Hall et al. (2004) to compute data-dependent bandwidths. The median relative MSPE over the 100 splits of the data is 1.13 (lower quartile=1.03, upper quartile=1.20), indicating that the nonparametric approach is producing superior out-of-sample quantile estimates. Figure 6.1 presents a density estimate summarizing these results for the 100 random splits of the data.

Figure 6.1 reveals that 76% of all sample splits (i.e., the area to the right of the vertical bar) had a relative efficiency greater than 1, or, equivalently, in 76 out of 100 splits, the nonparametric quantile model yields better predictions of the median housing price than the parametric quantile model. Given the small sample size and the fact that there exist three covariates, we feel this is a telling application for the nonparametric method. Of course, we are not suggesting that we will outperform an approximately correct parametric model. Rather, we only wish to suggest that we can often outperform common parametric specifications that can be found in the literature.

6.8.2   Adolescent Growth Charts

Growth charts are used by pediatricians and parents alike for comparing children's growth to a standard range. Height, weight, and body mass index (BMI) measurements are used to document a child's height and weight based on age in months. Measurements are compared to the standard or normal range for children of the same sex and age.

Growth charts provide an early warning that the child has a medical problem. For instance, too rapid growth may indicate the presence of a hydrocephalus (an accumulation of liquid within the cavity of the cranium), a brain tumor or other conditions that cause macrocephaly (the condition of having an unusually large head; it differs from hydrocephalus because there is no increase in intracranial pressure), while too slow growth may indicate malformations of the brain, early fusion of sutures or other problems. Insufficient gain in weight, height or a combination may indicate failure-to-thrive, chronic illness, neglect or other problems.

For the application that follows, data is taken from the Center for Disease Control (CDC) and Prevention's National Health and Nutrition Examination Survey. A variety of methods have been used for constructing growth curves, and results are typically presented as quantiles. For instance, the U.S. Center for Disease Control and Prevention use a two stage approach. In the first stage, empirical percentiles are smoothed by a variety of parametric and nonparametric procedures. To obtain corresponding percentiles and z scores, the smoothed percentiles are then approximated using a modified least median of squares estimation procedure in the second stage. We consider the direct application of mixed data quantile methods using the estimator defined in (6.19), and by way of example construct weight-for-age quantiles. We report the 25th, 50th, and 75th quantiles and plot those for males in Figure 6.2. Bandwidths were obtained via least squares cross-validation, with $\hat{h}_{\text{weight}} = 1.22$, $\hat{h}_{\text{age}} = 8.11$, and $\hat{\lambda}_{\text{sex}} = 0.12$.

Figure 6.2 readily reveals many features present in this dataset, including heteroskedasticity that increases with age and asymmetry in the conditional CDF of weight.

6.8.3   Conditional Value at Risk

Financial instruments are subject to many types of risk, including interest risk, default risk, liquidity risk, and market risk. Value at risk

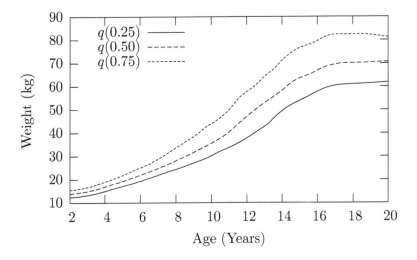

Figure 6.2: Weight-for-age quantiles for males.

(VaR) seeks to measure the latter; it is a single estimate of the amount by which one's position in an instrument could decline due to general market movements over a specific holding period. One can think of VaR as the maximal loss of a financial position during a given time period for a given probability; hence VaR is simply a measure of loss arising from an unlikely event under normal market conditions (Tsay (2002, p. 257)). For what follows, we report on the application outlined in Li and Racine (forthcoming).

Letting $\Delta V(l)$ denote the change in value of a financial instrument from time t to $t+l$, we define VaR over a time horizon l with probability p as

$$p = \mathrm{P}[\Delta V(l) \le \mathrm{VaR}] = F_l(\mathrm{VaR}),$$

where $F_l(\mathrm{VaR})$ is the unknown CDF of $\Delta V(l)$. VaR assumes negative values when p is small since the holder of the instrument suffers a loss.[2] Therefore, the probability that the holder will suffer a loss greater than or equal to VaR is p, and the probability that the maximal loss is VaR

---

[2]For a long position we are concerned with the lower tail of returns, i.e., a loss due to a fall in value. For a short position we are concerned with the upper tail, i.e., a loss due to a rise in value. In the latter case we simply model $1 - F_l(\mathrm{VaR})$ rather than $F_l(\mathrm{VaR})$. Of course, in either case we are modeling the tails of a distribution.

is $1 - p$. The quantity

$$\text{VaR}_p = \inf\{\text{VaR}|F_l(\text{VaR}) \geq p\}$$

is the pth quantile of $F_l(\text{VaR})$; hence VaR_p is simply the pth quantile of the CDF $F_l(\text{VaR})$. The convention is to drop the subscript p and refer to, e.g, "the 5% VaR" ($\text{VaR}_{0.05}$). Obviously the CDF $F_l(\text{VaR})$ is unknown in practice and must be estimated.

Conditional value at risk (CVaR) seeks to measure VaR when covariates are involved, which simply conditions one's estimate on a vector of covariates, X. Of course, the conditional CDF $F_l(\text{VaR}|X)$ is again unknown and must be estimated. A variety of parametric methods can be found in the literature. In what follows, we compare results from five popular parametric approaches with the nonparametric quantile estimator defined in (6.19).

We consider data used in Tsay (2002) for IBM stock (r_t, daily log returns (%) from July 3, 1962, through December 31, 1998) plotted in Figure 6.3. Log returns correspond approximately to percentage changes in the value of a financial position, and are used throughout. The CVaR computed from the quantile of the distribution of r_{t+1} conditional upon information available at time t is therefore in percentage terms, and so the dollar amount of CVaR is the cash value of one's position multiplied by the CVaR of the log return series. For what follows, we compute CVaR for a one day horizon ($l = 1$).

Following Tsay (2002), we model CVaR for daily log returns of IBM stock using the following explanatory variables:

(i) X_{1t}: an indicator variable for October, November, and December, equaling 1 if t is in the fourth quarter. This variable takes care of potential fourth-quarter effects (or year-end effects), if any, on the daily IBM stock returns.

(ii) X_{2t}: an indicator variable for the behavior of the previous trading day, equaling 1 if and only if the log return on the previous trading day was $\leq 2.5\%$. This variable captures the possibility of panic selling when the price of IBM stock dropped 2.5% or more on the previous trading day.

(iii) X_{3t}: a qualitative measurement of volatility, measured as the number of days between $t - 1$ and $t - 5$ having a log return with magnitude exceeding a threshold ($|r_{t-i}| \geq 2.5\%$, $i = 1, 2, \ldots, 5$).

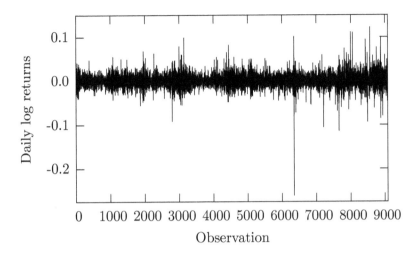

Figure 6.3: Time plot of daily log returns of IBM stock from July 3, 1962, through December 31, 1998.

(iv) X_{4t}: an annual trend defined as (year of time t-1961)/38, used to detect any trend behavior of extreme returns of IBM stock.

(v) X_{5t}: a volatility series based on a Gaussian GARCH(1,1) model for the mean corrected series, equaling σ_t where σ_t^2 is the conditional variance of the GARCH(1,1) model.

Table 6.2 presents results reported in Tsay (2002, pp. 282, 295) along with the estimator defined in (6.19) for a variety of existing approaches to measuring CVaR for December 31, 1998. The explanatory variables assumed values of $X_{1,9190} = 1$, $X_{2,9190} = 0$, $X_{3,9190} = 0$, $X_{4,9190} = 0.9737$, and $X_{5,9190} = 1.7966$. Values are based on an assumed long position of \$10 million, hence if value at risk is -2%, then we obtain VaR $= \$10,000,000 \times 0.02 = \$200,000$.

Observe that, depending on one's choice of parametric model, one can obtain estimates that differ by as much 82% for 5% CVaR and 63% for 1% for this example. Of course, this variation arises due to model uncertainty. One might take a Bayesian approach to deal with this uncertainty, averaging over models, or alternatively consider nonparametric methods that are robust to functional specification. The kernel quantile approach provides guidance yielding sensible estimates that might be of value to practitioners. Another use for the nonparametric

Table 6.2: Conditional value at risk for a long position in IBM stock

Model	5% CVaR	1% CVaR
Inhomogeneous Poisson, GARCH(1,1)	$303,756	$497,425
Conditional normal, IGARCH(1,1)	$302,500	$426,500
AR(2)-GARCH(1,1)	$287,700	$409,738
Student-t_5 AR(2)-GARCH(1,1)	$283,520	$475,943
Extreme value	$166,641	$304,969
LSCV CDF	$258,727	$417,192

quantile estimator might be to evaluate the CDF nonparametrically at the values produced by the parametric estimators above to assess which quantile the parametric values in fact correspond to, presuming of course that the parametric models are misspecified.

Interestingly, Tsay (2002) finds that X_{1t} and X_{2t} are irrelevant explanatory variables. The LSCV bandwidths are consistent with this. However, X_{3t} is also found to be irrelevant; hence only one volatility measure is relevant.

6.8.4   Real Income in Italy, 1951–1998

We again consider the Italian GDP panel discussed previously in Section 1.13.5, a panel containing data for income in Italy for 21 regions for the period 1951–1998 (millions of lire, 1990=base). We consider the estimator defined in (6.19) and model the 25th, 50th, and 75th income quantiles treating time as an ordered discrete regressor. Figure 6.4 plots the resulting quantile estimates.

Recall that Figure 1.9 presented in Chapter 1 revealed that the distribution of income evolved from a unimodal one in the early 1950s to a markedly bimodal one in the 1990s. This feature is clearly captured by the nonparametric quantile estimator, as can be seen in Figure 6.4.

6.8.5   Multivariate Y Conditional CDF Example: GDP Growth and Population Growth Conditional on OECD Status

In Section 5.5.5 of Chapter 5 we modeled a multivariate Y conditional PDF with data-driven methods of bandwidth selection, the sample size

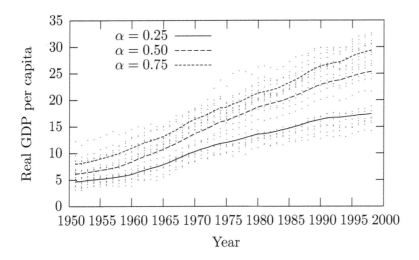

Figure 6.4: Income quantiles for Italian real GDP.

was $n = 616$, and Y consisted of the following variables: y_1, the growth rate of income per capita during each period; y_2, the annual rate of population growth during each period; x, OECD status $(0/1)$. We now estimate the conditional CDF $F(y_1, y_2|x)$ and present the resulting conditional PDF in Figure 5.5, that is, we plot $\hat{F}(y_1, y_2|X = 0)$ and $\hat{F}(y_1, y_2|X = 1)$ again using Hall et al.'s (2004) least squares cross-validation method.

Figure 6.5 presents a clear picture of this multivariate Y conditional CDF. A stochastic dominance relationship is evident in that OECD countries tend to have lower population growth rates and higher GDP growth rates than their non-OECD counterparts.

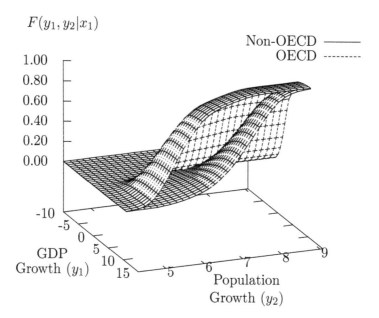

Figure 6.5: Multivariate Y conditional CDF with Y consisting of GDP and population growth rates and X being OECD status.

6.9 Proofs

6.9.1 Proofs of Theorems 6.1, 6.2, and 6.4

Proof of Theorem 6.1 (i).

$$
\begin{aligned}
\mathrm{E}[\tilde{F}(y|x)\hat{\mu}(x)] &= \mathrm{E}[\mathbf{1}(Y_i \le y)W_h(X_i, x)] \\
&= \mathrm{E}[W_h(X_i, x)\mathrm{E}(\mathbf{1}(Y_i \le y)|X_i)] \\
&= \mathrm{E}[W_h(X_i, x)F(y|X_i)] \\
&= (h_1 \ldots h_q)^{-1} \int \mu(z)W\left(\frac{z-x}{h}\right)F(y|z)dz \\
&= \int \mu(x+hv)F(y|x+hv)W(v)dv \\
&= \int \left[\mu(x) + \sum_{s=1}^{q}\mu_s(x)h_s v_s + \frac{1}{2}\sum_{s=1}^{q}\sum_{t=1}^{q}\mu_{ts}(x)h_s h_t v_s v_t\right] \\
&\quad \times \left[F(y|x) + \sum_{s=1}^{q}F_s(y|x)h_s v_s\right. \\
&\quad \left. + \frac{1}{2}\sum_{s=1}^{q}\sum_{t=1}^{q}F_{ts}(y|x)h_s h_t v_s v_t\right] W(v)\,dv + o(|h|^2) \\
&= \mu(x)F(y|x) + \frac{1}{2}\kappa_2 \sum_{s=1}^{q}h_s^2\left[\mu(x)F_{ss}(y|x)\right. \\
&\quad \left. + 2\mu_s(x)F_s(y|x) + F(y|x)\mu_{ss}(x)\right] + o(|h|^2). \qquad (6.36)
\end{aligned}
$$

Similarly,

$$
\mathrm{E}[\hat{\mu}(x)] = \mathrm{E}[W_h(X_i, x)] = \mu(x) + (1/2)\kappa_2 \sum_{s=1}^{q}h_s^2\mu_{ss}(x) + o(|h|^2). \qquad (6.37)
$$

By noting that $\mathrm{E}[\tilde{M}(y,x)] = \mathrm{E}[\tilde{F}(y|x)\hat{\mu}(x)] - F(y|x)\mathrm{E}[\hat{\mu}(x)]$, Theorem 6.1 (i) follows from (6.36) and (6.37). $\qquad \square$

Proof of Theorem 6.1 (ii).

$$
\begin{aligned}
\mathrm{var}(\tilde{M}(y,x)) &= n^{-1}\mathrm{var}[(\mathbf{1}(Y_i \leq y) - F(y|x))W_h(X_i,x)] \\
&= n^{-1}\{\mathrm{E}[(\mathbf{1}(Y_i \leq y) - F(y|x))^2]W_h(X_i,x)^2 + O(1)\} \\
&= n^{-1}\mathrm{E}\{\mathrm{E}[(\mathbf{1}(Y_i \leq y) - F(y|x))^2|X_i]W_h(X_i,x)^2\} + O(n^{-1}) \\
&= n^{-1}\mathrm{E}\{[F(y|X_i) - 2F(y|x)F(y|X_i) + F(y|x)^2]W_h(X_i,x)^2\} \\
&\quad + O(n^{-1}) \\
&= n^{-1}\int \mu(z)[F(y|z) - 2F(y|x)F(y|z) + F(y|x)^2]W_h(z,x)^2dz \\
&\quad + O(n^{-1}) \\
&= (nh_1\ldots h_q)^{-1}\int \mu(x - hv)[F(y|x - hv) - 2F(y|x)F(y|x - hv) \\
&\quad + F(y|x)^2]W(v)^2dv + O(n^{-1}) \\
&= \kappa^q(nh_1\ldots h_q)^{-1}\mu(x)[F(y|x) - F(y|x)^2] \\
&\quad + O\left((nh_1\ldots h_q)^{-1}|h|^2 + n^{-1}\right),
\end{aligned}
$$

where $\kappa = \int w(v)^2dv$. $\qquad\square$

Proof of Theorem 6.1 (iii). Define $B_n(y,x) = \sum_{s=1}^{q}h_s^2B_s(y,x)$. Then

$$
\begin{aligned}
[\tilde{F}(y|x) - F(y|x) - B_n(y,x)] &= [\tilde{F}(y|x) - F(y|x) - B_n(y,x)]\hat{\mu}(x)/\hat{\mu}(x) \\
&= [\tilde{F}(y|x) - F(y|x) - B_n(y,x)]\hat{\mu}(x)/\mu(x) + o_p(1) \\
&\equiv \tilde{A}(y,x)/\mu(x) + o_p(1),
\end{aligned}
$$

where $\tilde{A}(y,x) = [\tilde{F}(y|x) - F(y|x) - B_n(y,x)]\hat{\mu}(x)$. By Theorem 6.1 (i) and (ii) we know that $\mathrm{E}[\tilde{A}(y,x)] = O(|h|^3)$ and that $\mathrm{var}[\tilde{A}(y,x)] = (nh_1\ldots h_q)^{-1}\mu(x)^2\mathrm{var}(y,x) + O(\eta_n)$ $(\eta_n = (nh_1\ldots h_q)^{-1}|h|^2)$. By virtue of a CLT argument one can show that

$$
(nh_1\ldots h_q)^{1/2}\tilde{A}(y,x) \to N\left(0,\mu(x)^2\Sigma_{y|x}\right) \text{ in distribution.}
$$

Hence,

$$
\begin{aligned}
(nh_1\ldots h_q)^{1/2}&[\tilde{F}(y|x) - F(y|x) - B_n(y,x)] \\
&= (nh_1\ldots h_q)^{1/2}\tilde{A}(y,x)/\mu(x) + o_p(1) \\
&\xrightarrow{d} \mu(x)^{-1}N\left(0,\mu(x)^2\Sigma_{y|x}\right) = N(0,\Sigma_{y|x}).
\end{aligned}
$$

$\qquad\square$

Proof of Theorem 6.2 (i). Using Lemma 6.1 we have

$$
\begin{aligned}
\mathrm{E}[\hat{M}(y,x)] &= \mathrm{E}\left[G\left(\frac{y-Y_i}{h_0}\right)W_h(X_i,x)\right] \\
&= \mathrm{E}\left\{\mathrm{E}[G\left(\frac{y-Y_i}{h_0}\right)|X_i]W_h(X_i,x)\right\} \\
&= \mathrm{E}\left\{\left[F(y|X_i)+\frac{\kappa_2 h_0^2}{2}F_{00}(y|X_i)\right]W_h(X_i,x)\right\}+o(h_0^2) \\
&= \int \mu(z)\left[F(y|z)+\frac{\kappa_2 h_0^2}{2}F_{00}(y|z)\right]W_h(z,x)dz+o(h_0^2) \\
&= \int \mu(x+hv)\left[F(y|x+hv)\right. \\
&\quad \left.+\frac{\kappa_2 h_0^2}{2}F_{00}(y|x+hv)\right]W(v)dv+o(h_0^2) \\
&= \mu(x)F(y|x)+\frac{\kappa_2 h_0^2}{2}\mu(x)F_{00}(y|x)+\kappa_2\sum_{s=1}^{q}h_s^2\mu_s(x)F_s(y|x) \\
&\quad +\frac{\kappa_2}{2}F(y|x)\sum_{s=1}^{q}\mu_{ss}(x)+o(|\bar{h}|^2). \qquad (6.38)
\end{aligned}
$$

Theorem 6.2 (i) follows from (6.37) and (6.38). $\qquad\square$

Proof of Theorem 6.2 (ii). Let $H_q = h_1 \ldots h_q$. By using Lemma 6.1 we

have

$$\mathrm{var}[\hat{M}(y,x) - F(y|x)\hat{\mu}(x)]$$

$$= n^{-1}\mathrm{var}\left[\left(G\left(\frac{y-Y_i}{h_0}\right) - F(y|x)\right)W_h(X_i,x)\right]$$

$$= \mathrm{E}\left\{\mathrm{E}\left[G^2\left(\frac{y-Y_i}{h_0}\right)|X_i\right]\right.$$

$$\left. - 2F(y|x)\mathrm{E}\left[G\left(\frac{y-Y_i}{h_0}\right)|X_i\right] + F(y|x)^2 W_h^2(X_i,x)\right\} + O(1)$$

$$= \mathrm{E}\{[F(y|X_i) - h_0 C_k F_0(y|X_i) - 2F(y|X_i)F(y|x) + F(y|x)^2$$

$$+ O(|\bar{h}|^2)]W_h^2(X_i,x)\} + O(n^{-1})$$

$$= \int \mu(z)[F(y|z) - h_0 C_k F_0(y|z) + 2F(y|z)F(y|x)$$

$$+ F(y|x)^2]W_h^2(z,x)dz + (s.o.)$$

$$= (nH_q)^{-1}\int \mu(x+hv)[F(y|x+hv) - h_0 C_k F_0(y|x+hv)$$

$$+ 2F(y|x+hv)F(y|x) + F(y|x)^2]W^2(v)dv + O(n^{-1})$$

$$= (nH_q)^{-1}\mu(x)\kappa^q\{F(y|x)[1 - F(y|x)] - h_0 C_k \mu(x)F_0(y|x)\}$$

$$+ O(|\bar{h}|^2(nH_q)^{-1} + n^{-1})$$

$$\equiv (nH_q)^{-1}\mu(x)^2[\Sigma_{y|x} - h_0\Omega(y,x)] + O(|\bar{h}|^2(nH_q)^{-1} + n^{-1}).$$

$\square$

Proof of Theorem 6.2 (ii). Part (iii) follows from (i) and (ii) and the Liapunov CLT. $\square$

Lemma 6.1.

(i) $\mathrm{E}\left[G\left(\frac{y-Y_i}{h_0}\right)|X_i\right] = F(y|X_i) + (1/2)\kappa_2 h_0^2 F_{00}(y|X_i) + o(h_0^2).$

(ii) $\mathrm{E}\left[G^2\left(\frac{y-Y_i}{h_0}\right)|X_i\right] = F(y|X_i) - h_0 C_k F_0(y|X_i) + o(h_0),$ *where* $C_k = 2\int G(v)w(v)v\,dv.$

Proof. This is left as an exercise. $\square$

Lemma 6.2. $\hat{F}(y+\epsilon_n|x) - \hat{F}(y|x) = f(y|x)\epsilon_n + O_p(h_0^2) + o_p(\epsilon_n + (nh_1\dots h_q)^{-1/2}).$

Proof. Let $A_n(\epsilon_n) = [\hat{F}(y + \epsilon_n|x) - \hat{F}(y|x)]\hat{\mu}(x)/\mu(x)$. Then $\hat{F}(y + \epsilon_n|x) - \hat{F}(y|x) = A_n(\epsilon_n)[1 + o_p(1)]$. By Lemma 6.1 we have

$$
\begin{aligned}
\mathrm{E}[A_n(\epsilon_n)] &= \mathrm{E}\left\{\mathrm{E}\left[G\left(\frac{y + \epsilon_n - Y_i}{h_0}\right) - G\left(\frac{y - Y_i}{h_0}\right)|X_i\right]\frac{K_\gamma(X_i, x)}{\mu(x)}\right\} \\
&= \mathrm{E}\left\{[F(y + \epsilon_n|x) - F(y|x) + O(h_0^2)]K_\gamma(X_i, x)\right\} \\
&= \mathrm{E}\left\{[f(y|X_i)\epsilon_n + O(\epsilon_n^2) + O(h_0^2)]K_\gamma(X_i, x)\right\} \\
&= f(y|X_i)\epsilon_n/\mu(x) + O(\epsilon_n^2 + h_0^2).
\end{aligned}
$$

Similarly,

$$
\begin{aligned}
\mathrm{var}[A_n(\epsilon_n)] &\leq n^{-1}\mu(x)^{-2}\mathrm{E}\Bigg\{\left[G\left(\frac{y + \epsilon_n - Y_i}{h_0}\right) - G\left(\frac{y - Y_i}{h_0}\right)\right]^2 \\
&\qquad \times K_\gamma^2(X_i, x)\Bigg\} = O(\epsilon_n(nh_1\ldots h_q)^{-1}).
\end{aligned}
$$

Therefore,

$$
\begin{aligned}
\hat{F}(y + \epsilon_n|x) - \hat{F}(y|x) &= A_n(\epsilon_n)[1 + o_p(1)] \\
&= f(y|x)\epsilon_n + O_p(h_0^2) + o_p(\epsilon_n + (nh_1\ldots h_q)^{-1/2}).
\end{aligned}
$$

$\square$

Proof of Theorem 6.4. We know that $\hat{F}(y|x) \to F(y|x)$ in probability by Theorem 6.2. It follows by Theorem 1 of Tucker (1967) that

$$
\sup_{y \in \mathbb{R}}|\hat{F}(y|x) - F(y|x)| \to 0 \text{ in probability} \tag{6.39}
$$

because $F(y|x)$ is a conditional CDF.

Since $q_\alpha(x)$ is unique, this implies that

$$
\delta = \delta(\epsilon) = \min\{\alpha - F(q_\alpha(x) - \epsilon|x), F(q_\alpha(x) + \epsilon|x) - \alpha\} > 0.
$$

It is easy to see that

$$
\begin{aligned}
\mathrm{P}\left[|\hat{q}_\alpha(x) - q_\alpha(x)| > \epsilon\right] &\leq \mathrm{P}\left[|F(\hat{q}_\alpha(x)|x) - F(y|x)| > \delta\right] \\
&\leq \mathrm{P}\left[\sup_y|\hat{F}(y|x) - F(y|x)| > \delta\right], \tag{6.40}
\end{aligned}
$$

which goes to zero by (6.39). Therefore, $\hat{F}(y|x) - F(y|x) \xrightarrow{p} 0$. We now prove Theorem 6.4. For any v, let $\epsilon_n = B_\alpha(x) + (nh)^{-1/2}\sigma_\alpha(x)v$. Then

$$Q_\alpha(v) \stackrel{\text{def}}{=} \mathrm{P}\left[(nH^q)^{1/2}\sigma_\alpha^{-1}(x)[\hat{q}_\alpha(x) - q_\alpha(x) - B_{n,\alpha}(x)\right.$$
$$\left. + o_p(|h|^2 + |\lambda|)] \le v\right]$$
$$\sim \mathrm{P}\left[\hat{q}_\alpha(x) \le q_\alpha(x) + \epsilon_n\right]$$
$$= \mathrm{P}\left[\hat{F}(q_\alpha(x) + \epsilon_n|x) \ge \alpha\right]$$
$$\sim \mathrm{P}\left[\hat{F}(q_\alpha(x)|x) \ge -f(q_\alpha(x)|x)\epsilon_n + \alpha\right] \quad (6.41)$$

by Lemma 6.2 and the assumption that $h_0 = o((nh_1 \ldots h_q)^{1/2})$. Therefore,

$$Q_n(v) \sim \mathrm{P}\left[(nh_1 \ldots h_q)^{1/2}\sigma^{-1}(q_\alpha(x)|x) \times \right.$$
$$\left. \left\{\hat{F}(q_\alpha(x)|x) - \alpha - B_n(q_\alpha(x)|x)\right\} \ge -v\right] \sim \Phi(v),$$

where $\Phi(\cdot)$ is the standard normal distribution.   □

6.9.2 Proofs of Theorems 6.5 and 6.6 (Mixed Covariates Case)

Theorem 6.5 is proved in Lemmas 6.3 and 6.4 below, while Theorem 6.6 is proved in Lemmas 6.5 and 6.6.

Lemma 6.3.

   (i) $\mathrm{E}[\tilde{M}(y,x)] = \mu(x)\sum_{s=1}^{q} h_s^2 B_{1s}(y,x) + \mu(x)\sum_{s=1}^{r} \lambda_s B_{2s}(y,x) + o(|\lambda| + |h|^2)$.

   (ii) $\mathrm{var}(\tilde{M}(y,x)) = \kappa^q \mu(x) F(y|x)[1 - F(y|x)]$, where $B_{1s}(y,x)$ and $B_{2s}(y,x)$ are defined in Theorem 6.5.

Proof. See Li and Racine (forthcoming).   □

Lemma 6.4.

$$(nh_1 \ldots h_q)^{1/2}\left[\tilde{F}(y|x) - F(y|x) - \sum_{s=1}^{q} h_s^2 B_{1s}(y,x) - \sum_{s=1}^{r} \lambda_s B_{2s}(y,x)\right]$$
$$\to N(0, V),$$

where $V = \kappa^q F(y|x)[1 - F(y|x)]/\mu(x)$.

Proof. By noting that $\tilde{F}(y|x) - F(y|x) = \tilde{M}(y,x)/\hat{\mu}(x) = \tilde{M}(y,x)/\mu(x)$ $+ o_p(1)$, Lemma 6.4 follows from Lemma 6.3 and the Liapunov CLT. $\square$

Lemma 6.5.

(i) $\mathrm{E}[\hat{M}(y,x)] = \mu(x) \sum_{s=0}^{q} h_s^2 B_{1s}(y,x) + \mu(x) \sum_{s=1}^{r} \lambda_s B_{2s}(y,x) + o(|\lambda| + |h|^2)$.

(ii) $\mathrm{var}(\hat{M}(y,x)) = \kappa^q (nh_1 \ldots h_q)^{-1} \mu(x)$

$$\times [F(y|x) - F(y|x)^2 - h_0 C_k F_0(y|x)].$$

Proof. This is left as an exercise. $\square$

Lemma 6.6.

$$(nh_1 \ldots h_q)^{1/2} [\hat{F}(y|x) - F(y|x) - \sum_{s=1}^{q} h_s^2 B_{1s}(y,x) - \sum_{s=1}^{r} \lambda_s B_{2s}(y,x)]$$

$$\xrightarrow{d} N(0, V),$$

where $V = \kappa^q [F(y|x) - F(y|x)^2]/\mu(x)$.

Proof. By noting that

$$\hat{F}(y|x) - F(y|x) = \hat{M}(y,x)/\hat{\mu}(x) = \hat{M}(y,x)/\mu(x) + o_p(1),$$

Lemma 6.6 follows from Lemma 6.5 and the Liapunov CLT. $\square$

6.10 Exercises

Exercise 6.1. Prove Lemma 6.1.

Hint: Use the change of variable and integration by parts arguments as we did in Section 1.4. Also note that $2 \int G(v)w(v)dv = \int dG^2(v) = G^2(v)|_{-\infty}^{\infty} = 1$.

Exercise 6.2. Prove Lemma 6.5.

Exercise 6.3. Prove Theorem 6.3.

Hint: Mimic the proof of Theorem 6.4 but without introducing λ_0.

Exercise 6.4. Show that for the general q and r case, the optimal smoothing parameters that minimize IMSE$[\hat{F}(y|x)]$ require that $h_s \sim n^{-1/(4+q)}$ for $s = 1, \ldots, q$, $\lambda_s \sim n^{-2/(4+q)}$ for $s = 1, \ldots, r$, and $h_0 \sim n^{-2/(4+q)}$.

Hint: Use arguments similar to those used in the two paragraphs immediately following (6.6) and (6.7).

Exercise 6.5. Derive (6.13).

Hint: Write the Lagrange function as

$$\mathcal{L} = \sum_{i=1}^{n} \ln p_i(x) - \gamma_1 \left[\sum_{i=1}^{n} p_i(x) - 1 \right] - \gamma_2 \sum_{i=1}^{n} (X_i - x) p_i(x) K_h(X_i, x).$$

The first order conditions are

$$\frac{\partial \mathcal{L}}{\partial \gamma_1} = \sum_{i=1}^{n} p_i(x) - 1 \overset{\text{set}}{=} 0, \tag{6.42}$$

$$\frac{\partial \mathcal{L}}{\partial \gamma_2} = \sum_{i=1}^{n} p_i(x)(X_i - x) K_h(X_i, x) \overset{\text{set}}{=} 0, \tag{6.43}$$

$$\frac{\partial \mathcal{L}}{\partial p_i(x)} = \frac{1}{n p_i(x)} - \gamma_1 - \gamma_2 (X_i - x) K_h(X_i, x) \overset{\text{set}}{=} 0, \tag{6.44}$$

Equation (6.43) leads to $1 = n p_i(x)[\gamma_1 + \gamma_2(X_i - x) K_h(X_i, x)]$. Summing this over i and using (6.42) and (6.43) gives

$$n = \gamma_1 \sum_{i=1}^{n} p_i(x)\gamma_1 + \gamma_2 \sum_{i=1}^{n} p_i(x)(X_i - x) K_h(X_i, x) = \gamma_1.$$

Substituting $\gamma_1 = n$ into (6.44), we get ($\gamma_2 = \gamma$)

$$p_i(x) = \frac{1}{n[1 + \gamma(X_i - x) K_h(X_i, x)]}.$$

This proves (6.5).

Hence, one can choose γ to maximize the log-likelihood function given by

$$\mathcal{L}(\gamma) = \sum_{i=1}^{n} \ln p_i(x) = - \sum_{i=1}^{n} \ln[1 + \gamma(X_i - x) K_h(X_i, x)].$$

Exercise 6.6.

(i) Derive (6.32).

Hint:

$$
\begin{aligned}
h(t) &= \lim_{\Delta t \to 0} \left(\frac{1}{\Delta t} \mathrm{P}(t \leq T < t + \Delta t | T \geq t) \right) \\
&= \lim_{\Delta t \to 0} \left(\frac{1}{\Delta t} \int_t^{t+\Delta t} f(v|T \geq t) dv \right) \\
&= \lim_{\Delta t \to 0} \left(\frac{1}{\Delta t} \int_t^{t+\Delta t} f_T(v) dv / \mathrm{P}(T \geq t) \right) \\
&= f_T(t) / \mathrm{P}(T \geq t) \\
&= f_T(t) / [1 - F_T(t)].
\end{aligned}
$$

(ii) Show that $f_X(x) = h(x) \exp(-\int_0^x h(y) dy)$.

Hint:

$$
\begin{aligned}
\int_0^y h(v) dv &= \int_0^v \frac{f_T(v)}{1 - F_T(v)} dv \\
&= -\ln[1 - F_T(v)]|_{v=0}^{v=t} \\
&= -\ln[1 - F_T(v)],
\end{aligned}
$$

which implies that

$$
1 - F_T(t) = e^{-\int_0^t h(v) dv}.
$$

Substituting this into (i), we obtain (ii).

Part II

Semiparametric Methods

Chapter 7

Semiparametric Partially Linear Models

In this chapter we discuss a relatively simple and popular semipara-metric model, the semiparametric partially linear regression model; see Härdle, Liang and Gao (2000) for a thorough treatment of partially lin-ear models. Roughly speaking, a semiparametric model is one for which some components are parametric, while the remaining components are left unspecified. These models therefore have a finite dimensional pa-rameter of interest, yet also contain some unknown functions which can be viewed as functions characterized by infinite dimensional parame-ters.

The partially linear model is one of the simplest semiparametric models used in practice. We shall use this model to introduce semi-parametric models because its estimation is straightforward, involv-ing nothing more than basic kernel estimation of regression functions along with least squares regression. This model also serves to illustrate a number of somewhat subtle issues which arise in the estimation of semiparametric models in general. For example, the finite dimensional parameter (the parametric part of the model) can usually be estimated with a parametric $\sqrt{n}$-rate, though we usually need stronger regularity conditions along with stricter conditions on the smoothing parameters in order to achieve the $\sqrt{n}$-rate for the parametric part of the model.

7.1   Partially Linear Models

A semiparametric partially linear model is given by

$$Y_i = X_i'\beta + g(Z_i) + u_i, \quad i = 1, \ldots, n, \tag{7.1}$$

where X_i is a $p \times 1$ vector, β is a $p \times 1$ vector of unknown parameters, and $Z_i \in \mathbb{R}^q$. The functional form of $g(\cdot)$ is not specified. The finite dimensional parameter β constitutes the parametric part of the model and the unknown function $g(\cdot)$ the nonparametric part. The data is assumed to be i.i.d. with $\mathrm{E}(u_i|X_i, Z_i) = 0$, and we allow for a conditionally heteroskedastic error process $\mathrm{E}(u_i^2|x, z) = \sigma^2(x, z)$ of unknown form. We focus our discussion on how to obtain a $\sqrt{n}$-consistent estimator of β, as once this is done, an estimator of $g(\cdot)$ can be easily obtained.

7.1.1   Identification of β

Some identification conditions will be required in order to identify the parameter vector β. Observe that X cannot contain a constant (i.e., β cannot contain an intercept) because, if there were an intercept, say α, it could not be identified separately from the unknown function $g(\cdot)$. That is, for any constant $c \neq 0$, observe that $\alpha + g(z) = [\alpha + c] + [g(z) - c] \equiv \alpha_{\mathrm{new}} + g_{\mathrm{new}}(z)$, thus the sum of the new intercept and the new $g(\cdot)$ function are observationally equivalent to the sum of the old ones in (7.1). Since the functional form of $g(\cdot)$ is not specified, this immediately tells us that an intercept term cannot be identified in a partially linear model. After we derive the asymptotic distribution of our semiparametric estimator of β in Section 7.2, it will be apparent that the identification condition for β becomes the requirement that $\Phi \stackrel{\mathrm{def}}{=} \mathrm{E}\{[X - \mathrm{E}(X|Z)][X - \mathrm{E}(X|Z)]'\}$ be a positive definite matrix, implying that X cannot contain a constant and that none of the components of X can be a deterministic function of Z for, otherwise, $X - \mathrm{E}(X|Z) \equiv 0$ for that component and Φ will be singular.

7.2   Robinson's Estimator

We first present an *infeasible* estimator of (7.1) to illustrate the mechanics involved in the estimation of β. Taking the expectation of (7.1) conditional on Z_i, we get

$$\mathrm{E}(Y_i|Z_i) = \mathrm{E}(X_i|Z_i)'\beta + g(Z_i). \tag{7.2}$$

Subtracting (7.2) from (7.1) yields

$$Y_i - \mathrm{E}(Y_i|Z_i) = (X_i - \mathrm{E}(X_i|Z_i))'\,\beta + u_i. \tag{7.3}$$

Defining the shorthand notation $\tilde{Y}_i = Y_i - \mathrm{E}(Y_i|Z_i)$ and $\tilde{X}_i = X_i - \mathrm{E}(X_i|Z_i)$, and applying the least squares method to (7.3), we obtain an estimator of β given by

$$\hat{\beta}_{\mathrm{inf}} = \left[\sum_{i=1}^{n} \tilde{X}_i \tilde{X}_i'\right]^{-1} \sum_{i=1}^{n} \tilde{X}_i \tilde{Y}_i. \tag{7.4}$$

By the Lindeberg-Levy CLT we immediately have (see Exercise 7.1)

$$\sqrt{n}(\hat{\beta}_{\mathrm{inf}} - \beta) \xrightarrow{d} N(0, \Phi^{-1}\Psi\Phi^{-1}), \tag{7.5}$$

provided that Φ is positive definite, where $\Psi = \mathrm{E}[\sigma^2(X_i, Z_i)\tilde{X}_i\tilde{X}_i']$, $\Phi = [\mathrm{E}(\tilde{X}_i\tilde{X}_i')]$.

The basic idea underlying this procedure is to first eliminate the unknown function $g(\cdot)$ by subtracting (7.2) from (7.1). Although the unknown function $g(\cdot)$ washes out in (7.3), two new unknown functions are introduced, namely $\mathrm{E}(Y_i|Z_i)$ and $\mathrm{E}(X_i|Z_i)$. Therefore, the above estimator $\hat{\beta}_{\mathrm{inf}}$ is not feasible because $\mathrm{E}(Y_i|Z_i)$ and $\mathrm{E}(X_i|Z_i)$ are unknown. However, we know that these conditional expectations can be consistently estimated using kernel methods, so we can replace the unknown conditional expectations that appear in $\hat{\beta}_{\mathrm{inf}}$ with their kernel estimators, thereby obtaining a feasible estimator of β. That is, we replace $\tilde{Y}_i = Y_i - \mathrm{E}(Y_i|Z_i)$ and $\tilde{X}_i = X_i - \mathrm{E}(X_i|Z_i)$ by $Y_i - \hat{Y}_i$ and $X_i - \hat{X}_i$, respectively, where

$$\hat{Y}_i \equiv \hat{\mathrm{E}}(Y_i|Z_i) \stackrel{\mathrm{def}}{=} n^{-1} \sum_{j=1}^{n} Y_j K_h(Z_i, Z_j)/\hat{f}(Z_i), \tag{7.6}$$

$$\hat{X}_i \equiv \hat{\mathrm{E}}(X_i|Z_i) \stackrel{\mathrm{def}}{=} n^{-1} \sum_{j=1}^{n} X_j K_h(Z_i, Z_j)/\hat{f}(Z_i), \tag{7.7}$$

and

$$\hat{f}(Z_i) = n^{-1} \sum_{j=1}^{n} K_h(Z_i, Z_j), \tag{7.8}$$

where $K_h(Z_i, Z_j) = \prod_{s=1}^{q} h_s^{-1} k\left(\frac{Z_{is}-Z_{js}}{h_s}\right)$.

The presence of the random denominator $\hat{f}(Z_i)$ can cause some technical difficulties when deriving the asymptotic distribution of the feasible estimator of β. We will consider two different approaches to handling the presence of the random denominator, one that uses a function that "trims out" observations for which the denominator is small, and another that uses a density-weighted method for getting rid of the random denominator altogether. We begin with a discussion of the trimming method. Define a feasible estimator of β given by

$$\hat{\beta} = \left\{ \sum_i (X_i - \hat{X}_i)(X_i - \hat{X}_i)' \right\}^{-1} \sum_i (X_i - \hat{X}_i)(Y_i - \hat{Y}_i) \mathbf{1}_i, \quad (7.9)$$

where $\mathbf{1}_i = \mathbf{1}(\hat{f}(Z_i) \geq b)$, which equals 1 if $\hat{f}(Z_i) \geq b$, 0 otherwise, and where the trimming parameter $b = b_n > 0$ and satisfies $b_n \to 0$ as $n \to \infty$.

To derive the asymptotic distribution of $\hat{\beta}$, we first provide a definition and state some assumptions. We shall use $\mathcal{G}_\nu^\alpha$, where $\alpha > 0$ and $\nu \geq 2$ is an integer, to denote the class of smooth functions such that if $g \in \mathcal{G}_\nu^\alpha$, then g is ν times differentiable; g and its partial derivative functions (up to order ν) all satisfy some Lipschitz-type conditions such as $|g(z) - g(z')| \leq H_g(z)\|z' - z\|$, where $H_g(z)$ is a continuous function having finite αth moment, and where $\|\cdot\|$ denotes Euclidean norm, i.e., $\|z\| = \sqrt{\sum_{j=1}^q z_j^2}$.

Condition 7.1.

(i) (Y_i, X_i, Z_i), $i = 1, 2, \ldots, n$ are i.i.d. observations, Z_i admits a PDF $f \in \mathcal{G}_{\nu-1}^\infty$ (i.e., f is bounded), $g(\cdot) \in \mathcal{G}_\nu^4$, and $\mathrm{E}(X|z) \in \mathcal{G}_\nu^4$, where $\nu \geq 2$ is an integer.

(ii) $\mathrm{E}(u|X, Z) = 0$, $\mathrm{E}(u^2|x, z) = \sigma^2(x, z)$ is continuous in z, both X and u have finite fourth moments.

(iii) $K(\cdot)$ is a product kernel, the univariate kernel $k(\cdot)$ is a bounded νth order kernel, and $k(v) = O\left(1/[1 + |v|]^{\nu+1}\right)$.

(iv) As $n \to \infty$, $n(h_1 \ldots h_q)^2 b^4 \to \infty$, $nb^{-4} \sum_{s=1}^q h_s^{4\nu} \to 0$.

Condition 7.1 (i) states a set of smoothness and moment conditions. The unknown functions $g(z)$ and $\mathrm{E}(X|z)$ are assumed to be νth order differentiable. These, together with a νth order kernel of 7.1 (iii), ensure that the bias of the kernel estimator is of order $O\left(\sum_{s=1}^{q} h_s^{\nu}\right)$.

Condition 7.1 (iv) is used in Robinson (1988). One can ignore the trimming parameter b in empirical applications as one can let $b \to 0$ at an extremely slow rate. Thus, Condition 7.1 (iv) is basically equivalent to

$$\sqrt{n}\left[\sum_{s=1}^{q} h_s^{2\nu} + (nh_1 \ldots h_q)^{-1}\right] \to 0 \text{ as } n \to \infty.$$

This condition is easy to understand; $O\left(\sum_{s=1}^{q} h_s^{2\nu} + (nh_1 \ldots h_q)^{-1}\right)$ is the order of the nonparametric MSE. The difference between the feasible estimator $\hat{\beta}$ and the infeasible estimator $\hat{\beta}_{\text{inf}}$ is proportional to an average of squared nonparametric estimation errors. Therefore, for $\hat{\beta}$ to be a $\sqrt{n}$-consistent estimator of β, one needs the squared estimation error terms to be smaller than $n^{-1/2}$, i.e., for $\sum_{s=1}^{q} h_s^{2\nu} + (nh_1 \ldots h_q)^{-1}$ to be of order $o(n^{-1/2})$, resulting in Condition 7.1 (iv).

Theorem 7.1. *Under Condition 7.1, we have*

$$\sqrt{n}(\hat{\beta} - \beta) \xrightarrow{d} N\left(0, \Phi^{-1}\Psi\Phi^{-1}\right), \qquad (7.10)$$

provided that Φ *is positive definite, where*

$$\Phi = \mathrm{E}[\tilde{X}_i \tilde{X}_i'], \ \Psi = \mathrm{E}[\sigma^2(X_i, Z_i)\tilde{X}_i \tilde{X}_i'] \ and \ \tilde{X}_i = X_i - \mathrm{E}(X_i|Z_i).$$

The proof of Theorem 7.1 can be found in Robinson (1988). A consistent estimator of the asymptotic variance of $\hat{\beta}$ is given in Exercise 7.1.

Comparing Theorem 7.1 with the distributional result given in (7.5), we see that the feasible estimator $\hat{\beta}$ has exactly the same asymptotic distribution as that of the infeasible estimator $\hat{\beta}_{\text{inf}}$. The intuition underlying this result is quite simple. If we ignore the trimming parameter b, then in essence $\hat{\beta} - \hat{\beta}_{\text{inf}} = O_p\left(\sum_{s=1}^{q} h_s^{2\nu} + (nh_1 \ldots h_q)^{-1}\right)$, the MSE rate of the nonparametric estimator, which is $o_p(n^{-1/2})$ by Condition 7.1 (iv). Hence, $\sqrt{n}(\hat{\beta} - \hat{\beta}_{\text{inf}}) = o_p(1)$, which implies that the two estimators have the same asymptotic distribution.

Suppose one uses a second order kernel, i.e., assume $\nu = 2$. With $h_s \sim h,$[1] Condition 7.1 (iv) becomes $n^{1/2}\left[\sum_{s=1}^{q} h_s^4 + (nh_1 \ldots h_q)^{-1}\right] \sim n^{1/2}\left[h^4 + (nh^q)^{-1}\right] = o(1)$, which requires that $q < 4$ (or that $q \leq 3$

---

[1] $h_s \sim h$ means that $(h_s - h)/h = o(1)$ or, equivalently, $h_s = h + o(h)$.

since q is a positive integer, where q is the dimension of Z). This is the condition invoked by Robinson (1988).

Thus, Condition 7.1 (iv) requires one to use a higher order kernel if $q \geq 4$. However, Li (1996) showed that Condition 7.1 (iv) can be replaced by a weaker condition given below.

Condition 7.2. *As $n \to \infty$, we have $nb^{-4}(h_1 \ldots h_q)^2/(\sum_{s=1}^q h_s^4) \to \infty$, $nb^{-4}(h_1 \ldots h_q) \to \infty$, and $nb^4 \sum_{s=1}^q h_s^{4\nu} \to 0$.*

Li (1996) shows that

$$\hat{\beta} - \hat{\beta}_{\text{inf}} = O_p\left(\sum_{s=1}^q h_s^{2\nu} + \sum_{s=1}^q h_s^2 (nh_1 \ldots h_q)^{-1} + n^{-1/2}(nh_1 \ldots h_q)^{-1}\right).$$

If this term is of order $o_p(n^{-1/2})$, we obtain Condition 7.2. A detailed explanation as to why the estimation error has this order rather than the more familiar order $O_p\left(\sum_{s=1}^q h_s^{2\nu} + (nh_1 \ldots h_q)^{-1}\right)$ can be found in Li (1996) (see also Exercise 7.5 for further explanation).

Considering the case for which all h_s have the same order ($h_s \sim h$ for all s), then Condition 7.2 becomes $n \max\{h^{2q-4}, h^q\} \to \infty$ and $nh^{4\nu} \to 0$. If one uses a second order kernel ($\nu = 2$), this condition requires that $4\nu = 8 > \max(2q - 4, q)$, leading to the requirement that $q < 6$, or that $q \leq 5$ since q is a positive integer. Therefore, a nonnegative second order kernel can lead to $\sqrt{n}$-consistent estimation of β as long as $q \leq 5$.

This following corollary is proved in Li (1996).

Corollary 7.1. *Under the same conditions given in Theorem 7.1, except that Condition 7.1 (iv) is replaced by Condition 7.2, then Theorem 7.1 still holds true.*

One undesirable feature of the semiparametric estimator described above is the use of a trimming function which requires the researcher to choose a nuisance parameter, the trimming parameter b. However, one can instead use the density-weighted approach to avoid a random denominator in the kernel estimator as follows.

Multiplying (7.3) by $f_i = f(Z_i)$, we get

$$(Y_i - \text{E}(Y_i|Z_i))f_i = (X_i - \text{E}(X_i|Z_i))'\beta f_i + u_i f_i. \qquad (7.11)$$

One can estimate β using the least squares method by regressing $(Y_i - \text{E}(Y_i|Z_i))f_i$ on $(X_i - \text{E}(X_i|Z_i))f_i$. Letting $\hat{\beta}_{\text{inf},f}$ denote the resulting infeasible estimator of β, then by the Lindeberg-Levy CLT (see Exercise 7.1) we know that $\hat{\beta}_{\inf,f}$ is $\sqrt{n}$-consistent and asymptotically normal, i.e.,

$$\sqrt{n}\left(\hat{\beta}_{\inf,f}-\beta\right) \xrightarrow{d} N\left(0,\Phi_f^{-1}\Psi_f\Phi_f^{-1}\right), \tag{7.12}$$

where $\Phi_f = \mathrm{E}[\tilde{X}_i\tilde{X}_i'f_i^2]$ and $\Psi_f = \mathrm{E}[\sigma^2(X_i,Z_i)\tilde{X}_i\tilde{X}_i'f_i^4]$, where $\tilde{X}_i = X_i - \mathrm{E}(X_i|Z_i)$.

A feasible estimator of β is obtained by replacing $(Y_i - \mathrm{E}(Y_i|Z_i))f_i$ and $(X_i - \mathrm{E}(X_i|Z_i))f_i$ with $(Y_i - \hat{Y}_i)\hat{f}_i$ and $(X_i - \hat{X}_i)\hat{f}_i$, where $\hat{Y}_i$, $\hat{X}_i$ and $\hat{f}_i$ are the kernel estimators of $\mathrm{E}(Y_i|Z_i)$, $\mathrm{E}(X_i|Z_i)$ and $f(X_i)$ defined in (7.6) to (7.8). Because $\hat{Y}_i\hat{f}_i = n^{-1}\sum_i Y_i K_h(Z_i,Z_j)$ (and $\hat{X}_i\hat{f}_i$) does not have a random denominator ($\hat{f}_i$), after removing the trimming parameter b, Condition 7.1 (iv) can be replaced by the following:

Condition 7.3. *As $n \to \infty$, $n(h_1 \ldots h_q)^2 \to \infty$, and $n\sum_{s=1}^q h_s^{4\nu} \to 0$,*

while Condition 7.2 can be replaced by

Condition 7.4. *As $n \to \infty$,*

$$n \min\left\{(h_1 \ldots h_q)/(\sum_{s=1}^q h_s^4), (h_1 \ldots h_q)^2\right\} \to \infty,$$

and $n\sum_{s=1}^q h_s^{4\nu} \to 0$.

The next theorem gives the asymptotic distribution of the feasible density-weighted estimator.

Theorem 7.2. *Letting $\hat{\beta}_f$ denote the feasible density-weighted estimator of β, then, under the same conditions as in Theorem 7.1, except that Condition 7.1 (iv) is replaced by either Condition 7.3 or Condition 7.4, we have*

$$\sqrt{n}(\hat{\beta}_f - \beta) \xrightarrow{d} N(0,\Phi_f^{-1}\Psi_f\Phi_f^{-1}),$$

where Φ_f and Ψ_f are defined in (7.12).

Theorem 7.2, under the weaker Condition 7.4, is proved in Li (1996). In Section 7.5 we provide a proof using the stronger Condition 7.3. As will be seen, the stronger Condition 7.3 yields a relatively simple proof.

Theorem 7.2 states that the feasible estimator $\hat{\beta}_f$ has the same asymptotic distribution as the infeasible estimator $\hat{\beta}_{\inf,f}$.

Note that the use of the specific weight function $f(Z_i)$ for avoiding the random denominator when estimating β is *not* based on any efficiency arguments. In fact, when the error is conditionally homoskedastic, the unweighted estimator $\hat{\beta}$ can be shown to be semiparametrically efficient.

When the error is conditionally heteroskedastic, i.e., $\mathrm{E}(u_i^2|X_i, Z_i) = \sigma^2(X_i, Z_i)$, one might be lured by analogy into thinking that an efficient estimator of β could be obtained by choosing $w_i = 1/\sigma(X_i, Z_i)$ as a weight function. In general, however, this intuition is incorrect. This approach will not lead to efficient estimation of β except in the special case for which the conditional variance is only a function of Z_i. That is, only when $\mathrm{E}(u_i^2|X_i, Z_i) = \sigma^2(Z_i)$ will the choice of weight $1/\sigma(Z_i)$ lead to efficient estimation of β. Efficient estimation of β in the general case is more complex and will be discussed in Section 7.4.

7.2.1   Estimation of the Nonparametric Component

From (7.2) we know that $g(Z_i) = \mathrm{E}(Y_i - X_i'\beta|Z_i)$. Therefore, after obtaining a $\sqrt{n}$-consistent estimator of β (i.e., $\hat{\beta}$), a consistent estimator of $g(z)$ is given by

$$\hat{g}(z) = \frac{\sum_{j=1}^n (Y_j - X_j'\hat{\beta}) K_h(z, Z_j)}{\sum_{j=1}^n K_h(z, Z_j)}, \tag{7.13}$$

where $\hat{\beta}$ can be replaced by $\hat{\beta}_f$. We know that the nonparametric kernel estimator has a convergence rate that is slower than the parametric $\sqrt{n}$-rate. Therefore, it is easy to see that, asymptotically, $\hat{g}(z)$ is equivalent to the following infeasible estimator that makes use of the true value of β:

$$\tilde{g}(z) = \frac{\sum_{j=1}^n (Y_j - X_j'\beta) K_h(z, Z_j)}{\sum_{j=1}^n K_h(z, Z_j)}. \tag{7.14}$$

The convergence rate and the asymptotic distribution of $\tilde{g}(z)$, from which one can immediately obtain the asymptotic distribution of $\hat{g}(z)$ (see Exercise 7.2), is discussed in Chapter 2.

Note that the choice of h_s's for estimating $g(z)$ can be quite different from those for estimating β. In order to obtain a $\sqrt{n}$-consistent estimator of β, a higher order kernel is needed if $q \geq 6$. However, when estimating $g(z)$, there is no need to use a higher order kernel regardless of the value of q. Therefore, one can always use a nonnegative second order kernel to estimate $g(z)$, and one could choose the smoothing parameters by least squares cross-validation (in estimating $g(z)$); i.e., one can always choose $h_1, \ldots, h_q$ to minimize

$$\sum_{i=1}^{n} \left[Y_i - X_i'\hat{\beta} - \hat{g}_{-i}(Z_i, h) \right]^2, \qquad (7.15)$$

where $\hat{g}_{-i}(Z_i, h) = \hat{g}_{-i}(Z_i)$ as defined in (7.13) with z replaced by Z_i, and $\sum_{j=1}^{n}$ replaced by $\sum_{j=1, j \neq i}^{n}$.

Note that in (7.15) the dependent variable is $Y_i - X_i'\hat{\beta}$ rather than Y_i. Because $\hat{\beta} - \beta = O_p\left(n^{-1/2}\right)$ has a faster rate of convergence than any nonparametric estimator, one can replace $\hat{\beta}$ in (7.15) with β to study the asymptotic behavior of the cross-validation selected $\hat{h}_s$'s. The rate of convergence of the $\hat{h}_s$'s is the same as discussed in Chapter 2.

One can also select $\hat{\beta}$ and h simultaneously by minimizing

$$\sum_{i=1}^{n} \left[Y_i - X_i'\beta - \hat{g}_{-i}(Z_i, h) \right]^2.$$

Under general conditions, including the use of a second order kernel, the cross-validation choice of h will be of order $O_p\left(n^{-1/(q+4)}\right)$. This order satisfies Conditions 7.1 (iv), 7.2, 7.3 and 7.4 if $q \leq 3$. Therefore, when $q \leq 3$, one can choose the h_s's and β simultaneously by minimizing $\sum_{i=1}^{n} [Y_i - X_i'\beta - \hat{g}(Z_i, h)]^2$. The resulting $\hat{h}_s$'s will be of order $O_p\left(n^{-1/(q+4)}\right)$, and the resulting $\hat{\beta}$ will be $\sqrt{n}$-consistent having asymptotic variance given in Theorem 7.1. One can also use second order expansion results (in the h_s's) in a partially linear model to select the smoothing parameters so as to minimize the estimation MSE up to second order; see Linton (1995).

The partially linear estimator has been applied in a range of settings. For example, Anglin and Gencay (1996) used it for the semiparametric modeling of hedonic price functions; Blundell, Duncan and Pendakur (1998) considered partially linear models for the semiparametric estimation of Engel curves; Engle, Granger, Rice and Weiss (1986) used a partially linear specification for estimating the relationship between weather and electricity sales; Stock (1989) considered the problem of predicting the mean effect of a change in the distribution of certain policy-related variables on a dependent variable in a partially linear framework; Adams, Berger and Sickles (1999) apply a partially linear specification to study the production frontier of the U.S. banking industry; and Yatchew and No (2001) estimated price and income elasticities allowing for endogeneity of prices in a partially linear model with price and age entering nonparametrically.

7.3 Andrews's MINPIN Method

Andrews (1994) provides a general framework for proving the $\sqrt{n}$-consistency and asymptotic normality of a wide class of semiparametric estimators. Andrews names the estimators MINPIN because they are estimators that MINimize a criterion function that may depend on Preliminary Infinite dimensional Nuisance parameter estimators. Andrews's method can be used to derive the asymptotic distribution of many semiparametric estimators, including an estimator of β in a partially linear model. We briefly discuss this method below.

Let $\theta \in \Theta \subset \mathbb{R}^p$ denote a finite dimensional parameter, and let τ denote some infinite dimensional function. Further, let $\hat{\tau}$ be some preliminary nonparametric estimator of $\tau \in \mathcal{H}$, where $\mathcal{H}$ is a class of smooth functions the specifics of which depend on the particular semiparametric model being considered. We use θ_0 and τ_0 to denote the true parameter and the true unknown function. Let $\hat{\theta}$ denote an estimator of θ_0 that is a solution to a minimization problem where the objective function depends on θ and $\hat{\tau}$, with $\hat{\tau}$ being a preliminary nonparametric estimator of τ_0. Suppose that $\hat{\theta}$ is a consistent estimator of θ_0 that solves a minimization problem resulting in the following first order condition:

$$\sqrt{n}\bar{m}_n(\theta, \hat{\tau}) = 0, \qquad (7.16)$$

where $\bar{m}_n(\theta, \hat{\tau}) = n^{-1} \sum_i m(W_i, \theta, \hat{\tau})$.

We consider the case where $m(W_i, \theta, \tau)$ is differentiable with respect to θ. If τ were finite dimensional, one could establish the asymptotic normality of $\hat{\theta}$ by expanding $\sqrt{n}\bar{m}_n(\hat{\theta}, \hat{\tau})$ about (θ_0, τ_0) using element by element mean value expansions. Since τ is infinite dimensional, however, a mean value expansion in (θ, τ) is unavailable. Andrews (1994) suggests expanding $\sqrt{n}\bar{m}_n(\hat{\theta}, \hat{\tau})$ about θ_0 only and using the concept of stochastic equicontinuity (see Appendix A) to handle $\hat{\tau}$. A mean value expansion in $\hat{\theta}$ about θ_0 yields

$$o_p(1) = \sqrt{n}\bar{m}_n\left(\hat{\theta}, \hat{\tau}\right) = \sqrt{n}\bar{m}_n\left(\theta_0, \hat{\tau}\right) + \frac{\partial}{\partial\theta'}\bar{m}_n\left(\bar{\theta}, \hat{\tau}\right)\sqrt{n}\left(\hat{\theta} - \theta_0\right),$$

$$(7.17)$$

where $\bar{\theta}$ lies on a line segment between $\hat{\theta}$ and θ_0. Under some regularity assumption, one can show that

$$\frac{\partial}{\partial \theta'} \bar{m}_n(\bar{\theta}, \hat{\tau}) \equiv n^{-1} \sum_i \frac{\partial}{\partial \theta'} m\left(W_i, \bar{\theta}, \hat{\tau}\right)$$

$$\xrightarrow{p} \mathrm{E}\left[n^{-1} \sum_i \frac{\partial}{\partial \theta'} m\left(W_i, \theta_0, \tau_0\right)\right]$$

$$= \mathrm{E}\left[\frac{\partial}{\partial \theta'} m\left(W_i, \theta_0, \tau_0\right)\right]$$

$$\equiv M.$$

Thus, provided that M is nonsingular, from (7.17) and (7.18) we get

$$\sqrt{n}\left(\hat{\theta} - \theta_0\right) = \left(M^{-1} + o_p(1)\right) n^{-1/2} \sum_i m(W_i, \theta_0, \hat{\tau}). \qquad (7.18)$$

Therefore, if

$$n^{-1/2} \sum_i m(W_i, \theta_0, \hat{\tau}) - n^{-1/2} \sum_i m(W_i, \theta_0, \tau_0) = o_p(1), \qquad (7.19)$$

then we will have

$$\sqrt{n}(\hat{\theta} - \theta_0) = M^{-1} n^{-1/2} \sum_i m(W_i, \theta_0, \tau_0) + o_p(1) \xrightarrow{d} N(0, M^{-1} S M^{-1}),$$

$$(7.20)$$

by the Lindeberg-Levy CLT, where $S = \mathrm{var}(m(W_i, \theta_0, \tau_0))$.

In practice, (7.19) can be difficult to verify for general semiparametric models that are more complicated than the simple partially linear model. Andrews (1994) suggests using the concept of "stochastic equicontinuity" to establish (7.19). Stochastic equicontinuity can be used to establish (7.19) because if $\rho(\hat{\tau}, \tau_0) \to 0$ ($\rho(\cdot, \cdot)$ is a pseudometric; see Definition A.32 in the appendix) as $n \to \infty$ and $\nu_n(\tau)$ is stochastic equicontinuous for $\tau \in \Lambda$, where Λ is a bounded set that contains τ_0 as an interior point, then

$$|\nu_n(\tau) - \nu(\tau_0)| \xrightarrow{p} 0. \qquad (7.21)$$

See Andrews (1994, eq. (2.10)) for a proof of (7.21). Recall that $\nu(\tau) \overset{\text{def}}{=} \sqrt{n} \bar{m}_n(\theta_0, \tau)$. Thus, (7.19) holds if $\nu_n(\cdot)$ is stochastically equicontinuous.

The following assumptions can be used to establish the $\sqrt{n}$-normality result for $\hat{\theta}$.

Suppose that the MINPIN estimator $\hat{\theta}$ solves the minimization problem of $\hat{\theta} = \inf_{\theta \in \Theta} d(\theta, \hat{\tau})$ for some objective function $d(\theta, \hat{\tau})$, and as a result the first order condition is $\bar{m}_n(\theta, \hat{\tau}) = n^{-1} \sum_i m(W_i, \theta, \hat{\tau}) = 0$. The population moment condition is $\mathrm{E}[m(W_i, \theta_0, \tau_0)] = 0$. Defining $\nu_n(\tau) = n^{1/2} \bar{m}_n(\theta_0, \tau)$, we make the following assumption.

Assumption 7.1. *(Normality) Assume that*

(i) $\hat{\theta} \xrightarrow{p} \theta_0 \in \Theta$, Θ *is a compact subset of* $\mathbb{R}^r$.

(ii) $\hat{\tau} \xrightarrow{p} \tau_0 \in \mathcal{G}$.

(iii) $\sqrt{n} \nu_n(\tau_0) \to N(0, S)$.

(iv) $\{\nu_n(\cdot)\}$ *is stochastically equicontinuous at* τ_0.

(v) $m(\theta, \tau)$ *is twice continuously differentiable in* $\theta \in \Theta$, *while*

$$n^{-1} \sum_i m(W_t, \theta, \tau) \to \mathrm{E}[m(W_t, \theta, \tau)],$$

$$n^{-1} \sum_i (\partial/\partial\theta) m(W_t, \theta, \tau) \xrightarrow{p} \mathrm{E}[m(W_t, \theta, \tau)], \;\; and$$

$$n^{-1} \sum_i (\partial/\partial\theta) m(W_t, \theta, \tau) \xrightarrow{p} \mathrm{E}[(\partial/\partial\theta) m(W_t, \theta, \tau)],$$

uniformly over $\Theta \times \mathcal{G}$ *(i.e., uniform weak law of large numbers).*

Theorem 7.3. *Under Assumption 7.1,*

$$\sqrt{n} \left(\hat{\theta} - \theta_0 \right) \xrightarrow{d} N \left(0, M^{-1} S M^{-1} \right).$$

Proof. The above theorem is a special case of Theorem 1 of Andrews (1994) and is therefore omitted. In fact, Andrews does not assume i.i.d. data; rather, he allows for weakly dependent time series data and allows for nonidentically distributed data. We discuss weakly dependent data in Chapter 18. □

In practice, the stochastic equicontinuity condition (Assumption 7.1 (iv)) is the most difficult part to verify, especially for highly nonlinear semiparametric models. Andrews (1994) uses Theorem 7.3 to establish the $\sqrt{n}$-normality result for a partially specified nonlinear model (see also Ai and McFadden (1997)). We discuss verification of Assumption 7.1 (iv) for partially linear models in Section 7.5.

One maintained assumption above is that the objective function is smooth in its arguments; see Chen, Linton and van Keilegom (2003) on estimation of semiparametric models when the criterion function is not smooth.

7.4 Semiparametric Efficiency Bounds

7.4.1 The Conditionally Homoskedastic Error Case

In this section we discuss the (local) semiparametric efficiency bound for (7.1) and consider two approaches. We begin by deriving the (local) semiparametric lower bound under the assumption that the errors are conditionally homoskedastic, i.e., that $\mathrm{E}(u_i^2|X_i, Z_i) = \mathrm{E}(u_i^2)$, where u_i is normally distributed. This approach uses parametric maximum likelihood estimation and is easy to understand, and we follow the arguments found in Newey (1990b) and Rilstone (1993). The discussion here will be informal, while a rigorous approach can be found in Newey; also see Begun, Hall, Huang and Wellner (1983) and Tripathi and Severina (2001) for a general treatment of efficiency bounds of semiparametric models, and the related work of Pakes and Olley (1995).

Let $m(z, \delta)$ be a parametric submodel such that $m(z, \delta_0) = g(z)$ for some δ_0, where δ is a $k \times 1$ vector of nuisance parameters ($k \geq q$). The parameters of this parametric submodel are $\psi = (\beta', \delta')$, and the parameter vector of interest is β_0. For each parametric submodel there is a vector-valued score function l_ψ, which one can partition with respect to the parameter of interest β_0 and the nuisance parameter δ so that $l_\psi' = (l_\beta', l_\delta')$. The semiparametric bound can be interpreted as the supremum of the covariance matrices over the parametric submodels. Define the tangent set $\mathcal{J}$ for the nuisance function as the mean square closure of all $k \times 1$ linear combinations of l_δ. Let $\mathcal{P}[l_\theta|\mathcal{J}]$ denote the projection of l_θ onto the space $\mathcal{J}$ and define $l_\theta^* = l_\theta - \mathcal{P}[l_\theta|\mathcal{J}]$. Then the semiparametric lower bound for the model is given by $\mathcal{V}_\theta = \left\{ \mathrm{E}[l_\theta^* l_\theta^{*'}] \right\}^{-1}$.

The log-likelihood function corresponding to the parametric submodel is

$$\mathcal{L}(\beta, \delta) = \text{Constant} - \frac{(Y - X'\beta_0 - g(Z, \delta))^2}{2\sigma^2}.$$

The score function when evaluated at the true model is

$$\begin{pmatrix} l_\beta \\ l_\delta \end{pmatrix} \equiv \begin{pmatrix} \frac{\partial \mathcal{L}}{\partial \beta} \\ \frac{\partial \mathcal{L}}{\partial \delta} \end{pmatrix} = \begin{pmatrix} (1/\sigma^2)u\,X \\ -(1/\sigma^2)u\,g^{(1)}(Z) \end{pmatrix},$$

where we used $\partial g(z, \delta_0)/\partial z = g^{(1)}(z)$. Since $g(\eta)$ is not specified, $g^{(1)}(z)$ cannot be identified either. We obtain the tangent set $\Lambda(\cdot)$, the mean square closure of all $k \times 1$ linear combinations of l_δ, given by

$$\Lambda = \left\{ u\Delta(z) : \quad \text{with } \mathrm{E}\left\{ [\Delta(Z)]^2 \right\} < \infty \right\}.$$

The projection of l_β on $\Lambda(\cdot)$ is $(1/\sigma^2)u\mathrm{E}(X|Z)$, therefore, we obtain the efficient score as

$$l_\beta^* \stackrel{\text{def}}{=} l_\beta - \mathrm{E}(l_\beta|\Lambda(\cdot)) = (1/\sigma^2)u(X - \mathrm{E}(X|Z)).$$

Therefore, the semiparametric efficiency bound for (7.1) is

$$\mathcal{V}_\beta = \{\mathrm{E}[l_\beta^* l_\beta^{*\prime}]\}^{-1} = \sigma^2\{\mathrm{E}[(X - \xi)(X - \xi)']\}^{-1}, \tag{7.22}$$

where $\xi = \mathrm{E}(X|Z)$.

Thus, $\hat{\beta}$ defined in (7.9) is semiparametrically efficient in the sense that the asymptotic covariance matrix Σ equals to the semiparametric lower bound $\mathcal{V}_\beta$ for the partially linear model.

We can also compare V_R with the asymptotic variance of the least squares estimator of β_0 when (7.1) is a linear regression model, i.e., $g(z) = \alpha + z'\gamma$, α is a scalar and $\gamma \in \mathbb{R}^q$,

$$y_i = X_i'\beta_0 + \alpha + Z_i'\gamma + u_i. \tag{7.23}$$

Letting $\hat{\beta}_{\text{ols}}$ denote the ordinary least squares estimator of β_0 based on (7.23), then it is easy to show that

$$\sqrt{n}(\hat{\beta}_{\text{ols}} - \beta_0) \stackrel{d}{\to} N(0, V_{\text{ols}}), \tag{7.24}$$

where $V_{\text{ols}} = \sigma^2 \mathrm{E}\left\{ [X_i - a - bZ_i][X_i - a - bZ_i]' \right\}^{-1}$ (see Exercise 7.6), where a and b are constant matrices of dimensions $p \times 1$ and $p \times q$, respectively, and $a + bZ_i$ is the best linear projection of X_i on a space that is linear in Z_i. Now compare V_R with V_{ols}. We see that if $\mathrm{E}(X_i|Z_i) =$

$a + bZ_i$ is a linear function in Z_i, then $V_R = V_{\text{ols}}$. However, if $\mathrm{E}(X_i|Z_i)$ is not a linear function in Z_i, then $\mathrm{E}\left\{[X_i - \mathrm{E}(X_i|Z_i)][X_i - \mathrm{E}(X_i|Z_i)]'\right\} - \mathrm{E}\left\{[X_i - s(Z_i)][X_i - s(Z_i)]'\right\}$ is negative semidefinite for any function $s(Z_i)$ (by Theorem A.3). Thus, $V_R - V_{\text{ols}}$ is positive definite when $\mathrm{E}(X_i|z)$ is not linear in z. In this latter case, the semiparametrically efficient estimator $\hat{\beta}_R$ is asymptotically less efficient than the *parametric* estimator $\hat{\beta}_{\text{ols}}$, which uses the extra information that $g(z) = \alpha + z'\gamma$.

7.4.2 The Conditionally Heteroskedastic Error Case

The derivation of the semiparametric efficiency bound for a partially linear model can be found in Chamberlain (1992) under the general conditionally heteroskedastic error case, while Ai and Chen (2003) consider efficient estimation for general semiparametric models which includes the partially linear model as a special case. The discussion below is based on Ai and Chen. The results presented in this section include a conditionally homoskedastic error model as a special case.

Consider the partially linear model

$$Y_i = X_i'\beta_0 + g(Z_i) + u_i, \quad i = 1, \ldots, n, \tag{7.25}$$

where $\mathrm{E}(u_i^2|X_i, Z_i) = \sigma^2(X_i, Z_i)$ is of unknown form.

In order to derive the semiparametric efficiency bound of β_0 allowing for conditionally heteroskedastic errors, we first assume that $\sigma^2(X_i, Z_i)$ is known, and then proceed to discuss how to obtain a feasible semiparametrically efficient estimator when $\sigma^2(x, z)$ is of unknown form. Ai and Chen (2003) show that β_0 can be efficiently estimated by minimizing the following objective function *simultaneously* (jointly) over β_0 and the unknown function g:

$$\inf_{\beta \in \mathcal{B}, g \in \mathcal{G}} \mathrm{E}\left\{[Y_i - X_i'\beta_0 + g(Z_i)]^2/\sigma^2(X_i, Z_i)\right\}, \tag{7.26}$$

where $\mathcal{B}$ is a compact subset in $\mathbb{R}^r$ and $\mathcal{G}$ is a class of smooth functions.

In practice, one works with the sample mean rather than with the population mean (7.26), thereby minimizing the following:

$$\inf_{\beta \in \mathcal{B}, g \in \mathcal{G}} \sum_{i=1}^{n} [Y_i - X_i'\beta_0 + g(Z_i)]^2/\sigma^2(X_i, Z_i). \tag{7.27}$$

The minimization can be done by first concentrating out the unknown function $f(\cdot)$. That is, we first treat β_0 as a fixed constant, and by application of calculus of variations to (7.26) over $g(\cdot)$, we obtain

$$2\mathrm{E}\left\{\mathrm{E}\left[(Y_i - X_i'\beta_0 + g(Z_i))/\sigma^2(X_i, Z_i)|Z_i\right]\delta(Z_i)\right\} = 0, \qquad (7.28)$$

where $\delta(Z_i)$ is a arbitrary function of Z_i. Solving for $g(Z_i)$ in (7.28) leads to

$$g(Z_i) = \frac{1}{\mathrm{E}\left(\frac{1}{\sigma_i^2}|Z_i\right)}\left[\mathrm{E}\left(\frac{Y_i}{\sigma_i^2}|Z_i\right) - \mathrm{E}\left(\frac{X_i'}{\sigma_i^2}|Z_i\right)\right]\beta, \qquad (7.29)$$

where $\sigma_i^2 = \sigma^2(X_i, Z_i)$.

Substituting (7.29) into (7.27), we get

$$\sum_i \left\{Y_i - \frac{\mathrm{E}\left(\frac{Y_i}{\sigma_i^2}|Z_i\right)}{\mathrm{E}\left(\frac{1}{\sigma_i^2}|Z_i\right)} - \left[X_i - \frac{\mathrm{E}\left(\frac{X_i}{\sigma_i^2}|Z_i\right)}{\mathrm{E}\left(\frac{1}{\sigma_i^2}|Z_i\right)}\right]'\beta\right\}^2 /\sigma_i^2. \qquad (7.30)$$

By using the shorthand notation $\mathcal{Y}_i = Y_i - \mathrm{E}(Y_i/\sigma_i^2)/\mathrm{E}(1/\sigma_i^2|Z_i)$ and $\mathcal{X}_i = X_i - \mathrm{E}(X_i/\sigma_i^2)/\mathrm{E}(1/\sigma_i^2|Z_i)$, (7.30) becomes $\sum_i[\mathcal{Y}_i - \mathcal{X}_i'\beta_0]^2/\sigma_i^2$. Minimizing this objective function over β_0 gives an (infeasible) efficient estimator of β_0:

$$\tilde{\beta}_{\mathrm{eff}} = \left[\sum_i \mathcal{X}_i\mathcal{X}_i'/\sigma_i^2\right]^{-1}\sum_i \mathcal{X}_i\mathcal{Y}_i/\sigma_i^2$$

$$= \beta + \left[\sum_i \mathcal{X}_i\mathcal{X}_i'/\sigma_i^2\right]^{-1}\sum_i \mathcal{X}_i u_i/\sigma_i^2.$$

A standard law of large numbers along with the Lindeberg-Levy CLT leads to

$$\sqrt{n}\left(\hat{\beta}_{\mathrm{eff}} - \beta_0\right) \to N\left(0, V_0^{-1}\right) \text{ in distribution}, \qquad (7.31)$$

where

$$V_0 = \mathrm{E}\left[\mathcal{X}_i\mathcal{X}_i'/\sigma_i^2\right]$$

$$\equiv \mathrm{E}\left\{\left[X_i - \frac{\mathrm{E}\left(\frac{X_i}{\sigma_i^2}|Z_i\right)}{\mathrm{E}\left(\frac{1}{\sigma_i^2}|Z_i\right)}\right]\left[X_i - \frac{\mathrm{E}\left(\frac{X_i}{\sigma_i^2}|Z_i\right)}{\mathrm{E}\left(\frac{1}{\sigma_i^2}|Z_i\right)}\right]'/\sigma_i^2\right\}. \qquad (7.32)$$

Equation (7.32) is the semiparametric efficiency bound derived by Chamberlain (1992, p. 569, eq. 1.9).

When $\sigma^2(X_i, Z_i) = \sigma^2(Z_i)$, (7.32) can be simplified to

$$V_0 = \mathrm{E}\left\{[X_i - \mathrm{E}(X_i|Z_i)]\,[X_i - \mathrm{E}(X_i|Z_i)]'/\sigma^2(Z_i)\right\}. \qquad (7.33)$$

When $\sigma_i^2 = \sigma^2$, a constant, (7.32) further reduces to the asymptotic variance of $\sqrt{n}(\hat{\beta} - \beta_0)$ covered by Theorem 7.1.

The above estimator $\hat{\beta}_{\mathrm{eff}}$ is not feasible. A feasible efficient estimator of β_0 can be obtained from $\hat{\beta}_{\mathrm{eff}}$ by replacing the unknown conditional expectations with their respective kernel estimators, e.g., by replacing $\mathrm{E}[Y_i/\sigma_i^2|Z_i]$ with $\hat{\mathrm{E}}[Y_i/\sigma_i^2|Z_i] = \sum_j Y_j/\hat{\sigma}_j^2 K_{ij}/\sum_j K_{ij}$, where $K_{ij} = K((Z_i - Z_j)/h)$, and by further replacing σ_i^2 with $\hat{\sigma}_i^2 = \sum_j \hat{u}_j^2 \bar{K}_{h,ij}/\sum_j \bar{K}_{h,ij}$ where $\bar{K}_{h,ij} = K((X_i - X_j)/h_x)K((Z_i - Z_j)/h_z)$ with $\hat{u}_i = \hat{\mathrm{E}}(Y_i|Z_i) - \hat{\mathrm{E}}(X_i|Z_i)'\hat{\beta}$ being a consistent estimator of u_i defined in Exercise 7.1. Some additional regularity conditions, such as the density $f(x, z)$ being bounded away from zero in its support or, alternatively, the use of a trimming function, are needed to establish that the feasible estimator indeed has the same asymptotic distribution as the efficient infeasible estimator $\tilde{\beta}_{\mathrm{eff}}$. We point out that an efficient semiparametric estimator of β_0 is quite complex. It requires estimation of a nonparametric model with dimension $p + q$ (the dimension of (X_i, Z_i)), while the estimation of β_0 and $g(\cdot)$ involves only nonparametric estimation with dimension q. Therefore, the "curse of dimensionality" may prevent researchers from applying efficient estimation procedures to a partially linear model when the error is conditionally heteroskedastic.

In this chapter we only cover the case in which (Y, X, Z) are all observed without error. For estimation of a semiparametric partially linear model with errors-in-variables, see Liang, Härdle and Carroll (1999) and Liang and Wang (2004).

7.5   Proofs

7.5.1   Proof of Theorem 7.2

Proof. We first provide a consistent estimator of the asymptotic variance of $\hat{\beta}_f$. It can be shown that

$$\hat{\Phi}_f = \frac{1}{n}\sum_i (X_i - \hat{X}_i)(X_i - \hat{X}_i)'\hat{f}_i^2 \text{ and}$$

$$\hat{\Psi} = \frac{1}{n}\sum_i \left[(\tilde{u}_i\hat{f}_i)^2(X_i - \hat{X}_i)(X_i - \hat{X}_i)'\hat{f}_i^2\right]$$

(7.34)

are consistent estimators of Φ and Ψ respectively, where $\tilde{u}_i \equiv (y_i - \hat{y}_i) - (X_i - \hat{X}_i)'\hat{\beta}_f$ is a consistent estimator of u_i.

Throughout, we use $\sum_i$ to denote $\sum_{i=1}^n$ and $\sum_{j\neq i}$ to denote $\sum_{j=1, j\neq i}^n$.

From $Y_i = X_i'\beta_0 + g_i + u_i$, we get $\hat{Y}_i = \hat{X}_i'\beta_0 + \hat{g}_i + \hat{u}_i$, where $\hat{A}_i = n^{-1}\sum_{j\neq i} A_j K_{h,ij}/\hat{f}_i$ ($A = Y, X, g, u$). Define $S_{A\hat{f},B\hat{f}} = n^{-1}\sum_i A_i\hat{f}_i B_i'\hat{f}_i$, and $S_{A\hat{f},A\hat{f}} = S_{A\hat{f}}$. Using $Y_i - \hat{Y}_i = (X_i - \hat{X}_i)\beta + g_i - \hat{g}_i + u_i - \hat{u}_i$ we get

$$\hat{\beta}_f = S_{(x-\hat{x})\hat{f}}^{-1} S_{(x-\hat{x})\hat{f},(Y-\hat{Y})\hat{f}} = \beta_0 + S_{(x-\hat{x})\hat{f}}^{-1} S_{(x-\hat{x})\hat{f},(g-\hat{g}+u-\hat{u})\hat{f}}. \quad (7.35)$$

Hence, we have

$$\sqrt{n}(\hat{\beta}_f - \beta_0) = S_{(x-\hat{x})\hat{f}}^{-1}\sqrt{n}S_{(x-\hat{x})\hat{f},(g-\hat{g}+u-\hat{u})\hat{f}}. \quad (7.36)$$

In Propositions 7.1 to 7.4 below, we show that

(i) $\sqrt{n}S_{(x-\hat{x})\hat{f},(g-\hat{g})\hat{f}} = o_p(1)$,

(ii) $S_{(x-\hat{x})\hat{f}} \xrightarrow{p} \Phi_f$,

(iii) $\sqrt{n}S_{(x-\hat{x})\hat{f},\hat{u}\hat{f}} = o_p(1)$, and

(iv) $\sqrt{n}S_{(x-\hat{x})\hat{f},u\hat{f}} = \sqrt{n}S_{vf,uf} + o_p(1) \xrightarrow{d} N(0, \Psi_f)$.

Using (i)-(iv), from (7.36) we obtain

$$\sqrt{n}(\hat{\beta}_f - \beta_0) = S^{-1}_{(x-\hat{x})\hat{f}} \sqrt{n} S_{(x-\hat{x})\hat{f},(g-\hat{g}+u-\hat{u})\hat{f}}$$

$$= S^{-1}_{(x-\hat{x})\hat{f}} \sqrt{n} \left\{ S_{(x-\hat{x})\hat{f},(g-\hat{g})\hat{f}} + S_{(x-\hat{x})\hat{f},u\hat{f}} - S_{(x-\hat{x})\hat{f},\hat{u}\hat{f}} \right\}$$

$$= [\Phi_f + o_p(1)]^{-1} \{ o_p(1) + [\sqrt{n} S_{vf,uf} + o_p(1)] + o_p(1) \}$$

$$\xrightarrow{d} \Phi_f^{-1} N(0, \Psi_f)$$

$$= N\left(0, \Phi_f^{-1} \Psi_f \Phi_f^{-1} \right).$$

This completes the proof of Theorem 7.2. $\square$

In the lemmas presented below, we assume that the support of (X_i, Z_i) is a bounded set to simplify the proof. All results for $g_i = g(Z_i)$ also hold true for $\xi_i = \xi(Z_i) \equiv E(X_i|Z_i)$. Letting $\epsilon = v_i$ or u_i, then $g(Z_i)$, $\xi(x_i, z_i)$ and $\sigma_\epsilon^2(X_i, Z_i) = E[\epsilon_i^2|X_i, Z_i]$ are all bounded functions with bounded derivatives up to order ν, though the support of u_i need not be bounded.

We will use the shorthand notation $E_1(A) = E(A|X_1, Z_1)$ and $K_{ij} = K((Z_i - Z_j)/h)$ below.

Lemmas 7.1 to 7.5 below hold true if one replaces g with ξ. The only difference between g and ξ is that g is a scalar function, while ξ is of dimension $r \times 1$. The proofs below hold true for each component of ξ and, therefore, hold true for the vector function ξ since r is finite.

Also, we assume that $h_1 = \cdots = h_q = h$ for notational simplicity. Alternatively, we can interpret the results of $O\left(h^2\right)$ as $O\left(\sum_{s=1}^{q} h_s^2\right)$ and $O\left(h^q\right)$ as $O(h_1 \ldots h_q)$ to obtain the results that correspond to the case where we do not impose the condition that all of the h_s's are equal.

Also, in order to simplify the proof, we use the leave-one-out estimators for $\hat{X}_i$ and $\hat{Y}_i$ in the proof below. Note that Theorem 7.2 remains valid without using leave-one-out kernel estimators.

Lemma 7.1. *Let $m_i = g(Z_i)$ or $m_i = \xi(Z_i)$. Then*

$$E_1[(m_i - m_1)K_{h,i1}] = O(h^\nu).$$

Proof. Note that $g(z)$ has bounded derivatives. It follows by using the Taylor expansion and a change of variables argument. $\square$

Lemma 7.2.

(i) $S_{(\hat{m}-m)\hat{f}} = O_p\left(h^{2\nu} + h^2(nh^q)^{-1}\right)$ *($m_i = g_i$ or $m_i = \xi_i$).*

(ii) Let $\epsilon_i = u_i$ or v_i; then $S_{\hat{\epsilon}\hat{f}} = O_p\left((nh^q)^{-1}\right)$.

Proof of (i). (we ignore the difference between $(n-1)^{-1}$ and n^{-1}):

$$\mathrm{E}\left[\left|S_{(\hat{m}-m)\hat{f}}\right|\right] = n^{-1}\sum_i \mathrm{E}\left[(\hat{m}_i - m_i)^2 \hat{f}_i^2\right]$$

$$= \mathrm{E}\left[(\hat{m}_1 - m_1)^2 \hat{f}_1^2\right]$$

$$= n^{-2}\sum_{i\neq 1}\sum_{j\neq 1} \mathrm{E}\left[(m_i - m_1)K_{h,i1}(m_j - m_1)K_{h,j1}\right]$$

$$= n^{-2}\sum_{i\neq 1}\left\{\mathrm{E}\left[(m_i - m_1)^2 K_{h,i1}^2\right]\right.$$

$$+ \sum_{j\neq 1, j\neq i} \mathrm{E}\left\{\mathrm{E}_1\left[(m_i - m_1)K_{h,i1}\right]\right.$$

$$\left.\left.\times \mathrm{E}_1\left[(m_j - m_1)K_{h,j1}\right]\right\}\right\}$$

$$= n^{-1}\left\{O\left(h^2 h^{-q}\right) + nO\left(h^{2\nu}\right)\right\}$$

$$= O\left(\left(nh^{q-2}\right)^{-1} + h^{2\nu}\right)$$

by Lemma 7.1. $\square$

Proof of (ii).

$$\mathrm{E}\left[\left|S_{\hat{\epsilon}\hat{f}}\right|\right] = n^{-1}\sum_i \mathrm{E}\left[\hat{\epsilon}_i^2 \hat{f}_i^2\right]$$

$$= \mathrm{E}\left[\hat{\epsilon}_1^2 \hat{f}_1^2\right]$$

$$= n^{-2}\sum_{i\neq 1}\sum_{j\neq 1} \mathrm{E}\left[\epsilon_i\epsilon_j K_{h,i1}K_{h,j1}\right]$$

$$= n^{-2}\sum_{i\neq 1} \mathrm{E}\left[\epsilon_i^2 K_{h,i1}^2\right]$$

$$= n^{-1}\mathrm{E}\left[\sigma_\epsilon^2(X_i, Z_i)K_{h,i1}^2\right]$$

$$\leq Cn^{-1}\mathrm{E}\left(K_{h,i1}^2\right)$$

$$= O\left((nh^q)^{-1}\right).$$

$\square$

Lemma 7.3. $S_{(\hat{m}-m)\hat{f},\epsilon\hat{f}} = o_p\left(n^{-1/2}\right)$ *($m_i = g_i$ or $m_i = \xi_i$).*

Proof.

$$S_{(\hat{m}-m)\hat{f},\epsilon\hat{f}} = S_{(\hat{m}-m)\hat{f},\epsilon f} + S_{(\hat{m}-m)\hat{f},\epsilon(\hat{f}-f)}$$
$$= S_{(\hat{m}-m)\hat{f},\epsilon f} + (s.o.).$$

$$\mathrm{E}\left\{\left[S_{(\hat{m}-m)\hat{f},\epsilon f}\right]^2\right\} = n^{-2}\sum_i \mathrm{E}\left[(\hat{m}_i - m_i)^2 \hat{f}_i^2 \epsilon_i^2 f_i^2\right]$$
$$= n^{-1}\mathrm{E}\left[(\hat{m}_1 - m_1)^2 \hat{f}_1^2 \sigma_\epsilon^2(X_1, Z_1) f_1^2\right]$$
$$\leq Cn^{-1}\mathrm{E}\left[(\hat{m}_1 - m_1)^2 \hat{f}_1^2\right]$$
$$= Cn^{-1}\mathrm{E}\left[S_{(\hat{m}-m)\hat{f}}\right]$$
$$= n^{-1}o(1)$$
$$= o(n^{-1})$$

by Lemma 7.2.
    Hence,

$$S_{(\hat{m}-m)\hat{f},\epsilon\hat{f}} = S_{(\hat{m}-m)\hat{f},\epsilon f} + (s.o.) = o_p\left(n^{-1/2}\right).$$

$\square$

Lemma 7.4. $S_{(\hat{m}-m)\hat{f},\hat{\epsilon}\hat{f}} = O_p\left(h(nh^q)^{-1} + h^\nu(nh^q)^{-1/2}\right) = o_p\left(n^{-1/2}\right).$

Proof. By the Cauchy inequality,

$$\left|S_{(\hat{m}-m)\hat{f},\hat{\epsilon}f}\right| \leq \left\{\left|S_{(\hat{m}-m)\hat{f}}\right|\left|S_{\hat{\epsilon}\hat{f}}\right|\right\}^{1/2}$$
$$= \left\{O_p\left(h^2(nh^q)^{-1} + h^{2\nu}\right)O_p\left((nh^q)^{-1}\right)\right\}^{1/2}$$
$$= O_p\left(h(nh^q)^{-1} + h^\nu(nh^q)^{-1/2}\right)$$
$$= o_p\left(n^{-1/2}\right).$$

$\square$

Lemma 7.5.

(i) $S_{u\hat{f},\hat{v}\hat{f}} = O_p\left((nh^{q/2})^{-1}\right),$

(ii) $S_{v\hat{f},\hat{u}\hat{f}} = O_p\left((nh^{q/2})^{-1}\right),$

(iii) $S_{v\hat{f},\hat{v}\hat{f}} = O_p(n^{-1}h^{q/2})$,

(iv) $S_{\hat{u}\hat{f},\hat{v}\hat{f}} = O_p\left((nh^q)^{-1}\right)$,

(v) $S_{\hat{v}\hat{f}} = o_p(1)$.

The proof of (ii) and (iii) are the same as (i).

Proof of (i).

$$S_{u\hat{f},\hat{v}\hat{f}} = S_{uf,\hat{v}\hat{f}} + S_{u(\hat{f}-f),\hat{v}\hat{f}}$$
$$= S_{uf,\hat{v}\hat{f}} + (s.o.).$$

$$\mathrm{E}\left\{\left[S_{uf,\hat{v}\hat{f}}\right]^2\right\} = n^{-2}\sum_i \mathrm{E}\left[u_i^2 f_i^2 \left|\hat{v}_i\hat{f}_i\right|^2\right]$$
$$= n^{-1}\mathrm{E}\left[\sigma^2(X_1,Z_1)f_1^2\left|\hat{v}_1\hat{f}_1\right|^2\right]$$
$$\leq Cn^{-1}\mathrm{E}\left[\left|\hat{v}_1\hat{f}_1\right|^2\right] = O\left(n^{-1}(nh^q)^{-1}\right)$$
$$= O\left((n^2h^q)^{-1}\right)$$

by Lemma 7.2. Hence, $S_{uf,\hat{v}\hat{f}} = O_p\left((nh^{q/2})^{-1}\right)$. $\square$

(ii) The proof of (ii) is the same as (i).

(iii) The proof of (iii) is the same as (i).

(iv) By the Cauchy inequality,

$$\left|S_{\hat{u}\hat{f},\hat{v}\hat{f}}\right| \leq \left\{\left|S_{\hat{u}\hat{f}}\right|\left|S_{\hat{v}\hat{f}}\right|\right\}^{1/2} = \left\{O_p\left((nh^q)^{-1}\right)O_p\left((nh^q)^{-1}\right)\right\}^{1/2}$$
$$= O_p\left((nh^q)^{-1}\right) = o_p\left(n^{-1/2}\right).$$

(v) Follows from Lemma 7.2.

Proposition 7.1. $S_{(X-\hat{X})\hat{f},(g-\hat{g})\hat{f}} = o_p(n^{-1/2})$.

Proof. Define $\xi_i = \mathrm{E}(X_i|Z_i)$, $V_i = X_i - \mathrm{E}(X_i|Z_i) = X_i - \xi_i$. Then $X_i = \xi_i + V_i$ and $\hat{X}_i = \hat{\xi}_i + \hat{V}_i$.

$$
\begin{aligned}
S_{(X-\hat{X})\hat{f},(g-\hat{g})\hat{f}} &= S_{(\xi-\hat{\xi}+V-\hat{V})\hat{f},(g-\hat{g})\hat{f}} \\
&= S_{(\xi-\hat{\xi})\hat{f},(g-\hat{g})\hat{f}} + S_{V\hat{f},(g-\hat{g})\hat{f}} - S_{\hat{V}\hat{f},(g-\hat{g})\hat{f}} \\
&= O_p\left(h^2(nh^q)^{-1} + h^{2\nu}\right) + O_p\left(h(nh^{q/2})^{-1} + n^{-1/2}h^\nu\right) \\
&= o_p\left(n^{-1/2}\right)
\end{aligned}
$$

by Lemmas 7.2, 7.3, and 7.4.   □

Proposition 7.2. $S_{(X-\hat{X})\hat{f}} \xrightarrow{p} \Phi$.

Proof.

$$
\begin{aligned}
S_{(X-\hat{X})\hat{f}} &= S_{(\xi-\hat{\xi})\hat{f}+V\hat{f}-\hat{V}\hat{f}} \\
&= S_{(\xi-\hat{\xi})\hat{f}} + S_{V\hat{f}} + S_{\hat{V}\hat{f}} \\
&\quad + 2S_{(\xi-\hat{\xi})\hat{f},V\hat{f}} - 2S_{(\xi-\hat{\xi})\hat{f},\hat{V}\hat{f}} \\
&\quad - 2S_{V\hat{f},\hat{V}\hat{f}} = S_{V\hat{f}} + o_p(1) \\
&= S_{Vf} + o_p(1) \\
&= n^{-1}\sum_{i=1}^n V_i V_i' f_i^2 + o_p(1) \xrightarrow{p} \mathrm{E}(V_1 V_1' f_1^2) = \Phi_f
\end{aligned}
$$

by Lemmas 7.1 to 7.5 and a law of large numbers argument.   □

Proposition 7.3. $S_{(X-\hat{X})\hat{f},\hat{U}\hat{f}} = o_p\left(n^{-1/2}\right)$.

Proof.

$$
\begin{aligned}
S_{(X-\hat{X})\hat{f},\hat{U}\hat{f}} &= S_{(\xi-\hat{\xi})\hat{f},\hat{U}\hat{f}} + S_{V\hat{f},\hat{U}\hat{f}} - S_{\hat{V}\hat{f},\hat{U}\hat{f}} \\
&= O_p\left(h(nh^q)^{-1} + h^\nu(nh^q)^{-1/2}\right) \\
&\quad + O_p\left((nh^q)^{-1}\right) + O_p\left((nh^q)^{-1}\right) \\
&= o_p\left(n^{-1/2}\right)
\end{aligned}
$$

by Lemmas 7.4 and 7.5.   □

Proposition 7.4. $\sqrt{n}S_{(X-\hat{X})\hat{f},U\hat{f}} \xrightarrow{d} N(0,\Psi)$.

Proof.

$$\sqrt{n}S_{(\hat{X}-X)\hat{f},U\hat{f}} = \sqrt{n}\left\{S_{(\xi-\hat{\xi})\hat{f},U\hat{f}} + S_{V\hat{f},U\hat{f}} - S_{\hat{V}\hat{f},U\hat{f}}\right\}$$

$$= \sqrt{n}S_{V\hat{f},U\hat{f}} + o_p(1)$$

$$= \sqrt{n}S_{Vf,Uf} + o_p(1)$$

$$= n^{-1/2}\sum_i V_iU_if_i^2 \xrightarrow{d} N(0,\Psi_f)$$

by Lemmas 7.3, 7.5 and the Lindeberg-Levy CLT. $\qquad\qquad\square$

7.5.2　Verifying Theorem 7.3 for a Partially Linear Model

We will consider the density-weighted estimator $\hat{\beta}$. The objective function is

$$d(\theta,\hat{\tau}) = (1/2)\sum_i [Y_i - \hat{Y}_i - (X_i - \hat{X}_i)'\beta_0]^2 \hat{f}_i^2,$$

and the necessary first order conditions are

$$\bar{m}_n(\beta,\hat{\tau}) = n^{-1}\sum_i (X_i - \hat{X}_i)'\hat{f}_i\left[Y_i - \hat{Y}_i - (X_i - \hat{X}_i)'\beta_0\right]\hat{f}_i = 0 \quad (7.37)$$

and

$$Y_i - \hat{Y}_i = (X_i - \hat{X}_i)'\beta_0 + (g_i - \hat{g}_i) + u_i - \hat{u}_i. \quad (7.38)$$

Using (7.38), we can rewrite (7.37) as

$$\frac{1}{n}\sum_i (X_i - \hat{X}_i)'\hat{f}_i\left[g_i - \hat{g}_i + u_i - \hat{u}_i\right]\hat{f}_i$$

$$-\frac{1}{n}\sum_i (X_i - \hat{X}_i)(X_i - \hat{X}_i)'(\hat{\beta} - \beta_0) = 0. \quad (7.39)$$

Comparing (7.39) with (7.17), we know that

$$\nu_n(\hat{\tau}) = n^{1/2}S_{(\xi-\hat{\xi}+v-\hat{v})\hat{f},(g-\hat{g}+u-\hat{u})\hat{f}}.$$

Note that $\hat{\xi}$, $\hat{g}$, $\hat{v}$, $\hat{u}$ and $\hat{f}$ estimate ξ, $\hat{g}$, $E(v|z) = 0$, $E(u|z) = 0$, and f, respectively. Thus, replacing $\hat{\tau}$ with τ_0 in $\nu_n(\hat{\tau})$, we obtain $\nu_n(\tau_0) = n^{1/2}S_{vf,uf}$.

Assumption 7.1 (v) is satisfied because

$$n^{-1} \sum_i (\partial/\partial\beta_0) m(W_i, \beta_0, \hat\tau) = n^{-1} \sum_i (X_i - \hat X_i)(X_i - \hat X_i)' \hat f_i^2$$

$$\xrightarrow{p} \mathrm{E}\left[(X_i - \mathrm{E}(X_i|Z_i))(X_i - \mathrm{E}(X_i|Z_i))' f_i^2 \right]$$

$$\equiv \mathrm{E}\left[(\partial/\partial\beta_0) m(W_i, \beta_0, \tau_0) \right]$$

by a proof similar to Proposition 7.2.

To check Assumption 7.1 (iv), we have

$$\nu_n(\hat\tau) - \nu_n(\tau_0) = n^{1/2} S_{(\xi - \hat\xi - \hat v)\hat f, (g - \hat g + u - \hat u)\hat f} + n^{1/2} S_{v\hat f, (g - \hat g - \hat u)\hat f}$$

$$\equiv \nu_{n,1}(\hat\tau, \tau_0) + \nu_{n,2}(\hat\tau, \tau_0),$$

where

$$\nu_{n,1}(\hat\tau, \tau_0) = n^{1/2} S_{(\xi - \hat\xi - \hat v)\hat f, (g - \hat g + u - \hat u)\hat f}$$

and

$$\nu_{n,2}(\hat\tau, \tau_0) = n^{1/2} S_{v\hat f, (g - \hat g - \hat u)\hat f}.$$

We define the pseudometric $\rho_n(\hat\tau, \tau_0) = \mathrm{E}\,|\nu_{n,1}(\hat\tau, \tau_0)| + \mathrm{E}\left[\nu_{n,2}(\hat\tau, \tau_0)^2\right]$ and $\rho(\hat\tau, \tau_0) \stackrel{\mathrm{def}}{=} \lim_{n\to\infty} \rho_n(\hat\tau, \tau_0)$. Then

$$\rho_n(\hat\tau, \tau_0) = \mathrm{E}\,|\nu_{n,1}(\hat\tau, \tau_0)| + \mathrm{E}\left[\nu_{n,2}(\hat\tau, \tau_0)^2\right]$$

$$\leq \mathrm{E}\left\{ n^{-1/2} \sum_i \left[(\xi_i - \hat\xi_i)^2 \hat f_i^2 + \hat v_i^2 \hat f_i^2 + (g_i - \hat g_i)^2 \hat f_i^2 + \hat u_i^2 \hat f_i^2 \right] \right\}$$

$$+ n^{-1} \sum_i \mathrm{E}\left\{ v_i^2 \left[(g_i - \hat g_i)^2 \hat f_i^2 + \hat u_i^2 \hat f_i^2 \right] \right\} \to 0$$

by the proofs of Lemma 7.2.

Thus, Assumption 7.1 (iv) holds.

Note that for the partially linear model $m(\hat\theta, \hat\tau)$ is linear in $\hat\tau$, so stochastic equicontinuity is relatively easy to verify. The stochastic equicontinuity property is substantially more difficult to verify for classes of nonlinear functions.

By Theorem 7.3, we know that

$$\sqrt{n}(\hat\beta - \beta_0) \xrightarrow{d} N\left(0, M^{-1} S M^{-1}\right),$$

which is, of course, the same as Theorem 7.1 since $M = \Phi_f$ and $\Psi_f = S$.

7.6   Exercises

Exercise 7.1. Prove (7.5).

Hint: Write $W_i = X_i - \mathrm{E}(X_i|Z_i)$, then

$$\sqrt{n}(\hat{\beta}_{\mathrm{inf}} - \beta_0) = \left[n^{-1} \sum_{i=1}^{n} W_i W_i' \right]^{-1} n^{-1/2} \sum_{s=1}^{n} W_i u_i \equiv A_n^{-1} B_n$$

By Khinchin's law of large numbers (see Appendix A), we have $A_n = n^{-1} \sum_i W_i W_i' \xrightarrow{p} \mathrm{E}[W_i W_i'] \equiv \Phi$. Also, $\mathrm{E}[W_i u_i] = 0$ and $\mathrm{var}(W_i u_i) = \mathrm{E}\left[\sigma^2(X_i, Z_i) W_i W_i'\right] \equiv \Psi$. By the Lindeberg-Levy CLT, we have

$$n^{-1/2} \sum_i W_i u_i \xrightarrow{d} N(0, \Psi).$$

These results imply that

$$\sqrt{n}(\hat{\beta} - \beta_{\mathrm{inf}}) = [A_n]^{-1} B_n \to \Phi^{-1} N(0, B) = N\left(0, \Phi^{-1} B \Phi^{-1}\right).$$

Exercise 7.2. Prove that a consistent estimator of the asymptotic variance of $\hat{\beta}$ is given by $\hat{\Phi}^{-1} \hat{\Psi} \hat{\Phi}^{-1}$, where $\hat{\Phi} = \frac{1}{n} \sum_i (X_i - \hat{X}_i)'(X_i - \hat{X}_i)\mathbf{1}_i$, $\hat{\Psi} = \frac{1}{n} \sum_i \left[\hat{u}_i^2 (X_i - \hat{X}_i)'(X_i - \hat{X}_i)\mathbf{1}_i \right]$, $\hat{u}_i = (y_i - \hat{y}_i) - (X_i - \hat{X}_i)'\hat{\beta}$ is a consistent estimator for u_i, and where $\hat{y}_i$ and $\hat{X}_i$ are kernel estimators of $\mathrm{E}(y_i|Z_i)$ and $\mathrm{E}(X_i|Z_i)$ respectively, defined in Section 7.2.

Exercise 7.3. Prove that a consistent estimator of the asymptotic variance of $\hat{\beta}_f$ is given by $\hat{\Phi}_f^{-1} \hat{\Psi}_f \hat{\Phi}_f^{-1}$, where $\hat{\Phi}_f = n^{-1} \sum_i (X_i - \hat{X}_i)'(X_i - \hat{X}_i)\hat{f}_i^2$, $\hat{\Psi}_f = n^{-1} \sum_i \left[\hat{u}_i^2 (X_i - \hat{X}_i)'(X_i - \hat{X}_i)\hat{f}_i^4 \right]$, $\tilde{u}_i = (Y_i - \hat{Y}_i) - (X_i - \hat{X}_i)'\hat{\beta}_f$ is a consistent estimator for u_i, and $\hat{Y}_i$ and $\hat{X}_i$ are kernel estimators of $\mathrm{E}(y_i|Z_i)$ and $\mathrm{E}(X_i|Z_i)$ respectively, defined in Section 7.2.

Exercise 7.4. Show that, under the conditions $\hat{\beta} - \beta_0 = O_p(n^{-1/2})$,

$$(nh_1 \ldots h_q)^{1/2} \left(\hat{g}(z) - g(z) - \sum_{s=1}^{q} h_s^2 B_s(z) \right) \to N(0, V(z))$$

in distribution, where $\hat{g}(z)$ is defined in (7.13), $B_s(z)$ is defined in Theorem 7.1, and $V(z) = \kappa^q \left[\sigma^2(z)/f(z) \right]$.

Hint: $(nh_1 \ldots h_q)^{1/2} \left(\tilde{g}(z) - g(z) - \sum_{s=1}^{q} h_s^2 B_s(z) \right) \to N(0, V(z))$ by Theorem 7.1, $\tilde{g}(z)$ is defined in (7.14). From $\hat{\beta} - \beta_0 = O_p(n^{-1/2})$, one can show that $\hat{g}(z) - \tilde{g}(z) = O_p(n^{-1/2}) = o_p\left((nh_1 \ldots h_q)^{-1/2} + \sum_{s=1}^{q} h_s^2\right)$.

Exercise 7.5.

(i) Show that the result of Lemma 7.4 can be sharpened to
$$S_{(\hat{g}-g)\hat{f},\hat{\epsilon}\hat{f}} = O_p\left(h(nh^{q/2})^{-1} + n^{-1/2}h^{\nu}\right) = o_p\left(n^{-1/2}\right).$$

(ii) Show that the result of Lemma 7.5 (iii) can be sharpened to
$$S_{\hat{u}\hat{f},\hat{v}\hat{f}} = O_p\left(n^{-1}h^{-q/2}\right).$$

Hint: Do not use Cauchy's inequality, rather, show that

$$\mathrm{E}\left[S^2_{(\hat{g}-g)\hat{f},\hat{\epsilon}\hat{f}}\right] = O\left(h^2(n^{-1}h^q)^{-1} + n^{-1}h^{2\nu}\right)$$

for (i), and $\mathrm{E}\left[S^2_{\hat{u}\hat{f},\hat{v}\hat{f}}\right] = O(n^{-2}h^{-q})$ for (ii).

Note that with the above sharpened rate, Condition 7.3 can be replaced by the weaker Condition 7.4.

Exercise 7.6. Prove (7.24).

Hint: Use the Frisch-Waugh-Lovell Theorem (see Davidson and MacKinnon (1993, pp. 19-24)). Define $\mathcal{M}_z = I_n - P_z(P'_z P_z)^{-1}P'_z$, where P_z is an $n \times (q+1)$ matrix with ith row given by $(1, Z'_i)$. Project the matrix form of (7.24) on $\mathcal{M}_z$ to wipe out $\alpha + Z'_i\gamma$, then use a standard law of large numbers and CLT arguments as we did in the proof of Exercise 7.1.

Exercise 7.7.

(i) Assume that $\mathrm{E}(u_i^2|X_i, Z_i) = \sigma^2(Z_i)$. Using arguments similar to those we used when deriving (7.33), show that the semiparametric efficiency bound of β_0 is given by (7.33).

(ii) When $\mathrm{E}(u_i^2|X_i, Z_i) = \sigma^2(X_i Z_i)$, is $V_0 - V_{0,R}$ positive definite?

Hint: No calculation is needed for answering (ii). A simple logical argument is sufficient.

Chapter 8

Semiparametric Single Index Models

In this section we consider another popular semiparametric model, the so-called semiparametric single index model. This model has been widely used by applied econometricians and has been deployed in a variety of settings.

A semiparametric single index model is of the form

$$Y = g(X'\beta_0) + u, \tag{8.1}$$

where Y is the dependent variable, $X \in \mathbb{R}^q$ is the vector of explanatory variables, β_0 is the $q \times 1$ vector of unknown parameters, and u is the error satisfying $\mathrm{E}(u|X) = 0$. The term $x'\beta_0$ is called a "single index" because it is a scalar (a single index) even though x is a vector. The functional form of $g(\cdot)$ is unknown to the researcher. This model is semiparametric in nature since the functional form of the linear index is specified, while $g(\cdot)$ is left unspecified.

Semiparametric single index models arise naturally in binary choice settings, and so for illustrative purposes we first discuss this popular example. In a binary choice model, if one is willing to accept the parametric linear index governing choices but unwilling to specify the unknown distribution of the error term, then one arrives at a semiparametric single index model. Specifically, when considering the relationship between a binary dependent variable (Y) and some other covariates (X), one might model this relationship as follows:

$$Y_i = \begin{cases} 1 & \text{if } Y_i^* \overset{\text{def}}{=} \alpha + X_i'\beta + \epsilon_i > 0 \\ 0 & \text{if } Y_i^* = \alpha + X_i'\beta + \epsilon_i \leq 0, \end{cases} \tag{8.2}$$

where Y^* is a latent variable. Note that here $\epsilon = Y^* - \mathrm{E}(Y^*|X)$, which differs from $u = Y - \mathrm{E}(Y|X)$ defined in (8.1) because $Y \neq Y^*$.

For example, Y could represent a labor force participation decision where if Y equals 1, an individual participates in the labor market, while if Y equals 0, the individual does not. The explanatory variables X contain a set of economic factors that could influence the participation decision, such as age, marital status, education, work history, and number of children. Model (8.2) assumes a linear parametric link function between the decision regarding whether to participate in the labor market (Y) and the explanatory variables X. We are mainly interested in estimating β, which reflects the impact of changes in X on the probability of participating in the labor market.

Parametric methods for estimating β require one to specify the (unknown) distribution of the error term ϵ. A popular assumption is that ϵ has a normal distribution, i.e., $\epsilon \sim N(0, \sigma^2)$. It can be shown that β and σ^2 cannot be jointly identified without additional identification conditions (see Maddala (1986) for further details). For instance, if we assume that $\sigma = 1$, then β is identified, and we can use maximum likelihood estimation to estimate β. However, if the error term does not possess a normal distribution, then the parametric approach will in general produce inconsistent estimates, i.e., of $\mathrm{P}(Y = 1|x) = \mathrm{E}(Y|x)$; see Exercise 8.1. To see this, let $F_\epsilon(\cdot)$ denote the true CDF of ϵ. From (8.2) we have

$$
\begin{aligned}
\mathrm{E}(Y|x) &= \sum_{y=0,1} y\mathrm{P}(y|x) \\
&= 1 \times \mathrm{P}(Y = 1|x) + 0 \times \mathrm{P}(Y = 0|x) \\
&= \mathrm{P}(Y = 1|x) \\
&= \mathrm{P}(\alpha + x'\beta + \epsilon > 0) \\
&= \mathrm{P}(\epsilon > -(\alpha + x'\beta)) \\
&= 1 - \mathrm{P}(\epsilon < -(\alpha + x'\beta)) \\
&= 1 - F(-(\alpha + x'\beta)) \\
&\equiv m(\alpha + x'\beta),
\end{aligned}
$$

where $F(\cdot)$ is the CDF of ϵ. Note that if ϵ has a symmetric distribution, then $F(\alpha + x'\beta) = 1 - F(-(\alpha + x'\beta))$, and we have $m(\cdot) = F(\cdot)$ in this case. For example, if $\epsilon \sim N(0,1)$ $(\sigma = 1)$, then (8.2) becomes a Probit model:

$$
\mathrm{E}(Y|x) = \mathrm{P}(Y = 1|x) = \Phi(\alpha + x'\beta), \tag{8.3}
$$

where $\Phi(\cdot)$ is the CDF of a standard normal variable. If, on the other hand, ϵ has a symmetric logistic distribution, then (8.3) results in a logistic model of the form

$$\mathrm{E}(Y|x) = \mathrm{P}(Y = 1|x) = \frac{1}{1 + e^{\alpha + x'\beta}}. \tag{8.4}$$

From (8.3) and (8.4), we see that different distributional assumptions for ϵ lead to different functional forms for the conditional probability of $Y = 1$. Hence, consistent parametric estimation of $\mathrm{P}(Y = 1|x) = \mathrm{E}(Y|x)$ requires the *correct* distributional specification of ϵ. A semiparametric single index model therefore avoids the problem of error distribution misspecification. Moreover, the semiparametric single index model (8.1) is more general than the binary choice model since we do not require that the dependent variable necessarily be binary in nature. As we will see in Section 8.1, the location parameter α cannot be identified when the functional form of $g(\cdot)$ is unknown, which is why we write our semiparametric model (8.1) only as a function of $X_i'\beta_0$. We discuss this and other identification conditions in Section 8.1. Note that model (8.1) implies that $\mathrm{E}(Y|x) = g(x'\beta_0)$, hence y depends on x only through the linear combination $x'\beta_0$, and the relationship is characterized by the link function $g(\cdot)$.

We would like to emphasize here that, like the partially linear model, the semiparametric single index model is an alternative approach designed to mitigate effects arising from the curse of dimensionality. Also, we emphasize that Y can be continuous or discrete, i.e., there is no no reason to restrict Y to be a binary variable.

8.1 Identification Conditions

For the semiparametric single index model, we have

$$\mathrm{E}(Y|x) = g(x'\beta_0).$$

Ichimura (1993), Manski (1988) and Horowitz (1998, pp. 14–20), provide excellent intuitive explanations of the identifiability conditions underlying semiparametric single index models (i.e., the set of conditions under which the unknown parameter vector β_0 and the unknown function $g(\cdot)$ can be sensibly estimated). We briefly discuss these conditions and then summarize them in a proposition.

First, $g(\cdot)$ cannot be a constant function, for otherwise it is obvious that β_0 is not identified. Next, as is the case for linear regression, the different components of x cannot have a perfect linear relationship (perfect multicollinearity). Another restriction is that x contain at least one continuous random variable. Intuitively this can be understood via the following line of reasoning. If x contains only discrete variables, say some 0-1 dummy variables, then the support of x is finite, and so is the support of the scalar variable $v = x'\beta$ for any vector of β. Obviously then there will exist an infinite number of functions $g(\cdot)$ which differ in terms of their β vectors such that $g(x'\beta) = E(Y|x)$. This is so simply because $E(Y|x) = g(x'\beta)$ imposes only a finite number of restrictions on the unknown function $g(\cdot)$, therefore, there exist an infinite number of different choices of $g(\cdot)$ and β that satisfy the finite set of restrictions imposed by $E(Y|x) = g(x'\beta)$. See Horowitz (1998) for a specific example and illustration of this point. Also, x cannot contain a constant. That is, β_0 cannot contain a location parameter, and β_0 is identifiable only up to a scale. This follows because, for *any* nonzero constants α_1 and α_2 and for any $g(\cdot)$ function and fixed vector β, we can always find another function, say $g_2(\cdot)$, defined by $g_2(\alpha_1 + \alpha_2 x'\beta) = g(x'\beta)$. Therefore, β_0 is not identified without some location and scale restrictions (normalizations). One popular normalization is that x does not contain a constant, the so-called location normalization. For the so-called scale normalization, one approach is to assume that the vector β has unit length, i.e., $||\beta|| = 1$, where $||\beta|| = \{\sum_{j=1}^{q} \beta_j^2\}^{1/2}$ is the Euclidean norm (length) of β. Another popular scale normalization is to assume that the first component of x has a unit coefficient, and this first component is assumed to be a continuous variable.

We summarize the above conditions in the following proposition.

Proposition 8.1. *(Identification of a Single Index Model). For the semiparametric single index model (8.1), identification of β_0 and $g(\cdot)$ requires that*

(i) *x should not contain a constant (intercept), and x must contain at least one continuous variable. Moreover, $||\beta_0|| = 1$.*

(ii) *$g(\cdot)$ is differentiable and is not a constant function on the support of $x'\beta_0$.*

(iii) *For the discrete components of x, varying the values of the discrete variables will not divide the support of $x'\beta_0$ into disjoint subsets.*

We have already discussed how, when x contains only discrete variables, β_0 and $g(\cdot)$ are not identified. However, when $g(\cdot)$ is assumed to be an increasing function, then one can obtain identified *bounds* on the components of β. For a detailed discussion of how to characterize the bounds when all components of x are discrete, see Horowitz (1998, pp. 17-20).

8.2 Estimation

8.2.1 Ichimura's Method

In this section we review the semiparametric estimation method proposed by Ichimura (1993).

If the functional form of $g(\cdot)$ were known, (8.1) would become a standard nonlinear regression model, and we could use the nonlinear least squares method to estimate β_0 by minimizing

$$\sum_{i=1} [Y_i - g(X_i'\beta)]^2 \qquad (8.5)$$

with respect to β.

In the case of an unknown function $g(\cdot)$, we first need to estimate $g(\cdot)$. However, the kernel method does not estimate $g(X_i'\beta_0)$ directly because not only is $g(\cdot)$ unknown, but so too is β_0. Nevertheless, for a given value of β we can estimate

$$G(X_i'\beta) \stackrel{\text{def}}{=} \mathrm{E}(Y_i|X_i'\beta) = \mathrm{E}[g(X_i'\beta_0)|X_i'\beta] \qquad (8.6)$$

by the kernel method, where the last equality follows from the fact that $\mathrm{E}(u_i|X_i'\beta) = 0$ for all β since $\mathrm{E}(u_i|X_i) = 0$.

Note that when $\beta = \beta_0$, $G(X_i'\beta_0) = g(X_i'\beta_0)$, while in general, $G(X_i'\beta) \neq g(X_i'\beta_0)$ if $\beta \neq \beta_0$. A leave-one-out nonparametric kernel estimator of $G(X_i'\beta)$ is given by

$$\hat{G}_{-i}(X_i'\beta) \equiv \hat{\mathrm{E}}_{-i}(Y_i|X_i'\beta) = \frac{(nh)^{-1} \sum_{j=1, j \neq i}^n Y_j K\left(\frac{X_j'\beta - X_i'\beta}{h}\right)}{\hat{p}_{-i}(X_i'\beta)}, \qquad (8.7)$$

where $\hat{p}_{-i}(X_i'\beta) = (nh)^{-1} \sum_{j=1, j \neq i}^n K\left(\frac{X_j'\beta - X_i'\beta}{h}\right)$.

Ichimura (1993) suggests estimating $g(X_i'\beta_0)$ in (8.5) by $\hat{G}_{-i}(X_i'\beta)$ of (8.7) and choosing β by (semiparametric) nonlinear least squares.

There is one technical problem though, being that (8.7) has a random denominator, i.e., $\hat{p}(X_i'\beta) = (nh)^{-1}\sum_{j=1,j\neq i}^n K((X_j'\beta - X_i'\beta)/h)$. Ichimura uses a trimming function to trim out small values of $\hat{p}(X_i'\beta)$. Let $p(x'\beta)$ denote the PDF of $X_i'\beta$. Define A_δ and A_n to be the following sets:

$$A_\delta = \{x : p(x'\beta) \geq \delta, \text{ for all } \beta \in \mathcal{B} \}$$

where $\delta > 0$ is a constant, $\mathcal{B}$ is a compact subset in $\mathbb{R}^q$, and

$$A_n = \{x : ||x - x^*|| \leq 2h \text{ for some } x^* \in A_\delta \}.$$

The set A_δ ensures that the denominator in (8.7) does not get too close to zero for $x \in A_\delta$. The A_n set is slightly larger than A_δ, but as $n \to \infty$, $h \to 0$ and A_n shrinks to A_δ.

Ichimura (1993) suggests choosing β by minimizing the following objective function:

$$S_n(\beta) = \sum_{i=1}^n \left[Y_i - \hat{G}_{-i}(X_i'\beta)\right]^2 w(X_i)\mathbf{1}(X_i \in A_n), \qquad (8.8)$$

where $\hat{G}_{-i}(X_i'\beta)$ is defined in (8.7), $w(X_i)$ is a nonnegative weight function, and $\mathbf{1}(\cdot)$ is the usual indicator function. That is, $\mathbf{1}(X_i \in A_n)$ is a trimming function which equals one if $X_i \in A_n$, zero otherwise.

The trimming function ensures that the random denominator in the kernel estimator is positive with high probability so as to simplify the asymptotic analysis.

Let $\hat{\beta}$ denote the semiparametric estimator of β_0 obtained from minimizing (8.8). To derive the asymptotic distribution of $\hat{\beta}$, the following conditions are needed:

Assumption 8.1. *The set A_δ is compact, and the weight function $w(\cdot)$ is bounded and positive on A_δ. Define the set $D_z = \{z : z = x'\beta, \beta \in \mathcal{B}, x \in A_\delta\}$. Letting $p(\cdot)$ denote the PDF of $z \in D_z$, $p(\cdot)$ is bounded below by a positive constant for all $z \in D_z$.*

Assumption 8.2. *$g(\cdot)$ and $p(\cdot)$ are three times differentiable with respect to $z = x'\beta$. The third derivatives are Lipschitz continuous uniformly over $\mathcal{B}$ for all $z \in D_z$.*

Assumption 8.3. *The kernel function is a bounded second order kernel having bounded support, is twice differentiable, and its second derivative is Lipschitz continuous.*

Assumption 8.4. $\mathrm{E}|Y^m| < \infty$ *for some* $m \geq 3$. $\mathrm{cov}(Y|x)$ *is bounded and bounded away from zero for all* $x \in A_\delta . q \ln(h)/[nh^{3+3/(m-1)}] \to 0$ *and* $nh^8 \to 0$ *as* $n \to \infty$.

Ichimura (1993) has proven the following result:

Theorem 8.1. *Under Assumptions 8.1 through 8.4,*

$$\sqrt{n}(\hat{\beta} - \beta_0) \to N(0, \Omega_I) \text{ in distribution,}$$

where $\Omega_I = V^{-1}\Sigma V^{-1}$, *and where*

$$\Sigma = \mathrm{E}\Big\{ w(X_i)\sigma^2(X_i) \left(g_i^{(1)}\right)^2 \left(X_i - \mathrm{E}_A(X_i|X_i'\beta_0)\right)$$
$$\times \left(X_i - \mathrm{E}_A(X_i|X_i'\beta_0)\right)' \Big\},$$

with $g_i^{(1)} = [\partial g(v)/\partial v]|_{v=X_i'\beta_0}$, $\mathrm{E}_A(X_i|v) = \mathrm{E}(X_i|x_A'\beta_0 = v)$ *with* x_A *having the distribution of* X_i *conditional on* $X_i \in A_\delta$, *and*

$$V = \mathrm{E}\left[w(X_i) \left(g_i^{(1)}\right)^2 \left(X_i - \mathrm{E}_A(X_i|X_i'\beta_0)\right) \left(X_i - \mathrm{E}_A(X_i|X_i'\beta_0)\right)' \right].$$

A consistent estimator of Ω_I is given by

$$\hat{\Omega}_I = \hat{V}^{-1}\hat{\Sigma}\hat{V}^{-1},$$

where $\hat{V} = n^{-1}\sum_i w(X_i)\hat{g}^{(1)}(X_i'\hat{\beta})(X_i - \hat{\mathrm{E}}(X_i|X_i'\beta))(X_i - \hat{\mathrm{E}}(X_i|X_i'\beta))'$, $\hat{\Sigma} = n^{-1}\sum_i w(X_i)\hat{u}_i^2\hat{g}^{(1)}(X_i'\hat{\beta})(X_i - \hat{\mathrm{E}}(X_i|X_i'\beta))(X_i - \hat{\mathrm{E}}(X_i|X_i'\beta))'$, $\hat{u}_i = Y_i - \hat{g}(X_i'\hat{\beta})$, $\hat{g}^{(1)}(X_i'\hat{\beta}) = [\partial\hat{g}_{-i}(X_i'\beta)/\partial\beta]|_{\beta=\hat{\beta}}$, $\hat{g}_{-i}(X_i'\beta)$ is defined in (8.7), $\hat{\mathrm{E}}(X_i|X_i'\beta)' = \sum_j X_j K((X_i - X_j)'\hat{\beta})/\sum_j K((X_i - X_j)'\hat{\beta})$.

The proof of Theorem 8.1 is quite technical, and we refer readers to Ichimura (1993). Horowitz (1998) provides an excellent heuristic outline for proving Theorem 8.1, using only the familiar Taylor series methods, a standard law of large numbers, and the Lindeberg-Levy CLT arguments.

When $\mathrm{E}(u_i^2|X_i) = \sigma^2$ is a constant (i.e., when $u_i = Y_i - g(X_i'\beta_0)$ has conditionally homoskedastic errors), it can be shown that the optimal choice of $w(X_i)$ is $w(X_i) = 1$, and in this case $\hat{\beta}$ is semiparametrically efficient in the sense that Ω_I is the semiparametric variance lower bound (conditional on $X \in A_\delta$).

In general, however, $\mathrm{E}(u_i^2|X_i) = \sigma^2(X_i)$, and the semiparametrically efficient estimator of β has a complicated structure. If one assumes that $E(u_i^2|X_i) = \sigma^2(X_i'\beta_0)$, that is, that the conditional variance depends only on the single index, then the choice of $w(X_i) = 1/\sigma^2(X_i'\beta_0)$ can lead to a semiparametrically efficient estimator for β_0. However, this choice is infeasible since, in practice, $\sigma^2(X_i'\beta_0)$ is unknown. One could therefore adopt a two-step procedure as follows. Suppose that the conditional variance is a function of $X_i'\beta_0$ only. In this case, for the first step, use $w(X_i) = 1$ to obtain a $\sqrt{n}$-consistent estimator of β_0, say $\tilde{\beta}_0$, then using $\tilde{u}_i = Y_i - \hat{g}(X_i'\tilde{\beta}_0)$ one can obtain a consistent nonparametric estimator of $\sigma^2(X_i'\beta_0)$, say $\hat{\sigma}^2(X_i'\tilde{\beta}_0) = \text{vâr}(\tilde{u}_i|X_i\tilde{\beta}_0)$. In the second step choose $w(X_i) = 1/\hat{\sigma}^2(X_i'\beta_0)$ to estimate β_0 again. Provided that $\hat{\sigma}^2(v) - \sigma^2(v)$ converges to zero at a particular rate uniformly over $v \in D_v$ (D_v is the support of $X_i'\beta_0$), the resulting second step estimator $\hat{\beta}_0$ will be semiparametrically efficient.

For what follows below, we ignore the trimming set A_δ, the weight function $w(\cdot)$, and also assume that the minimization over β is, in fact, done over a shrinking set $\mathcal{B}_n = \{\beta : \|\beta - \beta_0\| \le Cn^{-1/2}\}$ for some constant $C > 0$. This type of argument is used by Härdle, Hall and Ichimura (1993). The requirement that β lie in a set with $\beta - \beta_0 = O\left(n^{-1/2}\right)$ may appear to be an overly strong assumption; however, given Ichimura's (1993) result, we know that $\hat{\beta}$ is a $\sqrt{n}$-consistent estimator of β, and we can look at a minimum of $S(\beta)$ for β with $O\left(n^{-1/2}\right)$ distance from β_0. With this assumption, together with the assumption that $h \in \mathcal{H}_n = \{h : C_1 n^{-1/5} \le h \le C_2 n^{-1/5}\}$ for some $C_2 > C_1 > 0$, then an alternative proof can establish the result of Theorem 8.1 as follows. First, it can be shown that the nonparametric sum of squared residuals can be written as (we omit $w_i = 1$ and omit the trimming indicator function for notational simplicity)

$$S_n(\beta) = \frac{1}{n} \sum_i \left[Y_i - \hat{G}_{-i}(X_i'\beta)\right]^2 = S(\beta) + T_n + o_p(1), \qquad (8.9)$$

where $S(\beta) = n^{-1} \sum_i [Y_i - G(X_i'\beta)]^2$, where

$$T_n = \sum_{i=1}^{n} \left[\hat{G}_{-i}(X_i'\beta_0) - g(X_i'\beta_0)\right]^2$$

is a term that is independent of β, and where $o_p(1)$ denotes terms of order $o_p(1)$ uniformly in $\beta \in \mathcal{B}_n$. The proof of (8.9) can be found in Härdle et al. (1993), who in fact consider a more general setting where they choose β and h simultaneously by cross-validation methods.

In Section 8.12 we show that $S(\beta) = O(1)$. Therefore, minimizing (8.9) with respect to β is asymptotically equivalent to minimizing $S(\beta)$. Letting $\bar{\beta}$ denote the value of β that minimizes $S(\beta)$ then, using Taylor expansion arguments, we can easily show that (see Section 8.12) $\bar{\beta}$ satisfies the following first order condition:

$$W_0 \left(\bar{\beta} - \beta_0 \right) = V_0 + (s.o.), \tag{8.10}$$

where

$$W_0 = \sum_{i=1}^{n} u_i \left[f^{(1)}(X_i'\beta_0) \right]^2 \left[X_i - \mathrm{E}(X_i|X_i'\beta_0) \right] \left[X_i - \mathrm{E}(X_i|X_i'\beta_0) \right]'$$

and

$$V_0 = \sum_{i=1}^{n} u_i f^{(1)}(X_i'\beta_0) \left[X_i - \mathrm{E}(X_i|X_i'\beta_0) \right].$$

Hence, by a standard law of large numbers and CLT argument, we have

$$\sqrt{n}(\bar{\beta} - \beta_0) = (W_0/n)^{-1} n^{-1/2} V_0 + o_p(1) \xrightarrow{d} N(0, \Omega_0), \tag{8.11}$$

where Ω_0 is the same as Ω_I except that $w(X_i)$ is replaced by 1.

Up to now we have restricted ourselves to the normalization rule, $\|\beta\| = 1$. We could also use a different normalization rule if desired. Instead of assuming that β has unit length, we can assume that the first component of β is one. Assume that the first component of x is a continuous variable, and write $X_i = (X_{1i}, \tilde{X}_i')'$, where $\tilde{X}_i$ is X_i excluding the first component of X_i. Also, define $\tilde{\beta}$ as the coefficient of $\tilde{X}_i$, i.e., $\beta = (1, \tilde{\beta}')'$. Then we could choose $\tilde{\beta}$ to minimize

$$S_2(\tilde{\beta}) = n^{-1} \sum_i \left[Y_i - \hat{G}_{-i}(X_{1i} + \tilde{X}_i'\beta) \right]^2 w(X_i) \mathbf{1}(X_i \in A_x).$$

In this case it can be shown that the asymptotic variance of $\sqrt{n}(\hat{\beta} - \tilde{\beta}_0)$ is $\Omega_2 = V_2^{-1} \Sigma_2 V_2^{-1}$, with

$$\Sigma_2 = \mathrm{E} \left\{ w(X_i)\sigma^2(X_i) \left(g_i^{(1)} \right)^2 \right.$$

$$\left. \times \left(\tilde{X}_i - \mathrm{E}_A(\tilde{X}_i|X_i'\beta) \right) \left(\tilde{X}_i - \mathrm{E}_A(\tilde{X}_i|X_i'\beta) \right)' \right\},$$

with $g_i^{(1)} = [\partial g(v)/\partial \tilde{\beta}]|_{v=X_i'\beta}$, $\mathrm{E}_A(\tilde{X}_i|v) = \mathrm{E}(\tilde{X}_i|X_A'\beta = v)$ with X_A having the distribution of X conditional on $X \in A_x$, and

$$V_2 = \mathrm{E} \left[W(X_i) \left(g_i^{(1)} \right)^2 \left(\tilde{X}_i - \mathrm{E}_A(\tilde{X}_i|X_i'\beta) \right) \left(\tilde{X}_i - \mathrm{E}_A(\tilde{X}_i|X_i'\beta) \right)' \right].$$

8.3 Direct Semiparametric Estimators for β

Ichimura's (1993) semiparametric nonlinear least squares estimator can be computationally costly in practice since the objective function is likely to be multimodal and may require extensive searching to avoid local minima. This section discusses a direct estimation method that does not require solving an optimization problem involving iterative solutions. The computational cost is less than the semiparametric non-linear least squares method of Ichimura; however, this does not come for free, and we will discuss some of the problems associated with the direct estimation method at the end of this section.

8.3.1 Average Derivative Estimators

When X_i is a vector of continuous variables, we can also estimate the single index model by estimating the average derivative of the conditional mean function $\mathrm{E}(Y|x)$. From $\mathrm{E}(Y|x) = g(x'\beta_0)$, we get

$$\frac{\partial \mathrm{E}(Y|x)}{\partial x} = g^{(1)}(x'\beta_0)\beta_0. \qquad (8.12)$$

Therefore, the average of (8.12) (the average derivative) is proportional to β_0, i.e.,

$$\mathrm{E}\left[\frac{\partial \mathrm{E}(Y|x)}{\partial x}\right] = \mathrm{E}\left[g^{(1)}(x'\beta_0)\right]\beta_0 \equiv C\beta_0. \qquad (8.13)$$

One can also consider a weighted average derivative of the form

$$\mathrm{E}\left[w(x)\frac{\partial \mathrm{E}(Y|x)}{\partial x}\right] = \mathrm{E}\left[w(x)g^{(1)}(x'\beta_0)\right]\beta_0 \equiv C_2\beta_0, \qquad (8.14)$$

which is also proportional to β_0.

Under the assumption that the kernel function is differentiable, one can estimate β_0 by estimating the average derivative $\mathrm{E}[\partial \mathrm{E}(Y|x)/\partial x]$, say

$$\tilde{\beta}_{\mathrm{ave}} = \frac{1}{n}\sum_{i=1}^{n}\frac{\partial \hat{\mathrm{E}}(Y_i|X_i)}{\partial X_i}, \qquad (8.15)$$

where the subscript ave denotes that it is an *average* derivative-based estimator, $\hat{\mathrm{E}}(Y_i|X_i) = \sum_{j=1}^{n} Y_j K_{ij}/\sum_j K_{ij}$ is the local constant kernel estimator of $\mathrm{E}(Y_i|X_i)$, $K_{ij} = K((X_i - X_j)/a)$ is a product kernel function, and a is the vector of smoothing parameters. The scale normalization can be obtained by dividing the estimated $\tilde{\beta}_{\text{ave}}$ by $|\tilde{\beta}_{\text{ave}}| = \left\{ \sum_{j=1}^{q} \tilde{\beta}_{\text{ave},j}^2 \right\}^{1/2}$ if one uses $|\beta| = 1$ as the normalization rule or by dividing $\tilde{\beta}_{\text{ave}}$ by $\tilde{\beta}_{\text{ave},1}$ if one chooses to normalize the coefficient of the first variable to be one.

One difficulty encountered in the derivation of the asymptotic distribution of $\tilde{\beta}_{\text{ave}}$ is the presence of a random denominator, which can be arbitrarily close to zero at some points. Rilstone (1991) suggests using a trimming function to avoid the "small denominator problem," and establishes the $\sqrt{n}$-normality result for $\tilde{\beta}_{\text{ave}}$ defined in (8.15).

When $f(x) = 0$ at the boundary of the support of X (for example, if X has unbounded support), Powell, Stock and Stoker (1989) suggest using the weighted average derivative estimator defined in (8.14) using the weight function $w(x) = f(x)$. Then, using integration by parts, we obtain

$$
\begin{aligned}
\delta &\stackrel{\text{def}}{=} \text{E}\left[f(X)g^{(1)}(X) \right] \\
&= \int g^{(1)}(x)f^2(x)dx \\
&= \int \left(\frac{\partial g(x'\beta_0)}{\partial x} \right) f^2(x)dx \\
&= 0 - 2\int g(x'\beta_0)f(x)f^{(1)}(x)dx \\
&= -2\text{E}\left[g(X'\beta_0)f^{(1)}(X) \right] \\
&= -2\text{E}\left[Y f^{(1)}(X) \right].
\end{aligned}
\tag{8.16}
$$

One can estimate (8.16) by

$$
\hat{\delta} = -\frac{2}{n}\sum_i Y_i \hat{f}^{(1)}(X_i),
\tag{8.17}
$$

where $\hat{f}^{(1)}(X_i)$ is a $q \times 1$ vector with its sth component given by $\partial \hat{f}(X_i)/\partial X_{is} = n^{-1}\sum_{j=1}^{n} a_s^{-2}k^{(1)}((X_{is} - X_{js})/a_s)\prod_{t \neq s}^{q} a_t^{-1}k((X_{it} - X_{jt})/a_t)$. In order to avoid potential confusion with the smoothing parameter h used for the estimation of the semiparametric index function, here we use a to denote the smoothing parameter used in the average derivative estimator. Note that by choosing $w(x) = f(x)$, $\hat{\delta}$ defined in (8.17) does not have a random denominator, and therefore, one does not need to introduce a trimming nuisance parameter. Härdle and

Stoker (1989) consider the average derivative estimator based on an unweighted quantity $E[g^{(1)}(X)] = -2E[Yf^{(1)}(X)/f(X)]$, and they use the trimming method to avoid the small random denominator problem. Powell et al. (1989) establish the $\sqrt{n}$-normality result for $\hat{\delta}$ defined by (8.17). We summarize their result below.

As mentioned above, the key assumption is that $f(x) = 0$ at the boundary of the support of X. Other smoothness and moments conditions can be found in Powell et al. (1989), or else see conditions (a)-(d) in Horowitz (1998, pp. 37–38). These conditions include smoothness of moment conditions on the unknown functions $g(\cdot)$ and $f(\cdot)$, the use of a νth order kernel function, as well as $n \sum_{s=1}^{q} a_s^{2\nu} \to 0$ and $n(a_1 \ldots a_q) \sum_{s=1}^{q} a_s^2 \to \infty$ as $n \to \infty$. The last two conditions require that $\nu > 1 + q/2$. Therefore, a higher order kernel ($\nu > 2$) is needed since $q \geq 2$. In the case of a single index model we need $q \geq 2$ since, otherwise, β is not identified. Powell et al. (1989) prove the following result:

$$\sqrt{n}(\hat{\delta} - \delta) \to N(0, \Omega_{PNS}), \qquad (8.18)$$

where $\Omega_{PNS} = 4E[\sigma^2(X)f^{(1)}(X)f^{(1)}(X)'] + 4\text{var}(f(X)g^{(1)}(X))$. A normalized vector β can be obtained via $\hat{\delta}/|\hat{\delta}|$.

The proof of (8.18) requires the use of U-statistic decompositions for variable kernel functions (some of these are collected in Appendix A).

In Chapter 2 we discussed using local polynomial methods to estimate an unknown conditional mean function and its derivatives. Since $\tilde{\beta}$ given in (8.15) is based on the derivative of a local constant kernel estimator of $E(Y|x)$, we could also use the local polynomial method to estimate $\partial E(Y|x)/\partial x$. This approach is considered by Li, Lu and Ullah (2003). Letting $\hat{g}^{(1)}(X_i)$ denote the kernel estimator of $g^{(1)}(X_i)$ obtained from an mth order local polynomial regression, Li, Lu and Ullah suggest using

$$\hat{\beta}_{\text{ave}} = \frac{1}{n} \sum_i \hat{g}^{(1)}(X_i) \qquad (8.19)$$

to estimate $\beta = E[g^{(1)}(X)]$. $\hat{\beta}_{\text{ave}}$ estimates β directly without assuming that $f(x) = 0$ at the boundary of the support of X. In this sense, it is similar to $\tilde{\beta}$ defined in (8.15). However, the price of not imposing the condition $f(x) = 0$ at the boundary of its support is that, as in Li, Lu and Ullah, one usually has to assume that the support of X is a compact set and that the density $f(x)$ is bounded below by a positive constant at the support of X, i.e., their conditions rule out the case of unbounded support. In the case of unbounded support, one needs to introduce a trimming function to trim out small values of the random denominator. With the assumptions of bounded support and the density being bounded away from zero in its support, one can avoid the use of a trimming function. Li, Lu and Ullah use the uniform convergence rate result of Masry (1996a) to handle the random denominator. Under some smoothness and moment conditions similar to those used in Powell et al. (1989), but with their boundary assumption replaced by compact support and the density being bounded away from zero in its support, the use of a second order kernel, and with $n \sum_{s=1}^{q} a_s^{2m} \to 0$ and $n(a_1 \ldots a_q) \sum_{s=1}^{q} a_s^2 / \ln(n) \to \infty$ as $n \to \infty$, where m is the order of polynomial in the local polynomial estimation and q is the dimension of x, Li, Lu and Ullah establish the following result:

$$\sqrt{n}(\hat{\beta}_{\text{ave}} - \beta) \to N\left(0, \Phi + \text{var}\left(g^{(1)}(X)\right)\right), \qquad (8.20)$$

where $\Phi = \mathrm{E}[\sigma^2(X) f^{(1)}(X) f^{(1)}(X)' / f^2(X)]$ and $\beta = \mathrm{E}[g^{(1)}(X)]$.

The reason why $\hat{\delta}$ and $\hat{\beta}_{\text{ave}}$ differ in their variances is because $\hat{\delta}$ estimates $\delta = \mathrm{E}\left[f(X) g^{(1)}(X)\right]$, while $\hat{\beta}_{\text{ave}}$ estimates $\beta = \mathrm{E}\left[g^{(1)}(X)\right]$. While neither $\hat{\delta}$ nor $\hat{\beta}_{\text{ave}}$ given above is normalized to have unit length, should normalization be applied, the variances of the normalized vectors obtained from $\hat{\delta}$ and $\hat{\beta}_{\text{ave}}$ would be identical. This is what one should expect given the result of Newey (1994b), who shows that the asymptotic variance of a $\sqrt{n}$-consistent estimator in a semiparametric model should not depend on the specific nonparametric estimation method used. Indeed, Newey also shows that the asymptotic variance of an average derivative estimator remains the same should one use nonparametric series methods rather than kernel methods. We discuss series methods in Chapter 15.

The proof of (8.20) is similar to the proof of (8.18) in that one uses the U-statistic decomposition with variable kernels developed in Powell et al. (1989) and makes extensive use of results contained in Masry (1996a). Rather than repeating detailed proofs contained in Li, Lu and Ullah (2003) here, we provide a brief outline of the proof of (8.20) intended to provide readers with an intuitive understanding. Defining $\bar{\beta} = n^{-1} \sum_{l=1}^{n} g^{(1)}(X_l)$, we write

$$\sqrt{n}\left(\hat{\beta}_a - \beta\right) = \sqrt{n}\left(\hat{\beta} - \bar{\beta}\right) + \sqrt{n}\left(\bar{\beta} - \beta\right).$$

Note that $\sqrt{n}\left(\bar{\beta} - \beta\right) \xrightarrow{d} N\left(0, \text{var}\left(g^{(1)}(X)\right)\right)$ by the Lindeberg-Levy

CLT. It can be shown that $\sqrt{n}\left(\hat{\beta}_a - \bar{\beta}\right) \xrightarrow{d} N(0, \Phi)$ in distribution. Finally, the two terms are asymptotically independent. Hence,

$$\sqrt{n}\left(\hat{\beta}_a - \beta\right) \to N\left(0, \Phi + \text{var}\left(g^{(1)}(X)\right)\right)$$

in distribution.

Hristache, Juditsky and Spokoiny (2001) propose an iterative procedure that improves upon the original (noniterative) average derivative estimator. Their idea is to use prior information about the vector β for improving the quality of the gradient estimate by extending a weighting kernel in the direction of small directional derivatives, and they demonstrate that the whole procedure requires at most $2\log(n)$ iterations. The resulting estimator is $\sqrt{n}$-consistent under relatively mild assumptions.

8.3.2   Estimation of $g(\cdot)$

We use β_n to denote a generic $\sqrt{n}$-consistent estimator of β or δ (i.e., it could be $\tilde{\beta}$, $\hat{\beta}$, $\tilde{\beta}_a$, $\hat{\beta}_a$, or $\hat{\delta}$ defined earlier). With β_n, we can estimate $E(Y|x) = g(x\beta_0)$ by

$$\hat{g}(x'\beta_n) = \frac{\sum_{j=1}^{n} Y_j K\left(\frac{(X_j - x)'\beta_n}{h}\right)}{\sum_{j=1}^{n} K\left(\frac{(X_j - x)'\beta_n}{h}\right)}. \tag{8.21}$$

Since $\beta_n - \beta_0 = O_p(n^{-1/2})$, which converges to zero faster than standard nonparametric estimators, the asymptotic distribution of $\hat{g}(x'\beta_0)$ is the same as the case with β_n being replaced by β_0. Therefore, it is covered by Theorem 2.2 of Chapter 2 with $q = 1$ (since $v = x'\beta_0$ is a scalar). Thus, we have

Corollary 8.1. *Assume that $\beta_n - \beta = O_p(n^{-1/2})$ and under conditions similar to those given in Theorem 2.2, we have*

$$\sqrt{nh}\left[\hat{g}(x'\beta_n) - g(x'\beta_0) - h^2 B(x'\beta_0)\right] \xrightarrow{d} N\left(0, \kappa\sigma^2(x'\beta_0)/f(x'\beta_0)\right), \tag{8.22}$$

where $B(x'\beta_0)$ is defined immediately following (2.8).

The direct average derivative estimation method discussed above is applicable only when x is a q-vector of continuous variables since the derivative with respect to discrete variables is not defined. Horowitz and

Härdle (1996) discuss how direct (noniterative) estimation can be generalized to cases for which some components of x are discrete. Horowitz (1998) provides an excellent overview of this method, and we refer readers to the detailed discussions contained in Horowitz and Härdle (1996) and Horowitz (1998, pp. 41–48).

The advantage of the direct average derivative estimation method is that one can estimate β_0 and $g(x'\beta_0)$ directly without using nonlinear iteration procedures. This computational simplicity is particularly attractive in large-sample settings; however, it gives rise to a potential finite-sample problem. The direct estimators all involve multidimensional nonparametric estimation in the initial estimation stage, and we know that nonparametric estimators suffer from the curse of dimensionality. In the second stage, the multidimensional nonparametric estimator is averaged over all sample points, resulting in a $\sqrt{n}$-consistent estimator of β_0. Therefore, *asymptotically*, the curse of dimensionality problem disappears because the second stage estimate has a parametric $\sqrt{n}$-rate of convergence and the dimension of x does not affect the rate of convergence of the average derivative estimator obtained at the second stage. However, in *finite-sample* applications, inaccurate estimation in the first stage may affect the accuracy of the second stage estimator unless the sample size is sufficiently large. Therefore, with relatively large sample sizes, the direct estimator is more attractive due to its computational ease. However, in small-sample settings, the iterative method of Ichimura (1993) may be more appealing as it avoids having to conduct high-dimensional nonparametric estimation.

Carroll, Fan, Gijbels and Wand (1997) proposed a method related both to the material in Chapter 7 (i.e., partially linear models) and in this chapter (i.e., single index models). In particular, Carroll et al. considered the problem of estimating a general partially linear single index model which contains both a partially linear model and a single index model as special cases.

8.4 Bandwidth Selection

8.4.1 Bandwidth Selection for Ichimura's Method

Ichimura's (1993) approach estimates β by the (iterative) nonlinear least squares method, where the unknown function $g(X_i'\beta_0)$ is replaced by the nonparametric kernel estimator $\hat{g}(X_i'\beta)$ defined in (8.7). The smoothing parameter is chosen to satisfy the conditions $nh^8 \to 0$, and

$\ln(h)/\left[nh^{3+3/(\nu-1)}\right] \to 0$ as $n \to \infty$, where $\nu \geq 3$ is a positive integer whose specific value depends on the existence of a number of finite moments of Y along with smoothness of the unknown function $g(\cdot)$. The range of permissible smoothing parameters allows for optimal smoothing, i.e., $h = O\left(n^{-1/5}\right)$. Therefore, Härdle et al. (1993) suggest selecting h and β simultaneously by the nonlinear least squares cross-validation method of Ichimura. Specifically, they suggest choosing β and h simultaneously by minimizing

$$M(\beta, h) = \sum_i \left[Y_i - \hat{G}_{-i}(X_i'\beta, h)\right]^2 \mathbf{1}(X_i \in A_\delta), \qquad (8.23)$$

where $\hat{G}_{-i}(X_i'\beta, h) = \hat{G}_{-i}(X_i'\beta)$ is defined in (8.7), and A_δ is the trimming set introduced earlier.

Under some regularity conditions including Y having finite moments of any order, the use of a second order kernel function, the unknown functions $g(x'\beta)$ and $p(x'\beta)$ being twice differentiable, $f(x)$ being bounded away from zero on A_δ, and the assumption that $\beta \in \mathcal{B}_n = \left\{\beta : |\beta - \beta_0| \leq C_0 n^{-1/2}\right\}$, where $h \in H_n = \left[C_1 n^{-1/5}, C_2 n^{-1/5}\right]$, and where $C_0, C_2 > C_1$ are three positive constants, then Härdle et al. (1993) show that $M(\beta, h)$ has the following decomposition:

$M(\beta, h) = M(\beta) + T(h) +$ {terms of smaller order than $T(h)$ and not dependent on β} + {terms of smaller order than either $M(\beta)$ or $T(h)$ },   (8.24)

where

$$M(\beta) = \sum_i \left[Y_i - g(X_i'\beta)\right]^2 \mathbf{1}(X_i \in A_x),$$

and

$$T(h) = \sum_i \left[\hat{G}_{-i}(X_i'\beta_0) - g(X_i'\beta_0)\right]^2,$$

and where $\hat{G}_{-i}(X_i'\beta_0)$ is defined in (8.7) with β being replaced by β_0.

Therefore, minimizing $M(\beta, h)$ simultaneously over both $(\beta, h) \in \mathcal{B}_n \times H_n$ is equivalent to first minimizing $M(\beta)$ over $\beta \in \mathcal{B}_n$ and then minimizing $T(h)$ over $h \in H_n$.

Let $(\hat{\beta}, \hat{h})$ denote the estimators that minimize (8.23). The asymptotic distribution of $\hat{\beta}$ is given by Theorem 8.1. For $\hat{h}$, with the use of a second order kernel function, it is easy to show that the leading term of the nonstochastic objective function $\mathrm{E}[T(h)]$ equals $A_1 h^4 + A_2(nh)^{-1}$ by the standard MSE calculation of a nonparametric estimator discussed in Chapter 2, where A_1 and A_2 are two positive constants. Hence, $h_o = [A_1/(4A_2)]^{1/5} n^{-1/5} = O(n^{-1/5})$ minimizes $A_1 h^4 + A_2(nh)$. Härdle et al. (1993) show that $\hat{h}/h_o \to 1$ in probability.

We now briefly compare the regularity conditions used in Ichimura (1993) with those in Härdle et al. (1993). The regularity conditions used to prove Theorem 8.1 and to establish (8.24) are somewhat different. For example, the conditions used in Theorem 8.1 require a higher order kernel, while for deriving (8.11), Härdle et al. use a second order kernel with an optimal smoothing parameter $h = O(n^{-1/5})$. In (8.24), the minimization is done within a restricted shrinking set $(\beta, h) \in \mathcal{B}_n \times H_n$ so that $\beta - \beta_0 = O(n^{-1/2})$. This condition makes the kernel estimation bias smaller than it would be under the conditions of Theorem 8.1, thus one can establish (8.11) without resorting to higher order kernels. Another difference in regularity conditions is that a stronger moment condition, namely, Y having moments of any order, is used to obtain (8.11). This is because Härdle et al. need to establish that the small order terms in (8.11) hold *uniformly* in $\mathcal{B}_n \times H_n$. Demonstrating uniform rates of convergence usually requires stronger moment conditions, while, in Theorem 8.1, h is treated as being nonstochastic, and minimization is done with respect to β only, therefore, a weaker moment condition suffices.

8.4.2 Bandwidth Selection with Direct Estimation Methods

For the direct average derivative estimation method, the estimation of β_0 involves the q-dimensional multivariate nonparametric estimation of the first order derivatives. Härdle and Tsybakov (1993) suggest choosing the smoothing parameters $a_1, \ldots, a_q$ to minimize the MSE of $\hat{\delta}$, that is, choosing h to minimize $E[|\hat{\delta} - \delta|^2]$. Härdle and Tsybakov show that the asymptotically optimal bandwidth is of the form (for all $s = 1, \ldots, q$)

$$a_s = c_s n^{-2/(2q+\nu+2)},$$

where c_s is a constant, ν is the order of kernel, and q is the dimension of x.

Powell and Stoker (1996) provide a method for estimating c_s, while Horowitz (1998, pp. 50–52) considers selecting a_s based on bootstrap resampling.

Having selected a_s optimally, one can then obtain an average derivative estimator of β. Using β_n to denote a generic estimator, one then estimates $E(Y|x) = g(x'\beta_0)$ by $\hat{g}(x'\beta_n, h) \equiv \hat{g}(x'\beta_n)$ defined in (8.7). The smoothing parameter h associated with the scalar index $x'\beta_n$ can be selected by least squares cross-validation, i.e., by choosing h to minimize $\sum_{i=1}^{n} [Y_i - \hat{g}_{-i}(X_i'\beta_n, h)]^2$. Under some regularity conditions, the cross-validated selection of h is of order $O_p\left(n^{-1/5}\right)$.

One can also combine a partially linear model and a single index model to obtain a "partially linear single index model" of the form $E(Y|X, Z) = X'\alpha + g(Z'\beta)$. For the estimation of a partially linear single index model see Carroll et al. (1997), Xia, Tong and Li (1999), and Liang and Wang (2005).

8.5   Klein and Spady's Estimator

When the single index model is derived from the binary choice model (8.2), and under the assumption that ϵ_i and X_i are independent, Klein and Spady (1993) suggested estimating β by maximum likelihood methods. The estimated log-likelihood function is

$$\mathcal{L}(\beta) = \sum_i (1 - Y_i) \ln(1 - \hat{g}(X_i'\beta)) + \sum_i Y_i \ln[\hat{g}(X_i'\beta)], \qquad (8.25)$$

where $\hat{g}(X_i'\beta)$ is defined in (8.7). Maximizing (8.25) with respect to β leads to the semiparametric maximum likelihood estimator of β, say $\hat{\beta}_{KS}$, proposed by Klein and Spady. Like Ichimura's (1993) estimator, maximization must be performed numerically by solving the first order condition obtained from (8.25).

Under some regularity conditions, including introducing a trimming function to trim out observations near the boundary of the support of X_i, and the use of higher order kernels, Klein and Spady (1993) showed that $\hat{\beta}_{KS}$ is $\sqrt{n}$-consistent and has an asymptotic normal distribution given by

$$\sqrt{n}(\hat{\beta}_{KS} - \beta) \to N(0, \Omega_{KS}),$$

where

$$\Omega_{KS} = \left[E\left\{ \frac{\partial P}{\partial \beta} \left(\frac{\partial P}{\partial \beta} \right)' \left[\frac{1}{P(1-P)} \right] \right\} \right]^{-1},$$

and $P = P(\epsilon < x'\beta) = F_{\epsilon|x}(x'\beta)$, where $F_{\epsilon|x}(\cdot)$ is the CDF of ϵ_i conditional on $X_i = x$.

Klein and Spady (1993) also showed that their proposed estimator is semiparametrically efficient in the sense that the asymptotic variance of their estimator attains the semiparametric efficiency bound.

We compare the asymptotic variance of the semiparametric estimator, Ω_{KS}, with the parametric counterpart Ω_{nls}. The parametric model has two additional parameters, $\eta = (\gamma_0, \gamma_1)'$. Partitioning the parameter γ into $\gamma = (\eta', \beta')'$, then the asymptotic variance for $n^{1/2}(\hat{\beta}_{nls} - \beta)$ is $V_{nls} \overset{\text{def}}{=} \left(\mathcal{I}_{\beta\beta}^0 - \mathcal{I}_{\beta\eta}^0 (\mathcal{I}^0)^{-1} \mathcal{I}_{\eta\beta}^0 \right)^{-1}$. Comparing this with V_{KS}^{-1}, one can show that (e.g., Pagan and Ullah (1999, p. 278)) if $E(X_i | X_i'\beta) = c_0 + c_1(X_i'\beta)$, where c_0 and c_1 are two $q \times 1$ vector of constants, then

$$V_{KS}^{-1} = V_{nls}^{-1} \text{ or, equivalently, } V_{KS} = V_{nls}.$$

That is, the semiparametric estimator is asymptotically as efficient as the parametric nonlinear least squares estimator based on the known true functional form of $g(\cdot)$ when $E(X_i | X_i'\beta)$ is linear in $X_i'\beta$ ("first order efficiency"). This is similar to the partially linear model case. However, when $E(X_i | X_i'\beta)$ is not a linear function of $X_i'\beta$, it can be shown that $V_{KS} - V_{mle}$ is positive definite. Therefore, the semiparametric estimator is asymptotically less efficient compared with the parametric nonlinear least squares estimator based on the true function $g(\cdot)$. The asymptotic variance $V_{KS} - V_{nls}$ is positive definite unless $E(X_i | X_i'\beta) = c_0 + c_1(X_i'\beta)$. Moreover, in this case the result cannot be improved since V_{KS} already attains the semiparametric efficiency bound. The efficiency loss of the semiparametric model compared with a parametric nonlinear least squares estimator arises because the functional form of $g(\cdot)$ (or, equivalently, $F_{\epsilon|x}(\cdot)$) is unknown. Of course, in practice, the true functional form $g(\cdot)$ it typically unknown, and in this case, the semiparametric estimator is robust to functional form misspecification of $g(\cdot)$.

8.6 Lewbel's Estimator

Lewbel (2000) considers the following *binary* choice model:

$$Y_i = \mathbf{1}(v_i + X_i'\beta + \epsilon_i > 0), \tag{8.26}$$

where v_i is a (special) continuous regressor whose coefficient is normalized to be one and X_i is of dimension q. Let $f(v|x)$ denote the conditional density of v_i given X_i, and let $F_\epsilon(\epsilon|v, x)$ denote the conditional

CDF of ϵ_i given (v_i, X_i). Under the condition that $F_\epsilon(\epsilon|v, x) = F_\epsilon(x)$, that is, conditional on x, ϵ is independent of the special regressor v, and that $\mathrm{E}[X_i \epsilon_i] = 0$, then Lewbel shows that

$$\beta = \left[\mathrm{E}(X_i X_i')\right]^{-1} \mathrm{E}[X_i \tilde{Y}_i], \qquad (8.27)$$

where $\tilde{Y}_i = [Y_i - \mathbf{1}(v_i > 0)]/f(v_i|X_i)$.

Equation (8.26) suggests that one can estimate β by regressing $\tilde{Y}_i$ on X_i. $\tilde{Y}_i$ involves the unknown quantity $f(v_i|X_i)$, which can be consistently estimated using, say, the nonparametric kernel method discussed in Chapter 5. Letting $\hat{\beta}$ denote the resulting feasible estimator of β, Lewbel (2000) establishes the $\sqrt{n}$-normality result of his proposed estimator of β.

Lewbel (2000) further extends his result to the case where ϵ_i and X_i are uncorrelated so that $\mathrm{E}(\epsilon_i X_i) \neq 0$. Assuming that there exists a p-vector of instrumental variables Z_i such that $\mathrm{E}(\epsilon_i Z_i) = 0$, $\mathrm{E}(Z_i X_i')$ is nonsingular, and $F_{\epsilon x}(\epsilon, x|v, z) = F_{\epsilon x}(\epsilon, x|z)$, where $F_{\epsilon x}(\epsilon, x|\cdot)$ denotes the distribution function of (ϵ, x) conditional on the data $\cdot$, Lewbel shows that

$$\beta = [\mathrm{E}(Z_i X_i')]^{-1} \mathrm{E}\left[Z_i \frac{Y_i - \mathbf{1}(v_i > 0)}{f(v_i|Z_i)}\right].$$

Hence, one can estimate β by replacing the above expectations with sample means and by replacing $f(v_i|Z_i)$ with a consistent estimator thereof.

The above approach can be extended to cover the ordered response model defined as

$$Y_i = \sum_{j=0}^{J-1} j \mathbf{1}(a_j < v_i + X_i'\beta + \epsilon_i \leq a_{j+1}), \qquad (8.28)$$

where $a_0 = -\infty$ and $a_J = +\infty$. The response variable Y_j takes values in $\{0, 1, \ldots, J-1\}$, and $Y_i = j$ if $v_i + X_i\beta + \epsilon_i$ lies between a_j and a_{j+1}. Let $X_{1i} = 1$ (the intercept) and without loss of generality let $\beta_1 = 0$ (since otherwise one can redefine a_j as $a_j - \beta_1$). Let $Y_{ji} = \mathbf{1}(Y_i \geq j)$ for $j = 1, \ldots, J-1$, and define $\Delta = [\mathrm{E}(X_i X_i')]^{-1}$. Also, let Δ_j equal the jth row of Δ. Then Lewbel (2000) shows that

$$\alpha_j = -\Delta_1 \mathrm{E}\left(X_i \frac{Y_{ji} - \mathbf{1}(v_i > 0)}{f(v_i|X_i)}\right), \quad j = 1, \ldots, J-1, \text{ and} \qquad (8.29)$$

$$\beta_l = -\Delta_j \mathrm{E}\left(X_i \frac{\sum_{j=1}^{J-1} Y_{ji}/(J-1) - \mathbf{1}(v_i > 0)}{f(v_i|X_i)}\right), \quad l = 2, \ldots, q. \quad (8.30)$$

From (8.29) and (8.30), one can easily obtain feasible estimators for the α_j's and β_l's, i.e., by replacing the expectations with sample means and by replacing $f(v_i|X_i)$ with a consistent estimator. Lewbel (2000) establishes the asymptotic normality results for the resulting estimators. Lewbel further shows that his results can be extended to deal with multinomial choices, partially linear latent variable models, and threshold and censored regression models.

8.7 Manski's Maximum Score Estimator

Manski's (1975) maximum score[1] estimator involves choosing β to maximize the following objective function:

$$S_M(\beta) = \sum_{i=1}^{n} Y_i \mathbf{1}(X_i'\beta \geq 0) + (1 - Y_i)\mathbf{1}(X_i'\beta < 0). \qquad (8.31)$$

This estimator seeks to maximize the number of correct predictions. For $Y_i = 1$, $S_M = 1$ if $X_i'\beta \geq 0$, and $S_M(\beta) = 0$ if $X_i'\beta < 0$. The correct prediction gets weight one, and an incorrect prediction gets weight zero. Similarly, for $Y_i = 0$, $S_M = 1$ if $X_i'\beta < 0$, and $S_M = -1$ if $X_i'\beta \geq 0$. In this case, a correct prediction gets weight one, an incorrect prediction gets weight minus one. Manski (1975) demonstrates strong consistency of $\hat{\beta}$ assuming that $\text{median}(Y_i|X_i) = X_i'\beta$ (or $\text{median}(\epsilon_i|X_i) = 0$), that the first component of β is one, and that the first component of x is a continuous variable. Kim and Pollard (1990) show that the maximum score estimator has a convergence rate of $n^{-1/3}$, not the usual $n^{-1/2}$. Because the objective function is discontinuous, the standard Taylor series expansion method of asymptotic theory cannot be applied to the maximum score estimator. Kim and Pollard show that the limiting distribution of $n^{1/3}(\hat{\beta}_{\text{m-score}} - \beta)$ is that of a maximum of a multidimensional Brownian motion with quadratic drift. This asymptotic distribution is quite complex and therefore quite inconvenient for applied inference. Manski and Thompson (1986) propose using a bootstrap procedure to approximate the asymptotic distribution of $\hat{\beta}_{\text{m-score}}$. This bootstrap method is easy to implement and the simulations reported in Manski and Thompson show that their proposed bootstrap method works well in finite-sample applications.

---

[1]Note that Manski uses the term "score" as in "keeping score," e.g., the score of a baseball game, and not the statistical score function (e.g., the sum of gradients of a log-likelihood function).

8.8   Horowitz's Smoothed Maximum Score Estimator

Though Manski (1975) demonstrates that his maximum score estimator is consistent under fairly weak distributional assumptions, it has a slow rate of convergence and has a complicated asymptotic distribution. Horowitz (1992) proposes a modified maximum score estimator obtained by maximizing a smoothed version of Manski's score function, which has a rate approaching $\sqrt{n}$ depending on the strength of certain smoothness assumptions. In essence, the problems associated with Manski's approach are due mainly to the lack of continuity of the indicator function used in (8.31). Horowitz proposes replacing the indicator function $\mathbf{1}(A)$ with a twice continuously differentiable function that retains the essential features of the indicator function. Horowitz proposes estimating β by maximizing the following smooth objective function:

$$\max_{\beta \in \mathcal{B}, \beta_1 = 1} S_{\mathrm{sms}}(\beta) \equiv \frac{1}{n} \sum_{i=1}^{n} (2Y_i - 1) G\left(\frac{X_i'\beta}{h}\right), \qquad (8.32)$$

where $G(\cdot)$ is a p-times continuously differentiable CDF, $h = h_n > 0$ and $h \to 0$ as $n \to \infty$. It is easy to see that $G(X_i'\beta/h) \to \mathbf{1}(X_i'\beta \geq 0)$ as $h \to 0$. For example, one can choose $G(x) = \int_{-\infty}^{x} k(v)dv$, where $k(\cdot)$ is a $(p-1)$-times differentiable kernel function. Under some regularity assumptions including some smoothness conditions on the conditional PDF of y given $x'\beta$, Horowitz shows his proposed smoothed maximum score estimator, say $\hat{\beta}_{\mathrm{sm-score}}$, has a rate of convergence equal to $\hat{\beta}_{\mathrm{sm-score}} - \beta = (nh)^{-1/2}$ and an asymptotic normal distribution. If $h = (c/n)^{1/(2p+1)}$ for some $0 < c < \infty$, then $\hat{\beta}_{\mathrm{sm-score}} - \beta$ has a rate of convergence equal to $n^{-p/(2p+1)}$, which can be made arbitrarily close to $n^{-1/2}$ for sufficiently large p.

8.9   Han's Maximum Rank Estimator

Rather than maximizing the score function given in (8.31), Han (1987) considers maximizing the rank correlation between the binary outcome Y_i and the index function $X_i'\beta$. This is achieved by maximizing

$$G_H(\beta) = \frac{2}{n(n-1)} \sum_{i=1}^{n} \sum_{j>i}^{n} \mathbf{1}(Y_i \geq Y_j)\mathbf{1}(X_i'\beta \geq X_j'\beta), \qquad (8.33)$$

with the summation being taken over all $\binom{n}{2} = n(n-1)/2$ combinations of the distinct elements $\{i, j\}$. A simple principle motivates this estimator. The monotonicity of F and the independence of the ϵ_i's and the X_i's ensure that

$$\mathrm{P}(Y_i > Y_j | X_i, X_j) \geq \mathrm{P}(Y_i \leq Y_j | X_i, X_j) \text{ whenever } X_i'\beta_0 \geq X_j'\beta_0.$$

That is, when $X_i'\beta_0 \geq X_j'\beta_0$, more likely than not $Y_i \geq Y_j$. Han (1987) shows that $\mathrm{E}[G_H(\beta)]$ is maximized at $\beta = \beta_0$, the true value of β. Han furthers establishes the strong consistency of his proposed maximum rank correlation (MRC) estimator, but Han did not provide the asymptotic distribution of his MRC estimator. The main difficulty in determining the limiting distribution of the MRC estimator is the nonsmooth nature of the objective function $G_H(\beta)$. Note that $G_H(\beta)$ is a second order U-statistic (or U-process, indexed by β). Using a U-statistic decomposition and a uniform bound for degenerate U-processes, Sherman (1993) shows that the MRC estimator is $\sqrt{n}$-consistent and has an asymptotic normal distribution.

Up to now we have considered a semiparametric binary choice model in which the distribution of the error term is modeled nonparametrically and the linear index $x'\beta$ is the parametric part of the model. Matzkin (1992) considers a more general binary choice model without imposing any parametric structure on either the systematic function of the observed exogenous variable or on the distribution of the random error term. Matzkin provides identification conditions and demonstrates consistency of her nonparametric maximum likelihood estimator.

8.10   Multinomial Discrete Choice Models

Pagan and Ullah (1999, pp. 296–299) provide an excellent overview of the semiparametric estimation of multinomial discrete choice models. For what follows, consider the case where an individual faces J ($J > 2$) choices. Define $Y_{ij} = 1$ if individual i selects alternative j ($j = 1, \ldots, J$) and $Y_{ij} = 0$ otherwise. Let $F_{ij} = \mathrm{P}(Y_{ij} = 1 | X_i) \equiv \mathrm{E}(Y_{ij} | X_i)$; then the multiple choice equation is

$$Y_{ij} = F_{ij} + \epsilon_{ij} \tag{8.34}$$

and the likelihood function is

$$\sum_{i=1}^{n}\sum_{j=1}^{J} Y_{ij} \ln F_{ij}. \tag{8.35}$$

Parametric approaches specify a functional form for F_{ij}. For example, to obtain a multinomial Logit model one sets

$$F_{ij} = \exp(X_{ij}'\beta)/\sum_{j=1}^{J}\exp(X_{ij}'\beta).$$

The semiparametric approach sets $F_{ij} = \mathrm{E}(Y_{ij}|X_i) = \mathrm{E}(Y_{ij}|v_{i1},\ldots,v_{iJ})$ $= g(v_{i1},\ldots,v_{iJ})$, where the functional form of $g(\cdot)$ is unknown, and where $v_{ij} = X_{ij}'\beta_j$. The estimation procedure is similar to the semiparametric single index model case discussed earlier. Ichimura and Lee (1991) extend Ichimura's (1993) method to the multi-index case and derive the asymptotic distribution of their semiparametric least squares estimator. Lee (1995) proposes using semiparametric maximum likelihood methods to estimate the multi-index model (8.35). Ai (1997) considers a general semiparametric maximum likelihood approach which covers many semiparametric models such as multi-index models and partially linear models as special cases. We now turn to Ai's general approach.

8.11   Ai's Semiparametric Maximum Likelihood Approach

Ai (1997) considers a general semiparametric maximum likelihood estimation approach. Let $q(Y|X,\theta_0,g_0)$ denote the conditional PDF of Y given X, where θ_0 is a finite dimensional parameter (the parametric part), and $g_0(\cdot)$ is an infinite dimensional unknown function. Ai further assumes that the conditional density satisfies an index restriction, i.e., that there exist some known functions $v_1(z,\theta)$, $v_2(x,\theta)$ such that

$$q(Y|X,\theta_0,g_0) = J(Z,\theta_0)f\left(v_1(Z,\theta_0)|v_2(X,\theta_0),\theta_0\right), \tag{8.36}$$

where $f(.|.,\theta)$ is the conditional density of v_1 given v_2 for arbitrary θ, and $J(z,\theta)$ is a known Jacobian of the transformation from $v_1(z,\theta)$ to y.

Model (8.36) contains many familiar semiparametric models as special cases. For example, consider a partially specified regression model $\eta_1(Y) = X_1'\theta_1 + \eta_2(X_2'\theta_2 + X_3) + u$, where $\eta_1(\cdot)$ and $\eta_2(\cdot)$ are functions of *unknown* form, and u is independent of $x = (X_1, X_2, X_3)$ and has an unknown density $\eta_3(\cdot)$. $\theta = (\theta_1, \theta_2)$ is the parametric part of the model, and $\eta = (\eta_1, \eta_2, \eta_3)$ is the nonparametric part of the model. The conditional density of y given x in this example is

$$q(Y|X, \theta, \eta) = \eta_3 \left[\eta_1(Y) - X_1'\theta_1 - \eta_2(X_2'\theta_2 + X_3) \right] |\eta_1^{(1)}(y)|, \quad (8.37)$$

which is also the conditional density of $v_1 = Y$ given $v_2 = (X_1'\theta_1, X_2'\theta_2 + X_3)$, where $\eta_1^{(1)}(y)$ denotes the derivative of $\eta_1(y)$ with respect to y, and $|\eta_1^{(1)}(y)|$ is the Jacobian.

For the partially linear multi-index model considered in Ichimura and Lee (1991), $\eta_1(Y) = Y$ (hence Jacobian $J = 1$), $v_1 = Y - X_1'\theta_1$ and $v_2 = X_2'\theta$, and for this case (8.37) becomes (with Jacobian $= 1$)

$$f(v_1|v_2) = \eta_3 \left(Y - X_1'\theta - \eta_2(X_2'\theta_2) \right), \quad (8.38)$$

where $\eta_3(\cdot)$ is the density of $u = Y - X_1'\theta_1 - \eta_2(X_2'\theta)$, and $\eta_2(X_2'\theta_2) = E[Y - X_1'\theta_1|X_2'\theta]$. If one uses $\theta_1 = 0$ in (8.38), it collapses to Ichimura's (1993) single index model (see Chapter 8).

For the partially linear model considered in Chapter 7, $\eta_1(Y) = Y$, $v_1 = Y - X_1'\theta_1$, $\theta_2 = 0$, $v_2 = X_3$, and (8.37) becomes $(J = 1)$

$$f(v_1|v_2) \equiv \eta_3 \left(Y - X_1'\theta - \eta_2(X_3) \right),$$

where $\eta_3(\cdot)$ is the density of $u = Y - X_1'\theta_1 - \eta_2(X_3)$ and $\eta_2(X_3) = E[Y - X_1'\theta_1|X_3]$.

We now turn to the issue of estimating this class of models. Define $m(z, \theta, f) = \partial \ln[q(y|x, \theta, f)]/\partial\theta$. If the functional form of f is known, we could estimate θ by solving for θ from the score equation

$$S_n(\tilde{\theta}) = \sum_{i=1}^{n} m\left(Z_i, \tilde{\theta}, f \right) = 0. \quad (8.39)$$

The $\sqrt{n}$-normality result of $\tilde{\theta}$ follows from standard laws of large number and CLT arguments. When f is unknown, Ai (1997) suggests estimating it using nonparametric kernel methods. Letting $f_1(v(z, \theta), \theta)$ and $f_2(v_2(x, \theta), \theta)$ denote the joint density of v and the marginal density of v_2, respectively, we have

$$f\left(v_1(z, \theta)|v_2(x, \theta), \theta \right) = \frac{f_1\left(v(z, \theta), \theta \right)}{f_2\left(v_2(x, \theta), \theta \right)}.$$

Substituting this into $m(z, \theta, f) = \partial \ln[q(y|x, \theta, f)]/\partial\theta$ gives

$$m(z, \theta, f) = m_1(z, \theta, f_1, f_2) m_2(z, \theta, f_1, f_2),$$

where

$$
\begin{aligned}
m_1(z, \theta, f_1, f_2) = {} & \frac{d \ln |J(z, \theta)|}{d\theta} f_1[v(z, \theta), \theta] f_2[v_2(z, \theta), \theta] \\
& + \frac{df_1[v(z, \theta), \theta]}{d\theta} f_2[v_2(z, \theta), \theta] \\
& - \frac{df_2[v_2(z, \theta), \theta]}{d\theta} f_1[v(z, \theta), \theta],
\end{aligned}
$$

and

$$m_2(z, \theta, f_1, f_2) = \frac{1}{f_1[v(z, \theta), \theta] f_2[v_2(z, \theta), \theta]}.$$

Letting q and q_2 denote the dimension of v and v_2, respectively, then a kernel estimator of $f_i(\theta) \equiv f(v_1(Z_i\, \theta)|v_2(X_i, \theta), \theta)$ is given by

$$\hat{f}(v_1(Z_i, \theta)|v_2(X_i, \theta), \theta) = \frac{\hat{f}_1(v, \theta)}{\hat{f}_2(v_2, \theta)}, \qquad (8.40)$$

where

$$\hat{f}_1(v, \theta) = \frac{1}{n} \sum_{j=1}^{n} K_{h_1}\left(\frac{v - v(Z_j, \theta)}{h_1}\right) \qquad (8.41)$$

and

$$\hat{f}_2(v_2, \theta) = \frac{1}{n} \sum_{j=1}^{n} K_{h_2}\left(\frac{v_2 - v_2(X_j, \theta)}{h_2}\right), \qquad (8.42)$$

with product kernels defined by

$$K_h\left(\frac{v - v(Z_j, \theta)}{h_1}\right) = \prod_{s=1}^{q} h_s^{-1} k\left(\frac{v_s - v_s(Z_j, \theta)}{h_s}\right) \text{ and}$$

$$K_{h_2}\left(\frac{v_2 - v_2(X_j, \theta)}{h_2}\right) = \prod_{s=1}^{q_2} h_{2s}^{-1} k\left(\frac{v_{2s} - v_{2s}(X_j, \theta)}{h_{2s}}\right).$$

Then an estimator of $\hat{f}_i(\theta) = f_i(\theta) \equiv f(v_1(Z_i\, \theta)|v_2(X_i, \theta), \theta)$ is given by

$$\hat{f}_i(\theta) = \frac{\hat{f}(v(Z_i, \theta), \theta)}{\hat{f}_2(v_2(X_i, \theta), \theta)}.$$

Finally, one estimates θ, say $\hat{\theta}$, by solving the following first order condition:

$$S_n(\hat{\theta}) = \sum_{i=1}^{n} m\left(Z_i, \hat{\theta}, \hat{f}_i(\theta)\right) = 0. \qquad (8.43)$$

For the single index model example, the Jacobian $= 1$, $\theta_{10} = 0$, and $v_1 = y$, X_3 is empty. We write $X_2 = x$ and $\theta_2 = \theta$ so that $v_2 = x'\theta$. Then we have

$$\hat{f}_{1i} = f_1(v_i, \theta) \equiv f_1(Y_i, X_i'\theta) = n^{-1} \sum_{j=1}^{n} \mathbf{1}(Y_j = Y_i) K_h\left(\frac{(X_j - X_i)'\theta}{h}\right)$$

and

$$\hat{f}_{2i} = f_2(v_{2i}, \theta) \equiv f_2(x'\theta) = n^{-1} \sum_{j=1}^{n} K_h\left(\frac{(X_j - X_i)'\theta}{h}\right).$$

Substituting these into

$$m(Z_i, \theta, \hat{f}_{1i}, \hat{f}_{2i}) = m_1(Z_i, \theta, \hat{f}_{1i}, \hat{f}_{2i}) m_2(Z_i, \theta, \hat{f}_{1i}, \hat{f}_{2i}),$$

we get exactly the same first order condition as for Klein and Spady's (1993) estimator;[2] we leave the verification of this as an exercise (see Exercise 8.4).

Ai (1997) shows that the feasible estimator $\hat{\theta}$ has the same asymptotic distribution as the infeasible estimator $\tilde{\theta}$, and that $\hat{\theta}$ is semiparametrically efficient in the sense that the inverse of its asymptotic variance equals the semiparametric efficiency bound for this type of semiparametric model.

8.12   A Sketch of the Proof of Theorem 8.1

We first derive (8.45).

Note that $G(X_i'\beta) = \mathrm{E}[g(X_i'\beta_0)|X_i'\beta]$. By Taylor expansion of $g(X_i'\beta_0)$ at $\beta_0 = \beta$, and using $\beta_0 - \beta = O(n^{-1/2})$, we have

$$g(X_i'\beta_0) - G(X_i'\beta) \equiv g(X_i'\beta_0) - \mathrm{E}\left[g(X_i'\beta_0)|X_i'\beta\right]$$
$$= g(X_i'\beta_0) - g(X_i'\beta) - g^{(1)}(X_i'\beta)\mathrm{E}\left[X_i'(\beta_0 - \beta)|X_i'\beta\right] + O(n^{-1})$$
$$= g^{(1)}(X_i'\beta)\left[X_i - \mathrm{E}(X_i|X_i'\beta)\right](\beta_0 - \beta) + O\left(n^{-1}\right).$$
$$\qquad (8.44)$$

---

[2]For expositional simplicity, we omitted the trimming functions; see Ai (1997, p. 938) for the details on introducing trimming functions.

Substituting (8.44) into $S(\beta) = \sum_{i=1}^{n} [g(X_i'\beta_0) + u_i - G(X_i'\beta_0)]^2$, we obtain

$$S(\beta) = (\beta_0 - \beta)'W_0(\beta_0 - \beta) - 2V_0(\beta_0 - \beta) + \sum_{i=1}^{n} u_i^2 + o(1), \quad (8.45)$$

where W_0 and V_0 are defined by (8.10). The first order condition of (8.45) yields (8.10).

It can be shown that the leading terms can be obtained by replacing $\hat{\mathrm{E}}(Y_i|X_i'\beta)]$ with $\mathrm{E}[g(X_i'\beta_0)|X_i'\beta]$ in (8.9). We have, uniformly in $\beta \in \mathcal{B}_n$,

$$S_{1n}(\beta) = \frac{1}{n}\sum_i \left\{ g(X_i'\beta_0) - \mathrm{E}\left[g(X_i'\beta_0)|X_i'\beta\right]\right\}^2$$

$$+ 2\frac{1}{n}\sum_i u_i \left\{ g(X_i'\beta_0) - \mathrm{E}\left[g(X_i'\beta_0)|X_i'\beta\right]\right\}$$

$$+ \{\text{terms independent of } \beta\} + o_p\left(n^{-1}\right). \quad (8.46)$$

Since $\hat{\beta} \in \mathcal{B}_n$, we have $|\hat{\beta} - \beta_0| = O(n^{-1/2})$. Using a Taylor expansion of $g(X_i'\beta_0)$ at $\beta_0 = \beta$ (use it twice below), we have

$$g(X_i'\beta_0) - \mathrm{E}[g(X_i'\beta_0)|X_i'\beta] = g(X_i'\beta_0) - g(X_i'\beta)$$

$$- g^{(1)}(X_i'\beta)\mathrm{E}(X_i'|X_i'\beta)(\beta_0 - \beta) + O_p(n^{-1})$$

$$= g^{(1)}(X_i'\beta)\left\{ X_i' - \mathrm{E}(X_i'|X_i'\beta)\right\}(\beta_0 - \beta) + O_p\left(n^{-1}\right).$$

$$(8.47)$$

Substituting (8.47) into (8.46) we get

$$S_{1n}(\beta) = (\beta_0 - \beta)'\left[\frac{1}{n}\sum_i (g_i^{(1)})^2 v_i v_i'\right](\beta_0 - \beta)$$

$$+ 2\frac{1}{n}\sum_i u_i g_i^{(1)} v_i'(\beta_0 - \beta)$$

$$+ \{\text{terms independent of } \beta\} + o_p(n^{-1}), \quad (8.48)$$

where $g_i^{(1)} = g^{(1)}(X_i'\beta)$ and $v_i = X_i - \mathrm{E}(X_i|X_i'\beta)$.

Minimizing $S_{1n}(\beta)$ with respect to β, and ignoring the term which is independent of β and the $o_p(n^{-1})$ term, we obtain the first order condition

$$2(\beta_0 - \beta)\frac{1}{n}\sum_i \left(g_i^{(1)}\right)^2 v_i v_i' - 2\frac{1}{n}\sum_i u_i g_i^{(1)} v_i = 0, \quad (8.49)$$

which leads to

$$\sqrt{n}(\beta_0 - \beta) = \left[\frac{1}{n} \sum_i \left(g_i^{(1)} \right)^2 v_i v_i' \right]^{-1} \frac{1}{\sqrt{n}} \sum_i u_i g_i^{(1)} v_i$$

$$= \left[\frac{1}{n} \sum_i \left(g_{i0}^{(1)} \right)^2 v_{i0} v_{i0}' \right]^{-1} \frac{1}{\sqrt{n}} \sum_i u_i g_{i0}^{(1)} v_{i0} + o_p(1),$$

$$(8.50)$$

where $g_{i0}^{(1)} = g^{(1)}(X_i'\beta_0)$, $v_{i0} = X_i - \mathrm{E}(X_i|X_i'\beta_0)$, and the second equality in (8.50) uses the fact that $\hat{\beta} - \beta_0 = O_p(n^{-1/2})$.

A standard law of large numbers and the Lindeberg-Levy CLT argument leads to

$$\sqrt{n}(\beta_0 - \beta) \to N(0, V_0) \text{ in distribution,} \qquad (8.51)$$

where

$$V_0 = \Omega_0^{-1} \Sigma_0 \Omega^{-1},$$

$$\Omega_0 = \mathrm{E}\left\{ \left(g_{i0}^{(1)} \right)^2 v_{i0} v_{i0}' \right\},$$

$$\Sigma_0 = \mathrm{E}\left\{ \sigma^2(X_i) \left(g_{i0}^{(1)} \right)^2 v_{i0} v_{i0}' \right\}, \text{ and}$$

$$v_{i0} = X_i - \mathrm{E}(X_i|X_i'\beta_0).$$

Equation (8.51) matches the result of Theorem 8.1 if one replaces $w(X_i) = 1$ there.

8.13 Applications

8.13.1 Modeling Response to Direct Marketing Catalog Mailings

Direct marketing is often used to target individuals who, on the basis of observable characteristics such as demographics and their past purchase decisions, are most likely to be repeat customers. For example, one might think of mailing catalogs only to those who are highly likely to be repeat customers or who most "closely resemble" repeat customers.[3]

---

[3]Bult and Wansbeek (1995), in a profit maximization framework, point out that in fact one might want to do the opposite, thereby saving costs by avoiding repeated

The success or failure of direct marketing, however, hinges directly upon the ability to identify those consumers who are most likely to make a purchase.

Racine (2002) considers an industry-standard database obtained from the Direct Marketing Association (DMA)[4] that contains data on a reproduction gift catalog company, "an upscale gift business that mails general and specialized catalogs to its customer base several times each year." The base time period covers December 1971 through June 1992. Data collected by the DMA includes orders, purchases in each of fourteen product groups, time of purchase, and purchasing methods. Then a three month gap occurs in the data after which customers in the existing database are sent at least one catalog in early Fall 1992. Then from September 1992 through December 1992 the database was updated. This provides a setting in which models can be constructed for the base time period and then evaluated on the later time period. A random subset of 4,500 individuals from the first time period was created, and various methods for predicting the likelihood of a consumer purchase was undertaken followed by evaluation of the forecast accuracy for the independent hold-out sample consisting of 1,500 randomly selected individuals drawn from the later time period.

Parametric index models (Logit, Probit) and semiparametric index models (Ichimura (1993); Ichimura and Lee (1991)) were fitted to the estimation sample of size $n_1 = 4,500$ and evaluated on the hold-out sample of size $n_2 = 1,500$.

Data Description

We have two *independent* estimation and evaluation datasets of sizes $n_1 = 4,500$ and $n_2 = 1,500$ respectively having one record per customer. We restrict our attention to one product group and thereby select the middle of the 14 product groups, group 8. The variables involved in the study are listed below, while their properties are summarized in Tables 8.1 and 8.2.

(i) Response: whether or not a purchase was made

---

mailings to those who in fact are highly likely to make a purchase. Regardless of the objective, it is the ability to identify those most likely to make a purchase that has proven problematic in the past.

[4]This database contains customer buying history for about 100,000 customers of nationally known catalog and nonprofit database marketing businesses.

Table 8.1: Summary of the estimation dataset ($n_1 = 4,500$)

Variable	Mean	Std Dev	Min	Max
Response	0.09	0.28	0	1
LTDFallOrders	1.36	1.38	0	15
LastPurchSeason	1.62	0.53	-1	2
Orders4YrsAgo	0.26	0.55	0	5
LTDPurchGrp8	0.09	0.31	0	4
DateLastPurch	37.31	27.34	0	117

Table 8.2: Summary of the evaluation dataset ($n_2 = 1,500$)

Variable	Mean	Std Dev	Min	Max
Response	0.08	0.27	0	1
LTDFallOrders	1.32	1.38	0	14
LastPurchSeason	1.63	0.51	-1	2
Orders4YrsAgo	0.25	0.52	0	4
LTDPurchGrp8	0.08	0.29	0	3
DateLastPurch	36.44	26.95	0	116

(ii) LTDFallOrders: life-to-date Fall orders

(iii) LastPurchSeason: the last season in which a purchase was made[5]

(iv) Orders4YrsAgo: orders made in the latest five years

(v) LTDPurchGrp8: life-to-date purchases

(vi) DateLastPurch: the date of the last purchase[6]

Each model was evaluated in terms of its out-of-sample performance based upon the measure of McFadden, Puig and Kirschner (1977)[7]

---

[5]This is recorded in the database as 1 if the purchase was made in January through June, 2 if the purchase was made in July through December, and –1 if no purchase was made.

[6]12/71 was recorded as 0, 1/72 as 1 and so on.

[7]$p_{11} + p_{22} - p_{21}^2 - p_{12}^2$ where p_{ij} is the ijth entry in the 2×2 confusion matrix expressed as a fraction of the sum of all entries. A "confusion matrix" is simply a

Table 8.3: Confusion matrix and classification rates for the Logit model

	Predicted Nonpurchase	Predicted Purchase
Actual Nonpurchase	1378	1
Actual Purchase	108	9
Predictive Performance		91.95%
Overall correct classification rate		92.47%
Correct nonpurchase classification rate		99.64%
Correct purchase classification rate		7.69%

Table 8.4: Confusion matrix and classification rates for the semiparametric index model

	Predicted Nonpurchase	Predicted Purchase
Actual Nonpurchase	1361	22
Actual Purchase	75	42
Predictive Performance		93.26%
Overall correct classification rate		93.53%
Correct nonpurchase classification rate		98.41%
Correct purchase classification rate		35.90%

along with the correct purchase classification rate.[8] Results for the Logit model[9] are presented in the form of a confusion matrix given in Table 8.3 while those for the semiparametric index model are given in Table 8.4.

The semiparametric single index model delivers better predictive performance for the hold-out data than the parametric Logit model. Note also that, although the parametric models appear to perform fairly well in terms of McFadden et al.'s (1977) measure, they yield poor predictions for the class of persons who actually make a purchase.

---

tabulation of the actual outcomes versus those predicted by a model. The diagonal elements contain correctly predicted outcomes while the off-diagonal ones contain incorrectly predicted (confused) outcomes.

[8] The fraction of correctly predicted purchases among those who actually made a purchase.

[9] Results for the Probit model are not as good as those for the Logit model and are omitted for space considerations.

8.14   Exercises

Exercise 8.1.

(i) Suppose that Y is a $\{0,1\}$ binary variable. Show that $P(Y = 1|x) = E(Y|x)$.

(ii) If Y is a binary variable taking values in $\{1,2\}$, is $P(Y = 1|x)$ still equal to $E(Y|x)$ or not?

Exercise 8.2. In deriving (8.51), for the second term on the right-hand side of (8.51), we used the fact that

(i) $\frac{1}{n}\sum_i u_i \hat{E}(u_i|X_i'\beta) = $ terms independent of $\beta + o_p(n^{-1})$, and that

(ii) $\frac{1}{n}\sum_i u_i \left\{ E[g(X_i'\beta_0)] - \hat{E}[g(X_i'\beta_0)|X_i'\beta] \right\} = o_p\left(n^{-1}\right)$, where

$$\hat{E}(u_i|X_i'\beta) = (nh)^{-1}\sum_{j \neq i} u_j K((X_i - X_j)'\beta/h)/\hat{p}(X_i'\beta),$$

$$\hat{E}(u_i|X_i'\beta) = (nh)^{-1}\sum_{j \neq i} u_j K((X_i - X_j)'\beta/h)/\hat{p}(X_i'\beta), \text{ and}$$

$$\hat{p}(X_i'\beta) = (nh)^{-1}\sum_{j \neq i} K((X_i - X_j)'\beta/h).$$

Prove (i) and (ii).

Hint: For (i), apply a Taylor series expansion at $\beta = \beta_0$, and use $\beta - \beta_0 = O_p(n^{-1/2})$. The first term in the Taylor expansion will be independent of β. The second term is a second order U-statistic, and is of order $o_p\left(n^{-1}\right)$ by using the H-decomposition.

Exercise 8.3. Prove that

$$\frac{1}{n}\sum_i \left[g(X_i'\beta_0) - \hat{E}(Y_i|X_i'\beta) \right]^2 = \frac{1}{n}\sum_i \left[g(X_i'\beta_0) - E(g(X_i'\beta_0)|X_i'\beta) \right]^2$$

$$+ \text{ terms independent of } \beta + o_p(n^{-1}).$$

Hint: Write

$$\hat{E}(Y_i|X_i'\beta) = \hat{E}(g(X_i'\beta_0)|X_i'\beta) + \hat{E}(u_i|X_i'\beta)$$

$$= E(g(X_i'\beta_0)|X_i'\beta) + \left[\hat{E}(g(X_i'\beta_0)|X_i'\beta) - E(g(X_i'\beta_0)|X_i'\beta) \right]$$

$$+ \hat{E}(u_i|X_i'\beta),$$

where $\hat{E}(g(X_i'\beta_0)|X_i'\beta)$ and $\hat{E}(u_i|X_i'\beta)$ are defined in Section 8.12.

Exercise 8.4. Verify that when applying Ai's (1997) general approach to the single index model with a binary variable y, Ai's first order condition coincides with that of Klein and Spady (1993) as given in (8.52).

Hint: Klein and Spady's (1993) estimator solves the first order condition (see Pagan and Ullah (1999, p. 283)) $\sum_{i=1}^{n} \hat{m}_i(\theta) = 0$, where

$$\hat{m}_i(\theta) = \hat{g}(x'\theta)^{-1} \left[1 - \hat{g}(X_i'\theta)\right]^{-1} \frac{\partial \hat{g}(X_i'\theta)}{\partial \theta} \left[Y_i - \hat{g}(X_i'\theta)\right] \qquad (8.52)$$

with $\hat{g}(X_i'\theta) = \hat{E}(Y_i|X_i'\theta) = \dfrac{\sum_{j=1}^{n} Y_j K\left(\frac{(X_j - X_i)'\theta}{h}\right)}{\sum_{j=1}^{n} K\left(\frac{(X_j - X_i)'\theta}{h}\right)}.$

Chapter 9

Additive and Smooth (Varying) Coefficient Semiparametric Models

In this chapter we consider some popular semiparametric regression models that appear in the literature. The rationale for using these, rather than fully nonparametric models, is to reduce the dimension of the nonparametric component in order to mitigate the curse of dimensionality. Of course, these models are liable to the same critique of functional misspecification as are fully parametric models, but they have proven to be extremely popular in applied settings and tend to be simpler to interpret than fully nonparametric models.

9.1 An Additive Model

We first consider the semiparametric additive model

$$Y_i = c_0 + g_1(Z_{1i}) + g_2(Z_{2i}) + \cdots + g_q(Z_{qi}) + u_i, \qquad (9.1)$$

where c_0 is a scalar parameter, the Z_{li}'s are all univariate continuous variables, and $g_l(\cdot)$ $(l = 1, \ldots, q)$ are unknown smooth functions. The observations $\{Y_i, Z_{1i}, \ldots, Z_{qi}\}_{i=1}^{n}$ are presumed to be i.i.d.

For kernel-based methods, two approaches are commonly used for estimating an additive model: the "backfitting" method (see Buja, Hastie and Tibshirani (1989) and Hastie and Tibshirani (1990)) and the "marginal integration" method independently proposed by Linton and Nielsen (1995), Newey (1994b), and Tjøstheim and Auestad (1994); see also Chen, Härdle, Linton and Severance-Lossin (1996), and Linton (1997, 2000). Due to its iterative nature, the backfitting method is more difficult to analyze than the marginal integration method, hence we begin with a discussion of the relatively simple marginal integration method.

9.1.1   The Marginal Integration Method

First, note that for any constant c, $[g_1(z_1) + c] + [g_2(z_2) - c] = g_1(z_1) + g_2(z_2)$. Therefore, we need some identification conditions for the $g_l(\cdot)$ functions to be identified. With kernel methods it is convenient to impose the condition $\mathrm{E}[g_l(Z_l)] = 0$ so that the individual components $g_l(\cdot)$ are identified $(l = 1, \ldots, q)$. This also leads to $\mathrm{E}(Y_i) = c_0$.

Let $Z_{\underline{\alpha}i} = (Z_{1i}, \ldots, Z_{\alpha-1,i}, Z_{\alpha+1,i} \ldots, Z_{qi})$. That is, $Z_{\underline{\alpha}i}$ is obtained from $(Z_{1i}, Z_{2i}, \ldots, Z_{qi})$ by removing $Z_{\alpha i}$. Define $G_{\underline{\alpha}}(z_{\underline{\alpha}}) = g_1(z_1) + \cdots + g_{\alpha-1}(z_{\alpha-1}) + g_{\alpha+1}(z_{\alpha+1}) + \cdots + g_q(z_q)$. With this notation, (9.1) can be written as

$$Y_i = c_0 + g_\alpha(Z_{\alpha i}) + G_{\underline{\alpha}}(Z_{\underline{\alpha}i}) + u_i. \qquad (9.2)$$

Define $\xi(z_\alpha, Z_{\underline{\alpha}j}) = \mathrm{E}(Y_j | Z_{\alpha j} = z_\alpha, Z_{\underline{\alpha}j})$, and also let $\eta(z_\alpha, Z_{\underline{\alpha}j}) = \mathrm{E}(X_j | Z_{\alpha j} = z_\alpha, Z_{\underline{\alpha}j})$. Applying $\mathrm{E}[\cdot | Z_{\alpha j} = z_\alpha, Z_{\underline{\alpha}j}]$ to both sides of (9.2), we get

$$\xi_\alpha(z_\alpha, Z_{\underline{\alpha}j}) = c_0 + g_\alpha(z_\alpha) + G_{\underline{\alpha}}(Z_{\underline{\alpha}j}). \qquad (9.3)$$

Define $m_\alpha(z_\alpha) = \mathrm{E}[\xi(z_\alpha, Z_{\underline{\alpha}j})]$, and note that the marginal expectation is with respect to $Z_{\underline{\alpha}j}$. Applying the expectation (with respect to $Z_{\underline{\alpha}j}$) to (9.3), we obtain

$$m_\alpha(z_\alpha) = c_0 + g_\alpha(z_\alpha), \qquad (9.4)$$

where we have used $\mathrm{E}[G_{\underline{\alpha}}(Z_{\underline{\alpha}j})] = 0$. From (9.4), we get

$$g_\alpha(z_\alpha) = m_\alpha(z_\alpha) - \mathrm{E}[m_\alpha(Z_{\alpha i})]. \qquad (9.5)$$

The above approach is infeasible. However, a feasible estimator can be obtained by replacing expectations by sample means, marginal expectation (integration) by marginal averaging, and conditional mean functions by local linear kernel estimators. Specifically, a feasible counterpart of (9.5) is

$$\tilde{g}_\alpha(z_\alpha) = \tilde{m}_\alpha(z_\alpha) - n^{-1} \sum_{i=1}^{n} \tilde{m}_\alpha(Z_{\alpha i}), \qquad (9.6)$$

where

$$\tilde{m}_\alpha(z_\alpha) = n^{-1} \sum_{j=1}^{n} \tilde{a}_\alpha(Z_\alpha, Z_{\underline{\alpha}j}), \qquad (9.7)$$

and $\tilde{a}_\alpha(z_\alpha, Z_{\underline{\alpha}j})$ is the solution to a in the following minimization problem,

$$\min_{\{a,b\}} \sum_{l=1}^{n} [y_l - a - (Z_{\alpha l} - z_\alpha)b]^2 k_{h_\alpha}(Z_{\alpha l} - z_\alpha) K_{h_{\underline{\alpha}}}(Z_{\underline{\alpha}l} - Z_{\underline{\alpha}j}).$$

Note that $\tilde{a}_\alpha(z_\alpha, Z_{\underline{\alpha}j})$ is a kernel estimator of $\mathrm{E}[Y_j | Z_{\alpha j} = z_\alpha, Z_{\underline{\alpha}j}]$, which applies the local linear method only to the component z_α, and the local constant method to $z_{\underline{\alpha}}$.

Fan, Härdle and Mammen (1998) assume that $k(\cdot)$ is a univariate second order kernel, and $K(\cdot)$ is a νth order product kernel, where ν is a positive integer satisfying $\nu \geq (q-1)/2$. Therefore, a higher order kernel is needed ($\nu > 2$) if $q > 4$; see Section 1.11 regarding the construction of higher order kernel functions. The following theorem gives the asymptotic distribution of $\tilde{g}_\alpha(z_\alpha)$, and for expositional simplicity, we assume that $h_1 = \cdots = h_{\alpha-1} = h_{\alpha+1} = \cdots = h_q = h_{\underline{\alpha}}$. Fan et al. prove the following result.

Theorem 9.1. *Under the conditions given in Fan et al. (1998), and also assuming that $nh_\alpha h_{\underline{\alpha}}^{q-1}/\ln n \to \infty$, $h_{\underline{\alpha}}^\nu/h_\alpha^2 \to 0$, $h_\alpha \to 0$ and that $h_{\underline{\alpha}} \to 0$, then*

$$\sqrt{nh_\alpha} \left\{ \tilde{g}_\alpha(z_\alpha) - g_\alpha(z_\alpha) - c_0 - \frac{1}{2}h_\alpha^2 \kappa_2 g_\alpha^{(2)}(z_\alpha) + o(h_\alpha^2) \right\}$$
$$\to N(0, v_\alpha(z_\alpha)),$$

where $g_\alpha^{(2)}(\cdot)$ is the second order derivative of $g_\alpha(\cdot)$, $\kappa_2 = \int u^2 k(u)du$,

$$v_\alpha(z_\alpha) = f_\alpha(z_\alpha) \left[\int k^2(u)du \right] \mathrm{E} \left\{ \frac{\sigma^2(z_\alpha, Z_{\underline{\alpha}i})f_{\underline{\alpha}}^2(z_\alpha)}{f^2(z_\alpha, z_{\underline{\alpha}})} | Z_{\alpha i} = z_\alpha \right\},$$

and $\sigma^2(z_\alpha, z_{\underline{\alpha}}) = \mathrm{E}(u_i^2 | Z_{\alpha i} = z_\alpha, Z_{\underline{\alpha}i} = z_{\underline{\alpha}})$.

Theorem 9.1 shows that $\tilde{g}_\alpha(z_\alpha)$ reaches the one-dimensional optimal rate of convergence.

A disadvantage of the marginal integration method is that it is computationally costly. One has to estimate $\mathrm{E}[Y_l | Z_{\alpha l} = Z_{\alpha i}, Z_{\underline{\alpha}l} = Z_{\underline{\alpha}j}]$ for all $i, j = 1, \ldots, n$, which has a computational order involving n^2 calculations, whereas the computational cost of estimating a nonadditive model is only of order n. In the next section we discuss a computationally efficient method for estimating additive models.

9.1.2   A Computationally Efficient Oracle Estimator

The marginal integration method discussed above is computationally costly as it requires one to estimate $g(Z_{\alpha i}, Z_{\underline{\alpha} j})$ for $i, j = 1, \ldots, n$. Kim, Linton and Hengartner (1999) propose an alternative method which reduces the estimation time to order n. Consider the nonparametric regression of Y on Z_α,

$$E(Y|Z_\alpha = z_\alpha) = c_0 + g_\alpha(z_\alpha) + \sum_{s \neq \alpha}^{q} E[g_s(Z_s)|Z_\alpha = z_\alpha], \qquad (9.8)$$

which shows that $E(Y|Z_\alpha = z_\alpha)$ is a biased estimator of $c_0 + g_\alpha(z_\alpha)$ due to the presence of $\sum_{s \neq \alpha} E[g_s(Z_s)|Z_\alpha = z_\alpha]$. Kim et al. suggest choosing an instrumental variable $w_\alpha(z)$ such that

$$E[w_\alpha(Z)|Z_\alpha = z_\alpha] = 1 \text{ and}$$
$$E[w_\alpha(Z)g_s(X_s)|Z_\alpha = z_\alpha] = 0 \text{ for } s \neq \alpha. \qquad (9.9)$$

Then one would obtain $E[w_\alpha(Z_i)Y_i|Z_{\alpha i} = z_\alpha] = c_0 + g_\alpha(z_\alpha)$. It is easy to check that $w_\alpha(z) = f_\alpha(z_\alpha)f_{\underline{\alpha}}(z_{\underline{\alpha}})/f(z_\alpha, z_{\underline{\alpha}})$ is such a function, where $f_{\underline{\alpha}}(z_{\underline{\alpha}})$ is the joint PDF of $z_{\underline{\alpha}} = (z_1, \ldots, z_{\alpha-1}, z_{\alpha+1}, \ldots, z_q)$. In fact, for any random variable ξ, we have

$$E[\xi \, w_\alpha(z)|z_\alpha] = \int \xi \, w_\alpha(z) \frac{f(z_\alpha, z_{\underline{\alpha}})}{f_\alpha(z_\alpha)} dz_{\underline{\alpha}}$$
$$= \int \xi \frac{f_\alpha(z_\alpha)f_{\underline{\alpha}}(z_{\underline{\alpha}})}{f(z_\alpha, z_{\underline{\alpha}})} \frac{f(z_\alpha, z_{\underline{\alpha}})}{f_\alpha(z_\alpha)} dz_{\underline{\alpha}}$$
$$= \int \xi \, f_{\underline{\alpha}}(z_{\underline{\alpha}}) dz_{\underline{\alpha}}, \qquad (9.10)$$

which is exactly the marginal integration of ξ over the $z_{\underline{\alpha}}$ components. Replacing ξ in (9.10) by $\xi = 1$ we obtain $E[w_\alpha(Z)|Z_{\alpha i}] = \int f_{\underline{\alpha}}(z_{\underline{\alpha}})dz_{\underline{\alpha}} = 1$. Also, if we replace ξ by $g_s(Z_{si})$ for $s \neq \alpha$, then $E[w_\alpha(Z_i)g_s(Z_{si})|Z_{\alpha i}] = \int g_s(Z_{si})f_{\underline{\alpha}}(z_{\underline{\alpha}})dz_{\underline{\alpha}} = E[g_s(Z_{si})] = 0$. Thus, (9.9) holds true.

It is easy to see that

$$
\tilde{\gamma}_\alpha(z_\alpha, h_o) = \frac{1}{nh_o} \sum_{j=1}^n k\left(\frac{Z_{\alpha j} - z_\alpha}{h_o}\right) \frac{\hat{f}_{\underline{\alpha}}(Z_{\underline{\alpha}j})}{\hat{f}(Z_{\alpha j}, Z_{\underline{\alpha}j})} Y_j
$$

$$
= \frac{1}{n^2 h_o^q} \sum_{j=1}^n \sum_{l=1}^n \frac{k\left(\frac{Z_{\alpha j} - z_\alpha}{h_o}\right) K_{\underline{\alpha}}\left(\frac{Z_{\underline{\alpha}l} - Z_{\underline{\alpha}j}}{h_o}\right)}{\hat{f}(z_{\alpha j}, Z_{\underline{\alpha}j})} Y_j \quad (9.11)
$$

is a consistent estimator of $E[w_\alpha(Z)Y|Z_\alpha = z_\alpha] = c_0 + g_\alpha(z_\alpha)$, where $w_\alpha(z) = f_\alpha(z_\alpha) f_{\underline{\alpha}}(z_{\underline{\alpha}})/f(z_\alpha, z_{\underline{\alpha}})$.

Note that $\tilde{\gamma}_\alpha(z_\alpha)$ can be interpreted as a one-dimensional standard local constant estimator obtained by regressing the adjusted $\hat{Y}_{\alpha j}$ on $Z_{\alpha j}$, where $\hat{Y}_{\alpha j} = Y_j \hat{f}_\alpha(z_\alpha) \hat{f}_{\underline{\alpha}}(Z_{\underline{\alpha}j})/\hat{f}(Z_{\alpha j}, Z_{\underline{\alpha}j})$. Since $\tilde{\gamma}(z_\alpha)$ estimates $c_0 + g_\alpha(z_\alpha)$, naturally one can estimate $g_\alpha(z_\alpha)$ by $\tilde{g}_\alpha(z_\alpha) = \tilde{\gamma}_\alpha(z_\alpha) + n^{-1} \sum_{j=1}^n \tilde{\gamma}_\alpha(z_{\alpha j})$. The leading bias, variance and asymptotic normal distribution of $\tilde{g}_\alpha(z_\alpha)$ are given in Theorem 1 of Kim et al. (1999). Kim et al. show that the asymptotic variance of $\tilde{g}_\alpha(z_\alpha)$ has an extra term compared with the asymptotic variance of the marginal integration estimator of $g_\alpha(z_\alpha)$. Therefore, $\tilde{g}_\alpha(z_\alpha)$ is less efficient than the marginal integration estimator. Kim et al. further propose an efficient oracle estimator which we discuss below.

An oracle (efficient) estimator for $g_\alpha(z_\alpha)$ is defined as an estimator that has the same leading bias and variance terms as in the case when all other additive functions are known. Define $Y_{\alpha i}^{\text{oracle}} = Y_i - \sum_{s \neq \alpha} g_s(Z_{si}) - c_0$, and consider a univariate kernel estimator of $g_\alpha(z_\alpha)$ using $\{Z_{\alpha i}, Y_{\alpha i}^{\text{oracle}}\}_{i=1}^n$. That is,

$$
\tilde{g}_\alpha^{\text{oracle}}(z_\alpha) = \frac{\sum_{j=1}^n k\left(\frac{Z_{\alpha j} - z_\alpha}{h_\alpha}\right) Y_{\alpha j}^{\text{oracle}}}{\sum_{j=1}^n k\left(\frac{Z_{\alpha j} - z_\alpha}{h_\alpha}\right)}, \quad (9.12)
$$

with $h_\alpha = \delta_1 n^{-1/5}$ ($\delta_1 > 0$ is a constant). Then using results derived in Chapter 2, we know that (using a second order kernel function)

$$
\sqrt{nh_\alpha} \left\{ \tilde{g}_\alpha^{\text{oracle}}(z_\alpha) - g_\alpha(z_\alpha) - h_\alpha^2 b_\alpha(z_\alpha) \right\} \to N(0, V_\alpha(z_\alpha)) \quad (9.13)
$$

in distribution, where $b(z_\alpha) = \kappa_2 \left[\frac{1}{2} g_\alpha^{(2)}(z_\alpha) + g_\alpha^{(1)}(z_\alpha) f_\alpha^{(1)}(z_\alpha) \right] / f_\alpha(z_\alpha)$ and where $V_\alpha(z_\alpha) = \kappa \sigma_\alpha^2(z_\alpha)/f_\alpha(z_\alpha)$ ($\sigma_\alpha^2(z_\alpha) = \text{var}(Y|Z_\alpha = z_\alpha)$).

Instead of using a local constant estimator, a local linear estimator can be used to estimate $g_\alpha(z_\alpha)$. That is, letting $\tilde{a}$ and $\tilde{b}$ be the values of a and b that minimize the objective function

$$\sum_{i=1}^{n} k\left(\frac{Z_{\alpha i} - z_\alpha}{h_\alpha}\right)\left[Y_{\alpha i}^{\text{oracle}} - a - b(Z_{\alpha i} - z_\alpha)\right]^2,$$

then $\tilde{a}$ is the local linear oracle estimate of $g_\alpha(z_\alpha)$, and its asymptotic distribution is the same as that given in Chapter 2, which is basically the same as (9.13) except that the leading bias term should be changed to $(1/2)\kappa_2 g_\alpha^{(2)}(z_\alpha)/f_\alpha(z_\alpha)$.

The estimator $\tilde{g}_\alpha^{\text{oracle}}(z_\alpha)$ given above is not feasible because c_0 and the $g_s(z_s)$'s are unknown for $s \neq \alpha$. We can replace $g_s(z_s)$ by $\tilde{\gamma}_s(z_s)$ and c_0 by $\bar{Y}$. Thus, we can use

$$Y_{\alpha i}^{2-\text{step}} = Y_i - \sum_{s \neq \alpha}^{q} \tilde{\gamma}_s(Z_{si}, h_\alpha) + (q-1)\bar{Y}$$

to replace $Y_{\alpha i}^{\text{oracle}} = Y_i - \sum_{s \neq \alpha}^{q} g_s(Z_{si}) - c_0$, where

$$\tilde{\gamma}_s(z_s, h_\alpha) = \frac{1}{nh_\alpha}\sum_{j=1}^{n} k\left(\frac{Z_{sj} - z_s}{h_\alpha}\right)\frac{\hat{f}_{\underline{s}}(Z_{\underline{s}j})}{\hat{f}(Z_{sj}, Z_{\underline{s}j})}Y_j \qquad (9.14)$$

is a consistent estimator of $\mathrm{E}[w_s(Z)Y|Z_s = z_s] = c_0 + g_s(z_s)$, $s = 1, \ldots, q$.

Letting $\hat{g}_\alpha^{\text{oracle}}$ be defined as was $\tilde{g}_\alpha^{\text{oracle}}$ in (9.12) but with $Y_{\alpha i}^{\text{oracle}}$ being replaced by $Y_{\alpha i}^{2-\text{step}}$, Kim et al. (1999) showed that $\hat{g}_\alpha^{\text{oracle}}$ has the same leading bias and variance terms as $\tilde{g}_\alpha^{\text{oracle}}$; therefore, it has the same asymptotic distribution. Kim et al. assume that $h_\alpha = an^{-1/5}$ for some $a > 0$ and that $h_o = o(n^{-1/5})$. Note that here one chooses h_o to be of smaller order than h_α. They show that if a local linear estimator is used, then

$$\sqrt{nh_\alpha}\left\{\hat{g}_\alpha^{\text{oracle}}(z_\alpha) - g_\alpha(z_\alpha) - \frac{\kappa_2}{2}h_\alpha^2 g_\alpha^{(2)}(z_\alpha)/f_\alpha(z_\alpha)\right\} \xrightarrow{d} N(0, V_\alpha(z_\alpha))$$

$$(9.15)$$

in distribution, where the definition of $V_\alpha(z_\alpha)$ appears directly below (9.13).

Equation (9.15) shows that the feasible estimator $\hat{g}_\alpha^{\text{oracle}}(z_\alpha)$ has the same first order efficiency as for the case where all other $g_s(z_s)$'s are known (for $s \neq \alpha$).

Kim et al. (1999) further show that a wild bootstrap procedure can be used to better approximate the finite-sample distribution of $\hat{g}_\alpha^{\text{oracle}}(\cdot)$. Define an estimated additive function

$$\hat{g}_{add}(z; h_\alpha, h_o) = \bar{Y} + \sum_{\alpha=1}^{q} \hat{g}_\alpha(z_\alpha; h_\alpha, h_o),$$

where $\hat{g}_\alpha(z_\alpha; h_\alpha, h_o) = \hat{g}_\alpha(z_\alpha)$ is the initial additive function estimator of $g_\alpha(z_\alpha)$. Then u_i is estimated by $\hat{u}_i = Y_i - \hat{g}_{add}(Z_i; h_\alpha, h_o)$ $(i = 1, \ldots, n)$. Define the centered residual by $\tilde{u}_i = \hat{u}_i - n^{-1} \sum_{l=1}^{n} \hat{u}_l$. The bootstrap error u_i^* is generated by the two-point wild bootstrap method,[1] i.e., $u_i^* = [(1 + \sqrt{5})/2]\tilde{u}_i$ with probability $r = (1 + \sqrt{5})/(2\sqrt{5})$ and $u_i^* = [(1 - \sqrt{5})/2]\tilde{u}_i$ with probability $1 - r$. Next generate

$$Y_i^* = \hat{g}_{add}(Z_i; \bar{h}_\alpha, h_o) + u_i^*,$$

where in the above another bandwidth $\bar{h}_\alpha$ is used. Kim et al. show that $\bar{h}_\alpha$ should have an order larger than h_α for the bootstrap method to work. Kim et al. suggest choosing $h_\alpha \sim n^{-1/5}$, $h_o = o(h_\alpha)$, and letting $\bar{h}_\alpha$ assume values in $[n^{-1/5+\delta}, n^{-\delta}]$ for some $0 < \delta < 1/5$. One can use the bootstrap sample $\{Z_i, Y_i^*\}_{i=1}^{n}$ to compute $\hat{g}_\alpha^{*,oracle}(z_\alpha)$, where $\hat{g}_\alpha^{*,oracle}(z_\alpha)$ is the same as $\hat{g}_\alpha^{\text{oracle}}(z_\alpha)$ except that one replaces Y_i by Y_i^* wherever it occurs. Kim et al. show that one can repeatedly generate, say, B bootstrap estimates of $\hat{g}_\alpha^{*,oracle}(z_\alpha)$ and use their empirical distribution to approximate the finite-sample distribution of $\hat{g}_\alpha^{\text{oracle}}(z_\alpha)$.

9.1.3   The Ordinary Backfitting Method

By taking the conditional expectation of (9.1), conditional on $Z_{\alpha i} = z_\alpha$, we get $(\alpha = 1, \ldots, q)$

$$g_\alpha(z_\alpha) = \text{E}(Y_i | Z_{\alpha i} = z_\alpha) - c_0 - \sum_{s \neq \alpha}^{q} \text{E}[g_s(Z_{si}) | Z_{\alpha i} = z_\alpha]. \qquad (9.16)$$

Equation (9.16) suggests that an iterative procedure is appropriate. Let $\hat{g}_\alpha^{[0]}(z_\alpha)$ be some initial estimators for $g_\alpha(z_\alpha)$, say, $\hat{g}_\alpha^{[0]}(z_\alpha) = 0$, or let $\hat{g}_\alpha^{[0]}(z_\alpha)$ be the marginal integration estimator of $g_\alpha(z_\alpha)$. Also,

---

[1] We provide more detailed discussion of the wild bootstrap method in Chapter 12.

$\hat{c}_0 = n^{-1} \sum_{i=1}^{n} Y_i$. Then the iterative procedure is given as follows. For $\alpha = 1, \ldots, q$, and for $l = 1, 2, 3, \ldots$, compute the lth-step $\hat{g}_\alpha^{[l]}(z_\alpha)$ by

$$\hat{g}_\alpha^{[l]}(z_\alpha) = \hat{\mathrm{E}}(Y_i | Z_{\alpha i} = z_\alpha) - \hat{c}_0 - \sum_{s=1}^{\alpha-1} \hat{\mathrm{E}} \left[\hat{g}_s^{[l]}(Z_{si}) | Z_{\alpha i} = z_\alpha \right]$$

$$- \sum_{s=\alpha+1}^{q} \hat{\mathrm{E}} \left[\hat{g}_s^{[l-1]}(Z_{si}) | Z_{\alpha i} = z_\alpha \right], \tag{9.17}$$

where, for a random variable A_i, $\hat{\mathrm{E}}[A_i | Z_{\alpha i} = z_\alpha]$ is the (univariate) kernel estimator of $\mathrm{E}(A_i | Z_{\alpha i} = z_\alpha)$. $\hat{\mathrm{E}}[A_i | Z_{\alpha i} = z_\alpha]$ could be the local constant estimator given by $\sum_{j=1}^{n} A_j k_{\alpha,z,z_j} / \sum_{j=1}^{n} k_{\alpha,z,z_j}$, where $k_{\alpha,z,z_j} = k((Z_{\alpha j} - z_\alpha)/h_\alpha)$, or it could be a local linear estimator of $\mathrm{E}(A_i | Z_{\alpha i} = z_\alpha)$.

Iteration ends when a prespecified convergence criterion is reached, say, when $\sum_{i=1}^{n} [\hat{g}_\alpha^{[l]}(Z_{\alpha i}) - \hat{g}^{[l-1]}(Z_{\alpha i})]^2 / \sum_{i=1}^{n} (\hat{g}_\alpha^{[l-1]}(Z_{\alpha i}))^2$ is less than some small number, say, 10^{-4}.

By using a local linear smoother in the above procedure, Opsomer and Ruppert (1998) and Opsomer (2000) showed that estimation bias is of order $O(\sum_{\alpha=1}^{q} h_\alpha^2)$, and the leading variance term of $\hat{g}_\alpha(z_\alpha)$ is given by ($\kappa = \int k^2(v) dv$)

$$\mathrm{var}\, (\hat{g}_\alpha(z_\alpha)) = \frac{\kappa \sigma^2}{n h_\alpha f_\alpha(x_\alpha)} + o \left(\frac{1}{n h_\alpha} \right),$$

where $\sigma^2 = \mathrm{E}(u_i^2 | Z_i) = \mathrm{E}(u_i^2)$ (assuming conditionally homoskedastic errors).

9.1.4   The Smoothed Backfitting Method

Mammen, Linton and Nielsen (1999) propose a smoothed backfitting procedure for estimating the additive model (9.1). The idea is to project Y (or $\mathrm{E}(Y|z)$) on the space of additive functions. Let $\tilde{g}(z) = \sum_{i=1}^{n} Y_i K_h(Z_i, z) / \sum_{i=1}^{n} K_h(Z_i, z)$ and $\tilde{f}(z) = n^{-1} \sum_{i=1}^{n} K_h(Z_i, z)$ denote the multidimensional kernel estimators of $\mathrm{E}(Y | Z = z)$ and $f(z)$, respectively, where $z = (z_1, \ldots, z_q)$. The local constant smoothed backfitting estimators of $g_1(z_1), \ldots, g_q(z_q)$ are defined as those $g_1, \ldots, g_q$ that minimize the objective function

$$\int [\tilde{g}(z) - g_1(z_1) - \cdots - g_q(z_q)]^2 \, \tilde{f}(z) dz, \tag{9.18}$$

where the minimization runs over all functions $g(z) = c_0 + \sum_{\alpha=1}^{q} g_\alpha(z_\alpha)$ with $\int g_\alpha(z_\alpha) \tilde{f}_\alpha(z_\alpha) dz_\alpha = 0$, where $\tilde{f}_\alpha(z_\alpha) = \int \tilde{f}(z) dz_{\underline{\alpha}}$ is the kernel estimator of the marginal PDF $f_\alpha(z_\alpha)$, $z_{\underline{\alpha}} = (z_1, \ldots, z_{\alpha-1}, z_{\alpha+1}, \ldots, z_q)$.

The solution to (9.18) is characterized by the following system of equations ($\alpha = 1, \ldots, q$; $\bar{Y} = n^{-1} \sum_{i=1}^{n} Y_i$):

$$\hat{g}_\alpha(z_\alpha) = \int \tilde{g}(z) \frac{\tilde{f}(z)}{\tilde{f}_\alpha(z_\alpha)} dz_{\underline{\alpha}} - \sum_{s \neq \alpha}^{q} \int \hat{g}(z_s) \frac{\tilde{f}(z)}{\tilde{f}_\alpha(z_\alpha)} dz_{\underline{\alpha}} - \bar{Y}, \qquad (9.19)$$

$$0 = \int \hat{g}_\alpha(z_\alpha) \tilde{f}_\alpha(z_\alpha) dz_\alpha. \qquad (9.20)$$

Note that

$$\int \tilde{g}(z) \frac{\tilde{f}(z)}{\tilde{f}_\alpha(z_\alpha)} dz_{\underline{\alpha}} = \frac{(nh_\alpha)^{-1} \sum_{i=1}^{n} Y_i k(z_\alpha, Z_{\alpha i})}{\tilde{f}_\alpha(z_\alpha)} \equiv \tilde{g}_\alpha(z_\alpha), \qquad (9.21)$$

because $\int \prod_{s \neq \alpha} h_s^{-1} k((z_s - Z_{si})/h_s) dz_{\underline{\alpha}} = 1$, where $\tilde{g}_\alpha(z_\alpha)$ is the local constant estimator of $\mathrm{E}(Y_i | Z_{\alpha i} = z_\alpha)$. Also, using the additive structure of $\hat{g}_\alpha(z_\alpha)$ and the fact that $\int h_s^{-1} k((z_s - Z_{si})/h_s) dz_s = 1$, the $q - 1$ dimensional integration $\int dz_{\underline{\alpha}}$ can be reduced to double integration, hence

$$\sum_{s \neq \alpha} \int \hat{g}_\alpha(z) \frac{\tilde{f}(z)}{\tilde{f}_\alpha(z_\alpha)} dz_{\underline{\alpha}} = \sum_{s \neq \alpha} \int \hat{g}_\alpha(z) \frac{\tilde{f}_{\alpha,s}(z_\alpha, z_s)}{\tilde{f}_\alpha(z_\alpha)} dz_s, \qquad (9.22)$$

where $\tilde{f}_{\alpha,s}(z_\alpha, z_s) = (nh_s h_\alpha)^{-1} \sum_{i=1}^{n} k((Z_{\alpha i} - z_\alpha)/h_\alpha) k((Z_{si} - z_s)/h_s)$ is the kernel estimator of the two-dimensional marginal PDF of (z_α, z_s).

Equations (9.19), (9.21), and (9.22) lead to the following iterative procedure:

$$\hat{g}_\alpha^{[r+1]}(z_\alpha) = \tilde{g}_\alpha(z_\alpha) - \sum_{s=1}^{\alpha-1} \int \hat{g}_s^{[r+1]}(z_s) \frac{\tilde{f}_{\alpha,s}(z_\alpha, z_s) dz_s}{\tilde{f}_\alpha(z_\alpha)}$$

$$- \sum_{s=\alpha+1}^{q} \int \hat{g}_s^{[r]}(z_s) \frac{\tilde{f}_{\alpha,s}(z_\alpha, z_s) dz_s}{\tilde{f}_\alpha(z_\alpha)},$$

where $l = 1, 2, \ldots,$ denote the number of iterations.

Mammen et al. (1999) derived the asymptotic distribution of $\hat{g}_\alpha(x_\alpha)$. To present their result we first define a constant β_0 and univariate functions $\beta_\alpha(z_\alpha)$ (with $\int \beta_\alpha(z_\alpha)dz_\alpha = 0$, $\alpha = 1, \ldots, q$) by

$$
\begin{aligned}
&(\beta_0, \ldots, \beta_q) \\
&= \arg \min_{\beta_0, \ldots, \beta_q} \left[\int \{\beta(z) - \beta_0 - \beta_1(z_1) - \cdots - \beta_q(z_q)\}^2 f(z)dz \right]
\end{aligned}
\tag{9.23}
$$

for a given function $\beta(z)$.

Under regularity conditions given in Mammen et al. (1999) (see also Nielsen and Sperlich (2005)), it can be shown that

$$
(nh_\alpha)^{1/2}[\hat{g}_\alpha(z_\alpha) - g_\alpha(z_\alpha) - h_\alpha^2 \beta_\alpha(z_\alpha)] \xrightarrow{d} N(0, v_\alpha(z_\alpha)),
\tag{9.24}
$$

where β_α is defined in (9.23) with $\beta(z)$ defined by

$$
\beta(z) = \kappa_2 \sum_{s=1}^{q} \left[\frac{g_s^{(1)}(z_s)}{f(z)} \frac{\partial f(z)}{\partial z_s} + \frac{1}{2}g_s^{(2)}(z_s) \right],
$$

and $v_\alpha(z_\alpha) = \kappa \sigma_\alpha^2(z_\alpha)/f_\alpha(z_\alpha)$ ($\kappa_2 = \int k(v)v^2 dv$, $\kappa = \int k^2(v)dv$).

Finally, one can estimate $g(z) = c_0 + \sum_{\alpha=1}^{q} g_\alpha(z_\alpha)$ by

$$
\hat{g}(z) = \bar{Y} + \sum_{\alpha=1}^{q} \hat{g}_\alpha(z_\alpha).
\tag{9.25}
$$

Moreover, Mammen et al. (1999) show that different components of $\hat{g}_\alpha(z_\alpha)$ are asymptotically independent; therefore, the asymptotic distribution of $\hat{g}(x)$ follows readily from (9.24) (see Exercise 9.1). Mammen et al. also discuss using boundary corrected kernels when Z has compact support.

Mammen et al. (1999) also consider using a local linear estimator of $g_\alpha(z_\alpha)$, so that the objective function (9.18) becomes

$$
\int \left[Y_i - \hat{c}_0 - \sum_{\alpha=1}^{q} \hat{g}_\alpha(z_\alpha) - \sum_{\alpha=1}^{q} \hat{\theta}_\alpha(z_\alpha)(z_\alpha - Z_{\alpha i}) \right]^2 K_h(z, Z_i)dz,
\tag{9.26}
$$

where the minimization is over the additive components $\hat{c}_0$, all $\hat{g}_\alpha(z_\alpha)$'s (with $\int \hat{g}_\alpha(z_\alpha)\tilde{f}_\alpha(z_\alpha)dz_\alpha = 0$), and also over all $\hat{\theta}_\alpha(z_\alpha)$'s, where $\theta_\alpha(z_\alpha)$ is the first order derivative of $g_\alpha(z_\alpha)$.

Mammen et al. (1999) (see also Mammen and Park (2005)) show that the $\hat{g}_\alpha$'s and $\hat{\theta}_\alpha$'s satisfy the following equation:

$$
\begin{pmatrix} \hat{g}_\alpha(z_\alpha) \\ \hat{\theta}_\alpha(z_\alpha) \end{pmatrix} = - \begin{pmatrix} \hat{c}_0 \\ 0 \end{pmatrix} + \begin{pmatrix} \tilde{g}_\alpha(z_\alpha) \\ \tilde{\theta}_\alpha(z_\alpha) \end{pmatrix}
$$

$$
= -\hat{M}_\alpha(z_\alpha)^{-1} \sum_{s \neq \alpha}^{q} \int \hat{S}_{s\alpha}(z_s, z_\alpha) \begin{pmatrix} \hat{g}_\alpha(z_\alpha) \\ \hat{\theta}_\alpha(z_\alpha) \end{pmatrix} dz_\alpha,
$$

with

$$
\hat{c}_0 = \frac{1}{n} \sum_{i=1}^{n} Y_i - \sum_{\alpha=1}^{q} \int \hat{g}_\alpha(z_\alpha) \hat{f}_\alpha(z_\alpha) dz_\alpha
$$

$$
- \sum_{\alpha=1}^{q} \int \hat{\theta}_\alpha(z_\alpha) \hat{f}_\alpha^1(z_\alpha, z_\alpha) dz_\alpha, \tag{9.27}
$$

$$
\hat{M}_\alpha(z_\alpha) = n^{-1} \sum_{i=1}^{n} k_{h_\alpha}(z_\alpha, Z_{\alpha i}) \begin{pmatrix} 1 & Z_{\alpha i} - z_\alpha \\ Z_{\alpha i} - z_\alpha & (Z_{\alpha i} - z_\alpha)^2 \end{pmatrix}, \tag{9.28}
$$

$$
\hat{S}_{s\alpha}(z_s, z_\alpha) = n^{-1} \sum_{i=1}^{n} k_{h_\alpha}(z_s, Z_{si}) k_{h_\alpha}(z_\alpha, z_{\alpha i})
$$

$$
\times \begin{pmatrix} 1 & Z_{si} - z_s \\ Z_{\alpha i} - z_\alpha & (z_s - Z_{si})(Z_{\alpha i} - z_\alpha) \end{pmatrix}, \tag{9.29}
$$

$$
\hat{f}_\alpha^1(z_\alpha) = n^{-1} \sum_{i=1}^{n} k_{h_\alpha}(z_s, Z_{si})(Z_{\alpha i} - z_\alpha), \text{ and}
$$

$$
\hat{f}_\alpha(z_\alpha) = n^{-1} \sum_{i=1}^{n} k_{h_\alpha}(z_s, Z_{si}).
$$

Also, $\tilde{g}_\alpha(z_\alpha)$ and $\tilde{\theta}_\alpha(z_\alpha)$ are the local linear fits obtained by regressing Y_i on $Z_{\alpha i}$; that is, they minimize the objective function

$$
\sum_{i=1}^{n} \left[Y_i - \tilde{g}_\alpha(z_\alpha) - \tilde{\theta}_\alpha(z_\alpha)(Z_{\alpha i} - z_\alpha) \right]^2 k_{h_\alpha}(z_s, Z_{si}). \tag{9.30}
$$

The definition of $\hat{c}_0, \hat{g}_1(z_1), \ldots, \hat{g}_q(z_q)$, and $\hat{\theta}_1(z_1), \ldots, \hat{\theta}_q(z_q)$ can be made unique by imposing the normalization condition

$$
\int \hat{g}_\alpha(z_\alpha) \hat{f}_\alpha(z_\alpha) dz_\alpha + \int \hat{\theta}_\alpha(z_\alpha) \hat{f}_\alpha^1(z_\alpha) dz_\alpha = 0. \tag{9.31}
$$

The smooth backfitting estimates are obtained via the iterative application of (9.27) where, when the left-hand side is the iteration step $[l+1]$, the right-hand quantities are either $[l+1]$ or $[l]$, depending on whether $s < \alpha$ or $s > \alpha$. Note that (9.31) yields $\hat{c}_0 = n^{-1} \sum_{i=1}^{n} Y_i$.

The asymptotic distribution of $\hat{g}_\alpha(z_\alpha)$ is derived by Mammen et al. (1999). Below we state a simple version given by Nielsen and Sperlich (2005).

$$\sqrt{nh_\alpha}\left[\hat{g}_\alpha(z_\alpha) - g_\alpha(z_\alpha) - \nu_\alpha - h_\alpha^2 \frac{\kappa_2}{2} \mu_\alpha(z_\alpha)\right] \xrightarrow{d} N(0, V_\alpha(z_\alpha)), \quad (9.32)$$

where

$$\nu_\alpha = \int g_\alpha(z_\alpha) k_{h_\alpha}(z_\alpha, v) f_\alpha(v) dv dz_\alpha,$$

$$\mu_\alpha(z_\alpha) = g_\alpha^{(2)}(z_\alpha) - \int g_\alpha^{(2)}(z_\alpha) f_\alpha(z_\alpha) dz_\alpha,$$

$$V_\alpha(z_\alpha) = \kappa \sigma_\alpha^2(z_\alpha) / f_\alpha(z_\alpha),$$

$$\kappa_2 = \int k(v) v^2 dv, \quad \kappa = \int k^2(v) dv.$$

One can also present the joint distribution using matrices, i.e.,

$$\begin{pmatrix} \sqrt{nh_1}[\hat{g}_1(z_1) - g_1(z_1) - \nu_1 - h_1^2 \frac{\kappa_2}{2} \mu_1(z_1)] \\ \vdots \\ \sqrt{nh_q}[\hat{g}_q(z_q) - g_q(z_q) - \nu_q - h_q^2 \frac{\kappa_2}{2} \mu_q(z_q)] \end{pmatrix} \xrightarrow{d} N\left(\mathbf{0}, \mathrm{diag}(V_\alpha(z_\alpha))\right),$$

$$(9.33)$$

where $\mathbf{0} = (0, \ldots, 0)'$ is a $q \times 1$ vector of zeros, and $\mathrm{diag}(V_\alpha(z_\alpha))$ is a $q \times q$ diagonal matrix with the αth diagonal element equal to $V_\alpha(z_\alpha)$ $(\alpha = 1, \ldots, q)$ and all off-diagonal elements being zero.

Equation (9.33) shows that the different components of $\hat{g}_\alpha(z_\alpha)$ are asymptotically independent of one another.

Nielsen and Sperlich (2005) suggest using leave-one-out least squares cross-validation to select the smoothing parameters, while Mammen and Park (2005) recommend minimizing the penalized sum of squared residuals, i.e., they recommend choosing $h_1, \ldots, h_q$ to minimize the objective function

$$PLS(h) = RSS(h)\left[1 + 2 \sum_{\alpha=1}^{q} \frac{1}{nh_\alpha} k(0)\right], \quad (9.34)$$

where

$$RSS(h) = n^{-1} \sum_{i=1}^{n} \left[Y_i - \hat{c}_0 - \sum_{\alpha=1}^{q} \hat{g}_\alpha(z_{\alpha i}) \right]^2. \qquad (9.35)$$

In this chapter we do not discuss kernel estimation of an additive model with interaction terms, or derivative estimation in generalized additive models. However, readers can find a discussion of these issues in Sperlich, Tjøstheim and Yang (2002) and Yang, Sperlich and Härdle (2003). Also, for efficient and fast spline-backfitted kernel smoothing of additive regression models, see Wang and Yang (2005).

9.1.5 Additive Models with Link Functions

A more general additive function is an additive model with a known link function given by

$$Y_i = G \left[c_0 + \sum_{\alpha=1}^{q} g_\alpha(Z_{\alpha i}) \right] + u_i, \qquad (9.36)$$

where $G(\cdot)$ is a known link function. When $G(\cdot)$ is the identity function, (9.36) collapses to (9.1). In practice, $G(\cdot)$ could be the exponential or logistic function, etc.

Linton and Härdle (1996) propose a marginal integration approach to estimate (9.36). Let $m(z) = E(Y|z)$ and let $M(\cdot) = G^{-1}(\cdot)$; then (9.36) can be written as

$$M[m(z)] = c_0 + \sum_{\alpha=1}^{q} g_\alpha(z_\alpha). \qquad (9.37)$$

Define

$$\phi_\alpha(z_\alpha) = \int M[m(z_\alpha, z_{\underline{\alpha}})] f_{\underline{\alpha}}(z_{\underline{\alpha}}) dz_{\underline{\alpha}}, \qquad (9.38)$$

where $z_{\underline{\alpha}} = (z_1, \ldots, z_{\alpha-1}, z_{\alpha+1}, \ldots, z_q)$, $f_{\underline{\alpha}}(z_{\underline{\alpha}})$ is the PDF of $z_{\underline{\alpha}}$. From (9.38) we know that ϕ_α differs from g_α only by an additive constant c_0. Linton and Härdle (1996) suggest estimating ϕ_α based on the multidimensional local constant kernel estimator

$$\hat{m}(z_\alpha, z_{\underline{\alpha}}) = \frac{n^{-1} \sum_i Y_i k_{h_\alpha}(z_\alpha, Z_{\alpha i}) W_{h_{\underline{\alpha}}}(z_{\underline{\alpha}}, Z_{\underline{\alpha} i})}{n^{-1} \sum_i k_{h_\alpha}(z_\alpha, Z_{\alpha i}) W_{h_{\underline{\alpha}}}(z_{\underline{\alpha}}, Z_{\underline{\alpha} i})}, \qquad (9.39)$$

where $k(\cdot)$ is a univariate second order kernel function, and where $W_{h_{\underline{\alpha}}}(v) = \prod_{s \neq \alpha}^{q} \bar{h}_s^{-1} w((z_s - Z_{si})/\bar{h}_s)$ with $w(\cdot)$ being a kernel function of order $d > q - 1$ (a higher order kernel when $q > 2$).

Then $\phi_\alpha(z_\alpha)$ is estimated by the sample analogue of (9.38) given by

$$\tilde{\phi}_\alpha(z_\alpha) = \frac{1}{n}\sum_{i=1}^{n} M[\hat{m}(z_\alpha, Z_{\underline{\alpha}i})]f_{\underline{\alpha}}(Z_{\underline{\alpha}i}). \qquad (9.40)$$

When M is the identity function, then $\tilde{\phi}_\alpha(z_\alpha)$ is linear in the Y_i's. In general, however, $\tilde{\phi}_\alpha(z_\alpha)$ is a nonlinear function of the Y_i's. The constant term c_0 is estimated by

$$\tilde{c}_0 = \frac{1}{nq}\sum_{\alpha=1}^{q}\sum_{i=1}^{n} \tilde{\phi}_\alpha(Z_{\alpha i}), \qquad (9.41)$$

and $g_\alpha(z_\alpha)$ is estimated by

$$\tilde{g}_\alpha(z_\alpha) = \tilde{\phi}_\alpha(z_\alpha) - \tilde{c}_0. \qquad (9.42)$$

The final estimate for $m(z)$ is given by ($G = M^{-1}$)

$$\hat{m}(z) = G\left[\sum_{\alpha=1}^{q} \tilde{g}_\alpha(z_\alpha) + \tilde{c}_0\right]. \qquad (9.43)$$

Under some regularity conditions, Linton and Härdle (1996) prove the following results.

$$\sqrt{nh_\alpha}\left[\tilde{\phi}_\alpha - \phi_\alpha(z_\alpha) - h_\alpha^2 \mu_\alpha(z_\alpha)\right] \xrightarrow{d} N(0, V_\alpha(z_\alpha)), \qquad (9.44)$$

where

$$\mu_\alpha(z_\alpha) = (\kappa_2/2)\left\{g_\alpha^{(2)}(z_\alpha)\int M^{(1)}[m(z)]f_{\underline{\alpha}}(z_{\underline{\alpha}})dz_{\underline{\alpha}}\right.$$
$$\left. +2g_\alpha^{(1)}(z_\alpha)\int M^{(1)}[m(z)]\frac{\partial \ln f(z)}{\partial z_\alpha}f_{\underline{\alpha}}(z_{\underline{\alpha}})dz_{\underline{\alpha}}\right\},$$
$$V_\alpha(z_\alpha) = \kappa\int\left(M^{(1)}[m(z)]\right)^2\sigma^2 f_{\underline{\alpha}}^2(z_{\underline{\alpha}})\frac{1}{f_\alpha(z_\alpha)}dz_{\underline{\alpha}}.$$

A consistent estimator of $V_\alpha(z_\alpha)$ is given by

$$\tilde{V}_\alpha = \sum_{i=1}^{n} \tilde{\delta}_i^2 \tilde{u}_i^2,$$

where

$$\tilde{\delta}_i = n^{-1} \sum_{i=1}^{n} M^{(1)}[\tilde{m}(z_\alpha, Z_{\underline{\alpha}i})] w_i(z_\alpha, Z_{\underline{\alpha}i}),$$

$$w_i(z_\alpha, Z_{\underline{\alpha}i}) = \frac{k_{h_\alpha}(z_\alpha - Z_{\alpha i}) W_{h_{\underline{\alpha}}}(z_{\underline{\alpha}} - Z_{\underline{\alpha}i})}{\sum_{j=1}^{n} k_{h_\alpha}(z_\alpha - Z_{\alpha j}) W_{\bar{h}}(z_{\underline{\alpha}} - Z_{\underline{\alpha}j})},$$

and where $\tilde{u}_i = Y_i - \tilde{m}(Z_i)$.

As observed by Horowitz and Mammen (2004), one undesirable property of the above marginal integration based estimator is that a higher order kernel must be used for $w(\cdot)$, with the order of the kernel depending on q (i.e., the larger is q, the higher the order of $w(\cdot)$). This arises because, at the initial stage, one has to estimate a q-dimensional function $m(z)$ nonparametrically (i.e., the additive structure is *not* imposed at the initial stage). Horowitz and Mammen suggest using series methods at the initial stage when estimating $m(z)$, then using a kernel local linear method to estimate the individual functions $g_\alpha(\cdot)$. We discuss Horowitz and Mammen's approach in Chapter 15, where we introduce nonparametric series methods. Horowitz and Lee (2005) further extend Horowitz and Mammen's result to additive quantile regression models.

Horowitz (2001) generalizes the above result to the case in which the functional form of the link function $G(\cdot)$ is unknown.

9.2 An Additive Partially Linear Model

While the additive model outlined above has the advantage of not suffering from the curse of dimensionality, it is, however, a very restrictive model since it does not allow for the presence of interaction terms. An additive partially linear model can avoid this problem and maintain the "one-dimensional" nonparametric rate of convergence. Consider a model of the form

$$Y_i = \beta_0 + X_i'\beta + g_1(Z_{1i}) + \cdots + g_q(Z_{qi}) + u_i, \qquad (9.45)$$

where X_i is a $p \times 1$ vector of random variables, $\beta = (\beta_1, \ldots, \beta_p)'$ is a $p \times 1$ vector of unknown parameters, X_i can contain interaction terms involving $(Z_{1i}, \ldots, Z_{qi})$, β_0 is a scalar parameter, the $Z_{\alpha i}$'s are all univariate continuous variables, and the $g_\alpha(\cdot)$'s ($\alpha = 1, \ldots, q$) are unknown smooth functions. The observations $\{Y_i, X_i', Z_{1i}, \ldots, Z_{qi}\}_{i=1}^n$ are i.i.d. We impose the condition $\mathrm{E}[g_\alpha(Z_{\alpha i})] = 0$ for $\alpha = 1, \ldots, q$ in order to identify the individual components $g_1(\cdot), \ldots, g_q(\cdot)$.

Defining $v_i = X_i - \mathrm{E}(X_i | Z_i)$, we say that X is not a deterministic function of $(Z_1, \ldots, Z_q)$ if

$$\mathrm{E}[v_i v_i'] \text{ is positive definite.} \qquad (9.46)$$

Under (9.46), one can use the method discussed in Chapter 6 to obtain a $\sqrt{n}$-consistent estimator of β, say $\tilde{\beta}$. One then can estimate the additive functions by rewriting the model as

$$Y_i - X_i' \tilde{\beta} = c + \sum_{\alpha=1}^q g_\alpha(Z_{\alpha i}) + \epsilon_i,$$

where $\epsilon_i = u_i + X_i'(\beta - \tilde{\beta})$. Since $\tilde{\beta} - \beta = O_p(n^{-1/2})$ has a faster rate of convergence than the nonparametric additive function estimators, the resulting nonparametric estimator of $g_\alpha(z_\alpha)$ has the same asymptotic properties as when β is known. Thus, they have the same asymptotic distribution as the nonparametric additive model discussed in Section 9.1 (without the linear components).

We formally summarize this estimator below. Define $v_i = X_i - \mathrm{E}(X_i | Z_i)$. When $\mathrm{E}(v_i v_i')$ is positive definite, one can use the following simple two-step method to estimate this model:

(i) First, ignore the additive structure of the model and estimate β using Robinson's (1988) approach, i.e., regress $Y_i - \hat{\mathrm{E}}(Y_i | Z_i)$ on $X_i - \hat{\mathrm{E}}(X_i | Z_i)$ to obtain a semiparametric estimator of β, say $\tilde{\beta}$, where $\hat{\mathrm{E}}(Y_i | Z_i)$ and $\hat{\mathrm{E}}(X_i | Z_i)$ are the kernel estimators of $\mathrm{E}(Y_i | Z_i)$ and $\mathrm{E}(X_i | Z_i)$, respectively.

(ii) Next, rewrite the model as $Y_i - X_i' \tilde{\beta} = g_1(Z_{1i}) + \cdots + g_q(Z_{qi}) + \epsilon_i$, and estimate the additive functions $g_l(\cdot)$ as discussed in Section 9.1.

The asymptotic distribution of $\tilde{\beta}$ is discussed in Chapter 7, and the asymptotic distribution of the resulting estimator of $g_\alpha(z_\alpha)$, say $\tilde{g}_\alpha(z_\alpha)$, is the same as that discussed in Section 9.1. This is because $\tilde{\beta} - \beta = O_p(n^{-1/2})$, which is faster than the nonparametric rate of convergence; therefore, replacing $\tilde{\beta}$ by β does not affect the asymptotic distribution of $\hat{g}_\alpha(z_\alpha)$.

The advantage of the above procedure is that it is computationally simple. However, there is one problem with this approach. When $\mathrm{E}(v_i v_i')$ is not positive definite, the procedure fails to estimate β. Consider the simple case where $q = 2$, and consider a model of the form

$$Y_i = \beta_0 + (Z_{1i} Z_{2i})\beta + g_1(Z_{1i}) + g_2(Z_{2i}) + u_i, \qquad (9.47)$$

where we have $X_i = Z_{1i} Z_{2i}$. In this case, X_i is a deterministic function of Z_i, and we have $v_i = X_i - \mathrm{E}(X_i|Z_i) = X_i - X_i = 0$. That is, the above procedure cannot apply in such cases.

However, (9.46) is a strong assumption as it rules out cases for which X_i is a deterministic (but nonadditive) function of $(Z_{1i}, \ldots, Z_{qi})$. For example, when $q = 2$ we may wish to let X_i contain interaction terms such as $X_i = Z_{1i} Z_{2i}$, but then (9.46) fails to hold.

Fan et al. (1998) and Fan and Li (2003) proposed an alternative $\sqrt{n}$-consistent estimator of β based on marginal integration methods. Their method has the advantage that it does not rely upon condition (9.46). As discussed earlier, the marginal integration method is computationally costly. Schick (1996) and Manzan and Zerom (2005) suggest using a computationally efficient method for estimating β. We describe Manzan and Zerom's procedure below.

9.2.1 A Simple Two-Step Method

For any random variable (vector) ξ_i, define $\xi_{\alpha i} = \mathrm{E}[\xi_i w_\alpha(Z_i)|Z_{\alpha i}] \equiv \int \mathrm{E}[\xi_i|Z_i = z]f_{\underline{\alpha}}(z_{\underline{\alpha}})dz_{\underline{\alpha}}$, where $w_\alpha(z) = f_\alpha(z_\alpha)f_{\underline{\alpha}}(z_{\underline{\alpha}})/f(z_\alpha, z_{\underline{\alpha}})$, $\alpha = 1, \ldots, q$, and define the projection of ξ_i on the additive functional space by

$$\mathrm{E}_A(\xi_i) = \sum_{\alpha=1}^{q} \xi_{\alpha i}. \qquad (9.48)$$

Applying the projection (9.48) to (9.45) we obtain

$$\mathrm{E}_A(Y_i) = \mathrm{E}_A(X_i)'\beta + \sum_{s=1}^{q} g(Z_{si}). \qquad (9.49)$$

Subtracting (9.49) from (9.45) we get

$$Y_i - \mathrm{E}_A(Y_i) = (X_i - \mathrm{E}_A(X_i))'\beta + u_i. \qquad (9.50)$$

We can estimate β by applying least squares methods. However, we must first obtain consistent estimators for $\mathrm{E}_A(Y_i)$ and $\mathrm{E}_A(X_i)$. By the results given in Section 9.1 we know that they can be consistently estimated by

$$\hat{E}_A(Y_i) = \sum_{\alpha=1}^{q} \hat{Y}_{\alpha i} \text{ and } \hat{E}_A(X_i) = \sum_{\alpha=1}^{q} \hat{X}_{\alpha i}, \qquad (9.51)$$

where

$$\hat{\xi}_{\alpha i} = \frac{1}{n h_\alpha} \sum_{j=1}^{n} \xi_j k\left(\frac{Z_{\alpha j} - Z_{\alpha i}}{h_\alpha}\right) \frac{\hat{f}_\alpha(Z_{\alpha j})}{\hat{f}(Z_{\alpha j}, Z_{\underline{\alpha} j})}, \quad \alpha = 1, \dots, q, \quad (9.52)$$

and, with $\xi_i = Y_i$ or $\xi_i = X_i$ in (9.52), we obtain $\hat{E}_A(Y_i)$ and $\hat{E}_A(X_i)$, respectively.

Therefore, a feasible estimator of β is given by

$$\hat{\beta} = S^{-1}_{X-\hat{E}_A(X)} S_{X-\hat{E}_A(X),Y-\hat{E}_A(Y)}, \qquad (9.53)$$

where $S_{C,D} = n^{-1}\sum_{i=1}^{n} C_i D_i'$, $S_C = S_{C,C}$. The asymptotic distribution of $\hat{\beta}$ is given in Manzan and Zerom (2005) and is as follows.

Theorem 9.2. *Under the same regularity conditions given in Manzan and Zerom (2005),*

$$\sqrt{n}(\hat{\beta} - \beta) \to N(0, \Sigma) \text{ in distribution,}$$

where $\Sigma = \Phi^{-1}\Omega\Phi^{-1}$, $\Phi = E[\eta_i \eta_i']$, $\eta_i = X_i - E_A(X_i)$, *and* $\Omega = E[u_i^2 \eta_i \eta_i']$.

A consistent estimator of Σ is given by $\hat{\Sigma} = \hat{\Phi}^{-1}\hat{\Omega}\hat{\Phi}^{-1}$ where $\hat{\Phi} = n^{-1}\sum_{i=1}^{n}[X_i - \hat{E}_A(X_i)][X_i - \hat{E}_A(X_i)]'$, $\hat{\Omega} = n^{-1}\sum_{i=1}^{n} \hat{u}_i^2[X_i - \hat{E}_A(X_i)][X_i - \hat{E}_A(X_i)]'$, and $\hat{u}_i = Y_i - \hat{E}_A(Y_i) - (X_i - \hat{E}_A(X_i))'\hat{\beta}$.

When the error is conditionally homoskedastic, $\hat{\beta}$ is semiparametrically efficient in the sense that its asymptotic variance reaches the semiparametric efficiency bound for this model (see Chamberlain (1992)).

Positive definiteness of Φ is an identification condition for β. It allows for X_i to be a deterministic function of $(Z_{1i}, \dots, Z_{qi})$ provided it is not an additive function of the $Z_{\alpha i}$'s. More specifically, consider the simple case of $q = 2$ in (9.47) with $X_i = Z_{1i}Z_{2i}$ given by

$$Y_i = \beta_0 + (Z_{1i}Z_{2i})\beta + g_1(Z_{1i}) + g_2(Z_{2i}) + u_i. \qquad (9.54)$$

Model (9.54) is immune to the curse of dimensionality since it only involves a one-dimensional nonparametric function $g_\alpha(\cdot)$ ($\alpha = 1, 2$).

Also, it is more general than an additive model that does not have interaction terms (i.e., (9.45) allows interaction terms to enter the model parametrically).

Continuing with this simple case ($q = 2$), we next estimate the individual nonparametric components $g_\alpha(z_\alpha)$. Given the $\sqrt{n}$-consistent estimator $\hat\beta$, we can rewrite (9.45) as

$$Y_i - X_i'\hat\beta = \beta_0 + \sum_{\alpha=1}^{q} g_\alpha(Z_{\alpha i}) + \epsilon_i, \qquad (9.55)$$

where $\epsilon_i = u_i + X_i'(\beta - \hat\beta)$.

Equation (9.55) is essentially an additive regression model with $Y_i - X_i'\hat\beta$ as the new dependent variable and $[u_i + X_i'(\beta - \hat\beta)]$ as the new (composite) error. Hence, one can estimate $g_\alpha(z_\alpha)$ by marginally integrating a local linear model as discussed in (9.6) and (9.7), with Y_i replaced by $Y_i - X_i'\hat\beta$. Let $\hat g_\alpha(z_\alpha)$ denote the resulting estimator of $g_\alpha(z_\alpha)$. From Theorem 9.1 and the fact that $\hat\beta - \beta = O_p(n^{-1/2})$, it is easy to see that the asymptotic distribution of $\hat g_\alpha(z_\alpha)$ is the same as that of $\tilde g_\alpha(z_\alpha)$, which was given in Theorem 9.1.

The intercept term β_0 can be $\sqrt{n}$-consistently estimated by $\hat\beta_0 = \bar Y - \bar X'\hat\beta$, where $\bar Y = n^{-1}\sum_{i=1}^{n} Y_i$ and $\bar X = n^{-1}\sum_{i=1}^{n} X_i$. The conditional mean function $\mathrm{E}[Y_i|X_i = x, Z_{1i} = z_1, \ldots, Z_{qi} = z_q]$ can be estimated by $\hat\beta_0 + x'\hat\beta + \sum_{\alpha=1}^{q} \hat g_\alpha(z_\alpha)$, and the error can be estimated by $\hat u_i = Y_i - \hat\beta_0 - X_i'\hat\beta - \sum_{\alpha=1}^{q} \hat g_\alpha(Z_{\alpha i})$.

9.3 A Semiparametric Varying (Smooth) Coefficient Model

In the previous section we discussed a partially linear model of the form

$$Y_i = \alpha(Z_i) + X_i'\beta_0 + u_i, \qquad (9.56)$$

where $\alpha(\cdot)$ is an unknown function and β_0 is an $r \times 1$ vector of unknown parameters.

In this section we consider a more general semiparametric regression model, the so-called semiparametric smooth coefficient model, which nests a partially linear model as a special case. The smooth coefficient model is given by

$$Y_i = \alpha(Z_i) + X_i'\beta(Z_i) + u_i, \qquad (9.57)$$

where $\beta(z)$ is a vector of unspecified smooth functions of z. When $\beta(z) = \beta_0$, (9.57) collapses to the partially linear model (9.56).

By way of example, the smooth coefficient model would be appropriate when, say, modeling a cross-sectional production function where the right-hand side variables are, say, labor, capital and the firm's R&D inputs. If we let $X_i = (labor_i, capital_i)$ and $Z_i = R\&D_i$, then (9.57) suggests that the labor and capital input coefficients may vary directly with the firm's R&D input. Thus, both the marginal productivity of labor and capital depend on the firm's R&D values. As a result, returns to scale may also be a function of R&D. The partially linear model (9.56) assumes that the slope coefficients β are invariant with respect to R&D, hence the R&D variable can only shift the level of the production frontier. In this case, the R&D variable is said to have "neutral" effects on the production frontier. In contrast to (9.56), the smooth coefficient model (9.57) allows R&D to affect the stochastic frontier "nonneutrally."

9.3.1   A Local Constant Estimator of the Smooth Coefficient Function

To avoid introducing superfluous notation, we abuse notation slightly and express (9.57) more compactly as

$$Y_i = X_i'\beta(Z_i) + u_i, \qquad (9.58)$$

where now X_i is a $p \times 1$ vector which may contain a constant as its first component (so that it is equivalent to (9.57)), $\beta(z)$ is a $p \times 1$ dimension function of z, and Z_i is of dimension q.

Premultiplying (9.58) by X_i and taking $\mathrm{E}(.|Z_i)$ leads to $\mathrm{E}[X_i Y_i | Z_i] = \mathrm{E}[X_i X_i']\beta(Z_i)$, yielding

$$\beta(z) = \left[\mathrm{E}(X_i X_i'|z)\right]^{-1} \mathrm{E}[X_i Y_i|z]. \qquad (9.59)$$

Equation (9.59) suggests the following local constant least squares estimator for $\beta(z)$:

$$\hat{\beta}(z) = \left[\sum_{j=1}^{n} X_j X_j' K\left(\frac{Z_j - z}{h}\right)\right]^{-1} \sum_{j=1}^{n} X_j Y_j K\left(\frac{Z_j - z}{h}\right). \qquad (9.60)$$

The intuition underlying the above local least squares estimator should be apparent. In the case where z is a scalar and $K(\cdot)$ is a uniform kernel, (9.60) becomes

$$\hat{\beta}(z) = \left[\sum_{|Z_j - z| \leq h} X_j X_j' \right]^{-1} \sum_{|Z_j - z| \leq h} X_j Y_j. \qquad (9.61)$$

Here, $\hat{\beta}(z)$ is simply a least squares estimator obtained by regressing Y_j on X_j using the observations (X_j, Y_j) where the corresponding Z_j is close to z ($|Z_j - z| \leq h$). Since $\beta(z)$ is a smooth function of z, $|\beta(Z_j) - \beta(z)|$ is small when $|Z_j - z|$ is small. The condition that nh is large ensures that we have a sufficient number of observations within the interval $|Z_j - z| \leq h$ when $\beta(Z_j)$ is close to $\beta(z)$. Therefore, under conditions such as $h \to 0$ and $nh \to \infty$ ($nh_1 \ldots h_q \to \infty$ if $Z_i \in \mathbb{R}^q$), we can show that the local least squares estimator $\hat{\beta}(z)$ provides a consistent estimator of $\beta(z)$.

The following theorem establishes the consistency and asymptotic normality of $\hat{\beta}(z)$.

Theorem 9.3. *Under some regularity conditions (see Li, Huang, Li and Fu (2002)), and for a fixed value of z with $f_z(z) > 0$ ($f_z(\cdot)$ is the marginal PDF of Z_i), we have*

$$\sqrt{nh_1 \ldots h_q} \left(\hat{\beta}(z) - \beta(z) - \sum_{s=1}^{q} h_s^2 B_s(z) \right) \to N(0, \Omega_z) \text{ in distribution,}$$

provided that $M_z \overset{\text{def}}{=} f_z(z) \mathrm{E}[X_i X_i' | Z_i = z]$ is positive definite, $B_s(z) = \kappa_2 M_z^{-1} \mathrm{E}[X_i X_i' \{\delta_s(z) f_s(X_i, Z_i) / f(X_i | Z_i = z) + (1/2) f_z(Z_i) \beta_{ss}(Z_i)\} | z]$, $\kappa_2 = \int k(v) v^2 dv$, $\beta_s(z) = \partial \beta(z) / \partial z_s$, $\beta_{ss}(z) = \partial^2 \beta(z) / \partial z_s^2$, $\Omega_z = M_z^{-1} V_z M_z^{-1}$, $V_z = \kappa^q f_z(z) \mathrm{E}[X_i X_i' \sigma^2(X_i, Z_i) | Z_i = z]$, and $\sigma^2(X_i, Z_i) = \mathrm{E}(u_i^2 | X_i, Z_i)$. A consistent estimator of Ω_z is given in Exercise 9.2.

The proof of Theorem 9.3 is presented in Section 9.3.5.

9.3.2 A Local Linear Estimator of the Smooth Coefficient Function

For what follows, the model is identical to that given in (9.58). For expositional simplicity, we assume that Z_i is a scalar, and so the local linear estimator of $\beta_s(z)$ is $\hat{\beta}_s(z) = \hat{a}_s(z)$, where $\{(\hat{a}_s(z), \hat{b}_s(z))\}_{s=1}^{p}$ minimizes the following weighted sum of squares:

$$\sum_{i=1}^{n} \left[Y_i - \sum_{s=1}^{p} \{a_s + b_s(Z_i - z)\} X_{is} \right]^2 K_h(Z_i, z), \qquad (9.62)$$

where $k_h(\cdot) = h^{-1}K(./h)$.

Let $\delta(z) = (a_1(z), \ldots, a_p(z), b_1(z), \ldots, b_p(z))'$, let $\mathcal{X}$ denote an $n \times 2p$ matrix having $(X_i', X_i'(Z_i - z))$ as its ith row, and let $\mathcal{K}$ be a diagonal matrix (of dimension n) with the ith diagonal element being $K_h(Z_i - z)$, while $\mathcal{Y} = (Y_1, \ldots, Y_n)'$. Then, from (9.62), it follows from least squares theory that the estimator of $\delta(z)$ is given by

$$\hat{\delta}(z) = (\mathcal{X}'\mathcal{K}\mathcal{X})^{-1}\mathcal{X}\mathcal{K}\mathcal{Y}. \tag{9.63}$$

Note that $\hat{\delta}(z) = (\hat{a}_1(z), \ldots, \hat{a}_p(z), \hat{b}_1(z), \ldots, \hat{b}_p(z))'$, where $\hat{a}_s(z)$ estimates $\beta_s(z)$ and $\hat{b}_s(z)$ estimates $\partial\beta(z)/\partial z_s$.

To derive the asymptotic distribution for the local linear estimator $\hat{\delta}(z)$, we first introduce some notation. Let

$$\mathbf{S}_n = \mathbf{S}_n(z) = \begin{pmatrix} S_{n,0} & S_{n,1} \\ S_{n,1} & S_{n,2} \end{pmatrix} \text{ and } \mathbf{T}_n = \mathbf{T}_n(z) = \begin{pmatrix} T_{n,0} \\ T_{n,1} \end{pmatrix},$$

where, for $j = 1, 2$,

$$S_{n,j} = S_{n,j}(z) = n^{-1}\sum_{i=1}^{n} X_i X_i'((Z_i - z)/h)^j K_h(Z_i, z)$$

and $T_{n,j} = T_{n,j}(z) = n^{-1}\sum_{i=1}^{n} X_i Y_i\left((Z_j - z)/h\right)^j K_h(Z_i, z)$. Also, let

$$\delta(z) = (a_1, \ldots, a_p, b_1, \ldots, b_p)' \text{ and let}$$
$$\hat{\delta} = \hat{\delta}(z) = (\hat{a}_1(z), \ldots, \hat{a}_p(z), \hat{b}_1(z), \ldots, \hat{b}_p(z)).$$

Using this notation we can write $\hat{\delta}(z)$ as

$$\hat{\delta}(z) = \mathbf{H}^{-1}\mathbf{S}_n^{-1}\mathbf{T}_n, \tag{9.64}$$

where $\mathbf{H} = \text{diag}\{1, \ldots, 1, h, \ldots, h\}$ with p-diagonal ones and p-diagonal h's.

To facilitate notation, we denote, for nonnegative integers j,

$$\mu_j = \int_{-\infty}^{\infty} v^j k(v)dv \text{ and } \nu_j = \int_{-\infty}^{\infty} v^j k^2(v)dv.$$

Furthermore,

$$\Omega(z) = (w_{l,m})_{p \times p} = \mathbb{E}[\mathcal{X}_i\mathcal{X}_i'|Z_i = z].$$

We will assume that the kernel function $k(\cdot)$ is symmetric, so that $\mu_1 = \int u k(u) du = 0$, while we also assume that $\mu_0 = \int k(u) du = 1$. Then it can be shown that (see Exercise 9.4)

$$\mathrm{E}[\mathbf{S}_{n,j}(z)] \to f(z)\Omega(z)\mu_j \text{ and } nh\,\mathrm{var}(\mathbf{S}_{n,j}(z)_{l,m}) \to f(z)\nu_{2j}w_{l,m}$$
$$(9.65)$$

for each $0 \leq j \leq 3$ and $1 \leq l, m \leq p$, where $f(\cdot)$ is the PDF of Z_i. A consequence of (9.65) is that

$$\mathbf{S}_n \xrightarrow{p} f(z)\mathbf{S} \text{ and } \mathbf{S}_{n,3} \xrightarrow{p} \mu_3 f(z)\Omega(z), \qquad (9.66)$$

where

$$\mathbf{S} = \begin{pmatrix} \Omega(z) & 0 \\ 0 & \mu_2\Omega(z) \end{pmatrix}.$$

Cai, Fan and Yao (2000) proved the following result:

Theorem 9.4. *Under some smoothness and moment regularity conditions, and also assuming that $f(z) > 0$, then $(\hat{a}(z) = (\hat{a}_1(z), \ldots, \hat{a}_p(z))')$*

$$\sqrt{nh}\left[\hat{a}(z) - a(z) - \frac{h^2}{2}\mu_2 a^{(2)}(z)\right] \to N(0, \Theta(z)) \text{ in distribution,}$$

where $a^{(2)}(z)$ is a $p \times 1$ vector whose s^{th} component is given by $a_s^{(2)}(z) = \partial^2 a_s(z)/\partial z^2$, where

$$\Theta(z) = \nu_0 \Omega(z)^{-1}(z)\Omega^*(z)\Omega(z)/f(z) \text{ and where}$$
$$\Omega^*(z) = \mathrm{E}[X_i X_i' \sigma^2(X_i, Z_i)|Z_i = z].$$

Theorem 9.4 implies that

$$\sqrt{nh}[\hat{a}_s(z) - a_s(z) - \frac{h^2}{2}\mu_2 a_s^{(2)}(z)] \to N(0, V_{s0}) \text{ in distribution,}$$

where $V_{s,0} = \nu_0 e'_{s,p}\Omega^{-1}(z)\Omega^*(z)\Omega(z)e_{s,p}/f(z)$, $e_{s,p}$ is the $p \times 1$ vector with 1 at the sth position and 0 for other positions.

Xue and Yang (forthcoming, 2006) provide alternative approaches to estimating a semiparametric varying coefficient model (e.g., polynomial splines).

9.3.3   Testing for a Parametric Smooth Coefficient Model

When $\beta(z) = \beta_0(z)$ is of known functional form, one can estimate the model by parametric methods. For example, if $\beta(z) = \beta_0$, a vector of parameter constants, we can estimate the model via ordinary least squares. If $\beta(z) = \beta_0(z, \gamma)$, where $\beta_0(\cdot)$ has a known functional form with γ being a finite dimensional parameter, we can estimate the model via nonlinear least squares if the model is nonlinear in parameters. Below we discuss how to test $\beta(z) = \beta_0(z, \gamma)$ a.e. (in z).

A Local Constant Estimator-Based Test

Letting $\hat{\gamma}$ be a $\sqrt{n}$-consistent estimator of γ and letting $\hat{\beta}_0(z) = \beta_0(z, \hat{\gamma})$, one can construct a test statistic based on a weighted integrated square difference between $\hat{\beta}(z)$ and $\hat{\beta}_0(z)$ given by

$$I_n = \int \left\{ \left[\hat{\beta}(z) - \hat{\beta}_0(z)\right]' A_n \left[\hat{\beta}(z) - \hat{\beta}_0(z)\right] \right\} dz,$$

where A_n is a positive definite matrix. $\hat{\beta}(z)$ is the local constant estimator which has a random denominator $D_n(z)^{-1}$ and this will complicate the asymptotic analysis of I_n. Li et al. (2002) suggest choosing $A_n = D_n(z)' D_n(z)$ to remove the random denominator in I_n. With this choice of A_n we have

$$
\begin{aligned}
I_n &= \int \left\{ D_n(z) \left[\hat{\beta}(z) - \hat{\beta}_0(z)\right] \right\}' D_n(z) \left[\hat{\beta}(z) - \hat{\beta}_0(z)\right] dz \\
&= \frac{1}{n^2} \sum_i \sum_j \int X_i' \left[Y_i - X_i'\hat{\beta}_0(z)\right] X_j \left[y_j - X_j'\hat{\beta}_0(z)\right] K_{h,z_i,z} K_{h,z_j,z} dz \\
&= \frac{1}{n^2} \sum_i \sum_j X_i' X_j \hat{u}_i \hat{u}_j \bar{K}_{h,z_i,z_j},
\end{aligned}
$$

where $\hat{u}_i = Y_i - X_i'\hat{\beta}_0(z)$, $\bar{K}_{h,z_i,z_j} = \prod_{s=1}^q h_s^{-1}\bar{k}((Z_{is} - Z_{js})/h_s)$, and $\bar{k}(v) = \int k(u)k(u-v)du$ is the twofold convolution kernel derived from $k(\cdot)$.

In fact there is no need to compute the convolution kernel, as one can simply replace $\bar{K}(\cdot)$ by a standard second order kernel $K(\cdot)$. Also, one can remove the $i = j$ term in I_n so that the test statistic will be asymptotically centered at zero under the null hypothesis. Therefore, the final test statistic proposed by Li et al. (2002) is given by

$$\hat{I}_n = \frac{1}{n^2} \sum_{i=1}^{n} \sum_{j \neq i}^{n} X_i' X_j \hat{u}_i \hat{u}_j K_{h,z_i,z_j}.$$

Li et al. (2002) further showed that

$$\hat{J}_n = n(h_1 \ldots h_q)^{1/2} \hat{I}_n / \sqrt{\hat{\sigma}_0^2} \xrightarrow{d} N(0,1)$$

under the null hypothesis, where[2]

$$\hat{\sigma}_0^2 = \frac{2h_1 \ldots h_q}{n^2} \sum_{i=1}^{n} \sum_{j \neq i}^{n} (X_i' X_j)^2 \hat{u}_i^2 \hat{u}_j^2 K_{h,z_i,z_j}^2.$$

One can also use the wild bootstrap method to approximate the null distribution of $\hat{J}_n$. The exact steps for computing the bootstrap test statistic are left as an exercise.

A Local Linear Estimator-Based Test

Cai, Fan and Yao (2000) suggest testing a parametric varying coefficient function based on the comparison of parametric and semiparametric sum of squared residuals. Define

$$RSS_{\text{para}} = n^{-1} \sum_{i=1}^{n} [Y_i - \beta_1(Z_i, \hat{\gamma}) X_{i1} - \cdots - \beta_p(Z_i, \hat{\gamma}) X_{ip}]^2$$

and

$$RSS_{\text{semi}} = n^{-1} \sum_{i=1}^{n} [Y_i - \hat{\beta}_1(Z_i) X_{i1} - \cdots - \hat{\beta}_p(Z_i) X_{ip}]^2,$$

where $\hat{\beta}_s(z) = \hat{a}_s(z)$ is the local linear estimator of $\beta_s(z)$ discussed in Section 9.3.2. Cai, Fan and Yao propose using the test statistic

$$TS_n = [RSS_{\text{para}} - RSS_{\text{semi}}]/RSS_{\text{semi}} = RSS_{\text{para}}/RSS_{\text{semi}} - 1$$

to test null hypothesis of $\beta(z) = \beta_0(z, \gamma)$ a.e. In practice, one rejects the null hypothesis for large value of TS_n. Cai, Fan and Yao propose using the following nonparametric bootstrap procedure to evaluate the P-value of the TS_n test.

---

[2]The expressions here are the same as in Li et al. (2002) by noting that $K_{h,ij} = (h_1 \ldots h_q)^{-1} K((z_j - z_i)/h)$.

(i) Generate the bootstrap residuals u_i^* from the empirical distribution of the centered residuals $\{\hat{u}_i - n^{-1} \sum_{j=1} \hat{u}_j\}_{i=1}^n$, where

$$\hat{u}_i = Y_i - \hat{\beta}_1(Z_i)X_{i1} - \cdots - \hat{\beta}_p(Z_i)X_{ip}.$$

Define

$$Y_i^* = \hat{\beta}_1(Z_i)X_{i1} + \cdots + \hat{\beta}_p(Z_i)X_{ip} + u_i^*.$$

(ii) Calculate the bootstrap statistic TS_n^* based on the bootstrap sample $\{Z_i, X_i', Y_i^*\}_{i=1}^n$, and repeat steps (i) and (ii) a large number of times, say $B = 399$.

(iii) Reject the null hypothesis when TS_n is greater than the upper-α percentile of the bootstrap statistics $\{TS_{n,j}^*\}_{j=1}^B$.

One can also use the two-point distribution of the wild bootstrap method in generating u_i^* in step (i) above, i.e., $u_i^* = [(1 - \sqrt{5})/2]\hat{u}_i$ with probability $r = (1 + \sqrt{5})/(2\sqrt{5})$ and $u_i^* = [(1 + \sqrt{5})/2]\hat{u}_i$ with probability $1 - r$ so that the resulting bootstrap statistic is robust to the presence of conditionally heteroskedastic errors.

We direct the interested reader to Yang, Park, Xue and Härdle (forthcoming), who provide an alternative testing procedure for varying coefficient structures in an additive model based on marginal integration methods. Fan and Zhang (2000) derive simultaneous confidence bands in a varying coefficient model which can also be used for testing hypothesis.

9.3.4 Partially Linear Smooth Coefficient Models

We can generalize this to a partially linear framework by considering models of the form

$$Y_i = W_i'\gamma + X_i'\beta(Z_i) + u_i, \tag{9.67}$$

where γ is a vector of unknown (constant) parameters, and $\beta(z_i)$ is the smooth coefficient function.

If γ were known, we could rewrite (9.67) as

$$Y_i - W_i'\gamma = X_i'\beta(Z_i) + u_i, \tag{9.68}$$

and estimate $\beta(Z_i)$ as discussed before treating $Y_i - W_i'\gamma$ as the new dependent variable, i.e.,

$$\hat{\beta}(Z_i) = \left[\sum_j X_j X_j' K_{h,z_i,z}\right]^{-1} \sum_j X_j \left[Y_j - W_j'\gamma\right] K_{h,z_i,z} \qquad (9.69)$$
$$\equiv \hat{\beta}_y(Z_i) - \hat{\beta}_w(Z_i)'\gamma,$$

where

$$\hat{\beta}_y(Z_i) = \left[\sum_j X_j X_j' K_{h,z_j,z_i}\right]^{-1} \sum_j X_j Y_j K_{h,z_j,z_i} \quad \text{and}$$

$$\hat{\beta}_w(Z_i) = \left[\sum_j X_j X_j' K_{h,z_j,z_i}\right]^{-1} \sum_j X_j W_j K_{h,z_j,z_i}.$$

Replacing $\beta(z_i)$ in (9.68) by the estimator $\hat{\beta}(z_i)$ given in (9.69), we get

$$Y_i - X_i'\hat{\beta}_y(Z_i) = \left(W_i' - X_i'\hat{\beta}_w(Z_i)'\right)\gamma + \text{ error.} \qquad (9.70)$$

We can now estimate γ via the ordinary least squares method by regressing $Y_i - X_i'\hat{\beta}_y(Z_i)$ on $\left(W_i' - X_i'\hat{\beta}_w(Z_i)'\right)$. Letting $\hat{\gamma}$ denote the resulting (semiparametric) estimator of γ, Fan and Huang (2005) showed that

$$\sqrt{n}(\hat{\gamma} - \gamma) \to N(0, V) \quad \text{in distribution,} \qquad (9.71)$$

where $V = A^{-1}BA^{-1}$, where $A = \mathrm{E}[\zeta_i\zeta_i']$, $B = \mathrm{E}[\sigma^2(X_i, Z_i W_i)\zeta_i\zeta_i']$, $\zeta_i = w_i - \mathrm{E}_{sm}(w_i)$, and where $\mathrm{E}_{sm}(W_i)$ denotes the projection of W_i into the smooth coefficient functional space, i.e., $\mathrm{E}_{sm}(W_i) = X_i'\beta_w(Z_i)$, where $\beta_{ws}(\cdot) = \inf_{\beta(\cdot)} \mathrm{E}\{[W_{is} - X_i'\beta(Z_i)]'[W_{is} - X_i'\beta(Z_i)]\}$. The above approach is called a "profile likelihood" method. Exercise 9.3 provides a consistent estimator of $\beta_w(Z_i)$, from which it should be easy for the reader to construct a consistent estimator for V, which can be accomplished by replacing the population mean $\mathrm{E}(\cdot)$ by sample mean $n^{-1}\sum_{i=1}^n (\cdot)$.

When the error term is conditionally homoskedastic, i.e., when $\sigma_u^2 = \mathrm{E}(u_i^2|X_i, Z_i, W_i) = \mathrm{E}(u_i^2)$, V simplifies to $V = \sigma_u^2 A^{-1}$, which is the same as the lower bound for the asymptotic variance of a (regular) estimator of γ. Thus, $\hat{\gamma}$ is a semiparametrically efficient estimator of γ when the error is conditionally homoskedastic.

9.3.5   Proof of Theorem 9.3

Proof.

$$
\hat{\beta}(z) = \left[\sum_j X_j X_j' K_{z_j,z} \right]^{-1} \sum_j X_j Y_j K_{z_j,z}
$$

$$
= \left[\sum_j X_j X_j' K_{z_j,z} \right]^{-1} \sum_j X_j \left[X_j' \beta(Z_j) + u_j \right] K_{z_j,z}
$$

$$
= \left[\sum_j X_j X_j' K_{z_j,z} \right]^{-1} \sum_j X_j \left[X_j' \beta(z) + X_j'(\beta(X_j) - \beta(z)) + u_j \right] K_{z_j,z}
$$

$$
= \beta(z) + \left[\sum_j X_j X_j' K_{z_j,z} \right]^{-1} \sum_j X_j \left[X_j'(\beta(X_j) - \beta(z)) + u_j \right] K_{z_j,z}
$$

$$
= \beta(z) + [D_n(z)]^{-1} \left\{ A_{1n}(z) + A_{2n}(z) \right\},
$$

where

$$
D_n(z) = n^{-1} \sum_j X_j X_j' K_{h,z_j,z},
$$

$$
A_{1n}(z) = n^{-1} \sum_j X_j X_j'(\beta(X_j) - \beta(z)) K_{h,z_j,z},
$$

$$
A_{2n}(z) = n^{-1} \sum_j X_j u_j K_{h,z_j,z}.
$$

Statements (i)–(iii) below imply Theorem 9.3.

(i) $D_n(z) = n^{-1} \sum_j X_j X_j' K_{h,z_j,z} \xrightarrow{p} M_z.$

(ii) $A_{1n}(z) = M_z \sum_{s=1}^{q} h_s^2 B_s(z) + o_p \left(\sum_{s=1}^{q} h_s^2 \right).$

(iii) $\sqrt{n h_1 \ldots h_q} A_{2n}(z) \xrightarrow{d} N(0, V_z).$

We prove these results next. Writing $H_q = h_1 \ldots h_q$, $H_q^{-1} =$

$(h_1 \ldots h_q)^{-1}$ and $h^2 = \sum_{s=1}^{q} h_s^2$, we have

(i) $\mathrm{E}(D_n(z)) = H_q^{-1} \mathrm{E}[X_i X_i' K_{z_i,z}]$

$$= H_q^{-1} \int \int x_1 x_1' K((z_1 - z)/h) f(x_1, z_1) dx_1 dz_1$$

$$= \int \int x_1 x_1' K(v) f(x_1, z + hv) dv dx_1$$

$$= \left[\int x_1 x_1' f(x_1, z) dx_1 \right] \left[\int K(v) dv + O(h^2) \right]$$

$$= f_z(z) \left[\int x_1 x_1' f(x_1 | z_1 = z) dx_1 \right] [1 + O(h^2)]$$

$$= f_z(z) \mathrm{E}[X_i X_i' | Z_i = z] + o(1) = M_z + o(1).$$

Similarly, we can show that $\mathrm{var}(D_n(z)) = O\left((nh_1 \ldots h_q)^{-1}\right) = o(1)$. Therefore, we have shown that

$$D_n(z) = M_z + o_p(1). \tag{9.72}$$

(ii) $\mathrm{E}[A_{1n}(z)] = \mathrm{E}[X_i X_i'(\beta(Z_i) - \beta(z)) K_{h,z_i,z}]$

$$= \int x_1 x_1'(\beta(z_1) - \beta(z)) K_{h,z_1,z} f(z_1, x_1) dx_1 dz_1$$

$$= \int x_1 x_1'(\beta(z + hv) - \beta(z)) f(z + hv, x_1) K(v) dx_1 dv$$

$$= \int x_1 x_1' \left[\sum_{s=1}^{q} h_s \beta_s(z) v_s + (1/2) \sum_{s=1}^{q} h_s^2 \beta_{ss}(z) v_s^2 \right]$$

$$\times \left[f(x_1, z) + \sum_{s=1}^{q} f_s(x_1, z) h_s v_s \right] K(v) dx_1 dv + O\left(\sum_{s=1}^{q} h_s^3 \right)$$

$$= M_z \sum_{s=1}^{q} h_s^2 B_s(z) + O\left(\sum_{s=1}^{q} h_s^3 \right),$$

where $B_s(z)$ is defined in Theorem 9.3. Similarly, one can show that $\mathrm{var}(A_{1n}(z)) = O\left(\sum_{s=1}^{q} h_s^2 (nh_1 \ldots h_q)^{-1} + \sum_{s=1}^{q} h_s^5 \right)$. Hence,

$$\left(A_{1n}(z) - M_z \sum_{s=1}^{q} h_s^2 B_s(z) \right) = o_p \left(\sum_{s=1}^{q} h_s^2 + (nh_1 \ldots h_q)^{-1/2} \right). \tag{9.73}$$

(iii) $\sqrt{nh_1 \ldots h_q} A_{2n}(z)$ has mean zero and its variance is

$$nH_q n^{-2} \sum_{i=1}^{n} E\left[X_i X_i' u_i^2 K_{h,z_i,z}^2\right]$$

$$= H_q \int f(x_1,z_1)\sigma_u^2(x_1,z_1)x_1 x_1' K_{h,z_1,z}^2 dx_1 dz_1$$

$$= \left[\int x_1 x_1' \sigma_u^2(x_1,z)f(x_1,z)dx_1\right]\left[\int K^2(v)dv\right] + O\left(\sum_{s=1}^{q} h_s\right)$$

$$= \kappa^q f_z(z) E\left[X_i X_i' \sigma_u^2(X_i,Z_i)|Z_i = z\right] + o(1) = V_z + o(1)$$

where $\kappa^q = \int K^2(v)dv$ and $H_q = h_1 \ldots h_q$.

It is straightforward to check that the conditions of Liapunov's CLT hold. Thus,

$$\sqrt{nH_q} A_{2n}(z) \xrightarrow{d} N(0, V_z). \tag{9.74}$$

Summarizing (9.73), (9.72), and (9.74), we have shown that

$$\sqrt{nH_q}\left(\hat{\beta}(z) - \beta(z) - \sum_{s=1}^{q} h_s^2 B_s(z)\right)$$

$$= [D_n(z)]^{-1}\sqrt{nH_q}\left\{A_{1n}(z) - M_z \sum_{s=1}^{q} h_s^2 B_s(z) + A_{2n}(z)\right\}$$

$$= [M_z + o_p(1)]^{-1}\left\{\sqrt{nH_q} A_{2n}(z) + o_p(1)\right\}$$

$$\xrightarrow{d} M_z^{-1} N(0, V_z) = N\left(0, M_z^{-1} V_z M_z^{-1}\right).$$

$\square$

9.4 Exercises

Exercise 9.1. Letting $\hat{g}(z)$ be defined as in (9.25), and assuming that $h_1 = \cdots = h_q$, show that

$$\sqrt{nh}\left[\hat{g}(z) - g(z) - \frac{\kappa_2}{2}h^2 \sum_{s=1}^{q} g_{ss}(z_s)\right] \xrightarrow{d} N\left(0, \sum_{s=1}^{q} v_s(z_s)\right).$$

Hint: Since $\hat{c}_0 - c_0 = O_p(n^{-1/2}) = o_p((nh)^{-1/2})$, one can replace $\hat{c}_0$ by c_0 without changing the asymptotic distribution of $\hat{g}(z)$. Also, use the fact that $\hat{g}_\alpha(z_\alpha)$ and $\hat{g}_s(z_s)$ are asymptotically independent of one another for $\alpha \neq s$.

Exercise 9.2. Show that $\hat{\Omega}_z = \hat{M}_z^{-1} \hat{V}_z \hat{M}_z^{-1}$ is a consistent estimator for Ω_z defined in Theorem 9.3, where $\hat{M}_z = n^{-1} \sum_i X_i X_i' K_{h,z_i,z}$ with

$$K_{h,z_i,z} \equiv \prod_{s=1}^{q} h_s^{-1} k\left(\frac{Z_{is} - z_s}{h_s}\right),$$

$$\hat{V}_z = (h_1 \ldots h_q/n) \sum_{i=1}^{n} X_i X_i' \hat{u}_i^2 K_{h,z_i,z}^2,$$

and $\hat{u}_i = Y_i - X_i' \hat{\beta}(Z_i)$.

Exercise 9.3. Construct a consistent estimator for the asymptotic variance V defined in (9.71).

Hint: No proof is needed. Construct consistent estimators of A and B, respectively, say $\hat{A}$ and $\hat{B}$, then $\hat{V} = \hat{A}^{-1} \hat{B} \hat{A}^{-1}$. Note that $\beta_w(z_i)$ can be consistently estimated from the semiparametric varying coefficient model

$$W_i = X_i' \beta_w(Z_i) + \text{ error},$$

so that $\hat{\beta}_w(Z_i) = [\sum_{j=1}^{n} X_j X_j' K_{h,z_i,z_j}]^{-1} \sum_{j=1}^{n} X_j W_j K_{h,z_i,z_j}$.

Exercise 9.4. Prove the first part of (9.65), i.e., show that

$$E[\mathbf{S}_{n,j}(z)] \to f(z)\Omega(z)\mu_j$$

for $j = 0, 1, 2$.

Chapter 10

Selectivity Models

Sample selection issues frequently arise in the course of applied work. For instance, in the medical field, those who elect to enroll in clinical trials may be more (or less) likely to respond to a treatment than someone randomly selected from the general population due to, say, past treatment. In the social sciences, analogous situations arise when those who, say, elect to enroll in a job training program are more (or less) likely to benefit from the program than a randomly selected individual. In either case, one might worry that the impact of the treatment (training) for those who "selected into" a program will differ from persons randomly selected from the general population, hence the measured treatment effect may be confounded by the nonrepresentative sample used for analysis. Or the researcher may be interested in the extent to which socioeconomic characteristics affect some outcome of interest, again worrying whether the impact of such characteristics based on the subsample will hold for the general population.

Pioneering parametric approaches for dealing with sample selectivity can be found in Heckman (1976, 1979), who suggested a widely used procedure in which a process describing the outcome is implemented and information from this is used, in a second stage, to obtain consistent estimates of the relevant parameters. Many ingenious methods have been proposed for dealing with sample selectivity, and in this chapter we consider a number of semiparametric and nonparametric approaches that have been proposed to handle its presence.

10.1   Semiparametric Type-2 Tobit Models

Consider the following set of latent variable equations:

$$Y_{1i}^* = X_{1i}'\beta_1 + u_{1i}, \tag{10.1}$$
$$Y_{2i}^* = X_{2i}'\beta_2 + u_{2i}, \tag{10.2}$$

where Y_{1i}^* and Y_{2i}^* are (unobservable) latent variables. The observed dependent variables are Y_{1i} and Y_{2i} defined as

$$Y_{1i} = \mathbf{1}(Y_{1i}* > 0), \tag{10.3}$$
$$Y_{2i} = Y_{2i}^*\mathbf{1}(Y_{i1} = 1), \tag{10.4}$$

where $\mathbf{1}(A)$ represents the indicator function of the event A. We only observe the sign of Y_{1i}^*, and we observe Y_{2i} only when $Y_{1i} = 1$ ($Y_{1i}^* > 0$), (X_{1i}, X_{2i}) are always observed. Equations (10.1) through (10.4) are termed "Type-2" Tobit models in the econometrics literature. A typical application for these models arises when modeling labor supply decisions, which we briefly describe by way of example. In the labor supply context, if $Y_{1i} = 1$, the individual enters the labor force, and Y_{1i}^* would be the optimal number of working hours. However, we do not observe Y_{1i}^*'s exact value even when the individual works. The individual will remain out of the labor force if $Y_{1i}* \leq 0$. Y_{2i} is individual's (logarithm) wage, which we observe only when the individual works ($Y_{1i} = 1$). The covariates (X_{1i}, X_{2i}) contain observable characteristics on individual workers.

Interest lies in estimating (10.2), bearing in mind that Y_{2i} is observed only when $Y_{i1} = 1$. The expectation of Y_{2i} conditional on $Y_{1i} = 1$ and X_i is therefore

$$E(Y_{2i}|X_i, Y_{1i} = 1) = X_{2i}'\beta_2 + E(u_{2i}|X_i, Y_{1i} = 1), \tag{10.5}$$

which, combined with (10.2), gives

$$Y_{2i} = X_{2i}'\beta_2 + E(u_{2i}|X_i, Y_{1i} = 1) + \epsilon_{2i}, \tag{10.6}$$

where $\epsilon_{2i} = Y_{2i} - E(Y_{2i}|X_i, Y_{1i} = 1)$ so that $E(\epsilon_{2i}|X_i, Y_{1i} = 1) = 0$. Hence, one can estimate β_2 from (10.6) provided that $E(Y_{2i}|X_i, Y_{1i} = 1)$ can be consistently estimated. In a parametric framework, one usually assumes that (u_{1i}, u_{2i}) has a joint normal distribution $N(0, \Sigma)$, where

$$\Sigma = \begin{pmatrix} \sigma_{11} & \sigma_{12} \\ \sigma_{21} & \sigma_{22} \end{pmatrix}.$$

Then it can be shown that (see Exercise 10.1)

$$E(u_{2i}|X_i, Y_{1i} = 1) = \sigma_{11}^{-1/2}\sigma_{12}\phi(X_{1i}'\beta_1/\sigma_{11}^{1/2})\Phi^{-1}(X_{1i}'\beta_1/\sigma_{11}^{1/2}), \quad (10.7)$$

where $\phi(\cdot)$ and $\Phi(\cdot)$ are the PDF and CDF of a standard normal variable (Amemiya (1985, p. 367)). Substituting (10.7) into (10.6) leads to an equation which can be used to estimate β_2 either by a two-stage procedure as suggested by Heckman (1974, 1979), or by maximum likelihood methods; see Pagan and Ullah (1999, p. 303) for a detailed comparison of parametric two-stage and maximum likelihood estimation methods.

10.2 Estimation of a Semiparametric Type-2 Tobit Model

Without imposing parametric distributional assumptions on the joint distribution of u_{1i} and u_{2i}, under the assumption that X_i is independent of (u_{1i}, u_{2i}), one can obtain the following results:

$$\begin{aligned} E(u_{2i}|X_i, Y_{1i} = 1) &= E(u_{2i}|X_i, u_{1i} > -X_{1i}'\beta_1) \\ &= g(X_{1i}'\beta_1), \end{aligned} \quad (10.8)$$

where $g(z) = E(u_{2i}|u_{1i} > -z) = 1 - F_{u_2|u_1}(-z)$, and $F_{u_2|u_1}$ is the conditional CDF of u_{2i} given u_{1i}. Thus, the functional form of $g(\cdot)$ is unknown. Substituting (10.8) into (10.6) yields

$$Y_{2i} = X_{2i}'\beta_2 + g(X_{1i}'\beta_1) + u_{2i}. \quad (10.9)$$

Equation (10.9) is a partially linear single index model. Powell (1987) suggests a two-step estimation procedure to estimate (10.9) where one first estimates β_1 by, say, Powell's (1984) CLAD estimator outlined in Section 11.2, which we denote by $\tilde{\beta}_1$, and then one proceeds to estimate β_2 along the lines of Robinson's (1988) approach discussed in Chapter 7, except that now $X_{1i}'\tilde{\beta}$ is a generated regressor, therefore, the asymptotic variance will differ from the result presented in Chapter 7. Equation (10.9) is a special case of the semiparametric multi-index model considered by Ichimura and Lee (1991), and it is also covered by the general semiparametric model considered in Ai (1997). Identification conditions are, however, required when using this approach. As was the case for the partially linear model discussed in Chapter 7, we know that an intercept term is not identified in (10.9), hence the potential intercept term has to be incorporated into $g(\cdot)$. Also, identification conditions for a single index model discussed in Chapter 8 are required in order for β_1 to be identified.

Letting $\theta = (\beta_1', \beta_2')'$, Ichimura and Lee (1991) propose estimating θ by minimizing the objective function

$$Q_n(\theta) = \frac{1}{n} \sum_{i=1}^{n} \mathbf{1}(X_i \in \mathcal{X}) \left[Y_i - X_{2i}'\beta_2 - \hat{g}(X_i'\beta_1) \right]^2,$$

where

$$\hat{g}(X_{1i}'\beta_1) = \frac{\sum_{j=1}^{n} [Y_{2j} - X_{2j}'\beta_2] K_h((X_{1i} - X_{1j})'\beta_1/h)}{\sum_{j=1}^{n} K_h((X_{1i} - X_{1j})'\beta_1/h)},$$

which is a kernel estimator of $E[Y_{2i} - X_{2i}'\beta_2 | X_{1i}'\beta_1]$, and where $K_h(v) = h^{-1}K(v/h)$, and $\mathcal{X}$ is a trimming set discussed in Chapter 8. Letting $\hat{\theta}$ denote the resulting estimator of θ, under regularity conditions similar to those given in Chapter 8, Ichimura and Lee derive the following result:

$$\sqrt{n}(\hat{\theta} - \theta) \xrightarrow{d} N(0, A^{-1}\Sigma A^{-1}), \qquad (10.10)$$

where $A = E[\mathbf{1}(X_i \in \mathcal{X})\Delta(X_i)\Delta(X_i)']$, $\Sigma = E(u_{2i}^2 B_i B_i')$, $B_i = \mathbf{1}(X_i \in \mathcal{X}) - E[\mathbf{1}(X_i \in \mathcal{X})|X_{1i}'\beta_1]$, and $\Delta(X_i) = X_{2i}[X_{2i} - E(X_{2i}|X_{1i}'\beta_1)]' + X_{1i}[X_{1i} - E(X_{1i}|X_{1i}'\beta_1)]'g(X_{1i}'\beta_1)$. Ichimura and Lee (1991, p. 21) also provide consistent estimators for A and Σ.

10.2.1 Gallant and Nychka's Estimator

Gallant and Nychka (1987) suggest approximating the joint density of $f(u_1, u_2)$ by a series expansion, where (u_1, u_2) are the error terms defined in (10.1) and (10.2). They propose approximating $f(.,.)$ by

$$\tilde{f}(u_{1i}, u_{2i}) = \exp\left[-u_{1i}^2/(2\sigma_1^2) - u_{2i}^2/(2\sigma_2^2) \right] \left[\sum_{j=0}^{K} \sum_{k=0}^{K} \gamma_{jk} u_{1i}^j u_{2i}^k \right].$$
$$(10.11)$$

The idea is to use a joint normal expression as a baseline distribution, accompanied by a power series expansion allowing for a general form of the CDF. Using the above joint density formula, one can compute $f(u_{2i}|u_{2i})$ and then construct a log-likelihood function and obtain estimates for β_1 and other parameters by maximizing the log-likelihood function. Gallant and Nychka established the consistency of their proposed estimator under the conditions $K \to \infty$ and $K/n \to 0$

as $n \to \infty$. Coppejans and Gallant (2002) show that one can use data-driven methods to select the power series expansion terms when estimating $f(u_1, u_2)$.

Newey (1999) proposes an alternative two-step series-based estimation method in which one first estimates β_1 efficiently and then estimates β_2 by solving an efficient score equation. Pagan and Ullah (1999, pp. 311–314) provide a detailed discussion of Newey's series-based estimation method and its asymptotic distribution. We discuss general series methods in Chapter 15.

10.2.2   Estimation of the Intercept in Selection Models

As discussed earlier, estimation methods based on (10.9) cannot identify an intercept since it cannot be separated from the function $g(\cdot)$. If one is mainly interested in the partial effect of X_i on Y_{2i}, then the intercept is irrelevant. However, the intercept may also be of interest in other cases: when determining "wage gaps" between unionized and nonunionized workers, decomposing wage differentials between different socioeconomic groups, and so forth. Letting μ denote the intercept, we write $X_{2i} = (1, \tilde{X}_{2i}')'$ and $\beta_2 = (\mu, \delta')'$. Heckman (1990) suggests estimating the intercept μ by averaging those observations for which $E(u_{2i}|Y_{1i} = 1) = g(X_{1i}'\beta_1)$ is zero. This leads to

$$\tilde{\mu} = \frac{\sum_{i=1}^{n}(Y_{2i} - \tilde{X}_{2i}'\hat{\delta})Y_{1i}\mathbf{1}(X_{1i}'\hat{\beta}_1 > \gamma_n)}{\sum_{i=1}^{n} Y_{1i}\mathbf{1}(X_{1i}'\hat{\beta}_1 > \gamma_n)},$$

where γ_n is a bandwidth satisfying $\gamma_n \to \infty$ as $n \to \infty$.

Because the indicator function $\mathbf{1}(\cdot)$ is not differentiable, it is difficult to examine the asymptotic distribution of $\tilde{\mu}$ defined above. Andrews and Schafgans (1998) suggest replacing the indicator function in $\tilde{\mu}$ with a smoothed nondecreasing CDF function which satisfies the conditions $s(z) = 0$ for $z \leq 0$, $s(z) = 1$ for $z \geq b$ for some $0 < b < \infty$, and $s(\cdot)$ having three bounded derivatives. Andrews and Schafgans propose estimating μ by

$$\hat{\mu} = \frac{\sum_{i=1}^{n}(Y_{2i} - \tilde{X}_{2i}'\hat{\delta})Y_{1i}s(X_{1i}'\hat{\beta}_1 > \gamma_n)}{\sum_{i=1}^{n} Y_{1i}s(X_{1i}'\hat{\beta}_1 > \gamma_n)}.$$

Andrews and Schafgans (1998) prove consistency and derive the asymptotic distribution of $\hat{\mu}$. The rate of convergence of $\hat{\mu} - \mu$ (to zero) depends on the distribution of $v_i = X'_{1i}\beta_1$. In some cases, the rate of convergence can be arbitrarily close to $n^{-1/2}$.

Other methods for estimating semiparametric Type-2 Tobit models include the series-based estimators of Newey (1991a, 1999), the approximate likelihood-based estimator of Cosslett (1983), and the kernel-based partially linear single index model estimator of Powell (1987).

10.3   Semiparametric Type-3 Tobit Models

In this section we study the semiparametric estimation of a Type-2 Tobit model which is defined in Section 10.3.1 below. Vella (1992) proposes a test for sample selection bias using a Type-3 Tobit residual as a generated regressor. Using a similar idea, Wooldridge (1994) proposed a two-stage estimator which is simple to use and is more robust than Heckman's (1979) procedure. Li and Wooldridge (2002) generalized Wooldridge's method to allow for nonnormality in the error distribution, which results in a semiparametric partially linear model having generated regressors that enter the model nonparametrically. Alternative semiparametric two-stage methods that do not require knowledge of the error distribution have been proposed by various authors including Chen (1997), Honoré, Kyriazidou and Udry (1997), and Lee (1994).

10.3.1   Econometric Preliminaries

Consider the Type-3 Tobit model defined by the latent variables

$$Y_1^* = X'_1\beta_1 + u_1, \qquad\qquad (10.12)$$
$$Y_2^* = X'_2\beta_2 + u_2, \qquad\qquad (10.13)$$

where the first equation is the selection equation and the second equation is the main equation of interest. The dependent variable Y_2^* can be observed only when the selection variable Y_1^* is positive. Thus we observe Y_1 and Y_2 which satisfy

$$Y_1 = \max\{Y_1^*, 0\}, \qquad\qquad (10.14)$$
$$Y_2 = Y_2^* \mathbf{1}(Y_1 > 0), \qquad\qquad (10.15)$$

where Y_1 and Y_2 are the observable dependent variables, X_1 and X_2 are vectors of exogenous variables with dimension p_1 and p_2 respectively, and β_1 and β_2 are conformable column vectors of unknown parameters. In, say, labor market applications, Y_1 would be the working hours of an individual and Y_2 the (logarithm of the) hourly wage rate. In contrast to the Type-2 Tobit model discussed in Section 10.1, here one observes working hours when it is positive, whereas in a Type-2 Tobit model, one knows only whether working hours are positive or zero, i.e., one does not observe the exact number of working hours.

Under the selection rule described by (10.14) and (10.15), we have

$$\mathrm{E}(Y_2^*|X_1, X_2, Y_1^* > 0) = X_2'\beta_2 + \mathrm{E}(u_2|u_1 > -X_1'\beta_1, X_1, X_2). \quad (10.16)$$

Hence, the least squares method of regressing Y_2 on X_2 yields an inconsistent estimator of β_2 if the second term on the right-hand side of (10.16) is nonzero. Under the assumption of the joint normality of (u_1, u_2), Heckman (1976, 1979) proposed a simple two-stage method to estimate Type-2 or Type-3 Tobit models. Heckman's suggestion was to restore a zero conditional mean in (10.15) by including an estimate of the selection bias term, $\mathrm{E}(u_2|u_1 > -X_1'\beta_1, X_1, X_2)$. Under normality, this term is proportional to the inverse Mills ratio and depends only on the unknown parameters of (10.12), which can be estimated by a Probit or Tobit maximum likelihood method.

Vella (1992, 1993) and Wooldridge (1994) suggest alternative two-stage estimation methods that may have better finite-sample properties. Under the assumption that (X_1, X_2) are independent of (u_1, u_2), they note that $\mathrm{E}(u_2|x, u_1, Y_1 > 0) = \mathrm{E}(u_2|u_1, Y_1 > 0)$. If one further assumes that $\mathrm{E}(u_2|u_1) = \gamma_1 u_1$, then the selection bias correction term is $\gamma_1 u_1$. One can estimate u_1 by $\hat{u}_1 = Y_1 - X_1'\hat{\beta}_1$, where $\hat{\beta}_1$ is the Tobit estimator of β_1. Thus one can use u_1, rather than Heckman's (1979) inverse Mills ratio, as an additional variable in the conditional expectation. The advantage is that even when X_2 and the inverse Mills ratio are nearly collinear, u_1 has more variation than X_2, thereby rendering the Vella-Wooldridge estimator more stable and therefore more efficient; see Wooldridge (2002, p. 573) for further details.

There is no need to assume that the joint distribution of (u_1, u_2) is known, or to assume that $\mathrm{E}(u_2|u_1) = \gamma_1 u_1$. When the joint distribution of (u_1, u_2) is unknown, one has $\mathrm{E}(u_2|u_1) = g(u_1)$, where $g(\cdot)$ is an unknown function. In this case one can easily show that $\mathrm{E}(Y_{2i}|X_i, u_{1i}) = X_{2i}'\beta_2 + g(u_{1i})$. Thus we have

$$Y_{2i} = X_{2i}'\beta_2 + g(u_{1i}) + v_{2i}, \quad (10.17)$$

where v_{2i} satisfies $\mathrm{E}(v_{2i}|u_{1i}, Y_{1i} > 0) = 0$.

Following Robinson (1988) and using those observations for which $Y_{1i} > 0$, from (10.17) we get

$$Y_{2i} - \mathrm{E}(Y_{2i}|u_{1i}) = [X_{2i} - \mathrm{E}(X_2|u_{1i})]'\beta_2 + v_{2i} \qquad (10.18)$$

or, alternatively, a density-weighted counterpart,

$$[Y_{2i} - \mathrm{E}(Y_{2i}|u_{1i})]f_i = f_i[X_{2i} - \mathrm{E}(X_2|u_{1i})]'\beta_2 + f_i v_{2i}, \qquad (10.19)$$

where $f_i = f(u_{1i})$ is the PDF of u_1.

Li and Wooldridge (2002) suggest a multistep method to estimate β_2, which proceeds as follows:

(i) Estimate u_{1i} by $\hat{u}_{1i} = Y_{1i} - X_{1i}\hat{\beta}_1$, where $\hat{\beta}_1$ is a first stage estimator of β_1.

(ii) Use $\{Y_{2i}, X_{2i}, \hat{u}_{1i}\}_{i=1}^{n_1}$ to obtain nonparametric kernel estimates of $\mathrm{E}(Y_{2i}|u_{1i})$ and $\mathrm{E}(X_{2i}|u_{1i})$, say, $\hat{Y}_{2i} = \hat{\mathrm{E}}(Y_{2i}|\hat{u}_{1i})$ and $\hat{X}_{2i} = \hat{\mathrm{E}}(Y_{xi}|\hat{u}_{1i})$.

(iii) Apply a least squares method to estimate β_2 based on (10.18) (e.g., Robinson (1988)), i.e.,

$$\hat{\beta}_2 = \left[\sum_{i=1}^n (X_{2i} - \hat{X}_{2i})(X_{2i} - \hat{X}_{2i})'\right]^{-1} \sum_{i=1}^n (X_{2i} - \hat{X}_{2i})(Y_{2i} - \hat{Y}_{2i}).$$

We assume that for the first stage, there is a $\sqrt{n}$-consistent and asymptotic normally distributed estimator for β_1, say $\hat{\beta}_1$, which is characterized by the following equation:

$$\sqrt{n}\left(\hat{\beta}_1 - \beta_1\right) = \frac{1}{\sqrt{n}}\sum_{i=1}^n r_i + o_p(1) \to N(0, \Omega_2) \text{ in distribution,}$$

$$(10.20)$$

where $\Omega_2 = \mathrm{E}[r_i r_i']$, and where $\hat{r}_i$ is an estimator of r_i; hence, $\hat{\Omega}_2 = n^{-1}\sum_i \hat{r}_i \hat{r}_i'$ is a consistent estimator of Ω_2.

For example, Powell's (1984) CLAD estimator satisfies (10.20) and is defined by

$$\hat{\beta}_1 = \arg\min_{\beta_1} \frac{1}{n}\sum_{i=1}^n |Y_{1i} - \max\{0, X_{1i}'\beta_1\}|. \qquad (10.21)$$

For this case, the specific definitions of r_i (defined in (10.20) and $\hat{\Omega}$ are given in Powell (1984)).

Li and Wooldridge (2002) established the $\sqrt{n}$-normality of their estimator for β_2, which is given by

$$\sqrt{n}\left(\hat{\beta}_2 - \beta_2\right) \to N(0, \Sigma) \text{ in distribution},$$

where $\Sigma = \Phi^{-1}[\Omega_1 + \Psi\Omega_2\Psi']\Phi^{-1}$, $\Phi = \mathrm{E}[v_i'v_if_i^2]$, $v_i = X_{2i} - \xi_i$, $\xi_i = \mathrm{E}(X_{2i}|u_{1i})$, $\Psi = \mathrm{E}\{v_if^2(u_{1i})g^{(1)}(u_{1i})[X_{1i} - \mathrm{E}(X_{1i}|u_{1i})]\}$, $\Omega_1 = \mathrm{E}[v_i'v_i\sigma_u^2(X_{2i}, u_{1i})f_i^4]$, $u_{1i} = Y_{1i} - X_{1i}'\beta_1$, $g^{(1)}(u_1) = dg(u_1)/du_1$, and Ω_2 is given in (10.20).

Li and Wooldridge (2002) also provide a consistent estimator for the asymptotic variance Σ and further derive the semiparametric efficiency bound for this model. The above multistep method is not semiparametrically efficient in the sense that the difference between Σ and the semiparametric lower bound is a positive definite matrix. Efficient estimation can usually be achieved by a one-step procedure, where β_1 and β_2 are estimated simultaneously as in Ai (1997).

In the approach outlined above, the generated regressor is estimated from a parametric model. Ahn and Powell (1993) consider a more general case where the generated regressor is estimated from a nonparametric regression model. Their method can also be used to estimate β_2 in the semiparametric Type-3 Tobit model.

10.3.2 Alternative Estimation Methods

A number of authors have also suggested the semiparametric estimation of Type-3 Tobit models without requiring knowledge of the joint distribution of (u_1, u_2); see Chen (1997), Honoré et al. (1997), and Lee (1994), among others. Below, we briefly discuss some of the these estimators.

Chen (1997) observes that under the condition that (u_1, u_2) is independent of (X_1, X_2),

$$\mathrm{E}(Y_2|X_1, X_2, u_1 > 0, X_1'\beta_1 > 0, Y_1 > 0) = \mathrm{E}(Y_2|u_1 > 0, x) = X_2'\beta_2 + \alpha_0, \tag{10.22}$$

where α_0 is a constant. However, α_0 is not the intercept of the original model because an intercept is not identified without further assumptions. Based on (10.22), Chen then suggests a simple least squares procedure applied to a trimmed subsample to estimate β_2 by

$$\hat{\beta}_{2,Chen} = \arg\min_{\beta_2,\alpha} \frac{1}{n} \sum_{i=1}^{n} \mathbf{1}_{\{Y_{1i}-X'_{1i}\hat{\beta}_1>0, X'_{1i}\hat{\beta}_1>0\}} (Y_{2i} - X'_{2i}\beta_2 - \alpha)^2,$$

(10.23)

where $\hat{\beta}_1$ is a $\sqrt{n}$-consistent estimator of β_1 in a first step, say the estimator proposed by Honoré and Powell (1994), or Powell's (1984) CLAD estimator. As discussed in Chen, one problem with the estimator given by (10.23) is that it may trim out too many observations and hence lead to inefficient estimation. Chen therefore suggests an alternative estimator that trims far fewer data points in finite-sample applications (see equation (11) of Chen (1997) for details).

Honoré et al. (1997) consider an alternative approach. To relax the normality assumption of Heckman (1979), Honoré et al. consider the case where the underlying errors are symmetrically distributed conditional on the regressors, with arbitrary heteroskedasticity permitted. The effect of sample selection in this case is that the errors are no longer symmetrically distributed conditional on the sample selection. Honoré et al. note that if one estimates β_2 using observations for which $-X'_1\beta_1 < u_1 < X'_1\beta_1$ (which is equivalent to $0 < Y_1 < 2X'_1\beta_1$), then u_2 is symmetrically distributed around 0. Hence, the following least absolute deviations estimator consistently estimates β_2:

$$\hat{\beta}_{2,\text{HKU}} = \arg\min_{\beta_2} \frac{1}{n} \sum_{i=1}^{n} \mathbf{1}_{\{0<Y_{1i}<2X'_{1i}\hat{\beta}_1\}} |Y_{2i} - X'_{2i}\beta_2|,$$

(10.24)

where $\hat{\beta}_1$ is a first stage $\sqrt{n}$-consistent estimator of β_1 such as Powell's (1984) CLAD estimator. Honoré et al. also establish the $\sqrt{n}$-normality of their proposed estimator $\hat{\beta}_{2,\text{HKU}}$.

Under the assumption of independence between the errors and the regressors, Lee (1994, equation 2.12) shows that

$$\begin{aligned} Y_{2i} - \mathrm{E}(Y_2|u_1 > -X'_{1i}\beta_1, X'_1\beta > X'_{1i}\beta_1) \\ = [X'_{2i} - \mathrm{E}(X'_2|X'_1\beta_1 > X'_{1i}\beta_1)]\beta_2 + u_{2i}, \end{aligned}$$

(10.25)

where u_{2i} satisfies $\mathrm{E}(u_{2i}|u_1 > -X'_{1i}\beta_1, X'_1\beta > X'_{1i}\beta_1) = 0$. Lee suggests first replacing the conditional expectations in (10.25) by kernel estimators (also β_1 needs to be replaced by a first stage estimator) and then applying a least squares procedure to estimate β_2 (which we denote by $\hat{\beta}_{2,Lee}$). Lee establishes the asymptotic normality of $\hat{\beta}_{2,Lee}$.

Chen's (1997) and Honoré et al.'s (1997) methods do not require nonparametric techniques, while Li and Wooldridge (2002) and Lee (1994) use nonparametric kernel methods. While nonparametric kernel methods are, in general, sensitive to the choice of smoothing parameters, Monte Carlo simulations reported in Lee and Min, Sheu and Wang (2003) suggest that the estimators of Lee and Li and Wooldridge are fairly insensitive to the choice of smoothing parameter. The reason is that the semiparametric estimator β_2 depends on the *average* of the nonparametric estimators, and an *average* nonparametric estimator is less sensitive to different values of the smoothing parameters than, say, a pointwise nonparametric kernel estimator.

One can also use a semiparametric Type-2 Tobit model where one uses Ichimura's (1993) semiparametric nonlinear least squares method to estimate β_1 based on a single index model with, say, a binary labor force participation variable. Using only data for which $Y_{1i} > 0$, the corresponding semiparametric wage equation is a partially linear single index model (see Ichimura and Lee (1991)) of the form

$$Y_{2i} = X'_{2i}\beta_2 + \theta(X'_{1i}\beta_1) + \eta_{2i}, \tag{10.26}$$

where $\theta(X'_{1i}\beta_1) = \mathrm{E}(u_2 | u_1 > -X'_{1i}\beta)$ is of unknown functional form, and η_{2i} satisfies the condition $\mathrm{E}(\eta_{2i}|X_i) = 0$. Ichimura and Lee propose a semiparametric nonlinear least squares method to estimate (10.26) and they established the asymptotic distribution of their proposed estimator.

We direct the interested reader to Christofides, Li, Liu and Min (2003), who considered the relative performance of five semiparametric estimators in an applied setting. The estimators used were (i) Chen's (1997) semiparametric estimator, (ii) Honoré et al.'s (1997) semiparametric estimator, (iii) Lee's (1994) semiparametric estimator, (iv) Li and Wooldridge's (2002) semiparametric estimator, and (v) the semiparametric Type-2 Tobit estimator based on Ichimura (1993) and Ichimura and Lee (1991). Note that Honoré et al. require that u_2 have a (conditional) symmetric distribution, but they do not require (u_1, u_2) to be independent of (X_1, X_2); on the other hand, Chen, Ichimura, Ichimura and Lee, Lee, and Li and Wooldridge assume that (u_1, u_2) is independent of (X_1, X_2), but u_2 need not be symmetrically distributed. The symmetry condition is neither weaker nor stronger than the independence condition.

Turning to tests for selection bias, we consider testing for no selection bias, or for parametric selection bias as described in Vella (1992) and Wooldridge (1994), against general semiparametric selection bias as described in Li and Wooldridge (2002). Let H_0^a denote the null hypothesis of no selection bias. If H_0^a is rejected, it is necessary to test whether the parametric selection model is adequate, that is, whether H_0^b: $\mathrm{E}(u_2|u_1) = u_1\gamma$ a.e. If the errors are normally distributed, then $g(u_1) = u_1\gamma$ and one can test for no selection bias by testing whether $\gamma = 0$. However, when $g(u_1) \neq u_1\gamma$, the parametric test for no selection bias based upon testing $\gamma = 0$ can give misleading results because two types of mistakes can occur. First, when H_0^a is true, the parametric test may reject the null hypothesis when $g(u_1) \neq u_1\gamma$. Second, when H_0^a is false, the parametric test can have no power, even as the sample size tends to infinity, because it is not a consistent test (see Chapter 12 for the definition of a consistent test).

The test statistic we describe below is robust to distributional assumptions regarding (u_1, u_2). That is, no matter what the joint distribution of (u_1, u_2) is, if there is selection bias, the probability of detecting this will converge to one as the sample size goes to infinity. The null hypothesis of no selection bias (H_0^a) can be stated as $\mathrm{E}(u_2|u_1) = 0$. The alternative hypothesis (H_1^a) can be stated as $\mathrm{E}(u_2|u_1) \equiv g(u_1) \neq 0$. If H_0^a is true, then the ordinary least squares regression of the observed Y_2 on X_2 gives a consistent estimator for β_2 under H_0^a (which we denote by $\hat{\beta}_{2,ols}$), and the least squares residual, $\hat{u}_{2i} = Y_{2i} - X_{2i}'\hat{\beta}_{2,ols}$, is a consistent estimator of u_{2i} (under H_0^a). Like the test statistic for parametric model specification proposed by Li and Wang (1998) and Zheng (1996) (see Chapter 12 for a more detailed discussion of this type of test), a test statistic for H_0^a is given by

$$\tilde{I}_n^a = \frac{1}{n_1(n_1 - 1)} \sum_{i=1}^{n_1} \sum_{j \neq i, j=1}^{n_1} \hat{u}_{2i}\hat{u}_{2j}K_h\left(\hat{u}_{1i} - \hat{u}_{1j}\right), \qquad (10.27)$$

where n_1 denotes the the sample size of the observed sample (i.e., observations with $Y_{2i} > 0$) and $\hat{u}_{1i} = Y_{1i} - X_{1i}'\hat{\beta}_1$.

We now provide some regularity conditions under which one can derive the asymptotic distribution of $\tilde{I}_n^a$, as well as another test, I_n^b, defined below.

Condition 10.1. $(Y_{2i}, X_i, u_{1i}, u_{2i})$ *are i.i.d. as* (Y_2, x, u_1, u_2). x, u_1 *and* u_2 *all have finite fourth moments.* $\partial g(u_1)/\partial u_1$, $\partial^2 g(u_1)/\partial u_1^2$ *are continuous in* u_1 *and dominated by a function (say* $M(u_1)$*) with finite second moment.* $\hat{\beta}_1 - \beta_1 = O_p(n^{-1/2})$.

Condition 10.2. *The kernel function $K(\cdot)$ is bounded, symmetric and three times differentiable with bounded derivative functions. $\int K(v)dv = 1$ and $\int K(v)v^4 dv < \infty$.*

Condition 10.3. *As $n_1 \to \infty$, $h \to 0$ and $n_1 h \to \infty$.*

Drawing on proofs in Theorem 12.1 of Chapter 12, one can show that

Proposition 10.1. *Under Conditions 10.1 to 10.3, we have (as $n_1 \to \infty$)*

(i) *If H_0^a is true,*

$$n_1 h^{1/2} \tilde{I}_n^a / \hat{\sigma}_a \xrightarrow{d} N(0,1).$$

(ii) *If H_1^a is true,*

$$\mathrm{P}\left[|n_1 h^{1/2} \tilde{I}_n^a / \hat{\sigma}_a| > C\right] \to 1, \text{ for any } C > 0,$$

where $\hat{\sigma}_a^2 = \frac{2h}{n_1(n_1-1)} \sum_{i=1}^{n_1} \sum_{j \neq i}^{n_1} \hat{u}_{2i}^2 \hat{u}_{2j}^2 K_h^2 (\hat{u}_{1i} - \hat{u}_{1j}).$

If H_0^a is rejected, one should estimate either a parametric or a semiparametric selection model. It is, therefore, important to test whether the parametric model is appropriate. The null hypothesis of correct parametric specification can be stated as H_0^b: $\mathrm{E}(Y_2|X_2, u_1) = X_2'\beta_2 + u_1\gamma$, and the alternative hypothesis is that $\mathrm{E}(Y_2|X_2, u_1) = X_2'\beta_2 + g(u_1)$ with $g(u_1) \neq u_1\gamma$. Thus, it is necessary to test a linear regression model versus a partially linear regression model. Li and Wang (1998) propose just such a test when u_1 is observable. Replacing u_{1i} by $\hat{u}_{1i} = Y_{1i} - X_{1i}'\hat{\beta}_1$ in the test proposed by Li and Wang will give a valid method for testing H_0^b versus H_1^b. Let $\tilde{u}_{2i} = Y_{2i} - X_{2i}'\hat{\beta}_2 - \hat{u}_{1i}\hat{\gamma}$, where $\hat{\beta}_2$ is the semiparametric estimator of β_2 as suggested in Li and Wooldridge (2002) and $\hat{\gamma}$ is the ordinary least squares estimator of γ based on $Y_{2i} = X_{2i}'\beta_2 + \hat{u}_{1i}\gamma +$ error. Then the test statistic is given by

$$\tilde{I}_n^b = \frac{1}{n_1(n_1-1)} \sum_{i=1}^{n_1} \sum_{j \neq i, j=1}^{n_1} \tilde{u}_{2i} \tilde{u}_{2j} K_h (\hat{u}_{1i} - \hat{u}_{1j}).$$

Proposition 10.2. *Under Conditions 10.1 to 10.3, we have (as $n_1 \to \infty$)*

(i) *If H_0^b is true, $n_1 h^{1/2} \tilde{I}_n^b / \hat{\sigma}_b \xrightarrow{d} N(0,1)$.*

(ii) If H_1^b is true, $\mathrm{P}\left[|n_1 h^{1/2} \tilde{I}_n^b / \hat{\sigma}_b| > c\right] \to 1$, for any $c > 0$, where
$$\hat{\sigma}_b^2 = \frac{2h}{n_1(n_1-1)} \sum_{i=1}^{n_1} \sum_{j \neq i}^{n_1} \tilde{u}_{2i}^2 \tilde{u}_{2j}^2 K_h^2 (\hat{u}_{1i} - \hat{u}_{1j}).$$

The proof of Proposition 10.2 is similar to the proof of Theorem 12.1 of Chapter 12, and is thus omitted here.

Note that both $\tilde{I}_n^a$ and $\tilde{I}_n^b$ involve only one-dimensional kernel estimation and thus do not suffer from the curse of dimensionality. When dealing with large datasets, the test statistics $\tilde{I}_n^a$ and $\tilde{I}_n^b$ should provide powerful ways of detecting possible sample selection bias and determining whether a semiparametric selection model is needed to correct for this bias.

It should be mentioned that the above tests are designed to test for no selection bias or parametric selection bias under the maintained assumption that the model is linear and additive. If the linearity or additivity assumptions fail to hold, the $\tilde{I}_n^a$ and $\tilde{I}_n^b$ tests may reject the null models due to these violations. Ideally, one should further test a semiparametric selection model versus a general nonparametric alternative that does not rely on linearity and additivity. However, such a test is likely to suffer from the curse of dimensionality.

10.4   Das, Newey and Vella's Nonparametric Selection Model

Das, Newey and Vella (2003) consider the following nonparametric sample selection problem. Let Y be the dependent variable and X be the vector of right-hand side variables of interest. Suppose that

$$\begin{aligned} Y_i^* &= g(X_i) + \epsilon_i, \\ Y_i &= d_i Y_i^*, \end{aligned} \qquad (10.28)$$

where the functional form of $g(\cdot)$ is not specified, and where ϵ_i is a disturbance and d_i is a binary selection indicator. This generalizes the usual sample selection model by allowing $g(\cdot)$ to have unknown functional form rather than being a linear function of X_i. If d_i and ϵ_i are correlated, one needs to correct for selection bias in order to estimate $g(\cdot)$. Let Z_i denote a vector of variables that determines selection and define $p_i \stackrel{\text{def}}{=} \mathrm{E}(d_i | X_i, Z_i)$ (the propensity score). Das et al. make the following assumptions.

Assumption 10.1.

(i) $\mathrm{E}(\epsilon|X, Z, d = 1) = m(p)$.

(ii) *For any random variables $l(X)$ and $b(p)$, $\mathrm{P}[l(X) + b(p) = 0|d = 1] = 1$ implies that $l(x)$ is a constant.*

Das et al. (2003) show that if $d = \mathbf{1}(\alpha_0(Z) - \eta > 0)$ (the functional form of $\alpha_0(\cdot)$ need not be specified) and (ϵ, η) is independent of (Z, X), then Assumption 10.1 holds true. Assumption 10.1 (i) immediately implies that

$$\mathrm{E}(Y|X, Z, d = 1) = g(X) + m(p). \qquad (10.29)$$

Equation (10.29) identifies $g(\cdot)$ up to an additive constant. One can estimate $g(\cdot)$ by nonparametrically regressing selected (observed) Y on X and p in an additive regression model. Therefore, Das et al. (2003) propose a two-step series-based estimation method for estimating $g(\cdot)$. In the first step one estimates p by estimating the propensity score $p = \mathrm{E}(d|X, Z)$ nonparametrically (say $\hat{p}$), while in the second step, one regresses the observed Y on X and $\hat{p}$ with the additive restriction imposed. The reason for using nonparametric series methods is that it is easy to impose additive restrictions (see Chapter 15 for detailed discussion on series methods). One can also use kernel methods to estimate the additive model (10.29), say by marginal integration or backfitting methods.

Das et al. (2003) further extend their selection model (10.28) to allow for endogeneity of X using the approach presented in Newey, Powell and Vella (1999). Here, we partition $X = (Z_1, X_2)$ and $Z = (Z_1, Z_2)$. The model is given by

$$\begin{aligned}
Y_i^* &= g(Z_{1i}, X_{2i}) + \epsilon_i, \\
X_{2i} &= \pi(Z_{1i}, Z_{2i}) + v_i, \\
Y_i &= d_i Y_i^*.
\end{aligned} \qquad (10.30)$$

Assumption 10.1 is modified as follows.

Assumption 10.2.

(i) $\mathrm{E}(\epsilon|v, Z, d = 1) = m(p, v)$.

(ii) *For any random variables $l(X)$ and $b(p, v)$, $\mathrm{P}[l(X) + b(p, v) = 0|d = 1] = 1$ implies that $l(x)$ is a constant.*

Under assumption 10.2, Das et al. (2003) show that

$$E(Y|X, Z, d = 1) = g(X) + m(p, v). \qquad (10.31)$$

Equation (10.31) provides the basis for estimating $g(\cdot)$. One first estimates p and v based on nonparametric estimators of $E(d|X, Z)$ and $E(X_2|Z)$, respectively (since $p = E(d|X, Z)$ and $v = X_2 - E(X|Z)$). Then one estimates $g(\cdot)$ (along with m) by nonparametric regression of the observed Y on X and (p, v) with the additive restriction imposed, i.e., one estimates (10.31) using Y, X and estimated values of v and p. Das et al. (2003) establish the asymptotic distribution of the resulting estimator. They then apply their proposed method to estimate the impact of education on wages for Australian youth.

10.5 Exercises

Exercise 10.1. Derive (10.7).

Exercise 10.2. Derive (10.17).

Exercise 10.3. Consider $\tilde{I}_n^a$ defined (10.27).

   (i) Show that $\tilde{I}_n^a \xrightarrow{p} 0$ under H_0^a.

   (ii) Show that $\tilde{I}_n^a \xrightarrow{p} C$, where $C > 0$ is a positive constant.

   (iii) Discuss intuitively why $\tilde{I}_n^a$ would be expected to have power if H_0^a is false.

   Hint: The power of a test statistic is defined as the probability that the test rejects H_0 given that H_0 is false.

Chapter 11

Censored Models

Data collected by economists is sometimes incomplete in one way or another. In this chapter we consider one such instance in which data is said to be "censored." Censoring occurs when we do not observe, say, a dependent variable having values above or below some particular value, although we do indeed observe the associated explanatory variables. That is, the observed data on the dependent variable is cut off outside of some range, and multiple observations exist at the endpoints of this range. In such cases, we know both the number of observations for which the dependent variable takes, say, zero values and the value of the explanatory variables for those observations.[1] Strictly speaking, a sample has been censored if no observations have been systematically excluded, but some of the information has been suppressed. Envision a censor who reads your mail and blacks out part of it – you still get your mail, although some parts of it are illegible.

A variety of situations can give rise to censored data. A common source of censoring arises from "top coding" which exists, for example, in publicly available CPS data. For publicly available data, the Census Bureau currently caps the top of the earnings distribution at \$99,999 a year. Thus, all earners above that level appear in the CPS public use database as earning \$99,999 a year, whatever their actual earnings may be. Another example, taken from Long (1997, p. 189), involves a model in which the dependent variable is the prestige of a scientist's first academic job, prestige being rated on a continuous scale in the range $[1.0, 5.0]$. However, the prestige of the job was not available for

---

[1]Truncation, on the other hand, occurs if the observations for both the dependent *and* explanatory variables lying outside some range are totally lost.

graduate programs rated below a 1.0 on the prestige scale or for depart-
ments lacking a graduate program. These records appear as a recorded
prestige of 1.0, whatever the actual prestige might be.

We first consider a popular traditional parametric approach to handling the presence of censoring, which then provides the backdrop for
a number of innovative semiparametric and nonparametric approaches
that have been proposed over the past two decades.

11.1 Parametric Censored Models

Parametric approaches deal with the presence of censoring by providing
an adjustment mechanism that overcomes the bias that would otherwise arise from the direct application of, say, least squares methods.
Often this is accomplished by prescribing a particular PDF for the
model's residuals, which yields a correction term that, when consistently estimated, leads to consistent estimation of the parameters of
interest. We briefly review one popular approach, which then sets the
stage for a range of semiparametric and nonparametric methods that
can be found in the literature.

Consider the "latent variable model" given by

$$Y_i^* = X_i'\beta + \epsilon_i, \quad i = 1, \ldots, n, \tag{11.1}$$

where $X_i \in \mathbb{R}^q$, β is a $q \times 1$ vector of parameters, and ϵ_i is a mean zero
disturbance term. However, we do not observe Y_i^*, rather, we observe
Y_i given by

$$Y_i = \left\{ \begin{array}{ll} Y_i^* & \text{if } Y_i^* > 0 \\ 0 & \text{if } Y_i^* \leq 0 \end{array} \right. \quad i = 1, \ldots, n, \tag{11.2}$$

which is a simple "left-censoring mechanism,"[2] i.e.,

$$Y_i = \max\{X_i'\beta + \epsilon_i, 0\}. \tag{11.3}$$

This model can be readily modified to admit censoring from the right
or both right and left, and it admits nonzero censoring points c by

---

[2]This model is sometimes referred to as the "Tobit model" (Tobin (1958)). Tobin modeled household durable goods expenditure noting that expenditure is not
continuous, purchases being made only when "desire" exceeds a certain level. Expenditures therefore will be nonzero only if the good is actually purchased, households
with no purchases recording zero expenditure. See also Heckman (1976, 1979).

simply subtracting c from Y_i and $X_i'\beta$. For what follows, we assume a left censoring mechanism is present.

We therefore are forced to work with (11.3), i.e., without loss of generality, Y_i is censored at zero and therefore ϵ_i is censored at $-X_i'\beta$ (i.e., $\epsilon_i > -X_i'\beta$). Clearly the mean of Y_i differs from the mean of Y_i^*. For censored data, the variation in the Y_i will understate the variation in the true Y_i^*, and the application of classical least squares methods will, in general, yield parameter estimates that are biased toward zero.

The simplest traditional parametric approaches that deal with censoring estimate β by likelihood methods involving a particular density specification for u_i, the normal being the most common. A popular parametric approach is that of Heckman (1979), who proposed a two-step procedure that involves using only those observations for which $Y_i > 0$. Given n_1 observations for which $Y_i^* > 0$, where $n_1 < n$, the regression equation for these observations is ($Y_i = Y_i^*$ when $Y_i^* > 0$)

$$Y_i = X_i'\beta + \epsilon_i, \quad i = 1, 2, \ldots, n_1.$$

Now consider the conditional expectation of Y_i given that $Y_i^* > 0$, i.e.,

$$\begin{aligned}\mathrm{E}[Y_i|X_i, Y_i > 0] &= X_i'\beta + \mathrm{E}[\epsilon_i|Y_i > 0] \\ &= X_i'\beta + \mathrm{E}[\epsilon_i|\epsilon_i > -X_i'\beta].\end{aligned}$$

The PDF for the disturbance ϵ_i conditional on X_i and $Y_i^* > 0$ (i.e., for $\epsilon_i > -X_i'\beta$) assuming that $\epsilon_i \sim N(0, \sigma^2)$ is given by

$$f(\epsilon_i|\epsilon_i > -X_i'\beta) = \frac{\phi(\epsilon_i/\sigma)}{1 - \Phi(-X_i'\beta/\sigma)} \quad \text{for } \epsilon_i > -X_i'\beta,$$

where ϕ and Φ are PDF and CDF of a standard normal random variable. The conditional mean of ϵ_i is therefore given by

$$\begin{aligned}\mathrm{E}[\epsilon_i|\epsilon_i > -X_i'\beta] &= \int_{-X_i'\beta/\sigma}^{\infty} \frac{\epsilon f(\epsilon)}{1 - F(-X_i'\beta/\sigma)} \, d\epsilon \\ &= \sigma \frac{\phi(X_i'\beta/\sigma)}{\Phi(X_i'\beta/\sigma)} \\ &= \sigma \lambda_i,\end{aligned} \qquad (11.4)$$

where $\lambda_i = \phi(X_i'\beta/\sigma)/\Phi(X_i'\beta/\sigma)$.

To allow for the nonzero mean of ϵ_i, the regression equation for the m observations for which $Y_i^* > 0$ can therefore be written as

$$Y_i = X_i'\beta + \sigma \lambda_i + u_i, \quad i = 1, 2, \ldots, n_1,$$

where, clearly, $\mathrm{E}(u_i|X_i, Y_i > 0) = 0$ because $\mathrm{E}(Y_i|X_i, Y_i > 0) = X_i'\beta + \sigma\lambda_i$. If λ_i was observable, one could simply apply least squares methods to estimate β (and σ), and the resulting estimator would be unbiased. However, though λ_i is not observable, it can be consistently estimated presuming correct parametric specification, leading to Heckman's (1979) famous two-step estimation procedure, with λ_i often being referred to as "Heckman's lambda." Heckman's approach involves first estimating the unobserved term λ_i via maximum likelihood using a Probit model with outcome 0 if the observation is censored, 1 otherwise, denoted $\hat{\lambda}_i$, and then estimating $Y_i = X_i'\beta + \sigma\hat{\lambda}_i + \varepsilon_i$ using only those observations for which $Y_i^* > 0$ (see Amemiya (1985) for details). If we let $\gamma = (\beta, \sigma)'$ and $\hat{Z}_i = (X_i, \hat{\lambda}_i)$, this produces a least squares estimator of the form

$$\hat{\gamma} = \begin{pmatrix} \hat{\beta} \\ \hat{\sigma} \end{pmatrix} = \left(\frac{1}{n_1} \sum_{i=1}^{n_1} \hat{Z}_i \hat{Z}_i' \right)^{-1} \frac{1}{n_1} \sum_{i=1}^{n_1} \hat{Z}_i Y_i.$$

Clearly the properties of $\hat{\beta}$ depend on correct specification of both the regression function and the density of ϵ_i. When the density of ϵ_i is misspecified, the conditional mean will itself be misspecified leading to inconsistent estimation of β.

Potential inconsistency of maximum likelihood estimators when ϵ_i is heteroskedastic has been widely studied (see Arabmazar and Schmidt (1981) and the references therein), which contrasts with a classical regression model in which the maximum likelihood estimator under normality is of course generally consistent.

Powell (1984) proposed a popular semiparametric approach that is robust to the presence of conditional heteroskedasticity and to distributional misspecification of ϵ_i, which is discussed in Section 11.2. Powell's estimator is an L_1 norm approach, which he termed "censored least absolute deviations" (CLAD). Though popular, this estimator breaks down under heavy censoring, and a kernel-based solution proposed by Chen and Khan (2000) is outlined in Section 11.3.

We now consider the rich array of semiparametric estimators which have been recently developed for handling censored data.

11.2 Semiparametric Censored Regression Models

Powell's (1984) censored least absolute deviations (CLAD) estimator takes a markedly different approach from that of, say, Heckman (1979). Rather than using the L_2-norm method of least squares, Powell considers the L_1-norm method of least absolute deviations, beginning from the observation that, were one to observe the true Y_i^*, its median would coincide with the regression model $X_i'\beta$ under the assumption that the median of the error term ϵ_i is zero. In the presence of data that is left censored at, say, zero, this remains true provided that the typical (i.e., median) value of the true dependent variable Y_i^* is nonnegative for a positive fraction of individuals in the sample, which may be reasonable for many populations but may fail to hold for heavily censored populations. That is, when Y_i is censored, its median is unaffected by the presence of censoring *provided* that the regression function $X_i'\beta$ lies in the uncensored range; otherwise the median of Y_i will be the censoring point.

Exploiting the zero conditional median restriction on ϵ_i, Powell's (1984) CLAD estimator is defined as the minimizer of

$$S_n(\beta) = \frac{1}{n}\sum_{i=1}^{n} |Y_i - \max\{X_i'\beta, 0\}|. \qquad (11.5)$$

It can be seen that (11.5) is equivalent to minimizing

$$S_n(\beta) = \frac{1}{n}\sum_{i=1}^{n} \mathbf{1}(X_i'\beta > 0)|Y_i - X_i'\beta|, \qquad (11.6)$$

since, for observations with $X_i'\beta < 0$, we have $\max\{X_i'\beta, 0\} = 0$ and therefore $|Y_i - \max\{X_i'\beta, 0\}| = |Y_i|$, which does not depend on β. Letting $\hat{\beta}$ denote the estimator of β that minimizes (11.6), Powell has proved the following result:

$$\sqrt{n}(\hat{\beta} - \beta) \xrightarrow{d} N(0, V_{CLAD}^{-1}),$$

where $V_{CLAD} = 4f^2(0)\mathrm{E}[\mathbf{1}(X_i'\beta > 0)X_iX_i']$, and where $f(0)$ is the density of ϵ_i at the origin. Assuming that ϵ_i and X_i are independent, then $f(0) = \lim_{h\to 0} \mathrm{P}(0 \leq \epsilon_i < h) = \lim_{h\to 0} \mathrm{P}(0 \leq \epsilon_i < h | X_i'\beta > 0)$. Hence, Powell suggests estimating $f(0)$ by

$$\hat{f}(0) = \frac{\mathbf{1}(X_i'\hat{\beta} > 0)\mathbf{1}(0 \leq \hat{\epsilon}_i < h)}{h\sum_{i=1}^{n}\mathbf{1}(X_i'\hat{\beta} > 0)}.$$

Horowitz and Neumann (1987) propose an alternative estimator for estimating $f(0)$ that uses data with $X_i'\hat{\beta} \in [-h/2, h/2]$ given by

$$\hat{f}(0) = \frac{\sum_{i=1}^n \mathbf{1}(-\frac{h}{2} \le \hat{\epsilon}_i \le \frac{h}{2})\mathbf{1}(Y_i > 0)}{h\left[\sum_{i=1}^n \mathbf{1}\left(X_i'\hat{\beta} > \frac{h}{2}\right) + \frac{1}{2}\left(1 + \frac{X_i'\hat{\beta}}{(h/2)}\right)\mathbf{1}\left(-\frac{h}{2} < X_i'\hat{\beta} \le \frac{h}{2}\right)\right]}. \tag{11.7}$$

Hall and Horowitz (1990) suggest replacing the indicator function by a kernel function. Newey and Powell (1990) modify the objective function, yielding

$$\sum_{i=1}^n w_i|Y_i - \max\{X_i'\beta, 0\}|,$$

and show that the optimal weight should be $w_i = 2f(0|X_i)$. The resulting estimator has an asymptotic variance that can be shown to be $\{4\mathrm{E}[\mathbf{1}(X_i'\beta > 0)f^2(0|X_i)X_iX_i']\}^{-1}$, and Newey and Powell show that this equals the semiparametric efficiency bound for the censored regression model under the zero conditional median restriction. Of course, if ϵ_i and X_i are independent, then $f(0|X_i)$ equals a constant, $f(0)$, and Newey and Powell's estimator collapses to $\hat{\beta}$.

Powell (1986) also proposes a symmetrically censored least squares estimator for β. Assuming that ϵ_i is symmetrically distributed around zero, then ϵ_i has a nonzero conditional mean because the observations with $\epsilon_i > -X_i'\beta$ are censored; hence if one also drops the observations with $\epsilon_i < X_i'\beta$, then the zero mean condition for ϵ_i is restored. Therefore, one can use observations with $\epsilon_i \in [-X_i'\beta, X_i'\beta]$ or, equivalently, with $Y_i \in [0, 2X_i'\beta]$ to estimate β consistently. Other estimation methods include the GMM-based estimation method of Newey (1991b), who proposes estimating β based on the efficient score that exploits the conditional symmetry of the error term to obtain an efficient estimator, and Honoré and Powell's (1994) identically censored least absolute deviation (ICLAD) and identically censored least squares (ICLS) estimators.

11.3 Semiparametric Censored Regression Models with Nonparametric Heteroskedasticity

Chen and Khan (2000) consider estimation procedures for heteroskedastic censored linear regression models that have weaker requirements for identification than Powell's (1984) CLAD estimator, and that allow for various degrees of censoring. Chen and Khan observe that a serious empirical problem arises with the CLAD estimator when the matrix $E[\mathbf{1}(X_i'\beta > 0)X_iX_i']$ is not of full rank and hence β cannot be identified. This arises typically in cases where the index $X_i'\beta$ is negative with high probability, as often occurs under heavy censoring of the data. Chen and Khan, by restricting the conditional heteroskedasticity to be multiplicative, allow for less stringent identification conditions than required by Powell's CLAD estimator. Their approach models the error term as the product of a homoskedastic error and a scale function of the regressors that can be estimated using kernel methods. They assume that

$$\epsilon_i = \sigma(X_i)v_i, \quad P(v_i \le \lambda | X_i) \equiv P(v_i \le \lambda) \ \forall \lambda \in \mathbb{R}, \ X_i \text{ a.s.}$$

with $E(v_i) = 0$ and $\mathrm{var}(v_i) = 1$.

Note that for any $\alpha \in (0, 1)$, from (11.3) we have

$$q_\alpha(X_i) = \max\{X_i'\beta + c_\alpha\sigma(X_i), 0\},$$

where $q_\alpha(\cdot)$ denotes the αth conditional quantile function of Y_i given X_i, and c_α denotes the αth quantile from the (unknown) distribution of v_i. Thus, for any $q_{\alpha_j}(X_i) > 0$ for two distinct α_1 and α_2, we have

$$q_{\alpha_j}(X_i) = X_i'\beta + c_{\alpha_j}\sigma(X_i) \text{ for } j = 1, 2. \tag{11.8}$$

Chen and Khan (2000) propose two estimators of β, one assuming that v_i has a known parametric distribution, and one that does not require such assumptions. We discuss only the latter estimator, which constitutes the more general case since it does not assume that the distribution of v_i is known a priori.

From (11.8) one can show that (see Exercise 11.2)

$$\bar{q}_\alpha(X_i) = X_i'\beta + \frac{\bar{c}}{\Delta c}\Delta q_{\alpha(X_i)} \text{ for } j = 1, 2, \tag{11.9}$$

where $\bar{q}_\alpha(\cdot) = (q_{\alpha_2}(\cdot) + q_{\alpha_1}(\cdot))/2$, $\Delta q_\alpha(\cdot) = q_{\alpha_2}(\cdot) - q_{\alpha_1}(\cdot)$, $\bar{c} = (c_{\alpha_2} + c_{\alpha_1})/2$, and $\Delta c = c_{\alpha_2} - c_{\alpha_1}$. Equation (11.9) suggests that one can estimate β (and the nuisance parameter $\gamma_1 = \bar{c}/\Delta c$) by regressing $\hat{\bar{q}}(\cdot)$ on X_i and $\Delta\hat{q}(\cdot)$, where $\hat{q}_{\alpha_j}(\cdot)$ is some nonparametric estimator of $q_{\alpha_j}(\cdot)$ $(j = 1, 2)$. Hence, Chen and Khan (2000) suggest estimating β (and γ_1) by minimizing

$$\frac{1}{n}\sum_{i=1}^n \tau(X_i)w(\hat{q}_{\alpha_1}(X_i))\left[\hat{\bar{q}}(X_i) - X_i'\beta - \gamma_1\Delta\hat{q}_\alpha(X_i)\right]^2, \tag{11.10}$$

where $w(\cdot)$ is a "smooth" weighting function that keeps observations only for which the first stage estimation values exceed the censoring value,[3] and $\tau(\cdot)$ is a trimming function having compact support. Under a series of regularity conditions, the estimator $\hat{\beta}$ is shown to have the parametric $\sqrt{n}$ rate of convergence and possess a limiting normal distribution.

Cosslett (2004) proposes (alternative) asymptotically efficient likelihood-based semiparametric estimators for censored and truncated regression models. His approach is based on estimating the density function of the residuals in a partially observed regression, which is similar to a nonparametric maximum likelihood estimator, and allows for estimation of the semiparametrically efficient score.

11.4   The Univariate Kaplan-Meier CDF Estimator

There exists a class of semiparametric estimators that employ the so-called Kaplan-Meier estimator of a CDF in the presence of censored data. We briefly describe this estimator and provide an illustrative example of its application.

In many applications, making complete measurements on all members of a random sample is often impossible. For example, in medical follow-up studies to determine the distribution of survival times after receiving treatment, contact with some individuals may be lost before their death. Similarly, observation of the life of a vacuum tube may be ended by the use of the test facilities for other purposes. In both examples the data may be censored.

Kaplan and Meier (1958) propose a novel product-limit estimator for estimating a CDF $F(\cdot)$ or survival function $S(\cdot) = 1 - F(\cdot)$. Let $Y_1, \ldots, Y_n$ be the random sample of interest drawn from a distribution F or S (e.g., survival duration in months of patients). Let $L_1, \ldots, L_n$ be a (random or fixed) censoring variable that is independent of the Y_i's. Define

$$Z_i = \min\{Y_i, L_i\} \text{ and } \delta_i = \mathbf{1}(Y_i \le L_i). \qquad (11.11)$$

Then we observe Z_i and δ_i; however, the exact value of Y_i is unknown if $\delta_i = 0$. In the medical duration example in which Y_i is survival duration, if we observe the death of a patient prior to the end of the

---

[3]It is a smoothed version of $\mathbf{1}(\hat{q}_{\alpha_1}(X_i) > 0)$.

study, then Y_i is observed ($\delta_i = 1$). However, if contact with a patient is lost at time L_i (i.e., during the study period), then we do not know the exact value of Y_i; rather, we only know that $Y_i > L_i$. Also, if a patient remains alive at the end of the study, we will not observe the exact value of Y_i.

Define the ascending points $c_0, c_1, \ldots, c_m$ at which the CDF F (or survival function S) is to be evaluated, and define $I_j = \mathbf{1}(Y > c_j)$ which takes value 1 if Y exceeds c_j, and 0 otherwise. Because I_j is a random variable, by the conditional probability formula we have (because $I_j = 1$ implies $I_{j-1} = 1$)

$$\mathrm{P}(I_j = 1 | I_{j-1} = 1) = \frac{\mathrm{P}(I_j = 1)}{\mathrm{P}(I_{j-1} = 1)}$$

$$= 1 - \frac{\mathrm{P}(c_{j-1} < Y \leq c_j)}{\mathrm{P}(Y > c_{j-1})}. \qquad (11.12)$$

By choosing c_1 small enough, say below the smallest observation in the data, we can always ensure that $\mathrm{P}(I_0 = 1)$. That is, all items survive initially. In the case of no censoring, we would estimate (11.12) by

$$\tilde{\mathrm{P}}(I_j = 1 | I_{j-1} = 1) = \frac{\tilde{\mathrm{P}}(I_j = 1)}{\tilde{\mathrm{P}}(I_{j-1} = 1)} = \frac{[\#Y_i > c_j]}{[\#Y_i > c_{j-1}]}$$

$$= 1 - \frac{[\# \text{ of } Y_i \text{ in the range } c_{j-1} < Y_i \leq c_j]}{[\#Y_i \geq c_{j-1}]}. \qquad (11.13)$$

Repeated application of $\tilde{\mathrm{P}}(I_j = 1) = \tilde{\mathrm{P}}(I_j = 1 | I_{j-1} = 1)\tilde{\mathrm{P}}(I_{j-1} = 1)$ leads to the following estimator of the survival function $S(c_j) = \mathrm{P}(I_j = 1)$ ($\mathrm{P}(I_0 = 1) = 1$ is used in (11.14) below):

$$\tilde{\mathrm{P}}(I_j = 1) = \prod_{s=2}^{j} \tilde{\mathrm{P}}(I_s = 1 | I_{s-1} = 1) = \frac{[\#Y_i > c_j]}{[\#Y_i > c_{j-1}]} \cdots \frac{[\#Y_i > c_1]}{[\#Y_i > c_0]}$$

$$= \frac{[\#Y_i > c_j]}{[\#Y_i > c_1]} = \frac{1}{n}[\#Y_i > c_j] = 1 - \hat{F}^n(c_j), \qquad (11.14)$$

where $\hat{F}^n(c_j) = n^{-1}[\#Y_i \leq c_j]$ is the standard empirical CDF.

When the data is censored, Kaplan and Meier (1958) propose modifying (11.13) as follows:

$$\hat{P}(I_j = 1 | I_{j-1} = 1) = 1 - \frac{[\# \text{ uncensored } Y_i \text{ in the range } c_{j-1} < Y_i \le c_j]}{[\# Y_i \ge c_{j-1}]},$$

(11.15)

for $j = 1, \ldots, m$.

The survival probability is computed by

$$\hat{S}(c_j) \equiv \hat{P}(I_j = 1) = \prod_{s=1}^{j} \hat{P}(I_{j-1} = 1 | I_{j=1}).$$

(11.16)

The CDF is estimated by

$$\hat{F}(c_j) = 1 - \hat{S}(c_j) = 1 - \prod_{s=1}^{j} \hat{P}(I_{j-1} = 1 | I_{j=1}).$$

(11.17)

We borrow an example from Kaplan and Meier (1958) to illustrate the use of (11.15) and (11.16) for estimating survival probabilities. Assume that there are 100 items (say, patients) initially. Define $n_j = $ number of items that survive beyond c_{j-1}, $\gamma_j = $ number of deaths between c_{j-1} and c_j, and $\lambda_j = $ number of items that are censored (get lost) at time c_j (assuming the corresponding $Y_i > c_j$). The detailed data is given in Table 11.1, along with estimates based on Kaplan and Meier's product-limit estimator and the conventional estimator that ignores the censoring, where we assume that censoring (missing observations) occurs only at 1.7, 3.6, and 5.

In Table 11.1 the Kaplan-Meier conditional survival probability $\hat{P}_{I_j | I_{j-1}}^{km} = \hat{P}(I_j = 1 | I_{j-1} = 1)$ is computed using (11.15). For example, $\hat{P}(I_2 = 1 | I_1 = 1) = 1 - 5/97 = 92/97$ because there are 97 items that survive beyond c_1, and there are 5 deaths (not including censored items) that occurred between c_1 and c_2. The survival function $\hat{S}^{km}$ can be obtained as the product of conditional probabilities using (11.16). For example, $\hat{S}^{km}(c_2) = (97/100)(92/97) = 0.92$. Note that the conventional method $\tilde{S}^n(c_j)$, which ignores the censoring, would lead to $\hat{P}_{I_j | I_{j-1}}^n = 1 - 25/97 = 72/97$, because it treats censored and uncensored items identically, i.e, both are deemed to be deaths ($20 + 5 = 25$ deaths), resulting in an *underestimate* of the true survival probability, i.e., $\tilde{S}^n(c_2) = (97/100)(72/97) = 0.72 < \hat{S}^{km}(c_2)$.

Table 11.1: Frequency and Kaplan-Meier estimators of survivor and CDFs for censored survival time data. The superscript km denotes Kaplan-Meier, and n denotes the conventional estimator that ignores censoring

c_{j-1} to c_j	n_j	γ_j	λ_j	$\hat{P}^{km}_{I_j \mid I_{j-1}}$	$\hat{S}^{km}(c_j)$	$\hat{P}^n_{I_j \mid I_{j-1}}$	$\hat{S}^n(c_j)$
0 to 1	100	3	0	97/100	0.97	97/100	0.97
1 to 1.7	97	5	20	92/97	0.92	72/97	0.72
1.7 to 2	72	4	0	68/72	0.87	68/72	0.68
2 to 3	68	10	0	58/68	0.74	58/68	0.58
3 to 3.6	58	9	12	49/58	0.63	37/58	0.37
3.6 to 4	37	6	0	31/37	0.52	31/37	0.31
4 to 5	31	15	16	16/31	0.27	0/31	0

The Kaplan-Meier product-limit estimator has been applied to a variety of nonparametric and semiparametric models with censored data. For example, Horowitz (1986, 1988) applies Kaplan and Meier's (1958) method to construct an estimator a linear regression model with censored data. Before we discuss the estimation of nonparametric and semiparametric regression models with censored data, we first turn to a discussion of multivariate CDF estimation with censored data.

11.5   The Multivariate Kaplan-Meier CDF Estimator

For what follows we retain the notation from the previous section, i.e., $Z_i = \min\{Y_i, L_i\}$ and $\delta_i = \mathbf{1}(Y_i \leq L_i)$. Let $Z_{i:n}$ denote the ordered Z-values such that $Z_{1:n} \leq Z_{2:n} \leq \cdots \leq Z_{n:n}$ and let $\delta_{[i:n]}$ denote the δ-value associated with $Z_{i:n}$. With this notation, the Kaplan-Meier estimator of $F(y)$ discussed in the last section is the following product-limit estimator $\hat{F}_n(y)$ given by

$$1 - \hat{F}_n(y) = \prod_{i=1}^{n} \left[1 - \frac{\delta_{[i:n]}}{n - i + 1} \right]^{\mathbf{1}(Z_{i:n} \leq y)}. \tag{11.18}$$

Kaplan and Meier (1958) show that $\hat{F}_n(\cdot)$ defined in (11.18) is the maximum likelihood estimator of $F(\cdot)$.

Stute (1993) extends the product-limit estimator to the multivariate framework. Let $F(y, x)$ denote the joint CDF for (Y, X), where X is a q-dimensional continuous random variable. Stute proposes estimating $F(y, x)$ by

$$\hat{F}_n(y, x) = \sum_{i=1}^{n} W_{in} \mathbf{1}(X_{[i:n]} \leq x, Z_{i:n} \leq y), \qquad (11.19)$$

where

$$W_{in} = \frac{\delta_{[i:n]}}{n - i + 1} \prod_{j=1}^{i-1} \left[\frac{n - j}{n - j + 1} \right]^{\delta_{[j:n]}} \qquad (11.20)$$

is the mass attached to $Z_{i:n}$ under the Kaplan-Meier estimator and $X_{[i:n]}$ the observed value of X that is paired with $Z_{i:n}$.

Stute (1993) proves the consistency of $\hat{F}_n(y, x)$. In fact, Stute shows that $S(\hat{F}_n) \to S(F)$ with probability 1 for a large class of statistical functionals S. Stute (1996) further establishes the asymptotic distribution of $\hat{F}_n(\cdot)$ by considering a general linear functional of $\hat{F}_n$ defined by

$$S_n^{\phi} \stackrel{\text{def}}{=} \sum_{i=1}^{n} W_{in} \phi(X_{[i:n]}, Z_{i:n}) \equiv \int \phi \, d\hat{F}_n, \qquad (11.21)$$

where $\hat{F}_n$ is the Kaplan-Meier estimator of $F(y, x)$ defined in (11.19) and $\phi(.,.)$ is a smooth function of $(X_{[i:n]}, Z_{i:n})$.

Under some regularity conditions, Stute (1996) shows that

$$\sqrt{n}(S_n^{\phi} - S^{\phi}) \to N(0, \sigma_{\phi}^2) \text{ in distribution,} \qquad (11.22)$$

where σ_{ϕ}^2 is the asymptotic variance of $\sqrt{n} S_n^{\phi}$ (the explicit expression of σ_{ϕ}^2 can be found in Stute (1996, p. 464)).

Note that by removing x from (11.19) one obtains an alternative estimator for $F(y)$ as follows:

$$\tilde{F}_n(y) = \sum_{i=1}^{n} W_{in} \mathbf{1}(Z_{i:n} \leq y), \qquad (11.23)$$

where W_{in} is defined by (11.20). Exercise 11.3 asks the reader to show that $\hat{F}_n(y)$ defined in (11.18) and $\tilde{F}_n(y)$ defined in (11.23) are indeed identical.

Cai (2001) generalizes Kaplan and Meier's (1958) product-limit estimator to the dependent data case and establishes the strong consistency of the estimator for α-mixing data. Lai and Ying (1991) and Lin and Ying (1999) also treat the problem of nonparametric estimation of distribution functions with censored data.

11.5.1 Nonparametric Regression Models with Random Censoring

Next, we discuss estimation of a nonparametric regression model with random censored dependent data. We focus on the local linear estimator proposed by Fan and Gijbels (1992) and Cai (2003). The model is given by

$$Y_i = g(X_i) + u_i, \tag{11.24}$$

where Y_i is the dependent variable which may be the survival time of an individual or an object under some experimental study, and X_i is the associated q-dimensional covariates. For expositional simplicity, we assume that X_i is a q-vector of continuous random variables. Under the censoring scheme, rather than observing Y_i, we observe $Z_i = \min\{Y_i, L_i\}$ and $\delta_i = \mathbf{1}(Y_i \leq L_i)$. Therefore, the observations are $\{Z_i, X_i, \delta_i\}_{i=1}^n$, a random sample from $\{Z, X, \delta\}$.

First note that the conventional local linear estimator of $g(\cdot)$ with *uncensored* data can be obtained by minimizing the objective function with respect to a and b (a estimates $g(x_0)$):

$$\int \left[y - a - (x - x_0)'b\right]^2 K_{h,x,x_0} dF_n(x, y)$$
$$\equiv \frac{1}{n} \sum_{i=1}^n \left[Y_i - a - (X_i - x_0)'b\right]^2 K_{h,X_i,x_0}, \tag{11.25}$$

where $K_{h,x,x_0} = K_h(x, x_0)$ is the product kernel function, and $F_n(x, y)$ is the (standard) empirical distribution of $\{X_i, Y_i\}_{i=1}^n$ when there is no censoring. With censored data, Fan and Gijbels (1992) and Cai (2003) suggest replacing the empirical CDF $F_n(.,.)$ in (11.25) by $\hat{F}_n(.,.)$, Kaplan and Meier's (1958) estimator for $F(.,.)$. Hence, we estimate $g(x_0)$ by minimizing the objective function

$$\int \left[y - a - (x - x_0)'b\right]^2 K_h(x, x_0) d\hat{F}_n(x, y)$$
$$= \sum_{i=1}^n W_{in} \left[Z_{i:n} - a - (X_{[i:n]} - x_0)'b\right]^2 K_{h,X_{[i:n]},x_0}, \tag{11.26}$$

where W_{in}, $Z_{i:n}$ and $X_{[i:n]}$ are all defined in Section 11.5.

Letting $\hat{a}(x_0)$ and $\hat{b}(x_0)$ denote the values of a and b that minimize (11.26), then $\hat{a}(x_0)$ estimates $g(x_0)$. By the standard least squares formula, we have (replacing x_0 by x)

$$
\begin{pmatrix} \hat{a}(x) \\ \hat{b}(x) \end{pmatrix} = \left[\sum_{i=1}^{n} W_{in} K_h(X_{[i:n]}, x)[1, (X_{[i:n]} - x)']'[1, (X_{[i:n]} - x)'] \right]^{-1}
$$
$$
\times \left[\sum_{i=1}^{n} W_{in} K_h(X_{[i:n]}, x)[1, (X_{[i:n]} - x)']' Z_{i:n} \right]. \quad (11.27)
$$

Fan and Gijbels (1992) and Cai (2003) prove the following result, where $\hat{g}(x) = \hat{a}(x)$ is defined in (11.27).

Theorem 11.1. *Under some regularity conditions.*

$$
\sqrt{nh_1 \dots h_q} \left[\hat{g}(x) - g(x) - \frac{\kappa_2}{2} \sum_{s=1}^{q} h_s^2 g_{ss}(x) \right] \xrightarrow{d} N(0, \Sigma_x),
$$

where $g_{ss}(x) = \partial^2 g(x)/\partial x_s^2$, $\Sigma_x = \kappa^q v(x)/f(x)$ with $v(x) = \mathrm{E}[Y^2\{1 - G(Y)\}^{-1}]$, and $G(\cdot)$ is the CDF of L_i (i.e., the censoring variable).

It is interesting to note that the asymptotic bias is the same as that for the local linear estimator with uncensored data. However, the asymptotic variance for the censored case is larger than its counterpart for the uncensored situation. When there is no censoring at all, one may set $G = 0$ and Σ_x reduces to $\kappa^q \mathrm{E}(Y_i^2|X_i = x)/f(x)$, which is the asymptotic variance without censoring.

Cai (2003) further shows that $\lim_{n\to\infty} \mathrm{var}(\xi_{n,i}(x)) = \kappa^q v(x) f(x)$, where $\xi_{n,i}(x) = \sqrt{h_1 \dots h_q} K_h(X_i, x)[1 - G(Z_i)]^{-1}\delta_i$, which involves the unknown censoring distribution $G(\cdot)$. Under the assumption that the censoring variable L_i does not depend on the covariates X_i, one can also use the Kaplan-Meier product-limit estimator for estimating $G(\cdot)$, that is, $1 - \hat{G}(x) = \prod_{j, Z_{j:n} \leq z} \{(n-j)/(n-j+1)\}^{1-\delta_{[j:n]}}$. This leads to an estimator of $\xi_{n,i}(x)$ given by $\hat{\xi}_{n,i}(x) = \sqrt{h_1 \dots h_q} K_h(X_i, x)[1 - \hat{G}(Z_i)]^{-1}\delta_i$. Therefore, a consistent estimator of Σ_x is given by $n^{-1}\sum_{i=1}^{n}\{\hat{\xi}_{n,i}(x) - \bar{\xi}_n(x)\}^2\delta_i$, where $\bar{\xi}_n(x) = n^{-1}\sum_{i=1}^{n}\hat{\xi}_{n,i}(x)$.

Other related work includes Fan, Gijbels and King (1997), who propose a local likelihood and partially local likelihood method to estimate a semiparametric hazard function, and Cai and Sun (2003), who apply the partial likelihood approach to estimate a semiparametric varying coefficient hazard function.

11.6 Nonparametric Censored Regression

11.6.1 Lewbel and Linton's Approach

Lewbel and Linton (2002) consider censored regression models of the form $Y_i = \max\{g(X_i) - \epsilon_i, c\}$, where $g(\cdot)$ is the conditional expectation for the uncensored population, and the censoring point c is presumed to be a known constant (writing the model as $g - \epsilon$ instead of the more usual $g + \epsilon$ simplifies later results). If $\mathrm{E}(\epsilon_i) = 0$, then the function $g(X_i)$ equals the regression function of the uncensored population

Lewbel and Linton (2002) consider fully nonparametric estimation of the function $g(\cdot)$ and $F(\cdot)$ (the distribution of ϵ_i), both of which are assumed to be unknown. Conditions are given under which $g(\cdot)$ can be consistently estimated, while F can be estimated given $g(\cdot)$.

For what follows, we define the following functions: $r(x) = \mathrm{E}(Y|x)$ and $q(r) = \mathrm{E}[\mathbf{1}(Y > 0)|r(X) = r]$. Lewbel and Linton (2002) show that

$$g(x) = \lambda_0 - \int_{r(x)}^{\lambda_0} \frac{1}{q(r)} dr \tag{11.28}$$

for some large constant λ_0.

Equation (11.28) provides the basis for estimating $g(\cdot)$. Lewbel and Linton (2002) propose the following two-step procedure. First, estimate the regression function $\mathrm{E}(Y_i|X_i) = r(X_i)$ using a local polynomial estimator, which we call $\hat{r}(X_i)$. Next, let $\hat{q}(r)$ be the one-dimensional nonparametric regression of $\mathbf{1}(Y_i > 0)$ on the generated regressor $\hat{r}(X_i)$. Then let

$$\hat{g}(X_i) = \lambda_0 - \int_{\hat{r}(X_i)}^{\lambda_0} \frac{1}{\hat{q}(r)} dr$$

for some fixed positive λ_0. This univariate integral can be readily evaluated using numerical methods; hence $\hat{g}(X_i)$ can itself be readily computed. Let $\lambda_r = \sup_{x \in \Omega} r(x)$ and $\lambda_\epsilon = \sup_{\epsilon \in \Omega_\epsilon} \epsilon$, where Ω and Ω_ϵ are the supports of x and ϵ, respectively. If $\lambda_r > \lambda_\epsilon$, then in practice, one can use $\hat{\lambda} \equiv \max_{i=1,\ldots,n} \hat{r}(X_i)$ or $\hat{\lambda}_Y = \max_{i=1,\ldots,n} Y_i$ to replace λ_0.

Letting $r_l(x) = \partial r(x)/\partial x_l$ ($l = 1, \ldots, q$) and $s(x) = \mathrm{E}[\mathbf{1}(Y_i^* > 0)|X_i = x]$, partial derivative estimates are given by

$$\hat{g}_l(x) = \frac{\hat{r}_l(x)}{\hat{s}(x)},$$

where $\hat{r}_l(x)$ and $\hat{s}(x)$ are local polynomial estimators of $r_l(x)$ and $s(x)$, respectively.

Lewbel and Linton (2002) provide conditions under which $\hat{g}(x)$ and $\hat{g}_l(x)$ provide consistent and asymptotically normal estimates of $g(x)$ and $g_l(x)$, respectively. In particular, letting $\sigma_r^2(x) = \text{var}(Y|X = x)$, $f(x)$ be the PDF of X, Lewbel and Linton prove that

$$\sqrt{nh_1 \dots h_q} \left(\hat{g}(x) - g(x) - \sum_{s=1}^{q} h_s^2 b_s(x) \right) \xrightarrow{d} N \left(0, \frac{\kappa^q \sigma^2(x)}{f(x)s^2(x)} \right),$$

$$(11.29)$$

where $\kappa = \int k(v)^2 dv$, $k(\cdot)$ is the univariate kernel function used in the product kernel in the local linear kernel estimator, and the $b_s(\cdot)$'s are some smooth and bounded functions. The conditions on the smoothing parameters are that $h_l \to 0$ (all $l = 1, \dots, q$) and $(nh_1 \dots h_q) \sum_{s=1}^{q} h_s^4$ $< \infty$. If instead one imposes an undersmoothing condition of the form $(nh_1 \dots h_q) \sum_{s=1}^{q} h_s^4 \to 0$, then the leading bias term can be ignored, and the estimator $\hat{g}(x) - g(x)$ becomes correctly centered at zero.

11.6.2   Chen, Dahl and Khan's Approach

Chen, Dahl and Khan (2005) propose an alternative estimation method for a nonparametric censored regression model. Motivated by classes of problems in which interest lies in the estimation of a location function in regions where it is *less* than the censoring point, Chen, Dahl and Khan propose an extension of the nonparametric location-scale model to handle censored data. They consider the model

$$Y_i^* = g(X_i) + \sigma(X_i)\epsilon_i,$$
$$Y_i = \max\{Y_i^*, 0\},$$

where Y_i^* is an unobserved latent dependent variable, Y_i is the observed dependent variable equal to Y_i^* if it exceeds the fixed censoring point (of zero) and equals zero otherwise, X_i is an observed q-dimensional random vector, and ϵ_i is a mean zero, unit variance i.i.d. random disturbance term that is distributed independently of X_i.

Chen, Dahl and Khan (2005) present conditions under which $g(x)$ can be identified and estimated after imposing a location restriction, namely that the median of ϵ_i is zero, and they are able to identify $g(x)$ on the entire support of X, not just the region exceeding the censoring point. Their approach is based on a structural relationship between the conditional mean and upper quantiles for those X_i for which $g(X_i) \geq 0$, and they require the condition $\text{P}(g(X) \geq 0) > 0$.

Under the assumption that ϵ_i and X_i are independent, and also assuming that the PDF of ϵ_i is positive on $\mathbb{R}$, then there exist quantiles $\alpha_1 < \alpha_2 < 1$ such that

$$q_{\alpha_j}(x) = g(x) + c_{\alpha_j}\sigma(x) > 0, \text{ for } j = 1, 2, \qquad (11.30)$$

where $q_\alpha(x)$ is the α conditional quantile of Y_i, conditional on $X_i = x$, and c_α is the αth quantile value of ϵ_i.

Equation (11.30) gives the regression framework for estimating $g(\cdot)$ and $\sigma(\cdot)$. Once we obtain estimators for $q_\alpha(\cdot)$ and $c_\alpha(\cdot)$, say $\hat{q}_\alpha(\cdot)$ and $\hat{c}_\alpha(\cdot)$, we regress $\hat{q}_\alpha(\cdot)$ on $\hat{c}_\alpha(\cdot)$ to obtain estimates of $g(\cdot)$ and $\sigma(\cdot)$.

Note that (11.30) together with the fact that $q_{0.5}(x) = g(x)$ (since ϵ_i has median zero) leads to $q_{\alpha_j}(x) = q_{0.5}(x) + c_{\alpha_j}\sigma(x)$ $(j = 1, 2)$, and solving for c_{α_2} from these two equations gives

$$c_{\alpha_2} = \frac{q_{\alpha_2}(x) - q_{0.5}(x)}{q_{\alpha_1}(x) - q_{0.5}(x)}. \qquad (11.31)$$

We are now ready to discuss the three-step estimation procedure of Chen, Dahl and Khan (2005).

(i) Estimate $q_{0.5}(X_i)$ using a local constant method for each observation point X_i. Let $\bar{q}_{0.5}(X_i)$ denote the estimated values which are used to determine those observations whose median exceeds the censoring value c.

(ii) Compute a weighted average of local polynomial estimators to estimate the unknown disturbance quantiles denoted c_{α_l}, $l = 1, \ldots, N$, where $\hat{c}_{\alpha_l}$ equals

$$\frac{1}{n}\sum_{i=1}^{n} \tau(X_i)w(\bar{q}_{0.5}(X_i)) \frac{(\tilde{q}_{\alpha_l}(X_i) - \tilde{q}_{0.5}(X_i))/(\tilde{q}_{\alpha_s}(X_i) - \tilde{q}_{\alpha_l}(X_i))}{\frac{1}{n}\sum_{j=1}^{n} \tau(X_j)w(\bar{q}_{0.5}(X_j))},$$

where $w(\cdot)$ is a weight function, and where the tilde notation stands for the second step estimators (it differs from the first step (bar) estimator $\bar{q}_{0.5}(x)$).

(iii) Using a local polynomial method, estimate $a_\alpha(\cdot)$ at the point of interest x (x may not be an observation point), i.e.,

$$q_{\alpha_l}(x) = g(x) + c_{\alpha_l}\sigma(x),$$

which holds true for any α_l such that $q_{\alpha_l}(x) > 0$. Let $\theta(x) = (g(x), \sigma(x))'$ and let $\hat{\theta}(x) = (\hat{g}(x), \hat{\sigma}(x))'$. Letting $\hat{\mathbf{c}}_{\alpha_l} = (1, \hat{c}_{\alpha_l})$, and letting $\hat{\tilde{d}}_{\alpha_l}$ denote the indicator $\mathbf{1}[\hat{q}_{\alpha_l} \geq \epsilon]$, where $\epsilon > 0$ is a small constant, the estimator of $\theta(x)$ is given by

$$\hat{\theta}(x) = \left(\sum_{l=1}^{N} \hat{\tilde{d}}_{\alpha_l} \hat{\mathbf{c}}_{\alpha_l} \hat{\mathbf{c}}'_{\alpha_l} \right)^{-1} \sum_{l=1}^{N} \hat{\tilde{d}}_{\alpha_l} \hat{\mathbf{c}}_{\alpha_l} \hat{q}_{\alpha_l}(x), \qquad (11.32)$$

where $\hat{g}_\alpha(x)$ is the nonparametric estimator of $g_\alpha(x)$ in the third step.

Letting h_{js}, $j = 1, 2, 3$, denote the smoothing parameters used in the jth step for X_{is} ($s = 1, \ldots, q$), Chen, Dahl and Khan (2005) assume that, for all $s = 1, \ldots, q$,

(i) $h_{1s} \to 0$ and $nh_{11} \ldots h_{1q} / \ln(n) \to \infty$.

(ii) $h_{2s} = o(n^{-1/(2p+q)})$ and $nh_{21} \ldots h_{2q} / \ln(n) \to \infty$.

(iii) $h_{3s} = c_s n^{-1/(2p+q)}$ for some finite positive constant c_s.

Note that the first step estimators are only used in $w(\bar{q}_{0.5}(X_i))$ (using h_{1s}) when computing $\hat{c}_{\alpha_l}$, where $w(\cdot)$ selects observations whose median is positive. The second step estimators are $\tilde{q}_\alpha(X_i)$ (with h_{2s}) and they are also used to compute $\hat{c}_{\alpha_l}$. Finally, the third step estimator is $\hat{g}(x)$ (that uses h_{3s}), which is used to compute $\hat{\theta}(x)$ as defined in (11.32).

Asymptotic properties of this estimator can be found in Chen, Dahl and Khan (2005).

11.7 Exercises

Exercise 11.1. Derive (11.4).

Exercise 11.2. Derive (11.9).

Exercise 11.3. Prove that $\hat{F}_n(y)$ defined in (11.18) and $\tilde{F}_n(y)$ defined in (11.23) are identical.

Exercise 11.4. Derive (11.31).

Part III

Consistent Model Specification Tests

Chapter 12

Model Specification Tests

As we first discussed in Chapter 1, correctly specified parametric models are a "first-best" solution to the problem of estimation and inference, but unfortunately theory rarely if ever provides guidance on the appropriate functional specification. Therefore, in practice one must confront the possibility that one's parametric model might be misspecified, and this typically takes the form of a "model specification test." Many popular parametric model specification tests, by their nature, require the user to specify the set of parametric alternatives for which the null hypothesis will be rejected if the data generating process indeed follows the specified alternative models, and if there exist some alternative models that the test cannot detect, then the test is said to be an "inconsistent test" since it lacks power in certain directions. A popular application of nonparametric methods turns out to be for the detection of incorrectly specified parametric models, and we now turn to the discussion of how to construct consistent model specification tests using nonparametric techniques.

We first provide the definition of a "consistent test." Let H_0 denote a null hypothesis whose validity we wish to test. A test is said to be a *consistent* test if

$$P(\text{Reject } H_0 \mid H_0 \text{ is false}) \to 1 \text{ as } n \to \infty.$$

The power of a test is defined as $P(\text{Reject } H_0 \mid H_0 \text{ is false})$. Therefore, a consistent test has asymptotic power equal to one. Suppose we are interested in testing whether the income distribution of two regions (or perhaps of the same region over two different time periods) is the same, and let $f(\cdot)$ and $g(\cdot)$ denote the two income distributions.

Then the null hypothesis is $f(x) = g(x)$ for almost all $x \in \mathbb{R}$. A parametric approach would begin by presuming a parametric family for $f(\cdot)$ and $g(\cdot)$, for example, presuming that both $f(\cdot)$ and $g(\cdot)$ belong to the normal family of distributions. Since a normal distribution is completely characterized by its mean and variance, we can proceed to test whether the means and the variances of the two distributions are the same or not, and of course this parametric approach works if the normality assumption is correct. However, when the underlying distribution is misspecified, a parametric test can give misleading results. For example, $f(\cdot)$ and $g(\cdot)$ may not belong to the same family of distributions, although the two distributions may in fact have the same means and variances. In this case the parametric test based on the normality assumption may fail to reject an incorrect null, i.e., can lack power. Thus, the parametric test is not a consistent test. In this example, the parametric test has asymptotic power equal to one when the normality assumption is correct, but it may lack power when the assumed distribution is misspecified. That is, it does not have asymptotic power equal to one for every possible departure from the null hypothesis.

Unlike their parametric counterparts, nonparametric methods can be used to construct consistent tests that have power in every direction. One can estimate $f(\cdot)$ and $g(\cdot)$ using nonparametric techniques and then test whether or nor $f(x) = g(x)$ for almost all x. One convenient distance measure between two distributions $f(\cdot)$ and $g(\cdot)$ is their integrated square difference given by

$$J = \int [f(x) - g(x)]^2 \, dx.$$

Observe that $J = 0$ under H_0, and $J > 0$ if H_0 is false. Thus, J provides a sound basis for consistently testing H_0. We discuss how to test H_0 based on a kernel estimate of J in Section 12.2.

Let us consider another example in which we wish to test for correct specification of a linear regression model of the form

$$Y_i = \alpha + X_i'\beta + u_i, \tag{12.1}$$

where X_i is of dimension $q \times 1$, $\beta = (\beta_1, \ldots, \beta_q)'$ and α (a scalar) are unknown parameters.

The conventional F-test or t-test for testing omitted variables can be used to check the correctness of (12.1) by nesting (12.1) in a larger *parametric* model. However, these parametric model-based tests have power only in certain directions as we demonstrate below.

For expositional simplicity we assume that X_i is a scalar. A standard t-test (or F-test) can be used to test the hypothesis

$$H_{p0} : Y_i = \alpha + \beta_1 X_i + u_i \qquad (12.2)$$

against the alternative hypothesis

$$H_{p1} : Y_i = \alpha + \beta_1 X_i + \beta_2 X_i^2 + u_i. \qquad (12.3)$$

If H_{p1} is the true model, a parametric t or $f(\cdot)$ test will possess power to detect the fact that the true model is H_{p1}. Thus, a parametric test is expected to have good power when the deviation from the null model lies in the direction of H_{p1}.

Note, however, that H_{p1} is not the complement of H_{p0}. That is, when H_{p0} is false, *this does not necessarily imply that H_{p1} is true.* Assume that, in fact, the following equation represents the true model:

$$H_{p2} : Y_i = \alpha + \beta_1 X_i + \beta_3 X_i^3 + u_i. \qquad (12.4)$$

If H_{p2} is the true model, then neither H_{p0} nor H_{p1} is correctly specified. Now let us further assume that X_i is symmetrically distributed around zero (so that $\mathrm{E}(X_i^l) = 0$ for $l = 1, 3, 5$). Then it can be shown that $\hat{\beta}_2 \xrightarrow{p} 0$ (see Exercise 12.1), where $\hat{\beta}_2$ is the least squares estimator of β_2 based on Model (12.3). This implies that a standard t-test (or F-test) based on estimating Model (12.3) will lack power, and in practice is likely to fail to reject the false null Model (12.2). Thus, when the null hypothesis is false, a parametric test does not have power in *every* direction, and thus cannot form the basis for a consistent test. Nonparametric methods, however, can be used to construct a model specification test that has power in *all* directions that depart from the null model, which explains why they are so appealing. Bierens (1982) appears to be the first to propose a consistent (nonsmoothing) test for correct parametric regression functional form, while Ullah (1985) considered consistent model specification tests using nonparametric smoothing techniques.

In the remaining part of this chapter we discuss how to use nonparametric methods to construct consistent kernel-based model specification tests. Model specification tests can also be constructed without using nonparametric techniques, and we shall refer to this second class of tests as "nonsmoothing tests" (we discuss such tests in Chapter 13). Consistent k-nn and series-based model specification tests are covered in Chapters 14 and 15, respectively.

12.1   A Simple Consistent Test for Parametric Regression Functional Form

One can test for correct specification of a linear regression model based upon $\int [\hat{g}(x) - \hat{\alpha} - x'\hat{\beta}]^2 \, dx$, where $\hat{g}(x)$ is a nonparametric estimate of $g(x) = \mathrm{E}(Y|x)$, and $\hat{\alpha}$ and $\hat{\beta}$ are the least squares estimators of α and β based on a linear regression model. However, as we shall show, it is desirable to cast such regression-based tests in the form of a conditional moment test whose null is H_0^a: $\mathrm{E}(u|x) = 0$ for almost all x, where the definition of u and x depend upon the particular model and null hypothesis being tested. In the example above where we considered testing a linear regression model, we can define $u = Y - \alpha - X'\beta$; hence $\mathrm{E}(u|x) = 0$ a.e. is equivalent to $\mathrm{E}(Y|x) = \alpha + x'\beta$ a.e.

We now consider a conditional moment test constructed from $I = \mathrm{E}[u\mathrm{E}(u|X)M(X)]$, where $M(\cdot)$ is a nonnegative weight function. This statistic is used because, by the law of iterated expectations, we observe that $I = \mathrm{E}\{[\mathrm{E}(u|X)]^2 M(X)\} \geq 0$ with equality holding if and only if H_0^a is true. Thus, I serves as a proper candidate for consistently testing H_0^a. The commonly used weight functions are (i) $M(x) = f(x)$ ($f(\cdot)$ is the PDF of X) and (ii) $M(x) \equiv 1$. The choice of $M(x) = f(x)$ serves to avoid a random denominator problem, thereby simplifying the asymptotic analysis. Therefore, to simplify the theoretical analysis we mainly focus on case (i), which uses $M(x) = f(x)$.

Using $M(\cdot) = f(\cdot)$, the sample analogue of $\mathrm{E}[u\mathrm{E}(u|X)f(X)]$ is given by $n^{-1}\sum_{i=1}^{n} u_i\mathrm{E}(u_i|X_i)f(X_i)$, and a feasible statistic can be obtained by replacing u_i and $\mathrm{E}(u_i|X_i)f(X_i)$ by consistent estimators thereof. The resulting test statistic has a simpler form than that based upon the sample analogue of $\mathrm{E}\{[\mathrm{E}(u|X)]^2 f(X)\}$ because the sample analogue of the latter is $n^{-1}\sum_{i=1}^{n} u_i^2[\mathrm{E}(u_i|X_i)]^2 f(X_i)$. When the conditional mean function is replaced by a nonparametric kernel estimator, this test statistic will contain three summations, while the former contains only two. The former test statistic is also simpler than a test based on integrated squared differences between a parametric and nonparametric estimator (see Section 12.1.2 for further details).

12.1.1 A Consistent Test for Correct Parametric Functional Form

For testing the correctness of a parametric regression model, the null hypothesis is

$$H_0^a : \mathrm{E}(Y|x) = m(x, \gamma_0), \text{ for almost all } x \text{ and for some } \gamma_0 \in \mathcal{B} \subset \mathbb{R}^p, \tag{12.5}$$

where $m(x, \gamma)$ is a known function with γ being a $p \times 1$ vector of unknown parameter (which clearly includes a linear regression model as a special case) and where $\mathcal{B}$ is a compact subset of $\mathbb{R}^p$. The alternative hypothesis is the negation of H_0^a, i.e., H_1^a: $\mathrm{E}(Y|x) \equiv g(x) \neq m(x, \gamma)$ for all $\gamma \in \mathcal{B}$ on a set (of x) with positive measure. If we define $u_i = Y_i - m(X_i, \gamma_0)$, then the null hypothesis can be equivalently written as

$$\mathrm{E}(u_i | X_i = x) = 0 \text{ for almost all } x. \tag{12.6}$$

We will construct a consistent model specification test based on non-parametric kernel estimation of (12.6).

Using (12.6) and the discussion at the beginning of this chapter, one can construct a consistent test statistic based on $\mathrm{E}\{u_i \mathrm{E}(u_i|X_i)f(X_i)\}$, where $f(x)$ is the joint PDF of X. Density weighting is used here simply to avoid a random denominator that would otherwise appear in the kernel estimator.

The sample analogue of $\mathrm{E}[u_i\mathrm{E}(u_i|X_i)f(X_i)]$ is given by the formula $n^{-1}\sum_{i=1}^{n} u_i\mathrm{E}(u_i|X_i)f(X_i)$. To obtain a feasible test statistic, we replace u_i by $\hat{u}_i$, where $\hat{u}_i = Y_i - m(X_i, \hat{\gamma})$ is the residual obtained from the parametric null model, and $\hat{\gamma}$ is a $\sqrt{n}$-consistent estimator of γ based on the null model (say, the nonlinear least squares estimator of γ). We estimate $\mathrm{E}(u_i|X_i)f(X_i)$ by the leave-one-out kernel estimator $(n-1)^{-1}\sum_{j\neq i}\hat{u}_j K_{h,ij}$, where $K_{h,ij} = \prod_{s=1}^{q} h_s^{-1}k((X_{is} - X_{js})/h_s)$ and we assume that X_i is a continuous variable of dimension q. We will discuss the case for which X_i is a vector of mixed discrete and continuous variables in Section 12.1.2. Our test statistic is based upon

$$I_n^a \stackrel{\text{def}}{=} \frac{1}{n}\sum_{i=1}^{n}\hat{u}_i\left\{\frac{1}{n-1}\sum_{j=1,j\neq i}^{n}\hat{u}_j K_{h,ij}\right\}$$

$$= \frac{1}{n(n-1)}\sum_{i=1}^{n}\sum_{j=1,j\neq i}^{n}\hat{u}_i\hat{u}_j K_{h,ij}. \tag{12.7}$$

Condition 12.1.

(i) $f(x)$, $g(x) = \mathrm{E}(Y|x)$, $\sigma^2(x) = \mathrm{E}(u_i^2|x)$, and $\mu_4(x) = \mathrm{E}(u_i^4|x)$ are all bounded and continuous functions. $m(x, \gamma)$ is continuous in x and twice differentiable in γ, and $m(\cdot)$ and its derivative functions are bounded by functions having finite second moments.

(ii) $k(\cdot)$ is a bounded second order kernel. As $n \to \infty$, $h_s \to 0$ ($s = 1, \ldots, q$) and $nh_1 \ldots h_q \to \infty$.

The asymptotic null distribution of I_n^a is given in the following theorem.

Theorem 12.1. *Assuming that Condition 12.1 holds, then under H_0^a,*

$$T_n^a \stackrel{\text{def}}{=} n(h_1 \ldots h_q)^{1/2} I_n^a / \sqrt{\hat{\sigma}_a^2} \stackrel{d}{\to} N(0,1),$$

where $\hat{\sigma}_a^2 = \frac{2h_1 \ldots h_q}{n(n-1)} \sum_{i=1}^n \sum_{j \neq i}^n \hat{u}_i^2 \hat{u}_j^2 K_{h,ij}^2$ *is a consistent estimator of* $\sigma_a^2 = 2\kappa^q \mathrm{E}[\sigma^4(X)f(X)]$.

The proof of Theorem 12.1 is given in Section 12.6. The next theorem shows that T_n^a is a consistent test.

Theorem 12.2. *Assume that Condition 12.1 holds. Then if H_0^a is false, we have, for any positive constant $C > 0$,*

$$\mathrm{P}(T_n^a > C) \to 1 \ as \ n \to \infty.$$

The proof of Theorem 12.2 is sketched out in Section 12.6.2. The T_n^a statistic was proposed independently by Li (1994) and Zheng (1996), and a version of it was also used in Fan and Li (1996).

Note that because T_n^a is a one-sided test, in practice H_0^a is rejected at level α if $T_n^a > Z_\alpha$, where Z_α is the upper α-percentile of a standard normal variable. For example, we reject H_0^a at the 5% level if $T_n^a > 1.645$.

Theorems 12.1 and 12.2 place only minimal requirements on the permissible range of the h_s's. Thus, I_n^a admits a wide range of smoothing parameter values. For example, it allows one to use least squares cross-validation methods, plug-in methods, and some ad hoc methods for selecting the h_s's. Theorems 12.1 and 12.2 remain valid when one replaces the unknown optimal nonstochastic smoothing parameters by any of the aforementioned methods so long as they result in $h_s \to 0$ and $nh_1 \ldots h_q \to \infty$ as $n \to \infty$.

It can be shown that under H_0^a, $n(h_1 \ldots h_q)^{1/2} I_n^a$ converges to a zero mean normal random variable at a slow rate, $O_p\left((h_1 \ldots h_q)^{1/2}\right)$ (see (12.41) of Section 12.6.1). If we consider the case for which $q = 1$ and $h \sim n^{-1/5}$ (the optimal rate for nonparametric estimation with $q = 1$), then $O(h^{1/2}) = O(n^{-1/10})$, which converges to zero extremely slowly. The simulation study in Li and Wang (1998) indeed shows that the I_n^a test converges to a normal variable very slowly, and the test is significantly undersized even for samples of size $n = 1,000$. However, they demonstrate that a wild bootstrap procedure (Liu (1988)) can be used to greatly improve the finite-sample performance of the I_n^a test (see Exercise 12.2 for further insight into the workings of the wild bootstrap method).

The steps involved in computing the wild bootstrap statistic are as follows:

(i) For $i = 1, \ldots, n$, generate the two-point wild bootstrap error $u_i^* = [(1 - \sqrt{5})/2]\hat{u}_i$ with probability $r = (1 + \sqrt{5})/(2\sqrt{5})$, and $u_i^* = [(1 + \sqrt{5})/2]\hat{u}_i$ with probability $1 - r$.

(ii) Obtain $Y_i^* = m(X_i, \hat{\gamma}) + u_i^*$ ($i = 1, \ldots, n$). The resulting sample $\{X_i, Y_i^*\}_{i=1}^n$ is called the bootstrap sample. Then obtain the bootstrap residuals $\hat{u}_i^* = Y_i^* - m(X_i, \hat{\gamma}^*)$ ($i = 1, \ldots, n$), where $\hat{\gamma}^*$ is the nonlinear least squares estimator of γ estimated for the bootstrap sample.

(iii) Use the bootstrap residuals to compute the test statistic $T_n^{a*} = n(h_1 \ldots h_q)^{1/2} I_n^{a*}/\sqrt{\hat{\sigma}_a^{*2}}$, where I_n^{a*} and $\hat{\sigma}_a^{*2}$ are the same as I_n^a and $\hat{\sigma}_a^2$ except that $\hat{u}_i$ is replaced by $\hat{u}_i^*$.

(iv) Repeat steps (i) through (iii) a large number of times, say $B = 399$ times, and then construct the empirical distribution of the B bootstrap test statistics, $\{T_{nj}^{a*}\}_{j=1}^B$. This bootstrap empirical distribution is used to approximate the null distribution of the test statistic T_n^a. We reject H_0^a if $T_n^a > T_{n(\alpha B)}^{a*}$, where $T_{n(\alpha B)}^{a*}$ is the upper α-percentile of $\{T_{nj}^{a*}\}_{j=1}^B$.

Heuristically, steps (ii) and (iii) above ensure that, conditional on the random sample $\{X_i, Y_i\}_{i=1}^n$, the bootstrap sample is generated by the null model because, conditional on $\{X_i, Y_i\}_{i=1}^n$, u_i^* has zero mean and the bootstrap statistic obtained in step (iii) approximates the *null* distribution of the test statistic T_n^a whether the null hypothesis is true or not.

The next theorem confirms this intuition and proves that the wild bootstrap works.

Theorem 12.3. *Under the same conditions as in Theorem 12.1, except that we do not impose the null hypothesis H_0^a, then*

$$\sup_{z \in \mathbb{R}} |P(T_n^{a*} \le z|\{X_i, Y_i\}_{i=1}^n) - \Phi(z)| = o_p(1), \qquad (12.8)$$

where $\Phi(\cdot)$ is the CDF of a standard normal random variable.

Theorem 12.3 says that the bootstrap statistic T_n^{a*} converges to an $N(0,1)$ random variable in distribution in probability. See Li, Hsiao and Zinn (2003), who give an alternative formulation of the concept of "convergence in distribution in probability."

Note that $\Phi(z)$, the CDF of an $N(0,1)$ random variable, is a continuous function. By Polyā's theorem (see Bhattacharya and Rao (1986)), we know that in order to prove (12.8) it suffices to show that, for any fixed value of $z \in \mathbb{R}$,

$$|P(T_n^{a*} \le z|\{X_i, Y_i\}_{i=1}^n) - \Phi(z)| = o_p(1). \qquad (12.9)$$

The proof of (12.9) is similar to the proof of Theorem 12.1 except that one needs to utilize a different CLT argument because, conditional on the data, the leading term of T_n^{a*} is a U-statistic with a kernel function (the U-statistic kernel function, not the nonparametric kernel function $k(\cdot)$) that depends on i and j. In this case, one can use de Jong's (1987) CLT for quadratic forms to prove Theorem 12.3. See Fan, Li and Min (2006) and Hsiao et al. (forthcoming) for more detailed discussion on this issue.

The simulations reported in Li and Wang (1998) show that the T_n^{a*} test performs well in practice, with its empirical level not differing significantly from its nominal level in moderate sample sizes (e.g., $n = 100$). Li and Wang further show that, under H_0, $|T_n^{a*} - T_n^a| = O_p(n^{-1/2}(h_1 \dots h_q)^{1/2})$. Thus, the bootstrap method indeed provides a much better approximation to the null distribution than does the asymptotic normal approximation. Again, considering the case for which $q = 1$ and $h = O(n^{-1/5})$, the bootstrap approximation error rate is $O_p(n^{-1/2}h^{1/2}) = O_p(n^{-11/20})$, which is much smaller than the asymptotic normal approximation rate of $O_p(h^{1/2}) = O_p(n^{-1/10})$. Fan and Linton (2003) provide further analysis on the accuracy of the bootstrap statistic T_n^{a*}.

We now briefly discuss the choice of the weight function $M(x) = 1$. In this case the test statistic is modified as follows:

$$I_{n,m}^a = \frac{1}{n(n-1)} \sum_{i=1}^{n} \sum_{j \neq i}^{n} \hat{u}_i \hat{u}_j K_{h,ij} / \hat{f}_{-i}(X_i), \qquad (12.10)$$

where $\hat{f}_{-i}(X_i) = (n-1)^{-1} \sum_{j \neq i}^{n} K_{h,ij}$ is the leave-one-out kernel estimator of $f(X_i)$. Theorem 12.1 is modified to

Theorem 12.4. *Under conditions similar to those stated in Theorem 12.1, and further assuming that X has a bounded support and that $f(\cdot)$ is bounded below by a positive constant in the support of X, then under H_0^a,*

$$T_{n,m}^a \overset{\text{def}}{=} n(h_1 \dots h_q)^{1/2} I_{n,m}^a / \sqrt{\hat{\sigma}_{a,m}^2} \overset{d}{\to} N(0,1),$$

where $\hat{\sigma}_{a,m}^2 = \frac{2h_1 \dots h_q}{n(n-1)} \sum_{i=1}^{n} \sum_{j \neq i}^{n} \hat{u}_i^2 \hat{u}_j^2 K_{h,ij}^2 / \hat{f}_{-i}(X_i)^2$ is a consistent estimator of $\sigma_{a,m}^2 = 2\kappa^q E[\sigma^4(X)/f(X)]$.

Theorem 12.4 requires that X has bounded support and that $f(\cdot)$ is bounded from below because, otherwise, the asymptotic variance $E[\sigma^2(X)/f(X)]$ may not be finite. Alternatively, one can use a fixed trimming set to trim out extremely large values of the X_i's so that one uses data from a bounded set only. Modifying the bootstrap procedure for the $T_{n,m=1}^a$ test is straightforward. The steps (i) and (ii) for generating u_i^*, Y_i^* and $\hat{u}_i^*$ remain the same. In steps (iii) and (iv), one computes the bootstrap statistic $T_{n,m}^{a*}$ in the same manner as $T_{n,m}^a$ (not T_n^a) except that $\hat{u}_i$ is replaced by $\hat{u}_i^*$.

Alternatively, one could test for correct parametric regression functional form based upon a difference of sums of squared residuals, i.e., $SSR_P - SSR_N$ as suggested by Ullah (1985), where $SSR_N = n^{-1} \sum_{i=1}^{n} \tilde{u}_i^2$, $\tilde{u}_i = Y_i - \hat{g}_{-i}(X_i)$, $\hat{g}_{-i}(X_i)$ is the leave-one-out kernel estimator of $E(Y_i|X_i)$, and $SSR_P = n^{-1} \sum_{i=1}^{n} \hat{u}_i^2$, $\hat{u}_i = Y_i - m(X_i, \hat{\gamma})$. Dette (1999) derives the asymptotic null distribution of a squared residual-based test for the univariate X case, while Fan and Huang (2001) and Fan and Li (2002) consider squared residual-based tests for the general multivariate X case. Fan and Li (2002) showed that, under H_0,

$$\hat{T}_{n,SSR} \overset{\text{def}}{=} n(h_1 \dots h_q)^{1/2} [SSR_P - SSR_N + \hat{c}_n] / \hat{\sigma}_{SSR} \overset{d}{\to} N(0,1), \qquad (12.11)$$

where $\hat{c}_n = \hat{c}_{2n}$ if $q \leq 3$, and $\hat{c}_n = \hat{c}_{1n} + \hat{c}_{2n}$ if $q \geq 4$, with

$$\hat{c}_{1n} = \frac{1}{n^3} \sum_{i=1}^{n} \sum_{j \neq i}^{n} [m(x_i, \hat{\gamma}) - m(x_j, \hat{\gamma})]^2 K_{h,ij}^2 / \hat{f}_{-i}(X_i)^2,$$

$$\hat{c}_{2n} = \frac{1}{n^3} \sum_{i=1}^{n} \sum_{j \neq i}^{n} \hat{u}_i^2 K_{h,ij}^2 / \hat{f}_{-i}(X_i)^2,$$

$$\hat{\sigma}_{SSR}^2 = \frac{2(h_1 \ldots h_q)}{n(n-1)} \sum_{i=1}^{n} \sum_{j \neq i}^{n} \hat{u}_i^2 \hat{u}_j^2 (\bar{K}_{h,ij} - 2K_{h,ij})^2 / \hat{f}_{-i}(X_i)^2,$$

$$\hat{f}_{-i}(X_i) = \frac{1}{n-1} \sum_{j \neq i}^{n} K_{h,ij},$$

where $K_{h,ij} = \prod_{s=1}^{q} h_j^{-1} k((X_{js} - X_{is})/h_s)$, $\bar{K}_{h,ij} = \prod_{s=1}^{q} h_j^{-1} \bar{k}((X_{js} - X_{is})/h_s)$, and $\bar{k}(v) = \int k(u+v)k(u)du$.

Note that when $q = 1$ (12.11) collapses to the result given in Theorem 2.3 of Dette (1999) except that (12.11) only has one center term $\hat{c}_{2n}$ because (12.11) uses the *leave-one-out* kernel estimator which removes a center term as compared with Dette, who did not use the leave-one-out estimator.

Fan and Li (2002) recommend using a bootstrap method to better approximate the null distribution of the $\hat{T}_{n,SSR}$ test. Let $\hat{u}_i^* = Y_i^* - m(X_i, \hat{\gamma}^*)$ be the bootstrap residual discussed above, and define $\tilde{u}_i^* = Y_i^* - \hat{Y}_i^*$, where $\hat{Y}_i^* = \sum_{j \neq i} Y_j^* K_{h,ij} / \sum_{j \neq i} K_{h,ij}$. Then the bootstrap statistic is $T_{n,SSR}^* = n(h_1 \ldots h_q)^{1/2}[SSR_P^* - SSR_N^* + \hat{c}_n^*]/\hat{\sigma}_{SSR}^*$, where SSR_P^*, SSR_N^*, $\hat{c}_n^*$ and $\hat{\sigma}_{SSR}^*$ are obtained from SSR_P, SSR_N, $\hat{c}_n$ and $\hat{\sigma}_{SSR}$ with $\tilde{u}_i$ and $\hat{u}_i$ being replaced by $\tilde{u}_i^*$ and $\hat{u}_i^*$, respectively.

For seminal work on the theory of bootstrap methods see Efron (1982) and Hall (1992); for related work on the appropriate number of bootstrap replications see Davidson and MacKinnon (2000) and Andrews and Buchinsky (2002).

12.1.2   Mixed Data

In this section we consider the case for which $X = (X^c, X^d)$, where X^c is a continuous variable of dimension q, and X^d is a discrete variable of dimension r. If the sample size is much larger than the number of discrete cells and the dimension of q is small, then one can use the frequency method outlined in Chapter 3 to handle the presence of the discrete variables. In this case the test statistic remains unchanged except that the kernel function $K_{h,ij}$ needs to be replaced by $K_h(X_i^c, X_j^c)\mathbf{1}(X_i^d = X_j^d)$, where $\mathbf{1}(X_i^d = X_j^d) = \prod_{s=1}^r \mathbf{1}(X_{is}^d = X_{js}^d)$, which equals 1 if $X^d = X_j^d$, and 0 otherwise. With this modification, the results of Theorems 12.1 and 12.2 remain valid.

One can also smooth the discrete variables as outlined in Chapter 4. Then the test statistic I_n^a needs to be modified by replacing $K_{h,ij}$ by $K_{\gamma,ij} = K_h(X_i^c, X_j^c)L(X_i^d, X_j^d, \lambda)$, where $L(X_i^d, X_j^d, \lambda) = \prod_{s=1}^r l(X_{is}^d, X_{js}^d, \lambda_s)$ is defined in Chapter 4, $\gamma = (h, \lambda)$. One can choose the smoothing parameters $(h_1, \ldots, h_q, \lambda_1, \ldots, \lambda_r)$ by the (local constant) least squares cross-validation method, or by an ad hoc method. Letting $I_n^a(\hat{h}, \hat{\lambda})$ denote the resulting test statistic, then Theorems 12.1 and 12.2 remain valid. For example, Theorem 12.1 becomes

$$T_n^a = n(\hat{h}_1 \ldots \hat{h}_q)^{1/2} I_n^a(\hat{h}, \hat{\lambda})/\hat{\sigma}_a \xrightarrow{d} N(0,1) \text{ under } H_0,$$

where

$$I_n^a \stackrel{\text{def}}{=} \frac{1}{n(n-1)} \sum_{i=1}^n \sum_{j=1, j\neq i}^n \hat{u}_i \hat{u}_j K_{\hat{h}}\left(X_i^c, X_j^c\right) L(X_i^d, X_j^d, \hat{\lambda})$$

and

$$\hat{\sigma}_a^2 = \frac{2\hat{h}_1 \ldots \hat{h}_q}{n(n-1)} \sum_{i=1}^n \sum_{j\neq i}^n \hat{u}_i^2 \hat{u}_j^2 K_{\hat{h}}\left(X_i^2, X_j^c\right)^2 L(X_i^d, X_j^d, \hat{\lambda})^2.$$

The simulations reported in Hsiao et al. (forthcoming) show that the "wild bootstrap method" yields a test having correct level. Furthermore, the cross-validation method tends to select relatively large values of the h_s's for slowly changing functions (low frequency alternatives) and relatively small values for rapidly changing functions (high frequency alternatives). Therefore, the cross-validation-based T_n^a test has better power than the T_n^a test based upon ad hoc bandwidth selection rules such as $h_s = X_{s,sd} n^{-1/(q+4)}$ and $\lambda_s = 0$.

In addition to the tests discussed in this section, many alternative nonparametric tests for testing for correct parametric regression functional form have been proposed in the literature. See, for example, Azzalini, Bowman and Härdle (1989), Wooldridge (1992), Yatchew (1992), Eubank and Spiegelman (1990), Härdle and Mammen (1993), Eubank and Hart (1992), Ait-Sahalia, Bickel and Stoker (2001), Ellison and Ellison (2000), Liu, Stengos and Li (2000), and Stengos and Sun (2001). Tripathi and Kitamura (2003), Chen, Härdle and Li (2003), and Chen and Gao (forthcoming) consider empirical likelihood goodness-of-fit tests. Hart (1997) provides a general treatment for testing correct parametric regression functional form based on nonparametric estimation techniques. Horowitz (2006) constructs a consistent test for correct parametric regression functional form against a general nonparametric alternative model in an instrumental variable regression model framework. We discuss nonparametric instrumental variable estimation in Chapter 17.

12.2   Testing for Equality of PDFs

In this section we consider the problem of testing whether two random samples are drawn from the same distribution. Suppose we have two i.i.d. data sets $\{X_i\}_{i=1}^{n_1}$ and $\{Y_i\}_{i=1}^{n_2}$, each being drawn from q-dimensional continuous random vectors. Assuming that X has PDF $f(\cdot)$ and Y has PDF $g(\cdot)$, then the null hypothesis we wish to test is

$$H_0^b : f(x) = g(x) \text{ for almost all } x.$$

We construct a test statistic based on the integrated squared difference between $f(\cdot)$ and $g(\cdot)$, which is given by

$$I^b = \int [f(x) - g(x)]^2 dx$$
$$= \int \left[f^2(x) + g^2(x) - 2f(x)g(x) \right] dx$$
$$= \int f(x)dF(x) + \int g(x)dG(x) - 2 \int f(x)dG(x),$$

where $F(\cdot)$ and $G(\cdot)$ are the CDFs of X and Y, respectively. A feasible test statistic can be obtained by replacing $f(\cdot)$, $g(\cdot)$, $F(\cdot)$ and $G(\cdot)$ by $\hat{f}(\cdot)$, $\hat{g}(\cdot)$, $F_n(\cdot)$ and $G_n(\cdot)$, where $\hat{f}(x) = n_1^{-1} \sum_{i=1}^{n_1} K_h(X_i, x)$, $\hat{g}(x) = n_2^{-1} \sum_{i=1}^{n_2} K_h(Y_i, x)$, and where $F_n(\cdot)$ and $G_n(\cdot)$ are the empirical CDFs of $\{X_i\}_{i=1}^{n_1}$ and $\{Y_i\}_{i=1}^{n_2}$. Note that, using the Dirac δ function approach (see definition A.15 in the appendix), we know that for any (measurable) function $M(\cdot)$, $\int M(x)dF_n(x) = n_1^{-1} \sum_{j=1}^{n_1} M(X_j)$, and $\int M(x)dG_n(x) = n_2^{-1} \sum_{j=1}^{n_2} M(Y_j)$. Therefore, we obtain a feasible statistic given by

$$I_n^b = \int \hat{f}(x)dF_n(x) + \int \hat{g}(x)dG_n(x) - 2\int \hat{f}(x)dG_n(x)$$

$$= \left\{ \frac{1}{n_1^2}\sum_{i=1}^{n_1}\sum_{j=1}^{n_1}K_{h,ij}^x + \frac{1}{n_2^2}\sum_{i=1}^{n_2}\sum_{j=1}^{n_2}K_{h,ij}^y - \frac{2}{n_1 n_2}\sum_{i=1}^{n_1}\sum_{j=1}^{n_2}K_{h,ij}^{xy} \right\},$$

where $K_{h,ij}^x = \prod_{s=1}^q h_s^{-1}k((X_{is} - X_{js})/h_s)$, $K_{h,ij}^y = \prod_{s=1}^q h_s^{-1}k((Y_{is} - Y_{js})/h_s)$, and $K_{h,ij}^{x,y} = \prod_{s=1}^q h_s^{-1}k((X_{is} - Y_{js})/h_s)$. The following condition is needed to derive the asymptotic distribution of I_n^b.

Condition 12.2.

(i) Both $f(\cdot)$ and $g(\cdot)$ are bounded and continuous functions.

(ii) $k(\cdot)$ is a bounded, nonnegative second order kernel function.

Theorem 12.5. *When Condition 12.2 holds, under H_0^b we have*

$$T_n^b \stackrel{\text{def}}{=} (n_1 n_2 h_1 \dots h_q)^{1/2}\frac{(I_n^b - c_{n,b})}{\hat{\sigma}_b} \stackrel{d}{\to} N(0,1), \qquad (12.12)$$

where $c_{n,b} = \frac{k(0)^q}{h_1\dots h_q}[\frac{1}{n_1} + \frac{1}{n_2}]$ and where $\hat{\sigma}_b^2$ equals

$$\frac{h_1\dots h_q}{n_1 n_2}\left\{ \sum_{i=1}^{n_1}\sum_{j=1}^{n_1}\frac{(K_{h,ij}^x)^2}{(n_1/n_2)} + \sum_{i=1}^{n_2}\sum_{j=1}^{n_2}\frac{(K_{h,ij}^y)^2}{(n_2/n_1)} + 2\sum_{i=1}^{n_1}\sum_{j=1}^{n_2}(K_{h,ij}^{x,y})^2 \right\}.$$

The proof of Theorem 12.5 is given in Section 12.6.3. Note that $\hat{\sigma}_b^2$ given in Theorem 12.5 is different from the one given in Li (1996). Exercise 12.4 shows that $\hat{\sigma}_b^2$ is asymptotically equivalent to the variance estimator given in Li.

It can be shown that T_n^b is indeed a consistent test, having power in all directions when H_0^b is false, i.e., if H_0 is false, then

$$\text{P}\left(T_n^b > C\right) \to 1, \text{ for any positive constant } C. \qquad (12.13)$$

T_n^b is a one-sided test, therefore in practice one rejects H_0^b at level α if $T_n^b > Z_\alpha$, where Z_α is the upper α-percentile of a standard normal variable.

Note that the I_n^b test has a nonzero center term $c_{n,b}$, which needs to be subtracted in order to obtain an asymptotic zero mean test (under H_0^b). In the proof of Theorem 12.5 we know that the center term comes from the presence of the $i = j$ terms in I_n^b. Li (1996) also considers a center-free test statistic obtained by removing the $i = j$ terms in I_n^b. Define

$$
I_{1n}^b = \left\{ \frac{1}{n_1^2} \sum_{i=1}^{n_1} \sum_{j\neq i,j=1}^{n_1} K_{h,ij}^x + \frac{1}{n_2^2} \sum_{i=1}^{n_2} \sum_{j\neq i,j=1}^{n_2} K_{h,ij}^y \right.
$$
$$
\left. - \frac{2}{n_1 n_2} \sum_{i=1}^{n_1} \sum_{j\neq i,j=1}^{n_2} K_{h,ij}^{x,y} \right\} \quad (12.14)
$$

By the proof of Theorem 12.5 we immediately have the following corollary:

Corollary 12.1. *Under the same conditions given in Theorem 12.5, we have*

$$
T_{1n}^b \overset{\text{def}}{=} (n_1 n_2 h_1 \dots h_q)^{1/2} I_{1n}^b / \hat{\sigma}_b \overset{d}{\to} N(0,1) \ \text{under } H_0^b. \quad (12.15)
$$

The simulations reported in Li (1996) show that the center-free T_{1n}^b test has slightly better finite-sample size and power than the T_n^b test; however, the center-free test T_{1n}^b presents one problem. In finite samples, the value of this statistic depends on the ordering of X_i and Y_j ($i = 1, \dots, n_1; j = 1, \dots, n_2$). To see this note that

$$
I_{1n}^b = I_n^b - \left(\frac{1}{n_1} + \frac{1}{n_2} \right) \frac{k(0)^q}{h_1 \dots h_q} - \frac{2}{n_1 n_2} \sum_{i=1}^{\min\{n_1,n_2\}} K_{ii}^{x,y}. \quad (12.16)
$$

While I_n^b is invariant to the ordering of the data, the third term in (12.16), $2(n_1 n_2)^{-1} \sum_{i=1}^{\min\{n_1,n_2\}} K_{ii}^{x,y}$, depends on how the data is ordered. This implies that I_{1n}^b must depend on the order of the data. This last term in (12.16) is asymptotically negligible, and so different orderings will not affect the *asymptotic* distribution of I_{1n}^b but may affect the outcome of the I_{1n}^b test procedure in finite-sample applications.

As there is no natural ordering for cross-sectional data sets and as one may obtain different test results by randomly reordering the data, in practice one should be cautious when using the T_{1n}^b test. In contrast, however, the T_n^b test is invariant with respect to different orderings of the data.

The test in (12.12) is basically the same as a test proposed by Mammen (1992) except that the test in Mammen requires the computation of twofold and fourfold convolutions of the kernel function. Anderson, Hall and Titterington (1994) also propose a test similar to T_n^b but with a fixed smoothing parameter (a nonsmoothing test), which leads to their test statistic having a nonstandard distribution. They suggest using bootstrap methods to approximate the null distribution of their test statistic. We discuss nonsmoothing tests in Chapter 13.

Mammen (1992) suggests using bootstrap methods to better approximate the null distribution of the test statistic. This is accomplished by randomly sampling with replacement from the pooled data. Letting Z_i denote the ith sample realization for the pooled data, randomly draw n_1 observations from $\{Z_i\}_{i=1}^{n_1+n_2}$ with replacement, call this sample $\{X_i^*\}_{i=1}^{n_1}$, then randomly draw n_2 observations with replacement from $\{Z_i\}_{i=1}^{n_1+n_2}$ and call this $\{Y_i^*\}_{i=1}^{n_2}$. Compute the test statistic T_n^{b*} the same way as T_n^b except with X_i and Y_i being replaced by X_i^* and Y_i^*, respectively. This procedure is repeated a large number of times, say $B = 399$ times, and the resulting bootstrap statistics $\{T_{nj}^{b*}\}_{j=1}^B$ are called the bootstrap sample of the test statistic. One rejects H_0^b if $T_n^b > T_{n(\alpha B)}^{b*}$, where $T_{n(\alpha B)}^{b*}$ is the upper α-percentile of $\{T_{nj}^{b*}\}_{j=1}^B$. For example, for an $\alpha = 5\%$ level test and for $B = 399$, put the 399 bootstrap statistics in an ascending order $T_{n(1)}^{b*} \leq T_{n(2)}^{b*} \leq \cdots \leq T_{n(399)}^{b*}$, hence $T_{n(1-\alpha(B+1))}^{b*} = T_{n(380)}^{b*}$. Or one can compute the bootstrap P-value given by m/B, where m is the number of the bootstrap statistics (T_n^{b*}) that exceed the original test statistic T_n^b.

Other related tests for checking the equality of two PDFs include Fan and Gencay (1993) and Ahmad (1980). For related metric entropy tests of equality of univariate densities, see Robinson (1991), Maasoumi and Racine (2002), and Granger, Maasoumi and Racine (2004).

12.3 More Tests Related to Regression Functions

12.3.1 Härdle and Mammen's Test for a Parametric Regression Model

Härdle and Mammen (1993) propose a consistent test for parametric regression functional form based on the sample analogue of

$$I_{HM} = \int [\hat{g}(x) - m(x, \hat{\gamma})]^2 w(x)dx,$$

where $w(x)$ is a weight function.

If one chooses $w(x) = f^2(x)$ and uses $\hat{f}(x) = n^{-1} \sum_{i=1}^{n} K_h(X_i, x)$ to replace $f(x)$, then the above statistic becomes

$$
\begin{aligned}
I_{n,HM} = \frac{1}{n} \sum_{i=1}^{n} \sum_{j=1}^{n} [Y_i - m(X_i, \hat{\gamma})] \, [Y_j - m(X_j, \hat{\gamma})] \\
\times \int K_h(X_i, x) K_h(X_j, x) \, dx \\
= \frac{1}{n} \sum_{i=1}^{n} \sum_{j=1}^{n} \hat{u}_i \hat{u}_j \bar{K}_h(X_i, X_j),
\end{aligned}
\tag{12.17}
$$

where $\hat{u}_i = Y_i - m(X_i, \hat{\gamma})$, $\bar{K}_h(X_i, X_j) = \prod_{s=1}^{q} h_s^{-1} \bar{k}((X_{is} - X_{js})/h_s)$, and $\bar{k}(v) = \int k(u)k(v+v)du$ is the twofold convolution kernel derived from k.

Comparing I_n^a and $I_{n,HM}$, we see that the only difference between them is that the latter includes the $i = j$ terms in the double summation and that K is replaced by $\bar{K}$. Therefore, by the result of Theorem 12.1 we immediately have the following corollary.

Theorem 12.6. *Under the same conditions as in Theorem 12.1, we have under H_0^a,*

$$n(h_1 \ldots h_q)^{1/2}(I_{n,HM} - c_{n,a})/\tilde{\sigma}_a^2 \xrightarrow{d} N(0, 1),$$

where $c_{n,a} = \frac{\bar{k}(0)^q}{nh_1 \ldots h_q} \sum_{i=1}^{n} \hat{u}_i^2$ and

$$\tilde{\sigma}_a^2 = \frac{2h_1 \ldots h_q}{n^2} \sum_{i=1}^{n} \sum_{j \neq i}^{n} \hat{u}_i^2 \hat{u}_j^2 \bar{K}_h (X_i, X_j)^2.$$

Proof. Note that $I_{n,HM} - c_{n,a}$ equals I_n^a except that the kernel K in I_n^a is replaced by the convolution kernel $\bar{K}$. $\bar{K}$ is also a second order kernel. Therefore, Theorem 12.6 follows from Theorem 12.1. $\square$

If one chooses $w(x) = f(x)$ in $I_{n,HM}$ and replaces the population mean with the sample mean, this gives yet another version of Härdle and Mammen's (1993) test,

$$\tilde{I}_{n,HM} = n^{-1} \sum_{i=1}^{n} [\hat{g}(X_i) - m_h(X_i, \hat{\gamma})]^2. \qquad (12.18)$$

The early literature on nonparametric testing relied upon rule-of-thumb bandwidth selection methods to construct consistent model specification tests (see, e.g., Härdle and Mammen (1993), Zheng (1996), and Li and Wang (1998)). Unfortunately, this ad hoc approach to selecting the smoothing parameters has been shown to lead to a loss of power, which has in turn led to more recent developments; see Hsiao et al. (forthcoming), who suggest using data-driven cross-validation methods for selecting the smoothing parameters, and Horowitz and Spokoiny (2001), who propose a rate-optimal adaptive test based on (12.18), which is the subject of next section.

12.3.2 An Adaptive and Rate Optimal Test

Smoothing parameter choice is a key component of nonparametric kernel analysis, and it is also extremely important when constructing nonparametric model specification tests. For nonparametric kernel-based tests, both empirical size and power are sensitive to the value of the bandwidth. When bootstrap methods are used, the empirical size of nonparametric tests is usually not that sensitive to some variation in the smoothing parameters; however, empirical power can be sensitive to such variation. Thus, an important question is how to best choose the smoothing parameters so that the resulting test will have high power against all deviations from the null model. Intuitively, one can appreciate that for low frequency data one should use a relatively large bandwidth in order to accurately estimate the deviation from the null model. However, for high frequency alternatives, a large bandwidth value will oversmooth the data and obscure deviations from the null model. Therefore, one should use a relatively small bandwidth value for high frequency alternatives (see Fan and Li (2000) for a more detailed discussion).

Horowitz and Spokoiny (2001) propose an adaptive test statistic offering the advantage of having high power against both low and high frequency alternatives. They consider a test based on a studentized version of $\tilde{I}_{n,HM}$ given in (12.18). Under the assumption that the X_i's are nonstochastic, it is easy to show that

$$N_h \stackrel{\text{def}}{=} \mathrm{E}(\tilde{I}_{n,HM}) = \sum_{i=1}^{n} a_{ii,h}\sigma^2(X_i) \text{ and}$$

$$V_h^2 \stackrel{\text{def}}{=} \mathrm{var}(\tilde{I}_{n,HM}) = 2\sum_{i=1}^{n}\sum_{j=1}^{n} a_{ij,h}^2\sigma^2(X_i)\sigma^2(X_j),$$

where $a_{ij,h} = \sum_{l=1}^{n} w_{il}w_{lj}$ with $w_{ij} \equiv K((X_i - X_j)/h)/\sum_{l=1}^{n} K((X_i - X_l)/h)$. Thus, a studentized test is given by

$$\tilde{T}_h = \frac{\tilde{I}_{n,HM} - N_h}{V_h},$$

and a feasible test is given by

$$\hat{T}_h = \frac{\tilde{I}_{n,HM} - \hat{N}_h}{\hat{V}_h},$$

where $\hat{N}_h = \sum_{i=1}^{n} a_{ii,h}\hat{\sigma}^2(X_i)$ and

$$\hat{V}_h^2 = 2\sum_{i=1}^{n}\sum_{j=1}^{n} a_{ij,h}^2\hat{\sigma}^2(X_i)\hat{\sigma}^2(X_j),$$

with $\hat{\sigma}^2(x)$ being a consistent estimator of $\sigma^2(x)$ under either H_0^a or H_1^a (see Horowitz and Spokoiny for a detailed discussion on the construction of $\hat{\sigma}^2(x)$).

To obtain an adaptive test, Horowitz and Spokoiny (2001) propose using several different smoothing parameter values $h \in H_n = \{h_{n1}, h_{n2}, \ldots, h_{nm}\}$, where m is a finite number. An example of H_n would be $H_n = \{h_s = h_{s,\max}a^k : h_s \geq h_{s,\min}, s = 1, \ldots, q; k = 0, 1, 2, \ldots\}$, where $0 < h_{s,\min} < h_{s,\max}$, and $0 < a < 1$. The test statistic is then chosen as the maximal value over all values of h considered, i.e.,

$$\hat{T} = \max_{\{h \in H_n\}} T_h. \tag{12.19}$$

Horowitz and Spokoiny (2001) suggest using bootstrap methods to approximate the critical values of the test statistic $\hat{T}$. The bootstrap steps are:

(i) Generate $Y_i^* = m(X_i, \hat{\gamma}) + u_i^*$, $i = 1, \ldots, n$, where u_i^* is a random draw from $N(0, \hat{\sigma}^2(X_i))$.

(ii) Use the bootstrap sample $\{X_i, Y_i^*\}_{i=1}^n$ to estimate γ and $\sigma^2(X_i)$, and call the resulting estimators $\hat{\gamma}^*$ and $\hat{\sigma}^{2*}(X_i)$. Compute $\hat{T}^*$ the same way as $\hat{T}$ defined in (12.19), but replace Y_i, $\hat{\gamma}$ and $\hat{\sigma}^2(X_i)$ by Y_i^*, $\hat{\gamma}^*$ and $\hat{\sigma}^{2*}(X_i)$.

(iii) Let t_α denote the asymptotic null critical value of the test at level α. Estimate t_α by the $1-\alpha$ quantile of the empirical distribution of $\hat{T}^*$ that is obtained by repeating steps (i) and (ii) a large number of times.

Horowitz and Spokoiny (2001) proved the following result:

Theorem 12.7. *Under the regularity conditions given in in Horowitz and Spokoiny (2001), letting H_0^e be true, then*

$$\lim_{n \to \infty} \mathrm{P}\left(\hat{T}^* > t_\alpha\right) = \alpha.$$

The simulations in Horowitz and Spokoiny (2001) show that their test has better power than the T_n^a test, particularly in the direction of high frequency alternatives.

12.3.3 A Test for a Parametric Single Index Model

The parametric single index model introduced in Chapter 8 is of the form

$$Y_i = g(X_i'\beta) + u_i, \quad \text{with } \mathrm{E}(u_i|X_i) = 0,$$

where $g(\cdot)$ is a known function and β is a vector of unknown parameters. For example, if $g(\cdot) = \Phi(\cdot)$, the CDF of a standard normal variable, we obtain the popular Probit model.

The null hypothesis is therefore H_0^c: $\mathrm{E}(Y_i|X_i) = g(X_i'\beta)$ or, equivalently, $\mathrm{E}(u_i|X_i) = 0$, where $u_i = Y_i - g(X_i'\beta)$. Along the lines of the analysis in Section 12.1.1, one can construct a test statistic based on $\mathrm{E}[u\mathrm{E}(u|X'\beta)f(X'\beta)]$ of the form

$$I_n^c = \frac{1}{n(n-1)} \sum_{i=1}^n \sum_{j \neq i, j=1}^n \hat{u}_i \hat{u}_j K_h\left(X_i, X_j\right), \qquad (12.20)$$

where $\hat{u}_i = Y_i - g(X_i'\hat{\beta})$, and $\hat{\beta}$ is a $\sqrt{n}$-consistent estimator of β_0 based on the parametric null model. It can be the nonlinear least squares estimator, or, in the case of a Probit or Logit model, it can be the maximum likelihood estimator of β_0.

Condition 12.3.

(i) $g(X)$ and u all have finite fourth moments. $g(\cdot)$ is twice differentiable, and $\sigma^2(v) = \mathrm{E}(u^2|x\beta = v)$ is continuous.

(ii) $k(\cdot)$ is a nonnegative second order kernel function that is m times differentiable ($m \geq 3$ is an integer).

(iii) As $n \to \infty$, $h \to 0$ and $n^{(m-2)}h^{(2m-1)} \to \infty$.

(iv) $\hat{\beta} - \beta = O_p(n^{-1/2})$ under H_0^c.

Fan and Liu (1997) proved the following result.

Theorem 12.8. *Under Condition 12.3 and H_0^c we have*

$$nh^{1/2}I_n^c/\hat{\sigma}_c^2 \xrightarrow{d} N(0,1),$$

where $\hat{\sigma}_c^2 = \frac{2h}{n(n-1)} \sum_{i=1}^n \sum_{j\neq i}^n \hat{u}_i^2 \hat{u}_j^2 K_h \left((X_i - X_j)'\hat{\beta} \right)^2$.

As was the case in Section 12.1.1, one could also use bootstrap methods to better approximate the null distribution of I_n^c.

Using an approach similar to Härdle and Mammen (1993), Horowitz and Härdle (1994) propose an approach to testing a general parametric index model versus semiparametric alternatives, which can also be used as a consistent test for H_0^c. Hristache et al. (2001) propose an alternative goodness-of-fit test for single-index models.

12.3.4 A Nonparametric Omitted Variables Test

The "test of significance" is probably the most frequently used test in applied regression analysis and is often used to confirm or refute economic theories. Sound parametric inference hinges on the correct functional specification of the underlying data generating process (DGP); however, the likelihood of misspecification in a parametric framework cannot be ignored, particularly in light of the fact that applied researchers tend to choose parametric models on the basis of parsimony and tractability. Significance testing in a nonparametric kernel framework would therefore have obvious appeal given that nonparametric techniques are consistent under much less restrictive assumptions than those required for a parametric approach.

In this section we outline an approach that allows for applied researchers to test hypotheses in a fully nonparametric and robust framework, thereby deflecting potential criticism that a particular finding is driven by an arbitrary parametric specification.

Let $X \in \mathbb{R}^q$ be a $q \times 1$ vector of continuous random variables, and partition $X = (W, Z) \in \mathbb{R}^p \times \mathbb{R}^{q-p}$ $(1 \le p < q)$. The null hypothesis is that the conditional mean of Y does not depend on Z, i.e.,

$$H_0^d : \mathrm{E}(Y|w, z) = \mathrm{E}(Y|w) \text{ a.e.}$$

Define $u = Y - \mathrm{E}(Y|W)$. Then $\mathrm{E}(u|X) = 0$ a.e. under H_0^d, and we can construct a test statistic based on $\mathrm{E}\{uf_w(W)\mathrm{E}[uf_w(W)|X]f(X)\}$, where $f_w(\cdot)$ and $f(\cdot)$ are the PDFs of W and X, respectively. Let $\hat{f}_{w_i}$ and $\hat{Y}_i$ denote the leave-one-out kernel estimators of $f_w(W_i)$ and $\mathrm{E}(Y_i|W_i)$, respectively, i.e.,

$$\hat{f}_{w_i} = \frac{1}{(n-1)} \sum_{\substack{j \ne i}}^{n} K_{h_w}(W_i, W_j),$$

$$\hat{Y}_i = \frac{1}{(n-1)} \sum_{\substack{j \ne i}}^{n} Y_j K_{h_w}(W_i, W_j)/\hat{f}_{w_i}, \text{ and}$$

$$K_{h_w}(W_i, W_j) = \prod_{s=1}^{p} h_{w,s}^{-1} k_w \left(\frac{W_{is} - W_{js}}{h_{w,s}} \right),$$

where $k_w(\cdot)$ is a univariate kernel function, and where $h_{w,s}$ is the smoothing parameter associated with W_{is}. A feasible test statistic is given by

$$I_n^d = \frac{1}{n(n-1)} \sum_{i=1}^{n} \sum_{\substack{j \ne i}}^{n} (Y_i - \hat{Y}_i)\hat{f}_{w_i}(Y_j - \hat{Y}_j)\hat{f}_{w_j} K_h(X_i, X_j),$$

where $K_h(X_i, X_j) = \prod_{s=1}^{q} h_s^{-1} k\left((X_{is} - X_{js})/h_s\right)$ is the kernel function used to estimate $\mathrm{E}(uf_w(W)|X)f(X)$.

The following condition is used to derive the asymptotic null distribution of I_n^d.

Condition 12.4.

(i) *Define* $u_i = Y_i - \mathrm{E}(Y_i|W_i)$ *and let* $\mu_4(x) = \mathrm{E}(u_i^4|x)$, f_z, $f(\cdot)$, σ^2 *and* μ_4 *all satisfy some Lipschitz type conditions, i.e.,* $|m(u + v) - m(u)| \leq C|v|$. *Let* $\mathrm{E}(Y|x)$ *be* ν *times differentiable, and let* $\mathrm{E}(Y|w)$ *be a continuous function.*

(ii) *Let* $k_w(\cdot)$ *be a* ν*th order kernel and let* $k(\cdot)$ *be a nonnegative second order kernel.*

(iii) *As* $n \to \infty$, $h_{w,s} \to 0$ ($s = 1, \ldots, p$), $h_s \to 0$ ($s = 1, \ldots, q$), $nh_{w,1} \ldots h_{w,p} \to \infty$, $nh_1 \ldots h_q \to \infty$, $n(h_1 \ldots h_q)^{1/2}(\sum_{s=1}^p h_{w,s}^{2\nu}) \to 0$, *and* $(h_1 \ldots h_q)/(h_{w,1}^2 \ldots h_{w,p}^2) \to 0$.

Condition 12.4 (i) contains standard smoothness conditions placed on the unknown functions. Condition 12.4 (ii) assumes that one uses a νth order kernel to estimate the null model. This implies that the MSE of the null model is of order $O\left(\sum_{s=1}^q h_{w,s}^{2\nu} + (nh_{w,1} \ldots h_{w,q})^{-1}\right)$. Consistent model specification tests usually involve a second order degenerate U-statistic, and the normalization constant for such a U-statistic is $n(h_1 \ldots h_q)^{1/2}$. Condition 12.4 (iii) assumes that the MSE from the null model is of smaller order than $\left(n(h_1 \ldots h_q)^{1/2}\right)^{-1}$, i.e., $n(h_1 \ldots h_q)^{1/2}\left(\sum_{s=1}^p h_{w,s}^{2\nu} + (nh_{w,1} \ldots h_{w,q})^{-1}\right) = o(1)$. Note that if $p \leq q/2$, the last condition implies that h_s has an order smaller than $h_{w,s}$, implying that we must undersmooth the alternative regression model relative to the null model.

Theorem 12.9. *Under Condition 12.4, and* H_0^d, *we have*

$$T_n^d \stackrel{\text{def}}{=} (nh_1 \ldots h_q)^{1/2} I_n^d/\hat{\sigma}_d \stackrel{d}{\to} N(0,1),$$

where $\hat{\sigma}_d^2 = \frac{2h_1 \ldots h_q}{n^2} \sum_{i=1}^n \sum_{j=1}^n \tilde{u}_i^2 \hat{f}_{wi}^2 \tilde{u}_j^2 \hat{f}_{wj}^2 K_h(X_i, X_j)^2$, $\tilde{u}_i = Y_i - \hat{Y}_i$, *and where* $K_h(X_i, X_j) = \prod_{s=1}^q h_s^{-1} k((X_{is} - X_{js})/h_s)$.

It can be shown that if H_0^d does not hold, then $\mathrm{P}(T_n^d > C) \to 1$ as $n \to \infty$, and therefore is a consistent test.

The test statistic T_n^d has an asymptotic standard normal distribution under the null hypothesis. However, simulation results reported in Li (1999) and Lavergne and Vuong (2000) reveal that the normal approximation does not work well for small to moderate samples. Also the test statistic T_n^d depends on two sets of smoothing parameters, the $h_{w,s}$'s and h_s's, and is sensitive to the choice of smoothing parameters. Lavergne and Vuong therefore suggest a modified version of the T_n^d test which has better finite-sample performance than the I_n^d test. Alternatively, one could use bootstrap methods to better approximate the null distribution of I_n^d.

In order to apply the T_n^d test in practice, first the regressor X must be partitioned into two parts, W and Z. We recommend using the local constant least squares cross-validation method to help determine which variables should belong in Z. Letting $h_s = c_s X_{s,sd} n^{-1/(4+q)}$ ($X_{s,sd}$ is the sample standard deviation of $\{X_{is}\}_{i=1}^n$), then we can search over c_s to minimize the cross-validation function. From the result of Theorem 2.4 of Chapter 2 we know that c_s should diverge to (positive) infinity when x_s is an irrelevant regressor. Therefore, x_s can be chosen to be part of Z when c_s is large, say when c_s exceeds n^{4+q} (which is equivalent to $h_s > X_{s,sd}$).

A Bootstrap Procedure for T_n^d

We use u_i^* to denote the wild bootstrap error which is obtained from the fitted residual $\tilde{u}_i = Y_i - \hat{Y}_i$, i.e., $u_i^* = [(1-\sqrt{5})/2]\tilde{u}_i$ with probability $r = (1+\sqrt{5})/(2\sqrt{5})$, and $u_i^* = [(1+/\sqrt{5})/2]\tilde{u}_i$ with probability $1-r$.

The bootstrap test statistic is obtained via the following steps.

(i) Use the wild bootstrap error u_i^* to obtain $Y_i^* = \hat{Y}_i + u_i^*$, then obtain the kernel estimator of $E^*(Y_i^*|w_i)f_{w_i}$ via

$$\hat{Y}_i^* \hat{f}_{w_i} = (n-1)^{-1} \sum_{j \neq i}^n Y_j^* K_{h_w,ij}.$$

The estimated density-weighted bootstrap residual is $\tilde{u}_i^* \hat{f}_{w_i} = (Y_i^* - \hat{Y}_i^*)\hat{f}_{w_i} = Y_i^* \hat{f}_{w_i} - \hat{Y}_i^* \hat{f}_{w_i}$.

(ii) Compute the bootstrap test statistic

$$I_n^{d*} = \frac{1}{n(n-1)} \sum_{i=1}^n \sum_{j \neq i}^n \tilde{u}_i^* \hat{f}_{w_i} \tilde{u}_j^* \hat{f}_{w_j} K_{h,ij},$$

and the estimated asymptotic variance is

$$\hat{\sigma}_d^{*2} = 2(n^2 h_1 \ldots h_q)^{-1} \sum_{i=1}^n \sum_{j \neq i}^n \tilde{u}_i^{*2} \tilde{u}_j^{*2} K \left(\frac{X_i - X_j}{h} \right)^2.$$

The standardized bootstrap statistic is therefore given by $T_n^{d*} = n(h_1 \ldots h_q)^{1/2} I_n^{d*}/\hat{\sigma}_d^*$.

(iii) Repeat steps (i) and (ii) a number of times, say $B = 399$ times, and obtain the empirical distribution of the B test statistics T_n^{d*}. Let $T_{n,\alpha}^{d*}$ denote the α percentile of the bootstrap distribution. We will reject the null hypothesis at significance level α if $T_n^d > T_{n,\alpha}^{d*}$.

The simulation results reported in Gu and Li (2006) show that the above bootstrap test successfully overcomes the size distortion present when using the asymptotic normal approximation. The estimated size is close to the nominal size and the results are relatively insensitive to the selection of smoothing parameters.

The use of density-weighting when constructing the statistic I_n^d avoids a random denominator, thereby simplifying the asymptotic analysis. Similar to the statistic $I_{n,m}^a$ discussed in Section 12.1.1, one can also use a nondensity-weighted version that results in the following modified test statistic:

$$I_{n,m}^d = \frac{1}{n(n-1)} \sum_{i=1}^n \sum_{j \neq i}^n (Y_i - \hat{Y}_i)(Y_j - \hat{Y}_j) K_h(X_i, X_j)/\hat{f}(X_i). \quad (12.21)$$

Theorem 12.9 is then modified as follows.

Theorem 12.10. *Under similar conditions as in Theorem 12.9, and also assuming that $f_e(\cdot)$ and $f(\cdot)$ are both bounded below by some positive constants in the support of W and X, then under H_0^d, we have*

$$T_{n,m}^d \stackrel{\text{def}}{=} (nh_1 \ldots h_q)^{1/2} I_{n,m}^d/\sqrt{\hat{\sigma}_{d,m}^2} \stackrel{d}{\rightarrow} N(0,1),$$

where $\hat{\sigma}_{d,m}^2 = (2h_1 \ldots h_q/n^2) \sum_{i=1}^n \sum_{j=1}^n \tilde{u}_i^2 \tilde{u}_j^2 K_h(X_i, X_j)^2/\hat{f}(X_i)^2$.

The bootstrap statistic $T_{n,m}^{d*}$ can be obtained from $T_{n,m}^d$ by replacing $\tilde{u}_i$ by $\tilde{u}_i^*$, where $\tilde{u}_i^* = Y_i^* - \hat{Y}_i^*$, Y_i^* is the same as that discussed when constructing the (density-weighted) T_n^{d*} statistic, with $\hat{Y}_i^* = (n-1)^{-1} \sum_{j \neq i}^n Y_j^* K_{h_w,ij}/\hat{f}_{w_i}$.

Related work includes Lavergne and Vuong (1996), who considered the problem of selecting nonparametric regressors in a nonnested regression model framework, and Donald (1997), who proposed a nonparametric test for selecting the factors in a multivariate nonparametric relationship, which is closely related to the nonparametric significance test discussed in this section.

12.3.5   Testing the Significance of Categorical Variables

In this section we consider the problem of testing the significance of categorical variables in a nonparametric regression model. The test discussed in the last section can be extended to the case of testing the significance of categorical variables using the conventional nonparametric frequency estimation method; however, such a test is likely to suffer finite-sample power loss because the conventional frequency approach splits the sample into a number of "discrete cells" or subsamples and uses only those observations within each cell to generate a nonparametric estimate. This efficiency loss is unfortunate because, under the null hypothesis, some discrete variables are irrelevant regressors and should therefore be removed from the regression model, i.e., the corresponding discrete cells should be smoothed out as opposed to splitting the sample into different cells.

Consider a nonparametric regression model with mixed categorical and continuous regressors, where interest lies in testing whether some of the categorical regressors are irrelevant, i.e., redundant. Let z denote the categorical explanatory variables that might be redundant, let X denote the remaining explanatory variables in the regression model, and let Y denote the dependent variable. Then the null hypothesis can be written as

$$H_0^e : \mathrm{E}(Y|x, z) = \mathrm{E}(Y|x) \text{ a.e.}$$

The alternative hypothesis is the negation of the null hypothesis H_0^e, i.e., H_1^e: $\mathrm{E}(Y|x, z) \neq \mathrm{E}(Y|x)$ on a set with positive measure. We allow X to contain both categorical (discrete) and continuous variables. We will first focus on the case where Z is a univariate categorical variable. We discuss multivariate Z at the end of this section.

Let $g(x) = \mathrm{E}(Y|x)$ and let $m(x, z) = \mathrm{E}(Y|x, z)$. The null hypothesis is $m(x, z) = g(x)$ a.e. Suppose that the univariate Z assumes c different values, $\{0, 1, 2, \ldots, c - 1\}$. If $c = 2$, then Z is a 0-1 dummy variable, which in practice is probably the most frequently encountered situation.

Note that we have assumed that Z is a univariate categorical variable, while if Z is an ordinal (ordered) categorical variable, the kernel function for Z is given by $l(Z_i, Z_j, \lambda_z) = 1$ if $Z_i = Z_j$, and $l(Z_i, Z_j, \lambda_z) = \lambda_z^{|Z_i - Z_j|}$ if $Z_i \neq Z_j$. If Z is nominal (i.e., unordered), then $l(Z_i, Z_j, \lambda_z) = 1$ if $Z_i = Z_j$, and λ_z otherwise.

We use the same shorthand notation $K_{h,ij} = \prod_{s=1}^{q} h_s^{-1} k((X_{is}^c - X_{js}^c)/h_s)$, $L_{\lambda,ij} = \prod_{s=1}^{r} l(X_{is}^d, X_{js}^d, \lambda_s)$, and $l_{\lambda_z,ij} = l(Z_i, Z_j, \lambda_z)$ to denote the kernel functions. We choose $(h_1, \ldots, h_q, \lambda_1, \ldots, \lambda_r, \lambda_z)$ by the least squares cross-validation method outlined in Chapter 4.

We use $\hat{h}_s$, $\hat{\lambda}_s$ and $\hat{\lambda}_z$ to denote the cross-validation choices of h_s, λ_s, and λ_z. When H_1^e is true, from Theorem 4.7 we know that $\hat{\lambda}_z = O_p\left(n^{-2/(q+4)}\right)$ because consistent nonparametric estimation requires that $\hat{\lambda}_z \to 0$ as $n \to \infty$. However, when H_0^e is true, $\hat{\lambda}_z$ will converge to its upper bound value, one. In this case, the cross-validation method will smooth out the irrelevant regressor Z, which is more efficient than the conventional frequency method, which splits the sample into a number of subsets even when the discrete variable is irrelevant.

Note that the null hypothesis H_0^e is equivalent to $m(x, z = l) = m(x, z = 0)$ for all X and for $l = 1, \ldots, c - 1$. The test statistic is an estimator of

$$I^e = \sum_{l=1}^{c-1} \mathrm{E}\left\{ [m(x, z = l) - m(x, z = 0)]^2 \right\}.$$

Obviously $I^e \geq 0$ and $I^e = 0$ if and only if H_0^e is true. Therefore, I^e serves as a proper measure for testing H_0^e. A feasible test statistic is given by

$$I_n^e = \frac{1}{n} \sum_{i=1}^{n} \sum_{l=1}^{c-1} [\hat{m}(X_i, Z_i = l) - \hat{m}(X_i, Z_i = 0)]^2, \qquad (12.22)$$

where

$$\hat{m}(X_i, Z_i = l) = \frac{\sum_{j=1}^{n} Y_j W_{\hat{h},ij} L_{\hat{\lambda},ij} l_{Z_j, z=l, \hat{\lambda}_z}}{\sum_{j=1}^{2} W_{\hat{h},ij} L_{\hat{\lambda},ij} l_{Z_j, z=l, \hat{\lambda}_z}}. \qquad (12.23)$$

It is easy to show that I_n^e is a consistent estimator of I^e. Therefore, $I_n^e \to 0$ in probability under H_0^e and $I_n^e \to I > 0$ in probability under H_1^e. In practice one should reject H_0^e if I_n^e assumes "too large" a value.

Generalizing the test statistic (12.22) to handle the case where Z is multivariate is straightforward. Suppose Z is of dimension d. Let z_s and z_{is} denote the sth components of Z and Z_i, respectively, and assume that z_s assumes $c_{z,s}$ different values in $\{0, 1, \ldots, c_{z,s} - 1\}$ $(s = 1, \ldots, d)$. For multivariate Z the test statistic I_n^e becomes

$$I_n^e = \frac{1}{n} \sum_{i=1}^{n} \sum_{z} [\hat{m}(X_i, z) - \hat{m}(X_i, z_1 = 0, \ldots, z_r = 0)]^2, \qquad (12.24)$$

where $\sum_z$ denote summation over all of the possible values of $z \in \prod_{s=1}^{q}\{0, 1, \ldots, c_{z,s} - 1\}$. The definition of $\hat{m}(X_i, z)$ is similar to (12.23) except that the univariate kernel $\bar{l}(Z_i, Z_j, \hat{\lambda}_z)$ should be replaced by the product kernel $\prod_{s=1}^{d} l(Z_{s,i}, Z_{s,j}, \hat{\lambda}_{z,s})$, and the $\hat{\lambda}_{z,s}$'s are the cross-validated values of $\lambda_{z,s}$, the smoothing parameters associated with z_s ($s = 1, \ldots, d$). We now turn our attention to a bootstrap method used to approximate the finite-sample null distribution of the test statistic.

The asymptotic null distribution of the I_n^e test is quite complex (it depends on the null distribution of $\hat{\lambda}_z$). Racine et al. (forthcoming) suggest using a bootstrap method to approximate the null distribution of I_n^e. Note that in this testing problem, one cannot resample from $\{Y_i, X_i, Z_i\}_{i=1}^{n}$ as this will not impose the null hypothesis.

Define the nonparametric residuals

$$\hat{u}_i = Y_i - \hat{m}(X_i) - \bar{\delta}, \quad i = 1, \ldots, n,$$

where $\hat{m}(X_i) = \sum_{z=0}^{c-1} \hat{m}(X_i, z)/c$ and $\bar{\delta} = \sum_{i=1}^{n}(Y_i - \hat{m}(X_i))/n$. The following simple bootstrap method is suggested by Racine et al. (forthcoming).

(i) Let $u_1^*, \ldots, u_n^*$ be the wild bootstrap errors generated by $u_i^* = [(1 - \sqrt{5})/2]\hat{u}_i$ with probability $r = (1 + \sqrt{5})/(2\sqrt{5})$, and $u_i^* = [(1 + \sqrt{5})/2]\hat{u}_i$ with probability $1 - r$. Next, generate Y_i^* by $Y_i^* = \hat{m}(X_i) + u_i^*$. The bootstrap sample is (Y_i^*, X_i, Z_i), $i = 1, \ldots, n$, i.e., $X_i^* = X_i$ and $Z_i^* = Z_i$, which we shall denote by $\{Y_i, X_i, Z_i^*\}_{i=1}^{n}$.

(ii) Use the bootstrap sample to compute the bootstrap statistic I_n^{e*}, where I_n^{e*} is the same as I_n^e except that Z_i is replaced by Z_i^*, i.e., using the same cross-validation-selected $\hat{h}$, $\hat{\lambda}$ and $\hat{\lambda}_z$ obtained initially.

(iii) Repeat steps (i) and (ii) a large number of times, say $B = 399$ times. Let $\{I_{n,j}^{e*}\}_{j=1}^{B}$ be the ordered (in an ascending order) statistic of the B bootstrap statistics, and let $I_{n,(\alpha)}^{e*}$ denote the αth percentile of $\{I_{n,j}^*\}_{j=1}^{B}$. We reject H_0 if $I_n^{e*} > \hat{I}_{n,(\alpha)}^{e*}$ at the level α.

An advantage of the bootstrap method described above is that it is computationally simple. One only need apply cross-validation once, and need not recompute the cross-validated smoothing parameters for each bootstrap sample. Another advantage of using wild bootstrap, rather than the naïve i.i.d. bootstrap, is that the test will be robust to the presence of conditional heteroskedasticity. The above procedure pairs the X_i's and Z_i's so that any correlation between them is preserved.

Simulations reported in Racine et al. (forthcoming) reveal that the bootstrap test performs well, having significantly better power than a conventional frequency-based nonparametric test.

Lavergne (2001) proposed a test of equality across a group of nonparametric regression functions. His test can also be used to test for the significance of a discrete variable. Hall and Hart (1990), King, Hart and Wehrly (1991), Delgado (1993), and Dette and Neumeyer (2001) propose test statistics for testing the equality of regression curves.

12.4 Tests Related to PDFs

12.4.1 Testing Independence between Two Random Variables

Let $(X, Y)'$ be a $(p+q) \times 1$ random vector with joint CDF $F(x, y)$ and joint PDF $f(x, y)$. Furthermore, let $F_1(x)$ $(F_2(y))$ denote the marginal CDF of X (Y) having marginal PDF $f_1(x)$ $(f_2(y))$. We are interested in testing the null hypothesis H_0^f: $f(x, y) = f_1(x)f_2(y)$ for almost all (x, y). Under H_0^f, X and Y are independent of each other. We construct a test based on the integrated square difference between $f(.,.)$ and $f_1(\cdot)f_2(\cdot)$ given by

$$
\begin{aligned}
I^f &= \int [f(x,y) - f_1(x)f_2(y)]^2 \, dxdy \\
&= \int [f^2(x,y) + f_1^2(x)f_2^2(y) - 2f_1(x)f_2(y)f(x,y)] \, dxdy \\
&= \int f(x,y)dF(x,y) + \int f_1(x)dF_1(x) \int f_2(y)dF_2(y) \\
&\quad - 2\int f_1(x)f_2(y)dF(x,y) \\
&= \mathrm{E}[f(X,Y)] + \mathrm{E}[f_1(X)]\mathrm{E}[f_2(Y)] - 2\mathrm{E}[f_1(X)f_2(Y)]. \quad (12.25)
\end{aligned}
$$

Replacing the unknown population means by their sample analogues and replacing $f(X_i, Y_i)$, $f_1(X_i)$, and $f_2(Y_i)$ in (12.25) by the corresponding leave-one-out kernel estimators, we obtain a feasible test statistic given by

$$I_n^f = \frac{1}{n^2} \sum_{i=1}^n \sum_{j \neq i, j=1}^n K_{h_x,ij}^x K_{h_y,ij}^y + \frac{1}{n^4} \sum_{i=1}^n \sum_{j \neq i, j=1}^n K_{h_x,ij}^x \sum_{l=1}^n \sum_{r \neq l, r=1}^n K_{h_y,lr}^y$$

$$- \frac{2}{n^3} \sum_{i=1}^n \sum_{j \neq i, j=1}^n \sum_{l \neq i, l=1}^n K_{h_x,ij}^x K_{h_y,il}^y,$$

$$(12.26)$$

where again $K_{h_x,ij}^x = \prod_{s=1}^p h_{x,s}^{-1} k \left((X_{is} - X_{js})/h_{x,s} \right)$ and where $K_{h_y,ij}^y = \prod_{s=1}^q h_{y,s}^{-1} k \left((Y_{is} - Y_{js})/h_{y,s} \right)$. Here we use the same set of smoothing parameters, i.e., the $h_{x,s}$'s and $h_{y,s}$'s, to estimate the joint PDF $f(x,y)$ and the marginal PDFs $f_1(x)$ and $f_2(y)$.

Condition 12.5.

(i) *$f(x,y)$, $f_1(x)$ and $f_2(x)$ are continuous and bounded functions, $|f_l(u+v) - f_l(u)| \leq C|v|$ $(l=1,2)$.*

(ii) *The univariate kernel function k is a bounded, symmetric, non-negative second order kernel function.*

(iii) *As $n \to \infty$, $h_{x,s} \to 0$ for $s = 1, \ldots, p$, $h_{y,s} \to 0$ for $s = 1, \ldots, q$, and $n h_{x,1} \ldots h_{x,p} h_{y,1} \ldots h_{y,q} \to \infty$.*

Ahmad and Li (1997b) prove the following result.

Theorem 12.11. *Letting $H_{x,p} = h_{x,1} \ldots h_{x,p}$ and $H_{y,q} = h_{y,1} \ldots h_{y,q}$, then under Condition 12.3, and H_0^f, we have*

$$n(H_{x,p} H_{y,q})^{1/2} I_n^f / \hat{\sigma}_f \xrightarrow{d} N(0,1), \qquad (12.27)$$

where $\hat{\sigma}_f^2 = \frac{2}{n(n-1)} \sum_{i=1}^n \sum_{j \neq i}^n (K_{h,ij}^x)^2 (K_{h,ij}^y)^2$.

Ahmad and Li (1997a) proved Theorem 12.11, although they used a different variance estimator given by

$$\tilde{\sigma}_f^2 = 2\kappa^{p+q} \left[\frac{1}{n} \sum_{i=1}^n \hat{f}_1(X_i) \right] \left[\frac{1}{n} \sum_{i=1}^n \hat{f}_2(Y_i) \right].$$

The $\hat{\sigma}_f^2$ given in Theorem 12.11 is somewhat easier to compute than $\tilde{\sigma}_f^2$ because the former does not require one to compute κ ($\kappa = \int k(v)^2 dv$).

12.4.2   A Test for a Parametric PDF

Fan (1994) considers the problem of testing for a particular parametric PDF, i.e., testing

$$H_0^g : \quad f(x) = f_0(x, \delta) \text{ for almost all } x,$$

where f_0 is a unknown PDF and δ is a vector of unknown parameters. Fan considers a test based upon

$$
\begin{aligned}
I^g &= \int \left[f(x) - f_0(x, \delta) \right]^2 dx \\
&= \int \left[f^2(x) + f_0^2(x, \delta) - 2f(x)f_0(x, \delta) \right] dx \\
&= \int f(x)dF(x) + \int f_0^2(x, \delta)dx - 2 \int f_0(x, \delta)dF(x) \\
&= \mathrm{E}[f(X)] + \int f_0^2(x, \delta)dx - 2\mathrm{E}[f_0(X, \delta)].
\end{aligned}
$$

Let $\hat{\delta}$ denote the maximum likelihood estimator of δ_0 based on the null distribution. A feasible statistic is obtained by replacing $f(X_i)$ and δ by $\hat{f}_{-i}(X_i)$ and $\hat{\delta}$, and is given by

$$
I_n^g = \frac{1}{n} \sum_{i=1}^n \hat{f}_{-i}(X_i) + \int f_0^2(x, \hat{\delta})dx - \frac{2}{n} \sum_{i=1}^n f_0(X_i, \hat{\delta}),
$$

where $\hat{f}_{-i}(X_i) = (n-1)^{-1} \sum_{j \neq i}^n K_h(X_j, X_i)$ and where $K_h(X_j, X_i) = \prod_{s=1}^q h_s^{-1} k \left(\frac{X_{is} - X_{js}}{h_s} \right)$.

Fan (1994) showed that the I_n^g statistic has three different asymptotic distributions depending on whether the data is undersmoothed ($nh_1 \ldots h_q \eta_2^2 \to 0$, $\eta_2 = \sum_{s=1}^q h_s^2$), optimally smoothed ($nh_1 \ldots h_q \eta_2^2 \to c > 0$), or oversmoothed ($nh_1 \ldots h_q \eta_2^2 \to \infty$); see also Pagan and Ullah (1999, p. 63).

Fan (1994) also suggests a bias-corrected test statistic which has a simple asymptotic distribution under the general conditions $h_s \to 0$ and $nh_1 \ldots h_q \to \infty$, hence the data can be undersmoothed, optimally smoothed, or oversmoothed. We present the bias-corrected test below.

The bias-corrected test involves replacing $f_0(x, \hat{\delta})$ in I_n^g by a kernel smoothed version, $K_h * f(x, \hat{\delta}) = \int K_h(x, v) f_0(v, \hat{\delta}) dv$ where the asterisk

$(*)$ denotes convolution, and the test statistic is given by

$$I_n^g = n^{-1} \sum_{i=1}^{n} \hat{f}_{-i}(X_i) + \int \left[K_h * f(x, \hat{\delta}) \right]^2 dx - 2n^{-1} \sum_{i=1}^{n} K_h * f_0(X_i, \hat{\delta}).$$

$$(12.28)$$

The asymptotic null distribution of I_n^g is given in the next theorem.

Theorem 12.12. *Under Condition 12.4, we have under H_0^g,*

$$n(h_1 \ldots h_q)^{1/2} I_n^g / \hat{\sigma}_g \xrightarrow{d} N(0, 1),$$

where $\hat{\sigma}_g^2 = \frac{2h_1 \ldots h_q}{n^2} \sum_{i=1}^{n} \sum_{j=1}^{n} K_h(X_i, X_j)^2$.

Proof. See Theorem 4.1 of Fan (1994). □

It is important to note that the test statistic we present here is slightly different from the T_n-statistic presented in Theorem 4.1 of Fan (1994). Fan replaces $\int f^2(x) dx$ with $\int \hat{f}^2(x) dx$, where

$$\int \hat{f}^2(x) dx = \frac{1}{n^2} \sum_{i=1}^{n} \sum_{j=1}^{n} \int K_h(X_i, x) K_h(X_j, x) dx$$

$$\equiv \frac{1}{n^2} \sum_{i=1}^{n} \bar{K}_h(X_i, X_j),$$

where $\bar{K}_h(X_i, X_j) = \prod_{s=1}^{q} h_s^{-1} \bar{k}((X_{is} - X_{js})/h_s)$, and where $\bar{k}(v) = \int k(u)k(v + u) du$ is the twofold convolution kernel. The center term $(nh_1 \ldots h_q)^{-1} \int K(v)^2 dv$ in Fan is equal to $(nh_1 \ldots h_q)^{-1} \bar{K}(0)$ $(\bar{K}(0) = \bar{k}(0)^q)$. In (12.28) we use $\int \hat{f}(x) dF_n(x) = n^{-1} \sum_{i=1}^{n} \hat{f}_{-i}(X_i) = [n(n - 1)]^{-1} \sum_{i=1}^{n} \sum_{j \neq i}^{n} K_h(X_i, X_j)$ to replace $\int f^2(x) dx = \int f(x) dF(x)$. In our statistic, $K(\cdot)$ plays the same role as the convolution kernel $\bar{K}(\cdot)$ in Fan's T_n-statistic. Therefore, if we did not use the leave-one-out kernel estimator, our test would have a center term equal to $(nh_1 \ldots h_q)^{-1} k(0)^q$, i.e., the $i = j$ term in $n^{-2} \sum_{i=1}^{n} \sum_{j=1}^{n} K_h(X_i, X_j)$. But since we choose to use a leave-one-out kernel estimator, our test I_n^g does not have an asymptotic nonzero center term. In general, a center-free test should have better finite-sample properties than a test with a nonzero center because one needs to estimate the center for the latter which usually introduces some finite-sample bias.

12.4.3 A Kernel Test for Conditional Parametric Distributions

Let $\{Y_i, X_i\}_{i=1}^n$ denote i.i.d. data having a joint PDF given by $f(y, x)$. Let $f(y|x)$ denote the conditional PDF of Y given X. We are interested in testing whether $f(y|x)$ belongs to a particular parametric family. Let $p(y|x, \theta)$ denote a parametric conditional PDF with θ being a $k \times 1$ parameter vector. The null hypothesis is given by

$$H_0^i: \mathrm{P}[f(Y_i|X_i) = p(Y_i|X_i, \theta)] = 1 \qquad \text{for some } \theta \in \Theta,$$

where Θ is a compact subset of the parameter space. The alternative hypothesis is the negation of the null, $H_1: \mathrm{P}[f(Y_i|X_i) = p(Y_i|X_i, \theta)] < 1$ for all $\theta \in \Theta$.

The Kullback-Leibler information criterion that measures the discrepancy between two conditional CDFs is defined as

$$I(p, f) = \mathrm{E}\left\{\ln\left[\frac{f(Y_i|X_i)}{p(Y_i|X_i, \theta)}\right]\right\} = \int f(y, x) \ln\left[\frac{f(y|x)}{p(y|x, \theta_0)}\right] dy dx.$$
$$(12.29)$$

It is well known that $I(p, f) \geq 0$ and $I(p, f) = 0$ if and only if $f(y|x) = p(y|x, \theta_0)$ a.e. Thus, $I(p, f)$ serves as a proper measure to test H_0. Zheng (2000) considered a first order expansion of the information function, that is,

$$\mathrm{E}\left\{\ln\left[\frac{f(Y_i|X_i)}{p(Y_i|X_i, \theta)}\right]\right\} \stackrel{\sim}{=} \mathrm{E}\left[\frac{f(Y_i|X_i)}{p(Y_i|X_i, \theta)} - 1\right]$$
$$= \mathrm{E}\left[\frac{f(Y_i|X_i) - p(Y_i|X_i, \theta)}{p(Y_i|X_i, \theta)}\right].$$
$$(12.30)$$

Weighting (12.30) by the density $f_1(x)$ leads to

$$I_1(p, f) = \mathrm{E}\left[\frac{f(Y_i|X_i) f_1(X_i) - p(Y_i|X_i, \theta) f_1(X_i)}{p(Y_i|X_i, \theta)}\right].$$
$$(12.31)$$

Zheng (2000) showed that $I_1(f, p) \geq 0$ with equality holding if and only if H_0 is true. Therefore, $I_1(f, p)$ also serves as a proper measure for testing H_0. Zheng considered the case for which both Y and X are continuous variables. Fan et al. (2006) extend Zheng's test to the discrete dependent variable and mixed conditional covariates case. Below we first discuss the case for which the dependent variable Y is discrete (X contains mixed data types). This covers many interesting cases, such as testing for correct specification of parametric binary or multinomial response models. Let $X = (X^c, X^d)$, where X^c is a $q \times 1$ continuous variable, and X^d is an $r \times 1$ discrete variable. We use X_{is}^c (X_{is}^d) to denote the sth component of X^c (X^d). Letting $l(X_{is}^d, X_{js}^d, \lambda_s)$ be the kernel introduced in Chapter 4 for the discrete variable X_s^d, then the product kernel for the discrete variable is $L(X_i^d, X_j^d, \lambda) = \prod_{s=1}^r l(X_{is}^d, X_{js}^d, \lambda_s)$. For the continuous component X^c, we still use the standard (second order) product kernel function discussed earlier. Therefore, for the mixed data variable $X = (X^c, X^d)$, the kernel function is defined by ($\gamma = (h, \lambda)$)

$$K_{\gamma,ij} \stackrel{\text{def}}{=} W_h \left(\frac{X_i^c - X_j^c}{h} \right) L(X_i^d, X_j^d, \lambda). \qquad (12.32)$$

When Y_i is a discrete variable, we estimate $f(Y_i, X_i)$ and $f_1(X_i)$ by the following leave-one-out kernel estimators (we do not smooth y):

$$\hat{f}(Y_i, X_i) = \frac{1}{n} \sum_{\substack{j \neq i}}^n \mathbf{1}(Y_i = Y_j) K_n(X_i, X_j), \qquad (12.33)$$

$$\hat{f}_1(X_i) = \frac{1}{n} \sum_{\substack{j \neq i}}^n K_n(X_i, X_j). \qquad (12.34)$$

We estimate $p(Y_i|X_i, \theta_0)$ by a kernel weighted version of $p(.|., \hat{\theta}_0)$ given by

$$\tilde{f}(Y_i, X_i) = \frac{1}{n} \sum_{j=1}^n K_{\gamma,ij} p(Y_j | X_j, \hat{\theta}), \qquad (12.35)$$

where $\hat{\theta}$ is the maximum likelihood estimator of θ_0 based on the null model.

With $\hat{f}(Y_i, X_i)$, $\hat{f}_1(X_i)$ and $\tilde{f}(Y_i, X_i)$ defined above, we obtain our test statistic given by

$$I_{n,d}^i = \frac{1}{n(n-1)} \sum_{i=1}^n \sum_{\substack{j=1, j \neq i}}^n \left\{ \frac{K_{\gamma,ij}}{p(Y_i|X_i, \hat{\theta})} \left[\mathbf{1}(Y_i = Y_j) - p(Y_j|X_j, \hat{\theta}) \right] \right\}.$$
$$(12.36)$$

Fan et al. (2006) recommend using the cross-validation procedure discussed in Chapter 5 to select the smoothing parameters $h_1, \ldots, h_q$, $\lambda_1, \ldots, \lambda_r$. The asymptotic null distribution of $I_{n,d}^i$ is given in the next theorem.

Theorem 12.13. *Under the conditions given in Fan et al. (2006), then under H_0^i we have*

$$T_{n,d}^i \overset{\text{def}}{=} n(h_1 \dots h_q)^{1/2} I_{n,d}^i / \hat\sigma_i \to N(0,1) \text{ in distribution,}$$

where

$$\hat\sigma_i^2 = \frac{2(h_1 \dots h_q)}{n(n-1)} \sum_i \sum_{j \neq i} K_n(X_i, X_j)^2 \left\{ \frac{\left[\mathbf{1}(Y_i = Y_j) - p(Y_i | X_j, \hat\theta) \right]}{\hat p(Y_i | X_i, \hat\theta)} \right\}^2$$

is a consistent estimator of $\sigma_0^2 = [\int W^2(v)dv] \mathrm{E}[(1-p_i)p_i^{-1} f_1(X_i)]$, the asymptotic variance of $n(h_1 \dots h_q)^{1/2} I_{n,d}^i$.

It can be shown that under H_1^i, $T_{n,d}^i$ diverges to $+\infty$, hence this is a consistent test. The simulations in Fan et al. (2006) show that the $T_{n,d}^i$ test suffers from finite-sample size distortions if one uses the asymptotic standard normal critical values. Fan et al. recommend using the following bootstrap procedure to better approximate the finite-sample null distribution of $T_{n,d}^i$.

   (i) Generate Y_i^* based on the parametric conditional distribution $p(Y_i^* | X_i, \hat\theta)$. Call $\{X_i, Y_i^*\}_{i=1}^n$ the bootstrap sample.

  (ii) Based on the parametric null model, estimate θ using the bootstrap sample. Let $\hat\theta^*$ denote the resulting estimator. Compute the bootstrap statistic $T_{n,d}^{i*}$ the same way as $T_{n,d}^i$ except that Y_i and $\hat\theta$ are replaced by Y_i^* and $\hat\theta^*$, respectively.

 (iii) Repeat steps (i) and (ii) a large number of times, say $B = 399$ times, and obtain the empirical distribution of $\{T_{n,d}^{i*}\}_{j=1}^B$. Let $T_{n,\alpha}^{i*}$ denote the α percentile of the bootstrap distribution. We will reject the null hypothesis at significance level α if $T_{n,d}^i > T_{n,\alpha}^{i*}$.

Next we discuss the case for which the dependent variable Y is continuous. For expositional simplicity we consider only the case in which Y is a scalar. Zheng (2000) suggested using a smoothed density estimator $\tilde f(Y_i, X_i)$ to estimate $p(Y_i | X_i, \theta_0) f_1(X_i)$, where

$$\tilde f(Y_i, X_i) = \frac{1}{n} \sum_{j=1}^n \int W_{2,h_y}\left(\frac{Y_i - y}{h_y} \right) K_h\left(\frac{X_i - X_j}{h} \right) f(y | X_j, \hat\theta) dy,$$

$$(12.37)$$

and where $W_{2,h_y}(\cdot) = h_y^{-1}W_2(\cdot)$, where $W_2(\cdot)$ is a (specially defined) univariate kernel function. Zheng suggested first transforming the dependent variable Y to lie in the range $[0,1]$, and then choosing a special kernel function for $W_2(\cdot)$ having the property that $h_y^{-1} \int_0^1 W_2((Y_i - y)/h_y)^2 dy \to 1$ as $n \to \infty$. Zheng proposed the following test statistic:

$$I_{n,c}^i = \frac{1}{n(n-1)} \sum_{i=1}^n \sum_{j=1, j\neq i}^n$$

$$\left[\frac{W_{2,h_y}\left(\frac{Y_i-Y_j}{h_y}\right) K_{\gamma,ij} - \int W_{2,h_y}\left(\frac{Y_i-y}{h_y}\right) K_{\gamma,ij} f(y|X_j,\widehat{\theta})dy}{f(Y_i|X_i,\widehat{\theta})} \right].$$

$$\tag{12.38}$$

The asymptotic distribution of $I_{n,c}^i$ is given in the following theorem.

Theorem 12.14. *Under the conditions given in Fan et al. (2006), under H_0^i we have*

$$T_{n,c}^i \overset{\text{def}}{=} n(h_y h_1 \dots h_q)^{1/2} I_{n,c}^i / \hat{\sigma}_{i,c} \to N(0,1) \text{ in distribution,}$$

where

$$\hat{\sigma}_{i,c}^2 = \frac{2(h_y h_1 \dots h_q)}{n(n-1)} \sum_{i=1}^n \sum_{j\neq i}^n K_{\gamma,ij}^2.$$

Other model specification tests include Gozalo and Linton (2001) and Härdle, Sperlich and Spokoiny (2001), who propose a kernel-based test for testing additivity in a general nonparametric regression model, and Sun (2006), who proposes a test for equality of conditional quantile functions.

12.5 Applications

12.5.1 Growth Convergence Clubs

Quah (1996), Maasoumi et al. (forthcoming), and others have examined the issue of whether there exist "convergence clubs," that is, whether growth rates differ for members of clubs such as the Organization for Economic Cooperation and Development (OECD). We do not attempt to review this vast literature here; rather, we refer the interested reader to Mankiw, Romer and Weil (1992), Liu and Stengos (1999), Durlauf and Quah (1999), and the references therein. For what follows, we follow the analysis contained in Maasoumi et al.

We apply the test statistic in (12.22) to determine whether OECD countries and non-OECD countries follow the same growth model. This is done by testing whether OECD membership (a binary categorical variable) is a relevant regressor in a nonparametric framework. The null hypothesis is that OECD membership is an irrelevant regressor, thus under the null hypothesis OECD and non-OECD countries' growth rates are all determined by the same growth model. The alternative hypothesis is the negation of the null hypothesis, i.e., that OECD and non-OECD countries have different growth rate (regression) models.

Following Liu and Stengos (1999), we employ panel data over seven 5-year periods for 88 countries (1960–1964, 1965–1969, 1970–1974, 1975–1979, 1980–1984, 1985–1989 and 1990–1994) yielding a total of $88 \times 7 = 616$ observations in the panel. We then construct our test based on the following model:

$$
\begin{aligned}
\text{Growth}_{it} = m\big(&\text{OECD}_{it}, \text{dT}_t, \ln(\text{inv}_{it}), \ln(\text{popgro}_{it}), \ln(\text{inigdp}_{it}), \\
&\ln(\text{humancap}_{it})\big) + \epsilon_{it},
\end{aligned}
$$

$$(12.39)$$

where Growth_{it} refers to the growth rate of income per capita during each period, dT_t the seven period dummies, inv_{it} the ratio of investment to gross domestic product (GDP), popgro_{it} growth of the labor force, inigdp_{it} per capita income at the beginning of each period, and humancap_{it} human capital. Initial income estimates are from the Summers-Heston data base, as are the estimates of the average investment/GDP ratio for 5-year periods. The average growth rate of per capita GDP and the average annual population growth rate for each period are from the World Bank. Finally, the average years of schooling in the population above 15 years of age is obtained from Barro and Lee (2000).

Before we report results for the smoothing-based nonparametric test, we first consider some popular parametric methods for approaching this problem. A common parametric approach is to employ a linear regression model with the OECD dummy variable being one possible regressor, and then to test whether the coefficient on this dummy variable is significant. We consider a parametric specification suggested by Liu and Stengos (1999) which contains dummy variables for OECD status and year and is nonlinear in the initial GDP and human capital variables given by

$$\text{Growth}_{it} = \beta_0 \text{OECD}_{it} + \sum_{s=1}^{7} \beta_s d\text{T}_s + \beta_8 \ln(\text{inv}_{it}) + \beta_9 \ln(\text{popgro}_{it})$$

$$+ \sum_{s=1}^{4} \alpha_s [\ln(\text{inigdp}_{it})]^s + \sum_{s=1}^{3} \gamma_s [\ln(\text{humancap})_{it})]^s + \epsilon_{it}.$$

$$(12.40)$$

Estimation results for Model (12.40) yield a t-statistic for the OECD dummy equal to -0.973 having a P-value of 0.33. Thus, the parametric test fails to reject the null.

Next, we follow the conventional frequency approach and implement the nonparametric test, i.e., our test is based on Model (12.39) with sample splitting on the OECD and the dT dummies. Using $B = 999$ bootstrap resamples we obtain a P-value of 0.113, and once again we fail to reject the null at the conventional 1%, 5%, and 10% levels.

We now report the results for the smoothing-based nonparametric test (see Section 12.3.5). For each bootstrap test we employed $B = 999$ bootstrap resamples, while for cross-validation we employed 5 restarts of the numerical search algorithm and retained those smoothing parameters that yielded the lowest value of the cross-validation function. The P-value generated from inverting the empirical CDF at I_n^e is 0.006, which constitutes strong evidence against the validity of the null.

The inconsistency of the parametric test and the nonparametric test also suggests that the parametric model is misspecified. We therefore applied the consistent nonparametric test I_n^a (see Section 12.1.1) for correct specification of the parametric model. The P-value from this test was 0.001 and we therefore reject the null of correct parametric specification.

The reason why the conventional frequency-based nonparametric test also fails to reject the null is because it splits the sample into $2 \times 7 = 14$ parts (the number of discrete cells arising from the discrete variables OECD and dT) when estimating the nonparametric regression functions, thus the much smaller (sub)sample sizes lead to substantial finite-sample power loss for the conventional frequency-based test.

We conclude that robust nonparametric evidence supports the existence of convergence clubs, a feature that may remain undetected when using both common parametric specifications and conventional nonparametric approaches. That is, growth rates for OECD countries appear to be generated by a different process than those for non-OECD countries.

12.6 Proofs

12.6.1 Proof of Theorem 12.1

Proof. We will prove Theorem 12.1 for the case where $m(X_i, \gamma) = \alpha + X_i'\beta \equiv Z_i'\gamma$, where $Z_i = (1, X_i')$ and $\gamma = (\alpha, \beta')'$. The general case can be similarly proved and is left as an exercise (see Exercise 12.4). Using $\hat{u}_i = Y_i - Z_i'\hat{\gamma} = u_i - Z_i'(\hat{\gamma} - \gamma)$, we have (using $n(n-1) \sim n^2$)

$$I_n^e = n^{-2} \sum_{i=1}^{n} \sum_{j \neq i}^{n} u_i u_j K_{h,ij} - 2(\hat{\gamma} - \gamma)' n^{-2} \sum_{i=1}^{n} \sum_{j \neq i}^{n} u_i Z_j K_{h,ij}$$

$$+ (\hat{\gamma} - \gamma)' n^{-2} \sum_{i=1}^{n} \sum_{j \neq i}^{n} Z_i Z_j K_{h,ij} (\hat{\gamma} - \gamma)$$

$$\equiv I_{1n}^a - (\hat{\gamma} - \gamma)' I_{2n}^a + (\hat{\gamma} - \gamma)' I_{3n}^a (\hat{\gamma} - \gamma),$$

where the definition of I_{jn}^a should be apparent ($j = 1, 2, 3$).

By writing $I_{1n}^a = 2n^{-2} \sum_{i=1}^{m} \sum_{j>i}^{n} u_i u_j K_{h,ij}$, it is easy to show that

$$\mathrm{E}\left[(I_{1n}^a)^2\right] = 4n^{-4} \sum_{i} \sum_{j>i} \mathrm{E}\left[u_i^2 u_j^2 K_{h,ij}^2\right]$$

$$= \frac{2}{n^2 H_q^2} \left\{ \mathrm{E}\left[\sigma^2(X_1)\sigma^2(X_2)K((X_1 - X_2)/h)^2\right] + o(1) \right\}$$

$$= \frac{2}{n^2 H_q^2} \left\{ \int f(x_1)f(x_2)\sigma^2(x_1)\sigma^2(x_2)K((x_1 - x_2)/h)^2 dx_1 dx_2 + o(1) \right\}$$

$$= \frac{2}{n^2 H_q} \left\{ \int f(x_1)f(x_1 + hv)\sigma^2(x_1)\sigma^2(x_1 + hv)K(v)^2 dx_1 dv + o(1) \right\}$$

$$= \frac{2}{n^2 H_q} \left\{ \kappa^q \int f^2(x_1)\sigma^4(x_1) dx_1 dx_1 dv + o(1) \right\}$$

$$= \frac{2}{n^2 H_q} \left\{ \kappa^q \mathrm{E}\left[f(X_1)\sigma^4(X_1)\right] + o(1) \right\} \equiv (n^2 H_q) \left\{ \sigma_a^2 + o(1) \right\}.$$

Hence, $n H_q^{1/2} I_{1n}^a$ has mean zero and asymptotic variance σ_a^2. By Hall's (1984) CLT (see Lemma A.16 in Appendix A), we know that

$$n H_q^{1/2} I_{1n}^a \xrightarrow{d} N(0, \sigma_a^2).$$

Let $I_{2n,t}^a$ and $I_{3n,ts}^a$ denote the tth and (t,s)th components of I_{2n}^a and I_{3n}^a. One can easily show that $\mathrm{E}[|I_{2n,t}^a|^2] = O(n^{-1})$ for all t, which implies that $I_{2n}^a = O_p(n^{-1/2})$. Also, for all t, s, $\mathrm{E}[|I_{3n,ts}^a|] = O(1)$, which implies that $I_{3n}^a = O_p(1)$. These results together with $\hat{\gamma} - \gamma = O_p(n^{-1/2})$ lead to

$$nH_q^{1/2}I_n^a = nH_q^{1/2}I_{1n}^a + O_p(H_q^{1/2}) \xrightarrow{d} N(0, \sigma_a^2). \qquad (12.41)$$

Exercise 12.3 asks the reader to show that $\hat{\sigma}_a^2 = \sigma_a^2 + o_p(1)$. This completes the proof of Theorem 12.1. □

12.6.2 Proof of Theorem 12.2

Proof. We only consider the case where $m(X_i, \gamma) = \alpha + X_i'\beta = Z_i'\gamma$. Let $g(X_i) = \mathrm{E}(Y_i|X_i)$, and let $\bar{\gamma}$ to denote the probability limit of $\hat{\gamma}$ under H_1. Then similar to the proof of Theorem 12.1, we can show that under H_1, $I_n^a = I_{n,0} + o_p(1)$, where

$$I_{n,0} = \frac{1}{n^2} \sum_i \sum_{j \neq i} [u_i + g(X_i) - Z_i'\bar{\gamma}][u_j + g(X_j) - Z_j'\bar{\gamma}]K_h(X_i - X_j).$$

In Exercise 12.4 the reader is asked to show that $I_{n,0} = C + o_p(1)$, where $C = \mathrm{E}[(g(X_i) - Z_i'\bar{\gamma})^2] > 0$. Hence, $nH_q^{1/2}I_n^a = nH_q^{1/2}C + o_p(nH_q^{1/2})$, which implies Theorem 12.2. □

12.6.3 Proof of Theorem 12.5

Proof. The test statistic I_n^b can be written as $I_n^b = I_{1n}^b + I_{2n}^b$, where

$$I_{1n}^b = c_{n,b} - 2(n_1 n_2)^{-1} \sum_{i=1}^n K_{h,ii}^{xy}$$

where $c_{n,b} = k(0)^q(h_1 \dots h_q)^{-1}[n_1^{-1} + n_2^{-1}]$, $n = \min\{n_1, n_2\}$, and

$$I_{2n}^b = \sum_i \sum_{j \neq i} \left[\frac{1}{n_1^2}K_{h,ij}^x + \frac{1}{n_2^2}K_{h,ij}^y - \frac{1}{n_1 n_2}K_{h,ij}^{xy} - \frac{1}{n_1 n_2}K_{h,ij}^{yx} \right],$$

where $\sum_i = \sum_{i=1}^{n_1}$ if the summand contains X_i, and $\sum_i = \sum_{i=1}^{n_2}$ if the summand contains Y_i, while $\sum_j$ is similarly defined.

Define $H_q = h_1 \dots h_q$. It is easy to show that

$$\mathrm{E}[I_{1n}^b] = c_{n,b} + (n_1 n_2)^{-1}O(nH_q) = c_{n,b}[1 + O(n^{-1}H_q)],$$

and that

$$\mathrm{var}(I_{1n}^b) = (n_1 n_2 H_q)^{-2} O(n^2 H_q^2 + n H_q) = O(n^{-2})$$

(see Exercise 12.4). Hence,

$$I_{1n}^b = c_{n,b} + O_p(n^{-1}). \tag{12.42}$$

Let $z_i = (X_i, Y_i)$ and define $H_n(z_i, z_j) = K_{h,ij}^x + K_{h,ij}^y - K_{ij}^{h,xy} - K_{ij}^{h,yx}$. For $i \neq j$, we have

$$E[H_n(z_i, z_j)|z_i] = \left\{ E[k_{h,ij}^x|X_i] - E[k_{h,ij}^{xy}|X_i] \right\}$$
$$+ \left\{ E[k_{h,ij}^y|Y_i] - E[k_{h,ij}^{yx}|Y_i] \right\} = 0$$

under H_0^b (since $f = g$). Therefore, I_{1n}^b is a degenerate U-statistic (see Appendix A for a definition). It is easy to see that $E[(I_{2n}^b)^2] = \mathrm{var}(I_{2n}^b) = O\left((n_1 n_2 H_q)^{-1}\right)$, and that

$$\mathrm{var}\left[(n_1 n_2 H_q)^{1/2} I_{2n}^b\right] = E\left\{ \left[(n_1 n_2 H_q)^{1/2} I_{2n}^b\right]^2 \right\}$$

$$= (n_1 n_2 H_q) \sum_i \sum_{j \neq i} \left\{ n_1^{-4} E[(k_{h,ij}^x)^2] + n_2^{-4} E[(k_{h,ij}^y)^2] \right.$$

$$\left. + (n_1 n_2)^{-2} E[(k_{h,ij}^{x,y})^2] + (n_1 n_2)^{-2} E[(k_{h,ij}^{y,x})^2] + O(n^{-4}) \right\}$$

$$\sim (n_1 n_2 H_q) \sum_i \sum_{j \neq i} \left\{ n_1^{-4} (k_{h,ij}^x)^2 + n_2^{-4} (k_{h,ij}^y)^2 + 2(n_1 n_2)^{-2} (k_{h,ij}^{x,y})^2 \right\}$$

$$\equiv \tilde{\sigma}_a^2 = O_p(1).$$

In the above $A \sim B$ means that $A = B + o_p(1)$. Thus, $\tilde{\sigma}_a^2$ is a consistent estimator for $E[(n_1 n_2 H_q)^{1/2} I_{2n}^b]^2$. Note that

$$\hat{\sigma}_a^2 - \tilde{\sigma}_a^2 = \frac{n_1 n_2}{h_1 \ldots h_q} \sum_{i=1}^{n} \left\{ \frac{k(0)^{2q}}{n_1^4} + \frac{k(0)^{2q}}{n_2^4} + \frac{2h_1 \ldots h_q}{(n_1 n_2)^2} k_h (X_i, Y_i)^2 \right\}$$

$$= O_p\left((n h_1 \ldots h_q)^{-1}\right) = o_p(1).$$

Therefore, $\hat{\sigma}_a^2$ is also a consistent estimator of $\mathrm{var}[(n_1 n_2 H_q)^{1/2} I_{2n}^b]$.

Finally, it is straightforward to check that the condition of Hall's (1984) CLT for degenerate U-statistics holds (see Appendix A). Thus, we have

$$(n_1 n_2 H_q)^{1/2} I_{2n}^b / \hat{\sigma}_b \xrightarrow{d} N(0, 1). \tag{12.43}$$

Equations (12.42) and (12.43) lead to $(n_1 n_2 H_q)^{1/2}[I_n^b - c_{n,b}]/\hat{\sigma}_b = (n_1 n_2 H_q)^{1/2} I_{2n}^b/\hat{\sigma}_b + o_p(1) \overset{d}{\to} N(0,1)$. This completes the proof of Theorem 12.5. $\qquad\square$

12.6.4 Proof of Theorem 12.9

Let $r_i = r(W_i) \equiv E(Y_i|W_i)$. Then using $\tilde{U}_i = Y_i - \hat{Y}_i = (r_i - \hat{r}_i) + u_i - \hat{u}_i$, where $\hat{r}_i = n^{-1} \sum_{j \neq i} r_j L_{h_w, ij}/\hat{f}_{w_i}$, and $\hat{u}_i = n^{-1} \sum_{j \neq i} u_j L_{h_w, ij}/\hat{f}_{w_i}$, we have the following expression for I_n^d:

$$I_n^d = \frac{1}{n(n-1)} \sum_i \sum_{j \neq i} \left\{ (r_i - \hat{r}_i)(r_j - \hat{r}_j) + u_i u_j + \hat{u}_i \hat{u}_j + 2u_i(r_j - \hat{r}_j) \right.$$
$$\left. - 2\hat{u}_i(r_j - \hat{r}_j) - 2u_i \hat{u}_j \right\} K_{h,ij}$$
$$\overset{\text{def}}{=} I_{n1}^d + I_{n2}^d + I_{n3}^d + 2I_{n4}^d - 2I_{n5}^d - 2I_{n6}^d.$$

For notational simplicity, we will assume that $h_1 = \cdots = h_q$ and $h_{w,1} = \cdots = h_{w,p} = h_w$ in the proofs that follow. We shall complete the proof of Theorem 12.9 by showing that $I_{ni}^d = o_p\left((nh^{q/2})^{-1}\right)$ for $i = 1, 3, 4, 5, 6$ and that $nh^{q/2} I_{n2}^d/\hat{\sigma}_d \to N(0,1)$ in distribution. These results are proved in Lemmas 12.1 through 12.6 below.

Lemma 12.1. $J_{n1}^d = o_p\left((nh^{q/2})^{-1}\right)$.

Proof. Noting that $K(\cdot)$ is *nonnegative* and $\hat{f}_{X_i} = n^{-1} \sum_{j \neq i} K_{h,ij}$ ($n - 1 \sim n$), we have

$$I_{n1}^d = n^{-2} \sum_i \sum_{j \neq i} (r_i - \hat{r}_i)(r_j - \hat{r}_j) K_{h,ij}$$
$$\leq (1/2) n^{-2} \sum_i \sum_{j \neq i} \left[(r_i - \hat{r}_i)^2 + (r_j - \hat{r}_j)^2 \right] K_{h,ij}$$
$$= n^{-2} \sum_i \sum_{j \neq i} (r_i - \hat{r}_i)^2 K_{h,ij} = n^{-1} \sum_i (r_i - \hat{r}_i)^2 \hat{f}_{X_i}$$
$$\sim n^{-1} \sum_i (r_i - \hat{r}_i)^2 f_{X_i} = O_p\left(h_w^{2\nu} + (nh_w^p)^{-1}\right)$$
$$= o\left((nh^{q/2})^{-1}\right),$$

the second last line following from Lemma 7.2 in Chapter 7. $\qquad\square$

Lemma 12.2.

(i) $nh^{q/2}I_{n2}^d \to N(0, \sigma_d^2)$ in distribution.

(ii) $\hat{\sigma}_d^2 = \sigma_d^2 + o_p(1)$.

Part (i) is proved by Theorem 12.1, while (ii) can be proved easily using Lemma A.16.

Lemma 12.3. $I_{n3}^d = o_p\left((nh^{q/2})^{-1}\right).$

Proof.

$$
\begin{aligned}
J_{n3} &= n^{-2}\sum_i \sum_{j \neq i} \hat{u}_i \hat{u}_j K_{h,ij} \\
&\leq (1/2)n^{-2}\sum_i \sum_{j \neq i} \left[\hat{u}_i^2 + \hat{u}_j^2\right] K_{h,ij} \\
&= (n^2 h^d)^{-1}\sum_i \sum_{j \neq i} \hat{u}_i^2 K_{h,ij} \\
&= n^{-1}\sum_i \hat{u}_i^2 \hat{f}_{X_i} \\
&= n^{-1}\sum_i \hat{u}_i^2 f_{X_i} + n^{-1}\sum_i \hat{u}_i^2(\hat{f}_i - f_i) \\
&= [O(1) + o_p(1)]O\left((nh_w^p)^{-1}\right) \\
&= o\left((nh^{q/2})^{-1}\right)
\end{aligned}
$$

by Lemma 7.2 of Chapter 7.   □

Lemma 12.4. $I_{n4}^d = o_p\left((nh^{q/2})^{-1}\right).$

Proof. Using the identity $\hat{f}_j^{-1} = f_j^{-1}[1 + (f_j - \hat{f}_j)/\hat{f}_j]$, we have

$$
\begin{aligned}
I_{n4}^d &= n^{-2} \sum_i \sum_{j \neq i} u_i (r_j - \hat{r}_j) K_{h,ij} \\
&= (n^2 h^d)^{-1} \sum_i \sum_{j \neq i} u_i (r_j - \hat{r}_j) \hat{f}_j K_{h,ij} \hat{f}_j^{-1} \\
&\sim n^{-2} \sum_i \sum_{j \neq i} u_i (r_j - \hat{r}_j) \hat{f}_j K_{h,ij} f_j^{-1} \\
&\equiv I_{n4,1}^d, \text{ say, where} \\
I_{n4,1}^d &= n^{-2} \sum_i \sum_{j \neq i} u_i (r_j - \hat{r}_j) \hat{f}_j K_{h,ij} f_j^{-1} \\
&= O_p(h_w^{2\nu} + (nh_w^p)^{-1}) = o_p\left((nh^{q/2})^{-1}\right)
\end{aligned}
$$

by Lemma 7.5. □

Lemma 12.5. $I_{n5}^d = o_p\left((nh^{q/2})^{-1}\right).$

Proof.

$$
\begin{aligned}
I_{n5}^d &= n^{-2} \sum_i \sum_{j \neq i} \hat{u}_i (r_j - \hat{r}_j) \\
&\leq (1/2)(n^2 h^d)^{-1} \sum_i \sum_{j \neq i} [(r_j - \hat{r}_j)^2 K_{h,ij} + \hat{u}_i^2 K_{h,ij}] \\
&= O_p(h_w^{2\nu} + (nh_w^p)^{-1}) = o\left((nh^{q/2})^{-1}\right)
\end{aligned}
$$

by the proofs of Lemmas 12.1 and 12.3. □

Lemma 12.6. $I_{n6}^d = o_p\left((nh^{q/2})^{-1}\right).$

Proof.

$$I_{n6}^d = n^{-2} \sum_i \sum_{j \neq i} u_i \hat{u}_j K_{h,ij}$$

$$= (n^2 h^d)^{-1} \sum_i \sum_{j \neq i} u_i \hat{u}_j \hat{f}_j K_{h,ij} \hat{f}_j^{-1}$$

$$= n^{-2} \sum_i \sum_{j \neq i} u_i \hat{u}_j \hat{f}_j K_{h,ij} f_j^{-1} [1 + (\hat{f}_j - f_j)/\hat{f}_j]$$

$$\sim n^{-2} \sum_i \sum_{j \neq i} u_i \hat{u}_j \hat{f}_j K_{h,ij} f_j^{-1} \equiv I_{n6,1}^d, \text{ say, where}$$

$$I_{n6,1}^d = n^{-2} \sum_i \sum_{j \neq i} u_i \hat{u}_j \hat{f}_j K_{h,ij} f_j^{-1}$$

$$= O_p \left((nh_w p)^{-1} \right) = o \left((nh^{q/2})^{-1} \right)$$

by Lemma 7.5. $\qquad\qquad\qquad\qquad\qquad\qquad\qquad\qquad\qquad\qquad\qquad\qquad$ $\square$

12.7 Exercises

Exercise 12.1. Assume that (12.4) is the true model, but instead one tests Model (12.2) against Model (12.3). Also assume that $E(X_i^3) = E(X_i^5) = E(X_i) = 0$.

(i) Show that $\hat{\beta}_2 \xrightarrow{p} 0$, where $\hat{\beta}_2$ is the least squares estimator of β_2 based on Model (12.3).

(ii) Show that a standard t-test will not have asymptotic power equal to 1 (i.e., is not a consistent test).

Exercise 12.2. For the wild bootstrap procedure discussed in Section 12.1.1, show that $E^*(u_i^*) = 0$ and that $E^*(u^{*j}) = \hat{u}_i^j$ for $j = 2, 3$, where $E^*(\cdot) = E(.|\{X_i, Y_i\}_{i=1}^n)$.

Exercise 12.3. Assume $g(X_i, \gamma) = \alpha + X_i'\beta \equiv Z_i'\gamma$, where $Z_i' = (1, X_i')$

and $\gamma = (\alpha, \beta')'$. Using $\hat{u}_i = u_i - Z_i'(\hat{\gamma} - \gamma)$, we have

$$I_n^a = \frac{1}{n(n-1)} \sum_{i=1}^{n} \sum_{j \neq i}^{n} u_i u_j K_{h,ij} - \frac{2(\hat{\gamma} - \gamma)'}{n(n-1)} \sum_{i=1}^{n} \sum_{j \neq i}^{n} u_i Z_i K_{h,ij}$$

$$+ (\hat{\gamma} - \gamma)' \left[\frac{1}{n(n-1)} \sum_{i=1}^{n} \sum_{j \neq i}^{n} Z_i Z_j' K_{h,ij} \right] (\hat{\gamma} - \gamma)$$

$$\equiv I_{1n} - 2(\hat{\gamma} - \gamma) I_{2n} + (\hat{\gamma} - \gamma)' I_{3n} (\hat{\gamma} - \gamma), \qquad (12.44)$$

where the definition of I_{jn} should be apparent.

(i) Show that $I_{2n} = O_p(n^{-1/2})$ and that $I_{3n} = O_p(1)$.

Hint: Show that $\mathrm{E}[|I_{2n}|^2] = O(n^{-1})$ and that $\mathrm{E}[|I_{3n,ts}|] = O(1)$ for all $t, s = 1, \ldots, q+1$, where $I_{3n,ts}$ is the (t,s) element of I_{3n} (I_{3n} is of dimension $(q+1) \times (q+1)$).

(ii) Show that $\hat{\sigma}_a^2 = \sigma_a^2 + o_p(1)$.

Hint: Show $\mathrm{E}[\hat{\sigma}_a^2] = \sigma_a^2 + o(1)$, and use the H-decomposition result (Lemma A.15).

(iii) Show that $n H_q^{1/2} I_{1n} \xrightarrow{d} N(0, \sigma_a^2)$.

Hint: First show that $\mathrm{E}(I_{1n}) = 0$ and that $\mathrm{var}(n H_q^{1/2} I_{1n}) = \sigma_a^2 + o(1)$.

Verify that conditions given in Hall's (1984) Theorem 1 hold for the I_{1n} test, i.e., define $H_n(W_i, W_j) = u_i u_j K((X_i - X_j)/h)$, $W_i = (u_i, X_i)$, $G_n(W_i, W_j) = \mathrm{E}[H_n(W_i, W_l) H_n(W_j, W_l) | W_i, W_j]$. Show that

$$\frac{\mathrm{E}[G_n(W_1, W_2)] + n^{-1} \mathrm{E}[H_n^4(W_1, W_2)]}{\{\mathrm{E}[H_n^2(W_1, W_2)]\}^2}$$

$$= \frac{O(H_q^3) + n^{-1} O(H_q)}{O(H_q^2)}$$

$$= O(H_q + (n H_q)^{-1}) = o(1).$$

(iv) Using the results from (i) and (ii), show that $n H_q^{1/2} I_n^a / \sqrt{\hat{\sigma}_a^2} \xrightarrow{d} N(0, 1)$.

Exercise 12.4. Let $I_{n,0} = n^{-2} \sum_i \sum_{j \neq i} [u_i + g(X_i) - Z_i' \bar{\gamma}][u_j + g(X_j) - Z_j' \bar{\gamma}] K_h(X_i, X_j)$ be defined as in the proof of Theorem 12.2.

(i) Show that $\mathrm{E}[I_{n,0}] = \mathrm{E}[(g(X_i) - Z_i'\bar{\gamma})^2] + o(1)$.

(ii) Show that $I_{n,0} = \mathrm{E}[(g(X_i) - Z_i'\bar{\gamma})^2] + o_p(1)$.

Hint: Note that $I_{n,0}$ can be written as a second order U-statistic, then use H-decomposition of U-statistics (see Appendix A), while (ii) follows trivially from (i).

Exercise 12.5. Let $\hat{\gamma}^*$ be defined as in Section 12.1.1. Show that $\hat{\gamma}^* - \gamma = O_p(n^{-1/2})$.

Hint: Write $\hat{\gamma}^* - \gamma = \hat{\gamma}^* - \hat{\gamma} + \hat{\gamma} - \gamma$. Show that $\mathrm{E}^*[(\hat{\gamma}^* - \hat{\gamma})^2] = O_p(n^{-1})$.

Exercise 12.6. Let I_n^b, $\hat{\sigma}_b^2$ and σ_b^2 be those defined in Theorem 12.5. Consider the case where $n_1 = n_2 = n$.

(i) Show that I_n^b is a degenerate U-statistic, i.e., show that

$$\mathrm{E}\left[K_{h,ij}^x + K_{h,ij}^y - 2K_{h,ij}^{x,y} \middle| X_i, Y_i\right] = 0.$$

(ii) Show that $\mathrm{var}(n(h_1 \dots h_q)^{1/2} I_n^b) = \sigma_b^2 + o(1)$.

(iii) Prove that $\hat{\sigma}_b^2 = \sigma_b^2 + o_p(1)$.

(iv) Using the results of (i)-(iii) above, prove Theorem 12.5.

Hint: In (ii) write $\sum_i \sum_{j \neq i} = 2 \sum_i \sum_{j < i}$ and use the result of (i). Use Lemma A.16 to prove (iii). Check Hall's (1984) CLT condition for (iv).

Exercise 12.7. Show that

$$\hat{\sigma}_f^2 = \frac{2}{n(n-1)} \sum_{i=1}^n \sum_{j \neq i}^n (K_{h,ij}^x)^2 (K_{h,ij}^y)^2.$$

defined in Theorem 12.11 is a consistent estimator of

$$\sigma_f^2 = \kappa^{p+q} \mathrm{E}[f_1(X_1)^2] \mathrm{E}[f_2(Y_i)^2].$$

Hint: Note that under H_0^f, X and Y are independent,

$$\mathrm{E}[\hat{\sigma}_f^2] = 2\mathrm{E}\left[K_{h_x}(X_i - X_j)\right]\mathrm{E}\left[K_{h_y}(Y_i - Y_j)\right]$$
$$= 2\kappa^p \left\{\mathrm{E}[f_1(X_i)^2] + o(1)\right\} \kappa^q \left\{\mathrm{E}[f_2(Y_i)^2] + o(1)\right\}$$
$$= \sigma_f^2 + o(1).$$

Use Lemma A.16 to show that $\mathrm{var}(\hat{\sigma}_h^2) = o(1)$.

Chapter 13

Nonsmoothing Tests

The conditional moment tests discussed in Chapter 12 are based on nonparametric kernel estimation of conditional mean functions. However, instead of estimating the conditional mean by nonparametric kernel methods, one could instead construct a consistent test based on the estimation of unconditional moments which results in a class of so-called nonsmoothing tests.

Note that the null hypothesis for conditional moment tests, H_0: $\mathrm{E}(u_i|X_i) = 0$ a.s., is equivalent to $\mathrm{E}[u_i M(X_i)] = 0$ for *all* $M(\cdot) \in \mathcal{M}$, where $\mathcal{M}$ denotes the class of bounded Borel measurable (or a.e. continuous) functions. Following Bierens (1982), Bierens and Ploberger (1997), Stinchcombe and White (1998), and Stute (1997), consider the following unconditional moment test

$$\mathrm{E}[u_i \mathcal{H}(X_i, x)] = 0 \text{ for almost all } x \in \mathcal{S} \subset \mathbb{R}^q \ , \qquad (13.1)$$

where $\mathcal{S}$ is the support of X_i. Equation (13.1) is equivalent to the condition $\mathrm{E}[u_i M(X_i)] = 0$ for all $M(\cdot) \in \mathcal{M}$ provided the linear span of $\{\mathcal{H}(X_i, x) : x \in \mathcal{S}\}$ is dense (see Definition A.36 in the appendix) in the space of bounded and continuous functions on $\mathcal{S}$. We assume that the weight function $\mathcal{H}(.,.)$ is bounded on $\mathcal{S} \times \mathcal{S}$. A popular choice of weight functions in the nonparametric statistics literature is $\mathcal{H}(X_i, x) = \mathbf{1}(X_i \leq x)$, where $\mathbf{1}(\cdot)$ is the usual indicator function; see Stute (1997). Other choices of weight functions include the exponential function $\mathcal{H}(X_i, x) = \exp(\iota X_i'x)$, $(\iota = \sqrt{-1})$ and the logistic function $\mathcal{H}(X_j, x) = 1/[1 + \exp(c - X_i'x)]$ with $c \neq 0$; see Stinchcombe and White (1998) for further discussion. By converting the conditional moment test given in (12.5) to the unconditional moment test given in (13.1), we avoid the need for nonparametric estimation when constructing the test. Hence, a test based on (13.1) alleviates the curse of dimensionality problem.

A feasible test can be obtained by multiplying the sample analogue of $E[u_i\mathcal{H}(X_i,x)]$ by $\sqrt{n}$, as in

$$J_n(x) = \sqrt{n}\left[\frac{1}{n}\sum_{j=1}^n u_j\mathcal{H}(X_j,x)\right] = \frac{1}{\sqrt{n}}\sum_j u_j\mathcal{H}(X_j,x). \qquad (13.2)$$

It is easy to see that for a fixed value of x, $J_n(x)$ converges to a zero mean finite variance normal random variable by the Lindeberg-Levy CLT. To decide whether H_0^a holds true one needs to examine whether (13.1) holds true *for all* x. Therefore, in order to obtain a consistent test based on (13.2), one needs to consider $J_n(x)$ for all x, and one way to do this is the so-called integrated conditional moment test (a Cramer-von Mises type test) of the form

$$CM = \int J_n(x)^2 dF(x) = \int\left[n^{-1}\sum_i u_i\mathcal{H}(X_i,x)\right]^2 dF(x). \qquad (13.3)$$

By applying a functional CLT, it can be shown that $J_n(\cdot)$ converges to a zero mean Gaussian process (say $J_\infty(\cdot)$). Then by the continuous mapping theorem one can show that $CM \to \int J_\infty(x)^2 dF(x)$, which provides the basis for a consistent nonsmoothing test. In practice, u_i is unobservable, and we therefore replace u_i by some consistent estimate thereof. Below we discuss several consistent model specification tests based on (13.2) and (13.3) that appear in the literature.

13.1   Testing for Parametric Regression Functional Form

When testing for correct specification of a parametric regression function, i.e., testing H_0^a: $E(Y_i|x) = m(x,\gamma)$ a.e., we replace u_i by $\hat{u}_i = Y_i - m(X_i,\hat{\gamma}_0)$ and construct a feasible version of (13.2). Thus, the test statistic for H_0^a is based upon

$$\hat{J}_n^a(x) = \frac{1}{\sqrt{n}}\sum_i \mathcal{H}(X_i,x)\hat{u}_i. \qquad (13.4)$$

To derive the asymptotic distribution of $\hat{J}_n^a(x)$, typically one first chooses a norm under which weak convergence will be defined. Commonly used norms include the Skorohod norm (see Stute (1997)) and some L_2 norms. Using an L_2-norm makes the asymptotic analysis much simpler than using the Skorohod norm, therefore we will use an L_2-norm to establish the weak convergence of $\hat{J}_n(\cdot)$. In Section 13.7 we prove the following result:

Theorem 13.1. *Under some standard regularity conditions, $\hat{J}_n(\cdot)$ converges weakly to a zero mean Gaussian process $J_\infty(\cdot)$ with covariance structure given in Section 13.7.*

With $\hat{J}_n^a(x)$ we can construct a Cramer-von Mises (CM) type statistic for testing H_0^a given by

$$CM_n^a = \int \left[\hat{J}_n^a(x)\right]^2 dF_n(x) = \frac{1}{n} \sum_{i=1}^n \left[\hat{J}_n^a(X_i)\right]^2, \qquad (13.5)$$

where $F_n(\cdot)$ is the empirical distribution of $X_1, \dots, X_n$. Given that $\hat{J}_n^a(\cdot)$ converges weakly to $J_\infty^a(\cdot)$ and employing the continuous mapping theorem (see Exercise 13.2), one gets $CM_n^a \xrightarrow{d} \int [J_\infty^a(x)]^2 F(dx)$, where $F(\cdot)$ is the CDF of X_i.

As in Bierens and Ploberger (1997), Stute (1997), and Whang (2000), we can show that $\int [J_\infty^a(x)]^2 F(dx)$ can be written as an infinite sum of weighted (independent) χ_1^2 random variables with weights depending on the unknown distribution of (X_i, Y_i). Therefore it is impossible to tabulate critical values for CM_n; however, the residual-based wild bootstrap method can be used to approximate the critical values for the limiting null distribution of CM_n^a. The wild bootstrap error u_i^* is generated via a two-point distribution $u_i^* = [(1 - \sqrt{5})/2]\hat{u}_i$ with probability $(1 + \sqrt{5})/[2\sqrt{5}]$ and $u_i^* = [(\sqrt{5} + 1)/2]\hat{u}_i$ with probability $(\sqrt{5} - 1)/[2\sqrt{5}]$. With $\{u_i^*\}_{i=1}^n$, we generate Y_i^* according to the null model $Y_i^* = m(X_i, \hat{\gamma}) + u_i^*$. Using the bootstrap sample $\{(Y_i^*, X_i)\}_{i=1}^n$, we estimate γ based on the null model, and let $\hat{\gamma}^*$ denote the resulting estimator. We obtain the bootstrap residual $\hat{u}_i^* = Y_i^* - m(X_i, \hat{\gamma}^*)$, and the bootstrap statistic $\hat{J}_n^{a*}(x)$ is obtained by replacing $\hat{u}_i$ in $\hat{J}_n^a(x)$ by $\hat{u}_i^*$. Using $\hat{J}_n^*(\cdot)$ we can compute a bootstrap version of the CM_n^a statistic, i.e., $CM_n^{a*} = n^{-1} \sum_i [\hat{J}_n^{a*}(X_i)]^2$. Conditional on the random sample $\{X_i, Y_i\}_{i=1}^n$, CM_n^{a*} converges to $\int [J_\infty^a(x)]^2 dx$ in distribution in probability under H_0. Therefore, CM_n^{a*} can be used to approximate the null distribution of CM_n^a. The definition of "convergence in distribution in probability" is given by (12.8).

It can be shown that the CM_n^a test can detect Pitman local alternatives that approach the null model at the rate $O_p(n^{-1/2})$. The smoothing and nonsmoothing tests look quite different in that they are derived from different principles. However, Fan and Li (2000) showed that the two types of test are in fact closely related. In particular, they show that if one fixes h_s to be a constant in the kernel test statistic I_n^a defined in Chapter 12, say $h_s = 1$ ($s = 1, \ldots, q$), and provided that the kernel function $w(\cdot)$ satisfies some additional conditions, then I_n^a becomes a nonsmoothing test, i.e.,

$$I_n^a(h = 1) = \frac{1}{n(n-1)} \sum_i \sum_{j \neq i} \hat{u}_i \hat{u}_j K(X_i - X_j) \qquad (13.6)$$

is a nonsmoothing test, where $K(X_i - X_j) = \prod_{s=1}^q k(X_{is} - X_{js})$ is the product kernel function with $h_s = 1$ for all $s = 1, \ldots, q$. Fan and Li showed that for commonly used kernel functions including the uniform, standard normal, triangular, and Epanechnikov kernels, the $I_n^a(h = 1)$ test is indeed a consistent test. Therefore, the only difference between a smoothing test and a nonsmoothing test is that the former uses shrinking h_s ($h_s \to 0$ as $n \to \infty$). Analysis based on Pitman local alternatives suggests that the nonsmoothing test is more powerful than the smoothing test since the former can detect Pitman local alternatives that approach the null model at the rate of $O_p(n^{-1/2})$, while the latter can only detect Pitman local alternatives that approach the null at the rate of $O_p\left((n(h_1 \ldots h_q)^{1/2})^{-1/2}\right)$, which is slower than $O_p(n^{-1/2})$. However, Fan and Li show that under high frequency local alternatives (Rosenblatt (1975)), the smoothing test can be more powerful than the nonsmoothing test. The Monte Carlo simulations in Fan and Li show that this indeed is the case (see also Andrews (1997)). Therefore, nonsmoothing tests and smoothing tests complement each other.

One problem with the nonsmoothing test given in (13.6) is that it is not invariant with respect to the scale of the data.[1] To remedy this, we suggest using

$$I_n^a(h = 1) = \frac{1}{n(n-1)} \sum_i \sum_{j \neq i} \hat{u}_i \hat{u}_j K\left(\frac{X_i - X_j}{x_{sd}}\right) \qquad (13.7)$$

---

[1]It is straightforward to use, say, $h = n^{-1/5}$ versus $h = x_{sd} n^{-1/5}$, where x_{sd} is the sample standard deviation of $\{X_i\}_{i=1}^n$. The latter is preferred since it is invariant with respect to the scale (i.e., standard deviation) of X.

where $K((X_i - X_j)/x_{sd}) = \prod_{s=1}^{q} k((X_{is} - X_{js})/x_{s,sd})$, where $x_{s,sd}$ is the sample standard deviation of $\{X_{is}\}_{i=1}^{n}$.

13.2 Testing for Equality of PDFs

We discussed testing the equality of two unknown PDFs in Section 12.2. The null hypothesis is H_0^b: $f(x) = g(x)$ a.e. Anderson et al. (1994) suggest using a fixed bandwidth h for testing H_0^b. Without loss of generality we can use $h = 1$ in I_n^b, resulting in a nonsmoothing test statistic given by

$$J_n^b = \frac{1}{n_1^2} \sum_{i=1}^{n_1} \sum_{j=1}^{n_1} K_{ij}^x + \frac{1}{n_2^2} \sum_{i=1}^{n_1} \sum_{j=1}^{n_1} K_{ij}^y - \frac{2}{n_1 n_2} \sum_{i=1}^{n_1} \sum_{j=1}^{n_2} K_{ij}^{x,y}, \quad (13.8)$$

where $K_{ij}^x = K(X_i - X_j)$, $K_{ij}^y = K(Y_i - Y_j)$, and $K_{ij}^{x,y} = K(X_i - Y_j)$. Under the assumption that n_1 and $n_2 \to \infty$ with n_1/n_2 being bounded away from zero and infinity, Anderson et al. show that $T_{n,ns}^b = n_1 \left[J_n^b - \left(\frac{1}{n_1} + \frac{1}{n_2} \right) k(0)^q \right]$ converges to an infinite sum of independent χ_1^2 distributions. The bootstrap version of J_n^b can be generated in exactly the same manner as in Section 13.1 (with $h_j = 1$ for all $j = 1, \ldots, q$). Let J_n^{b*} denote the resulting bootstrap version of J_n^b. The bootstrap statistic will be $T_{n,ns}^{*b} = n_1 \left[J_n^{*b} - \left(\frac{1}{n_1} + \frac{1}{n_2} \right) k(0)^q \right]$, and again the empirical distribution of the bootstrap statistic can be used to approximate the null distribution of T_n^b. Again, in practice, one may want to replace $K_{ij}^x = K(X_i - X_j)$ by $K((X_i - X_j)/x_{sd})$, K_{ij}^y by $K((Y_i - Y_j)/y_{sd})$, and K_{ij}^{xy} by $K(X_i/x_{sd} - Y_j/y_{sd})$ to make the test invariant with respect to the scale of the data.

13.3 A Nonparametric Significance Test

For what follows, the null hypothesis is the same as H_0^d discussed in Chapter 12, i.e., H_0^d: $E(Y_i|w, z) = r(w)$ a.e., where $r(w) = E(Y_i|w)$. Define $u_i = (Y_i - r(W_i))f(X_i)$ $(x = (w, z))$. Then H_0^d is equivalent to $E(u_i|X_i) = 0$ a.s. Thus, one can construct a test statistic based on $J_n^d(x) = n^{-1} \sum_i u_i \mathcal{H}(X_i, x)$. Chen and Fan (1999) used a smooth weight function $\mathcal{H}(X_i, x)$, and Delgado and Manteiga (2001) used $\mathcal{H}(X_i, x) = \mathbf{1}(X_i \leq x)$. To obtain a feasible test statistic, one can use kernel estimators $\hat{r}(X_i) = n^{-1} \sum_i Y_j K_{h_w, ij}/\hat{f}_w(W_i)$ and

$\hat{f}_w(W_i) = n^{-1} \sum_i Y_j K_{h_w,ij}$ to replace $r(W_i)$ and $f_w(W_i)$, yielding

$$\hat{J}_n^d(x) = \frac{1}{n} \sum_{i=1}^{n} \hat{u}_i \hat{f}(X_i) \mathcal{H}(X_i, x), \qquad (13.9)$$

where $\hat{u}_i \hat{f}(X_i) = (Y_i - \hat{r}(W_i)) \hat{f}_w(W_i)$. Chen and Fan used an L_2-norm, and Delgado and Manteiga worked with the Skorohod norm, and it can be shown that $\hat{J}_n^d(\cdot)$ converges to a zero mean Gaussian process under H_0^d under either a L_2-norm or the Skorohod norm.

Note that the $\hat{J}_n^d(\cdot)$ test is a partially nonsmoothing test since one still needs to smooth the null model in order to obtain consistent estimates of u_i and $f_w(\cdot)$. But unlike the smoothing test $\hat{I}_n^d$ considered in Chapter 12, it does not smooth the alternative model. Therefore, it alleviates the curse of dimensionality problem. A CM-type statistic is given by

$$CM_n^d = \int \left[\hat{J}_n^d(x)\right]^2 F_n(dx) = \frac{1}{n} \sum_i \left[\hat{J}_n^d(X_i)\right]^2. \qquad (13.10)$$

The bootstrap version of CM_n^d is given by

$$CM_n^{d*} = \frac{1}{n} \sum_i \left[\hat{J}_n^{d*}(X_i)\right]^2, \qquad (13.11)$$

where $\hat{J}_n^{d*}(X_i) = n^{-1} \sum_{j=1}^{n} \hat{u}_j^* \mathcal{H}(X_j, X_i)$, $\hat{u}_j^* = Y_i^* - \hat{r}^*(W_i)$, $Y_i^* = \hat{r}(W_i) + u_i^*$, $\hat{r}^*(W_i) = n^{-1} \sum_j Y_j^* K_{h_w,ij}/\hat{f}_w(W_i)$, and u_i^* is the two-point wild bootstrap error generated from $\hat{u}_i = Y_i - \hat{m}(W_i)$. Delgado and Manteiga (2001) showed that the bootstrap method works well in this setting for moderate sample sizes.

13.4   Andrews's Test for Conditional CDFs

Andrews (1997) proposed a nonsmoothing test to test for correct specification of a parametric conditional CDF. Andrews refers to his approach as a conditional Kolmogorov (CK) test. Let $f(y|x,\theta)$ denote the parametric conditional PDF. The parametric conditional CDF is given by

$$F(y|x,\theta) = \int \mathbf{1}(v < y) f(v|x,\theta) d\mu(v), \qquad (13.12)$$

where $d\mu(v) = dv$ and Y is a continuous variable, while when Y is a discrete variable and letting $\mathcal{Z}_y$ denote the range of Y, then $\int d\mu(v) = \sum_{v \in \mathcal{D}_y}$. Y can also consist of mixed continuous and discrete values. Let $H(.|.)$ denote the conditional CDF of Y_i given X_i and let $G(\cdot)$ be the marginal CDF of X_i. The null hypothesis is

$$H_0^i : H(y|x) = F(y|x, \theta) \text{ a.e. (in } (y,x)) \text{ for some } \theta \in \Theta, \quad (13.13)$$

where Θ is a compact subset of $\mathbb{R}^L$. Let $\hat{H}_n(z)$ denote the empirical CDF of $Z_i = (X_i, Y_i), i \le n$, i.e.,

$$\hat{H}_n(z) = \frac{1}{n} \sum_{i=1}^n \mathbf{1}(Z_i < z). \quad (13.14)$$

Let $\hat{G}_n(x)$ denote the empirical CDF of X_i, $i \le n$, i.e.,

$$\hat{G}_n(x) = \frac{1}{n} \sum_{i=1}^n \mathbf{1}(X_i < x). \quad (13.15)$$

Let $\hat{\theta}$ denote an estimator of θ based on the null model, and let $\hat{F}_n(z, \hat{\theta})$ denote the semiparametric/semiempirical CDF of $\{Z_i, i \le n\}$ based on the parametric conditional CDF $F(.|., \hat{\theta})$ and the empirical CDF $\hat{G}_n(\cdot)$ given by

$$\hat{F}_n(z, \hat{\theta}) = \frac{1}{n} \sum_{i=1}^n F(y|X_i, \hat{\theta}) \mathbf{1}(X_i \le x). \quad (13.16)$$

Andrews (1997) proposed the following CK test statistic:

$$CK_n = \sqrt{n} \max_{1 \le j \le n} \left| \hat{H}_n(Z_j) - \hat{F}_n(Z_j, \hat{\theta}) \right|$$

$$= \max_{1 \le j \le n} \left| \frac{1}{\sqrt{n}} \sum_{i=1}^n \left[\mathbf{1}(Y_i \le Y_j) - F(Y_j|X_i, \hat{\theta}) \right] \mathbf{1}(X_i \le X_j) \right|.$$

$$(13.17)$$

Andrews (1997) showed that the asymptotic null distribution of CK_n is nuisance-parameter-dependent as it depends on θ_0 and $G(\cdot)$. As a consequence, asymptotic critical values for CK_n cannot be tabulated. Andrews suggested using the following parametric bootstrap procedure to obtain the critical values for CK_n:

(i) For $i = 1, \ldots, n$, generate Y_i^* according to the parametric conditional PDF $f(Y_i|X_i, \hat{\theta})$ (or $F(Y_i|X_i, \hat{\theta})$).

(ii) Compute the bootstrap test CK_n^*, where CK_n^* is the same as CK_n except that Y_i in CK_n is replaced by Y_i^*.

(iii) Repeat (i) and (ii) a large number of times, say $B = 399$ times, and obtain the empirical distribution of $\{CK_n^{*j}\}_{j=1}^B$, which can then be used to obtain critical values for CK_n.

Andrews (1997) provided justification for the above bootstrap procedure and reported simulations which show that the parametric bootstrap method performs well in finite-sample settings.

13.5   Hong's Tests for Serial Dependence

Hong (1999) proposes a class of generalized spectrum tests that can be used to test for various patterns of serial dependence. Let $\{X_t\}$ be a strictly stationary process with a marginal characteristic function $\phi(u) = \mathrm{E}(e^{iuX_t})$ and a pairwise joint characteristic function $\phi_j(u, v) = \mathrm{E}[e^{i(uX_t + vX_{t-|j|})}]$, where $i = \sqrt{-1}$, $u, v \in (-\infty, \infty)$, and $j = 0, \pm 1, \ldots$ Define the covariate function between the transformed variables e^{iuX_t} and $e^{ivX_{t-|j|}}$ to be

$$\sigma_j(u, v) \equiv \mathrm{cov}(e^{iuX_t}, e^{ivX_{t-|j|}}). \qquad (13.18)$$

It is straightforward to show that $\sigma_j(u, v) = \phi_j(u, v) - \phi(u)\phi(v)$. Because $\phi_j(u, v) = \phi(u)\phi(v)$ for all u, v if and only if X_t and $X_{t-|j|}$ are independent, $\sigma_j(u, v)$ can capture any kind of (serial) dependence between X_t and $X_{t-|j|}$. Assuming that $\sup_{u,v \in (-\infty,\infty)} \sum_{j=-\infty}^{\infty} |\sigma_j(u, v)| < \infty$, then the Fourier transform of $\sigma_j(u, v)$ exists, i.e.,

$$f(w, u, v) \equiv \frac{1}{2\pi} \sum_{j=-\infty}^{\infty} \sigma_j(u, v)e^{-ijw}, \quad w \in [-\pi, \pi]. \qquad (13.19)$$

$f(w, u, v)$ contains information on all pairwise serial dependencies in $\{X_t\}$ over all lags. Therefore, one can construct test statistics based on $f(\cdot)$ for testing various patterns of serial dependence.

Hong (1999, Theorem 1) shows that $f(w, u, v)$ can be consistently estimated by

$$\hat{f}(w, u, v) = \frac{1}{2\pi} \sum_{j=1-n}^{n-1} k(j/p)\hat{\sigma}_j(u, v)e^{-ijw}, \qquad (13.20)$$

where $\hat{\sigma}_j(u, v) = \hat{\phi}_j(u, v) - \hat{\phi}(u, 0)\hat{\phi}(0, v)$, and where $\hat{\phi}_j(u, v) = (n - |j|)^{-1} \sum_{t=|j|+1}^{n} e^{i(uX_t + vX_{t-|j|})}$ is the empirical (pairwise) characteristic function, $p = p_n$ is a bandwidth or lag order, and $k(\cdot)$ is a kernel function. The optimal choice of p (i.e., that minimizes the IMSE of $\hat{f}(\cdot)$) depends on the smoothness of $f(\cdot)$ and the choice of k. For the Bartlett kernel $p \sim n^{1/3}$ and for the Daniell and Parzen kernels, $p \sim n^{2/5}$. Hong also proposes a data-driven method for the optimal selection of p. Note that the Daniell kernel is given by $k(z) = \sin(\pi z)/\pi z$, $z \in (-\infty, \infty)$.

If $\{X_t\}$ is an i.i.d sequence, then $\sigma_j(u, v) = 0$ for all $|j| \geq 1$; hence, $f(w, u, v)$ becomes a constant function in w:

$$f_{(0)}(w, u, v) = \frac{1}{2\pi}\sigma_0(u, v), \quad w \in [-\pi, \pi].$$

Thus, one can test serial dependence by comparing $\hat{f}(w, u, v)$ defined in (13.20) and $\hat{f}_{(0)}(w, u, v) = \frac{1}{2\pi}\hat{\sigma}_0(u, v)$ (see the $M(0, 0)$ test defined below). If the i.i.d. hypothesis is rejected, one can further test other specific types of serial dependence by comparing the derivative estimators of $f(w, u, v)$ and $\hat{f}_{(0)}(w, u, v)$ given by

$$\hat{f}_n^{(0,m,l)}(w, u, v) = \frac{1}{2\pi} \sum_{j=1-n}^{n-1} \left(1 - \frac{|j|}{n}\right)^{1/2} k(j/p)\hat{\sigma}_j^{(m,l)}(u, v)e^{-ijw},$$

$$(13.21)$$

$$\hat{f}_{(0)}^{(0,m,l)}(w, u, v) = \frac{1}{2\pi}\hat{\sigma}_0^{(m,l)}(u, v), \tag{13.22}$$

where $\hat{\sigma}_j^{(m,l)}(u, v) = \partial^{m+l}\hat{\sigma}_j(u, v)/\partial^m u \partial^l v$ for $m, l \geq 0$.

Hong (1999) proposes a class of tests based on a weighted integrated squared difference between $\hat{f}_n^{(0,m,l)}(w, u, v)$ and $\hat{f}_{(0)}^{(0,m,l)}(w, u, v)$ given by

$$\int \int \left|\hat{f}^{(0,m,l)}(w, u, v) - \hat{f}_{(0)}^{(m,l)}(w, u, v)\right|^2 dw \, dW_1(u)dW_2(v)$$

$$= \frac{1}{\pi} \int \sum_{j=1}^{n-1} k^2(j/p)(1 - \frac{j}{n})|\hat{\sigma}^{(m,l)}(u, v)|^2 dW_1(u)dW_2(v), \quad (13.23)$$

where the equality follows from Parseval's identity, and where $W_1(\cdot)$ and $W_2(\cdot)$ are weight functions that will be discussed below.

The test statistic is a standardized version of the above quadratic form:

$$M(m, l) = \left[\int \sum_{j=1}^{n-1} k^2(j/p)(n-j)|\hat{\sigma}_j^{(m,l)}(u,v)|^2 dW_1(u)dW_2(v) \right.$$

$$\left. - \hat{C}_0^{(m,l)} \sum_{j=1}^{n-1} k^2(j/p) \right],$$

$$(13.24)$$

where $W_1(\cdot)$ and $W2(\cdot)$ are chosen weight functions,

$$\hat{C}_0^{(m,l)} = \int \hat{\sigma}^{(m,m)}(u,-u)dW_1(u) \int \hat{\sigma}^{(l,l)}(v,-v)dW_2(v),$$

and

$$\hat{D}_0^{(m,l)} = 2 \int |\hat{\sigma}_0^{(m,m)}(u,u')|^2 dW_1(u)dW_2(u')$$

$$\times \int |\hat{\sigma}_0^{(m,m)}(v,v')|^2 dW_1(v)dW_2(v').$$

For given (m, l), $M(m, l)$ is asymptotically (one-sided) $N(0,1)$ under the null hypothesis of serial independence.

Commonly used hypotheses include choosing $(m, l) = (0, 0)$ to test for any type of serial dependence. Once one rejects the null of general serial independence, one may proceed to test for a specific type of serial dependence. For example, choosing $(m, l) = (1, 0)$ tests the null of $E(X_t|X_{t-j}) = E(X_t)$ for all $j > 0$, and this will be called a test for martingale differences. Similarly, $(m, l) = (1, l)$ for $l = 1, 2, 3, 4$ test whether $\text{cov}(Y_t, Y_{t-j}^l) = 0$ for all $j > 0$, which tests for linear in mean, ARCH in mean, skewness-in-mean and kurtosis-in-mean effects, respectively. Below we provide further details on the application of the general $M(m, l)$ statistic given above in (13.24) to the cases for which $(m, l) = (0, 0)$ and $(m, l) = (1, 0)$.

With $(m, l) = (0, 0)$, Hong (1999) suggests choosing $W_1(\cdot) = W_2(\cdot) = W_0(\cdot)$, where $W_0(\cdot)$ is the CDF of a standard normal random variable.

Then it can be shown that

$$
M(0,0) = \left\{ \int \left[\sum_{j=1}^{n-1} k^2(j/p)(n-j) |\hat{\sigma}_j(u,v)|^2 \right] dW_0(u)dW_0(v) \right.
$$
$$
\left. - \hat{C}^{(0,0)} \sum_{j=1}^{n-1} k^2(j/p) \right\} / \hat{\sigma}_{(0,0)},
$$

$$(13.25)$$

where $\hat{C}^{(0,0)} = [\int \hat{\sigma}_0(u,-u)dW_0(u)]^2$ and

$$
\hat{\sigma}_{(0,0)}^2 = 2 \left[\int |\hat{\sigma}_0(u,v)|^2 \, dW_0(u)dW_0(v) \right]^2 \sum_{j=1}^{n-2} k^4(j/p).
$$

To test for martingale differences with $(m,l) = (1,0)$, Hong (1999) suggests using $W_1(\cdot) = \delta(\cdot)$, the Dirac δ-function (see Definition A.15 in the appendix), where $W_2(\cdot) = W_0(\cdot)$. Then

$$
M(1,0) = \left\{ \int \left[\sum_{j=1}^{n-1} k^2(j/p)(n-j) \left| \hat{\sigma}_j^{(1,0)}(0,v) \right|^2 \right] dW_0(v) \right.
$$
$$
\left. - \hat{C}^{(1,0)} \sum_{j=1}^{n-1} k^2(j/p) \right\} / \hat{\sigma}_{(1,0)},
$$

$$(13.26)$$

where

$$
\hat{C}_0^{(1,0)} = \hat{R}_{1,0} \int \hat{\sigma}_0(u,-u)dW_0(u),
$$

$$
\hat{\sigma}_{(1,0)} = \left[2\hat{R}_{1,0}^2 \int \left| \hat{\sigma}_0^2(u,u) \right|^2 dW_0(u) \sum_{j=1}^{n-2} k^4(j/p) \right]^{1/2},
$$

$$
\hat{\sigma}_j^{(1,0)} = (n-j)^{-1} \sum_{t=j+1}^{n} X_t \left[e^{ivX_{t-j}} - \hat{\phi}_j(0,v) \right],
$$

$$
\hat{R}_{1,j} = (n-j)^{-1} \sum_{t=j+1}^{n} \left[X_t - \bar{X}_t(j) \right] \left[X_{t-j} - \bar{X}_2(j) \right],
$$

$$
\bar{X}_1(j) = (n-j)^{-1} \sum_{t=j+1}^{n} X_t, \text{ and}
$$

$$
\bar{X}_2(j) = (n-j)^{-1} \sum_{t=j+1}^{n} X_{t-j}.
$$

Hong and Lee (2003) recommend using bootstrap methods to better approximate the finite-sample null distribution of the test statistic $M(m, l)$. Let $\hat{M}_{m,l}$ denote the statistic based on the original sample $\{X_t\}_{t=1}^n$, and let $\hat{M}_{m,l}^b$ denote the statistic using the bootstrap sample $\{X_t^b\}_{t=1}^n$. Then the bootstrap P-value of $\hat{M}_{m,l}$ can be approximated by $p_B = B^{-1} \sum_{b=1}^B \mathbf{1}(\hat{M}_{m,l}^b \geq \hat{M}_{m,l})$, where B is the number of bootstrap replications and $\mathbf{1}(\cdot)$ is an indicator function. For the case of testing the null of i.i.d. $((m, l) = (0, 0))$, one can use the naïve (resampling) bootstrap, and for testing the null of martingale differences, one can use the wild bootstrap: $Y_t^b = aY_t$ with probability r and $Y_t^b = (1 - a)Y_t$ with probability $1 - r$, $a = (1 + \sqrt{5})/2$ and $r = a/\sqrt{5}$. Hong and Lee show that the bootstrap method performs well with sample sizes of $n = 100$.

Hong and Lee (2003) applied Hong's (1999) general spectrum tests for a variety of (m, l) values; see Table 1 of Hong and Lee for the choices of $W_1(\cdot)$ and $W_2(\cdot)$ for different (m, l) cases. Hong and Lee apply the tests to daily exchange rate data for Canada, Germany, the United Kingdom, Japan, and France. The general findings are that the changes of all five exchange rates show strong serial dependence (rejecting the null of case $(m, l) - (0, 0)$), while the changes are often serially uncorrelated (i.e., they fail to reject the null for the case of $(m, l) = (1, 1)$), but they are clearly not martingale difference processes (rejecting the null with $(m, l) = (1, 0)$). Their findings suggest that it should be possible to forecast the mean of the changes of exchange rates. They further use various nonlinear time series models to forecast the change in exchange rates, and find that the method of combining several different forecasting models often provides the best forecasts.

13.6   More on Nonsmoothing Tests

In principle, all consistent model specification tests can be constructed using nonsmoothing methods. For example, Delgado (1993) proposed a nonsmoothing test for the equality of two nonparametric regression curves, Bai and Ng (2001) considered a nonsmoothing test for conditional symmetry, Fan (1994) proposed a nonsmoothing test for parametric PDFs, and Fan and Gencay (1995) proposed a consistent test for symmetry in linear regression models.

13.7 Proofs

13.7.1 Proof of Theorem 13.1

We first present a lemma.

Lemma 13.1. *Let $Z_1(\cdot), \ldots, Z_n(\cdot)$ be independent and identically distributed zero mean random elements on the L_2 space (a Hilbert space) with norm $||Z_i(\cdot)||_\nu^2 = \int |Z_i(x)|^2 d\nu(x)$, where $\nu(\cdot)$ is a finite measure on $\mathcal{S}$, the support of X_i. If $\mathrm{E}[||Z_i(\cdot)||_\nu^2] < \infty$, then $n^{-1/2} \sum_{i=1}^n Z_i(\cdot)$ converges weakly to a zero mean Gaussian process with covariance function given by $\Omega(x, x') = \mathrm{E}[Z_i(x)Z_i(x')]$.*

Proof. See Theorem 2.1 of Politis and Romano (1994), or van der Vaart and Wellner (1996, ex. 1.8.5, p. 50). Note that $\mathrm{E}[||Z_i(\cdot)||_\nu^2] < \infty$ is a sufficient condition that ensures that the process $n^{-1/2} \sum_{i=1}^n Z_i(\cdot)$ is tight.

To prove Theorem 13.1, we first write

$$n^{-1/2} \sum_i Z_i(\cdot) = n^{-1/2} \sum_i \hat{u}_i \mathcal{H}(X_i, .),$$

where $\hat{u}_i = Y_i - m(X_i, \hat{\gamma})$. Assume that $\hat{\gamma}$ is the nonlinear least squares estimator of γ. Letting $m_i^{(1)} = [\partial m(X_i, \gamma)/\partial \gamma]|_\gamma = \gamma_0$, and by the fact that $\hat{\gamma} - \gamma_0 = O_p(n^{-1/2})$ and using a Taylor series expansion, we have $\hat{u}_i = Y_i - m(X_i, \gamma_0) - m_i^{(1)}(\hat{\gamma} - \gamma_0) + O_p(n^{-1})$. Also, from nonlinear least squares theory, we know that

$$\hat{\gamma} - \gamma_0 = \left[n^{-1} \sum_i m_i^{(1)'} m_i^{(1)} \right]^{-1} \sum_i m_i^{(1)} u_i + O_p\left(n^{-1}\right)$$

$$= \left\{ \mathrm{E}\left[m_i^{(1)'} m_i^{(1)} \right] \right\}^{-1} \sum_i m_i^{(1)} u_i + O_p\left(n^{-1}\right).$$

(13.27)

Letting $B = \mathrm{E}\left[m_i^{(1)'} m_i^{(1)} \right]$ and $\Phi(X_i, .) = \mathrm{E}\left[m_i^{(1)} \mathcal{H}(X_i, .) \right] B m_i^{(1)}$, we have

$$\hat{J}_n^a(\cdot) = n^{-1/2} \sum_i \hat{u}_i \mathcal{H}(X_i, .)$$

$$= n^{-1/2} \sum_i u_i \mathcal{H}(X_i, .)$$

$$+ \left[n^{-1} \sum_i m_i^{(1)} \mathcal{H}(X_i, .) \right] B \left[n^{-1/2} \sum_i m_i^{(1)} u_i \right] + O_p(n^{-1})$$

$$= n^{-1/2} \sum_i u_i \mathcal{H}(X_i, .)$$

$$+ \mathrm{E}\left[m_i^{(1)} \mathcal{H}(X_i, .) \right] B \left[n^{-1/2} \sum_i m_i^{(1)} u_i \right] + O_p(n^{-1/2})$$

$$= n^{-1/2} \sum_i [\mathcal{H}(X_i, .) + \phi(X_i, .)] u_i$$

$$\equiv n^{-1/2} \sum_i Z_i(\cdot) + O_p(n^{-1/2}),$$

where $Z_i(\cdot) = [\mathcal{H}(X_i, .) + \phi(X_i, .)] u_i$. It is easy to see that $\mathrm{E}[\|Z_i(\cdot)\|_\nu^2] < \infty$ (see Exercise 13.1). Therefore, by Lemma 13.1 we know that $\hat{J}_n^a(\cdot)$ converges to a zero mean Gaussian process with covariance structure given by $\Omega(x, x') = \mathrm{E}[Z_i(x) Z_i(x')]$ with $Z_i(x) = [\mathcal{H}(X_i, x) + \phi(X_i, .)] u_i$. $\square$

13.8   Exercises

Exercise 13.1. Letting $Z_i(\cdot) = [\mathcal{H}(X_i, .) + \phi(X_i, .)] u_i$, show that $\mathrm{E}[\|Z_i(\cdot)\|_\nu^2] < \infty$.

Exercise 13.2. By Theorem 13.1, we know that $\hat{J}_n^a(\cdot)$ converges to $J_\infty^a(\cdot)$ and by the continuous mapping theorem (see Appendix A), we know that

$$\int [\hat{J}_n^a(x)]^2 d\nu(x) \to \int [J_\infty^a(x)]^2 d\nu(x). \tag{13.28}$$

Under the assumption that $F(\cdot)$ is absolutely continuous with respect to ν, (13.28) implies that (changing ν to $F(\cdot)$)

$$\int [\hat{J}_n^a(x)]^2 dF(x) \to \int [J_\infty^a(x)]^2 dF(x). \tag{13.29}$$

Prove that $(dF_n(\cdot)$ versus $dF(\cdot))$

$$\int [\hat{J}_n^a(x)]^2 dF_n(x) - \int [\hat{J}_n^a(x)]^2 dF(x) = o_p(1). \qquad (13.30)$$

Note that (13.29) and (13.30) imply that

$$CM^a \equiv \int [\hat{J}_n^a(x)]^2 dF_n(x)$$

$$= \int [\hat{J}_n^a(x)]^2 dF(x) + o_p(1) \to \int [J_\infty^a(x)]^2 dF(x)$$

in distribution.

Part IV

Nonparametric Nearest Neighbor and Series Methods

Chapter 14

K-Nearest Neighbor Methods

In Chapter 15 we will study nonparametric series methods which constitute an alternative to the nonparametric kernel methods that form the core of this book. In this chapter we consider yet another alternative, the so-called nearest neighbor methods that constitute one of the established nonparametric approaches that also enjoy widespread use.

The main benefit arising from the use of nearest neighbor methods is that they automatically adapt to the amount of local information that is available. That is, the greater the amount of local information, the smaller the range in which smoothing occurs. This is a feature not shared by the fixed bandwidth estimator that underlies much existing applied work. However, the k-nearest neighbor method (henceforth simply "k-nn") also has some disadvantages relative to kernel methods. For example, k-nn methods lack the ability to completely smooth out irrelevant variables. Therefore, the k-nn method should be viewed as a complement to the popular kernel methods that we have seen in previous chapters.

14.1   Density Estimation: The Univariate Case

The uniform kernel estimator defined in (1.6) uses observations that fall inside the interval $[x - h, x + h]$ to estimate $f(x)$. One feature of this estimator is that it uses a fixed smoothing parameter h, that is, h is constant and unrelated to x. When $f(x)$ is large at a given point x, more data points fall inside the interval $[x - h, x + h]$ than when $f(x)$

is small, say, in the tail of a distribution where far fewer data points fall inside $[x - h, x + h]$. The use of fixed bandwidths, however, may lead to oversmoothing in some range of the support of the data and undersmoothing in others, say, in the tails.

An alternative nonparametric estimator, the so-called nearest neighbor density estimator, can be used to circumvent this problem. Rather than use a constant bandwidth whereby the number of observations lying in the interval $[x - h, x + h]$ will vary, a simple nearest neighbor method instead uses the k observations lying nearest x to estimate $f(x)$, where k is a fixed integer. That is, this simple estimator instead keeps the number of observations used to construct the density estimate fixed by using a bandwidth that may vary with x. One advantage of this approach is that it is locally adaptive, that is, if $f(x)$ is small, then the interval will be large, and vice versa, a property not enjoyed by fixed bandwidth kernel methods.

One difference between the kernel estimator and the k-nn estimator is that the bandwidth R_x defined in (14.12) below is now stochastic. Hence the asymptotic analysis of a k-nn estimator is more complex than that for the fixed bandwidth kernel estimator.

Let $X_1, X_2, \ldots, X_n$ be i.i.d. random observations with bounded continuous density $f(x)$. The simplest form of a k-nn estimator is to use k nearest observations (to x) to estimate $f(x)$. When x is a q-vector, we will use Euclidean distance to measure the distance between data points.

Definition 14.1. *Let $R_x = R_n(x)$ denote the Euclidean distance between x and the kth nearest neighbor of x among the x_i's.*

Though $R_x = R_n(x)$ depends on n, we shall suppress the dependence on n for notational simplicity. A simple k-nn estimator, for a fixed value x ($x \in \mathbb{R}$), is given by

$$\tilde{f}(x) = \frac{1}{nR_x} \sum_{i=1}^{n} \left(\frac{1}{2}\right) \mathbf{1}\left(\frac{|x - X_i|}{R_x} \le 1\right) = \frac{k}{2nR(x)}, \qquad (14.1)$$

where $\mathbf{1}(\cdot)$ is the usual indicator function that ensures that only the k observations nearest x are used to estimate $f(x)$.

To obtain a consistent estimator of $f(x)$, we need to choose $k = k(n)$ such that $k \to \infty$ and $k/n \to 0$ as $n \to \infty$. Here, k/n plays a role similar to the fixed smoothing parameter h for the kernel estimator.

The conditions $k \to \infty$ and $k/n \to 0$ correspond to $nh \to \infty$ and $h \to 0$ in kernel estimation.

For multivariate estimation, $x \in \mathbb{R}^q$, we shall use $||.||$ to denote the Euclidean norm, i.e.,

$$||x - X_i|| = \sqrt{(x_1 - X_{1i})^2 + \cdots + (x_q - X_{qi})^2}.$$

A simple k-nn density estimator is therefore given by

$$\tilde{f}(x) = \frac{1}{nR_x^q} \sum_{i=1}^{n} \frac{1}{c_0} \mathbf{1}\left(\frac{||x - X_i||}{R_x} \leq 1\right) = \frac{k}{c_0 n R_x^q}, \qquad (14.2)$$

where $c_0 = \pi^{q/2}/[\Gamma(\frac{q+2}{2})]$ is the volume of the unit ball in $\mathbb{R}^q$, and $\Gamma(\cdot)$ is the Γ function defined by $\Gamma(\alpha) = \int_0^\infty t^{\alpha-1} e^{-t} dt$. Using $\Gamma(z+1) = z\Gamma(z)$, $\Gamma(1/2) = \sqrt{\pi}$ and $\Gamma(1) = 1$, one can easily compute c_0 for any positive integer q.

$\tilde{f}(x)$ defined in (14.2) gives equal weight $(1/c_0)$ to observations lying inside the sphere $||X_i - x|| \leq R(x)$ and zero weight to observations lying outside the sphere, while the weight function is discontinuous at the boundary of the sphere. A continuous weight function such as a standard normal PDF, i.e., $w(v) = (2\pi)^{-q/2} e^{-||v||^2/2}$, can also be used so that the weight function $w(v)$ is monotonically decreasing as $||v||$ increases. Using a general weight function $w(\cdot)$, one can estimate $f(x)$ by

$$\hat{f}(x) = \frac{1}{nR_x^q} \sum_{i=1}^{n} w\left(\frac{||x - X_i||}{R_x}\right), \qquad (14.3)$$

where $w(\cdot)$ is a bounded, symmetric, nonnegative integrable weight function with

$$\int_{\mathbb{R}^q} w(v) dv = 1.$$

When $w(\cdot)$ is the uniform PDF (i.e., $w(v) = 1/c_0$ if $||v|| \leq 1$, and $w(v) = 0$ if $||v|| > 1$), $\hat{f}(x)$ given in (14.3) collapses to $\tilde{f}(x)$ defined in (14.2). To simplify the derivation below we impose the restriction that $w(v) = 0$ for $||v|| \geq 1$.

Assumption 14.1. $w(\cdot)$ is a bounded symmetric nonnegative function, $w(v) = 0$ for $||v|| \geq 1$, $\int w(v) dv = 1$, $\int w(v) vv' dv = \kappa_2 I_q$, $\int w^2(v) dv = \kappa$ and $\int w^2(v) vv' du = \kappa_{22} I_q$, and I_q is an identity matrix of dimension q. κ_2, κ and κ_{22} are all finite positive constants.

We impose the following mild conditions on $f(x)$ and k.

Assumption 14.2.

(i) $f(x)$ is twice differentiable.

(ii) $k \to \infty$, and $k/n \to 0$ as $n \to \infty$.

Theorem 14.1. *Under Assumptions 14.1 and 14.2, we have*

(i) $\operatorname{bias}(\hat{f}(x)) = \frac{c_1 \operatorname{tr}[f^{(2)}(x)]}{f(x)^{2/q}} \left(\frac{k}{n}\right)^{2/q} + O\left((k/n)^{3/q}\right).$

(ii) $\operatorname{var}(\hat{f}(x)) = \frac{c_2 f(x)^2}{k} + o(1/k)$, *where* $c_1 = (1/2)\kappa_2 c_0^{-2/q}$, $\kappa_2 = \int w(v)^2 v_s^2 dv$, v_s *is the sth component of* v, *and* $c_2 = c_0[\int w^2(v)dv]$.

The proof of Theorem 14.1 is given in Section 14.9.

Comparing Theorem 14.1 with the results given in (1.23) and (1.24), we observe that $(k/n)^{1/q}$ corresponds to the bandwidth h (or $(k/n) \sim h^q$) used in the kernel estimator of $f(x)$. It is easy to see that the optimal rate for k that balances the squared bias and variance is of order $O(n^{4/(4+q)})$. If we use this optimal order for k, then from Theorem 14.1 we immediately have

$$\operatorname{MSE}(\hat{f}(x)) = \frac{[c_1 \operatorname{tr}(f^{(2)}(x))]^2}{[f(x)]^{4/q}} \left(\frac{k}{n}\right)^{4/q} + \frac{c_2 f^2(x)}{k} + (s.o.)$$

$$= O\left((k/n)^{4/q} + (1/k)\right). \tag{14.4}$$

For the kernel density estimator outlined in Chapter 1, the bias term is $O(h^2)$, which does not depend on q, the dimension of x. The variance is $O\left((nh^q)^{-1}\right)$, which depends on q and thereby leads to the curse of dimensionality in kernel estimation. However, results differ for the k-nn method because the variance term is $O(1/k)$, which does not depend on q, while the bias term is $O((\frac{k}{n})^{2/q})$, which does depend on q, giving rise to the curse of dimensionality.

One can see that the bias term contains the factor $f(x)^{2/q}$ in its denominator, thus, in the tails of a distribution where $f(x)$ is small, the squared bias will be the dominant MSE component.

Mack and Rosenblatt (1979) establish the following asymptotic normality result for $\hat{f}(x)$.

Theorem 14.2. *Assuming, in addition to Assumption 14.1, that $f(x)$ is three times differentiable and that $k^{1/2}(k/n)^{3/q} \to 0$ as $n \to \infty$, then we have*

$$k^{1/2}\left(\hat{f}(x) - f(x) - (k/n)^{2/q}\frac{c_1 \operatorname{tr}[f^{(2)}(x)]}{[f(x)]^{2/q}}\right) \xrightarrow{d} N(0, c_2 f^2(x)). \quad (14.5)$$

An excellent overview of the relationship between kernel density estimators and k-nn density estimators can be found in Mack and Rosenblatt (1979, pp. 13–14).

One problem with k-nn methods is that they treat all components symmetrically. To appreciate this, consider the case for which $q = 2$. If the data range (support) of X_1 is much larger than that for X_2, then $||X_i - x|| \leq R_x$ may contain points mostly with the same X_{i1} and x_1 but different in X_{i2} and x_2, which is undesirable. In practice, one could first standardize the data so that each component has sample mean zero and sample unit variance (e.g., $(X_{is} - \bar{x}_s)/sd(X_{is})$), or standardize each variable so that they assume values between 0 and 1, i.e., $(X_{is} - \min_i X_{is})/(\max_i X_{is} - \min_i X_{is})$. This latter transformation symmetrizes the data components in terms of their range, which should lead to better finite-sample performance relative to that based on the untransformed data. However, this still will not solve the problem of x_s potentially having a different impact on $f(x)$ when, say, $f(x)$ is relatively flat in x_1 but changes rapidly as x_2 varies. Ideally, one ought to use a different k_s for each variable x_s, and we will discuss this possibility in Section 14.8.

14.2 Regression Function Estimation

For the nonparametric regression model given by

$$Y_i = g(X_i) + u_i, \quad (14.6)$$

one can estimate the regression function $g(x) = E(Y|x)$ using k-nn methods by

$$\hat{g}(x) = \frac{(nR_x^q)^{-1}\sum_{i=1}^{n} Y_i w\left(\frac{x-X_i}{R_x}\right)}{(nR_x^q)^{-1}\sum_{i=1}^{n} w\left(\frac{x-X_i}{R_x}\right)}. \quad (14.7)$$

Note that the assumption $\int w(v)dv = 1$ in (14.1) can be replaced by $\int w(v)dv = a > 0$ since the weight function can be multiplied by any positive constant without changing the regression estimator.

The next theorem gives the leading bias and variance terms for $\hat{g}(x)$.

Theorem 14.3. *In addition to Assumptions 14.1 and 14.2, and assuming that $g(x)$ is twice differentiable, then we have*

$$\text{bias}(\hat{g}(x)) = c_3 \left(\frac{k}{n}\right)^{2/q} \frac{g^{(1)}(x)' f^{(1)}(x) + 2f(x) \,\text{tr}[g^{(2)}(x)]}{f(x)^{(2+q)/q}}$$

$$+ o(k^{-1/2}) + o\left((k/n)^{q/2}\right) \quad \text{and}$$

$$\text{var}(\hat{g}(x)) = \frac{c_4 \sigma^2(x)}{k} + o(k^{-1}),$$

where $c_3 = \kappa_2/[2c_0^{2/q}]$, $\kappa_2 = \int w(v) v_s^2 dv$, $c_4 = c_0[\int w^2(v) dv]$.

The proof can be found in Mack (1981).

Comparing Theorem 14.3 with Theorem 2.2, we see once again that $(k/n)^{1/q}$ corresponds to h for the kernel estimator of $g(x)$.

Theorem 14.3 implies the MSE rate

$$\text{MSE}(\hat{g}(x)) = [\text{bias}(\hat{g}(x))]^2 + \text{var}(\hat{g}(x)) = O\left(\left(\frac{k}{n}\right)^{4/q} + k^{-1}\right). \quad (14.8)$$

Mack (1981) also established the following asymptotic normality result:

Theorem 14.4. *In addition to Assumptions 14.1 and 14.2, and assuming that $g(x)$ is three-times differentiable and that $k^{1/2}(k/n)^{3/q} \to 0$ as $n \to \infty$, then we have*

$$k^{1/2}\left(\hat{g}(x) - g(x) - (k/n)^{2/q} B_g(x)\right) \xrightarrow{d} N(0, c_4 \sigma^2(x)), \quad (14.9)$$

where $B_g(x) = c_3 \left\{g^{(1)}(x)' f^{(1)}(x) + 2g(x) \,\text{tr}[f^{(2)}(x)]\right\} / \left[f(x)^{(2+q)/q}\right]$.

As noted earlier, with multivariate X one should not apply the k-nn method directly to the raw data. This is because the range of different components of x will differ in general. A common practice is to first standardize X_{is} to have, say, zero mean and unit standard deviation so that X_{is} all have comparable ranges, and then to apply Euclidean distance to the standardized variables to obtain the k-nn smoothing parameters.

14.3   A Local Linear k-nn Estimator

In this section we consider the problem of using a local linear k-nn method to estimate an unknown regression function. We consider the nonparametric regression model

$$Y_i = g(X_i) + u_i, \quad i = 1, \ldots, n, \tag{14.10}$$

where $X_i \in \mathbb{R}^q$. We are interested in estimating the unknown function $g(x)$ and its derivative, $\beta(x) \stackrel{\text{def}}{=} \partial g(x)/\partial x \equiv g^{(1)}(x)$. Let $\delta(x) = (g(x), (\beta(x))')'$. Using a Taylor series expansion of $g(X_i)$ at x, we get $g(X_i) = g(x) + (X_i - x)'\beta(x) + T(X_i, x)$, where $T(X_i, x) = g(X_i) - g(x) - (X_i - x)'\beta(x)$. Thus, we may write

$$Y_i = (1, (X_i - x)')\delta(x) + T(X_i, x) + u_i. \tag{14.11}$$

Let $w(\cdot)$ be a bounded, symmetric weight function with $\int w(v)dv = 1$ and $w(v) = 0$ for $||v|| \geq 1$. A local linear k-nn estimator of $\delta(x)$ is given by $\hat{\delta}(x)$ which is equal to

$$\left[\sum_i w_{i,x} \begin{pmatrix} 1, & (X_i - x)' \\ X_i - x, & (X_i - x)(X_i - x)' \end{pmatrix} \right]^{-1} \sum_i w_{i,x} \begin{pmatrix} 1 \\ X_i - x \end{pmatrix} Y_i, \tag{14.12}$$

where $w_{i,x} = w((X_i - x)/R_x)$.

We make the following assumptions.

Assumption 14.3. (X_i, Y_i) are i.i.d., $u_i = Y_i - g(X_i)$, $\mathrm{E}(u_i^4)$ is finite, $g(x)$ and $f(x)$ are both differentiable up to the third order, and $\sigma^2(x) = \mathrm{E}(u_i^2 | X_i = x)$ is continuous in x.

Assumption 14.4. As $n \to \infty$, $k \to \infty$, $k^{q+2}/n^2 \to \infty$ and $k^{q+6}/n^6 \to 0$.

The next theorem gives the asymptotic normality result for $\hat{\delta}(x)$.

Theorem 14.5. *Under Assumptions 14.3 and 14.4,*

$$D(n)\left(\hat{\delta}(x) - \delta(x) - \begin{pmatrix} (k/n)^{2/q}\mu_L(x) \\ 0 \end{pmatrix} \right) \to N(0, \Sigma_x) \text{ in distribution,}$$

where

$$D(n) = \begin{pmatrix} k^{1/2}, & 0 \\ 0, & d_n I_q \end{pmatrix}$$

with

$$d_n = k^{1/2}(k/n)^{1/q},$$

$$\mu_L(x) = (1/2)\kappa_2 \operatorname{tr}\{g^{(2)}(x)\}/(c_0 f(x))^{q/2}, \text{ and}$$

$$\Sigma_x = \begin{pmatrix} c_0\kappa\sigma^2(x), & 0 \\ 0, & c_0\kappa_{22}\sigma^2(x)I_q/\kappa_2^2 \end{pmatrix}.$$

The proof of Theorem 14.5 is given in Section 14.9.

The asymptotic distribution of $\hat{g}(x)$ (the first element of $\hat{\delta}(x)$) is obtained as a corollary.

Corollary 14.1. *Under the same conditions as in Theorem 14.5, we have*

$$k^{1/2}\left(\hat{g}(x) - g(x) - (k/n)^{2/q}\mu_L(x)\right) \to N\left(0, c_0\kappa\sigma^2(x)\right) \text{ in distribution.}$$

14.4 Cross-Validation with Local Constant k-nn Estimation

We consider the nonparametric regression model

$$Y_i = g(X_i) + u_i, \quad i = 1, 2, \ldots, n.$$

Define the k-nn distance centered at X_i as follows:

Definition 14.2. $R_i \equiv R_n(X_i) \overset{\text{def}}{=}$ *the k-nn Euclidean distance to X_i among all the X_j's for $j \neq i$.*

We impose a stronger condition on the weight function to simplify the proof. We assume that $w(\cdot) : \mathbb{R}^q \to \mathbb{R}$ is a bounded nonnegative weight function, $w(v) = w(-v)$, $\int w(v)dv = 1$, and $w(v) = 0$ for $||v|| \geq 1$, where $||v||$ denotes the Euclidean norm of v. It can be shown that all of the results discussed in this chapter remain unchanged if the condition $w(v) = 0$ for $||v|| \geq 1$ is relaxed to $w(v) = 0$ for $||v|| > 1$. However, the proofs will become lengthy since we have to consider an extra term. Note that when changing variables in the proofs, $||v|| = 1$ corresponds to the kth nearest neighbor, which is of order k^{-2} in the MSE calculation, while the leading MSE term is of order $k^{-1} + (k/n)^{2/q}$, which is smaller than k^{-2}. Thus, the kth nearest neighbor has an asymptotically negligible contribution to the MSE calculation.

Hence, whether we assume $w(v) = 0$ for $||v|| \geq 1$ or for $||v|| > 1$ will not affect the asymptotic analysis of the k-nn estimator.

Let $\hat{G}_k$ denote the $n \times 1$ vector with its ith element being $\hat{g}(X_i)$. Then we know that $\hat{G}_k = M_n(k)Y$, where M_n is an $n \times n$ matrix with its (i, j)th element given by $w_{ij} / \sum_{l=1}^n w_{il}$, where $w_{ij} = w((X_i - X_j)/R_i)$ and R_i depends on k.

The following three well-known procedures for selecting k were studied by Li (1987).

(i) Mallows's C_L (or C_p) (Mallows (1973)): Select $\hat{k}$ that minimizes the following objective function:

$$\hat{k}_C = \arg\min_k n^{-1} \sum_{i=1}^n [Y_i - \hat{g}(X_i)]^2 + 2\sigma^2 \operatorname{tr}[M_n(k)]/n, \quad (14.13)$$

where σ^2 is the variance of u_i. In practice one can estimate σ^2 by $\hat{\sigma}^2 = n^{-1} \sum_{i=1}^n \hat{u}_i^2$, where $\hat{u}_i = Y_i - \hat{g}(X_i)$.

(ii) Generalized cross-validation (Craven and Wahba (1979)): Select $\hat{k}$ by minimizing

$$\hat{k}_{GCV} = \arg\min_k \frac{n^{-1} \sum_{i=1}^n [Y_i - \hat{g}(X_i)]^2}{(1 - n^{-1} \operatorname{tr}[M_n(k)])^2}. \quad (14.14)$$

(iii) Leave-one-out cross-validation (Stone (1974)): Select $\hat{k}$ to minimize

$$CV_k = \sum_{i=1}^n [Y_i - \hat{g}_{-i}(X_i)]^2 \quad (14.15)$$

where $\hat{g}_{-i}(X_i) = \sum_{j \neq i} Y_j w_{ij} / \sum_{j \neq i} w_{ij}$ ($w_{ij} = w((X_i - X_j)/R_i)$) is the leave-one-out k-nn estimator of $g(X_i)$.

GCV and C_L methods are computationally simpler than the leave-one-out CV method.

Li (1987) showed that the above three procedures are asymptotically equivalent and all of them lead to optimal smoothing in the sense that

$$\frac{\int [\hat{g}_{\hat{k}}(x) - g(x)]^2 dF(x)}{\inf_k \int [\hat{g}_k(x) - g(x)]^2 dF(x)} \xrightarrow{p} 1, \quad (14.16)$$

where $\hat{g}_k(x) = \hat{g}(x)$ as defined in (14.7) with a generic k, and where $\hat{g}_{\hat{k}}(x)$ is the k-nn estimator of $g(x)$ using one of the above procedures to select k, i.e., in (14.16), $\hat{k} = \hat{k}_C$, or $\hat{k} = \hat{k}_{GCV}$, or $\hat{k} = \hat{k}_{CV}$.

Equation (14.16) states that each of the above three procedures leads to optimally selected k in the sense that the resulting asymptotic weighted integrated square error equals the smallest possible weighted integrated square error.

To establish the asymptotic normality of $\hat{g}(x)$ with data-driven $\hat{k}$, one needs to obtain a nonstochastic k, say k_0, such that $\hat{k}/k_0 \overset{p}{\to} 1$. We turn to this derivation below for the leave-one-out cross-validation method.

Assumption 14.5. (X_i, Y_i) *are i.i.d.,* $u_i = Y_i - g(X_i)$, $\mathrm{E}(u_i^4)$ *is finite,* $g(x)$ *and* $f(x)$ *are both continuous and differentiable up to the third order, and* $\sigma^2(x) = \mathrm{E}(u_i^2 | X_i = x)$ *is continuous in* x. *Letting* $\mathcal{S}$ *denote the support of* $M(\cdot)$, *then* $\inf_{x \in \mathcal{S}} f(x) \geq \delta$ *for some* $\delta > 0$.

Assumption 14.6. $w(\cdot)$ *is a bounded symmetric nonnegative function,* $w(v) = 0$ *for* $||v|| \geq 1$, $\int w(v)dv = \int_{||v|| \leq 1} w(v)dv = 1$, $\int w(v)vv'dv = \kappa_2 I_q$, $\int w^2(v)dv = \kappa$ *and* $\int w^2(v)vv'du = \kappa_{22} I_q$, *where* I_q *is an identity matrix of dimension* q. κ_2, κ *and* κ_{22} *are all finite positive constants.*

Assumption 14.7. $k \in \Lambda = [n^\epsilon, n^{1-\epsilon}]$ *for some arbitrarily small* $\epsilon \in (0, 1/2)$.

The condition that $w(v) = 0$ for $||v|| \geq 1$ can be relaxed to $w(v) = 0$ for $||v|| > 1$ without changing these results, but it requires lengthier proofs. Assumption 14.7 implies that $k/n \to 0$ and $k \to \infty$ as $n \to \infty$, which ensures that the bias and variance of the k-nn estimator converge to zero as the sample size increases.

Denote the $q \times 1$ first derivative vector and the $q \times q$ second derivative matrix of $g(x)$ by $g^{(1)}(x)$ and $g^{(2)}(x)$, respectively. Also, let $g_s(x)$ ($f_s(x)$) denote the partial derivative of $g(\cdot)$ ($f(\cdot)$) with respect to x_s, the sth component of x ($s = 1, \ldots, q$).

Ouyang, Li and Li (forthcoming) showed that, uniformly in $k \in \Lambda$, the leading term of $CV_k(k)$ defined in (14.15) is of the form $\Phi_1(k/n)^{4/q} + \Phi_2 k^{-1}$, where

$$\Phi_1 = c_0^{-4/q} \kappa_2^2 \int \left(\left[\frac{1}{2} f(x) \operatorname{tr} \left[{}^{(2)} g(x) \right] + \sum_{s=1}^{q} f_s(x) g_s(x) \right] \right)^2 \tag{14.17}$$
$$\times [f(x)]^{-(q+4)/q} M(x) dx$$

and

$$\Phi_2 = c_0 \kappa \int \sigma^2(x) M(x) f(x) dx. \tag{14.18}$$

Thus, we have

$$CV_{kC}(k) = \Phi_1(k/n)^{4/q} + \Phi_2 k^{-1} + o\left((k/n)^{4/q} + k^{-1}\right) \qquad (14.19)$$

uniformly in $k \in \Lambda$. Let k_0 denote the value of k that minimizes $\Phi_1(k/n)^{4/q} + \Phi_2 k^{-1}$, the leading term of $CV_k(k)$. Then it is easy to show that $k_0 = a_0 n^{4/(4+q)}$, where $a_0 = [q\Phi_2/(4\Phi_1)]^{q/(4+q)}$. Recalling that $\hat{k}$ is the cross-validated k, then from (14.19) we immediately have the following result.

Theorem 14.6. *Under Assumptions 14.5 to 14.7, we have*

$$\hat{k} = k_0 + o_p(k_0) \text{ or, equivalently, } \hat{k}/k_0 \xrightarrow{p} 1.$$

The proof of Theorem 14.6 is given in Ouyang et al. (forthcoming).
Let $\hat{g}_{\hat{k}}(x)$ denote $\hat{g}(x)$ with $k = \hat{k}$. The next theorem gives the asymptotic distribution of $\hat{g}_{\hat{k}}(x)$.

Theorem 14.7. *Under the same condition as in Theorem 14.6, for $x \in \mathbb{R}^q$ with $f(x) > 0$, we have*

$$\hat{k}^{1/2}(\hat{g}_{\hat{k}}(x) - g(x) - (\hat{k}/n)^{2/q}\mu_L(x)) \to N(0, c_0 \kappa \sigma^2(x)) \text{ in distribution,}$$

where

$$\mu_L(x) = (1/2)\kappa_2 \left\{ \sum_{s=1}^{q} f_s(x) g_s(x) + f(x) \operatorname{tr}[^{(2)}g(x)] \right\} / [c_0^{q/2} f(x)^{(q+2)/2}].$$

The proof of Theorem 14.7 follows from Theorem 14.4, Theorem 14.6, and a stochastic equicontinuity argument; see Ichimura (2000) for a detailed proof.

14.5 Cross-Validation with Local Linear k-nn Estimation

The nonparametric regression model is the same as that considered earlier, i.e.,

$$Y_i = g(X_i) + u_i, \quad i = 1, \ldots, n.$$

Recall that $\delta(X_i) = (g(X_i), g^{(1)}(X_i)')'$. The leave-one-out k-nn estimator for $\delta(X_i)$ is given by

$$\hat{\delta}_{-i}(X_i) = \left[\sum_{j \neq i}^{n} w_{R_i,ij} \begin{pmatrix} 1, & (X_j - X_i)' \\ X_j - X_i, & (X_j - X_i)(X_j - X_i)' \end{pmatrix} \right]^{-1}$$

$$\times \sum_{j \neq i}^{n} w_{R_i,ij} \begin{pmatrix} 1 \\ X_j - X_i \end{pmatrix} Y_j, \qquad (14.20)$$

where $w_{R_i,ij} = R_i^{-q} w((X_j - X_i)/R_i)$.

The leave-one-out k-nn estimator of $g(X_i)$ is given by $\hat{g}_{-i,L}(X_i) = e_1' \hat{\delta}_{-i}(X_i)$, where e_1 is a $q \times 1$ vector whose first element is one with all remaining elements being zero. We choose k to minimize the cross-validation objective function

$$CV_L(k) = n^{-1} \sum_{i=1}^{n} (Y_i - \hat{g}_{-i,L}(X_i))^2 M(X_i), \qquad (14.21)$$

where $\hat{g}_{-i,L}(X_i) = e_1' \hat{\delta}_{-i}(X_i)$ and $M(\cdot)$ is a weight function.

Ouyang et al. (forthcoming) showed that, uniformly in $k \in \Lambda$,

$$CV_{kL}(k) = \Phi_{1,L} \left(\frac{k}{n} \right)^{4/q} + \Phi_2 k^{-1} + o_p \left(\left(\frac{k}{n} \right)^{4/q} + k^{-1} \right),$$

where Φ_2 is the same as defined in (14.18) and

$$\Phi_{1,L} = c_0^{-4/q} \kappa_2^2 \int \left(\frac{1}{2} f(x) \operatorname{tr} \left[g^{(2)}(x) \right] \right)^2 [f(x)]^{-(q+4)/q} M(x) \, dx. \qquad (14.22)$$

We observe that, similar to the pointwise results, the local linear cross-validation objective function has a simple form for the leading bias term.

Letting $k_{0,L}$ denote the value of k that minimizes $\Phi_{1,L} \left(\frac{k}{n} \right)^{4/q} + \Phi_2 k^{-1}$, the leading term of $C_L(k)$, then it is easy to show that $k_{0,L} = a_L n^{4/(4+q)}$, where $a_L = [q\Phi_2/(4\Phi_{1,L})]^{q/(4+q)}$ is a positive constant. The next theorem shows that the cross-validated k is asymptotically equivalent to $k_{0,L}$.

Theorem 14.8. *Under Assumptions 14.5 through 14.7, and letting $\hat{k}_L$ denote the local linear cross-validated value of k, then*

$$\hat{k}_L = k_{0,L} + o(k_{0,L}) \quad \text{or, equivalently,} \quad \hat{k}_L / k_{0,L} \xrightarrow{p} 1.$$

Let $\hat{\delta}_{\hat{k}}(x)$ be defined as in $\hat{\delta}(x)$ except that $k = \hat{k}_L$; then the asymptotic distribution of $\hat{\delta}_{\hat{k}}(x)$ is given in the following theorem.

Theorem 14.9. *Under the same conditions as given in Theorem 14.8,*

$$\hat{D}(n)\left(\hat{\delta}_{\hat{k}}(x) - \delta(x) - \left(\begin{array}{c} (\hat{k}/n)^{2/d}\mu_L(x) \\ 0 \end{array}\right)\right) \rightarrow N(0, \Sigma_x) \ in \ distribution,$$

where

$$\hat{D}(n) = \left(\begin{array}{cc} \hat{k}_L^{1/2}, & 0 \\ 0, & \hat{d}_n I_q \end{array}\right),$$

$$\hat{d}_n = \hat{k}_L^{1/2}(\hat{k}_L/n)^{1/q},$$

$$\mu_L(x) = (1/2)\kappa_2 \, \mathrm{tr}\{g^{(2)}(x)\}/(c_0 f(x))^{q/2}, \ and$$

$$\Sigma_x = \left(\begin{array}{cc} c_0\kappa\sigma^2(x), & 0 \\ 0, & c_0\kappa_{22}\sigma^2(x)I_q/\kappa_2^2 \end{array}\right).$$

The proof of Theorem 14.9 follows from Theorem 14.8 and arguments similar to those found in the proof of Theorem 14.7 and is thus omitted here.

The asymptotic distribution of $\hat{g}_{L,\hat{k}}(x)$, the first element of $\hat{\delta}_{\hat{k}}(x)$, is given as a corollary to Theorem 14.9.

Corollary 14.2. *Under the same conditions as in Theorem 14.9, we have*

$$\hat{k}_L^{1/2}\left(\hat{g}_{L,\hat{k}}(x) - g(x) - (\hat{k}_L/n)^{2/q}\mu_L(x)\right) \xrightarrow{d} N\left(0, c_0\kappa\sigma^2(x)\right).$$

14.6   Estimation of Semiparametric Models with *k*-nn Methods

Each of the semiparametric models that we discussed earlier using kernel methods can be estimated using *k*-nn methods. For example, using the *k*-nn estimation method, Newey (1994*a*) considers estimation of average derivatives, Liu and Lu (1997) study the estimation of a partially linear model, and Yatchew, Sun and Deri (2003) estimate a single (multiple) index model. In this section we discuss the estimation of one popular semiparametric model, the partially linear model considered in Chapter 7.

The partially linear model is given by

$$Y_i = X_i'\beta + \theta(Z_i) + u_i, \tag{14.23}$$

where $Z_i \in \mathbb{R}^q$ is a vector of continuous random variable.

As was the case for the derivation of the kernel-based estimator of β, we can estimate β by k-nn-based methods using

$$\hat{\beta} = S_{X-\hat{X}}^{-1} S_{X-\hat{X}, Y-\hat{Y}}, \tag{14.24}$$

where $S_{X-\hat{X}} = n^{-1} \sum_i (X_i - \hat{X}_i)(X_i - \hat{X}_i)'$, $S_{X-\hat{X}, Y-\hat{Y}} = n^{-1} \sum_i (X_i - \hat{X}_i)(Y_i - \hat{Y}_i) I_i$, $I_i = \mathbf{1}(\hat{f}_i > b)$, $b = b_n(> 0)$ is a trimming parameter, $\hat{X}_i = \sum_{j=1}^n X_j w_{ij} / \sum_{j=1}^n w_{ij}$, $\hat{Y}_i = \sum_{j=1}^n Y_j w_{ij} / \sum_{j=1}^n w_{ij}$, $\hat{f}_i = (nR_i^q)^{-1} \sum_{j=1}^n w_{ij}$, $w_{ij} = w((X_i - X_j)/R_i)$, and $\hat{X}_i$, $\hat{Y}_i$, and $\hat{f}_i$ are k-nn estimators of $\mathrm{E}(X_i|Z_i)$, $\mathrm{E}(Y_i|Z_i)$ and $f(X_i)$, respectively.

Condition 14.1. *w is a νth order weight function (i.e., a νth order kernel function); as $n \to \infty$, $k \to \infty$, $b \to 0$, $n^{-1}k^2b^4 \to \infty$, $n^{q-4}k^{4-2q}b^{-4q} \to 0$, $k^{4\nu}n^{q-4\nu}b^{-4q} \to 0$ and $k^4n^{-4}b^{-4q} \to 0$.*

Theorem 14.10. *Under the same conditions as given in Theorem 7.1 (kernel method) and Condition 14.1 above, we have*

$$\sqrt{n}(\hat{\beta} - \beta) \to N(0, V) \text{ in distribution,}$$

where $V = \mathrm{E}[\tilde{X}_i \tilde{X}_i']\{\mathrm{E}[\sigma^2(X_i, Z_i)\tilde{X}_i\tilde{X}_i']\}^{-1}\mathrm{E}[\tilde{X}_i\tilde{X}_i']$, $\tilde{X}_i = X_i - \mathrm{E}(X_i|Z_i)$, and $\sigma^2(X_i, Z_i) = \mathrm{E}(u_i^2|X_i, Z_i)$.

A sketch of the proof of Theorem 14.10 is given in Section 14.9.

Theorem 14.10 shows that the k-nn-based semiparametric estimator $\hat{\beta}$ has the same asymptotic distribution as the kernel-based estimator. This is, of course, what one would expect given Newey's (1994a) result.

14.7 Model Specification Tests with k-nn Methods

There is a rich literature on constructing consistent model specification tests such as those outlined in Chapter 12, though most existing tests are based on kernel, series, spline or wavelet methods. While the k-nn method is one of the most popular nonparametric estimation techniques, the only k-nn-based tests that we are aware of are Stute and

Manteiga (1996) and Li (2006). Stute and Manteiga consider a *univariate* regression model, and they use a monotone transformation to make their k-nn test equivalent to a kernel test, while Li proposes a test for general multivariate regression models.

Consider a parametric regression model of the form

$$Y_i = m(X_i, \beta) + u_i, \tag{14.25}$$

where $x \in \mathbb{R}^q$ and β is a $p \times 1$ vector of unknown parameters. We are interested in testing the null hypothesis of correct specification of (14.25), i.e., H_0^a: $\mathrm{E}(Y_i | X_i = x) = m(x, \beta)$ a.e. for some $\beta \in \mathcal{B} \subset \mathbb{R}^p$, where $\mathcal{B}$ is a compact subset of $\mathbb{R}^p$. Given $u_i = Y_i - m(X_i, \beta)$, the null hypothesis can be equivalently written as

$$H_0 : \mathrm{E}(u_i | X_i = x) = 0 \text{ a.e. for some } \beta \in \mathcal{B}.$$

The alternative hypothesis is the negation of H_0, i.e., H_1: $\mathrm{E}(u_i | X_i = x) \neq 0$ for any $\beta \in \mathcal{B}$ on a set with positive measure. We construct our test statistic based on $I = \mathrm{E}[u_i \mathrm{E}(u_i | X_i) f(X_i)]$. The sample analogue of I is $I_n = \frac{1}{n} \sum_i u_i \mathrm{E}(u_i | X_i) f(X_i)$. To obtain a feasible test statistic, we estimate u_i by $\hat{u}_i = Y_i - m(X_i, \hat{\beta})$, where $\hat{\beta}$ is any $\sqrt{n}$-consistent estimator of β under H_0, say the nonlinear least squares estimator of β based on (14.25).

First we define a shorthand notation R_i as follows:

$R_i = R_n(X_i)$

$\quad$ = the Euclidean distance of the kth nearest neighbor to X_i.

Then we estimate $\mathrm{E}(\epsilon_i | X_i)$ and $f(X_i)$ by the leave-one-out k-nn estimators

$$\hat{\mathrm{E}}_{-i}(u_i | X_i) = \frac{1}{n-1} \sum_{\substack{j \neq i}}^{n} \frac{1}{R_i^q} \hat{u}_j w\left(\frac{X_i - X_j}{R_i}\right) / \hat{f}_{-i}(X_i)$$

and

$$\hat{f}_{-i}(X_i) = \frac{1}{n-1} \sum_{\substack{j \neq i}}^{n} \frac{1}{R_i^q} w\left(\frac{X_i - X_j}{R_i}\right). \tag{14.26}$$

Replacing u_i, $\mathrm{E}(u_i | X_i)$ and $f(X_i)$ by $\hat{u}_i$, $\hat{\mathrm{E}}_{-i}(u_i | X_i)$ and $\hat{f}_{-i}(X_i)$ in I_n leads to a feasible test statistic given by

$$\hat{I}_n = \frac{1}{n(n-1)} \sum_{i=1}^{n} \sum_{\substack{j \neq i}}^{n} \frac{1}{R_i^q} \hat{u}_i \hat{u}_j w_{ij}, \tag{14.27}$$

where $w_{ij} = w((X_i - X_j)/R_i)$. Note that $w_{ij} \neq w_{ji}$ since $R_i \neq R_j$.

The condition $w(v) = 0$ if $||v|| > 1$ can be replaced by the condition $\int w(v)||v||^4 dv < \infty$ without changing the results of this section. For example, a standard normal kernel can be used in practice, although the proofs will be more tedious.

Under the same conditions as in Theorem 12.1 (using kernel methods) together with Assumptions 14.1 and 14.2, Li (2006) shows that the asymptotic null distribution of $\hat{I}_n$ is determined by the leading term $\hat{I}_{n1}$, where $\hat{I}_{n1}$ is given by

$$
\begin{aligned}
\hat{I}_{n1} &= \frac{2}{n(n-1)} \sum_{i=1}^{n} \sum_{j>i}^{n} \frac{1}{2} u_i u_j \left(\frac{w_{ij}}{R_i^q} + \frac{w_{ji}}{R_j^q} \right) \\
&\equiv \frac{2}{n(n-1)} \sum_{i=1}^{n} \sum_{j>i}^{n} H_{1n}(Z_i, Z_j),
\end{aligned}
\tag{14.28}
$$

where $H_{1n}(Z_i, Z_j) = (1/2)u_i u_j ((w_{ij}/R_i^q) + (w_{ji}/R_j^q))$ and where $Z_i = (u_i, X_i, R_i)$. $\mathrm{E}(u_i|X_i) = 0$ implies that $\mathrm{E}[H_{1n}(Z_i, Z_j)|Z_i] = 0$. Hence, $\hat{I}_{n1}$ is a second order degenerate U-statistic. The asymptotic distribution of $\hat{I}_{n1}$ can be derived using Hall's (1984) CLT for degenerate U-statistics.

Li (2006) shows that under H_0^a, $\hat{I}_{n1} = O_p\left((nk)^{-1/2}\right)$ and $\hat{I}_n - \hat{I}_{n1} = O_p(n^{-1}) = o_p\left((nk)^{-1/2}\right)$. Therefore, $\hat{I}_{n1}$ is the leading term of $\hat{I}_n$ under H_0, i.e., $\hat{I}_{n1}$ and $\hat{I}_n$ have the same asymptotic null distribution. Define

$$
\hat{\sigma}_n^2 = \frac{1}{n(n-1)} \sum_{i=1}^{n} \sum_{j>i}^{n} \hat{u}_i^2 \hat{u}_j^2 (w_{ij}/R_i^q + w_{ji}/R_j^q)^2.
\tag{14.29}
$$

Li (2006) proves the following result.

Theorem 14.11. *Under Lemmas A.15 and A.16, and under H_0, then*

$$
\begin{aligned}
\hat{T}_n &\stackrel{\text{def}}{=} n\hat{I}_n/\{\hat{\sigma}_n^2\}^{1/2} \\
&\equiv (nk)^{1/2}\hat{I}_n/\{(k/n)\hat{\sigma}_n^2\}^{1/2} \stackrel{d}{\to} N(0,1).
\end{aligned}
$$

It can be shown that $(k/n)\hat{\sigma}_n^2 = O_p(1)$ under either H_0 or H_1. When the null hypothesis is true, the leading term of $\hat{I}_n$ is a degenerate U-statistic which converges to 0 at the rate of $(nk)^{-1/2}$. It can be shown that when H_1 is true, $\hat{I}_n$ converges to a positive constant, say $C > 0$. Consequently, $\hat{T}_n$ diverges to infinity at the rate $(nk)^{1/2}$ under H_1. Thus, a test based upon $\hat{T}_n$ is a consistent test.

14.7.1   A Bootstrap Test

It can be shown that under H_0 the $\hat{T}_n$ test converges to its asymptotic standard normal distribution at the fairly slow rate $O_p\left((k/n)^{1/2}\right)$. This is the same rate as kernel-based tests if one chooses $k/n \sim h^q$, where h is the smoothing parameter in a kernel test. Various bootstrap methods have been used to better approximate the null distributions of a number of existing nonparametric tests; see Härdle and Mammen (1993), Li and Wang (1998), and the references therein.

One can also approximate the null distribution of $\hat{T}_n$ by the wild bootstrap method. Let u_i^* denote the bootstrap error (based on $\hat{u}_i$) that satisfies the following conditions:

$$(i)\,\mathrm{E}^*(u_i^*) = 0, \quad (ii)\,\mathrm{E}^*(u_i^{*2}) = \hat{u}_i^2, \quad (iii)\,\mathrm{E}^*(u_i^{*3}) = \hat{u}_i^3, \qquad (14.30)$$

where $\mathrm{E}^*(\cdot) = \mathrm{E}(\cdot|\mathcal{X}_n)$ and $\mathcal{X}_n = \{(X_i, Y_i)\}_{i=1}^n$. For example, the two-point wild bootstrap error given by $u_i^* = a\hat{u}_i$ with probability $r = (\sqrt{5}+1)/(2\sqrt{5})$ and $u_i^* = b\hat{u}_i$ with probability $1 - r$, where $a = (1 - \sqrt{5})/2$ and $b = (1 + \sqrt{5})/2$, satisfies the three conditions given in (14.30).

Next, generate $Y_i^* = m(X_i, \hat{\beta}) + u_i^*$, and then estimate β by nonlinear least squares using the bootstrap sample $\{X_i, Y_i^*\}_{i=1}^n$ based on the null model $Y_i^* = m(X_i, \beta) + \text{error}$. Let $\hat{\beta}^*$ denote the resulting estimator. The bootstrap residual is obtained via $\hat{u}_i^* = Y_i^* - m(X_i, \hat{\beta}^*)$. Define $\hat{T}_n^*$ the same way as in $\hat{T}_n$ but with $\hat{u}_i^*$ replacing $\hat{u}_i$. In practice one repeats the above process many times, say $B = 399$ times, to obtain B bootstrap statistics $\{\hat{T}_{n,j}^*\}_{j=1}^B$. One rejects H_0 if $\hat{T}_n > \hat{T}_{n,(\alpha)}^*$ at level α, where $\hat{T}_{n,(\alpha)}^*$ is the upper αth percentile of $\{\hat{T}_{n,j}^*\}_{j=1}^B$.

Simulations reported in Li (2006) show that the k-nn-based test is quite similar to kernel-based tests; see, e.g., Härdle and Mammen (1993) and Li and Wang (1998). In particular, the $\hat{T}_n$ test is generally undersized if one uses the asymptotic normal critical values, while the bootstrap test works quite well. Therefore, we recommend the use of the bootstrap method in practice.

The result for the k-nn-based test given above can be readily extended to the case of testing for correct parametric regression functional form for weakly dependent time series models (using k-nn methods). In this case, one can use a CLT for degenerate U-statistics with weakly dependent data (e.g., Fan and Li (1999a)) to show that the test has the same asymptotic null distribution for weakly dependent data. One can also extend these results to test more complex null models using k-nn methods, e.g., a nonparametric omitted variable test, a test for single index models, or a test for partially linear models versus general nonparametric models; see by way of example Fan and Li (1999a) and Delgado and Manteiga (2001).

See also the related work of Delgado and Stengos (1994), who use k-nn methods to construct a model specification test for testing a parametric null model against nonnested nonparametric alternative models, and Robinson (1987), who constructed a k-nn-based adaptive (efficient) estimation method in a linear regression model with conditionally heteroskedastic errors of unknown form.

14.8 Using Different k for Different Components of x

Up to now we have considered only the case of using a scalar k. In practice we may use a product kernel $W((X_i - x)/R_x) = \prod_{s=1}^{q} w((X_{is} - X_s)/R_{xs})$, where R_{xs} is the distance between x_s and the k_sth nearest neighbor to x_s among X_{is} for $i = 1, \ldots, n$ and $s = 1, \ldots, q$. Such an approach allows for different k_s to be used for different x_s (similar to kernel estimation using different h_s for different x_s) and is expected to lead to more accurate finite-sample estimates. In practice we can also choose k_s by Mallows's C_L method, the CV method, and the GCV method discussed in Section 14.4. As expected, using different k_s for different components of x_s yields more accurate nonparametric estimates than using a scalar k (associated with using a Euclidean distance). However, when allowing k_s to differ across covariates, the asymptotic analysis is quite complex and currently such cases fall in a theoretical void.

14.9 Proofs

We will not distinguish between n and $(n - 1)$ as they both produce identical asymptotic results. For example, we may simply write $n^{-2} \sum_{i=1}^{n} \sum_{j=1, j \neq i}^{n} \mathrm{E}(A_{ij}) = \mathrm{E}(A_{12})$ instead of $[n(n - 1)/n^2]\mathrm{E}(A_{12})$ to simplify our analysis.

Let $S_r = \{v : ||v - x|| < r\}$ (a ball centered at x with radius r), $G(r) = \mathrm{P}[X_i \in S_r]$, $S_x = \{v : ||v - x|| < R_x\}$ and $\mathrm{P}(S_x) = \mathrm{P}[X_i \in S_x]$. Obviously $G(R_x) = \mathrm{P}(S_x)$.

Lemma 14.1. *Letting* $\Phi(r) = 1/[r^\lambda G^\gamma(r)]$, *and letting* λ *and* γ *be integers such that* $\mathrm{E}[\Phi(R_i)]$ *exists, then*

$$\mathrm{E}[\Phi(R_i)|X_i] = (c_0 f(X_i))^{\lambda/q} \left(\frac{k}{n}\right)^{-\lambda/q-\gamma} + (s.o.)$$

where $c_0 = \pi^{q/2}/\Gamma((q+2)/2)$ *is the volume of a unit ball in* $\mathbb{R}^q$, *and* (*s.o.*) *denotes terms having probability order smaller than* $(k/n)^{-\lambda/q-\gamma}$.

Proof. Using Equation (12) of Mack and Rosenblatt (1979), Liu and Lu (1997, Lemma 1) showed that, for $m = (\lambda+\eta)/q$ where m is an integer and η is a nonnegative integer less than or equal to $q-1$ ($0 \le \eta \le q-1$),

$$\mathrm{E}[\Phi(R_i)|X_i] = (c_0 f(X_i))^{\lambda/q} \frac{n!}{k!} \frac{(k-m-\gamma)!}{(n-m-\gamma)!} \left(\frac{k-m-\gamma}{n-m-\gamma}\right)^{\eta/q} + (s.o.).$$

$$(14.31)$$

Note that

$$\frac{n!}{k!} \frac{(k-m-\gamma)!}{(n-m-\gamma)!} \left(\frac{k-m-\gamma}{n-m-\gamma}\right)^{\eta/q} = \left(\frac{n}{k}\right)^{m+\gamma} \left(\frac{k}{n}\right)^{\eta/q} + (s.o.)$$

$$= \left(\frac{k}{n}\right)^{\eta/q-m-\gamma} + (s.o.)$$

$$= \left(\frac{k}{n}\right)^{-\lambda/q-\gamma} + (s.o.).$$

Substituting this into (14.31) proves Lemma 14.1.   □

Note that Lemma 14.1 implies that (with $\gamma = 0$ and $\lambda = -1$) $R_i \sim (c_0 f(X_i)q)^{-1/q} (k/n)^{1/q}$. This is an expected result because R_i corresponds to the smoothing parameter h in kernel estimation and $h \sim (k/n)^{1/q}$. Lemma 14.1 also implies that $G(R_i) \sim (k/n)$.

Lemma 14.2. *Let* $A(x)$ *be a measurable function of* x. *Then*

$$\mathrm{E}\left[A(X_j)w\left(\frac{X_j - X_i}{R_i}\right)\Big|X_i, R_i\right] = \frac{k-1}{n} \frac{1}{G(R_i)}$$

$$\times \int_{\|X_j-X_i\|<R_i} f(X_j)A(X_j)w\left(\frac{X_j - X_i}{R_i}\right) dX_j. \quad (14.32)$$

Proof. This follows directly from Mack and Rosenblatt (1979, eq. 22) and the fact that $w((X_j - X_i)/R_i) = 0$ for $\|X_j - X_i\| \ge R_i$.   □

We know that

$$G(R_i) = \mathrm{P}[||X_j - X_i|| < R_i|R_i]$$

$$= \int_{||x_j - x_i|| < R_i} f(x_i|R_i)f(x_j)dx_idx_j$$

$$= \int f(x_i|R_i)\mathrm{P}[||X_j - x_i|| < R_i|x_i, R_i]dx_i$$

$$= \int f(x_i|R_i)(k/n)dx_i = k/n.$$

By Lemma 14.1 we know that we can replace $G(R_i)$ by k/n. If we replace $G(R_i)$ in (14.32) by k/n, we obtain

$$\mathrm{E}\left[A(X_j)w\left(\frac{X_j - X_i}{R_i}\right)\Big|X_i, R_i\right] = \int_{||x_j - X_i|| < R_i} f(x_j)A(x_j)$$

$$\times w\left(\frac{x_j - X_i}{R_i}\right)dx_j.$$

$$(14.33)$$

On the other hand, we know that

$$\mathrm{E}\left[A(X_j)w\left(\frac{X_j - Xx_i}{R_i}\right)\Big|X_i, R_i\right] = \int_{||x_j - X_i|| < R_i} f(x_j|R_i)A(x_j)$$

$$\times w\left(\frac{x_j - X_i}{R_i}\right)dx_j.$$

$$(14.34)$$

Comparing (14.33) with (14.34) we obtain

$$\int_{||x_j - X_i|| < R_i} f(x_j|R_i)A(x_j)w\left(\frac{x_j - X_i}{R_i}\right)dx_j$$

$$= \int_{||x_j - X_i|| < R_i} f(x_j)A(x_j)w\left(\frac{x_j - X_i}{R_i}\right)dx_j.$$

$$(14.35)$$

Equation (14.35) shows that we can effectively replace $f(x_j|R_i)$ by $f(x_j)$ in the calculations.

14.9.1   Proof of Theorem 14.1

Proof. Using (14.33) we have

$$
\mathrm{E}[\hat{f}(x)|R_x] = \mathrm{E}\left[R_x^{-q}w\left(\frac{X_1 - x}{R_x}\right)|R_x\right]
$$

$$
= R_x^{-q}\int w\left(\frac{x_1 - x}{R_x}\right)f(x_1)dx_1
$$

$$
= \int w(v)f(x + vR_x)dv
$$

$$
= f(x) + (1/2)R_x^2\int w(v)v'f^{(2)}(x)vdv + O(R_x^3).
$$

Hence, $\mathrm{E}(\hat{f}(x)) = f(x) + (1/2)\kappa_2\,\mathrm{tr}[f^{(2)}(x)]\mathrm{E}(R_x^2) + O(\mathrm{E}(R_x^3))$. We now compute $\mathrm{E}(R_x^2)$. Using Lemma 14.1 with $\lambda = -2$, $\gamma = 0$, we get

$$
\mathrm{E}(R_x^2) = (c_0 f(x))^{-2/q}(k/n)^{2/q} + (s.o.). \tag{14.36}
$$

Similarly, we can show that $\mathrm{E}(R_x^3) = O\left((k/n)^{3/q}\right)$. Thus, we have

$$
\mathrm{bias}(\hat{f}(x)) = (1/2)\kappa_2\,\mathrm{tr}[f^{(2)}(x)](cf(x))^{-2/q}(k/n)^{2/q} + O\left((k/n)^{3/q}\right).
$$

Next,

$$
\mathrm{var}(\hat{f}(x)|R_x) = (nR_x^{2q})^{-1}\left\{\mathrm{E}\left[w\left(\frac{X_1 - x}{R_x}\right)^2|R_x\right] + (s.o.)\right\}
$$

$$
= (nR_x^q)^{-1}f(x)\int w(v)^2 dv + (s.o.).
$$

Also, $\mathrm{E}(R_x^{-q}) = c_0 f(x)(n/k) + o(n/k)$ by Lemma 14.1 (with $\lambda = q$, $\gamma = 0$). Hence, $\mathrm{var}(\hat{f}(x)) = k^{-1}c_2 f(x)^2 + o(k^{-1})$ $(c_2 = c\int w(v)^2 dv)$. $\square$

14.9.2   Proof of Theorem 14.5

Proof. Similar to the proof of Theorem 2.7 (kernel case), inserting the identity matrix $I_{q+1} = \mathcal{G}_n^{-1}\mathcal{G}_n$ in the middle of (14.12), where

$$
\mathcal{G}_n = (nR_x^{q+2})^{-1}\begin{pmatrix} R_x^2, & 0 \\ 0, & I_q \end{pmatrix},
$$

we get

$$
\hat{\delta}(x) = \delta(x) + [A^{1,x}]^{-1}\{A^{2,x} + A^{3,x}\} + (s.o.),
$$

where

$$A^{1,x} = \frac{1}{nR^{q+2}} \sum_i w_{i,x} \begin{pmatrix} R_x^2, & R_x^2(X_i - x)' \\ X_i - x, & (X_i - x)(X_i - x)' \end{pmatrix}$$
$$= \begin{pmatrix} A_{11}^{1,x}, & A_{12}^{1,x} \\ A_{21}^{1,x}, & A_{22}^{1,x} \end{pmatrix}, \tag{14.37}$$

$$A^{2,x} = \frac{1}{nR_x^{q+2}} \sum_i w_{i,x} \begin{pmatrix} R_x^2 \\ X_i - x \end{pmatrix} (x_i - x)' g^{(2)}(x)(X_i - x)/2$$
$$= \begin{pmatrix} A_1^{2,x} \\ A_2^{2,x} \end{pmatrix}, \tag{14.38}$$

and

$$A^{3,x} = \frac{1}{nR_x^{q+2}} \sum_i w_{i,x} \begin{pmatrix} R_x^2 \\ X x_i - x \end{pmatrix} u_i = \begin{pmatrix} A_1^{3,x} \\ A_2^{3,x} \end{pmatrix}. \tag{14.39}$$

$\square$

Lemma 14.3. *Under the conditions of Theorem 14.5, we have*

(i) $A_{11}^{1,x} = f(x) + o_p(1)$,

(ii) $A_{21}^{1,x} = \kappa_2 f^{(1)}(x) + o_p(1)$,

(iii) $A_{12}^{1,x} = O_p\left((k/n)^{2/q}\right)$,

(iv) $A_{22}^{1,x} = \kappa_2 f(x) I_q + o_p(1)$,

(v) $A^{1,x} = M + o_p(1)$, *where* $M = \begin{pmatrix} f(x), & 0 \\ \kappa_2 f^{(1)}(x), & \kappa_2 f(x) I_q \end{pmatrix}$.

Proof of (i). $A_{11}^{1,x} = \hat{f}(x)$ *is a* k-nn *density estimator,* $\hat{f}(x) = f(x) + o_p(1)$ *is proved in Theorem 14.1.* $\square$

Proof of (ii). Using (14.33) we have

$$E[A_{21}^{1,x}] = E\left[R_x^{-(q+2)}w\left(\frac{X_1-x}{R_x}\right)(X_1-x)\right]$$

$$= E\left\{E\left[R_x^{-(q+2)}w\left(\frac{X_1-x}{R_x}\right)(X_1-x)|R_x\right]\right\}$$

$$= E\left\{R_x^{-1}\int w(v)vf(x+vR_x)dv\right\}$$

$$= E\left\{R_x^{-1}\int w(v)v\left[f(x)+v'f^{(1)}(x)R_x\right]dv\right\} + (s.o.)$$

$$= \kappa_2 f^{(1)}(x) + O\left((k/n)^{2/q}\right) \text{ since } (s.o.) = O(E(R_x^2))$$

$$= O\left((k/n)^{2/q}\right).$$

Exercise 14.1 shows that $\mathrm{var}(A_{21}^{1,x}) = O(n^{-1})$. Hence, $A_{21}^{1,x} = E(A_{21}^{1,x}) + O_p(n^{-1/2}) = \kappa_2 f^{(1)}(x) + O_p\left((k/n)^{2/q} + n^{-1/2}\right)$. □

Proof of (iii). By Lemma 14.1 we have $E[R_x^2] = O\left((k/n)^{2/q}\right)$ by (14.36). Hence, $A_{12}^{1,x} = R_x^2(A_{21}^{1,x})' = O_p\left((k/n)^{2/q}\right)O_p(1)$ because $A_{12}^{1,x} = O_p(1)$ by Lemma 14.3 (ii). □

Proof of (iv). Using (14.33) we have

$$E[A_{22}^{1,x}|R_x] = E\left[R^{-(q+2)}(X_i-x)(X_i-x)'w\left(\frac{X_i-x}{R_x}\right)|R_x\right]$$

$$= R_x^{-(q+2)}\int (x_1-x)(x_1-x)'w\left(\frac{x_1-x}{R_x}\right)f(x_1)dx_1$$

$$= \int vv'w(v)f(x)dv + O(R_x^2).$$

Therefore, $E[A_{22}^{1,x}] = E\left\{E\left[A_{22}^{1,x}|R_x\right]\right\} = \kappa_2 f(x)I_q + O\left((k/n)^{2/q}\right)$ by Lemma 14.1.

By the *same* arguments as in the proof of (ii) one can show that $E\left[||A_{22}^{1,x} - \kappa_2 f(x)I_q||^2\right] = o(1)$. Hence, $A_{22}^{1,x} = \kappa_2 f(x)I_q + o_p(1)$. □

Proof of (v). $A^{1,x} = M + o_p(1)$ follows from (i)-(iv) above. □

Lemma 14.4.

(i) $A_1^{2,x} = (k/n)^{2/q}[f(x)\mu_L(x) + o_p(1)]$.

(ii) $A_2^{2,x} = O_p((k/n)^{2/q})$.

Proof of (i).

$$E[A_1^{2,x}|R_x] = R_x^{-q} \int w\left(\frac{x_1 - x}{R_x}\right)(x_1 - x)'g^{(2)}(x_1)(x_1 - x)f(x_1)dx_1$$

$$= R_x^2 f(x) \int w(v)v'g^{(2)}(x)vdv + (s.o.)$$

$$= \kappa_2 R_x^2 f(x)\,\mathrm{tr}\left[g^{(2)}(x)\right] + (s.o.).$$

Therefore,

$$E[A_1^{2,x}] = E\left\{E\left[A_1^{2,x}|R_x\right]\right\}$$

$$= \kappa_2 f(x)\,\mathrm{tr}\left\{g^{(2)}(x)\right\}(k/n)^{2/q} + (s.o.)$$

$$= (k/n)^{2/q}[f(x)\mu_L(x) + o(1)]$$

by Lemma 14.1.

Similar to the proof of Lemma 14.3 (ii), one can show that

$$E\left\{\left[(k/n)^{-2/q}A_1^{2,x} - f(x)\mu_L(x)\right]^2\right\} = o(1).$$

Hence, $(k/n)^{-2/q}A_1^{2,x} = f(x)\mu_L(x) + o_p(1)$.   □

Proof of (ii). Defining $\mathcal{W}_{i,x} = w_{i,x}(X_i - x)(X_i - x)'g^{(2)}(x)(X_i - x)$, we have

$$E\left[||A_2^{2,x}||^2|R_x\right] = E\left[(A_2^{2,x})'(A_2^{2,x})|R_x\right]$$

$$= (2nR_x)^{-2}\sum_i\sum_j E\{[\mathcal{W}_{i,x}]'[\mathcal{W}_{i,x}]|R_x\}$$

$$= (4nR_x^2)^{-1}E\left\{\left[\mathcal{W}_{1,x}'\mathcal{W}_{1,x}|R_x\right]\right\}$$

$$\quad + \frac{n-1}{4nR_x^2}E\left\{E\left[\mathcal{W}_{1,x}'|R_x\right]E\left[\mathcal{W}_{2,x}|R_x\right]\right\}$$

$$\equiv C_{1n} + C_{2n}.$$

Using (14.33) and Lemma 14.1, it is easy show that

$$C_{1n} = O_p\left((k/n)^{2/q}k^{-1}\right) = o_p\left((k/n)^{4/q}\right)$$

and that $C_{2n} = O\left((k/n)^{4/q}\right)$ (see Exercise 14.2). Therefore, we see that $E[||A_2^{2,x}||^2] = E\{E[||A_2^{2,x}||^2|R_x]\} = C_{1n} + C_{2n} = O_p\left((k/n)^{4/q}\right)$, which implies $A_2^{2,x} = O_p\left((k/n)^{2/q}\right)$.   □

Lemma 14.5.

(i) $\operatorname{var}(k^{1/2}A_1^{3,x}) = c_0\kappa f^2(x)\sigma^2(x) + o(1).$

(ii) $\operatorname{var}(d_n A_2^{3,x}) = c_0\kappa_{22}f^2(x)\sigma^2(x)I_q + o(1).$

(iii) $\operatorname{cov}(k^{1/2}A_1^{3,x}, d_n A_2^{3,x}) = O\left((k/n)^{1/q}\right).$

Proof of (i).

$$
\begin{aligned}
\mathrm{E}[(A_1^{3,x})^2|R_x] &= R_x^{-2q}\mathrm{E}\left[w^2\left(\frac{X_1 - x}{R_x}\right)u_1^2|R_x\right] \\
&= n^{-1}R_x^{-2q}\int w^2\left(\frac{x_1 - x}{R_x}\right)\sigma^2(x_1)f(x_1)dx_1 \\
&= n^{-1}R_x^{-q}\left[\kappa\sigma^2(x)f(x) + (s.o.)\right].
\end{aligned}
$$

Hence,

$$
\operatorname{var}(A_1^{3,x}) = \mathrm{E}\left\{\mathrm{E}\left[(A_1^{3,x})^2|R_x\right]\right\} = (1/k)\kappa f^2(x)\sigma^2(x) + o(1/k)
$$

by Lemma 14.1. □

Proof of (ii).

$$
\begin{aligned}
\mathrm{E}\left[(A_2^{3,x})(A_2^{3,x})'|R_x\right] &= \frac{1}{nR_x^{2q+4}} \\
&\quad \times \mathrm{E}\left[w^2\left(\frac{X_i - x}{R_x}\right)\right. \\
&\quad \left. \times \sigma^2(X_i)(X_i - x)(X_i - x)'|R_x\right] \\
&= (nR_x^{q+2})^{-1}\left[\kappa_{22}f(x)\sigma^2(x)I_q + o(1)\right].
\end{aligned}
$$

Hence,

$$
\begin{aligned}
\operatorname{var}(d_n A_2^{3,x}) &= d_n^2\mathrm{E}\left\{\mathrm{E}\left[A_2^{3,x}(A_2^{3,x})'|R_x\right]\right\} \\
&= d_n^2 n^{-1}(k/n)^{(q+2)/q}\left[\kappa_{22}f(x)\sigma^2(x)I_q + o(1)\right] \\
&= \left[\kappa_{22}f(x)\sigma^2(x)I_q + o(1)\right]
\end{aligned}
$$

by Lemma 14.1. □

Proof of (iii).

$$\text{cov}(k^{1/2}A_1^{3,x}, d_n A_2^{3,x}|R_x) = k^{1/2}d_n\text{E}\left[A_1^{3,x}A_2^{3,x}|R_x\right]$$

$$= k^{1/2}d_n(nR_x^{2q+2})^{-1}$$

$$\times \int w^2\left(\frac{x_1 - x}{R_x}\right)$$

$$\times (x_1 - x)\sigma^2(x_1)f(x_1)dx_1$$

$$= k^{1/2}d_n(nR_x^q)^{-1}$$

$$\times \int w^2(v)vv'dv m^{(1)}(x) + (s.o.),$$

where $m(x) = \sigma^2(x)f(x)$.

Hence by Lemma 14.1 we have

$$\text{cov}(k^{1/2}A_1^{3,x}, d_n A_2^{3,x}) = Ck^{1/2}d_n n^{-1}\text{E}(R_x^{-q}) + (s.o.)$$

$$= k^{1/2}d_n n^{-1}O(n/k) + (s.o.)$$

$$= O\left((k/n)^{1/q}\right) = o(1)$$

$$(\text{since } d_n = k^{1/2}(k/n)^{1/q}).$$

Theorem 14.5 follows from Lemmas 14.3 to 14.5. $\square$

14.9.3   Proof of Theorem 14.10

Lemma 14.6. *Letting* $\text{E}_1(\cdot) = \text{E}(.|Z_1 = z_1, R_1)$, *and letting* $g(z)$ *and* $h(x,z)$ *belong to* $\mathcal{G}_\nu^\alpha$ *for some* $\alpha > 0$ *and integer* $\nu \geq 2$, *then*

(i) $\left|\text{E}_1\left\{(g(Z_2) - g(z_1))W\left(\frac{z_1 - Z_2}{R_1}\right)\right\}\right| \leq D_g(z_1)\left(\frac{R_1^{q+\nu}}{G(R_1)}\right),$

(ii) $\left|\text{E}_1\left\{h(X_2, Z_2)w^s\left(\frac{z_1 - Z_2}{R_1}\right)\right\}\right| \leq L_h(z_1)\left(\frac{R_1^q}{G(R_1)}\right) + M_h(z_1)\left(\frac{R_1^{q+1}}{G(R_1)}\right),$
   $(s = 1, 2),$

   where $Z_1 \neq z_1$ *is one of the* $(k-1)$-*nn samples that fall inside* $\{z : ||z - z_1|| < R_1\}$, *also* $|h(x, z + u) - h(x, z)| \leq H_h(x, z)|u|$ *for all* $(x, z + u)$ *and* (x, z), *while* $D_g(\cdot), L_h(\cdot), M_h(\cdot)$ *and* $H_h(.,.)$ *all have finite* α*th moments.*

Proof.

(i) Note that, conditional on (X_1, Z_1, R_1), Z_2 has density $f(z)/G(R_1)$. Hence,

$$\mathrm{E}_1 \left\{ (g(Z_2) - g(z_1)) w \left(\frac{z_1 - Z_2}{R_1} \right) \right\}$$

$$= \int [g(z_1 + R_1 v) - g(z_1)] w(v) f(z_1 + R_1 v) G(R_1)^{-1} R_1^q dv$$

$$\leq D_g(z_1) \left(\frac{R_1^{q+\nu}}{G(R_1)} \right)$$

by Lemma 5 of Robinson (1988).

(ii)

$$\mathrm{E}_1 \left\{ h(X_2, Z_2) w^s \left(\frac{z_1 - Z_2}{R_1} \right) \right\}$$

$$= \frac{R^q}{G(R_1)} \int \int h(x, z_1 - v R_1) w^s(v) f(x, z + R_1 v) dv dx$$

$$\leq C_1 \frac{R_1^q}{G(R_1)} \int \int \left[|h(x, z_1)| + |H_h(x, z_1) v R_1| \right] w^s(v) dv dx$$

$$\leq L_h(z_1) \left(\frac{R_1^q}{G(R_1)} \right) + M_h(z_1) \left(\frac{R_1^{q+1}}{G(R_1)} \right),$$

where $L_h(z) = C \int |h(x, z)| dx$ and $M_h(z) = C \int |H_h(x, z)| dx$.

$\square$

Lemma 14.7.

$$\mathrm{E}[S_{g-\hat{g}}] = O \left((k/n)^{2/q} k^{-1} b^{-2} + (k/n)^{2\nu/q} b^{-2} = o(n^{-1/2}) \right),$$

where $g(z) = \theta(z)$ *or* $\mathrm{E}(X|z)$.

Proof. See Exercise 14.3. $\square$

Lemma 14.8. $S_{g-\hat{g},\epsilon} = O_p \left((nk)^{-1/2} (k/n)^{1/q} b^{-1} + n^{-1/2} (k/n)^{\nu/q} b^{-1} \right)$, *where* $\epsilon = u$ *or* $\epsilon = v \stackrel{\text{def}}{=} X - \mathrm{E}(X|Z)$.

Proof. We prove only the case for which $g = \theta$ and $\epsilon = u$. The vector case follows by the Cauchy inequality. $\mathrm{E}\{S_{\hat{g}-g,\epsilon}^2\} = n^{-2} \sum_i \mathrm{E}[(\hat{g}_i - g_i)^2 \epsilon_i^2 I_i] = n^{-1} \mathrm{E}[(\hat{g}_1 - g_1)^2 \epsilon_1^2 I_1]$.

$E[(\hat{g}_1 - g_1)^2 \sigma^2(X_1, Z_1) I_1]$ has the same order as $E[(\hat{g}_1 - g_1)^2 I_1]$. Using Lemma 14.7 we have

$$n^{-1}E[(\hat{g}_1 - g_1)^2 I_1] = O\left((nk)^{-1}(k/n)^{2/q}b^{-2} + n^{-1}(k/n)^{2\nu/q}b^{-2}\right),$$

and Lemma 14.8 follows.   □

Lemma 14.9.

(i) $S_{u,\hat{v}} = O_p\left((nk)^{-1/2}b^{-1}\right).$

(ii) $S_{v,\hat{u}} = O_p\left((nk)^{-1/2}b^{-1}\right).$

Proof. We prove (i) only for the case where $v = v(x, z)$ is a scalar, and the vector case follows from the Cauchy inequality.

(i) $E[S_{u,\hat{v}}^2] = n^{-1}E[u_1^2 \hat{v}_1^2 I_1] = n^{-1}E[\sigma^2(X_1, Z_1)\hat{v}_1^2 I_1]$, which has the same order as $n^{-1}E[\hat{v}_1^2 I_1] = O\left((nk)^{-1}b^{-2}\right)$ by Exercise 14.4, and Lemma 14.9 follows.

(ii) The proof of (ii) is the same as (i) (by interchanging u and v); hence we provide a proof of (i) only.

                                                                          □

Lemma 14.10.

(i) $S_{\hat{\epsilon}} = O_p(k^{-1}b^{-2})$ $(\epsilon = u \ or \ v).$

(ii) $S_{\hat{u},\hat{v}} = O_p(k^{-1}b^{-2}).$

Proof of (i).

$$E\left[|S_{\hat{\epsilon}}|\right] = E\left[\hat{\epsilon}_1^2 I_1\right]$$

$$= n^{-2}E\left\{\left[R_1^{-q}\sum_{j\neq 1}\epsilon_j w_{1j}I_1/\hat{f}_1\right]^2\right\}$$

$$\leq n^{-2}b^{-2}E\left[R_1^{-2q}\sum_{j\neq 1}\epsilon_j^2 w_{1j}^2 I_1\right]$$

$$\leq C_1(k-1)n^{-2}b^{-2}E\left[R_1^{-2q}w^2\left(\frac{Z_1-\tilde{Z}_1}{R_1}\right)\right]$$

$$\leq C\,k\,n^{-2}b^{-2}E\left\{E\left[(R_1^{-q}G(R_1))^{-1}|R_1\right]\right\}$$

$$= k\,n^{-2}b^{-2}O\left((n/k)^2\right)$$

$$= O(k^{-1}b^{-2})$$

by Lemma 14.1 and Lemma 14.6 (ii).

The proof of (ii) follows from (i) and the Cauchy inequality. □

Lemma 14.11. $S_{\hat{g}-g,\hat{\epsilon}} = O_p(k^{-1}(k/n)^{1/q}b^{-2} + k^{-1/2}(k/n)^{\nu/q}b^{-2})$ $(\epsilon = u\ or\ v)$.

Proof. This lemma follows from 14.7, Lemma 14.10 (i) and the Cauchy inequality. □

Lemma 14.12. $P[\hat{f}_1 < b] = E(1 - I_1) = o(1)$.

Proof. See Exercise 14.5. □

Lemma 14.13.

(i) $S_v = n^{-1}\sum_i v_i v_i' + o_p(1)$.

(ii) $S_{v,u} = n^{-1}\sum_i v_i u_i + o_p(n^{-1/2})$.

Proof. This follows from the Cauchy inequality and Lemma 14.12. □

By exactly the same arguments we used when proving Theorem 7.1, Lemmas 14.6 through 14.13 can be shown to imply Theorem 14.10.

14.10   Exercises

Exercise 14.1. Show that $\mathrm{var}(A_{21}^{1,x}) = O(n^{-1})$.
  Hint: Apply Lemma 14.1.

Exercise 14.2. Show that $\mathrm{E}[A_2^{2,x}] = O_p\left((k/n)^{2/q}\right)$.

Exercise 14.3. Prove Lemma 14.7.
  Hint: Show that $\mathrm{E}[S_{g-\hat{g}}] = O\left((k/n)^{2/q}k^{-1}b^{-2} + (k/n)^{2\nu/q}b^{-2}\right) = o(n^{-1/2})$.

Exercise 14.4. Prove that $\mathrm{E}[\hat{v}_1^2 I_1] = O(k^{-1}b^{-2})$.

Exercise 14.5. Prove Lemma 14.12
  Hint: This is Lemma 8 of Liu and Lu (1997).

Chapter 15

Nonparametric Series Methods

The kernel methods that form the backbone of this book are but one of a variety of nonparametric techniques that have been developed to date. In this chapter we consider an alternative nonparametric approach that often goes by the moniker "series methods." Series methods are easily identified by their use of approximating functions such as splines or power series. Series methods require the user to select the number of "knots" or number of terms of power series, where the number of knots or power series terms is analogous to the size of the bandwidth for kernel methods. In particular, as the number of knots (or number of power series terms) increases, the resulting fit becomes more flexible (i.e., having less pointwise bias but greater variability), which is equivalent to letting the bandwidth associated with a kernel estimator shrink.

One advantage arising from the use of series methods relative to kernel methods is the ease with which structure (e.g., restrictions) can be imposed on the resulting estimate (see Section 15.3.1). We view series methods as complementary nonparametric approaches that are particularly well-suited to certain classes of problems, for instance, the estimation and testing of restricted nonparametric models such as additive and varying coefficient structures that we studied in Chapter 9. In this chapter we will only consider series estimators that are linear in their series base functions. For an in-depth treatment of general series (sieve) estimation, see Chen (2006).

15.1   Estimating Regression Functions

Consider a nonparametric regression model of the form

$$Y_i = g(X_i) + u_i, \quad i = 1, \ldots, n, \tag{15.1}$$

where $g(x) = \mathrm{E}(Y_i|x)$ is the (unspecified) conditional expectation function.

For ease of exposition, we first consider the case for which X_i is a scalar. Assuming i.i.d. data $\{X_i, Y_i\}_{i=1}^n$, we can estimate $g(\cdot)$ using series approximating functions which we denote by $\{p_s(x)\}_{s=1}^K$,[1] where $K = K_n$. The approximating function should have the property that, as K gets large, a linear combination of the base functions $\{p_s(x)\}_{s=1}^K$, say $\sum_{s=1}^K \beta_s p_s(x)$, can approximate any smooth function $g(x)$ arbitrarily well in the MSE sense, i.e., there exists $\beta_1, \ldots, \beta_K$ such that $\mathrm{E}\{[\sum_{s=1}^K \beta_s p_s(X_i) - g(X_i)]^2\} \to 0$ as $K \to \infty$ for all smooth functions $g(x)$. In fact, we often need to impose stronger conditions, such as $\sup_{x \in \mathcal{S}} |\sum_{s=1}^K \beta_s p_s(x) - g(x)| = O(K^{-\alpha})$ for some $\alpha > 0$, where $\mathcal{S}$ is a compact set. This usually requires that the unknown function $g(x)$ be differentiable up to a certain order. Many series functions are known to satisfy the necessary approximating properties. For example, the power series function $\{x^s\}_{s=0}^\infty$ ($p_s(x) = x^s$), trigonometric function, and spline functions are all perfectly acceptable. A spline function is a piecewise polynomial function, and the piecewise linear and piecewise cubic polynomial (spline) functions are popular choices. When using a power series, one needs to choose the value K for the highest term in the series; when using a spline function, one needs to choose the number of knots, say, a total of K knots. We show below that the consistent estimation of $g(x)$ requires that as $n \to \infty$, $K \to \infty$ and $K/n \to 0$. Here the role of K/n is similar to that played by the smoothing parameter h for kernel methods.

The simplest series base function is the power series, $\{1, x, x^2, \ldots\}$. However, estimation based on power series can be sensitive to outliers and, for this reason, the power series is not typically used for nonparametric series estimation. Instead, the piecewise local polynomial spline is the most popular choice. An rth order univariate B-spline base func-

---

[1] The base function may depend on K, and ought to be written as $\{p_{sK}(x_i)\}_{s=1}^K$; however, for what follows we suppress the K subscript for notational simplicity.

tion is given by (see Chui (1992, Chapter 4))

$$B_r(x|t_0, \ldots, t_r) = \frac{1}{a^{r-1}(r-1)!} \sum_{j=0}^{r} (-1)^j \binom{r}{j} [\max(0, x - t_j)]^{r-1},$$

(15.2)

where $t_0, \ldots, t_r$ are the evenly spaced design knots on the support of X. When $r = 2$ (15.2) delivers a piecewise linear spline, and when $r = 4$ it delivers a piecewise cubic spline (i.e., third order polynomial).

Consider the case for which X takes values in the unit interval $[0, 1]$. Suppose we decide to divide the support of X into five equally spaced ($m = 5$ is the number of subintervals in the support of X) intervals (with six knots), hence the distance between knots will be $a = 1/m = 1/5 = 0.2$. For $r = 2$ (piecewise linear splines), we can have four functions completely lying inside the unit interval. But the linear combination of these four base functions cannot generate nonzero function values for $x = 0$ and $x = 1$. To relax this restriction, we add two more knots outside each side of the support to have a total of eight knots. This results in a total of eight knots with six base functions, i.e., $K = 6 = r + m - 1$ ($r = 2$, $m = 5$). Figure 15.1 graphs the six base functions. If we choose $r = 4$ (cubic spline), since each base function will take four subintervals, we have only two base functions that completely lie inside the unit interval. We extend three additional knots on each side of the unit interval, resulting in a total of 12 knots, which allows for eight base functions, i.e., $K = 8 = r + m - 1$ ($r = 4$, $m = 5$), which is plotted in Figure 15.2. Note that as $n \to \infty$, the number of intervals m should go to infinity, and since r is fixed, the number of base functions ($K = r + m - 1$) goes to infinity.

It can be seen from Figures 15.1 and 15.2 that the base functions sum to one for all values of x.

For general multivariate regression models, $X \in \mathbb{R}^q$, one can use multivariate series functions to approximate $g(x)$. For example, one can use the product of univariate spline functions (i.e., the tensor spline) to form the multivariate base function. When $q = 2$, the power series base function becomes $\{1, x_1, x_2, x_1^2, x_1 x_2, x_2^2, \ldots\}$. For spline functions, if the domain of (x_1, x_2) is bounded, then one can transform the data so that (x_1, x_2) lies in a rectangle, say $(x_1, x_2) \in [a, b] \times [c, d]$, and then one can use the product of univariate spline functions to form the multivariate spline base function. If the domain cannot be transformed into a rectangle, one can use a general multivariate spline base function to approximate $g(x)$; see Chui (1988) and Eubank (1999) on the

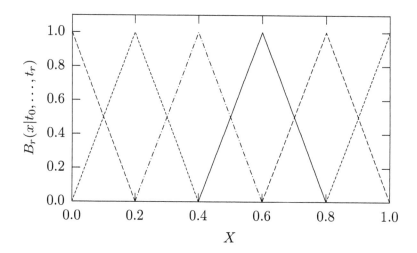

Figure 15.1: An rth order B-spline base function with k subintervals, $X \in [0, 1]$, $r = 2$, $K = 5$.

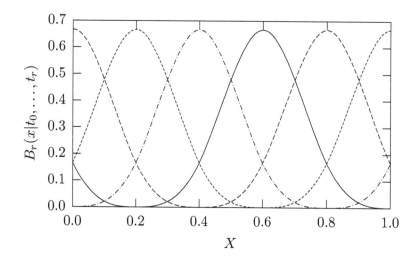

Figure 15.2: An rth order B-spline base function with k subintervals, $X \in [0, 1]$, $r = 4$, $K = 5$.

construction of general multivariate spline functions.

We now discuss how to estimate $g(x)$ using series methods. Letting $p^K(\cdot)$ denote the $K \times 1$ vector of the first K approximating functions (assuming that $x \in \mathbb{R}^q$ is a continuous variable),

$$p^K(x) = (p_1(x), \dots, p_K(x))', \qquad (15.3)$$

and letting P denote the $n \times K$ matrix whose ith row is given by $p^K(X_i)'$, i.e., $P = [p^K(X_1), \dots, p^K(X_n)]'$, we rewrite (15.1) as

$$Y_i = p^K(X_i)'\beta + \epsilon_i, \qquad (15.4)$$

where $\epsilon_i = g(X_i) - p^K(X_i)'\beta + u_i$. By the approximation property of the base function, we know that there exists a $K \times 1$ vector β such that $p^K(x)'\beta - g(x) \to 0$ for all x. We estimate β by the least squares regression of Y on P, i.e.,

$$\hat{\beta} = (P'P)^- P'Y, \qquad (15.5)$$

where $(\cdot)^-$ denotes the generalized inverse of $(\cdot)$, and Y is an $n \times 1$ vector with ith row given by Y_i. We estimate $g(x)$ by

$$\hat{g}(x) = p^K(x)'\hat{\beta}. \qquad (15.6)$$

15.1.1 Convergence Rates

Some of the early results on rates of convergence for series estimators (e.g., spline-based estimation) are given in Stone (1985, 1986), while more recent work on series estimation includes Andrews (1991a), Stone (1994), Kooperberg, Stone and Truong (1995), Newey (1995, 1997), Huang (1998a, 1998b, 2001), and de Jong (2002).

Andrews (1991a) provides general rates of convergence and asymptotic normality results for nonparametric series estimators under possibly nonidentically distributed data. In this section we deal only with i.i.d. data, and we follow Newey's (1997) approach. To establish the consistency of $\hat{g}(x)$, we adopt the following assumptions from Newey.

Assumption 15.1. $\{X_i, Y_i\}$ *is i.i.d. as* (X, Y), $\mathrm{var}(Y|x)$ *is bounded on* $\mathcal{S}$, *the compact support of* X.

Assumption 15.2. *For every* K *there is a nonsingular matrix of constants* B *such that, for* $P^K(x) = Bp^K(x)$,

  (i) *The smallest eigenvalue of* $\mathrm{E}[P^K(X_i)P^K(X_i)']$ *is bounded away from zero uniformly in* K.

(ii) *There exists a sequence of constants $\zeta_0(K)$ that satisfy the condition $\sup_{x \in S} \|P^K(x)\| \leq \zeta_0(K)$, where $K = K(n)$ such that $\zeta_0(K)^2/n \to 0$ as $n \to \infty$.*

(iii) *There exists $\alpha > 0$, such that*

$$\sup_{x \in S} |g(x) - p^K(x)'\beta_K| = O(K^{-\alpha}).$$

(iv) *As $n \to \infty$, $K \to \infty$ and $K/n \to 0$.*

The following theorem establishes the consistency of $\hat{g}(x)$.

Theorem 15.1. *Under Assumptions 15.1 and 15.2, we have*

(i) $\int [\hat{g}(x) - g(x)]^2 dF(x) = O_p(K/n + K^{-2\alpha})$.

(ii) $n^{-1} \sum_{i=1}^{n} [\hat{g}(X_i) - g(X_i)]^2 = O_p(K/n + K^{-2\alpha})$.

(iii) $\sup_{x \in S} |\hat{g}(x) - g(x)| = O_p(\zeta_0(K)(\sqrt{K}/\sqrt{n} + K^{-\alpha}))$, *where $F(\cdot)$ is the CDF of X.*

Theorem 15.1 is proved by Newey (1997); therefore, we only provide the proof for (i) in Section 15.6. In Section 15.6 we show that the $O_p(K/n)$ term corresponds to the variance term, and $K^{-2\alpha}$ corresponds to the squared bias term. For spline and power series, the variance term does not depend on q directly, whereas the bias term does since it can be shown that if $g(x)$ is m-times differentiable, then for splines and power series, $\alpha = m/q$. This differs from kernel methods but is similar to k-nn methods (since, in kernel estimation, the bias term does not depend on q, while the variance term does). Thus, in Theorem 15.1 $\alpha = m/q$. Theorem 15.1 (i) and (ii) above show that the optimal rates for power series and splines are $O_p(n^{-q/(q+2m)})$, which equals Stone's (1982) bound.

Newey (1997) gives primitive conditions for power series and regression splines (B-splines) such that Assumptions 15.1 and 15.2 hold.

Assumption 15.3.

(i) *The support of X is a Cartesian product of compact connected intervals on which X has an absolutely continuous probability PDF that is bounded above by a positive constant and bounded away from zero.*

(ii) $g(x)$ is continuously differentiable of order m on the support of X.

Assumption 15.4. *The support of X is $[-1, 1]^q$.*

When the support of X is known and Assumption 15.3 (i) is satisfied, X can always be rescaled so that Assumption 15.4 holds.

Newey (1997, p. 167) shows that for power series, Assumption 15.3 (i) implies that the smallest eigenvalue of $\mathrm{E}[P^K(X_i)P^K(X_i)']$ is bounded for all K ($P^K(x) = Bp^K(x)$; see Assumption 15.2) and that $\zeta_0(K) = O(K)$. Also, it follows from Assumption 15.3 (ii) and from Lorentz (1966) that Assumption 15.2 (iii) holds with $\alpha = m/q$. Thus Assumption 15.3 gives primitive conditions underlying Assumptions 15.1 and 15.2 for power series. Also Newey (1997) showed that Assumptions 15.3 and 15.4 imply that Assumptions 15.1 and 15.2 hold for B-splines with $\zeta_0(K) = O(\sqrt{K})$. We summarize these results in the following corollary.

Corollary 15.1.

(i) *For power series, if Assumptions 15.1 and 15.3 are satisfied and $K^3/n \to 0$ as $n \to \infty$, then Theorem 15.1 holds true with $\zeta_0(K)$ replaced by K.*

(ii) *For B-splines, if Assumptions 15.1, 15.3 and 15.4 are satisfied and $K^2/n \to 0$ as $n \to \infty$, then Theorem 15.1 holds true with $\zeta_0(K)$ replaced by $\sqrt{K}$.*

Corollary 15.1 shows that the conclusion of Theorem 15.1 holds under primitive conditions for power series and splines.

15.2 Selection of the Series Term K

The following three well-known procedures for selecting K have been studied by Li (1987) (also see Wahba (1985)).

(i) Mallows's C_L (or C_p) (Mallows (1973)): Select $\hat{K}$ to minimize

$$\hat{K}_C = \arg\min_K n^{-1} \sum_{i=1}^{n} [Y_i - \hat{g}(X_i)]^2 + 2\sigma^2(K/n), \qquad (15.7)$$

where σ^2 is the variance of u_i. In practice one can estimate σ^2 by $\hat{\sigma}^2 = n^{-1} \sum_{i=1}^{n} \hat{u}_i^2$, $\hat{u}_i = Y_i - \hat{g}(X_i)$.

(ii) Generalized cross-validation (Craven and Wahba (1979)): Select $\hat{K}$ to minimize

$$\hat{K}_{GCV} = \arg\min_K \frac{n^{-1}\sum_{i=1}^{n}[Y_i - \hat{g}(X_i)]^2}{(1 - (K/n))^2}. \qquad (15.8)$$

(iii) Leave-one-out cross-validation (Stone (1974)): Select $\hat{K}$ to minimize

$$CV_K = \sum_{i=1}^{n}[Y_i - \hat{g}_{-i}(X_i)]^2, \qquad (15.9)$$

where $\hat{g}_{-i}(X_i) = p^k(X_i)'\hat{\beta}_{-i}$, $\hat{\beta}_{-i} = [P'_{-i}P_{-i}]^{-1}P'_{-i}Y_{-i}$ obtained by removing (X_i, Y_i).

Note that GCV and C_L methods are computationally simpler than the leave-one-out CV method.

Let $\hat{G}_K$ denote an $n \times 1$ vector whose ith element is $\hat{g}(X_i)$. Then we know that $\hat{G}_K = P(P'P)^{-1}P'Y \equiv M_nY$, where $M_n = P(P'P)^{-1}P'$ is the $n \times n$ projection matrix. In fact, in the original form of the C_L and GCV objective functions, K was $\text{tr}[M_n]$. However, since M_n is a projection matrix, we have $\text{tr}[M_n] = \text{tr}[P(P'P)^{-1}P'] = \text{tr}[P'P(P'P)^{-1}] = \text{tr}(I_K) = K$.

Li (1987) showed that the foregoing three procedures are asymptotically equivalent and that all of them lead to optimal smoothing in the sense that

$$\frac{\int[\hat{g}_{\hat{K}}(x) - g(x)]^2 dF(x)}{\inf_K \int[\hat{g}_K(x) - g(x)]^2 dF(x)} \xrightarrow{p} 1, \qquad (15.10)$$

where $\hat{g}_K(x) = \hat{g}(x)$ as defined in (15.6) with a generic K, and where $\hat{g}_{\hat{K}}(x)$ is the series estimator of $g(x)$ using one of the above procedures to select K, i.e., in (15.10), $\hat{K} = \hat{K}_C$, or $\hat{K} = \hat{K}_{GCV}$, or $\hat{K} = \hat{K}_{CV}$.

Equation (15.10) states that each of the above three procedures leads to optimally selected K in the sense that the resulting asymptotic weighted integrated square error equals the smallest possible weighted integrated square error.

When K is selected optimally, the asymptotic normality result for series estimators is quite difficult to establish. This is because the leading bias term is hard to compute. We know that $\text{bias}(\hat{g}(x)) = O(K^{-\alpha})$ ($\alpha = m/q$, $g(\cdot)$ is m-times differentiable) but it is difficult to obtain an exact result for the leading bias term such as $B(x)$ in $\text{bias}(\hat{g}(x)) =$

$B(x)K^{-\alpha} + o(K^{-\alpha})$. Zhou, Shen and Wolfe (1998) obtained an asymptotic leading bias expression for univariate spline regression functions that belong to C^p (that is, for regression functions having continuous pth derivatives) under somewhat stringent conditions such as the knots being asymptotically equally spaced, and the degree of the spline m being equal to $p-1$. See Huang (2003) for a more detailed discussion on difficulties associated with obtaining the asymptotic bias for general cases using splines. Therefore, asymptotic normality results are not available for general series estimators when K is selected optimally. However, if one imposes an undersmoothing condition, one can derive the asymptotic normality of a series estimator quite easily.

15.2.1 Asymptotic Normality

Given that the leading bias expression of $\hat{g}(x)$ is not available, we shall impose undersmoothing conditions in order to derive the asymptotic distribution of $\hat{g}(x)$, i.e., we assume that $K^{-2\alpha} = o(K/n)$. Thus, the squared bias has an order smaller than the variance term so that $\sqrt{K/n}[\hat{g}(x) - g(x)]$ has an asymptotic zero mean.

Assumption 15.5.

(i) $\mathrm{E}\{[y - g(x)]^4 | x\}$ is bounded, and $\mathrm{var}(y|x)$ is bounded away from zero.

(ii) $K^{-\alpha} = o\left((K/n)^{1/2}\right)$.

Given the undersmoothing condition, and using $(P'P/n) = Q + o_p(1) \equiv I + o_p(1)$ by Lemma 15.2, it is easy to check that the asymptotic variance of $\hat{g}(x)$ is $n^{-1}V_K$, where

$$V_K = n^{-1}p^K(x)'Q^{-1}\Sigma Q^{-1}p^K(x)$$
$$= n^{-1}\Sigma$$

because $Q = \mathrm{E}[p^K(X_i)p^K(X_i)'] = I_K$, $\Sigma = \mathrm{E}[p^K(X_i)p^K(X_i)'\sigma^2(X_i)]$, and $\sigma^2(X_i) = \mathrm{E}(u_i^2|X_i)$. Note that $V_K = O(K)$; for example, if the error is conditionally homoskedastic, i.e., $\mathrm{E}[u_i^2|X_i] = \mathrm{E}(u_i^2) = \sigma^2$, then $V_K = \sigma^2 p^K(x)'p^K(x) = O(K)$. Hence, $\mathrm{var}(\hat{g}(x)) = O(K/n)$.

Theorem 15.2. *Under Assumptions 15.1, 15.2 and 15.5,*

$$\sqrt{n}\hat{V}_K^{-1/2}(\hat{g}(x) - g(x)) \xrightarrow{d} N(0, 1),$$

where

$$\hat{V}_K = p^K(x)'\hat{Q}^{-1}\hat{\Sigma}\hat{Q}^{-1}p^K(x),$$

$$\hat{Q} = n^{-1}\sum_{i=1}^{n} p^K(X_i)p^K(X_i)',$$

$$\hat{\Sigma} = n^{-1}\sum_{i=1}^{n} p^K(X_i)p^K(X_i)'\hat{u}_i^2, \ and$$

$$\hat{u}_i = Y_i - p^K(X_i)'\hat{\beta}.$$

Theorem 15.2 is a special case of Theorem 2 of Newey (1997), who also covers the case of a general linear functional of $\hat{g}$. The proof of Theorem 15.2 for the case of conditionally homoskedastic errors is left as an exercise (see Exercise 15.1).

15.3   A Partially Linear Model

Donald and Newey (1994) consider using series methods to estimate a partially linear model of the form

$$Y_i = Z_i'\gamma + g(X_i) + u_i, \tag{15.11}$$

where Z_i is of dimension r and X_i of dimension q.

The series method involves approximating the unknown function $g(x)$ by a linear combination of $p^K(x) = (p_1(x), p_2(x), \ldots, p_K(x))'$, say $p^K(x)'\beta$, for some $K \times 1$ vector β. Rewriting (15.11) as

$$Y_i = Z_i'\gamma + p^K(X_i)'\beta + \epsilon_i, \tag{15.12}$$

where $\epsilon_i = g(X_i) - p^K(X_i)'\beta + u_i$, we estimate γ and β by the least squares regression of Y_i on $(Z_i', p^K(X_i)')$, i.e.,

$$\hat{\delta} = \begin{pmatrix} \hat{\gamma} \\ \hat{\beta} \end{pmatrix} = (\mathcal{W}'\mathcal{W})^{-1}\mathcal{W}'y, \quad \mathcal{W} = (Z, P), \tag{15.13}$$

where Z is of dimension $n \times r$ and P is $n \times K$.

Using the partitioned inverse one can show that (see Exercise 15.2)

$$\hat{\gamma} = [(Z - \hat{Z})'(Z - \hat{Z})]^{-1}(Z - \hat{Z})'(Y - \hat{Y}), \tag{15.14}$$

where $\hat{Z}$ is an $n \times r$ vector whose ith row is $\hat{Z}_i = p^K(X_i)'(P'P)^{-1}P'Z$, the series estimator of $\mathrm{E}(Z_i|X_i)$, while $\hat{Y}$ is an $n \times 1$ vector whose ith element is given by $\hat{Y}_i = p^K(X_i)'(P'P)^{-1}P'Y$, i.e., the series estimator of $E(Y_i|X_i)$.

Equation (15.14) has the same form as the semiparametric kernel (or k-nn) estimator given in Chapter 7. Donald and Newey (1994) proved the following result.

Theorem 15.3. *Under Assumptions 15.1 and 15.2, and also assuming that* $(K/n + K^{-2\alpha}) = o(n^{-1/2})$, *then*

$$\sqrt{n}(\hat{\gamma} - \gamma) \rightarrow N(0, V) \text{ in distribution,}$$

where V is the same as that defined in Theorem 7.1 in Chapter 7.

The proof of Theorem 15.3 is given in Section 15.6.

Besides Assumptions 15.1 and 15.2, Theorem 15.3 requires the additional assumption that $K/n + K^{-2\alpha} = o(n^{-1/2})$, i.e., that the nonparametric series estimation MSE has an order smaller than $n^{-1/2}$. This is similar to conditions used for the semiparametric kernel method introduced in Chapter 7 where we also assume that the nonparametric estimation MSE is smaller than $n^{-1/2}$.

The nonparametric estimator for $g(x)$ is given by

$$\hat{g}(x) = p^K(x)'\hat{\beta}. \tag{15.15}$$

It can be shown that $\hat{\beta} = (P'P)^{-1}P'(Y - Z\hat{\gamma})$. By noting that $\hat{\gamma} - \gamma = O_p(n^{-1/2})$, the asymptotic distribution of $\hat{g}(x)$ is determined by $\tilde{g}(x) = p^K(x)'\tilde{\beta}$, where $\tilde{\beta} = (P'P)^{-1}P'(Y - Z\gamma)$. Obviously, $\tilde{g}(x)$ has the same asymptotic distribution as given in Theorem 15.1. Hence, we know that Theorem 15.1 holds true with $\hat{g}(x)$ defined in (15.15). That is, with $F(\cdot)$ denoting the CDF of X, then

(i) $\int [\hat{g}(x) - g(x)]^2 dF(x) = O_p(K/n + K^{-2\alpha})$.

(ii) $n^{-1} \sum_{i=1}^n [\hat{g}(X_i) - g(X_i)]^2 = O_p(K/n + K^{-2\alpha})$.

(iii) $\sup_{x \in \mathcal{S}} |\hat{g}(x) - g(x)| = O_p(\zeta_0(K)(\sqrt{K}/\sqrt{n} + K^{-\alpha}))$.

15.3.1 An Additive Partially Linear Model

We discussed the estimation of additive partially linear models via kernel methods in Chapter 9. In this section we consider instead using series methods for estimating such models. Several advantages are associated with the use of series methods when estimating additive partially linear models rather than using kernel methods that require marginal integration. The kernel approach involves first estimating a high dimension nonparametric model, and then using the method of marginal integration to obtain a lower dimensional estimator of the underlying function. This approach, however, may cause some finite-sample efficiency loss due to the fact that the additive structure is not used in the initial estimation stage. In contrast, series methods can easily impose additive structure throughout the entire estimation procedure.

Consider the following additive partially linear regression model,

$$Y_i = Z_i'\gamma + g_1(X_{1i}) + g_2(X_{2i}) + \cdots + g_L(X_{Li}) + u_i, \qquad (15.16)$$

where the prime denotes transpose, Z_i is an $r \times 1$ vector of random variables that contains a constant term, $\gamma = (\gamma_1, \ldots, \gamma_r)'$ is an $r \times 1$ vector of unknown parameters, and X_{li} is of dimension q_l ($q_l \geq 1$, $l = 1, \ldots, L$). Let X_i denote the nonoverlapping variables obtained from $(X_{1i}, \ldots, X_{Li})$. X_i is of dimension q with $L \leq q \leq \sum_{l=1}^{L} q_l$. $E(u_i|X_i, Z_i) = 0$, and $g_1(\cdot), \ldots, g_L(\cdot)$ are unknown smooth functions.

The individual functions $g_l(\cdot)$ ($l = 1, \ldots, L$) cannot be identified without imposing some identification conditions. For kernel methods, a convenient identification condition is to impose $E[g_l(X_{li})] = 0$ for all $l = 2, \ldots, L$. The identification conditions for series methods can be obtained by choosing some normalization rules that are easy to impose on series approximating base functions. For instance, in the case of an additive model without interaction terms,

$$g(x_1, \ldots, x_q) = c + g_1(x_1) + \cdots + g_q(x_q),$$

where $x_j \in \mathbb{R}$, we can use $g_j(x_j = 0) \equiv g_j(0) = 0$ as the identification condition.

Similarly, for the case of an additive model with second order interaction terms, we have

$$g(x_1, \ldots, x_q) = c + \sum_{j=1}^{q} m_j(x_j) + \sum_{j=1}^{q-1} \sum_{l>j}^{q} m_{jl}(x_j, x_l). \qquad (15.17)$$

The representation in (15.17) is not unique, but it can be made so by imposing the following identification conditions:

$m_j(x_j = 0) \equiv m_j(0) = 0$, $j = 1, \ldots, q$, and

$m_{jl}(0, x_l) = m_{jl}(x_j, 0) = 0$ for all values of x_j, x_l ($1 \leq j < l \leq q$). $\qquad (15.18)$

In principle one can always impose the identification conditions on the approximating base functions. Let $\mathcal{N}_1 = \{1, 2, \ldots\}$ denote the set of positive integers. If one uses a finite linear combination of $\{\phi_t(x_j)\}_{t\in\mathcal{N}_1}$, $j = 1, \ldots, q$, as the base function to approximate the additive function $m_j(x_j)$, the above identification condition implies that one should use a finite linear combination of $\{\phi_t(x_j)\}_{t\in\mathcal{N}_1}$ to approximate $m_j(x_j)$ with $\phi_t(x_j = 0) = \phi_t(0) = 0$ for all $t \in \mathcal{N}_1$. Then one can use a finite linear combination of $\{\phi_t(x_j)\phi_s(x_l)\}_{s>t\in\mathcal{N}_1}$ to approximate $m_{jl}(x_j, x_l)$. For example, consider the case of polynomial (power) series with $\phi_t(x_j) = x_j^t$. The approximating function for $m_j(x_j)$ is a finite linear combination of $\{x_j^t\}_{t\in\mathcal{N}_1} = \{x_j, x_j^2, x_j^3, \ldots\}$ (without the constant term) so that $\phi_t(0) = 0^t = 0$ is satisfied. And the base function for approximating $m_{jl}(x_j, x_l)$ is a finite linear combination of $\{x_j^t x_l^s\}_{t,s\in\mathcal{N}_1} = \{x_j x_l, x_j^2 x_l, x_j x_l^2, x_j^2 x_l^2, \ldots\}$. The approximating functions have the property that $\phi_t(x_j = 0)\phi_s(x_l) = \phi_t(x_j)\phi_s(x_l = 0) = 0$ as imposed by (15.18). It is straightforward to generalize the above identification conditions to additive models with higher order interaction terms.

We now discuss the identification condition for γ. For any random variable (vector) $\mathcal{A}_i$, let $\mathrm{E}_\mathcal{G}(\mathcal{A}_i)$ denote the projection of $\mathcal{A}_i$ onto the linear additive functional space $\mathcal{G}$. Then $\mathrm{E}_\mathcal{G}(\mathcal{A}_i)$ is the closest function to $\mathcal{A}_i$ (in the MSE sense) among all functions in the class of additive functions $\mathcal{G}$.

Remark 15.1. *Letting $\mathcal{V}_i = \mathcal{A}_i - \mathrm{E}_\mathcal{G}(\mathcal{A}_i)$, then $\mathrm{E}_\mathcal{G}(\mathcal{V}_i) = 0$. That is, for any random variable (vector) $\mathcal{A}_i$, we have the orthogonal decomposition of $\mathcal{A}_i = \mathrm{E}_\mathcal{G}(\mathcal{A}_i) + \mathcal{V}_i$ with $\mathrm{E}_\mathcal{G}(\mathcal{A}_i) \in \mathcal{G}$ and $\mathcal{V}_i \perp \mathcal{G}$, i.e., $\mathrm{E}_\mathcal{G}(\mathcal{V}) = 0$.*

Next we give the definition of the class of additive functions.

Definition 15.1. *We say that a function $\xi(x)$ belongs to an additive class of functions $\mathcal{G}_A$ ($\xi \in \mathcal{G}_A$) if (i) $\xi(x) = \sum_{l=1}^L \xi_l(x_l)$, $\xi_l(x_l)$ is continuous in its support $\mathcal{S}_l$, where $\mathcal{S}_l$ is a compact subset of $\mathbb{R}^{q_l}$ ($l = 1, \ldots, L$), (ii) $\sum_{l=1}^L \mathrm{E}[\xi_l(x_l)]^2 < \infty$, and (iii) $\xi_l(0) = 0$ for $l = 2, \ldots, L$.*

When $\xi(x)$ is a vector-valued function, we say $\xi \in \mathcal{G}_A$ if each component of ξ belongs to $\mathcal{G}_A$. In vector-matrix notation, we can write (15.16) as

$$\mathcal{Y} = \mathcal{Z}\gamma + g_1 + g_2 + \cdots + g_L + U \equiv \mathcal{Z}\gamma + g + U, \qquad (15.19)$$

where $\mathcal{Y}$ and U are both $n \times 1$ vectors whose ith components are given by Y_i and u_i, respectively, $\mathcal{Z}$ is $n \times r$ with its ith row given by Z_i', and g is $n \times 1$ with the ith component given by $g_i = g(X_i) \equiv \sum_{l=1}^{L} g_l(X_{li})$.

We use a linear combination of K_l functions,

$$p_l^{K_l}(x_l) = \left(p_{l1}^{K_l}(x_l), \ldots, p_{lK_l}^{K_l}(x_l)\right)',$$

to approximate $g_l(x_l)$ ($l = 1, \ldots, L$). Hence, we use a linear combination of $K = \sum_{l=1}^{L} K_l$ functions $(p_1^{K_1}(x_1)', \ldots, p_L^{K_L}(x_L)') \equiv p^K(z)'$ to approximate $g(x) = g(x_1, \ldots, x_L) = \sum_{l=1}^{L} g_l(x_l)$. The approximating function $p^K(x)$ has the following properties: (i) $p^K(x) \in \mathcal{G}_A$ and (ii) as K_l grows (for all $l = 1, \ldots, L$), a linear combination of $p^K(x)$ can approximate any $g \in \mathcal{G}_A$ arbitrarily well in the MSE sense.

We introduce some notation. Define

$$p_l = (p_l^{K_l}(x_{l1}), \ldots, p_l^{K_l}(x_{ln}))' \ (l = 1, \ldots, L), \text{ and } P = (p_1, \ldots, p_L).$$
$$(15.20)$$

Note that p_l is of dimension $n \times K_l$ and P is of dimension $n \times K$.

Let $M = P(P'P)^- P'$, where $(\cdot)^-$ denotes any symmetric generalized inverse of $(\cdot)$. For an $n \times 1$ or an $n \times r$ matrix A, define $\tilde{A} = MA$. Then premultiplying (15.19) by M leads to

$$\tilde{\mathcal{Y}} = \tilde{\mathcal{Z}}\gamma + \tilde{g} + \tilde{U}. \qquad (15.21)$$

Subtracting (15.21) from (15.19) gives

$$\mathcal{Y} - \tilde{\mathcal{Y}} = (\mathcal{Z} - \tilde{\mathcal{Z}})\gamma + g - \tilde{g} + U - \tilde{U}. \qquad (15.22)$$

We estimate γ by the least squares regression of $\mathcal{Y} - \tilde{\mathcal{Y}}$ on $\mathcal{Z} - \tilde{\mathcal{Z}}$, i.e.,

$$\hat{\gamma} = [(\mathcal{Z} - \tilde{\mathcal{Z}})'(\mathcal{Z} - \tilde{\mathcal{Z}})]^- (\mathcal{Z} - \tilde{\mathcal{Z}})'(\mathcal{Y} - \tilde{\mathcal{Y}}). \qquad (15.23)$$

Then $g(x) = \sum_{l=1}^{L} g_l(x_l)$ is estimated by $\hat{g}(x) = p^K(x)'\hat{\beta}$, where $\hat{\beta}$ is given by

$$\hat{\beta} = (P'P)^- P'(\mathcal{Y} - \mathcal{Z}\hat{\gamma}). \qquad (15.24)$$

Under the conditions given below, both $(P'P)$ and $(\mathcal{Z} - \tilde{\mathcal{Z}})'(\mathcal{Z} - \tilde{\mathcal{Z}})$ are asymptotically nonsingular. Hence, all the generalized inverses are in fact inverses when we take the limit of $\min\{K_1, \ldots, K_n\} \to \infty$ (as $n \to \infty$). Note that when both $(\mathcal{Z} - \tilde{\mathcal{Z}})'(\mathcal{Z} - \tilde{\mathcal{Z}})$ and $(P'P)$ are nonsingular, $\hat{\gamma}$ and $\hat{\beta}$ given in (15.23) and (15.24) are numerically identical to the least squares estimator obtained by regressing $\mathcal{Y}$ on $(\mathcal{Z}, P)$. In finite-sample applications, it is possible for $(\mathcal{Z} - \tilde{\mathcal{Z}})'(\mathcal{Z} - \tilde{\mathcal{Z}})$ and/or $(P'P)$ to be singular. However, one can always drop the redundant regressors to make these matrices nonsingular.

The following assumptions are needed to establish the asymptotic distribution of $\hat{\gamma}$ as well as the rate of convergence of $\hat{g}(x) = p^K(x)'\hat{\beta}$ to $g(x)$.

Assumption 15.6.

(i) $(Y_1, X_1, Z_1), \ldots, (Y_n, X_n, Z_n)$ *are i.i.d. as* (Y, X, Z), *the support of* (X, Z) *is a compact subset of* $\mathbb{R}^{r+q}$.

(ii) *Define* $\theta(x) = \mathrm{E}(Z|X = x)$. *Both* $\theta(x)$ *and* $\mathrm{var}(Y|X = x, Z = z)$ *are bounded functions on the support of* (X, Z).

Assumption 15.7.

(i) *For* $f = g$ *or* $f = \theta_s$ *(where* $s = 1, \ldots, r$, *and where* $\theta(x) = \mathrm{E}(Z_i|x) = (\theta_1(x), \ldots, \theta_r(x))')$, *there exists some* $\delta_l > 0$ *($l = 1, \ldots, L$), $\beta_f = \beta_{fK} = (\beta'_{fK_1}, \ldots, \beta'_{fK_L})'$, such that* $\sup_{z \in \mathcal{Z}} |f(x) - P^K(x)'\beta_f| = O(\sum_{l=1}^{L} K_l^{-\delta_l})$ *as* $\min\{K_1, \ldots, K_L\} \to \infty$.

(ii) $\sqrt{n}(\sum_{l=1}^{L} K_l^{-\delta_l}) \to 0$ *as* $n \to \infty$.

Assumptions 15.6 and 15.7 (i) are standard in the literature of estimating additive models. Assumption 15.7 (ii) requires that the data is undersmoothed, hence the estimation bias has an order smaller than $n^{-1/2}$.

Let $\mathrm{E}_A(Z_i)$ denote the projection of Z_i onto the additive functional space $\mathcal{G}_A$ (under the L_2-norm). That is, $\mathrm{E}_A(Z_i)$ is an element that belongs to $\mathcal{G}_A$ (it has an additive structure) and it is the closest to Z_i in the MSE sense among all the random functions in $\mathcal{G}_A$. The following theorem gives the asymptotic distribution of $\hat{\gamma}$.

Theorem 15.4. *Defining* $\epsilon_i = Z_i - \mathrm{E}_A(Z_i)$, *and assuming that* $\Phi \overset{\text{def}}{=} \mathrm{E}[\epsilon_i \epsilon'_i]$ *is positive definite, then under Assumptions 15.1, 15.2, 15.6 and 15.7, we have*

(i) $\sqrt{n}(\hat{\gamma} - \gamma) \to N(0, \Sigma)$ *in distribution, where* $\Sigma = \Phi^{-1}\Omega\Phi^{-1}$, $\Omega = \mathrm{E}[\sigma_u^2(X_i, Z_i)\epsilon_i \epsilon'_i]$ *and* $\sigma_u^2(x, z) = \mathrm{E}(u_i^2|X_i = x, Z_i = z)$.

(ii) A consistent estimator of Σ is given by $\hat{\Sigma} = \hat{\Phi}^{-1}\hat{\Omega}\hat{\Phi}^{-1}$, where $\hat{\Phi} = n^{-1}\sum_i (Z_i - \tilde{Z}_i)(Z_i - \tilde{Z}_i)'$, $\hat{\Omega} = n^{-1}\sum_i \hat{u}_i^2 (Z_i - \tilde{Z}_i)(Z_i - \tilde{Z}_i)'$, $\tilde{Z}_i'$ is the ith row of $\tilde{\mathcal{Z}} = M\mathcal{Z}$ $(M = P(P'P)^- P')$ and $\hat{u}_i = Y_i - Z_i'\hat{\gamma} - \hat{g}(X_i)$.

The proof of Theorem 15.4 is given in Li (2000).

The requirement that $\Phi = \mathrm{E}(\epsilon_i \epsilon_i')$ be positive definite is an identification condition for γ. As discussed in Chapter 9, this condition is weaker than the condition needed to identify γ when one ignores the additive structure of $\sum_{l=1}^{L} g_l(x_l)$.

Recall that $v_i = Z_i - \mathrm{E}(Z_i|X_i)$ and define $\eta_i = \mathrm{E}(X_i|X_i) - \mathrm{E}_A(Z_i)$. Then $\epsilon_i = v_i + \eta_i$. Using $\mathrm{E}(v_i|X_i) = 0$, we get

$$\Phi = \mathrm{E}[(v_i + \eta_i)(v_i + \eta_i)'] = \mathrm{E}(v_i v_i') + \mathrm{E}(\eta_i \eta_i').$$

Hence, either $\mathrm{E}(v_i v_i')$ is positive definite, or $\mathrm{E}(\eta_i \eta_i')$ being positive definite will imply that Φ is positive definite. Note that $\mathrm{E}(v_i v_i')$ being a positive definite matrix would be the required identification condition (for γ) if one ignores the additive structure of $\sum_{l=1}^{L} g_l(x_l)$ when estimating γ. Thus, by using the information that the model has an additive partially linear structure, one can weaken the identification condition for γ to Φ being a positive definite matrix.

When the error is conditionally homoskedastic, i.e., $\mathrm{E}(u_i^2|X_i, Z_i) = \mathrm{E}(u_i^2) = \sigma_u^2$, then $\hat{\gamma}$ is semiparametrically efficient in the sense that the inverse of the asymptotic variance of $\sqrt{n}(\hat{\gamma} - \gamma)$ equals the semiparametric efficiency bound.

It is interesting to observe that when $\mathrm{E}(X|z)$ is not an additive function, γ is identified even if X is a deterministic function of Z (i.e., $\mathrm{E}(Z|X) = Z$). Consider a simple case of $L = 2$, where X_{1i} and X_{2i} are scalars. Letting $Z_i = X_{1i}X_{2i}$, then Model (15.16) becomes

$$Y_i = Z_i\gamma + g_1(X_{1i}) + g_2(X_{2i}) + u_i. \qquad (15.25)$$

The parameter γ in (15.25) is identified since $Z_i = X_{1i}X_{2i}$ is not an additive separable function in X_{1i} and X_{2i}. Model (15.25) has the advantage that it involves one-dimensional nonparametric regression functions only, hence it does not suffer from the curse of dimensionality. Also it allows an interaction term (entering the model parametrically) and is therefore more general than an additive model that does not allow for interaction terms. In practice, one can replace the interaction term $Z_i = X_{1i}X_{2i}$ by any other known (nonadditive) function of (X_{1i}, X_{2i}). Clearly γ in (15.25) is not identified if one ignores the additive structure of $g(x) = g_1(x_1) + g_2(x_2)$.

The next theorem gives the convergence rates of $\hat{g}(x) = p^K(x)'\hat{\beta}$ to $g(x) = \sum_{l=1}^{L} g_l(x_l)$.

Theorem 15.5. *Under Assumptions 15.6 and 15.7, and letting $\mathcal{S}$ denote the support of z, we have*

(i) $\sup_{x \in \mathcal{S}} |\hat{g}(x) - g(x)| = O_p(\zeta_0(K))[\sqrt{K}/\sqrt{n} + \sum_{l=1}^{L} K_l^{-\delta_l}]$.

(ii) $n^{-1} \sum_{i=1}^{n} [\hat{g}(X_i) - g(X_i)]^2 = O_p(K/n + \sum_{l=1}^{L} K_l^{-2\delta_l})$.

(iii) $\int [\hat{g}(x) - g(x)]^2 dF(x) = O_p(K/n + \sum_{l=1}^{L} K_l^{-2\delta_l})$, *where $F(\cdot)$ is the CDF of Z.*

Theorem 15.5 basically says that the rate of convergence of $\hat{g}(x)$ to $g(x)$ is the same regardless of whether γ is known or one uses the estimate $\hat{\gamma}$ in constructing $\hat{g}(x)$. This is to be expected because $\hat{\gamma} - \gamma = O_p(n^{-1/2})$, which is faster than the convergence rate of nonparametric (series) estimators such as $\hat{g}(x)$.

We can also estimate $g_l(x_l)$ by $\hat{g}_l(x_l) = p_l^{K_l}(x_l)'\hat{\beta}_l$, where $\hat{\beta}_l$ is a $K_l \times 1$ vector obtained from $\hat{\beta} = (\hat{\beta}_1', \ldots, \hat{\beta}_L')'$, and $\mathcal{S}_l$ denotes its support.

When the x_l's are all scalars and each of the unknown functions ($g_l(\cdot)$'s) is c-order differentiable, then we can choose all of the K_l to have the same order, say $K_l = K/L$ for all $l = 1, \ldots, L$, and the condition on K becomes $K^3/n \to 0$ and $nK^{-2c} \to 0$ for power series (one needs $c > (3/2)$), and $K^2/n \to 0$ and $nK^{-2c} \to 0$ for splines, requiring $c > 1$.

15.3.2 Selection of Nonlinear Additive Components

Consider an additive model with dependent data given by

$$Y_t = \beta_0 + \sum_{j=1}^{d} g_j(X_{tj}) + u_t, \qquad (15.26)$$

where the functional forms of the $g_j(\cdot)$'s are unknown. We can again impose $g_j(0) = 0$ $(j = 1, \ldots, d)$ as the identification conditions. We assume that only a subset of variables $\{X_{tj}, j \in s\}$, $s \in \{1, \ldots, d\}$, with cardinality $q \leq d$ as small as possible, provide (almost) the same information on Y_t as $X_t = (X_{t1}, \ldots, X_{td})$, i.e.,

$$\mathrm{E}(Y_t | x_{tj} = x_j, j \in s) = \mathrm{E}(Y_t | X_t = x), \text{ for almost all } x. \qquad (15.27)$$

The selected variables are called "significant variables." If X_t only contains lagged values of Y_t, the selected lags are called "significant lags." Huang and Yang (2004) suggest using splines (i.e., nonparametric series methods) to estimate the unknown functions (i.e., the $g_j(\cdot)$'s). To be specific we write

$$
g_j(X_{tj}) \cong \sum_{l=1}^{L_j} \gamma_{lj} B_{lj}(X_{tj}), \tag{15.28}
$$

where $B_{lj}(\cdot)$, $l = 1, \ldots, L_j$, is the B-spline base function for a given degree and knot sequence satisfying the identification condition with $B_{lj}(0) = 0$. We estimate β_0 and the γ coefficients by the least squares method, which minimizes the criterion function

$$
\sum_{t=1}^{n} \left[Y_t - \beta_0 - \sum_{j=1}^{d} \sum_{l=1}^{L_j} \gamma_{lj} B_{lj}(X_{tj}) \right]^2 . \tag{15.29}
$$

Letting $\hat{\beta}_0$ and the $\hat{\gamma}_{lj}$'s denote the minimizers of (15.29), the spline-based estimator of $g(x_t)$ is given by

$$
\hat{g}(X_t) = \hat{\beta}_0 + \sum_{j=1}^{d} \sum_{l=1}^{L_j} \hat{\gamma}_{lj} B_{lj}(X_{tj}). \tag{15.30}
$$

Let MSE_s denote the estimation MSE using the subset of variables in the set s, i.e.,

$$
\mathrm{MSE}_s = \frac{1}{n} \sum_{t=1}^{n} \left[Y_t - \tilde{\beta}_0 - \sum_{j \in s} \sum_{l=1}^{L_j} \tilde{\gamma}_{tj} B_{lj}(X_{tj}) \right]^2 , \tag{15.31}
$$

where $\tilde{\beta}_0$ and the $\tilde{\gamma}_{lj}$'s are the least square estimators of β_0 and the γ_{lj}'s using only the subset of base functions $B_{lj}(X_{tj})$ for $j \in s$ and $l = 1, \ldots, L_j$.

Huang and Yang (2004) suggest using the BIC criterion to select the set of significant variables, i.e., choose the set of variables s that minimize

$$
BIC_s = \ln(\mathrm{MSE}_s) + \frac{N_s}{n} \ln(n), \tag{15.32}
$$

where $N_s = 1 + \sum_{j \in s} L_j$ is the number of parameters to be estimated in the series estimator (with the set of variables s).

For technical reasons, Huang and Yang (2004) restricted the above estimation problem to a compact set. Letting $\hat{s}$ denote the set of variables selected by the BIC criterion, and letting s_0 denote the true set of significant variables, Huang and Yang showed that the BIC selection criterion is consistent, i.e., that

$$\lim_{n \to \infty} P[\hat{s} = s_0] = 1. \tag{15.33}$$

That is, the probability that the BIC method selects the correct set of variables converges to one as sample size increases to infinity.

Of course, (15.33) relies on the set of significant variables s_0 being uniquely defined. Huang and Yang (2004)) proved that s_0 is indeed uniquely defined provided that the joint density of $X_t = (X_{t1}, \ldots, X_{td})$ is continuous in X_t.

Simulations reported in Huang and Yang (2004) show that the BIC criterion works well for selecting the correct set of significant variables. Huang and Yang also applied the method to select significant lags using U.S. quarterly unemployment rate data (1948:4 to 2003:1), taking a fourth difference of the data in order to eliminate nonstationarity. Letting $Y_t = r_{t+4} - r_t$, then the total sample size was $n = 217$, $\{Y_t\}_{t=1}^{217}$. They leave out the last 10 observations for producing rolling out-of-sample forecasts for periods 208 through 217. The BIC method selects two significant lags with a mean square prediction error (MSPE) of 0.023, while a linear model with five lags also selected by BIC gives an MSPE of 0.058. Thus, a nonparametric additive model with two lags produces an MSPE that is less than 50% less than that obtained from a linear model with five lags, suggesting significant nonlinearity in U.S. unemployment rate data.

Härdle et al. (2001) proposed an alternative (wavelet-based) method to test whether some of the additive components are of polynomial structure (e.g., linear) without specifying the structure of the remaining components, which also covers the problem of selecting the significant covariates.

15.3.3 Estimating an Additive Model with a Known Link Function

Horowitz and Mammen (2004) consider estimating an additive function with a known link function given by

$$Y_i = G[c_0 + g_1(Z_{1i}) + \cdots + g_q(Z_{qi})] + u_i, \quad i = 1, \ldots, n, \tag{15.34}$$

where $G(\cdot)$ is a known link function, and where the g_α's are unknown univariate functions. We discussed how to estimate (15.34) based on marginal integration methods in Chapter 9. One problem with the marginal integration method is that one has to estimate a q-dimensional function $g(z) = \mathrm{E}(Y_i|Z_i = z)$ at the initial estimation stage.

The series estimation method can easily impose additive structure by using additive base functions. However, one disadvantage of the series method is that its asymptotic distribution is usually unknown when the number of series terms is selected optimally because the exact leading bias is, in general, unknown. Horowitz and Mammen's (2004) approach is to combine the advantages of both the series and the kernel methods. They suggest using series methods at the first stage so that the additive structure can be easily imposed. Then, at the second stage, one can employ a kernel method to estimate the individual function g_α.

Assuming that the support of z is $[-1,1]^q$, Horowitz and Mammen (2004) require the identification condition that $\int_{-1}^{1} g_\alpha(z_\alpha) dz_\alpha = 0$ for all $\alpha = 1, \ldots, q$. Let $\{p_l : l = 1, \ldots\}$ denote a basis for smooth functions on $[-1,1]$. The conditions imposed on the p_l's are that $\int_{-1}^{1} p_l(v) dv = 0$, that the delta function $\int_{-1}^{1} p_l(v) p_j(v) dv = \delta_{lj}$ equals 1 if $l = j$ and 0 otherwise, and that (the base function is complete)

$$g_\alpha(z_\alpha) = \sum_{l=1}^{\infty} \theta_{\alpha l} p_l(z_\alpha) \tag{15.35}$$

for all $\alpha = 1, \ldots, q$, for $z_\alpha \in [-1,1]$ and for some suitable coefficients $\theta_{\alpha l}$. It is easy to check that $\theta_{lj} = \int_{-1}^{1} g_\alpha(z_\alpha) p_l(z_\alpha) dz_\alpha$ (see Exercise 15.5). Let $P^K(z)$ denote the additive base function defined by

$$P^K(z) = [1, p_1(z_1), \ldots, p_k(z_1), p_1(z_2), \ldots, p_k(z_2), \ldots, p_1(z_q), \ldots, p_k(z_q)]'. \tag{15.36}$$

Note that P^K is of dimension $(kq+1) \times 1$. Let $P^K(z)'\theta$ approximate $c_0 + \sum_{\alpha=1}^{q} g_\alpha(z_\alpha)$. In the first stage we estimate θ by

$$\hat{\theta} = \arg \min_{\theta \in \Theta_k} n^{-1} \sum_{i=1}^{n} \{Y_i - G[P^K(Z_i)'\theta]\}^2, \tag{15.37}$$

where $\Theta \in \mathbb{R}^{qk+1}$ is a compact parameter set. The series estimator of $c_0 + g(z)$ is $P^K(z)'\hat{\theta} = \tilde{c}_0 + \tilde{g}(z)$, where $\tilde{c}_0$ is the first element of $\hat{\theta}$.

To obtain the second stage estimate for $g_\alpha(z_\alpha)$, let $Z_{\underline{\alpha}i}$ denote Z_i with $Z_{\alpha i}$ removed and define $\tilde{g}_{\underline{\alpha}}(Z_{\underline{\alpha}i}) = \sum_{s \neq \alpha}^{q} \tilde{g}_s(Z_{si})$, where $\tilde{g}_s(Z_{si}) =$

$p^k(Z_{si})'\hat{\theta}_s$, $p^k(Z_{si}) = (p_1(Z_{si}), \ldots, p_k(Z_{si}))'$, and θ_s is the $k\times 1$ vector of coefficients corresponding to $p^k(z_s) = (p_1(z_s), \ldots, p_k(z_s))'$. Let $w_h(v) = w(v/h)$ be a univariate second order kernel function. Let $G^{(j)}(v) = \partial^j G(v)/\partial v^j$, $j = 1, 2$, and define

$$S_{nj\alpha}^{(1)}(z_\alpha, \tilde{g}) = -2 \sum_{i=1}^{n} \{Y_i - G[\tilde{c}_0 + \tilde{g}_\alpha(Z_\alpha) + \tilde{g}_{\underline{\alpha}}(Z_{\underline{\alpha}i})]\}$$
$$\times G^{(1)}[\tilde{c}_0 + \tilde{g}_\alpha(z_\alpha) + \tilde{g}_{\underline{\alpha}}(Z_{\underline{\alpha}i})](Z_{\alpha i} - z_\alpha)w_h(z_\alpha - Z_{\alpha i}) \tag{15.38}$$

for $j = 0, 1$, and also define

$$S_{nj\alpha}^{(2)}(z_\alpha, \tilde{g}) = 2 \sum_{i=1}^{n} -G[\tilde{c}_0 + \tilde{g}_\alpha(z_\alpha) + \tilde{g}_{\underline{\alpha}}(Z_{\underline{\alpha}i})](Z_{\alpha i} - z_\alpha)^j w_h(z_\alpha - Z_{\alpha i})$$
$$- 2 \sum_{i=1}^{n} \{Y_i - G[\tilde{c}_0 + \tilde{g}_\alpha(z_\alpha) + \tilde{g}_{\underline{\alpha}}(Z_{\underline{\alpha}i})]\}$$
$$\times G^{(2)}[\tilde{c}_0 + \tilde{g}_\alpha(z_\alpha) + \tilde{g}_{\underline{\alpha}}(Z_{\underline{\alpha}i})](Z_{\alpha i} - z_\alpha)^j w_h(z_\alpha - Z_{\alpha i}) \tag{15.39}$$

for $j = 0, 1, 2$. The second stage estimator for $g_\alpha(z_\alpha)$ is

$$\hat{g}_\alpha(z_\alpha) = \tilde{g}_\alpha(z_\alpha)$$
$$- \frac{S_{n2\alpha}^{(2)}(z_\alpha, \tilde{g})S_{n0\alpha}^{(1)}(z_\alpha, \tilde{g}) - S_{n1\alpha}^{(2)}(z_\alpha, \tilde{g})S_{n1\alpha}^{(1)}(z_\alpha, \tilde{g})}{S_{n0\alpha}^{(2)}(z_\alpha, \tilde{g})S_{n2\alpha}^{(2)}(z_\alpha, \tilde{g}) - S_{n1\alpha}^{(2)}(z_\alpha, \tilde{g})}. \tag{15.40}$$

The estimator given in (15.40) has a nice intuitive interpretation. If $\tilde{c}_0$ and $\tilde{g}_{\underline{\alpha}}$ were the true values of c_0 and $g_{\underline{\alpha}}$, the local linear estimator of $g_\alpha(z_\alpha)$ would be the value b_0 given below, where (b_0, b_1) minimize the following objective function

$$S_{n\alpha}(z_\alpha, b_0, b_1) = \sum_{i=1}^{n} \{Y_i - G[\tilde{c}_0 + b_0 - b_1(Z_{\alpha i} - z_\alpha)$$
$$+ \tilde{g}_{\underline{\alpha}}(Z_{\underline{\alpha}i})]\}^2 w_h(z_\alpha - Z_{\alpha i}). \tag{15.41}$$

Also note that $S_{nj\alpha}^{(1)} = \partial S_{n\alpha}/\partial b_j$ $(j = 0, 1)$ evaluated at $b_0 = \tilde{g}_\alpha(z_\alpha)$ and $b_1 = 0$. $S_{nj\alpha}^{(2)}$ gives the second derivatives of $S_{n\alpha}$ evaluated at the same point. The estimator (15.40) is the result of taking one Newton step from the starting values $b_0 = \tilde{g}_\alpha(z_\alpha)$, $b_1 = 0$ toward the minimum of the right-hand side of (15.41).

In order to obtain the asymptotic distribution of $\hat{g}_\alpha(z_\alpha)$, we first define some related quantities. Define

$$D_0(z_\alpha) = 2 \int G^{(1)}[c_0 + g_\alpha(z_\alpha) + g_{\underline{\alpha}}(z_{\underline{\alpha}})]^2 f_z(z_\alpha, z_{\underline{\alpha}}) dz_{\underline{\alpha}},$$

$$D_1(z_\alpha) = 2 \int G^{(1)}[c_0 + g_\alpha(z_\alpha) + g_{\underline{\alpha}}(z_{\underline{\alpha}})]^2 [\partial f_z(z_\alpha, z_{\underline{\alpha}})/\partial z_\alpha] dz_{-\alpha},$$

$$m(z) = G^{(2)}[c_0 + g_\alpha(z_\alpha) + g_{\underline{\alpha}}(z_{\underline{\alpha}})]g_\alpha^{(1)}(z_\alpha)$$
$$+ G^{(1)}[c_0 + g_\alpha(z_\alpha) + g_{\underline{\alpha}}(z_{\underline{\alpha}})]g_\alpha^{(2)}(z_\alpha),$$

$$\beta_\alpha(z_\alpha) = 2C_h^2 \kappa_2 D_0(z_\alpha)^{-1} \int m(z_\alpha, z_{\underline{\alpha}})$$
$$\times G^{(1)}[c_0 + g_\alpha(z_\alpha) + g_{\underline{\alpha}}(z_{\underline{\alpha}})]f_z(z_\alpha, z_{\underline{\alpha}}) dz_{\underline{\alpha}},$$

$$V_\alpha(z_\alpha) = \kappa C_h^2 D_0(z_\alpha)^{-1} \int \text{var}(u_i|z) G^{(1)}[g(z)] f_z(z) dz_{\underline{\alpha}},$$

where $\kappa_2 = \int w(v)v^2 dv$ and where $\kappa = \int w(v)^2 dv$.

Under some regularity conditions, including $h_\alpha = c_h n^{-1/5}$, $k = c_k n^{4/15+\nu}$, for some constant $0 < c_h, c_k < \infty$ and $0 < \nu < 1/30$, and G and the g_α's being twice continuously differentiable, Horowitz and Mammen (2004) prove the following result:

$$\sqrt{nh_\alpha}[\hat{g}_\alpha(z_\alpha) - g_\alpha(z_\alpha) - h_\alpha^2 \mu_\alpha(z_\alpha)] \xrightarrow{d} N(0, V_\alpha(z_\alpha)). \qquad (15.42)$$

Moreover, for $\alpha \neq s$, $\sqrt{nh_\alpha}[\hat{g}_\alpha(z_\alpha) - g_\alpha(z_\alpha)]$ and $\sqrt{nh_s}[\hat{g}_s(z_s) - g_s(z_s)]$ are asymptotically independent.

Horowitz and Lee (2005) further extend the result of Horowitz and Mammen (2004) to the case of estimating an additive quantile regression model where they suggest first using nonparametric series methods (with additive base functions) to estimate all of the additive quantile functions. Then, at the second stage, a local polynomial kernel method is used to estimate an individual quantile function. They show that the resulting estimator has the oracle property under quite mild conditions.

15.4   Estimation of Partially Linear Varying Coefficient Models

In Chapter 7 we discussed a partially linear model of the form

$$Y_i = v_i' \gamma + \delta(X_i) + u_i, \quad i = 1, \ldots, n, \qquad (15.43)$$

where $v_i'\gamma$ is the parametric component and $\delta(x_i)$ is an unknown function that constitutes the nonparametric part of the model. This model can be generalized to the semiparametric varying coefficient model

$$Y_i = v_i'\gamma(X_i) + \delta(X_i) + u_i, \quad i = 1, \ldots, n, \qquad (15.44)$$

where $\gamma(x)$ is a vector of unknown smooth functions of x. Define $X_i = (1, v_i')'$ and let $\beta(x) = (\delta(x), \gamma(x)')'$. Then (15.44) can be written more compactly as

$$Y_i = Z_i'\beta(X_i) + u_i, \quad i = 1, \ldots, n. \qquad (15.45)$$

The varying coefficient model is appropriate in a variety of settings, for example, in a cross-sectional production function framework where $v_i = (Labor_i, Capital_i)'$ represents firm's labor and capital inputs, and $x_i = R\&D_i$ is the firm's research and development expenditure. The varying coefficient model suggests that the labor and capital input coefficients may vary directly with a firm's R&D input, so the marginal productivity of labor and capital depend on the firm's level of R&D. The partially linear model (15.43), on the other hand, only allows the R&D variable to have a neutral effect on the production function, i.e., it only shifts the level of the production frontier but does not affect the marginal productivity of labor and/or capital.

However, when some of the β coefficients are in fact constants, one should model them as constants and thereby obtain more efficient estimates by incorporating this information. Consider again the production function example. If one further separates capital into liquid and fixed capital, it is reasonable to expect that the level of R&D will affect the marginal productivity of fixed but not liquid capital. This gives rise to a partially linear varying coefficient model of the form

$$Y_i = W_i'\gamma + Z_i'\beta(X_i) + u_i, \quad i = 1, \ldots, n, \qquad (15.46)$$

where W_i is a $d \times 1$ vector of random variables, γ is a $d \times 1$ vector of unknown parameters, z_i is of dimension $r \times 1$, $X_i = (X_{i1}, \ldots, X_{iq})$ is of dimension q, $\beta(\cdot) = (\beta_1(\cdot), \ldots, \beta_r(\cdot))'$ is an $r \times 1$ vector of unknown varying coefficient functions, and u_i is an error term satisfying $E(u_i|W_i, X_i, Z_i) = 0$.

We estimate (15.46) using series methods. For $l = 1, \ldots, r$, we approximate the varying coefficient function $\beta_l(z)$ by $p_l^{k_l}(x)'\alpha_l^{k_l}$, a linear combination of k_l base functions, where $p_l^{k_l}(x) = [p_{l1}(x), \ldots, p_{lk_l}(x)]'$ is a $k_l \times 1$ vector of base functions and $\alpha_l^{k_l} = (\alpha_{l1}, \ldots \alpha_{lk_l})'$ is a $k_l \times 1$ vector of unknown parameters.

Define the $K \times 1$ matrices

$$p^K(X_i, Z_i) = (Z_{i1} p_1^{k_1}(X_i)', \ldots, Z_{id} p_r^{k_r}(X_i)')'$$

and $\alpha = (\alpha_1^{k_1'}, \ldots, \alpha_r^{k_r'})'$, where $K = \sum_{l=1}^r k_l$. We use a linear combination of K functions, $p^K(Z_i, X_i)'\alpha$, to approximate $Z_i'\beta(X_i)$, hence we can rewrite (15.46) as

$$Y_i = W_i'\gamma + p^K(Z_i, X_i)'\alpha + (Z_i'\beta(X_i) - p^K(Z_i, X_i)'\alpha) + u_i$$
$$= W_i'\gamma + p_i^K(Z_i, X_i)'\alpha + \text{error}_i, \qquad (15.47)$$

where the definition of error_i should be apparent.

We now introduce some matrix notation. Let $\mathcal{Y} = (Y_1, \ldots, Y_n)'$, $u = (u_1, \ldots, u_n)'$, $\mathcal{W} = (W_1, \ldots, W_n)'$, and

$$P = (p^K(Z_1, X_1), \ldots, p^K(Z_n, X_n))'.$$

Hence, Model (15.47) can be written using vector-matrix notation as

$$\mathcal{Y} = \mathcal{W}\gamma + P\alpha + \text{error}. \qquad (15.48)$$

Letting $\hat{\gamma}$ and $\hat{\alpha}$ denote the least squares estimators of γ and α obtained by regressing $\mathcal{Y}$ on (W, P) from (15.48), we estimate $\beta_l(x)$ by $\hat{\beta}_l(x) \stackrel{\text{def}}{=} p_l^{k_l}(x)'\hat{\alpha}_l$ $(l = 1, \ldots, r)$. We will establish the $\sqrt{n}$-normality result for $\hat{\gamma}$ and derive the rate of convergence for $\hat{\beta}_l(x)$.

We present an alternative form for $\hat{\gamma}$ and $\hat{\alpha}$ that is convenient for the asymptotic analysis given below. In matrix form, (15.46) can be written as

$$\mathcal{Y} = \mathcal{W}\gamma + G + u, \qquad (15.49)$$

where $G = (X_1'\beta(Z_1), \ldots, X_n'\beta(Z_n))'$.

Define $M = P(P'P)^-P'$, where $(\cdot)^-$ denotes any symmetric generalized inverse of $(\cdot)$. For an $n \times m$ matrix A, define $\tilde{A} = MA$. Then premultiplying (15.49) by M leads to

$$\tilde{Y} = \tilde{W}\gamma + \tilde{G} + \tilde{u}. \qquad (15.50)$$

Subtracting (15.50) from (15.49) yields

$$\mathcal{Y} - \tilde{\mathcal{Y}} = (\mathcal{W} - \tilde{\mathcal{W}})\gamma + (G - \tilde{G}) + u - \tilde{u}. \qquad (15.51)$$

$\hat{\gamma}$ can also be obtained as the least squares regression of $\mathcal{Y} - \tilde{\mathcal{Y}}$ on $\mathcal{W} - \tilde{\mathcal{W}}$, i.e.,

$$\hat{\gamma} = [(\mathcal{W} - \tilde{\mathcal{W}})'(\mathcal{W} - \tilde{\mathcal{W}})]^-(\mathcal{W} - \tilde{\mathcal{W}})'(\mathcal{Y} - \tilde{\mathcal{Y}}). \qquad (15.52)$$

Also, $\hat{\alpha}$ can be obtained from (15.48) with γ being replaced by $\hat{\gamma}$,

$$\hat{\alpha} = (P'P)^- P'(\mathcal{Y} - \mathcal{W}\hat{\gamma}), \qquad (15.53)$$

from which we obtain $\hat{\beta}_l(x) = p_l^{k_l}(x)'\hat{\alpha}_l^{k_l}$, $l = 1, \ldots, r$.

Under the assumptions given below, both $(\mathcal{W} - \tilde{\mathcal{W}})'(\mathcal{W} - \tilde{\mathcal{W}})$ and $P'P$ are asymptotically nonsingular. Hence, $\hat{\gamma}$ and $\hat{\alpha}$ given in (15.52) and (15.53) are well-defined and are numerically identical to the least squares estimator obtained by regressing $\mathcal{Y}$ on $(\mathcal{W}, P)$.

Next, we give a definition and some assumptions that are used to derive the main results presented below.

Definition 15.2. *$g(x, z)$ is said to belong to the varying coefficient class of functions $\mathcal{G}$ if (i) $g(x, z) = z'h(x) \equiv \sum_{l=1}^r z_l h_l(x)$ for some continuous functions $h_l(x)$, where $h(x) = (h_1(x), \ldots, h_r(x))'$, and (ii) $\sum_{l=1}^r \mathrm{E}[z_{il}^2 h_l(x_i)^2] < \infty$, where z_l (z_{il}) is the lth component of z (z_i).*

For any function $f(x, z)$, let $\mathrm{E}_\mathcal{G}[f(x, z)]$ denote the projection of $f(x, z)$ onto the varying coefficient functional space $\mathcal{G}$ (under the L_2-norm). That is, $\mathrm{E}_\mathcal{G}[f(x, z)]$ is an element that belongs to $\mathcal{G}$ and it is the closest function to $f(x, z)$ among all functions in $\mathcal{G}$. More specifically (x_l is the lth component of x, $l = 1, \ldots, r$),

$$\mathrm{E}\left\{(f(x, z) - \mathrm{E}_\mathcal{G}[f(x, z)])(f(x, z) - \mathrm{E}_\mathcal{G}[f(x, z)])'\right\}$$
$$= \inf_{\sum_l z_l h_l(x) \in \mathcal{G}} \mathrm{E}\left\{\left(f(x, z) - \sum_{l=1}^r z_l h_l(x)\right)\left(f(x, z) - \sum_{l=1}^r z_l h_l(x)\right)'\right\}. \qquad (15.54)$$

Define $\theta(x, z) = \mathrm{E}[W|x, z]$, and let $m(x, z) = \mathrm{E}_\mathcal{G}[\theta(x, z)]$. The following assumptions will be used to establish the asymptotic distribution of $\hat{\gamma}$ and the rate of convergence of $\hat{\beta}(z)$.

Assumption 15.8.

(i) *$(Y_i, W_i, X_i, Z_i)_{i=1}^n$ are i.i.d. as (Y_1, W_1, X_1, Z_1) and the support of (W_1, X_1, Z_1) is a compact subset of $\mathbb{R}^{d+q+r}$.*

(ii) *Both $\theta(x_1, z_1)$ and $\mathrm{var}(Y_1|w_1, x_1, z_1)$ are bounded functions on the support of (w_1, x_1, z_1).*

Assumption 15.9.

(i) *For* $f(x, z) = \sum_{l=1}^{r} x_l \beta_l(z)$ *or* $f(x, z) = m_j(x, z)$ *(m_j is the jth component of m ($j = 1, \ldots, d$)), there exists some* $\delta_l > 0$ *($l = 1, \ldots, r$),* $\alpha_f = \alpha_{fK} = (\alpha_1^{k_1 \prime}, \ldots, \alpha_r^{k_r \prime})'$, *such that*

$$\sup_{(x,z)\in\mathcal{S}} \left| f(x, z) - P^K(x, z)'\alpha_f \right| = O\left(\sum_{l=1}^{r} k_l^{-\delta_l} \right).$$

(ii) $\min\{k_1, \ldots, k_r\} \to \infty$, $\sqrt{n}(\sum_{l=1}^{r} k_l^{-2\delta_l}) \to 0$ *as* $n \to \infty$.

Under the above assumptions, we can now state our main theorem.

Theorem 15.6. *Defining* $\varepsilon_i = w_i - m(X_i, Z_i)$, *where* $m(X_i, Z_i) = \mathrm{E}_{\mathcal{G}}(W_i)$, *and assuming that* $\Phi \equiv \mathrm{E}[\varepsilon_i \varepsilon_i']$ *is positive definite, then under Assumptions 15.8 and 15.9, we have*

(i) $\sqrt{n}(\hat{\gamma} - \gamma) \to N(0, \Sigma)$ *in distribution, where* $\Sigma = \Phi^{-1}\Omega\Phi^{-1}$, $\Omega = \mathrm{E}[\sigma^2(W_i, X_i, Z_i)\varepsilon_i \varepsilon_i']$ *and* $\sigma^2(W_i, X_i, Z_i) = \mathrm{E}[u_i^2 | W_i, X_i, Z_i]$.

(ii) *A consistent estimator of* Σ *is given by* $\hat{\Sigma} = \hat{\Phi}^{-1}\hat{\Omega}\hat{\Phi}^{-1}$, *where* $\hat{\Phi} = n^{-1}\sum_{i=1}^{n}(W_i - \tilde{W}_i)(W_i - \tilde{W}_i)'$, $\hat{\Omega} = n^{-1}\sum_{i=1}^{n} \hat{u}_i^2 (W_i - \tilde{W}_i)(W_i - \tilde{W}_i)'$, $\tilde{W}_i$ *is the ith row of* $\tilde{\mathcal{W}}$ *and* $\hat{u}_i = Y_i - W_i'\hat{\gamma} - p^K(X_i, Z_i)'\hat{\alpha}$.

The proof of Theorem 15.6 is given in Section 15.6.

Under the conditionally homoskedastic error assumption (i.e., that $\mathrm{E}[u_i^2 | W_i, X_i, Z_i] = \mathrm{E}(u_i^2) = \sigma^2$), the estimator $\hat{\gamma}$ is semiparametrically efficient in the sense that the inverse of the asymptotic variance of $\sqrt{n}(\hat{\gamma} - \gamma)$ equals the semiparametric efficiency bound (see Chamberlain (1992)).

The next theorem gives the convergence rate of $\hat{\beta}_l(x) = p_l^{k_l}(x)'\hat{\alpha}_l^{k_l}$ to $\beta_l(x)$ for $l = 1, \ldots, r$.

Theorem 15.7. *Under Assumptions 15.8 and 15.9, letting* $\mathcal{S}_x$ *denote the support of* x_i, *then we have, for* $l = 1, \ldots, r$,

(i) $\sup_{x \in \mathcal{S}_x} |\hat{\beta}_l(x) - \beta_l(x)| = O_p\left(\zeta_0(K)(\sqrt{K}/\sqrt{n} + \sum_{l=1}^{r} k_l^{-\delta_l}) \right).$

(ii) $\frac{1}{n}\sum_{i=1}^{n}(\hat{\beta}_l(x) - \beta_l(x))^2 = O_p(K/n + \sum_{l=1}^{r} k_l^{-2\delta_l}).$

(iii) $\int(\hat{\beta}_l(x) - \beta_l(x))^2 dF_x(x) = O_p(K/n + \sum_{l=1}^{r} k_l^{-2\delta_l})$, *where* F_x *is the CDF of* x_i.

The proof of Theorem 15.7 is similar to the proof of Theorem 15.1 and is therefore omitted here.

The asymptotic normality result for a varying coefficient model can be directly applied to obtain the asymptotic distribution of $\hat{\beta}(z)$ in a partially linear varying coefficient model. This is because $\hat{\gamma} - \gamma = O_p(n^{-1/2})$, which converges to zero faster than any nonparametric estimation convergence rate. Therefore, $\hat{\beta}(z)$ has the same asymptotic distribution whether one uses the estimator $\hat{\gamma}$ or the true γ, the latter becoming a varying coefficient model (when γ is unknown) and the results of Huang and Shen (2004) and Huang, Wu and Zhou (2004) apply. See also Chen and Conley (2001) for related work on semiparametric spatial models for panel time series.

We have shown that nonparametric series estimation methods can be used to readily impose shape restrictions such as additivity and varying coefficient structures. Nonparametric series methods can also be used to impose other types of restrictions such as monotonicity; see He and Shi (1998) on the construction of monotone B-splines for nonparametric estimation.

15.4.1   Testing for Correct Parametric Regression Functional Form

Consider the null hypothesis of testing for correctly specified parametric regression functional form, i.e., H_0^a: $E(Y|x) = m(x, \gamma)$ for almost all x. Let $\hat{\gamma}$ denote a $\sqrt{n}$-consistent estimator of γ based on the parametric null model, and let $\hat{g}(x)$ denote the nonparametric series estimator of $g(x) = E(Y|x)$, i.e., $\hat{g}(x) = p^K(x)'(P'P)^{-1}P'Y$, where $p^K(x)$, P and Y are the same as defined in Section 15.1. Define $\hat{u}_i = Y_i - m(X_i, \hat{\gamma})$ and let $\hat{\nu}_i = \hat{g}(X_i) - m(X_i, \hat{\gamma})$. Hong and White (1995) suggest testing H_0^a based on

$$\hat{I}_{se}^a = \frac{1}{n} \sum_{i=1}^{n} \hat{\nu}_i \hat{u}_i. \tag{15.55}$$

The rationale behind (15.55) is that

$$E\left[u_i(g(X_i) - m(X_i, \gamma))\right] = E\left[(g(X) - m(X, \gamma))^2\right] \geq 0$$

with equality holding if and only if H_0^a is true.

Assumption 15.10. $\{X_i', Y_i\}_{i=1}^n$ *is an i.i.d. process with* $E(Y_i^4) < \infty$. X_i *has a continuous and positive PDF* f *on* $\mathcal{S}$, *where* $\mathcal{S}$ *is the compact support of* X_i. *The error is conditionally homoskedastic.*

Hong and White (1995) prove the following result.

Theorem 15.8. *Under Assumptions 15.2 and 15.10, if H_0^a is true, then*

$$\hat{J}_{se}^a = (n\hat{I}_{se}^a/\hat{\sigma}_{se,a}^2 - K)/(2K)^{1/2} \xrightarrow{d} N(0,1), \qquad (15.56)$$

where $\hat{\sigma}_{se,a}^2 = n^{-1}\sum_{i=1}^n \hat{u}_i^2$, $\hat{u}_i = Y_i - m(x_i,\hat{\gamma})$.

Hong and White (1995) also discuss how to extend their test to handle the conditionally heteroskedastic error case.

Hong and White (1995) propose an alternative series-based test statistic for H_0^a based on the difference between sums of squared residuals from a parametric and a nonparametric regression model, i.e.,

$$\tilde{I}_{se}^a = \frac{1}{n}\sum_{i=1}^n \hat{\nu}_i \hat{u}_i^2 - \frac{1}{n}\sum_{i=1}^n \hat{\nu}_i \hat{\eta}_i^2, \qquad (15.57)$$

where $\hat{\eta}_i = Y_i - \hat{g}(x_i)$ is the residual from the nonparametric estimator. Similar to Theorem 15.8, Hong and White show that under H_0^a,

$$\tilde{J}_{se}^a = (n\tilde{I}_{se}^a/\hat{\sigma}_{se,a}^2 - K)/(2K)^{1/2} \xrightarrow{d} N(0,1). \qquad (15.58)$$

If H_0^a is false, both $\hat{I}_{se}^a$ and $\tilde{I}_{se}^a$ will converge to some positive constants in probability; hence, both $\hat{J}_{se}^a$ and $\tilde{J}_{se}^a$ will diverge to $+\infty$ at the rate $\sqrt{n}/\sqrt{K}$, i.e., they are consistent tests.

In Chapter 12 we constructed kernel tests based upon $E[u_i E(u_i|X_i)]$. One can also construct series-based tests using this measure. We estimate $r(x) \equiv E(u|x)$ by $\hat{r}(x) = p^K(x)'[P'P]^- P'\hat{u}$, and we define the leave-one-out estimator of $r(X_i)$ by

$$\hat{r}_{-i}(X_i) = p^K(X_i)'[P'P]^- \sum_{j\neq i} p^K(X_j)\hat{u}_j. \qquad (15.59)$$

One can construct a test statistic based on the sample analogue of $E[u_i E(u_i|X_i)]$ given by

$$\bar{I}_{se}^a = \frac{1}{n}\sum_{i=1}^n \hat{u}_i \hat{r}_{-i}(X_i) = \frac{1}{n}\sum_{i=1}^n \sum_{j\neq i}^n \hat{u}_i p^K(X_i)'(P'P)^- p^K(X_j)\hat{u}_j.$$

Sun and Li (forthcoming) showed that under H_0^a,

$$\bar{J}_{se}^a \stackrel{\text{def}}{=} n\bar{I}_{n,se}^a / \left[(2K)^{1/2}\hat{\sigma}_{se,a}^2\right] \xrightarrow{d} N(0,1). \qquad (15.60)$$

The proof of 15.60 is left as an exercise (see Exercise 15.6).

In practice one can compute $I_{n,se}^a$ by

$$\bar{I}_{n,se}^a = \frac{1}{n^2} \sum_{i=1}^{n} \sum_{j=1}^{n} \hat{u}_i p^K(X_i)'[P'P]^- p^K(X_j)\hat{u}_j$$

$$- \frac{1}{n^2} \sum_{i=1}^{n} \hat{u}_i^2 p^K(X_i)'[P'P]^- p^K(X_i).$$

Under H_0^a, Hong and White (1995) require that

$$\mathrm{E}\left\{ \left[\theta_0(X_i) - p^K(X_i)'\beta_K \right]^2 \right\} = o\left(K^{1/4} n^{1/2} \right),$$

while this condition is not required for the $\bar{J}_{se}^a$ statistic (under H_0^a). Also, $\bar{J}_{se}^a$ does have a nonzero center term. Therefore, it may exhibit better finite-sample properties than tests having nonzero center terms. Indeed the simulation results reported in Sun and Li (forthcoming) show that the $\bar{J}_{n,se}$ test is better behaved in finite samples than the $\hat{J}_{n,se}$ and the $\tilde{J}_{n,se}$ tests. These tests can all be generalized to handle conditionally heteroskedastic errors. For the sake of brevity, we give only the result for the $\bar{J}_{n,se}$ test.

Theorem 15.9. *Under Assumptions 15.2 and 15.10, but allowing for conditionally heteroskedastic errors, i.e., $\mathrm{E}(u_i^2|X_i) = \sigma^2(X_i)$, where $\sigma^2(x)$ is a smooth (but unspecified) function of x, then*

(i) Under H_0^a, $\hat{J}_{se}^a \stackrel{\text{def}}{=} n\bar{I}_{se}^a/\hat{S}_{n,a} \stackrel{d}{\rightarrow} N(0,1)$, where

$$\hat{S}_{n,a}^2 = 2 \sum_{i=1}^{n} \sum_{j=1}^{n} \left[p^K(X_i)'(P'P)^{-1} p^K(X_j) \right]^2 \hat{u}_i^2 \hat{u}_j^2.$$

(ii) Under H_1, $\mathrm{P}(\bar{J}_{n,se}^a > C_n) \rightarrow 1$ for any $C_n = o(nK^{1/2})$.

The proof of Theorem 15.9 is given in Section 15.6.

Note that when the error is conditionally homoskedastic, one can replace $\hat{u}_i^2$ and $\hat{u}_j^2$ in $\hat{S}_n^2$ by $\hat{\sigma}^2 = n^{-1} \sum_{i=1}^{n} \hat{u}_i^2$, and $\hat{S}_{n,se}$ then simplifies to $2\hat{\sigma}^4 K$.

Eubank and Hart (1992) proposed an alternative series-based test for correct parametric regression functional form. They nest the parametric null model (e.g., a linear model) in a more general nonparametric series regression model and then test for significance of the series coefficients in the nonparametric part of the model. Their approach has the advantage that when the null hypothesis is rejected, the estimated series coefficients provide indications as to which nonlinear terms should be added to the model.

15.4.2 A Consistent Test for an Additive Partially Linear Model

Given the relative ease of implementing nonparametric series estimators subject to restrictions, for example, subject to additivity or monotonicity constraints, we now consider constructing test statistics based upon series methods. In particular, we focus on the problem of testing model adequacy via additive partially linear models.

The test statistic considered in this section has a number of desirable properties, including (i) it avoids estimating the alternative model nonparametrically so as to partially circumvent the curse of dimensionality, (ii) it can detect local alternatives of order $O_p(n^{-1/2})$, and (iii) it is computationally simple.

We consider a consistent test for the following additive partially linear null model:

$$H_0^b : \mathrm{E}(Y_i|X_i) = z_0(X_i)'\gamma + \sum_{l=1}^{L} m_l(X_{li}) \text{ a.s.}$$

$$\text{for some } \gamma \in \mathcal{B}, \quad \sum_{l=1}^{L} m_l(\cdot) \in \mathcal{G}, \tag{15.61}$$

where $\mathcal{B}$ is a compact subset of $\mathbb{R}^r$ and $\mathcal{G}$ is the class of additive functions defined below.

The alternative hypothesis H_1^b is the negation of H_0^a, i.e.,

$$H_1^b : \mathrm{E}(Y_i|X_i) \neq z_0(X_i)'\gamma + \sum_{l=1}^{L} m_l(X_{li}) \tag{15.62}$$

on a set with positive measure for any $\gamma \in \mathcal{B}$, and any $\sum_{l=1}^{L} m_l(\cdot) \in \mathcal{G}$.

The null hypothesis H_0^b is equivalent to $\mathrm{E}(u_i|X_i) = 0$ almost surely (a.s.), where u_i is defined in (15.61). Note that $\mathrm{E}(u_i|X_i) = 0$ a.s. if and only if $\mathrm{E}[u_i M(X_i)] = 0$ for all $M(\cdot) \in \mathcal{M}$, the class of bounded $\sigma(X_i)$-measurable functions. Instead of considering the conditional moment test of (15.61), following Bierens and Ploberger (1997), Stinchcombe and White (1998), and Stute (1997), we consider the following unconditional moment test:

$$\mathrm{E}[u_i \mathcal{H}(X_i, x)] = 0 \text{ for almost all } x \in \mathcal{S} \subset \mathbb{R}^q , \qquad (15.63)$$

where $\mathcal{H}(.,.)$ is a proper choice of a weight function chosen so as to render (15.63) and (15.61) equivalent. See Assumption 15.11 (i) and (ii) below for specific conditions on $\mathcal{H}$.

We assume that the weight function $\mathcal{H}(.,.)$ is bounded on $\mathcal{S} \times \mathcal{S}$. Stinchcombe and White (1998) showed that there exists a wide class of weight functions $\mathcal{H}(.,.)$ that makes (15.63) equivalent to $\mathrm{E}(u_i | X_i) = 0$ a.s. Choices of weight functions include the exponential function $\mathcal{H}(X_i, x) = \exp(X_i' x)$, the logistic function $\mathcal{H}(X_i, x) = 1/[1 + \exp(c - X_i' x)]$ with $c \neq 0$, and $\mathcal{H}(X_i, x) = \cos(X_i' x) + \sin(X_i' x)$; see Stinchcombe and White (1998) and Bierens and Ploberger (1997) for further discussion.

Multiplying the sample analogue of $\mathrm{E}[u_i \mathcal{H}(X_i, x)]$ by $\sqrt{n}$, we have

$$J_n^0(x) = \sqrt{n} \left[\frac{1}{n} \sum_i u_i \mathcal{H}(X_i, x) \right] = \frac{1}{\sqrt{n}} \sum_i u_i \mathcal{H}(X_i, x). \qquad (15.64)$$

J_n^0 can be viewed as a random element taking values in the separable space $\mathcal{L}_2(\mathcal{S}, \nu)$ of all real, Borel measurable functions f on $\mathcal{S}$ such that $\int_{\mathcal{S}} f(x)^2 \nu(dx) < \infty$, which is endowed with the L_2-norm $\|f\|_\nu^2 = \int_{\mathcal{S}} f(x)^2 \nu(dx)$. The theory of probability on Hilbert spaces, developed in the 1960s and 1970s, greatly simplified the problem of studying the asymptotic distribution of statistics like $\|J_n^0\|_{L_2(\nu)}$ because sufficient conditions for CLTs for random elements taking values in $\mathcal{L}_2(\mathcal{S}, \nu)$ were obtained that are easy to check. For example, for a sequence $\{Z_n(\cdot)\}_n$ of i.i.d. $\mathcal{L}_2(\mathcal{S}, \nu)$-valued elements, Araujo and Giné (1980, p. 205), van der Vaart and Wellner (1996, p. 50), and Chen and White (1998) assert that $n^{-1/2} \sum_{i=1}^n Z_i(\cdot)$ converges to $\mathcal{Z}(\cdot)$ under the L_2-norm $(\mathcal{L}_2(\mathcal{S}, \nu), \|.\|_{L_2(\nu)})$ if and only if $\int_{\mathcal{S}} \mathrm{E}[Z_1(x)^2] \nu(dx) < \infty$, where $\mathcal{Z}$ is a Gaussian element with the same covariance function as Z_1. We will formally summarize this result in a lemma below.

We assume that $\nu(\mathcal{S}) < \infty$. Since we will only consider the case for which $\mathcal{S}$ is a bounded subset of $\mathbb{R}^d$, we will choose $\nu(\cdot)$ to be the Lebesgue measure on $\mathcal{S}$. Then $J_n^0(\cdot)$ is a Hilbert-valued random element in $\mathcal{L}_2(\mathcal{S}, \nu)$. We present a Hilbert-valued CLT in a lemma below.

Lemma 15.1. *Let $Z_1(\cdot)$, ..., $Z_n(\cdot)$ be Hilbert-valued, i.i.d. zero mean random elements on $\mathcal{L}_2(\mathcal{S}, \nu)$ such that $\mathrm{E}[\|Z_i(\cdot)\|_\nu^2] < \infty$. Then we can show that $n^{-1/2} \sum_{i=1}^n Z_i(\cdot)$ converges weakly[2] to a zero mean Gaussian process with covariance (kernel) function given by*

$$\Omega(x, x') = \mathrm{E}[Z_i(x)Z_i(x')].$$

Proof. See Theorem 2.1 of Politis and Romano (1994), or van der Vaart and Wellner (1996, ex. 1.8.5, p. 50). Note that $\mathrm{E}[\|Z_i(\cdot)\|_\nu^2] < \infty$ is a sufficient condition that ensures the process $n^{-1/2} \sum_{i=1}^n Z_i(\cdot)$ is tight. $\square$

It is straightforward to check that $J_n^0(\cdot)$ is tight using Lemma 15.1. Letting $Z_i(\cdot) = u_i \mathcal{H}(X_i, \cdot)$, we have

$$\mathrm{E}[\|Z_i(\cdot)\|_\nu^2] = \mathrm{E}\left\{ \int u_i^2 [\mathcal{H}(X_i, x)]^2 \nu(dx) \right\}$$

$$= \mathrm{E}\left\{ \sigma^2(X_i) \int [\mathcal{H}(X_i, x)]^2 \nu(dx) \right\}$$

$$\leq \mathrm{E}[\sigma^2(X_i)] \left\{ C \int_{\mathcal{S}} \nu(dx) \right\} < \infty,$$

where $\sigma^2(X_i) = \mathrm{E}(U_i^2 | X_i)$.

Thus by Lemma 15.1, we know that

$$J_n^0(\cdot) \text{ converges weakly to } J_\infty^0(\cdot) \text{ in } \mathcal{L}_2(\mathcal{S}, \nu, \|.\|_\nu),$$

where J_∞^0 is a Gaussian process centered at zero and with covariance function Ω given by

$$\Omega(x, x') = \mathrm{E}[Z_i(x)Z_i(x')] = \mathrm{E}[\sigma^2(X_i)\mathcal{H}(X_i, x)\mathcal{H}(X_i, x')], \quad (15.65)$$

where x and $x' \in \mathcal{S}$.

Since u_i is unobservable, we must replace u_i by $\hat{u}_i$, the definition of which is given in (15.67) below, which leads to a feasible version of (15.64) given by

$$\hat{J}_n(x) = \frac{1}{\sqrt{n}} \sum_i \hat{u}_i \mathcal{H}(X_i, x). \quad (15.66)$$

---

[2] A sequence of H-valued random elements $\mathcal{Z}_n$ converges weakly to $\mathcal{Z}$ if $\mathrm{E}[h(\mathcal{Z}_n)] \to \mathrm{E}[h(\mathcal{Z})]$ for all real-valued bounded continuous functions h.

We use a linear combination of K_l functions given by

$$p_l^{K_l}(x_l) = (p_{l1}^{K_l}(x_l), \ldots, p_{lK_l}^{K_l}(x_l))'$$

to approximate $m_l(x_l)$ ($l = 1, \ldots, L$). That is, we use a linear combination of $K = \sum_{l=1}^{L} K_l$ functions $(p_1^{K_1}(x_1)', \ldots, p_L^{K_L}(x_L)') \equiv p^K(x)'$ to approximate an additive function $\sum_{l=1}^{L} m_l(x_l)$.

We use $||.||$ to denote the usual Euclidean norm ($||.||_\nu$ denotes the L_2 norm). We assume that

Assumption 15.11.

(i) *The weight function* $\mathcal{H}(X_i, x) = w(X_i'x)$ *with* $w(\cdot)$ *being an analytic, nonpolynomial function.*[3]

(ii) $\mathcal{H}(.,.)$ *is bounded on* $\mathcal{S} \times \mathcal{S}$ *and satisfies a Lipschitz condition, i.e., for all* $x_1, x_2 \in \mathcal{S}$, $|\mathcal{H}(X_i, x_1) - \mathcal{H}(X_i, x_2)| \leq G(X_i)||x_1 - x_2||$ *with* $\mathrm{E}[G^2(X_i)] < \infty$.

(iii) $\nu(\cdot)$ *is the Lebesgue measure.*

Let p_l and P be those defined in (15.20) and let Z_0 be the $n \times r$ matrix whose ith row is given by $z_0(X_i)'$. Then in vector-matrix notation, we can write (15.61) as

$$\mathcal{Y} = Z_0\gamma + m + U = Z_0\gamma + P\beta + (m - P\beta) + U$$
$$= \mathcal{X}\alpha + (m - P\beta) + U,$$

where $\mathcal{X} = (Z_0, P)$, $\alpha = (\gamma', \beta')'$, Y and U are both $n \times 1$ vectors whose ith components are given by Y_i and u_i, respectively, and m is $n \times 1$ with the ith component given by $m_i = \sum_{l=1}^{L} m_l(X_{li})$. P is of dimension $n \times K$ and $\beta = \beta_m$ is a $K \times 1$ vector that satisfies Assumption 15.2 (iii) (with $f = m$).

We estimate $\alpha = (\gamma', \beta')'$ by regressing Y on $\mathcal{X}$ using least squares, yielding

$$\hat{\alpha} = \begin{pmatrix} \hat{\gamma} \\ \hat{\beta} \end{pmatrix} = (\mathcal{X}'\mathcal{X})^- \mathcal{X}'\mathcal{Y},$$

where $(\mathcal{X}'\mathcal{X})^-$ is the generalized inverse of $(\mathcal{X}'\mathcal{X})$. Li (2000) showed that $\hat{\gamma} - \gamma = O_p(n^{-1/2})$. Also $\hat{m}(x) - m(x) = O_p((K/n)^{1/2} + \sum_{l=1}^{L} K_l^{-\delta_l})$

---

[3]An analytic function is one locally equal to its Taylor expansion at each point of its domain, such as $\exp(\cdot)$, the logistic, the hyperbolic tangent, the sine and cosine, etc.

by the results of Andrews and Whang (1990) and Newey (1995, 1997), where $\hat{m}(x) = p^K(x)'\hat{\beta}$. Hence, we estimate u_i by

$$\hat{u}_i = Y_i - z_0(X_i)'\hat{\gamma} - p^K(X_i)'\hat{\beta}. \tag{15.67}$$

Our test statistic for H_0^b is based on

$$\hat{J}_n(x) = \frac{1}{\sqrt{n}} \sum_i \mathcal{H}(X_i, x)\hat{u}_i,$$

where $\hat{u}_i$ is given in (15.67). With $\hat{J}_n(x)$ we can construct a Cramer-von Mises (CM) type statistic for testing H_0^b:

$$CM_n = \int [\hat{J}_n(x)]^2 F_n(dx) = \frac{1}{n} \sum_i [\hat{J}_n(X_i)]^2,$$

where $F_n(\cdot)$ is the empirical distribution of $X_1, \ldots, X_n$.

The next theorem establishes the weak convergence of $\hat{J}_n(\cdot)$ and CM_n under H_0^b.

Theorem 15.10. *Suppose that Assumptions 15.6, 15.7 and 15.11 hold. Then, under H_0^b,*

(i) *$\hat{J}_n(\cdot)$ converges weakly to $J_\infty(\cdot)$ in $\mathcal{L}_2(\mathcal{S}, \nu, ||.||_\nu)$, where J_∞ is a Gaussian process with zero mean and covariance function given by $\Sigma_1(x, x') = \mathrm{E}[\sigma^2(X_i)\eta_i(x)\eta_i(x')]$, where $\eta_i(x) = \mathcal{H}(X_i, x) - \phi_i(x) - \psi_i(x)$, with*

$$\phi_i(x) = \mathrm{E}_\mathcal{G}[\mathcal{H}(X_i, x)],$$
$$\psi_i(x) = \mathrm{E}[\mathcal{H}(X_i, x)\epsilon_i]\{\mathrm{E}[\epsilon_i\epsilon_i']\}^{-1}\epsilon_i, \text{ and}$$
$$\epsilon_i = z_0(X_i) - \mathrm{E}_\mathcal{G}(z_0(X_i)).$$

(ii) *CM_n converges to $\int [J_\infty(x)]^2 F(dx)$ in distribution, where $F(\cdot)$ is the CDF of X_i.*

The proof of Theorem 15.10 (i) is given in Section 15.6.

As advocated by Bierens and Ploberger (1997) and Chen and Fan (1999), one can show that $\int [J_\infty(x)]^2 F(dx)$ can be written as an infinite sum of weighted (independent) χ_1^2 random variables with weights depending on the unknown distribution of (X_i, Y_i). Therefore, obtaining critical values is difficult. We suggest using a residual-based wild bootstrap method to approximate the critical values for the null limiting distribution of CM_n. The wild bootstrap error u_i^* is generated via a two-point distribution, i.e., $u_i^* = [(1 - \sqrt{5})/2]\hat{u}_i$ with probability $(1+\sqrt{5})/[2\sqrt{5}]$ and $u_i^* = [(\sqrt{5}+1)/2]\hat{u}_i$ with probability $(\sqrt{5}-1)/[2\sqrt{5}]$. Note that u_i^* satisfies

$$\mathrm{E}^*(u_i^*) = 0, \quad \mathrm{E}^*(u_i^{*2}) = \hat{u}_i^2, \quad \text{and} \quad \mathrm{E}^*(u_i^{*3}) = \hat{u}_i^3,$$

where $\mathrm{E}^*(\cdot) = \mathrm{E}(.|\mathcal{W}_n)$ and $\mathcal{W}_n = \{Y_i, X_i\}_{i=1}^n$. From $\{u_i^*\}_{i=1}^n$, we generate Y_i^* according to the null model

$$Y_i^* = z_0(X_i)'\hat{\gamma} + p^K(X_i)'\hat{\beta} + u_i^*, \quad i = 1, \dots, n.$$

Then, using the bootstrap sample $\{(Y_i^*, X_i)\}_{i=1}^n$, we obtain

$$\begin{pmatrix} \hat{\gamma}^* \\ \hat{\beta}^* \end{pmatrix} = (\mathcal{X}'\mathcal{X})^- \mathcal{X}'\mathcal{Y}^*,$$

where $\mathcal{X} = (Z_0, P)$ and $\mathcal{Y}^*$ is an $n \times 1$ vector whose jth element is given by Y_i^*. The bootstrap residual is given by $\hat{u}_i^* = Y_i^* - z_0(X_i)'\hat{\gamma}^* - p^K(X_i)'\hat{\beta}^*$ and the bootstrap statistic $\hat{J}_n^*(x)$ is obtained by replacing $\hat{u}_i$ in $\hat{J}_n(x)$ by $\hat{u}_i^*$, i.e.,

$$\hat{J}_n^*(x) = \frac{1}{\sqrt{n}} \sum_i \hat{u}_i^* \mathcal{H}(X_i, x).$$

Using $\hat{J}_n^*(\cdot)$ we can compute a bootstrap version of the CM_n statistic, i.e.,

$$CM_n^* = \frac{1}{n} \sum_i [\hat{J}_n^*(X_i)]^2.$$

Li, Hsiao and Zinn (2003) showed that CM_n^* converges to the same limiting distribution as the null limiting distribution of CM_n. The simulation results in Li, Hsiao and Zinn show that the bootstrap statistic CM_n^* performs well in finite-sample applications.

15.5 Other Series-Based Tests

Li, Hsiao and Zinn (2003) also consider series-based approaches to testing the null hypothesis of an additive regression model without the parametric partially linear component, which can be thought of as a special case of testing an additive partially linear model with $\gamma = 0$.

Li, Hsiao and Zinn further consider testing the null of a partially linear model, which can be thought of as a special case of testing an additive partially linear model but with one ($L = 1$) nonparametric function (instead of having $L > 1$ nonparametric additive functions). In principle, series-based tests can be constructed for all types of hypotheses, including nonparametric omitted variable tests and testing for equality of two unknown densities.

Donald, Imbens and Newey (2003) propose a novel approach to constructing a consistent conditional moment test based upon series estimation of an empirical likelihood function. Their test statistic is based on the efficient estimation of the finite dimensional parameters that appear in the conditional moment restrictions. Their approach admits endogenous regressors and also allows for a large number of moment conditions.

15.6   Proofs

Following arguments given in Newey (1997), we assume that $B = I$ in Assumption 15.2. Hence $p^K(\cdot) = P^K(\cdot)$ since all nonparametric series estimators are invariant with respect to nonsingular transformations of $p^K(\cdot)$. Also we assume that $Q \overset{\text{def}}{=} \mathrm{E}[p^K(X_i)p^K(X_i)'] = I$. This is because, for a symmetric square root $Q^{-1/2}$ of Q^{-1}, $Q^{-1/2}p^K(\cdot)$ is a nonsingular transformation of $p^K(\cdot)$ and, by using Assumption 15.2 (ii), it is easy to show that $\tilde{\zeta}_0(K) \overset{\text{def}}{=} \sup_{x \in \mathcal{S}} \|Q^{-1/2}p^K(\cdot)\| \le C\zeta_0(K)$. Further, if we change $p^K(\cdot)$ to $\bar{p}^K(\cdot) \equiv Q^{-1/2}p^K(\cdot)$ and define $\bar{\beta} = Q^{1/2}\beta$, then Assumption 15.2 (iii) is satisfied since $|g(\cdot) - p^K(\cdot)'\beta| = |f(\cdot) - \bar{p}^K(\cdot)'\bar{\beta}|$. Thus all assumptions hold when $p^K(\cdot)$ is changed to $Q^{-1/2}p^K(\cdot)$.

15.6.1   Proof of Theorem 15.1

We prove only Theorem 15.1 (i) here. Theorem 15.1 (ii) and (iii) can be proved in a similar manner.

Proof of (i). By the triangle inequality $(||A + B|| \leq ||A|| + ||B||)$,

$$1_n \int [\hat{g}(x) - g(x)]^2 dF(x)$$

$$= 1_n \int [p^K(x)'(\hat{\beta} - \beta) + p^K(x)'\beta - g(x)]^2 dF(x)$$

$$\leq 21_n \int [p^K(x)'(\hat{\beta} - \beta)]^2 dF(x) + 21_n \int [p^K(x)'\beta - g(x)]^2 dF(x)$$

$$= 21_n||\hat{\beta} - \beta||^2 + 21_n \int [p^K(x)'\beta - g(x)]^2 dF(x)$$

$$\leq O_p(K/n + K^{-2\alpha}) + O(K^{-2\alpha}) = O_p(K/n + K^{-2\alpha})$$

by Lemma 15.3 (see below) and Assumption 15.2. In the second equality above we used

$$\int [p^K(x)'(\hat{\beta} - \beta)]^2 dF(x) = (\hat{\beta} - \beta)' \int p^K(x)p^K(x)'dF(x)(\hat{\beta} - \beta)$$

$$= ||\hat{\beta} - \beta||^2,$$

because $\int p^K(x)p^K(x)'dF(x) = \mathrm{E}[p^K(X)p^K(X)] = I_K$. $\square$

We now prove the lemma used in the proof of Theorem 15.1.

Lemma 15.2. $\mathrm{E}[||\hat{Q} - I||^2] = O(\zeta_0(K)^2 K/n)$ $(Q = I_K)$.

Proof. Recall that, for any matrix A, $||A||^2$ is defined by $||A||^2 = \mathrm{tr}(A'A)$. For a $K \times K$ matrix, letting A_{jl} denote the element appearing in the jth row and lth column of A, we have $\mathrm{tr}(A'A) = \sum_{j=1}^K \sum_{l=1}^K A_{jl}^2$. Letting δ_{jl} denote $(I_K)_{jl}$, and noting that the assumption that $Q = I$

implies that $\mathrm{E}[p_{jK}(x_i)p_{lK}(x_i)] = \delta_{jl}$, we have

$$
\begin{aligned}
\mathrm{E}[||\hat{Q} - I||^2] &= \mathrm{E}||(P'P/n) - I||^2 \\
&= \sum_{j=1}^{K}\sum_{l=1}^{K}\mathrm{E}\left[\left\{n^{-1}\sum_{i=1}^{n}p_{jK}(x_i)p_{lK}(X_i) - \delta_{js}\right\}^2\right] \\
&\quad (\text{by } ||A||^2 = \mathrm{tr}(A'A) = \sum_{j=1}^{K}\sum_{l=1}^{K}A_{jl}^2) \\
&= \sum_{j=1}^{K}\sum_{l=1}^{K}n^{-1}\mathrm{E}\left\{[p_{jK}(X_i)p_{lK}(x_i) - \delta_{jl}]^2\right\} \\
&\quad (\text{because } \mathrm{E}[p_{jK}(X_i)p_{lK}(x_i)] = \delta_{jl}) \\
&\le \sum_{j=1}^{K}\sum_{l=1}^{K}\mathrm{E}\left[p_{jK}(X_i)^2 p_{lK}(x_i)^2\right]/n \\
&\quad (\text{since } \mathrm{var}(A) \le \mathrm{E}(A^2) \text{ with } A = p_{jK}(X_i)p_{lK}(X_i)) \\
&= \mathrm{E}\left[||p^K(X_i)||^2\sum_{j=1}^{K}p_{jK}(X_i)^2\right]/n \\
&\le \zeta_0(K)^2\mathrm{E}\left[\sum_{j=1}^{K}p_{jK}(X_i)^2\right]/n \\
&\quad (\text{by Assumption 15.2}) \\
&= \zeta_0(K)^2\mathrm{E}\left\{\mathrm{tr}\left[p^K(x_i)p^K(X_i)'\right]\right\}/n \\
&= \zeta_0(K)^2\,\mathrm{tr}(I_K)/n = \zeta_0(K)^2 K/n.
\end{aligned}
$$

Note that Lemma 15.2 implies that $||\hat{Q} - I|| = O_p(\zeta_0(K)\sqrt{K/n}) = o_p(1)$. Also, since the smallest eigenvalue of $\hat{Q} - I$ is bounded by $||\hat{Q} - I||$, this implies that the smallest eigenvalue of $\hat{Q}$ converges to one in probability. Letting $\mathbf{1}_n$ be the indicator function for the smallest eigenvalue of $\hat{Q}$ being greater than $1/2$, then $\mathrm{P}(\mathbf{1}_n = 1) \to 1$. $\square$

Lemma 15.3. $\mathbf{1}_n||\hat{\beta} - \beta|| = O_p(K^{1/2}/n^{1/2} + K^{-\alpha})$.

Proof. Letting $u = (u_1, \ldots, u_n)'$, we have

$$
\begin{aligned}
\mathrm{E}[\mathbf{1}_n \|\hat{Q}^{-1/2} P' u / n\|^2 | X] &= \mathbf{1}_n \mathrm{E}[u' P \hat{Q}^{-1} P' u | X] / n^2 \\
&= \mathbf{1}_n \mathrm{E}[u' P (P'P)^{-1} P' u | X] / n \\
&= \mathbf{1}_n \mathrm{E}[\mathrm{tr}\{u' P (P'P)^{-1} P' u\} | X] / n \\
&= \mathbf{1}_n \, \mathrm{tr}\{P (P'P)^{-1} P' \mathrm{E}[uu' | X]\} / n \\
&\leq C \mathbf{1}_n \, \mathrm{tr}\{P (P'P)^{-1} P'\} / n \\
&= \mathbf{1}_n C K / n.
\end{aligned}
$$

Hence, by the Markov inequality,

$$
\begin{aligned}
\mathbf{1}_n \|\hat{Q}^{-1} P' u / n\| &= \mathbf{1}_n \left\{ (u' P / n) \hat{Q}^{-1/2} \hat{Q}^{-1} \hat{Q}^{-1/2} (P' u / n) \right\}^{1/2} \\
&\leq O_p(1) \mathbf{1}_n \|\hat{Q}^{-1/2} P' u / n\| \\
&= O_p((K/n)^{1/2}).
\end{aligned} \tag{15.68}
$$

Let $\beta = \beta_K$ be that given in Assumption 15.2, and let G be an $n \times 1$ matrix whose ith row is given by $g(X_i)$. Then, noting that $\mathbf{1}_n P (P'P)^{-1} P'$ is idempotent, we have

$$
\begin{aligned}
\mathbf{1}_n &\|\hat{Q}^{-1} P' (G - P\beta) / n\| \\
&= \mathbf{1}_n \left[(G - P\beta)' P \hat{Q}^{-1/2} \hat{Q}^{-1} \hat{Q}^{-1/2} P' (G - P\beta) / n^2 \right]^{1/2} \\
&\leq O_p(1) \mathbf{1}_n \left[(G - P\beta)' \hat{Q}^{-1/2} \hat{Q}^{-1/2} P' (G - P\beta) / n^2 \right]^{1/2} \\
&= O_p(1) \mathbf{1}_n \left[(G - P\beta)' P (P'P)^{-1} P' (G - P\beta) / n \right]^{1/2} \\
&\leq O_p(1) \mathbf{1}_n \left[(G - P\beta)' (G - P\beta) / n \right]^{1/2} \\
&= O_p(K^{-\alpha}),
\end{aligned} \tag{15.69}
$$

where, in the last inequality above, we used $z' A z \leq z' z$ if A is an idempotent matrix, and the last equality follows from Assumption 15.2.

Therefore, by using the triangle inequality, we have

$$
\begin{aligned}
\|\mathbf{1}_n(\hat{\beta} - \beta)\| &= \|\mathbf{1}_n \hat{Q}^{-1} P' y / n - \mathbf{1}_n \hat{Q}^{-1} P' P\beta / n\| \\
&= \|\mathbf{1}_n \hat{Q}^{-1} P' (y - G) / n + \mathbf{1}_n \hat{Q}^{-1} P' (G - P\beta) / n\| \\
&\leq \mathbf{1}_n \|\hat{Q}^{-1} P' u / n\| + \mathbf{1}_n \|\hat{Q}^{-1} P' (G - P\beta) / n\| \\
&= O_p \left((K/n)^{1/2} + K^{-\alpha} \right),
\end{aligned}
$$

where the last equality follows from (15.68) and (15.69). $\qquad \square$

15.6.2   Proof of Theorem 15.3

Recalling that $\theta(X_i) = E(Z_i|X_i)$, $v_i = Z_i - \theta(X_i)$, we will use the following shorthand notation: $\theta_i = \theta(X_i)$, $g_i = g(X_i)$, and $v_i = Z_i - \theta_i$.

To avoid introducing too much notation for vector-matrix variables, we will use the same notation without subscripts to denote a vector or a matrix. For example, θ is the $n \times r$ matrix with the ith row given by $\theta(Z_i)'$. This convention applies to g, v, u, etc.

Recall that we define $\tilde{A}$ by $\tilde{A} = (P'P)^- P'A$. This definition applies to any $n \times 1$ or $n \times r$ matrix considered below. For example, $\tilde{\theta} = (P'P)^- P'\theta$, while $\tilde{u}$ and $\tilde{v}$ are similarly defined.

From $X_i = \theta_i + v_i$, we get $\tilde{Z}_i = \tilde{\theta}_i + \tilde{v}_i$. Or, in vector-matrix notation, $Z = \theta + v$ and $\tilde{Z} = \tilde{\eta} + \tilde{v}$. Thus we have

$$Z - \tilde{Z} = (\theta - \tilde{\theta}) + v - \tilde{v}. \tag{15.70}$$

For scalars or column vectors A_i and B_i, let us define $S_{A,B} = n^{-1}\sum_i A_i B_i'$. Also we let $S_{A,A} = S_A$.

Note that if $S_{Z-\tilde{Z}}^{-1}$ exists, then we have

$$\sqrt{n}(\hat{\gamma} - \gamma) = S_{Z-\tilde{Z}}^{-1} \sqrt{n} S_{Z-\tilde{Z}, g-\tilde{g}+u-\tilde{u}}.$$

We will prove Theorem 15.3 by showing that

(i) $S_{Z-\tilde{Z}} = \Phi + o_p(1)$ (hence $S_{Z-\tilde{Z}}$ is asymptotically nonsingular).

(ii) $S_{Z-\tilde{Z}, g-\tilde{g}} = o_p(n^{-1/2})$.

(iii) $S_{Z-\tilde{Z}, \tilde{u}} = o_p(n^{-1/2})$.

(iv) $\sqrt{n} S_{Z-\tilde{Z}, u} \to N(0, \Omega)$ in distribution.

These are proved below.

Proof of (i) $S_{Z-\tilde{Z}} = \Phi + o_p(1)$. Using (15.70), we have

$$S_{Z-\tilde{Z}} = S_{v+(\theta-\tilde{\theta})-\tilde{v}} = S_v + S_{(\theta-\tilde{\theta})-\tilde{v}} + 2S_{v,(\theta-\tilde{\theta})-\tilde{v}}.$$

First, $S_v = n^{-1}\sum_i v_i v_i' = \Phi + o_p(1)$ by virtue of a law of large numbers.

Next, $S_{(\theta-\tilde{\theta})-\tilde{v}} \leq 2\{S_{\theta-\tilde{\theta}} + S_{\tilde{v}}\} = o_p(1)$ by Lemma 15.7 and Lemma 15.8 (i) and (iii).

Finally, $S_{v,\theta-\tilde{\theta}-\tilde{v}} \leq \{S_v S_{\theta-\tilde{\theta}-\tilde{v}}\}^{1/2} = \{O_p(1)o_p(1)\}^{1/2} = o_p(1)$ by the above results. $\qquad\square$

Proof of (ii) $S_{Z-\tilde{Z},g-\tilde{g}} = O_p(K^{-\delta}) = o_p(n^{-1/2})$. Using (15.70),

$$S_{Z-\tilde{Z},g-\tilde{g}} = S_{v+(\theta-\tilde{\theta})-\tilde{v},g-\tilde{g}} = S_{v,g-\tilde{g}} + S_{\theta-\tilde{\theta},g-\tilde{g}} - S_{\tilde{v},g-\tilde{g}},$$

and we consider the three terms on the right-hand side separately.

(i) $E[||S_{v,g-\tilde{g}}||^2|X] = n^{-2}\operatorname{tr}[(g-\tilde{g})(g-\tilde{g})'E(vv'|X)] \leq Cn^{-2}\operatorname{tr}[(g-\tilde{g})(g-\tilde{g})'] = Cn^{-1}\operatorname{tr}(S_{g-\tilde{g}}) = n^{-1}O_p(K^{-2\delta}) = o_p(n^{-1})$. Hence, $S_{v,g-\tilde{g}} = o_p(n^{-1/2})$.

(ii) $S_{\theta-\tilde{\theta},g-\tilde{g}} \leq \{S_{\theta-\tilde{\theta}}S_{g-\tilde{g}}\}^{1/2} = O_p(K^{-2\delta})$ by Lemma 15.7.

(iii) $S_{\tilde{v},g-\tilde{g}} \leq \{S_{\tilde{v}}S_{g-\tilde{g}}\}^{1/2} = o_p(1)O_p(K^{-\delta})$ by Lemmas 15.7 and 15.8 (i).

$\square$

Proof of (iii) $S_{Z-\tilde{Z},\tilde{u}} = o_p(n^{-1/2})$. Using (15.70),

$$S_{Z-\tilde{Z},\tilde{u}} = S_{v+(\theta-\tilde{\theta})-\tilde{v},\tilde{u}} = S_{v,\tilde{u}} + S_{\theta-\tilde{\theta},\tilde{u}} - S_{\tilde{v},\tilde{u}}.$$

We consider these three terms separately.

(i) By Lemma 15.8 (i),

$$\begin{aligned}
E[||S_{v,\tilde{u}}||^2|X,Z] &= n^{-2}\operatorname{tr}[P(P'P)^- P'vv'P(P'P)^- P'E(uu'|X,Z)] \\
&\leq Cn^{-2}\operatorname{tr}[P(P'P)^{-1}P'vv'P(P'P)^{-1}P'] \\
&= Cn^{-2}\operatorname{tr}[\tilde{v}\tilde{v}'] = Cn^{-1}\operatorname{tr}(S_{\tilde{v}}) = O(K/n^2).
\end{aligned}$$

Hence $S_{v,\tilde{u}} = O_p(\sqrt{K}/n)$.

(ii) $S_{\theta-\tilde{\theta},\tilde{u}} \leq \{S_{h-\tilde{h}}S_{\tilde{u}}\}^{1/2} = O_p(K^{-\delta})O_p(\sqrt{K}/\sqrt{n})$ by Lemma 15.7 and Lemma 15.8 (ii).

(iii) $S_{\tilde{v},\tilde{u}} \leq \{S_{\tilde{v}}S_{\tilde{u}}\}^{1/2} = O_p(K/n)$ by Lemma 15.8 (i) and (ii).

$\square$

Proof of (iv) $\sqrt{n}S_{Z-\tilde{Z},u} \to N(0,\Omega)$ *in distribution.*

$$S_{Z-\tilde{Z},u} = S_{v+(\theta-\tilde{\theta})-\tilde{v},u} = S_{v,u} + S_{\theta-\tilde{\theta},u} - S_{\tilde{v},u}.$$

We consider these three terms separately.

(i) $\sqrt{n}S_{v,u} = n^{-1/2}\sum_i[\eta_i + v_i]u_i \to N(0,\Omega)$ in distribution by the Lindeberg-Levy CLT.

(ii) $\mathrm{E}[\|S_{\theta-\tilde{\theta},u}\|^2|X] = n^{-2}\,\mathrm{tr}[(\theta-\tilde{\theta})(\theta-\tilde{\theta})'\mathrm{E}(uu'|X)] \le Cn^{-1}\,\mathrm{tr}[(\theta-\tilde{\theta})'(\theta-\tilde{\theta})/n] = Cn^{-1}\,\mathrm{tr}(S_{\theta-\tilde{\theta}}) = o_p(n^{-1})$ by Lemma 15.7. Hence, $S_{\theta-\tilde{\theta},u} = o_p(n^{-1/2})$.

By exactly the same arguments as in (ii) above, we have

(iii) $\mathrm{E}[\|S_{\tilde{v},u}\|^2|X] \le Cn^{-1}\,\mathrm{tr}(S_{\tilde{v}}) = o_p(n^{-1})$ by Lemma 15.8 (i). Thus, $S_{\tilde{v},u} = o_p(n^{-1/2})$, and (i)-(iv) above imply that $\sqrt{n}(\hat{\gamma}-\gamma) = \Phi^{-1}N(0,\Omega) + o_p(1) \to N(0,\Phi^{-1}\Omega\Phi^{-1})$ in distribution.

$\square$

Proof of $\hat{\Sigma} = \Sigma + o_p(1)$. $\hat{\Sigma} = \hat{\Phi}^{-1}\hat{\Omega}\hat{\Phi}^{-1}$. $\hat{\Phi} \equiv S_{X-\tilde{X}} = \Phi + o_p(1)$ was proved above. Below we provide a sketch of a proof of $\hat{\Omega} = \Omega + o_p(1)$ since the detailed proof is very similar to the proof of $\hat{\Phi} = \Phi + o_p(1)$.

Using $\hat{\gamma}-\gamma = O_p(n^{-1/2})$ and $\hat{g}(X_i)-g(X_i) = o_p(1)$, it is easy to see that $\hat{u}_i = u_i + o_p(1)$. Also, by Lemma 15.7 and Lemma 15.8 (i) and (iii), we know that $\theta_i - \tilde{\theta}_i = o_p(1)$, $\tilde{v}_i = o_p(1)$ and $\tilde{\eta}_i = o_p(1)$. Hence, from (15.70), we know that $Z_i - \tilde{Z}_i = v_i + (\theta_i - \tilde{\theta}_i) - \tilde{v}_i = v_i + o_p(1)$. These results lead to $\hat{\Omega} = n^{-1}\sum_i \hat{u}_i^2(Z_i - \tilde{Z}_i)(Z_i - \tilde{Z}_i)' = n^{-1}\sum_{i=1}^n u_i^2 v_i v_i' + o_p(1) = \Omega + o_p(1)$ by virtue of a law of large numbers. $\square$

We use $\mathbf{1}_n$ to denote an indicator function that takes value one if $(P'P)$ is invertible and zero otherwise. We will explicitly use the indicator function $\mathbf{1}_n$ only in the proof of Lemma 15.5 and will omit it in the proofs of Lemmas 15.6 through 15.8 (iii) to simplify notation. Whenever we have $(P'P)^{-1}$, it should be understood as $\mathbf{1}_n(P'P)^{-1}$ and since $\mathrm{P}(\mathbf{1}_n = 1) \to 1$ in probability, we will often omit the indicator function $\mathbf{1}_n$.

Lemma 15.4. $\hat{Q} - I = O_p(\zeta_0(K)\sqrt{K}/\sqrt{n})$, *where* $\hat{Q} = (P'P/n)$.

Proof. See the proof of Theorem 1 of Newey (1997, pp. 161–162). $\square$

Lemma 15.5. $\|\tilde{\beta}_f - \beta_f\| = O_p(K^{-\delta})$, *where* $\tilde{\beta}_f = (P'P)^-P'f$, β *satisfies Assumption 15.2,* $f = g$ *or* $f = \theta$.

Proof.

$$\mathbf{1}_n||\tilde{\beta}_f - \beta_f|| = \mathbf{1}_n||(P'P)^{-1}P'(f - P\beta_f)||$$
$$= \mathbf{1}_n\{(f - P\beta_f)'P(P'P)^{-1}(P'P/n)^{-1}P'(f - P\beta_f)/n\}^{1/2}$$
$$= \mathbf{1}_n O_p(1)\{(f - P\beta_f)'P(P'P)^{-1}P'(f - P\beta_f)/n\}^{1/2}$$
$$\leq O_p(1)\{(f - P\beta_f)'(f - P\beta_f)/n\}^{1/2} = O_p(K^{-\delta}),$$

by Lemma 15.2, Assumption 15.2, and the fact that $P(P'P)^{-1}P'$ is idempotent. Finally $||\tilde{\beta}_f - \beta_f|| = O_p(K^{-\delta})$ since $\mathrm{P}(\mathbf{1}_n = 1) \to 1$. $\square$

Lemma 15.6.

$$(P'\eta/n) = O_p(\zeta_0(K)/\sqrt{n}) = o_p(1), \text{ where } \eta = u \text{ or } \eta = v.$$

Proof. Noting that $\mathrm{E}[P_i\eta_i] = 0$, we have

$$\mathrm{E}||P'\eta/n||^2 = n^{-2}\left\{\sum_i\sum_j\mathrm{E}[P_i'P_j\eta_i\eta_j]\right\}$$
$$= n^{-2}\left\{\sum_i\mathrm{E}[P_iP_i'\eta_i^2] + \sum_i\sum_{j\neq i}\mathrm{E}[P_i'\eta_i]\mathrm{E}[P_j\eta_j]\right\}$$
$$= n^{-2}\sum_i\mathrm{E}[P_i'P_i\eta_i^2]$$
$$\leq Cn^{-1}\mathrm{E}[P_i'P_i] = O((\zeta_0(K))^2/n).$$

Hence, $(P'\eta/n) = O_p(\zeta_0(K)/\sqrt{n})$. $\square$

Lemma 15.7. $S_{f-\tilde{f}} = O_p(K^{-2\delta}) = o_p(n^{-1/2})$, where $f = g$ or $f = h$.

Proof. Noting that $\tilde{f} \equiv P\tilde{\beta}_f$, we have $S_{f-\tilde{f}} = 2n^{-1}||f - \tilde{f}||^2 \leq n^{-1}\{||f - P\beta_f||^2 + ||P(\beta_f - \tilde{\beta}_f)||^2\} = O(K^{-2\delta}) + (\beta_f - \tilde{\beta}_f)'(P'P/n)(\beta_f - \tilde{\beta}_f) = O(K^{-2\delta}) + O_p(1)||\beta_f - \tilde{\beta}_f||^2 = O_p(K^{-2\delta})$ by Assumption 15.2 and Lemmas 15.2 and 15.5. $\square$

Lemma 15.8.

(i) $S_{\tilde{v}} = O_p(K/n)$.

(ii) $S_{\tilde{u}} = O_p(K/n)$.

Proof of (i). Similar to the proof of Lemma 15.2, we have

$$
\begin{aligned}
\mathrm{E}[S_{\tilde{v}}|Z] &= n^{-1}\mathrm{E}\{v'P(P'P)^{-1}P'v|Z\} \\
&= n^{-1}\operatorname{tr}[P(P'P)^{-1}P'\mathrm{E}(vv'|Z)] \\
&\leq Cn^{-1}\operatorname{tr}[P(P'P)^{-1}P'] \\
&= O(K/n), \text{ which implies } S_{\tilde{v}} = O_p(K/n).
\end{aligned}
$$

$\square$

Proof of (ii). Follow the same proof as in the proof of Lemma 15.8 (i).

$\square$

15.6.3   Proof of Theorem 15.6

Recall that $\theta(X_i, Z_i) = \mathrm{E}[W_i|X_i, Z_i]$, that $m(X_i, Z_i) = \mathrm{E}_{\mathcal{G}}(W_i) = \mathrm{E}_{\mathcal{G}}(\theta(X_i, Z_i))$, and that $\varepsilon_i = W_i - m(Z_i, X_i)$. Define $v_i = W_i - \theta(X_i, Z_i)$, and $\eta_i = \theta(Z_i, X_i) - m(X_i, Z_i)$. We will use the following shorthand notation: $\theta_i = \theta(X_i, Z_i)$, $g_i = X_i'\beta(Z_i)$, and $m_i = m(X_i, Z_i)$. Hence, $v_i = W_i - \theta_i$, $\varepsilon_i = \theta_i + v_i - m_i$, $\eta_i = \theta_i - m_i$. Finally, the variables without the subscript represent matrices, e.g., $\theta = (\theta_1, \ldots, \theta_n)'$ is of dimension $n \times 1$.

Also recall that for any matrix A having n rows, we define $\tilde{A} = P(P'P)^- P'A$ (P is defined below (15.47)). Applying this definition to θ, m, g, η, u, v, we get $\tilde{\theta}, \tilde{m}, \tilde{g}, \tilde{\eta}, \tilde{u}, \tilde{v}$.

Since $W_i = \theta_i + v_i$ and $\theta_i = m_i + \eta_i$, we get $W_i = \eta_i + v_i + m_i$ and $\tilde{W}_i = \tilde{\eta}_i + \tilde{v}_i + \tilde{m}_i$. In matrix notation, $\mathcal{W} = \eta + v + m$ and $\tilde{\mathcal{W}} = \tilde{\eta} + \tilde{v} + \tilde{m}$. Therefore, we have

$$
\mathcal{W} - \tilde{\mathcal{W}} = \eta + v + (m - \tilde{m}) - \tilde{v} - \tilde{\eta}. \tag{15.71}
$$

For both scalars or column vectors A_i and B_i, we define $S_{A,B} = n^{-1}\sum_i A_i B_i'$ and $S_A = S_{A,A}$. We also define a scalar function $\bar{S}_A = n^{-1}\sum_i A_i'A_i$, which is the sum of diagonal elements of S_A. Using $ab \leq (a^2 + b^2)/2$, it is easy to see that each element of $S_{A,B}$ is less than or equal to $\bar{S}_A + \bar{S}_B$. When we evaluate the probability order of $S_{A,B}$, we often write $S_{A,B} \leq \bar{S}_A + \bar{S}_B$. The scalar bound $\bar{S}_A + \bar{S}_B$ bounds each of the elements in $S_{A,B}$. Therefore, if $\bar{S}_A + \bar{S}_B = O_p(a_n)$ (for some positive sequence a_n), then each element of $S_{A,B}$ is at most $O_p(a_n)$, which implies that $S_{A,B} = O_p(a_n)$. Similarly, using the Cauchy-Schwarz inequality, we have $S_{A,B} \leq (\bar{S}_A \bar{S}_B)^{1/2}$. Here again, the scalar bounds all elements in $S_{A,B}$.

Note that if $S_{W-\tilde{W}}^{-1}$ exists, then from (15.51) and (15.52), we get

$$
\sqrt{n}(\hat{\gamma} - \gamma) = \left[n^{-1} \sum_i (W_i - \tilde{W}_i)(W_i - \tilde{W}_i)' \right]^{-1}
$$

$$
\times \sqrt{n} \left\{ n^{-1} \sum_i (W_i - \tilde{W}_i)(g_i - \tilde{g}_i + u_i - \tilde{u}_i) \right\} \quad (15.72)
$$

$$
= S_{W-\tilde{W}}^{-1} \sqrt{n} S_{W-\tilde{W}, g-\tilde{g}+u-\tilde{u}},
$$

where $g_i = x_i' \beta(z_i)$.

For the first part of the theorem, we will prove the following: (i) $S_{W-\tilde{W}} = \Phi + o_p(1)$, (ii) $S_{W-\tilde{W},g-\tilde{g}} = o_p(n^{-1/2})$, (iii) $S_{W-\tilde{W},\tilde{u}} = o_p(n^{-1/2})$ and (iv) $\sqrt{n} S_{W-\tilde{W},u} \to N(0,\Omega)$ in distribution.

Proof of (i). For a matrix A and scalar sequence a_n, $A = O_p(a_n)$ $(o_p(a_n))$ means that each element of A is of order $O_p(a_n)$ $(o_p(a_n))$. Using (15.71), we have

$$
S_{W-\tilde{W}} = S_{\eta+v+(m-\tilde{m})-\tilde{v}-\tilde{\eta}} = S_{\eta+v} + S_{(m-\tilde{m})-\tilde{v}-\tilde{\eta}} + 2S_{\eta+v,(m-\tilde{m})-\tilde{v}-\tilde{\eta}}
$$

The first term, $S_{\eta+v} = \frac{1}{n} \sum_i (\eta_i + v_i)(\eta_i + v_i)' = \frac{1}{n} \sum_i \varepsilon_i \varepsilon_i' = \Phi + o_p(1)$ by virtue of the law of large numbers.

The second term, $S_{(m-\tilde{m})-\tilde{v}-\tilde{\eta}} \le 3(\bar{S}_{(m-\tilde{m})} + \bar{S}_{\tilde{v}} + \bar{S}_{\tilde{\eta}}) = o_p(1)$ by Lemma 15.10 and Lemma 15.11 (i), and (iii) is stated and proved at the end of this section.

The last term,

$$
S_{\eta+v,(m-\tilde{m})-\tilde{v}-\tilde{\eta}} \le \{\bar{S}_{\eta+v} \bar{S}_{(m-\tilde{m})-\tilde{v}-\tilde{\eta}}\}^{1/2} = (O_p(1)o_p(1))^{1/2} = o_p(1)
$$

by the preceding results, where for an $m \times m$ matrix A, $\mathrm{diag}(A)$ is an $m \times 1$ matrix constructed from the diagonal elements of A, and $A^{1/2}$ has the same dimension as A by taking the square root of each element of A. $\qquad\square$

Proof of (ii). Using (15.71), we have

$$
S_{W-\tilde{W},g-\tilde{g}} = S_{\eta+v+(m-\tilde{m})-\tilde{v}-\tilde{\eta},g-\tilde{g}}
$$

$$
= S_{\eta+v,g-\tilde{g}} + S_{m-\tilde{m},g-\tilde{g}} - S_{\tilde{v},g-\tilde{g}} - S_{\tilde{\eta},g-\tilde{g}}.
$$

For the first term, by noting that $\eta_i + v_i$ is orthogonal to the varying coefficient functional space $\mathcal{G}$, and noting that $g_i - \tilde{g}_i$ belongs to $\mathcal{G}$, we use Lemma 15.10 to get $\mathrm{E}[||S_{\eta+v,g-\tilde{g}}||^2] = n^{-2}\sum_{i=1}^n \mathrm{E}[(\eta_i + v_i)(\eta_i + v_i)'(g_i - \tilde{g}_i)^2] \leq Cn^{-1}(\sum_{l=1}^d k_l^{2\delta_l})\mathrm{E}[||\eta_1 + v_1||^2] = O(n^{-1}\sum_{l=1}^d k_l^{2\delta_l}) = o(n^{-1})$, which implies that $S_{\eta+v,g-\tilde{g}} = O_p(n^{-1/2}\sum_{l=1}^d k_l^{-\delta_l})$.

The second term, $S_{m-\tilde{m},g-\tilde{g}} \leq (\bar{S}_{m-\tilde{m}}\bar{S}_{g-\tilde{g}})^{1/2} = O_p(\sum_{l=1}^r k_l^{-2\delta_l})$ by Lemma 15.10.

The third term, $S_{\tilde{v},g-\tilde{g}} \leq (\bar{S}_{\tilde{v}}\bar{S}_{g-\tilde{g}})^{1/2} = O_p(K/n)O_p(\sum_{l=1}^r k_l^{-\delta_l})$ by Lemma 15.10 and Lemma 15.11 (i). The last term, $S_{\tilde{\eta},g-\tilde{g}} \leq (\bar{S}_{\tilde{\eta}}\bar{S}_{g-\tilde{g}})^{1/2} = O_p(K/n)O_p(\sum_{l=1}^r k_l^{-\delta_l})$ by Lemmas 15.10 and 15.11 (iii).

Combining the above four terms, we have

$$S_{W-\tilde{W},g-\tilde{g}} = O_p\left(n^{-1/2} + (K/n)^{1/2}\right)\left(\sum_{l=1}^d k_l^{-\delta_l} + \sum_{l=1}^d k_l^{-2\delta_l}\right)$$

$$= o_p\left(n^{-1/2}\right)$$

by Assumption 15.9.   □

Proof of (iii). Using (15.71), we have

$$S_{W-\tilde{W},\tilde{u}} = S_{\eta+v+(m-\tilde{m})-\tilde{v}-\tilde{\eta},\tilde{u}} = S_{\eta+v,\tilde{u}} + S_{m-\tilde{m},\tilde{u}} - S_{\tilde{v},\tilde{u}} - S_{\tilde{\eta},\tilde{u}}.$$

The first term, $S_{\eta+v,\tilde{u}} \leq (\bar{S}_{\eta+v}\bar{S}_{\tilde{u}})^{1/2} = O_p(K/n)$ by Lemma 15.11 (ii).

The second term (using $\mathrm{tr}(AB) = \mathrm{tr}(BA)$)

$$S_{m-\tilde{m},\tilde{u}} \leq (\bar{S}_{m-\tilde{m}}\bar{S}_{\tilde{u}})^{1/2} = O_p\left(\sum_{l=1}^r k_l^{-\delta_l}\right)O_p(\sqrt{K}/\sqrt{n})$$

by Lemmas 15.10 and 15.11 (ii).

The third term, $S_{\tilde{v},\tilde{u}} \leq (\bar{S}_{\tilde{v}}\bar{S}_{\tilde{u}})^{1/2} = O_p(K/n)$ by Lemma 15.10 (i) and (ii).

The last term, $S_{\tilde{\eta},\tilde{u}} \leq (\bar{S}_{\tilde{\eta}}\bar{S}_{\tilde{u}})^{1/2} = O_p(K/n)$ by Lemmas 15.11 (ii) and (iii).

Combining all four terms, we get

$$S_{W-\tilde{W},\tilde{u}} = O_p\left(K/n + n^{-1/2}\sum_{l=1}^d k_l^{-\delta_l}\right) = o_p(n^{-1/2})$$

by Assumption 15.9.   □

Proof of (iv). Using (15.71), we have

$$\sqrt{n}S_{W-\tilde{W},u} = \sqrt{n}S_{\eta+v+(m-\tilde{m})-\tilde{v}-\tilde{\eta},u}$$
$$= \sqrt{n}S_{\eta+v,u} + \sqrt{n}(S_{m-\tilde{m},u} - S_{\tilde{v},u} - S_{\tilde{\eta},u})$$

The first term, $\sqrt{n}S_{\eta+v,u} = \sqrt{n}\sum_{i=1}^{n}(\eta_i + v_i)u_i = \sqrt{n}\sum_{i=1}^{n}\varepsilon_i u_i \to N(0,\Omega)$ in distribution by the Lindeberg-Feller CLT.

The second term,

$$\mathrm{E}[S_{m-\tilde{m},u}^2|X,Z] = \frac{1}{n^2}\operatorname{tr}\{(m-\tilde{m})(m-\tilde{m})'\mathrm{E}[uu'|X,Z]\}$$
$$\leq (C/n)\operatorname{tr}[(m-\tilde{m})'(m-\tilde{m})/n]$$
$$= (C/n)S_{m-\tilde{m}} = O_p(n^{-1})O_p\left(\sum_{l=1}^{r}K_l^{-2\delta_l}\right)$$

by Lemma 15.10. Hence, $S_{m-\tilde{m},u} = O_p\left(n^{-1/2}\sum_{l=1}^{r}K_l^{-\delta_l}\right)$.

The third term,

$$\mathrm{E}[S_{\tilde{v},u}^2|X,Z] = \frac{1}{n^2}\operatorname{tr}(P(P'P)^{-1}P'vv'P(P'P)^{-1}P'\mathrm{E}[uu'|X,Z])$$
$$\leq (C/n^2)\operatorname{tr}[P(P'P)^{-1}P'vv'P(P'P)^{-1}P']$$
$$= (C/n)\operatorname{tr}(\tilde{v}\tilde{v}'/n)$$
$$= (C/n)S_{\tilde{v}} = o_p(n^{-1})$$

by Lemma 15.11 (i). Hence, $S_{\tilde{v},u} = o_p(n^{-1/2})$.   □

The last term $S_{\tilde{\eta},u} = o_p(n^{-1/2})$ can be proved by the same proof as $S_{\tilde{v},u} = o_p(n^{-1/2})$ by citing Lemma 15.11 (iii) rather than citing Lemma 15.11 (i).

Combining the proofs of (i), (ii), (iii) and (iv) with (15.72), we conclude that $\sqrt{n}(\hat{\gamma} - \gamma) \to N(0, \Phi^{-1}\Omega\Phi^{-1})$ in distribution.

For the second part of the theorem, we need to show that $\hat{\Sigma} = \Sigma + o_p(1)$, where $\hat{\Sigma} = \hat{\Phi}^{-1}\hat{\Omega}\hat{\Phi}^{-1}$. But $\hat{\Phi} = S_{W-\tilde{W}} = \Phi + o_p(1)$ is proved in the proof of (i) above. By similar arguments it is easy to show that $\hat{\Omega} = \Omega + o_p(1)$. Therefore, $\hat{\Sigma} = \Sigma + o_p(1)$.

Lemma 15.9. $\|\tilde{\alpha}_f - \alpha_f\| = O_p(\sum_{l=1}^{r}k_l^{-\delta_l})$, where $\tilde{\alpha}_f = (P'P)^{-1}P'f$, α_f satisfies Assumption 15.9, where $f = G$ or $f = m$.

Lemma 15.10. $S_{f-\tilde{f}} = O_p(\sum_{l=1}^{r}k_l^{-2\delta_l})$, where $f = G$ or $f = m$.

Lemma 15.11. *(i)* $S_{\tilde{v}} = O_p(K/n)$, *(ii)* $S_{\tilde{u}} = O_p(K/n)$, *(iii)* $S_{\tilde{\eta}} = O_p(K/n)$.

The proofs of Lemmas 15.9, 15.10, and 15.11 are similar to the proofs of Lemmas 15.5, 15.7, and 15.8, and therefore are omitted here.

15.6.4   Proof of Theorem 15.9

Proof of (i). Noting that

$$\hat{u}_i = Y_i - m(X_i, \hat{\gamma}) = u_i - [m(X_i, \hat{\gamma}) - m(X_i, \gamma_0)],$$

we have

$$
\begin{aligned}
\bar{I}_{se}^a = \; & n^{-1} \sum_{i=1}^{n} \sum_{j=1, j \neq i}^{n} u_i p^K(X_i)'(P'P)^{-1} p^K(X_j) u_j \\
& - 2n^{-1} \sum_{i=1}^{n} \sum_{j=1, j \neq i}^{n} [m(X_i, \hat{\gamma}) - m(X_i, \gamma_0)] \\
& \times p^K(X_i)'(P'P)^{-1} p^K(X_j) u_j \\
& + n^{-1} \sum_{i=1}^{n} \sum_{j=1, j \neq i}^{n} [m(X_i, \hat{\gamma}) - m(X_i, \gamma_0)] \\
& \times p^K(X_i)'(P'P)^{-1} p^K(X_j) \\
& \times [m(X_j, \hat{\gamma}) - m(X_j, \gamma_0)] \\
\equiv \; & I_{1n} - 2I_{2n} + I_{3n}.
\end{aligned}
$$

As in Newey (1997), we can show that $\hat{I}_n$, $\hat{S}_n$, S_n, S_n^* are all invariant to nonsingular linear transformations of $p^K(\mathbf{x})$, thus we assume throughout that $B = I_K$, i.e., that $p^K(x) = \mathbf{P}^K(x)$ defined in Assumption 15.2, and that $\mathrm{E}[p^K(\mathbf{x}) p^K(x)'] = I_K$ (I_K is the identity matrix of dimension K). Thus the smallest eigenvalue of $P'P/n$ converges in probability to one and

$$\sup_{1 \leq i \leq n} p^K(X_i)'(P'P)^{-1} p^K(X_i) \leq \lambda_{\min}^{-1}(P'P/n) \sup_{1 \leq i \leq n} p^K(X_i) p^K(X_i)/n$$

$$\leq \lambda_{\min}^{-1}(P'P/n) \xi_0^2(K)/n \xrightarrow{p} 0.$$

It follows from reasoning analogous to the proof of Theorem A.3 in Hong and White (1995) that

$$nI_{1n}/S_n \xrightarrow{d} N(0,1).$$

Now we show that both I_{2n} and I_{3n} are of the order $O_p(n^{-1})$. By using a Taylor series expansion, we have

$$
I_{2n} = n^{-1} \sum_{i=1}^{n} \sum_{j=1}^{n} (\hat{\gamma} - \gamma_0)' \nabla_\gamma m(X_i, \gamma_0) p^K(X_i)'(P'P)^{-1} p^K(X_j) u_j
$$

$$
- n^{-1} \sum_{i=1}^{n} (\hat{\gamma} - \gamma_0)' \nabla_\gamma m(X_i, \gamma_0) p^K(X_i)'(P'P)^{-1} p^K(X_i) u_i
$$

$$
+ (1/2) n^{-1} \sum_{i=1}^{n} \sum_{j=1}^{n} (\hat{\gamma} - \gamma_0)' \nabla_\gamma^2 m(X_i, \tilde{\gamma})(\hat{\gamma} - \gamma_0)
$$

$$
\times p^K(X_i)'(P'P)^{-1} p^K(X_j) u_j
$$

$$
- (1/2) n^{-1} \sum_{i=1}^{n} (\hat{\gamma} - \gamma_0)' \nabla_\gamma^2 m(X_i, \tilde{\gamma})(\hat{\gamma} - \gamma_0)
$$

$$
\times p^K(X_i)'(P'P)^{-1} p^K(X_i) u_i
$$

$$
\equiv (\hat{\gamma} - \gamma_0)' (I_{2n,1} - I_{2n,2}) + (1/2)(\hat{\gamma} - \gamma_0)'(I_{2n,3} - I_{2n,4})(\hat{\gamma} - \gamma_0).
$$

By $P(P'P)^{-1}P'$ being idempotent, we have

$$
\mathrm{E}\left(\|I_{2n,1}\|^2\right) \le \sum_{k=1}^{K} Cn^{-2} \mathrm{E}\Bigg\{ \sum_{i=1}^{n} \sum_{i'=1}^{n} \frac{\partial m(X_i, \gamma_0)}{\partial \gamma_k}
$$

$$
\times p^K(X_i)'(P'P)^{-1} p^K(X_{i'}) \frac{\partial m(X_{i'}, \gamma_0)}{\partial \gamma_k} \Bigg\}
$$

$$
\le \sum_{k=1}^{K} C n^{-2} \mathrm{E}\left\{ \sum_{i=1}^{n} \left[\frac{\partial m(X_i, \gamma_0)}{\partial \gamma_k} \right]^2 \right\}
$$

$$
= Cn^{-2} \sum_{i=1}^{n} \mathrm{E}\left\{ \|\nabla m(X_i, \gamma_0)\|^2 \right\} = O(n^{-1})
$$

and

$$
\mathrm{E}\left(\|I_{2n,2}\|^2\right) \le \sum_{k=1}^{K} Cn^{-2} \mathrm{E}\Bigg\{ \sum_{i=1}^{n} \left[\frac{\partial m(X_i, \gamma_0)}{\partial \gamma_k} \right]^2
$$

$$
\times \left[\sup_i p^K(X_i)'(P'P)^{-1} p^K(X_i) \right]^2 \Bigg\}
$$

$$
= Cn^{-2} \sum_{i=1}^{n} \mathrm{E}\left\{ \|\nabla m(x_i, \gamma_0)\|^2 \right\} o_p(1) = o(n^{-1}).
$$

It follows that $\|I_{2n,1} - I_{2n,2}\| \leq O_p(n^{-1/2})$ by Chebyshev's inequality. For $I_{2n,3}$ and $I_{2n,4}$, Cauchy's inequality and $P(P'P)^{-1}P'$ being idempotent lead to

$$
\|I_{2n,3}\|^2 = \sum_{k=1}^{K}\sum_{l=1}^{K}\left(n^{-1}\sum_{i=1}^{n}\sum_{j=1}^{n}\frac{\partial^2 m(X_i,\tilde{\gamma})}{\partial\gamma_k\partial\gamma_l}p^K(X_i)'(P'P)^{-1}p^K(X_j)u_j\right)^2
$$

$$
\leq \sum_{k=1}^{K}\sum_{l=1}^{K}\left(n^{-1}\sum_{i=1}^{n}\sum_{j=1}^{n}\frac{\partial^2 m(X_i,\tilde{\gamma})}{\partial\gamma_k\partial\gamma_l}p^K(X_i)'(P'P)^{-1}p^K(X_j)\frac{\partial^2 m(X_j,\tilde{\gamma})}{\partial\gamma_k\partial\gamma_l}\right)
$$

$$
\times \left(n^{-1}\sum_{j=1}^{n}u_j^2\right)
$$

$$
\leq \sum_{k=1}^{K}\sum_{l=1}^{K}\left(n^{-1}\sum_{i=1}^{n}\left[\frac{\partial^2 m(X_i,\tilde{\gamma})}{\partial\gamma_k\partial\gamma_l}\right]^2\right)\left(n^{-1}\sum_{i=1}^{n}\left(u_i^2-\sigma_i^2\right)+n^{-1}\sum_{i=1}^{n}\sigma_i^2\right)
$$

$$
= O_p(1),
$$

where the last inequality follows from Chebyshev's inequality. Thus, we have

$$
\|I_{2n,4}\|^2 Y = \sum_{k=1}^{K}\sum_{l=1}^{K}\left(n^{-1}\sum_{i=1}^{n}\frac{\partial^2 m(X_i,\tilde{\gamma})}{\partial\gamma_k\partial\gamma_l}p^K(X_i)'(P'P)^{-1}p^K(X_i)u_i\right)^2
$$

$$
\leq \sum_{k=1}^{K}\sum_{l=1}^{K}\left(n^{-1}\sum_{i=1}^{n}\left[\frac{\partial^2 m(X_i,\tilde{\gamma})}{\partial\gamma_k\partial\gamma_l}\right]^2\right)
$$

$$
\times \left(n^{-1}\sum_{j=1}^{n}u_j^2\right)\left[\sup_i p^k(X_i)'(P'P)^{-1}p^K(X_i)\right]^2 = o_p(1).
$$

So $\|I_{2n,3} - I_{2n,4}\| \leq O_p(1)$ and thus

$$
|I_{2n}| \leq \|\hat{\gamma} - \gamma_0\|\,\|I_{2n,1} - I_{2n,2}\| + (1/2)\,\|\hat{\gamma} - \gamma_0\|^2\,\|I_{2n,3} - I_{2n,4}\|
$$

$$
\leq O_p(n^{-1}).
$$

By the mean value expansion,

$$
m(X_i,\hat{\gamma} - m(fX_i,\gamma_0)) = \nabla_\gamma m(fX_i,\overline{\gamma})'(\hat{\gamma} - \gamma_0),\quad i=1,\ldots,n,
$$

where $\bar{\gamma} \in \Gamma$ is such that $\|\tilde{\gamma} - \gamma_0\| \leq \|\hat{\gamma} - \gamma_0\|$, we can write

$$I_{3n} = n^{-1} \sum_{i=1}^{n} \sum_{j=1}^{n} (\hat{\gamma} - \gamma_0)' \nabla m(X_i, \bar{\gamma}) p^K(x_i)' (P'P)^{-1} p^K(X_j)$$
$$\times \nabla m(X_j, \bar{\gamma})' (\hat{\gamma} - \gamma_0)$$
$$- n^{-1} \sum_{i=1}^{n} (\hat{\gamma} - \gamma_0)' \nabla m(X_i, \bar{\gamma}) p^K(x_i)' (P'P)^{-1} p^K(X_j)$$
$$\times \nabla m(x_i, \bar{\gamma})' (\hat{\gamma} - \gamma_0)$$
$$= (\hat{\gamma} - \gamma_0)' (I_{3n,1} - I_{3n,2})(\hat{\gamma} - \gamma_0).$$

Similarly, by Cauchy inequality and $P(P'P)^{-1}P'$ being idempotent, we have

$$\|I_{3n,1}\|^2 \leq \sum_{k=1}^{K} \sum_{l=1}^{K} \left(n^{-1} \sum_{i=1}^{n} \left[\frac{\partial m(x_i, \bar{\gamma})}{\partial \gamma_k} \right]^2 \right) \left(n^{-1} \sum_{i=1}^{n} \left[\frac{\partial m(x_i, \bar{\gamma})}{\partial \gamma_l} \right]^2 \right)$$
$$= O_p(1)$$

and

$$\|I_{3n,2}\|^2 \leq \left[\sup_i p^K(X_i)' (P'P)^{-1} p^K(X_i) \right]^2$$
$$\times \sum_{k=1}^{K} \sum_{l=1}^{K} \left(n^{-1} \sum_{i=1}^{n} \left[\frac{\partial m(X_i, \bar{\gamma})}{\partial \gamma_k} \right]^2 \right)$$
$$\times \left(n^{-1} \sum_{i=1}^{n} \left[\frac{\partial m(X_i, \bar{\gamma})}{\partial \gamma_l} \right]^2 \right)$$
$$= o_p(1).$$

So we get $\|I_{3n,1} - I_{3n,2}\| = O_p(1)$. Therefore

$$|I_{3n}| \leq \|\hat{\gamma} - \gamma_0\|^2 \|I_{3n,1} - I_{3n,2}\| = O_p(n^{-1}).$$

Summarizing the above results and using $S_n = O_p(K^{1/2})$ and $\hat{S}_n = S_n + o_p(S_n)$ under H_0, we complete the proof of (i), i.e.,

$$\bar{J}_{se}^a = n\bar{I}_{se}^a / \hat{S}_n + o_p(1) \xrightarrow{d} N(0,1).$$

$\square$

Proof of (ii). Under H_1^a,

$$\hat{u}_i = Y_i - m(X_i, \hat{\gamma}) = u_i - [m(X_i, \hat{\gamma}) - m(X_i, \gamma^*)] - [m(X_i, \gamma^*) - \theta_0(X_i)].$$

Since $\hat{\gamma} - \gamma^* = o_p(1)$ and $E(u_i|X_i) = 0$, one can easily show that the terms related to $[m(X_i, \hat{\gamma}) - m(X_i, \gamma^*)]$ and u_i are all $o_p(1)$. Hence, under H_1^a, the leading term is the following term that does not contain either u_i or $[m(X_i, \hat{\gamma}) - m(X_i, \gamma^*)]$. Hence, we have

$$\bar{I}_{se}^a = A_n + (1), \tag{15.73}$$

where

$$A_n = n^{-1} \sum_i \sum_{j \neq i} [m(X_i, \gamma^*) - \theta_0(X_i)] p^K(X_i)'(P'P)^{-1} p^K(X_j)$$
$$\times [m(X_j, \gamma^*) - \theta_0(X_j)].$$

Since there exists a $K \times 1$ vector β_K such that as $K \to \infty$,

$$E\left[\{m(\mathbf{x}, \gamma^*) - \theta_0(\mathbf{x}) - \mathbf{p}^K(\mathbf{x})'\beta_K\}^2\right] \to 0,$$

through adding and subtracting terms, we get

$$\sum_{j=1}^n p^K(X_i)'(P'P)^{-1} p^K(X_j)[m(X_j, \gamma^*) - \theta_0(X_j)]$$
$$= [m(X_i, \gamma^*) - \theta_0(X_i)] + \left[p^K(X_i)'\beta_K - m(X_i, \gamma^*) + \theta_0(X_i)\right]$$
$$+ \sum_{j=1}^n p^K(x_i)'(P'P)^{-1} p^K(X_j)[m(X_j, \gamma^*) - \theta_0(X_j) - p^K(X_j)'\beta_K].$$

$$\tag{15.74}$$

Substituting (15.74) into (15.73), and noting that the terms related to $\left[p^K(fX_i)'\beta_K - m(X_i, \gamma^*) + \theta_0(X_i)\right]$ are all $o_p(1)$, we have

$$A_n = n^{-1} \sum_i [m(X_i, \gamma^*) - \theta_0(X_i)]^2$$
$$+ n^{-1} \sum_i [m(X_i, \gamma^*) - \theta_0(X_i)]$$
$$\times [p^K(X_i)'\beta_K - m(X_i, \gamma^*) + \theta_0(X_i)] \tag{15.75}$$
$$= n^{-1} \sum_i \sum_j [m(X_i, \gamma^*) - \theta_0(x_i)] p^K(X_i)'(P'P)^{-1} p^K(X_j)$$
$$\times \left[m(X_j, \gamma^*) - \theta_0(X_j) - p^K(X_j)'\beta_K\right].$$

Since $\mathrm{E}\{[p^K(x)'\beta_K - m(x,\gamma^*) + \theta_0(x)]^2\} = o(1)$, we obtain

$$\bar{I}^a_{se} \xrightarrow{p} \mathrm{E}\left\{[m(X_i,\gamma^*) - \theta_0(X_i)]^2\right\} \equiv C > 0.$$

Hence, from (15.75), the fact that $S^*_n = O_p(K^{1/2})$ and $\hat{S}_n = S^*_n + o_p(S^*_n)$, we obtain $\bar{J}^a_{se} = n\bar{I}_{se}/\hat{S}_n = O_p(n/K^{1/2})$ under H^a_1. Part (ii) follows immediately from this. □

15.6.5 Proof of Theorem 15.10

In this section we use (typically capital) letters without the subscript i to denote vectors or matrices. For example, $\mathcal{H}(X,x)$, U, $\hat{U}$, m and $\phi(x)$ are $n \times 1$ vectors whose ith elements are given by $\mathcal{H}(X_i,x)$, u_i, $\hat{u}_i$, $m(X_i)$ and $\phi_i(x)$, respectively. Also for an $n \times 1$ (or $d \times 1$) vector $\mathcal{A}$, we use $||\mathcal{A}||$ to denote its Euclidean norm.

Proof of Theorem 15.10 (i). Note that

$$\begin{aligned}
\hat{u}_i &= Y_i - z_0(X_i)'\hat{\gamma} - p^K(X_i)\hat{\beta} \\
&= u_i - z_0(X_i)'(\hat{\gamma} - \gamma) + m(X_i) - \hat{m}(X_i), \text{ and} \\
\hat{m}(X_i) &\equiv p_K(X_i)'\hat{\beta} = p^K(X_i)'(P'P)^- P'(Y - Z_0\hat{\gamma}).
\end{aligned}$$

Hence we have, in vector-matrix notation,

$$\begin{aligned}
\hat{m} &= P(P'P)^- P'(Y - Z_0\hat{\gamma}) = M_n(Y - Z_0\hat{\gamma}) \\
&= M_n[U - Z_0(\hat{\gamma} - \gamma) + m] \text{ and} \qquad\qquad (15.76) \\
\hat{U} &= U - M_nU - (I_n - M_n)Z_0(\hat{\gamma} - \gamma) + (I_n - M_n)m.
\end{aligned}$$

Using (15.76), we get

$$\begin{aligned}
\hat{J}_n(x) &= n^{-1/2}\sum_i \mathcal{H}(X_i,x)\hat{u}_i = n^{-1/2}(\mathcal{H}(X,x))'\hat{U} \\
&= n^{-1/2}(\mathcal{H}(X,x))'U - n^{-1/2}(\mathcal{H}(X,x))'M_nU \\
&\quad - n^{-1/2}(\mathcal{H}(X,x))'(I_n - M_n)Z_0(\hat{\gamma} - \gamma) \qquad (15.77) \\
&\quad + n^{-1/2}(\mathcal{H}(X,x))'(I_n - M_n)m \\
&\equiv J_{n1}(x) - J_{n2}(x) - J_{n3}(x) + J_{n4}(x).
\end{aligned}$$

Lemma 15.12 shows that $||J_{n2}(\cdot) - n^{-1/2}\phi(\cdot)'U||_\nu = o_p(1)$, where $\phi(x)$ is an $n \times 1$ vector with the ith component given by $\phi_i(x) = \mathrm{E}_\mathcal{G}[\mathcal{H}(X_i,x)]$. Lemma 15.14 establishes that $||J_{n4}(\cdot) - n^{-1/2}\psi(\cdot)'U||_\nu =$

$o_p(1)$, where $\psi(x)$ is an $n \times 1$ vector with the ith component given by $\psi_i(x) = \mathrm{E}[\mathcal{H}(X_i, x)\epsilon_i']\{\mathrm{E}[\epsilon_i\epsilon_i']\}^{-1}\epsilon_i$ and $\epsilon_i = z_0(X_i) - \mathrm{E}_{\mathcal{G}}[z_0(X_i)]$. Lemma 15.13 proves that $||J_{n3}(\cdot)||_\nu = o_p(1)$

Define

$$J_n(x) = n^{-1/2} \sum_i [\mathcal{H}(X_i, x) - \phi_i(x) - \psi_i(x)]u_i$$

$$\equiv n^{-1/2} \sum_i Z_i(x).$$

Then by Lemmas 15.12 through 15.14, we have

$$||\hat{J}_n(\cdot) - J_n(\cdot)||_\nu = o_p(1). \tag{15.78}$$

It is easy to see that $\mathrm{E}[||J_n(\cdot)||_\nu^2] < \infty$, i.e., $J_n(\cdot)$ is tight. Hence, by the CLT for Hilbert-valued random arrays we have that

$$J_n(\cdot) \text{ converges weakly to } J_\infty(\cdot) \text{ in } \mathcal{L}_2(\mathcal{S}, \nu, ||.||_\nu), \tag{15.79}$$

where $J_\infty(\cdot)$ is a Gaussian process with mean zero and covariance function given by

$$\Sigma(x, x') = \mathrm{cov}(J_n(x), J_n(x')) = \mathrm{E}[Z_i(x)Z_i(x')]$$

$$= \mathrm{E}\Big\{\sigma^2(X_i)[\mathcal{H}(X_i, x) - \phi_i(x) - \psi_i(x)]$$

$$\times \big[\mathcal{H}(X_i, x') - \phi_i(x') - \psi_i(x')\big]\Big\}.$$

Equation (15.78) implies that $\hat{J}_n(\cdot)$ and $J_n(\cdot)$ have the same limiting distribution, thus this and (15.79) imply that $\hat{J}_n(\cdot)$ converges weakly to $J_\infty(\cdot)$. This completes the proof of Theorem 15.10 (i). □

Proof of Theorem 15.10 (ii). Clearly $h(J) \stackrel{\mathrm{def}}{=} \int [J(x)]^2 F(dx)$ is a continuous function in $\mathcal{L}_2(S, F)$. Given that F is absolutely continuous with respect to the Lebesgue measure ν, $h(J)$ is also continuous in $\mathcal{L}_2(S, \nu)$. Therefore, by Theorem 15.10 (i) and the continuous mapping theorem, we have $\int [\hat{J}_n(x)]^2 F(dx)$ converges to $\int [J_\infty(x)]^2 F(dx)$ in distribution.

Now, define $A_n = CM_n - h(\hat{J}_n^2)$. Li, Hsiao and Zinn (2003) have shown that $A_n = o_p(1)$.

Therefore, we have

$$CM_n = \int [\hat{J}_n(x)]^2 F(dx) + A_n = \int [\hat{J}_n(x)]^2 F(dx) + o_p(1)$$

$$\to \int [J_\infty(x)]^2 F(dx)$$

in distribution by the result of Theorem 15.10 (i) and the continuous mapping theorem. This completes the proof of Theorem 15.10 (ii). $\square$

Below we present some lemmas that are used in the proofs of Theorem 15.10. For an $n \times d$ matrix A, we denote $\tilde{A} = M_n A$ and let $\tilde{A}_i$ be the ith component of $\tilde{A}$. For example, $\tilde{m} = M_n m$ and $\tilde{Z}_0 = M_n Z_0$.

Lemma 15.12. $||J_{n2}(\cdot) - n^{-1/2}\phi(\cdot)'U||_\nu^2 = o_p(1)$, where $\phi(x)$ is an $n \times 1$ vector with the ith element given by $\phi_i(x) = \mathrm{E}_\mathcal{G}[\mathcal{H}(X_i, x)]$.

Proof. Define $V_i(x) = \mathcal{H}(X_i, x) - \phi_i(x)$. Then $\mathrm{E}_\mathcal{G}(V_i(x)) = 0$ and $\mathrm{E}_\mathcal{G}(V_i^2(x))$ is bounded for any $x \in \mathcal{S}$, and we have

$$\mathrm{E}[||J_{n2}(\cdot) - n^{-1/2}\phi(\cdot)'U||_\nu^2 | X]$$

$$= n^{-1} \int [(\mathcal{H}(X, x))'M_n - \phi(x)']\mathrm{E}(UU'|X)[M_n\mathcal{H}(X, x) - \phi(x)]\nu(dx)$$

$$\leq Cn^{-1} \int [M_n\mathcal{H}(X, x) - \phi(x)]'[M_n\mathcal{H}(X, x) - \phi(x)]\nu(dx)$$

$$= Cn^{-1}||M_n\mathcal{H}(X, x) - \phi(x)||_\nu^2$$

$$= Cn^{-1}||M_n(\phi(x) + V(x)) - \phi(x)||_\nu^2$$

$$\leq 2Cn^{-1}\left\{||M_n\phi(x) - \phi(x)||_\nu^2] + ||M_nV(x)||_\nu^2\right\}$$

$$= O_p\left(\sum_{l=1}^L K_l^{-2\delta_l} + K/n\right)$$

$$= o_p(1) \text{ by Lemmas 15.15, and 15.16.}$$

$\square$

Lemma 15.13. $||J_{n3}(\cdot) - n^{-1/2}\psi(\cdot)U||_\nu^2 = o_p(1)$.

Proof. Note that $z_0(X_i) - \tilde{z}_0(X_i)$ estimates $\epsilon_i = z_0(X_i) - \mathrm{E}_\mathcal{G}[z_0(X_i)]$, or in matrix notation $Z_0 - M_n Z_0$ estimates ϵ. From Lemma 15.17 we know that $(\hat{\gamma} - \gamma) = \{\mathrm{E}[\epsilon_i\epsilon_i']\}^{-1}n^{-1}\sum_i \epsilon_i u_i + o_p(n^{-1/2})$. Using Lemmas 15.15 and 15.16 we have $||n^{-1}\mathcal{H}(X, .)'(I_n - M_n)Z_0 - \mathrm{E}[\mathcal{H}(X_i, .)'\epsilon_i]||_\nu^2 = o_p(1)$. Hence,

$$J_{n3}(\cdot) = n^{-1/2}\mathcal{H}(X, .)'(I_n - M_n)Z_0(\hat{\gamma} - \gamma)$$

$$= \mathrm{E}[\mathcal{H}(X_i, .)\epsilon_i][n^{1/2}(\hat{\gamma} - \gamma)] + o_p(1)$$

$$= \mathrm{E}[\mathcal{H}(X_i, .)\epsilon_i]\{\mathrm{E}[\epsilon_i\epsilon_i']\}^{-1}[n^{-1/2}\sum_i \epsilon_i u_i] + o_p(1)$$

$$= n^{-1/2}\psi(\cdot)U + o_p(1).$$

□

Lemma 15.14. $||J_{n4}(\cdot)||_\nu^2 = o_p(1)$.

Proof.

$$||J_{n4}(\cdot)||_\nu^2 \leq n^{-1} \sum_i \sum_j \int \mathcal{H}(X_i, x)\mathcal{H}(X_j, x)(m_i - \tilde{m}_i)(m_j - \tilde{m}_j)\nu(dx)$$

$$\leq C \sum_i \int \left[(m_i - \tilde{m}_i)^2\right] \nu(dx)$$

$$= C \left[||m - \tilde{m}||_\nu^2\right] = nO_p \left(\sum_{l=1}^{L} K_l^{-2\delta_l}\right) = o_p(1)$$

by Lemma 15.15.   □

Lemma 15.15. *Let $f_i(x) \equiv f_0(x, X_i) \in \mathcal{G}$ (the class of additive functions), where $f_0(x, X_i)$ is of dimension $d \times 1$ (d is a finite positive integer). Let $f_X(x)$ denote the $n \times d$ matrix with the ith row given by $f_i(x)'$. Define $\tilde{f}_X(x) = M_n f_X(x)$. Then*

$$n^{-1}||f_X(x) - M_n f_X(x)||_\nu^2 = O_p \left(\sum_l K_l^{-2\delta_l}\right) = o_p(1).$$

Proof.

$$n^{-1}\mathrm{E}\left[||f_X(x) - M_n f_X(x)||_\nu^2\right] \equiv n^{-1}\mathrm{E}[||f_X(x) - \tilde{f}_X(x)||_\nu^2]$$

$$= n^{-1} \int \mathrm{E}\left[||f_X(x) - \tilde{f}_X(x)||^2\right] \nu(dx)$$

$$= O \left(\sum_l K_l^{-2\delta_l}\right)$$

by the result of Andrews and Whang (1990), Newey (1995, 1997), or by Lemma A.4 of Li (2000).   □

Lemma 15.16. *Let $v_i(x) \equiv V(x, X_i)$ with $\mathrm{E}_\mathcal{G}(v_i(x)) = 0$ and with $\mathrm{E}_\mathcal{G}([v_i(x)]^2)$ being uniformly bounded in $x \in \mathcal{S}$. Also, define $V(x) = (v_1(x), \ldots, v_n(x))'$ and $\tilde{V}(x) = M_n V(x)$. Then we have*

$$n^{-1}||M_n V(\cdot)||_\nu^2 = n^{-1}||\tilde{V}(\cdot)||_\nu^2 = O_p(K/n) = o_p(1).$$

Proof. Without loss of generality we can assume $\mathrm{E}[p^K(X_i)p^K(X_i)'] = I_K$ (see the arguments at the beginning of Section 15.6, before the proof of Theorem 15.1). First we show that $\mathrm{E}[\|P'V(\cdot)/n\|_\nu^2] = O((K/n)^{1/2})$. Note that $p^K(X_i) \in \mathcal{G}$ and $v_i(\cdot) \perp \mathcal{G}$ imply that $\mathrm{E}[p^K(X_i)v_i(\cdot)] = 0$. We have

$$
\begin{aligned}
\mathrm{E}[\|P'V(\cdot)/n\|_\nu^2] = n^{-2}\Bigg\{ &\sum_i \int \mathrm{E}\left[v_i(x)^2 p^K(X_i)' p^K(X_i)\right] \nu(dx) \\
&+ \sum_i \sum_{j \neq i} \int \mathrm{E}\left[v_i(x)p^K(X_i)'\right] \\
&\times \mathrm{E}\left[v_j(x)p^K(X_j)\right] \nu(dx) \Bigg\} \\
= &\; n^{-1} \int \mathrm{E}\left[v_1(x)^2 p^K(X_1)' p^K(X_1)\right] \nu(dx) \\
\leq &\; Cn^{-1}\mathrm{E}\left[p^K(X_1)' p^K(X_1)\right] = O(K/n).
\end{aligned}
$$

This implies that

$$\|P'V(x)/n\|_\nu^2 = O_p(K/n) = o_p(1). \tag{15.80}$$

Then

$$
\begin{aligned}
n^{-1}\|M_n V(\cdot)\|_\nu^2 &= n^{-1} \int V(x)' M_n V(x)\nu(dx) \\
&= \int (V(x)'P/n)(P'P/n)^-(P'V(x)/n)\nu(dx) \\
&= \int (V(x)'P/n)[I + (P'P/n)^- - I](P'V(x)/n)\nu(dx) \\
&= \int \|P'V(x)/n\|^2[1 + o_p(1)]\nu(dx) \\
&= \int O_p(K/n)[1 + o_p(1)]\nu(dx) \\
&= O_p(K/n) = o_p(1)
\end{aligned}
$$

by (15.80) and the fact that $\|(P'P/n)^- - I\| = O_p(\zeta_0(K)\sqrt{K}/\sqrt{n}) = o_p(1)$ (see the proof of Theorem 1 of Newey (1997, pp. 161–162)). $\quad\square$

Lemma 15.17.

$$(\hat{\gamma} - \gamma) = \left\{\mathrm{E}\left[\epsilon_i \epsilon_i'\right]\right\}^{-1}\left\{n^{-1}\sum_i \epsilon_i u_i\right\} + o_p(n^{-1/2}),$$

where $\epsilon_i = z_0(X_i) - \mathrm{E}_{\mathcal{G}}(z_0(X_i))$.

This was proved in Theorem 2.1 of Li (2000). Note that Lemma 15.17 implies that $\hat{\gamma} - \gamma = O_p\left(n^{-1/2}\right)$.

15.7 Exercises

Exercise 15.1. Assuming that $\mathrm{E}(u_i^2|X_i) = \mathrm{E}(u_i^2) = \sigma^2$, prove Theorem 15.2.

Hint: Define $A_n = n^{1/2} V_k^{-1/2}(\hat{g}(x) - g(x))$. Then show that (i) $\mathrm{E}[A_n] = O\left((nK)^{1/2}K^{-\alpha}\right) = o(1)$ by Assumption 15.2, $\mathrm{var}[A_n] = nV_K^{-1}\mathrm{var}(\hat{g}(x)) = nV_K^{-1}[n^{-1}V_K + o(1)] = 1 + o(1)$. It can be verified that Liapunov's CLT conditions hold for A_n. Thus, $A_n \xrightarrow{d} N(0,1)$. Further, show that (ii) $\hat{V}_K = V_K + o_p(1)$.

Theorem 15.2 follows from (i) and (ii).

Exercise 15.2. Derive (15.14).

The next three exercises refer to Section 15.3.2 (Selection of Nonlinear Additive Components).

Exercise 15.3. Write a program for additive models using a power series estimator and use Huang and Yang's (2004) BIC criterion to select the significant variables.

Exercise 15.4. Repeat Exercise 15.3 but use the leave-one-out method to select the number of series terms.

Exercise 15.5. Show that $\theta_{\alpha l}$ defined in (15.35) is given by $\theta_{lj} = \int_{-1}^{1} g_\alpha(z_\alpha) p_l(z_\alpha) dz_\alpha$.

Hint: Multiply both sides of (15.35) by $p_s(z_\alpha)$, integrate over z_α and use $\int p_l(z_\alpha) p_s(z_\alpha) dz_\alpha = \delta_{ls}$.

Exercise 15.6. Prove (15.60).

Hint: (i) Define $I_{n,se}^{a,0} = n^{-2} \sum_i \sum_{j \neq i} u_i p^K(x_i)'(P'P)^- p^K(x_j) u_j = 2n^{-2} \sum_i \sum_{j>i} u_i p^K(x_i)'(P'P)^- p^K(x_j) u_j$. Compute $\mathrm{E}[(n/K^{1/2})I_{n,se}^{a,0}]$ and $\mathrm{var}[(n/K^{1/2})I_{n,se}^{a,0}]$, and show that $(n/K)^{1/2} I_{n,se}^{a,0}/\hat{\sigma}_{se,a}^2 \xrightarrow{d} N(0,1)$ under H_0^a. (ii) show that $I_{n,se}^a - I_{se,n}^{a,0} = o_p(K^{1/2}/n)$. Equation (15.60) follows from (i) and (ii).

Part V

Time Series, Simultaneous Equation, and Panel Data Models

Chapter 16

Instrumental Variables and Efficient Estimation of Semiparametric Models

The assumption that the regressors and the disturbances are uncorrelated in a parametric regression model (i.e., that the regressors are exogenous) is a crucial assumption for deriving consistency. Even when all other classical assumptions hold, without this assumption least squares loses its appeal as an estimator. In many social science applications, this assumption may be violated. An alternative method often used in such cases is known as the method of "instrumental variables" or simply "IV estimation." Parametric models, however, are not the only class of models that suffer when the regressors are endogenous. In this chapter, we consider a set of semiparametric estimators that have been developed to handle the presence of endogenous regressors.

16.1 A Partially Linear Model with Endogenous Regressors in the Parametric Part

We first consider a semiparametric partially linear time series model of the form[1]

$$Y_t = X_t'\beta + \theta(Z_t) + u_t, \quad t = 1, \dots, n, \qquad (16.1)$$

---

[1] See Chapter 18 for the asymptotic theory underlying nonparametric estimation with dependent data.

where X_t is of dimension $p \times 1$, β is a $p \times 1$ vector of unknown parameters, Z_t is of dimension q, and $\theta(\cdot)$ is an unspecified smooth function. We allow X_t to contain lagged values of Y_t; for instance, the first element of X_t might be Y_{t-1}, hence (16.1) constitutes a semiparametric dynamic model. We shall assume that Z_t is weakly exogenous in the sense that $E(u_t|Z_s) = 0$ for $s \leq t$. The asymptotic theory of nonparametric estimation with dependent data (i.e., time series) is discussed in Chapter 18.

We allow for the possibility that the error u_t is serially correlated. If $\theta(z) = z'\gamma$ is linear in z, (16.1) becomes a parametric linear model, and one may choose a linear combination of Z_{t-1}, say $Z'_{t-1}\alpha$, as an instrument for Y_{t-1} (α is a $q \times 1$ vector of constants), because it can be shown that $E(Y_{t-1}Z'_{t-1}\alpha) \neq 0$ in general, and that $E(u_t Z'_{t-1}\alpha) = 0$ by our assumption that Z_t is weakly exogenous. Thus, $Z'_{t-1}\alpha$ is a legitimate instrument for Y_{t-1} if the model is linear in Z_t. However, for the general function $\theta(\cdot)$, it is possible that Y_{t-1} and Z_{t-1} are uncorrelated. For example, assume that Z_t is a scalar for expositional simplicity, and assume that $\theta(Z_t) = Z_t^2$, the data is strictly stationary, and $E(Z_t^3) = 0$. Then it can be shown that $E(Y_{t-1}Z_{t-1}) = 0$ (Exercise 16.1). Hence, one should not use Z_{t-1} as an instrument for Y_{t-1} when the functional form of $\theta(\cdot)$ is unknown. From (16.1) it is obvious that Y_{t-1} is correlated with some function of Z_{t-1}, say $\theta(Z_{t-1})$. If we restrict ourselves to constructing an instrument from a function of Z_{t-1}, then following Newey (1990a), it can be shown that the optimal instrument in this case is $E(Y_{t-1}|Z_{t-1})$. This optimal instrument function is unknown, but it can be consistently estimated by any nonparametric method such as kernel, k-nn or series methods.

Equation (16.1) contains an unknown function $\theta(\cdot)$. Following Robinson (1988), we first eliminate $\theta(\cdot)$. Taking the expectation of (16.1) conditional on Z_t, then subtracting it from (16.1), we get

$$Y_t - E(Y_t|Z_t) = (X_t - E(X_t|Z_t))'\beta + u_t \equiv v_t'\beta + u_t, \qquad (16.2)$$

where we have used $E(u_t|Z_t) = 0$, and $v_t \stackrel{\text{def}}{=} X_t - E(X_t|Z_t)$. Note that v_t and u_t may be correlated because v_t contains lagged values of Y_t, and u_t could be serially correlated. Suppose there exists a $d \times 1$ ($d \geq p$) instrumental variable W_t that is correlated with X_t and uncorrelated with u_t (see (16.5) below for details). Writing (16.2) in vector-matrix notation, X and v ($v = X - E(X|Z)$) are $n \times p$, W is $n \times d$, and Y, $E(Y|Z)$, and u are all $n \times 1$. Multiplying the matrix version of (16.2) by W', we get

$$W'(Y - \mathrm{E}(Y|Z)) = W'v\beta + W'u. \tag{16.3}$$

Applying the method of least squares to (16.3), we obtain an IV-OLS estimator for β given by

$$\begin{aligned}
\tilde{\beta}_{IVO} &= (v'WW'v)^{-1}v'WW'(Y - \mathrm{E}(Y|Z)) \\
&= \beta + (v'WW'v)^{-1}v'WW'u,
\end{aligned} \tag{16.4}$$

where W and v are of dimension $n \times d$ and $n \times p$, respectively, with typical rows given by W_t' and v_t'.

We impose the following conditions to derive the asymptotic distribution of $\tilde{\beta}_{IVO}$:

$$W'v/n \xrightarrow{p} \mathrm{E}\left[W_t v_t'\right] \equiv A,$$

$$\frac{1}{n}\sum_{t=1}^{n}\sum_{s=1}^{n} \mathrm{E}\left[W_t W_s' u_t u_s\right] \xrightarrow{p} B, \tag{16.5}$$

$$W'u/\sqrt{n} \xrightarrow{d} N(0, B),$$

where we require that A has full column rank and that B is a finite positive definite matrix. Note that when the data are i.i.d. across t (e.g., cross-sectional data) or u_t is a martingale difference process, then $B = \mathrm{E}\left[\sigma^2(W_t)W_t W_t'\right]$ ($\sigma^2(W_t) = \mathrm{E}(u_t^2|W_t)$) in (16.5). For general time series data where u_t is not a martingale difference process, the expression for B depends on the specific error process for u_t.

Using (16.5), one can easily show that

$$\sqrt{n}\left(\tilde{\beta}_{IVO} - \beta\right) \to N(0, V_O) \text{ in distribution}, \tag{16.6}$$

where $V_O = Q^{-1}A'BAQ^{-1}$, and $Q = A'A$ with A and B defined in (16.5). The proof of (16.6) is left as an exercise (see Exercise 16.2).

Next we consider the case for which the error u_t is a martingale difference process and is conditionally homoskedastic, i.e., the error u_t is one for which $\mathrm{E}(u_t|W_t, Z_t, \Omega_{t-1}) = 0$ (Ω_τ denotes the information set up to time period τ), and $\mathrm{E}(u_t^2|W_t, Z_t, \Omega_{t-1}) = \mathrm{E}(u_t^2) = \sigma^2$. The error $w'u/\sqrt{n}$ in (16.3) has variance $B = \sigma^2\mathrm{E}[W_t W_t']$. In this case, we can estimate β using the following IV-GLS estimator:

$$\tilde{\beta}_{IVG} = (v'W(W'W)^{-1}W'v)^{-1}v'W(W'W)^{-1}W'(Y - \mathrm{E}(Y|Z)). \tag{16.7}$$

To derive the asymptotic distribution of $\tilde{\beta}_{IVG}$, we make the following assumptions:

$$w'v/n \xrightarrow{p} \mathrm{E}[W_t'v_t] \equiv \bar{A},$$
$$W'W/n \xrightarrow{p} \mathrm{E}[W_t W_t'] = \bar{B},$$
$$W'u/n \xrightarrow{p} \mathrm{E}[W_t u_t] = 0, \tag{16.8}$$
$$W'u/\sqrt{n} \xrightarrow{d} N(0, \sigma^2 \bar{B}).$$

If we use (16.8), it is straightforward to show that

$$\sqrt{n}\left(\tilde{\beta}_{IVG} - \beta\right) \to N(0, V_G) \text{ in distribution}, \tag{16.9}$$

where $V_G = \sigma^2(\bar{A}\bar{B}^{-1}\bar{A}')^{-1}$ where $\bar{A}$ and $\bar{B}$ are defined in (16.8).

It can be shown that $V_G - V_O$ is negative semidefinite (see, e.g., White (1984)). Hence, $\tilde{\beta}_{IVG}$ is asymptotically more efficient than $\tilde{\beta}_{IVO}$. When the conditionally homoskedastic error assumption is violated, $\tilde{\beta}_{IVG}$ is still a $\sqrt{n}$-consistent estimator for β, but it will have a different asymptotic variance and may not be more efficient than $\hat{\beta}_{IVO}$.

Write $X_t' = (Y_{t-1}, \dots, Y_{t-d_1}, X_{t2}')$, where the dimension of X_{t2} is $d - d_1$. Suppose that X_{t2} is weakly exogenous, i.e., $\mathrm{E}(u_s | X_{t2}) = 0$ for all $t \leq s$. Then we need to find instruments for $X_{t1}' = (Y_{t-1}, \dots, Y_{t-d_1})$ only if we want to construct an instrument for Y_{t-s} using a function of Z_{t-s}. As discussed above, $W_{ts} = \mathrm{E}(Y_{t-s} | Z_{t-s})$ should be chosen as an instrument for Y_{t-s}. Let $\hat{W}_t = (\hat{W}_{t1}, \dots, \hat{W}_{td_1})$, where $\hat{W}_{ts} = \hat{\mathrm{E}}(Y_{t-s} | Z_{t-s})$ for $s = 1, \dots, d_1$. Let $\hat{v}_t = X_t - \hat{\mathrm{E}}(X_t | Z_t)$ and $\hat{Y}_t = \hat{\mathrm{E}}(Y_t | Z_t)$ denote the nonparametric estimators of $X_t - \mathrm{E}(X_t | Z_t)$ and $\mathrm{E}(Y_t | Z_t)$, respectively. Then the feasible IV-OLS estimator is given by

$$\hat{\beta}_{IVO} = \left(\hat{v}'\hat{W}\hat{W}'\hat{v}\right)^{-1} \hat{v}'\hat{W}\hat{W}'\left(Y - \hat{\mathrm{E}}(Y|Z)\right). \tag{16.10}$$

If the error is conditionally homoskedastic, we can estimate β by the feasible IV-GLS estimator given by

$$\hat{\beta}_{IVG} = \left(\hat{v}'\hat{W}\left(\hat{W}'\hat{W}\right)^{-1}\hat{W}'\hat{v}\right)^{-1} \hat{v}'\hat{W}\left(\hat{W}'\hat{W}\right)^{-1}\hat{W}'\left(Y - \hat{\mathrm{E}}(Y|Z)\right). \tag{16.11}$$

Under the condition that the nonparametric estimation MSE has an order smaller than $n^{-1/2}$, then it can be shown that

$$\sqrt{n}\left(\hat{\beta}_{IVO} - \beta\right) \to N(0, V_O) \text{ in distribution}, \tag{16.12}$$

where V_O is that defined in (16.6). If the error u_t is a martingale difference process and conditionally homoskedastic, then

$$\sqrt{n}\left(\hat{\beta}_{IVG} - \beta\right) \to N(0, V_G) \text{ in distribution,} \qquad (16.13)$$

where V_G is the same as that defined in (16.9).

If instead we were to use nonparametric kernel methods, the proofs of (16.12) and (16.13) would be similar to the proof of Theorem 7.1 of Chapter 7. Let $\tilde{\beta}$ denote $\tilde{\beta}_{IVO}$ or $\tilde{\beta}_{IVG}$, and $\hat{\beta}$ denote $\hat{\beta}_{IVO}$ or $\hat{\beta}_{IVG}$. One can write $\sqrt{n}(\hat{\beta} - \beta) = \sqrt{n}(\hat{\beta} - \tilde{\beta}) + \sqrt{n}(\tilde{\beta} - \beta)$. $\hat{\beta} - \tilde{\beta}$ is of order $(\sum_{s=1}^{q} h_s^{2\nu} + (nh_1 \ldots h_q)^{-1})$ (ν is the order of the kernel function). If $\hat{\beta} - \tilde{\beta}$ is $o_p(n^{-1/2})$, then we have $\sqrt{n}(\hat{\beta} - \beta) = \sqrt{n}(\tilde{\beta} - \beta) + o_p(1) \to N(0, V)$ by (16.6) or (16.13). Thus, the feasible estimator $\hat{\beta}$ has the same (first order) asymptotic distribution as the infeasible estimator $\tilde{\beta}$.

16.2 A Varying Coefficient Model with Endogenous Regressors in the Parametric Part

We consider a varying coefficient model with either cross-sectional or time series data of the form

$$Y_t = X_t'\beta(Z_t) + u_t, \quad t = 1, \ldots, n, \qquad (16.14)$$

where X_t is of dimension $p \times 1$, β is a $p \times 1$ vector of unknown functions, and Z_t is of dimension q. We allow X_t to contain endogenous variables such that $E(u_t|X_t) \neq 0$. We assume that Z_t is (weakly) exogenous in the sense that $E(u_t|Z_s) = 0$ for $s \leq t$ if it is a time series, or simply that $E(u_t|Z_t) = 0$ if we have independent data (say, cross-sectional data).

Suppose there exists a vector of instrumental variables v_t such that $E(u_t|v_t) = 0$, and suppose that $E[E(X_t|v_t)X_t']$ is nonsingular. Then we can use $W_t = E(X_t|v_t)$ as an instrument for X_t. For example, for time series data, if $X_t = Y_{t-1}$ and Z_t is exogenous, then we can use choose $v_t = Z_{t-1}$, which leads to $W_t = E(Y_{t-1}|Z_{t-1})$.

Letting W and X be $n \times p$ matrices, Y and u be $n \times 1$ matrices, and $K_{h,z}$ be an $n \times n$ diagonal matrix with tth diagonal element given by $K_{h,tz} = \prod_{s=1}^{q} h_s^{-1}k((Z_{ts} - Z_s)/h_s)$, then

$$\tilde{\beta}(z) = (W'K_{h,z}X)^{-1}W'K_{h,z}Y = \beta(z) + (W'K_{h,z}X)^{-1}W'K_{h,z}u$$

$$= \beta(z) + \left[\sum_{t=1}^{n} W_t X_t' K_{h,tz}\right]^{-1} \left[\sum_{t=1}^{n} W_t u_t K_{h,tz}\right].$$

$$(16.15)$$

Under the assumption that the data is i.i.d., that some smoothness assumptions on $\beta(z)$ and $f(x,w,z)$ hold, and that some moment conditions on (x_t, w_t, z_t, u_t) hold, then we show in Section 16.4 that

$$\sqrt{nh_1 \ldots h_q}\left[\tilde{\beta}(z) - \beta(z) - \sum_{s=1}^{q} h_s^2 B_s(z)\right] \xrightarrow{d} N(0, \Omega_z), \qquad (16.16)$$

where

$$B_s(z) = (1/2)\kappa_2 M_z^{-1}\{f_z(z)\beta_{ss}(z)\mathrm{E}[W_t X_t'|Z_t = z]$$
$$+ 2\beta_s(z)\mathrm{E}[W_t X_t' f_s(X_t, W_t, Z_t)f(X_t, W_t|Z_t = z)^{-1}|Z_t = z]\},$$
$$M_z = f_z(z)\mathrm{E}[W_t X_t'|Z_t = z],$$
$$\Omega_z = M_z^{-1}V_z M_z^{-1},$$
$$V_z = \kappa^q f_z(z)\mathrm{E}[W_t X_t' \sigma^2(W_t, X_t, Z_t)|Z_t = z],$$
and $\sigma^2(W_t, X_t, z) = \mathrm{E}(u_t^2|X_t, W_t, Z_t = z).$

Note that if X_t is exogenous, then we can choose $W_t = X_t$, and (16.16) reduces to the result considered in Chapter 9.

The normality result given in (16.16) remains valid for weakly dependent mixing data provided that the mixing coefficients satisfy certain decay rates and that the error u_t is a martingale difference process.

The optimal instrument function $W_t = \mathrm{E}(X_t|v_t)$ is unknown, but can be consistently estimated by any nonparametric method such as kernel, k-nn, or series methods. If one uses the kernel method, then a feasible estimator for $\beta(z)$ can be obtained by replacing W_t by $\hat{W}_t = \hat{\mathrm{E}}(X_t|v_t) = \sum_{j=1}^{n} X_j K((v_j - v_t)/b)/\sum_{j=1}^{n} K((v_j - v_t)/b)$ in (16.15). Letting $\hat{\beta}(z)$ denote the resulting feasible estimator of $\beta(z)$, then under regularity conditions similar to those given in Cai, Das, Xiong and Wu (2006), Cai and Li (2005), and Das (2005), such as $\sum_{s=1}^{q} b_s^2 = o(\sum_{s=1}^{q} h_s^2)$, one can show that $\hat{\beta}(z)$ has the same asymptotic distribution as $\tilde{\beta}(z)$ given in (16.16).

In the semiparametric models above, we consider only the case for which the parametric components are endogenous, while the nonparametric components remain exogenous. When the nonparametric components are endogenous, the asymptotic analysis will be much more complex. In the next section we discuss general semiparametric models with endogenous variables possibly appearing in the nonparametric components. We address endogenous regressors in a fully nonparametric setting in Chapter 17.

16.3   Ai and Chen's Efficient Estimator with Conditional Moment Restrictions

Ai and Chen (2003) consider a general framework for estimating an econometric model under conditional moment restrictions of the form

$$\mathrm{E}\left[\rho\left(Z,\theta_0,g_0(\cdot)\right)|X\right]=0, \qquad (16.17)$$

where the error $\rho(\cdot)$ is a scalar of known functional form,[2] θ_0 is a $d \times 1$ vector of finite dimensional parameters (the parametric part of the model), and $g_0(\cdot) = (g_{01}, g_{02}, \ldots, g_{0q})$ is vector of unknown functions. The inclusion of unknown functions $g_0(\cdot)$ allows (16.17) to encompass many important classes of semiparametric and nonparametric models. For example, it includes as special cases the partially linear model, $\rho(Z, \theta_0, g_0) = Y - X_1'\theta_0 - g_0(X_2)$, studied in Chapter 7, and the single index model, $\rho(Z, \theta_0, g_0) = Y - g_0(X'\theta_0)$, studied in Chapter 8.

A leading example considered in Ai and Chen (2003) is the partially linear model with an endogenous variable entering the nonparametric part of the model, i.e., $\rho(Z, \theta_0, g_0(\cdot)) = Y_1 - X_1'\theta_0 - g_0(Y_2)$, with the corresponding regression model being $Y_1 = X_1'\theta_0 + g_0(Y_2) + u$, but $\mathrm{E}(u|X_1, Y_2) \neq 0$ since Y_2 is endogenous. In this case we need to assume that there exists a vector of instrumental variables X_2 such that $\mathrm{E}(u|X_1, X_2) \equiv \mathrm{E}[Y_1 - X_1'\theta_0 - g_0(Y_2)|X_1, X_2] = 0$ (X_2 serves as an instrument for Y_2).

16.3.1   Estimation Procedures

When Z contains endogenous variables, one cannot estimate $\alpha_0 \overset{\text{def}}{=} (\theta_0, g_0)$ by the standard minimum distance or generalized method of

---

[2] Ai and Chen (2003) consider the general case in which ρ is a vector-valued function. Here, for expositional simplicity, we consider only the case in which ρ is a scalar function.

moments (hereafter GMM) type estimation methods applied to ρ. Under the assumption that (16.17) identifies $\alpha_0 = (\theta_0, g_0)$, Ai and Chen (2003) suggest that one first project $\rho(Z, \alpha)$ onto the space of exogenous variables X. Defining $m(x, \alpha) = \mathrm{E}[\rho(Z, \alpha)|X = x]$, one can then estimate $\alpha = (\theta, g)$ by a minimum distance estimator that minimizes $\mathrm{E}[m(X, \alpha)^2/\sigma^2(X)]$, where $\sigma^2(X) = \mathrm{var}(\rho(Z, \alpha_0)|X)$. Note that, in practice, $m(\cdot)$ is unknown for two reasons: (i) $g_0(\cdot)$ has an unknown functional form, and (ii) even if we know g_0, the conditional expectation of ρ given X is still unknown.

If g were known, one could estimate $m(\cdot)$ nonparametrically using, say, series methods. Letting $p_j(X)$, $j = 1, 2, \ldots$, denote a sequence of known basis functions (power series, splines, Fourier series, etc.) and letting $p^{K_n}(X) = (p_1(X), \ldots, p_{K_n}(X))'$, then the nonparametric series estimator of $m(X, \alpha)$ is given by

$$\hat{m}(X, \alpha) = p^{K_n}(X)'\hat{\pi}, \tag{16.18}$$

where $\hat{\pi} = (P'P)^{-1}P'\rho(., \alpha)$, $\mathrm{P} = (p^{K_n}(X_1), \ldots, p^{K_n}(X_n))'$ is of dimension $n \times K_n$, and $\rho(., \alpha)$ is of dimension $n \times 1$ with the ith row given by $\rho(Z_i, \alpha)$. Using the nonparametric series estimator $\hat{m}(X, \alpha)$ of $m(X, \alpha)$, if g were known one could estimate θ by minimizing

$$\frac{1}{n}\sum_{i=1}^{n}[\hat{m}(X_i, \theta, g)]^2/\hat{\sigma}^2(X_i),$$

where $\hat{\sigma}^2(X)$ is a consistent estimator of $\sigma^2(X)$ that is introduced to address potential heteroskedasticity.

However, in practice g is also unknown. Ai and Chen (2003) suggest using B-splines, Fourier series, or wavelet sieve bases to approximate $g(Z)$. Letting $q^{L_n}(\cdot) = (q_1(\cdot), \ldots, q_{L_n}(\cdot))'$ denote the first L_n basis functions, then one can approximate $g(Z)$ using $q^{L_n}(Z)'\beta$, where β is of dimension $L_n \times 1$ under the assumption that $\theta_0 \in \Theta$, where Θ is a compact subset of $\mathbb{R}^d$. This assumes that the base function $q^{L_n} \in \mathcal{H}_n$, where $\mathcal{H}_n$ is a sieve space which is a computable, finite dimensional compact parameter space that becomes dense in the space of continuous functions as n increases.

For a given value of K_n in (16.18), the estimation of (θ, g) becomes the estimation of (θ, β). One can estimate (θ, β) by $(\hat{\theta}, \hat{\beta})$, which is defined as the solution of the following minimization problem:

$$\begin{pmatrix} \hat{\theta} \\ \hat{\beta} \end{pmatrix} = \arg\min_{(\theta,\beta)\in\Theta\times\mathbb{R}^{L_n}} n^{-1}\sum_{i=1}^{n}\hat{m}(X_i, \theta, q^{L_n}(Z_i)'\beta)^2/\hat{\sigma}^2(X_i). \tag{16.19}$$

The resulting estimator of $g(z)$ is $\hat{g}(z) = q^{L_n}(z)'\hat{\beta}$.

The weighting function $\sigma^2(X)$ is used for efficiency considerations. If the error is conditionally homoskedastic, one can simply replace σ^2 by 1. Or, if one is mainly interested in obtaining a consistent estimator for (θ, g) and cares less about (asymptotic) efficiency, one can also replace $\sigma^2(X)$ by 1. In this case, one simply minimizes (with respect (θ, β)) the following:

$$n^{-1} \sum_{i=1}^{n} \left[\hat{m}(X_i, \theta, q^{L_n}(Z_i)'\beta) \right]^2.$$

The above semiparametric estimator can be interpreted as a GMM estimator. Letting $(\tilde{\theta}, \tilde{\beta})$ denote the resulting estimator, combining (16.18) with (16.19) but with $\hat{\sigma}^2(X)$ replaced by 1, we obtain

$$\begin{pmatrix} \tilde{\theta} \\ \tilde{\beta} \end{pmatrix} = \min_{(\theta, \beta) \in \Theta \times \mathbb{R}^{L_n}} \left(\sum_{j=1}^{n} \rho(Z_j, \theta, q^{L_n}(Z_j)'\beta) p^{K_n}(X_j) \right)' (P'P)^{-1}$$

$$\times \left(\sum_{j=1}^{n} \rho(Z_j, \theta, q^{L_n}(Z_j)'\beta) p^{K_n}(X_j) \right).$$

$$(16.20)$$

We shall study the asymptotic distribution of $\hat{\theta}$ in the next section.

16.3.2 Asymptotic Normality for $\hat{\theta}$

Suppose that for almost all Z, $\rho(Z, (1-\tau)\alpha_0 + \tau\alpha_0)$ is continuously differentiable at $\tau = 0$. Denote the first pathwise derivative in the direction $[\alpha - \alpha_0]$ evaluated at α_0 by

$$\frac{d\,\rho(Z, \alpha_0)}{d\alpha}[\alpha - \alpha_0] \stackrel{\text{def}}{=} \frac{d\rho(Z, (1-\tau)\alpha_0 + \tau\alpha)}{d\tau}\Big|_{\tau=0},$$

and define

$$\frac{d\,m(X, \alpha_0)}{d\alpha}[\alpha_1 - \alpha_2] \stackrel{\text{def}}{=} \mathrm{E}\left\{ \frac{d\rho(Z, \alpha_0)}{d\alpha}[\alpha_1 - \alpha_2] \,|\, X \right\}.$$

Let $\mathcal{A} = \mathbb{R}^d \times \mathcal{W}$ denote the permissible range for $\alpha = (\theta, g)$, where $\mathcal{W}$ is a Hölder-continuous class of functions that excludes g_0; see Ai and Chen (2003) for further details. For any $\alpha_1, \alpha_2 \in \mathcal{A}$, we have

$$\frac{d\,\rho(Z, \alpha_0)}{d\alpha}[\alpha_1 - \alpha_2] = \frac{d\rho(Z, \alpha_0)}{d\alpha}[\alpha_1 - \alpha_0] + \frac{d\rho(Z, \alpha_0)}{d\alpha}[\alpha_2 - \alpha_0].$$

To study the convergence rate of $\hat{\alpha}$ to α, one must define a metric, commonly used ones including the sup and L_2 metrics. Ai and Chen (2003) define a weaker metric $||.||_w$ as follows:

$$||\alpha_1 - \alpha_2||_w = \sqrt{E\left\{\left[\frac{dm(X, \alpha_0)}{d\alpha}(\alpha_1 - \alpha_2)\right]^2 / \sigma^2(X)\right\}},$$

and the L_2 metric is (changing $m(X, .)$ to $\rho(Z, .)$ in $||.||_w$)

$$||\alpha_1 - \alpha_2||_2 = \sqrt{E\left\{\left[\frac{d\rho(Z, \alpha_0)}{d\alpha}(\alpha_1 - \alpha_2)\right]^2 / \sigma^2(X)\right\}}.$$

It can be shown that $||\alpha - \alpha_0||_w \le ||\alpha - \alpha_0||_2$ for all $\alpha \in \mathcal{A}$.

When the unknown functions g depend on the endogenous variable Y, one could have slow convergence rates under the usual L_2 metric and fast convergence rates under $||.||_w$. Ai and Chen (2003) show that for the $\sqrt{n}$-normality of the semiparametric estimator $\hat{\theta}_n$, it suffices to have a fast convergence rate under the weaker metric $||.||_w$.

Define

$$\frac{dm(X, \alpha_0)}{d\alpha}[\alpha - \alpha_0] = \frac{dm(X, \alpha_0)}{d\theta'}(\theta - \alpha_0) + \frac{dm(X, \alpha_0)}{dg}[g - g_0].$$

For each component of θ_j (of θ), $j = 1, \ldots, d$, let $w_j^* \in \mathcal{W}$ denote the solution to following optimization problem:

$$\min_{w_j \in \mathcal{W}} E\left\{\left(\frac{dm(X, \alpha_0)}{d\theta_j} - \frac{dm(X, \alpha_0)}{dg}[w_j]\right)^2 / \sigma^2(X)\right\}. \qquad (16.21)$$

Defining $w^* = (w_1^*, \ldots, w_d^*)$, we have

$$\frac{dm(X, \alpha_0)}{dg}[w^*] = \left(\frac{dm(X, \alpha_0)}{dg}[w_1^*], \ldots, \frac{dm(X, \alpha_0)}{dg}[w_d^*]\right)$$

and

$$D(X) \stackrel{\text{def}}{=} \frac{dm(X, \alpha_0)}{d\theta'} - \frac{dm(X, \alpha_0)}{dg}[w^*].$$

Ai and Chen (2003) prove the following results.

Theorem 16.1. *Under the regularity conditions given in Ai and Chen (2003), we have*

$$\sqrt{n}(\hat{\theta}_n - \theta_0) \to N(0, V_0) \text{ in distribution,}$$

where $V_0 = \left\{E[D(X)D(X)'/\sigma^2(X)]\right\}^{-1}$.

Ai and Chen (2003) also show that V_0 equals the semiparametrically efficient lower bound for the asymptotic variance of any $\sqrt{n}$-consistent semiparametric estimator of θ_0.

16.3.3   A Partially Linear Model with the Endogenous Regressors in the Nonparametric Part

For the partially linear model with an endogenous nonparametric component, we have

$$\rho(Z_i, \alpha) = Y_{1i} - X_{1i}'\theta - g(Y_{2i}), \text{ with } \mathrm{E}[\rho(Z_i, \alpha_0)|X_{1i}, X_{2i}] = 0, \quad (16.22)$$

where $\alpha = (\theta, g)$, Y_1 is a scalar, and $Z = (Y_1, Y_2', X_1')'$, $X = (X_1', X_2')'$. The functional form of $g(\cdot)$ is unknown, and Ai and Chen (2003) suggest using a spline-wavelet sieve basis to approximate $g(Y_2)$. Letting $q^{L_n}(\cdot) = (q_1(\cdot), \ldots, q_{L_n}(\cdot))'$ denote the first L_n basis functions, then we can approximate $g(Y_2)$ using $q^{L_n}(Y_2)'\beta$, where β is of dimension $L_n \times 1$. By (16.20) we know that $(\hat{\theta}, \hat{\beta})$ minimizes the following objective function:

$$\rho_\alpha P(P'P)^{-1}P'\rho_\alpha,$$

where ρ_α is an $n \times 1$ vector whose i^{th} element is given by ($\alpha = (\theta, g)$)

$$\rho_{i,\theta,\beta} = Y_{1i} - X_{1i}'\theta - q^{L_n}(Y_{2i})'\beta, \quad (16.23)$$

and P is of dimension $n \times K_n$ with the ith row given by $p^{K_n}(X_i)' = (p_{K_n 1}(X_i), \ldots, p_{K_n K_n}(X_i))$.

It is easy to show that one can also interpret $(\hat{\theta}, \hat{\beta})$ as the solution to the following minimization problem:

$$\begin{pmatrix} \hat{\theta} \\ \hat{\beta} \end{pmatrix} = \arg \min_{(\theta, \beta) \in \Theta \times \mathbb{R}^{L_n}} \sum_{j=1}^{n} \hat{\rho}_{i,\theta,\beta}^2, \quad (16.24)$$

where

$$\hat{\rho}_{i,\theta,\beta} = p^{K_n}(X_i)'(P'P)^{-1}P\left(Y_{1i} - X_{1i}'\theta - q^{L_n}(Y_{2i})'\beta\right). \quad (16.25)$$

Note that $\hat{\rho}_{i,\theta,\beta}$ is the fitted value which is obtained by regressing $\rho(Z_i, \theta, q^{L_n}(Y_{2i})'\beta) \equiv Y_{1i} - X_{1i}'\theta - q^{L_n}(Y_{2i})'\beta$ on $p^{K_n}(X_i)$.

Note that (16.23) (or equivalently (16.24)) leads to a closed form solution for $\hat{\theta}$ and $\hat{\beta}$ because ρ is linear in θ and g and the sieve estimator of g is linear in β (since we use linear sieves). In fact, the semiparametric estimation procedure with an identity weight function is simply 2SLS estimation applied to $Y_{1i} = X'_{1i}\theta_0 + q^{L_n}(Y_{2i})'\beta + u_i$ with $p^{K_n}(X_i)$ serving as an instrument for $q^{L_n}(Y_{2i})$.

To derive the asymptotic distribution of $\hat{\theta}_n$, note that for the partially linear model with identity weighting (i.e., $m(X,\alpha) = X'_1\theta + E[g(Y_2)|X]$), (16.21) becomes

$$\min_{w_j \in \mathcal{W}} E\left\{(X_{1j} - [w_j(Y_2)])'\,(X_{1j} - [w_j(Y_2)])\right\}, \qquad (16.26)$$

and we get $w_j^* = E[w_j(Y_2)|X]$.

The corollary below follows by applying Theorem 16.1 to the partially linear model with an endogenous nonparametric component.

Corollary 16.1. *Let w^* be the solution to*

$$\min_{w_j} E\left\{[X_{1j} - E\,(w_j(Y_2)|X)]^2\right\} \ \textit{for } j = 1, \ldots, d,$$

and assume that $E[g_0(Y_2)|X]$ is not in the linear span of X_1.[3] Then

$$\sqrt{n}(\hat{\theta}_n - \theta_0) \to N(0, V_0) \ \textit{in distribution,}$$

where $V_0 = \{E[D(X)D(X)'/\sigma^2(X)]\}^{-1}$, and $D(X) = X'_1 - E[w^*(Y_2)|X]$.

Ai and Chen (2003) also show that $\hat{g}(y_2) = q^{L_n}(y_2)'\hat{\beta}$ is a consistent estimator for $g(y_2)$ with a convergence rate smaller than $O_p(n^{-1/4})$, i.e., that $\hat{g}(y_2) - g(y_2) = o_p(n^{-1/4})$.

So far we have focused attention on Y_2 being endogenous. However, if $Y_2 = X_2$ is exogenous, and assuming that $\text{var}(Y_1 - X'_1\theta - g(X_2)|X) = \sigma^2$ (i.e., conditionally homoskedastic errors), then the above result collapses to

$$
\begin{aligned}
D(X) &= \min_g E\{[X_1 - E(g(X_2)|X)]'[X_1 - E(g(X_2)|X)]\} \\
&= \min_g E\{[X_1 - g(X_2)]'[X_1 - g(X_2)]\} \\
&= E\{[X_1 - E(X_2|X_1)]'[X_1 - E(X_1|X_2)]\},
\end{aligned}
$$

where the second equality follows from the fact that $E(g(X_2)|X_1, X_2) = g(X_2)$, and the last equality follows from Theorem 2.1 that $E(X_1|X_2)$ is the optimal prediction of X_1 as a function of X_2 in the MSE sense. Thus, in the case of Y_2 being exogenous, we obtain $V = \sigma^2\{E[DD']\}^{-1}$ with $D = X_1 - E(X_1|X_2)$, which is Robinson's (1988) result that was discussed in Chapter 7.

---

[3]That is, $E\{[X'_1\theta - g_0(Y_2)]^2\} > 0$ for all $\theta \in \mathbb{R}^d$.

16.4   Proof of Equation (16.16)

For what follows we use $||\cdot||$ to denote the Euclidean norm. We observe that

$$
\tilde{\beta}(z) = \left[\sum_j W_j X_j' K_{h,z_j,z}\right]^{-1} \sum_j W_j Y_j K_{h,z_j,z}
$$

$$
= \left[\sum_j W_j X_j' K_{h,z_j,z}\right]^{-1} \sum_j W_j (X_j' \beta(Z_j) + u_j) K_{h,z_j,z}
$$

$$
= \left[\sum_j W_j X_j' K_{h,z_j,z}\right]^{-1}
$$
$$
\times \sum_j w_j \left[X_j' \beta(z) + X_j'(\beta(Z_j) - \beta(z)) + u_j\right] K_{h,z_j,z}
$$

$$
= \beta(z) + \left[\sum_j W_j X_j' K_{h,z_j,z}\right]^{-1}
$$
$$
\times \sum_j W_j \left[X_j'(\beta(Z_j) - \beta(z)) + u_j\right] K_{h,z_j,z}
$$

$$
= \beta(z) + [D_n(z)]^{-1} \{A_{1n}(z) + A_{2n}(z)\},
$$

where

$$
D_n(z) = n^{-1} \sum_j W_j X_j' K_{h,z_j,z},
$$

$$
A_{1n}(z) = n^{-1} \sum_j W_j X_j'(\beta(Z_j) - \beta(z)) K_{h,z_j,z},
$$

$$
A_{2n}(z) = n^{-1} \sum_j W_j u_j K_{h,z_j,z}.
$$

Points (i)–(iii) below imply (16.16).

(i) $D_n(z) = n^{-1} \sum_j W_j X_j' K_{h,z_j,z} \xrightarrow{p} M_z.$

(ii) $A_{1n}(z) = \sum_{s=1}^q h_s^2 B_s(z) + o_p \left(\sum_{s=1}^q h_s^2\right).$

(iii) $\sqrt{nh_1 \ldots h_q} A_{2n}(z) \xrightarrow{d} N(0, V_z).$

We prove these results next.

Proof of (i). Letting $||h||^2 = \sum_{s=1}^{q} h_s^2$, we have

$$
\begin{aligned}
\mathrm{E}(D_n(z)) &= \mathrm{E}[W_1 W_1' K_{h,z_1,z}] \\
&= \int q_1 x_1' K_h(z_1 - z) f(x_1, w_1, z_1) dx_1 dz_1 dw_1 \\
&= \int w_1 x_1' K(v) f(x_1, w_1, z + hv) dv dx_1 dw_1 \\
&= \left[\int w_1 x_1' f(x_1, w_1, z) dx_1 dw_1 \right] \left[\int K(v) dv + O(|h|^2) \right] \\
&= f_z(z) \left[\int w_1 x_1' f(x_1, w_1 | z_1 = z) dx_1 dw_1 \right] \left[1 + O(|h|^2) \right] \\
&= f_z(z) \mathrm{E}[w_1 x_1' | z_1 = z] + o(1) = M_z + o(1).
\end{aligned}
$$

Similarly, one can easily show that

$$
\mathrm{var}(D_n(z)) = O\left((nh_1 \ldots h_q)^{-1} \right) = o(1).
$$

Therefore, we have shown that

$$
D_n(z) = M_z + o_p(1). \tag{16.27}
$$

$\square$

Proof of (ii).

$$E[A_{1n}(z)] = E[W_i X_i'(\beta(Z_i) - \beta(z))K_{h,z_i,z}]$$

$$= \int w_1 x_1'(\beta(z_1) - \beta(z))K_{h,z_1,z}f(x_1, w_1, z_1)dx_1 dw_1 dz_1$$

$$= \int w_1 x_1'(\beta(z + hv) - \beta(z))f(x_1, w_1, z + hv)K(v)dx_1 dw_1 dv$$

$$= \int w_1 x_1' \left[\sum_{s=1}^{q} h_s \beta_s(z)v_s + (1/2)\sum_{s=1}^{q} h_s^2 \beta_{ss}(z)v_s^2\right]$$

$$\times \left[f(x_1, w_1, z) + \sum_{s=1}^{q} f_s(x_1, w_1, z)h_s v_s\right]K(v)dx_1 dw_1 dv$$

$$+ O\left(\sum_{s=1}^{q} h_s^3\right)$$

$$= \kappa_2 \sum_{s1}^{q} h_s^2 \int w_1 x_1'[\beta_s(z)f_s(x_1, w_1, z)/f(x_1, w_1|z_1 = z)$$

$$+ (1/2)f_z(z)\beta_{ss}(z)]f(x_1, w_1|z_1 = z)dx_1 dw_1$$

$$+ O\left(\sum_{s=1}^{q} h_s^3\right) = M_z \sum_{s=1}^{q} h_s^2 B_s(z) + O\left(\sum_{s=1}^{q} h_s^3\right),$$

where M_z and $B_s(z)$ are defined in (16.16).

Similarly, one can show that

$$\text{var}(A_{1n}(z)) = O\left(\sum_{s=1}^{q} h_s^2(nh_1 \ldots h_q)^{-1} + \sum_{s=1}^{q} h_s^5\right).$$

Hence,

$$\left(A_{1n}(z) - \sum_{s=1}^{q} h_s^2 B_s(z)\right) = o_p\left(\sum_{s=1}^{q} h_s^2 + (nh_1 \ldots h_q)^{-1/2}\right). \quad (16.28)$$

$\square$

Proof of (iii). $\sqrt{nH_q}A_{2n}(z)$ has mean zero and its variance is ($H_q =$

$h_1 \ldots h_q$)

$$(nH_q)^{-1}\left\{\sum_{j=1}^{n}\mathrm{E}[W_jW_j'u_j^2K_{h,z_j,z}^2]\right\}$$

$$= H_q^{-1}\int f(w_1,z_1)\sigma_u^2(w_1,z_1)w_1x_1'K_{h,z_1,z}^2dw_1dz_1$$

$$= \left[\int w_1w_1'\sigma_u^2(w_1,z)f(w_1,z)dw_1\right]\left[\int K^2(v)dv\right]+O\left(\sum_{s=1}^{q}h_s\right)$$

$$= \kappa^q f_z(z)\mathrm{E}\left[W_iW_i'\sigma_u^2(W_i,Z_i)|Z_i=z\right]+o(1)=V_z+o(1)$$

where $\kappa^q=\int K^2(v)dv$.

It is straightforward to check that the conditions of Liapunov's CLT hold. Thus,

$$\sqrt{nH_q}A_{2n}(z)\overset{d}{\to}N(0,V_z). \qquad (16.29)$$

□

Summarizing (16.27), (16.28), and (16.29), we have shown that

$$\sqrt{nH_q}\left(\hat{\beta}(z)-\beta(z)-\sum_{s=1}^{q}h_s^2B_s(z)\right)$$

$$= [D_n(z)]^{-1}\sqrt{nH_q}\left\{A_{1n}(z)-M_z\sum_{s=1}^{q}h_s^2B_s(z)+A_{2n}(z)\right\}$$

$$= [M_z+o_p(1)]^{-1}\left\{\sqrt{nH_q}A_{2n}(z)+o_p(1)\right\}\overset{d}{\to}M_z^{-1}N(0,V_z)$$

$$= N\left(0,M_z^{-1}V_zM_z^{-1}\right).$$

16.5   Exercises

Exercise 16.1. Presuming that $\theta(Z_t) = Z_t^2$ ($q = 1$) in (16.1), that $X_t = Y_{t-1}$ ($p = 1$), and that the data is strictly stationary, show that $\mathrm{E}(Y_{t-1}Z_{t-1}) = 0$.

Exercise 16.2. (i) Prove (16.6), (ii) prove (16.9).

Exercise 16.3. For $||\cdot||_w$ and $||\cdot||_2$ defined in Section 16.3.2, show that $||\alpha-\alpha_0||_w\leq||\alpha-\alpha_0||_2$ for all $\alpha\in\mathcal{A}$.

Chapter 17

Endogeneity in Nonparametric Regression Models

The two general types of econometric models are single-equation and multiple-equation models. A set of equations is said to be "simultaneous" in nature when variables which appear as dependent variables in one equation also appear as explanatory variables in other equations. In this chapter we consider a variety of approaches for modeling simultaneous equations in nonparametric settings.

17.1 A Nonparametric Model

We consider the following nonparametric regression model,

$$Y_i = g(X_i) + \epsilon_i, \quad i = 1, \dots, n, \tag{17.1}$$

where $g(\cdot)$ is a function of unknown form. Our aim is to estimate $g(\cdot)$. However, unlike the regression models presented in Chapter 2, the error term ϵ_i is now acknowledged to be correlated with the explanatory variable X_i so that $\mathrm{E}(\epsilon_i|X_i) \neq 0$. Thus, the conditional mean no longer coincides with the object of interest, i.e., $\mathrm{E}(Y_i|X_i) \neq g(X_i)$. As explained in Hall and Horowitz (2003), this may occur if a third variable causes variation in both X_i and Y_i but is not included in the model. For example, suppose that Y_i denotes the hourly wage of individual i, and X_i includes the individual's level of education, among other variables.

The error term ϵ_i would include unobserved personal characteristics, for example, "ability." High-ability individuals are likely to choose high levels of education and, therefore, ability and education are correlated, that is, ϵ_i is correlated with at least some components of X_i. In this case, direct application of the estimators presented in Chapter 2 will yield inconsistent estimates of the objects of interest.

As was the case for linear parametric regression models, when there exist endogenous regressors we need to assume that there exists some instrumental variable, say Z_i, such that

$$E(\epsilon_i | Z_i) = 0, \tag{17.2}$$

which is sometimes called "instrument exogeneity," while we also need to assume that there is a strong relationship between Z_i and X_i, which is sometimes called "instrument relevance." Given the existence of Z_i and given a set of regularity conditions, it is possible to obtain consistent estimates of $g(\cdot)$. However, the problem of estimating $g(\cdot)$ is quite complicated because the mapping from the reduced form $E(Y_i | Z_i)$ to the structural form $g(X_i)$ turns out to be discontinuous, making it difficult to construct a consistent estimator. For the moment, we will postpone the discussion of estimating (17.1) under the assumption that (17.2) holds, and we shall first consider a simple triangular semiparametric simultaneous model.

17.2 A Triangular Simultaneous Equation Model

Newey et al. (1999) consider the following triangular nonparametric simultaneous equation model:

$$Y_i = g_1(X_i, Z_{1i}) + \epsilon_i, \tag{17.3}$$
$$X_i = \Pi(Z_i) + u_i \equiv E(X_i | Z_i) + u_i, \tag{17.4}$$

where Y_i is a scalar, X_i and u_i are of dimension d_x, Z_{1i} is of dimension d_1 and is part of $Z_i = (Z_{1i}, Z_{2i})$, which is of dimension q. Z_i is assumed to be exogenous in the sense that $E(u_i | Z_i) = 0$ and $E(\epsilon_i | u_i, Z_i) = E(\epsilon_i | u_i)$. That is, (17.4) is a reduced-form equation. The functional forms of $g_1(\cdot)$ and $\Pi(\cdot)$ are unspecified. Our main interest lies in the consistent estimation of $g_1(\cdot)$.

We shall let $g_2(u_i) = \mathrm{E}(\epsilon_i | u_i)$. Noting that (17.4) implies that $\mathrm{E}(\cdot | X_i, Z_i) = \mathrm{E}(\cdot | u_i, Z_i)$ since X_i is a deterministic function of (Z_i, u_i), this together with (17.3) leads to

$$
\begin{aligned}
\mathrm{E}(Y_i | X_i, Z_i) &= g_1(X_i, Z_{1i}) + \mathrm{E}(\epsilon_i | X_i, Z_i) \\
&= g_1(X_i, Z_{1i}) + \mathrm{E}(\epsilon_i | u_i) \\
&= g_1(X_i, Z_{1i}) + g_2(u_i) \equiv g(W_i),
\end{aligned}
\tag{17.5}
$$

where $W_i = (X_i', Z_{1i}', u_i')'$. Equation (17.5) shows that $\mathrm{E}(Y_i | X_i, Z_i)$ is an additive regression model that we discussed in Chapter 9 with the difference being that, here, u_i is not observable. However, u_i can be consistently estimated from (17.4) by either nonparametric kernel or series methods. Given that series methods are more convenient for imposing additive structure, Newey et al. (1999) suggest using series methods for estimating $g_1(\cdot)$ from (17.5) with u_i being estimated from (17.4).

Newey et al. (1999) showed that if there is no functional relationship between (x, z_1) and u, then $g_1(x, z_1)$ is identified up to an additive constant. This is similar to the identification condition discussed in Chapter 9. This is sufficient for many applications, say, when interest lies in the change in y due to changes in x and z_1. However, in other cases, such as when forecasting quantity demanded, it is also desirable to know the level of $g_1(x, z_1)$, which can be identified if one also assumes that $\mathrm{E}(\epsilon) = 0$, so that $\mathrm{E}(Y) = \mathrm{E}[g_1(X, Z_1)]$.

More formally, Newey et al. (1999) proved the following identification condition:

Lemma 17.1. *If $g_1(\cdot)$, $g_2(\cdot)$ and Π are differentiable, the boundary of the support of (z_i, u_i) has zero probability, and, with probability one, the rank of $\partial \Pi(z_i)/\partial z_{2i}$ is d_x, then $g_1(x, z_1)$ is identified.*

Newey et al. (1999) suggest a two-stage estimation procedure for estimating $g_1(\cdot)$. In the first stage, let $r^L(z) = (r_{1L}(z), \ldots, r_{LL}(z))'$ be a vector of the approximating (base) functions, and let $\hat{\Pi}(z)$ be the predicted value from a regression of X_i on $r_i = r^L(Z_i)$, i.e.,

$$
\hat{\Pi}(z) = r^L(z)' \hat{\gamma}, \quad \hat{\gamma} = (R'R)^{-1} R'(X_1, \ldots, X_n)', \quad R = (r_1, \ldots, r_n)'.
\tag{17.6}
$$

For the second stage, let $p^K(w) = (p_{1K}(w), \ldots, p_{KK}(w))'$ be a vector of approximating functions of $w = (x', z_1', u')'$ with an additive structure such that each $p_{kK}(w)$ depends either on (x, z_1) or on u, but not both. That is, the approximating base functions have the same additive structure as in (17.5), i.e., there are no interaction terms between (x, z_1) and u in the base function. Let $\hat{u}_i = X_i - \hat{\Pi}(Z_i)$, $\hat{W}_i = (X_i', Z_{1i}', \hat{u}_i')'$, and let $\mathbf{1}(\mathcal{A})$ denote the indicator function for the event $\mathcal{A}$. We introduce a trimming function of the form

$$\tau(w) = \prod_{j=1}^{d+d_x} \mathbf{1}(a_j \leq w_j \leq b_j), \tag{17.7}$$

where a_j and b_j are some finite constants, and where w_j is the jth component of w. The use of a trimming function is solely for the purpose of simplifying the asymptotic theory. The second stage involves regressing Y_i on $\hat{p}_i = p^K(\hat{W}_i)$, which, restricted to the trimmed data, gives

$$\hat{g}(w) = p^K(w)'\hat{\beta},$$
$$\hat{\beta} = (\hat{P}'\hat{P})^{-1}\hat{P}'\mathcal{Y},$$
$$\hat{P} = (\hat{\tau}_1 \hat{p}_1, \ldots, \hat{\tau}_n \hat{p}_n)', \text{ and}$$
$$\mathcal{Y} = (Y_1, \ldots, Y_n)', \tag{17.8}$$

where $\hat{\tau}_i = \tau(\hat{W}_i)$, $\hat{W}_i = (X_i', Z_{1i}', \hat{u}_i)'$.

The estimator $\hat{g}(w)$ can be used to construct estimates of $g_1(x, z_1)$ and $g_2(u)$ by collecting those terms that depend only on (x, z_1) and those that depend only on u. If $p_{1K}(w) = 1$, then $p_{kK}(w)$ depends on (x, z_1) for the next K_g term, and the remaining terms depend only on u. The estimators for $g_1(\cdot)$ and $g_2(\cdot)$ are then given by

$$\hat{g}_1(x, z_1) = \hat{c}_1 + \sum_{j=2}^{K_g+1} \hat{\beta}_j p_j(x, z_1) \text{ and}$$
$$\hat{g}_2(x, z_1) = \hat{c}_2 + \sum_{j=K_g+2}^{K} \hat{\beta}_j p_j(u), \tag{17.9}$$

with $\hat{c}_1 + \hat{c}_2 = \hat{\beta}_1$, and all of the coefficients except the constant terms, $\hat{c}_1$ and $\hat{c}_2$, are uniquely defined. If one is interested in estimating the marginal effects, then the constant terms are unimportant. One can also estimate the constant terms but, since the trimming function is used, one cannot use $\mathrm{E}(\epsilon) = 0$ to identify them because when ϵ is restricted to the trimming set it no longer has zero mean. Nevertheless, one may impose other restrictions to help identify the constant term. For example, the restriction $g_2(0) = 0$ can help to identify the constant because $E(Y|x, z_1, u = 0) = g_1(x, z_1) + g_2(0) = g_1(x, z_1)$. This amounts to $\hat{c}_1 = \hat{\beta}_1 - \hat{c}_2$ and $\hat{c}_2 = -\sum_{j=K_g+2}^{K} \hat{\beta}_j p_j(0)$.

The following assumptions are used by Newey et al. (1999) to derive the asymptotic distribution of $\hat{g}(w)$.

Assumption 17.1. $\Pi(z)$ *is continuously differentiable of order* s_1, *and* $g(x, z_1)$ *are Lipschitz and continuously differentiable of order* s.

Assumption 17.2. *For power series,* $((K^3 + K^2 L)(L/n)^{1/2} + L^{-s_1/d_1})$ $\to 0$; *for splines,* $((K^2 + K L^{1/2})(L/n)^{1/2} + L^{-s_1/d_1}) \to 0$.

Newey et al. (1999) proved the following result.

Theorem 17.1. *Under Assumptions 17.1 and 17.2 and some additional regularity conditions, setting* $q = 1/2$ *for splines and* $q = 1$ *for power series, then*

$$(i) \int \tau(w) \left[\hat{g}(w) - g(w)\right]^2 dF(w)$$

$$= O_p\left((K/n) + K^{-2s/d} + (L/n) + L^{-2s_1/d_1}\right) \ and$$

$$(ii) \sup_{(x, z_1) \in \mathcal{W}} |\hat{g}(w) - g(w)|$$

$$= O_p\left(K^q \left[(K/n)^{1/2} + K^{-s/d} + (L/n)^{1/2} + L^{-s_1/d_1}\right]\right),$$

where $F(\cdot)$ *is the CDF of* w.

The convergence rate is the sum of the two terms and depends on the series numbers L in the first stage estimation and K in the second stage estimation. Also, (ii) follows from Theorem 15.1 with $\zeta_0(K) = K$ for power series, and $\zeta_0(K) = K^{1/2}$ for splines.

To compute the asymptotic variance of $\hat{g}(w) = p^K(w)'\hat{\beta}$, one can apply the formula for parametric two-stage estimators (e.g., Newey (1994a)). Letting $\otimes$ denote the Kronecker product and defining $\hat{Q} = \hat{P}'\hat{P}/n$, $\hat{\Sigma} = \sum_{i=1}^{n} \hat{\tau}_i \hat{p}_i \hat{p}_i'[Y_i - \hat{g}(\hat{W}_i)]^2/n$, $\hat{Q}_1 = I_{d-k_1} \otimes (R'R/n)$, $\hat{\Sigma}_1 = \sum_{i=1}^{n}(\hat{u}_i \hat{u}_i') \otimes (r_i r_i')/n$, and $\hat{H} = \sum_{i=1}^{n} \hat{\tau}_i[\partial \hat{g}(\hat{W}_i)/\partial u_i]' \otimes \hat{p}_i r_i'/n$, the variance estimate for $\hat{g}(w)$ is given by

$$\hat{V}(w) = p^K(w)'\hat{Q}^{-1}\left[\hat{\Sigma} + \hat{H}\hat{Q}_1^{-1}\hat{\Sigma}_1\hat{Q}_1^{-1}\hat{H}'\right]\hat{Q}^{-1}p^K(w). \qquad (17.10)$$

Since the exact leading bias term is quite difficult to obtain, Newey et al. (1999) suggest undersmoothing the data, which leads to the bias-squared term being of smaller order than the variance term so that the nonparametric series estimator is properly centered. In particular they assume that as $n \to \infty$,

$$\sqrt{n}K^{-s/d} \to 0, \quad \sqrt{n}L^{-s_1/d_1} \to 0. \tag{17.11}$$

Equation (17.11) ensures that the series estimation bias-squared term is smaller than the variance term. In order for estimation variance to converge to zero, Newey et al. (1999) assume that

$$(K^9 L + K^8 L^2 + K^6 L^3 + K^2 L^6)/n \to 0 \text{ for power series,}$$
$$(K^5 L + K^4 L^2 + K^3 L^3 + K L^4)/n \to 0 \text{ for splines.} \tag{17.12}$$

Newey et al. (1999) proved the following asymptotic normality result.

Theorem 17.2. *Under the undersmoothing conditions (17.11) and (17.12) and some smoothness and moment conditions on $g_1(\cdot)$, $\Pi(\cdot)$ and $E(v_i^2|X_i, Z_i)$ ($v_i = \epsilon_i$ or u_i), then*

$$\sqrt{n}\hat{V}(w)^{-1/2}\left(\hat{g}(w) - g(w)\right) \xrightarrow{d} N(0,1).$$

Note that it can be shown that $\sqrt{\max\{K, L\}}\hat{V}(w) = O_p(1)$. Hence, (17.2) implies that $(\hat{g}(w) - g(w)) = O_p\left(\sqrt{n}/\sqrt{\max\{K, L\}}\right)$.

Alternatively, one can use bootstrap methods to approximate the finite-sample distribution of $\hat{g}(w)$. In fact, Newey et al. (1999) considered more general cases of linear functions of $\hat{g}(\cdot)$, which in turn are linear functions of $\hat{\beta}$ (since $\hat{g}(\cdot)$ is linear in $\hat{\beta}$), say, $\hat{\theta} = A\hat{\beta}$, where A is an $m \times K$ matrix (m is a finite positive constant). The asymptotic distribution of $\hat{\theta}$ is

$$\sqrt{n}\hat{V}_A^{-1/2}\left(\hat{\theta} - \theta\right) \xrightarrow{d} N(0, I_m), \tag{17.13}$$

where $\hat{V}_A = A\hat{Q}^{-1}[\hat{\Sigma} + \hat{H}\hat{Q}_1^{-1}\hat{\Sigma}_1\hat{Q}_1^{-1}\hat{H}']\hat{Q}^{-1}A'$, and all matrices in $\hat{V}_A$, except A, are defined above (17.10). This estimator is similar to parametric two-stage regression. It equals a term $A\hat{Q}^{-1}\hat{\Sigma}\hat{Q}^{-1}A'$, a heteroskedasticity consistent estimator, plus an additional nonnegative definite term that accounts for the presence of $\hat{u}$. The convergence rate of $\hat{\theta}$ to θ depends on how fast $\hat{V}_A$ goes to infinity. When $A = p^K(w)'$, (17.13) leads to Theorem 17.2.

17.3 Newey-Powell Series-Based Estimator

Newey and Powell (2003) consider a more general simultaneous equation model of the form

$$Y_i = g(X_i, Z_{1i}) + \epsilon_i, \quad \mathrm{E}(\epsilon_i | Z_i) = 0, \quad Z_i = (Z_{11}, Z_{2i}), \qquad (17.14)$$

where Y_i is a scalar, and X_i, Z_{1i} and Z_{2i} are of dimension d_x, d_1 and d_2, respectively. Note that without further assuming that $\mathrm{E}(\epsilon_i | Z_i, u_i) = \mathrm{E}(\epsilon_i | u_i)$, one cannot obtain a triangular equation system such as (17.5) from (17.14). This makes the consistent estimation of $g_1(\cdot)$ more difficult.

The conditional expectation of (17.14) yields the integral equation

$$\Pi(z) \equiv \mathrm{E}(Y_i | Z_i = z) = \mathrm{E}[g(X_i, Z_{1i}) | Z_i = z] = \int g(x, z_1) F(dx|z),$$
$$(17.15)$$

where F denotes the conditional CDF of x given z. The identification of $g(\cdot)$ depends on the existence of a unique solution to the integral equation (17.15). Letting $\hat{\Pi}$ and $\hat{F}$ denote the nonparametric estimators of Π and F, one needs to obtain an estimator of $g(\cdot)$ based on

$$\hat{\Pi}(z) = \int g(x, z_1) \hat{F}(dx|z). \qquad (17.16)$$

Letting $\hat{g}(\cdot)$ denote a solution for $g(\cdot)$ obtained from (17.16), the lack of continuity of $\hat{g}(\cdot)$ in $\hat{\Pi}$ and $\hat{F}$ means that small changes in the reduced form estimates can cause large changes in $\hat{g}(\cdot)$. Thus, unlike conventional estimators, consistency of $\hat{g}(\cdot)$ does not follow from the consistency of $\hat{\Pi}$ and $\hat{F}$. This is the so-called ill-posed inverse problem. In the literature on integral equations, various methods have been proposed to deal with the noncontinuity problem, and they are often referred to as "regularization methods." Newey and Powell (2003) impose the restriction that $g(\cdot)$ belongs to a compact set, where the compactness is defined under the Sobolev norm (see A.31 in Appendix A for the definition of Sobolev norm).

Letting $w = (x, z_1)$ and letting $\{p_1(w), p_2(w), \dots\}$ be a sequence of base functions, Newey and Powell (2003) assume that the structural function $g(\cdot)$ can be well-approximated by a linear combination of some series base functions of the form

$$g_0(w) \cong g_J(w) = \sum_{j=1}^{J} \gamma_j p_j(x), \qquad (17.17)$$

where the γ_j is the coefficient corresponding to $p_j(\cdot)$, and $p_j(\cdot)$ is the jth chosen (known) base functions (e.g., polynomials or trigonometric functions) having the property that as J grows, $g_J(x)$ can approximate $g(x)$ arbitrarily well in the MSE sense. Substituting (17.17) into (17.14) we get

$$E(Y_i|Z_i) = E[g_0(W_i)|Z_i)] \cong \sum_{j=1}^{J} \gamma_j E[p_j(W_i)|Z_i]. \qquad (17.18)$$

Equation (17.18) suggests that one can estimate $\{\gamma_j\}_{j=1}^{J}$ based on the least squares regression of Y_i on the $E[p_j(W_i)|Z_i]$'s. However, these conditional expectation functions are unknown. Newey and Powell (2003) suggest using a two-stage method where, in the first stage, one estimates $E[p_j(W_i)|Z_i]$ by a nonparametric series estimator, say $\hat{E}[p_j(W_i)|Z_i]$, then, in the second stage, one regresses Y_i on $\hat{E}[p_j(W_i)|Z_i]$ to estimate γ_j's.

However, this two-stage method may suffer from the aforementioned ill-posed inverse problem. To avoid this problem, Newey and Powell (2003) impose the restriction that $g_0(w)$ belongs to a compact set under the Sobolev norm. This assumption places strong limitations on the tail behavior of $g_0(w)$. To alleviate this, Newey and Powell assume that the $g(\cdot)$ function has a semiparametric form given by $g(w) = a(w)'\beta + g_0(w)$, where $a(w)$ and β are $r \times 1$ vectors of known functions and unknown parameters, respectively. This specification admits unbounded w through the parametric component $a(w)'\beta$. If, for a given problem, w is bounded, then one could instead drop the parametric part and obtain a fully nonparametric specification. With the semiparametric specification $g(w) = a(w)'\beta + g_0(w)$, (17.16) becomes

$$\hat{\Pi}(z) \cong \hat{E}(a(W)|z)'\beta + \sum_{j=1}^{J} \gamma_j \hat{E}(p_j(W)|z), \qquad (17.19)$$

where $\hat{E}(a(W)|z)$ and $\hat{E}(p_j(W)|z)$ are the (first stage) nonparametric series estimators of $E(a(W)|z)$ and $E(p_j(W)|z)$, respectively. In the second stage, one can estimate the unknown β and the γ_j's by minimizing the objective function

$$Q(\beta,\gamma) \stackrel{\text{def}}{=} \frac{1}{n} \sum_{i=1}^{n} \left[Y_i - \hat{E}(a(W_i)|Z_i)'\beta - \sum_{j=1}^{J} \gamma_j \hat{E}(p_j(W_i)|Z_i) \right]^2. \qquad (17.20)$$

A nonparametric two-stage least squares estimator can be obtained by minimizing (17.20) subject to restrictions on the parameters yielding

$$\hat{g}(w) = a(w)'\hat{\beta} + \hat{g}_0(w), \quad \hat{g}_1(w) = \sum_{j=1}^{J} \hat{\gamma}_j p_j(w),$$

with

$$(\hat{\beta}, \hat{\gamma}) = \arg\min_{\beta,\gamma} Q(\beta, \gamma) \text{ subject to } \beta'\beta \le B_\beta \text{ and } \gamma'\Lambda_J\gamma \le B_1,$$

where B_β and B_1 are some positive constants, $\gamma'\Lambda_J\gamma$ is the square of the Sobolev norm of the linear approximating function g_J, and Λ_J is a known matrix constructed using integrals involving the basis functions p_j and their derivatives. Newey and Powell (2003) established the uniform consistency of the nonparametric estimator $\hat{g}(w)$, i.e., $\sup_w |\hat{g}(w) - g(w)| = o(1)$ almost surely, where the sup is taken over a compact set with the PDF $f(w)$ being uniformly bounded from above and below in the compact set; see Newey and Powell (2003) for details on the regularity conditions that are used to prove the uniform consistency of $\hat{g}(w)$ to $g(w)$.

17.4 Hall and Horowitz's Kernel-Based Estimator

For what follows, the nonparametric regression model is the same as that given in (17.1), namely,

$$Y_i = g(X_i) + u_i, \tag{17.21}$$

where, for expositional simplicity, we first consider the case for which X_i is a scalar. Since $\mathrm{E}(u_i|X_i) \ne 0$, we need to assume that there exists a scalar instrumental variable Z_i such that

$$\mathrm{E}(u_i|Z_i) = 0, \tag{17.22}$$

and that Z_i and X_i are strongly correlated. However, estimation of the unknown function $g(\cdot)$ is nontrivial, as will be demonstrated below.

Let f_x, f_z, and f_{xz} denote the marginal densities of X and Z and the joint density of (X, Z), respectively. Define an operator T on the space of square-integrable functions as follows:

$$(T\psi)(w) = \int t(x, w)\psi(x)dx, \tag{17.23}$$

where

$$t(x, w) = \int f_{xz}(x, z) f_{xz}(w, z) dz. \qquad (17.24)$$

From (17.23) and (17.24), it can be shown that (see Exercise 17.1)

$$E\{E(Y|Z) f_{xz}(w, Z)\} = (Tg)(w). \qquad (17.25)$$

If we assume that T is nonsingular (i.e., that the inverse T^{-1} exists), then multiplying both sides of (17.25) by T^{-1}, we get

$$g(x) = E\{E(Y|Z)(T^{-1} f_{xz})(x, Z)\}. \qquad (17.26)$$

Equation (17.26) shows that the relationship that identifies $g(\cdot)$ is a Fredholm equation of the first kind,

$$Tg = \phi, \qquad (17.27)$$

where T is a linear operator, which leads to an ill-posed inverse problem if zero is a limit point of the eigenvalues of T so that T^{-1} is not a bounded, continuous operator. Hall and Horowitz (2003) suggest using a ridge-type regularization to avoid the unboundedness of T^{-1}, i.e., replace T^{-1} by $(T + a_n)^{-1}$, where a_n is a positive ridge parameter converging to zero as $n \to \infty$.

We now consider the multivariate case, with a model given by

$$Y_i = g(X_i, Z_{1i}) + u_i, \quad E(u_i|Z_{1i}, Z_{2i}) = 0, \qquad (17.28)$$

where X is endogenous and Z is exogenous. Hall and Horowitz (2003) further assume that X and Z have connected compact support, that is, $X_i, Z_{2i} \in [0, 1]^p$ and $Z_{1i} \in [0, 1]^q$.

Let $k_h(u, t)$ denote an rth order boundary kernel function, i.e., if h is small and t is not close to either 0 or 1, then $k_h(u, t) = h^{-1} k(u/h)$, while if t is close to 1, $k_h(u, t) = h^{-1} l(u/h)$ with $\int_0^\infty u^j l(u) = \delta_{0j}$ for $j = 0, 1$ ($\delta_{jl} = 1$ if $j = l$, 0 otherwise), and if t is close to 0, $k_h(u, t) = l_h(-u/h)$. We can estimate the joint density of (X, Z), f_{xz}, by

$$\hat{f}_{xz}(x, z)$$

$$= \frac{1}{n} \sum_{i=1}^n K_{p,h_x}(x - X_i, x) K_{q,h_z}(z_1 - Z_{1i}, z_1) K_{p,h_x}(z_2 - Z_{2i}, z_2),$$

where $K_{p,h_x}(u,t) = \prod_{s=1}^{p} h_{x,s}^{-1} k(u_s, t_s)$, $K_{q,h_z}(u,t) = \prod_{s=1}^{q} h_{z,s}^{-1} k(u_s, t_s)$, and the leave-one-out estimator is given by

$$\hat{f}_{xz,-i}(x,w,z)$$

$$= \frac{1}{(n-1)} \sum_{i=1}^{n} K_{p,h_x}(x - X_i, x) K_{q,h_z}(z_1 - Z_{1i}, z_1) K_{p,h_x}(z_2 - Z_{2i}, z_2).$$

Hence, we have

$$\hat{t}_{z_1}(x_1, x_2) = \int \hat{f}_{xz}(x_1, z) \hat{f}_{xz}(x_2, z) dz$$

and

$$(\hat{T}_{z_1})(\psi)(x, z) = \int \hat{t}_{z_1}(\xi, x) \psi(\xi, z) d\xi,$$

where ψ is a function that maps $\mathbb{R}^{2p+q}$ to the real line. The estimator of $g(x, z_1)$ is then given by

$$\hat{g}(x, z_1) = \frac{1}{n} \sum_{i=1}^{n} \hat{T}_{z_2}^{+} \hat{f}_{xz,-i}(x, z) Y_i K_{q,h_z}(z_2 - Z_{2i}, z_2).$$

Because consistent estimation of $g(\cdot)$ depends upon the invertibility of T, the rate of convergence of $\hat{g}(\cdot)$ depends on the rate at which the eigenvalues of T converge to 0. Let $\phi_1, \phi_2, \ldots$, denote the orthonormal basis for the square-integral functions on $[0, 1]$. Then $t(\cdot)$, f_{XW} and $g(\cdot)$ have the following expansions:

$$t(x, z) = \sum_{j=1}^{\infty} \lambda_j \phi_j(x) \phi_j(z),$$

$$t(x, z) = \sum_{j=1}^{\infty} \sum_{l=1}^{\infty} d_{jl} \phi_j(x) \phi_l(z),$$

$$g(x) = \sum_{j=1}^{\infty} b_j \phi_j(x),$$

where d_{jl} and b_j are the generalized Fourier coefficients of f_X and $g(\cdot)$, respectively.

Let α and β be constants satisfying $\alpha > 1$. With $\beta > 1/2$ and $\beta - 1/2 \leq \alpha < 2\beta$, where $|b_j| \leq C j^{-\beta}$, $j^{-\alpha} \leq C \lambda_j$ and $\sum_{l \geq j} |d_{jl}| \leq$

$Cj^{-\alpha/2}$ for all $j > 1$, Hall and Horowitz (2003) proved the following uniform rate of convergence result:

$$\sup_{G \in \mathcal{M}} \int_{[0,1]^q} \mathrm{E}_G \{\hat{g}(t) - g(t)\}^2 \, dt = O\left(n^{-(2\beta-1)/(2\beta+\alpha)}\right).$$

Letting $\tau = 2r/(2r + q)$, Hall and Horowitz (2003) further show that the optimal convergence rate is $n^{-\tau(2\beta-1)/(2\beta+\alpha)}$ in the following minimax sense:

$$\liminf_{n \to \infty} n^{\tau(2\beta-1)/(2\beta+\alpha)} \inf_{\hat{g}} \sup_{G \in \mathcal{C}} \int_{[0,1]^q} \mathrm{E}_G \{\hat{g}(x, z_1) - g(x, z_1)\}^2 dx > 0.$$

Under slightly stronger conditions, including requiring that α converge to 0 at a rate faster than the asymptotically optimal rate, and also restricting the smoothing parameter h to a slightly narrower range, Horowitz (2005) establishes the pointwise asymptotic normality result of $\hat{g}(x, z_1)$.

17.5 Darolles, Florens and Renault's Estimator

Darolles, Florens and Renault (2002) consider the same nonparametric regression model, i.e.,

$$Y = g(X) + u \text{ with } \mathrm{E}(u|Z) = 0, \tag{17.29}$$

where Z is the instrumental variable. Therefore, $g(\cdot)$ is defined as a solution of the functional equation

$$\mathrm{E}(Y - g(X)|Z) = 0. \tag{17.30}$$

In order to estimate the unknown function $g(\cdot)$, Darolles et al. (2002) begin by noting that $g(\cdot)$ is the solution to the following equation:

$$g(\cdot) = \arg \min_{\phi(\cdot)} \mathrm{E}\left[\left|\left|\mathrm{E}(Y|z) - \int \phi(x) F(dx|z)\right|\right|^2\right].$$

Next, define two linear operators $T_F(g)$ and $T_F^*(\psi)$ by $T_F(g) = \mathrm{E}[g(x)|z]$ and $T_F^*(\psi) = \mathrm{E}[\psi(x)|z]$. Using this notation, $g(\cdot)$ corresponds to any solution of the functional equation

$$A(g, F) = T_F(g) - r_F = 0, \tag{17.31}$$

where $r_F(z) = E(Y|z)$. Letting $f(y, x, z)$ be the PDF of (Y, X, Z), then (17.31) is an integral Fredholm type I equation given by

$$\int g(x) \frac{f(., x, z)}{f(., ., z)} dx - r_F(z) = 0, \qquad (17.32)$$

where $r_F(z) = \int y \frac{f(y, ., z)}{f(., ., z)} dy$.

In order for $g(\cdot)$ to be identified, Darolles et al. (2002) impose the condition that $E(g(X)|Z) = 0$ a.s., which implies that $g(X) = 0$ a.s. Under this condition, $g(\cdot)$ is identified. Let ϕ_j, $j \geq 1$, be an orthonormal sequence of $L_F^2(z)$, i.e., $\int \phi_j(w) \phi_l(w) dF(w) = \delta_{jl}$. For $j \geq 1$, $T_F(\phi_j) = \lambda_j \psi_j$, $T_F^*(\psi_j) = \lambda_j \phi_j$, $\phi_1 = 1$, $\psi_1 = 1$ and $\int \phi_j(x) \psi_l(x) dF(z, x) = \lambda_j \delta_{jl}$, it can be shown that (see Exercise 17.2)

$$T_F[g(X)](z) = E[g(X)|z] = \sum_{j=1}^{\infty} \lambda_j < g(x), \phi_j(x) > \psi_j(z). \qquad (17.33)$$

Then

$$g(x) = \sum_{j=1}^{\infty} \frac{1}{\lambda_j} < r_F, \psi_j > \phi_j(x).$$

The ill-posed inverse problem corresponds to $\lambda_j \to 0$ as $j \to \infty$. Small estimation errors may cause substantial changes in the estimated $g(\cdot)$ function. Darolles et al. (2002) suggest using a "cutoff estimator" that uses only ϕ_j's and ψ_j's with $\lambda_j^2 \geq \alpha_n$, where $\alpha_n > 0$ is a sequence of positive numbers with $\alpha_j \to 0$ as $j \to \infty$, hence

$$\hat{g}_{\alpha_n}(x) = \left(\alpha_n I + T_{\hat{F}_n}^* T_{\hat{F}_n} \right)^{-1} r_{\hat{F}_n}^*,$$

with $r_{\hat{F}_n}^* = T_{\hat{F}_n}^* r_{\hat{F}_n}$, and where $\hat{F}_n$ is the kernel smoothed empirical CDF. Darolles et al. provide rates of convergence of $\hat{g}_{\alpha_n}(w)$ to $g(w)$ and an asymptotic normality result for $\hat{g}_{\alpha_n}(w)$.

This approach has been used by Blundell, Chen and Kristensen (2003), who considered the estimation of semiparametric Engel curves in the presence of endogenous expenditures.

17.6   Exercises

Exercise 17.1. Derive (17.25) from (17.23) and (17.24).

Exercise 17.2. Derive (17.33).

Chapter 18

Weakly Dependent Data

Up to now we have restricted our attention to independent data. In this chapter, we show that all of the earlier results can be extended to the stationary weakly dependent data setting. For what follows, "weak dependence" means that the dependence between Z_t and $Z_{t+\tau}$ goes to zero as τ goes to infinity. Moreover, we also need to impose certain rates of convergence as $\tau \to \infty$. Thus, weakly dependent data rule out nonstationary processes (e.g., unit-roots), or processes possessing so-called long-range dependence. In this chapter we mainly focus on strictly stationary weakly dependent data. In Section 18.9 we briefly discuss nonparametric estimation of regression models with nonstationary data. To describe weakly dependent processes we make use of a variety of so-called mixing processes, which we define below.

Let $\mathcal{M}_t^{t+\tau}$ denote the σ-algebra generated from $\{Z_s\}_{s=t}^{t+\tau}$, let $\mathbb{N}$ denote the set of integers, and define

$$\phi_\tau = \phi(\tau) = \sup_{t \in \mathbb{N}} \sup_{A \in \mathcal{M}_{t+\tau}^\infty, B \in \mathcal{M}_{-\infty}^t} |P(A|B) - P(A)|,$$

$$\alpha_\tau = \alpha(\tau) = \sup_{t \in \mathbb{N}} \sup_{A \in \mathcal{M}_{t+\tau}^\infty, B \in \mathcal{M}_{-\infty}^t} |P(A \cap B) - P(A)P(B)|,$$

$$\beta_\tau = \beta(\tau) = \sup_{t \in \mathbb{N}} \sup_{A \in \mathcal{M}_{t+\tau}^\infty, B \in \mathcal{M}_{-\infty}^t} |E(A|B) - E(A)|, \text{ and} \qquad (18.1)$$

$$\rho_\tau = \rho(\tau) = \sup_{t \in \mathbb{N}} \sup_{A \in \mathcal{M}_{t+\tau}^\infty, B \in \mathcal{M}_{-\infty}^t} \left| \frac{\operatorname{cov}(A, B)}{\sqrt{\operatorname{var}(A)\operatorname{var}(B)}} \right|.$$

The sequence $\{Z_t\}_{t=-\infty}^\infty$ is said to be a ϕ-mixing, or α-mixing, or β-mixing, or ρ-mixing if ϕ_τ, or α_τ, or β_τ, or ρ_τ goes to zero, respectively, as $\tau \to \infty$. Note that α-mixing is also called "strong mixing."

Note that for independent data, ϕ_τ, α_τ, β_τ and ρ_τ are all zero for $\tau \geq 1$. Mixing processes can be viewed as asymptotically independent processes.

It can be shown that

$$\alpha_\tau \leq \beta_\tau \leq \phi_\tau \text{ and } \alpha_\tau \leq \rho_\tau \leq \phi_\tau. \qquad (18.2)$$

However, in general one cannot order β_τ and ρ_τ. See Carrasco and Chen (2002), and Chen, Hansen and Scheinkman (2005) for further discussion on the properties of different mixing processes.

Ibragimov and Linnik (1971) show that a Gaussian autoregressive moving average $ARMA(p,q)$ process $(p, q \in \mathbb{N}_+)$ is one for which $\alpha_\tau \to 0$ as $\tau \to \infty$ but ϕ_τ does not. Moreover, $\alpha_\tau \to 0$ exponentially fast.[1] Perhaps the most convenient property of mixing processes is that measurable functions of mixing processes are themselves mixing, provided that the function depends on only a finite number of lagged values of the mixing process. However, when Y_t depends on the entire history of the underlying process, a measurable function of Y_t may not be a mixing process even if Y_t itself is mixing. In this case, the concept of a mixing process has been generalized to that of a "mixingale" process by McLeish (1975). For a more detailed treatment of mixingales and other weakly dependent processes, we refer the reader to Gallant and White (1988) and Andrews (1988).

In a seminal paper on kernel estimation, Robinson (1983) established the consistency and asymptotic normality result for nonparametric density, regression, and conditional density estimators with strong mixing (α-mixing) data. Since the other three mixing processes imply α-mixing, α-mixing processes are therefore the strongest of the dependent processes among the aforementioned weakly dependent processes.

In this chapter we focus our attention mainly on stationary ρ-mixing or β-mixing processes because, mathematically, ρ-mixing and β-mixing processes are the easiest to handle. For example, a standard $AR(1)$ model of the form $Y_t = \alpha Y_{t-1} + u_t$, where u_t is a white noise error term with finite variance σ^2, is ρ-mixing provided that $|\alpha| < 1$ because $\rho_\tau = \text{cov}(Y_{t+\tau}, Y_t)/\sqrt{\text{var}(Y_t)\text{var}(Y_{t+\tau})} = \alpha^\tau \to 0$ as $\tau \to \infty$. Carrasco and Chen (2002) showed that many known nonlinear time series processes are β-mixing (or ρ-mixing).

We shall provide detailed proofs for pointwise consistency along with asymptotic normality results for kernel estimators of density and

---

[1] For non-Gaussian processes, Andrews (1984) shows that a simple $AR(1)$ processes can fail to be either ϕ-mixing or α-mixing.

regression functions. We also discuss the estimation of various semi-parametric models and we discuss consistent model specification tests with weakly dependent data.

The main purpose of this chapter is to demonstrate that results obtained in earlier chapters which relied upon independence assumptions, e.g., rates of convergence and asymptotic normality, remain unchanged when the independence assumption is relaxed to allow for weak dependence.

18.1   Density Estimation with Dependent Data

For expositional simplicity, we consider only the case for which $x \in \mathbb{R}^q$ is a vector-valued continuous variable. It is fairly straightforward to generalize the results to the mixed discrete and continuous variable case, as we did in Chapter 4. Suppose that we have stationary and ρ-mixing observations $X_1, X_2, \ldots, X_n$. As in Chapter 1, we estimate the PDF of X_t, $f(x)$, for a given fixed value of $x \in \mathbb{R}^q$ by

$$\hat{f}(x) = \frac{1}{n} \sum_{t=1}^{n} K_h \left(X_t - x \right),$$

where $K_h \left(X_t - x \right) = \prod_{s=1}^{q} h_s^{-1} k \left((X_{ts} - x_s)/h_s \right)$ is the product kernel.

The next theorem shows that the MSE convergence rate of $\hat{g}(x)$ with weakly dependent data is the same as the independent case discussed in Chapter 1.

Theorem 18.1. *Assuming that a ρ-mixing process satisfies $\rho(\tau) = O\left(\tau^{-(1+\epsilon)}\right)$ for some (small) $\epsilon > 0$ (which implies that $\sum_{\tau=1}^{\infty} \rho(\tau) < \infty$), that the same smoothness and moments conditions on $f(\cdot)$ and $k(\cdot)$ as given in Theorem 1.3 hold, and that $h_s \to 0$ $(s = 1, \ldots, q)$, $nh_1 \ldots h_q \to \infty$, as $n \to \infty$, then $(||h||^2 = \sum_{s=1}^{q} h_s^2)$*

$$\mathrm{E}\left\{ \left[\hat{f}(x) - f(x) \right]^2 \right\} = O\left(||h||^4 + (nh_1 \ldots h_q)^{-1} \right).$$

Proof. Letting $K_{h,tx} = K_h(X_t - x) = \prod_{s=1}^{q} h_s^{-1} k((X_{ts} - x_s)/h_s)$, then by the stationary assumption, we have

$$
\begin{aligned}
\text{bias}(\hat{f}(x)) = \mathrm{E}\left[\hat{f}(x)\right] - f(x) &= \mathrm{E}(K_{h,1x}) - f(x) \\
&= \int K_h(x_1 - x)f(x_1)dx_1 - f(x) \\
&= \int K(v)f(x + hv)dv - f(x) \\
&= (1/2)\kappa_2 \sum_{s=1}^{q} h_s^2 f_{ss}(x) + O\left(\sum_{s=1}^{q} h_s^3\right).
\end{aligned}
\tag{18.3}
$$

Note that the above bias calculation is exactly the same as with the i.i.d. data case because stationarity implies identical distribution.

Next, we compute the variance term given by

$$
\begin{aligned}
\text{var}\left(\hat{f}(x)\right) = n^{-2}\text{var}\left(\sum_{t=1}^{n} K_{h,tx}\right) \\
= n^{-2}\left\{\sum_{t=1}^{n} \text{var}(K_{h,tx}) + 2\sum_{t=1}^{n}\sum_{s>t}^{n} \text{cov}(K_{h,tx}, K_{h,sx})\right\}.
\end{aligned}
\tag{18.4}
$$

Below we compute $\text{var}(K_{h,tx})$ and $\text{cov}(K_{h,tx}, K_{h,sx})$ separately. The calculation of $\text{var}(K_{h,tx})$ is the same as with the i.i.d. data case. By stationarity we have (denoting by $H_q = h_1 \ldots h_q$)

$$
\begin{aligned}
\text{var}(K_{h,tx}) = \mathrm{E}\left[K_{h,tx}^2\right] - [\mathrm{E}(K_{h,tx})]^2 \\
= \int K_h^2\left(x_t - x\right) f(x_t)dx_t - \left[\int K_h\left(x_t - x\right) f(x_t)dx_t\right]^2 \\
= H_q^{-1} \int K^2(v)f(x + hv)dv - \left[\int K(v)f(x + hv)dv\right]^2 \\
= H_q^{-1}f(x)\int K^2(v)dv + O\left(H_q^{-1}\sum_{s=1}^{q} h_s^2 + 1\right).
\end{aligned}
\tag{18.5}
$$

By the stationarity property, (18.5), and presuming ρ-mixing, we

have

$$|\text{cov}(K_{h,tx}, K_{h,sx})| \leq \rho(s-t)\text{var}(K_{h,tx})$$

$$= H_q^{-1}\rho(s-t)f(x)\int K^2(v)dv + O\left(H_q^{-1}\sum_{s=1}^{q}h_s^2 + 1\right).$$

$$(18.6)$$

Using $\sum_{t=1}^{n-1}\sum_{s>t}^{n}\rho(s-t) = \sum_{t=1}^{n-1}\sum_{j=1}^{n-t}\rho(j) \leq n\sum_{j=1}^{\infty}\rho(j)$ (where $j = s - t$), we have

$$\text{var}(\hat{f}(x)) = n^{-2}\left\{\sum_{t}\text{var}(K_{h,tx}) + 2\sum_{t}\sum_{s>t}\text{cov}(K_{h,tx}, K_{h,sx})\right\}$$

$$\leq n^{-2}\left\{n\text{var}(K_{h,tx}) + 2n\text{var}(K_{h,tx})\sum_{j=1}^{\infty}\rho(j)\right\}$$

$$= O((nh_1 \ldots h_q)^{-1}),$$

$$(18.7)$$

where the last equality used $\text{var}(K_{h,tx}) = O((h_1 \ldots h_q)^{-1})$ by (18.5), and the fact that $\sum_{j=1}^{\infty}\rho(j) < \infty$.

Summarizing (18.3) and (18.7), we have

$$\text{MSE}(\hat{f}(x)) = O\left(\left(\sum_{s=1}^{q}h^2\right)^2 + (nh_1 \ldots h_q)^{-1}\right). \qquad (18.8)$$

$$\square$$

We have shown that for weakly dependent processes, the kernel density estimator $\hat{f}(x)$ has the same order MSE as for the i.i.d. case. In fact, we will show that the asymptotic distribution of $\hat{f}(x)$ is also the same as that for the i.i.d. case which, in particular, implies that both the leading bias and variance terms are the same as in the i.i.d. setting.

In Section 18.10.1 we show that

$$\text{var}\left((nh_1 \ldots h_q)^{1/2}\hat{f}(x)\right) = \kappa^q f(x) + o(1). \qquad (18.9)$$

Equation (18.9) shows that for ρ-mixing processes whose mixing coefficient satisfies $\sum_{\tau=1}^{\infty}\rho(\tau) < \infty$, the leading term of the asymptotic variance of $\hat{f}(x)$ is the same as that in the i.i.d. data case.

Given that the leading bias and variance terms of $\hat{f}(x)$ are the same as those of the i.i.d. data case, it is natural to expect that the pointwise asymptotic normality result also holds true for mixing data. We give this result in the next theorem.

Theorem 18.2. *Under conditions similar to those given in Theorem 2.2 for $f(\cdot)$ and $k(\cdot)$, but replacing the i.i.d. assumption by either ρ-mixing with $\rho(\tau) = O\left(\tau^{-(1+\epsilon)}\right)$ or α-mixing with $\rho(\tau) = O\left(\tau^{-(1+\epsilon)}\right)$, and also assuming that as $n \to \infty$, $h_s \to 0$ $(s = 1, \ldots, q)$, $nh_1 \ldots h_q \to 0$, and $nh_1 \ldots h_q \sum_{s=1}^{q} h_s^6 \to \infty$, then we have*

$$\sqrt{nh_1 \ldots h_q} \left(\hat{f}(x) - f(x) - \frac{1}{\kappa_2} \sum_{s=1}^{q} h_s^2 f_{ss}(x) \right) \xrightarrow{d} N\left(0, \kappa^q f_J(x)\right).$$

The proof of Theorem 18.2 under ρ-mixing is given in Section 18.10. For a proof under α-mixing, see Robinson (1983) and Masry (1996*b*).

Theorem 18.2 says that the (first order) asymptotic distribution of $\hat{f}(x)$ for weakly dependent processes is the same as in the i.i.d. data case.

One can also consider estimating a vector of joint PDFs evaluated at m different points. Let $\mathbf{x} = (x_{1+\tau_1}, \ldots, x_{1+\tau_m})$, where $0 \leq \tau_1 < \tau_2 < \cdots < \tau_m$ are some positive integers. Define an $m \times 1$ vector function $f_J(\mathbf{x})$ by

$$f_J(\mathbf{x}) \stackrel{\text{def}}{=} (f(x_{1+\tau_1}), f(x_{1+\tau_2}), \ldots, f(x_{1+\tau_m}))'.$$

Define the kernel estimator of $f_J(\mathbf{x})$ by

$$\hat{f}_J(\mathbf{x}) \stackrel{\text{def}}{=} (\hat{f}(x_{1+\tau_1}), \hat{f}(x_{1+\tau_2}), \ldots, \hat{f}(x_{1+\tau_m}))'.$$

Then it can be shown that $\hat{f}_J(\mathbf{x})$ converges to $f_J(\mathbf{x})$. Indeed one can show that

$$\sqrt{nH^q} \left(\hat{f}_J(\mathbf{x}) - f_J(\mathbf{x}) - \frac{1}{\kappa_2} \sum_{s=1}^{q} h_s^2 f_{J,ss}(\mathbf{x}) \right) \xrightarrow{d} N(0, \kappa^q f_J(x)),$$

$$(18.10)$$

where $f_{J,ss}(\mathbf{x})$ is an $m \times 1$ vector whose j^{th} element is given by

$$f_{ss}(x_{1+\tau_j}) = \left[\partial^2 f(x)/\partial x_s^2\right]|_{x=x_{1+\tau_j}}.$$

We observe that the $\hat{f}(x_{1+\tau_j})$'s are asymptotically independent for different j's. Robinson (1983) provides a proof of (18.10) for α-mixing data.

18.1.1 Uniform Almost Sure Rate of Convergence

As was the case for i.i.d. data, the uniform almost sure convergence rate remains unchanged for weakly dependent data.

Theorem 18.3. *Under conditions on $f(\cdot)$ and $k(\cdot)$ similar to those given in Theorem 1.4, and also assuming that the data is ρ-mixing with $\rho(\tau) = O(\tau^{-(1+\epsilon)})$ or α-mixing with $\alpha(\tau) = O(\tau^{-(1+\epsilon)})$, then*

$$\sup_{x \in D} \left| \hat{f}(x) - f(x) \right| = O \left(|h|^2 + \left(\frac{\ln(n)}{nh_1 \ldots h_q} \right)^{1/2} \right) \quad \text{almost surely.}$$

Proof. See Masry (1996*b*). □

Theorem 18.3 tells us that the almost sure uniform rate of $\hat{f}(x)$ is the same as for the i.i.d. data case (see Theorem 1.4).

18.2 Regression Models with Dependent Data

18.2.1 The Martingale Difference Error Case

Consider a nonparametric regression model of the form

$$Y_t = g(X_t) + u_t, \tag{18.11}$$

where, as in Chapter 2, $g(\cdot)$ is an unknown smooth function, and we assume that u_t is a martingale difference process (hence u_t is serially uncorrelated). We assume that $\{Y_t, X_t'\}_{t=1}^n$ is a strictly stationary β-mixing process with mixing coefficient β_τ. We estimate $g(x)$ by the local constant kernel method, hence

$$\hat{g}(x) = n^{-1} \frac{\sum_{t=1}^n Y_t K_h (x - X_t)}{\hat{f}(x)}. \tag{18.12}$$

We will assume that the error term u_t is a martingale difference process, i.e., we assume that $\mathrm{E}(u_t | X_t, \mathcal{M}_{-\infty}^{t-1}) = 0$ ($\mathcal{M}_{-\infty}^{t-1}$ contains $(Y_{t-\tau}, X_{t-\tau})$ for all $\tau \geq 1$). The martingale difference assumption implies that the error u_t is serially uncorrelated, but it allows the error to be of unknown conditionally heteroskedastic form. Also, when X_t contains lagged values of Y_t, say $Y_{t-1}, \ldots, y_{t-d}$, then $\mathrm{E}(u_t | X_t) = 0$ implies that $\mathrm{E}(u_t | Y_{t-1}, \ldots, Y_{t-d}) = 0$, which suggests that u_t is likely to be serially uncorrelated. Therefore, the martingale difference condition on

u_t is a reasonable assumption for nonparametric time series regression models.

To derive the asymptotic distribution of $\hat{g}(x)$, we write, as we did with the i.i.d. data case,

$$\hat{g}(x) - g(x) = [\hat{g}(x) - g(x)]\hat{f}(x)/\hat{f}(x) \equiv \hat{m}(x)/\hat{f}(x),$$

where

$$\hat{m}(x) = [\hat{g}(x) - g(x)]\hat{f}(x) = \hat{m}_1(x) + \hat{m}_2(x),$$

with

$$\hat{m}_1(x) = n^{-1}\sum_t [g(x_t) - g(x)]K_{h,tx} \text{ and}$$

$$\hat{m}_2(x) = n^{-1}\sum_t u_t K_{h,tx}.$$

By exactly the same proof as for the i.i.d. data case, one can show that $(|h|^j = \sum_{s=1}^q h_s^j)$

$$\mathrm{E}[\hat{m}_1(x)] = \sum_{s=1}^q h_s^2 B_s(x) + O\left(||h||^3\right), \qquad (18.13)$$

where $B_s(x) = (1/2)\kappa_2\left[f(x)g_{ss}(x) + 2f_s(x)g_s(x)\right]$.

By the same calculation used in computing $\mathrm{var}(\hat{f}(x))$, one can show that (see Exercise 18.2)

$$\mathrm{var}\left[\hat{m}_1(x)\right] = O\left(|h|^2(nH_q)^{-1}\right) = o\left((nH_q)^{-1}\right). \qquad (18.14)$$

Equations (18.13) and (18.13) imply that

$$\hat{m}_1(x) = \sum_{s=1}^q h_s^2 B_s(x) + o\left(|h|^2 + (nH_q)^{-1/2}\right). \qquad (18.15)$$

By assuming that u_t follows a martingale difference process, we have $\mathrm{E}(u_t u_s|X_t, X_s) = 0$ for $t \neq s$, hence,

$$\mathrm{E}[(\hat{m}_2(x))^2] = n^{-2}\sum_t\sum_s \mathrm{E}[u_t u_s K_h(x - X_t)K_h(x - X_s)]$$

$$= n^{-2}\sum_t \mathrm{E}\left[u_t^2 K_h^2(x - X_t)\right] \text{ (since } \mathrm{E}(u_t u_s|X_t, X_s) = 0 \text{ if } t \neq s)$$

$$= n^{-2}\mathrm{E}\left[\sigma^2(X_t)K_h^2(x - X_t)\right]$$

$$= (nh_1 \ldots h_q)^{-1}\left\{\kappa^q \sigma^2(x)f(x) + o_p(1)\right\}$$

$$\qquad (18.16)$$

by exactly the same proof as in the i.i.d. data case (see Chapter 2).

Equation (18.16) implies that $(H_q = h_1 \ldots h_q)$

$$\hat{m}_2(x) = O_p\left((nH_q)^{-1/2}\right). \qquad (18.17)$$

Theorem 18.1 and (18.17) lead to (assuming that $f(x) > 0$)

$$\begin{aligned}
\hat{g}(x) - g(x) &= \frac{\hat{m}(x)}{\hat{f}(x)} \\
&= \frac{O_p\left(|h|^2 + (nH_q)^{-1/2}\right)}{f(x) + o_p(1)} \\
&= O_p\left(|h|^2 + (nH_q)^{-1/2}\right). \qquad (18.18)
\end{aligned}$$

One can further establish the asymptotic distribution of $\hat{g}(x)$.

Theorem 18.4. *Assuming that $h \to 0$, $nh^q \to \infty$, and $nh^{q+8} \to 0$ as $n \to \infty$, we have*

$$\sqrt{nH_q}\left(\hat{g}(x) - g(x) - \sum_{s=1}^{q} h_s^2 B_s(x)\right) \xrightarrow{d} N(0, \kappa^q \sigma^2(x)/f(x)).$$

One can prove Theorem 18.4 using the same "small block" and "big block" approaches used in the proof of Theorem 18.2 (see Section 18.10 below for details); therefore, we omit this proof here.

Theorem 18.4 states that the (first order) asymptotic distribution of $\hat{g}(x)$ is the same as that for the i.i.d. data case.

From the derivation of (18.16) we see that the martingale difference error assumption makes the asymptotic variance calculation as simple as for the independent data case. Theorem 18.4 still holds true without the martingale difference assumption, provided the error u_t is a mixing process and that the mixing coefficient satisfies a decay rate such as the one used when proving Theorem 18.2.

As was the case for i.i.d. data, one can also select the smoothing parameters by the least squares cross-validation method, i.e., by choosing $h_1, \ldots, h_q$ to minimize

$$CV(h) = n^{-1}\sum_{t=1}^{n}[Y_t - \hat{g}_{-t}(X_t)]^2 M(X_t),$$

where $\hat{g}_{-t}(X_t) = \sum_{s\neq t}^{n} Y_s K_h(X_s - X_t) / \sum_{s\neq t}^{n} K_h(X_s - X_t)$ is the leave-one-out kernel estimator of $g(X_t)$, and $M(\cdot)$ is a compactly supported nonnegative weight function. Under the assumption that the data is some mixing process whose mixing coefficients decay to zero at certain rates, one can show that the CV-selected smoothing parameters have the same asymptotic behavior as in the independent data case (e.g., see Chapter 2). This is not surprising as we have already shown that the estimation MSE has the same leading term expansion whether the data is independent or weakly dependent.

18.2.2   The Autocorrelated Error Case

Xiao, Linton, Carroll and Mammen (2003) consider the following regression model:

$$Y_t = g(X_t) + u_t, \quad t = 1, \ldots, n, \tag{18.19}$$

where $X_t \in \mathbb{R}^q$ is strictly exogenous, i.e., $\mathrm{E}(u_t|X_1, \ldots, X_n) = 0$ for all t. Xiao et al. allow u_t to be serially correlated, and we write

$$u_t = \sum_{j=0}^{\infty} c_j \epsilon_{t-j}, \tag{18.20}$$

where the ϵ_j's are i.i.d. with zero mean and finite variance σ_ϵ^2, and the c_j's are unknown coefficients. Note that Xiao et al. assume that X_t and u_t are orthogonal, i.e., that $\mathrm{E}(u_t|X_t) = 0$. Since u_t is serially correlated, this implies that X_t cannot contain lagged values of Y_t. Letting L denote the lag operator and $c(L) = \sum_{j=0}^{\infty} c_j L^j$, inverting $c(L)$ yields

$$c(L)^{-1} = a(L) = a_0 - a_1 L - \cdots - a_j L^j - \cdots = a_0 - \sum_{j=1}^{\infty} a_j L^j.$$

Applying $a(L)$ to (18.19) leads to

$$a(L)Y_t = a(L)g(X_t) + \epsilon_t. \tag{18.21}$$

The error term in (18.21) is uncorrelated. Define

$$\underline{Y}_t = Y_t - \sum_{j=1}^{\infty} a_j \left(Y_{t-j} - g(X_{t-j}) \right).$$

Then (18.21) can be rewritten as

$$\underline{Y}_t = g(X_t) + \epsilon_t. \tag{18.22}$$

Equation (18.22) is a valid regression equation since the error ϵ_t is serially uncorrelated. Xiao et al. (2003) first consider an infeasible estimator of $g(\cdot)$ based on the assumption that $\underline{Y}_t$ is known. Xiao et al. consider the general local polynomial method. Here, for expositional simplicity, we consider only the local linear method. Letting $\bar{g}(x)$ denote the local linear estimator of $g(x)$ based on (18.22), then under some additional assumptions such as the data being α-mixing with the mixing coefficient satisfying a particular decay rate, Xiao et al. show that

$$\sqrt{nh_1 \dots h_q}\left(\bar{g}(x) - g(x) - \frac{1}{\kappa_2}\sum_{s=1}^{q} g_{ss}(x)\right) \xrightarrow{d} N\left(0, \sigma_\epsilon^2 \kappa^q / f(x)\right),$$

(18.23)

where $f(\cdot)$ is the PDF of X_t. Note that (18.23) is the same as the independent data case studied in Chapter 2. Also note that $\bar{g}(x)$ is more efficient than an estimator based on (18.19) because $\sigma_\epsilon^2 < \sigma_u^2 = \sigma_\epsilon^2 \sum_{j=0}^{\infty} c_j^2$. Xiao et al. further consider a feasible estimation procedure which can be described as follows: (i) estimate $g(\cdot)$ based on (18.19) (say $\hat{g}(X_t)$), (ii) obtain $\hat{u}_t = Y_t - \hat{g}(X_t)$, then estimate a τ-th order autoregression of $\hat{u}_t$, i.e., $\hat{u}_t = \hat{a}_1\hat{u}_{t-1} + \cdots + \hat{a}_\tau\hat{u}_{t-\tau} + \text{residual}$, (iii) construct an approximation to $\underline{Y}_t$ using $\hat{\underline{Y}}_t = Y_t - \sum_{t=1}^{\tau} \hat{a}_j(Y_{t-j} - \hat{g}(X_{t-j}))$, and, finally, (iv) estimate $g(\cdot)$ again based on $\hat{\underline{Y}}_t = g(X_t) + \text{error}$. This procedure may be iterated to achieve better finite-sample performance. Letting $\tilde{g}(x)$ denote the resulting feasible estimator of $g(\cdot)$, Xiao et al. show that $\tilde{g}(x)$ has the same asymptotic distribution as $\bar{g}(x)$ described in (18.23).

One can easily allow the error term to follow a finite order nonparametric ARCH process, say $\text{var}(u_t|Y_{t-1}, \dots, Y_{t-p}) = m(Y_{t-1}, \dots, Y_{t-p})$, where the functional form of $m(\cdot)$ is unspecified. One can consistently estimate $m(\cdot)$ by the nonparametric regression of $\hat{u}_t^2$ on $(Y_{t-1}, \dots, Y_{t-p})$, where $\hat{u}_t$ is the estimated residual; for theory and applications of nonparametric ARCH(p) models see Pagan and Schwert (1990) and Härdle and Tsybakov (1997). Estimating GARCH or ARCH(∞) models constitutes a more difficult problem. Recently, Linton and Mammen (2005) proposed a novel method for consistently estimating semiparametric ARCH(∞) models of the form $\text{var}(Y_t|I_{t-1}) = \sum_{j=1}^{\infty} \psi_j(\theta)m(Y_{t-j})$, where θ is a finite dimensional parameter and the functional form of $m(\cdot)$ is unspecified.[2] Linton and Mammen established the asymptotic

---

[2]See Engle (1982) and Bollerslev (1986) for seminal work on ARCH and GARCH

theory for the parametric components and the pointwise distribution of the nonparametric component of the model.

Su and Ullah (2006) consider nonparametric regression models having nonlinear errors of unknown form. They suggest estimating the error serial correlation structure by nonparametric kernel methods and then correcting for serial correlation to obtain more efficient estimates of the regression function. Peng and Yao (2004) consider nonparametric regression under dependent errors having infinite variance.

18.2.3   One-Step-Ahead Forecasting

Consider a simple nonparametric regression model of the form

$$Y_t = g(Y_{t-1}, \ldots, Y_{t-q}) + u_t, \tag{18.24}$$

which is a special case of (18.11) with $X_t = (Y_{t-1}, \ldots, Y_{t-q})$. Suppose we want to make one-step-ahead forecasts using this model with a rolling estimation sample of size $n - q$. We forecast Y_{n+t}, for $t = 1, \ldots, m$, by

$$\hat{Y}_{n+t,1} \equiv \hat{E}(Y_{n+t}|X_{n+t}) = \frac{\sum_{j=q+t}^{n+t-1} Y_j K_h (X_j - X_{n+t})}{\sum_{j=q+t}^{n+t-1} K_h (X_j - X_{n+t})}, \tag{18.25}$$

where $K_h(X_j - X_{n+t}) = \prod_{s=1}^{q} h_s^{-1} k((Y_{j-s} - Y_{n+t-s})/h_s)$ because $X_j = (Y_{j-1}, \ldots, Y_{j-q})$ and $X_{n+t} = (Y_{n+t-1}, \ldots, Y_{n+t-q})$.

Note that (18.25) forecasts Y_{n+t} using the previous $n - q$ observations to compute $E(Y_{n+t}|X_{n+t})$. On the right-hand side of (18.25), the summation upper limit is $j = n + t - 1$, so the latest Y_j is Y_{n+t-1}, which is one period before the forecast period, $n + t$. Therefore, the right-hand side of (18.25) uses information only up to period $n + t - 1$ to forecast the value Y_{n+t}. This is exactly the one-step-ahead forecast we want to make. After m periods we would obtain m one-step-ahead forecasts, $\hat{Y}_{n+t}$ for $t = 1, \ldots, m$, and the mean square forecasting error is given by

$$MSFE = \frac{1}{m} \sum_{t=1}^{m} (\hat{Y}_{n+t,1} - Y_{n+t})^2. \tag{18.26}$$

In practice, researchers often also compute MSFE based on some popular parametric models, say $Y_{n+t} = \alpha_0 + \alpha_1 Y_{n+t-1} + \cdots + \alpha_q Y_{n+t-q} + u_t$.

models.

If the nonparametric MSFE is (significantly) smaller than the MSFE obtained using a simple parametric model, this indicates that the parametric model is misspecified, and one should then search for a more flexible parametric model or use the nonparametric model to improve one's forecasts.

18.2.4 d-Step-Ahead Forecasting

To make a d-step-ahead forecast, one could consider the regression model given by

$$Y_t = g(Y_{t-d}, \ldots, Y_{t-d-q+1}) + u_t, \qquad (18.27)$$

which is also a special case of (18.11) with $X_t = (Y_{t-d}, \ldots, Y_{t-d-q+1})$. Suppose we want to make d-step-ahead forecasts using this model with a rolling estimation sample of size $n - q - d$. We forecast Y_{n+t}, for $t = 1, \ldots, m$, by

$$\hat{Y}_{n+t,d} \equiv \hat{E}(Y_{n+t}|X_{n+t}) = \frac{\sum_{j=q+d-1+t}^{n+t-d} Y_j K_h\left(X_j - X_{n+t}\right)}{\sum_{j=q+d-1+t}^{n+t-d} K_h\left(X_j - X_{n+t}\right)}, \qquad (18.28)$$

where $K_h(X_j - X_{n+t}) = \prod_{s=1}^{q} h_s^{-1} k((Y_{j+1-d-s} - Y_{n+t+1-d-s})/h_s)$. Note that when $d = 1$, (18.28) reduces to (18.25), as it should.

Note that (18.25) forecasts Y_{n+t} using the previous $n - q - d$ observations to compute $E(Y_{n+t}|X_{n+t})$. On the right-hand side of (18.25), the summation upper limit is $n+t-d$, so the latest Y_j is Y_{n+t-d}, which is measured d periods before the forecast period, i.e., $n + t$. Therefore, the right-hand side of (18.25) uses only information up to $n + t - d$ to forecast the value of Y_{n+t}. The d-step-ahead MSFE over m periods is given by

$$MSFE_d = \frac{1}{m} \sum_{t=1}^{m} (\hat{Y}_{n+t,d} - Y_{n+t})^2, \qquad (18.29)$$

where $\hat{Y}_{n+t,d}$ is defined in (18.28).

In practice researchers can compare this with the MSFE based on some popular parametric models such as $Y_{n+t} = \alpha_0 + \alpha_1 Y_{n+t-d} + \cdots + \alpha_q Y_{n+t-d-q+1} + u_t$.

See Chen and White (1999) and Chen, Racine and Swanson (2001) for related work on semiparametric neural network models in a forecasting framework.

18.2.5   Estimation of Nonparametric Impulse Response Functions

Consider the following nonparametric conditionally heteroskedastic autoregresssive model:

$$Y_t = g(X_{t-1}) + \sigma(X_{t-1})u_t, \quad t = q+1, \ldots, n, \qquad (18.30)$$

where $X_{t-1} = (Y_{t-1}, \ldots, Y_{t-q})'$ denotes a vector of lagged observations up to lag q, $g(\cdot)$ and $\sigma(\cdot)$ denote the conditional mean and conditional standard deviation, respectively, and u_t is an i.i.d. series with zero mean, unit variance, and a finite fourth moment. Following Koop, Pesaran and Potter (1996), Yang and Tschernig (2005) define the generalized impulse response for horizon k (GIR_k) as the quantity by which a prespecified shock u in period t changes the k-step-ahead prediction based on information up to period $t-1$ only. That is,

$$GIR_k(x, u) = \mathrm{E}(Y_{t+k-1}|X_{t-1} = x, u_t = u) - \mathrm{E}(Y_{t+k-1}|X_{t-1} = x)$$
$$= \mathrm{E}(Y_{t+k-1}|Y_t = g(x) + \sigma(x)u, X_{t-1} = x) - \mathrm{E}(Y_{t+k-1}|X_{t-1} = x).$$
$$(18.31)$$

Note that GIR_k depends on both x and the shock u. An alternative definition of a nonlinear impulse response function is given by Gallant, Rossi and Tauchen (1993). Yang and Tschernig (2005) suggest using nonparametric kernel methods to estimate the multi-step-ahead predictions contained in GIR_k. We first introduce some notation. For $k \geq 1$, we write

$$g_k(x) = \mathrm{E}[Y_{t+k-1}|X_{t-1} = x] \text{ and}$$
$$g_k(x, u) = \mathrm{E}[Y_{t+k-1}|X_{t-1} = x, u_t = u],$$

and write

$$Y_{t+k-1} = g_k(X_{t-1}) + \sigma_k(X_{t-1})u_{t,k},$$

where $\sigma_k^2(x) = \mathrm{var}(Y_{t+k-1}|X_{t-1} = x)$ and $u_{t,k}$ is a martingale difference process (because $\mathrm{E}(u_{t,k}|X_{t-1}) = \mathrm{E}(u_{t,k}|Y_{t-1}, \ldots, Y_{t-q}) = 0$) having a unit conditional variance, i.e., $\mathrm{var}(u_{t,k}|X_{t-1}) = 1$. Also, let

$$\sigma_{k',k}(x) = \mathrm{cov}[(Y_{t+k'-1}, Y_{t+k-1})|X_{t-1} = x] \text{ and}$$
$$\sigma_{k'k',k}(x) = \mathrm{cov}\big\{[(Y_{t+k'-1} - g_{k'}(X_{t-1}))^2, Y_{t+k-1} - g_k(X_{t-1})]$$
$$|X_{t-1} = x\big\}.$$

Then we can write GIR_k defined in (18.31) more compactly as

$$GIR_k(x, u) = g_{k-1}(g(x) + \sigma(x)u, x) - g_k(x) = g_{k-1}(x_u) - g_k(x),$$

where $x_u = (g(x) + \sigma(x)u, x)$. Replacing the multistep forecasting functions by their local linear kernel estimators, we obtain the estimator of GIR_k given by

$$\widehat{GIR}_k(x, u) = \hat{g}_{k-1}(\hat{x}_u) - \hat{g}_k(x),$$

where $\hat{x} = (\hat{g}(x) + \hat{\sigma}(x)u, x')$, and we describe the local linear estimators $\hat{g}(x)$, $\hat{g}_k(x)$ and $\hat{\sigma}(x)$ below.

Define

$$e = (1, 0_{1 \times q})', \quad Z_k = \begin{pmatrix} 1 & \cdots & 1 \\ X_{q-1} - x & \cdots & X_{n-k} - x \end{pmatrix}',$$

$W_k = n^{-1} \operatorname{diag}\{K_h(X_{t-1}, x)\}_{i=q}^{n-k+1}$, and $Y_k = (Y_{q+k-1}, \ldots, Y_n)'$. Then the local linear estimator of $g_k(x)$ is given by

$$\hat{g}_k(x) = e'(Z_k' W_k Z_k)^{-1} Z_k' W_k Y_k, \qquad (18.32)$$

while

$$\hat{\sigma}_k(x) = \left\{ e'(Z_k' W_k Z_k)^{-1} Z_k' W_k Y_k^2 - \hat{g}_k(x)^2 \right\}^{1/2}. \qquad (18.33)$$

Note that $\hat{g}(x) = \hat{g}_1(x)$ and $\hat{\sigma}(x) = \hat{\sigma}_1(x)$. Under the assumptions that $h_s = cn^{-1/(q+4)}$, $c > 0$, and that X_t is a stationary β-mixing process with the mixing coefficient satisfying $\beta(\tau) \le c_0 \rho^{-\tau}$ for some $c_0 > 0$ and $0 < \rho < 1$, and with additional smoothness and moment conditions on $g(\cdot)$, σ and $f(\cdot)$ (the density of X_t), Yang and Tschernig (2005) derive the asymptotic distribution of $\widehat{GIR}_k$, i.e.,

$$\sqrt{nh_1 \ldots h_q} \left\{ \widehat{GIR}_k(x, u) - GIR_k(x, u) - \sum_{s=1}^{q} b_{g,k,s}(x, u) \right\}$$

$$\xrightarrow{d} N(0, \Sigma_k(x, u)),$$

where the leading bias term is given by

$$b_{g,k,s}(x, u) = b_{g,k-1,s}(x_u) - b_{g,k,s}(x) + \frac{\partial g_{k-1}(x_u)}{\partial x_1}[b_{g,s}(x) + b_{\sigma,s}(x)u],$$

with $b_{g,k,s}(x) = (\kappa_2/2)\partial^2 g_k(x)/\partial x_s^2$, and with $b_{\sigma,k,s} = \kappa_2[\partial^2/\partial x_s^2(g_k^2(x) + \sigma_k^2(x)) - 2g_k(x)\partial^2/\partial x_s^2 g_k(x)]/[4\sigma_k(x)]$. The asymptotic variance is given by

$$
\Sigma_k(x,u) = \frac{\kappa^q \sigma^2(x)}{f(x)} \left[\frac{\sigma_{k-1}^2(x_u)f(x)}{f(x_u)\sigma^2(x)} + \left(\frac{\partial g_{k-1}(x_u)}{\partial x_1} \right)^2 \right.
$$

$$
\times \left\{ 1 + u\mu_3 + \frac{u^2(\mu_4 - 1)}{4} \right\} \frac{\sigma_k^2(x)}{\sigma^2(x)}
$$

$$
\left. - \frac{\partial g_{k-1}(x_u)}{\partial x_1} \left\{ \frac{2\sigma_{1,k}(x)}{\sigma^2(x)} + \frac{u\sigma_{11,k}(x)}{\sigma^3(x)} \right\} \right]
$$

$$
- \frac{\kappa^q}{f(x)} \mathbf{1}(x = x_u) \left\{ 2\sigma_{k-1,k}(x) - 2\frac{\partial g_{k-1}(x_u)}{\partial x_1} \sigma_{1,k-1}(x) \right.
$$

$$
\left. + u \frac{\partial g_{k-1}(x_u)}{\partial x_1} \frac{\sigma_{11,k-1}(x)}{\sigma(x)} \right\},
$$

where $\mu_j = \mathrm{E}(u_t^j)$ ($j = 3,4$).

Yang and Tschernig (2005) also suggest an alternative estimator for $\sigma_k^2(x)$ that is based on the estimated nonparametric residuals given by

$$
\tilde{\sigma}_k^2(x) = e'(Z_k' W_k Z_k)^{-1} Z_k' W_k V_k, \tag{18.34}
$$

where $V_k = ([Y_{q+k-1} - \hat{g}_k(X_{q-1})]^2, \ldots, [Y_n - \hat{g}_k(X_{n-k})]^2)'$.

The estimation procedure described above is simple to implement. However, it may be overly noisy due to noise accumulated over the k prediction periods. To estimate $g_k(x)$ more efficiently, Yang and Tschernig (2005) suggest an alternative multistage method proposed by Chen, Yang and Hafner (2004) for estimating GIR_k, which we briefly describe below. Let $Y_t^{(0)} = Y_t$, and repeating the following steps for $j = 1, \ldots, k$, compute

$$
\tilde{g}_j(x) = \frac{\sum_{t=m-1}^{n-k} K_h(X_t - x) Y_{t+j}^{(j-1)}}{\sum_{t=m-1}^{n-k} K_h(X_t - x)}, \tag{18.35}
$$

where $Y_{t+j}^{(j)} = \tilde{f}_j(X_t)$. The last step $j = k$ gives $\tilde{g}_k(x)$. Chen et al. showed that

$$
\sqrt{nh_1 \ldots h_q} \left[\tilde{g}_k(x) - g_k(x) - \sum_{s=1}^q b_{g,k,s}(x)h_s^2 \right] \xrightarrow{d} N(0, \kappa^q s_k(x)/f(x)),
$$

where $s_k(x) = \mathrm{var}(\tilde{f}_{k-1}(X_t)|X_{t-1} = x)$. This leads to an alternative estimator for GIR_k given by

$$\widetilde{GIR}_k(x, u) = \tilde{f}_{k-1}(\tilde{x}_u) - \tilde{g}_k(x),$$

with the multistep predictor $\tilde{f}_k(x)$ and the conditional standard deviation estimator $\tilde{\sigma}_k(x)$ given by (18.35) and (18.34) (with $k = 1$, $\sigma(x) = \sigma_1(x)$), respectively. The simulation results reported in Yang and Tschernig (2005) show that the multistep estimator $\widetilde{GIR}_k$ performs better than the direct estimator $\widehat{GIR}_k$ in the MISE sense.

18.3 Semiparametric Models with Dependent Data

18.3.1 A Partially Linear Model with Dependent Data

Andrews (1994) considers a general class of semiparametric models that includes a semiparametric partially linear model as a special case. We consider a partially linear model with dependent data in this section given by

$$Y_t = X_t'\gamma + \theta(X_t) + u_t.$$

We consider the β-mixing case. Therefore, we assume that (X_t', Z_t') is a β-mixing process with mixing coefficient β_τ, and u_t is a martingale difference process. We estimate γ by the same method as in the independent data case. That is, we estimate γ based on the following regression equation (see (7.11) of Chapter 7):

$$(Y_t - \hat{Y}_t)\hat{f}_t + (X_t - \hat{X}_t)'\hat{f}_t\gamma + \text{ error},$$

where $\hat{X}_t = n^{-1}\sum_{s=1}^n X_s K_{h,ts}/\hat{f}_t$ is the kernel estimator of $\hat{E}(X_t|Z_t)$, $\hat{Y}_t = n^{-1}\sum_{s=1}^n Y_s K_{h,ts}/\hat{f}_t$ is the kernel estimator of $\hat{E}(Y_t|Z_t)$, and $\hat{f}_t = \hat{f}(X_t)$.

As in Chapter 7, the semiparametric estimator of γ is the least squares estimator obtained by regressing $(Y_t - \hat{Y}_t)\hat{f}_t$ on $(X_t - \hat{X}_t)\hat{f}_t$, i.e.,

$$\hat{\gamma} = \left\{ \sum_{t=1}^n (X_t - \hat{X}_t)\hat{f}_t(X_t - \hat{X}_t)'\hat{f}_t \right\}^{-1} \sum_{t=1}^n (X_t - \hat{X}_t)\hat{f}_t(Y_t - \hat{Y}_t)\hat{f}_t. \tag{18.36}$$

We give a lemma regarding a β-mixing process.

Lemma 18.1. *Suppose that $X_1, \ldots, X_n$ is a random vector ($X_i \in \mathbb{R}^q$) β-mixing process. Let $g(x)$ be a Borel measurable function, and assume that $\mathrm{E}|g_n(X_1)g_n(X_{1+\tau})| \leq M_n$ and $\mathrm{E}|g_n(X_1)|^{1+\delta}\mathrm{E}|g_n(X_{1+\tau})|^{1+\delta} \leq M_n$ for some $\delta > 0$ and $M_n > 0$. Then*

$$|\mathrm{E}[g_n(X_1)g_n(X_{1+\tau})] - \mathrm{E}[g_n(X_1)]\mathrm{E}[g_n(X_{1+\tau})]| \leq 4M_n^{1/(1+\delta)}|\beta(\tau)|^{\delta/(1+\delta)}.$$

Proof. See Lemma 1 of Yoshihara (1976). $\qquad\qquad\qquad\qquad\qquad\qquad\square$

Using Lemma 18.1, Fan and Li (1999*b*) prove the following result.

Theorem 18.5. *Under conditions on $g(\cdot)$ and $f(\cdot)$ similar to those given in Theorem 7.2, but replacing the i.i.d. condition with the condition that $\{Y_t, X_t, Z_t\}_{t=1}^n$ is a β-mixing process with the β-mixing coefficient β_τ satisfying the condition that $\beta_\tau^{\delta/(2+\delta)} = O\left(\tau^{-2+\epsilon}\right)$ for some $0 < \epsilon < 1$ and $0 < \delta < \max\{1/2, 2/(q-2)\}$, then*

$$\sqrt{n}(\hat{\gamma} - \gamma) \to N(0, \Sigma) \text{ in distribution,}$$

where

$$\Sigma = \left\{\mathrm{E}\left[v_t v_t' f^2(Z_t)\right]\right\}^{-1} \mathrm{E}\left[\sigma^2(X_t, Z_t)v_t v_t' f^4(Z_t)\right] \left\{\mathrm{E}\left[v_t v_t' f^2(Z_t)\right]\right\}^{-1}$$
$$\equiv \Phi^{-1}\Omega\Phi^{-1}.$$

Note that the expressions $\hat{\Phi} = n^{-1}\sum_t (X_t - \hat{X}_t)(X_t - \hat{X}_t)'\hat{f}_t^2$ and $\hat{\Omega} = n^{-1}\sum_t (\hat{u}_t\hat{f}_t)^2(X_t - \hat{X}_t)\hat{f}_t(X_t - \hat{X}_t)'\hat{f}_t$ are consistent estimators for Φ and Ω, respectively, where $\hat{u}_t = (Y_t - \hat{Y}_t) - (X_t - \hat{X}_t)'\hat{\gamma}$.

Comparing Theorems 18.5 and 7.2, we see that the asymptotic distribution of $\hat{\gamma}$ is the same for weakly dependent data and independent data. This arises not only because of the weakly dependent data assumption but, more important, because we have assumed that u_t is a martingale difference process (hence is serially uncorrelated). If u_t is serially correlated, the asymptotic variance of $\hat{\gamma}$ may have a different form; see Newey and West (1987), Andrews (1991*b*), and Kiefer and Vogelsang (2002) for recent work on heteroskedasticity and autocorrelation robust covariance matrix estimation.

18.3.2 Additive Regression Models

Consider an additive model of the form

$$Y_t = g_1(X_{t1}) + \cdots + g_q(X_{tq}) + u_t. \tag{18.37}$$

The estimation procedure under weak dependence is the same as with the independent data case discussed in Chapter 9, i.e., we can estimate (18.37) by the kernel-based backfitting methods, marginal integration methods, or by nonparametric series methods.

Letting $X_{ts} = Y_{t+1-d-s}$ for $s = 1, \ldots, d$, then (18.37) becomes

$$Y_t = g_1(Y_{t-d}) + \cdots + g_q(Y_{t-d-q+1}) + u_t, \qquad (18.38)$$

and one can impose the identification condition that $\mathrm{E}[g_s(Y_{t-d-s})] = 0$ for $s = 1, \ldots, q - 1$ if one uses kernel methods (see, e.g., Kim et al. (1999)), or one can require that $g_s(0) = 0$ for $s = 1, \ldots, q - 1$ when using series (e.g., spline) methods. Model (18.38) can then be used to make d-step-ahead forecasts.

One shortcoming of additive models is that they do not allow for general interaction terms among $(X_{t1}, \ldots, X_{tq})$. To allow for interaction terms and also keep the nonparametric additive structure to avoid the curse of dimensionality, one may consider a partially linear additive model of the type discussed in Chapter 9. For example, when $q = 2$ and $X_{ts} = Y_{t-d-s}$ $(s = 0, 1)$, one could consider the model

$$Y_t = Z_t \alpha + g_1(Y_{t-d}) + g_2(Y_{t-d-1}) + u_t, \qquad (18.39)$$

where $Z_t = Y_{t-d} Y_{t-d-1}$.

The estimation method for this model is the same as that discussed in Chapter 9. Model (18.39) allows for an interaction term to enter the model as a parametric component.

Gao and Tong (2004) consider the model selection problem in a general partially linear model with dependent data. They propose a novel cross-validation procedure for selecting the number of lagged variables in both the parametric and nonparametric components.

18.3.3 Varying Coefficient Models with Dependent Data

The varying coefficient model considered in Chapter 9 has the following form:

$$Y_t = X_t' \beta(Z_t) + u_t, \qquad (18.40)$$

where $X_t = (X_{t1}, \ldots, X_{tp})'$ is of dimension p, $\beta(z) = (\beta_1(z), \ldots, \beta_p(z))'$ is a $p \times 1$ vector of unknown smoothing functions, and $Z_t = (Z_{t1}, \ldots, Z_{tq})$ is of dimension q.

The estimation method is the same as with the independent data case. One can use local constant or local linear methods to estimate $\beta(z)$. For example, the local constant estimator of $\beta(z)$ is given by

$$\hat{\beta}(z) = \left[\sum_{j=1}^{n} X_j X_j' K_{h,jz}\right]^{-1} \sum_{j=1}^{n} X_j Y_j K_{h,jz}, \qquad (18.41)$$

where $K_{h,jz} = \prod_{s=1}^{q} h_s^{-1} k\left((Z_{js} - Z_s)/h_s\right)$ is the product kernel.

For a local linear estimator of $\beta(z)$ along with its derivative function estimator, under various mixing conditions Cai, Fan and Yao (2000), Cai, Fan and Li (2000), and Fan, Yao and Cai (2003) show that the estimation methods as well as the asymptotic distributions of the local linear estimators are identical to the independent data case discussed in Chapter 9.

In (18.40) we could have $X_t = (Y_{t-d}, \ldots, Y_{t-d-p+1})$, although Z_t could also be a vector of variables. However, in practice researchers often choose Z_t to be a scalar for two reasons: first, this avoids the curse of dimensionality problem; and second, one can easily draw a two-dimensional graph of z-$\beta_s(z)$ (for $s = 1, \ldots, p$) in order to visually inspect the (possibly nonlinear) functional form of $\beta_s(z)$ for $s = 1, \ldots, p$.

18.4 Testing for Serial Correlation in Semiparametric Models

18.4.1 The Test Statistic and Its Asymptotic Distribution

We again consider the semiparametric partially linear models that were developed in Section 18.3.1. Recall that these models were of the form

$$Y_t = X_t'\gamma + \theta(Z_t) + u_t, \quad t = -L+1, \ldots, 0, 1, \ldots, n, \qquad (18.42)$$

where X_t is $d \times 1$, Z_t is $q \times 1$, γ is a $d \times 1$ parameter, and $\theta(\cdot)$ is an unknown smooth function. The hypothesis of interest is whether the error term u_t exhibits zero first order serial correlation or zero finite order serial correlation.

In order to test for zero (finite order) serial correlation of u_t as discussed in Chapter 7, we use a two-step procedure in which we first estimate γ by

$$\hat{\gamma} = S_{(x-\hat{x})\hat{f}}^{-1} S_{(x-\hat{x})\hat{f},(y-\hat{y})\hat{f}},$$

where for scalar or column-vector sequences with tth elements $A_t \hat{f}_t$ and $B_t \hat{f}_t$, we use the notation $S_{A\hat{f},B\hat{f}} = \frac{1}{n} \sum_t A_t \hat{f}_t B_t' \hat{f}_t$ and $S_{A\hat{f}} = S_{A\hat{f},A\hat{f}}$, and let $\hat{X}_t = \hat{\mathrm{E}}(X_t|Z_t)$ and $\hat{Y}_t = \hat{\mathrm{E}}(Y_t|Z_t)$ denote the kernel estimators of $\mathrm{E}(X_t|t)$ and $\mathrm{E}(Y_t|Z_t)$, respectively. With $\hat{\gamma}$ we can estimate u_t by

$$\tilde{u}_t = Y_t - \hat{Y}_t - (X_t - \hat{X}_t)'\hat{\gamma}. \qquad (18.43)$$

18.4.2 Testing Zero First Order Serial Correlation

Li and Stengos (2003) suggest a density-weighted test statistic to test for the absence of first order serial correlation. They derive the asymptotic distribution of their test statistic under a stronger condition for the error u_t than a martingale difference process. Under this condition we have $\rho_f = \mathrm{E}(u_t f_t u_{t-1} f_{t-1}) = 0$ and $\rho = \mathrm{E}(u_t u_{t-1}) = 0$. The construction of the test statistic for testing first order serial correlation can be based on either of the sample analogues of ρ_f or ρ. Li and Stengos construct a test statistic based on the sample analogue of ρ_f because it avoids technical difficulties arising from the presence of a random denominator in the kernel estimator. The test statistic is based on

$$J_n \overset{\text{def}}{=} \frac{1}{\sqrt{n}} \sum_t \tilde{u}_t \tilde{u}_{t-1} \hat{f}_t \hat{f}_{t-1}. \qquad (18.44)$$

Li and Stengos (2003) prove the following result.

Theorem 18.6. *Assuming that the error u_t is a martingale difference process, then*

(i) $J_n \to N(0, \sigma_0^2)$ *in distribution,*

   where $\sigma_0^2 = \mathrm{E}[\{(u_{t-1} f_{t-1} - v_t' f_t B^{-1} \Phi) u_t f_t\}^2]$, $\Phi = \mathrm{E}[v_t f_t u_{t-1} f_{t-1}]$, $v_t = X_t - \mathrm{E}(X_t|Z_t)$, and $B = \mathrm{E}[(X_t - \hat{X}_t)(X_t - \hat{X}_t)'(f_t)^2]$.

(ii) $\hat{\sigma}_0^2 = \frac{1}{n}\sum_t\{[\tilde{u}_{t-1}\hat{f}_{t-1} - (X_t - \hat{x}_t)'\hat{f}_t \hat{B}^{-1}\hat{\Phi}]\tilde{u}_t \hat{f}_t\}^2$ *with $\hat{\Phi} = \frac{1}{n}\sum_t(X_t - \hat{x}_t)\hat{f}_t \tilde{u}_{t-1}\hat{f}_{t-1}$ and $\hat{B} = \frac{1}{n}\sum_t(X_t - \hat{X}_t)(X_t - \hat{X}_t)'(\hat{f}_t)^2$, is a consistent estimator for σ_0^2.*

   Hence

$$J_n/\hat{\sigma}_0 \overset{d}{\to} N(0,1).$$

Note that when X_t and Z_t are strictly exogenous, the J_n statistic is analogous to Durbin and Watson's (1950) test statistic, whereas when

Z_t contains lagged Y_t, say Y_{t-1}, it is analogous to Durbin's (1970) h-statistic. Li and Stengos (2003) also consider testing for higher order serial correlation.

The above test for serial correlation allows for flexible regression functional forms. However, it is designed only to detect specific types of serial correlation (e.g., $AR(1)$), i.e., it is not a consistent test for detecting serial correlation of unknown form. Hong (1996) and Pinkse (1998) propose some test statistics that are consistent against any type of error serial correlation under parametric regression functional form assumption.

Robinson (1989) introduced a general testing procedure in semi-parametric and nonparametric models for economic time series and applied it to the rational expectations "surprise model" and the market disequilibrium model. His approach involves writing the null hypothesis in terms of a conditional moment restriction. One can also use Robinson's approach to test for zero finite order serial correlation or, more generally, to test the correct specification of a partially linear model of the form $\mathrm{E}[Y_t|X_t, Z_t] = X_t'\gamma + \theta(Z_t)$ a.e.

18.5 Model Specification Tests with Dependent Data

In this section we consider testing the null hypotheses of correct parametric regression functional form along with a nonparametric significance test in the presence of weakly dependent data. All other tests considered in Chapters 12 and 13 can be extended to allow for weakly dependent data.

18.5.1 A Kernel Test for Correct Parametric Regression Functional Form

For expositional simplicity we restrict attention to testing a linear null model. The null hypothesis we consider is therefore

$$H_0^a : \mathrm{E}(Y_t|X_t = x) = x'\gamma \text{ for almost all } x. \qquad (18.45)$$

As with the independent data case, we construct our test based upon $I^a = \mathrm{E}[u_t \mathrm{E}(u_t|X_t) f(X_t)]$. A sample analogue of I^a is given by

$$\hat{I}_n^a = \frac{1}{n(n-1)} \sum_{t=1}^{n} \sum_{s \neq t}^{n} \hat{u}_t \hat{u}_s K_h\left(X_t - X_s\right),$$

where $\hat{u}_t = Y_t - X_t'\hat{\gamma}$, $\hat{\gamma}$ is the least squares estimator of γ based on the (null) linear model. Recall that we used Hall's (1984) CLT to establish the null distribution of $\hat{I}_n^a$ under H_0^a. Hall's CLT has been extended to allow for weakly dependent (β-mixing) data by Fan and Li (1999a), and Hjellvik, Yao and Tjøstheim (1998). The following theorem is proved by Fan and Li.

Theorem 18.7. *Assuming that $h_s \to 0$ ($s = 1, \ldots, q$), $nH_q^{(7/8)} \to \infty$ as $n \to \infty$, and also assuming some moment and smoothness conditions on $f(X_t)$ and $E(Y_t|X_i)$ (see Fan and Li (1999a) for details), under H_0^a we have*

$$T_n^a \equiv n(h_1 \ldots h_q)^{1/2} \hat{I}_n^a / \hat{\sigma}_a \to N(0, 1) \; \text{in distribution,}$$

where $\hat{\sigma}_a^2 = \frac{2h_1 \ldots h_q}{n(n-1)} \sum_{t=1}^n \sum_{s \neq t}^n \hat{u}_t^2 \hat{u}_s^2 K_h^2 (X_t - X_s)$.

Comparing Theorem 18.7 with Theorem 12.1, we see that the asymptotic distribution of $\hat{T}_n^a$ is the same whether the data is independent or weakly dependent.

Fan and Li (1999a) have also shown that if H_0^a is false, T_n^a diverges to $+\infty$ at the rate $n(h_1 \ldots h_q)^{1/2}$. Hence, T_n^a is a consistent test, i.e., the probability of rejecting the null approaches one as $n \to \infty$ if H_0^a is false. Li (2005) has established the validity of a bootstrap procedure to approximate the null distribution of the T_n^a test. Alternatively, one can relax the assumption that the error is serially uncorrelated and use the resampling algorithms proposed by Berkowitz, Kilian and Birgean (1999) to compute a bootstrap statistic which will be robust to serial correlation of unknown form.

18.5.2   Nonparametric Significance Tests

The nonparametric omitted variable tests (i.e., significance tests) considered by Fan and Li (1996) and Lavergne and Vuong (2000) (discussed in Section 12.3.4) were shown to be valid with β-mixing data by Li (1999). Under the assumption that the error terms follow a martingale difference process, the construction of the test statistics and their asymptotic null distributions are identical to those presented in Section 12.3.4 and therefore are not reproduced here.

There is a rich literature on model specification tests with time series (i.e., dependent) data. Juhl and Xiao (2005) propose a robust nonparametric test for structural change in a parametric time trend model (see also Delgado and Hidalgo (2000) on alternative tests for detecting structural breaks in time series models). Kuan and Lee (2004) suggest testing the martingale difference hypothesis based on the empirical characteristic function. Chen, Chou and Kuan (2000) propose a method for testing time reversibility, again based on the characteristic function methodology (this has the advantage of not imposing any moment restrictions because a characteristic function is always bounded), while Fan (1997) uses the empirical characteristic function to test for correct parametric specification of a multivariate distribution function.

18.6 Nonsmoothing Tests for Regression Functional Form

One can also test the null hypothesis H_0^a: $\mathrm{E}(Y_t|X_t) = m(X_t, \gamma)$ a.e., using a nonsmoothing test. This can be easily done using a Hilbert space CLT given in Lemma A.19 (which covers stationary processes).

Bierens and Ploberger (1997) consider a statistic based upon

$$\hat{J}_n(x) = n^{-1/2} \sum_{t=1}^{n} \hat{u}_t \mathcal{H}(X_t, x),$$

where $\hat{u}_t = Y_t - m(X_t, \hat{\gamma})$, and where $\hat{\gamma}$ is an estimator (usually $\sqrt{n}$-consistent) of γ based on the null model. The resulting conditional moment (CM) test is given by

$$CM_n = \frac{1}{n} \sum_{j=1}^{n} \left[\hat{J}_n(X_j) \right]^2. \tag{18.46}$$

For example, one can use $\mathcal{H}(X_t, x) = \mathbf{1}(X_t \leq x)$, or other choices discussed in Chapter 13. Bierens and Ploberger (1997) show that CM_n converges to $\int [J_\infty(x)]^2 F(dx)$ in distribution under H_0^a, where $J_\infty(\cdot)$ is a well-defined zero mean Gaussian process, and $F(\cdot)$ is the CDF of X_t.

Chen and Fan (1999) consider a CM_n-type nonparametric significance test with β-mixing data, and they also show that one can use a stationary bootstrap method (Politis and Romano (1994)) to approximate the null distribution of their test statistic. One can also apply the stationary bootstrap method to approximate the null distribution of the CM_n test defined in (18.46).

18.7 Testing Parametric Predictive Models

18.7.1 In-Sample Testing of Conditional CDFs

Probability Integral Transformation Approach

Let $F(y|\mathcal{I}_{t-1}) = F_t(y|\mathcal{I}_{t-1})$ denote the true CDF of Y_t conditional on the information set up to $t-1$, and let $F(Y_t|\mathcal{I}_{t-1}, \theta_0) = F_t(Y_t|\mathcal{I}_{t-1}, \theta_0)$ be a parametric conditional CDF with θ_0 being a finite dimensional parameter. We will suppress the subscript t in $F(\cdot)$ for notational simplicity. We want to check whether the chosen parametric CDF equals the true CDF. Thus, the null hypothesis is

$$H_0 : \mathrm{P}(Y_t \leq y|\mathcal{I}_{t-1}) = F(Y_t|\mathcal{I}_{t-1}, \theta_0) \text{ a.s. for some } \theta_0 \in \Theta, \quad (18.47)$$

where $\mathcal{I}_{t-1}$ contains all relevant variables up to time $t-1$, The alternative hypothesis is the negation of H_0.

Diebold, Gunther and Tay (1998) suggest checking whether $U_t = F(Y_t|\mathcal{I}_{t-1}, \theta_0)$ is uniformly distributed. This is based on the fact that $V_t = F(Y_t|\mathcal{I}_{t-1})$ is i.i.d. uniformly distributed on the unit interval $[0,1]$. Therefore, if $F(Y_t|\mathcal{I}_{t-1}, \theta_0)$ is correctly specified, $F(Y_t|\mathcal{I}_{t-1}, \theta_0)$ will also be uniformly distributed in the unit interval. Diebold, Hahn and Tay (1999) extend the testing procedure to the multivariate Y case so that it can be used to evaluate the accuracy of density forecasts involving cross-variable interactions. The asymptotic distribution of Diebold et al.'s (1998) test is nonstandard and one needs to use either simulation or bootstrap methods to compute the critical values of the test statistic. Bai (2003) proposes using a martingale transformation to obtain a nuisance parameter free test; see also Pesaran and Timmermann (1992) for an alternative predictive test. We briefly discuss Bai's testing procedure below. Under the Markov assumption, there exists a finite dimensional variable Z^{t-1} such that $F(Y_t|Z^{t-1}, \theta_0) = F(Y_t|\mathcal{I}_{t-1}, \theta_0)$. Let $\hat{\theta}$ denote a $\sqrt{n}$-consistent estimator of θ_0 based on the null model. Defining $\hat{U}_t = F(r|Z^{t-1}, \hat{\theta})$, then for $r \in [0,1]$, one can estimate $F(r|Z^{t-1}, \theta_0)$ by $n^{-1/2} \sum_{t=1}^{n} \mathbf{1}(\hat{U}_t \leq r)$ and compare it with the true conditional CDF $F(r|Z^{t-1}) = r$. Thus, one can test H_0 based on $\hat{V}_n(r) \stackrel{\text{def}}{=} n^{-1/2} \sum_{t=1}^{n} [\mathbf{1}(\hat{U}_t \leq r) - r]$. Bai shows that

$$\hat{V}_n(r) = \frac{1}{\sqrt{n}} \sum_{t=1}^{n} [\mathbf{1}(U_t \leq r) - r] + \bar{g}(r)' \sqrt{n}(\hat{\theta} - \theta_0) + o_p(1), \quad (18.48)$$

where

$$\bar{g}(r) = \plim_{n \to \infty} n^{-1} \sum_{t=1}^{n} \frac{\partial F}{\partial \theta}(x|Z^{t-1}, \theta)|_{x=F^{-1}(r|Z^{t-1}, \theta_0)}.$$

The second term on the right side of (18.48) depends on both the un-known $F(\cdot)$ and $(\hat{\theta} - \theta_0)$. Hence, the asymptotic distribution of $\hat{V}_n(\cdot)$ depends on these nuisance parameters and one cannot tabulate critical values for this test. However, by applying a martingale transformation, one can remove the term $\bar{g}^{(1)}(r)\sqrt{n}(\hat{\theta} - \theta_0)$ and the transformed pro-cess will have a nuisance parameter free limiting distribution. Let $g^{(1)}$ denote the derivative of $g(\cdot)$ and define $C = \int_r^1 g^{(1)}(\tau)g^{(1)}(\tau)'d\tau$. Bai (2003) suggests the following nuisance parameter distribution free test statistic:

$$\hat{W}_n(r) = \hat{V}_n(r) - \int_0^r \left(g^{(1)}(s)'C^{-1}(s) \int_s^1 g^{(1)}(\tau)d\hat{V}_n(\tau) \right) ds. \quad (18.49)$$

The second term on the right side of (18.49) involves integration; Bai (2003, Appendix B) provides a numerical method for computing the integral.

Under some regularity conditions, Bai (2003, Corollary 1) proved the following result:

$$\sup_{r \in [0,1]} |\hat{W}_n(r)| \xrightarrow{d} \sup_{r \in [0,1]} |W(r)| \text{ under } H_0, \quad (18.50)$$

where $W(r)$ is a standard Brownian motion. Thus, the limiting distribu-tion is nuisance parameter free and the critical values can be tabulated; see Bai. If H_0 is false, the statistic $\sup_{r \in [0,1]} |\hat{W}_n(r)|$ will diverge to $+\infty$ at a $\sqrt{n}$ rate and hence it is a consistent test. Bai further discusses how to apply his test for testing specific parametric conditional CDFs, including general GARCH(p, q) processes as well as some parametric nonlinear time series models.

Corradi and Swanson's Bootstrap-Based Test

Corradi and Swanson (forthcoming) propose a test for correct specifica-tion of a parametric conditional CDF. One distinct feature of Corradi and Swanson's test is that they allow for dynamic misspecification. That is, Corradi and Swanson do not assume that the chosen set of variables Z^{t-1} contain all relevant historical information. Define

$$\tilde{U}_t = F(Y_t|Z^{t-1}, \tilde{\theta}),$$

where

$$\tilde{\theta} = \arg\min_{\theta \in \Theta} \frac{1}{n} \sum_{t=1}^{n} \ln \, f(Y_t | Z^{t-1}, \theta),$$

and where $f(.|.,.)$ is the corresponding parametric conditional PDF. Now define

$$\tilde{V}_n(r) = \frac{1}{\sqrt{n}} \sum_{t=1}^{n} \left(\mathbf{1}(\tilde{U}_t \leq r) - r \right).$$

Under some mild conditions, including allowing for dynamic misspecification (Z^t may not be equal to $\mathcal{I}_t$), Corradi and Swanson (forthcoming) show that under H_0,

$$\tilde{V}_n \overset{\text{def}}{=} \sup_{r \in [0,1]} |\tilde{V}_n(r)| \overset{d}{\to} \sup_{r \in [0,1]} |V(r)|, \tag{18.51}$$

where $V(\cdot)$ is a Gaussian process with zero mean and a covariance function depending on errors arising from both parameter estimation and possible dynamic misspecification.

The above $\tilde{V}_n$ is not nuisance parameter free. Corradi and Swanson (forthcoming) suggest using a bootstrap procedure to compute the critical values of the $\tilde{V}_n$ test. This involves comparing the empirical CDF of the resampled series evaluated at the bootstrap estimator with the empirical CDF of the actual series evaluated at the estimator based on the actual data. They use the following overlapping block resampling scheme: At each replication, draw b blocks (with replacement) of length l from the original sample $\{W_t\}_{t=1}^{n-1}$, where $W_t = (Y_t, Z^{t-1})$. For example, the first block is $W_{i_1+1}, \ldots, W_{i_1+l}$ for some $i_1 \in \{1, \ldots, n-1-l\}$ with probability $1/(n-l-1)$, the second block is $W_{i_2+1}, \ldots, W_{i_2+l}$ for some i_2 with probability $1/(n-l-1)$ (i_2 can equal to i_1), and so on. Thus, the resampled series W_t^* is such that $W_1^*, \ldots, W_l^*, W_{l+1}^*, \ldots, W_n^* = W_{i_1+1}, \ldots, W_{i_1+l}, W_{i_2+1}, \ldots, W_{i_b+l}$. Let $\tilde{\theta}^*$ denote the estimator of θ using the bootstrap sample, and define

$$\tilde{V}_n^*(r) = n^{-1/2} \sum_{t=1}^{n} \left(\mathbf{1}\{F(Y_t^* | Z^{*,t-1}, \tilde{\theta}^*) \leq r\} - \mathbf{1}\{F(Y_t | Z^{t-1}, \tilde{\theta}) \leq r\} \right).$$

Then the bootstrap statistic is given by

$$\tilde{V}_n^* = \sup_{r \in [0,1]} |\tilde{V}_n^*(r)|. \tag{18.52}$$

Corradi and Swanson (forthcoming) establish the validity of the above bootstrap procedure. Let $\{\tilde{V}_{n,j}^*\}_{j=1}^B$ denote the B bootstrap statistics, and let $\tilde{V}_{n,(\alpha)}^*$ denote the $(1-\alpha)$th percentile of $\{\tilde{V}_{n,j}^*\}_{j=1}^B$. Then for a level α test, one rejects H_0 if $\hat{V}_n \geq \tilde{V}_{n,(\alpha)}^*$; otherwise, one fails to reject H_0.

18.7.2   Out-of-Sample Testing of Conditional CDFs

The previous section deals with in-sample tests for correct specification of the conditional CDF. However, if interest lies with out-of-sample forecasts, one should be more interested in assessing the out-of-sample predictive accuracy.

For out-of-sample testing, one needs to split the sample into two parts, R observations for the estimation sample and P observations for the forecast sample ($n = R + P$). When making a forecast, a model is estimated either recursively, or using a rolling estimation sample. Corradi and Swanson (2006) provide detailed discussions on using both estimation schemes. Below we discuss only the case of recursive estimation for Bai's (2003) test and Corradi and Swanson's test.

Bai's (2003) V_n-statistic is defined as before, i.e.,

$$\hat{V}_P(r) = \frac{1}{\sqrt{P}} \sum_{t=R}^{n-1} \left(\mathbf{1}\{F(Y_{t+1}|Z^t, \hat{\theta}_{t,rec}) \leq r\} - r \right),$$

where $\hat{\theta}_{t,rec}$ is the estimator of θ_0 using the recursive sample, i.e.,

$$\hat{\theta}_{t,rec} = \arg\min_{\theta \in \Theta} \frac{1}{t} \sum_{j=1}^t q(Y_j, Z^{j-1}, \theta), \quad t = R, \ldots, n-1, \qquad (18.53)$$

and where $q(Y_j, Z^{j-1}, \theta)$ is the objective function, say, the quasi-MLE of $q(Y_j, Z^{j-1}, \theta) = -\ln f(Y_j, Z^{j-1}, \theta)$ with $f(\cdot)$ being the (pseudo) density of Y_t given Z^{t-1}.

Applying the martingale transformation to $\hat{V}_p(r)$ gives

$$\hat{W}_{P,rec}(r) = \hat{V}_P(r) - \int_0^r \left(g^{(1)}(s) C^{-1}(s) g^{(1)}(s)' \int_s^1 g(\tau) d\hat{V}_p(\tau) \right) ds.$$

Under the assumption that R and $P \to \infty$, $(\hat{\theta}_{t,rec} - \theta_0) = O_p(P^{-1/2})$ uniformly in t (this requires that $P/R \to \lambda$ with $\lambda < \infty$) and conditions similar to those used in the in-sample testing case, then under H_0,

$$\sup_{\tau \in [0,1]} \hat{W}_{p,rec}(r) \xrightarrow{d} \sup_{\tau \in [0,1]} W(r), \tag{18.54}$$

where, as before, $W(\cdot)$ is a standard Brownian motion.

We now turn to Corradi and Swanson's (2006) out-of-sample test. First, define $\hat{U}_{t+1,rec} = F(Y_{t+1}|Z^t, \hat{\theta}_{t,rec})$ and let

$$V_{p,rec} = P^{-1/2} \sum_{t=R}^{n-1} (\mathbf{1}(\hat{U}_{t+1,rec} \le r) - r).$$

Then under some regularity conditions, including R and $P \to \infty$ and $P/R \to \lambda$ with $0 < \lambda < \infty$, Corradi and Swanson (2006) showed that, under H_0,

$$\hat{V}_{p,rec} \stackrel{\text{def}}{=} \sup_{\tau \in [0,1]} \hat{V}_{p,rec}(r) \xrightarrow{d} \sup_{\tau \in [0,1]} V(r), \tag{18.55}$$

where $V(\cdot)$ is a Gaussian process with zero mean and a well-defined covariance function. Since V is not nuisance parameter free, we could instead rely on resampling procedures to approximate its null distribution.

The block bootstrap scheme of generating $W_t^* = (Y_t^*, Z^{*,t-1})$, $t = 1, \dots, n$, is exactly the same as that discussed earlier for the in-sample test case. The resampled series consists of b blocks which, conditional on the sample, are discrete i.i.d. uniform random variables. Define $\tilde{\theta}_{t,rec}^*$ by

$$\tilde{\theta}_{t,rec}^* = \arg \min_{\theta \in \Theta} \frac{1}{t} \sum_{t=1}^{t} \left(q(Y_j^*, Z^{*,j-1}, \theta) \right.$$

$$\left. - \theta' \left(\frac{1}{T} \sum_{k=1}^{n-1} \nabla_\theta q(Y_k, Z^{k-1}, \hat{\theta}_{t,rec}) \right) \right), \tag{18.56}$$

for $R \le t \le n - 1$. Note that it is important that (18.56) is recentered around the (full) sample mean, for otherwise the bootstrap procedure will have a nonnegligible bias term, even asymptotically.

Defining

$$V^*_{P,rec}(r) = \frac{1}{\sqrt{P}} \sum_{t=R}^{n-1} \left(\mathbf{1}[F(Y^{*,t}, \tilde{\theta}^*_{t,rec}) \leq r] \right.$$

$$\left. - \frac{1}{n} \sum_{j=1}^{n-1} \mathbf{1}[F(Y_{j+1}|Z^j, \hat{\theta}_{t,rec}) \leq r] \right), \qquad (18.57)$$

the bootstrap statistic is given by

$$\hat{V}^*_{p,rec} = \sup_{r \in [0,1]} |V^*_{P,rec}(r)|. \qquad (18.58)$$

Corradi and Swanson (2006) show that the bootstrap distribution of $\hat{V}^*_{p,rec}$ provides a first order approximation to the null distribution of $\hat{V}_{p,rec}$. Letting $\{\hat{V}^*_{p,rec,j}\}_{j=1}^B$ denote the B bootstrap statistics, and letting $\hat{V}^*_{p,rec,(\alpha)}$ denote the $(1 - \alpha)$th percentile of $\{\hat{V}^*_{p,rec,j}\}_{j=1}^B$, one rejects H_0 if $\hat{V}_{p,rec} \geq \hat{V}^*_{p,rec,(\alpha)}$; otherwise, one fails to reject H_0.

18.8   Applications

18.8.1   Forecasting Short-Term Interest Rates

Explaining the term structure of interest rates has a rich history in monetary economics; see Campbell (1995) and the references therein for a detailed discussion. Arbitrage arguments imply that long-term rates must be cointegrated with short-term rates (Campbell and Shiller (1987)). Anderson (1997) and Hansen and Seo (2000) provide related evidence using parametric nonlinear models, while Bachmeier and Li (2002) estimate a semiparametric error correction model (ECM) using U.S. interest rate data finding evidence of nonlinearity in the term structure. See also White (2000) for statistical issues surrounding the reuse of time-series data and a procedure for testing the null hypothesis that the best model encountered in a specification search has no predictive superiority over a given benchmark model.

Bachmeier and Li (2002) consider the following benchmark linear ECM using BIC to select the appropriate number of lags:

$$\Delta r_t = \mu + \alpha \widehat{W}_{t-1} + \gamma_1 \Delta R_{t-1} + \gamma_2 \Delta r_{t-1} + u_t, \qquad (18.59)$$

where R is the long-term interest rate, r is the short-term interest rate, $\widehat{W}_{t-1} = R_{t-1} - \hat{\beta}r_{t-1}$ is the error correction term, and $\hat{\beta}$ is the estimated cointegration coefficient.

As argued in Anderson (1997) and Hansen and Seo (2000), linearity is not implied by term structure theory. Li and Wooldridge (2002) explore the possibility that a semiparametric ECM may provide a better empirical description of the underlying process. The semiparametric ECM considered in Li and Wooldridge is of the form

$$\Delta r_t = \theta(\widehat{W}_{t-1}) + \gamma_1 \Delta R_{t-1} + \gamma_2 \Delta r_{t-1} + u_t, \tag{18.60}$$

where $\theta(\cdot)$ is of unknown functional form. Hence, (18.60) is a semiparametric partially linear model. Model (18.60) differs from the one discussed in Chapter 7 in that the component $\hat{w}_{t-1}$ is a generated regressor. Li and Wooldridge provide theory for estimation and inference based on (18.60). The difference between (18.59) and (18.60) is that the error correction term enters linearly in (18.59) but nonlinearly and nonparametrically in (18.60).

Following Bachmeier and Li (2002), we consider the term structure data used in McCulloch and Kwon (1993). We compare the out of sample predictive performance of (18.59) and (18.60) using monthly data. We use 60 and 120 month rates to predict the 1, 2, 3, 6, 12 and 24 month rates over the period 1952-1991. The sample size is $n = 480$. The long-term rates should contain all of the information in the shorter-term rates.

As discussed in Chapter 7, we first regress $Y_t - \hat{E}(Y_t|W_t)$ on $X_t - \hat{E}(X_t|W_t)$ to estimate $(\gamma_1, \gamma_2)'$, where for $s = 0, 1$, $\hat{E}(Y_{t-s}|W_{t-1}) = \sum_{j \neq t} Y_{j-s} K((\widehat{W}_{t-1} - \widehat{W}_{j-1})/h) / \sum_{j \neq t} K((\widehat{W}_{t-1} - \widehat{W}_{j-1})/h)$, and where $\hat{E}(X_{t-1}|W_{t-1}) = \sum_{j \neq t} X_{j-1} K((\widehat{W}_{t-1} - \hat{W}_{j-1})/h) / \sum_{j \neq t} K((\widehat{W}_{t-1} - \widehat{W}_{j-1})/h)$, where $\widehat{W}_{t-1} = Y_{t-1} - \hat{\beta}X_{t-1}$. Letting $\hat{\gamma} = (\hat{\gamma}_1, \hat{\gamma}_2)'$ denote the resulting semiparametric estimators of (γ_1, γ_2), Li and Wooldridge (2002) show that $\hat{\gamma}$ is $\sqrt{n}$-consistent and has an asymptotic normal distribution. One estimates $\theta(W_{t-1})$ by $\hat{\theta}(W_{t-1}) = \hat{E}(Y_t|W_{t-1}) - \hat{\gamma}_1 \hat{E}(Y_{t-1}|W_{t-1}) - \hat{\gamma}_2 \hat{E}(X_{t-1}|W_{t-1})$.

The predicted value of Y_t based on the semiparametric ECM is $\hat{y}_{t,semi} = \hat{\theta}(W_{t-1}) + Y_{t-1}\hat{\gamma}_1 + X_{t-1}\hat{\gamma}_2$, and the average squared prediction error is $n_2^{-1} \sum_{t=n_1+1}^{n} (\hat{y}_{t,semi} - Y_t)^2$, where $n_1 = 400$ and $n_2 = 80$ ($n = n_1 + n_2 = 480$). We use a normal kernel and the smoothing parameter is chosen via the method of least squares cross-validation.

Table 18.1: Average prediction MSE using 10 year rates

	1 Month	2 Month	3 Month	6 Month	12 Month
Linear	0.323	0.157	0.136	0.149	0.159
Semipar	0.316	0.141	0.129	0.135	0.144

For comparison purposes, we also compute the one-period-ahead linear predictions of Y_t given by $\hat{Y}_{t,linear} = \tilde{\mu} + \tilde{\alpha}\widehat{W}_{t-1} + \tilde{\gamma}_1 Y_{t-1} + \tilde{\gamma}_2 X_{t-1}$, where $(\tilde{\mu}, \tilde{\alpha}, \tilde{\gamma}_1, \tilde{\gamma}_2)$ are the ordinary least squares estimators of $(\mu, \alpha, \gamma_1, \gamma_2)$ using data from period 1 up to $t-1$. The linear model prediction error is $Y_t - \hat{y}_{t,L}$, and the average squared prediction error is $n_2^{-1} \sum_{t=n_1+1}^{n} (\hat{y}_{t,linear} - Y_t)^2$.

As Table 18.1 shows, the one-step-ahead prediction MSE for the semiparametric ECM using 10 year rates is always better than the linear model, hence the semiparametric ECM provides improved MSE prediction for short-term rates. This suggests that there are nonlinear adjustments in the error correction term.

18.9   Nonparametric Estimation with Nonstationary Data

The only nonparametric asymptotic analysis dealing with nonstationary data that we are aware of are the papers by Phillips and Park (1998), Juhl (2005), and Cai and Li (2006). Phillips and Park is apparently the first paper to deal with nonparametric estimation of a regression function with nonstationary data, while Juhl considers the problem of semiparametric estimation of a regression function with nonstationary data. Both Phillips and Park and Juhl consider the case for which the true DGP is a *linear* unit root process.

Cai and Li (2006) consider a varying coefficient semiparametric regression model of the form

$$Y_t = X_t'\beta(Z_t) + u_t, \tag{18.61}$$

where Y_t and u_t are scalar variables, $X_t = (X_{t1}, \ldots, X_{tp})'$ is a vector of covariates with dimension p, and $Z_t = (Z_{t1}, \ldots, Z_{tq})$ is a (row) vector of covariates of dimension q. Cai and Li discuss various scenarios including (i) X_t is nonstationary and Z_t is stationary, and (ii) X_t

is stationary and Z_t is nonstationary. Y_t can be either stationary or nonstationary. Consider the case where X_t is nonstationary while Z_t and Y_t are stationary. In this case, model (18.61) describes a nonlinear co-integrating relationship between different components of X_t. The estimation method is the same as that discussed in Chapter 9 (Section 9.3.1). However, the asymptotic theory differs substantially from the independent or stationary data case. Readers interested in the theory underlying nonparametric estimation with nonstationary data should consult Phillips and Park, Juhl, and Cai and Li for further details.

18.10   Proofs

18.10.1   Proof of Equation (18.9)

Proof. More detailed calculations show that the leading term of the variance of $\hat{f}(x)$ is the same as in the i.i.d. data case. Using (see Exercise 18.1)

$$\sum_{t=1}^{n-1}\sum_{s>t}^{n}\text{cov}(K_{h,tx},K_{h,sx}) = \sum_{t=1}^{n-1}\sum_{j=1}^{n-t}\text{cov}(K_{h,tx},K_{h,t+j,x})$$

$$= n\sum_{j=1}^{n-1}(1-j/n)\text{cov}(K_{h,1x},K_{h,1+j,x}),$$

we have $(H_q = h_1 \ldots h_q)$

$$\text{var}\left((nH_q)^{1/2}\hat{f}(x)\right)$$

$$= (H_q/n)\left\{\sum_{t=1}^{n}\text{var}(K_{h,tx}) + 2\sum_{t=1}^{n-1}\sum_{s>t}^{n}\text{cov}(K_{h,tx},K_{h,sx})\right\}$$

$$= (H_q/n)\left\{n\text{var}(K_{h,tx}) + 2n\sum_{j=1}^{n}\left(1-\frac{j}{n}\right)\text{cov}(K_{h,1x},K_{h,1+j,x})\right\}$$

$$= H_q\text{var}(K_{h,tx}) + 2H_q\sum_{j=1}^{n}\left(1-\frac{j}{n}\right)\text{cov}(K_{h,1x},K_{h,1+j,x})$$

$$= J_{1n} + J_{2n}. \tag{18.62}$$

By (18.5) we have

$$J_{1n} = \kappa^q f(x) + O(|h|^2), \tag{18.63}$$

where $\kappa = \int k(v_s)^2 dv_s$ (hence $\kappa = \int k(v)^2 dv$). Letting $\pi_n = [H_q^{-1/2}]$, the integer part of $H_q^{-1/2}$, and using $\sum_{j=1}^n = \sum_{j=1}^{\pi_n} + \sum_{j=\pi_n+1}^n$, we can write J_{2n} as

$$J_{2n} = 2H_q \sum_{j=1}^{\pi_n} \left(1 - \frac{j}{n}\right) \mathrm{cov}(K_{h,1x}, K_{h,1+j,x})$$

$$+ 2H_q \sum_{j=\pi_n+1}^{n} \left(1 - \frac{j}{n}\right) \mathrm{cov}(K_{h,1x}, K_{h,1+j,x}) \tag{18.64}$$

$$= J_{2n,1} + J_{2n,2}.$$

Letting $f_{1,1+j}(X_1, X_{1+j})$ denote the joint PDF of (X_1, X_{1+j}), we have

$$|\mathrm{cov}(K_{h,1x}, K_{h,1+j,x})| \le |E[K_{h,1x}K_{h,1+j,x}]|$$
$$= \left| \int K_h((x_1 - x)/h)K_h((x_{1+j} - x)/h)f_{1,1+j}(x_1, x_{1+j})dx_1 dx_{1+j} \right|$$
$$= \left[f_{1,1+j}(x, x) \int K(u)K(u + v)dudv + O(|h|) \right]$$
$$= [f_{1,1+j}(x, x) + O(|h|)] = O(1).$$

Hence,
$$J_{2n,1} = H_q O\left(\pi_n\right) = O(\pi_n H_q) = o(1) \tag{18.65}$$

because $\pi_n = O\left(H_q^{-1/2}\right)$. By the ρ-mixing property we have

$$\mathrm{cov}(K_{1x}, K_{1+j,x}) \le \rho(j)\mathrm{var}(K_{1x}) = \rho(j)H_q^{-1}[f(x) \int K^2(v)dv + O(|h|)].$$

Therefore,

$$J_{2n,2} \le \left[f(x) \int K^2(v)dv + o(1) \right] \sum_{j=\pi_n+1}^{\infty} \rho(j) \to 0 \tag{18.66}$$

since $\sum_{j=\pi_n+1}^{\infty} \rho(j) \to 0$ because $\pi_n \to \infty$.
Summarizing (18.62) to (18.66), we have shown that

$$\mathrm{var}\left((nh_1 \ldots h_q)^{1/2}\hat{f}(x)\right) = \kappa^q f(x) + o(1).$$

This completes the proof.   □

18.10.2 Proof of Theorem 18.2

Proof. We adopt the proof of Castellana and Leadbetter (1986) and Masry (1996a). Write $\hat{f}(x) - f(x) = \hat{f}(x) - \mathrm{E}(\hat{f}(x)) + \mathrm{E}(\hat{f}(x)) - f(x)$. We have already shown that the leading bias variance terms of $\hat{f}(x)$ are the same as for the independent data case (see (18.3) and (18.62)). To prove the asymptotic normality result, we first introduce some notation.

Let $Z_{n,t} = H_q^{1/2}[K_h(X_t, x) - \mathrm{E}(K_h(X_t, x))]$, and let $W_n = \sum_{t=1}^n Z_{n,t}$. Then

$$(nH_q)^{1/2}\left[\hat{f}(x) - \mathrm{E}(\hat{f}(x))\right] = n^{-1/2}\sum_t Z_{n,t} = n^{-1/2}W_n.$$

We use "big-small block" arguments. Partition the set $\{1, \ldots, n\}$ into $2k+1$ subsets ($k = k(n)$) with large block size $a = a_n$ and small block size $b = b_n$, where $k = k_n = [n/(a_n + b_n)]$ ($[.]$ denotes the integer part of .).

We ask that, as $n \to \infty$, $b_n \to \infty$ and $a_n \to \infty$ such that

$$b_n/a_n = o(1), \quad a_n = o\left((nH_q)^{1/2}\right), \quad \frac{n}{a_n}\rho(b_n) = o(1). \qquad (18.67)$$

Equation (18.67) only imposes a mild condition on $\rho(\cdot)$. For example, one can choose $a_n = [(nH_q)^{1/2}/\ln(n)]$, $b_n = a_n/\ln(n)$, so the first two conditions of (18.67) hold. If one further chooses h_s by optimal smoothing, i.e., $h_s = O(n^{-1/(4+q)})$, then a sufficient condition for the third condition in (18.67) to hold is $\tau^{1+q/2}\rho(\tau) \to 0$ as $\tau \to \infty$, which is only slightly stronger than the condition $\rho(\tau) = O(\tau^{-(1+\epsilon)})$ (for arbitrarily small $\epsilon > 0$) that is used to prove rate of convergence result (Theorem 18.1).

Define the random variables

$$\eta_j = \sum_{i=j(a+b)}^{j(a+b)+a-1} Z_{n,i}, \quad 0 \le j \le k-1 \qquad (18.68)$$

$$\zeta_j = \sum_{i=j(a+b)+a}^{(j+1)(a+b)-1} Z_{n,i}, \quad 0 \le j \le k-1, \text{ and} \qquad (18.69)$$

$$\xi_k = \sum_{i=k(a+b)}^{n} Z_{n,i}. \qquad (18.70)$$

η_j has a larger length of a_n, ζ_j has a smaller length of b_n, and ξ_k has a length smaller than a_n.

Write

$$W_n = \sum_{j=0}^{k-1} \eta_j + \sum_{j=0}^{k-1} \zeta_j + \xi_k \equiv W_{1n} + W_{2n} + W_{3n}.$$

Then obviously W_{1n} is the leading term of W_n since it contains $k_n a_n$ terms, while W_{2n} contains $k_n b_n$ terms and W_{3n} contains no more than a_n terms.

Below we will show that

$$n^{-1}\mathrm{E}\left[W_{2n}^2\right] = o(1) \text{ and } n^{-1}\mathrm{E}\left[W_{3n}^2\right] = o(1), \tag{18.71}$$

which imply that $n^{-1/2}W_{2n} = o_p(1)$ and $n^{-1/2}W_{3n} = o_p(1)$.

For W_{1n} (note that $\exp(itW_{1n}) = \prod_{j=0}^{k} \exp(it\eta_j)$ $(i = \sqrt{-1})$) we will show that

$$\left| \mathrm{E}\left[\exp(itW_{1n})\right] - \prod_{j=0}^{k-1} \mathrm{E}\left[\exp(it\eta_j)\right] \right| \to 0, \tag{18.72}$$

$$\frac{1}{n}\sum_{j=0}^{k-1} \mathrm{E}\left[\eta_j^2\right] \to \Omega(x), \tag{18.73}$$

$$\frac{1}{n}\sum_{j=0}^{k-1} \mathrm{E}\left[\eta_j^2 \mathbf{1}(|\eta_j| > \epsilon\Omega(x)/\sqrt{n})\right] \to 0, \tag{18.74}$$

for every $\epsilon > 0$. Equation (18.72) says that the characteristic function of W_{1n} is asymptotically the same as a process with η_j's being independent across j, which in turn implies that the summands $\{\eta_j\}$ in W_{1n} are asymptotically independent. Equations (18.73) and (18.74) are the standard Lindeberg-Feller condition for asymptotic normality for W_{1n} under independence. Thus, (18.72) to (18.74) imply that $\sqrt{n}W_{1n} \xrightarrow{d} N(0, \Omega(x))$.

We now prove these results. We first consider W_{2n}.

$$\mathrm{E}\left[W_{2n}^2\right] = \mathrm{var}\left[\sum_{j=0}^{k-1}\zeta_j\right] = \sum_{j=0}^{k-1}\mathrm{var}(\zeta_j) + \sum_{i=0}^{k-1}\sum_{j=0,j\neq i}^{k-1}\mathrm{cov}(\zeta_i,\zeta_j) \tag{18.75}$$
$$\equiv F_{1n} + F_{2n}.$$

There are b_n terms in ζ_i, and using the same arguments we used in deriving (18.62), we have

$$\mathrm{var}(\zeta_i) = b_n\mathrm{var}(Z_{n,i}) + 2b_n\sum_{i=1}^{b_n-1}(1 - b_n^{-1})\mathrm{cov}(Z_{n,1}, Z_{n,t})$$
$$= b_n\Omega(x)[1 + O(b_nH_q)] = b_n\Omega(x)[1 + o(1)]. \qquad (18.76)$$

Hence, by (18.75) and (18.76) we know that

$$F_{1n} = k_nb_n\Omega(x)[1 + o(1)] = O(k_nb_n) = o(n), \qquad (18.77)$$

because $k_n(a_n + b_n) = O(n)$ and $b_n = o(a_n)$ imply $k_nb_n = o(n)$.

Similarly, we have

$$|F_{2n}| \le 2\sum_{i_1=0}^{n-a_n-1}\sum_{i_2=i_1+a_n}^{n-1}|\mathrm{cov}(Z_{n,i_1}, Z_{n,i_2})| \le 2n\sum_{j=a_n}^{\infty}|\mathrm{cov}(Z_{n,1}, Z_{n,1+j})|$$
$$\le 2n\,\mathrm{var}(Z_{n,1})\sum_{j=a_n}^{n}\rho(j) = o(n),$$
$$\qquad (18.78)$$

because $\mathrm{var}(Z_{n,1}) = \Omega(x) + o(1) = O(1)$ and $\sum_{j=a_n}^{\infty}\rho(j) \to 0$ because $a_n \to \infty$.

Hence, $n^{-1}\mathrm{E}[W_{2n}^2] = o(1)$, which implies that $n^{-1/2}W_{2n} = o_p(1)$.

For W_{3n}, it is obvious that W_{3n} has an order smaller than that of W_{1n} because W_{1n} sums over a_nk_n while W_{3n} sums over no more than a_n terms. We will show below that $\sqrt{n}W_{1n} = O_p(1)$, which implies that $\sqrt{n}W_{3n} = o_p(1)$. We will use the following inequality for the ρ-mixing process.

Lemma 18.2. *Let $V_1,\ldots,V_J$ be α-mixing random variables belonging to $\mathcal{F}_{i_1}^{j_1},\ldots,\mathcal{F}_{i_J}^{j_J}$, respectively, with $1 \le i_1 < j_1 < i_2 < \cdots < j_J \le n$, $i_{l+1} - j_l \ge \tau$, and $|V_j| \le 1$ for $j = 1,\ldots,J$. Then*

$$\left|\mathrm{E}\left[\prod_{j=1}^{J}V_j\right] - \prod_{j=1}^{J}\mathrm{E}[V_j]\right| \le 16(J-1)\alpha(\tau).$$

Proof. See Volkonskii and Rozanov (1959) or Hall and Heyde (1980, Theorem A.5). $\qquad\square$

The above result also holds true for ρ, β, and ϕ mixing processes because $\alpha(\tau)$ is no larger than any of the other mixing coefficients.

Applying Lemma 18.2 to $\exp[itW_n] = \prod_{j=0}^{k-1} \exp(it\eta_j)$ (where $V_j = \exp(it\eta_j)$), we have

$$|\mathrm{E}[\exp(itW_{1n})] - \sum_{j=0}^{k-1} \mathrm{E}[\exp(it\eta_j)]| \le Ck_n\rho(a_n) = O\left(\frac{n}{a_n}\right)\rho(b_n) = o(1)$$

by Condition (18.67).

We can choose $a_n = (nH_q)^{1/2}/\ln(n)$, $b_n = (nH_q)^{1/2}/[\ln(n)]^2$, and $h = O(n^{-1/(4+q)})$ (optimal smoothing), so a sufficient condition for $O(\frac{n}{a_n})\rho(b_n) = o(1)$ is $\tau^{1+q/2}\rho(\tau) \to 0$ as $\tau \to \infty$.

By stationarity and by the same arguments used to derive (18.76), we have

$$\mathrm{var}(\eta_j) = \mathrm{var}(\eta_0) = a_n\Omega(x)[1 + o(1)].$$

Hence,

$$\frac{1}{n}\sum_{j=0}^{k-1} \mathrm{E}\left[\eta_j^2\right] = \frac{k_na_n}{n}\Omega(x)[1 + o(1)] \to \Omega(x)$$

because $k_na_n/n \to 1$ (since $b_n/a_n \to 0$). Also,

$$|Z_{n,t}| = H_q^{-1/2}\left|K\left(\frac{X_t - x}{h}\right) - \mathrm{E}\left[K\left(\frac{X_t - x}{h}\right)\right]\right| \le CH_q^{-1/2}$$

because $K(\cdot)$ is bounded. This implies that

$$\max_{0 \le j < k-1} |\eta_j|/\sqrt{n} \le Ca_n/(nH_q)^{1/2} \to 0 \qquad (18.79)$$

by (18.68). Hence when n is large, (18.79) implies that the set $\{|\eta_j| \ge \epsilon\Omega(x)\sqrt{n}\}$ becomes an empty set and thus (18.74) holds. This completes the proof of Theorem 18.2. $\qquad\square$

18.11   Exercises

Exercise 18.1. Show that

$$\sum_{t=1}^{n-1}\sum_{j=1}^{n-t} \mathrm{cov}(K_{h,tx}, K_{h,t+j,x}) = n\sum_{j=1}^{n-1}(1 - j/n)\mathrm{cov}(K_{h,1x}, K_{h,1+j,x}).$$

Exercise 18.2. Prove (18.14), i.e., show that

$$\text{var}[\hat{m}_1(x)] = O(||h||^2(nH_q)^{-1}).$$

Exercise 18.3. Using Lemma 18.1, prove that

$$\hat{f}(x) - f(x) = O_p(||h||^2 + (nH_q)^{-1/2})$$

for a stationary β-mixing process with mixing coefficient satisfying

$$\sum_{j=1}^{\infty} \beta(j)^{\delta/(1+\delta)} < \infty.$$

Hint: The bias calculation remains the same as in the independent data case. Using Lemma 18.1, one has

$$|\text{cov}(K_{h,tx}, K_{h,sx})| = |\text{E}\{[K_{h,tx} - \text{E}(K_{h,tx})][K_{h,sx} - \text{E}(K_{h,sx})]\}|$$
$$\leq 0 + 4M_n^{1/(1+\delta)}.$$

One can further show that

$$M_n \sim \text{E}[(K_{h,tx}K_{h,sx})^{1+\delta}] = \int (K_{h,tx}K_{h,sx})^{1+\delta} f(x_t, x_s) dx_t dx_s$$
$$\leq CH_q^{-2\delta}.$$

Then,

$$\left| \sum_t \sum_{s \neq t} \text{cov}(K_{h,tx}, K_{h,sx}) \right| \leq 4M_n^{1/(1+\delta)} \sum_t \sum_{s>t} \beta(s-t)^{\delta/(1+\delta)}$$
$$\leq 4M_n^{1/(1+\delta)} n \sum_{j=1}^{\infty} \beta(j)^{\delta/(1+\delta)}$$
$$= O(H^{-2q/(1+\delta)}) = o(H^{-q})$$

because $\delta < 1$. The remaining steps are trivial.

Chapter 19

Panel Data Models

A "panel" is a sample formed by drawing observations on N cross-sectional units for T consecutive periods yielding a dataset of the form $\{Y_{it}, Z_{it}\}_{i=1,t=1}^{N,T}$. A panel is therefore simply a collection of N individual time series that may be short ("small T") or long ("large T"). For example, the U.S. Panel Study of Income Dynamics (PSID)[1] is a nationally representative longitudinal study consisting of more than 7,000 U.S families originating in 1968, while the Canadian Survey of Labour and Income Dynamics (SLID)[2] is a longitudinal household survey conducted by Statistics Canada that tracks representative samples of around 15,000 Canadian households for six year periods, the earliest panel beginning in 1993. Like its U.S. counterpart, the SLID panel is designed to capture changes in the economic well-being of individuals and families over time along with the determinants of their well-being.

A number of interesting statistical issues arise when modeling panels, including how one models cross-sectional effects (i.e., whether to take so-called unobserved heterogeneity into account), whether to pool the data, and how to model potential dependence, to name but a few. A number of excellent texts on panel data models exist, and we direct the interested reader to Arellano (2003) for a thorough treatment. In this chapter we consider a number of flexible approaches that have been proposed for modeling panel datasets.

We will focus on two types of semiparametric and nonparametric models: (i) partially linear semiparametric and fully nonparametric panel data models and (ii) panel discrete choice and censored regression

---

[1]See http://psidonline.isr.umich.edu/.

[2]See http://www.statcan.ca/english/sdds/3889.htm.

models with unknown error distributions. We will cover both random effects and fixed effects nonparametric panel data models.

Throughout this chapter, we will let the subscript $i = 1, 2, \ldots, N$ index individuals and $t = 1, 2, \ldots, T$ index time. Typically, T is small relative to N. For clarity of exposition, we shall restrict discussion to balanced panels (i.e., T does not vary with i). However, the results we develop are easily extended to unbalanced panel settings.

We shall also see in Section 19.8 that a partially linear model of the form

$$Y_{it} = X'_{it}\alpha + g(Z_{it}) + u_{it} \qquad (19.1)$$

can occur quite naturally in panel data settings.

One popular error specification for panel data models is the so-called one-way error component model, whose error process is given by $u_{it} = \mu_i + \nu_{it}$, where μ_i is the (random or fixed) individual effect and ν_{it} is an idiosyncratic error term. ν_{it} is usually assumed to be an independent process across both the i and t indices. For the random effects model, the existence of the individual effects μ_i makes the error term u_{it} serially correlated. In this case, if Z_{it} contains a lagged dependent variable, say $Y_{i,t-1}$, then $\mathrm{E}(u_{it}|Z_{it}) \neq 0$ and some IV approach is needed in order to estimate (19.1) (see Chapter 16 for an overview of nonparametric and semiparametric IV methods). However, if the error u_{it} in (19.1) is serially uncorrelated, for instance, if u_{it} is a martingale difference process (which rules out an error component model), then one can estimate (19.1) as discussed in Chapter 18 (with $\sum_t$ being replaced by $\sum_i \sum_t$). Therefore, in practice one may want to first test for zero serial correlation or test for the absence of individual effects prior to deciding whether an error component model is appropriate for the data at hand.

19.1   Nonparametric Estimation of Panel Data Models: Ignoring the Variance Structure

A general nonparametric panel data model is given by

$$Y_{it} = g(Z_{it}) + u_{it}, \quad i = 1, 2, \ldots, N, \, t = 1, 2, \ldots, T, \qquad (19.2)$$

where, for expositional simplicity, we consider only the case in which Z_{it} is a continuous random vector of dimension q.

We assume that the data is *independent* across the i index. If N is large and T is small, there is no need to assume that the data is stationary in the t index. However, if T is large, then one usually needs to assume that the data is stationary and follows some sort of mixing process (see Chapter 18 for definitions of various mixing processes).

A standard approach is to introduce an individual effect μ_i. We first consider the random individual effects case; however, in this section we shall maintain the assumption that Z_{it} is strictly exogenous, i.e., that $E(u_{it}|Z_{i1}, Z_{i2}, \ldots, Z_{iT}) = 0$ for all t. Under this assumption one can estimate $g(\cdot)$ using a standard nonparametric approach, say, the local constant method, i.e.,

$$\hat{g}(z) = \frac{\sum_{j=1}^{N} \sum_{s=1}^{T} Y_{js} K_{h,js,z}}{\sum_{j=1}^{N} \sum_{s=1}^{T} K_{h,js,z}}, \tag{19.3}$$

where $K_{h,js,z} = \prod_{l=1}^{q} h_l^{-1} k((Z_{js,l} - Z_l)/h_l)$.

If, for a fixed i, u_{it} is a mixing process that satisfies the conditions given in Chapter 18, then the asymptotic distribution of $\hat{g}(x)$ is the same as in the independent data case. Below we consider the case of a one-way error component model for which

$$u_{it} = \mu_i + \nu_{it},$$

where μ_i is i.i.d. $(0, \sigma_\mu^2)$ and ν_{it} is a zero mean finite variance β-mixing process. We also assume that X_{it} is a (stationary) mixing process with mixing coefficient satisfying $\sum_{\tau=1}^{\infty} \beta_\tau^{\delta/(1+\delta)} < \infty$. Then, under smoothness conditions similar to those imposed on $g(\cdot)$ and $f(\cdot)$ that we introduced in Section 2.1 of Chapter 2, we have the following result:

Theorem 19.1. *Assume that $NTH_q \to \infty$ as $NT \to \infty$ ($H_q = h_1 \ldots h_q$). Also assume that one of the following conditions holds true: (i) N is large, T is small; (ii) both N and T are large, and $TH_q \to 0$ as $T \to \infty$. Then*

$$\sqrt{NTH_q} \left[\hat{g}(z) - g(z) - \sum_{s=1}^{q} h_s^2 B_s(z) \right] \xrightarrow{d} N\left(0, \frac{\kappa^q \sigma^2(z)}{f(z)}\right), \tag{19.4}$$

where $B_s(z)$ is the same as that defined in Section 2.1.

The proof of Theorem 19.1 is given in Section 19.10.

Note that when T is small, there is no need to impose mixing conditions on (Z_{it}, ν_{it}). When T is large we make the additional assumption that $TH_q \to 0$ as $T \to \infty$. This condition is used to control the covariance $\text{var}(\hat{g}(z))$ (due to the existence of μ_i).

Theorem 19.1 does not cover the small N and large T case because the one-way (random effects) error component modeling does not seem to be a reasonable approach in this setting. When T is large and N is small, one may not need to pool the data since there exists a lengthy time series for each individual unit. In such cases, one can simply estimate $g_i(Z_{it})$ for each individual unit i using the T individual time series available for each individual unit, and the asymptotic distributions of the resulting estimators are discussed in Chapter 18. To allow for the possibility that the data is in fact poolable, one can introduce an *unordered* discrete variable, say $\delta_i = i$ for $i = 1, 2, \ldots, N$, and estimate $E(Y_{it}|Z_{it}, \delta_i) = g(Z_{it}, \delta_i)$ nonparametrically using the mixed discrete and continuous kernel approach introduced in Chapter 4. Letting $\hat{\lambda}$ denote the cross-validated smoothing parameter associated with δ_i, then if $\hat{\lambda} = 1$, one gets $g(Z_{it}, \delta_i) = g(Z_{it})$ and the data is thereby pooled in the resulting estimate of $g(\cdot)$. If, on the other hand, $\hat{\lambda} = 0$ (or is close to 0), then this effectively estimates each $g_i(\cdot)$ using only the time series for the ith individual unit. Finally, if $0 < \hat{\lambda} < 1$, one might interpret this as a case in which the data is partially poolable.

One can also apply the nonparametric poolability tests proposed by Baltagi, Hidalgo and Li (1996) and Lavergne (2001) to test whether data is poolable.

19.2   Wang's Efficient Nonparametric Panel Data Estimator

Wang (2003) considers the following nonparametric panel data regression model:

$$Y_{it} = g(Z_{it}) + u_{it}, \quad i = 1, 2 \ldots, N, \ t = 1, 2, \ldots, T, \qquad (19.5)$$

where $g(\cdot)$ is an unknown smooth function, $Z_{it} = (Z_{it,1}, \ldots, Z_{it,q})$ is of dimension q, all other variables are scalars, and $E(u_{it}|Z_{i1}, \ldots, Z_{iT}) = 0$.

We will consider only the large N and small T case in this section, and we assume that the data is independent across the i index and strictly stationary across the t index. For what follows, we let $u_i = (u_{i1}, \ldots, u_{iT})'$ and let $\Sigma = \text{cov}(u_i|Z_{i1}, \ldots, Z_{iT})$. Wang (2003) proposes a novel method for estimating $g(\cdot)$ that utilizes the information contained in Σ. We will first discuss the estimation method for known Σ, and then discuss the case in which we estimate Σ when u_{it} has a one-way error component structure.

Wang (2003) suggests choosing the criterion function for individual i by

$$\mathcal{L}_i(\cdot) = \mathcal{L}(Y_i, g_i) = -\frac{1}{2}\left[Y_i - g_i\right]' \Sigma^{-1}\left[Y_i - g_i\right], \qquad (19.6)$$

where $Y_i = (Y_{i1}, \ldots, Y_{iT})'$, and where $g_i = (g_{i1}, \ldots, g_{iT})'$, $g_{it} = g(Z_{it})$.

We shall let $\mathcal{L}_{i,tg} = \partial\mathcal{L}_i(\cdot)/\partial g_{it}$, and let $\mathcal{L}_{i,tsg} = \partial^2\mathcal{L}_i(\cdot)/(\partial g_{it}\partial g_{is})$. Then from (19.6) we obtain

$$\mathcal{L}_{i,tg} = c_t'\Sigma^{-1}\left[Y_i - g_i\right] = \sum_{s=1}^{T} \sigma^{ts}(Y_{is} - g(Z_{is})), \qquad (19.7)$$

where c_t is a vector of dimension $T \times 1$ whose t^{th} element equals 1 and all other elements equal 0, and where σ^{ts} is the $(t,s)^{\text{th}}$ element of Σ^{-1}. Also, we have

$$\mathcal{L}_{i,tsg} = -c_t'\Sigma^{-1}c_s = -\sigma^{ts}. \qquad (19.8)$$

We will maximize a kernel-weighted objective function. Define the product kernel $K_h(v) = \prod_{j=1}^{q} h_j^{-1}k(v_j/h_j)$, where $k(\cdot)$ is a univariate kernel function. Let $f(\cdot)$ denote the PDF of Z_{it}. Define $G_{it}(z,h) = (1, (Z_{it,1} - Z_1)/h_1, \ldots, (Z_{it,q} - Z_q)/h_q)'$ (note that $G_{it}(z,h)$ is of dimension $(q+1) \times 1$) and define $g^{(1)}(z) = \partial g(z)/\partial z$, the first order derivative of $g(\cdot)$ with respect to z (which is of dimension $q \times 1$). Wang (2003) suggests estimating the unknown function $g(z)$ by $\alpha_0(z)$, where $\alpha_0(z)$ and $\alpha_1(z)$ solve the first order condition

$$0 = \sum_{i=1}^{N}\sum_{t=1}^{T} K_h(Z_{it}, z)G_{it}(z,h)\mathcal{L}_{tg}(Y_i, \hat{g}(Z_{i1}), \ldots, \alpha_0(z)$$
$$+ \left[(Z_{it} - z)/h\right]'\alpha_1(z), \ldots, \hat{g}(Z_{iT})), \qquad (19.9)$$

where $\hat{g}(Z_{is})$, $s \neq t$, is an initial estimator of $g(Z_{is})$, and $[(Z_{it} - z)/h]' = ((Z_{it,1} - z_1)/h_1, \ldots, (Z_{it,q} - z_q)/h_q)$. Note that (19.9) is an equation of dimension $(q+1) \times 1$, from which we solve for the $(q+1)$ parameters $\hat{\alpha}_0(z)$ (a scalar) and $\hat{\alpha}_1(z)$ (a $q \times 1$ vector), which estimate $g(z)$ and $g^{(1)}(z)$, respectively.

An Iterative Procedure

Equation (19.9) suggests the following iterative estimation procedure. Suppose the current estimate of $g(\cdot)$ at the $[l-1]^{\text{th}}$ step is $\hat{g}_{[l-1]}(\cdot)$. We use $\hat{g}_{[l]}(z)$ to denote the next stage estimator of $g(z)$, where $\hat{g}_{[l]}(z)$ and $\hat{g}_{[l]}^{(1)}(z)$ are solutions to the following equation (by (19.7) and (19.9)):

$$
\begin{aligned}
0 &= \sum_{i=1}^{N} \sum_{t=1}^{T} K_h(Z_{it}, z) G_{it}(z, h) \\
&\quad \times \mathcal{L}_{tg}\big(Y_i, \hat{g}_{[l-1]}(Z_{i1}), \ldots, \hat{g}_{[l]}(z) \\
&\quad + [(Z_{it} - z)/h]' \hat{g}_{[l]}^{(1)}(z), \ldots, \hat{g}_{[l-1]}(Z_{iT})\big)
\end{aligned}
\tag{19.10}
$$

$$
= \sum_{i=1}^{N} \sum_{t=1}^{T} K_h(Z_{it}, z) G_{it}(z, h) \Bigg[\sum_{s \neq t} \sigma^{ts} \big(Y_{is} - \hat{g}_{[l-1]}(Z_{is}) \big)
$$

$$
+ \sigma^{tt} \big(Y_{it} - \hat{\alpha}_0(z) - [(Z_{it} - z)/h]' \hat{\alpha}_1(z) \big) \Bigg].
\tag{19.11}
$$

Equation (19.10) is linear in $\hat{g}_{[l]}(z)$ and $\hat{g}_{[l]}^{(1)}(z)$ and it leads to

$$
\begin{pmatrix} \hat{g}_{[l]}(z) \\ \hat{g}_{[l]}^{(1)}(z) \end{pmatrix} = D_1(z)^{-1} D_2(z),
\tag{19.12}
$$

where

$$
D_1(z) = \sum_{i=1}^{N} \sum_{t=1}^{T} K_h(Z_{it}, z) \sigma^{tt} G_{it}(z, h) G_{it}(z, h)',
$$

and where

$$
D_2(z) = \sum_{i=1}^{N} \sum_{t=1}^{T} K_h(Z_{it}, z) G_{it}(z, h)
$$

$$
\times \Bigg[\sigma^{tt} Y_{it} + \sum_{s \neq t}^{T} \sigma^{ts} \big(Y_{is} - \hat{g}_{[l-1]}(Z_{is}) \big) \Bigg].
$$

Equation (19.12) yields $\hat{g}_{[l]}(z)$ as the next stage estimate of $g(\cdot)$, while $\hat{g}_{[l]}^{(1)}(z)$ is the next step estimate of $g^{(1)}(z) = \partial g(z)/\partial z$. Upon convergence, we obtain the final estimator $\hat{g}(z)$ of $g(z)$.

The above iterative procedure requires an initial estimate of $g(\cdot)$. One could choose the standard local constant or local linear estimator that ignores the variance-covariance structure of Σ. Since the initial estimate is already a consistent estimator of $g(\cdot)$, convergence can usually be achieved in a few steps.

Define

$$\Omega(z) = -f(z) \sum_{t=1}^{T} \mathrm{E}[\mathcal{L}_{i,ttg}(\cdot)|Z_{it} = z] = f(z) \sum_{t=1}^{T} \mathrm{E}\left[\sigma^{tt}|Z_{it} = z\right],$$

(19.13)

where the second equality follows from (19.8).

Also, for $r = 1, \ldots, q$, define $b_r(z)$ to be a bounded smooth function that is determined by

$$b_r(z) = \frac{\kappa_2}{2} g_{rr}(z) + \Omega(z)^{-1} f(z) \sum_{t=1}^{T} \mathrm{E}\left[\sum_{s \neq t}^{T} \sigma^{js} b_r(Z_{is})|Z_{it} = z\right],$$

(19.14)

where $\kappa_2 = \int k(v)v^2 dv$, and where $g_{rr}(z) = \partial^2 g(z)/\partial z_r^2$.

Under standard regularity conditions such as $g(\cdot)$ being twice continuously differentiable, Wang (2003) shows that

$$\hat{g}(z) - g(z) = \sum_{s=1}^{q} h_r^2 b_r(z) + v_N(z) + o_p\left(\sum_{s=1}^{q} h_r^2 + (Nh_1 \ldots h_q)^{-1/2}\right),$$

(19.15)

where

$$v_N(z) = \Omega(z)^{-1}\left\{\frac{1}{N}\sum_{i=1}^{N}\sum_{t=1}^{T} K_h(Z_{it}, z)c_t'\Sigma^{-1}u_i\right\}.$$

(19.16)

Obviously, $\mathrm{E}(v_N(z)) = 0$, and it can be shown that the asymptotic variance of $v_N(z)$ is (see Exercise 19.2)

$$\mathrm{var}(v_N(z)) = \frac{\kappa^q}{\Omega(z)Nh_1 \ldots h_q} + o(Nh_1 \ldots h_q)^{-1},$$

(19.17)

where $\kappa = \int k^2(v)dv$.

Assuming that $h_r \propto N^{-1/(4+q)}$ and using (19.14) and (19.17), one can show that

$$\sqrt{Nh_1 \ldots h_q}\left(\hat{g}(z) - g(z) - \sum_{s=1}^{q} h_r^2 b_r(z)\right) \xrightarrow{d} N\left(0, \frac{\kappa^q}{\Omega(z)}\right), \quad (19.18)$$

where $\Omega(z)$ is defined in (19.13).

Wang (2003) shows that the once-iterated estimator has the same asymptotic behavior as the fully iterated estimator. Her simulations also support this result, so in practice one can choose to iterate once only. In this case the leading bias term has a closed form expression given by

$$
b_r(z) = \frac{1}{2} g_{rr}(z) + \Omega(z)^{-1} f(z) \sum_{t=1}^{T} \mathrm{E} \left[\sum_{s \neq t}^{T} \sigma^{js} g_{rr}(Z_{is}) \Big| Z_{it} = z \right].
$$
(19.19)

Next we consider a specific form for Σ. We assume that u_{it} follows a one-way error component structure of the form u_{it}, i.e., $u_{it} = \mu_i + \nu_{it}$, where μ_i is i.i.d. $(0, \sigma_\mu^2)$, and where ν_{it} is i.i.d. $(0, \sigma_\nu^2)$. We further assume that u_{it} is conditionally homoskedastic. Hence, $\Sigma = \mathrm{cov}(u_i | Z_{i1}, \dots, Z_{iT}) = \mathrm{cov}(u_i)$ given by

$$
\Sigma = \sigma_\nu^2 I_T + \sigma_\mu^2 e_T e_T' = \sigma_\nu^2 [I_T - \bar{J}_T] + \sigma_1^2 \bar{J}_T,
$$
(19.20)

where $\sigma_1^2 = T\sigma_\mu^2 + \sigma_\nu^2$, I_T is an identity matrix of dimension $T \times T$, e_T is a column vector of ones of dimension $T \times 1$, and $\bar{J}_T = e_T e_T'/T$. It is easy to verify that (see Wansbeek and Kapteyn (1982))

$$
\Sigma^{-1} = \frac{1}{\sigma_\nu^2} \left[I_T - \bar{J}_T \right] + \frac{1}{\sigma_1^2} \bar{J}_T.
$$

Given that $\mathcal{L}_i(\cdot)$ is quadratic in $g(\cdot)$, $\mathcal{L}_{i,tsg}$ is a constant given by

$$
\mathcal{L}_{i,ttg} = -c_t' \Sigma^{-1} c_t = -\sigma^{tt} \equiv -c_1,
$$

where

$$
c_1 \equiv \sigma^{tt} = \frac{1}{\sigma_\nu^2} \left(1 - \frac{1}{T} \right) + \frac{1}{T\sigma_1^2} = \frac{(T-1)\sigma_\mu^2 + \sigma_\nu^2}{\sigma_\nu^2 \sigma_1^2}.
$$

Therefore, we have

$$
\Omega(z) = -f(z) \sum_{t=1}^{T} \mathrm{E}[\mathcal{L}_{i,ttg}(\cdot)|Z_t = z] = c_1 T f(z).
$$
(19.21)

Note that $\mathcal{L}_{i,tsg}$ is also a constant given by

$$
\mathcal{L}_{i,tsg} = -c_t' \Sigma^{-1} c_s = -\sigma^{ts} = -\frac{\sigma_\mu^2}{\sigma_1^2 \sigma_\nu^2} \equiv -c_2 \text{ for } t \neq s.
$$
(19.22)

Hence, we have

$$b_r(z) = \frac{\partial^2 g(z)}{\partial z_r^2} - \frac{c_2}{Tc_1} \sum_{t=1}^{T} \sum_{s \neq t}^{T} \mathrm{E}[b_r(Z_{is})|Z_{it} = z]. \qquad (19.23)$$

The asymptotic variance of $(Nh_1 \ldots h_q)^{1/2} \hat{g}(z)$ is given by

$$\mathrm{avar}\left[(Nh_1 \ldots h_q)^{1/2} \hat{g}(z)\right] = \frac{\kappa^q}{c_1 Tf(z)} = \frac{\kappa^q \sigma_\nu^2 \sigma_1^2}{Tf(z) \left[(T-1)\sigma_\mu^2 + \sigma_\nu^2\right]}$$

$$= \frac{\kappa^q \sigma_\nu^2}{Tf(z)} \left[1 + \frac{\rho}{(T-1)\rho + 1}\right], \qquad (19.24)$$

where $\rho = \sigma_\mu^2 / \sigma_\nu^2$.

The conventional kernel estimator of $g(z)$ that ignores the variance structure of Σ, for instance, the local constant estimator given by

$$\bar{g}(z) = \frac{\sum_{i=1}^{N} \sum_{t=1}^{T} Y_{it} K_h(Z_{it}, z)}{\sum_{i=1}^{N} \sum_{t=1}^{T} K_h(Z_{it}, z)}, \qquad (19.25)$$

has asymptotic variance given by[3]

$$\mathrm{avar}\left[(Nh_1 \ldots h_q)^{1/2} \bar{g}(z)\right] = \frac{\kappa^q[\sigma_\nu^2 + \sigma_\mu^2]}{Tf(z)} = \frac{\kappa^q \sigma_\nu^2}{Tf(z)}[1 + \rho]. \qquad (19.26)$$

The relative asymptotic variance is given by

$$\frac{\mathrm{avar}\left[(Nh_1 \ldots h_q)^{1/2} \hat{g}(z)\right]}{\mathrm{avar}\left[(Nh_1 \ldots h_q)^{1/2} \bar{g}(z)\right]} = \frac{1 + \frac{\rho}{(T-1)\rho + 1}}{1 + \rho} < 1, \qquad (19.27)$$

where $\rho = \sigma_\mu^2 / \sigma_\nu^2$. The above ratio gets smaller as either ρ or T increases. For example, for $\rho = 1$, (19.27) becomes $(T+1)/(2T)$, which takes values in $[3/4, 1/2)$ since $T \geq 2$. For the case of $T = 2$ and an arbitrary ρ, (19.27) becomes $1 - \rho^2/(1+\rho)^2$, which takes values in $(0, 1)$ since $\rho \in (0, +\infty)$. For large values of ρ, the efficiency gain arising from using $\hat{g}(z)$ over $\bar{g}(z)$ can be substantial.

In practice, σ_μ^2 and σ_ν^2 are unknown and need to be estimated. It can be shown that $\hat{\sigma}_\nu^2 = \frac{1}{N(T-1)} \sum_{i=1}^{N} \hat{u}_i'(I_T - \bar{J}_T)\hat{u}_i$ is a consistent estimator of σ_ν^2 and that $\hat{\sigma}_1^2 = \frac{1}{N} \sum_{i=1}^{N} \hat{u}_i' \bar{J}_T \hat{u}_i$ consistently estimates σ_1^2,

---

[3]The local linear estimator has the same asymptotic variance as the local constant kernel estimator. See Chapter 2 for details.

where $\hat{u}_i = (\hat{u}_{i1}, \ldots, \hat{u}_{iT})'$ with $\hat{u}_{it} = Y_{it} - \bar{g}(Z_{it})$, and where $\bar{g}(Z_{it})$ is the initial estimate of $g(Z_{it})$ given in (19.25) that ignores the structure of Σ. In fact, $\hat{\sigma}_\mu^2 - \sigma_\mu^2 = O_p(N^{-1/2})$, and $\hat{\sigma}_1^2 - \sigma_1^2 = O_p(N^{-1/2})$. Defining $\hat{\Sigma}^{-1}$ to be Σ^{-1} with σ_μ^2 and σ_1^2 replaced by $\hat{\sigma}_\mu^2$ and $\hat{\sigma}_1^2$, we obtain a feasible estimator of $g(z)$. The asymptotic distribution of the resulting estimator is the same as the one that uses the true Σ^{-1} because $\hat{\Sigma}^{-1} - \Sigma^{-1} = O_p(N^{-1/2})$, which converges to zero faster than the nonparametric estimator $\hat{g}(z)$.

19.3 A Partially Linear Model with Random Effects

In this section we consider a semiparametric partially linear panel data regression model with random effects of the form

$$Y_{it} = X_{it}'\alpha + g(Z_{it}) + \mu_i + \nu_{it}, \quad i = 1, 2, \ldots, N, \ t = 1, 2, \ldots, T, \quad (19.28)$$

where X_{it} is of dimension $d \times 1$, while the other variables are the same as those defined in Section 19.2.

The criterion function for individual i is modified as

$$\mathcal{L}_i(\cdot) = \mathcal{L}(Y_i, X_i, \alpha, g_i) = -\frac{1}{2} \left[Y_i - X_i'\alpha - g_i \right]' \Sigma^{-1} \left[Y_i - X_i'\alpha - g_i \right],$$
$$(19.29)$$

where $X_i = (X_{i1}, \ldots, X_{iT})'$. Letting $\mathcal{L}_{i,tg} = \partial\mathcal{L}_{i,tg}(\cdot)/\partial g_{it}$, then we have

$$\mathcal{L}_{i,tg} = -c_t'\Sigma^{-1} \left[Y_i - X_i'\alpha - g_i \right].$$

Presuming for the moment that α is known, then we simply estimate $g(\cdot)$ as in Section 19.2 but with $Y_i - X_i'\alpha$ replacing Y_i wherever it occurs. We use $\hat{g}(z, \alpha)$ to denote the resulting estimator. Let $\hat{g}_y(\cdot)$ be the nonparametric estimator of (19.12) (the $\hat{g}_{[l]}(z)$) and let $\hat{g}_{x,r}(\cdot)$ be the nonparametric estimator of (19.12) with Y_{it} being replaced by the rth component of X_{it}. Furthermore, let $\hat{g}_x(z) = \{\hat{g}_{x,1}(z), \ldots, \hat{g}_{x,d}(z)\}'$. Then it is immediately obvious by the linearity (in y) of the smoother and from (19.28) that

$$\hat{g}(z, \alpha) = \hat{g}_y(z) - \hat{g}_x(z)'\alpha, \quad (19.30)$$

which means that

$$\frac{\partial}{\partial \alpha} \hat{g}(z, \alpha) = -\hat{g}_x(z).$$

Define $\hat{g}_i(\alpha) = (\hat{g}(Z_{i1}, \alpha), \ldots, \hat{g}(Z_{iT}, \alpha))'$. For given estimated values of $\hat{g}_i(\alpha)$, $i = 1, 2, \ldots, N$, we estimate α by the maximization of

$$-\sum_{i=1}^{N} \left[Y_i - X_i'\alpha - \hat{g}_i(\alpha) \right]' \Sigma^{-1} \left[Y_i - X_i'\alpha - \hat{g}_i(\alpha) \right]$$

$$= -\sum_{i=1}^{N} \left[\hat{Y}_i - \hat{X}_i'\alpha \right]' \Sigma^{-1} \left[\hat{Y}_i - \hat{X}_i'\alpha \right], \qquad (19.31)$$

where $\hat{Y}_i = (\hat{Y}_{i1}, \ldots, \hat{Y}_{iT})'$ with $\hat{Y}_{it} = Y_{it} - \hat{g}_y(Z_{it})$, and where $\hat{X}_i = (\hat{X}_{i1}, \ldots, \hat{X}_{iT})'$ with $\hat{X}_{it} = X_{it} - \hat{g}_x(Z_{it})$.

Since both $\hat{g}_y(Z_{it})$ and $\hat{g}_x(Z_{it})$ are unrelated to α, we can obtain $\hat{g}_y(Z_{it})$ and $\hat{g}_x(Z_{it})$ using the method discussed in Section 19.2. Given $\hat{g}_y(Z_{it})$ and $\hat{g}_x(Z_{it})$, maximizing (19.31) over α yields a closed form solution for $\hat{\alpha}$ given by

$$\hat{\alpha} = \left[\sum_{i=1}^{N} \hat{X}_i \Sigma^{-1} \hat{X}_i \right]^{-1} \sum_{i=1}^{N} \hat{X}_i \Sigma^{-1} \hat{Y}_i. \qquad (19.32)$$

We then have

$$\sqrt{N}(\hat{\alpha} - \alpha) \to N(0, V) \text{ in distribution,}$$

where V is a positive definite matrix. Moreover, a consistent estimator of V is given by $\hat{V} = \left[N^{-1} \sum_{i=1}^{N} \hat{X}_i \Sigma^{-1} \hat{X}_i \right]^{-1}$.

Wang, Carroll and Lin (2005) show that $\hat{\alpha}$ is a semiparametrically efficient estimator of α in the sense that V reaches the semiparametric lower bound for a regular $\sqrt{N}$-consistent estimator of α.

Given $\hat{\alpha}$ we can rewrite (19.28) as

$$Y_{it} - X_{it}'\hat{\alpha} = g(Z_{it}) + \mu_i + \nu_{it} + X_{it}'(\alpha - \hat{\alpha}). \qquad (19.33)$$

Equation (19.33) suggests we can estimate $g(z)$ using the method discussed in Section 19.2 except that we need to replace Y_{it} by $Y_{it} - X_{it}'\hat{\alpha}$.

More specifically, for the current stage estimator of $g(\cdot)$, $(\hat{g}_{[l-1]}(\cdot))$, we estimate the next stage estimator of $g(\cdot)$ by

$$\begin{pmatrix} \hat{g}_{[l]}(z) \\ \hat{g}_{[l]}^{(1)}(z) \end{pmatrix} = D_1(z)^{-1} D_2(z, \hat{\alpha}), \qquad (19.34)$$

where $D_1(z)$ is the same as that defined in (19.12), i.e., $D_1(z) = \sum_{i=1}^{N} \sum_{t=1}^{T} K_h(Z_{it}, z) \sigma^{tt} G_{it}(z, h) G_{it}(z, h)'$, and $D_2(z, \hat{\alpha})$ is given by

$$D_2(z, \hat{\alpha}) = \sum_{i=1}^{N} \sum_{t=1}^{T} K_h(Z_{it}, z) G_{it}(z, h)$$

$$\times \left[\sigma^{tt} Y_{it} + \sum_{s \neq t}^{T} \sigma^{ts} \left(Y_{is} - X'_{is} \hat{\alpha} - \hat{g}_{[l-1]}(Z_{is}) \right) \right].$$

Upon convergence we obtain the final estimator $\hat{g}(z)$ (along with $\hat{g}^{(1)}(z)$). Since $\hat{\alpha}$ is $\sqrt{N}$-consistent for α, the asymptotic distribution of $\hat{g}(z)$ is the same as that given in Section 19.2 (i.e., the same as the case in which α is known).

19.4   Nonparametric Panel Data Models with Fixed Effects

Consider the following nonparametric panel data regression model with fixed effects:

$$Y_{it} = g(Z_{it}) + \mu_i + \nu_{it}, \quad i = 1, 2, \ldots, N, \, t = 1, 2, \ldots, T, \qquad (19.35)$$

where $g(\cdot)$ is an unknown smooth function, μ_i is the fixed effect,[4] $Z_{it} = (Z_{it,1}, \ldots, Z_{it,q})$ is of dimension q, and all other variables are scalars. In considering the case of large N and small T, we assume that the data is independent across the i index, and we assume that ν_{it} is independent of X_{is} for all i, t, and s.

We shall take first differences to remove the fixed effects, i.e.,

$$Y_{it} - Y_{i1} = g(Z_{it}) - g(Z_{i1}) + \nu_{it} - \nu_{i1},$$
$$i = 1, 2, \ldots, N, \, t = 2, 3, \ldots, T. \qquad (19.36)$$

We consider two cases for ν_{it}: (i) ν_{it} is i.i.d. with zero mean and finite (conditionally homoskedastic) variance σ_ν^2; and (ii) ν_{it} has zero mean and may be serially correlated with an unknown correlation structure. We discuss two nonparametric estimators for $g(\cdot)$, one that utilizes the variance structure Σ, the other that ignores the structure of Σ.

---

[4]The fixed effects should be thought of as random error terms that are correlated with Z_{it} with unknown correlation structure.

19.4.1 Error Variance Structure Is Known

We let $\epsilon_{it} = v_{it} - v_{i1}$, and let $\epsilon_i = (\epsilon_{i2}, \ldots, \epsilon_{iT})'$. In this section we assume that the error v_{it} is conditionally homoskedastic. Then $\Sigma = \text{cov}(\epsilon_i | Z_{i1}, \ldots, Z_{iT}) = \text{cov}(\epsilon_i)$ and is given by

$$\Sigma = \sigma_v^2 (I_{T-1} + e_{T-1} e'_{T-1}), \qquad (19.37)$$

where I_{T-1} is an identity matrix of dimension $(T-1) \times (T-1)$, and where e_{T-1} is a $(T-1) \times 1$ vector of ones. It is easy to check that

$$\Sigma^{-1} = \frac{1}{\sigma_v^2} \left[I_{T-1} - \frac{1}{T} e_{T-1} e'_{T-1} \right]. \qquad (19.38)$$

Henderson, Carroll and Li (2006) suggest using a profile likelihood approach by choosing the criterion function for individual i as

$$\mathcal{L}_i(\cdot) = \mathcal{L}(Y_i, g_i) = -\frac{1}{2} \left[\tilde{Y}_i - g_i + g_{i1} e_{T-1} \right]' \Sigma^{-1} \left[\tilde{Y}_i - g_i + g_{i1} e_{T-1} \right], \qquad (19.39)$$

where $\tilde{Y}_i = (\tilde{Y}_{i2}, \ldots, \tilde{Y}_{iT})'$, $\tilde{Y}_{it} = Y_{it} - Y_{i1}$, $g_{it} = g(Z_{it})$, and $g_i = (g_{i2}, \ldots, g_{iT})'$.

Define the product kernel $K_h(v) = \prod_{j=1}^{q} h_j^{-1} k(v_j / h_j)$, where $k(\cdot)$ is a univariate kernel function. Let $f(\cdot)$ denote the PDF of Z_{it}, let $(Z_{it} - z)/h = [(Z_{it,1} - z_1)/h_1, \ldots, (Z_{it,q} - z_q)/h_q]'$ and define $G_{it}(z,h) = (1, [(Z_{it} - z)/h]')'$ (G_{it} is of dimension $(q+1) \times 1$), and let $g^{(1)}(z) = \partial g(z)/\partial z$, the first order derivative of $g(\cdot)$ with respect to z (of dimension $q \times 1$). We estimate the unknown function $g(z)$ by $\alpha_0(z)$, where $\alpha_0(z)$ and $\alpha_1(z)$ solve the following first order condition:

$$0 = \sum_{i=1}^{N} \sum_{t=1}^{T} K_h(Z_{it}, z) G_{it}(z, h)$$
$$\times \mathcal{L}_{i,tg} \left(Y_i, \hat{g}(Z_{i1}), \ldots, \alpha_0(z) + [(Z_{it} - z)/h]' \alpha_1(z), \ldots, \hat{g}(Z_{iT}) \right), \qquad (19.40)$$

where $\mathcal{L}_{i,tg} = \partial \mathcal{L}_i(\cdot)/\partial g_{it}$. The argument in $\mathcal{L}_{i,tg}$ is $\hat{g}(Z_{is})$ for $s \neq t$ and $\alpha_0(z) + [(Z_{it} - z)/h]' \alpha_1(z)$ when $s = t$.

Note that (19.40) is of dimension $(q+1) \times 1$, which we solve to obtain estimators for the $(q+1)$ parameters $\alpha_0(z)$ (a scalar), and $\alpha_1(z)$ (a $q \times 1$ vector).

An Iterative Procedure for Nonparametric Estimation

Henderson et al. (2006) show that one can use the following iterative algorithm for estimating $g(\cdot)$, where we also need to impose the restriction that $\sum_{i=1}^{N} \sum_{t=1}^{T} \{Y_{it} - \hat{g}(Z_{it})\} = 0$ in order for $g(\cdot)$ to be uniquely defined based on (19.36). The algorithm is linear in the Y_{it} and is described below.

Define some current stage variables (at stage $l-1$) by

$$H_{i,[l-1]} = \begin{pmatrix} Y_{i2} - \hat{g}_{[l-1]}(Z_{i2}) \\ \cdots \\ Y_{iT} - \hat{g}_{[l-1]}(Z_{iT}) \end{pmatrix} - [Y_{i1} - \hat{g}_{[l-1]}(Z_{i1})]e_{T-1},$$

$$D_1 = \frac{1}{N} \sum_{i=1}^{N} \left[e'_{T-1} \Sigma^{-1} e_{T-1} K_h(Z_{i1}, z) G_{i1} G'_{i1} \right.$$
$$\left. + \sum_{t=2}^{T} c'_{t-1} \Sigma^{-1} c_{t-1} K_h(Z_{it}, z) G_{it} G'_{it} \right],$$

$$D_{2,[l-1]} = \frac{1}{N} \sum_{i=1}^{N} \left[e'_{T-1} \Sigma^{-1} e_{T-1} K_h(Z_{i1}, z) G_{i1} \hat{g}_{[l-1]}(Z_{i1}) \right.$$
$$\left. + \sum_{t=2}^{T} c'_{t-1} \Sigma^{-1} c_{t-1} K_h(Z_{it}, z) G_{it} \hat{g}_{[l-1]}(Z_{it}) \right],$$

$$D_{3,[l-1]} = \frac{1}{N} \sum_{i=1}^{N} \left[\sum_{t=2}^{T} K_h(Z_{it}, z) G_{it} c'_{t-1} \Sigma^{-1} H_{i,[l-1]} \right.$$
$$\left. - K_h(Z_{i1}, z) G_{i1} e'_{T-1} \Sigma^{-1} H_{i,[l-1]} \right]. \tag{19.41}$$

Henderson et al. (2006) show that the next stage (stage l) estimator is given by (see Exercise 19.3)

$$\begin{pmatrix} \hat{g}_{[l]}(z) \\ \hat{g}_{[l]}^{(1)}(z) \end{pmatrix} = D_1^{-1} \left[D_{2,[l-1]} + D_{3,[l-1]} \right]. \tag{19.42}$$

In practice Σ is unknown, and one can replace Σ by an identity matrix in the initial estimate. However, even when Σ is replaced by an identity matrix, (19.42) remains an iterative estimation procedure. Henderson et al. (2006) show that the procedure usually takes three to four steps to converge. Alternatively, one can use nonparametric series methods to obtain a consistent initial estimate of $g(\cdot)$. We will discuss nonparametric series estimation of a fixed effects model in Section 19.8.

Let $b_r(z)$ be a bounded and continuous function that is the solution to

$$b_r(z) = \frac{\kappa_2}{2} g_{rr}(z) - \frac{\sigma_\nu^2 f(z)}{T-1} \sum_{t=1}^{T} \sum_{s \neq t}^{T} \mathrm{E}[\mathcal{L}_{i,tsg}(\cdot) b_r(Z_{is}) | Z_{it} = z], \quad (19.43)$$

where $g_{rr}(z) = \partial^2 g(z)/\partial z_r^2$ $(r = 1, \ldots, q)$ and $\mathcal{L}_{i,tsg} = \partial^2 \mathcal{L}_i(\cdot)/\partial g_{it} \partial g_{is}$. It is easy to show that (see Exercise 19.4)

$$\mathcal{L}_{i,1tg} = -c'_{t-1} \Sigma^{-1} e_{T-1} = -\frac{1}{T\sigma_\nu^2} \quad \text{for } t \geq 2 \qquad (19.44)$$

and that

$$\mathcal{L}_{i,tsg} = -c'_{t-1} \Sigma^{-1} c_{s-1} = \frac{1}{T\sigma_\nu^2} \quad \text{for } t, s \geq 2 \text{ and } t \neq s. \qquad (19.45)$$

In general, $b_r(\cdot)$ does not have a closed form expression. However, if one uses a consistent initial estimator of $g(\cdot)$, then a one-step iteration has a closed form expression for $b_r(\cdot)$ and is given by (replacing $b_r(\cdot)$ by $g_{rr}(\cdot)$ at the right-hand side of the equation)

$$b_r(z) = \frac{\kappa_2}{2} g_{rr}(z) - \frac{\sigma_\nu^2 f(z)}{T-1} \sum_{t=1}^{T} \sum_{s \neq t}^{T} \mathrm{E}[\mathcal{L}_{i,tsg}(\cdot) g_{rr}(Z_{is}) | Z_{it} = z]. \quad (19.46)$$

Letting $\hat{g}(z)$ denote the convergent estimator of $g(z)$, Henderson et al. (2006) show that

$$\mathrm{E}[\hat{g}(z)] - g(z) = (\kappa_2/2) \sum_{r=1}^{q} h_r^2 b_r(z) + o\left(\sum_{r=1}^{q} h_r^2\right) \quad \text{and that}$$

$$\mathrm{var}(\hat{g}(z)) = \frac{\kappa^q}{Nh_1 \ldots h_q} \frac{\sigma_\nu^2}{(T-1)f(z)} + o\left((Nh_1 \ldots h_q)^{-1}\right). \qquad (19.47)$$

Under the assumption that $h_r \propto N^{-1/(4+q)}$, we have the following asymptotic distribution for $\hat{g}(z)$ $(\kappa = \int k(v)^2 dv)$:

$$\sqrt{Nh_1 \ldots h_q} \left[\hat{g}(z) - g(z) - \sum_{r=1}^{q} h_r^2 b_r(z)\right] \xrightarrow{d} N\left(0, \frac{\sigma_\nu^2}{(T-1)f(z)}\right).$$

Obviously, $f(z)$ and σ_ν^2 can be consistently estimated by $\hat{f}(z) = (NT)^{-1} \sum_{i=1}^N \sum_{t=1}^T K_h(Z_{it}, z)$, $\hat{\sigma}_\nu^2 = \frac{1}{2N(T-1)} \sum_{i=1}^N \sum_{t=2}^T \hat{u}_{it}^2$, $\hat{u}_{it} = Y_{it} - Y_{i1} - (\hat{g}(Z_{it}) - \hat{g}(Z_{i1}))$.

To estimate the leading bias term, we need a consistent estimator of $b_r(z)$, which is given by

$$\hat{b}_r(z) = \frac{\kappa_2}{2}\hat{g}_{rr}(z) - \frac{\hat{\sigma}_\nu^2}{N(T-1)} \sum_{i=1}^N \sum_{t=1}^T \sum_{s \neq t}^T K_h(Z_{it}, z)\mathcal{L}_{i,tsg}\hat{g}_{rr}(Z_{is}),$$

where $\hat{g}_{rr}(z)$ is a consistent estimator of $g_{rr}(z)$, which can be obtained, say, by local quadratic regression based on (19.36).

19.4.2   The Error Variance Structure Is Unknown

When Σ is of unknown form, one can still obtain a consistent estimate of Σ by estimating each component, σ_{jl}, for $1 \leq j \leq l \leq T$. There are only finitely many parameters to be estimated since T is finite; therefore, the resulting estimator will be $\sqrt{N}$-consistent. The asymptotic distribution of the estimator $\hat{g}(z)$ described in the last section remains unchanged when we use a $\sqrt{N}$-consistent estimator of Σ^{-1}. However, one can also choose to ignore the variance structure Σ. In this section we derive the asymptotic distribution of a fixed effects estimator that ignores the variance structure Σ. In this case the objective function (19.39) is modified as follows (by replacing Σ^{-1} by I_{T-1}):

$$\mathcal{L}_i(\cdot) = \mathcal{L}(Y_i, g_i) = -\frac{1}{2}\left[\tilde{Y}_i - g_i + g_{i1}e_{T-1}\right]'\left[\tilde{Y}_i - g_i + g_{i1}e_{T-1}\right]. \tag{19.48}$$

Like the definitions of D_1, D_2 and D_3 given in (19.41) but with Σ^{-1} now being replaced by I_{T-1}, we define (where we also use $e'_{T-1}e_{T-1} =$

$T - 1$ and $c'_{t-1} c_{t-1} = 1$)

$$J_1 = \frac{T-1}{N} \sum_{i=1}^{N} \left[K_h(Z_{i1}, z) G_{i1} G'_{i1} + \sum_{t=2}^{T} K_h(Z_{it}, z) G_{it} G'_{it} \right],$$

$$J_{2,[l-1]} = \frac{T-1}{N} \sum_{i=1}^{N} \left[K_h(Z_{i1}, z) G_{i1} \hat{g}_{[l-1]}(Z_{i1}) \right.$$
$$\left. + \sum_{t=2}^{T} K_h(Z_{it}, z) G_{it} \hat{g}_{[l-1]}(Z_{it}) \right],$$

$$J_{3,[l-1]} = \frac{1}{N} \sum_{i=1}^{N} \left[\sum_{t=2}^{T} K_h(Z_{it}, z) G_{it} c'_{t-1} H_{i,[l-1]} \right.$$
$$\left. - K_h(Z_{i1}, z) G_{i1} e'_{T-1} H_{i,[l-1]} \right].$$

The next step estimators of $g(z)$ and $g^{(1)}(z)$ are then given by

$$\begin{pmatrix} \tilde{g}_{[l]}(z) \\ \tilde{g}^{(1)}_{[l]}(z) \end{pmatrix} = J_1^{-1} \left[J_{2,[l-1]} + J_{3,[l-1]} \right]. \tag{19.49}$$

One can use the result given in Section 19.4.1 to derive the asymptotic distribution of $\tilde{g}(z)$ by replacing Σ^{-1} by I_{T-1}. In particular, the leading bias term is still given by (19.43) with $\mathcal{L}_{i,ts} = -1$ for all t, s (by replacing Σ^{-1} by I_{T-1} in (19.44) and (19.45)). Henderson et al. (2006) show that the asymptotic variance of $\tilde{g}(z)$ is given by

$$\text{var}(\tilde{g}(z)) = \frac{\sigma_\nu^2 \kappa^q (2+T)}{4(T-1) f(z) N h_1 \ldots h_q} + o\left((N h_1 \ldots h_q)^{-1} \right). \tag{19.50}$$

Henderson et al. (2006) also propose methods for testing a nonparametric random effects model versus a nonparametric fixed effects model (i.e., a "nonparametric Hausman test"). Letting $\hat{g}_{ran}(\cdot)$ and $\hat{g}_{fix}(\cdot)$ denote nonparametric random effects and fixed effects estimates of $g(\cdot)$, one test statistic proposed by Henderson et al. is based on the average squared difference between $\hat{g}_{ran}$ and $\hat{g}_{fix}$, which is given by $\frac{1}{NT} \sum_{i=1}^{N} \sum_{t=1}^{T} [\hat{g}_{ran}(Z_{it}) - \hat{g}_{fix}(Z_{it})]^2$. A bootstrap counterpart can be obtained by using a residual-based bootstrap method (the wild bootstrap).

19.5 A Partially Linear Model with Fixed Effects

As noted in Chapter 7, nonparametric regression suffers from the curse of dimensionality, hence practitioners often gravitate toward semiparametric approaches when confronted with a large number of regressors. In this section we consider a semiparametric partially linear model in which only a subset of the regressors enter the model nonparametrically. A partially linear panel data regression model with fixed effects is given by

$$Y_{it} = X_{it}'\alpha + g(Z_{it}) + \mu_i + \nu_{it}, \quad i = 1, 2, \ldots, N, \ t = 1, 2, \ldots, T, \quad (19.51)$$

where X_{it} and α are of dimension $d \times 1$, while the remaining variables are the same as those defined in Section 19.4.

Again we take the first differences to eliminate the fixed effects, thus

$$\tilde{Y}_{it} = \tilde{X}_{it}'\alpha + g(Z_{it}) - g(Z_{i1}) + \epsilon_{it}, \quad i = 1, 2, \ldots, N, \ t = 2, 3, \ldots, T, \quad (19.52)$$

where $\tilde{Y}_{it} \equiv Y_{it} - Y_{i1}$, $\tilde{X}_{it} \equiv X_{it} - X_{i1}$, and $\epsilon_{it} = \nu_{it} - \nu_{i1}$.

The criterion function for individual i is modified as follows:

$$\mathcal{L}_i(\cdot) = \mathcal{L}(Y_i, X_i, \alpha, g_i)$$
$$= -\frac{1}{2}\left[\tilde{Y}_i - \tilde{X}_i'\alpha - g_i + g_{i1}e_{T-1}\right]'\Sigma^{-1}\left[\tilde{Y}_i - \tilde{X}_i'\alpha - g_i + g_{i1}e_{T-1}\right], \quad (19.53)$$

where $\tilde{X}_i = (\tilde{X}_{i2}, \ldots, \tilde{X}_{iT})'$. The derivative functions become

$$\mathcal{L}_{i,1g} = -e_{T-1}\Sigma^{-1}\left[\tilde{Y}_{i,-1} - \tilde{X}_i\alpha - g_i + g_{i1}e_{T-1}\right],$$

and

$$\mathcal{L}_{i,tg} = c_{t-1}\Sigma^{-1}\left[\tilde{Y}_i - \tilde{X}_i\alpha - g_i - g_{i1}e_{T-1}\right], \quad \text{for } t \geq 2.$$

Henderson et al. (2006) suggest estimating $g(\cdot)$ and α by a profile-kernel approach. For a given value of α and current stage estimator $\hat{g}_{[l-1]}(\cdot)$, we estimate the next stage $g(z)$ by $\hat{g}_{[l]}(z)$, where $\hat{g}_{[l]}(z)$ and

$\hat{g}_{[l]}^{(1)}(z)$ satisfy the first order condition

$$
0 = \sum_{i=1}^{N} \sum_{t=1}^{T} K_h(Z_{it}, z) G_{it}(z, h) \mathcal{L}_{tg}\Big(Y_i, X_i, \alpha, \hat{g}_{[l-1]}(Z_{i1}, \alpha), \dots, \hat{g}_{[l]}(z)
$$
$$
+ \left[(Z_{it} - z)/h\right]' \hat{g}_{[l]}^{(1)}(z), \dots, \hat{g}(Z_{iT,\alpha})\Big).
$$
$$
\tag{19.54}
$$

Comparing (19.52) with (19.36), let $\hat{g}_y(\cdot)$ be the nonparametric estimator of (19.36) and let $\hat{g}_{x,r}(\cdot)$ be the nonparametric estimator of (19.36) in which Y_{it} is replaced by the rth component of X_{it}. Furthermore, let $\hat{g}_x(z) = \{\hat{g}_{x,1}(z), \dots, \hat{g}_{x,d}(z)\}'$. Then it is obvious by the linearity of the smoother and from (19.52) that

$$
\hat{g}(z, \alpha) = \hat{g}_y(z) - \hat{g}_x(z)'\alpha. \tag{19.55}
$$

Define $\hat{Y}_{it}^* = \tilde{Y}_{it} - \{\hat{g}_y(Z_{it}) - \hat{g}_y(Z_{i1})\}$, $\hat{Y}_i^* = (\hat{Y}_{i2}^*, \dots, \hat{Y}_{iT}^*)'$, $\hat{X}_{it}^* = \tilde{X}_{it} - \{\hat{g}_x(Z_{it}) - \hat{g}_x(Z_{i1})\}$ and $\hat{X}_i^* = (\hat{X}_{i2}^*, \dots, \hat{X}_{iT}^*)$. Henderson et al. (2006) suggest estimating α by minimizing

$$
\sum_{i=1}^{N} \left[\hat{Y}_i^* - \hat{X}_i^{*'}\alpha\right]' \Sigma^{-1} \left[\hat{Y}_i^* - \hat{X}_i^{*'}\alpha\right], \tag{19.56}
$$

which leads to the following closed form solution:

$$
\hat{\alpha} = \left[\sum_{i=1}^{N} \hat{X}_i^* \Sigma^{-1} \hat{X}_i^{*'}\right]^{-1} \sum_{i=1}^{N} \hat{X}_i^* \Sigma^{-1} \hat{Y}_i^*. \tag{19.57}
$$

Note that since we have a closed form solution for $\hat{\alpha}$, no iteration is needed for estimating $\hat{\alpha}$.

The asymptotic distribution of $\hat{\alpha}$ is

$$
\sqrt{N}(\hat{\alpha} - \alpha) \to N(0, V_1) \text{ in distribution,} \tag{19.58}
$$

where V_1 is a positive definite matrix. Moreover, a consistent estimator of V_1 is given by $\hat{V}_1 = \left[N^{-1} \sum_{i=1}^{N} \hat{X}_i^* \Sigma^{-1} \hat{X}_i^{*'}\right]^{-1}$.

With $\hat{\alpha}$ given by (19.57) we can estimate $g(\cdot)$ based on

$$
\tilde{Y}_{it} - \tilde{X}_{it}'\hat{\alpha} = g(Z_{it}) - g(Z_{i1}) + \text{error} \tag{19.59}
$$

by the method outlined in Section 19.4 except that now $\tilde{Y}_{it}$ is replaced by $\tilde{Y}_{it} - \tilde{X}_{it}'\hat{\alpha}$ whenever it occurs. Upon convergence, the resulting $\hat{g}(z)$

has the same asymptotic distribution as that given in Section 19.4. This is because replacing $\hat{\alpha}$ by the true value α in (19.59) simply gives us the nonparametric regression model covered in Section 19.4. Next, notice that $\hat{\alpha} - \alpha = O_p(N^{-1/2})$, which converges to zero faster than the nonparametric estimator $\hat{g}(z) - g(z)$. Therefore, replacing the true α by $\hat{\alpha}$ will not affect the asymptotic distribution of $\hat{g}(z)$.

One can also estimate α by ignoring the variance structure Σ. This approach also has the advantage of being computationally simple. Let $\tilde{Y}_i^*$ and $\tilde{X}_i^*$ denote $N \times 1$ and $N \times d$ matrices whose i^{th} rows are given by $\tilde{Y}_{it}^* = \tilde{Y}_{it} - [\tilde{g}_y(Y_{it}) - \tilde{g}_y(Z_{i1})]$ and $\tilde{X}_{it}^* = \tilde{X}_{it} - [\tilde{g}_x(Z_{it}) - \tilde{g}_x(Z_{i1})]$, respectively, where $\tilde{g}_y(\cdot)$ and $\tilde{g}_x(\cdot)$ are defined the same way as $\hat{g}_y(\cdot)$ and $\hat{g}_x(\cdot)$ except that we replace Σ^{-1} by I_{T-1}. Then one can estimate α by

$$\tilde{\alpha} = \left[\sum_{i=1}^{N} \tilde{X}_i^* \tilde{X}_i^{*'} \right]^{-1} \left[\sum_{i=1}^{N} \tilde{X}_i^* \tilde{Y}_i^* \right]. \qquad (19.60)$$

The asymptotic distribution of $\tilde{\alpha}$ is given by

$$\sqrt{N}(\tilde{\alpha} - \alpha) \rightarrow N(0, V_2) \text{ in distribution,} \qquad (19.61)$$

where $V_2 = A^{-1}BA^{-1}$ is a positive definite matrix. Moreover, $\hat{V}_2 = \hat{A}^{-1}\hat{B}\hat{A}^{-1}$ is a consistent estimator of V_2, where $\hat{A} = N^{-1}\sum_{i=1}^{N} \tilde{x}_i^* \tilde{x}_i^{*'}$ and $\hat{B} = N^{-1}\sum_{i=1}^{N}\sum_{t=1}^{T}\sum_{s=1}^{T} \tilde{\epsilon}_{it}\tilde{\epsilon}_{is}\tilde{X}_{it}^*\tilde{X}_{is}^*$, and where $\tilde{\epsilon}_{it} = \tilde{Y}_{it}^* - \tilde{X}_{it}^{*'}\tilde{\alpha}$.

19.6   Semiparametric Instrumental Variable Estimators

In this section we discuss estimation of a partially linear model of the form (19.1) where X_{it} maybe correlated with the error term u_{it}. We allow the error to be serially correlated (say, a random effects model) but we rule out a fixed effects model in this section.

19.6.1   An Infeasible Estimator

So far, we have considered only the case in which both X_{it} and Z_{it} are strictly exogenous for the partially linear panel data model (19.1) with a one-way random effects error structure. In this section we allow for the possibility that X_{it} is endogenous. However, we maintain the assumption that Z_{it} is strictly exogenous. For a partially linear model that allows Z_{it} to be endogenous, see Section 16.3.3 of Chapter 16. As in Chapter 7, we first eliminate $g(\cdot)$. Taking the expectation of (19.1) conditional on Z_{it}, then subtracting it from (19.1), gives

$$Y_{it} - \mathrm{E}(Y_{it}|Z_{it}) = (X_{it} - \mathrm{E}(X_{it}|Z_{it}))'\alpha + u_{it} \equiv v_{it}'\alpha + u_{it}, \quad (19.62)$$

where we have used $\mathrm{E}(u_{it}|Z_{it}) = 0$, and $v_{it} \overset{\text{def}}{=} X_{it} - \mathrm{E}(X_{it}|Z_{it})$. We allow for the possibility that X_{it} (hence v_{it}) and u_{it} are correlated. This will be the case if v_{it} contains lagged values of Y_{it} and/or u_{it} is serially correlated. Suppose that there exists a $p \times 1$ ($p \geq q$, $X_{it} \in \mathbb{R}^q$) vector of instruments W_{it} that is correlated with X_{it} and uncorrelated with u_{it} (see (19.64) below for details). Then we can estimate α using IV-OLS via

$$\tilde{\alpha}_{IV} = \left(v'ww'v\right)^{-1} v'ww' \left(y - \mathrm{E}(y|z)\right) = \alpha + \left(v'ww'v\right)^{-1} v'ww'u, \quad (19.63)$$

where w and v are of dimension $N \times p$ and $N \times q$, with typical rows given by W_{it}' and v_{it}'. Also, y, $\mathrm{E}(y|z)$ and u are all $N \times 1$ vectors with typical row elements given by Y_{it}, $\mathrm{E}(Y_{it}|Z_{it})$ and u_{it}. Let W_i and u_i denote $T \times p$ and $T \times 1$ matrices, with typical rows given by W_{it}' and u_{it}. The following conditions are needed to derive the asymptotic distribution of $\tilde{\alpha}_{IV}$ ($n = NT$):

$$w'v/n \overset{p}{\to} \mathrm{E}[W_{it}v_{it}'] \equiv A,$$
$$(w'uu'w)/n \overset{p}{\to} \mathrm{E}[W_i'u_iu_i'W_i]/T \equiv B, \; B \text{ is positive definite}, \quad (19.64)$$
$$w'u/n \overset{p}{\to} \mathrm{E}[W_{it}u_{it}] = 0.$$

Using (19.64) and a CLT argument, it is easy to show that

$$\sqrt{N}(\tilde{\alpha}_{IV} - \alpha) \to N(0, V) \text{ in distribution}, \quad (19.65)$$

where $V = Q^{-1}A'BAQ^{-1}$, and $Q = A'A$ with A and B defined in (19.64).

When X_{it} is in fact weakly exogenous, then one can simply choose $W_{it} = X_{it} - \mathrm{E}(X_{it}|Z_{it}) = v_{it}$, and $\tilde{\alpha}$ defined in (19.63) becomes the (infeasible) estimator defined by (7.5) discussed in Chapter 7.

19.6.2   The Choice of Instruments

We now turn to the fundamental problem of how one chooses the instruments W_{it}. Consider the simple case for which both X_{it} and Z_{it}

are scalars, where $X_{it} = Y_{i,t-1}$, and Z_{it} is exogenous. We note that one should *definitely not* choose $W_{it} = Z_{i,t-1}$ as an instrument for $v_{it} = Y_{i,t-1} - \mathrm{E}(Y_{i,t-1}|Z_{it})$ because, even though $Z_{i,t-1}$ is uncorrelated with u_{it}, there is no guarantee that it is correlated with v_{it} since the functional form of $g(\cdot)$ is unknown, hence $Z_{i,t-1}$ may be weakly correlated, or even uncorrelated, with v_{it}. By the assumption of the exogeneity of Z_{it}, we know that $\mathrm{E}(u_{it}|Z_{i,t-1}) = 0$, so that $Z_{i,t-1}$ is uncorrelated with the error term u_{it}. But we could also have $\mathrm{E}[v_{it}Z_{i,t-1}] = 0$, so that $Z_{i,t-1}$ is uncorrelated with v_{it}. Hence, $Z_{i,t-1}$ is not a legitimate instrument. To see that this is indeed possible, consider the case for which Z_{it} is an i.i.d. process satisfying

$$\mathrm{E}(Z_{it}) = 0 \text{ and } \mathrm{E}(Z_{it}^3) = 0, \tag{19.66}$$

and also assume that $g(Z_{it}) = Z_{it}^2$. In this case, we have

$$Y_{it} = \alpha Y_{i,t-1} + Z_{it}^2 + u_{it}. \tag{19.67}$$

From (19.67) it is easy to see that $Y_{i,t-1}$ and Z_{it} are independent of one another, hence $\mathrm{E}(Y_{i,t-1}|Z_{it}) = \mathrm{E}(Y_{i,t-1}) \stackrel{\text{def}}{=} \mu_y$. Using (19.66), (19.67) and $\mathrm{E}(u_{i,t-1}|Z_{i,t-1}) = 0$, we have

$$\mathrm{E}[v_{it}Z_{i,t-1}] = \alpha\mathrm{E}(Y_{i,t-2})\mathrm{E}(Z_{i,t-1}) + \mathrm{E}(Z_{i,t-1}^3) + \mathrm{E}(u_{i,t-1}Z_{i,t-1}) = 0. \tag{19.68}$$

This shows that $Z_{i,t-1}$ is not correlated with the endogenous regressor v_{it}, and hence cannot be a legitimate instrument. Of course we have made some strong assumptions in order to show that $Z_{i,t-1}$ is not a legitimate instrument. In practice, it is unlikely that $Z_{i,t-1}$ is uncorrelated with v_{it}, but it is certainly possible that the correlation between $Z_{i,t-1}$ and v_{it} is weak.

Given the structure of (19.62) with $X_{it} = Y_{i,t-1}$, we know that $v_{it} = Y_{i,t-1} - \mathrm{E}(Y_{i,t-1}|Z_{it})$ must be correlated with *some function* of $Z_{i,t-1}$, although it may not be correlated with the particular linear function of $Z_{i,t-1}$. Newey (1990a) discussed optimal IV estimation in general (parametric) nonlinear regression models with independent data. If we consider the unrealistic case whereby $\mathrm{E}(Y_{it}|Z_{it})$ and $\mathrm{E}(X_{it}|Z_{it})$ are known, then $v_{it} = X_{it} - \mathrm{E}(X_{it}|Z_{it})$ is known. In this case, (19.62) is a linear parametric model, and we can use Newey's result to obtain an instrument that has maximum correlation with the endogenous variable v_{it}. If we restrict ourselves to choosing instruments that are functions of $Z_{i,t-1}$, then the proper instrument is simply the optimal projection of v_{it} on $Z_{i,t-1}$, or the conditional mean function of v_{it} given $Z_{i,t-1}$. Thus, the proposed instrument is

$$W_{it} = \mathrm{E}(v_{it}|Z_{i,t-1})$$
$$= \mathrm{E}(Y_{i,t-1}|Z_{i,t-1}) - \mathrm{E}[\mathrm{E}(Y_{i,t-1}|Z_{it})|Z_{i,t-1}]. \qquad (19.69)$$

These conditional expectations are unknown in practice and we must use nonparametric methods to estimate them. Equation (19.69) is computationally demanding because it involves a double conditional expectation, i.e., $\mathrm{E}[\mathrm{E}(.|Z_{it})|Z_{i,t-1}]$. However, note that $Y_{i,t-1} = [Y_{i,t-1} - \mathrm{E}(Y_{i,t-1}|Z_{it})] + \mathrm{E}(Y_{i,t-1}|Z_{it}) \equiv v_{it} + \mathrm{E}(Y_{i,t-1}|Z_{it})$ and that $\mathrm{E}(Y_{i,t-1}|Z_{it})$ is orthogonal to v_{it}; therefore,

$$
\begin{aligned}
\mathrm{E}[v_{it}\mathrm{E}(Y_{i,t-1}|Z_{i,t-1})] &= \mathrm{E}(v_{it}\mathrm{E}[v_{it} + \mathrm{E}(Y_{i,t-1}|Z_{it})|Z_{i,t-1}]) \\
&= \mathrm{E}(v_{it}[\mathrm{E}(v_{it}|Z_{i,t-1}) + \mu_y]) \\
&= \mathrm{E}(v_{it}\mathrm{E}[v_{it}|Z_{i,t-1}]) + \mu_y\mathrm{E}[v_{it}] \\
&= \mathrm{E}(v_{it}\mathrm{E}[v_{it}|Z_{i,t-1}]), \qquad (19.70)
\end{aligned}
$$

where we used the assumption that Z_{it} is i.i.d. with $\mathrm{E}(Y_{i,t-1}|Z_{it}) = \mathrm{E}(Y_{i,t-1}) = \mu_y$ along with the fact that $\mathrm{E}(v_{it}) = 0$. Equation (19.70) tells us that $\mathrm{E}(Y_{i,t-1}|Z_{i,t-1})$ serves as an equivalent instrument for $\mathrm{E}(v_{it}|Z_{i,t-1})$. However, $\mathrm{E}(Y_{i,t-1}|Z_{i,t-1})$ is based upon a single conditional expectation and so is much easier to compute than $\mathrm{E}(v_{it}|Z_{i,t-1})$, which involves a double conditional expectation (see (19.70)). Therefore, instead of using (19.70), we suggest using

$$W_{it} = \mathrm{E}(Y_{i,t-1}|Z_{i,t-1})$$

as an instrument for v_{it}.

Even when Z_{it} is not an i.i.d. process, say when (Y_{it}, Z_{it}) is stationary with respect to t, it is easy to show that $\mathrm{E}(Y_{i,t-1}|Z_{i,t-1})$ and v_{it} are positively correlated and therefore $\mathrm{E}(Y_{i,t-1}|Z_{i,t-1})$ is a legitimate instrument.

In the general case we can have $X_{it} = (Y_{i,t-1}, X'_{2,it})'$, where $X_{2,it}$ is exogenous. Then our instrument will be $W_{it} = (W_{1,it}, W'_{2,it})'$, where $W_{1,it} = \mathrm{E}(Y_{i,t-1}|Z_{i,t-1})$ and $W_{2,it} = X_{2,it} - \mathrm{E}(X_{2,it}|Z_{it})$ (which is equivalent to $X_{2,it}$).

19.6.3 A Feasible Estimator

The estimator $\tilde{\alpha}_{IV}$ outlined in Section 19.6.1 is not feasible because the conditional mean functions $\mathrm{E}(Y_{it}|Z_{it})$, $\mathrm{E}(X_{it}|Z_{it})$ and $\mathrm{E}(W_{it}|Z_{it})$

are unknown. A feasible estimator can be obtained by replacing the unknown conditional mean functions by nonparametric estimators, say kernel estimators. For what follows, we shall use kernel methods to estimate the unknown conditional expectations listed above. Specifically, we estimate $f(Z_{it})$, $\xi_{it} \equiv \mathrm{E}(Y_{it}|Z_{it})$, $\mathrm{E}(X_{it}|Z_{it})$, and $W_{it} = \mathrm{E}(X_{it}|Z_{i,t-1})$ by $\hat{f}_{it}$, $\hat{\xi}_{it}$, $\hat{X}_{it}$ and $\hat{W}_{it}$, where (recall that $Z_{it} \in \mathbb{R}^q$)

$$\hat{f}_{it} = \frac{1}{NT} \sum_{j=1}^{N} \sum_{s=1}^{T} K_{h,it,js},$$

$$\hat{\xi}_{it} \equiv \hat{\mathrm{E}}(Y_{it}|Z_{it}) = \frac{1}{NT} \sum_{j=1}^{N} \sum_{s=1}^{T} Y_{js} K_{h,it,js}/\hat{f}_{it},$$

$$\hat{X}_{it} \equiv \hat{\mathrm{E}}(X_{it}|Z_{it}) = \frac{1}{NT} \sum_{j=1}^{N} \sum_{s=1}^{T} X_{js} K_{h,it,js}/\hat{f}_{it} \text{ and}$$

$$\hat{W}_{it} = (\hat{W}_{1,it}, \hat{W}'_{2,it})',$$

with

$$\hat{W}_{1,it} \equiv \hat{\mathrm{E}}(Y_{i,t-1}|Z_{i,t-1}) = \frac{1}{NT} \sum_{j=1}^{N} \sum_{s=1}^{T} Y_{j,s-1} K_{h,it-1,js}/\hat{f}_{i,t-1} \text{ and}$$

$$\hat{W}_{2,it} \equiv X_{2,it} - \hat{\mathrm{E}}(X_{2,it}|Z_{i,t-1})$$

$$= X_{2,it} - \frac{1}{NT} \sum_{j=1}^{N} \sum_{s=1}^{T} X_{2,js} K_{h,it-1,js}/\hat{f}_{i,t-1},$$

where $K_{h,it,js} = K_h((Z_{it} - Z_{js})/h)$ is a product kernel function.

We estimate $v_{it} = X_{it} - \mathrm{E}(X_{it}|Z_{it})$ by $\hat{v}_{it} = X_{it} - \hat{X}_{it}$. Then, using vector-matrix notation, the feasible version of $\tilde{\alpha}_{IV}$ is obtained from (19.63) by replacing $\xi_{it} \equiv \mathrm{E}(Y_{it}|Z_{it})$, $v_{it} = X_{it} - \mathrm{E}(X_{it}|Z_{it})$, and W_{it} by the kernel estimators $\hat{\xi}_{it}$, $\hat{v}_{it} = X_{it} - \hat{X}_{it}$ and $\hat{W}_{it}$, respectively, yielding, in matrix form,

$$\hat{\alpha}_{IV} = \left[\hat{v}'\hat{w}\hat{w}'\hat{v}\right]^{-1} \hat{v}'\hat{w}\hat{w}' \left(\mathcal{Y} - \hat{\xi}\right). \tag{19.71}$$

Baltagi and Li (2002) showed that $\hat{\alpha}_{IV}$ has the same asymptotic distribution as $\tilde{\alpha}_{IV}$ given in (19.65). After obtaining a $\sqrt{N}$-consistent estimator of α, one can estimate $g(z)$ based upon $Y_{it} - X'_{it}\hat{\alpha}_{IV} =$

$g(Z_{it}) + u_{it} + X'_{it}(\alpha - \hat{\alpha}_{IV}) \equiv g(Z_{it}) + \epsilon_{it}$, where $\epsilon_{it} = u_{it} + X'_{it}(\alpha - \hat{\alpha}_{IV})$.
A nonparametric kernel estimator of $g(z)$ is given by

$$\hat{g}(z) = \frac{1}{NT} \frac{\sum_i \sum_t (Y_{it} - X'_{it}\hat{\alpha}) K_h\left(\frac{Z_{it}-z}{h}\right)}{\hat{f}(Z_{it})}.$$

Because $\hat{\alpha}_{IV} - \alpha = O_p(N^{-1/2})$, which is faster than the usual nonparametric convergence rate, it can easily be shown that $\hat{g}(z)$ has the same asymptotic distribution as that for which α is known. We will not present the asymptotic distribution of $\hat{g}(z)$ here since it is a rather standard result.

Lin and Ying (2001) provide a general treatment of nonparametric and semiparametric estimation with panel data, and Fan and Li (2004) consider semiparametric varying coefficient panel data models and propose procedures that simultaneously select significant variables and estimate unknown parameters.

19.7 Testing for Serial Correlation and for Individual Effects in Semiparametric Models

Conventional statistics for testing for individual effects (or for zero serial correlation) are typically based on linear regression models. Such testing procedures are not robust to regression functional form misspecification. When one rejects the null of no individual effects (or zero serial correlation) based on a linear model, it is not clear whether the rejection is due to genuine individual effects (or error serial correlation) or to regression functional form misspecification. To obtain a robust test statistic, one can test for serially correlated errors based on an estimated semiparametric or nonparametric regression model.

Li and Hsiao (1998) considered the problem of testing error serial correlation in a semiparametric partially linear model of the form

$$Y_{it} = X'_{it}\alpha + g(Z_{it}) + u_{it}, \tag{19.72}$$

where the functional form of $g(\cdot)$ is unspecified, and where X_{it} may contain lagged values of Y_{it}. The main null hypothesis considered by Li and Hsiao is H_0: $\rho = \mathrm{E}[u_{it}u_{i,t-1}] = 0$ (against H_1: $\rho \neq 0$). They construct a test statistic based on estimated residuals from the partially linear model given above, and they derive the asymptotic distribution of their test statistic. They have also proposed methods to jointly test for higher order serial correlation and individual effects.

Li and Hsiao (1998) consider a density-weighted statistic given by $\rho_f = \mathrm{E}[u_{it}f_{it}u_{i,t-1}f_{i,t-1}]$, where $f_{it} = f(Z_{it})$ is the PDF of Z_{it}. One estimates $u_{it}f_{it}$ by $\hat{u}_{it}\hat{f}_{it}$, where $\hat{u}_{it} = Y_{it} - X'_{it}\hat{\alpha} - \hat{g}(Z_{it})$, where $\hat{\alpha}$ is the semiparametric estimator of α discussed in Chapter 18, and where $\hat{g}(Z_{it}) = \hat{\mathrm{E}}(Y_{it}|Z_{it}) - \hat{\mathrm{E}}(X_{it}|Z_{it})'\hat{\alpha}$. The test statistic is the sample analogue of I_f, i.e., $I_{f,n} = N^{-1}\sum_i \sum_t \hat{u}_{it}\hat{u}_{i,t-1}\hat{f}_{it}\hat{f}_{i,t-1}$.

Theorem 19.2. *Under the null hypothesis that the error u_{it} follows a martingale difference process, it can be shown that*

$$\frac{\sqrt{N}I_{N,f}}{\sqrt{\hat{V}_I}} \overset{d}{\to} N(0,1),$$

where

$$\hat{V}_I = N^{-1}\sum_i \sum_t \left[\left(\hat{u}_{i,t-1}\hat{f}_{i,t-1} - \hat{v}'_{it}\hat{f}_{it}\hat{B}^{-1}\hat{\Phi}\right)\hat{u}_{it}\hat{f}_{it}\right]^2,$$

$$\hat{B} = N^{-1}\sum_i \sum_t (X_{it} - \hat{X}_{it})(X_{it} - \hat{X}_{it})'\hat{f}_{it}^2, \hat{X}_{it} \equiv \hat{\mathrm{E}}(X_{it}|Z_{it}), \;\; and$$

$$\hat{\Phi} = N^{-1}\sum_i \sum_t (Z_{it} - \hat{Z}_{it})\hat{f}_{it}\hat{u}_{i,t-1}\hat{f}_{i,t-1}.$$

Li and Hsiao (1998) also propose a statistic for testing the null of no individual-specific effects based upon a density-weighted version of $\mathrm{E}[u_{it}u_{is}]$ for all $t \neq s$. The test statistic is given by

$$J_{N,f} = \frac{2}{N(T-1)}\sum_{i=1}^N \sum_{t=1}^T \sum_{s>t}^T \hat{u}_{it}\hat{u}_{is}\hat{f}_{it}\hat{f}_{is}.$$

Theorem 19.3. *Under the null hypothesis that the error u_{it} follows a martingale difference process,*

$$\sqrt{N}J_{N,f}/\sqrt{\hat{V}_J} \overset{d}{\to} N(0,1),$$

where

$$\hat{V}_J = \frac{2}{N(T-1)} \sum_{i=1}^{N} \sum_{t=1}^{T} \sum_{s>t}^{T} \sum_{s'>t}^{T} \hat{u}_{it}^2 \hat{f}_{it}^2 \left\{ \left[\hat{u}_{is}\hat{f}_{is} - \hat{v}_{is}'\hat{f}_{is}\hat{B}^{-1}\hat{\Phi}_{t-s} \right] \right.$$

$$\left. \times \left[\hat{u}_{is'}\hat{f}_{is'} - \hat{v}_{is'}'\hat{f}_{is'}\hat{B}^{-1}\hat{\Phi}_{t-s'} \right] \right\} \ \text{and}$$

$$\hat{\Phi}_{t-s} = N^{-1} \sum_{i} \sum_{s=t}^{T} \hat{v}_{it}\hat{f}_{it}\hat{u}_{i,t-s}\hat{f}_{i,t-s}.$$

Consider a semiparametric dynamic panel data model of the form

$$Y_{it} = X_{it}'\alpha + g(Z_{it}) + u_{it}, \quad i = 1, 2, \dots, N, \ t = 1, 2, \dots, T, \quad (19.73)$$

where X_{it} is of dimension $p \times 1$, α is a $p \times 1$ vector of unknown parameters, Z_{it} is of dimension q, and $g(\cdot)$ is an unspecified smooth function. We allow X_{it} to contain lagged values of Y_{it} (say, the first element of X_{it} is $Y_{i,t-1}$), so that (19.73) is a semiparametric dynamic panel data model. We assume that Z_{it} is weakly exogenous in the sense that $\mathrm{E}(u_{it}|Z_{is}) = 0$ for $s \leq t$. Also, we assume that the data is independent across the i index, so we have $\mathrm{var}(u) = I_N \otimes \Omega$, where $\Omega = \mathrm{var}(u_i)$, u is of dimension $NT \times 1$, and u_i is of dimension $T \times 1$. We consider the case of large N and fixed T, therefore, all asymptotics are for $N \to \infty$.

We allow for the possibility that the error u_{it} is serially correlated. For example, the error u_{it} could have a one-way error component specification of the form $u_{it} = \mu_i + \nu_{it}$, where μ_i is a random individual effect, which renders the errors serially correlated.

Kniesner and Li (2002) consider the estimation of a semiparametric dynamic panel model of the form

$$Y_{it} = Y_{i,t-1}\alpha + g(Z_{it}) + u_{it}, \quad (19.74)$$

where Y_{it} is the logarithm of hours worked by individual i during time period t, and Z_{it} contains ln(wage), education, age, number of children, etc. Kniesner and Li first estimated a linear model by specifying $g(Z_{it}) = Z_{it}'\gamma$. They tested for the null hypothesis of no individual effects based on ordinary least squares residuals and rejected the null hypothesis. If one takes this result as evidence of genuine serially correlated errors or as evidence of individual effects, one then needs to use some type of IV estimation method to estimate α. However, as argued above, the test outcome may in fact reflect regression functional form

misspecification. Kniesner and Li then estimate the semiparametric
model (19.74) and apply Li and Hsiao's (1998) $J_{N,f}$ test for no individual effects outlined above using estimated residuals from the partially
linear model, and they find no evidence for the existence of individual
effects. They further test whether $g(z) = z'\gamma$ using the test statistic
(12.7) outlined in Section 12.1.1, and the test strongly rejects the linear functional form for $g(\cdot)$. Thus, their application demonstrates how
the use of flexible functional forms can help to identify whether there
exist genuine individual effects or serially correlated errors, or whether
functional form misspecification exists.

19.8   Series Estimation of Panel Data Models

As we discussed in Chapter 15, one strength of series methods is the
ease with which restrictions, e.g., additivity, can be imposed. In the
remaining part of this chapter we focus on series estimation of panel
data models. The discussions draw heavily from the work of Ai and Li
(2006).

19.8.1   Additive Effects

We consider a general additive partially linear fixed effects model given
by

$$Y_{it} = X_{0it}'\alpha + \sum_{j=1}^{J} g_j(X_{jit}) + \mu_i + \nu_{it}, \tag{19.75}$$

where the functional forms of the $g_j(\cdot)$'s are unspecified.

Let $q_j(\cdot) = (q_{j1}(\cdot), q_{j2}(\cdot), \ldots, q_{jk_j}(\cdot))'$ denote *known* series base functions that can approximate $g_j(\cdot)$ well in the sense that

$$g_j(\cdot) = q_j(\cdot)'\pi_j + O\left(k^{-\tau_j}\right)$$

for some $\tau_j > 0$. Ignoring the approximation errors, the parameter vector α and the coefficient vector π_j's can be estimated by the following
nonlinear least squares estimator:

$$(\hat{\alpha}, \hat{\pi}) = \arg\min_{\alpha,\pi} \sum_{i=1}^{N} \sum_{t=2}^{T} \left[Y_{it} - Y_{i,t-1} - (X_{0it} - X_{0it-1})'\alpha \right.$$
$$\left. - \sum_{j=1}^{J} [q_j(X_{jit}) - q(X_{jit-1})]'\pi_j \right]^2. \tag{19.76}$$

Equation (19.76) is the series estimator of an additive partially linear model. $\hat{g}_j(\cdot) = q_j(\cdot)'\hat{\pi}_j$ is a consistent estimator of $g_j(\cdot)$ having the usual nonparametric rate of convergence. $\hat{\alpha}$ is $\sqrt{N}$-consistent and asymptotically normally distributed. A consistent estimator of the asymptotic variance of $\hat{\alpha}$ can be obtained by treating (19.76) as if it were a parametric regression model. More specifically, let $\theta = (\alpha', \pi_1', \ldots, \pi_J')' \equiv (\alpha', \pi')'$ and define

$$l_i(\theta) = \sum_{t=1}^{T} \Big[Y_{it} - Y_{it-1} - (X_{0it} - X_{0it-1})'\alpha$$

$$\times - \sum_{j=1}^{J} [q(X_{jit}) - q(X_{jit-1})]'\pi_j \Big]^2 \quad \text{and}$$

$$\hat{V} = \left(\sum_{i=1}^{N} \frac{\partial^2 l_i(\hat{\theta})}{\partial\theta\partial\theta'} \right)^{-1} \left(\frac{\partial l_i(\hat{\theta})}{\partial\theta} \frac{\partial l_i(\hat{\theta})}{\partial\theta'} \right) \left(\frac{\partial^2 l_i(\hat{\theta})}{\partial\theta\partial\theta'} \right)^{-1}$$

$$= \begin{pmatrix} \hat{V}_\alpha & \hat{V}_{\alpha\pi} \\ \hat{V}_{\pi\alpha} & \hat{V}_\pi \end{pmatrix}.$$

Note that $\hat{V}_\alpha$ would be the correct estimated variance of $\hat{\theta}$ if $q_j(\cdot)'\pi_j$ were the correct specification for $g_j(\cdot)$ for the *fixed* value of k_j (for all $j = 1, \ldots, J$). However, when $k_j \to \infty$, $\hat{V}$ is not the proper estimated variance of $\hat{\delta}$ because $q_j(\cdot)'\hat{\pi}_j$ is not a $\sqrt{N}$-consistent estimator of $g_j(\cdot)$. Nevertheless, the upper-left block $\hat{V}_\alpha$ always gives the correct (i.e., consistent) estimator of $\text{var}(\hat{\alpha})$.

The results of Ai and Chen (2003) can also be applied to estimate the more general model

$$Y_{it} = v_0(X_{it}, \alpha) + \sum_{j=1}^{J} g_j(v_j(X_{it}, \alpha)) + \mu_i + \nu_{it}, \tag{19.77}$$

where $v_j(\cdot)$, $j = 0, 1, \ldots, J$, are functions of known form, and the $g_j(\cdot)$'s are unknown functions. Let $q_j(\cdot) = (q_{j1}(\cdot), q_{j2}(\cdot), \ldots, q_{jk_j}(\cdot))'$ denote a *known* series that approximates $g_j(\cdot)$ well in the sense that

$$g_j(\cdot) = q_j(\cdot)'\pi_j + O\left(k_j^{-\tau_j}\right)$$

for some $\tau_j > 0$. Ignoring the approximation errors, the parameter vector α and the coefficient vector π are estimated by the nonlinear least squares estimator

$$(\hat{\alpha}, \hat{\pi}) = \arg\min_{\alpha, \pi} \sum_{i=1}^{N} \sum_{t=2}^{T} \left[Y_{it} - Y_{i,t-1} - v_0(X_{it}, \alpha) + v_0(X_{it-1}, \alpha) \right.$$

$$\left. - \sum_{j=1}^{J} [q_j(v_j(X_{it}, \alpha)) - q_j(v_j(X_{i,t-1}, \alpha))]' \pi_j \right]^2.$$

$$(19.78)$$

Under conditions similar to those of Ai and Chen (2003), $\hat{g}_j(\cdot) = q_j(\cdot)'\hat{\pi}_j$ can be shown to be a consistent estimator of $g_j(\cdot)$ with the usual nonparametric rate of convergence ($j = 1, \ldots, J$). $\hat{\alpha}$ is $\sqrt{N}$-consistent and asymptotically normally distributed. A consistent estimator of the asymptotic variance of $\hat{\alpha}$ can be obtained by treating (19.78) as if it were a parametric regression model. More specifically, letting $\theta = (\alpha, \pi)$, define

$$l_i(\theta) = \sum_{t=1}^{T} \left[Y_{it} - Y_{i,t-1} - [v_0(X_{it}, \alpha) - v_0(X_{it}, \alpha)] \right.$$

$$\left. - \sum_{j=1}^{J} [q_j(v_j(X_{it}, \alpha)) - q_j(v_j(X_{it-1}, \alpha))]' \pi_j \right]^2 \quad \text{and}$$

$$\hat{V} = \left(\sum_{i=1}^{N} \frac{\partial^2 l_i(\hat{\theta})}{\partial \theta \partial \theta'} \right)^{-1} \left(\frac{\partial l_i(\hat{\theta})}{\partial \theta} \frac{\partial l_i(\hat{\theta})}{\partial \theta'} \right) \left(\frac{\partial^2 l_i(\hat{\theta})}{\partial \theta \partial \theta'} \right)^{-1}$$

$$= \begin{pmatrix} \hat{V}_\alpha & \hat{V}_{\alpha\pi} \\ \hat{V}_{\pi\alpha} & \hat{V}_\pi \end{pmatrix}.$$

Then $\hat{V}_\alpha$ is the correct estimated variance of $\hat{\alpha}$.

19.8.2 Alternative Formulation of Fixed Effects

We consider a simple linear panel data model with fixed effects given by

$$Y_{it} = X_{it}'\alpha + \mu_i + \nu_{it}, \quad i = 1, 2, \ldots, N, \, t = 1, 2, \ldots, T. \quad (19.79)$$

In this section we do not take first differences to eliminate the fixed effects μ_i. Instead, we assume that there exists some time-invariant variable W_i such that $E(\mu_i | X_i, W_i) = g(X_i, W_i)$, where the functional form of $g(\cdot)$ is not specified. As we will show shortly, this will result in a semiparametric partially linear model. We interpret the so-called fixed effects model as a random effect μ_i such that the joint distribution of μ_i and X_i is unrestricted.[5] Moreover, suppose that the regressors satisfy the exogeneity condition $\mathrm{E}(\nu_i|X_i) = 0$ where $\nu_i = (\nu_{i1}, \ldots, \nu_{iT})$. Under this condition, it is known that the coefficients for the time-invariant regressors are not identified. Thus, for simplicity, we assume that X_{it} does not include time-invariant regressors. We shall use W_i to denote the time-invariant regressors, and we shall write the exogeneity condition as $\mathrm{E}(\nu_i|X_i, W_i) = 0$. The coefficient on the time-variant regressors, α, can be consistently estimated by the fixed effects estimator $\hat{\alpha}$. The advantage of the fixed effects estimator is that it does not require parameterization of the distribution of (X_i, W_i) and μ_i. The disadvantage is that it cannot estimate the effect of time-invariant regressors. To estimate the effect of the time-invariant regressors, applied researchers often resort to the restriction $\mathrm{E}(\mu_i|X_i, W_i) = W_i'\delta$ and apply the random effects estimator. This random effects estimator is consistent only if the restriction $\mathrm{E}(\mu_i|X_i, W_i) = W_i'\delta$ is satisfied.

If $\mathrm{E}(\mu_i|X_i, W_i) \equiv g(X_i, W_i) \neq W_i'\delta$, then one can simply treat $g(.,.)$ as an unknown nonparametric component in the model. In this way one can also identify and estimate the effect of the time-invariant regressors. To see this note that since the joint distribution of the individual effects and the regressors is unrestricted, the function $g(X_i, W_i)$ is unrestricted. Letting $\eta_i = \mu_i - g(X_i, W_i)$, then $\mathrm{E}(\eta_i|X_i, W_i) = 0$, and we can rewrite model (19.79) as

$$Y_i = X_i'\alpha + g(X_i, W_i) + u_{it}, \quad u_{it} = \eta_i + \nu_{it}, \quad \mathrm{E}(u_{it}|X_i, W_i) = 0. \tag{19.80}$$

Clearly, when α is identified the unknown function $g(X_i, W_i) = \mathrm{E}(Y_{it} - X_{it}'\alpha|X_i, W_i)$ is identified, and we can estimate α and $g(\cdot)$ using nonparametric series methods. To illustrate, let

$$p(x, w) = (p_1(x, w), p_2(x, w), \ldots, p_K(x, w))'$$

denote a *known* basis series (such as splines or power series functions) that, for a $K \times 1$ vector β and a scalar $\tau > 0$, satisfies

$$g(x, w) = p(x, w)'\beta + O(K^{-\tau}).$$

---

[5]That is, we view fixed effects as random effects, but the random effects term μ_i can be correlated with $X_i = (X_{i1}, \ldots, X_{iT})$ where the structure of the correlation is unspecified.

Ignoring the approximation error $O(K^{-\tau})$, we estimate the coefficients α and β by the least squares estimator

$$(\hat{\alpha}, \hat{\beta}) = \arg\min_{\alpha, \beta} \sum_{i=1}^{N} \sum_{t=1}^{T} \left(Y_{it} - X_{it}'\alpha - p(X_i, W_i)'\beta \right)^2, \qquad (19.81)$$

and the unknown function $g(\cdot)$ by $\hat{g}(x, w) = p(x, w)'\hat{\beta}$. $\hat{\alpha}$ is $\sqrt{N}$-consistent and asymptotically normally distributed. A consistent estimator of the asymptotic variance of $\hat{\alpha}$ can easily be obtained by the usual variance estimator by treating (19.81) as a parametric (linear) regression model.

The estimator $\hat{g}(x, w)$ can be used for analyzing the marginal effect of w and for testing the random effects assumption $\mathrm{E}(\mu_i | X_i, W_i) \neq W_i'\delta$. For instance, the average marginal effect of w is a special case of a general smooth functional of $\hat{g}(x, w)$, which is shown to be asymptotically normally distributed in Ai and Chen (2003). A consistent test for the hypothesis $g(x, w) = w'\delta$ is presented in Chapter 12.

19.9 Nonlinear Panel Data Models

A key feature of the linear panel data model which is exploited by each of the estimators discussed above is that the observed dependent variable is linear in the individual effects, hence the individual effects can be eliminated through simple time-differencing techniques. This structure also enables us to estimate the conditional mean $\mathrm{E}(\mu_i | X_i, W_i)$ under the condition that (X_i, W_i) is mean-independent of (η_i, ν_{it}), where $\eta_i = \mu_i - \mathrm{E}(\mu_i | X_i, W_i)$. If the observed dependent variable is, however, nonlinear in individual effects, the individual effects cannot be eliminated through simple time-differencing techniques and $\mathrm{E}(\mu_i | X_i, W_i)$ cannot be consistently estimated under the mean-independence condition. Limited and qualitative dependent variable panel data models are two important examples for which the observed dependent variable is nonlinear in the individual effects. In such models, "nonlinear differencing" techniques may be required to remove the individual effects. The aim of this section is to review those nonlinear differencing techniques that have been proposed in the literature. We review results for the panel data censored regression model (also known as a "Type-1 Tobit" model), for the panel data sample selection model (also known as a "Type-2 Tobit" model, which we discussed in Chapter 10) and finally for the panel data discrete choice model.

We will use $\mathbf{1}\{A\}$ to denote an indicator function that takes the value 1 if the event A occurs and 0 otherwise. We will also use the sign function, $\text{sgn}(A)$, which takes the value 1 if A is positive, 0 if A is zero, and -1 if A is negative. For each individual, we denote $X_i = (X_{i1}, X_{i2}, \ldots, X_{iT})$, $Y_i = (Y_{i1}, \ldots, Y_{iT})$, and $u_i = (u_{i1}, \ldots, u_{iT})$. Finally, variables superscripted by an asterisk $(*)$ are unobserved latent variables.

19.9.1 Censored Panel Data Models

We begin with the panel data censored regression model, which is given by

$$
\begin{aligned}
Y_{it}^* &= X_{it}'\alpha + \mu_i + \nu_{it}, \\
Y_{it} &= \max\{0, Y_{it}^*\}.
\end{aligned}
\tag{19.82}
$$

In this model, the latent dependent variable Y_{it}^* is linear in the individual effects μ_i, but the observed dependent variable Y_{it} is nonlinear in μ_i, with the nonlinearity being induced by censoring. Simple time-differencing of the observed dependent variable does not remove μ_i. To see why simple time-differencing does not remove the individual effects, for any period t and at the true value α write

$$
Y_{it} - X_{it}'\alpha = \max\{Y_{it}^* - X_{it}'\alpha, -X_{it}'\alpha\} = \max\{\mu_i + \nu_{it}, -X_{it}'\alpha\}. \tag{19.83}
$$

Clearly, $Y_{it} - X_{it}'\alpha$ is the censored version of the error term, $\mu_i + \nu_{it}$, with $-X_{it}'\alpha$ the censoring point. Similarly, for any period s,

$$
Y_{is} - X_{is}'\alpha = \max\{\mu_i + \nu_{is}, -X_{is}'\alpha\} \tag{19.84}
$$

is the censored version of the error term $\mu_i + \nu_{is}$, with $-X_{is}'\alpha$ as the censoring point. Applying simple time-differencing, we obtain

$$
Y_{it} - X_{it}'\alpha - (Y_{is} - X_{is}'\alpha) = \max\{\mu_i + \nu_{it}, -X_{it}'\alpha\} - \max\{\mu_i + \nu_{is}, -X_{is}'\alpha\}.
$$

Obviously, the individual effect is not eliminated by simple linear time-differencing.

In order to estimate the unknown parameter α, it is not necessary to remove the individual effects at every data point. If the differenced error term $\max\{\mu_i + \nu_{it}, -X_{it}'\alpha\} - \max\{\mu_i + \nu_{is}, -X_{is}'\alpha\}$ has a zero conditional mean given the regressors, then we can estimate α by standard regression techniques. Unfortunately, the differenced error term does not have a zero conditional mean when either (i) the error terms ν_{it} and ν_{is}, conditional on the regressors and the individual effects, are not identically distributed, or (ii) the censoring points $-X'_{it}\alpha$ and $-X'_{is}\alpha$ are not identical. Thus, to obtain consistent estimates of α, we must address both problems (i) and (ii). The first problem is usually dealt with by imposing the following condition:

Assumption 19.1. *The error terms ν_{it} and ν_{is} are identically distributed conditional on (X_{it}, X_{is}, μ_i).*

The second problem is solved by artificially censoring the observed dependent variables so that both error terms are censored at the same censoring point, namely, $\max\{-X'_{it}\alpha, -X'_{is}\alpha\}$. Specifically, define the artificially censored error terms as (the second inequality below uses (19.83))

$$
\begin{aligned}
e(Y_{it} - X'_{it}\alpha, X'_{is}\alpha) &\stackrel{\text{def}}{=} \max\{Y_{it} - X'_{it}\alpha, -X'_{is}\alpha\} \\
&= \max\{\mu_i + \nu_{it}, -X'_{it}\alpha, -X'_{is}\alpha\}; \\
e(Y_{is} - X'_{is}\alpha, X'_{it}\alpha) &= \max\{Y_{is} - X'_{is}\alpha, -X'_{it}\alpha\} \\
&= \max\{\mu_i + \nu_{is}, -X'_{it}\alpha, -X'_{is}\alpha\}.
\end{aligned}
$$

It then follows from Assumption 19.1 that $e(Y_{it} - X'_{it}\alpha, X'_{is}\alpha)$ and $e(Y_{is} - X'_{is}\alpha, X'_{it}\alpha)$, conditional on the regressors and the individual effect, are identically distributed. This in turn implies that (μ_i is canceled by differencing)

$$
\text{E}[e(Y_{it} - X'_{it}\alpha, X'_{is}\alpha) - e(Y_{is} - X'_{is}\alpha, X'_{it}\alpha)|X_{it}, X_{is}] = 0. \quad (19.85)
$$

Hence, α can be consistently estimated from the conditional moment restriction (19.85) by using standard regression techniques such as GMM. Since (19.85) is obtained by applying simple time-differencing after a nonlinear transformation of the observed dependent variables, we shall call this approach "nonlinear differencing."

Although the true value of α can be estimated from (19.85) by GMM, estimation based on a *conditional* zero mean restriction is more complex than that based on an *unconditional* zero mean restriction. Thus, a simpler approach would be to find a convex objective function whose first order condition coincides with some version of the unconditional moment condition implied by (19.85). For example, one might use the objective function

$$
A(\alpha) \stackrel{\text{def}}{=} \text{E}\left(r(Y_{it}, Y_{is}, (X_{it} - X_{is})'\alpha)\right),
$$

with

$$
r(Y_1, Y_2, \delta) = \begin{cases} Y_1^2 - \delta Y_1 - Y_1 Y_2 & \text{if } \delta \le -Y_2 \\ (Y_1 - Y_2 - \delta)^2 & \text{if } -Y_2 < \delta < Y_1 \\ Y_2^2 + \delta Y_2 - Y_1 Y_2 & \text{if } Y_1 \le \delta \end{cases}
$$

satisfying the unconditional moment restriction

$$
\frac{\partial A(\alpha)}{\partial \alpha} = \mathrm{E}\left(\left[e(Y_{it} - X'_{it}\alpha, X'_{is}\alpha) - e(Y_{is} - X'_{is}\alpha, X'_{it}\alpha)\right](X_{it} - X_{is})\right)
$$
$$
= 0.
$$

It is easy to see that $r(Y_1, Y_2, \delta) \ge 0$ for all (Y_1, Y_2, δ). Therefore, α can be estimated by minimizing the sample analogue of $A(\alpha)$ given by

$$
\widehat{\alpha} = \arg\min_{\alpha} \sum_{i=1}^{N} \sum_{t<s} r\left(Y_{it}, Y_{is}, (X_{it} - X_{is})'\alpha\right). \tag{19.86}
$$

This is exactly the approach suggested by Honoré (1992), who shows that this objective function identifies α, and he also shows that $\hat{\alpha}$ is $\sqrt{N}$-consistent and asymptotically normally distributed. One can estimate the asymptotic variance of $\hat{\alpha}$ by the usual formula given by

$$
\hat{V}_\alpha = \hat{A}^{-1} \hat{B} \hat{A}^{-1},
$$

where

$$
\hat{A} = \sum_{i=1}^{N} \sum_{t=1}^{T} \sum_{s<t}^{T} \frac{\partial^2 r(Y_{it}, Y_{is}, (X_{it} - X_{is})'\hat{\alpha})}{\partial \delta^2} (X_{it} - X_{is})(X_{it} - X_{is})',
$$

$$
\hat{B} = \sum_{i=1}^{N} \sum_{t} \sum_{s<t} D_{its} D'_{its},
$$

$$
D_{its} = \frac{\partial r(Y_{it}, Y_{is}, (X_{it} - X_{is})'\hat{\delta})}{\partial \alpha} (X_{it} - X_{is}), \text{ and}
$$

$$
\frac{\partial^2 r(.,.,a)}{\partial \delta^2} = \frac{\partial^2 r(.,.,\delta)}{\partial \delta^2}\Big|_{\delta=a}.
$$

Notice that Assumption 19.1 also implies that

$$
\mathrm{E}\left[\xi(e(Y_{it} - X'_{it}\alpha, X'_{is}\alpha)) - \xi(e(Y_{is} - X'_{is}\alpha, X'_{it}\alpha))|X_{it}, X_{is}\right] = 0 \tag{19.87}
$$

holds for any function $\xi(\cdot)$. Thus, a whole class of estimators indexed by ξ can be obtained from the conditional moment restrictions given above via GMM estimation; see Ai and Li (2006) on how to construct consistent estimators of α based on (19.87).

Under Assumption 19.1, the estimator described above can be extended to the additive partially linear panel data Tobit model given by

$$Y_{it} = \begin{cases} X'_{0,it}\alpha + \sum_{j=1}^{J} g_j(X_{j,it}) + \mu_i + \nu_{it} & \text{if the RHS} > 0 \\ 0 & \text{otherwise,} \end{cases}$$

where the $g_j(\cdot)$'s are unknown functions. For identification purposes, we assume that the unknown functions satisfy $g_j(0) = 0$ for all j. Define

$$e\left(Y_{it} - X'_{0,it}\alpha - \sum_{j=1}^{J} g_j(X_{j,it}), X'_{0,is}\alpha + \sum_{j=1}^{J} g_j(X_{j,is})\right)$$

$$= \max\left\{\mu_i + \nu_{it}, -X'_{0,it}\alpha - \sum_{j=1}^{J} g_j(X_{j,it}), -X'_{0,is}\alpha - \sum_{j=1}^{J} g_j(X_{j,is})\right\}.$$

Assumption 19.1 implies that

$$\mathrm{E}\left(\left[e\left(Y_{it} - X'_{0,it}\alpha - \sum_{j=1}^{J} g_j(X_{j,it}), X'_{0,is}\alpha + \sum_{j=1}^{J} g_j(X_{j,is})\right)\right]\right.$$

$$\left. - \left[e\left(Y_{is} - X'_{0,is}\alpha - \sum_{j=1}^{J} g_j(X_{j,is}), X'_{0,it}\alpha + \sum_{j=1}^{J} g_j(X_{j,it})\right)\right] \,\middle|\, X_{it}, X_{is}\right)$$

$$= 0$$

Following Ai and Chen (2003), we approximate $g_j(\cdot)$ by the linear sieve $p^{k_j}(\cdot)'\pi$, where $p^k(\cdot)$ is a vector of approximating functions. The unknown parameter vector α and the sieve coefficients π can be estimated by

$$(\widehat{\alpha}_\xi, \widehat{\pi}) = \arg\min_{\alpha,\pi} \sum_{i=1}^{N} \sum_{t<s} r\left[Y_{it}, Y_{is}, (X_{0,it} - X_{0,is})'\alpha\right.$$

$$\left. + \sum_{j=1}^{J} (p^{k_j}(X_{j,it}) - p^{k_j}(X_{j,is}))'\pi_j\right].$$

The unknown functions are estimated by $\hat{g}_j(\cdot) = p^{k_j}(\cdot)'\widehat{\pi}_j$. Ai and Li (2006) show that the estimators $\widehat{\alpha}$ and $\hat{g}_j(\cdot)$ are $\sqrt{N}$-consistent and asymptotically normally distributed, and that $\hat{g}_j(\cdot)$ consistently estimates $g_j(\cdot)$.

Assumption 19.1 is the key condition for all of the estimators discussed above. This condition is weaker than the one normally made for Tobit models. For instance, it permits dependent data and allows for dependence of the error term on the explanatory variables (e.g., heteroskedastic errors). It is still restrictive, however, and it rules out predetermined or endogenous regressors. For the case of predetermined or endogenous regressors, the conditional moment restriction (19.87) does not hold. In this case, the procedure described above needs to be modified. We now show how to modify the above procedure to consistently estimate the model's parameters. We begin with the case of predetermined regressors. Define $X_{it} = (X_{1it}', X_{2it}')'$ and decompose $\alpha = (\alpha_1', \alpha_2')'$ accordingly. Suppose that X_{1it} is exogenous and X_{2it} is predetermined (e.g., contains lagged dependent variables). Assumption 19.1 is modified as follows:

Assumption 19.2. *For any $t > s$, the error terms ν_{it} and ν_{is}, conditional on $(X_{1,it}, X_{is}, \mu_i)$, are identically distributed.*

Assumption 19.2 is weaker than Assumption 19.1. To see why Assumption 19.2 permits predetermined regressors, suppose for the moment that ν_{it} is independent of both $X_{1i} = (X_{1,i1}, X_{1,i2}, \ldots, X_{1,iT})$ and $X_{2i}^t = (X_{2,i1}, X_{2,i2}, \ldots, X_{2,it})$. Then, for any $s < t$, both ν_{it} and ν_{is} are independent of X_{1i} and X_{2i}^s and Assumption 19.2 is satisfied so long as ν_{it} and ν_{is} are identically distributed.

The problem with predetermined regressors is that the censoring point contains predetermined regressors so the censored error terms $e(Y_{it} - X_{it}'\alpha, X_{is}'\alpha)$ and $e(Y_{is} - X_{is}'\alpha, X_{it}'\alpha)$ are not identically distributed. A solution to this problem is to drop the predetermined regressors from the censoring point. To do so, Honoré and Hu (1999) assume that $X_{2it}'\alpha_2 \geq 0$ holds with probability one. Next, define

$$\epsilon(Y_{it} - X_{it}'\alpha, X_{1,it}'\alpha_1, X_{is}'\alpha) = \max\{Y_{it} - X_{it}'\alpha, -X_{1it}'\alpha_1, -X_{is}'\alpha\}$$
$$= \max\{\mu_i + \nu_{it}, -X_{1,it}'\alpha_1, -X_{is}'\alpha\};$$
$$\epsilon(Y_{is} - X_{is}'\alpha, X_{1,it}'\alpha_1) = \max\{Y_{is} - X_{is}'\alpha, -X_{1,it}'\alpha_1\}$$
$$= \max\{\mu_i + u_{is}, -X_{1it}'\alpha_1, -X_{is}'\alpha\}.$$

Assumption 19.2 along with the assumption that, with probability one, $X_{2,it}'\alpha_2 \geq 0$ imply that the error terms $\epsilon(Y_{it} - X_{it}'\alpha, X_{1,it}'\alpha_1, X_{is}'\alpha)$ and

$\epsilon(Y_{is} - X'_{is}\alpha, X'_{1,it}\alpha_1)$ are identically distributed given $(X_{1,it}, X_{is})$. This in turn implies that

$$\mathrm{E}\left(\epsilon(Y_{it} - X'_{it}\alpha, X'_{1,it}\alpha_1, X'_{is}\alpha) - \epsilon(Y_{is} - X'_{is}\alpha, X'_{1it}\alpha_1)|X_{1,it}, X_{is}\right) = 0.$$
$$(19.88)$$

The parameter α can now be estimated from the conditional moment condition (19.88) by GMM.

For the case of endogenous regressors $(X_{2,it}, X_{2,is})$, Assumption 19.2 does not hold. Let (Z_{it}, Z_{is}) denote instruments for $(X_{2,it}, X_{2,is})$. Depending on the restrictions we impose on the endogenous regressors, we may make one of the following two assumptions:

Assumption 19.3. *Conditional on $(X_{1,it}, X_{1,is}, Z_{it}, Z_{is}, \mu_i)$, the terms $(\nu_{it}, X_{2,it}, X_{2,is})$ and $(\nu_{is}, X_{2,it}, X_{2,is})$ are identically distributed.*

Assumption 19.4. *The error terms ν_{it} and ν_{is}, conditional on $(X_{1it}, X_{1is}, Z_{it}, Z_{is}, \mu_i)$, are identically distributed.*

Under Assumption 19.3, $e(Y_{it} - X'_{it}\alpha, X'_{is}\alpha)$ and $e(Y_{is} - X'_{is}\alpha, X'_{it}\alpha)$, conditional on $(X_{1it}, X_{1is}, Z_{it}, Z_{is}, \mu_i)$, are identically distributed. This in turn implies that

$$\mathrm{E}\left(e(Y_{it} - X'_{it}\alpha, X'_{is}\alpha) - e(Y_{is} - X'_{is}\alpha, X'_{it}\alpha)|X_{1it}, X_{1is}, Z_{it}, Z_{is}\right) = 0.$$
$$(19.89)$$

Hence, α can be consistently estimated from the conditional moment restriction (19.89) by GMM. Note that condition (19.89) does not require that $X'_{2,it}\alpha_2 \geq 0$ and that $X'_{2,is}\alpha_2 \geq 0$. Under the condition $X'_{2,it}\alpha_2 \geq 0$ with probability one and $X'_{2,is}\alpha_2 \geq 0$, we can drop $X_{2,is}$ from the censoring point and modify the censored error term as follows:

$$\upsilon(Y_{it} - X'_{it}\alpha, X'_{1,it}\alpha_1, X'_{1,is}\alpha_1) = \max\{Y_{it} - X'_{it}\alpha, -X'_{1,it}\alpha_1, -X'_{1,is}\alpha_1\}$$
$$= \max\{\mu_i + \nu_{it}, -X'_{1,it}\alpha_1, -X'_{1,is}\alpha_1\};$$
$$\upsilon(Y_{is} - X'_{is}\alpha, X'_{1,it}\alpha_1, X'_{1,is}\alpha_1) = \max\{Y_{is} - X'_{is}\alpha, -X'_{1,it}\alpha_1, -X'_{1,is}\alpha_1\}$$
$$= \max\{\mu_i + \nu_{is}, -X'_{1,it}\alpha_1, -X'_{1,is}\alpha_1\}.$$

Assumption 19.4 implies

$$\mathrm{E}\{\left[\upsilon(Y_{it} - X'_{it}\alpha, X'_{1,it}\alpha_1, X'_{1,is}\alpha_1) - \upsilon(Y_{is} - X'_{is}\alpha, X'_{1,it}\alpha_1, X'_{1,is}\alpha_1)\right]$$
$$|X_{1,it}, X_{1,is}, Z_{it}, Z_{is}\} = 0.$$
$$(19.90)$$

Again, α can be consistently estimated from the conditional moment restriction (19.90) by GMM.

The ideas described above can easily be applied to the following dynamic latent dependent variable panel data model:

$$Y^*_{it} = \rho Y^*_{it-1} + X'_{it}\alpha + \mu_i + \nu_{it}$$
$$Y_{it} = \max\{0, Y^*_{it}\}. \tag{19.91}$$

To illustrate, suppose that the regressor X_{it} is strictly exogenous. Note that this model differs from other Tobit models in that the lagged latent dependent variable may not be observed. First, we select a subsample for which $Y_{is-1} > 0$ for some $s < t$. Then

$$Y_{is} - \rho Y_{is-1} - X'_{is}\alpha = \max\{\mu_i + \nu_{is}, -\rho Y_{is-1} - X'_{is}\alpha\};$$
$$Y_{it} - \rho Y^*_{it-1} - X'_{it}\alpha = \max\{\mu_i + \nu_{it}, -\rho Y^*_{it-1} - X'_{it}\alpha\}.$$

It is reasonable to assume that the variable Y_{is-1} is independent of ν_{is} and ν_{it} ($t > s$). On the other hand, Y^*_{it-1}, and hence Y_{it-1}, is not independent of ν_{is}. Assuming that $\rho > 0$, then, conditional on $Y_{it-1} > 0$, denote

$$e(Y_{it} - \rho Y^*_{it-1} - X'_{it}\alpha, \rho Y_{is-1} + X'_{is}\alpha, X'_{it}\alpha)$$
$$= \max\{Y_{it} - \rho Y^*_{it-1} - X'_{it}\alpha, -\rho Y_{is-1} - X'_{is}\alpha, -X'_{it}\alpha\}$$
$$= \max\{\mu_i + \nu_{it}, -\rho Y_{is-1} - X'_{is}\alpha, -X'_{it}\alpha\};$$
$$e(Y_{is} - \rho Y_{is-1} - X'_{is}\alpha, X'_{it}\alpha) = \max\{Y_{is} - \rho Y_{is-1} - X'_{is}\alpha, -X'_{it}\alpha\}$$
$$= \max\{\mu_i + \nu_{is}, -\rho Y_{is-1} - X'_{is}\alpha, -X'_{it}\alpha\}.$$

Note that, conditional on $Y_{it-1} > 0$, $\max\{\mu_i + \nu_{it}, -\rho Y_{is-1} - X'_{is}\alpha, -X'_{it}\alpha\}$ and $\max\{\mu_i + \nu_{is}, -\rho Y_{is-1} - X'_{is}\alpha, -X'_{it}\alpha\}$ are not identically distributed. So, in order to restore symmetry, we require that both errors, ν_{is} and ν_{it}, satisfy the same constraint. For instance, we can require that they satisfy

$$\min\{\mu_i + \nu_{it-1}, \mu_i + \nu_{it}\} \geq \max\{-\rho Y_{it-2} - X'_{i2-1}\alpha, -X'_{it}\alpha\}, \tag{19.92}$$

and therefore

$$Y^*_{it-1} \geq \max\{0, \rho Y_{it-2} + X'_{it-1}\alpha - X'_{it}\alpha\} > 0;$$
$$Y^*_{it} \geq \max\{\rho Y_{it-1} + X'_{it}\alpha - \rho Y_{it-2} - X'_{it-1}\alpha, \rho Y_{it-1}\} > 0.$$

Assumption 19.5. *For any t, the error terms ν_{it} and ν_{it-1}, conditional on $(Y_{it-2} > 0, X_{it}, X_{is}, \mu_i)$, are identically distributed.*

Under Assumption 19.5, and conditional on

$$\mathcal{A}_{its} = \{Y_{it-2} > 0, Y_{it-1} \geq \max\{0, \rho Y_{it-2} + X'_{it-1}\alpha - X'_{it}\alpha\}\}$$

and

$$Y_{it} \equiv \max\{\rho Y_{it-1} + X'_{it}\alpha - \rho Y_{it-2} - X'_{it-1}\alpha, \rho Y_{it-1}\},$$

we have that

$$e(Y_{it} - \rho Y_{it-1} - X'_{it}\alpha, \rho Y_{it-2} + X'_{it-1}\alpha, X'_{it}\alpha)$$

and

$$e(Y_{it-1} - \rho Y_{it-2} - X'_{it-1}\alpha, \rho Y_{it-2} + X'_{it-1}\alpha, X'_{it}\alpha)$$

are identically distributed.

This leads to the following conditional moment restriction:

$$\begin{aligned}\mathrm{E}\big\{\mathbf{1}(\mathcal{A}_{its})\big[&e(Y_{it-1} - \rho Y_{it-2} - X'_{it-1}\alpha, X'_{it}\alpha)\\ &- e(Y_{it} - \rho Y_{it-1} - X'_{it}\alpha, \rho Y_{it-2} + X'_{it-1}\alpha, X'_{it}\alpha)\big]|X_{it}, X_{is}\big\} = 0.\end{aligned}$$

The parameter α can now be estimated from the above conditional moment restriction, and the asymptotic properties of the estimator can be derived exactly the same way as in Hu (2002).

19.9.2 Discrete Choice Panel Data Models

A key aspect of the nonlinear differencing approach that has been proposed for the Tobit model is that the latent dependent variable is partly observed so that trimming can be used to restore the symmetry of the distribution of the errors. This trick does not work for the panel data discrete choice model because the latent dependent variable is unobserved. A new nonlinear differencing approach must be developed. In this subsection, we review these new nonlinear differencing techniques. We begin with the panel data binary choice model given by

$$Y_{it} = 1\{X'_{it}\alpha + \mu_i + \nu_{it} > 0\}, \quad i = 1, 2, \ldots, N, \, t = 1, 2, \ldots, T,$$
(19.93)

where X_{it} is a vector of time-varying explanatory variables, μ_i is an individual specific intercept, and ν_{it} is an error term. Note that for any two time periods t and s, simple time-differencing gives

$$Y_{it} - Y_{is} = 1\{X'_{it}\alpha + \mu_i + \nu_{it} > 0\} - 1\{X'_{is}\alpha + \mu_i + \nu_{is} > 0\}.$$

Taking expectations, we obtain

$$E(Y_{it} - Y_{is}|X_{it}, X_{is}, \mu_i) = P(\nu_{it} > -X'_{it}\alpha - \mu_i|X_{it}, X_{is}, \mu_i)$$
$$- P(\nu_{is} > -X'_{is}\alpha - \mu_i|X_{it}, X_{is}, \mu_i).$$

Obviously, simple time-differencing does not eliminate the individual effects unless $X'_{it}\alpha = X'_{is}\alpha$. Manski (1987) observes that if the differenced probability on the right-hand side has the same sign as $X'_{it}\alpha - X'_{is}\alpha$, then $(Y_{it} - Y_{is})$ is positively correlated with $\text{sgn}(X'_{it}\alpha - X'_{is}\alpha)$. Based on this observation, Manski proposed a maximum score estimator that maximizes the sample correlation given by

$$\widehat{\alpha} = \arg\max_{\alpha} \sum_{i=1}^{N} \sum_{s<t} (Y_{it} - Y_{is}) \times \text{sgn}\left((X_{it} - X_{is})'\alpha\right).$$

Clearly, Manski's estimator is defined on differenced data via the sign function. Since the sign function is nonlinear, we shall refer to this approach as nonlinear differencing.

To ensure that the differenced probability has the same sign as $X'_{it}\alpha - X'_{is}\alpha$, we impose the following condition:

Assumption 19.6. *For any $t > s$, the error terms ν_{it} and ν_{is}, conditional on (X_{it}, X_{is}, μ_i), are identically distributed.*

Like Assumption 19.1 for the Tobit model, Assumption 19.6 is weak. It does not require specifying the error distribution, and it permits dependent data and heteroskedasticity. Under some additional conditions and a scale normalization on the model's parameters, Manski (1987) demonstrates consistency of the maximum score estimator. However, his estimator is neither $\sqrt{N}$-consistent nor asymptotically normally distributed. The nonnormal asymptotic distribution of his estimator arises due to the nonsmooth objective function. If the smoothing technique suggested by Horowitz (1992) is applied, the resulting estimator can be shown to be asymptotically normally distributed, although the rate is still slower than $\sqrt{N}$; see Kyriazidou (1997) and Charlier, Melenberg and van Soest (1995) for details.

It is straightforward to extend Manski's (1987) idea to the following nonparametric panel data model:

$$Y_{it} = 1\left\{g(X_{it}) + \mu_i + \nu_{it} > 0\right\}, \quad i = 1, 2, \ldots, N, \, t = 1, 2, \ldots, T,$$
$$(19.94)$$

where $g(\cdot)$ is of unknown form. Let $p^k(x)'\pi = p_1(x)\pi_1 + \cdots + p_k(x)\pi_k$ denote a nonparametric series function approximation to $g(x)$, let

$$\widehat{\pi} = \arg\max_{\pi} \sum_{i=1}^{N} \sum_{s<t} (Y_{it} - Y_{is}) \times \mathrm{sgn}((p^k(X_{it}) - p^k(X_{is}))'\pi),$$

and let $\widehat{g}(x) = p^k(x)'\widehat{\pi}$. Then using the techniques developed by Shen (1997) and Manski (1987), $\widehat{g}(x)$ can be shown to be consistent under the sup and L_2 norms.

Returning to (19.93), as was the case for Assumption 19.1, Assumption 19.5 rules out predetermined explanatory variables such as lagged dependent variables. If predetermined explanatory variables are allowed, the trick used by Honoré and Kyriazidou (2000) can be used here to estimate model (19.93). Specifically, decompose $X'_{it}\alpha = X'_{1it}\alpha_1 + X'_{2it}\alpha_2$, and suppose that X_{2it} are predetermined explanatory variables. Consider three periods $r < s < t$. The insight provided by Honoré and Kyriazidou yields the following estimator:

$$\widehat{\alpha} = \arg\max_{\alpha} \sum_{i=1}^{N} \sum_{r<s<t} K\left(\frac{X_{1is} - X_{1it}}{h_N}\right) (Y_{is} - Y_{ir})$$
$$\times \mathrm{sgn}((X_{1is} - X_{1ir})'\alpha_1 + (X_{2it} - X_{2ir})'\alpha_2),$$

where $K(\cdot)$ denotes the product kernel function. The consistency of this estimator is proved by Honoré and Kyriazidou.

For the nonparametric model (19.94) with $h(x) = g_1(X_1) + g_2(X_2)$, let $p_1^{k_1}(X_1)'\pi_1 = p_{11}(X_1)\pi_{11} + \cdots + p_{1k_1}(X_1)\pi_{1k_1}$ denote the approximation to $g_1(X_1)$ and let $p_2^{k_2}(X_2)'\pi_2 = p_{21}(X_2)\pi_{21} + \cdots + p_{2k_2}(X_2)\pi_{2k_2}$ denote the approximation to $g_2(X_2)$. Honoré and Kyriazidou's (2000) idea then gives rise to the following estimator:

$$\widehat{\pi} = \arg\max_{\alpha} \sum_{i=1}^{N} \sum_{r<s<t} K_{is,it}(Y_{is} - Y_{ir})$$
$$\times \mathrm{sgn}\left[\left(p_1^{k_1}(X_{1is}) - p_1^{k_1}(X_{1ir})\right)' \pi_1 \right.$$
$$\left. + \left(p_2^{k_2}(X_{2it}) - p_2^{k_2}(X_{2ir})\right)' \pi_2\right],$$

where $K_{is,it} = K((X_{1is} - X_{1it})/h_N)$. It can be shown that $\widehat{g}_j(\cdot) = p_j^{k_j}(\cdot)\widehat{\pi}_j$ consistently estimates $g_j(\cdot)$.

Manski's (1987) nonlinear differencing approach is general in the sense that it requires much weaker conditions than those normally made for binary choice models. The cost of such generality is that the estimator is neither $\sqrt{N}$-consistent nor asymptotically normally distributed. A natural question is therefore whether we can achieve $\sqrt{N}$-consistency and asymptotic normality by imposing a stronger condition. Andersen (1970) answered this question by considering a Logit version of model (19.93). His nonlinear differencing idea is based on the conditional maximum likelihood approach. Let $\gamma_i = \sum_{t=1}^{T} Y_{it}$, which takes values in $\{0, 1, \ldots, T\}$ because $Y_{it} \in \{0, 1\}$. Also, let γ_{it} take values in $\{0, 1\}$. Then Andersen suggested estimating α by

$$\widehat{\alpha} = \arg\max_{\alpha} \sum_{i=1}^{N} \ln \left(\frac{\exp\left(\sum_{t=1}^{T} Y_{it} X_{it}' \alpha\right)}{\sum_{\gamma_{i1}+\cdots+\gamma_{iT}=\gamma_i} \exp\left(\sum_{t=1}^{T} \gamma_{it} X_{it}' \alpha\right)} \right),$$

where $\sum_{\gamma_{i1}+\cdots+\gamma_{iT}=\gamma_i}$ denotes summation over all possible combinations of $(\gamma_{i1}, \ldots, \gamma_{iT})$ with $\sum_{t=1}^{T} \gamma_{it} = \gamma_i$.

Andersen (1970) showed that the conditional maximum likelihood estimator is $\sqrt{N}$-consistent and asymptotically normally distributed. This condition can easily be extended to the Logit version of (19.94), where

$$\widehat{\pi} = \arg\max_{\alpha} \sum_{i=1}^{N} \ln \left(\frac{\exp\left(\sum_{t=1}^{T} Y_{it} p^k (X_{it})' \pi\right)}{\sum_{\gamma_{i1}+\cdots+\gamma_{iT}=\gamma_i} \exp\left(\sum_{t=1}^{T} \gamma_{it} p^k (X_{it}) \pi\right)} \right)$$

and $\widehat{g}(x) = p^k(x)' \widehat{\pi}$. The consistency and asymptotic normality of smooth functionals of $\widehat{g}(x)$ can be proved exactly as in Shen (1997).

To allow for predetermined explanatory variables in a panel data Logit model, Honoré and Kyriazidou (2000) require at least three periods and propose the following estimator:

$$\widehat{\alpha} = \arg\max_{\alpha} \sum_{i=1}^{N} \sum_{r<s<t} 1\{Y_{ir} + Y_{is} = 1\} K_{is,it}$$

$$\times \ln \left(\frac{[\exp((X_{1ir} - X_{1is})' \alpha_1 + (X_{2ir} - X_{2it})' \alpha_2)]^{Y_{ir}}}{1 + \exp((X_{1ir} - X_{1is})' \alpha_1 + (X_{2ir} - X_{2it})' \alpha_2)} \right).$$

This estimator has the usual nonparametric rate of convergence.

Summarizing, we know that the maximum score estimator is not $\sqrt{N}$-consistent but it imposes only weak restrictions on the distribution of the error terms. On the other hand, the conditional maximum likelihood estimator is $\sqrt{N}$-consistent but requires a very strong assumption on the distribution of the error terms. It is natural to ask whether there exist other restrictions on the error distribution that lead to $\sqrt{N}$-consistent estimators for the model's parameters. Unfortunately, Chamberlain (1993) gives a surprisingly negative answer to this question. He shows that even if the errors are i.i.d. and independent of the explanatory variables and the individual effects, the model's parameters can be estimated $\sqrt{N}$-consistently only in the Logit case.[6] Therefore, to obtain a $\sqrt{N}$-consistent estimator for non-Logit models, some additional assumptions must be imposed on the correlation between the explanatory variables and the individual effects. Honoré and Lewbel (2002) require the existence of a "special regressor" that is continuous, has finite support, and is independent of the individual effects and the error terms. The role of this special regressor is to pull the individual effect out of the nonlinear function. Specifically, write $X'_{it}\alpha = X_{1it} + X'_{2it}\alpha_1$, where X_{1it} is a special regressor whose coefficient is normalized to unity for identification purposes, and where X_{2it} denotes the predetermined regressors. For any two periods $r > s$, let Z_{is} denote the instruments consisting of all predetermined variables up to time s. Under a set of regularity conditions, Honoré and Lewbel show that

$$\mathrm{E}\left(\frac{Z_{is}(Y_{it} - \mathbf{1}\{X_{1it} > 0\})}{f_t(X_{1it}|X_{2it}, Z_{is})}\right) = Z_{is}X'_{2it}\alpha_1 + \mathrm{E}(Z_{is}\mu_i), \quad t = r, s,$$

where f_t denotes the conditional density which is allowed to vary with time. The individual effects can now be eliminated through simple time-differencing between periods r and s, and the parameters can then be estimated by simple IV methods. For details see Honoré and Lewbel.

19.10 Proofs

19.10.1 Proof of Theorem 19.1

Since this proof is quite similar to the proof of Theorem 2.2 of Chapter 2, here we provide an outline only.

Proof. We write $\hat{g}(x) - g(x) = \hat{m}(x)/\hat{f}(x)$, where $\hat{m}(x) = [\hat{g}(x) - g(x)]\hat{f}(x)$. We further write $\hat{m}(x) = \hat{m}_1(x) + \hat{m}_2(x)$, where $\hat{m}_1(x) =$

---

[6]See Honoré and Tamer (2006) on how to place bounds on parameters in dynamic discrete choice panel data models when the parameters are not identified.

$\sum_i \sum_t (g(X_{it}) - g(x))K_{h,it,x}/NT$, and $\hat{m}_2(x) = \sum_i \sum_t u_{it} K_{h,it,x}/NT$. We will first consider $\hat{m}_2(x)$. Obviously, $E[\hat{m}_2(x)] = 0$ since $E(u_{it}|X_{it}) = 0$. To evaluate $var(\hat{m}_2(x))$, we consider the case in which both N and T are large, and we assume that $u_{it} = \mu_i + \nu_{it}$ with μ_i i.i.d. $(0, \sigma_\mu^2)$, ν_{it} i.i.d. $(0, \sigma_\nu^2)$ and μ_i and ν_{it} are independent of each other. Then we have

$$
\begin{aligned}
var(\hat{m}_2(x)) &= E[(\hat{m}_2(x))^2] \\
&= (NT)^{-2} \sum_{i=1}^{N} \sum_{t=1}^{T} \sum_{s=1}^{T} E[u_{it}u_{is}K_{h,it,x}K_{h,is,x}] \\
&= (NT^2)^{-1} \Bigg\{ TE(u_{it}^2 K_{h,it,x}^2) + \sum_t \sum_{s \neq t} E(\mu_i^2 K_{h,it,x}K_{h,is,x}) \\
&\quad + \sum_t \sum_{s \neq t} E(\nu_{it}\nu_{is}K_{h,it,x}K_{h,is,x}) \Bigg\} \\
&\equiv m_{2,1}(x) + m_{2,2}(x) + m_{2,3}(x).
\end{aligned}
$$

Now,

$$
\begin{aligned}
m_{2,1}(x) &= (NT)^{-1} E\left[u_{it}^2 K_{h,it,x}^2\right] = (NT)^{-1} E\left[\sigma^2(X_{it})K_{h,it,x}^2\right] \\
&= (NTH_q)^{-1}\left[\kappa^q \sigma^2(x)f(x) + o(1)\right].
\end{aligned}
$$

Using Lemma 18.1 of Chapter 18, we have

$$
\begin{aligned}
M_N &= E\left[|K_{h,it,x}K_{h,is,x}|^{1+\delta}\right] \\
&= \int |K_{h,it,x}K_{h,is,x}|^{1+\delta} f_{ts}(x_{it}, x_{is})dx_{it}dx_{is} \\
&= H_q^{-2\delta} \int |K(u)K(v)|^{1+\delta} f_{ts}(x + hu, x + hv)dudv \\
&\leq C_1 H_q^{-2\delta}.
\end{aligned}
$$

Also,

$$|m_{2,2}(x)| = (NT^2)^{-1} \left| \sum_t \sum_{s \neq t} \mathrm{E}(\mu_i^2 K_{h,it,x} K_{h,is,x}) \right|$$

$$\leq C_1 (NT^2)^{-1} \sum_t \sum_{s \neq t} \mathrm{E}[K_{h,it,x} K_{h,is,x})]$$

$$\leq C_1 (NT^2)^{-1} \left\{ \sum_t \sum_{s \neq t} \mathrm{E}(K_{h,it,x}) \mathrm{E}(K_{h,is,x}) \right.$$

$$\left. + \sum_t \sum_{s \neq t} M_N^{\delta/(1+\delta)} \beta_{t-s}^{\delta/(1+\delta)} \right\}$$

$$\leq C_2 N^{-1} f(x)^2 + C_3 N^{-1} H_q^{-2/(1+\delta)} \sum_{\tau=1}^{\infty} \beta_\tau^{\delta/(1+\delta)}$$

$$= O(N^{-1}) + O\left(\left(NH_q^{2/(1+\delta)} \right)^{-1} \right) = o(1)$$

because $TH_q = o(1)$ and $0 < \delta < 1$.
  Similarly, we can show that

$$|m_{2,3}| \leq C_3 N^{-1} H_q^{-2/(1+\delta)} \sum_{\tau=1}^{\infty} \beta_\tau^{\delta/(1+\delta)} = o(1).$$

Summarizing the above we have shown that

$$\mathrm{var}(\hat{m}_2(x)) = \frac{1}{NTH_q} \kappa^q \sigma^2(x) f(x)[1 + o(1)]. \tag{19.95}$$

By exactly the same proof as in Chapter 2, we can easily show that

$$\mathrm{E}[\hat{m}_1(x)] = \sum_{s=1}^{q} h_s^2 B_s(x) + o_p\left(\sum_{s=1}^{q} h_s^2 \right). \tag{19.96}$$

  By using the β-mixing inequality, as we did when deriving (19.95), we can show that $\mathrm{var}(\hat{m}_1(x)) = O(\sum_{s=1}^{q} h_s^2 (NTH^q)^{-1})$. Therefore, the leading variance and bias of $\hat{m}(x)$ are given in (19.95) and (19.96), which have the same forms as the independent data case considered in Chapter 2.

Similarly, one can show that

$$MSE[\hat{f}(x)] = O\left(\sum_{s=1}^{q} h_s^2 + (NTH_q)^{-1}\right),$$

which implies that $\hat{f}(x) - f(x) = o_p(1)$. Hence (conditions for the CLT to hold can also be verified)

$$\sqrt{NTH_q}\left[\hat{g}(x) - g(x) - \sum_{s=1}^{q} h_s B_s(x)\right]$$

$$\sim \sqrt{NTH_q}\left[\hat{m}(x) - m(x) - \sum_{s=1}^{q} h_s B_s(x)\right]/f(x)$$

$$\to N(0, \kappa^q \sigma^2(x)/f(x)) \text{ in distribution.}$$

$\square$

19.10.2   Leading MSE Calculation of Wang's Estimator

In this section we sketch a proof for calculating the leading bias and variance terms of Wang's (2003) estimator, $\hat{g}(z)$. We first prove a lemma.

Lemma 19.1. *Letting $\hat{g}_{[l]}(z)$ denote the lth-step estimator of $g(z)$, then*

$$\hat{g}_{[l]}(z) - g(z) = \frac{\kappa_2}{2}\sum_{r=1}^{q} h_r^2 g_{rr}(z) + \frac{1}{N\Omega(z)}\sum_{i=1}^{N}\sum_{t=1}^{T} K_h(Z_{it}, z)\epsilon_{it}$$

$$+\frac{1}{N\Omega(z)}\sum_{i=1}^{N}\sum_{t=1}^{T}\sum_{s\neq t}^{T} K_h(Z_{it}, z)\mathcal{L}_{i,tsg}(\cdot)\{\hat{g}_{[l-1]}(z) - g(z)\} + o_p(\eta_N),$$

$$(19.97)$$

where $\kappa_2 = \int k(v)v^2 dv$, $\epsilon_{it} = \mathcal{L}_{i,tg}\{Y_i, g(Z_{i1}), \ldots, g(Z_{iT})\} = c_t'\Sigma^{-1}u_i = \sum_{s=1}^{T}\sigma^{ts}u_{is}$ and $\eta_N = \sum_{r=1}^{q} h_r^2 + (Nh_1\ldots h_q)^{-1/2}$.

Proof. Using a Taylor expansion of the first order equation (19.10) for

$(\hat{g}_{[l]}(z), \hat{g}_{[l]}^{(1)}(z))$ at $(g(z), g^{(1)}(z))$, we have

$$0 = N^{-1} \sum_{i=1}^{N} \sum_{t=1}^{T} K_h(Z_{it}, z) G_{it}(z, h) \mathcal{L}_{i,tg}(\cdot)$$

$$+ N^{-1} \sum_{i=1}^{N} \sum_{t=1}^{T} K_h(Z_{it}, z) G_{it}(z, h) G_{it}(z, h)' \mathcal{L}_{i,ttg}(\cdot) \begin{pmatrix} \hat{g}_{[l]}(z) - g(z) \\ \hat{g}_{[l]}^{(1)}(z) - g^{(1)}(z) \end{pmatrix}$$

$$+ o_p(\eta_N), \tag{19.98}$$

where the argument $(\cdot)$ is given by

$$\{Y_i, \hat{g}_{[l-1]}(Z_{i1}), \ldots, g(z) + [(Z_{it} - z)/h]'g^{(1)}(z), \ldots, \hat{g}_{[l-1]}(Z_{iT})\}.$$

It is easy to show that

$$N^{-1} \sum_{i=1}^{N} K_h(Z_{it}, z) \mathcal{L}_{i,ttg} G_{it} G_{it}' \sim \mathrm{E}[K_h(Z_{it}, z) \mathcal{L}_{i,ttg} G_{it} G_{it}'],$$

which converges to $-\Omega(z) \begin{pmatrix} 1 & 0 \\ 0 & \kappa_2 I_q \end{pmatrix}$, where $\kappa_2 = \int k(v)v^2 dv$. Hence, (19.98) leads to

$$\Omega(z)(\hat{g}_{[l]}(z) - g(z)) = \frac{1}{N} \sum_{i=1}^{N} \sum_{t=1}^{T} K_h(Z_{it}, z) \mathcal{L}_{i,tg}(\cdot) + o_p(N^{-1/2})$$

$$\equiv A_N + o_p(\eta_N),$$

where

$$A_N(z) = \frac{1}{N} \sum_{i=1}^{N} \sum_{t=1}^{T} K_h(Z_{it}, z) \mathcal{L}_{i,tg}(\cdot) = \frac{1}{N} \sum_{i=1}^{N} \sum_{t=1}^{T} K_h(Z_{it}, z)$$

$$\times \left[\sigma^{tt} \left(Y_{it} - g(z) - [(Z_{it} - z)/h]'g^{(1)}(z) \right) \right.$$

$$\left. + \sum_{s \neq t}^{T} \sigma^{ts}(Y_{is} - \hat{g}_{[l-1]}(Z_{is})) \right].$$

We decompose A_N into $A_N = A_{1N} + A_{2N}$, where A_{1N} is obtained from A_N with $\hat{g}_{[l-1]}(\cdot)$ replaced by $g(\cdot)$ and $A_{2N} = A_N - A_{1N}$. By noting that $Y_{is} - g(Z_{is}) = u_{is}$, we have

$$A_{1N} = \frac{1}{N} \sum_{i=1}^{N} \sum_{t=1}^{T} K_h(Z_{it}, z) \left[\sigma^{tt} \left(g(Z_{it}) - g(z) - [(Z_{it} - z)/h]' g^{(1)}(z) \right) \right]$$

$$+ \frac{1}{N} \sum_{i=1}^{N} \sum_{t=1}^{T} K_h(Z_{it}, z) \sum_{s=1}^{T} \sigma^{ts} u_{is}$$

$$\equiv A_{1N1} + A_{1N2}, \tag{19.99}$$

where the definitions of A_{1N1} and A_{1N2} should be apparent.

Taylor expansion of $g(Z_{it})$ at z in A_{1N1} gives

$$A_{1N1} = \frac{1}{2N} \sum_{i=1}^{N} \sum_{t=1}^{T} K_h(Z_{it}, z) \sigma^{tt} [(Z_{it} - z)] g^{(2)}(z) [(Z_{it} - z)]'$$

$$+ o_p \left(\sum_{s=1} h_r^2 \right). \tag{19.100}$$

It can be shown that $A_{1N1} = E(A_{1N1}) + o_p(\eta_N)$ and that (see Exercise 19.6)

$$E(A_{1N1}) = \frac{\kappa_2}{2} \Omega(z) \sum_{r=1}^{q} h_r^2 g_{rr}(z) + o \left(\sum_{s=1}^{q} h_r^2 \right), \tag{19.101}$$

where $g_{rr}(z) = \partial^2 g(z)/\partial z_r^2$ $(r = 1, \ldots, q)$.

Next,

$$A_{2N} = A_N - A_{1N} = \frac{1}{N} \sum_{i=1}^{N} \sum_{t=1}^{T} K_h(Z_{it}, z) \sum_{s=1}^{T} \sigma^{ts} \left[\hat{g}_{[l-1]}(Z_{is}) - g(Z_{it}) \right] \tag{19.102}$$

This completes the proof of Lemma 19.1. □

The leading variance of $\hat{g}(z) - g(z)$ comes from $\Omega(z)^{-1} A_{1N2}$. It has zero mean and asymptotic variance given by (see Exercise 19.2)

$$\Omega(z)^{-2} \text{var}(A_{1N2}) = \frac{\kappa^q}{\Omega(z)} (Nh_1 \ldots h_q)^{-1} + o \left((Nh_1 \ldots h_q)^{-1} \right). \tag{19.103}$$

Repeated application of Lemma 19.1 leads to the leading bias of $\hat{g}(z) - g(z)$ being given by (19.14). If one only iterates one step, then the bias is given by A_{1N1} and A_{2N} with $l = 1$, while $\hat{g}_{[l-1]}(Z_{is}) = \hat{g}_{[0]}(Z_{is})$ is simply the conventional estimator of $g(Z_{is})$ that ignores the Σ structure. Hence, the leading bias term in this case becomes (see Exercise 19.7)

$$\frac{\kappa_2}{2} \sum_{r=1}^{q} h_r^2 \left\{ g_{rr}(z) + \Omega(z)^{-1} \sum_{t=1}^{T} \sum_{s=1}^{T} \mathrm{E}\left[\sigma^{ts} g_{rr}(Z_{is}) | Z_{it} = z\right] \right\}.$$

$$(19.104)$$

19.11 Exercises

Exercise 19.1. Derive the asymptotic variance of $\hat{g}(x)$ defined by (19.3) for the one-way error component error structure, i.e., $u_{it} = \mu_i + \nu_{it}$, where μ_i is i.i.d. $(0, \sigma_\mu^2)$ and ν_{it} is i.i.d. $(0, \sigma_\nu^2)$. Consider the following three cases:

(i) $N \to \infty$, T is finite.

(ii) $T \to \infty$ and N is finite.

(iii) Both N and T go to infinity.

Exercise 19.2. Verify that the asymptotic variance of v_N is indeed given by (19.17).
    Hint:

$$\mathrm{var}(v_N) = \Omega(z)^{-2} N^{-1} \sum_t \mathrm{E}[K_{h,Z_{it},z}^2 c_t' \Sigma^{-1} \mathrm{E}(u_i u_i'|z) \Sigma^{-1} c_t] + (s.o.)$$

$$= \Omega(z)^{-2} N^{-1} \kappa^q (h_1 \dots h_q)^{-1} \sum_{t=1}^{T} f(z) \mathrm{E}[\sigma^{tt} | Z_{it} = z] + (s.o.)$$

$$= \kappa^2 / [\Omega(z) N h_1 \dots h_q] + (s.o.),$$

where $(s.o.)$ comes from $s \neq t$ and $\mathrm{E}[K_{h,z_{it},z} K_{h,z_{is},z}] = O(1)$, which is smaller than $\mathrm{E}[K_{h,z_{it},z}^2] = O((h_1 \dots h_q)^{-1})$.

Exercise 19.3. Derive (19.42).
    Hint: Start from (19.40), then add and subtract $\alpha_0(z) + [(Z_{it} - z)/h]' \alpha_1(z)$, then combine terms and solve for $\begin{pmatrix} \hat{\alpha}_0(z) \\ \hat{\alpha}_1(z) \end{pmatrix} \equiv \begin{pmatrix} \hat{g}_{[l]}(z) \\ \hat{g}_{[l]}^{(1)}(z) \end{pmatrix}$.

Exercise 19.4. Derive (19.44) and (19.45).

Exercise 19.5. Use (19.64) to prove (19.65).

Exercise 19.6. Prove (19.101).

Hint: First, by Taylor expansion, we have

$$A_{1N1} = N^{-1} \sum_{i=1}^{N} \sum_{t=1}^{T} K_{h,it,z} \sigma^{tt} (Z_{it} - z)' g^{(2)}(z)(Z_{it} - z) + R_N$$

(R_N is the remainder term in Taylor expansion). Then $\mathrm{E}[A_{1N1}] = \kappa_2 \sum_{t=1}^{T} \sigma^{tt} \sum_{r=1}^{q} h_r^2 g_{rr}(z) + o(|h|^2)$.

Exercise 19.7. Prove (19.104).

Hint: The term from A_{1N1} is proved in Exercise 19.6. The term from A_{2N} follows by getting the leading bias term of $\hat{g}_{[0]}(Z_{is}) - g(Z_{is})$.

Chapter 20

Topics in Applied Nonparametric Estimation

In this chapter we consider some interesting applications of nonparametric methods that have appeared in the literature. Since these topics do not fit neatly into any of the previous chapters, we have instead elected to combine them into a separate chapter, with references to methods covered in previous chapters mentioned where appropriate. We hope that the applications contained herein will underscore the widespread potential application of nonparametric methods and will also encourage readers to undertake their own applications.

20.1 Nonparametric Methods in Continuous-Time Models

20.1.1 Nonparametric Estimation of Continuous-Time Models

In this section we discuss nonparametric methods for continuous-time diffusion models, and we focus on nonparametric estimation of diffusion processes and nonparametric testing of parametric diffusion models; see Cai and Hong (2003) and Fan (2005), who provide overviews of nonparametric methods for continuous-time financial models.

Continuous-time models have been widely used in finance to capture the dynamics of fundamental economic variables such as interest rates, exchange rates, and stock prices. The well-known "option pricing model" of Black and Scholes (1973) and the "term structure model" of

Cox, Ingersoll and Ross (1985), for example, assume that the underlying state variables follow a diffusion process that can be described by

$$dX_t = \mu(X_t)dt + \sigma(X_t)dW_t, \tag{20.1}$$

where $\mu(\cdot)$ and $\sigma^2(\cdot)$ are the "drift" (instantaneous mean) and "diffusion" (instantaneous variance) of X_t, respectively, and W_t is a standard Brownian motion. A parametric approach to modeling these processes would specify parametric functional forms for $\mu(\cdot)$ and $\sigma^2(\cdot)$, e.g., $\mu(X_t, \theta)$ and $\sigma^2(X_t, \theta)$, where θ is a finite dimensional parameter. Having specified functional forms for $\mu(\cdot)$ and $\sigma^2(\cdot)$, one then proceeds to estimate θ; see Gallant and Long (1997) for minimum distance estimation of θ and Ait-Sahalia (2002) for an approximate maximum likelihood approach. Like all parametric methods, however, the presumed specification may not be consistent with the DGP, hence one might instead gravitate toward nonparametric methods.

The drift and diffusion terms are the first two conditional moments of X_t for infinitesimal changes ($t \in [0, T]$), i.e.,

$$\mu(X_t) = \lim_{\Delta \to 0} \mathrm{E}\left[\frac{X_{t+\Delta} - X_t}{\Delta}\Big| X_t\right] \text{ and}$$

$$\sigma^2(X_t) = \lim_{\Delta \to 0} \mathrm{E}\left[\frac{(X_{t+\Delta} - X_t)^2}{\Delta}\Big| X_t\right]. \tag{20.2}$$

Suppose that the data is equispaced with $\{X_{\tau\Delta}\}_{\tau=1}^n$ being the observed discrete sample. The sample size is $n = T/\Delta$. With the discretized data, one can approximate $\mu(x)$ and $\sigma^2(x)$ by $\Delta^{-1}\mathrm{E}[X_{(\tau+1)\Delta} - X_{\tau\Delta}|X_{\tau\Delta}]$ and $\Delta^{-1}\mathrm{E}[(X_{(\tau+1)\Delta} - X_{\tau\Delta})^2|X_{\tau\Delta}]$, respectively. The approximation errors are $O(\Delta)$ in both cases; see Stanton (1997) and Fan and Zhang (2003) for further details. The above arguments suggest that one can estimate $\mu(\cdot)$ and $\sigma^2(\cdot)$ by

$$\hat{\mu}(x) = \frac{1}{\Delta}\frac{\sum_{\tau=1}^n (X_{(\tau+1)\Delta} - X_{\tau\Delta})k_h(x - X_{\tau\Delta})}{\sum_{\tau=1}^n k_h(x - X_{\tau\Delta})} \text{ and} \tag{20.3}$$

$$\hat{\sigma}^2(x) = \frac{1}{\Delta}\frac{\sum_{\tau=1}^n (X_{(\tau+1)\Delta} - X_{\tau\Delta})^2 k_h(x - X_{\tau\Delta})}{\sum_{\tau=1}^n k_h(x - X_{\tau\Delta})}, \tag{20.4}$$

where $k_h(v) = h^{-1}k(v/h)$, and where $k(\cdot)$ is a second order kernel with bounded support that satisfies (1.10).

Defining

$$\hat{m}_1(x) = [\hat{\mu}(x) - \mu(x)]\,\hat{f}(x), \tag{20.5}$$

where $\hat{f}(x) = \frac{1}{n\Delta} \sum_{t=1}^{n} k_h(X_{t\Delta} - x)$, then we have

$$\hat{\mu}(x) - \mu(x) = \hat{m}_1(x)/\hat{f}(x).$$

Using the same proof that we used for Theorem 1.4, we know that $\hat{f}(x) = f(x) + O(h^2 + [\ln(n)/(nh)]^{-1/2})$ a.s. Thus, we have $\hat{\mu}(x) - \mu(x) = \hat{m}_1(x)/f(x) + o(\hat{m}_1(x))$ a.s. Assuming that $f(x) > 0$, we will show that $\text{MSE}[\hat{m}_1(x)/f(x)] = O(\Delta^2 + h^4 + (nh\Delta)^{-1})$, which implies that $\hat{\mu}(x) - \mu(x) = O_p(\Delta + h^2 + (nh\Delta)^{-1/2})$. Similarly, if we define

$$\hat{m}_2(x) = (\hat{\sigma}^2(x) - \sigma^2(x))\hat{f}(x), \tag{20.6}$$

then $\hat{\sigma}^2(x) - \sigma^2(x) = \hat{m}_2(x)/\hat{f}(x) = \hat{m}_2(x)/f(x) + o(\hat{m}_2(x))$ a.s. We will also show that $\text{MSE}(\hat{m}_2(x)) = O(\Delta^2 + h^4 + (nh\Delta)^{-1})$, which implies that $\hat{\sigma}^2(x)$ is consistent.

The following results are established in Bandi and Phillips (2003) and Fan and Zhang (2003).

Theorem 20.1. *Assuming that X_t is a stationary β-mixing Markov process with mixing coefficient $\beta_\tau = \rho^\tau$ for some $0 < \rho < 1$, that the marginal PDF $f(x)$ is bounded and continuous, that $\mu(x)$ and $\sigma^2(x)$ are both twice continuously differentiable, and that $n \to \infty$, $T \to \infty$, $\Delta \to 0$, $h \to 0$ (recall that $\kappa_2 = \int v^2 k(v)\, dv$ and $\kappa = \int k^2(v)\, dv$), then $(g^{(s)}(x) = d^s g(x)/dx^s,\ s = 1, 2)$*

(i) $\quad \text{E}\left[\hat{m}_1(x)/f(x)\right] = \dfrac{h^2}{2}\kappa_2 \left[\mu^{(2)}(x) + 2\mu^{(1)}(x)f^{(1)}(x)/f(x)\right]$

$$+ \dfrac{\Delta}{2}\left[\mu^{(1)}(x)\mu(x) + \mu^{(2)}(x)\sigma^2(x)\right]$$

$$+ o(\Delta + h^2) \ and$$

$$\text{var}\left[\hat{m}_1(x)/f(x)\right] = (nh\Delta)^{-1}\kappa\sigma^2(x)/f(x)[1 + o(1)].$$

(ii) $\quad \text{E}\left[\hat{m}_2(x)/f(x)\right] = \dfrac{\Delta}{2}\left\{ \left[2\mu(x) + (\sigma^2)^{(1)}(x)\right]\mu(x) \right.$

$$\left. + \left[2\mu^{(1)}(x) + \dfrac{1}{2}(\sigma^2)^{(2)}(x)\right]\sigma^2(x)\right\}$$

$$+ \dfrac{h^2}{2}\kappa_2\left[(\sigma^2)^{(2)}(x) + 2\sigma^{(1)}(x)f^{(1)}(x)/f(x)\right]$$

$$+ o(\Delta + h^2) \ and$$

$$\text{var}\left[\hat{m}_2(x)/f(x)\right] = \dfrac{1}{nh}\kappa\sigma^4(x)/f(x)[1 + o(1)].$$

A proof of Theorem 20.1 (i) is given in Section 20.1.5. The proof for (ii) mirrors that for (i) and is thus omitted.

Note that Theorem 20.1 tells us that $\hat{\mu}(x)$ and $\hat{\sigma}^2(x)$ have differing rates of convergence. Consistency of $\hat{\sigma}^2(x)$ requires only that $h \to 0$ as $n \to \infty$ (T can be fixed), while consistency of $\hat{\mu}(x)$ requires a stronger condition, namely, that $T = n\Delta \to \infty$ (which implies that $n \to \infty$ because $\Delta \to 0$). Therefore, if T is not sufficiently large, the accurate estimation of $\mu(\cdot)$ is much more difficult than that for $\sigma^2(\cdot)$.

Bandi and Phillips (2003) established almost sure convergence and asymptotic distribution results for $\hat{\mu}(x)$ and $\hat{\sigma}^2(x)$. Under the same conditions as in Theorem 20.1 and also assuming that $\Delta = o(h^2)$, Bandi and Phillips proved that

$$\sqrt{Th}\left[\hat{\mu}(x) - \mu(x) - h^2\Gamma_\mu(x)\right] \to N\left(0, \frac{\kappa\sigma^2(x)}{f(x)}\right) \text{ in distribution,}$$

(20.7)

where $\Gamma_\mu(x) = \kappa_2[\mu^{(1)}(x)f^{(1)}(x)/f(x) + \frac{1}{2}\mu^{(2)}(x)]$, and where the asymptotic variance can be consistently estimated by $\kappa\hat{\sigma}^2(x)/\hat{f}(x)$. They also prove that

$$\sqrt{nh}\left[\hat{\sigma}^2(x) - \sigma^2(x) - h^2\Gamma_{\sigma^2}(x)\right] \to N\left(0, \frac{\kappa\sigma^4(x)}{f(x)}\right) \text{ in distribution,}$$

(20.8)

where $\Gamma_{\sigma^2}(x) = \kappa_2[(\sigma^2)^{(1)}(x)f^{(1)}(x)/f(x) + \frac{1}{2}(\sigma^2)^{(2)}(x)]$, and where the asymptotic variance can be consistently estimated by $\kappa\hat{\sigma}^4(x)/\hat{f}(x)$. Note that when $\Delta = o(h^2)$, the bias terms related to Δ are negligible. Therefore, (20.7) and (20.8) have leading bias terms that are proportional to h^2.

The proofs of (20.7) and (20.8) are given in Bandi and Phillips (2003) and Bandi and Moloche (2005). One key assumption used to derive the above results is the stationarity of X_t. For nonstationary data, Bandi and Phillips and Bandi and Moloche propose estimating $\mu(x)$ and $\sigma^2(x)$ by

$$\bar{\mu}(x) = \frac{\sum_{\tau=1}^n k_h(x - X_{\tau\Delta})\tilde{\mu}(X_{\tau\Delta})}{\sum_{\tau=1}^n k_h(x - Z_{\tau\Delta})} \text{ and}$$

$$\bar{\sigma}^2(x) = \frac{\sum_{\tau=1}^n k_h(x - X_{\tau\Delta})\tilde{\sigma}^2(X_{\tau\Delta})}{\sum_{\tau=1}^n k_h(x - Z_{\tau\Delta})},$$

(20.9)

where

$$\tilde{\mu}(x) = \Delta^{-1} \sum_{\tau=1}^{n-1} w_{i,n}(x)(X_{(\tau+1)\Delta} - X_{\tau\Delta}) \text{ and}$$

$$\tilde{\sigma}^2(x) = \Delta^{-1} \sum_{\tau=1}^{n-1} w_{i,n}(x)(X_{(\tau+1)\Delta} - X_{\tau\Delta})^2,$$

with $w_{i,n} = \mathbf{1}(|X_{\tau\Delta} - x| \le b)/\sum_{\tau=1}^{n} \mathbf{1}(|X_{\tau\Delta} - x| \le b)$, where, here, $b = b_n$ is a smoothing parameter that depends on both T and n. They also establish consistency and asymptotic distribution results for $\bar{\mu}(x)$ and $\bar{\sigma}^2(x)$.

With nonstationary data, $f(x)$ in (20.8) must be replaced by the so-called local time, i.e., $L_T(x) = \lim_{\Delta \to 0} \frac{1}{2\Delta} \int_0^1 \mathbf{1}(X_t \in A_\Delta)dt$, where $A_\Delta = (x - \Delta, x + \Delta)$, and the normal distribution must be replaced by a mixed normal distribution. For example, $\sqrt{Th}[\hat{\mu}(x) - h^2\Gamma_\mu]$ converges in distribution to a mixture of normal random variables, $\kappa^{1/2}[L_T(x)]^{-1}\mathcal{Z}$, where $\mathcal{Z}$ is a standard normal random variable independent of the local time $L_T(x)$.

One limitation of the time-homogeneous diffusion model given in (20.1) is that it does not allow for time effects. A more general time-dependent diffusion model is given by

$$dX_t = \mu(X_t, t) + \sigma(X_t, t)dW_t. \tag{20.10}$$

As was the case in (20.2), we have

$$\mu(X_t, t) = \lim_{\Delta \to 0} \mathrm{E}\left[\frac{X_{t+\Delta} - X_t}{\Delta}\Big|X_t\right] \text{ and}$$

$$\sigma^2(X_t, t) = \lim_{\Delta \to 0} \mathrm{E}\left[\frac{(X_{t+\Delta} - X_t)^2}{\Delta}\Big|X_t\right], \tag{20.11}$$

which suggests that a regression framework is appropriate for estimating $\mu(x, t)$ and $\sigma^2(x, t)$.

The time-heterogeneous model implies, however, that X_t is nonstationary, and asymptotic results for nonparametric methods will therefore be more difficult to establish. Asymptotic properties of nonparametric drift and diffusion estimators under general time-heterogeneity are unknown at this time and certainly deserve further study.

Related work includes Fan and Zhang (2003), who propose using local linear methods to estimate the following time-varying coefficient diffusion model.

$$dX_t = [\alpha_0(t) + \alpha_1(t)X_t]dt + \beta_0(t)dW_t, \qquad (20.12)$$

where the functional forms of $\alpha_0(\cdot)$, $\alpha_1(\cdot)$ and $\beta_0(\cdot)$ are unspecified.

20.1.2 Nonparametric Tests for Continuous-Time Models

The dynamics of interest rates, exchange rates and stock prices are often modeled as a continuous-time diffusion process. However, economic theory rarely, if ever, provides functional forms for continuous-time models. Therefore, it is important to test for the correct specification of parametric continuous-time models. Ait-Sahalia (1996) and Gallant and Tauchen (1996) develop nonparametric and semiparametric tests for diffusion models, while Fan, Zhang and Zhang (2001), Corradi and Swanson (2005), Hong and Li (2005), and Li and Tkacz (2006) propose alternative tests. In the next two sections we discuss Ait-Sahalia's and Hong and Li's tests.

20.1.3 Ait-Sahalia's Test

Ait-Sahalia (1996) considers the following continuous-time stationary diffusion process:

$$dX_t = \mu_0(X_t) + \sigma_0(X_t)dW_t,$$

where $\mu_0(X_t)$ and $\sigma_0(X_t)$ are the true drift and diffusion functions, and W_t is a standard Brownian motion. Ait-Sahalia considers the problem of testing the null hypothesis of $\mu_0(x) = \mu(x, \theta_0)$ and $\sigma_0(x) = \sigma^2(x, \theta_0)$ for all x and for some $\theta_0 \in \Theta$, where Θ is a compact subset of $\mathbb{R}^q$. He suggests testing the null hypothesis indirectly by testing a parametric marginal PDF derived from the parametric drift and diffusion functions $\mu(x, \theta)$ and $\sigma^2(x, \theta)$. Ait-Sahalia shows that the marginal PDF corresponding to (μ^2, σ^2) is

$$f(x, \theta) = \frac{\xi(\theta)}{\sigma^2(x, \theta)} \exp \left\{ \int_{x_0}^x \frac{2\mu(v, \theta)}{\sigma^2(v, \theta)} dv \right\}, \qquad (20.13)$$

where x_0 is an interior point of the support of X, and where $\xi(\theta)$ is a normalizing constant that ensures that the PDF integrates to one. Let $f_0(x)$ denote the true but unknown marginal PDF. One can estimate

$f_0(x)$ by kernel methods as discussed in Chapter 1, which we denote by $\hat{f}(\cdot)$. Ait-Sahalia suggests estimating θ by

$$\hat{\theta} = \arg\min_{\theta \in \Theta} \frac{1}{n} \sum_{i=1}^{n} \left[f(X_i, \theta) - \hat{f}(X_i) \right]^2 .$$

The test statistic for testing the null hypothesis that $f(x, \theta) = f_0(x)$ for almost all x is given by

$$\hat{M} = nh^{1/2} \left[\frac{1}{n} \sum_{i=1}^{n} \left(f(X_i, \hat{\theta}) - \hat{f}(X_i) \right)^2 \right]. \qquad (20.14)$$

Under some regularity conditions, Ait-Sahalia (1996) showed that under the null hypothesis $H_0 : f(x, \theta_0) = f_0(x)$ for almost all x,

$$[\hat{M} - \hat{\mathrm{E}}_M] / \hat{V}_M^{1/2} \xrightarrow{d} N(0, 1), \qquad (20.15)$$

where

$$\hat{\mathrm{E}}_M = n^{-1} \left[\sum_{i=1}^{n} \hat{f}(X_i) \right] \int_{-\infty}^{\infty} k^2(v) dv,$$

and where

$$\hat{V}_M = 2 \left[n^{-1} \sum_{i=1}^{n} \hat{f}(X_i)^2 \right] \int \left[\int k(u)k(u+v) du \right]^2 dv.$$

20.1.4 Hong and Li's Test

Suppose that a state variable X_t follows a continuous-time diffusion process of the form

$$dX_t = \mu_0(X_t, t) + \sigma_0(X_t, t) dW_t,$$

where $\mu_0(X_t, t)$ and $\sigma_0(X_t, t)$ are the true drift and diffusion functions, and W_t is a standard Brownian motion. We are interested in testing the null hypothesis that both μ_0 and σ_0 belong to some parametric family, say $\mu_0 \in \mathcal{M}_\mu = \{\mu(., ., \theta), \theta \in \Theta\}$ and $\sigma_0 \in \mathcal{M}_\sigma = \{\sigma(., ., \theta), \theta \in \Theta\}$, where Θ is a bounded finite dimensional parameter space. The null hypothesis is then given by

$$H_0 : \mathrm{P}[\mu(X_t, t, \theta_0) = \mu_0(X_t, t), \sigma_0(X_t, t, \theta_0) = \sigma_0(X_t, t)] = 1 \quad (20.16)$$

for some $\theta_0 \in \Theta$. The alternative hypothesis is that the above probability is strictly less than one. For estimating θ_0 based on (approximating) parametric models, see Gallant and Tauchen (1996) and Ait-Sahalia (2002).

We will test the above null hypothesis using $\{X_{\tau\Delta}\}_{\tau=1}^n$, a discrete sample of $\{X_t\}$ observed over a time span T at interval Δ so that the sample size is $n = T/\Delta$. Let $p_0(x, t|y, s)$ be the transition density of X_t, i.e., the conditional PDF of $X_t = x$ given $X_s = y$, $s < t$. Under H_0, $p_x(x, t|y, s, \theta_0) = p_{x,0}(x, t|y, s)$ a.e. Hence, one can also test H_0 by comparing parametric and nonparametric estimators of $p_x(x, t|y, s)$. However, a simpler way suggested by Hong and Li (2005) involves introducing the following dynamic probability integral transform:

$$Z_\tau(\theta) = \int_{-\infty}^{X_{\tau\Delta}} p[x, \tau\Delta|X_{(\tau-1)\Delta}, (\tau-1)\Delta, \theta]dx, \quad \tau = 1, \ldots, n.$$

(20.17)

Following Rosenblatt (1952), it can be shown that under H_0, $\{Z_t = Z_t(\theta_0)\}_{t=1}^n$ is i.i.d. $U[0,1]$ (i.e., uniform). Therefore, one can test H_0 by testing whether $\{Z_t\}$ is an i.i.d. $U[0,1]$ sequence, and in this way we can avoid estimating the null model, which can be difficult since closed form likelihood functions do not exist for most parametric diffusion models.

Hong and Li (2005) suggest testing whether, for some integer j, Z_t and Z_{t-j} are independent i.i.d. $U[0,1]$ random variables. Letting $g_j(z_1, z_2)$ denote the joint PDF of $\{Z_t, Z_{t-j}\}$, one can then test H_0 by comparing $\hat{g}_j(z_1, z_2)$ with a two-dimensional uniform PDF which equals the product of two $U[0,1]$ marginal PDFs, where

$$\hat{g}(z_1, z_2) = \frac{1}{n-j} \sum_{t=j+1}^n k_h(z_1, \hat{Z}_\tau)k_h(z_2, \hat{Z}_{\tau-j}), \quad (20.18)$$

where $\hat{Z}_\tau = Z_\tau(\hat{\theta})$, and where

$$k_h(x,y) = \begin{cases} h^{-1}k\left(\frac{y-x}{h}\right) / \int_{-x/h}^1 k(v)\,dv & \text{if } x \in [0, h) \\ h^{-1}k\left(\frac{y-x}{h}\right) & \text{if } x \in [h, 1-h] \\ h^{-1}k\left(\frac{y-x}{h}\right) / \int_{-1}^{(1-x)/h} k(v)\,dv & \text{if } x \in (1-h, 1]. \end{cases}$$

(20.19)

Note that $k_h(x,y)$ is a boundary-corrected kernel function, and $k(\cdot)$ is a second order kernel with support $[-1, 1]$ satisfying (1.10) (see (1.43) for a general boundary-corrected kernel not necessarily supported in $[-1, 1]$). Hong and Li (2005) suggest testing H_0 based on

$$\hat{M}(j) = \int_0^1 \int_0^1 [\hat{g}(z_1, z_2) - 1]^2 dz_1 dz_2$$

$$= \frac{1}{(n-j)^2} \sum_{t=j+1}^n \sum_{s=j+1}^n \int_0^1 \int_0^1 \left[k_h(z_1, \hat{Z}_t)k_h(z_2, \hat{Z}_{t-j}) - 1 \right]$$

$$\times \left[k_h(z_1, \hat{Z}_s)k_h(z_2, \hat{Z}_{s-j}) - 1 \right] dz_1 dz_2.$$

Below we suggest a slight modification of $\hat{M}(j)$ obtained by removing the $t = s$ terms in $\hat{M}(j)$, i.e.,

$$\tilde{M}(j) = \frac{1}{(n-j)^2} \sum_{t=j+1}^n \sum_{s \neq t, s=j+1}^n \int_0^1 \int_0^1 \left[k_h(z_1, \hat{Z}_t)k_h(z_2, \hat{Z}_{t-j}) - 1 \right]$$

$$\times \left[k_h(z_1, \hat{Z}_s)k_h(z_2, \hat{Z}_{s-j}) - 1 \right] dz_1 dz_2.$$

(20.20)

The following result is proved in Hong and Li (2005). Under H_0,

$$nh\tilde{M}(j)/\hat{\sigma}_{HL} \to N(0, 1) \text{ in distribution},$$

(20.21)

where $\hat{\sigma}_{HL}^2 = 2[\int_{-1}^1 [\int_{-1}^{1y} k(u + v)k(v) \, dv]^2 du]^2$.

The proof of (20.21) is given in the proof of Theorem 1 of Hong and Li (2005). The only difference between our modified test and Hong and Li's original test $\hat{M}(j)$ is that our modified test $\tilde{M}(j)$ does not have a nonzero center term.

Florens-Zmirou (1993) was the first to provide the asymptotic theory for the nonparametric estimation of diffusion $\sigma^2(\cdot)$; however, she did not consider the problem of estimating the drift term $\mu(\cdot)$. Jiang and Knight (1997) considered nonparametric estimation of both $\sigma^2(\cdot)$ and $\mu(\cdot)$. They obtained the consistency of $\hat{\mu}(x)$ but did not provide rates of convergence or the asymptotic distribution of $\hat{\mu}(x)$. Fan and Yao (1998) considered using local linear kernel regression to estimate $\sigma^2(\cdot)$. Ait-Sahalia (1996) proposed a semiparametric procedure for estimating the diffusion process under parametric specification of the drift function. Stanton (1997) provided high order approximations for estimating $\sigma^2(\cdot)$ and $\mu(\cdot)$ nonparametrically, while Fan and Zhang (2003) provided further analysis on high order approximations and derived rates of convergence for both the nonparametric diffusion and drift estimators. Bandi and Nguyen (1999) argued that approximations to the drift and diffusion of any order display the same rate of convergence and have the same asymptotic variance, so that asymptotic arguments in conjunction with computational issues suggest simply using the first order approximations in practice. Bandi and Phillips (2003) were the first to provide the asymptotic distribution theory for the nonparametric drift estimator under general conditions (e.g., allowing for nonstationarity). Bandi and Moloche (2005) extended Bandi and Phillips's work to multivariate diffusion models. The asymptotic theory for nonparametric estimation of a general time-heterogeneous diffusion process remains unknown.

Due to space limitations we shall not discuss jump diffusion models, which are, however, useful for modeling large shocks and volatility present in financial data; see Cai and Hong (2003) and the references therein on jump diffusion models.

20.1.5   Proofs

In this section we sketch the proof of Theorem 20.1 (i).

Proof of 20.1 (i). From (20.1), we have

$$
X_{(t+1)\Delta} - X_{t\Delta} = \int_{t\Delta}^{(t+1)\Delta} \mu(X_u)du + \int_{t\Delta}^{(t+1)\Delta} \sigma(X_u)dW_u.
$$

Substituting this into $\hat{g}(x) \stackrel{\text{def}}{=} \hat{\mu}(x)\hat{f}(x)$, by stationarity and the fact that

$$
\mathrm{E}\left[\int_{t\Delta}^{(t+1)\Delta} \sigma(X_u)dW_u | X_{t\Delta} \right] = 0
$$

(since $u \geq t\Delta$), we have

$$
\begin{aligned}
\mathrm{E}[\hat{g}(x)] &= \frac{1}{\Delta}\mathrm{E}\left[k_h(X_{t\Delta} - x) \int_{t\Delta}^{(t+1)\Delta} \mu(X_u)du \right] \\
&= \frac{1}{\Delta}\mathrm{E}\left\{ k_h(X_{t\Delta} - x) \int_{t\Delta}^{(t+1)\Delta} \left[\mu(X_u) - \mu(X_{t\Delta}) \right] du \right\} \\
&\quad + \mathrm{E}\left[k_h(X_{t\Delta} - x)\mu(X_{t\Delta}) \right] \\
&= A_{1n} + A_{2n},
\end{aligned}
\tag{20.22}
$$

where the definitions of A_{1n} and A_{2n} should be apparent.

Using Ito's lemma and adding and subtracting terms (see (A.14) in Appendix A), we have

$$
\begin{aligned}
\mu(X_u) - \mu(X_{t\Delta}) &= \int_{t\Delta}^{u} \mu^{(1)}(X_s)\mu(X_s)\,ds \\
&\quad + \frac{1}{2}\int_{t\Delta}^{u} \mu^{(2)}(X_s)\sigma^2(X_s)\,ds + B_n \\
&= \mu^{(1)}(X_{t\Delta})\mu(X_{t\Delta})(u - t\Delta) \\
&\quad + (1/2)\mu^{(2)}(X_{t\Delta})\sigma^2(X_{t\Delta})(u - t\Delta) \\
&\quad + \int_{t\Delta}^{u} \left[\mu^{(1)}(X_s)\mu(X_s) - \mu^{(1)}(X_{t\Delta})\mu(X_{t\Delta}) \right] ds \\
&\quad + (1/2)\int_{t\Delta}^{u} \left[\mu^{(2)}(X_s)\sigma^2(X_s) \right. \\
&\qquad \left. - \mu^{(2)}(X_{t\Delta})\sigma^2(X_{t\Delta}) \right] ds + B_n,
\end{aligned}
\tag{20.23}
$$

where $B_n = \int_{t\Delta}^{u} \mu^{(1)}(X_u)\sigma(X_u)dW_u$.

Integrating (20.23) gives (see Exercise 20.1)

$$
\begin{aligned}
&\int_{t\Delta}^{(t+1)\Delta} \left[\mu(X_u) - \mu(X_{t\Delta}) \right] du \\
&= \frac{\Delta^2}{2}\mu^{(1)}(X_{t\Delta})\mu(X_{t\Delta}) + \frac{\Delta^2}{4}\mu^{(2)}(X_{t\Delta})\sigma^2(X_{t\Delta}) \\
&\quad + \int_{t\Delta}^{(t+1)\Delta} \left[\int_{t\Delta}^{u} \left[\mu^{(1)}(X_s)\mu(X_s) - \mu^{(1)}(X_{t\Delta})\mu(X_{t\Delta}) \right] ds \right] du \\
&\quad + \frac{1}{2} \left[\int_{t\Delta}^{(t+1)\Delta} \int_{t\Delta}^{u} \left[\mu^{(2)}(X_s)\sigma^2(X_s) - \mu^{(2)}(X_{t\Delta})\sigma^2(X_{t\Delta}) \right] ds \right] du \\
&\quad + \int_{t\Delta}^{(t+1)\Delta} B_n du.
\end{aligned}
\tag{20.24}
$$

Substituting (20.24) back into A_{1n} and then noting that $\mathrm{E}(B_n) = \mathrm{E}[\mathrm{E}(B_n|X_{t\Delta})] = 0$, we obtain

$$
\begin{aligned}
A_{1n} &= \frac{\Delta}{2}\mathrm{E}\left\{ k_h(X_{t\Delta}, x) \left[\mu^{(1)}(X_{t\Delta})\mu(X_{t\Delta}) + \frac{1}{2}\mu^{(2)}(X_{t\Delta})\sigma^2(X_{t\Delta}) \right] \right\} \\
&\quad + O(\Delta^2),
\end{aligned}
$$

where the $O(\Delta^2)$ comes from the double integration terms because the the range of both integrations are $O(\Delta)$. Then by a change of variable argument, we have

$$
E\left\{k_h(X_{t\Delta} - x)\left[\mu^{(1)}(X_{t\Delta})\mu(X_{t\Delta}) + \frac{1}{2}\mu^{(2)}(X_{t\Delta})\sigma^2(X_{t\Delta})\right]\right\}
$$

$$
= \int f(x + hv)k(v)\left[\mu^{(1)}(x + hv)\mu(x + hv)\right.
$$

$$
\left. + \frac{1}{2}\mu^{(2)}(x + hv)\sigma^2(x + hv)\right]dv
$$

$$
= f(x)\left[\mu^{(1)}(x)\mu(x) + \frac{1}{2}\mu^{(2)}(x)\sigma^2(x)\right] + O(h^2).
$$

Hence, we get

$$
A_{1n} = \frac{\Delta}{2}f(x)\left[\mu^{(1)}(x)\mu(x) + (1/2)\mu^{(2)}(x)\sigma^2(x)\right] + o(\Delta).
$$

Similarly, we have

$$
\Delta A_{2n} = \int k_h(X_{t\Delta} - x)\mu(X_{t\Delta})f(X_{t\Delta})dX_{t\Delta}
$$

$$
= \int k(v)\mu(x + hv)f(x + hv)\, dv
$$

$$
= \mu(x)f(x) + \frac{h^2}{2}\left[\int k(v)v^2\, dv\right]
$$

$$
\times \left[\mu^{(2)}(x)f(x) + 2\mu^{(1)}(x)f^{(1)}(x) + \mu(x)f^{(2)}(x)\right]
$$

$$
+ o(h^2).
$$

Summarizing the above we have shown that

$$
E\left[\frac{\hat{m}_1(x)}{f(x)}\right] = f(x)^{-1}\left\{A_{1n} + A_{2n} - \mu(x)E[\hat{f}(x)]\right\}
$$

$$
= \frac{\Delta}{2}\left[\mu^{(1)}(x)\mu(x) + (1/2)\mu^{(2)}(x)\sigma^2(x)\right]
$$

$$
+ \frac{h^2}{2}\kappa_2\left[\mu^{(2)}(x) + 2\mu^{(1)}(x)f^{(1)}(x)/f(x)\right]
$$

$$
+ o(h^2 + \Delta).
$$

Next, let $Z_{nt} = k_h(X_{t\Delta} - x) \int_{t\Delta}^{(t+1)\Delta} \sigma(X_u)dW_u$. It can be shown that the leading term of $\text{var}(\hat{m}_1(x))$ comes from $\text{var}(\hat{m}_3(x))$ (see Exercise 20.2), where $\hat{m}_3(x) = (n\Delta)^{-1} \sum_{t=1}^{n} Z_{nt}$. Now, $\text{var}(\hat{m}_3(x)) = (n\Delta)^{-2} \{\sum_{t=1}^{n} \text{var}(Z_{nt}) + 0\} = (n\Delta^2)^{-1} \text{var}(Z_{nt})$ (which follows because $\text{cov}(Z_{nt}, Z_{ns}) = 0$ for $t \neq s$). Hence, we have

$$\text{var}(\hat{m}_3(x)) = (n\Delta^2)^{-1} \text{var} \left\{ \int_{t\Delta}^{(t+1)\Delta} k_h(X_{t\Delta} - x)\sigma(X_u)dW_u \right\}$$

$$= (n\Delta^2)^{-1} \left\{ \text{E} \left[\left(\int_{t\Delta}^{(t+1)\Delta} k_h(X_{t\Delta} - x)\sigma(X_u)dW_u \right)^2 \right] + (s.o.) \right\}$$

$$= (n\Delta^2)^{-1} \left\{ \text{E} \left[\int_{t\Delta}^{(t+1)\Delta} k_h^2(X_{t\Delta} - x)\sigma^2(X_u)\, du \right] + (s.o.) \right\}$$

$$= (n\Delta^2)^{-1} \left\{ \int f(x_{t\Delta})k_h^2 (x_{t\Delta} - x) \left[\int_{t\Delta}^{(t+1)\Delta} \sigma^2(x_{t\Delta})\, du \right] dx_{t\Delta} \right.$$

$$\left. + (s.o.) \right\}$$

$$= (n\Delta^2)^{-1} \left\{ \left[h^{-1}f(x)\sigma^2(x) \int k^2(v)\, dv \right] \Delta + (s.o.) \right\}$$

$$= (nh\Delta)^{-1} \{\kappa f(x)\sigma^2(x) + o(1)\}.$$

Hence, $\text{var}(\hat{m}_3(x)/f(x)) = (nh\Delta)^{-1}\kappa\sigma^2(x)/f(x)[1 + o(1)]$. This completes the proof of Theorem 20.1 (i). $\qquad\square$

20.2 Nonparametric Estimation of Average Treatment Effects

The measurement of average treatment effects, initially confined to the assessment of dose-response relationships in medical settings, is today widely used across a range of disciplines. Assessing human-capital losses arising from war (Ichino and Winter-Ebmer (1998)) and the effectiveness of job training programs (Lechner (1999), Black, Smith, Berger and Noel (2003)) are but two such examples.

One popular approach to the measurement of treatment effects involves estimation of a "propensity score." Estimation of the propensity

score (i.e., the conditional probability of receiving treatment) was originally undertaken with parametric index models such as the Logit or
Probit. More recently, Hahn (1998), and Hirano, Imbens and Ridder
(2003) proposed the nonparametric estimation of average treatment
effects, both approaches being based on series methods (see Chapter
15 for an overview). While series methods can readily handle discrete
covariates by using an indicator function approach, it is more difficult
to extend techniques that smooth discrete variables such as those outlined in Chapter 4 to the nonparametric series framework. Given that
datasets used to assess treatment effects frequently contain a prepon-
derance of categorical data, Li, Racine and Wooldridge (2005) suggest
estimating the treatment effects by kernel methods, smoothing both
the discrete and continuous covariates and using data-driven cross-
validation methods for selecting the smoothing parameters; we outline this treatment below. As discussed in Chapters 4 and 5, one of the
defining features of this approach is that it allows one to smooth out irrelevant covariates, be they continuous or discrete, leading to efficiency
gains in finite-sample settings.

For related literature involving matching versus estimation of a
propensity score see Heckman, Ichimura and Todd (1997, 1998), and
Dehejia and Wahba (1999). See also Vytlacil and Heckman (2005), who
propose using the marginal treatment effect to unify the nonparametric
literature on treatment effects with the econometric literature on structural estimation using a nonparametric analogue of a policy-invariant
parameter. Though we do not address potential endogeneity here, we
alert the interested reader to Abadie (2003), who considers semiparametric instrumental variable estimation of treatment response models.

20.2.1   The Model

We use a dummy variable, $t_i \in \{0, 1\}$, to indicate whether an individual
has received treatment, i.e., $t_i = 1$ for the treated and $t_i = 0$ for the
untreated. Letting $Y_i(t_i)$ denote the outcome, then,

$$Y_i = t_i Y_i(1) + (1 - t_i) Y_i(0), \quad i = 1, \ldots, n.$$

Interest lies in the average treatment effect defined by

$$\tau = \mathrm{E}[Y_i(1) - Y_i(0)].$$

Let X_i denote a vector of pretreatment variables. For each individual i, we observe either $Y_i(0)$ or $Y_i(1)$, but not both. Therefore, in

the absence of additional assumptions, the treatment effect is not consistently estimable. One popular assumption is the "unconfoundedness condition" (Rosenbaum and Rubin (1983)), which states that

Assumption 20.1. *Conditional on X_i, the treatment indicator t_i is independent of the potential outcome.*

In the presence of covariates, we define the conditional average treatment effect by $\tau(x) = \mathrm{E}[Y_i(1) - Y_i(0)|X = x]$. Under Assumption 20.1, we can easily show that

$$\tau(x) = \mathrm{E}[Y_i|t_i = 1, X_i = x] - \mathrm{E}[Y_i|t_i = 0, X_i = x]. \qquad (20.25)$$

The two terms on the right-hand side of (20.25) can be estimated consistently by any nonparametric estimation technique. Therefore, in the presence of covariates the average treatment effect can be obtained via simple averaging over $\tau(x)$, given by

$$\tau = \mathrm{E}[\tau(X_i)].$$

Letting $\mathrm{E}(Y_i|X_i, t_i)$ be denoted as $g(X_i, t_i)$, we then have

$$Y_i = g(X_i, t_i) + u_i, \qquad (20.26)$$

where $\mathrm{E}(u_i|X_i, t_i) = 0$.

Defining $g_0(X_i) = g(X_i, t_i = 0)$ and $g_1(X_i) = g(X_i, t_i = 1)$, we can rewrite (20.26) as

$$\begin{aligned} Y_i &= g_0(X_i) + [g_1(X_i) - g_0(X_i)]t_i + u_i \\ &= g_0(X_i) + \tau(X_i)t_i + u_i, \end{aligned} \qquad (20.27)$$

where $\tau(X_i) = g_1(X_i) - g_0(X_i)$.

From (20.27) we can show that $\tau(X_i) = \mathrm{cov}(Y_i, t_i|X_i)/\mathrm{var}(t_i|X_i)$. Letting $\mu_i \equiv \mu(X_i) = \mathrm{P}(t_1 = 1|X_i) \equiv \mathrm{E}(t_i|X_i)$ (because $t_i = \{0,1\}$), we may write

$$\tau = \mathrm{E}[\tau(X_i)] = \mathrm{E}\left\{\frac{(t_i - \mu_i)Y_i}{\mathrm{var}(t_i|X_i)}\right\}. \qquad (20.28)$$

Since $\mu(X_i) = \mathrm{P}(t_i = 1|X_i) = \mathrm{E}(t_i|X_i)$, one can use either a conditional probability estimator or a conditional mean estimator to estimate $\mu(X_i)$. We use the latter in this chapter. Let $\hat{t}(X_i)$ be the nonparametric estimator of μ_i defined by

$$\hat{t}(X_i) = \frac{\sum_{j=1}^{n} t_j K_{n,ij}}{\sum_{j=1}^{n} K_{n,ij}}, \qquad (20.29)$$

where $K_{n,ij}$ is a product kernel function for all of the conditional variables. By noting that $\text{var}(t_i|X_i) = \mu_i(1 - \mu_i)$, the average treatment effect can be estimated by

$$\hat{\tau} = \frac{1}{n}\sum_{i=1}^{n}\frac{(t_i - \hat{t}(X_i))Y_i M_{ni}}{\hat{t}(X_i)(1 - \hat{t}(X_i))} \equiv \frac{1}{n}\sum_{i=1}^{n}\left[\frac{t_i Y_i}{\hat{t}(X_i)} - \frac{(1 - t_i)Y_i}{1 - \hat{t}(X_i)}\right]M_{ni},$$

(20.30)

where $M_{ni} = M_n(X_i)$ is a trimming set that trims out observations near the boundary.

With the exception of the presence of the trimming function M_{ni} and the use of kernel rather than series methods, (20.30) is exactly the same as the estimator considered by Hirano et al. (2003). Li et al. (2005) show that $\hat{\tau}$ has the same asymptotic distribution as the series-method-based estimators proposed by Hahn (1998) and Hirano et al. We now turn to an empirical application.

20.2.2 An Application: Assessing the Efficacy of Right Heart Catheterization

The direct measurement of cardiac function via right-heart catheterization (RHC) is used both for diagnosis and to guide appropriate treatment for certain critically ill patients. The conventional wisdom is that the use of RHC leads to better outcomes.

Connors et al. (1996) reported a study designed to assess the effectiveness of RHC in critically ill patients involving 5,735 patients admitted to intensive care. They conducted a prospective cohort study which examined the relationship between the use of RHC during the first 24 hours of hospitalization and subsequent survival. They concluded that, in contrast to the conventional wisdom, the likelihood of death was *higher* among those who received RHC even after carefully controlling for a number of risk factors.

In a follow-up study, Lin, Psaty and Kronmal (1998) conducted further analysis to determine whether this result could be due to the presence of unmeasured confounders, and they concluded that this was not likely, though they also concluded that the risk of death may not be quite as high as was found by Connors et al. (1996).

The conclusions of both of these studies, however, are dependent upon the appropriateness of the parametric models which were used therein. Li et al. (2005) investigate whether these unexpected findings may in fact reflect the restrictive parametric specifications which were employed

For the analysis that follows, Li et al. (2005) use the following variables:

(i) Y: Outcome – 1 if death occurred within 180 days, 0 otherwise

(ii) T: Treatment – 1 if a Swan-Ganz catheter was received by patients when they were hospitalized, 0 otherwise

(iii) X_1: Sex – 0 for female, 1 for male

(iv) X_2: Race – 0 if black, 1 if white, 2 if other

(v) X_3: Income – 0 if under 11K, 1 if 11-25K, 2 if 25-50K, 3 if over 50K

(vi) X_4: Primary disease category – 1 if acute respiratory failure, 2 if congestive heart failure, 3 if chronic obstructive pulmonary disease, 4 if cirrhosis, 5 if colon cancer, 6 if coma, 7 if lung cancer, 8 if multiple organ system failure with malignancy, 9 if multiple organ system failure with sepsis

(vii) X_5: Secondary disease category – 1 if cirrhosis, 2 if colon cancer, 3 if coma, 4 if lung cancer, 5 if multiple organ system failure with malignancy, 6 if multiple organ system failure with sepsis, 7 if NA

(viii) X_6: Medical insurance – 1 if Medicaid, 2 if Medicare, 3 if Medicare and Medicaid, 4 if no insurance, 5 if private, 6 if private and Medicare

(ix) X_7: Age – age (converted to years from Y/M/D data stored with two-decimal accuracy)

We observe that the majority of these variables are categorical in nature, hence this application is well suited to the mixed-data kernel methods outlined in Chapter 4.

The parametric-propensity score based estimator gives an average treatment effect of 0.072, while the nonparametric propensity-score given by (20.30) yields an average treatment effect of -0.001. Li et al. (2005) also computed the confusion matrix for both the parametric and the nonparametric propensity score models and found that the nonparametric method correctly predicts 69.9% for whether a patient received the RHC treatment, while the parametric approach correctly predicted 66.7%. Thus for this dataset, even with the number of possible cells being 18,144, which far exceeds the number of records ($n = 5,735$), the nonparametric approach is able to predict who receives treatment and who does not better than the parametric Logit model. The parametric approach correctly predicts 3,828 of the 5,735 patients while the nonparametric approach correctly predicts 3,976 patients, thereby predicting an additional 148 patients correctly. The differences between the parametric and nonparametric versions of the weighting estimator reflect this additional number of correctly classified patients along with differences in the estimated probabilities of receiving treatment. The increased risk suggested by the parametric model drops from a 7% increase for those receiving RHC to roughly 0% when nonparametric methods are employed.

In order to assess whether such differences are due to chance, Li et al. (2005) use the following resampling procedure to construct the sampling distribution of $\hat{\tau}$. Letting $z = \{y, x\}$,

(i) Randomly draw Z_i^* from $\{Z_j\}_{j=1}^n$ with replacement, and call $\{Z_i^*\}_{i=1}^n$ the bootstrap sample.

(ii) Use the bootstrap sample to compute the bootstrap statistic $\hat{\tau}^*$ using the same cross-validated smoothing parameters as were used to obtain $\hat{\tau}$.

(iii) Repeat steps (i) and (ii) a large number of times, say $B = 399$ times. The empirical CDF of $\{\hat{\tau}*_j\}_{j=1}^B$ can then be used to approximate the finite-sample distribution of $\hat{\tau}$.

Li et al. (2005) obtained bootstrap 95% coverage error bounds of $[0.044, 0.099]$ for the parametric approach and $[-0.038, 0.011]$ for the nonparametric approach. Thus, they overturn the unexpected parametric results and conclude that, in agreement with the conventional wisdom, patients receiving RHC treatment do not appear to suffer an increased risk of mortality. To further investigate this result, Li et al. (2005) also conducted some sensitivity analysis. Using likelihood cross-validation rather than least squares cross-validation yielded 95% coverage error bounds of $[-0.034, 0.013]$. Out of concern that the nonparametric results might reflect "overfitting," they computed the leave-one-out kernel predictions, and again bootstrapped the error bounds. For the least squares cross-validated leave-one-out estimates they obtained

95% coverage error bounds of $[-0.015, 0.037]$, while for the likelihood cross-validated leave-one-out estimates they obtained 95% coverage error bounds of $[-0.007, 0.039]$.

These error bounds indicate that the parametric model suggests a statistically significant increased risk of death for those receiving RHC, while the nonparametric model yields no significant difference. This does not appear to reflect any loss of efficiency due to using the nonparametric rather than the parametric propensity score, as can be seen by a comparison of the out-of-sample prediction results of the confusion matrices, since a correctly specified parametric model would be expected to outperform the nonparametric model.

20.3 Nonparametric Estimation of Auction Models

20.3.1 Estimation of First Price Auction Models

Since the seminal work of Paarsch (1992), econometricians have adopted fully structural econometric approaches when estimating auction models. Early work was mostly based upon parametric models; see Donald and Paarsch (1993, 1996), and Laffont, Ossard and Vuong (1995). The first nonparametric approach of which we are aware is the work of Guerre, Perrigne and Vuong (2000). We refer the interested reader to Paarsch and Hong (2006) for a thorough treatment of the structural econometrics of auction data.

Suppose that a single and indivisible object is auctioned, and that all bids are collected simultaneously. The object is sold to the highest bidder provided that this bid is at least as high as a reservation price denoted by p_0. In the independent private values (IPV) paradigm, there are $i = 1, \ldots, I$ bidders. Individual i does not know other people's private value v_j $(j \neq i)$; however, all bidders' private values are assumed to be random draws from a known CDF $F(\cdot)$ with an absolutely continuous PDF $f(\cdot)$ having compact support $[\underline{v}, \bar{v}] \subset \mathbb{R}$, $p_0 \in [\underline{v}, \bar{v}]$.

The unique symmetric differential Bayesian Nash equilibrium with incomplete information is characterized by Riley and Samuelson (1981) as briefly described below. The equilibrium bid b_i of the ith bidder is

$$b_i = v_i - \frac{1}{(F(v_i))^{I-1}} \int_{p_0}^{v_i} (F(u))^{I-1} du \equiv s(v_i, F, I, p_0), \qquad (20.31)$$

provided $v_i \geq p_0$. This strategy is obtained by solving a first order differential equation in $s(\cdot)$ given by

$$1 = (v_i - s(v_i))\,(I - 1)\,\frac{f(v_i)}{F(v_i)}\frac{1}{s^{(1)}(v_i)}, \qquad (20.32)$$

with boundary condition $s(p_0) = p_0$. The equilibrium strategy (20.31) is strictly increasing in v_i on $[p_0, v]$.

In practice, bids are observed, while private values are unobserved. Assume that the reservation price p_0 is not binding, i.e., $p_0 = \underline{v}$ with $s(v_{\underline{v}}) = \underline{v}$. Let $G(\cdot)$ denote the CDF of b_i and let $g(\cdot)$ denote its PDF. For every $b \in [\underline{b}, \bar{b}] = [\underline{v}, s(\bar{v})]$ we have $G(b) = \mathrm{P}[\tilde{b} \leq b] = \mathrm{P}[\tilde{v} \leq s^{-1}(b)] = F(s^{-1}(b)) = F(v)$ because $b = s(v)$. $G(\cdot)$ is continuous and $g(b) = f(v)/s^{(1)}(v)$, where $v = s^{-1}(b)$. Taking the ratio gives $g(b)/G(b) = f(v)/[F(v)s^{(1)}(v)]$, and (20.32) becomes

$$v_i = b_i + \frac{1}{I - 1}\frac{G(b_i)}{g(b_i)} \equiv \xi(b_i, G, I). \qquad (20.33)$$

Equation (20.33) shows that the individual private value v_i can be expressed as a function of the individual's equilibrium bid b_i. Therefore, one can estimate the unobserved private value v_i through b_i by (20.33) provided that one can obtain consistent estimators for $G(\cdot)$ and $g(\cdot)$. Guerre et al. (2000) further show that $G(\cdot)$ is uniquely identified provided that $G(b_1, \ldots, b_I) = \prod_{i=1}^{I} G(b_i)$, that $\xi(., G, I)$ is strictly increasing on $[\underline{b}, \bar{b}]$, and that its inverse is differentiable. Guerre et al. (2000) suggest the following two-step estimation procedure. Suppose there are L homogeneous auctions with the same number of bidders I. In the first step one estimates $G(\cdot)$ and $g(\cdot)$ by

$$\tilde{G}(b) = \frac{1}{IL}\sum_{l=1}^{L}\sum_{i=1}^{I}\mathbf{1}(B_{il} \leq b),$$

$$\tilde{g}(b) = \frac{1}{ILh}\sum_{l=1}^{L}\sum_{i=1}^{I}k\left(\frac{B_{il} - b}{h}\right), \qquad (20.34)$$

where $k(\cdot)$ is a kernel function with compact support and h is the smoothing parameter.

To avoid estimation bias at the boundary, Guerre et al. (2000) suggest using the trimmed data defined by

$$\hat{V}_{il} = B_{il} + \tilde{G}(B_{il})/[(I - 1)\tilde{g}(B_{il})]$$

$$\text{if } B_{\min} + \rho/h/2 \leq B_{il} \leq B_{\max} - \rho h/2, \qquad (20.35)$$

where ρ is the (finite) length of the support of $k(\cdot)$, and $B_{\min}$ and $B_{\max}$ are the minimum and maximum bids. Then one estimates $f(\cdot)$ by

$$\hat{f}(v) = \frac{1}{ILh} \sum_{l=1}^{L} \sum_{i=1}^{I} k\left(\frac{\hat{V}_{il} - v}{h_f}\right), \tag{20.36}$$

where $\hat{V}_{il}$ is defined in (20.35) with boundary observations removed.

Supposing that $k(\cdot)$ is a νth order kernel and that $f(\cdot)$ has ν bounded continuous derivatives, we know that the optimal uniform convergence rate for estimating $f(\cdot)$ is $(n/\ln n)^{\nu/(2\nu+1)}$, where $n = IL$ (see Stone (1982)). However, in this case, b_i is observed but v_i is unobserved. Guerre et al. (2000) show that in this case the optimal uniform convergence rate of $\hat{f}(\cdot)$ to $f(\cdot)$ is $(n/\ln n)^{\nu/(2\nu+3)}$. Using $h = c(n/\ln n)^{1/(2\nu+3)}$ and $h_f = c_f(n/\ln n)^{1/(2\nu+3)}$, the above estimator $\hat{f}(\cdot)$ achieves this optimal rate. This change in convergence rates occurs because of the presence of a generated regressor. By a Lipschitz type of condition, the rate is the same as that achieved when estimating derivative functions using kernel methods.

Guerre et al. (2000) also extend their result to the heterogeneous auction case and the case where the bidders may change at different auctions. Consider L heterogeneous auctions. Let X_l denote the vector of relevant characteristics for the lth auctioned object, and let I_l be the number of bidders in the lth auction. Now, the distribution of bidders' private values V_{il} for the lth auction is the conditional CDF $F(.|X_l, I_l)$ of private values given (X_l, I_l). Similarly, $G(\cdot)$ becomes $G(.|X_l, I_l)$, and (20.31) and (20.33) become

$$B_{il} = V_{ii} - \frac{1}{(F(V_{il}|X_l, I_l))^{I-1}} \int_{p_0}^{V_{il}} (F(u|X_l, I_l))^{I-1} du$$

$$\equiv s(V_{il}, X_l, I_l), \tag{20.37}$$

$$V_{il} = B_{il} + \frac{1}{I_l - 1} \frac{G(B_{il}|X_l, I_l)}{g(B_{il}|X_l, I_l)} = B_{il} + \frac{1}{I_l - 1} \frac{G(B_{il}, X_l, I_l)}{g(B_{il}, X_l, I_l)}$$

$$\equiv \xi(B_{il}, X_l, I_l), \tag{20.38}$$

where, in (20.38), we cancel the marginal PDF of (X_i, I_l) so that it becomes a ratio of an unconditional CDF to a PDF.

Assuming that X_l has q continuous components and r discrete components, we can then estimate $G(b, x, i)$ and $g(b, x, i)$ by (20.34).

When auctions are heterogeneous, Guerre et al. (2000) suggest estimating $G(\cdot)$ and $g(\cdot)$ by

$$
\tilde{G}(b, x, i) = \frac{1}{L} \sum_{l=1}^{L} \frac{1}{I_l} \sum_{i=1}^{I} \mathbf{1}(B_{il} \leq b) K_h(X_l, x) L(I_l, i, \lambda),
$$

$$
\tilde{g}(b) = \frac{1}{L} \sum_{l=1}^{L} \frac{1}{I_l} \sum_{i=1}^{I_l} k_{h_b}(B_{il}, b) K_h(X_l, x) L(I_l, i, \lambda).
$$

(20.39)

The private value V_{il} is then estimated by

$$
\hat{V}_{il} = B_{il} - \frac{1}{I_l - 1} \hat{\psi}(B_{il}, X_l, I_l),
$$

(20.40)

where $\hat{\psi}(b, x, i) = \tilde{G}(n, x, i)/\tilde{g}(b)$. However, $\tilde{\psi}$ is an asymptotically biased estimator of ψ at the boundaries of the support of (B, X, I). Guerre et al. further introduce a trimming function that trims out observations near the boundary of support; for details on the trimming function, see Guerre et al.

20.3.2 Conditionally Independent Private Information Auctions

Li, Perrigne and Vuong (2000) extend the IPV model to a conditionally independent private information (CIPI) setting. Let σ_i denote the private value for bidder i ($i = 1, \ldots, n$) and let v denote the common value. Let $F_\sigma(\cdot)$ and $F_{\sigma|v}(.|.)$ denote the CDF and conditional CDF of v and σ given v, respectively, with corresponding PDFs $f_\sigma(\cdot)$ and $f_{\sigma|v}(.|.)$ and nonnegative support $[\underline{v}, \bar{v}]$ and $[\underline{\sigma}, \bar{\sigma}]$. The CIPI model assumes that bidders' signals σ_i are conditionally independent given the common value v. Hence,

$$
f(\sigma_1, \ldots, \sigma_n, v) = f_v(v) \prod_{i=1}^{n} f_{\sigma|v}(\sigma_i|v).
$$

(20.41)

Li et al. (2000) consider the case of strictly increasing differentiable symmetric Bayesian Nash equilibrium strategies. Player i chooses his bid b_i to maximize $\mathrm{E}[(U_i - b_i) \mathbf{1}(B_i \leq b_i)|\sigma_i]$, where $B_i = s(Y_i)$, $Y_i = \max_{j \neq i} \sigma_j$, and $s(\cdot)$ is the equilibrium strategy. The first order condition is

$$
s^{(1)}(\sigma_i) = \frac{[V(\sigma_i, \sigma_i) - s(\sigma_i)] f_{Y|\sigma}(\sigma_i|\sigma_i)}{F_{Y|\sigma}(\sigma_i|\sigma_i)},
$$

(20.42)

where $V(\sigma_i, Y_i) = \mathrm{E}[U(\sigma_i, v)|\sigma_i, Y_i]$, $F_{Y|\sigma}(.|.)$ denotes the conditional CDF of Y_i given σ_i, and $f_{Y|\sigma}(.|.)$ is its PDF.

When the reservation price is nonbinding, the solution is given by

$$b_i = s(\sigma_i) = V(\sigma_i, \sigma_i) - \int_{\underline{\sigma}}^{\sigma_i} L(\alpha|\sigma_i) dV(\alpha, \alpha), \qquad (20.43)$$

where $L(\alpha|\sigma_i) = \exp\left[-\int_{\underline{\sigma}}^{\sigma_i} f_{Y|\sigma}(u|u)/F_{Y|\sigma}(u|u)du\right]$.

In this model it is assumed that $U(\sigma_i, v) = \sigma_i$ so that each bidders' private information is his own utility function. To achieve identification, Li et al. (2000) assume that $\sigma_i = v\eta_i$, the η_i's are i.i.d. with mean equal to one, and v and the η_i's are mutually independent.

Let $G_{B|b}(.|.)$ and $g_{B|b}(.|.)$ denote the conditional CDF and PDF, respectively, of B_i given b_i. Then

$$\begin{aligned} G_{B|b}(X_i|X_i) &= \mathrm{P}\left[B_i \le X_i|b_i = X_i\right] \\ &= \mathrm{P}\left[Y_i \le s^{-1}(X_i)|\sigma_i = s^{-1}(X_i)\right] \\ &= F_{Y|\sigma}\left(s^{-1}(X_i)|s^{-1}(X_i)\right) \qquad (20.44) \end{aligned}$$

and

$$g_{B|b}(X_i|X_i) = \frac{f_{Y|\sigma}\left(s^{-1}(X_i)|s^{-1}(X_i)\right)}{s^{(1)}\left(s^{-1}(X_i)\right)}. \qquad (20.45)$$

Using (20.44), (20.45) and $\sigma = s^{-1}(b)$, then (20.42) can be written as

$$V(\sigma, \sigma) = b + \frac{G_{B|b}(b|b)}{g_{B|b}(b|b)} \equiv \xi(b, G). \qquad (20.46)$$

One can use methods similar to those discussed in Section 20.3.1 to estimate σ_i from $\ln(\sigma_i) = \ln(v) + \ln(\eta_i) \equiv \ln c + \ln \epsilon_i$, where $\ln c = \ln v + \mathrm{E}[\ln \eta_i]$ and $\ln \epsilon_i = \ln \eta_i - \mathrm{E}[\ln \eta_i]$.

Based on the observed bids b_{il}, $i = 1, \ldots, n$, $l = 1, \ldots, L$, we estimate $G_{B_1|b_1}(.|.)/g_{B_1|b_1}(.|.)$ by $\hat{G}_{B_1|b_1}(.|.)/\hat{g}_{B_1|b_1}(.|.)$, where

$$\begin{aligned} \hat{G}_{B_1,b_1}(B, b) &= \frac{1}{L}\sum_{l=1}^{L}\frac{1}{n}\sum_{i=1}^{n}\mathbf{1}(B_{il} \le B)K_{h_1}(b_{il}, b), \\ \hat{g}_{B_1,b_1}(B, b) &= \frac{1}{L}\sum_{l=1}^{L}\frac{1}{n}\sum_{i=1}^{n}k_{h_2}(B_{il}, B)k_{h_1}(b_{il}, b). \end{aligned} \qquad (20.47)$$

Using (20.46) we estimate V_{il} by

$$\hat{V}_{il} = b_{il} + \frac{\hat{G}_{B|b}(b_{il}|b_{il})}{g_{B|b}(b_{il}|b_{il})} \equiv \hat{\xi}(b_{il}).$$

As discussed in Section 20.3.1, some trimming is necessary in order to avoid boundary effects. Li et al. (2000) recommend trimming out those $\hat{V}_{il}$ values that correspond to bids within a distance h_1 of the boundaries of the bid's support $[0, b_{max}]$.

Next, one estimates the joint characteristic function of any two bidders' $\ln V_{il}$ among n bidders by

$$\hat{\psi}(u_1, u_2) = \frac{1}{n(n-1)} \sum_{1 \le i \ne j \le n} \frac{1}{L_T} \sum_{l=1}^{L_T} \exp\left(iu_1 \ln \hat{V}_{il} + iu_2 \ln \hat{V}_{jl}\right).$$

Then one can estimate the PDF of c and ϵ by

$$\hat{f}_c(x) = \frac{1}{2\pi} \int_{-T}^{T} e^{-itx} \hat{\phi}_c(t) dt \text{ and} \tag{20.48}$$

$$\hat{f}_\epsilon(y) = \frac{1}{2\pi} \int_{-T}^{T} e^{-ity} \hat{\phi}_\epsilon(t) dt \tag{20.49}$$

for $x \in [\ln \underline{c}, \ln \bar{c}]$ and $y \in [\ln \underline{\epsilon}, \ln \bar{\epsilon}]$, where T is a smoothing parameter, and

$$\hat{\phi}_c(t) = \exp \int_0^t \frac{\partial \hat{\psi}(0, u_2)/\partial u_1}{\hat{\psi}(0, u_2)} du_2 \text{ and} \tag{20.50}$$

$$\hat{\phi}_\epsilon(t) = \hat{\psi}(t, 0)/\hat{\phi}_c(t). \tag{20.51}$$

Finally, we estimate $f_v(\cdot)$ and $f_\eta(\cdot)$ by

$$\hat{f}_v(x) = \hat{f}_c\left(x + \hat{E}(\ln \eta)\right) \text{ and } \hat{f}_\eta(x) = \hat{f}_\epsilon\left(x - \hat{E}(\ln \eta)\right), \tag{20.52}$$

where $\hat{E}(\ln \eta) = -\ln \hat{E}(\epsilon)$.

Li et al. (2000) established the uniform consistency of $\hat{f}_v(\cdot)$ to $f_v(\cdot)$ and $\hat{f}_\eta(\cdot)$ to $f_\eta(\cdot)$ under some regularity conditions, including T diverging appropriately to ∞ as $L \to \infty$.

An important practical question is how to choose between private and common values models of bidders' information. Haile, Hong and Shum (2003) developed tests for common values at first-price sealed-bid auctions. Their tests are nonparametric and require observations only on bids submitted at each auction. Empirical applications to U.S. Forest Service timber auctions reported in Haile et al. show mixed evidence against private values hypothesis.

20.4 Copula-Based Semiparametric Estimation of Multivariate Distributions

Recently, so-called copula have attracted much well-deserved attention, particular from those working in the finance and insurance communities. For an overview of the applications of copulas in finance, see Embrechts, McNeil and Straumann (1999).[1] In this section we discuss the estimation of copula-based semiparametric multivariate distributions.

20.4.1 Some Background on Copula Functions

It has been known since the seminal work of Sklar (1959) that the joint behavior of a random vector $(X_1, \ldots, X_p)$ having continuous marginal CDFs, $F_j(x_j) = \mathrm{P}(X_j \leq x_j)$ $(j = 1, \ldots, p)$, can be characterized uniquely by its associated "copula function" C, defined for all $(v_1, \ldots, v_p) \in [0, 1]^p$ by

$$C(v_1, \ldots, v_p) = \mathrm{P}\left(F_1(X_1) \leq v_1, \ldots, F_p(X_p) \leq v_p\right). \qquad (20.53)$$

Equation (20.53) shows that the copula function is itself a CDF. Moreover, each component $V_j = F_j(X_j)$ has a uniform marginal distribution by Theorem A.2 of Appendix A.

Letting $F(x_1, \ldots, x_p)$ denote the joint CDF of the random vector $(X_1, \ldots, X_p)$, then the copula function connects the marginals to the joint CDF as follows:

$$F(X_1, \ldots, X_p) = C\left(F_1(X_1), \ldots, F_p(X_p)\right). \qquad (20.54)$$

Let $f_j(\cdot)$, $j = 1, \ldots, p$, and $c(v_1, \ldots, v_p)$ denote the PDFs associated with $F_j(\cdot)$, $j = 1, \ldots, p$, and $C(v_1, \ldots, v_p)$, respectively. Letting $\mathcal{X}_j$ denote the support of X_j, then for any $(x_1, \ldots, x_p) \in \mathcal{X}_1 \times \cdots \times \mathcal{X}_p$, the PDF $f(\cdot)$ that corresponds to $F(\cdot)$ given by (20.54) has the following representation:

$$f(x_1, \ldots, x_p) = c(F_1(x_1), \ldots, F_p(x_p)) \prod_{j=1}^{p} f_j(x_j), \qquad (20.55)$$

or, equivalently, $c(v_1, \ldots, v_p) = f(x_1, \ldots, x_p) / \prod_{j=1}^{p} f_j(x_j)$, where $v_j = F_j(x_j)$, $j = 1, \ldots, p$.

---

[1] Copula have also been shown to be useful in microeconometrics. See, e.g., Lee (1983) and Trivedi and Zimmer (forthcoming) for their use in sample selection models and Heckman and Honoré (1989) on competing risk models.

Equation (20.55) shows that the copula function completely characterizes the dependence structure of the random vector $(X_1, \ldots, X_p)$. Obviously, $c(v_1, \ldots, v_p) \equiv 1$ if and only if $X_1, \ldots, X_p$ are independent of each other.

One commonly used copula function is the Gaussian copula. Let Φ denote the univariate standard normal CDF, and let $\Phi_{\Sigma,p}$ denote a p-dimensional normal CDF with zero mean and correlation matrix Σ. Then the p-dimensional Gaussian copula with correlation matrix Σ is given by $C(\mathbf{v}; \Sigma) = \Phi_{\Sigma,p}(\Phi^{-1}(v_1), \ldots, \Phi^{-1}(v_d))$, where $\mathbf{v} = (v_1, \ldots, v_p)$. Its copula density is

$$c(\mathbf{v}; \Sigma) = \frac{1}{\sqrt{\det(\Sigma)}} \times$$

$$\exp\left\{ \frac{-(\Phi^{-1}(v_1), \ldots, \Phi^{-1}(v_p))'(\Sigma^{-1} - I_p)(\Phi^{-1}(v_1), \ldots, \Phi^{-1}(v_p))}{2} \right\}.$$

Similarly, let T_ν be the scalar standardized t-distribution with degree of freedom $\nu > 2$, and let $T_{\Sigma,\nu}$ be the p-dimensional standardized t-distribution with correlation matrix Σ. Then the p-dimensional (standardized) t-copula with correlation matrix given by Σ is $C(\mathbf{v}; \Sigma, \nu) = T_{\Sigma,\nu}(T_\nu^{-1}(v_1), \ldots, T_\nu^{-1}(v_d))$ and the t-copula density is

$$c(\mathbf{v}; \Sigma, \nu) = \frac{\Gamma(\frac{\nu+p}{2})[\Gamma(\frac{\nu}{2})]^{p-1}}{\sqrt{\det(\Sigma)}[\Gamma(\frac{\nu+1}{2})]^p} \left(1 + \frac{x'\Sigma x}{\nu - 2}\right)^{-\frac{\nu+p}{2}} \prod_{j=1}^{p} \left(1 + \frac{x_i^2}{\nu - 2}\right)^{\frac{\nu+1}{2}},$$

where $x = (x_1, \ldots, x_p)'$ and $x_i = T_\nu^{-1}(v_i)$. See Joe (1997) and Nelsen (2006) for a wide variety of non-Gaussian, asymmetric copula functions.

20.4.2 Semiparametric Copula-Based Multivariate Distributions

In this section we discuss the semiparametric copula models studied by Genest, Ghoudi and Pivest (1995) and Chen, Fan and Tsyrennikov (forthcoming), among others. This class of distributions is characterized by a parametric copula function evaluated at nonparametric marginal distributions. It has two attractive properties: (i) it allows one to separately model the dependence structure and the marginal behavior of a multivariate random variable; and (ii) it avoids the curse of dimensionality problem since it involves only one-dimensional (unknown) univariate CDFs.

If one chooses a parametric copula function, say $c(v_1, \ldots, v_p; \theta)$, where $\theta \in \Theta$ is a finite dimensional parameter (say, Θ is a bounded subset of $\mathbb{R}^q$), and uses it to replace $c(v_1, \ldots, v_p)$ in (20.55) (leaving the marginal distributions, $f_j(\cdot)$, unspecified), then the resulting multivariate PDF $f(x_1, \ldots, x_p)$ involves only one-dimensional nonparametric functions $f_j(x_j)$, $j = 1, \ldots, p$. Thus, it achieves the aim of dimensionality reduction in its nonparametric components. There exist many flexible parametric copula functions, and by choosing different parametric copula functions, the resulting joint PDF $f(\cdot)$ can be symmetric or asymmetric, possess various tail dependence properties, etc. Next, we turn to the estimation of the semiparametric model given in (20.55).

20.4.3 A Two-Step Estimation Procedure

One convenient estimation method is the two-step estimation procedure proposed by Oakes (1994) and Genest et al. (1995), where one estimates θ via

$$\tilde{\theta} = \arg\max_{\theta \in \Theta} \left[\sum_{i=1}^n \ln c \left(\tilde{F}_{n1}(X_{1i}), \ldots, \tilde{F}_{np}(X_{pi}; \theta) \right) \right], \qquad (20.56)$$

where $\tilde{F}_{nj}(x_j) = \frac{1}{n+1} \sum_{i=1}^n \mathbf{1}(X_{ji} \leq x_j)$ is the rescaled empirical CDF estimator of $F_j(x_j)$, $j = 1, \ldots, p$. Note that here the factor is $1/(n+1)$ rather than $1/n$. This rescaling avoids difficulties arising from the potential unboundedness of $\ln\{c(v_1, \ldots, v_p; \theta)\}$ as some of the v_i's tend to one. Genest et al. establish the $\sqrt{n}$-normality of $\tilde{\theta}$ which we summarize below.

Let

$$l(v_1, \ldots, v_p; \theta) = \ln\{c(v_1, \ldots, v_p; \theta)\},$$

$$l_{\theta,\theta} = \frac{\partial^2 \ln c(v_1, \ldots, v_p; \theta)}{\partial \theta \partial \theta'},$$

$$l_{\theta,j} = \frac{\partial^2 \ln c(v_1, \ldots, v_p, \theta)}{\partial v_j \partial \theta}, \text{ and}$$

$$W_j(V_j) = \int_0^1 \cdots \int_0^1 [\mathbf{1}(V_j \leq v_1) - v_1]$$
$$\times l_{\theta,j}(v_1, \ldots, v_p, \theta) c(v_1, \ldots, v_p, \theta) \, dv_1 \ldots dv_p$$

for $j = 1, \ldots, p$.

Genest et al. (1995) prove the following result.

Theorem 20.2. *Under the regularity conditions given in Genest et al.* *(1995),*

$$\sqrt{n}(\tilde{\theta} - \theta) \rightarrow N(0, V) \text{ in distribution,}$$

where $V = B^{-1}\Sigma B^{-1}$, $B = -E[l_{\theta,\theta}(F_1(X_1), \ldots, F_p(X_p), \theta)]$, *and*

$$\Sigma = \text{var}\left[l_{\theta}(F_1(X_1), \ldots, F_p(X_p), \theta) + \sum_{j=1}^{p} W_j(X_j) \right].$$

Genest et al. (1995) also propose consistent estimators for B and Σ. B is estimated by

$$\tilde{B} = -\frac{1}{n} \sum_{i=1}^{n} l_{\theta,\theta}\left(\tilde{F}_{n1}(X_{1i}), \ldots, \tilde{F}_{np}(X_{ni}); \tilde{\theta} \right).$$

The rescaled empirical copula function can be estimated by

$$\tilde{C}_n(v_1, \ldots, v_p) = \frac{1}{n} \sum_{i=1}^{n} \prod_{j=1}^{p} \mathbf{1}(\tilde{F}_{nj}(X_{ji}) \le v_j).$$

Let $\tilde{U}_i = l_{\theta}(\tilde{F}_{n1}(X_{1i}), \ldots, \tilde{F}_{np}(X_{ni}), \tilde{\theta})$, and let

$$\tilde{V}_t = \tilde{U}_t - \sum_{j=1}^{p} \int \mathbf{1}\left(\tilde{F}_{nj}(X_{jt}) \le v_j \right)$$

$$\times l_{\theta}\left(v_1, \ldots, v_p, \tilde{\theta} \right) l_j \left(v_1, \ldots, v_p, \tilde{\theta} \right) d\tilde{C}_n(v_1, \ldots, v_p)$$

$$= \tilde{U}_t - n^{-1} \sum_{i=1}^{n} \sum_{j=1}^{p} \int \mathbf{1}\left[\tilde{F}_{nj}(X_{jt}) \le \tilde{F}_{nh}(X_{ji}) \right]$$

$$\times l_{\theta}\left(\tilde{F}_{h1}(X_{j1}), \ldots, \tilde{F}_{np}(X_{np}), \tilde{\theta} \right)$$

$$\times l_j \left(\tilde{F}_{n1}(X_{j1}), \ldots, \tilde{F}_{np}(X_{jp}); \tilde{\theta} \right).$$

Then Σ can be estimated using the sample variance of $\{\tilde{V}_t\}_{t=1}^{n}$, i.e., $\hat{\Sigma} = n^{-1} \sum_{i=1}^{n} A_{ni} A'_{ni}$, where $A_{ni} = \tilde{V}_i - n^{-1} \sum_{t=1}^{n} \hat{V}_t$.

The two-step estimation procedure discussed above is computationally simple; however, it is not efficient in general. We now discuss an efficient estimation procedure.

20.4.4 A One-Step Efficient Estimation Procedure

Chen et al. (forthcoming) propose a one-step sieve-based efficient estimation method. They suggest using a linear sieve (series) to approximate the square root of the marginal PDFs, i.e.,

$$\mathcal{F}_{nj} = \left\{ f_{K_{nj}}(x) = \left[\sum_{k=1}^{K_{nj}} a_k A_k(x) \right]^2 , \int f_{K_{nj}}(x) dx = 1 \right\}, \quad (20.57)$$

where $K_{nj} \to \infty$ and $K_{nj}/n \to 0$, where $\{A_k(\cdot) : k \geq 1\}$ consists of known base functions, and where $\{a_k : k \geq 1\}$ is the collection of unknown sieve coefficients.

If $\mathcal{X}_j = [0,1]$, then the approximating base functions $A_k(\cdot)$'s can be the B-spline sieve $Spl(K_n)$, or the polynomial sieve $Pol(K_n) = \{\sum_{k=1}^{K_n} a_k x^k, x \in [0,1] : a_k \in \mathbb{R}\}$, or the trigonometric sieve

$$TriPol(K_n) = \left\{ a_0 + \sum_{k=1}^{K_n} [a_k \cos(k\pi x) + b_k \sin(k\pi x)], x \in [0,1] : a_k \in \mathbb{R} \right\}.$$

If $\mathcal{X}_j = \mathbb{R}$, then if the PDF $f_j(\cdot)$ has close to exponential thin tails, one can use the Hermite polynomial sieve given by

$$\mathcal{F}_{nj} = \left\{ f_{K_{nj}}(x) = \sigma^{-1} \left[\epsilon_0 + \left\{ \sum_{k=1}^{K_{nj}} a_k \left(\frac{x - \zeta_0}{\sigma} \right)^k \right\}^2 \right] \right.$$

$$\left. \times \exp\left\{ -\frac{(x-\zeta_0)^2}{2\sigma^2} \right\} : \int f_{K_{nj}}(x) dx = 1 \right\}, \quad (20.58)$$

as in Gallant and Nychka (1987), where $\epsilon_0 > 0$, $\sigma > 0$, ζ_0, and $a_k \in \mathbb{R}$.

If, on the other hand, $f_j(\cdot)$ has polynomial fat tails, one can use the spline wavelet sieve given by

$$\mathcal{F}_{nj} = \left\{ f_{K_{nj}}(x) = \left[\sum_{k=0}^{K_{nj}} \sum_{l \in \mathcal{K}_n} a_{kl} 2^{k/2} B_\gamma(2^k x - l) \right]^2 , \int f_{K_{nj}}(x) dx = 1 \right\},$$

$$(20.59)$$

where $B_\gamma(\cdot)$ denotes the cardinal B-spline of order γ as given in (15.2) in Chapter 15.

Let $\alpha = (\theta', f_1, \ldots, f_p)'$ and let

$$l(\alpha, Z_i) = \ln\left\{ c(F_1(X_{1i}), \ldots, F_p(X_{pi}); \theta) \prod_{j=1}^{p} f_j(X_{ji}) \right\}.$$

Also, let $\mathcal{A}_n = \Theta \times \prod_{j=1}^{p} \mathcal{F}_{nj}$, where the linear sieve space could be one of the above discussed sieves. Chen et al. (forthcoming) propose the following sieve estimator of α:

$$\hat{\alpha} = \arg \max_{\alpha \in \mathcal{A}_n} \sum_{i=1}^{n} l(\alpha, Z_i). \qquad (20.60)$$

The resulting estimator for $F_j(\cdot)$ is obtained by $\hat{F}_{nj}(x_j) = \int \mathbf{1}(y \le x_j) \hat{f}_{hj}(y) dy$.

Chen et al. (forthcoming) showed that $\hat{\alpha}$ is semiparametrically efficient. More specifically, they showed that

$$\sqrt{n}(\hat{\theta} - \theta) \to N\left(0, I_0(\theta)^{-1}\right) \text{ in distribution,}$$

where $I_0(\theta)^{-1}/n$ is the semiparametric lower bound of the asymptotic variance of any regular estimator. However, $I_0(\theta)$ does not have a closed form expression in general. Nevertheless Chen et al. are able to construct a consistent estimator for $I_0(\theta)$ as follows. Letting $\hat{U}_i = (\hat{U}_{1i}, \ldots, \hat{U}_{pi})' = (\hat{F}_{n1}(X_{1i}), \ldots, \hat{F}_{np}(X_{pi}))'$, a consistent estimator of $I_0(\theta)$ is given by

$$\hat{I}_0(\theta) = \min_{g_j \in \mathcal{A}_n, j=1,\ldots,p} n^{-1} \sum_{i=1}^{n} \left\{ B_{ni}(\hat{\theta}, \hat{U}_1, \ldots, \hat{U}_p)' B_{ni}(\hat{\theta}, \hat{U}_1, \ldots, \hat{U}_p) \right\},$$

$$(20.61)$$

where

$$B_{ni}(\hat{\theta}, \hat{U}_1, \ldots, \hat{U}_p) = \frac{\partial \ln c(\hat{U}_i, \hat{\theta})}{\partial \theta}$$
$$- \sum_{j=1}^{p} \left[\frac{\partial \ln c(\hat{U}_i, \hat{\theta})}{\partial v_j} \int_0^{\hat{U}_{ji}} g_j(v) \, dv + g_j(\hat{U}_{ji}) \right].$$

Chen et al. showed that $\hat{I}_0(\theta) - I_0(\theta) = o_p(1)$. Note that (20.61) requires an optimization procedure because $I_0(\theta)$ does not have a closed form expression.

The marginal CDFs can be estimated by $\hat{F}_{nj}(x_j) = \int_{-\infty}^{x_j} \hat{f}_{nj}(v) \, dv$. Chen et al. (forthcoming) further show that the resulting estimator $\hat{F}_{nj}(x_j)$ is a $\sqrt{n}$-consistent and semiparametrically efficient estimator for $F_j(x_j)$, i.e., that $\sqrt{n}(\hat{F}_{nj}(x_j) - F_j(x_j)) \to N(0, V_{0j}(x_j))$ in distribution. However, in general $V_{0j}(x_j)$ does not have a closed form expression. Nevertheless, one can still obtain a sieve-based consistent estimator, say $\hat{V}_{0j}(x_j)$ such that $\hat{V}_{0j}(x_j) = V_{0j}(x_j) + o_p(1)$;

see Chen et al. for a detailed definition of $\hat{V}_{0j}(x_j)$. When $X_1, \ldots, X_p$ are independent of each other ($c(v_1, \ldots, v_p; \theta) \equiv 1$ in this case), then $V_{j0}(x_j) = F_j(x_j)(1 - F_j(x_j))$ has a closed form expression and coincides with the asymptotic variance of $\sqrt{n}\tilde{F}_{nj}(x_j)$ (the empirical estimator of $F_j(x_j)$). For the general case we have $V_{0j}(x_j) \leq F_j(x_j)(1 - F_j(x_j))$.

The estimation procedures in Sections 20.4.3 and 20.4.4 both assume that the chosen parametric copula function is correctly specified. In practice, one needs to test whether a chosen parametric copula is indeed close enough to the unknown true copula function. We discuss the problem of testing a parametric copula function in the next section.

20.4.5 Testing Parametric Functional Forms of a Copula

Let $\{C_0(v_1, \ldots, v_p; \theta) : \theta \in \Theta\}$ be a class of parametric copulas for $\mathbf{X} = (X_1, \ldots, X_p)$. We are interested in testing the following null hypothesis:

$$H_0 : \mathrm{P}\left[C(v_1, \ldots, v_p) = C_0(v_1, \ldots, v_p; \theta_0)\right] = 1 \text{ for some } \theta_0 \in \Theta,$$

where Θ is a bounded subset in $\mathbb{R}^q$. The alternative hypothesis is the negation of H_0, i.e., H_1: $\mathrm{P}(C(v_1, \ldots, v_p) = C_0(v_1, \ldots, v_p; \theta)) < 1$ for all $\theta \in \Theta$. Let $C_{0j}(v_1, \ldots, v_p; \theta_0)$ denote the joint CDF of $V_1, \ldots, V_j$ under H_0, i.e., $C_{0j}(v_1, \ldots, v_j; \theta_0) = C_0(v_1, \ldots, v_j, 1, \ldots, 1; \theta_0)$ ($V_l = 1$ for $l > j$). Also, let $C_{0j}(V_j; \theta_0 | V_1, \ldots, V_{j-1})$ denote the conditional CDF of V_j given $(V_1, \ldots, V_{j-1})$ under H_0. Then it is known that

$$C_{0j}(v_j; \theta_0 | v_1, \ldots, v_{j-1}) = \frac{\partial^{j-1} C_{0j}(v_1, \ldots, v_j; \theta_0)}{\partial v_1 \ldots \partial v_{j-1}}$$
$$\times \frac{\partial^{j-1} C_{0,j-1}(v_1, \ldots, v_{j-1}; \theta_0)}{\partial v_1 \ldots \partial v_{j-1}}.$$

Define new random variables Z_j as follows. First, let $Z_1 = V_1$, then let $Z_j = C_{0j}(V_j; \theta_0 | V_1, \ldots, V_{j-1})$ for $j = 2, \ldots, p$. Since the copula function is a multivariate CDF, it follows from Rosenblatt (1952) that H_0 holds if and only if $Z_1, \ldots, Z_p$ are i.i.d. $U[0, 1]$ random variables. Therefore, the null hypothesis can be equivalently written as H_0: $\mathrm{P}(g(Z_1, \ldots, Z_p) = 1) = 1$, where $g(z_1, \ldots, z_p)$ is the joint PDF of $Z_1, \ldots, Z_p$. One can estimate $g(z_1, \ldots, z_p)$ by

$$\tilde{g}(z_1, \ldots, z_p) = \frac{1}{nh_1 \ldots h_p} \sum_{t=1}^{n} \left[k_h(\hat{Z}_t, z)\right],$$

where $\bar{k}_h(\hat{Z}_t, z) = \prod_{j=1}^{p} k_{h_j}(\hat{Z}_{jt}, z_j)$, and where $k_h(x, y)$ is the univariate boundary-corrected kernel function (with support $[-1, 1]$) defined in (20.19) of Section 20.1.4. Let $\hat{Z}_{t1} = \hat{F}_1(Y_{1t})$, and let

$$\hat{Z}_{jt} = C_{0j}\left(\hat{F}_j(Y_{jt}); \hat{\theta}|\hat{F}_1(Y_{1t}), \ldots, \hat{F}_{j-1}(Y_{j-1,t})\right)$$

for $j = 2, \ldots, p$, where $\hat{\theta}$ is a $\sqrt{n}$-consistent estimator of θ_0 (not necessarily the efficient estimator) under the null hypothesis. The test statistic will be based on

$$\int_0^1 \cdots \int_0^1 [\hat{g}(z_1, \ldots, z_p) - 1]^2 \, dz_1 \ldots dz_p. \qquad (20.62)$$

Note that (20.62) involves two summations (since $\hat{g}(\cdot)$ contains one summation), i.e., $\sum_{t=1}^{n} \sum_{s=1}^{n}$, and if we remove the $t = s$ term, then we obtain the following test statistic ($\int_0^1 dz = \int_0^1 \cdots \int_0^1 dz_1 \ldots dz_p$):

$$\hat{I}_n = \frac{1}{n(n-1)} \sum_{t=1}^{n} \sum_{s \neq t}^{n} \int_0^1 k_h(\hat{Z}_t, z) k_h(\hat{Z}_t, z) \, dz$$

$$- \frac{2}{n} \sum_{t=1}^{n} \int_0^1 k_h(\hat{Z}_t, z) \, dz + 1. \qquad (20.63)$$

Chen et al. (forthcoming), have proved the following result.

Theorem 20.3. *Under regularity conditions given in Chen et al. (forthcoming), then under H_0, $\hat{T}_n = n(h_1 \ldots h_p)^{1/2} \hat{I}_n / \sigma_{n,0} \to N(0, 1)$ in distribution, where $\sigma_{n,0}^2 = 2\{\int_{-1}^{1} [\int_{-1}^{1} k(v)k(u+v) \, dv]^2 du\}^p$.*

Note that unlike the original test statistic considered in Chen et al. (forthcoming), there is no nonzero center term in the $\hat{T}_n$ test in Theorem 20.3 because in (20.63) we have removed the $i = j$ term.

The above $\hat{T}_n$ statistic requires the estimation of a multivariate PDF $g(z_1, \ldots, z_p)$. When p is large, it suffers from the curse of dimensionality problem. Chen et al. (forthcoming) also propose an alternative test that involves estimation of a univariate PDF only. It is based on the fact that under H_0, $W = \sum_{j=1}^{p} [\Phi^{-1}(Z_j)]^2$ has a χ_p^2 distribution. Letting $F_{\chi_p^2}(w)$ denote the CDF of a χ_p^2 random variable, then $F_{\chi_p^2}(W)$ has the $U[0, 1]$ distribution. This motivates Chen et al. to construct a test based on $\int_0^1 [\hat{g}_W(w) - 1]^2 dw$, where $\hat{g}(w) = \frac{1}{nh} \sum_{t=1}^{n} k_h(w, F_{\chi_p^2}(\hat{W}_t))$, and $\hat{W}_t = \sum_{j=1}^{p}[\Phi^{-1}(\hat{Z}_{jt})]^2$. As was the case when deriving the $\hat{I}_n$ test, by removing the $t = s$ term we obtain the following test statistic:

$$\hat{I}_{n,2} = \frac{1}{n(n-1)} \sum_{t=1}^{n} \sum_{s \neq t}^{n} \int_0^1 \int_0^1 k_h \left(F_{\chi_p^2}(\hat{W}_t), w \right) k_h \left(F_{\chi_p^2}(\hat{W}_s), w \right) dw$$

$$- \frac{2}{n} \sum_{t=1}^{n} \int k_h \left(F_{\chi_p^2}(\hat{W}_t), z \right) dz + 1.$$

Similar to the result of Theorem 20.3, Chen et al. (forthcoming) showed that, under H_0,

$$nh^{1/2}\hat{I}_{n,2}/\sigma_{n,2} \to N(0,1) \text{ in distribution}, \tag{20.64}$$

where $\sigma_{n,2}^2 = 2 \int_{-1}^{1}[\int_{-1}^{1} k(u+v)k(v)\,dv]^2 du$.

Copula functions are also used to model the dependence structure of time series regression models. Estimation of semiparametric copula time series regression models is discussed in Chen and Fan (forthcoming, 2006). See also Brendstrup and Paarsch (2004) who consider an application to auction settings and employ the Frank copula.

20.5 A Semiparametric Transformation Model

In this section we consider a transformation model of the form

$$\Lambda_0(Y) = X'\beta + u, \tag{20.65}$$

where Y is a scalar dependent variable, $\Lambda_0(\cdot)$ is a strictly increasing function, X is a vector of explanatory variables, β is a vector of coefficients, and u is the unobserved error term independent of X having a CDF denoted by $F(\cdot)$. Model (20.65) can generate many different models depending on the different forms of Λ_0 and $F(\cdot)$, including the Box-Cox transformation model, the accelerated failure time model, proportional hazards model, and the mixed proportional hazards model. In parametric settings, one needs to specify both Λ_0 and $F(\cdot)$, misspecification of either typically leading to inconsistent estimates. In this section we discuss nonparametric estimation of (20.65) without imposing functional form restrictions on Λ_0 and $F(\cdot)$. A $\sqrt{n}$-consistent estimator of β can be obtained by treating (20.65) as a single index model and is covered in Chapter 8; see Han (1987), Härdle and Stoker (1989), Ichimura (1993), Powell et al. (1989), and Sherman (1993) for different approaches to estimating β. In this section we discuss estimation of $\Lambda_0(\cdot)$ only.

Most of the existing nonparametric methods are two-step nonparametric smoothing approaches. For instance, Horowitz (1996) and Ye and Duan (1997) propose estimating Λ_0 and $F(\cdot)$ based on nonparametric estimation of conditional CDFs. Chen (2002) proposes a rank estimation method (e.g., Han (1987)) which avoids nonparametric smoothing techniques. We briefly discuss Horowitz's and Chen's methods below.

Some identification conditions are needed to identify Λ_0 and β. We assume that $\Lambda_0(y_0) = 0$ for some y_0 and that $|\beta_1| = 1$, where β_1 is the coefficient of the first component of X, whose probability distribution conditional on the remaining variables is absolutely continuous with respect to the Lebesgue measure. Let $\{X_i, Y_i\}_{i=1}^n$ be a random sample of (X, Y), and let $G(.|z)$ be the CDF of Y conditional on z, where $z = x'\beta$. Then it is easy to show that

$$
\begin{aligned}
G(y|z) &= \mathrm{P}[Y \leq y|z] \\
&= \mathrm{P}[T(Y) \leq T(y)|z] \\
&= \mathrm{P}[U + z \leq T(y)] \\
&= F[T(y) - z].
\end{aligned}
$$

Horowitz (1996) further shows that

$$
\Lambda(y) = -\int_{y_0}^{y} [G_y(v|z)/G_z(v|z)] \, dv,
$$

where $G_y(v|z) = \partial G(y|z)/\partial y$ and $G_z(v|z) = \partial G(y|z)/\partial z$.

Therefore, Horowitz (1996) suggests estimating $\Lambda(\cdot)$ by

$$
\Lambda_n(y) = -\int_{y_0}^{y} \int_{S_w} w(z) \, [G_{ny}(v|z)/G_{nz}(v|z)] \, dz \, dv, \qquad (20.66)
$$

where w is a weight function satisfying $\int_{S_w} w(z)dz = 1$, and $G_{ny}(v|z)$ and $G_{nz}(v|z)$ are kernel estimators of $G_y(v|z)$ and $G_z(v|z)$, respectively. Under some regularity conditions, Horowitz establishes that $\sqrt{n}(\Lambda_n(\cdot) - \Lambda_0(\cdot))$ converges to a zero mean Gaussian process having a well-defined covariance function.

Next, we turn to Chen's (2002) estimation procedure. Define $d_{iy} = \mathbf{1}(Y_i \geq y)$ and let $d_{i0} = \mathbf{1}(Y_i \geq 0)$. By the monotone property of $\Lambda_0(\cdot)$ we have $d_{iy} = \mathbf{1}(X_i\beta + u_i \geq \Lambda_0(y)\}$ and $\mathrm{E}(\mathbf{1}(d_{iy})|X_i) = 1 - F(\Lambda_0(y) - X_i\beta)$. Hence,

$$\mathrm{E}\left[(d_{iy} - d_{iy_0})|X_i, X_j\right] \geq 0 \text{ whenever } (X_i - X_j)\beta \geq \Lambda_0(y) \quad (20.67)$$

for $i \neq j$ (and $\Lambda_0(y_0) = 0$).

For a given initial consistent estimator of β that we denote $\hat{\beta}$, Chen (2002) proposes estimating $\Lambda(y)$ by

$$\hat{\Lambda}_n(y) = \arg\min_{\Lambda \in M_\Lambda} \frac{1}{n(n-1)} \sum_{i=1}^{n} \sum_{j \neq i}^{n} (d_{iy} - d_{jy_0}) \mathbf{1}(X_i\hat{\beta} - X_j\hat{\beta} \geq \Lambda),$$

$$(20.68)$$

where M_Λ is an appropriate compact set.

Chen (2002) shows that $\hat{\Lambda}_n(y)$ is a $\sqrt{n}$-consistent estimator for $\Lambda_0(y)$ and that $\sqrt{n}(\hat{\Lambda}_n(\cdot) - \Lambda_0(\cdot))$ converges weakly to a Gaussian process with zero mean and a well-defined covariance function.

The transformation model (20.65) has been extended to the censored data case, i.e., $\Lambda_0(y^*) = X'\beta + u$ where one only observes $y = \min\{Y^*, C\}$ and $\delta = \mathbf{1}(Y^* \leq C)$, but not Y^*. Gorgens and Horowitz (1999) propose a kernel-based estimation method for the censored transformation model, while Chen (2002) also extends his rank-based estimation method to the censored data case.

Khan and Tamer (forthcoming) consider the following generalized accelerated failure time (GAFT) model introduced in Ridder (1990),

$$\Lambda(Y_i) = X_i'\beta_0 + \epsilon_i, \quad i = 1, \ldots, n, \quad (20.69)$$

where $(Y_i, X_i')'$ is a $(q+1) \times 1$ vector, with Y_i being the dependent variable (say, survival times after receiving treatment), X_i being a vector of observed covariates, with $\Lambda(\cdot)$ being a monotone but otherwise unknown function. Instead of observing Y_i, one observes (v_i, d_i), where v_i is a scalar variable and d_i is a binary random variable (i.e., a "right censored" transformation model), i.e.,

$$\Lambda(v_i) = \min(X_i'\beta_0 + \epsilon_i, c_i),$$
$$d_i = \mathbf{1}(X_i'\beta_0 + \epsilon_i \leq c_i), \quad (20.70)$$

where $v_i = Y_i$ if the data is uncensored, and $v_i = c_i$ for censored observations. Khan and Tamer propose a rank regression estimation method analogous to Han (1987), and they establish the asymptotic normality of the resulting estimator of β_0.

20.6   Exercises

Exercise 20.1. Derive (20.24).

Exercise 20.2. Defining $Z_{n2,t} = k_h(X_{t\Delta} - x) \int_{t\Delta}^{(t+1)\Delta} \mu(X_u)du$, and defining $\hat{m}_4(x) = (n\Delta)^{-1} \sum_{t=1}^n Z_{n2,t}$, then we have $\hat{m}_1(x) = \hat{m}_3(x) + \hat{m}_4(x)$, where we have used the fact that $\text{var}(\hat{m}_1(x)) = \text{var}(\hat{m}_3(x)) + (s.o.) = O((nh\Delta)^{-1})$ in the proof of Theorem 20.1 (i).

Prove that this is indeed true, i.e., show that $\text{var}(\hat{m}_4(x))$ is of order $O((nh)^{-1})$, which is smaller than $\text{var}(\hat{m}_3(x))$, which is of order $O((nh\Delta)^{-1})$.

Appendix A

Background Statistical Concepts

Many of the theoretical results established in the literature make use of a number of fundamental statistical concepts. Below we present some core concepts that we rely upon to derive results contained in the preceding chapters.

1.1 Probability, Measure, and Measurable Space

Definition A.1 (Random Experiment). *A random experiment is an action or observation whose outcome is uncertain in advance of its occurrence. A popular random experiment is the "coin toss" since we cannot predict for certain prior to the toss whether a coin will land heads up or tails up.*

Definition A.2 (Sample Space, Ω). *The sample space, denoted by Ω, is defined as a set that contains all possible outcomes of a random experiment.*

Example A.1. *If one flips a coin twice, then the sample space is*

$$\Omega = \{HH, HT, TH, TT\} = \{w_1, w_2, w_3, w_4\},$$

where $w_1 = HH$, $w_2 = HT$ (i.e., first toss is H, second is T), etc. In this example there are four elementary events w_i, $i = 1, \ldots, 4$.

Definition A.3 (Countable and Uncountable Sets). *Let* $\mathbb{N}_+ = \{1, 2, 3, \ldots\}$ *denote the set of natural numbers. A set B is said to be* **countable** *if all of the elements in B can be arranged in a one-to-one correspondence with the elements in $\mathbb{N}_+$. If a set has a countable subset, but itself is not countable, we say that the set is* **uncountable**.

Example A.2. $\mathcal{B} = \{1, 3, 5, \ldots\}$ *is countable because $B = \{b_n\}_{n=1}^{\infty}$ with $b_n = 2n - 1$, then there is a 1-1 mapping: $n \to 2n - 1$ from $\mathbb{N}_+$ to B. Similarly, the set of rational numbers is countable. However, the set $[0, 1] \in \mathbb{R}$ is not countable because one cannot find a 1-1 mapping from $\mathbb{N}_+$ to $[0, 1]$. However, there are subsets in B that are countable, for example, $A = \{1/n\}_{n=1}^{\infty}$ is a subset of $[0, 1]$ that is countable.*

The set of all power functions $\{x^n\}_{n=0}^{\infty} = \{1, x, x^2, \ldots\}$ has countably (infinite) many functions, while the set of all bounded continuous functions with domain $[0, 1]$ is uncountable.

Definition A.4 (σ-Field Defined in Ω). *Letting $\mathcal{F}$ (which contains at least one nonempty set) be a collection of subsets of Ω, then $\mathcal{F}$ is called a σ-field (or σ-algebra) if the following two conditions hold:*

(i) If $A \in \mathcal{F}$, then $A^c \in \mathcal{F}$, where A^c is the complement of A.

(ii) If $A_1, A_2, \ldots, \in \mathcal{F}$, then $\cup_{i=1}^{\infty} A_i \in \mathcal{F}$.

(i) and (ii) above tell us that a σ-field is closed under complementation and under countable union operations.

It is easy to show that (a) $\Omega \in \mathcal{F}$, (b) $\emptyset \in \mathcal{F}$ ($\emptyset$ denotes the empty set), and (c) if $A_1, A_2, \ldots, \in \mathcal{F}$. Then $\cap_{i=1}^{\infty} A_i \in \mathcal{F}$.

Proof of (a). Let A be a nonempty set of $\mathcal{F}$. Then $A^c \in \mathcal{F}$ by (i) above, hence $\Omega = A \cup A^c \in \mathcal{F}$ by (ii). $\qquad\qquad\square$

Proof of (b). $\emptyset = \Omega^c \in \mathcal{F}$ by (i) and the fact that $\Omega \in \mathcal{F}$. $\qquad\qquad\square$

Proof of (c). We know that $(\cup_{i=1}^{\infty} A_i^c)^c \in \mathcal{F}$ by properties (i) and (ii). Hence, by DeMorgan's law, $\cap_{i=1}^{\infty} A_i = (\cup_{i=1}^{\infty} A_i^c)^c \in \mathcal{F}$. $\qquad\qquad\square$

The pair $(\Omega, \mathcal{F})$ is called a **measurable space**.

Example A.3.

(i) If $\{\mathcal{F}\} = \{\emptyset, \Omega\}$ is a σ-field containing only the empty set and the entire sample space, then it is called the "trivial σ-field" (an obviously uninteresting one).

(ii) If Ω contains n (where n is finite) elementary events ("elements"), then it has a total of 2^n subsets. The set containing all subsets (called a "power set") of Ω is a σ-field and is the largest σ-field defined in Ω.

Definition A.5 (DeMorgan's Law). *Let $A_1, A_2, \ldots, \in \mathcal{F}$ ($\mathcal{F}$ is the σ-field defined in Ω). Letting A_i^c denote the complement of A_i, then*

$$(\cup_{i=1}^{\infty} A_i)^c = \cap_{i=1}^{\infty} A_i^c.$$

Example A.4. *DeMorgan's law can be (easily) intuitively verified using a Venn diagram. For example, let A_1 be the set of basketball team members and let A_2 be the set of soccer team members in a high school. Then $\cup_{i=1}^{2} A_i = A_1 \cup A_2$ is the set of students who are either basketball team members or soccer team members, hence, its complement $(\cup_{i=1}^{2} A_i)^c$ is the set of students who are neither basketball nor soccer team members. DeMorgan's law asserts that this set is identical to $\cap_{i=1}^{n} A_i^c = A_1^c \cap A_2^c$, which is the set of students who are not basketball team member (A_1^c) and are not soccer team members, which is of course true.*

Definition A.6 *($\sigma(\mathcal{A})$, the σ-field generated by $\mathcal{A}$). Let $\mathcal{A}$ be a nonempty set of subsets of Ω. Then the σ-field generated by $\mathcal{A}$ denoted by $\sigma(\mathcal{A})$ is one that satisfies*

(i) $\mathcal{A} \in \sigma(\mathcal{A})$.

(ii) $\sigma(\mathcal{A})$ is the smallest σ-field containing $\mathcal{A}$.

Example A.5. *Letting A be a nonempty proper subset of Ω, then $\{A, A^c, \emptyset, \Omega\}$ is a σ-field, and is the smallest σ-field containing A.*

For the coin-flip example, if we choose $A = w_1 = HH$, then $\{w_1, \{w_2, w_3, w_4\}, \emptyset, \Omega\}$ is the σ-field generated by $A = w_1$. This σ-field does not contain $\{w_2\}$, $\{w_3\}$, etc. The power set (that contains all subsets of Ω) also contains $A = w_1$, but it is not the smallest σ-field containing A, so the power set is not $\sigma(A)$ (for $A = w_1$).

When the sample space contains an interval of $\mathbb{R}$, say $\Omega = \mathbb{R}$ (it contains uncountably many points), then the set of all subsets of $\mathbb{R}$ is too large, and one cannot define a proper measure for all subsets of $\mathbb{R}$ in this case. Therefore, it is necessary to impose some restrictions on the subsets of $\mathbb{R}$. This can be done by requiring that the subsets of $\mathbb{R}$ belong to the Borel σ-field as defined below.

Definition A.7 (Borel Fields and Borel Sets). *Let $\mathbb{R}$ denote the set of real numbers, i.e., $\mathbb{R} = \{y : -\infty < y < \infty\}$. Let $A_x = \{y : -\infty < y < x\} = (-\infty, x)$, and define $\mathcal{A} = \{A_x, x \in \mathbb{R}\}$. Then the σ-field generated by $\mathcal{A}$ is called the Borel (σ) field on $\mathbb{R}$.*

It can be shown that $\{a\}, [a,b], (a,b), [a,b), (a,b], [a,+\infty)$ all belong to Borel field. Thus, a Borel field contains all sets of practical interest.

Example A.6. *From $(-\infty, a) \in \sigma(\mathcal{A})$, we know that the following sets all belong to $\sigma(\mathcal{A})$: (i) $[a, \infty) = (-\infty, a)^c$; (ii) $[a, b) = (-\infty, b) \cap [a, \infty)$ $(b > a)$; (iii) $\{a\} = \cap_{i=1}^{\infty}[a, a + \frac{1}{i})$; and (iv) $(a, b) = [a, b) \cap a^c$.*

In Exercise A.1, the reader is asked to show that the collection of all rational numbers and of all irrational numbers are both Borel sets. Therefore, all familiar subsets in $\mathbb{R}$ are Borel sets. For an example of a non-Borel set, see Royden (1988, pp. 64–66). For applied researchers, one can ignore the rather odd case of non-Borel sets since, in applied research settings, one (almost) never encounters non-Borel sets.

One can define measures on Borel sets of $\mathbb{R}$.

Definition A.8 (Measure). *Given the class $\mathcal{F}$ of subsets of Ω, a measure μ is a map from $\Omega \to \mathbb{R}^+ = \{x \in \mathbb{R} : x \geq 0\}$, satisfying*

(i) $\mu(A) \geq 0$ for all $A \in \mathcal{F}$.

(ii) $\mu(\emptyset) = 0$.

(iii) If $\{A_i\}_{i=1}^{\infty}$ are mutually exclusive sets, then

$$\mu(\cup_{i=1}^{\infty} A_i) = \sum_{i=1}^{\infty} \mu(A_i).$$

If $\mu(\Omega) = 1$, then we say that μ is a **probability measure**.

Definition A.9 (Lebesgue Measure). **Lebesgue measure** *is one of the most useful measures in practice, and is also perhaps the most intuitive. A Lebesgue measure m is a measure defined on the real line $\mathbb{R}$ (in fact on the Borel set $\mathcal{B}$) with the property that for any interval $[a, b]$ $(b \geq a)$, $m([a, b]) = b - a$, that is, the Lebesgue measure of an interval equals the length of the interval. Any single point has Lebesgue measure zero. Also, the Lebesgue measure of a countable subset of $\mathbb{R}$ is zero. The Lebesgue measure of the real line $\mathbb{R}$ is ∞ (as it has infinite length).*

The Lebesgue measure of a subset A of $\mathbb{R}^2$ gives a measure of the area of A, and for a set $A \in \mathbb{R}^3$, it measures the volume of A. Higher dimension Lebesgue measure is similarly defined.

However, note that not all measures can be interpreted as measuring length, or area, or volumes of a set. For example, a probability measure (defined below) maps a set with infinite Lebesgue measure (say, infinite length or volume) to a number between 0 and 1, which is of course not a measure of the length (or volume) of the set.

Definition A.10 (Probability as a Set Function P). *A probability measure is a mapping from the sample space to the unit interval $[0,1]$, i.e., $P: \Omega \to [0,1]$ such that*

(i) $P(A) \geq 0$ for all $A \in \mathcal{F}$.

(ii) $P(\Omega) = 1$.

(iii) If $\{A_i\}_{i=1}^{\infty}$ are mutually exclusive events in $\mathcal{F}$, i.e., $A_i \cap A_j = \emptyset$ for all $i \neq j$, then $P(\cup_{i=1}^{\infty} A_i) = \sum_{i=1}^{\infty} P(A_i)$.

The triplet $(\Omega, \mathcal{F}, P)$ is called the probability space.

Definition A.11 (Almost Everywhere versus Null Set). *Let $\mathcal{F}$ be a σ-field defined in Ω and μ be a measure defined for all $A \in \mathcal{F}$; then we say that for any $A, B \in \mathcal{F}$, A equals B **almost everywhere** (under μ) if the set of elements for which $A \neq B$ has a (μ) measure zero. A measure zero set is also called a **null set**.*

Example A.7. *Consider two functions defined in $[0,1]$, $f(x) = 1$ for all $x \in [0,1]$, and $g(x) = 1$ if x is an irrational number and $g(x) = 0$ if x is a rational number. Then $f(x) = g(x)$ for almost all x (under the Lebesgue measure) because the set of x for which $f(x) \neq g(x)$ is the set of rational numbers in $[0,1]$, which has a Lebesgue measure zero.*

In Example A.7 we introduced Borel sets in $\mathbb{R}$. We now define Borel measurable sets in $\mathbb{R}^q$.

Definition A.12 (Borel Measurable Set). *We say that a collection of sets, $\mathcal{A} \in \mathbb{R}^q$, is a **Borel measurable set** if the following conditions hold:*

(i) If $A \in \mathcal{A}$, then $A^c \in \mathcal{A}$.

(ii) If $A_1, A_2, \cdots \in \mathcal{A}$, then $\cup_{i=1}^{\infty} A_i \in \mathcal{A}$.

All familiar subsets of $\mathbb{R}^q$, such as singletons, any open, closed, half open, half closed regions, their unions and/or intersections, are Borel sets.

Definition A.13 (Borel Measurable Functions). *Let $f(x)$ be a real-valued function that maps $\mathbb{R}^q :\to \mathbb{R}$ $(x \in \mathbb{R}^q)$. Then $f(\cdot)$ is said to be a **Borel measurable function** if, for every $a \in \mathbb{R}$, the set $\{x \in \mathbb{R}^q : f(x) \le a\}$ is a Borel measurable set.*

All familiar functions are Borel measurable functions. For example, any continuous function is Borel measurable. Also, a function with countably many discontinuity points is Borel measurable. In fact, an everywhere discontinuous function can also be a Borel measurable function (see Exercise A.2).

Letting X be a random variable (a mapping from Ω to $\mathbb{R}$), we use $F(\cdot)$ to denote the **cumulative distribution function** (CDF) of X, which is defined as $F(x) = \mathrm{P}[X \le x]$ for all $x \in \mathbb{R}$. If $F(\cdot)$ is differentiable (say, a continuous random variable), then the **probability density function** (PDF) is defined as $f(x) = dF(x)/dx$. Note that one can also define a PDF for discrete random variables using the Dirac delta function; see Definition A.40 and the discussion that follows.

Definition A.14 (Riemann Integral). *Let $f(x)$ be a continuous function in $[a, b] \subset \mathbb{R}$. Partition $[a, b]$ to $a = x_0 < x_1 < \cdots < x_n = b$, define $\Delta x_j = x_j - x_{j-1}$, $j = 1, \ldots, n$, and let $\Delta x = \max_{\{1 \le j \le n\}} \Delta x_j$, if the limit*

$$\lim_{\Delta x \to 0} \sum_{j=1}^{n} f(\tilde{x}_j) \Delta x_j \ \text{ exists,} \tag{A.1}$$

*where $\tilde{x}_j \in [x_{j-1}, x_j]$, then it is called the **Riemann integral** of $f(\cdot)$ over $[a, b]$ and is denoted as $\int_a^b f(x)dx \equiv \int_{[a,b]} f(x)dx$.*

It can be shown that the Riemann integral has the property that $\int_a^b f(x)dx = -\int_b^a f(x)dx$. Also, $\int_a^b f(x)dx = \int_a^c f(x)dx + \int_c^b f(x)dx$ provided that all the integrals are well defined and finite.

The Riemann integral is the integral usually encountered in calculus texts and used by applied researchers (physicists, engineers, economists, etc.).

Definition A.15 (Riemann-Stieltjes Integral). *Let $f(x)$ and $g(x)$ be real-valued bounded functions defined on $[a, b]$. Take a partition $a = x_0 < x_1 < \cdots < x_n = b$, defined $\Delta x_j = x_j - x_{j-1}$, $j = 1, \ldots, n$, and let $\Delta x = \max_{\{1 \leq j \leq n\}} \Delta x_j$. If the limit*

$$\lim_{\Delta x \to 0} \sum_{j=1}^{n} f(\tilde{x}_j)[g(x_{j+1}) - g(x_j)] \ exists, \tag{A.2}$$

where $\tilde{x}_j \in [x_{j-1}, x_j]$, then it is called the **Riemann-Stieltjes integral** *and is denoted $\int_a^b f(x)dg(x)$.*

Note that if $f(\cdot)$ and $g(\cdot)$ have a common point of discontinuity, then the integral does not exist. However, if $f(\cdot)$ is continuous and $g(\cdot)$ is differentiable and $g^{(1)}(x) = dg(x)/dx$ is Riemann integrable, then

$$\int_a^b f(x)dg(x) = \int_a^b f(x)g^{(1)}(x)dx. \tag{A.3}$$

The right-hand side of (A.3) is a Riemann integral (i.e., of $m(x) = f(x)g^{(1)}(x)$).

The Riemann-Stieltjes integral is a generalization of the Riemann integral. When $g(x) = x$, it reverts back to the Riemann integral.

Definition A.16 (Simple Function). *Let $A \subset \mathcal{B}$ (Borel set) and let $f = \mathbf{1}_A$ denote an indicator function such that $f(x) = 1$ for $x \in A$ and 0 otherwise. We say that $g(\cdot)$ is a* **simple function** *if it has the following form:*

$$g(x) = \sum_{j=1}^{m} c_j \mathbf{1}_{A_j}, \tag{A.4}$$

where $A_j \in \mathcal{B}$ for $j = 1, \ldots, m$.

Definition A.17 (Lebesgue-Stieltjes Integral). *Let $f(\cdot)$ be a (Borel) measurable function, and let $\mu(A)$ denote the Lebesgue measure of $A \in \mathcal{B}$. If $f = \sum_{j=1}^{m} c_j \mathbf{1}(A_j)$ is a simple function, then the Lebesgue-Stieltjes integral of $f(\cdot)$ is defined as*

$$\int f d\mu = \sum_{j=1}^{m} c_k \mu(A_j).$$

If $f(\cdot)$ is a nonnegative measurable function, then the **Lebesgue-Stieltjes integral** is defined as

$$\int_A f\mu(dx) = \sup \left\{ \int g\mu(dx) : g \text{ is a simple function with} \right.$$

$$\left. g(x) \leq f(x) \text{ for all } x \in A \right\}.$$

One can also replace the Lebesgue measure μ by any other measure ν in the above definition, say a probability measure. This leads to

$$\int_A f\nu(dx) = \sup \left\{ \int g\nu(dx) : g \text{ is a simple function with} \right.$$

$$\left. g(x) \leq f(x) \text{ for all } x \in A \right\}.$$

We can express any measurable function $f(\cdot)$ as $f = f_+ - f_-$, where $f_+ = \max(f, 0)$ and $f_- = \max(-f, 0)$ are both nonnegative functions, and the Lebesgue-Stieltjes integral is defined as $\int f d\mu = \int f_+ d\mu - \int f_- d\mu$.

Note that the Lebesgue-Stieltjes integral is a further extension of the Riemann-Stieltjes integral. Even an everywhere discontinuous function (which is of course not Riemann integrable) can be Lebesgue integrable (see Exercise A.7).

Even a Lebesgue-Stieltjes integrable function might not be Riemann integrable. The next theorem tells us that the Riemann and the Lebesgue-Stieltjes integrals are closely related.

Theorem A.1. *Supposing that $f(\cdot)$ is a bounded function that is Riemann integrable over A, which we denote by $(R)\int_A f$, then it is also Lebesgue-Stieltjes integrable and the two integrals are identical, i.e.,*

$$\int_A f(x)\mu(dx) = (R)\int_A f(x)dx,$$

where μ is the Lebesgue measure.

Proof. See Wheeden and Zygmund (1977, Theorem 5.52). □

Theorem A.1 states that all Riemann integrable functions are also Lebesgue-Stieltjes integrable. Moreover, the two integration results are identical. Given that a Riemann integral is generally much easier to compute than a Lebesgue integral, one can always use the former to obtain results for the latter provided that the Riemann integral exists (see Exercise A.8). However, there exist functions that are not Riemann integrable, but are Lebesgue-Stieltjes integrable. For example, the *Dirichlet* function is one such case (see Exercise A.2).

The expectation of a random variable X is defined as

$$E(X) = \int xF(dx) \equiv \int x dF(x),$$

where $F(\cdot)$ is the CDF of X. It is defined as a Lebesgue-Stieltjes integral. However, if the PDF $f(x)$ of X exists, then $E(X) = \int xf(x)dx$, the integral becomes a Riemann integral, which is usually easier to compute than a Lebesgue-Stieltjes integral.

Theorem A.2. *Let X have a continuous CDF $F_X(x)$ and let $Y = F_X(X)$. Then Y is uniformly distributed on $[0,1]$, that is, $P(Y \leq y) = y$ for any $y \in [0,1]$.*

Proof.

$$P(Y \leq y) = P[F_X(X) \leq y]$$
$$= P\left\{F_X^{-1}[F_X(X)] \leq F^{-1}(y)\right\} \quad (F_X^{-1} \text{ is increasing})$$
$$= P\left(X \leq F_X^{-1}(y)\right) \quad \text{(see arguments below)}$$
$$= F_X\left(F_X^{-1}(y)\right) \quad \text{(definition of } F_X(\cdot))$$
$$= y. \quad \text{(continuity of } F_X(\cdot))$$

$\square$

In the proof we used $P\{F_X^{-1}[F_X(X)] \leq F^{-1}(y)\} = P(X \leq F_X^{-1}(y))$, which is true when $F_X(\cdot)$ is strictly increasing. However, $F_X(\cdot)$ maybe flat; see Casella and Berger (2002, p. 55) for details when $F_X(\cdot)$ is flat.

Definition A.18 (Characteristic Function). *Let X be a random vector on $\mathbb{R}^q$ with CDF $F(\cdot)$. The* **characteristic function** *of X is a complex valued function defined by*

$$\phi(t) = E(e^{it'X}) = \int e^{it'x} dF(x), \qquad (A.5)$$

where $i = \sqrt{-1}$, $t'x = t_1 x_1 + \cdots + t_q x_q$. The integral always exists because $|e^{it'x}| = |\cos(it'x) + i\sin(it'x)| = \sqrt{\cos^2(it'x) + \sin^2(it'x)} = 1$.

For a continuous random variable, $\phi(\cdot)$ uniquely determines its PDF as the following inversion formula shows (provided that $\int |\phi(t)| dt < \infty$):

$$f(x) = \frac{1}{(2\pi)^q} \int e^{-it'x} \phi(t) dt. \qquad (A.6)$$

Proof. From (A.5) we know that $\phi(t) = \int f(v) e^{it'v} dv$, and substituting this into (A.6), we obtain (also change the order of the double integration)

$$\int e^{-it'x} \phi(t) dt = \frac{1}{2\pi} \int \left[\int e^{-it'(x-v)} dt \right] f(v) dv$$

$$= \int \delta(x-v) f(v) dv = f(x),$$

where we have used the fact that $(2\pi)^{-1} \int_{-\infty}^{\infty} e^{it'v} dt = \delta(v)$, the Dirac delta function, which we define in Definition A.40 and in Equation (A.15) below.   □

Definition A.19 (Lipschitz Function). *Let $g(\cdot)$ be a real valued function on $\mathbb{R}^q$. It is a Lipschitz function of order 1 if the following inequality is satisfied:*

$|g(x) - g(y)| \le c||x - y||$ *for all $x, y \in \mathbb{R}^q$, where c is a finite constant.*

1.2   Metric, Norm, and Functional Spaces

Definition A.20 (Linear Vector Space). *A set $\mathcal{V}$ of elements is called a **vector space** (or linear space, or linear vector space) over the real numbers if we define a + (addition) on $\mathcal{V} \times \mathcal{V}$ to $\mathcal{V}$ and a · (multiplication by scalars) on $\mathbb{R} \times \mathcal{V}$ to $\mathcal{V}$ that satisfy the following conditions:*

(i) $x + y = y + x$.

(ii) $(x + y) + z = x + (y + z)$.

(iii) *There is a vector θ such that $x + \theta = x$ for all $x \in \mathcal{V}$.*

(iv) $\alpha(x + y) = \alpha x + \alpha y$ *for all $\alpha \in \mathbb{R}$ and all $x, y \in \mathcal{V}$.*

(v) $(\alpha + \beta)x = \alpha x + \beta x$ *for all $\alpha, \beta \in \mathbb{R}$, and all $x \in \mathcal{V}$.*

(vi) $\alpha(\beta x) = (\alpha\beta)x$ *for all* $\alpha, \beta \in \mathbb{R}$, *and all* $x \in \mathcal{V}$.

(vii) $0 \cdot x = \theta$, $1 \cdot x = x$.

The θ *element defined above can be shown to be unique, and it is called the zero element.*

Definition A.21 (The $C[a,b]$ and $C^m[a,b]$ Spaces). *We use $C[a,b]$ to denote the collection of real-valued functions that are bounded and continuous in $[a,b]$. Similarly, we use $C^m[a,b]$ to denote functions that are m times continuously differentiable on $[a,b]$ (with bounded derivatives), where m is a nonnegative integer.*

Definition A.22 (The $L^p[a,b]$ Space). *Let p be a positive real number. A measurable function defined on $[a,b]$ is said to belong to the space $L^p = L^p[a,b]$ if $\int_a^b |f(x)|^p dx < \infty$.*

With the usual definition of addition and scalar multiplication, both $C^m[a,b]$ and $L^p[a,b]$ are linear vector spaces.

Definition A.23 (Linear Space). *A space X of real valued functions is called a **linear space** if it has the property that if both f and $g \in X$, then $\alpha f + \beta g \in X$, where α and β are arbitrary constants. For example, the L^p space is a linear space.*

Definition A.24 (Span and Spanning Sets). *Let $v_1,\ldots,v_n$ be vectors in a vector space V. A sum of the form $\alpha_1 v_1 + \alpha_2 v_2 + \cdots + \alpha_n v_n$, where $\alpha_1,\ldots,\alpha_n$ are scalars, is called a **linear combination** of $v_1,\ldots,v_n$. The set of all linear combinations of $v_1,\ldots,v_n$ will be denoted by $Span(v_1,\ldots,v_n)$. For example, letting $v_1 = (1,0)'$ and $v_2 = (0,1)$ be two vectors in $\mathbb{R}^2$ ($V = \mathbb{R}^2$), then $Span(v_1, v_2) = \mathbb{R}^2$. That is, the two vectors v_1, v_2 span $\mathbb{R}^2$, and $\{v_1, v_2\}$ is said to be a spanning set for $\mathbb{R}^2$.*

Definition A.25 (A Normed Linear Space). *A linear space is said to be a **normed linear space** if we have assigned a nonnegative real number (a **norm**) $\|f\|$ to each $f \in X$ such that*

(i) $\|\alpha f\| = |\alpha| \|f\|$.

(ii) $\|f + g\| \leq \|f\| + \|g\|$.

(iii) $\|f\| = 0$ if and only if $f \equiv 0$ a.e.

L^p space is a normed linear space with the norm defined by $||f|| = \{\int |f(x)|^p)dx\}^{1/p}$.

Let $|| \cdot ||_\nu$ be a norm on a vector space $\mathcal{V}$. A sequence $\{v_k\}_{k=1}^\infty$ is called a **Cauchy sequence** if $||v_j - v_k||_\nu \to 0$ whenever $j, k \to \infty$.

Definition A.26 (Banach Space). *A normed linear space is called complete if every Cauchy sequence in the space converges. A complete normed linear space is called a **Banach space**.*

Examples of Banach spaces include $C[a,b]$ with norm defined by $||f - g||_{\sup} = \sup_{x \in [a,b]} |g(x) - f(x)|$ or $L^2[a,b]$ with norm defined by $||g - f||_{L_2} = \{\int_a^b [g(x) - f(x)]^2 dx\}^{1/2}$.

An **inner product** is a function defined on $V \times V :\to \mathbb{R}$ with the property that, for all $x, y, z \in V$ and all $\alpha, \beta \in \mathbb{R}$,

  (i) $(\alpha x + \beta y, z) = \alpha(x, z) + \beta(y, z)$.

  (ii) $(x, y) = (y, x)$.

  (iii) $(x, x) = ||x||^2$.

Definition A.27 (Hilbert Space). *A **Hilbert space** is a Banach space in which the norm is defined via an inner product.*

Example A.8. *For example, $L^2[0,1]$ is a Hilbert space with inner product defined by $(g, f) = \int f(x)g(x)dx$, and the L_2-norm $||f - g||_{L_2} = \{(f - g, f - g)\}^{1/2}$. However, $C[a, b]$ with norm defined by $||g - f||_{\sup} = \sup_{x \in [a,b]} |g(x) - f(x)|$ is not a Hilbert space as there does not exist an inner product that can produce the sup-norm: $|| \cdot ||_{\sup}$.*

Definition A.28 (Orthonormal Basis). *Let $\mathcal{H}$ denote a Hilbert space, and let $e_1, e_2, \ldots$, be elements in $\mathcal{H}$ and let $(.,.)$ denote the inner product. We say that $\{e_j\}_{j=1}^\infty$ is a complete (countable) basis of $\mathcal{H}$ if for all $g \in \mathcal{H}$, we have*

$$g = \sum_{j=1}^\infty c_j e_j, \qquad (A.7)$$

where the c_j's are some constants.

*If $(e_i, e_j) = \delta_{ij}$ for all $i, j \in \mathbb{N}_+$ ($\delta_{ij} = 1$ if $i = j$ and 0 if $i \neq j$), we say that $\{e_i\}_{i=1}^\infty$ is an **orthonormal basis**.*

If $\{e_j\}$ is an orthonormal basis, then it is easy to show that $c_j = (e_j, g)$ in (A.7).

Note that we discuss only the case where the Hilbert space has a *countable* (complete) basis. In general, a Hilbert space may have an uncountable basis. However, in most applied scenarios, one encounters the former case only.

Definition A.29 (Parseval's Equality). *Letting $\{e_j\}_{j=1}^{\infty}$ be a complete basis of $\mathcal{H}$ (a Hilbert space), then for all $g \in \mathcal{H}$, we have*

$$||g||^2 \stackrel{\text{def}}{=} (g, g) = \sum_{j=1}^{\infty} (g, e_j)^2. \tag{A.8}$$

For example, letting $L^2[-\pi, \pi]$ denote the bounded continuous and square integrable functions on $[-\pi, \pi]$, then the sequence $\{1/\sqrt{2\pi}, \sin(\pi x)/\pi, \cos(\pi x)/\pi, \sin(2\pi x)/\pi, \cos(2\pi x)/\pi, \ldots\}$ forms a complete orthonormal basis for $\mathcal{H}$ (see Exercise A.10).

Another example of an orthonormal basis in $L^2[-1, 1]$ is the *Legendre polynomial* $P_n(x)$ (i.e., an orthonormal polynomial in $[-1, 1]$), which is defined by

$$P_n(x) = \frac{(2n+1)^{1/2}}{2^{n+1/2}n!} \frac{d^n}{dx^n} (x^2 - 1)^n \text{ for } n = 0, 1, 2, \ldots \tag{A.9}$$

Example A.9. $P_0(x) = 1/2$, $P_1(x) = \sqrt{3/2}x$, $P_2(x) = (3/2)\sqrt{5/2}(x^2 - 1/3)$, *and so on. It can be shown that $\int_{-1}^{1} P_j(x)P_l(x) = 0$ for $j \neq l$. It can also be shown that $\int_{-1}^{1} P_n^2(x)dx = 1$ so that $\{P_j(x)\}_{j=0}^{\infty}$ forms an orthonormal basis for $L^1[-1, 1]$.*

Definition A.30 (Bessel's Inequality). *Let $\{v_j\}_{j=1}^{\infty}$ be an orthonormal sequence in $\mathcal{H}$ (a Hilbert space). Then for any $g \in \mathcal{H}$, we have*

$$\sum_{j=1}^{\infty} (g, v_j)^2 \leq ||g||^2. \tag{A.10}$$

Definition A.31 (Sobolev Norm). *For differentiable functions defined on $[a, b]$, the (first order) **Sobolev norm** is defined by*

$$||f||_H = \left\{ \int_a^b f(x)^2 dx + \int_a^b \left(\frac{df}{dx}\right)^2 dx \right\}^{1/2}.$$

For multivariate functions ($f(x)$, $x \in \mathbb{R}^q$) that are p^{th} order differentiable, the Sobolev norm is defined as

$$\|f\|_{H^p} = \left\{ \sum_{0 \leq p_1 + \cdots + p_q \leq p} \int_a^b \left[\frac{\partial f(x)}{\partial x_1^{p_1} \ldots \partial x_q^{p_q}} \right]^2 dx \right\}^{1/2}.$$

Definition A.32 (Metric Space). *A **metric space** $\{X, \rho\}$ is a nonempty set X of elements together with a real valued function ρ defined on $X \times X$ such that for all x, y and z in X,*

(i) $\rho(x, y) \geq 0$.

(ii) $\rho(x, y) = 0$ if and only if $x = y$.

(iii) $\rho(x, y) = \rho(y, x)$.

(iv) $\rho(x, y) \leq \rho(x, z) + \rho(z, y)$.

*The function $\rho(\cdot, \cdot)$ is called a **metric**.*

The concept of metric is a generalization of distance. A simple example of a metric space is the set $\mathbb{R}^q$ of all numbers with $\rho(x, y) = \|x - y\| = \sqrt{x_1^2 + \cdots + x_q^2}$ ($\|.\|$ is the Euclidean norm). In fact, for any normed space (with norm $\|\cdot\|$) one can define a metric by $\rho(x, y) = \|x - y\|$, and this metric is said to be induced by the norm $\|\cdot\|$. When we remove condition (ii) in the definition of a metric space, i.e., when we allow for the possibility that $\rho(x, y) = 0$ for some $x \neq y$, then ρ is called a **pseudometric**. For example the space L^p with metric defined by $\rho(f, g) = \{\int |f(x) - g(x)|^p dx\}^{1/p}$ is a pseudometric defined in L^p. However, if we treat $f = g$ a.e. as $f = g$, then L^p becomes a metric space.

Definition A.33 (Open Set). *A set B in a metric space (X, ρ) is called **open** (an open set) if for every $x \in A$, there is a $\delta > 0$ such that each y with $\rho(y, x) < \delta$ belongs to A.*

Definition A.34 (Closure). *An element x is called a point of **closure** of a set B if for every $\delta > 0$ there is a $y \in B$ such that $\rho(y, x) < \delta$. We use $\bar{B}$ to denote the closure of B. Obviously, $B \subset \bar{B}$.*

Definition A.35 (Closed Set). *A set B in (X, ρ) is called **closed** (a closed set) if $B = \bar{B}$.*

For example, for the real line $\mathbb{R}$ with $\rho(x, y) = |x - y|$, we have $A = (0, 1)$ is an open set, and the closure of A: $\bar{A} = [0, 1]$ is a closed set.

Definition A.36 (Dense). *Let B be a closed set in a metric space (with metric ρ). A set $A \subset B$ is said to be **dense** in B if, for all (small) $\epsilon > 0$, and for every $x \in B$, there is a $y \in A$, such that $\rho(x, y) < \epsilon$.*[1]

For example, the set of rational numbers is dense in the set of real numbers (with $\rho(x, y) = |x - y|$). Also, $C^1[a, b]$ is dense in $C[a, b]$ with the metric induced by the L_2-norm (metric), i.e., $\rho(f, g) = \{\int_a^b [f(x) - g(x)]^2 dx\}^{1/2}$.

Definition A.37 (Absolutely Continuous). *A measure ν is said to be **absolutely continuous** with respect to a measure μ, if for any set $A \in \Omega$, $\mu(A) = 0$ implies that $\nu(A) = 0$.*

Letting $f(\cdot)$ be a nonnegative Borel measurable function, one can define the set function given by

$$\lambda(A) = \int_A f \, d\nu, \ A \in \mathcal{B},$$

which is a measure on $(\Omega, \mathcal{F})$. It can be shown that $\nu(A) = 0$ implies $\lambda(A) = 0$. Thus, λ is absolutely continuous with respect to ν. $f(\cdot)$ is called the **Radon-Nikodym derivative or density** of λ with respect to ν and is denoted by $f = d\lambda/d\nu$.

Example A.10. *Letting $f(\cdot)$ be a PDF, then the corresponding CDF is defined by $F(x) = \int_{(-\infty, x]} f(u) du$, and we know that $dF(x)/dx = f(x)$, that is, $f(\cdot)$ (a PDF) is the Radon-Nikodym derivative or density of $F(\cdot)$, while $F(\cdot)$ is a probability measure. Here $dx = d\nu$, where ν is the Lebesgue measure, and if $f(\cdot)$ is a measurable (say, continuous) function, then $F(\cdot)$ is absolutely continuous with respect to the Lebesgue measure.*

Note that if a CDF $F(x)$ has discontinuity points, as is the case for discrete random variables, then it is *not* absolutely continuous with respect to Lebesgue measure.

Absolutely continuous is weaker than differentiable, but stronger than continuous (for $F(\cdot)$).

---

[1]Usually, "A is dense in B" is defined as the closure of A equals B without using a distance (metric) concept; see Royden (1988, p. 142). Here we give an equivalent definition of "dense" in a metric space.

Definition A.38 (Standard Brownian Motion (or Weiner Process)). *We call a q-dimensional stochastic process $W(t)$ defined on $[0,1]$ a q-dimensional* **standard Brownian motion** *if*

(i) $P[W(0) = 0] = 1.$

(ii) $W(t_1) - W(t_0),\ W(t_2) - W(t_1),\ \ldots,\ W(t_n) - W(t_{n-1})$ *are independent for any positive integer n and the time partition* $0 \leq t_0 < t_1 < \cdots < t_n \leq 1.$

(iii) $W(t) - W(s) \sim N(0, (t-s)I_q)$ *for* $0 \leq s < t \leq 1.$

Definition A.39 (Gaussian Process). *A stochastic process $Z(\cdot)$ (or $Z(x)$, indexed by x, where x belongs to a compact set in $\mathbb{R}^q$) is called a* **Gaussian process** *if each of its finite-dimensional marginals $(Z(x_1), \ldots, Z(x_m))$ has a multivariate normal distribution on the Euclidean space $\mathbb{R}^m$.*

Note that $W(t)$ is a zero mean nonstationary Gaussian process with independent increments and a covariance structure $\mathrm{cov}(W(s), W(t)) = \min(s,t)I_q$. It is known that the sample path of $W(t)$ is continuous with probability 1, while it is nowhere differentiable on any interval subset of $[0,1]$.

Let $X(t)$ be a stochastic process that satisfies the following (Ito) stochastic differential equation:

$$dX(t) = \mu(X(t), t)dt + \sigma(X(t), t)dW(t), \quad 0 \leq t \leq 1. \qquad (A.11)$$

Lemma A.1 (Ito's lemma). *Letting $g(x,t)$ be a continuous function on $(-\infty, \infty) \times [0,1]$ (and assuming that some additional regularity conditions hold; see Tanaka (1996, p. 58)), then $g(x,t)$ satisfies the stochastic differential equation $(X_t \equiv X(t))$*

$$dg(X_t, t) = \frac{\partial g}{\partial X_t} dX_t + \left(\frac{\partial g}{\partial t} + \frac{1}{2} \frac{\partial g^2}{\partial X_t^2} \sigma^2(X_t, t) \right) dt. \qquad (A.12)$$

Replacing dX_t in (A.12) by (A.11), we obtain

$$dg(X_t, t) = \left[\frac{\partial g}{\partial t} + \frac{\partial g}{\partial X_t} \mu(X_t, t) + \frac{1}{2} \frac{\partial^2 g}{\partial X_t^2} \sigma^2(X_t, t) \right] dt$$

$$+ \frac{\partial g}{\partial X_t} \sigma(X_t, t) dW_t, \qquad (A.13)$$

Now, if $g(x,t) = \mu(x)$ and $\sigma^2(x,t) = \sigma^2(x)$ are both time-homogeneous processes, then (A.13) simplifies to

$$d\mu(x) = \mu(x)\mu^{(1)}(x)dt + \frac{1}{2}\mu^{(2)}(x)\sigma^2(x)dt + \mu^{(1)}(x)\sigma(x)dW_t. \quad (A.14)$$

Definition A.40 (Dirac delta Function). *The* **Dirac delta function** *is denoted by $\delta(x)$ and has the following properties ($x \in \mathbb{R}^q$):*

(i) $\delta(x) = 0$ for $x \neq 0$.

(ii) $\delta(0) = \infty$.

(iii) $\int_{-\infty}^{\infty} \delta(x)dx = 1$.

It can be shown that for any measurable function $g(x)$ we have

$$\int_{-\infty}^{\infty} \delta(x)g(x)dx = g(0).$$

Similarly, for any real number a, we have (see Exercise A.11)

$$\int_{-\infty}^{\infty} \delta(x-a)g(x)dx = g(a).$$

There are many (equivalent) expressions for the Dirac delta function. It can be show that (both $t, x \in \mathbb{R}^q$)

$$\delta(x) = \frac{1}{2\pi} \int_{-\infty}^{\infty} e^{it'x}dx. \quad (A.15)$$

One can also define the Dirac delta function as the derivative of a step function. Consider the step function $\mathbf{1}(x \geq 0)$, which equals 0 for $x < 0$ and equals 1 for $x \geq 1$. This function is discontinuous at 0; therefore, it is not differentiable at $x = 0$ in the usual sense. However, one can say that it has derivative 0 for all $x \neq 0$ and it has an infinite derivative at $x = 0$, which implies that the derivative of $\mathbf{1}(x \geq 0)$ is a Dirac delta function, i.e., $d\mathbf{1}(x \geq 0)/dx = \delta(x)$.

One can, therefore, use the Dirac delta function to define a PDF for a discrete random variable. Consider the case of the empirical CDF defined by $F_n(x) = n^{-1}\sum_{i=1}^{n} \mathbf{1}(X_i \leq x)$. The corresponding empirical PDF can be defined as $f_n(x) = dF_n(x)/dx = n^{-1}\sum_{i=1}^{n} \delta(X_i - x)$. Then we have $\int_{-\infty}^{x} f_n(v)dv = n^{-1}\sum_{i=1}^{n} \int_{-\infty}^{x} \delta(X_i - v)dv = n^{-1}\sum_{i=1}^{n} \mathbf{1}(X_i \leq$

x), which is exactly $F_n(x)$. Using this empirical PDF, it is easy to show that for any measurable function $g(x)$ we have

$$\int_{-\infty}^{\infty} g(x) dF_n(x) = \int_{-\infty}^{\infty} g(x) f_n(x) dx$$

$$= n^{-1} \sum_{i=1}^{n} \int g(x) \delta(X_i - x) dx = n^{-1} \sum_{i=1}^{n} g(X_i).$$

1.3   Limits and Modes of Convergence

1.3.1   Limit Supremum and Limit Infimum

Definition A.41 (Upper and Lower Bound). *A number b is said to be an* **upper bound** *of a set A if $b \geq x$ for all $x \in A$. A number c is said to be the* **least upper bound** *of a set A (denoted by $\sup A$), if c is an upper bound of A and $c \leq b$ for each upper bound b of A. Further, $\sup A$ is the maximum element of A if the maximum element exists; for example, if $A = [0, 1]$, then $\sup A = \max A = 1$. However, for $B = (0, 1)$, $\sup B = 1$ and $\max B$ does not exist because $1 \notin B$ ("$\sup$" means supremum).*

The **greatest lower bound** *of a set A: $\inf A$ is similarly defined. For the above example of $A = [0, 1]$, $\inf A = \min A = 0$, and for $B = (0, 1)$, $\inf B = 0$ and $\min B$ does not exist.*

Definition A.42 (Limit Supremum and Limit Infimum). *Let $\{a_n\}_{n=1}^{\infty}$ be a sequence of real numbers. For any positive integer k, letting $\beta_k = \sup\{a_k, a_{k+1}, \dots, \}$, which is obviously nonincreasing, and letting $\alpha_k = \inf\{a_k, a_{k+1}, \dots, \}$, then $\{\alpha_k\}$ is a nondecreasing sequence. If a_n is a bounded sequence, then both $\lim_{k \to \infty} \beta_k$ and $\lim_{k \to \infty} \alpha_k$ exist (bounded monotone sequences must convergence). They are called the* **limit supremum** *(superior) of a_n and the* **limit infimum** *(inferior) of a_n, respectively, and are denoted by*

$$\overline{\lim}_{n \to \infty} a_n \equiv \limsup a_n \overset{\text{def}}{=} \lim_{k \to \infty} \sup_{n \geq k} a_n \; \text{and}$$

$$\underline{\lim}_{n \to \infty} a_n \equiv \liminf a_n \overset{\text{def}}{=} \lim_{k \to \infty} \inf_{n \geq k} a_n,$$

respectively.

It can be shown that $\limsup a_n = \inf_n \sup_{k \geq n} a_k$, which is more intuitive as the least upper bound of $\{a_n\}$. Similarly, $\liminf a_n = \sup_n \inf_{k \geq n} a_k$.

Obviously, $\limsup a_n \geq \liminf a_n$, and the limit of a_n exists if and only if $\limsup a_n = \liminf a_n$ $(= \lim_{n \to \infty} a_n)$.

For example, if $a_n = (-1)^n = \{-1, 1, -1, 1, \dots\}$, then $\limsup a_n = 1$ and $\liminf a_n = -1$ and $\lim_{n \to \infty} a_n$ does not exist.

If $\lim_{n \to \infty} a_n$ does not exist, then $\{a_n\}_{n=1}^{\infty}$ usually has several convergent subsequences. If they converge to different values (as the above example shows), then $\limsup a_n$ equals the largest of them, and $\liminf a_n$ equals the smallest. In the limit as $n \to \infty$, or for sufficiently large values of n, a_n essentially takes values between these two limiting values.

For a general set $\{A_n\}_{n=1}^{\infty}$, $\limsup A_n$ is defined as follows: $x \in \limsup_n A_n$ if and only if $x \in A_n$ for infinite many n. Then $\liminf A_n$ is defined as $x \in \liminf_n A_n$ if and only if $x \in A_n$ for all n except perhaps for finitely many exceptions, i.e., there exist a fixed positive integer n_0 such that $x \in A_n$ for all $n \geq n_0$. Obviously, $\liminf A_n \subset \limsup A_n$.

It can be shown that

$$\limsup A_n = \cap_{n=1}^{\infty} \cup_{k=n}^{\infty} A_k \text{ and}$$
$$\liminf A_n = \cup_{n=1}^{\infty} \cap_{k=n}^{\infty} A_k.$$

In words, $x \in \limsup A_n$ if and only if, for all $n = 1, 2, \dots$ there exists a $k \geq n$ such that $x \in A_k$. Similarly, $x \in \liminf A_n$ if and only if there exists a positive integer n such that $x \in A_k$ for all $k \geq n$.

For example, defining $A_n = [0, 2]$ for $n = 1, 3, 5, \dots$, and $A_n = [0, 1]$ for $n = 2, 4, 6, \dots$, then $\limsup A_n = [0, 2]$ and $\liminf A_n = [0, 1]$.

1.3.2   Modes of Convergence

In order to define various modes of convergence, we first introduce the concept of the "Euclidean length" ("Euclidean norm") of a vector. Given a $q \times 1$ vector $x = (x_1, x_2, \dots, x_q)' \in \mathbb{R}^q$, we use $||x||$ to denote the Euclidean length of x defined as

$$||x|| = [x'x]^{1/2} \equiv \sqrt{x_1^2 + x_2^2 + \cdots + x_q^2}.$$

When $q = 1$ (a scalar), $||x||$ is simply the absolute value of x.

Definition A.43 (Convergence in Probability). *Let $\{X_n\}_{n=1}^{\infty}$ be a sequence of real random variables (possibly a finite dimensional vector or matrix-valued), and let X be a random variable having the same* *dimension as* $\mathcal{X}_n$. *We say that* $\mathcal{X}_n$ *converges to* X *in probability if, for every (small)* $\epsilon > 0$,

$$\lim_{n \to \infty} P(|\mathcal{X}_n - X| < \epsilon) = 1.$$

We use $\mathcal{X}_n \xrightarrow{p} X$ to indicate that $\mathcal{X}_n$ converges to X in probability.

Definition A.44 (Convergence in r^{th} Mean). *We say that* $\mathcal{X}_n$ *converges to* X *in the* r^{th} *mean if, for some* $r > 0$,

$$\lim_{n \to \infty} E\left[||\mathcal{X}_n - X||^r\right] = 0.$$

We use $\mathcal{X}_n \xrightarrow{rth} X$ to indicate convergence in the rth mean.

When $r = 2$, we also say that $\mathcal{X}_n$ converges to X in mean square error (MSE).

Definition A.45 (Convergence in Distribution). *We say that* $\mathcal{X}_n$ *converges to* X *in distribution, denoted by* $\mathcal{X}_n \xrightarrow{d} X$, *if*

$$\lim_{n \to \infty} F_n(x) = F(x),$$

for all continuous points of $F(x)$, *where* $F_n(x)$ *and* $F(x)$ *are the CDFs of* $\mathcal{X}_n$ *and* X, *respectively.*

Definition A.46 (Convergence Almost Surely). *We say that* $\mathcal{X}_n$ *converges to* X *almost surely (a.s.) (or with probability 1, almost everywhere (a.e.), or strongly), if*

$$P\left(\lim_{n \to \infty} \mathcal{X}_n = X\right) = 1$$

(see Serfling (1980, p. 6)).

    While we often use the concept of convergence in probability in this text, we point out that we rarely use Definition A.43 to evaluate the probability limit of a random variable. This is simply because computing the limiting MSE (or the rth mean in general) of a random variable is usually much easier than computing the probability limit of the random variable, and given Theorem A.3 below, convergence in MSE (or in the rth mean) implies convergence in probability. In practice, therefore, we resort to the simplest approach, convergence in the rth mean, when evaluating the probability limit of a random variable.

Theorem A.3. *If $\mathcal{X}_n \overset{rth}{\to} X$ (in the rth mean), then $\mathcal{X}_n \overset{p}{\to} X$.*

Proof. This follows by using Chebychev's inequality. For any $\epsilon > 0$, we have

$$P(\|X_n - X\| > \epsilon) \leq \frac{1}{\epsilon^r} E\left[\|X_n - X\|^r\right] \to 0$$

by the assumption that $X_n \to X$ in the rth mean. □

We emphasize that Theorem A.3 will be used most often, and only cases involving $r = 1$ and $r = 2$ will be used in this text. We provide an example below which illustrates how, by using Theorem A.3, the computation of probability limits can actually be fairly straightforward.

Example A.11.

(i) *Let Y_n be a sequence of i.i.d. random variables having zero mean and finite variance (say, i.i.d. $N(0,1)$). Define $\mathcal{X}_n = Y_n/n$. Find the MSE and probability limit of $\mathcal{X}_n$.*

Proof. $E(\mathcal{X}_n^2) = E(Y_n^2)/n^2 = 1/n^2 \to 0$ as $n \to \infty$. Thus $\mathcal{X}_n \to 0$ in MSE. By Theorem A.3 (with $r = 2$), we know that $\mathcal{X}_n \overset{p}{\to} 0$. □

(ii) *Let $X_1, \ldots, X_n$ be i.i.d. with mean μ and finite variance σ^2. Find the probability limit of $\bar{X}_n = \frac{1}{n}\sum_{i=1}^n X_i$.*

Proof. First, it makes intuitive sense to conjecture that the limit is the population mean μ. We verify this by computing $E[(\bar{X}_n - \mu)^2] = \frac{1}{n^2}\sum_{i=1}^n \sum_{j=1}^n E[(X_i - \mu)(X_j - \mu)] = \frac{1}{n^2}\{\sum_{i=1}^n E[(X_i - \mu)^2] + 0\} = \sigma^2/n \to 0$ as $n \to \infty$, where we used the fact that $\text{cov}(X_i, X_j) = 0$ since X_i and X_j are independent of one another for $i \neq j$. Thus $\bar{X}_n \overset{\text{MSE}}{\to} \mu$, and by Theorem A.3 $\bar{X}_n \overset{p}{\to} \mu$. □

Theorem A.4.

(i) *If $X_n \overset{d}{\to} X$, and $g(\cdot)$ is a bounded and continuous function, then $\int g\, dF_n \to \int g\, dF$ in distribution.*

(ii) *If $X_n \overset{d}{\to} X$, $Y_n \overset{p}{\to} c$, and $g(\cdot)$ is a continuous function, then $g(X_n, Y_n) \overset{d}{\to} g(X, c)$.*

The next theorem provides the relationship between convergence in probability and convergence in distribution.

Theorem A.5. *If $\mathcal{X}_n \overset{p}{\to} X$, then $\mathcal{X}_n \overset{d}{\to} X$.*

Proof. See Serfling (1980, p. 19). □

Note that the converse of Theorems A.3 and A.5 may not hold (see Serfling (1980) for some counterexamples).

In the following theorem we provide some useful properties regarding convergence in probability and convergence in distribution. These results are used frequently throughout this text.

Theorem A.6. *If $\mathcal{X}_n \overset{d}{\to} X$ and $\mathcal{Y}_n \overset{p}{\to} c$, where c is a constant, then*

(i) $\mathcal{X}_n + \mathcal{Y}_n \overset{d}{\to} X + c$.

(ii) $\mathcal{X}_n \mathcal{Y}_n \overset{d}{\to} cX$.

(iii) $\mathcal{X}_n / \mathcal{Y}_n \overset{d}{\to} X/c$ *(provided $c \neq 0$).*

Proof. See Serfling (1980, p. 19). □

The above properties are similar to the properties of ordinary limits. The proof of (i) under somewhat stronger conditions is left as an exercise (see Exercise A.4).

Definition A.47 (Order: Big $O(\cdot)$ and Small $o(\cdot)$). *For a positive integer n, we write $a_n = O(1)$ if, as $n \to \infty$, a_n remains bounded, i.e., $|a_n| \leq C$ for some constant C and for all large values of n (a_n is a bounded sequence).*

We write $a_n = o(1)$ if $a_n \to 0$ as $n \to \infty$.

Similarly, we write $a_n = O(b_n)$ if $a_n/b_n = O(1)$, or equivalently $a_n \leq Cb_n$ for some constant C and for all n sufficiently large.

We write $a_n = o(b_n)$ if $(a_n/b_n) \to 0$ as $n \to \infty$.

In the example below and the preceding chapters, when we say something holds for all n, we mean for all $n \in \mathbb{N}_+ = \{1, 2, \dots\}$, where we use $\mathbb{N}_+$ to denote the set of positive integers.

Example A.12.

(i) If $a_n = n/(n+1)$, then $a_n = O(1)$ since $a_n \leq 1$ for all n.

(ii) If $a_n = 10/(n+1)$, then $a_n = o(1)$ because $a_n \to 0$ as $n \to \infty$.

(iii) If $a_n = n + 5$, $b_n = n$, then $a_n = O(b_n)$ because $a_n \leq 2b_n$ for $n \geq 5$, or $a_n \leq 5b_n$ for all n.

(iv) If $a_n = 1/n$ and $b_n = 1/n^2$, then $b_n = o(a_n)$ because $b_n/a_n = (1/n) \to 0$.

Definition A.48 (Order in Probability: Big $O_p(\cdot)$ and Small $o_p(\cdot)$). *A sequence of real (possibly vector-valued) random variables $\{X_n\}_{n=1}^{\infty}$ is said to be bounded in probability if, for every $\epsilon > 0$, there exists a constant M and a positive integer N (usually $M = M_\epsilon$ and $N = N_\epsilon$), such that*

$$\mathrm{P}\left[||X_n|| > M\right] \leq \epsilon \qquad (A.16)$$

for all $n \geq N$. That is, we say that X_n is bounded in probability if, for any arbitrarily small positive number ϵ, we can always find a positive constant M such that the probability of the absolute value (or norm) of X_n being larger than M is less than ϵ.

Obviously, if $X_n = O(1)$ (bounded), then $X_n = O_p(1)$; however the converse is not true. Letting $\{X_n\}_{n=1}^{\infty}$ denote i.i.d. random draws from an $N(0,1)$ distribution, then $X_n \neq O(1)$, however, $X_n = O_p(1)$. In fact any random variable having a well-defined CDF is an $O_p(1)$ variable (see Exercise A.5).

Equation (A.16) can be equivalently written as

$$\mathrm{P}\left[||X_n|| \leq M\right] > 1 - \epsilon \qquad (A.17)$$

for all $n \geq N$.

We write $X_n = O_p(1)$ to indicate that X_n is bounded in probability.

We write $X_n = o_p(1)$ if $X_n \xrightarrow{p} 0$.

Similarly, we write $X_n = O_p(Y_n)$ if $(X_n/Y_n) = O_p(1)$, and $X_n = o_p(Y_n)$ if $(X_n/Y_n) = o_p(1)$.

Note that if $X_n = o_p(1)$, then it must be true that $X_n = O_p(1)$. However, when $X_n = O_p(1)$, X_n may not be $o_p(1)$.

As was the case when we obtained the probability limit of a random variable by computing its limiting MSE (or r^{th} mean), we can also evaluate the order in probability of a random variable by calculating the order of its second moment (or the order of its rth mean) as the next theorem shows.

Theorem A.7. *Let* $\{\mathcal{X}_n\}_{n=1}^{\infty}$ *be a sequence of real (possibly vector-valued) random variables, and let* a_n *and* b_n *be sequences of some non-stochastic, nonnegative numbers. Then*

(i) If $\mathrm{E}\|\mathcal{X}_n\| = O(a_n)$, *then* $\mathcal{X}_n = O_p(a_n)$.

(ii) If $\mathrm{E}\left[\|\mathcal{X}_n\|^2\right] = O(b_n)$, *then* $\mathcal{X}_n = O_p\left(b_n^{1/2}\right)$.

Proof of (i). From $\mathrm{E}\|\mathcal{X}_n\| = O(a_n)$ we know that $\mathrm{E}\|\mathcal{X}_n/a_n\| \leq M_0$ for some $M_0 > 0$. For any $\epsilon > 0$, choose $M = M_0/\epsilon$ (a finite positive constant). Then by Markov's inequality (see (A.24)) we have $\mathrm{P}\left(\|\mathcal{X}_n/a_n\| > M\right) \leq E\|\mathcal{X}_n/a_n\|/M \leq \epsilon$, which means $\|\mathcal{X}_n/a_n\| = O_p(1)$ or $\|\mathcal{X}_n\| = O_p(a_n)$. $\qquad\square$

Proof of (ii). The proof of (ii) follows in a similar fashion and is left as an exercise (see Exercise A.6). $\qquad\square$

Example A.13.

(i) *For any sequence of random variables* $\{\mathcal{X}_n\}_{n=1}^{\infty}$, *if* $\mathrm{E}|\mathcal{X}_n| \leq C < \infty$ *for all* n, *or if* $\mathrm{E}[|\mathcal{X}_n|^2] \leq C < \infty$ *for all* n, *then* $\mathcal{X}_n = O_p(1)$ *(this follows directly from Theorem A.7).*

(ii) *Letting* $\mathcal{X}_n$ *be a sequence of random variables with* $\mathrm{E}(\mathcal{X}_n) = o(1)$ *and* $\mathrm{var}(\mathcal{X}_n) = o(1)$, *then* $\mathcal{X}_n = o_p(1)$. *This follows from the fact that* $\mathrm{E}[\|\mathcal{X}_n\|^2] = \mathrm{tr}\{\mathrm{E}[\mathcal{X}_n\mathcal{X}_n']\} = \mathrm{E}(\mathcal{X}_n')\mathrm{E}(\mathcal{X}_n) + \mathrm{tr}\{\mathrm{var}(\mathcal{X}_n)\} = o(1)$ *and from Theorem A.7 (ii).*

Definition A.49 (Stochastic Equicontinuity). *Letting* $J_n(b)$ *denote a stochastic process indexed by* $b \in B$, *where* B *is a compact (closed and bounded) subset of* $\mathbb{R}^q$, *we say that* $J_n(b)$ *is stochastically equicontinuous for* $b \in B$ *if for all* $\epsilon > 0$, *we have*

$$\lim_{\delta \to 0} \limsup_{n \to \infty} \mathrm{P}\left[\sup_{b,b' \in B, \rho(b,b')<\delta} \left|J_n(b) - J_n(b')\right| > \epsilon\right] = 0, \qquad (A.18)$$

where $\rho(.,.)$ *is a metric, say* $\rho(b,b') = \|b - b'\|$, *the metric defined via the Euclidean norm.*

A simple sufficient condition for stochastic equicontinuity is given by the following theorem (assuming that the metric $\rho(x,y) = \|x - y\|$, the Euclidean norm).

Theorem A.8. *Let $J_n(b)$ be a stochastic process indexed by $b \in B$, where B is a compact subset of $\mathbb{R}^q$. If for all $b, b' \in B$ we have*

$$\mathrm{E}\left[\left|J_n(b') - J_n(b)\right|^\alpha\right] \leq C \left\|b - b'\right\|^\gamma, \qquad (A.19)$$

for some $\alpha > 0$, $\gamma > 1$ and C is a finite positive constant, then $J_n(b)$ is stochastically equicontinuous for $b \in B$.

Proof. It can be shown that (A.19) implies the following (see Exercise A.12).

For all $b, b', b'' \in B$,

$$\mathrm{E}\left[\left|J_n(b) - Jn(b')\right|^\beta \left|J_n(b) - J_n(b'')\right|^\beta\right] \leq C \left\|b'' - b'\right\|^\gamma \qquad (A.20)$$

for some $\beta > 0$, $\gamma > 1$, where C is a positive constant.

By Theorem 15.6 of Billingsley (1968, p. 128), we know that (A.20) is a sufficient condition that ensures that $J_n(b)$ is stochastically equicontinuous for $b \in B$. Hence, (A.19) implies that $J_n(b)$ is stochastically equicontinuous in $b \in B$. $\qquad \square$

In practice, when $J_n(\cdot)$ has mean zero, it is often convenient to choose $\alpha = 2$ and $\gamma = 2$ when applying (A.19).

Definition A.50 (Weak Convergence). *A sequence of (say, Banach-valued or Hilbert-valued) random elements $\mathcal{Z}_n(\cdot)$ converges weakly to $\mathcal{Z}(\cdot)$ if $\mathrm{E}[g(\mathcal{Z}_n)] \to \mathrm{E}[g(\mathcal{Z})]$ for all real-valued bounded continuous functions $g(\cdot)$.*

The expression "$\mathcal{Z}_n(\cdot)$ converges weakly to $\mathcal{Z}(\cdot)$" is also phrased as "$\mathcal{Z}_n(\cdot)$ converges in distribution to $\mathcal{Z}(\cdot)$" by some authors. One nonsmoothing test statistic that we considered in Chapter 13 is of the form $\mathcal{Z}_n(x) = n^{-1/2} \sum_{i=1}^n u_i \mathbf{1}(X_i \leq x)$ ($x \in \mathcal{S}$, $\mathcal{S}$ is a compact set, i.e., a closed and bounded set), where (X_i, u_i) is i.i.d. data with $\mathrm{E}(u_i|X_i) = 0$. $\mathcal{Z}_n(x)$ is a random process indexed by x (or a random element). If we define an L_2-norm by $\{\mathrm{E}[\|Z(\cdot)\|_\nu^2]\}^{1/2} = \{\mathrm{E}[\int_{\mathcal{S}} Z(x)^2 \nu(dx)]\}^{1/2}$, then $\mathcal{Z}_n(\cdot)$ is a Hilbert-valued random element. One can derive the asymptotic distribution of $\mathcal{Z}_n(\cdot)$ using the Hilbert-valued CLT as given in Section 1.4.

Definition A.51 (Continuous Mapping Theorem).

(i) *Let X_n be a sequence of random variables. If $g(\cdot)$ is a continuous function at every point of a Borel measurable set, and $X_n \to X$ in distribution (or in probability), then $g(X_n) \to g(X)$ in distribution (or in probability).*

(ii) *The continuous mapping theorem also holds true for random el-ements (random processes), where $X_n(\cdot)$ and $X(\cdot)$ are (Banach-valued or Hilbert-valued) random elements, and one replaces con-vergence in distribution above by weak convergence.*

1.4 Inequalities, Laws of Large Numbers, and Central Limit Theorems

Lemma A.2 (Khinchin's Law of Large Numbers). *If $X_1, \ldots, X_n$ are i.i.d. observations with mean $\mu < \infty$, then*

$$\bar{X}_n \equiv \frac{1}{n} \sum_{i=1}^{n} X_i \xrightarrow{p} \mathrm{E}\left[\frac{1}{n} \sum_{i=1}^{n} X_i\right] = \mathrm{E}(X_1) = \mu.$$

Proof. Note that the above lemma does not require that $\mathrm{var}(X_i)$ be finite. However, if $\mathrm{var}(X_i) = \sigma^2 < \infty$, then Example A.11 (ii) provides a proof of Lemma A.2. □

Lemma A.3 (Lindeberg-Levy Central Limit Theorem). *If $X_1, \ldots, X_n$ are i.i.d. observations with finite $\mu < \infty$ and variance σ^2 then*

$$\sqrt{n}\left\{\frac{1}{n} \sum_{i=1}^{n} (X_i - \mu)\right\} \equiv \frac{1}{\sqrt{n}} \sum_{i=1}^{n} (X_i - \mu) \xrightarrow{d} N(0, \sigma^2).$$

Proof. See Rao (1973, p. 127). □

Lemma A.4 (Lindeberg-Feller Central Limit Theorem). *Let $X_1, \ldots, X_n$ be independent observations with $\mathrm{E}(X_i) = \mu_i$, $\mathrm{var}(X_i) = \sigma_i^2$ and CDF $F_i(\cdot)$. Define $\bar{\sigma}_n = \left[n^{-1} \sum_{i=1}^{n} \sigma_i^2\right]^{1/2}$. If*

$$\lim_{n \to \infty}\left\{\max_{1 \le i \le n} \sigma_i / [\sqrt{n}\bar{\sigma}_n]\right\} = 0 \ and$$

$$\lim_{n \to \infty} \frac{1}{n\bar{\sigma}_n^2} \sum_{i=1}^{n} \int_{|x-\mu_i|>\epsilon\bar{\sigma}_n\sqrt{n}} (x - \mu_i)^2 dF_i(x) = 0, \ then$$

$$\frac{1}{\sqrt{n}\bar{\sigma}_n} \sum_{i=1}^{n} (X_i - \mu_i) \xrightarrow{d} N(0, 1).$$

Proof. See Rao (1973, p. 127). □

Lemma A.5 (Liapunov Central Limit Theorem). *Let $\{Z_{n,i}\}$ be a sequence of independent (double array) random variables such that $E(Z_{n,i}) = \mu_{n,i}$ and $\mathrm{var}(Z_{n,i}) = \sigma_{n,i}^2$, with $E|Z_{n,i}|^{2+\delta} < \infty$ for some $\delta > 0$. Let $S_n = \sum_{i=1}^n Z_{n,i}$, and let $\sigma_n^2 = \mathrm{var}(S_n) = \sum_{i=1}^n \sigma_{n,i}^2$. If $\sigma_n^2 = \sigma^2 + o(1)$ (σ^2 is a constant), and*

$$\lim_{n\to\infty} \sum_{i=1}^n E|(Z_{n,i} - \mu_{n,i})|^{2+\delta} = 0 \text{ for some } \delta > 0, \qquad (A.21)$$

then

$$\sigma_n^{-1}(S_n - E(S_n)) = \sigma_n^{-1} \sum_{i=1}^n [Z_{n,i} - E(Z_{n,i})] \xrightarrow{d} N(0,1). \qquad (A.22)$$

Lemma A.6 (Cramer-Wold Theorem). *The sequence of random vectors $\{X_n\}$, $X_n = \{X_{1n}, \ldots, X_{qn}\} \in \mathbb{R}^q$, converges in distribution to the random vector X with CDF $F(\cdot)$ if, for any real vector of constants $\lambda = (\lambda_1, \ldots, \lambda_q')$,*

$$\lambda' X_n \xrightarrow{d} \lambda' X.$$

The Cramer-Wold theorem can be used to derive the asymptotic distribution of a sequence of random vectors $X_n \in \mathbb{R}^q$ through studying a scalar sequence of random variables $\lambda' X_n$ as the follow corollary shows.

Corollary A.1. *If for all vectors $\lambda \in \mathbb{R}^q$, $\lambda' X_n \xrightarrow{d} \lambda' X \sim N(\lambda'\mu, \lambda'\Omega\lambda)$, then $X_n \xrightarrow{d} N(\mu, \Omega)$.*

Proof. This follows from Lemma A.6 directly. $\square$

Lemma A.7 (Borel-Cantelli lemma). *Let X_n be a sequence of random variables, and let a_n be a sequence of nonnegative numbers. If $\sum_{n=1}^\infty P(|X_n| > a_n)$ is finite, then*

$$X_n \leq a_n \text{ almost surely, or } X_n = O(a_n) \text{ almost surely.}$$

Lemma A.8 (Markov Inequality). *Suppose that $\phi\colon \mathbb{R}^q \to \mathbb{R}$, and that $\phi(x) \geq 0$ for all $x \in \mathbb{R}^q$. Letting $A \subset \mathbb{R}^q$ be a subset of $\mathbb{R}^q$, and defining $\phi_A = \inf_{x\in A} \phi(x)$, then*

$$\phi_A P(X \in A) \leq E[\phi(X)]. \qquad (A.23)$$

Proof.

$$\mathrm{E}[\phi(X)] = \int f(x)\phi(x)dx \geq \int_A f(x)\phi(x)dx \geq \phi_A \int_A f(x)dx$$
$$= \phi_A \mathrm{P}(X \in A).$$

$\square$

Note that when $x \in \mathbb{R}$, $\phi(x) = |x|^k$ and $A = \{x : |x| \geq \alpha\}$ $(\alpha > 0)$, then we have $\phi_A = \alpha^k$, $\mathrm{P}(X \in A) = \mathrm{P}(|X| \geq \alpha)$ and $\mathrm{E}[\phi(X)] = \mathrm{E}[|X|^k]$. Then (A.23) becomes

$$\mathrm{P}(|X| \geq \alpha) \leq \mathrm{E}[|X|^k]/\alpha^k. \tag{A.24}$$

Many textbooks refer to (A.24) as the "Markov inequality."

Note that when we choose $\phi(x) = \exp(ax)$ and $A = \{x : x > c\}$ $(a > 0, c > 0)$, then $\phi_A = \exp(ax)$, $\mathrm{P}(X \in A) = \mathrm{P}(X > c)$ and $\mathrm{E}[\phi(X)] = \mathrm{E}[\exp(aX)]$. By Markov's inequality we have

$$\mathrm{P}(|X| \geq c) \leq \mathrm{E}[\exp(aX)]/\exp(ac). \tag{A.25}$$

This is (1.55) used in the proof of Theorem 1.4.

Lemma A.9 (Chebychev's Inequality). *Let $g(x)$ be a positive Borel measurable function on $\mathbb{R}$ that is monotonically increasing on $(0, \infty)$ for which $g(x) = g(-x)$. Then for every random variable X on $\mathbb{R}$ and $\epsilon > 0$ we have*

$$\mathrm{P}[|X| > \epsilon] \leq \mathrm{E}[g(X)]/g(\epsilon).$$

When $g(X) = |X|^k$ $(k > 0)$, we have $\mathrm{P}[|X| > \epsilon] \leq \mathrm{E}(|X|^k)/\epsilon^k$.

Lemma A.10 (Hölder's Inequality). *Let X_1 and X_2 be two random variables. Then for $p > 1$ and $(1/p) + (1/q) = 1$,*

$$\mathrm{E}[|X_1 X_2|] \leq \{E|X_1|^p\}^{1/p}\{E|X_2|^q\}^{1/q}.$$

For $p = q = 2$ we obtain the well-known Cauchy (or Cauchy-Schwarz) inequality.

Lemma A.11 (Law of Iterated Expectations). *Let X and Y be two random variables, and let $\mathrm{E}(XY)$ be finite (and well defined). Then*

$$\mathrm{E}[XY] = \mathrm{E}[X\mathrm{E}(Y|X)].$$

Lemma A.12 (Convergence in r^{th} Mean). *If (i) $X_n \xrightarrow{p} X$ or $X_n \xrightarrow{d} X$, and (ii) $\{X_n^r\}$ is uniformly integrable, then*

$$\mathrm{E}[X_n^r] \to \mathrm{E}[X^r] \text{ and } E|X_n|^r \to E|X|^r.$$

A sufficient condition for X_n^r to be uniformly integrable is

$$\sup_n E|X_n|^{r+\epsilon} < \infty \text{ for some } \epsilon > 0.$$

Or, for all (sufficiently large) positive integers n, $\mathrm{E}[|X_n|^{r+\epsilon}] < C$ for some $\epsilon > 0$ and some positive constant C.

Here $\sup_n A_n$ is defined as follows. If $A = \sup_n A_n$, then $A_n \leq A$ for all sufficiently large n, and for any $\epsilon > 0$, there exists an n_0 such that $A_{n_0} > A - \epsilon$. That is, $A = \sup_n A_n$ is a tight upper bound for the sequence A_n.

Lemma A.13 (Dominated Convergence Theorem (I)). *Let g_n be a sequence of measurable functions defined on a set S, and suppose that $|g_n(x)| \leq m(x)$ for all $x \in S$ and that $\int_S m(x)dx$ is finite. If $\lim_{n\to\infty} g_n(x) = g(x)$ for all $x \in S$, then*

$$\lim_{n\to\infty} \int_S g_n(x)dx = \int_S \left[\lim_{n\to\infty} g_n(x)\right] dx = \int_S g(x)dx. \tag{A.26}$$

The dominated convergence theorem gives conditions under which one can interchange the order of limits and the integration operation. If S is a bounded set (i.e., having finite measure), then one can replace the bound function $m(x)$ by a finite constant C. Equation (A.26) still holds true under this condition, and this case is often referred to as the "bounded convergence theorem."

Lemma A.14 (Dominated Convergence Theorem (II)). *There is a stochastic version of the dominated convergence theorem. If $X_n \xrightarrow{p} X$ and if $|X_n| \leq Y$ a.s., where $\mathrm{E}(Y^r) < \infty$, then $\mathrm{E}[|X_n - X|^r] \to 0$ and $\mathrm{E}(X_n^r) \to \mathrm{E}(X^r)$.*

Proof. See Rao (1973). $\square$

Lemma A.15 (U-Statistic H-Decomposition with Variable Kernels). *Here we provide an intuitive explanation of H-decomposition for a second order U-statistic given by*

$$\mathcal{U}_n = \frac{2}{n(n-2)} \sum \sum_{1 \leq i < j \leq n} H_n(X_i, X_j), \tag{A.27}$$

where $H_n(.,.)$ is a symmetric function. Let

$$H_{1n}(X_i) = \mathrm{E}[H_n(X_i, X_j)|X_i].$$

Then the H-decomposition involves rewriting $\mathcal{U}_n$ in the form of uncorrelated terms of differing order, i.e.

$$\mathcal{U}_n = \mathrm{E}[H_n(X_i, X_j)] + \frac{2}{n}\sum_i \{H_{1n}(X_i) - \mathrm{E}[H_{1n}(X_i)]\}$$

$$+ \frac{2}{n(n-1)}\sum\sum_{1\leq i<j\leq n} \{H_n(X_i, X_j) - H_{1n}(X_i)$$

$$- H_{1n}(X_j) + \mathrm{E}[H_n(X_i, X_j)]\}. \qquad (A.28)$$

If $\mathrm{E}[H_n^2(X_i, X_j)] = O(1)$, then it is easy to see that the three terms in (A.28) are of order $O_p(1)$, $O_p(n^{-1/2})$ and $O_p(n^{-1})$, respectively. Moreover, the three terms are uncorrelated with each other. In our application of the H-decomposition below, usually $\mathrm{E}[H_n(X_i, X_j)] = O(a_n)$ (say $a_n = O((h^2 + \lambda)^2)$), the second term in the decomposition is of the order of $O_p(n^{-1/2}a_n)$, and the third term is of even smaller order. We also use the H-decomposition of a third order U-statistic, while Lee (1990, Section 1.6) provides a detailed result of H-decomposition for a general k^{th} order U-statistic. For U-statistics with variable kernels, see Powell et al. (1989).

Lemma A.16 (A Central Limit Theorem for Degenerate U-Statistics). *Consider a second order U-statistic given by*

$$\mathcal{U}_n = \binom{n}{2}^{-1} \sum_{i=1}^n \sum_{j>i}^n H_n(X_i, X_j),$$

where X_i is i.i.d., H_n is symmetric, centered $(\mathrm{E}[H_n(X_1, X_2)] = 0)$, degenerate $\mathrm{E}[H_n|X_1, X_2)|X_1] = 0$ a.s., and $\sigma_n^2 = \mathrm{E}[H_n^2(X_1, X_2)] < \infty$. Define $G(X_1, X_2) = \mathrm{E}[H_n(X_1, X_3)H_n(X_2, X_3)|X_1, X_2]$. Then if

$$\frac{\mathrm{E}[G_n^2(X_1, X_2)] + n^{-1}\mathrm{E}[H_n^4(X_1, X_2)]}{\{\mathrm{E}[H_n^2(X_1, X_2)]\}^2} \to 0$$

as $n \to \infty$, $\mathcal{U}_n/\sqrt{2\sigma_n^2} \xrightarrow{d} N(0, 1)$.

Proof. See Theorem 1 of Hall (1984). □

Lemma A.17. *Let*

$$U_n = \binom{n}{2}^{-1} \sum_{i=1}^{n} \sum_{j>i}^{n} H_n(Z_i, Z_j)$$

be a second order U-statistic. Define $r_n(Z_i) = \mathrm{E}[H_n(Z_i, Z_j)|Z_i]$, $\bar{r}_n = \mathrm{E}[r_n(Z_i)] = \mathrm{E}[H_n(Z_i, Z_j)]$, and $\bar{U}_n = \bar{r}_n + \frac{2}{n}\sum_{i=1}^{n}[r_n(Z_i) - \bar{r}_n]$. If $\mathrm{E}[|H_n(Z_i, Z_j)|^2] = o(n)$, then

(i) $U_n = \bar{r}_n + o_p(1)$.

(ii) $\sqrt{n}(U_n - \bar{U}_n) = o_p(1)$.

Proof. See Lemma 3.1 of Powell et al. (1989).   □

Lemma A.18. *For a kth order degenerate U-statistic,*

$$U_n = \binom{n}{k}^{-1} \sum_{(n,k)} H_n(X_{i_1}, \ldots, X_{i_k}),$$

where H_n is a symmetric (exchangeable) function that depends on n, X_i is i.i.d. random vector, and $\sum_{(n,k)}$ extends over all combinations $1 \le i_1 < \cdots < i_k \le n$ of $\{1, \ldots, n\}$. Assume that H_n is centered, degenerate ($\mathrm{E}[H_n(X_1, \ldots, X_k)|X_1] = 0$ a.s.), and define, for $c = 1, \ldots, k$,

$$H_{nc}(x_1, \ldots, x_c) = \mathrm{E}[H_n(X_1, \ldots, X_k)|X_1 = x_1, \ldots, X_c = x_c],$$

with their variance being $\sigma_{n,c}^2 = \mathrm{var}[H_{n,c}(\cdot)]$. Define $G_n(X_1, X_2) = \mathrm{E}[H_{nc}(X_1, X_3)H_{n2}(X_2, X_3)|X_1, X_2]$. If $\mathrm{E}[H_n^2(X_1, \ldots, X_k)] < \infty$ for each n, $\sigma_{nc}^2/\sigma_{n2}^2 = o(n^{(c-2)})$ for $c = 3, \ldots, k$ (when $k \ge 3$), and, as $n \to \infty$,

$$\frac{\mathrm{E}[G_n^2(X_1, X_2)] + n^{-1}\mathrm{E}[H_{n2}^4(X_1, X_2)]}{\{\mathrm{E}[H_{n2}^2(X_1, X_2)]\}^2} \to 0, \qquad (\mathrm{A}.29)$$

then nU_n is asymptotically normal with mean zero and variance $k^2(k-1)^2\sigma_{n2}^2/2$.

The above result is proved in Fan and Li (1996). When $k = 2$, it reduces to Theorem 1 of Hall (1984).

Let ν denote an L_2-norm and let $\mathcal{S}$ be the support of a Hilbert-valued random element with $\nu(\mathcal{S}) < \infty$. If $\mathcal{S}$ is a bounded subset of $\mathbb{R}^q$, then one can choose $\nu(\cdot)$ to be the Lebesgue measure on $\mathcal{S}$.

Lemma A.19 (Hilbert-Valued Central Limit Theorem). *Let $Z_1(\cdot), \ldots, Z_n(\cdot)$ be Hilbert-valued i.i.d. zero mean random elements on $\mathcal{L}_2(\mathcal{S}, \nu)$ such that $E[||Z_i(\cdot)||_\nu^2] = E[\int Z_i^2(x)\nu(dx)] < \infty$. Then $\mathcal{Z}_n(\cdot) \stackrel{def}{=} n^{-1/2} \sum_{i=1}^n Z_i(\cdot)$ converges weakly to (say, $\mathcal{Z}_\infty(\cdot)$) a zero mean Gaussian process with covariance function given by $\Omega(x, x') = E[Z_i(x)Z_i(x')]$.*

Proof. See Theorem 2.1 of Politis and Romano (1994), or see van der Vaart and Wellner (1996, ex. 1.8.5, p. 50). $\qquad\qquad\square$

Note that for weak convergence one usually needs to check two conditions: (i) finite dimensional convergence, i.e., that $(\mathcal{Z}_n(x_1), \ldots, \mathcal{Z}_n(x_m))$ converges weakly to $(\mathcal{Z}_n(x_1), \ldots, \mathcal{Z}_n(x_m))$ and (ii) that the process (indexed by $\cdot$) $\mathcal{Z}_n(\cdot)$ is tight.[2] Point (i) follows from the Lindeberg-Levi CLT and the Cramer-Wold device, while (ii) follows from $E[||Z_i(\cdot)||_\nu^2] < \infty$, which is a sufficient condition that ensures that the process $n^{-1/2} \sum_{i=1}^n Z_i(\cdot)$ is tight (under the L_2-norm $|| \cdot ||_\nu$).

If instead of using a CM-type statistic as we discussed in Chapter 13, one chooses to work with a statistic based on a sup-norm, say $I_n(x) \stackrel{def}{=} \sup_x |n^{-1/2} \sum_{i=1}^n \mathbf{1}(X_i \leq x)|$, then one works with a Banach-valued random element (i.e., not Hilbert-valued since the sup-norm cannot be induced from an inner product). For verification of tightness for a sequence of Banach-valued random elements, see Billingsley (1968) and Pollard (1984); see also Stute (1997), who discusses a specific statistic having the form of $I_n(\cdot)$.

1.5   Exercises

Exercise A.1.

(i) Prove that the collection of all rational numbers is a Borel set.

(ii) Prove that the collection of all irrational numbers is a Borel set.

   Hint:

(i) Note that the set of rational numbers is countable, i.e., it can be represented as $\sum_{i=1}^\infty \{a_i\}$, where each a_i is a distinct rational (single point) number.

---

[2]For a definition of a sequence of random elements to be tight, see Billingsley (1968, p. 40).

(ii) Irrational numbers are the complement of rational numbers.

Exercise A.2. Let $g(x)$ be defined as

$$g(x) = \begin{cases} 1 & \text{if } x \text{ is a irrational number} \\ 0 & \text{if } x \text{ is an rational number.} \end{cases}$$

This is called the Dirichlet function. Show that the Dirichlet function is a Borel measurable function.

Hint: Consider sets of the form $\{x : g(x) \le a\}$ for any constant $a < 0$, for $a = 0$, for $0 < a < 1$, for $a = 1$, and for $1 < a < +\infty$. Note that the empty set, the set of rational numbers, the set of irrational numbers, and $\mathbb{R}$ are all Borel sets.

Exercise A.3. Let A denote all rational numbers in $[0, 1]$, and B denote all irrational numbers in $[0, 1]$. What are the Lebesgue measures of A and B?

Hint: $[0, 1] = A \cup B$, $[0, 1]$ has Lebesgue measure of 1 and $1 = m([0, 1]) = m(A) + m(B)$ since $A \cap B = \emptyset$.

Exercise A.4. Prove Theorem A.6 (i) under the stronger conditions that $\mathrm{E}[(X_n - X)^2] \to 0$ and $\mathrm{E}[(Y_n - c)^2] \to 0$.

Exercise A.5. Prove that any random variable with a well-defined CDF, say $F(x)$, is an $O_p(1)$ variable.

Hint: A well-defined CDF possesses the following properties: (i) $\lim_{x \to \infty} F(x) = 1$, (ii) $\lim_{x \to -\infty} F(x) = 0$, (iii) $F(x)$ is a nondecreasing function, and (iv) $F(x)$ is right continuous. One only need use (i) and (ii) for this exercise.

Exercise A.6.

(i) Let a_n and b_n be two arbitrary positive sequences, and show that
$$O\left(\sqrt{a_n + b_n}\right) = O\left(\sqrt{a_n}\right) + O\left(\sqrt{b_n}\right).$$

(ii) Prove Theorem A.7 (ii).

Hint: (i) Use $\sqrt{a_n + b_n} \le \sqrt{a_n} + \sqrt{b_n} \le 2\sqrt{a_n + b_n}$ (by squaring each term one can easily see the inequalities hold). (ii) Use Chebychev's inequality.

Exercise A.7. Show that the Dirichlet function defined in Exercise A.2 is Lebesgue integrable and compute its Lebesgue integral over $x \in [0, 1]$.

Hint: The Dirichlet function is a simple function given by $g(x) = (1)\mathbf{1}(A) + (0)\mathbf{1}(B)$, where A is the set of irrational numbers and B is the set of rational numbers.

Note that the Dirichlet function is obviously not Riemann integrable.

Exercise A.8. Compute the Lebesgue integrals of (i) $\int_0^1 x^2 \mu(dx)$, and (ii) $\int_0^\pi \cos(x)\mu(dx)$, where μ is the Lebesgue measure.

Hint: Use the result of Theorem A.1.

Exercise A.9. Let $\{e_j\}$ be an orthonormal basis of a Hilbert space. Show that $c_j = (e_j, g)$, where c_j is defined in (A.7).

Hint: Consider (g, e_l), replacing $g(\cdot)$ by the right-hand side of (A.7) and use the orthonormal property of base functions.

Exercise A.10. Show that $\{1/\sqrt{2\pi}, \sin(\pi x)/\pi, \cos(\pi x)/\pi, \sin(2\pi x)/\pi,$ $\cos(2\pi x)/\pi, \ldots, \sin(n\pi x)/\sqrt{\pi}, \cos(n\pi x)/\sqrt{\pi}, \ldots\}$ is an orthonormal sequence for $x \in [-\pi, \pi]$.

Hint: For any positive integers k, l,

$$\int_\pi^\pi \sin(kx)dx = \int_{-\pi}^\pi \cos(lx)dx = 0;$$
$$\sin(kx)\cos(lx) = [\sin((k+l)x) + \sin((k-l)x)]/2;$$
$$\sin(kx)\sin(lx) = [\cos((k-l)x) - \cos((k+l)x)]/2;$$
$$\cos(kx)\cos(lx) = [\cos((k-l)x) + \cos((k+l)x)]/2;$$
$$\cos^2(kx) = [1 + \cos(2kx)]/2; \text{ and}$$
$$\sin^2(kx) = 1 - \cos^2(kx).$$

Exercise A.11. Show that $\int_{-\infty}^\infty \delta(x-a)g(x)dx = g(a)$, where $\delta(\cdot)$ is the Dirac delta function.

Hint: Write $g(x) = g(a) + [g(x) - g(a)]$ and note that $[g(x) - g(a)]\delta(x-a) = 0$.

Exercise A.12. Let $J_n(b)$ be a stochastic process as given in Theorem A.8. Show that (A.19) implies the following result:

For all $b, b' \in B$, b'' between the line segment of b and b',

$$E\left[|J_n(b) - Jn(b'')|^\beta |J_n(b') - J_n(b'')|^\beta\right] \le C||b'' - b'||^\gamma \qquad (A.30)$$

for some $\beta > 0$, $\gamma > 1$, and C is a positive constant.

Hint: Using $|ab| \le (1/2)(a^2 + b^2)$, choosing $\alpha = 2\beta$ and noticing that $\max\{||b' - b''||, ||b - b''||\} \le ||b' - b||$.

Bibliography

Abadie, A. (2003). Semiparametric instrumental variable estimation of treatment response models. *Journal of Econometrics* **113**, 231–263.

Abadir, K. M. and S. Lawford. (2004). Optimal asymmetric kernels. *Economics Letters* **83**, 61–68.

Adams, R. M, A. N. Berger and R. C. Sickles. (1999). Semiparametric approaches to stochastic panel frontiers with applications in the banking industry. *Journal of Business and Economic Statistics* **17**, 349–58.

Ahmad, I. A. (1980). Nonparametric estimation of an affinity measure between two absolutely continuous distributions with hypothesis testing applications. *Annals of the Institute of Statistical Mathematics* **32**, 223–240.

Ahmad, I. A. and P. B. Cerrito. (1994). Nonparametric estimation of joint discrete-continuous probability densities with applications. *Journal of Statistical Planning and Inference* **41**, 349–364.

Ahmad, I. A. and Q. Li. (1997*a*). Testing independence by nonparametric kernel method. *Statistics and Probability Letters* **34**, 201–210.

Ahmad, I. A. and Q. Li. (1997*b*). Testing symmetry of an unknown density function by kernel method. *Journal of Nonparametric Statistics* **7**, 279–293.

Ahn, H. and J. L. Powell. (1993). Semiparametric estimation of censored selection models with a nonparametric selection mechanism. *Journal of Econometrics* **58**, 3–29.

Ai, C. (1997). A semiparametric maximum likelihood estimator. *Econometrica* **65**(4), 933–963.

Ai, C. and D. McFadden. (1997). Estimation of some partially specified nonlinear models. *Journal of Econometrics* **76**, 1–37.

Ai, C. and Q. Li. (2006). Estimation of partly specified panel Tobit models. Unpublished manuscript University of Florida.

Ai, C. and X. Chen. (2003). Efficient estimation of models with conditional moment restrictions containing unknown functions. *Econometrica* **71**, 1795–1843.

Ait-Sahalia, Y. (1996). Testing continuous-time models of the spot interest rate. *Review of Financial Studies* **9**, 385–426.

Ait-Sahalia, Y. (2002). Maximum likelihood estimation of discrete sampled diffusions: A closed-form approximation approach. *Econometrica* **70**, 223–262.

Ait-Sahalia, Y., P. J. Bickel and T. M. Stoker. (2001). Goodness-of-fit tests for kernel regression with an application to option implied volatilities. *Journal of Econometrics* **105**, 363–412.

Aitchison, J. and C. G. G. Aitken. (1976). Multivariate binary discrimination by the kernel method. *Biometrika* **63**(3), 413–420.

Akaike, H. (1974). A new look at the statistical model identification +. *IEEE Transactions in Automatic Control* **19**(6), 716–723.

Altonji, J. and R. L. Matzkin. (2005). Cross section and panel data estimators for nonseparable models with endogenous regressors. *Econometrica* **73**, 1053–1102.

Amemiya, T. (1985). *Advanced econometrics.* Cambridge, MA: Harvard University Press.

Andersen, E. (1970). Asymptotic properties of conditional maximum likelihood estimators. *Journal of the Royal Statistical Society, Series B* **32**, 283–301.

Anderson, H. M. (1997). Transaction costs and nonlinear adjustment towards equilibrium in the us treasury bill market. *Oxford Bulletin of Economics and Statistics* **59**, 465–484.

Anderson, N. H., P. Hall and D. M. Titterington. (1994). Two-sample test statistics for measuring discrepancies between two multivariate probability density functions using kernel-based density estimates. *Journal of Multivariate Analysis* **50**, 41–54.

Andrews, D. W. K. (1984). Non-strong mixing autoregressive processes. *Journal of Applied Probability* **21**, 930–934.

Andrews, D. W. K. (1988). Laws of large numbers for dependent non-identically distributed random variables. *Econometric Theory* **4**, 458–467.

Andrews, D. W. K. (1991*a*). Asymptotic normality of series estimators for nonparametric and semiparametric regression models. *Econometrica* **59**, 307–345.

Andrews, D. W. K. (1991*b*). Heteroskedasticity and autocorrelation consistent covariance matrix estimation. *Econometrica* **59**, 817–858.

Andrews, D. W. K. (1994). Asymptotics for semiparametric models via stochastic equicontinuity. *Econometrica* **62**, 43–72.

Andrews, D. W. K. (1997). A conditional kolmogorov test. *Econometrica* **65**, 1097–1128.

Andrews, D. W. K. and M. Buchinsky. (2002). On the number of bootstrap repetitions for bc_a confidence intervals. *Econometric Theory* **18**, 962–984.

Andrews, D. W. K. and M. M. A. Schafgans. (1998). Semiparametric estimation of the intercept of a sample selection model. *Review of Economic Studies* **65**, 497–517.

Andrews, D. W. K. and Y. J. Whang. (1990). Additive interactive regression models: Circumvention of the curse of dimensionality. *Econometric Theory* **6**, 466–479.

Anglin, P. and R. Gencay. (1996). Semiparametric estimation of a hedonic price function. *Journal of Applied Econometrics* **11**, 633–648.

Arabmazar, A. and P. Schmidt. (1981). Further evidence on the robustness of the Tobit estimator to heteroscedasticity. *Journal of Econometrics* **17**, 253–258.

Araujo, A. and E. Giné. (1980). *The central limit theorem for real and banach valued random variables*. New York: Wiley.

Arellano, M. (2003). *Panel data econometrics*. Oxford University Press.

Azzalini, A. and A. W. Bowman. (1997). *Applied smoothing techniques for data analysis: The kernel approach with S-plus illustrations*. New York: Oxford University Press.

Azzalini, A., A. W. Bowman and W. Härdle. (1989). On the use of nonparametric regression for model checking. *Biometrika* **76**, 1–11.

Bachmeier, L. J. and Q. Li. (2002). Is the term structure nonlinear? a semiparametric investigation. *Applied Economics Letters* **9**, 151–153.

Bachmeier, L. J., S. Leelahanon and Q. Li. (forthcoming). Money growth and inflation in the united states. *Macroeconomic Dynamics*.

Bai, J. (2003). Testing parametric conditional distributions of dynamic models. *Review of Economics and Statistics* **85**, 531–549.

Bai, J. and S. Ng. (2001). A consistent test for conditional symmetry in time-series models. *Journal of Econometrics* **103**, 225–258.

Baiocchi, G. (2006). Economic applications of nonparametric methods. Ph.d. thesis University of York.

Baltagi, B. H., J. Hidalgo and Q. Li. (1996). A nonparametric test for poolability using panel data. *Journal of Econometrics* **75**, 345–367.

Baltagi, B. H. and Q. Li. (2002). On instrumental variable estimation of semiparametric dynamic panel data models. *Economics Letters* **76**, 1–9.

Bandi, F. and G. Moloche. (2005). On the functional estimation of multivariate diffusion processes. Working paper Graduate School of Business, The University of Chicago.

Bandi, F. and P. C. B. Phillips. (2003). Fully nonparametric estimation of scalar diffusion models. *Econometrica* **71**, 241–283.

Bandi, F. and T. H. Nguyen. (1999). Fully nonparametric estimators for diffusions: a small sample analysis. Working paper Graduate School of Business, The University of Chicago.

Barrett, G. and S. G. Donald. (2003). Consistent tests for stochastic dominance. *Econometrica* **71**, 71–104.

Barro, R. and J. W. Lee. (2000). International data on educational attainment: Updates and implications. Working paper 42 Center for International Development, Harvard University.

Begun, J. M., W. Hall, W. M. Huang and J. A. Wellner. (1983). Information and asymptotic efficiency in parametric-nonparametric models. *Annals of Statistics* **11**, 432–452.

Berkowitz, J., L. Kilian and I. Birgean. (1999). On the finite-sample accuracy of nonparametric resampling algorithms for economic time series. In *Advances in econometrics: Applying kernel and nonparametric estimation to economic topics*, ed. T. B. Fomby and R. C. Hill. Vol. 14 pp. 77–107.

Bhattacharya, R. N. and R. R. Rao. (1986). *Normal approximations and asymptotic expansions*. Malabar, FL: R.E. Krieger Publishing Company.

Bickel, P. J., C. A. J. Klaassen, Y. Ritov and J. A. Wellner. (1993). *Efficient and adaptive estimation for semiparametric models*. Baltimore: Johns Hopkins University Press.

Bierens, H. J. (1982). Consistent model specification tests. *Journal of Econometrics* **20**, 105–134.

Bierens, H. J. (1983). Uniform consistency of kernel estimators of a regression function under generalized conditions. *Journal of the American Statistical Association* **78**, 699–707.

Bierens, H. J. (1987). Kernel estimators of regression functions. In *Advances in econometrics: Fifth world congress*, ed. T. F. Bewley. Vol. I Cambridge: Cambridge University Press pp. 99–144.

Bierens, H. J. and W. Ploberger. (1997). Asymptotic theory of integrated conditional moment tests. *Econometrica* **65**, 1129–1151.

Billingsley, P. (1968). *Convergence of probability measures*. New York: Wiley.

Black, D., J. Smith, M. Berger and B. Noel. (2003). Is the threat of reemployment services more effective than the services themselves? evidence from random assignment in the UI system. *American Economic Review* **93**(4), 1313–27.

Black, F. and M. Scholes. (1973). The pricing of options and corporate liabilities. *Journal of Political Economy* **81**, 637–654.

Blundell, R., A. Duncan and K. Pendakur. (1998). Semiparametric estimation and consumer demand. *Journal of Applied Econometrics* **13**, 435–461.

Blundell, R., X. Chen and D. Kristensen. (2003). Semiparametric engel curves with endogenous expenditure. Unpublished manuscript University College London and New York University.

Bollerslev, T. (1986). Generalized autoregressive conditional heteroskedasticity. *Journal of Econometrics* **31**, 307–27.

Bowman, A. W. (1984). An alternative method of cross-validation for the smoothing of density estimates. *Biometrika* **71**, 353–360.

Bowman, A. W., P. Hall and T. Prvan. (1998). Bandwidth selection for the smoothing of distribution functions. *Biometrika* **85**, 799–808.

Brendstrup, B. and H. J. Paarsch. (2004). Semiparametric identification and estimation in multi-object, sequential, English auctions.
Working paper University of Iowa.

Buja, A., T. Hastie and R. Tibshirani. (1989). Linear smoothers and
additive models. *Annals of Statistics* **17**, 453–555.

Bult, J. R. and T. J. Wansbeek. (1995). Optimal selection for direct
mail. *Marketing Science* **14**(4), 378–394.

Cai, Z. (2001). Estimating a distribution function for censored time
series data. *Journal of Multivariate Analysis* **78**, 299–318.

Cai, Z. (2002). Regression quantiles for time series. *Econometric Theory*
18, 169–192.

Cai, Z. (2003). Weighted local linear approach to censored nonparametric regression. In *Recent advances and trends in nonparametric
statistics*, ed. M. G. Akritas and D. N. Politis. San Diego: Elsevier
Science B. V.

Cai, Z., J. Fan and Q. W. Yao. (2000). Functional-coefficient regression models for nonlinear time series. *Journal of the American
Statistical Association* **95**, 941–956.

Cai, Z., J. Fan and R. Li. (2000). Efficient estimation and inferences
for varying coefficient models. *Journal of the American Statistical
Association* **95**, 888–902.

Cai, Z., M. Das, H. Xiong and Z. Wu. (2006). Functional coefficient
instrumental variables models. *Journal of Econometrics* **133**, 207–
241.

Cai, Z. and Q. Li. (2005). Nonparametric estimation of varying coefficient dynamic panel models. Unpublished manuscript Texas A&M
University.

Cai, Z. and Q. Li. (2006). Functional-coefficient models for nonstationary time series data. Technical report University of North Carolina
at Charlotte.

Cai, Z. and Y. G. Sun. (2003). Local linear estimation for time-
dependent coefficients in cox's regression models. *Scandinavian
Journal of Statistics* **30**, 93–111.

Cai, Z. and Y. M. Hong. (2003). Nonparametric methods in continuous-
time finance: A selective review. In *Recent advances and trends in
nonparametric statistics*, ed. M. G. Akritas and D. N. Politis. San
Diego: Elsevier Sciences pp. 217–231.

Cameron, A. C. and P. K. Trivedi. (1998). *Regression analysis of count data*. New York: Cambridge University Press.

Campbell, J. Y. (1995). Some lessons from the yield curve. *Journal of Economic Perspectives* **9**, 129–152.

Campbell, J. Y. and R. J. Shiller. (1987). Cointegration and tests of present value models. *Journal of Political Economy* **95**, 1062–1088.

Carrasco, M. and X. Chen. (2002). Mixing and moment properties of various GARCH and stochastic volatility models. *Econometric Theory* **18**, 17–39.

Carroll, R. J., J. D. Maca and D. Ruppert. (1999). Nonparametric regression in the presence of measurement error. *Biometrika* **86**, 541–554.

Carroll, R. J. and P. Hall. (2004). Low order approximations in deconvolution and regression with errors in variables. *Journal of the Royal Statistical Society, B,* **66**, 31–46.

Carroll, R.J., J. Fan, I. Gijbels and M. P. Wand. (1997). Generalized partially linear single-index models. *Journal of American Statistical Association* **92**.

Casella, G. and R. L. Berger. (2002). *Statistical inference*. Second ed. Pacific Grove, CA: Thomson Learning.

Castellana, J. V. and M. R. Leadbetter. (1986). On smoothed probability density estimation for stationary processes. *Stochastic Processes and Their Applications* **21**, 179–193.

Chamberlain, G. (1992). Efficiency bounds for semiparametric regression. *Econometrica* **60**, 567–596.

Chamberlain, G. (1993). Feedback in panel data models. Unpublished manuscript Department of Economics, Harvard University.

Charlier, E., B. Melenberg and A. van Soest. (1995). A smoothed maximum score estimator for the binary choice panel data model with an application to labour force participation. *Statistica Nederlandica* **49**, 324–342.

Chaudhuri, P. (1991). Nonparametric estimates of regression quantiles and their local Bahadur representation. *Annals of Statistics* **19**, 760–777.

Chaudhuri, P., K. Doksum and A. Samarov. (1997). On average derivative quantile regression. *Annals of Statistics* **25**(2), 715–744.

Chen, R., L. Yang and C. Hafner. (2004). Nonparametric multi-step ahead prediction in time series analysis. *Journal of the Royal Statistical Society, Series B* **66**, 669–686.

Chen, R., W. Härdle, O. B. Linton and E. Severance-Lossin. (1996). Nonparametric estimation of additive separable regression models. In *Statistical theory and computational aspects of smoothing*, ed. W. Härdle and M. G. Schmeck. Physica Heidelberg pp. 247–265.

Chen, S. (1997). Semiparametric estimation of the Type-3 Tobit model. *Journal of Econometrics* **80**, 1–34.

Chen, S. (2002). Rank estimation of transformation models. *Econometrica* **70**, 1683–1697.

Chen, S., G. B. Dahl and S. Khan. (2005). Nonparametric identification and estimation of a censored location-scale regression model. *Journal of the American Statistical Association* **100**(469), 212–221.

Chen, S. and S. Khan. (2000). Estimating censored regression models in the presence of nonparametric multiplicative heteroskedasticity. *Journal of Econometrics* **98**, 283–316.

Chen, S. X. and J. Gao. (forthcoming). An adaptive empirical likelihood test for parametric time series regression models. *Journal of Econometrics*.

Chen, S. X., W. Härdle and M. Li. (2003). An empirical likelihood goodness-of-fit test for time series. *Journal of The Royal Statistical Society Series B* **65**, 663–678.

Chen, X. (2006). Large sample sieve estimation of semi-nonparametric models. In *The handbook of econometrics*, ed. J. J. Heckman and E. E. Leamer. Vol. 6 North-Holland.

Chen, X. and H. L. White. (1998). Central limit and functional central limit theorems for Hilbert-valued dependent heterogeneous arrays with applications. *Econometric Theory* **14**, 260–284.

Chen, X. and H. L. White. (1999). Improved rates and asymptotic normality for nonparametric neural network estimators. *IEEE Transactions on Information Theory* **45**, 682–691.

Chen, X., J. S. Racine and N. R. Swanson. (2001). Semiparametric ARX neural network models with an application to forecasting inflation. *IEEE Transactions on Neural Networks* **12**, 674–683.

Chen, X., L. P. Hansen and J. Scheinkman. (2005). Principal components and the long run. Unpublished manuscript New York University.

Chen, X., O. B. Linton and I. van Keilegom. (2003). Estimation of semiparametric models when the criterion function is not smooth. *Econometrica* **71**, 1591–1608.

Chen, X. and T. Conley. (2001). A new semiparametric spatial model for panel time series. *Journal of Econometrics* **105**, 59–83.

Chen, X. and Y. Fan. (1999). Consistent hypothesis testing in semiparametric and nonparametric models for econometric time series. *Journal of Econometrics* **91**, 373–401.

Chen, X. and Y. Fan. (2006). Estimation of copula-based semiparametric time series models. *Journal of Econometrics* **130**, 307–335.

Chen, X. and Y. Fan. (forthcoming). Estimation and model selection of semiparametric copula-based multivariate dynamic models under copula misspecification. *Journal of Econometrics*.

Chen, X., Y. Fan and V. Tsyrennikov. (forthcoming). Efficient estimation of semiparametric multivariate copula models. *Journal of the American Statistical Association*.

Chen, Y. T., R. Y. Chou and C. M. Kuan. (2000). Testing time reversibility without moment restrictions. *Journal of Econometrics* **95**, 199–218.

Cheng, M.-Y. (1997). A bandwidth selector for local linear density estimators. *Annals of Statistics* **25**, 1001–1013.

Cheng, M.-Y. and L. Peng. (2002). Regression modeling for nonparametric estimation of distribution and quantile functions. *Statistica Sinica* **12**, 1043–1060.

Chernozhukov, V. and H. Hong. (2002). Three-step censored quantile regression and extramarital affairs. *Journal of the American Statistical Association* **97**(459), 872–882.

Christofides, L., Q. Li, Z. Liu and I. Min. (2003). Recent two-stage sample selection procedures with an application to the gender wage gap. *Journal of Business and Economic Statistics* **21**, 396–405.

Chui, C. K. (1988). *Multivariate splines*. Philadelphia: , Society for Industrial and Applied Mathematics CBMS-NSF Regional Conference Series in Applied Mathematics #54.

Chui, C. K. (1992). *An introduction to wavelets*. Academic Press.

Cleveland, W. S. (1979). Robust locally weighted regression and smoothing scatterplots. *Journal of the American Statistical Association* **74**, 829–836.

Connors, A. F., T. Speroff, N. V. Dawson, C. Thomas, F. E Harrell Jr,
D. Wagner, N. Desbiens, L. Goldman, A. W. Wu, R. M. Califf,
W. J. Fulkerson, H. Vidaillet, S. Broste, P. Bellamy, J. Lynn and
W. A. Knaus. (1996). The effectiveness of right heart catheteriza-
tion in the initial care of critically ill patients. *The Journal of the
American Medical Association* **276**, 889–897.

Coppejans, M. and A. R. Gallant. (2002). Cross-validated SNP density
estimates. *Journal of Econometrics* **110**, 27–65.

Corradi, V. and N. R. Swanson. (2005). Bootstrap specification tests
for diffusion processes. *Journal of Econometrics* **124**, 117–148.

Corradi, V. and N. R. Swanson. (2006). Predictive density evaluation. In *Handbook of economic forecasting*, ed. G. Elliott, C. W. J.
Granger and A. Timmermann. Elsevier Sciences.

Corradi, V. and N. R. Swanson. (forthcoming). Bootstrap conditional
distribution tests in the presence of dynamic misspecification.
Journal of Econometrics.

Cosslett, S. R. (1983). Distribution-free maximum likelihood estimator
of the binary choice model. *Econometrica* **51**, 765–782.

Cosslett, S. R. (2004). Efficient semiparametric estimation of censored
and truncated regressions via a smoothed self-consistency equation. *Econometrica* **72**, 1277–1293.

Cox, J. C., J. E. Ingersoll and S. A. Ross. (1985). A theory of the term
structure of interest rate. *Econometrica* **53**, 385–407.

Craven, P. and G. Wahba. (1979). Smoothing noisy data with spline
functions. *Numerische Mathematik* **13**, 377–403.

Darolles, S., J. P. Florens and E. Renault. (2002). Nonparametric
instrumental regression. Cahiers de recherche 2002-05 Universite
de Montreal, Departement de sciences economiques. available at
http://ideas.repec.org/p/mtl/montde/2002-05. html.

Das, M. (2005). Instrumental variable estimators of nonparametric
models with discrete endogenous regressors. *Journal of Econometrics* **124**, 335–361.

Das, M., W. K. Newey and F. Vella. (2003). Nonparametric estimation
of sample selection models. *Review of Economics Studies* **70**, 33–
58.

Davidson, R. and J. G. MacKinnon. (1993). *Estimation and inference
in econometrics.* Oxford: Oxford University Press.

Davidson, R. and J. G. MacKinnon. (2000). Bootstrap tests: How many bootstraps? *Econometric Reviews* **19**, 55–68.

de Jong, P. (1987). A central limit theorem for generalized quadratic forms. *Probability Theory and Related Fields* **75**, 261–277.

de Jong, R. M. (2002). A note on convergence rates and asymptotic normality for series estimators: uniform convergence rates. *Journal of Econometrics* **111**, 1–9.

Dehejia, R. H. and S. Wahba. (1999). Causal effects in nonexperimental studies: Reevaluating the evaluation of training programs. *Journal of The American Statistical Association* **94**, 1053–1062.

Delgado, M. A. (1993). Testing the equality of nonparametric regressioni curves. *Statistics and Probability Letters* **17**, 199–204.

Delgado, M. A. and J. Hidalgo. (2000). Nonparametric inference on structural breaks. *Journal of Econometrics* **96**, 113–144.

Delgado, M. A. and T. Stengos. (1994). Semiparametric specification testing of nonnested econometric models. *Review of Economic Studies* **61**, 291–303.

Delgado, M. A. and W. G. Manteiga. (2001). Significance testing in nonparametric regression based on the bootstrap. *Annals of Statistics* **29**, 1469–1507.

Dette, H. (1999). A consistent test for the functional form of a regression based on a difference of variance estimators. *Annals of Statistics* **27**, 1012–1040.

Dette, H. and N. Neumeyer. (2001). Nonparametric analysis of covariance. *Annals of Statistics* **29**, 1361–1400.

Devroye, L. and L. Györfi. (1985). *Nonparametric density estimation: The L^1 view*. New York: Wiley.

Diebold, F. X., J. Hahn and A. S. Tay. (1999). Multivariate density forecast evaluation and calibration in financial risk management: High frequency returns on foreign exchange. *Review of Economics and Statistics* **81**, 661–673.

Diebold, F. X., T. Gunther and A. S. Tay. (1998). Evaluating density forecasts with applications to finance risk management. *International Economic Review* **39**, 863–883.

DiNardo, J. and J. L. Tobias. (2001). Nonparametric density and regression estimation. *Journal of Economic Perspectives* **15**(4), 11–28.

Donald, S. G. (1997). Inference concerning the number of factors in a multivariate nonparametric relationship. *Econometrica* **65**, 103–131.

Donald, S. G., G. W. Imbens and W. K. Newey. (2003). Empirical likelihood estimation and consistent tests with conditional moment restrictions. *Journal of Econometrics* **117**, 55–93.

Donald, S. G. and H. J. Paarsch. (1993). Piecewise pseudo-maximum likelihood estimation in empirical models of auctions. *International Economic Review* **34**, 121–148.

Donald, S. G. and H. J. Paarsch. (1996). Identification, estimation, and testing in parametric empirical models of auctions within the independent private values paradigm. *Econometric Theory* **12**, 517–567.

Donald, S. G. and W. K. Newey. (1994). Series estimation of semilinear models. *Journal of Multivariate Analysis* **50**, 30–40.

Duin, R. P. W. (1976). On the choice of smoothing parameters for Parzen estimators of probability density functions. *IEEE Transactions on Computing* **C-25**, 1175–1179.

Durbin, J. (1970). Testing for serial correlation in least squares regression when some of the regressors are lagged dependent variables. *Econometrica* **38**, 410–421.

Durbin, J. and G. S. Watson. (1950). Testing for serial correlation in least squares regression. I. *Biometrika* **37**, 409–428.

Durlauf, S. N. and D. T. Quah. (1999). The new empirics of economic growth. In *Handbook of macroeconomics I*, ed. J. B. Taylor and M. Woodford. New York: Elsevier Sciences pp. 235–308.

Efromovich, S. (1999). *Nonparametric curve estimation: Methods, theory and applications.* New York: Springer Verlag.

Efron, B. (1982). *The jackknife, the bootstrap, and other resampling plans.* Philadelphia, Pennsylvania 19103: Society for Industrial and Applied Mathematics.

Ellison, G. and S. F. Ellison. (2000). A simple framework for nonparametric specification testing. *Journal of Econometrics* **96**, 1–23.

Embrechts, P., A. McNeil and D. Straumann. (1999). Correlation and dependence in risk management: Properties and pitfalls. In *Risk management: Value at risk and beyond,* ed. M. Dempster. New York: Cambridge University Press.

Engle, R. F. (1982). Autoregressive conditional heteroscedasticity with estimates of the variance of uk inflation. *Econometrica* **50**, 987–1007.

Engle, R. F., C. W. J. Granger, J. Rice and A. Weiss. (1986). Semiparametric estimates of the relation between weather and electricity demand. *Journal of the American Statistical Association* **76**, 817–823.

Eubank, R. L. (1999). *Nonparametric regression and spline smoothing.* Second ed. New York: Marcel Dekker.

Eubank, R. L. and C. H. Spiegelman. (1990). Testing the goodness of fit of a linear model via nonparametric regression techniques. *Journal of the American Statistical Association* **85**, 387–392.

Eubank, R. L. and J. D. Hart. (1992). Testing goodness-of-fit in regression via order selection criteria. *Annals of Statistics* **20**, 1412–1425.

Fair, R. C. (1978). A theory of extramarital affairs. *Journal of Political Economy* **86**(1), 45–61.

Fan, J. (1992). Design-adaptive nonparametric regression. *Journal of the American Statistical Association* **87**, 998–1004.

Fan, J. (1993). Local linear regression smoothers and their minimax efficiencies. *Annals of Statistics* **21**, 196–216.

Fan, J. (2005). A selective overview of nonparametric methods in financial econometrics (with discussion). *Statistical Science* **20**(4), 317–337.

Fan, J. and C. M. Zhang. (2003). A reexamination of diffusion estimators with applications to financial model validation. *Journal of the American Statistical Association* **98**, 118–134.

Fan, J., C. M. Zhang and J. Zhang. (2001). Generalized likelihood ratio statistics and wilks phenomenon. *Annals of Statistics* **29**, 153–193.

Fan, J. and I. Gijbels. (1992). Variable bandwidth and local linear regression smoothers. *Annals of Statistics* **20**, 2008–2036.

Fan, J. and I. Gijbels. (1996). *Local polynomial modelling and its applications.* London: Chapman and Hall.

Fan, J., I. Gijbels and M. King. (1997). Local likelihood and local partial likelihood in hazard regression. *Annals of Statistics* **25**, 1661–1690.

Fan, J. and L. Huang. (2001). Goodness-of-fit tests for parametric regression models. *Journal of the American Statistical Association* **96**, 640–652.

Fan, J. and Q. W. Yao. (1998). Efficient estimation of conditional variance functions in stochastic regression. *Biometrika* **85**, 645–660.

Fan, J. and Q. W. Yao. (2005). *Nonlinear time series: Nonparametric and parametric methods.* Springer.

Fan, J., Q. W. Yao and Z. Cai. (2003). Adaptive varying-coefficient linear models. *Journal of the Royal Statistical Society, Series B* **65**, 57–80.

Fan, J. and R. Li. (2004). New estimation and model selection procedures for semiparametric modeling in longitudinal data. *Journal of the American Statistical Association* **99**, 710–723.

Fan, J., T. C. Hu and Y. K. Truong. (1994). Robust nonparametric function estimation. *Scandinavian Journal of Statistics* **21**, 433–446.

Fan, J. and T. Huang. (2005). Profile likelihood inferences on semiparametric varying-coefficient partially linear models. *Bernoulli* **11**, 1031–1057.

Fan, J., W. Härdle and E. Mammen. (1998). Direct estimation of low dimensional components in additive models. *Annals of Statistics* **26**, 943–971.

Fan, J. and W. Zhang. (2000). Simultaneous confidence bands and hypothesis testing in varying-coefficient models. *Scandinavian Journal of Statistics* **27**, 715–731.

Fan, J. and Y. K. Truong. (1993). Nonparametric regression with errors-in-variables. *Annals of Statistics* **21**, 1900–1925.

Fan, Y. (1994). Testing the goodness-of-fit of a parametric density function by kernel method. *Econometric Theory* **10**, 316–356.

Fan, Y. (1997). Goodness-of-fit tests for a multivariate distribution by the empirical characteristic function. *Journal of Multivariate Analysis* **62**, 36–63.

Fan, Y. and O. B. Linton. (2003). Some higher order theory for a consistent nonparametric model specification test. *Journal of Statistical Planning and Inference* **109**, 125–154.

Fan, Y. and Q. Li. (1996). Consistent model specification tests: omitted variables and semiparametric functional forms. *Econometrica* **64**, 865–90.

Fan, Y. and Q. Li. (1999a). Central limit theorem for degenerate u-statistics of absolutely regular processes with applications to model specification tests. *Journal of Nonparametric Statistics* **10**, 245–271.

Fan, Y. and Q. Li. (1999*b*). Root-n-consistent estimation of partially linear time series models. *Journal of Nonparametric Statistics* **11**, 251–269.

Fan, Y. and Q. Li. (2000). Consistent model specification tests: Kernel-based tests versus Bierens's icm tests. *Econometric Theory* **16**, 1016–1041.

Fan, Y. and Q. Li. (2002). A consistent model specification test based on the kernel sum of squares of residuals. *Econometric Reviews* **21**, 337–352.

Fan, Y. and Q. Li. (2003). A kernel-based method for estimating additive partially linear models. *Statistic Sinica* **13**, 739–762.

Fan, Y., Q. Li and I. Min. (2006). A nonparametric bootstrap test of conditional distributions. *Econometric Theory* **22**, 587–613.

Fan, Y. and R. Gencay. (1993). Hypothesis testing based on modified nonparametric estimation of an affinity measure between two distributions. *Journal of Nonparametric Statistics* **2**, 389–403.

Fan, Y. and R. Gencay. (1995). A consistent nonparametric test of symmetry in linear regression models. *Journal of the American Statistical Association* **90**, 551–557.

Fan, Y. and Z. Liu. (1997). A simple test for a parametric single index model. *The Journal of the Operationial Research Society of India* **34**, 186–195.

Florens-Zmirou, D. (1993). On estimating the diffusion coefficient from discrete observations. *Journal of Applied Probability* **30**, 790–804.

Fox, J. (2002). *An R and S-PLUS companion to applied regression.* Thousand Oaks, CA: Sage.

Gallant, A. R. and D. W. Nychka. (1987). Semi-nonparametric maximum likelihood estimation. *Econometrica* **55**, 363–390.

Gallant, A. R. and G. Tauchen. (1996). Which moments to match. *Econometric Theory* **12**, 657–681.

Gallant, A. R. and H. L. White. (1988). *A unified theory of estimation and inference for nonlinear dynamic models.* Oxford: Basil Blackwell Ltd.

Gallant, A. R. and J. R. Long. (1997). Estimating stochastic differential equations efficiently by minimum ch–squared. *Biometrika* **84**, 125–141.

Gallant, A. R., P. E. Rossi and G. Tauchen. (1993). Nonlinear dynamic structures. *Econometrica* **61**, 871–907.

Gan, L. and Q. Zhang. (2006). The thick market effect on local unemployment rate fluctuations. *Journal of Econometrics* **133**, 127–152.

Gao, J. and H. Tong. (2004). Semiparametric non-linear time series model selection. *Journal of the Royal Statistical Society Series B* **66**, 321–336.

Gasser, T. and H. G. Müller. (1979). Kernel estimation of regression functions. In *Smoothing techniques for curve estimation*. Berlin, Heidelberg, New York: Springer-Verlag pp. 23–68.

Genest, C., K. Ghoudi and L. P. Pivest. (1995). A semiparametric estimation procedure of dependence parameters in multivariate families of distributions. *Biometrika* **82**(3), 543–552.

Gerfin, M. (1996). Parametric and semiparametric estimation of the binary response model of labour market participation. *Journal of Applied Econometrics* **11**(3), 321–339.

Gorgens, T. and J. L. Horowitz. (1999). Semiparametric estimation of a censored regression model with an unknown transformation of the dependent variable. *Journal of Econometrics* **90**, 155–191.

Gozalo, P. and O. B. Linton. (2001). Testing additivity in generalized nonparametric regression models with estimated parameters. *Journal of Econometrics* **104**, 1–48.

Granger, C. W. J., E. Maasoumi and J. S. Racine. (2004). A dependence metric for possibly nonlinear processes. *Journal of Time Series Analysis* **25**(5), 649–669.

Greene, W. H. (2003). *Econometric analysis*. Fifth ed. Upper Saddle River, NJ: Prentice Hall.

Gu, J. and D. Li. (2006). A bootstrap nonparametric significance test. Unpublished manuscript Department of Economics, Texas A&M University.

Guerre, E., I. Perrigne and Q. Vuong. (2000). Optimal nonparametric estimation of first-price auctions. *Econometrica* **68**, 525–574.

Hahn, J. (1998). On the role of the propensity score in efficient semi-parametric estimation of average treatment effects. *Econometrica* **66**, 315–331.

Haile, P., H. Hong and M. Shum. (2003). Nonparametric tests for common values in first-price sealed-bid auctions. Unpublished manuscript NBER Working Paper Series.

Hall, P. (1981). On nonparametric multivariate binary discrimination. *Biometrika* **68**(1), 287–294.

Hall, P. (1984). Central limit theorem for integrated square error of multivariate nonparametric density estimators. *Journal of Multivariate Analysis* **14**, 1–16.

Hall, P. (1987*a*). On kullback-leibler loss and density estimation. *Annals of Statistics* **15**, 1491–1519.

Hall, P. (1987*b*). On the use of compactly supported density estimates in problems of discrimination. *Journal of Multivariate Analysis* **23**, 131–158.

Hall, P. (1992). *The bootstrap and edgeworth expansion.* New York: Springer Series in Statistics, Springer-Verlag.

Hall, P. and C. C. Heyde. (1980). *Martingale limit theory and its application.* Academic Press.

Hall, P. and J. D. Hart. (1990). Bootstrap test for difference between means in nonparametric regression. *Journal of the American Statistical Association* **85**, 1039–1049.

Hall, P. and J. L. Horowitz. (1990). Bandwidth selection in semiparametric estimation of censored linear regression models. *Econometric Theory* **6**, 123–150.

Hall, P. and J. L. Horowitz. (2003). Nonparametric methods for inference in the presence of instrumental variables. Unpublished manuscript Australian National University.

Hall, P., J. S. Racine and Q. Li. (2004). Cross-validation and the estimation of conditional probability densities. *Journal of the American Statistical Association* **99**(468), 1015–1026.

Hall, P., Q. Li and J. S. Racine. (2006). Nonparametric estimation of regression functions in the presence of irrelevant regressors. Unpublished manuscript Department of Economics, Texas A&M University.

Hall, P. and Q. W. Yao. (2005). Approximating conditional distribution functions using dimension reduction. *Annals of Statistics* **33**, 1404–1421.

Hall, P., R. C. L. Wolff and Q. W. Yao. (1999). Methods for estimating a conditional distribution function. *Journal of the American Statistical Association* **94**, 154–163.

Hall, P. and T. E. Wehrly. (1991). A geometrical method for removing edge effects from kernel-type nonparametric regression estimators. *Journal of the American Statistical Association* **86**(415), 665–672.

Han, A. K. (1987). A non-parametric analysis of transformations. *Journal of Econometrics* **35**, 191–209.

Hansen, B. (2004). Nonparametric estimation of smooth conditional distributions. Technical report University of Wisconsin, Madison.

Hansen, B. (2005). Exact mean integrated squared error of higher order kernel estimators. *Econometric Theory* **21**, 1031–1057.

Hansen, B. and B. Seo. (2000). Testing for threshold cointegration. Working paper University of Wisconsin, Madison.

Härdle, W. (1990). *Applied nonparametric regression.* New York: Cambridge University Press.

Härdle, W. and A. B. Tsybakov. (1993). How sensitive are average derivatives? *Journal of Econometrics* **58**, 31–48.

Härdle, W. and A. B. Tsybakov. (1997). Local polynomial estimators of the volatility function in nonparametric autoregression. *Journal of Econometrics* **81**, 223–242.

Härdle, W. and E. Mammen. (1993). Comparing nonparametric versus parametric regression fits. *Annals of Statistics* **21**, 1926–1947.

Härdle, W., H. Liang and J. Gao. (2000). *Partially linear models.* Heidelberg: Physica-Verlag.

Härdle, W., M. Müller, S. Sperlich and A. Werwatz. (2004). *Nonparametric and semiparametric models.* Berlin: Springer Series in Statistics.

Härdle, W., P. Hall and H. Ichimura. (1993). Optimal smoothing in single index models. *Annals of Statistics* **21**, 157–178.

Härdle, W., P. Hall and J. S. Marron. (1988). How far are automatically chosen regression smoothing parameters from their optimum? *Journal of The American Statistical Association* **83**, 86–101.

Härdle, W., S. Sperlich and V. Spokoiny. (2001). Structural tests in additive regression. *Journal of the American Statistical Association* **96**, 1333–1347.

Härdle, W. and T. M. Stoker. (1989). Investigating smooth multiple regression by the method of average derivatives. *Journal of the American Statistical Association* **84**, 986–995.

Hart, J. D. (1997). *Nonparametric smoothing and lack-of-fit tests*. New York: Springer Verlag.

Hastie, T. and R. Tibshirani. (1990). *Generalized additive models*. London: Chapman and Hall.

He, X. and L. X. Zhu. (2003). A lack-of-fit test for quantile regression. *Journal of the American Statistical Association* **98**.

He, X. and P. D. Shi. (1998). Monotone B-spline smoothing. *Journal of the American Statistical Association* **93**(442), 643–650.

Heckman, J. J. (1974). Shadow prices, market wages, and labor supply. *Econometrica* **42**, 679–694.

Heckman, J. J. (1976). The common structure of statistical models of truncation, sample selection and limited dependent variables and a simple estimator for such models. *Annals of Economic and Social Measurement* **5**, 475–492.

Heckman, J. J. (1979). Sample selection bias as a specification error. *Econometrica* **47**, 153–162.

Heckman, J. J. (1990). Varieties of selection bias. *American Economic Review* **80**, 313–318.

Heckman, J. J. and B. E. Honoré. (1989). The identifiability of the competing risks model. *Biometrika* **76**(2), 325–330.

Heckman, J. J., H. Ichimura and P. Todd. (1997). Matching as an econometric evaluation estimator: Evidence from evaluating a job training programme. *Review of Economic Studies* **64**, 605–654.

Heckman, J. J., H. Ichimura and P. Todd. (1998). Matching as an econometric evaluation estimator. *Review of Economic Studies* **65**, 261–294.

Henderson, D., R. J. Carroll and Q. Li. (2006). Nonparametric estimation and testing of fixed effects panel data models. Unpublished manuscript Texas A & M University.

Hirano, K., G. W. Imbens and G. Ridder. (2003). Efficient estimation of average treatment effects using the estimated propensity score. *Econometrica* **71**(4), 1161–1189.

Hjellvik, V., Q. W. Yao and D. Tjøstheim. (1998). Linearity testing using local polynomial approximation. *Journal of Statistical Planning and Inference* **68**(2), 295–321.

Honda, T. (2000). Nonparametric estimation of a conditional quantile for α-mixing processes. *Annals of the Institute of Statistical Mathematics* **52**, 459–470.

Hong, Y. M. (1996). Consistent specification testing for serial correlation of unknown form. *Econometrica* **64**, 837–864.

Hong, Y. M. (1999). Hypothesis testing in time series via the empirical characteristic function: a generalized spectral density approach. *Journal of the American Statistical Association* **94**, 1201–1220.

Hong, Y. M. and H. L. White. (1995). Consistent specification testing via nonparametric series regression. *Econometrica* **63**, 1133–1159.

Hong, Y. M. and H. Li. (2005). Nonparametric specification testing for continuous-time models with applications to term structure of interest rates. *Review of Financial Studies* **18**, 37–84.

Hong, Y. M. and T. Lee. (2003). Inference on predictability of exchange rates via generalized spectrum and nonlinear time series models. *Review of Economics and Statistics* **85**, 1048–1062.

Honoré, B. E. (1992). Trimmed LAD and least squares estimation of truncated and censored regression models with fixed effects. *Econometrica* **60**, 533–565.

Honoré, B. E. and A. Lewbel. (2002). Semiparametric binary choice panel data models without strictly exogenous regressors. *Econometrica* **70**, 2053–2063.

Honoré, B. E. and E. Kyriazidou. (2000). Panel data discrete choice models with lagged dependent variables. *Econometrica* **68**, 839–874.

Honoré, B. E., E. Kyriazidou and C. Udry. (1997). Estimation of Type-3 Tobit models using symmetric trimming and pairwise comparisons. *Journal of Econometrics* **76**, 107–28.

Honoré, B. E. and E. T. Tamer. (2006). Bounds on parameters in dynamic discrete choice models. *Econometrica* **74**(3), 611–629.

Honoré, B. E. and J. L. Powell. (1994). Pairwise difference estimators for censored and truncated regression models. *Journal of Econometrics* **64**, 241–278.

Honoré, B. E. and L. Hu. (1999). Estimation of cross-sectional and panel data censored regression models with endogeneity. Unpublished manuscript Princeton University.

Horowitz, J. L. (1986). A distribution-free least squares estimator for censored linear regression models. *Journal of Econometrics* **32**, 59–84.

Horowitz, J. L. (1988). Semiparametric M-Estimation of Censored Linear Regression Models. In *Advances in econometrics: Parametric and robust inference*, ed. G. F. Rhodes and T. B. Fomby. Vol. 7 New York: Elsevier pp. 45–83.

Horowitz, J. L. (1992). A smoothed maximum score estimator for the binary response model. *Econometrica* **60**, 505–531.

Horowitz, J. L. (1996). Semiparametric estimation of a regression model with an unknown transformation of the dependent variable. *Econometrica* **64**, 103–137.

Horowitz, J. L. (1998). *Semiparametric methods in econometrics*. New York: Springer-Verlag.

Horowitz, J. L. (1999). Semiparametric estimation of a proportional hazard model with unobserved heterogeneity. *Econometrica* **67**, 1001–1028.

Horowitz, J. L. (2001). Nonparametric estimation of a generalized additive model with an unknown link function. *Econometrica* **69**, 499–513.

Horowitz, J. L. (2005). Asymptotic normality of a nonparametric instrumental variable estimator. Unpublished manuscript Northwestern University.

Horowitz, J. L. (2006). Testing a parametric model against a nonparametric alternative with identification through instrumental variables. *Econometrica* **74**, 1238–1249.

Horowitz, J. L. and E. Mammen. (2004). Nonparametric estimation of an additive model with a link function. *Annals of Statistics* **32**, 2412–2443.

Horowitz, J. L. and G. R. Neumann. (1987). Semiparametric estimation of employment duration models. *Econometric Reviews* **6**, 5–40.

Horowitz, J. L. and S. Lee. (2005). Nonparametric estimation of an additive quantile regression model. *Journal of the American Statistical Association* **100**(472), 1238–1249.

Horowitz, J. L. and V. G. Spokoiny. (2001). An adaptive, rate-optimal test of a parametric mean-regression model against a nonparametric alternative. *Econometrica* **69**(3), 599–631.

Horowitz, J. L. and W. Härdle. (1994). Testing a parametric model against a semiparametric alternative. *Econometric Theory* **10**, 821–848.

Horowitz, J. L. and W. Härdle. (1996). Direct semiparametric estimation of single-index models with discrete covariates. *Journal of the American Statistical Association* **91**, 1632–1640.

Hristache, M., A. Juditsky and V. Spokoiny. (2001). Direct estimation of the index coefficient in a single-index model. *Annals of Statistics* **29**, 595–623.

Hsiao, C., Q. Li and J. S. Racine. (forthcoming). A consistent model specification test with mixed categorical and continuous data. *Journal of Econometrics.*

Hu, L. (2002). Estimation of a censored dynamic panel data model. *Econometrica* **70**, 2499–2517.

Huang, J. Z. (1998*a*). Functional ANOVA models for generalized regression. *Journal of Multivariate Analysis* **67**, 49–71.

Huang, J. Z. (1998*b*). Projection estimation in multiple regression with application to functional ANOVA models. *Annals of Statistics* **26**, 242–272.

Huang, J. Z. (2001). Concave extended linear modeling: a theoretical synthesis. *Statistica Sinica* **11**, 173–197.

Huang, J. Z. (2003). Local asymptotics for polynomial spline regression. *Annals of Statistics* **31**, 1600–1635.

Huang, J. Z., C. O. Wu and L. Zhou. (2004). Polynomial spline estimation and inference for varying coefficient models with longitudinal data. *Statistica Sinica* **14**(3), 763–788.

Huang, J. Z. and H. Shen. (2004). Functional coefficient regression models for nonlinear time series: a polynomial spline approach. *Scandinavian Journal of Statistics* **31**, 515–534.

Huang, J. Z. and L. Yang. (2004). Identification of non-linear additive autoregressive models. *Journal of the Royal Statistical Society Series B* **66**, 463–477.

Hurvich, C. M., J. S. Simonoff and C. L. Tsai. (1998). Smoothing parameter selection in nonparametric regression using an improved Akaike information criterion. *Journal of the Royal Statistical Society Series B* **60**, 271–293.

Ibragimov, I. and Y. Linnik. (1971). *Independent and stationary sequences of random variables.* Groningen: Wolters-Noordhoff.

Ichimura, H. (1993). Semiparametric least squares (SLS) and weighted SLS estimation of single-index models. *Journal of Econometrics* **58**, 71–120.

Ichimura, H. (2000). Asymptotic distribution of non-parametric and semiparametric estimators with data dependent smoothing parameters. Unpublished manuscript University College London.

Ichimura, H. and L. F. Lee. (1991). Semiparametric least squares single equation estimation of multiple index models. In *Nonparametric and semiparametric methods in econometrics and statistics*, ed. W. A. Barnett, J. L. Powell and G. Tauchen. Cambridge: Cambridge University Press pp. 3–49.

Ichino, A. and R. Winter-Ebmer. (1998). The long-run educational cost of world war II: An example of local average treatment effect estimation. CEPR publication DP1895 Center for Economic Policy Research.

Imbens, G. W. and C. F. Manski. (2004). Confidence intervals for partially identified parameters. *Econometrica* **72**, 1845–1857.

Jensen, H. H. and S. T. Yen. (1996). U. S. food expenditures away from home by type of meal. *Canadian Journal of Agricultural Economics* **44**, 67–80.

Jiang, G. and J. L. Knight. (1997). A nonparametric approach to the estimation of diffusion processes, with an application to a short-term interest rate model. *Econometric Theory* **13**, 615–645.

Joe, H. (1997). *Multivariate models and dependence concepts.* Vol. 73 London: Chapman and Hall. Monographs on Statistics and Applied Probability.

Jones, M. C. and P. Hall. (1990). Mean squared error properties of kernel estimates of regression quantiles. *Statistics and Probability Letters* **10**, 283–289.

Juhl, T. (2005). Functional coefficient models under unit root behavior. *Econometrics Journal* **8**, 197–213.

Juhl, T. and Z. Xiao. (2005). A nonparametric test for changing trends. *Journal of Econometrics* **127**, 179–199.

Juhn, C. and K. M. Murphy. (1997). Wage inequality and family labor supply. *Journal of Labor Economics* **15**(1), 72–97.

Kaplan, E. L. and P. Meier. (1958). Nonparametric estimation from incomplete observations. *Journal of the American Statistical Association* **53**, 457–481.

Khan, S. and E. T. Tamer. (forthcoming). Partial rank estimation of duration models with general forms of censoring. *Journal of Econometrics.*

Kiefer, N. M. and T. J. Vogelsang. (2002). Heteroskedasticity-autocorrelation robust standard errors using the bartlett kernel without truncation. *Econometrica* **70**, 2093–2095.

Kim, J. and D. Pollard. (1990). Cube root asymptotics. *Annals of Statistics* **18**, 191–219.

Kim, W., O. B. Linton and N. W. Hengartner. (1999). A computationally efficient oracle estimator for additive nonparametric regression with bootstrap confidence intervals. *Journal of Computational and Graphical Statistics* **8**, 278–297.

King, E. C., J. D. Hart and T. E. Wehrly. (1991). Testing the equality regression curves using linear smoothers. *Statistics and Probability Letters* **12**, 239–247.

Klein, R. W. and R. H. Spady. (1993). An efficient semiparametric estimator for binary response models. *Econometrica* **61**, 387–421.

Kniesner, T. and Q. Li. (2002). Nonlinearity in dynamic adjustment: Semiparametric estimation of panel labor supply. *Empirical Economics* **27**, 131–148.

Koenker, R. (2005). *Quantile regression.* New York: Cambridge University Press.

Koenker, R. and G. Bassett. (1978). Regression quantiles. *Econometrica* **46**, 33–50.

Koenker, R. and Z. Xiao. (2002). Inference on the quantile regression process. *Econometrica* **70**(4), 1583–1612.

Koop, G., M. H. Pesaran and S. M. Potter. (1996). Impulse response analysis in nonlinear multivariate models. *Journal of Econometrics* **74**, 119–147.

Kooperberg, C., C. J. Stone and Y. K. Truong. (1995). The l_2 rate of convergence for hazard regression. *Scandinavian Journal of Statistics* **22**, 143–157.

Kuan, C. M. and W. M. Lee. (2004). A new test for the martingale difference hypothesis. *Studies in Nonlinear Dynamics and Econometrics* **8**(4), 1–24.

Kyriazidou, E. (1997). Estimation of a panel data sample selection model. *Econometrica* **65**, 1335–1364.

Laffont, J. J., H. Ossard and Q. Vuong. (1995). Econometrics of first-price auctions. *Econometrica* **63**, 953–980.

Lai, T. and Z. Ying. (1991). Estimating a distribution function with truncated and censored data. *Annals of Statistics* **19**, 417–442.

Lavergne, P. (2001). An equality test across nonparametric regressions. *Journal of Econometrics* **103**, 307–344.

Lavergne, P. and Q. Vuong. (1996). Nonparametric selection of regressors: The nonnested case. *Econometrica* **64**, 207–219.

Lavergne, P. and Q. Vuong. (2000). Nonparametric significance testing. *Econometric Theory* **16**, 576–601.

Lechner, M. (1999). Earnings and employment effects of continuous off-the-job training in east germany after unification. *Journal of Business and Economic Statistics* **17**, 74–90.

Lee, J. (1990). *U-statistics: Theory and practice.* New York: Marcel Dekker.

Lee, L. F. (1983). Generalized econometric models with selectivity. *Econometrica* **51**, 507–512.

Lee, L. F. (1994). Semiparametric two-stage estimation of sample selection models subject to Tobit-type selection rules. *Journal of Econometrics* **61**, 305–344.

Lee, L. F. (1995). Semiparametric maximum likelihood estimation of polychotomous and sequential choice models. *Journal of Econometrics* **65**, 381–428.

Leeper, E. M. and J. E. Roush. (2003). Putting "M" back into monetary policy. *Journal of Money, Credit, and Banking* **35**(6), 1217–1256.

Lewbel, A. (2000). Semiparametric qualitative response model estimation with unknown heteroskedasticity or instrumental variables. *Journal of Econometrics* **97**, 145–177.

Lewbel, A. and O. B. Linton. (2002). Nonparametric censored and truncated regression. *Econometrica* **70**(2), 765–779.

Li, D. (2005). A simple bootstrap test for time series regression models. *Journal of Nonparametric Statistics* **17**, 513–520.

Li, D. and T. Stengos. (2003). Testing serial correlation in semiparametric time series models. *Journal of Time Series Analysis* **24**(3), 311–335.

Li, F. and G. Tkacz. (2006). A consistent bootstrap test for conditional density functions with time series data. *Journal of Econometrics* **133**, 863–886.

Li, K. C. (1987). Asymptotic optimality for c_p, c_l, cross-validation, and generalized cross-validation: Discrete index set. *Annals of Statistics* **15**, 958–975.

Li, Q. (1994). A consistent test for linearity in partially linear regression models. Working paper no. 1994-7 University of Guelph.

Li, Q. (1996). Nonparametric testing of closeness between two unknown distribution functions. *Econometric Reviews* **15**, 261–274.

Li, Q. (1999). Consistent model specification tests for time series econometric models. *Journal of Econometrics* **92**, 101–147.

Li, Q. (2000). Efficient estimation of additive partially linear models. *International Economic Review* **41**, 1073–1092.

Li, Q. (2006). Testing parametric regression functional forms using k-nearest-neighbor methods. Unpublished manuscript Texas A&M University.

Li, Q. and C. Hsiao. (1998). Testing serial correlation in semiparametric panel data models. *Journal of Econometrics* **87**, 207–237.

Li, Q., C. Hsiao and J. Zinn. (2003). Consistent specification tests for semiparametric/nonparametric models based on series estimation methods. *Journal of Econometrics* **112**, 295–325.

Li, Q., C. J. Huang, D. Li and T. T. Fu. (2002). Semiparametric smooth coefficient models. *Journal of Business and Economics Statistics* **20**, 412–422.

Li, Q., D. Ouyang and J. S. Racine. (2006). Nonparametric estimation of regression functions with discrete regressors. Unpublished manuscript Department of Economics, Texas A&M University.

Li, Q. and J. M. Wooldridge. (2002). Semiparametric estimation of partially linear models for dependent data with generated regressors. *Econometric Theory* **18**, 625–645.

Li, Q. and J. S. Racine. (2003). Nonparametric estimation of distributions with categorical and continuous data. *Journal of Multivariate Analysis* **86**, 266–292.

Li, Q. and J. S. Racine. (2004a). Cross-validated local linear nonparametric regression. *Statistica Sinica* **14**(2), 485–512.

Li, Q. and J. S. Racine. (2004b). Predictor relevance and extramarital affairs. *Journal of Applied Econometrics* **19**(4), 533–535.

Li, Q. and J. S. Racine. (forthcoming). Nonparametric estimation of conditional CDF and quantile functions with mixed categorical and continuous data. *Journal of Business and Economic Statistics*.

Li, Q., J. S. Racine and J. M. Wooldridge. (2005). Efficient estimation of average treatment effects with mixed categorical and continuous data. Unpublished manuscript Department of Economics, Texas A&M University.

Li, Q. and J. Zhou. (2005). The uniqueness of cross-validation selected smoothing parameters in kernel estimation of nonparametric models. *Econometric Theory* **21**(5), 1017–1025.

Li, Q. and S. Wang. (1998). A simple consistent bootstrap test for a parametric regression function. *Journal of Econometrics* **87**, 145–165.

Li, Q., X. Lu and A. Ullah. (2003). Multivariate local polynomial regression for estimating average derivatives. *Journal of Nonparametric Statistics* **15**, 607–624.

Li, T., I. Perrigne and Q. Vuong. (2000). Conditionally independent private information in OCS wildcat auctions. *Journal of Econometrics* **98**, 129–161.

Liang, H. and N. S. Wang. (2004). Estimation in partially linear models with missing covariates. *Journal of the American Statistical Association* **99**, 357–367.

Liang, H. and N. S. Wang. (2005). Partially linear single-index measurement error models. *Statistica Sinica* **15**, 99–116.

Liang, H., W. Härdle and R. J. Carroll. (1999). Estimation in a semiparametric partially linear errors-in-variables model. *Annals of Statistics* **27**, 1519–1535.

Lin, D. Y., B. M. Psaty and R. A. Kronmal. (1998). Assessing the sensitivity of regression results to unmeasured confounders in observational studies. *Biometrics* **54**, 948–63.

Lin, D. Y. and Z. Ying. (1999). Nonparametric estimation of the gap time distributions for serial events with censored data. *Biometrika* **86**, 59–70.

Lin, D. Y. and Z. Ying. (2001). Semiparametric and nonparametric regression analysis of longitudinal data. *Journal of the American Statistical Association* **96**, 103–126.

Linton, O. B. (1995). Second order approximation in the partially linear regression model. *Econometrica* **63**(5), 1079–1112.

Linton, O. B. (1997). Efficient estimation of additive nonparametric regression models. *Biometrika* **84**, 469–473.

Linton, O. B. (2000). Efficient estimation of generalized additive nonparametric regression models. *Econometric Theory* **16**, 502–523.

Linton, O. B. and E. Mammen. (2005). Estimating semiparametric ARCH(infinity) models by kernel smoothing methods. *Econometrica* **73**, 771–836.

Linton, O. B. and J. P. Nielsen. (1995). A kernel method of estimating structured nonparametric regression based on marginal integration. *Biometrika* **82**, 93–100.

Linton, O. B., J. P. Nielsen and S. van de Geer. (2003). Estimating multiplicative and additive hazard functions by kernel methods. *Annals of Statistics* **31**, 464–492.

Linton, O. B. and W. Härdle. (1996). Estimation of additive regression models with known links. *Biometrika* **83**, 529–540.

Linton, O. B., Y. J. Whang and E. Maasoumi. (2005). Consistent testing for stochastic dominance under general sampling schemes. *Review of Economic Studies* **73**(3), 735–765.

Liu, R. Y. (1988). Bootstrap procedures under some non i.i.d. models. *Annals of Statistics* **16**, 1696–1708.

Liu, Z. and T. Stengos. (1999). Non-linearities in cross country growth regressions: a semiparametric approach. *Journal of Applied Econometrics* **14**, 527–538.

Liu, Z., T. Stengos and Q. Li. (2000). Nonparametric model check based on polynomial fitting. *Statistics and Probability Letters* **48**, 327–334.

Liu, Z. and X. Lu. (1997). Root-n-consistent semiparametric estimation of partially linear models based on k-nn method. *Econometric Reviews* **16**, 411–420.

Loader, C. R. (1999). Bandwidth selection: Classical or plug-in? *Annals of Statistics* **27**(2), 415–438.

Long, J. S. (1997). *Regression models for categorical and limited dependent variables*. Vol. 7 Thousand Oaks, CA: Sage Publications.

Lorentz, G. G. (1966). *Approximation of functions*. New York: Holt, Rinehart and Winston.

Maasoumi, E. and J. S. Racine. (2002). Entropy and predictability of stock market returns. *Journal of Econometrics* **107**, 291–312.

Maasoumi, E., J. S. Racine and T. Stengos. (forthcoming). Growth and convergence: A profile of distribution dynamics and mobility. *Journal of Econometrics*.

Mack, Y. P. (1981). Local properties of k-NN regression estimates. *Society for Industrial and Applied Mathematics Journal on Algebraic and Discrete Methods* **2**(3), 311–323.

Mack, Y. P and M. Rosenblatt. (1979). Multivariate k-nearest neighbor density estimates. *Journal of Multivariate Analysis* **9**(97), 1–15.

Maddala, G. S. (1986). *Limited-dependent and qualitative variables in econometrics.* Cambridge: Cambridge University Press.

Mallows, C. L. (1973). Some comments on c_p. *Technometrics* **15**, 661–675.

Mammen, E. (1992). *When does bootstrap work? Asymptotic results and simulations.* New York: Springer-Verlag.

Mammen, E. and B. U. Park. (2005). Bandwidth selection for smooth backfitting in additive models. *Annals of Statistics* **33**, 1260–1294.

Mammen, E., O. B. Linton and J. P. Nielsen. (1999). The existence and asymptotic properties of a backfitting projection algorithm under weak conditions. *Annals of Statistics* **27**, 1443–1490.

Mankiw, N., D. Romer and D. Weil. (1992). A contribution to the empirics of economic growth. *Quarterly Journal of Economics* **107**, 407–437.

Manski, C. F. (1975). Maximum score estimation of the stochastic utility model of choice. *Journal of Econometrics* **3**(3), 205–228.

Manski, C. F. (1987). Semiparametric analysis of random effects linear models from binary panel data. *Econometrica* **55**(2), 357–362.

Manski, C. F. (1988). Identification of binary response models. *Journal of the American Statistical Association* **83**(403), 729–738.

Manski, C. F. (2003). *Partial identification of probability distributions.* New York: Spring-Verlag.

Manski, C. F. and E. T. Tamer. (2002). Inference on regressions with interval data on a regressor or outcome. *Econometrica* **70**, 519–546.

Manski, C. F. and T. S. Thompson. (1986). Operational characteristics of maximum score estimation. *Journal of Econometrics* **32**, 85–108.

Manzan, S. and D. Zerom. (2005). Kernel estimation of a partially linear additive model. *Statistics and Probability Letters* **72**, 313–327.

Marron, J. S., M. C. Jones and S. J. Sheather. (1996). A brief survey of bandwidth selection for density estimation. *Journal of the American Statistical Association* **91**, 401–407.

Masry, E. (1996*a*). Multivariate local polynomial regression for time series: uniform strong consistency and rates. *Journal of Time Series Analysis* **17**, 571–599.

Masry, E. (1996*b*). Multivariate regression estimation: local polynomial fitting for time series. *Stochastic Processes and Their Applications* **65**, 81–101.

Matzkin, R. L. (1992). Nonparametric and distribution-free estimation of the binary threshold crossing and the binary choice models. *Econometrica* **60**(2), 239–270.

Matzkin, R. L. (2003). Nonparametric estimation of nonadditive random functions. *Econometrica* **71**, 1339–1375.

McAdam, P. and O. Rummel. (2004). Corruption: A non-parametric analysis. *Journal of Economic Studies* **31**(6), 509–523.

McCulloch, J. H. and H. C. Kwon. (1993). US term structure data, 1947-1991. Working paper no. 93-6 Ohio State University.

McFadden, D., C. Puig and D. Kirschner. (1977). Determinants of the long-run demand for electricity. *Proceeedings of the American Statistical Association (Business and Economics Section)* pp. 109–117.

McLeish, D. L. (1975). A maximal inequality and dependent strong laws. *Annals of Probability* **3**, 829–839.

Min, I., C. Fang and Q. Li. (2004). Investigation of patterns in food-away-from-home expenditure for china: A nonparametric approach. *China Economic Review* **15**, 457–476.

Min, I., S. Sheu and Z. Wang. (2003). A monte carlo comparison of various semiparametric Type-3 Tobit estimators. *Annals of Economics and Finance* **4**.

Nadaraya, E. A. (1965). On nonparametric estimates of density functions and regression curves. *Theory of Applied Probability* **10**, 186–190.

Nelsen, R. B. (2006). *An introduction to copulas*. Second ed. New York: Springer-Verlag.

Newey, W. K. (1990*a*). Efficient instrumental variables estimation of nonlinear models. *Econometrica* **58**, 809–837.

Newey, W. K. (1990*b*). Semiparametric efficiency bounds. *Journal of Applied Econometrics* **5**, 99–135.

Newey, W. K. (1991*a*). Consistency and asymptotic normality of nonparametric projection estimators. Working paper no. 584 Department of Economics, MIT.

Newey, W. K. (1991*b*). Efficient estimation of Tobit models under conditional symmetry. In *Nonparametric and semiparametric methods* *in econometrics and statistics*, ed. W. A. Barnett, J. L. Powell and G. E. Tauchen. New York: Cambridge University Press pp. 291–336.

Newey, W. K. (1994*a*). The asymptotic variance of semiparametric estimators. *Econometrica* **62**, 1349–1382.

Newey, W. K. (1994*b*). Kernel estimation of partial means and a general variance estimator. *Econometric Theory* **10**, 233–253.

Newey, W. K. (1995). Convergence rates for series estimators. In *Statistical methods of economics and quantitative economics*, ed. G. S. Maddala, P. C. B. Phillips and T. N. Srinavsan. Cambridge: Cambridge University Press.

Newey, W. K. (1997). Convergence rates and asymptotic normality for series estimators. *Journal of Econometrics* **79**, 147–168.

Newey, W. K. (1999). Two-step series estimation of sample selection models. Working paper no. 99-04 MIT.

Newey, W. K. and J. L. Powell. (1990). Efficient estimation of linear and Type I censored regression models under conditional quantile restrictions. *Econometric Theory* **6**, 295–317.

Newey, W. K. and J. L. Powell. (2003). Instrumental variable estimation of nonparametric models. *Econometrica* **71**(5), 1565–1578.

Newey, W. K., J. L. Powell and F. Vella. (1999). Nonparametric estimation of triangular simultaneous equations models. *Econometrica* **67**, 565–603.

Newey, W. K. and K. D. West. (1987). A simple, positive semi-definite, heteroskedasticity and autocorrelation consistent covariance matrix. *Econometrica* **55**(3), 703–08.

Nielsen, J. P. and S. Sperlich. (2005). Smooth backfitting in practice. *Journal of the Royal Statistical Society, Series B* **67**, 43–61.

Oakes, D. (1994). Multivariate survival distributions. *Journal of Nonparametric Statistics* **3**, 343–354.

Opsomer, J. D. (2000). Asymptotic properties of backfitting estimators. *Journal of Multivariate Analysis* **73**, 166–179.

Opsomer, J. D. and D. Ruppert. (1998). A fully automated bandwidth selection method for fitting additive models. *Journal of the American Statistical Association* **93**, 605–619.

Ouyang, D., D. Li and Q. Li. (forthcoming). Cross-validation and estimation of regression functions with k-nn methods. *Econometrics Journal*.

Ouyang, D., Q. Li and J. S. Racine. (2006). Cross-validation and the estimation of probability distributions with categorical data. *Journal of Nonparametric Statistics* **18**(1), 69–100.

Paarsch, H. J. (1992). Deciding between the common and private value paradigms in empirical models of auctions. *Journal of Econometrics* **51**, 191–215.

Paarsch, H. J. and H. Hong. (2006). *An introduction to the structural econometrics of auction data*. Cambridge, MA: The MIT Press.

Pagan, A. and A. Ullah. (1999). *Nonparametric econometrics*. New York: Cambridge University Press.

Pagan, A. and F. Vella. (1989). Diagnostic tests for models based on individual data: A survey. *Journal of Applied Econometrics* **4**, S29–S59.

Pagan, A. and G. W. Schwert. (1990). Alternative models for conditional stock volatility. *Journal of Econometrics* **45**, 267–90.

Pakes, A. and S. Olley. (1995). A limit theorem for a smooth class of semiparametric estimators. *Journal of Econometrics* **65**, 295–332.

Parzen, E. (1962). On estimation of a probability density function and mode. *The Annals of Mathematical Statistics* **33**, 1065–1076.

Peng, L. and Q. W. Yao. (2004). Nonparametric regression under dependent errors with infinite variance. *Annals of the Institute of Statistical Mathematics* **56**, 73–86.

Pesaran, M. H. and A. Timmermann. (1992). A simple non-parametric test of predictive performance. *Journal of Business and Economic Statistics* **10**, 561–565.

Phillips, P. C. B. and J. Y. Park. (1998). Nonstationary density estimation and kernel autoregression. Technical report Yale University.

Pinkse, J. (1998). A consistent nonparametric test for serial independence. *Journal of Econometrics* **84**, 205–231.

Politis, D. N. and J. P. Romano. (1994). Limit theorems for weakly dependent Hilbert space valued random variables with applications to the stationary bootstrap. *Statistica Sinica* **4**, 461–476.

Pollard, D. (1984). *Convergence of stochastic processes*. New York: Springer-Verlag.

Powell, J. L. (1984). Least absolute deviations estimation for the censored regression model. *Journal of Econometrics* **25**, 303–325.

Powell, J. L. (1986). Symmetrically trimmed least squares estimation of Tobit models. *Econometrica* **54**, 1435–1460.

Powell, J. L. (1987). Semiparametric estimation of bivariate latent variable models. Working paper no. 8704 University of Wisconsin.

Powell, J. L., J. H. Stock and T. M. Stoker. (1989). Semiparametric estimation of index coefficients. *Econometrica* **57**(6), 1403–1430.

Powell, J. L. and T. M. Stoker. (1996). Optimal bandwidth choice for density-weighted averages. *Journal of Econometrics* **75**, 291–316.

Prakasa Rao, B. L. S. (1983). *Nonparametric functional estimation.* Orlando, FL: Academic Press.

Quah, D. T. (1996). Empirics for economic growth and convergence. *European Economic Review* **40**, 1353–1375.

R Development Core Team. (2006). *R: A language and environment for statistical computing.* Vienna, Austria: R Foundation for Statistical Computing. ISBN 3-900051-07-0.
URL: *http://www.R-project.org*

Racine, J. S. (2002). 'New and improved' direct marketing: A nonparametric approach. In *Econometric models in marketing,* ed. A. Montgomery and P. H. Franses. Vol. 16 New York: Elsevier pp. 141–164.

Racine, J. S., J. D. Hart and Q. Li. (forthcoming). Testing the significance of categorical predictor variables in nonparametric regression models. *Econometric Reviews.*

Racine, J. S. and Q. Li. (2004). Nonparametric estimation of regression functions with both categorical and continuous data. *Journal of Econometrics* **119**(1), 99–130.

Racine, J. S., Q. Li and X. Zhu. (2004). Kernel estimation of multivariate conditional distributions. *Annals of Economics and Finance* **5**(2), 211–235.

Rao, C. R. (1973). *Linear statistical inference and its applications.* Second ed. New York: Wiley.

Ridder, G. (1990). The nonparametric identification of generalized accelerated failure-time models. *Review of Economic Studies* **57**, 167–181.

Riley, J. G. and W. F. Samuelson. (1981). Optimal auctions. *American Economic Review* **71**, 381–392.

Rilstone, P. (1991). Nonparametric hypothesis testing with parametric rates of convergence. *International Economic Review* **32**, 209–227.

Rilstone, P. (1993). Calculating the (local) semiparametric efficiency bounds for the generated regressors problem. *Journal of Econometrics* **56**, 357–370.

Rilstone, P. and A. Ullah. (1989). Nonparametric estimation of response coefficients. *Communications in Statistics - Theory and Methods* **18**(7), 2615–2627.

Robinson, P. M. (1983). Nonparametric estimators for time series. *Journal of Time Series Analysis* **4**, 185–207.

Robinson, P. M. (1987). Asymptotically efficient estimation in the presence of heteroskedasticity of unknown form. *Econometrica* **55**, 875–891.

Robinson, P. M. (1988). Root-n consistent semiparametric regression. *Econometrica* **56**, 931–954.

Robinson, P. M. (1989). Hypothesis testing in semiparametric and nonparametric models for econometric time series. *Review of Economic Studies* **56**, 511–534.

Robinson, P. M. (1991). Consistent nonparametric entropy-based testing. *Review of Economic Studies* **58**, 437–453.

Rosenbaum, P. and D. Rubin. (1983). The central role of the propensity score in observational studies for causal effects. *Biometrika* **70**, 41–55.

Rosenblatt, M. (1952). Remarks on a multivariate transformation. *Annals of Mathematical Statistics* **23**, 470–472.

Rosenblatt, M. (1956). Remarks on some nonparametric estimates of a density function. *The Annals of Mathematical Statistics* **27**, 832–837.

Rosenblatt, M. (1975). A quadratic measure of deviation of two-dimensional density estimates and a test of independence. *Annals of Statistics* **3**, 1–14.

Royden, H. L. (1988). *Real analysis*. Third ed. Upper Saddle River, NJ: MacMillan Co.

Rudemo, M. (1982). Empirical choice of histograms and kernel density estimators. *Scandinavian Journal of Statistics* **9**, 65–78.

Ruppert, D. and M. P. Wand. (1994). Multivariate locally weighted least squares regression. *Annals of Statistics* **22**, 1346–1370.

Ruppert, D., R. J. Carroll and M. P. Wand. (2003). *Semiparametric regression modeling*. New York: Cambridge University Press.

Ruppert, D., S. J. Sheather and M. P. Wand. (1995). An effective bandwidth selector for local least squares regression. *Journal of the American Statistical Association* **90**, 1257–1270.

Schick, A. (1996). Root-n-consistent and efficient estimation in semi-parametric additive regression models. *Statistics and Probability Letters* **30**, 45–51.

Scott, D. W. (1992). *Multivariate density estimation: Theory, practice, and visualization.* New York: Wiley.

Serfling, R. J. (1980). *Approximation theorems of mathematical statistics.* New York: Wiley.

Shen, X. (1997). On methods of sieves and penalization. *Annals of Statistics* **25**, 2555–2591.

Sherman, R. P. (1993). The limiting distribution of the maximum rank correlation estimator. *Econometrica* **61**, 123–137.

Silverman, B. W. (1986). *Density estimation for statistics and data analysis.* New York: Chapman and Hall.

Simonoff, J. S. (1996). *Smoothing methods in statistics.* New York: Springer Series in Statistics.

Sklar, A. (1959). Fonctions de répartition an dimensions et leurs marges. *Publication Institite Statistics d'Université du Paris* **8**, 229–231.

Sperlich, S., D. Tjøstheim and L. Yang. (2002). Nonparametric estimation and testing of interaction in additive models. *Econometric Theory* **18**(2), 197–251.

Stanton, R. (1997). A nonparametric model of term structure dynamics and the market price of interest rate risk. *Journal of Finance* **53**, 1973–2002.

Stengos, T. and Y. Sun. (2001). A consistent model specification test for a regression function based on nonparametric wavelet estimation. *Econometric Reviews* **20**, 41–60.

Stinchcombe, M. and H. L. White. (1998). Consistent specification testing with nuisance parameters present only under the alternative. *Econometric Theory* **14**, 295–325.

Stock, J. H. (1989). Nonparametric policy analysis. *Journal of the American Statistical Association* **84**, 567–575.

Stock, J. H. and M. W. Watson. (1999). Forecasting inflation. *Journal of Monetary Economics* **44**, 293–335.

Stone, C. J. (1974). Cross-validatory choice and assessment of statistical predictions (with discussion). *Journal of the Royal Statistical Society* **36**, 111–147.

Stone, C. J. (1977). Consistent nonparametric regression. *Annals of Statistics* **5**, 595–645.

Stone, C. J. (1982). Optimal global rates of convergence for nonparametric regression. *Annals of Statistics* **10**(4), 1040–1053.

Stone, C. J. (1984). An asymptotically optimal window selection rule for kernel density estimates. *Annals of Statistics* **12**, 1285–1297.

Stone, C. J. (1985). Additive regression and other nonparametric models. *Annals of Statistics* **13**, 689–705.

Stone, C. J. (1986). The dimensionality reduction principle for generalised additive models. *Annals of Statistics* **14**, 590–606.

Stone, C. J. (1994). The use of polynomial splines and their tensor products in multivariate function estimation. *Annals of Statistics* **22**, 118–184.

Stute, W. (1993). Consistent estimation under random censorship when covariables are present. *Journal of Multivariate Analysis* **45**, 89–103.

Stute, W. (1996). Distributional convergence under random censorship when covariables are present. *Scandinavian Journal of Statistics* **23**, 461–471.

Stute, W. (1997). Nonparametric model checks for regression. *Annals of Statistics* **25**, 613–641.

Stute, W. and W. G. Manteiga. (1996). NN goodness-of-fit tests for linear models. *Journal of Statistical Planning and Inference* **53**, 75–92.

Su, L. and A. Ullah. (2006). More efficient estimation in nonparametric regression with nonparametric autocorrelated errors. *Econometric Theory* **22**, 98–126.

Sun, Y. (2006). A consistent nonparametric equality test of conditional quantile functions. *Econometric Theory* **22**, 614–632.

Sun, Y. and Q. Li. (forthcoming). An alternative series based consistent model specification test. *Economics Letters*.

Tanaka, K. (1996). *Time series analysis*. New York: Wiley.

Tjøstheim, D. and B. Auestad. (1994). Non-parametric identification of non-linear time series: projections. *Journal of the American Statistical Association* **89**, 1398–1409.

Tobin, J. (1958). Estimation of relationships for limited dependent variables. *Econometrica* **26**, 24–36.

Tripathi, G. and T. Severina. (2001). A simplified approach to computing efficiency bounds in semiparametric models. *Journal of Econometrics* **102**, 23–66.

Tripathi, G. and Y. Kitamura. (2003). Testing conditional moment restrictions. *Annals of Statistics* **31**, 2059–2095.

Trivedi, P. K. and D. M. Zimmer. (forthcoming). Using trivariate copulas to model sample selection and treatment effects: Application to family health care demand. *Journal of Business and Economic Statistics*.

Tsay, R. S. (2002). *Analysis of financial time series*. New York: Wiley.

Tucker, H. (1967). *A graduate course in probability*. New York: Academic Press.

Ullah, A. (1985). Specification analysis of econometric models. *Journal of Quantitative Economics* **1**, 187–209.

van der Vaart, A. W. and J. A. Wellner. (1996). *Weak convergence and empirical processes: With applications to statistics*. New York: Springer Series in Statistics.

van Dijk, M. and A. Szirmai. (2003). Technical efficiency trends in historical perspective: The indonesian pulp and paper industry. *Eindoven Center for Innovation Studies Working Paper*.

Vella, F. (1992). Simple tests for sample selection bias in censored and discrete choice models. *Journal of Applied Econometrics* **7**, 413–21.

Vella, F. (1993). A simple estimator for simultaneous models with censored endogenous regressors. *International Economic Review* **34**, 441–57.

Vinod, R. and A. Ullah. (1988). Flexible production function estimation by nonparametric kernel estimators. *Advances in Econometrics: Nonparametric and Robust Inference* **7**, 139–160.

Volkonskii, V. A. and Y. A. Rozanov. (1959). Some limit theorems for random functions I. *Theory of Probability and its Applications* **4**, 178–197.

Vytlacil, E. and J. J. Heckman. (2005). Structural equations, treatment effects and econometric policy evaluation. *Econometrica* **73**, 669–738.

Wahba, G. (1985). A comparison of GCV and GML for choosing the smoothing parameters in the generalized spline smoothing problem. *Annals of Statistics* **13**, 1378–1402.

Wand, M. P. and M. C. Jones. (1995). *Kernel smoothing*. London: Chapman and Hall.

Wang, J. and L. Yang. (2005). Efficient and fast spline-backfitted kernel smoothing of additive regression model. Statistics and probability RM 638 Michigan State University.

Wang, N. (2003). Marginal nonparametric kernel regression accounting for within-subject correlation. *Biometrika* **90**, 43–52.

Wang, N., R. J. Carroll and X. Lin. (2005). Efficient semiparametric marginal estimation for longitudinal/clustered data. *Journal of the American Statistical Association* **100**, 147–157.

Wansbeek, T. J. and A. Kapteyn. (1982). A class of decompositions of the variance-covariance matrix of a generalized error components model. *Econometrica* **50**, 713–724.

Watson, G. S. (1964). Smooth regression analysis. *Sankhya* **26:15**, 359–372.

Wei, Y. and X. He. (2006). Conditional growth charts. *Annals of Statistics* **34**.

Wells, C. (2003). Retesting Fair's (1978) model on infidelity. *Journal of Applied Econometrics* **18**, 237–239.

Western, B. (1996). Vague theory and model uncertainty in macrosociology. *Sociological Methodology* **26**, 165–192.

Whang, Y. J. (2000). Consistent bootstrap tests of parametric regression functions. *Journal of Econometrics* **98**, 27–46.

Whang, Y. J. (2006). Smoothed empirical likelihood methods for quantile regression models. *Econometric Theory* **22**, 173–205.

Wheeden, R. L. and A. Zygmund. (1977). *Measure and integral*. Nezw York: Marcel Dekker.

White, H. L. (1984). *Asymptotic theory for econometricians*. Orlando, FL: Academic Press.

White, H. L. (2000). A reality check for data snooping. *Econometrica* **68**, 1097–1126.

Wooldridge, J. M. (1992). A test for functional form against nonparametric alternatives. *Econometric Theory* **8**, 452–475.

Wooldridge, J. M. (1994). Selection corrections with a censored selection variable. Working paper Michigan State University.

Wooldridge, J. M. (2002). *Econometric analysis of cross section and panel data.* Cambridge: MIT Press.

Xia, Y., H. Tong and W. K. Li. (1999). On extended partially linear single-index models. *Biometrika* **86**, 831–842.

Xiao, Z., O. B. Linton, R. J. Carroll and E. Mammen. (2003). More efficient local polynomial estimation in nonparametric regression with autocorrelated errors. *Journal of the American Statistical Association* **98**, 980–992.

Xue, L. and L. Yang. (2006). Estimation of semiparametric additive model. *Journal of Statistical Planning and Inference* **136**, 2506–2534.

Xue, L. and L. Yang. (forthcoming). Additive coefficient modeling via polynomial spline. *Statistica Sinica.*

Yang, L. (2000). Root-n convergent transformation-kernel density estimation. *Journal of Nonparametric Statistics* **12**(4), 447–474.

Yang, L., B. U. Park, L. Xue and W. Härdle. (forthcoming). Estimation and testing for varying coefficients in additive models with marginal integration. *Journal of the American Statistical Association.*

Yang, L. and J. S. Marron. (1999). Iterated transformation-kernel density estimation. *Journal of the American Statistical Association* **94**(446), 580–589.

Yang, L. and R. Tschernig. (1999). Multivariate bandwidth selection for local linear regression. *Journal of the Royal Statistical Society, Series B* **61**(4), 793–815.

Yang, L. and R. Tschernig. (2005). Nonparametric estimation of generalized impulse response functions. Unpublished manuscript Michigan State University.

Yang, L., S. Sperlich and W. Härdle. (2003). Derivative estimation and testing in generalized additive models. *Journal of Statistical Planning and Inference* **115**(2), 521–542.

Yatchew, A. J. (1992). Nonparametric regression tests based on least squares. *Econometric Theory* **8**, 435–451.

Yatchew, A. J. (2003). *Semiparametric regression for the applied econometrician.* New York: Cambridge University Press.

Yatchew, A. J. and J. A. No. (2001). Household gasoline demand in canada. *Econometrica* **69**, 1697–1709.

Yatchew, A. J., Y. Sun and C. Deri. (2003). Efficient estimation of semiparametric equivalent scales with evidence from South Africa. *Journal of Business and Economic Statistics* **21**, 247–257.

Ye, J. and N. Duan. (1997). Nonparametric $\sqrt{n}$ consistent estimation for the general transformation models. *Annals of Statistics* **25**, 2682–2717.

Yoshihara, K. (1976). Limiting behavior of U-statistics for stationary, absolutely regular processes. *Zeitschrift für Wahrscheinlichkeitstheorie und Verwandte* **35**, 237–252.

Yu, K. and M. C. Jones. (1997). A comparison of local constant and local linear regression quantile estimators. *Computational Statistics and Data Analysis* **25**, 156–166.

Yu, K. and M. C. Jones. (1998). Local linear quantile regression. *Journal of the American Statistical Association* **93**(441), 228–237.

Zheng, J. X. (1996). A consistent test of functional form via nonparametric estimation techniques. *Journal of Econometrics* **75**, 263–289.

Zheng, J. X. (2000). A consistent test of conditional parametric distributions. *Econometric Theory* **16**, 667–691.

Zhou, S., X. Shen and D. A. Wolfe. (1998). Local asymptotics for regression splines and confidence regions. *Annals of Statistics* **26**(5), 1760–1782.

Zinde-Walsh, V. (2005). Kernel estimation when density does not exist. Unpublished manuscript McGill University.

Author Index

Subject Index

Cramer-Wold theorem, 689
cumulative distribution func-
         tion (CDF), 3,
         7
     cross-validation, 23
     frequency, 7
     nonsmooth, 182
     smooth, 20, 184
curse of dimensionality, xvii

density estimation
     least squares cross-
         validation bandwidth se-
         lection, 15,
         27
     likelihood cross-
         validation bandwidth se-
         lection, 18,
         28
     plug-in bandwidth selection,
         14, 26
     rule-of-thumb bandwidth se-
         lection, 14,
         26
Dirac delta function, 679

empirical distribution function, 19

fixed effects, 586
Fourier series, 512
frequency method, 6, 115

Gaussian process, 678
generalized method of mo-
         ments (GMM),
         512

hazard function, 198
Hilbert space, 674
hypothesis testing
     conditional parametric
         density function, 402
     conditional parametric distri-
         butions,
         382
     correct parametric func-
         tional form, 355, 365,
         398
     equality of density functions,
         362, 401

independence, 378
omitted variables, 370
parametric density function,
         380
parametric single index model,
         369
serial dependence, 404
significance, 375
significance test, 401

inequality
     Cauchy, 690
     Cauchy-Schwarz, *see* Cauchy
     Chebychev, 690
     Hölder, 690
     Markov, 689
     triangle, 481
instrumental variable, 506
integrated mean squared error
         (IMSE), 13
integrated square error (ISE), 157

Kaplan-Meier estimator, 338
kernel
     Aitchison and Aitken, 167
     Bartlett, 405
     convolution, 16
     Daniell, 405
     Epanechnikov, 35
     Gaussian, 34
     higher order, 33
     Parzen, 405
     triangular, 400
     uniform, 8
Khinchin's law of large numbers,
         688
knots, 446
Kullback-Leibler, 382

latent variable, 316
law of iterated expectations, 690
Lebesgue-Stieltjes integral, 670
Lebesgue measure, 666
link function, 250, 295, 463
Lipschitz function, 672
local average, 64
local constant estimator, 60
     AIC_c bandwidth selection, 72

GPSR Authorized Representative: Easy Access System Europe - Mustamäe tee
50, 10621 Tallinn, Estonia, gpsr.requests@easproject.com

www.ingramcontent.com/pod-product-compliance
Ingram Content Group UK Ltd.
Pitfield, Milton Keynes, MK11 3LW, UK
UKHW050155160325
456259UK00004B/22